THE COMPLETE MODERN

CROSSWORD
DICTIONARY

THE COMPLETE MODERN

CROSSWORD DICTIONARY

Norman G. Pulsford

OMEGA BOOKS

Originally published by Pan Books Ltd, Cavaye Place, London SW10.

This edition published 1987 by Omega Books Ltd,
14 Greville Street, Hatton Garden, London EC1, under licence
from the proprietor.

Copyright © Morley Adams Ltd 1967.

ISBN 1 85007 083 0

Printed and bound by Biddles Ltd, Walnut Tree House, Woodbridge Park,
Guildford, Surrey.

FOREWORD

The 'Phrase' section of this book is unique in its method of presentation. Within its pages you will find: Films, Novels, Plays, Fictional and Historical Characters, Musical Works, Song Titles, Pop Groups, Animals, Birds, Insects, Fish, Television and Radio Programmes, Buildings, Streets, Locations, Geographical Names, Celebrities, Games, Hobbies, Foreign Terms, Things to Eat, Drink and Wear, and tens of thousands of everyday terms, phrases and expressions.

All the items are tabulated according to the number of letters which they contain, and are set out in strictly alphabetical order for quick and easy reference.

The section has been especially compiled as an aid to solvers of the more difficult 'cryptic' crossswords published in *The Times*, *The Daily Telegraph*, the *Guardian*, the *Independent*, the *Sunday Times*, the *Sunday Telegraph*, and so on.

It frequently happens that a solver is held up by one particular clue, the answer to which is a phrase with one or two interlocking letters already inserted. Let us assume that the clue is: 'He might play one a single piece (8, 2, 5)', and that you have 'B' as the first letter. The second phrase under the heading 'B-15' at once gives you your answer: 'Bachelor of Music'. Naturally, when the first letter has not already been inserted, further research will be necessary.

In order to save space, most plurals and past participles have been omitted. Thus, when the 15-letter answer to a clue is obviously in the plural, it must, in most cases, be looked for under the '14' heading. A similar adjustment must be made when the answer is obviously a past participle. 'Backing down' and 'Holding over', for example, must be looked for under 'Back down' and 'Hold over'.

The 'Word' section will be extremely useful to solvers of the easier 'straightforward' crosswords as published in the *Evening Standard*, the *Daily Mirror*, and other popular papers.

The compilation of this book has taken a little under five years. Here are some of the sources from which we culled our information: three standard dictionaries; one American dictionary; one 20-volume encyclopaedia; *Roget's Thesaurus*; *Brewer's Dictionary of Phrase and Fable*; *Who's Who in The Theatre*; *Pears Cyclopaedia*; *Whitaker's Almanack*; *Philip's Gazetteer*, and more than 20,000 published crosswords.

Norman G. Pulsford

CONTENTS

PHRASES

A—8
A BAD TIME
A BIT MUCH
ABOVE ALL
ABOVE PAR
ACCEPT IT
ACES HIGH
ACES WILD
ACID BATH
ACID DROP
ACID TEST
ACT A PART
ACT BADLY
ACT OF GOD
ACT OF WAR
ACT THREE
ACUTE EAR
ADAM BEDE
ADAM'S ALE
ADAM'S RIB
ADDING UP
ADD WATER
ADMIT ONE
ADMIT TWO
A FAIR COP
A FAST ONE
AFTER ALL
AFTER TEA
AFTER YOU
AGE GROUP
A GOOD BUY
A GOOD FEW
A GOOD RUN
AIM A BLOW
AIR COVER
AIR FORCE
AIR LINER
AIR POWER
AIR RAIDS
AIR ROUTE
AIR SENSE
AIR SPACE
A LA CARTE
ALAN LADD
AL CAPONE
AL FRESCO
AL JOLSON

ALL ALIKE
ALL ALONE
ALL ALONG
ALL ASKEW
ALL AT SEA
ALL BLACK
ALL CLEAR
ALLEY CAT
ALL FARES
ALL FOUND
ALL FOURS
ALL HANDS
ALL HOURS
ALL IN ALL
ALL IN ONE
ALL KINDS
ALL MY EYE
ALL NIGHT
ALL QUIET
ALL READY
ALL RIGHT
ALL ROADS
ALL ROUND
ALL'S FAIR
ALL SIDES
ALL SORTS
ALL SOULS
ALL'S WELL
ALL THE GO
ALL THERE
ALL WRONG
ALPHA RAY
ALTER EGO
ANDY CAPP
A NEW LEAF
ANTS' NEST
ANZAC DAY
APPLE PIE
APPLE PIP
APTLY PUT
ARC LAMPS
ARC LIGHT
ARK ROYAL
ARMED MAN
ARM IN ARM
ARMS BEND
ARMS RACE

ARMY CAMP
ARMY LIFE
ARMY LIST
ARMY RANK
ARMY TYPE
ART CLASS
ART PAPER
ARTS CLUB
ARTY TYPE
ARUM LILY
AS A WHOLE
ASCOT HAT
AS GOOD AS
ASH GROVE
ASH TREES
AS IT WERE
ASK FOR IT
ASK LEAVE
ASK MERCY
AS STATED
ASWAN DAM
AS WELL AS
AT A GUESS
AT ANCHOR
AT A PARTY
AT A PINCH
AT A PRICE
AT BOTTOM
AT DINNER
AT HARROW
AT LENGTH
AT LOW EBB
AT NO TIME
ATOM BOMB
AT OXFORD
AT RANDOM
AT SCHOOL
AT SUNSET
AT THE BAR
AT THE END
AT THE OFF
AT THE TOP
AT THE ZOO
ATTIC WIT
AUDIT ALE
AU GRATIN
AU REVOIR

AUTO DA FE	BAD LIGHT	BATH BUNS
AVE MARIA	BAD LIVER	BATH CHAP
AWAY GAME	BAD LOGIC	BATH CUBE
AWAY TEAM	BAD LOSER	BATH ROBE
AWAY WINS	BADLY OFF	BATH SOAP
	BAD MARKS	BATTLE ON
B—8	BAD MIXER	BAY HORSE
BABE RUTH	BAD MONEY	BAY TREES
BABY CARE	BAD NIGHT	BEACH HUT
BABY CARS	BAD ODOUR	BEADY EYE
BABY DOLL	BAD PATCH	BEAR ARMS
BABY FACE	BAD PENNY	BEAR DOWN
BABY FOOD	BAD POINT	BEAR LEFT
BABY GIRL	BAD PRESS	BEAR PAIN
BABY LOVE	BAD SCORE	BEARS OUT
BABY MINE	BAD SHAPE	BEAR WITH
BABY SHOW	BAD SHOTS	BE A SPORT
BABY TALK	BAD SIGHT	BEAT BACK
BABY WOOL	BAD SMELL	BEAT DOWN
BACK AWAY	BAD SPORT	BEATEN UP
BACK AXLE	BAD START	BEAT IT UP
BACK DOOR	BAD STATE	BEATS OFF
BACK DOWN	BAD STORY	BEAT TIME
BACKED UP	BAD TASTE	BEAU NASH
BACK HAIR	BAD TERMS	BED LINEN
BACK KICK	BAD THING	BEEF STEW
BACK PAGE	BAD TIMES	BEER HALL
BACK RENT	BAD TOOTH	BEE STING
BACK ROOM	BAD TRADE	BEG LEAVE
BACK SEAT	BALD HEAD	BE IN DEBT
BACKS OUT	BALD PATE	BE IN LOVE
BACK SPIN	BALES OUT	BELL TENT
BACK STUD	BALL BOYS	BELOW PAR
BACK VIEW	BALL GAME	BE MY LOVE
BACK YARD	BALL GOWN	BEND DOWN
BACON FAT	BANK DOWN	BEND OVER
BAD ACTOR	BANK LOAN	BEN NEVIS
BAD BLOOD	BANK NOTE	BENNY LEE
BAD BOOKS	BANK ON IT	BE NO MORE
BAD CAUSE	BANK RATE	BENT BACK
BAD COUGH	BARE FEET	BE ON CALL
BAD DEBTS	BARE HEAD	BE ON EDGE
BAD DREAM	BARE IDEA	BE POLITE
BAD FAIRY	BARE LEGS	BE SEATED
BAD FAITH	BARE NECK	BE SILENT
BAD GRACE	BARE WORD	BEST CUTS
BAD HABIT	BASE COIN	BEST DAYS
BAD HEART	BASS CLEF	BEST EVER
BAD IMAGE	BASS DRUM	BEST FORM
BAD LANDS	BASS HORN	BEST GIRL
BAD LAYER	BASS NOTE	BEST LOVE

BEST PART	BLACK BOX	BODY BLOW
BEST SUIT	BLACK CAP	BODY HEAT
BEST TEAM	BLACK CAT	BOIL AWAY
BEST TIME	BLACK DOG	BOIL DOWN
BEST TOGS	BLACK EYE	BOIL OVER
BEST WINE	BLACK INK	BOLD DEED
BETEL NUT	BLACK KEY	BOLD FACE
BE UNKIND	BLACK MAN	BOLD MOVE
BEVIN BOY	BLACK OUT	BOLD TYPE
BIG APPLE	BLACK RAT	BOMB SITE
BIG BREAK	BLACK ROD	BONA FIDE
BIG BUILD	BLACK SEA	BONAR LAW
BIG BULLY	BLACK TEA	BONE IDLE
BIG CHIEF	BLACK TIE	BOOK CLUB
BIG CROWD	BLESS YOU	BOOKED UP
BIG DEALS	BLIND EYE	BOOK ENDS
BIG DRINK	BLIND MAN	BOOK SHOP
BIG FIGHT	BLOCK OUT	BOOM TOWN
BIG FILMS	BLOOD RED	BORN DEAD
BIG GIRLS	BLOOD TIE	BORN FOOL
BIG HOUSE	BLOTS OUT	BORN RICH
BIG IDEAS	BLOW AWAY	BOTH ENDS
BIG MATCH	BLOW COLD	BOTH WAYS
BIG MONEY	BLOW DOWN	BOTTLE UP
BIG MOUTH	BLOW HARD	BOTTOM UP
BIG NOISE	BLOWN OUT	BOUGHT IN
BIG PIECE	BLOW OVER	BOUGHT UP
BIG RACES	BLUE BABY	BOUNCE IN
BIG SCORE	BLUE BIRD	BOUNCE UP
BIG SHOTS	BLUE BOOK	BOW BELLS
BIG STAND	BLUE EYES	BOWL OVER
BIG STICK	BLUE FUNK	BOXER DOG
BIG STIFF	BLUE LAMP	BOYS' CLUB
BIG STORM	BLUE MOON	BOY SCOUT
BIG STUFF	BLUE NILE	BRAIN BOX
BIG WHEEL	BLUE ROOM	BRAIN FAG
BILLY BOY	BLUE RUIN	BRAND NEW
BILLY CAN	BLUE STAR	BRASS HAT
BIND OVER	BLUE SUIT	BRAVE MAN
BIRD CALL	BLUNT END	BREAD BIN
BIRD LIFE	BLURT OUT	BREAK OFF
BIRD LORE	BOARD OUT	BREAK OUT
BIRD SEED	BOAT CLUB	BREAKS IN
BIRD SONG	BOAT RACE	BREAKS UP
BIT BY BIT	BOBBY PIN	BREN GUNS
BITE INTO	BOBBY VEE	BRET HART
BITER BIT	BOB DYLAN	BRIAN RIX
BIT OF FUN	BOB MAJOR	BRICK RED
BLACK ART	BOB MINOR	BRIM OVER
BLACK BAG	BOB ROYAL	BRING OFF
BLACK BAT	BODE EVIL	BRING OUT

BRINGS IN
BRINGS ON
BRINGS TO
BRINGS UP
BROKEN IN
BROKEN UP
BROWN ALE
BROWN COW
BROWN EGG
BROWN OWL
BROWN RAT
BRUSH OFF
BUBBLE UP
BUCKLE ON
BUCKLE TO
BUCKLE UP
BULL NECK
BULL'S EYE
BULLY OFF
BUMP INTO
BUMPS OFF
BUN FIGHT
BUNGED UP
BUNNY HUG
BUN PENNY
BUOYED UP
BURN AWAY
BURN DOWN
BURNT OAK
BURNT OUT
BURST OUT
BUS DEPOT
BUS FARES
BUSH FIRE
BUS QUEUE
BUS STOPS
BUSY BEES
BUSY LIFE
BUSY TIME
BUSY TOWN
BUTTED IN
BUTTER UP
BUTTON UP
BUY BLIND
BUY CHEAP
BUZZ BOMB
BY A FLUKE
BY CHANCE
BY CHEQUE
BY GEORGE
BY HALVES

BY INCHES
BY ITSELF
BY LETTER
BY MYSELF
BY MY WILL
BY NATURE
BY RETURN
BY RIGHTS
BY STAGES
BY THE ARM
BY THE SEA
BY THE WAY

C—8

CABIN BOY
CABLE-CAR
CAB RANKS
CAFE NOIR
CALF LOVE
CALL A CAB
CALL AWAY
CALL BACK
CALL BOYS
CALL DOWN
CALLED IN
CALLED UP
CALL GIRL
CALL OVER
CALLS FOR
CALLS OFF
CALLS OUT
CALL TIME
CALL UPON
CALM DOWN
CAME DOWN
CAMP FIRE
CAMP SITE
CANON LAW
CAPE HORN
CAPE TOWN
CAP IT ALL
CAR CRASH
CARD GAME
CARD VOTE
CARE A LOT
CAR FERRY
CAR PARKS
CAR RALLY
CARRY OFF
CARRY OUT
CAR SMASH

CART AWAY
CARVE OUT
CASE BOOK
CASH BOOK
CASH DESK
CASH DOWN
CASHED IN
CASH SALE
CAST A FLY
CAST A NET
CAST AWAY
CAST DICE
CAST DOWN
CAST IRON
CAST LOTS
CASTS OFF
CASTS OUT
CATCH OUT
CAT LOVER
CATS' EYES
CATS' HOME
CAT SHOWS
CAT'S MEAT
CAUGHT ON
CAUGHT UP
CELL MATE
CHALK OUT
CHANCE IT
CHECK OFF
CHECK OUT
CHECKS IN
CHECKS UP
CHEERS UP
CHEESE IT
CHESS SET
CHEW OVER
CHEZ NOUS
CHINA CUP
CHINA EGG
CHINA SEA
CHINA TEA
CHIN CHIN
CHIP SHOT
CHOIR BOY
CHOKE OFF
CHOP DOWN
CHOP SUEY
CHUCK OUT
CHURN OUT
CIDER CUP
CIGAR ASH

CIGAR BOX
CISCO KID
CITY DESK
CITY GENT
CITY HALL
CITY LIFE
CITY WALL
CIVIL LAW
CIVIL WAR
CLASS WAR
CLAY PIPE
CLEAN CUT
CLEAN OUT
CLEANS UP
CLEAR DAY
CLEAR OFF
CLEAR OUT
CLEAR SKY
CLEARS UP
CLEAR WIN
CLOCK OUT
CLOCKS IN
CLOSED IN
CLOSE FIT
CLOSE RUN
CLOSE SET
CLOSES UP
CLOSE TIE
CLOTH CAP
CLUB BORE
CLUB FEES
CLUB LIFE
COAL CART
COAL DUST
COAL FIRE
COAL MINE
COAL SEAM
COCA COLA
CODE NAME
CODE WORD
CODS' ROES
COKE FIRE
COLD BATH
COLD BEEF
COLD CURE
COLD DISH
COLD DUCK
COLD FEET
COLD FISH
COLD FOOD
COLD LAMB

COLD MEAL
COLD MEAT
COLD MILK
COLD PACK
COLD PORK
COLD ROOM
COLD SNAP
COLD WAVE
COLD WIND
COLOUR UP
COME AWAY
COME BACK
COME DOWN
COME HERE
COME HOME
COME INTO
COME LAST
COME NEAR
COME NEXT
COME OVER
COMES OFF
COMES OUT
COME TRUE
COME UPON
COME UP TO
COMING IN
COMING ON
COMING TO
CON AMORE
COOL CARD
COOL DOWN
COOL FISH
COOL HAND
COOL HEAD
COOPED UP
COPE WITH
COPY DOWN
CORK TIPS
CORN CURE
CORN LAWS
COSY CAFE
COSY CHAT
COTTON ON
COUGHS UP
COUNT OUT
COUNT TEN
COUPLE UP
COVERS UP
COW'S MILK
CRACKS UP
CREAM BUN

CREAM TEA
CREEP OFF
CREEP OUT
CREW CUTS
CRIED OUT
CRIES OFF
CROCKS UP
CROSS NOW
CROSS OFF
CROSS OUT
CROWN HIM
CROW OVER
CRUDE OIL
CRUEL ACT
CRUEL SEA
CRY ALOUD
CRY "HAVOC"
CRY OF JOY
CRY QUITS
CRY "SHAME"
CUBE ROOT
CUP FINAL
CUP OF TEA
CURLED UP
CUSHY JOB
CUT A DASH
CUT GLASS
CUT GRASS
CUT IN TWO
CUT IT OFF
CUT IT OUT
CUT LOOSE
CUT NO ICE
CUT PRICE
CUT RATES
CUT ROUND
CUTS BACK
CUTS DEAD
CUTS DOWN
CUTS FINE
CUT SHORT

D—8
DAILY USE
DAIRY COW
DAME TROT
DAMP DOWN
DANNY BOY
DARK AGES
DARK BLUE
DARK DAYS

DARK DEED	DEATH RAY	DO HOMAGE
DARK GREY	DEED POLL	DOLLED UP
DARK HAIR	DEEP BLUE	DONE DOWN
DARK LADY	DEEP COMA	DO NO GOOD
DARK ROOM	DEEP DOWN	DO NO HARM
DARK SIDE	DEEP NOTE	DORIS DAY
DARK SKIN	DEEP SIGH	DO SCALES
DARK SUIT	DEEP SNOW	DO THE LOT
DART PAST	DEEP TONE	DOUBLE UP
DASH AWAY	DEER PARK	DOVE GREY
DASH DOWN	DEFY TIME	DO WISELY
DASH INTO	DE GAULLE	DOWN BEAT
DATE PALM	DE LA MARE	DOWN LINE
DAVE KING	DENSE FOG	DOWN TOWN
DAVID LOW	DERBY DAY	DOWN WIND
DAVIS CUP	DEREK ROY	DRAG DOWN
DAVY LAMP	DESK WORK	DRAG HUNT
DAY BOOKS	DE VALERA	DRAGS OUT
DAY BY DAY	DEVON MAN	DRAIN DRY
DAY DREAM	DICE GAME	DRAW AWAY
DAY NURSE	DID RIGHT	DRAW BACK
DAY OR TWO	DID WRONG	DRAW LOTS
DAY SHIFT	DIED AWAY	DRAW NEAR
DAY'S WORK	DIED DOWN	DRAW NIGH
DEAD BALL	DIED HARD	DRAWN OFF
DEAD BEAT	DIE HAPPY	DRAWN OUT
DEAD BODY	DIG A HOLE	DRAW REIN
DEAD CALM	DIG A MINE	DRAW WELL
DEAD CERT	DIGS DEEP	DREAM MAN
DEAD DUCK	DIM LIGHT	DRIED EGG
DEAD EASY	DINED OUT	DRIED OUT
DEAD FLAT	DINE LATE	DRINKS UP
DEAD HAND	DIRTY DOG	DRIVE MAD
DEAD HEAT	DIRTY SKY	DRIVE OFF
DEAD KEEN	DISHED UP	DRIVE OUT
DEAD LEAF	DIVAN BED	DROP AWAY
DEAD LOSS	DO A TRICK	DROP DEAD
DEAD NUTS	DO BATTLE	DROP DOWN
DEAD SHOT	DO BETTER	DROPS OFF
DEAD SLOW	DOCTOR NO	DROPS OUT
DEAD SPIT	DOG FIGHT	DRY BONES
DEAD SURE	DOG LATIN	DRY BREAD
DEAD WOOD	DOG LOVER	DRY CELLS
DEAF EARS	DOGS' HOME	DRY COUGH
DEAF MUTE	DOG SHOWS	DRY FACTS
DEAL WITH	DOG'S LIFE	DRY FRUIT
DEAN INGE	DOG'S NOSE	DRY GOODS
DEAR DEAR!	DOG'S TAIL	DRYING UP
DEAR LIFE	DOG TEAMS	DRY PLATE
DEAR SIRS	DOG TRACK	DRY TOAST
DEATH BED	DOG WATCH	DR. WATSON

DUCK DOWN
DUCK POND
DUCK'S EGG
DUCK SOUP
DUE NORTH
DUE SOUTH
DULL ACHE
DULL PAIN
DULL THUD
DULL WORK
DUMB SHOW
DUMMY RUN
DUST BOWL
DUST TRAP
DUTCH GIN
DUTCH HOE
DUTY CALL
DUTY FREE
DUTY LIST
DUTY PAID
DYED HAIR
DYING BED
DYING DAY
DYING MAN
DYING OUT

E—8
EAGLE EYE
EARL HAIG
EARLY AGE
EARLY MAN
EARN FAME
EARN LESS
EARN MORE
EAR PLUGS
EASED OFF
EASED OUT
EASE OVER
EAST SIDE
EAST WIND
EAST WING
EASY BEAT
EASY COME
EASY DROP
EASY GAME
EASY LIFE
EASY MIND
EASY PACE
EASY PREY
EASY ROAD
EASY TASK

EASY TIME
EASY WORD
EAT A MEAL
EATS AWAY
EATS DIRT
EAU DE VIE
ECCE HOMO
EDEN KANE
EDGE AWAY
EGG FLIPS
EGG PLANT
EGG SALAD
EGG SAUCE
EGG SPOON
EGG TIMER
EIGHT MEN
ELDER SON
EL DORADO
ELM TREES
EMIT RAYS
EMPTY BOX
EMPTY CAN
EMPTY TIN
END HOUSE
END IT ALL
END SEATS
END TO END
ENEMY SPY
ENTRY FEE
EPIC FILM
EPIC POEM
EPIC POET
EQUAL PAY
ET CETERA
ETON CROP
ETON SUIT
EVEN BEAT
EVEN DATE
EVEN KEEL
EVEN PACE
EVEN TIME
EVERY BIT
EVERY DAY
EVERY ONE
EVERY WAY
EVIL DAYS
EVIL DEED
EVIL HOUR
EVIL LIFE
EVIL OMEN
EVIL STAR

EXCUSE ME
EXTRA MAN
EXTRA PAY
EXTRA RUN
EYES LEFT
EYE TO EYE

F—8
FACE CARD
FACE DOWN
FACE LIFT
FACE ODDS
FACE PACK
FACE RUIN
FACE UP TO
FADE AWAY
FADED OUT
FAIR COPY
FAIR DEAL
FAIR GAME
FAIR HAIR
FAIR HAND
FAIR ISLE
FAIR LADY
FAIR MAID
FAIR NAME
FAIR PLAY
FAIR SKIN
FAIR SWOP
FAIR WAGE
FAIR WIND
FALL AWAY
FALL BACK
FALL DOWN
FALL FLAT
FALL FOUL
FALL OPEN
FALL OVER
FALL SICK
FALLS ILL
FALLS OFF
FALLS OUT
FALL UPON
FALSE GOD
FALSE RIB
FAN CLUBS
FANCY BOX
FAN DANCE
FAR ABOVE
FAR AHEAD
FAR APART

FAR BELOW	FIFTH SET	FIRST LAP
FARM EGGS	FIFTH TEE	FIRST MAN
FARM HAND	FIGHT FOR	FIRST OUT
FARM LAND	FIGHT OFF	FIRST ROW
FAR NORTH	FIGHT SHY	FIRST SET
FAR SIGHT	FILE AWAY	FIRST TEE
FAR SOUTH	FILE DOWN	FIR TREES
FAST AWAY	FILE PAST	FISH CAKE
FAST CARS	FILL A GAP	FISH DISH
FAST DAYS	FILLED IN	FISH FORK
FAST LIFE	FILM FANS	FISH POND
FAST RACE	FILM PLAY	FISH SHOP
FAST TIME	FILM SHOW	FISH TANK
FAST WORK	FILM STAR	FISH TEAS
FATAL DAY	FINAL BID	FIT STATE
FAT STOCK	FINAL DAY	FITS WELL
FATTEN UP	FIND A JOB	FITTED IN
FAT WOMAN	FIND A WAY	FITTED UP
FAWN UPON	FIND BAIL	FIVE DAYS
FEAST DAY	FIND ROOM	FIVE DEEP
FEED WELL	FINDS OUT	FIVE FEET
FEEL BLUE	FIND TIME	FIVE QUID
FEEL COLD	FINE AIRS	FIVE SETS
FEEL EASY	FINE ARTS	FIX A DATE
FEEL FINE	FINE BIRD	FIX A TIME
FEEL GOOD	FINE CHAP	FLAG DAYS
FEEL HURT	FINE DAYS	FLAG DOWN
FEEL LAZY	FINE DOWN	FLARED UP
FEEL LIKE	FINE EDGE	FLAT BEER
FEEL PAIN	FINE FARE	FLAT FACE
FEEL SAFE	FINE GOLD	FLAT FEET
FEEL SICK	FINE LADY	FLAT FISH
FEELS ILL	FINE RAIN	FLAT NOSE
FEEL SORE	FINE SHOW	FLAT RACE
FEEL SURE	FINE VIEW	FLAT RATE
FEEL WARM	FINISH UP	FLAT ROOF
FEEL WELL	FIR CONES	FLAT SPIN
FELL AN OX	FIRE AWAY	FLAT TYRE
FELL BACK	FIRE DAMP	FLAT WASH
FELL DOWN	FIRE RISK	FLEA PITS
FELL FLAT	FIRE UPON	FLEE FROM
FELO DE SE	FIRM DATE	FLEET ARM
FELT HATS	FIRM GRIP	FLEW AWAY
FEME SOLE	FIRM HAND	FLEW HIGH
FENCED IN	FIRM HOLD	FLEW HOME
FETCH OUT	FIRM HOPE	FLEW SOLO
FEW WORDS	FIRST ACT	FLICK OFF
FIELD DAY	FIRST AID	FLIES OFF
FIERY RED	FIRST BID	FLING OFF
FIFTH DAY	FIRST BUS	FLING OUT
FIFTH ROW	FIRST DAY	FLIP SIDE

FLIT PAST	FOUR TENS	FULL TOSS
FLOP DOWN	FOUR TWOS	FULL WELL
FLOUR BIN	FOWL PEST	FUMED OAK
FLOW BACK	FREE BEER	FUN FAIRS
FLOW OVER	FREE CITY	FUNNY HAT
FLUFF OUT	FREE COPY	FUNNY MAN
FLUSH OUT	FREE FLOW	FUR COATS
FLY ABOUT	FREE GIFT	FUR STOLE
FLY A KITE	FREE HAND	FUR TRADE
FLY APART	FREE KICK	FUR WRAPS
FOAM BATH	FREE LIFT	FUSE WIRE
FOG BOUND	FREE LIST	FUSS OVER
FOGGY DAY	FREE LOVE	G—8
FOIST OFF	FREE MEAL	GAD ABOUT
FOLD ARMS	FREE MILK	GAG BOOKS
FOLD BACK	FREE PASS	GAIN TIME
FOLD DOWN	FREE PLAY	GAIN UPON
FOLDED UP	FREE PORT	GAME BIRD
FOLD OVER	FREE RIDE	GAME LAWS
FOLK LORE	FREE SEAT	GAME PIES
FOLK SONG	FREE TIME	GAMMA RAY
FOLK TALE	FREE TO GO	GAMMY LEG
FOLLOW ON	FREE VOTE	GANG SHOW
FOLLOW UP	FREE WILL	GAOL BIRD
FOND HOPE	FRESH AIR	GAS BOARD
FOOD FISH	FRESH EGG	GAS FIRES
FOOL AWAY	FRESH TEA	GAS METER
FOR A JOKE	FRET AWAY	GAS PLANT
FOR A LARK	FRIED EGG	GAS POKER
FOR A SONG	FROM AFAR	GAS STOVE
FOR A TERM	FRONT MAN	GATHER IN
FOR A TIME	FRONT ROW	GATHER UP
FORCE OUT	FROZEN UP	GAVE A TUG
FORGET IT	FRUIT PIE	GAVE AWAY
FOR KEEPS	FUEL BILL	GAVE BACK
FOR KICKS	FUEL TANK	GAY PARTY
FORKS OUT	FULL BLUE	GAY SMILE
FOR SHAME	FULL CREW	GAY SPARK
FORT KNOX	FULL FACE	GET ABOUT
FORTY ALL	FULL LIFE	GET A GOAL
FOUL BLOW	FULL LOAD	GET AHEAD
FOUL DEED	FULL MEAL	GET A LIFT
FOUL PLAY	FULL MOON	GET ALONG
FOUND OUT	FULL OF GO	GET ANGRY
FOUR ACES	FULL PLAY	GET A RISE
FOUR DAYS	FULL SAIL	GET BELOW
FOUR DEEP	FULL SIZE	GET CLEAR
FOUR FEET	FULL STOP	GET CROSS
FOUR LAPS	FULL TIDE	GET DRUNK
FOUR ONES	FULL TILT	GET FRESH
FOUR QUID	FULL TIME	GET GOING

GET IDEAS	GO ABOARD	GOLD RING
GET LEAVE	GO ABROAD	GOLD RUSH
GET LOOSE	GO ABSENT	GOLD VASE
GET OLDER	GO ACROSS	GOLD VEIN
GET RATTY	GO ADRIFT	GOLD WIRE
GET READY	GO ALL OUT	GOLF BALL
GET RID OF	GO AND SEE	GOLF CLUB
GET RIGHT	GO AROUND	GO MODERN
GET ROUGH	GO ASHORE	GO NATIVE
GET ROUND	GO ASTERN	GONE AWAY
GETS AWAY	GO ASTRAY	GONE DOWN
GETS BACK	GOBBLE UP	GONE WEST
GETS EVEN	GO BEHIND	GOOD BALL
GETS OVER	GO BEYOND	GOOD BOOK
GETS RICH	GO BY BOAT	GOOD CASE
GETS WELL	GO BY RAIL	GOOD CAST
GET THERE	GO BY ROAD	GOOD CHAP
GET TIRED	GO BY SHIP	GOOD COOK
GET TOUGH	GO BY TAXI	GOOD COPY
GET UPSET	GO BY TRAM	GOOD CROP
GET WORSE	GO BY TUBE	GOOD DEAL
GIFT GOAL	GOD BLESS	GOOD DEBT
GIFT SHOP	GO DIRECT	GOOD DEED
GIN AND IT	GOD OF WAR	GOOD DRAW
GINGER UP	GOD'S ACRE	GOOD FACE
GINNED UP	GOD SPEED	GOOD FARE
GIN RUMMY	GOD'S WILL	GOOD FEED
GIN SLING	GOES AWAY	GOOD FIRE
GIVE AWAY	GOES BACK	GOOD FOLK
GIVE BACK	GOES DOWN	GOOD FOOD
GIVE HEED	GOES OVER	GOOD FORM
GIVE HOPE	GOES SLOW	GOOD GAME
GIVE IN TO	GOES WEST	GOOD GATE
GIVE IT UP	GOES WITH	GOOD GIRL
GIVEN OUT	GO FOR HIM	GOOD HAND
GIVE ODDS	GO HALVES	GOOD HAUL
GIVE OVER	GO HUNGRY	GOOD HOPE
GIVE PAIN	GO IN FEAR	GOOD HOST
GIVES EAR	GOING MAD	GOOD IDEA
GIVES WAY	GOING OFF	GOOD KING
GIVE VENT	GOING OUT	GOOD LADY
GIVING UP	GOINGS ON	GOOD LAND
GLAD HAND	GO IN RAGS	GOOD LIFE
GLAD NEWS	GO INSIDE	GOOD LUCK
GLAD RAGS	GOLD COIN	GOOD MEAL
GLASS EYE	GOLD DUST	GOOD MOOD
GLASS JAW	GOLD FOIL	GOOD MOVE
GLEE CLUB	GOLD LACE	GOOD NAME
GLUM FACE	GOLD LEAF	GOOD NEWS
GNAT BITE	GOLD MINE	GOOD OMEN
GNAW AWAY	GOLD REEF	GOOD PACE

GOOD PALS	GREAT JOY	H—8
GOOD PART	GREAT MAN	HAD WORDS
GOOD PLAN	GREAT TOM	HAIL A BUS
GOOD SEAT	GREAT WAR	HAIL A CAB
GOOD SHOT	GREAT WIT	HAIL MARY
GOOD SHOW	GREEK ART	HAIRY APE
GOOD SIGN	GREEK GOD	HALF A CUP
GOOD SOIL	GREEK URN	HALF A MAN
GOOD SORT	GREEN EYE	HALF A TON
GOOD SOUL	GREEN FEE	HALF DEAD
GOOD TIME	GREEN FLY	HALF EACH
GOOD TIPS	GREEN HAT	HALF FARE
GOOD TRIM	GREEN INK	HALF FULL
GOOD TURN	GREEN MAN	HALF MILE
GOOD TYPE	GREEN TEA	HALF MOON
GOOD VIEW	GREY COAT	HALF OVER
GOOD WASH	GREY DAWN	HALF TIME
GOOD WIFE	GREY EYES	HALL MARK
GOOD WILL	GREY HAIR	HALT SIGN
GOOD WINE	GREY MARE	HAM ACTOR
GOOD WORD	GREY SUIT	HAM HOUSE
GOOD WORK	GRIM FACE	HAMMER IN
GOOD YEAR	GRIM JOKE	HAM ROLLS
GO ON DECK	GRIM LOOK	HAM SALAD
GO ON FOOT	GRIM TASK	HAND BACK
GOON SHOW	GRIM VIEW	HAND DOWN
GO PLACES	GRIP HARD	HAND IT IN
GO PURPLE	GROPE FOR	HAND OVER
GO RACING	GROW COLD	HAND PUMP
GO SHARES	GROW COOL	HANDS OFF
GO STEADY	GROW DARK	HANDS OUT
GO SURETY	GROW LESS	HANG BACK
GO TO GAOL	GROWN MAN	HANG DOWN
GO TO HELL	GROW PALE	HANG FIRE
GO TOO FAR	GROW PEAS	HANG ON TO
GO TO SEED	GROW RICH	HANG OVER
GO TO TOWN	GROWS OLD	HANGS OUT
GO TO WORK	GROW UPON	HAPPY BOY
GOUGE OUT	GROW WEAK	HAPPY MAN
GRADE ONE	GROW WILD	HARD AT IT
GRADE TWO	GUARD DOG	HARD BALL
GRAF SPEE	GUESS HOW	HARD BLOW
GRAND AIR	GUESS WHO	HARD CASE
GRAND SUM	GUIDE DOG	HARD CASH
GRAY'S INN	GULP DOWN	HARD COAL
GREAT AGE	GUN FIGHT	HARD CORE
GREAT AUK	GUNGA DIN	HARD FACT
GREAT DAY	GUN METAL	HARD FATE
GREAT FUN	GYM DRESS	HARD GAME
GREAT GUY	GYM SHOES	HARD HEAD
GREAT HIT	GYM SLIPS	HARD KICK

HARD LIFE	HELP OVER	HIRED OUT
HARD LOOK	HELPS OUT	HIRED VAN
HARD LUCK	HEMMED IN	HIS GRACE
HARD ROES	HEN PARTY	HIT IT OFF
HARD SEAT	HENS' EGGS	HITS BACK
HARD TACK	HERB BEER	HITS HARD
HARD TASK	HERE GOES	HIT TO LEG
HARD TIME	HERE WE GO	HOCK SHOP
HARD TONE	HER GRACE	HOG'S BACK
HARD UPON	HERNE BAY	HOLD BACK
HARD WEAR	HIDE AWAY	HOLD DEAR
HARD WORD	HIGH AIMS	HOLD DOWN
HARD WORK	HIGH BALL	HOLD FAST
HARK BACK	HIGH CARD	HOLD GOOD
HARM'S WAY	HIGH COST	HOLD HARD
HARP UPON	HIGH DIVE	HOLD ON TO
HAT TRICK	HIGHER UP	HOLD OVER
HAUL BACK	HIGH FEES	HOLDS OFF
HAUL DOWN	HIGH GEAR	HOLDS OUT
HAULED IN	HIGH HAND	HOLD SWAY
HAVE A BET	HIGH HATS	HOLD WITH
HAVE A FAG	HIGH HOPE	HOLED OUT
HAVE A FIT	HIGH JUMP	HOLY CITY
HAVE A JOB	HIGH KICK	HOLY FEAR
HAVE A NAP	HIGH LAND	HOLY LAND
HAVE A PEW	HIGH LIFE	HOLY LOCH
HAVE A ROW	HIGH MASS	HOLY WARS
HAVE A RUN	HIGH NECK	HOLY WEEK
HAVE A TRY	HIGH NOON	HOLY WRIT
HAVE DONE	HIGH NOTE	HOME FARM
HAVE LIFE	HIGH RANK	HOME GAME
HAVE PITY	HIGH RATE	HOME HELP
HAY FEVER	HIGH RENT	HOME LIFE
HAZEL NUT	HIGH ROAD	HOME NEWS
HEAD BACK	HIGH SEAS	HOME PARK
HEAD COOK	HIGH SPOT	HOME RULE
HEAD GIRL	HIGH TEAS	HOME RUNS
HEADS OFF	HIGH TIDE	HOME SAFE
HEAD WIND	HIGH TIME	HOME TEAM
HEAR HEAR!	HIGH TONE	HOME TIES
HEAT SPOT	HIGH WAGE	HOME TOWN
HEAT WAVE	HIGH WALL	HOME WINS
HEAVED TO	HIGH WIND	HONEY BEE
HEAVY DAY	HILL FARM	HONEY POT
HEAVY DEW	HILL FOLK	HONG KONG
HEAVY SEA	HIND FOOT	HOOKED IT
HEAVY TAX	HIND LEGS	HOP ABOUT
HEEL OVER	HIP FLASK	HOP ALONG
HELD BACK	HIRED BUS	HOP FIELD
HELD OVER	HIRED CAR	HOT BATHS
HELP DOWN	HIRED MAN	HOT BLOOD

HOT CAKES	IDLE JACK	IN DETAIL
HOT COALS	IDLE RICH	IN DUBLIN
HOT DRINK	IDLE TALK	IN EFFECT
HOT JOINT	ILEX TREE	IN EMBRYO
HOT LUNCH	ILL GRACE	IN EUROPE
HOT MEALS	ILL TASTE	IN EXCESS
HOT MONEY	ILL USAGE	IN FAVOUR
HOT MUSIC	IN ACCORD	IN FLAMES
HOT NIGHT	IN A CROWD	IN FLIGHT
HOT PLATE	IN A CRUSH	IN FLOWER
HOT PUNCH	IN ACTION	INFRA DIG
HOT SCENT	IN A DREAM	IN FRANCE
HOT SPELL	IN A FAINT	INFRA RED
HOT STOVE	IN A FEVER	IN FRENCH
HOT STUFF	IN A FIELD	IN GERMAN
HOTTED UP	IN A FLASH	IN GROUPS
HOT TODDY	IN A FRAME	IN HEAVEN
HOT WATER	IN AFRICA	IN HIDING
HOUR HAND	IN A GROUP	IN HORROR
HOUSE BOY	IN A HURRY	INK SPOTS
HOUSE DOG	IN A JIFFY	INK STAIN
HOUSE FLY	IN AMBUSH	IN LAYERS
HOWL DOWN	IN AND OUT	IN LEAGUE
HOW'S THAT?	IN A PADDY	IN LONDON
HULL CITY	IN A PANIC	IN LUXURY
HULL DOWN	IN ARABIC	IN MADRID
HUMAN CRY	IN ARMOUR	IN MEMORY
HUM-AND HA	IN A SENSE	IN MID AIR
HUNT BALL	IN A SLING	IN MOSCOW
HUNT DOWN	IN A SNARE	IN MOTION
HURRY OFF	IN A STATE	IN MY VIEW
HURRY OUT	IN A SWEAT	INNER MAN
HURT LOOK	IN A SWOON	IN NORWAY
HUSHED UP	IN A TRICE	IN NO TIME
HYDE PARK	IN AUGUST	IN NO WISE
HYMN BOOK	IN AUTUMN	INN SIGNS
HYMN TUNE	IN A WHIRL	IN OFFICE
	IN CAMERA	IN OFF RED
I—8	IN CANADA	IN ONE WAY
IAN SMITH	IN CHAINS	IN ORDERS
ICE CREAM	IN CHARGE	IN PENCIL
ICE CUBES	IN CHORUS	IN PENURY
ICED CAKE	IN CHURCH	IN PERSON
ICY BLAST	IN CLOVER	IN PIECES
ICY PATCH	IN COLOUR	IN POCKET
ICY STARE	IN COLUMN	IN POLAND
ICY WASTE	IN COMMON	IN PRISON
ICY WATER	IN CONVOY	IN PUBLIC
IDEAL MAN	IN CREDIT	IN PURDAH
IDEAS MAN	IN DANGER	IN QUIRES
IDÉE FIXE	IN DEMAND	IN QUOTES

IN REASON	IRON BOOT	JUST A FEW
IN RECESS	IRON DUKE	JUST A SEC
IN RELIEF	IRON FIST	JUST GONE
IN REPAIR	IRON GATE	JUST LOSE
IN REPOSE	IRON GRIP	JUST MISS
IN REVOLT	IRON HAND	JUST THEN
IN RUSSIA	IRON HEEL	
IN SAFETY	IRON LUNG	K—8
IN SEASON	IRON MASK	KARL MARX
IN SECRET	IRON MINE	KEEL OVER
IN SERIES	IRON RULE	KEEN EDGE
IN SCHOOL	IRON SHOT	KEEN TYPE
IN SHREDS	IRON WILL	KEEN WIND
IN SPASMS	IT'S A CERT	KEEP A CAT
IN SPIRIT	IT'S A FACT	KEEP A DOG
IN SPRING		KEEP A LOG
IN SUMMER	J—8	KEEP AT IT
IN SWEDEN	JACK CADE	KEEP AWAY
IN TERROR	JAMMED IN	KEEP BACK
IN THE ACT	JAM PUFFS	KEEP CALM
IN THE AIR	JAM ROLLS	KEEP CAVE
IN THE ARK	JAM TARTS	KEEP COOL
IN THE BAG	JAM TIGHT	KEEP DARK
IN THE BAR	JANE EYRE	KEEP DOWN
IN THE BOX	JAR OF JAM	KEEP FINE
IN THE CUP	JAZZ BAND	KEEP GOAL
IN THE END	JAZZ CLUB	KEEP HOLD
IN THE GYM	JEST BOOK	KEEP IT UP
IN THE NET	JET BLACK	KEEP LEFT
IN THEORY	JET PLANE	KEEP OPEN
IN THE PIT	JEW'S HARP	KEEP PACE
IN THE RAW	JOE LOUIS	KEEP SAFE
IN THE RED	JOG ALONG	KEEPS FIT
IN THE SEA	JOHN ADAM	KEEP SHOP
IN THE SKY	JOHN BULL	KEEPS MUM
IN THE SUN	JOHN DORY	KEEPS OFF
IN THE VAN	JOHN KNOX	KEEPS OUT
IN THE WAR	JOHN NASH	KEEP STEP
IN THE WAY	JOHN PEEL	KEEP TIME
IN THE WET	JOINED IN	KEEP WARM
IN THE ZOO	JOKE BOOK	KEEP WELL
IN TIGHTS	JUMP AT IT	KEMP TOWN
IN UNISON	JUMP BACK	KEPT BACK
IN VENICE	JUMP DOWN	KEPT BUSY
IN VIENNA	JUMP INTO	KEW GREEN
IN WINTER	JUMP OVER	KEY ISSUE
IRISH ELK	JUMP TO IT	KEY MONEY
IRISH JIG	JUMP UPON	KEY MOVES
IRISH SEA	JUNK SHOP	KEY POINT
IRON BAND	JURY LIST	KEY POSTS
IRON BARS	JUST A BIT	KICK BACK

KICK OVER	LARGE RUM	LATIN TAG
KICKS OFF	LARGE SUM	LAUGH OFF
KICKS OUT	LAST BALL	LAW AGENT
KID STUFF	LAST BELL	LAW COURT
KILL PAIN	LAST BOUT	LAW SUITS
KILLS OFF	LAST CALL	LAY ABOUT
KILL TIME	LAST CAST	LAY A FIRE
KIM NOVAK	LAST DAYS	LAY AN EGG
KIND DEED	LAST DROP	LAY ASIDE
KIND FACE	LAST GASP	LAY A TRAP
KIND HOST	LAST HEAT	LAYS BARE
KIND LOOK	LAST HOLE	LAYS DOWN
KIND SOUL	LAST HOME	LAY SIEGE
KIND WORD	LAST HOPE	LAYS OPEN
KING COLE	LAST HOUR	LAY WASTE
KING JOHN	LAST JULY	LEAD MINE
KING KONG	LAST JUNE	LEAD PIPE
KING LEAR	LAST LEGS	LEAD SHOT
KING'S CUP	LAST LINE	LEADS OFF
KING SIZE	LAST LOOK	LEAD UP TO
KISS AWAY	LAST LOVE	LEAK AWAY
KNEE DEEP	LAST MEAL	LEAKS OUT
KNEE GRIP	LAST MOVE	LEAN BACK
KNOCK OFF	LAST NAME	LEAN DIET
KNOCK OUT	LAST OVER	LEAN MEAT
KNOCKS UP	LAST PAGE	LEAN OVER
KNOW BEST	LAST PART	LEAP OVER
KNOW WELL	LAST POST	LEAP YEAR
	LAST RACE	LEAST BIT
L—8	LAST REST	LEAVE OFF
LA BOHÈME	LAST ROSE	LEAVE OUT
LADLE OUT	LAST SEEN	LEEK SOUP
LADY HELP	LAST'S OUT	LEE SHORE
LADY LUCK	LAST TERM	LEFT BACK
LAID FLAT	LAST TEST	LEFT BANK
LAKE COMO	LAST TIME	LEFT FACE
LAKE ERIE	LAST TO GO	LEFT FLAT
LAMB CHOP	LAST WEEK	LEFT FOOT
LAME DOGS	LAST WILL	LEFT HALF
LAME DUCK	LAST WORD	LEFT HAND
LAND AHOY	LAST YEAR	LEFT HOME
LAND A JOB	LAS VEGAS	LEFT HOOK
LAND ARMY	LATE BIRD	LEFT OVER
LAND CRAB	LATE CALL	LEFT SIDE
LAND GIRL	LATE HOUR	LEFT TURN
LAND LINE	LATE MEAL	LEFT WING
LAND'S END	LATE NEWS	LEGAL AGE
LA PALOMA	LATE PASS	LEGAL AID
LARGE EGG	LATE POST	LEG BREAK
LARGE GAP	LATE SHOW	LEG DRIVE
LARGE GIN	LATE WIFE	LEG STUMP

LEMON TEA	LITA ROZA	LONG REST
LEMON PIE	LITTLE ME	LONG RIDE
LEND TONE	LITTLE MO	LONG ROAD
LENT TERM	LIVE A LIE	LONG ROOM
LET ALONE	LIVE BAIT	LONG ROPE
LET BLOOD	LIVE COAL	LONG SHOT
LET DRIVE	LIVED OUT	LONG SLIP
LET IT LIE	LIVE DOWN	LONG STAY
LET IT RIP	LIVE IT UP	LONG STOP
LET LOOSE	LIVE RAIL	LONG SUIT
LET ME SEE	LIVE SHOW	LONG TAIL
LETS DOWN	LIVE UP TO	LONG TERM
LETS FALL	LIVE WELL	LONG TIME
LETS FREE	LIVE WIRE	LONG VIEW
LET SLIDE	LIVING IN	LONG WAIT
LETS PASS	LOAN CLUB	LONG WALK
LETS SLIP	LOCAL INN	LONG WAVE
LEVEL OFF	LOCAL LAD	LONG WORD
LEVEL OUT	LOCAL PUB	LOOK ARCH
LEVELS UP	LOCAL RAG	LOOK AWAY
LEWIS GUN	LOCAL TAX	LOOK BACK
LIAR DICE	LOCH NESS	LOOK BLUE
LIE ABOUT	LOCK AWAY	LOOK COOL
LIE AWAKE	LOCKED IN	LOOK DOWN
LIE CLOSE	LOCKED UP	LOOKED AT
LIE DOGGO	LOG CABIN	LOOKED IN
LIE HEAVY	LOG FIRES	LOOKED ON
LIE IN BED	LOIN CHOP	LOOKED UP
LIES DOWN	LONE HAND	LOOK GLUM
LIES FLAT	LONE WOLF	LOOK GOOD
LIE STILL	LONG ACRE	LOOK GRIM
LIFE PEER	LONG DROP	LOOK HERE
LIFE SPAN	LONG FACE	LOOK INTO
LIFE WORK	LONG GONE	LOOK IT UP
LIGHT ALE	LONG HAIR	LOOK LEFT
LIGHT CAR	LONG HAUL	LOOK LIKE
LIGHT RAY	LONG JUMP	LOOK OVER
LIGHTS UP	LONG LANE	LOOK PALE
LIGHT TEA	LONG LEAD	LOOKS BIG
LIKE A MAN	LONG LEGS	LOOKS FOR
LIKE BEST	LONG LIFE	LOOK SICK
LIKE FURY	LONG LINE	LOOKS OUT
LILY POND	LONG LIST	LOOK SPRY
LILY PONS	LONG LOST	LOOK TRUE
LIMBER UP	LONG NOTE	LOOK UP TO
LINGER ON	LONG ODDS	LOOK WELL
LINKED UP	LONG POEM	LOOM OVER
LION CUBS	LONG PULL	LOOP LINE
LION'S DEN	LONG PUTT	LOOSE BOX
LIP SALVE	LONG RACE	LOOSE END
LISTEN IN	LONG READ	LOOSEN UP

LORD AVON	LUCKY DAY	MAKE FREE
LORD'S DAY	LUCKY DIP	MAKE GOOD
LOSE A LEG	LUCKY DOG	MAKE IT UP
LOSE FACE	LUCKY HIT	MAKE LAWS
LOSE HOPE	LUCKY JIM	MAKE LOVE
LOSE TIME	LUCKY MAN	MAKE NEWS
LOST BALL	LUCKY RUN	MAKE OVER
LOST CITY	LUCKY WIN	MAKE PLAY
LOST GAME	LUG ABOUT	MAKE PORT
LOST LOVE	LUMP SUMS	MAKE PUNS
LOST SOUL	LUNCH OUT	MAKE REAL
LOST TIME	LUTON HOO	MAKE ROOM
LOT'S WIFE	LYING LOW	MAKE RUNS
LOUD BANG	LYNCH LAW	MAKE SAFE
LOUD BOOM	LYRE BIRD	MAKE SAIL
LOUD PEAL		MAKES HAY
LOUD RING	**M—8**	MAKES OFF
LOUIS D'OR	MADE EASY	MAKES OUT
LOVED ONE	MADE OVER	MAKE SURE
LOVE GAME	MADLY GAY	MAKES WAY
LOVE NEST	MAD PARTY	MAKE TIME
LOVE POEM	MAGIC BOX	MAKE UP TO
LOVE SONG	MAGIC EYE	MAL DE MER
LOVE SUIT	MAIL BOAT	MALE HEIR
LOW BIRTH	MAIN BODY	MAN ALIVE
LOW CARDS	MAIN CROP	MAN A SHIP
LOW CLASS	MAIN DECK	MAN OF GOD
LOW DIVES	MAIN DISH	MAN OF LAW
LOW DUTCH	MAIN FILM	MAN POWER
LOWER JAW	MAIN HALL	MAN'S CLUB
LOWER LIP	MAIN IDEA	MAN TO MAN
LOWER SET	MAIN ITEM	MANX CATS
LOW GRADE	MAIN LINE	MANY A ONE
LOW HEELS	MAIN MEAL	MANY MORE
LOW JOINT	MAIN PART	MARCH OFF
LOW LATIN	MAIN ROAD	MARCH OUT
LOW MARKS	MAIN ROOM	MARK DOWN
LOW PITCH	MAJOR KEY	MARKS OFF
LOW POINT	MAJOR WAR	MARKS OUT
LOW POWER	MAKE A BED	MARK TIME
LOW PRICE	MAKE A BET	MARK WELL
LOW RATES	MAKE A BID	MARRY OFF
LOW RENTS	MAKE A BOW	MARSH GAS
LOW SCORE	MAKE A HIT	MARY RAND
LOW SOUND	MAKE A PUN	MARY ROSE
LOW SPEED	MAKE A ROW	MARY WEBB
LOW TIDES	MAKE A VOW	MATA HARI
LOW VOICE	MAKE BOLD	MAXIM GUN
LOW WAGES	MAKE EYES	MAY QUEEN
LOW WATER	MAKE FAST	MEAN TIME
LUCKY BOY	MAKE FIRM	MEAN WELL

MEAT BALL	MORAL LAW	NEAP TIDE
MEAT DISH	MORE TIME	NEAR BEER
MEAT LOAF	MORT SAHL	NEAR EAST
MEAT PIES	MOSS ROSE	NEAR HERE
MEAT SAFE	MOTH BALL	NEAR HOME
MELT AWAY	MOT JUSTE	NEAR MISS
MELT DOWN	MOTOR OIL	NEAR ONES
MEN OF OLD	MOURN FOR	NEAR SIDE
MENS SANA	MOVE AWAY	NEON LAMP
MEN'S WEAR	MOVE BACK	NEON SIGN
MERE IDEA	MOVED OFF	NEON TUBE
MERE LUCK	MOVED OUT	NEST EGGS
MERRY MEN	MOVE FAST	NET PRICE
MESS BILL	MOVE OVER	NET SALES
MESSED UP	MOVIE FAN	NET VALUE
MESS ROOM	MOVING UP	NEVER END
METAL BOX	MOWN DOWN	NEW ANGLE
METAL CAP	MR. PASTRY	NEW BALLS
MEWS FLAT	MUCH LESS	NEW BIRTH
MILD BEER	MUCH MORE	NEW BLOOD
MILE RACE	MUCH ROOM	NEW BRAND
MILES OUT	MUCH TIME	NEW BREAD
MILK BARS	MUD BATHS	NEW BREED
MILK BILL	MUDDLE ON	NEW BROOM
MILK DIET	MUFFLE UP	NEW CROSS
MILK JUGS	MUG'S GAME	NEW DELHI
MILK LOAF	MUSE UPON	NEW DRESS
MILK MAID	MUSK ROSE	NEW FACES
MILK PAIL	MUTE SWAN	NEW FLINT
MILKY WAY	MY CHOICE	NEW FRANC
MILL GIRL	MY FRIEND	NEW HEART
MILL HILL	MY OLD MAN	NEW HOUSE
MILL POND	MY PUBLIC	NEW IDEAS
MIME SHOW	MYRA HESS	NEW ISSUE
MIND'S EYE	MYRNA LOY	NEW LAMPS
MINE HOST		NEW LIGHT
MING VASE	**N—8**	NEW MODEL
MINK COAT	NAG'S HEAD	NEW MONEY
MINK FARM	NAIL A LIE	NEW NOVEL
MINK WRAP	NAIL DOWN	NEW ORDER
MINOR KEY	NAIL FILE	NEW OWNER
MINUS ONE	NAKED EYE	NEW PENNY
MINUS TWO	NAKED MAN	NEW PUPIL
MISS OTIS	NAME PART	NEW SHOES
MIXED BAG	NATAL DAY	NEW SHOOT
MIXED LOT	NAVAL ARM	NEWS ITEM
MOBY DICK	NAVAL GUN	NEWS ROOM
MODEL HAT	NAVAL MAN	NEW STAGE
MONA LISA	NAVY BLUE	NEW STOCK
MOOT CASE	NAVY LIST	NEW STYLE
MOPPED UP	NAVY WEEK	NEW SUITS

NEW TOWNS	NO MATTER	OFF STUMP
NEW TRAIL	NONE LEFT	OFF TO BED
NEW TRIAL	NO NERVES	OFF TO SEA
NEW TRICK	NO OBJECT	OIL DRUMS
NEW TYRES	NO OPTION	OIL LAMPS
NEW VISTA	NO QUORUM	OIL STOVE
NEW WOMAN	NO REMEDY	OIL WELLS
NEW WORLD	NO RETURN	OLD BIRDS
NEXT BEST	NORTH END	OLD BLUES
NEXT DOOR	NORTH SEA	OLD BONES
NEXT MOVE	NO SECRET	OLD BOOTS
NEXT PAGE	NOSED OUT	OLD CHINA
NEXT RACE	NOTA BENE	OLD CROCK
NEXT STEP	NOT A SOUL	OLD CRONY
NEXT TIME	NOT AS YET	OLD DEBTS
NEXT WEEK	NOT AT ALL	OLD DRESS
NEXT YEAR	NOT A WHIT	OLD DUTCH
NICE MESS	NOTE DOWN	OLD FACES
NICE TIME	NOTE WELL	OLD FLAME
NICE WORK	NO THANKS	OLD FOGEY
NIGHT AIR	NOT LEAST	OLD FOLKS
NIGHT OFF	NOT OFTEN	OLD FRUIT
NIGHT OUT	NOT QUITE	OLD GIRLS
NINE DAYS	NO TRUMPS	OLD GLORY
NINE DEEP	NOT SO BAD	OLD GUARD
NINE ELMS	NOT SO HOT	OLD HABIT
NINE FEET	NOT TODAY	OLD HANDS
NINE QUID	NOT VALID	OLD HARRY
NINTH DAY	NO WAY OUT	OLD HAUNT
NINTH ROW	NOW FOR IT	OLD HEADS
NINTH TEE	NO WONDER	OLD MAIDS
NIP OF GIN	NUT BROWN	OLD MOORE
NO ACCENT	NUT CASES	OLD ORDER
NOAH'S ARK		OLD ROGER
NO ANSWER	**O—8**	OLD SALTS
NO APPEAL	OAK CHEST	OLD SARUM
NO BETTER	OAK TREES	OLD SCORE
NOBLE ART	OCEAN BED	OLD SCREW
NO BOTHER	ODD MONEY	OLD STOCK
NO CHANCE	ODD SIGHT	OLD STORY
NO CHANGE	ODD TRICK	OLD STYLE
NO CHARGE	OF COURSE	OLD SWEAT
NO CHOICE	OFF AND ON	OLD THING
NO COLOUR	OFF BREAK	OLD TIMER
NO DESIRE	OFF DRINK	OLD TIMES
NO EFFECT	OFF DRIVE	OLD TRICK
NO EFFORT	OFF GUARD	OLD TUNES
NO ESCAPE	OFF PITCH	OLD WITCH
NO EXCUSE	OFF SALES	OLD WOMAN
NO FUTURE	OFF SHORE	OLD WORLD
NO LONGER	OFF STAGE	OLIVE OIL

ON A BINGE	ONLY ONCE	OPEN TART
ON A CHAIR	ON MONDAY	OPEN TOWN
ON A LEVEL	ON MY LIFE	OPEN VOTE
ON AND OFF	ON ONE LEG	OPEN WIDE
ON A PLATE	ON PARADE	OPEN WORK
ON A SLOPE	ON PAROLE	OPERA HAT
ON A TABLE	ON PATROL	OPIUM DEN
ON A VISIT	ON RECORD	OPTED OUT
ONCE A DAY	ON REMAND	ORB OF DAY
ONCE MORE	ON SAFARI	ORDER OFF
ONCE ONLY	ON SKATES	ORDER OUT
ONCE OVER	ON STILTS	ORDER TEA
ON COURSE	ON STRIKE	OUT AT SEA
ON CREDIT	ON SUNDAY	OUT FIRST
ON DEMAND	ON TARGET	OUT OF BED
ONE BY ONE	ON THE AIR	OUT OF GAS
ONE DOZEN	ON THE DOT	OUT OF OIL
ONE ENTRY	ON THE EBB	OUT OF USE
ONE FIFTH	ON THE HOB	OUT TO WIN
ONE GROSS	ON THE HOP	OVEN BIRD
ONE HEART	ON THE JOB	OVEN DOOR
ONE IN SIX	ON THE MAP	OVERDO IT
ONE IN TEN	ON THE MAT	OVER HERE
ONE IN TWO	ON THE NOD	OVER MUCH
ONE MATCH	ON THE RUN	OVER SEAS
ONE MONTH	ON THE SEA	OVER WE GO
ONE NINTH	ON THE SET	OWE MONEY
ONE OR TWO	ON THE SLY	OX TONGUE
ONE OUNCE	ON THE TOP	
ONE PENNY	ON THE WAY	P—8
ONE PIECE	ON TIP-TOE	PACK A GUN
ONE POINT	ON VELVET	PACKED UP
ONE POUND	ON WHEELS	PACK IT IN
ONE QUART	OPEN ARMS	PACK IT UP
ONE ROUND	OPEN BOAT	PAGAN GOD
ONE'S DUTY	OPEN BOOK	PAGE FIVE
ONE'S HOST	OPEN CITY	PAGE FOUR
ONE SIXTH	OPEN DOOR	PAGE NINE
ONE SPADE	OPENED UP	PAID BACK
ONE STONE	OPEN EYES	PAID CASH
ONE'S WORD	OPEN FIRE	PAID LESS
ONE TENTH	OPEN GAME	PAID MORE
ONE THIRD	OPEN GATE	PAINT OUT
ONE TRICK	OPEN GOAL	PAINT POT
ONE VERSE	OPEN HAND	PAIRS OFF
ONE VOICE	OPEN LAND	PALE BLUE
ONE WHEEL	OPEN MIND	PALE FACE
ON FRIDAY	OPEN NOTE	PALE PINK
ONLY A FEW	OPEN ROAD	PALL MALL
ONLY HOPE	OPEN SHOP	PALM TREE
ONLY JUST	OPENS OUT	PAPER BAG

PAPER HAT	PER ANNUM	PLAY SAFE
PAPER WAR	PERKED UP	PLAY SNAP
PARDON ME	PETER MAY	PLAYS OFF
PARK LANE	PETER OUT	PLAY SOLO
PART SONG	PETER PAN	PLAY UP TO
PART TIME	PET HOBBY	PLAY WELL
PART WITH	PET NAMES	PLAY WITH
PARTY MAN	PET SHOPS	PLEASE GO
PAR VALUE	PHASE ONE	PLUG AWAY
PASS A LAW	PHASE TWO	PLUM CAKE
PASS AWAY	PHONE BOX	PLUM DUFF
PASS BACK	PIANO KEY	PLUNGE IN
PASS BOOK	PICKED UP	PLUS SIGN
PASS DOWN	PICK IT UP	POINT OUT
PASSED BY	PICKS OFF	POKED FUN
PASSED ON	PICKS OUT	POLE JUMP
PASSED UP	PIG SWILL	POLE STAR
PASS IT ON	PILE ARMS	POLISH UP
PASS OVER	PILE IT ON	POLKA DOT
PAST CURE	PINE AWAY	POLO NECK
PAST HELP	PINE CONE	POLO PONY
PAST HOPE	PINE TREE	PONY CLUB
PAST LIFE	PINK COAT	PONY RACE
PAST TIME	PINK GINS	POOL ROOM
PAST WORK	PINK GLOW	POOLS WIN
PAUL MUNI	PINK SPOT	POOR CAST
PAY A CALL	PIN MONEY	POOR CHAP
PAY A FINE	PINNED IN	POOR CROP
PAY CLAIM	PINNED UP	POOR DEAL
PAY CORPS	PINS DOWN	POOR DEAR
PAY COURT	PINT POTS	POOR FISH
PAY EXTRA	PINT SIZE	POOR FOLK
PAY FOR IT	PIPE DOWN	POOR GAME
PAY PAUSE	PLACE BET	POOR HAND
PAYS BACK	PLAIN BOX	POOR JOHN
PAYS CASH	PLAIN MAN	POOR LAND
PAY SHEET	PLANT OUT	POOR LAWS
PAY WAGES	PLAN WELL	POOR MAKE
PEA GREEN	PLAY AWAY	POOR RATE
PEAK FORM	PLAY BACK	POOR RISK
PEAK HOUR	PLAY BALL	POOR SHOT
PEAR TREE	PLAY DICE	POOR SHOW
PEAT FIRE	PLAY DOWN	POOR SIDE
PEAT MOSS	PLAYED ON	POOR SOIL
PEER GYNT	PLAY FAIR	POOR SOUL
PEGGY LEE	PLAY FLAT	POOR VIEW
PEGS AWAY	PLAY GOLF	POPE JOHN
PEN NAMES	PLAY HARD	POPE PAUL
PENNY BUN	PLAY HIGH	POP MUSIC
PEP PILLS	PLAY HOST	POPPY DAY
PEP TALKS	PLAY POLO	POP SONGS

POP STARS	PUT ABOUT	RAW DEALS
PORE OVER	PUT ASIDE	RAW EDGES
PORK CHOP	PUT FORTH	RAW STEAK
PORK PIES	PUT ON TOP	REACH OUT
PORT ARMS	PUT RIGHT	READ OVER
PORT BEAM	PUTS AWAY	READ WELL
PORT ERIN	PUTS BACK	READY CUT
PORT SAID	PUTS DOWN	READY FOR
PORT SIDE	PUTS OVER	READY PEN
PORT WINE	PUTS UPON	READY WIT
POST FREE	PUT TO BED	REAL GOLD
POT HERBS	PUT TO SEA	REAL LIFE
POT OF JAM	PUT TO USE	REAL SELF
POT OF TEA	PUT-UP JOB	REAL SILK
POT ROAST		REAL TEST
POT SHOTS	**Q—8**	REAR RANK
POURS OUT	QUART POT	REAR VIEW
POWER CUT	QUEEN ANT	RECKON ON
PRESS BOX	QUEEN BEE	RECKON UP
PREY UPON	QUEEN MAB	RED BERET
PRICE CUT	QUEUED UP	RED BERRY
PRICE WAR	QUICK EAR	RED BIDDY
PRIME CUT	QUICK EYE	RED BLOOD
PRIX FIXE	QUICK ONE	RED BRICK
PRO FORMA	QUICK WIT	RED CHINA
PROUD DAY	QUIET END	RED CROSS
PROUD MAN	QUILL PEN	RED FACES
PUB CRAWL	QUITE MAD	RED LABEL
PUB HOURS	QUIT RENT	RED LIGHT
PUFF AWAY	QUIZ GAME	RED MAPLE
PUFFED UP	QUIZ KIDS	RED OCHRE
PULL AWAY	QUIZ TEAM	RED PAINT
PULL BACK	QUO VADIS?	RED PERIL
PULL DOWN		RED PIECE
PULLED IN	**R—8**	RED QUEEN
PULLED UP	RACE AWAY	RED ROSES
PULL HARD	RACE CARD	RED SAILS
PULL OVER	RADIO HAM	RED SHIRT
PULLS OFF	RADIO SET	RED SOCKS
PULLS OUT	RAG DOLLS	RED SPOTS
PUMPED UP	RAG TRADE	RED STAMP
PUPPY FAT	RAIN HARD	RED SUITS
PURE GOLD	RAINY DAY	REEF KNOT
PURE WOOL	RAKE OVER	REELS OFF
PUSH AWAY	RAMS HOME	REG DIXON
PUSH BACK	RANK HIGH	RELY UPON
PUSH DOWN	RARA AVIS	RENT ACTS
PUSH HARD	RARE BIRD	RENT BOOK
PUSH OVER	RARE GIFT	RENT FREE
PUSH PAST	RAT'S TAIL	RENT ROLL
PUSSY CAT	RATTLE ON	REST CAMP

REST CURE	ROAD RACE	RUM START
REST HOME	ROAD SHOW	RUN ABOUT
RHUM BABA	ROAD SIGN	RUN AFTER
RICE CROP	ROAD TEST	RUN AHEAD
RICE DISH	ROAST PIG	RUN ALONG
RICH AUNT	ROB A BANK	RUN A MILE
RICH FARE	ROCK CAKE	RUN AMUCK
RICH FOLK	ROD LAVER	RUN A RACE
RICH FOOD	ROLL BACK	RUN A RISK
RICH HAUL	ROLL CALL	RUN FOR IT
RICH JOKE	ROLLED IN	RUN RISKS
RICH LAND	ROLLED UP	RUN ROUND
RICH MILK	ROLL OVER	RUNS AWAY
RICH SEAM	ROMAN GOD	RUNS BACK
RICH SOIL	ROMAN LAW	RUNS DOWN
RICH VEIN	ROMP HOME	RUNS HARD
RICH WIFE	ROOM MATE	RUN SHORT
RIDE AWAY	ROOT CROP	RUNS INTO
RIDE DOWN	ROOTS OUT	RUNS OVER
RIDE HARD	ROPED OFF	RUNS RIOT
RIDE OVER	ROPE'S END	RUNS WILD
RIGHT ARM	ROSE BOWL	RUN THIRD
RIGHT EAR	ROSE BUSH	RUN TO FAT
RIGHT EYE	ROSE PINK	RUSH AWAY
RIGHT LEG	ROSY GLOW	RUSH HOUR
RIGHT MAN	ROUGH MAP	RUSH INTO
RIGHT OFF	ROUGH OUT	RUSH MATS
RIGHT OUT	ROUGH SEA	RYDER CUP
RIGHT SET	ROUND BOX	RYE BREAD
RIGHT WAY	ROUND OFF	
RING ROAD	ROUND ONE	S—8
RINGS OFF	ROUND PEG	SABRE JET
RINGS OUT	ROUND SIX	SACK RACE
RING TRUE	ROUND SUM	SADDLE UP
RINSE OUT	ROUNDS UP	SAD HEART
RIPE CORN	ROUND TEN	SAD SIGHT
RIPE LIPS	ROUND TIN	SAD SONGS
RISE LATE	ROUND TWO	SAD STORY
RISEN SUN	ROW A RACE	SAD TO SAY
RIVER CAM	ROYAL BOX	SAD WORLD
RIVER DAM	ROYAL OAK	SAFE SEAT
RIVER DEE	RUB ALONG	SAFE SIDE
RIVER DON	RUBBED IN	SAIL AWAY
RIVER EXE	RUB NOSES	SAINT DAY
RIVER GOD	RUBS DOWN	SALAD OIL
RIVER TAY	RUBS IT IN	SALE ROOM
RIVER USK	RUBY LIPS	SALES TAX
RIVER WYE	RUBY PORT	SALT AWAY
ROAD FUND	RUDE WORD	SALT BEEF
ROAD HOGS	RULED OUT	SALT LAKE
ROAD MAPS	RUM PUNCH	SALT MINE

SALT PORK	SEE STARS	SHARP EAR
SAM COSTA	SEIZED UP	SHARP END
SAME DATE	SELF HELP	SHARP EYE
SAME KIND	SELL DEAR	SHARP WIT
SAME MIND	SELLS OFF	SHEER OFF
SAME NAME	SELLS OUT	SHELL OUT
SAME TIME	SELL WELL	SHIN BONE
SAME VEIN	SEND AWAY	SHIP AHOY
SAM SMALL	SEND BACK	SHIP OARS
SAND DUNE	SEND DOWN	SHIP'S LOG
SANK DOWN	SEND HELP	SHOE LANE
SAVE FACE	SEND HOME	SHOE SHOP
SAVE TIME	SEND WORD	SHOO AWAY
SAVING UP	SENNA POD	SHOOT LOW
SAXE BLUE	SENNA TEA	SHOOT OUT
SAY GRACE	SERVE ILL	SHOOTS UP
SCALED UP	SERVE OUT	SHOP BELL
SCENE ONE	SET ABOUT	SHOP GIRL
SCENE TWO	SET AFOOT	SHORT CUT
SCENT OUT	SET APART	SHORT LEG
SCOOP OUT	SET ASIDE	SHORT ONE
SCORE OFF	SET A TRAP	SHORT RUN
SCORE OUT	SET BOOKS	SHOT AWAY
SCOT FREE	SET FORTH	SHOT DEAD
SCOUT OUT	SET GOING	SHOT DOWN
SCRAPE UP	SET IDEAS	SHOT SILK
SCRUB OUT	SET LUNCH	SHOUT OUT
SEA COAST	SET MEALS	SHOVE OFF
SEA FEVER	SET PAPER	SHOW A LEG
SEA FLOOR	SET PIECE	SHOW BOAT
SEA GREEN	SET PLANS	SHOW CASE
SEALED UP	SET POINT	SHOW DOWN
SEA LORDS	SET PRICE	SHOWED UP
SEA NYMPH	SET RIGHT	SHOW FEAR
SEA POWER	SET SCENE	SHOW GIRL
SEA SCOUT	SETS DOWN	SHOWN OFF
SEA SPRAY	SETS FOOT	SHOWN OUT
SEA STORY	SETS FREE	SHOW OVER
SEAT BELT	SET SMILE	SHOW PITY
SEA WATER	SETS SAIL	SHOW ROOM
SEA WINDS	SET STARE	SHRUG OFF
SEE ABOUT	SETS UPON	SHUT DOWN
SEE AFTER	SET TERMS	SHUTS OFF
SEE AHEAD	SETTLE IN	SHUTS OUT
SEED CAKE	SETTLE UP	SHY CHILD
SEE IT ALL	SEVEN MEN	SHY SMILE
SEE IT OUT	SEWER RAT	SHY THING
SEEKS OUT	SHAKEN UP	SHY WOMAN
SEEM REAL	SHAKE OFF	SICK JOKE
SEE NO ONE	SHAKE OUT	SICK LIST
SEES LIFE	SHARE OUT	SICK ROOM

SIDE ARMS	SIZE FOUR	SMELL OUT
SIDE BETS	SIZE NINE	SMOG MASK
SIDE DISH	SKIM OVER	SMOKE OUT
SIDE DOOR	SKIN DEEP	SNACK BAR
SIDE DRUM	SKIN GAME	SNAKE PIT
SIDE GATE	SKIP OVER	SNAP VOTE
SIDE LINE	SKY PILOT	SNATCH UP
SIDE ROAD	SLACK OFF	SNEAK OFF
SIDE SHOW	SLAG HEAP	SNEAK OUT
SIDE VIEW	SLAP DOWN	SNEAKS IN
SIDE WIND	SLEEP OFF	SNEAKS UP
SIDE WITH	SLEEP OUT	SNOWED IN
SIEGE CAP	SLEEPS IN	SNOWED UP
SIGN AWAY	SLEEPS ON	SNOW HILL
SIGNED ON	SLING OFF	SNOW LINE
SIGN HERE	SLING OUT	SNUB NOSE
SIGNS OFF	SLINGS IN	SNUFF BOX
SILK GOWN	SLIP AWAY	SNUFF OUT
SILLY ASS	SLIP BACK	SOBER MAN
SING HIGH	SLIP INTO	SOB STORY
SING SING	SLIP KNOT	SOB STUFF
SINGS OUT	SLIP PAST	SOFT BALL
SINK BACK	SLIPS OFF	SOFTEN UP
SINK DOWN	SLIPS OUT	SOFT EYES
SINN FEIN	SLIT OPEN	SOFT HAIR
SIT ABOUT	SLOG AWAY	SOFT ROES
SIT ERECT	SLOPE OFF	SOFT SEAT
SIT IT OUT	SLOPES UP	SOFT SKIN
SITS BACK	SLOP OVER	SOFT SOAP
SITS DOWN	SLOW BALL	SOFT SPOT
SIT STILL	SLOW BOAT	SOFT TOYS
SIT TIGHT	SLOW DOWN	SOFT WORD
SIT UNDER	SLOWED UP	SOHO FAIR
SITZ BATH	SLOW PACE	SOLD A PUP
SIX CLUBS	SLOW TIME	SOLE HEIR
SIX DOZEN	SLUM AREA	SOLO. CALL
SIX GROSS	SLY JOKES	SOME GOOD
SIX HOLES	SMALL ADS	SOME MORE
SIX HOURS	SMALL BOY	SONG BIRD
SIX MILES	SMALL CAR	SONG HITS
SIX PARTS	SMALL EGG	SONNY BOY
SIX PINTS	SMALL FRY	SON OF GOD
SIX SCORE	SMALL GIN	SORE EYES
SIXTH DAY	SMALL MAN	SORE FEET
SIXTH ROW	SMALL RUM	SORE HEAD
SIXTH TEE	SMALL SUM	SORE NEED
SIX TIMES	SMALL WAY	SORRY END
SIX TO ONE	SMART LAD	SORTS OUT
SIX WEEKS	SMART MAN	SO SIMPLE
SIX YEARS	SMART SET	SOUND BET
SIZE FIVE	SMASH HIT	SOUND BID

SOUND BOX	STANDS UP	ST. PETER'S
SOUND MAN	STAR PART	STRAW HAT
SOUR LOOK	START OFF	STRAY CAT
SOUR MILK	START OUT	STRAY DOG
SOUTH SEA	STARTS UP	STREAK BY
SPACE AGE	STAR TURN	STREAK IN
SPACE MAN	STAVE OFF	STREAM BY
SPACE OUT	STAY AWAY	STREAM IN
SPARE BED	STAY DOWN	STRIKE UP
SPARE MAN	STAYED IN	STRING UP
SPARE RIB	STAYED UP	STRIP OFF
SPARK OFF	STAY HERE	STROLL BY
SPEAK FOR	STAY OPEN	STRUCK ON
SPEAK OUT	STAYS PUT	STRUCK UP
SPEAKS UP	ST. BRIDE'S	STRUNG UP
SPEED COP	ST. DAVID'S	STUD BOOK
SPELL OUT	STEAK PIE	STUD FARM
SPILT INK	STEEL BAR	STUDY ART
SPIN A WEB	STEEL NIB	STUDY LAW
SPINS OUT	STEN GUNS	STUMPS UP
SPLIT PIN	STEP BACK	STUNT MAN
SPLITS UP	STEP DOWN	SUCK EGGS
SPONGE ON	STEP INTO	SUGAR RAY
SPOON FED	STEP IT UP	SUMMED UP
SPOT CASH	STEP ON IT	SUMMON UP
SPRING UP	STEP OVER	SUMS IT UP
SPRUCE UP	STEPS OUT	SUM TOTAL
SPUN GOLD	ST. GEORGE	SUNNY DAY
SPUN SILK	ST. GILES'S	SUNNY JIM
SPUN YARN	ST. HELENA	SUN SPOTS
SQUAD CAR	ST. HELEN'S	SUN'S RAYS
SQUARE UP	ST. HELIER	SURE CURE
STAFF CAR	STICK OUT	SURE GAIN
STAGE ONE	STICKS TO	SURE LOSS
STAGE SET	STICKS UP	SURE SHOT
STAG HUNT	STIFF LEG	SWAN LAKE
STAKE OUT	ST. JAMES'S	SWAN SONG
ST. ALBANS	ST. MORITZ	SWAP NEWS
STALE AIR	STOCK CAR	SWEAR OFF
STALE BUN	STONE AGE	SWEARS IN
STALL OFF	STOP AWAY	SWEEP OUT
STAMP ACT	STOP DEAD	SWEEPS UP
STAMP OUT	STOP HERE	SWEET AIR
STAND FOR	STOP HOME	SWEET PEA
STAND OFF	STOP OVER	SWEET SUE
STAND OUT	STOP PLAY	SWEET TEA
STAND PAT	STOPS OFF	SWELL MOB
ST. ANDREW	STOPS OUT	SWELL OUT
STANDS BY	STOP WORK	SWELLS UP
STANDS IN	STOUT MAN	SWIM SUIT
STANDS TO	STOW AWAY	SWING LOW

SWITCH ON	TAKING IN	TENSED UP
SWOP OVER	TALK A LOT	TENTH DAY
	TALK BACK	TENTH MAN
T—8	TALK BOSH	TENTH ROW
TABBY CAT	TALK DOWN	TENTH TEE
TABLE BAY	TALK OVER	TEN TIMES
TAG ALONG	TALKS BIG	TEN TO ONE
TAIL AWAY	TALK SHOP	TEN TO SIX
TAIL COAT	TALL GIRL	TEN TO TEN
TAIL WIND	TALL TALE	TEN TO TWO
TAJ MAHAL	TALL TALK	TEN WEEKS
TAKE A BOW	TALL TREE	TEN YEARS
TAKE A BUS	TANK TRAP	TERM TIME
TAKE A CAB	TAP DANCE	TEST CASE
TAKE A NAP	TAPER OFF	TEST TUBE
TAKE A NIP	TAP WATER	TEXAS TEA
TAKE A PEW	TAUT ROPE	TEXT BOOK
TAKE A TIP	TAWNY OWL	THANK GOD
TAKE A VOW	TAXI FARE	THANK YOU
TAKE AWAY	TAXI RANK	THAT SIDE
TAKE BACK	TEA BREAK	THE ANDES
TAKE BETS	TEA CADDY	THE ANGEL
TAKE CARE	TEACH ART	THE ASHES
TAKE DOWN	TEA DANCE	THE BELLS
TAKE FIRE	TEA IN BED	THE BENCH
TAKE FOOD	TEAMED UP	THE BIBLE
TAKE HEED	TEAM GAME	THE BLIND
TAKE HOLD	TEAM MATE	THE BLITZ
TAKE IT IN	TEAM WORK	THE BLUES
TAKE IT UP	TEA PARTY	THE BRAVE
TAKE LIFE	TEAR DOWN	THE BRIDE
TAKEN ILL	TEAR IT UP	THE BRINY
TAKEN OFF	TEAR OPEN	THE BRONX
TAKE NOTE	TEA ROSES	THE BUFFS
TAKEN OUT	TEARS OFF	THE BYRDS
TAKE ODDS	TEA SHOPS	THE CHAIR
TAKE OVER	TEDDY BOY	THE CHASE
TAKE PART	TED HEATH	THE CLOTH
TAKE PITY	TEE SHOTS	THE CONGO
TAKE ROOT	TELL A FIB	THE COUNT
TAKES AIM	TELL A LIE	THE CREED
TAKE SILK	TELL LIES	THE CROWN
TAKES OFF	TELLS OFF	THE DALES
TAKES OUT	TEN CENTS	THE DERBY
TAKE THAT	TEN DOZEN	THE DEVIL
TAKE THIS	TEN GROSS	THE DOWNS
TAKE TIME	TEN HOURS	THE DRAMA
TAKE TOLL	TEN MARKS	THE DUTCH
TAKE VOWS	TEN MILES	THE EARTH
TAKE WINE	TEN PARTS	THE ÉLITE
TAKE WING	TEN SCORE	THE ENEMY

THE FACTS	THE TWINS	TIED GAME
THE FATES	THE TWIST	TIGER BAY
THE FIELD	THE URALS	TIGER CUB
THE FILMS	THE USUAL	TIGER RAG
THE FIRST	THE VOLGA	TIGHT FIT
THE FLEET	THE WAITS	TILL THEN
THE FLOOD	THE WAY IN	TILT OVER
THE GOODS	THE WEALD	TIME BOMB
THE GOONS	THE WELSH	TIME CARD
THE GRAVE	THE WILDS	TIME FUSE
THE GREAT	THE WOLDS	TIME IS UP
THE GREYS	THE WORLD	TIME TEST
THE GROOM	THE WORKS	TIME TO GO
THE HAGUE	THE WORST	TIMOR SEA
THE HAVES	THICK EAR	TIN LIZZY
THE HOUSE	THICK FOG	TIN MINES
THE IDEAL	THIN COAT	TINY HAND
THE IDIOT	THIN DOWN	TINY MITE
THE IRISH	THIN EDGE	TINY TOTS
THE JOKER	THIN HAIR	TIPPED UP
THE KINKS	THINK BIG	TIP TO TOE
THE KORAN	THINK FIT	TIP TO WIN
THE LIMIT	THINK OUT	TIRED MAN
THE LOCAL	THINKS UP	TIRED OUT
THE LORDS	THIN SKIN	TIRED TIM
THE LOSER	THIN TIME	TO A FAULT
THE MAFIA	THIN WIRE	TO AND FRO
THE MITRE	THIRD ACT	TO BE SURE
THE MOORS	THIRD DAY	TOBY JUGS
THE MUSES	THIRD MAN	TODDLE IN
THE NORTH	THIRD ROW	TODDLE UP
THE NOVEL	THIRD SET	TOE TO TOE
THE PANEL	THIRD TEE	TOLL CALL
THE POINT	THIS IS IT	TOM BROWN
THE POOLS	THIS SIDE	TOM JONES
THE PRESS	THIS TIME	TOMMY GUN
THE RAINS	THIS WEEK	TOMMY ROT
THE RIGHT	THIS YEAR	TOM PINCH
THE ROPES	THREE MEN	TOM THUMB
THE SHAKE	THROWN IN	TOM WALLS
THE SHORE	THROW OFF	TO MY MIND
THE SOMME	THROW OUT	TONE DEAF
THE SOUTH	THUMBS UP	TONE DOWN
THE SPURS	TICK OVER	TONE POEM
THE STAGE	TICKS OFF	TON-UP BOY
THE STAKE	TIDE MARK	TOO EAGER
THE STARS	TIDE OVER	TOO EARLY
THE SUDAN	TIDIED UP	TOO LARGE
THE THING	TIDY MIND	TOO QUICK
THE TIMES	TIE A KNOT	TOO SHARP
THE TOWER	TIED DOWN	TOO SMALL

TOO STEEP	TRIED OUT	TWIN BEDS
TOOTH OUT	TRIM AWAY	TWIN BOYS
TOP BRASS	TRIP OVER	TWO BRACE
TOP FLOOR	TROOP OFF	TWO BY TWO
TOP LAYER	TROOP OUT	TWO CARDS
TOP MARKS	TROTS OFF	TWO CLUBS
TOP NOTCH	TROTS OUT	TWO DOZEN
TOP NOTES	TRUE BILL	TWO GROSS
TOPPED UP	TRUE BLUE	TWO HANDS
TOP PLACE	TRUE COPY	TWO HEADS
TOP PRICE	TRUE HEIR	TWO HOLES
TOP PRIZE	TRUE LOVE	TWO HOURS
TOP RATES	TRUE TIME	TWO IN ONE
TOP SCORE	TRUE WORD	TWO LUMPS
TOP SPEED	TRY AGAIN	TWO MILES
TOP SPOTS	TRY FOR IT	TWO MINDS
TOP STAIR	TRY IT OUT	TWO PAGES
TOP TABLE	TRY TO SAY	TWO PAIRS
TOP TO TOE	TUCK AWAY	TWO PARTS
TORY GAIN	TUCKED IN	TWO PINTS
TORY LOSS	TUCKED UP	TWO PUTTS
TOSS AWAY	TUCK SHOP	TWO RANKS
TOSSED UP	TUG ALONG	TWO SCORE
TOTAL SUM	TUG OF WAR	TWO SIDES
TOTAL WAR	TURN AWAY	TWO STARS
TOTE A GUN	TURN BACK	TWO TO ONE
TOTE ODDS	TURN BLUE	TWO WEEKS
TO THE BAD	TURN COLD	TWO WIVES
TO THE END	TURN DOWN	TWO WORDS
TO THE TOP	TURNED IN	TWO YARDS
TOT OF RUM	TURNED ON	TWO YEARS
TOTTED UP	TURNED UP	TYPE SIZE
TOTTER UP	TURN GREY	
TOUCH OFF	TURN INTO	U—8
TOUGH GUY	TURN IT IN	UGLY FACE
TOUGH JOB	TURN IT ON	UGLY LOOK
TOUGH NUT	TURN IT UP	UGLY MOOD
TOW ALONG	TURN LEFT	UGLY SCAR
TOWN HALL	TURN OVER	UNCLE MAC
TOWN LIFE	TURN PALE	UNCLE SAM
TOWN TALK	TURNS OFF	UNCLE TOM
TOY MAKER	TURN SOFT	UNCUT GEM
TOY SHOPS	TURN SOUR	UNDER AGE
TOY TRAIN	TURNS OUT	UNDER PAR
TRADE GAP	TURN TAIL	UNDER WAY
TRAIL OFF	TURN UPON	UNTIL NOW
TRAIN SET	TWICE ONE	UPAS TREE
TRAM STOP	TWICE SHY	UP AT DAWN
TRAP FIVE	TWICE SIX	UP IN ARMS
TRAP FOUR	TWICE TEN	UP ON HIGH
TRIAL RUN	TWICE TWO	UPON OATH

UPPER AIR	VINE LEAF	WATER RAT
UPPER CUT	VIVA VOCE	WAT TYLER
UPPER JAW	VIVID RED	WAVE AWAY
UPPER LIP	VOTE DOWN	WAVY HAIR
UPPER SET	VOTE TORY	WAVY LINE
UPPER TEN	VOUCH FOR	WAVY NAVY
UP STREAM		WAX MATCH
UP TO DATE	**W—8**	WAX MERRY
UP TO FORM	WADE INTO	WAX MODEL
UP TO TIME	WAGE BILL	WAX VESTA
UP TO TOWN	WAGED WAR	WAY AHEAD
USED CARS	WAIT A BIT	WEAK CASE
USED HALF	WAITED ON	WEAK CHIN
USED TO IT	WAIT HERE	WEAK EYES
USE FORCE	WAIT UPON	WEAK HEAD
USHER OUT	WALK AWAY	WEAK LINK
USHERS IN	WALK BACK	WEAK SIDE
USUAL WAY	WALK DOWN	WEAK SPOT
UTTER CAD	WALK INTO	WEAK WILL
	WALK OVER	WEAR AWAY
V—8	WALK PAST	WEAR DOWN
VAIN HOPE	WALKS OFF	WEARS OFF
VAIN SHOW	WALKS OUT	WEARS OUT
VAST SIZE	WALLED UP	WEAR WELL
VEER AWAY	WALL GAME	WEIGHS UP
VEER LEFT	WALTZ OUT	WELL AWAY
VERA CRUZ	WANGLE IT	WELL DONE
VERA LYNN	WAN SMILE	WELL HELD
VERSED IN	WANT A LOT	WELL MADE
VERY BEST	WANT MORE	WELL OVER
VERY COLD	WAR CRIME	WELL PAID
VERY DEAR	WAR DANCE	WELL READ
VERY FAIR	WARDS OFF	WELL SAID
VERY FULL	WAR FEVER	WELL TO DO
VERY GOOD	WAR HOUSE	WELL UP IN
VERY HARD	WAR LORDS	WELL USED
VERY KEEN	WARMED UP	WELL WELL!
VERY KIND	WARM OVEN	WENT AWAY
VERY LATE	WARM WORK	WENT BACK
VERY MANY	WAR PAINT	WENT DOWN
VERY MUCH	WAR PARTY	WENT EAST
VERY NEAR	WAR POEMS	WENT FREE
VERY NICE	WAR SCARE	WENT OVER
VERY POOR	WART HOGS	WENT WELL
VERY RICH	WAR YEARS	WENT WEST
VERY SLOW	WASH AWAY	WEST DOOR
VERY SOFT	WASH DOWN	WEST SIDE
VERY SOON	WASHED UP	WEST WIND
VERY TRUE	WATCH OUT!	WEST WING
VERY WARM	WATER ICE	WET PAINT
VERY WELL	WATER JUG	WET PLATE

WET SHEET	WINDY DAY	YEAR BOOK
WET SPELL	WINE BARS	YEARN FOR
WHALE OIL	WINE GUMS	YEARS AGO
WHAT A FAG	WINE LIST	YES AND NO
WHAT IS IT?	WINE SHOP	YET AGAIN
WHAT NEXT?	WING HALF	YOGI BEAR
WHAT OF IT?	WIN GLORY	YOU AND ME
WHAT'S NEW?	WIN MONEY	YOUNG BOY
WHEEL OFF	WINS OVER	YOUNG MAN
WHEEL OUT	WIPE AWAY	YOUNG ONE
WHICH WAY?	WIPED OUT	YOUR CALL
WHIP HAND	WIRE MESH	YOUR DEAL
WHISK OFF	WISE GUYS	YOUR MOVE
WHITE ANT	WISE HEAD	YOUR TURN
WHITE EGG	WISE MOVE	YULE LOGS
WHITE HOT	WITH CARE	
WHITE KEY	WITH EASE	**Z—8**
WHITE LIE	WITH LOVE	ZANE GREY
WHITE MAN	WITTY MAN	ZERO HOUR
WHITE SEA	WOLF CALL	
WHITE TIE	WOLF CUBS	**A—9**
WHIT WEEK	WOOD FIRE	AARON'S ROD
WHO DUN IT?	WOOD PULP	A BIT FISHY
WHOLE HOG	WORD GAME	A BIT STEEP
WHOLE LOT	WORKED UP	A BIT STIFF
WHO'S NEXT?	WORK EVIL	A BIT THICK
WHY WORRY?	WORK HARD	ABLE TO FLY
WIDE BALL	WORK LATE	ABLE TO PAY
WIDE BOYS	WORK OVER	ABOUT FACE
WIDE FAME	WORKS OFF	ABOUT TIME
WIDE GULF	WORKS OUT	ABOUT TURN
WIDE OPEN	WORKS WELL	ABOVE ZERO
WIDE ROAD	WORLD WAR	ACID REPLY
WIDE VIEW	WORN DOWN	ACKER BILK
WILD BIRD	WRAP IT UP	ACT AS HOST
WILD BLOW	WRING DRY	ACTED WELL
WILD BOAR	WRING OUT	ACT FAIRLY
WILD DUCK	WRITE OFF	ACTING FOR
WILD FOWL	WRITE OUT	ACT OF LOVE
WILD GOAT	WRITES UP	ACT WISELY
WILD LIFE	WRONG DAY	ACUTE PAIN
WILD LOOK	WRONG MAN	ADAM FAITH
WILD OATS	WRONG WAY	ADAM SMITH
WILD ROSE	WRY SMILE	ADAM STYLE
WILD TALK	WYCH ELMS	ADAM'S WINE
WILD WEST		ADD A RIDER
WILD WIND	**X—8**	ADD A TOUCH
WILY BIRD	X-RAY UNIT	ADD COLOUR
WIN A GAME		ADD FRILLS
WIN A RACE	**Y—8**	ADDLED EGG
WIND SOCK	YALE LOCK	AD NAUSEAM

A DOG'S LIFE	ALL THE WAY	ART DEALER
AD VALOREM	ALL THUMBS	ART EDITOR
AEGEAN SEA	ALL TIED UP	ARTIE SHAW
AER LINGUS	ALMA COGAN	ART MASTER
AFTER DARK	ALMA MATER	ART MUSEUM
AFTER TIME	ALMOND OIL	ART SCHOOL
AGILE MIND	ALMOST ALL	ART STUDIO
A GOOD DEAL	ALPHA PLUS	AS A RESULT
A GOOD MANY	ALPHA RAYS	ASCOT MILE
AGREE WITH	AMPLE ROOM	ASCOT WEEK
AHOY THERE	AMPLE TIME	ASH BLONDE
AIMED HIGH	ANDY PANDY	ASIA MINOR
AIM HIGHER	ANGEL CAKE	AS IT COMES
AIM TO KILL	ANGEL FACE	ASK ADVICE
AIR BATTLE	ANGEL FISH	ASK A PRICE
AIR LETTER	ANGORA CAT	ASK NICELY
AIR LOSSES	ANGRY LOOK	ASK PARDON
AIR POCKET	ANIMAL CRY	ASK THE WAY
AIR TRAVEL	ANIMAL FAT	AS ORDERED
ALARM BELL	ANIMAL OIL	ASPEN LEAF
ALARM CALL	ANITA LOOS	AS PER PLAN
ALEC WAUGH	ANKLE DEEP	AS PLANNED
ALERT MIND	ANNUAL FEE	AS THEY SAY
ALFIE BASS	ANY MOMENT	AT A CANTER
ALICE BAND	ANY OFFERS?	AT A GALLOP
ALIEN CORN	ANY TO COME	AT A GLANCE
ALIEN RACE	APPIAN WAY	AT A LOW EBB
ALL ABOARD	APPLE A DAY	AT AN ANGLE
ALL ACTION	APPLE CART	AT ANY RATE
ALL ADRIFT	APPLE TART	AT ANY TIME
ALL AGREED	APPLE TREE	AT A PROFIT
ALL AROUND	APRIL FOOL	AT LEISURE
ALL ASHORE	ARAB HORSE	AT LIBERTY
ALL AT ONCE	ARAB STEED	AT LOW TIDE
ALL BEHIND	ARCH ENEMY	ATOMIC AGE
ALL BLACKS	ARCH KNAVE	ATOMIC WAR
ALL BUT ONE	ARCH ROGUE	AT ONE BLOW
ALL CHANGE	ARCH SMILE	AT ONE TIME
ALL COMERS	AREA STEPS	AT PRESENT
ALL FOR ONE	ARID WASTE	AT THE BACK
ALL IN VAIN	ARMED BAND	AT THE BANK
ALL IS LOST	ARMS DEPOT	AT THE BEST
ALL IS WELL	ARMS LOWER	AT THE DOOR
ALL ON DECK	ARMS RAISE	AT THE FAIR
ALL ON EDGE	ARMY BOOTS	AT THE HEAD
ALLOW BAIL	ARMY CADET	AT THE HELM
ALL SAINTS	ARMY CORPS	AT THE MAIN
ALL SERENE	ARMY GROUP	AT THE MOST
ALL SQUARE	ARMY ISSUE	AT THE NETS
ALL THE DAY	ARNOLD BAX	AT THE OVAL
ALL THE LOT	ART CRITIC	AT THE PEAK

AT THE POST
AT THE REAR
AT THE SIDE
AT THE TIME
ATTIC SALT
AUGUR WELL
AU NATUREL
AUNT SALLY
AWAY MATCH
AZURE BLUE

B—9
BABY GRAND
BABY LINEN
BACK AGAIN
BACK ALLEY
BACK BACON
BACKED OUT
BACK OUT OF
BACK PEDAL
BACK SLANG
BACK STAGE
BACK TEETH
BACK TOOTH
BACK WATER
BACK WHEEL
BACON RIND
BAD ADVICE
BAD ATTACK
BAD CREDIT
BAD CUSTOM
BAD DRIVER
BAD ENOUGH
BAD EXCUSE
BAD FIGURE
BAD FOR ONE
BAD FRIEND
BAD HABITS
BAD HEALTH
BAD HUMOUR
BAD INTENT
BADLY DONE
BADLY DOWN
BADLY HURT
BAD MARKET
BAD MEMORY
BAD PLAYER
BAD POINTS
BAD POLICY
BAD RECORD
BAD REPORT

BAD REPUTE
BAD RESULT
BAD REVIEW
BAD SAILOR
BAD SCRAPE
BAD SEAMAN
BAD SECOND
BAD SPIRIT
BAD TEMPER
BAD TIMING
BAG OF GOLD
BAG O' NAILS
BAG THE LOT
BAKE A CAKE
BAKE A LOAF
BAKE BREAD
BALANCE UP
BALD FACTS
BALD PATCH
BALD TRUTH
BALLET FAN
BALLOT BOX
BALSA WOOD
BALTIC SEA
BAND WAGON
BANDY LEGS
BANK CLERK
BANK PAPER
BARE FACTS
BARE FISTS
BARE KNEES
BARE TRUTH
BARE WALLS
BARE WORDS
BARGE INTO
BARLEY MOW
BAR MAGNET
BARN DANCE
BAR OF IRON
BAR OF SOAP
BARROW BOY
BAR THE WAY
BASE METAL
BASIC NEED
BASIC PLAN
BASIC WAGE
BAS RELIEF
BASS NOTES
BASS VOICE
BATH BRICK
BATH NIGHT

BATH SALTS
BATH TOWEL
BATH WATER
BATTLE CRY
BAY LEAVES
BAY WINDOW
BEACH SUIT
BEACH WEAR
BE ADVISED
BE A MARTYR
BE AN ANGEL
BEAR FRUIT
BEARING UP
BEAR RIGHT
BE AT A LOSS
BE AT FAULT
BEAT MUSIC
BEAU GESTE
BEAU IDEAL
BEAU MONDE
BE A YES-MAN
BE CAREFUL
BE CERTAIN
BECOME DUE
BECOME ONE
BEDDED OUT
BED OF PAIN
BED SHEETS
BEECH TREE
BEEF CURRY
BEER MONEY
BEER ON TAP
BEER STAIN
BEET SUGAR
BEFORE ALL
BEFORE NOW
BEFORE TEA
BE FRIENDS
BEGGED OFF
BEG IN VAIN
BEGIN WELL
BEGIN WORK
BEG PARDON
BEL ESPRIT
BELL METAL
BELL TOWER
BELOW COST
BELOW ZERO
BELT ALONG
BEN JONSON
BEN LOMOND

BENNY HILL	BITING WIT	BLOOD CLOT
BE ONE'S AGE	BIT OF A JOB	BLOOD FEUD
BE ONESELF	BIT OF A LAD	BLOOD HEAT
BE ON GUARD	BIT OF LUCK	BLOOD TEST
BE PRESENT	BITTER CUP	BLOOD TYPE
BE PRUDENT	BITTER END	BLOW A FUSE
BERTA RUCK	BLACK ARTS	BLOW ALONG
BERYL GREY	BLACK BALL	BLOWING UP
BERYL REID	BLACK BEAR	BLUE ANGEL
BE SERIOUS	BLACK BELT	BLUE BLOOD
BEST CHINA	BLACK BESS	BLUE CHIPS
BEST DRESS	BLACK BOOK	BLUE GRASS
BEST ENTRY	BLACK FLAG	BLUE JEANS
BEST GRADE	BLACK GOLD	BLUE LIGHT
BEST OF ALL	BLACK HAIR	BLUE MOVIE
BEST SCORE	BLACK HAND	BLUE PAINT
BEST TASTE	BLACK HOLE	BLUE PETER
BEST THING	BLACK JACK	BLUE PRINT
BEST VALUE	BLACK KING	BLUE RINSE
BE SWEET ON	BLACK LACE	BLUE SKIES
BÊTE NOIRE	BLACK LEAD	BLUE SOCKS
BE THE BEST	BLACK LION	BLUE STAMP
BETTER MAN	BLACK LIST	BLUE STEEL
BETTER OFF	BLACK LOOK	BLUE STORY
BETTER 'OLE	BLACK MARK	BLUE WATER
BETWEEN US	BLACK MASS	BLUE WHALE
BEVIN BOYS	BLACK MONK	BLUNT EDGE
BEYOND ONE	BLACK MOOD	BOARD A BUS
BIG BERTHA	BLACK NOTE	BOARDED UP
BIG CHANCE	BLACK OPAL	BOARD GAME
BIG CHEESE	BLACK PAWN	BOARD ROOM
BIG DEMAND	BLACK ROOK	BO'AR'S HEAD
BIG DIPPER	BLACK RUIN	BOAT DRILL
BIG EFFORT	BLACK SPOT	BOAT TRAIN
BIG FREEZE	BLACK SUIT	BOB SAWYER
BIG HEADED	BLACK SWAN	BODY OF MEN
BIG MARGIN	BLANK FILE	BOIL AN EGG
BIG PROFIT	BLANK LOOK	BOILED EGG
BIG TALKER	BLANK MIND	BOILED HAM
BILL SIKES	BLANK PAGE	BOLD FRONT
BILLY FURY	BLANK WALL	BOLD LINES
BILLY GOAT	BLAZE AWAY	BOLD PRINT
BILLY LIAR	BLIND DATE	BOLSTER UP
BINGO CLUB	BLIND ROAD	BONA FIDES
BINGO HALL	BLIND SIDE	BON CHANCE
BIRCH TREE	BLIND SPOT	BONE CHINA
BIRD BRAIN	BLOCK PERM	BON MARCHÉ
BIRD'S NEST	BLOCK VOTE	BON VIVANT
BIRTH MARK	BLOND HAIR	BON VIVEUR
BIRTH RATE	BLOOD BANK	BON VOYAGE
BITE TO EAT	BLOOD BATH	BOOK A ROOM

BOOK A SEAT
BOOK LOVER
BOOK OF JOB
BOOK SEATS
BOOK STORE
BOOK TITLE
BOOK TOKEN
BORE A HOLE
BORN ACTOR
BORN AGAIN
BORN ALIVE
BORN MIMIC
BORN MIXER
BORN SLAVE
BOTANY BAY
BOTH HANDS
BOTH SIDES
BOTTOM DOG
BOTTOMS UP
BOUGHT OFF
BOUGHT OUT
BOUNCE OUT
BOUND BOOK
BOUND OVER
BOWED DOWN
BOWED HEAD
BOWL ALONG
BOWLED OUT
BOWLER HAT
BOW STREET
BOW TO FATE
BOW WINDOW
BOX AND COX
BOX CAMERA
BOX CLEVER
BOXING DAY
BOX NUMBER
BOX OFFICE
BOX OF FIGS
BOY FRIEND
BOYLE'S LAW
BRAIN WAVE
BRAKE DRUM
BRANCH OFF
BRANCH OUT
BRASS BALL
BRASS BAND
BRASS RING
BRASS TACK
BRAVE DEED
BRAVE FACE

BRAZEN OUT
BRAZIL NUT
BREAD LINE
BREAD ROLL
BREAK A LEG
BREAK AWAY
BREAK BACK
BREAK BAIL
BREAK CAMP
BREAK DOWN
BREAK EVEN
BREAK IT UP
BREAK JAIL
BREAK OPEN
BREAK STEP
BREATHE IN
BRENDA LEE
BRET HARTE
BRIAR PIPE
BRICK WALL
BRIDAL BED
BRIDE TO BE
BRIGHT BOY
BRIGHT LAD
BRIGHT RED
BRING BACK
BRING DOWN
BRING HOME
BRING OVER
BRING WORD
BRISK WALK
BRISTLE UP
BROAD BACK
BROAD BEAM
BROAD BEAN
BROAD GRIN
BROAD HINT
BROAD JOKE
BROAD MIND
BROAD VIEW
BROKEN ARM
BROKEN LEG
BROKEN MAN
BROKEN RIB
BROKEN SET
BROKE OPEN
BRONZE AGE
BROOD MARE
BROODY HEN
BROUGHT UP
BROWN BEAR

BROWN BESS
BROWN COAL
BROWN EYES
BROWN HAIR
BROWN LOAF
BROWN STEW
BROWN SUIT
BRUSH AWAY
BRUSHED UP
BRUSH DOWN
BRUSH OVER
BRUSH PAST
BUBBLE CAR
BUBBLE GUM
BUCK TEETH
BUDGET DAY
BUGLE CALL
BULLY BEEF
BUMBLE BEE
BUMPED OFF
BUNNY GIRL
BURKE'S LAW
BURMA ROAD
BURMA STAR
BURN A HOLE
BURN ALIVE
BURNT CORK
BURNT DOWN
BURST OPEN
BURST PIPE
BURST TYRE
BUS DRIVER
BUSH HOUSE
BUSH SHIRT
BUS STRIKE
BUS TICKET
BUSY PLACE
BUY A HOUSE
BUY A ROUND
BUY ON TICK
BUY SHARES
BUZZ ABOUT
BUZZ ALONG
BY ACCLAIM
BY AIR MAIL
BY AUCTION
BY COMMAND
BY CONSENT
BY DEFAULT
BY DEGREES
BY HERSELF

BY HIMSELF
BY NO MEANS
BY NUMBERS
BY ONESELF
BY REQUEST
BY STEALTH
BY THE ACRE
BY THE BOOK
BY THE HOUR
BY THE NOSE
BY THE YARD
BY THUNDER

C—9
CAB DRIVER
CADDIE CAR
CAFE ROYAL
CALF'S HEAD
CALL AGAIN
CALL A HALT
CALL A TAXI
CALLED FOR
CALLED OFF
CALLED OUT
CALL FORTH
CALL HEADS
CALL IT OFF
CALL TAILS
CALM CHEEK
CAME APART
CAME LOOSE
CAMERA SHY
CAMPED OUT
CANAL BANK
CANAL TURN
CANAL ZONE
CANCEL OUT
CANE CHAIR
CANE SUGAR
CANNY SCOT
CAN OF BEER
CAPE DUTCH
CAPE WRATH
CAP IN HAND
CARD INDEX
CARD PARTY
CARD SENSE
CARD TABLE
CARD TRICK
CARGO SHIP
CAROL REED

CARPET BAG
CARRIED ON
CARRY AWAY
CARRY OVER
CARRY SAIL
CAR TRIALS
CAR WINDOW
CARY GRANT
CASHEW NUT
CASH PRICE
CASH PRIZE
CASH TERMS
CAST ABOUT
CAST A LOOK
CAST AN EYE
CAST A SHOE
CAST A SHOW
CAST ASIDE
CAST A SLUR
CAST A VOTE
CAST DOUBT
CAST FORTH
CAST LOOSE
CASTOR OIL
CAT AND DOG
CATCH A BUS
CATCH COLD
CATCH FIRE
CATCH FISH
CAT FAMILY
CATTLE PEN
CAUGHT OUT
CAUSE LIST
CAUSE PAIN
CEASE FIRE
CEASE TO BE
CEASE WORK
CEDAR TREE
CEYLON TEA
CHA CHA CHA
CHAIN DOWN
CHAIN GANG
CHAIN MAIL
CHALKED UP
CHALK FARM
CHALK IT UP
CHANCE HIT
CHASE AWAY
CHEAP FARE
CHEAP GIFT
CHEAP JACK

CHEAP LINE
CHEAP MILK
CHEAP RATE
CHEAP TRIP
CHEAP WINE
CHECK MATE
CHECK OVER
CHEERED UP
CHERRY PIE
CHESS CLUB
CHIEF COOK
CHIEF HOPE
CHIEF MEAL
CHIEF PART
CHIEF PORT
CHIEF WHIP
CHILD CARE
CHILD STAR
CHILD WIFE
CHINA CLAY
CHINA DOLL
CHINA ROSE
CHINA SHOP
CHIPPED IN
CHOICE BIT
CHOKE BACK
CHOKE DAMP
CHOKE DOWN
CHOP HOUSE
CHOPPY SEA
CHOSEN FEW
CHUMP CHOP
CIRCUS ACT
CITY GATES
CITY STATE
CIVIC DUTY
CIVIL CASE
CIVIL CODE
CIVIL LIFE
CIVIL LIST
CIVIL SUIT
CLAIM BACK
CLAMP DOWN
CLAP HANDS
CLARA BUTT
CLARET CUP
CLASH WITH
CLEAN BILL
CLEAN BLOW
CLEAN DOWN
CLEANED UP

CLEAN LIFE	COIN MONEY	CONJURE UP
CLEAR AWAY	COLD AS ICE	COOL CHEEK
CLEAR CASE	COLD BLOOD	COOL DRINK
CLEARED UP	COLD CREAM	COOLED OFF
CLEAR HEAD	COLD DRINK	COOL WATER
CLEAR LEAD	COLD FRAME	COPIED OUT
CLEAR MIND	COLD FRONT	COPPER AGE
CLEAR NOTE	COLD HANDS	CORAL REEF
CLEAR ROAD	COLD HEART	CORDON OFF
CLEAR SOUP	COLD JOINT	CORNY JOKE
CLEAR VIEW	COLD NIGHT	COSMIC RAY
CLEVER DOG	COLD PLATE	COST PRICE
CLEVER MAN	COLD SCENT	COUGHED UP
CLIMB DOWN	COLD SNACK	COUNT DOWN
CLIMB OVER	COLD SOBER	COUNT UPON
CLIP JOINT	COLD SPELL	COUP D'ÉTAT
CLOCHE HAT	COLD STEEL	COURT CARD
CLOCKED IN	COLD SWEAT	COURT CASE
CLOCK GOLF	COLD WATER	COVERED UP
CLOG DANCE	COLLIE DOG	COVER GIRL
CLOSE CALL	COLOUR BAR	COVER OVER
CLOSE COPY	COLWYN BAY	COWES WEEK
CLOSE CROP	COME ABOUT	CRAB SALAD
CLOSED CAR	COME AFTER	CRACK A NUT
CLOSE DOWN	COME ALIVE	CRACKED UP
CLOSE GAME	COME ALONG	CRACK OPEN
CLOSE LOOK	COME AND GO	CRACK SHOT
CLOSE RACE	COME APART	CRASH DOWN
CLOSE UPON	COME CLEAN	CRAZY GANG
CLOSING IN	COME CLOSE	CREAM CAKE
CLOTH EARS	COME EARLY	CREAM PUFF
CLOTH FAIR	COME FIRST	CREEP AWAY
CLOUD OVER	COME FORTH	CRESTA RUN
CLOUDY SKY	COME LOOSE	CRIED DOWN
CLUB MONEY	COME OF AGE	CRIED WOLF
CLUB NIGHT	COME OFF IT	CRIME WAVE
COACH TOUR	COME RIGHT	CROPPED UP
COACH TRIP	COME ROUND	CROSS FIRE
COAL BLACK	COME THIRD	CROSS KEYS
COAL BOARD	COME UNDER	CROSS OVER
COAL FIELD	COMIC CUTS	CROSS WIND
COAL TRUCK	COMIC MASK	CROUCH END
COAST ROAD	COMIC MUSE	CROUCH LOW
COCKED HAT	COMIC SONG	CROWD WORK
COCK ROBIN	COMING MAN	CROWN CORK
COCOA BEAN	COMING OUT	CROWN LAND
CODE OF LAW	COMMON END	CROW'S FEET
COFFEE BAR	COMMON LAW	CROW'S NEST
COFFEE CUP	COMMON LOT	CRUDE JOKE
COFFEE POT	COMMON MAN	CRUDE SALT
COIN A WORD	CONGER EEL	CRUEL BLOW

CRUEL FATE
CRUMPLE UP
CRUSH DOWN
CRY FOR JOY
CUBAN HEEL
CUBE SUGAR
CUBIC FOOT
CUBIC INCH
CUBIC YARD
CUB MASTER
CUFF LINKS
CUPID'S BOW
CUP OF MILK
CURIO SHOP
CURTAIN UP
CURTIS CUP
CURLY HAIR
CURLY KALE
CUT A CAPER
CUT ACROSS
CUT ADRIFT
CUT AND RUN
CUT A TOOTH
CUT CAPERS
CUT IN HALF
CUT IT FINE
CUTTING IN
CUTTY SARK
CUT UP WELL
CYCLE TOUR

D—9
DAILY HELP
DAILY MAIL
DAILY WORK
DAIRY FARM
DAIRY HERD
DAIRY MAID
DAISY BELL
DALAI LAMA
DAMP PATCH
DAMP SQUIB
DAMSON JAM
DAN ARCHER
DANCE A JIG
DANCE AWAY
DANCE BAND
DANCE HALL
DANCE STEP
DANCE TUNE
DANDY DICK

DANNY KAYE
DARK BLUES
DARK BROWN
DARK CLOUD
DARK DEEDS
DARK DRESS
DARK GREEN
DARK HORSE
DARK NIGHT
DARTED OUT
DARTS TEAM
DASHED OFF
DASHED OUT
DATE STAMP
DATUM LINE
DAVY JONES
DAWN OF DAY
DAY BEFORE
DAY IS DONE
DAY OF DOOM
DAY OF REST
DAY SCHOOL
DAYS OF OLD
DEAD AHEAD
DEAD DRUNK
DEAD FAINT
DEAD LUCKY
DEADLY SIN
DEAD MARCH
DEAD QUIET
DEAD RIGHT
DEAD SLEEP
DEAD SOBER
DEAD TIRED
DEAD WATER
DEAD WRONG
DEAL A BLOW
DEAL TABLE
DEAN SWIFT
DEAR ENEMY
DEAR HEART
DEAR MADAM
DEATH BLOW
DEATH CELL
DEATH DUTY
DEATH MASK
DEATH RATE
DEATH ROLL
DEATH TRAP
DEATH WISH
DEBIT SIDE

DECK GAMES
DECOY DUCK
DEEP GRIEF
DEEP RIVER
DEEP SLEEP
DEEP SOUTH
DEEP VOICE
DEEP WATER
DEMON KING
DEN OF VICE
DEPOT ONLY
DEPOT SHIP
DE QUINCEY
DEREK BOND
DEREK HART
DE RIGUEUR
DESERT AIR
DESERT RAT
DEVIL'S OWN
DIANA DORS
DIESEL OIL
DIET SHEET
DIG DEEPLY
DIME NOVEL
DIM MEMORY
DINING CAR
DINING OUT
DINNER SET
DIRECT HIT
DIRECT TAX
DIRT CHEAP
DIRT TRACK
DIRTY DICK
DIRTY LOOK
DIRTY PLAY
DIRTY WORD
DIRTY WORK
DISH CLOUT
DISHED OUT
DISH OF TEA
DIXIE LAND
DO A BAD JOB
DO A FAVOUR
DO AS ASKED
DOCK BRIEF
DOCK GREEN
DOCTOR WHO
DODGE CITY
DOG COLLAR
DOG EAT DOG
DOG KENNEL

DOG RACING
DOGS OF WAR
DOG'S TOOTH
DOING FINE
DOING GOOD
DOING TIME
DOING WELL
DO IT AGAIN
DO JUSTICE
DOLLAR GAP
DOLL'S PRAM
DOLLY BIRD
DONE BROWN
DONE THING
DO NOTHING
DON'T WORRY
DO ONE DOWN
DO ONE'S BIT
DOPE FIEND
DO PENANCE
DORA BRYAN
DO REPAIRS
DORSAL FIN
DO THE DEED
DO THE TOWN
DO TO DEATH
DOUBLE ACT
DOUBLE BED
DOUBLED UP
DOUBLE GIN
DOUBLE ONE
DOUBLE ROW
DOUBLE RUM
DOUBLE SIX
DOUBLE TEN
DOUBLE TOP
DOUBLE TWO
DOVER ROAD
DOVER SOLE
DO WITHOUT
DOWN BELOW
DOWN GRADE
DOWN IN ONE
DOWN IN TWO
DOWN QUILT
DOWN RIVER
DOWN SOUTH
DOWN STAGE
DOWN THERE
DOWN TOOLS
DOWN TRAIN

DOWN UNDER
DO YOU MIND?
DRAIN AWAY
DRAW A BEAD
DRAW A LINE
DRAW APART
DRAW A VEIL
DRAW BLANK
DRAW BLOOD
DRAW FORTH
DRAW LEVEL
DRAW MONEY
DRAWN FACE
DRAWN GAME
DRAW TEARS
DRAW TIGHT
DRAW WATER
DRAY HORSE
DREAM BOAT
DREAM GIRL
DREAM LAND
DRESS COAT
DRESS DOWN
DRESSED UP
DRESS RING
DRESS SHOW
DRESS SUIT
DRESS WELL
DRIED EGGS
DRIED FIGS
DRIED MILK
DRIED PEAS
DRIFT AWAY
DRILL HALL
DRINK DEEP
DRIVE A BUS
DRIVE A CAR
DRIVE AWAY
DRIVE BACK
DRIVE HARD
DRIVE HOME
DRIVEN MAD
DRIVE PAST
DR. JOHNSON
DR. KILDARE
DROP A BOMB
DROP A HINT
DROP A LINE
DROP A NOTE
DROP OF GIN
DROP OF TEA

DROPPED IN
DROP SHORT
DRUG FIEND
DRUG HABIT
DRUG STORE
DRUM MAJOR
DRURY LANE
DRY AS DUST
DRY GINGER
DRY HUMOUR
DRY REMARK
DRY SEASON
DRY SHERRY
DRY SUMMER
DRY WICKET
DUBLIN BAY
DUD CHEQUE
DUDE RANCH
DUE NOTICE
DUE REWARD
DULL LIGHT
DULL SOUND
DU MAURIER
DUNCE'S CAP
DUST STORM
DUSTY ROAD
DUTCH BARN
DUTCH DOLL
DUTCH OVEN
DUTCH WIFE
DUTY BOUND
DUTY CALLS
DUTY FIRST
DUTY NURSE
DWARF BEAN
DWELL UPON
DYING DOWN
DYING DUCK
DYING RACE
DYING SWAN
DYING TO GO
DYING WISH
DYING YEAR

E—9
EACH OF TWO
EACH OTHER
EARLY BIRD
EARLY CALL
EARLY DAYS
EARLY DOOR

EARLY HOUR
EARLY LIFE
EARLY PART
EARLY WORM
EARN A NAME
EARN MONEY
EAR OF CORN
EASILY LED
EAST COAST
EASTER DAY
EASTER EGG
EASTER EVE
EAST INDIA
EAST LYNNE
EAST SHEEN
EASY AS PIE
EASY CATCH
EASY DEATH
EASY FIRST
EASY GOING
EASY MONEY
EASY PITCH
EASY TERMS
EASY THING
EASY TIMES
EASY TO RUN
EASY TO SEE
EATEN AWAY
EATING OUT
EAT NO MEAT
EDGED TOOL
EDGE ROUND
EDGE TOOLS
EIGHT DAYS
EIGHT DEEP
EIGHT FEET
EIGHTH DAY
EIGHTH MAN
EIGHTH ROW
EIGHTH TEE
EIGHT QUID
EITHER WAY
EL ALAMEIN
ELBOW ROOM
ELDER WINE
ELDEST SON
ELEVEN MEN
ELMER RICE
EMBER DAYS
EMILE ZOLA
EMIT WAVES

EMPIRE DAY
EMPTY LIFE
EMPTY ROOM
EMPTY SEAT
EMPTY SHOW
EMPTY TALK
EMPTY TANK
END IN GAOL
END IN VIEW
END OF PLAY
END OF TERM
END OF TIME
ENEMY FIRE
EN FAMILLE
ENJOY LIFE
EN PASSANT
EN PENSION
EN RAPPORT
ENTER INTO
ENTRE NOUS
ENTRY CARD
ENTRY FORM
EPIC VERSE
EQUAL RANK
ERIC SYKES
ERRAND BOY
ESKIMO DOG
ESTATE CAR
ET TU BRUTE
EVA BARTOK
EVEN MONEY
EVEN SCORE
EVEN TENOR
EVER AFTER
EVER SINCE
EVERY HOUR
EVERY INCH
EVERY SIDE
EVERY TIME
EVERY WEEK
EVERY WORD
EVERY YEAR
EXACT COPY
EXACT FARE
EXACT TIME
EXIT OMNES
EX OFFICIO
EXTRA COPY
EXTRA FOOD
EXTRA GOOD
EXTRA HELP

EXTRA ROOM
EXTRA SEAT
EXTRA TIME
EXTRA WORK
EYE APPEAL
EYE LOTION
EYE MAKE-UP
EYES FRONT
EYES RIGHT
EYE STRAIN
EZRA POUND

F—9

FACE ABOUT
FACE CREAM
FACE DEATH
FACE FACTS
FACE IT OUT
FACE NORTH
FACE SOUTH
FACE TOWEL
FACE VALUE
FADING OUT
FAGGED OUT
FAIL TO ACT
FAIL TO SEE
FAIL TO WIN
FAINT HOPE
FAINT LINE
FAIR BREAK
FAIR FIELD
FAIR FIGHT
FAIR JUDGE
FAIRLY NEW
FAIR OFFER
FAIR PRICE
FAIR'S FAIR
FAIR SHARE
FAIR START
FAIR TRADE
FAIR TRIAL
FAIR VALUE
FAIR WORDS
FAIRY CAKE
FAIRY DOLL
FAIRY FOLK
FAIRY KING
FAIRY RING
FAIRY TALE
FAIRY WAND

FAITH CURE	FATAL URGE	FIGURE TWO
FAKE ALIBI	FAT CATTLE	FILE A SUIT
FALL AMONG	FAT CHANCE	FILM ACTOR
FALL APART	FAT PROFIT	FILM EXTRA
FALLEN OUT	FEED A COLD	FILM STILL
FALL FOR IT	FEEL A NEED	FILM STUNT
FALL OF MAN	FEEL ANGRY	FILTER TIP
FALL SHORT	FEEL CHEAP	FINAL BOUT
FALL UNDER	FEEL FAINT	FINAL HEAT
FALSE CARD	FEEL FRESH	FINAL HOPE
FALSE CASE	FEEL FUNNY	FINAL MOVE
FALSE COIN	FEEL GIDDY	FINALS DAY
FALSE GODS	FEEL GREAT	FINAL STEP
FALSE HAIR	FEEL HAPPY	FINAL TEST
FALSE IDEA	FEEL QUEER	FIND A CLUE
FALSE MOVE	FEEL RIGHT	FIND A FLAT
FALSE NAME	FEEL SEEDY	FIND A HOME
FALSE NOSE	FEEL SHAME	FIND A WIFE
FALSE NOTE	FEEL SMALL	FIND FAULT
FALSE OATH	FEEL SORRY	FIND MEANS
FALSE PLEA	FEE SIMPLE	FIND PEACE
FALSE STEP	FEET APART	FIND WORDS
FAMILY CAR	FEET FIRST	FINE BIRDS
FAMILY MAN	FELL APART	FINE BLADE
FAMILY PEW	FELT A FOOL	FINE GRAIN
FAMILY ROW	FELT SILLY	FINE LINEN
FAMOUS MAN	FEMALE SEX	FINE POINT
FANCY CAKE	FEMME SOLE	FINE SPORT
FANCY FREE	FENCED OUT	FINE SPRAY
FANCY WORK	FERRET OUT	FINE TIMES
FAN DANCER	FERRY OVER	FINE TOUCH
FANNED OUT	FEUDAL LAW	FINE VOICE
FANNY HILL	FEUDAL TAX	FINE WOMAN
FAR AFIELD	FEVER HEAT	FINISH OFF
FAR BEHIND	FIELD ARMY	FIRE ALARM
FAR BETTER	FIELD GREY	FIRE A SHOT
FAR BEYOND	FIELD TEST	FIRE AT SEA
FAR CORNER	FIFTH FORM	FIRE DRILL
FAR ENOUGH	FIFTH HOLE	FIRE POWER
FARE STAGE	FIFTH PART	FIRM BASIS
FAR FROM IT	FIFTH RACE	FIRM FAITH
FARMED OUT	FIFTH TEST	FIRM GOING
FARM HORSE	FIFTH TIME	FIRM OFFER
FARTHER UP	FIFTY QUID	FIRM PRICE
FAR TOO FEW	FIGHT BACK	FIRM STAND
FAST TRAIN	FIGHT FAIR	FIRST ARMY
FAST WOMAN	FIGHT WITH	FIRST BALL
FATAL BLOW	FIG LEAVES	FIRST BASE
FATAL DOSE	FIGURE ONE	FIRST BELL
FATAL HOUR	FIGURE OUT	FIRST BLOW
FATAL MOVE	FIGURE TEN	FIRST COAT

FIRST COME	FIT TO DROP	FLYING FOX
FIRST COPY	FIVE CARDS	FLYING LOW
FIRST COST	FIVE CLUBS	FLYING MAN
FIRST CROP	FIVE DOZEN	FLY TO ARMS
FIRST FOOT	FIVE GROSS	FOBBED OFF
FIRST FORM	FIVE HOLES	FOG SIGNAL
FIRST GEAR	FIVE HOURS	FOLK DANCE
FIRST HALF	FIVE LUMPS	FOLK MUSIC
FIRST HAND	FIVE MILES	FOLLOW OUT
FIRST HEAT	FIVE OR SIX	FOOD STORE
FIRST HOLE	FIVE PARTS	FOOD VALUE
FIRST HOME	FIVE PINTS	FOOL ABOUT
FIRST LADY	FIVE SCORE	FOOL'S MATE
FIRST LEAD	FIVE TIMES	FOOT FAULT
FIRST LINE	FIVE TO ONE	FORAGE CAP
FIRST LORD	FIVE TO TEN	FOR A START
FIRST LOVE	FIVE TO TWO	FOR A WHILE
FIRST MATE	FIVE TOWNS	FORCE OPEN
FIRST MEAL	FIVE WEEKS	FOR EFFECT
FIRST MOVE	FIVE YEARS	FOREST LAW
FIRST NAME	FIX A PRICE	FOR EXPORT
FIRST PAGE	FIXED GAZE	FORKED OUT
FIRST PART	FIXED IDEA	FORK LUNCH
FIRST POST	FIXED LOOK	FORM A CORE
FIRST RACE	FIXED ODDS	FORMAL BOW
FIRST RATE	FIXED STAR	FORM A RING
FIRST SHOT	FIXED TIME	FORM FOURS
FIRST SIGN	FIXED TYPE	FOR MY PART
FIRST SLIP	FIXED WAYS	FORTY DAYS
FIRST STEP	FIZZLE OUT	FORTY LOVE
FIRST TEAM	FLAKED OUT	FOR VALOUR
FIRST TERM	FLARE PATH	FOSTER SON
FIRST TEST	FLASH BULB	FOUL CRIME
FIRST TIME	FLAT BROKE	FOUL FIEND
FIRST TO GO	FLAT TO LET	FOUL SMELL
FIRST TURN	FLAY ALIVE	FOUL THROW
FIRST WORD	FLESH PINK	FOUR AWAYS
FIRST YEAR	FLESH TINT	FOUR BY TWO
FISHED OUT	FLICK AWAY	FOUR CARDS
FISH KNIFE	FLING AWAY	FOUR CLUBS
FISH PASTE	FLING DOWN	FOUR DOZEN
FISH SLICE	FLING OPEN	FOUR FIVES
FISH STEAK	FLIRT WITH	FOUR FOURS
FISHY EYED	FLIT ABOUT	FOUR GROSS
FISHY LOOK	FLOAT DOWN	FOUR HOLES
FISHY TALE	FLOOD TIDE	FOUR HOURS
FIT FOR USE	FLOOR PLAN	FOUR IN ONE
FIT OF RAGE	FLOOR SHOW	FOUR JACKS
FIT PERSON	FLOUR MILL	FOUR KINGS
FITTED OUT	FLOW OF WIT	FOUR LUMPS
FIT TO BUST	FLY AT ZERO	FOUR MILES

FOUR NINES	FRESH FOOD	FULL SCORE
FOUR PAIRS	FRESH LOAF	FULL SKIRT
FOUR PARTS	FRESH MEAT	FULL SPEED
FOUR PINTS	FRESH MILK	FULL STEAM
FOUR SCORE	FRESH NEWS	FULL STORY
FOUR SIDES	FRESH PEAS	FULL SWING
FOUR SIXES	FRESH ROLL	FULL TABLE
FOURTH DAY	FRESH WIND .	FULL TITLE
FOURTH ROW	FRIAR TUCK	FULL VALUE
FOURTH SET	FRIED FISH	FULLY CLAD
FOURTH TEE	FRIED FOOD	FULLY PAID
FOUR TIMES	FRIED RICE	FULLY RIPE
FOUR TO ONE	FRIGID BOW	FUND OF WIT
FOUR WEEKS	FROCK COAT	FUNNY BONE
FOUR WINDS	FROM BELOW	FUNNY FACE
FOUR YEARS	FROM BIRTH	FUNNY FILM
FRANK MUIR	FROM NOW ON	FUNNY HA-HA
FRANS HALS	FRONT DOOR	FUNNY IDEA
FRED EMNEY	FRONT LINE	FUNNY JOKE
FRED KARNO	FRONT PAGE	FUNNY LIFE
FRED PERRY	FRONT RANK	FUNNY TIME
FREE AGENT	FRONT ROOM	FUN PALACE
FREE AS AIR	FRONT SEAT	FUR COLLAR
FREE BOARD	FRONT STEP	FUR GLOVES
FREE CHINA	FRONT STUD	FUR LINING
FREE DRINK	FRONT VIEW	FUR MARKET
FREE ENTRY	FROWN DOWN	FURTHER ON
FREE FIELD	FROWN UPON	FURTHER UP
FREE FIGHT	FROZEN SEA	FUR TRADER
FREE HOUSE	FRUIT BOWL	
FREE LUNCH	FRUIT CAKE	G—9
FREE OFFER	FRUIT TART	GAG WRITER
FREE OF TAX	FRUIT TREE	GAIN POWER
FREE PLACE	FULL BLAST	GALA DRESS
FREE PRESS	FULL BLOOM	GALA NIGHT
FREE RANGE	FULL BOARD	GALE FORCE
FREE SCOPE	FULL COVER	GALLOP OFF
FREE SPACE	FULL DRESS	GALWAY BAY
FREE STATE	FULL GLASS	GAME CHIPS
FREE STYLE	FULL GROWN	GAMES ROOM
FREE TRADE	FULL HEART	GAMING ACT
FREE UNION	FULL HOUSE	GAMMA RAYS
FREE VERSE	FULL MARKS	GANG AGLEY
FREE WHEEL	FULL OF FUN	GARDEN BED
FREE WORLD	FULL OF JOY	GAS ATTACK
FREEZE OUT	FULL OF PEP	GAS COOKER
FRESH BAIT	FULL OF WOE	GAS ENGINE
FRESH EGGS	FULL PITCH	GAS ESCAPE
FRESHEN UP	FULL PURSE	GAS HEATER
FRESH FACE	FULL QUOTA	GAS MANTLE
FRESH FISH	FULL SCOPE	GATE HOUSE

GATE MONEY	GIVEN TIME	GO FLAT OUT
GATHER WAY	GIVE PAUSE	GO FOR A CAB
GAVE CHASE	GIVE PLACE	GO FOR A DIP
GAY REVELS	GIVE TERMS	GO FOR A RUN
GENE AUTRY	GIVE VOICE	GO FOR HELP
GENOA CAKE	GIVING OUT	GO FORWARD
GENTLE SEX	GIVING WAY	GO HALF-WAY
GEORGE FOX	GLANCE OFF	GO HAYWIRE
GET A CHILL	GLASS CASE	GO HUNTING
GET ACROSS	GLASS TUBE	GO INDOORS
GET AROUND	GLASS VASE	GO IN FRONT
GET A START	GLIDE AWAY	GOING AWAY
GET BEHIND	GLOAT OVER	GOING BACK
GET BETTER	GLOBAL WAR	GOING BALD
GET CREDIT	GLOOMY DAY	GOING DOWN
GET KILLED	GLORY HOLE	GOING GREY
GET MOVING	GLOSS OVER	GOING HOME
GET THE PIP	GNAW IN TWO	GOING OVER
GETTING ON	GO AGAINST	GOING SLOW
GETTING UP	GO A-MAYING	GOING WELL
GET TO HEAR	GO AND LOOK	GOING WEST
GET TO KNOW	GOAT'S HAIR	GO IN ORBIT
GET UP LATE	GOAT'S MILK	GO IT ALONE
GET WIND OF	GO BEGGING	GOLD BRAID
GET WITH IT	GO BERSERK	GOLD BRICK
GHOST TOWN	GO BETWEEN	GOLD CHAIN
GIDDY GOAT	GO BOATING	GOLD COAST
GIFTED MAN	GO BY COACH	GOLDEN AGE
GIFT HORSE	GO BY PLANE	GOLDEN BOY
GIFT TOKEN	GO BY TRAIN	GOLDEN EGG
GIN AND PEP	GO BY WATER	GOLDEN KEY
GIN BOTTLE	GO DANCING	GOLDEN ROD
GINGER ALE	GOD FORBID	GOLD FEVER
GINGER CAT	GOD OF FIRE	GOLD INGOT
GINGER POP	GOD OF LOVE	GOLD MEDAL
GINGER TOM	GOD OF WINE	GOLD MINER
GIN PALACE	GOD'S IMAGE	GOLD PAINT
GIPSY LOVE	GOD'S TRUTH	GOLD PLATE
GIPSY MOTH	GOES ABOUT	GOLD TOOTH
GIRL GUIDE	GOES AFTER	GOLD WATCH
GIRLS' HOME	GOES AHEAD	GOLF LINKS
GIVE A HAND	GOES BELOW	GOLF MATCH
GIVE A HINT	GOES IN FOR	GOLF WIDOW
GIVE A LEAD	GOES ROUND	GONE TO BED
GIVE A LIFT	GOES TO BED	GONE TO POT
GIVE A TALK	GOES TO POT	GONE UNDER
GIVE BIRTH	GOES TO SEA	GOOD ACTOR
GIVE CHASE	GOES TO SEE	GOOD ALIBI
GIVE EAR TO	GOES UNDER	GOOD ANGEL
GIVE FORTH	GOES WRONG	GOOD BOOKS
GIVEN NAME	GO FISHING	GOOD CATCH

GOOD CAUSE	GOOD SPEED	GRAND TIME
GOOD CHEER	GOOD SPORT	GRAND TOUR
GOOD CLASS	GOOD START	GRAND VIEW
GOOD DEBTS	GOOD STATE	GRASS PLOT
GOOD DODGE	GOOD STOCK	GRAVEL PIT
GOOD EATER	GOOD STORY	GRAVE NEWS
GOOD FAIRY	GOOD STUFF	GRAVE NOTE
GOOD FAITH	GOOD TABLE	GREAT AUNT
GOOD FAULT	GOOD TASTE	GREAT BEAR
GOOD FIELD	GOOD TERMS	GREAT BLOW
GOOD FIGHT	GOOD THING	GREAT CARE
GOOD GOING	GOOD TIMES	GREAT DANE
GOOD GRACE	GOOD TO EAT	GREAT DEAL
GOOD GRIEF	GOOD TONIC	GREAT DEED
GOOD GUESS	GOOD TO SEE	GREAT DRAW
GOOD GUIDE	GOOD TRADE	GREAT FAME
GOOD HABIT	GOOD USAGE	GREAT FEAT
GOOD HANDS	GOOD VALUE	GREAT FIRE
GOOD HEART	GOOD VOICE	GREAT FOLK
GOOD HOTEL	GOOD WAGES	GREAT GAIN
GOOD HOURS	GOOD WOMAN	GREAT GUNS
GOOD HOUSE	GOOD WORKS	GREAT HALL
GOOD IMAGE	GOOD YIELD	GREAT HELP
GOOD JUDGE	GO OFF DUTY	GREAT IDEA
GOOD LAYER	GO ON A DIET	GREAT LIFE
GOOD LIGHT	GO ON AND ON	GREAT LOSS
GOOD LINES	GO ON BOARD	GREAT MANY
GOOD LIVER	GO ONE'S WAY	GREAT MIND
GOOD LOOKS	GO ON LEAVE	GREAT NAME
GOOD LOSER	GOOSE FAIR	GREAT NEWS
GOOD LUNCH	GO OUTSIDE	GREAT PAIN
GOOD LUNGS	GO QUIETLY	GREAT PITY
GOOD MARKS	GO SAILING	GREAT SCOT
GOOD MATCH	GO SKATING	GREAT SEAL
GOOD MIXER	GO THE PACE	GREAT SHIP
GOOD MONEY	GO THROUGH	GREAT TIME
GOOD MUSIC	GO TO EARTH	GREEDY PIG
GOOD NIGHT	GO TO GLORY	GREEK CITY
GOOD ODOUR	GO TO GRASS	GREEK FIRE
GOOD OFFER	GO TO HADES	GREEK FLAG
GOOD ORDER	GO TO PRESS	GREEK GIFT
GOOD PATCH	GO TO SLEEP	GREEK MYTH
GOOD POINT	GO TOWARDS	GREEK PLAY
GOOD PRICE	GO TO WASTE	GREEN BELT
GOOD REPLY	GO WITHOUT	GREEN EYES
GOOD SCORE	GRACE NOTE	GREEN FEES
GOOD SENSE	GRAND DUKE	GREEN FIGS
GOOD SHAPE	GRAND JURY	GREEN FLAG
GOOD SHAVE	GRAND LAMA	GREEN HILL
GOOD SIGHT	GRAND PRIX	GREEN LINE
GOODS LIFT	GRAND SLAM	GREEN PARK

GREEN PEAS	HALF A QUID	HARD GRIND
GREEN ROOM	HALF A TICK	HARD HEART
GRETA GYNT	HALF AWAKE	HARD KNOCK
GREY CLOUD	HALF A YARD	HARD LINES
GREY GOOSE	HALF CROWN	HARDLY ANY
GREY HAIRS	HALF DRUNK	HARD MONEY
GREY HORSE	HALF HITCH	HARD STEEL
GREY SKIES	HALF LIGHT	HARD STUFF
GRILL ROOM	HALF PRICE	HARD TIMES
GRIM DEATH	HALF SHARE	HARD TO GET
GRIM SMILE	HALF SPEED	HARD TO SAY
GRIM TRUTH	HALF TRUTH	HARD TO SEE
GRIND DOWN	HALF WAY UP	HARD USAGE
GRIP TIGHT	HALL CAINE	HARD VOICE
GROUND NUT	HALL TABLE	HARD WATER
GROW ANGRY	HAM AND EGG	HARD WORDS
GROW APART	HAM COMMON	HARE'S FOOT
GROW FRUIT	HAMMER OUT	HARRY LIME
GROWING UP	HAND BASIN	HARRY TATE
GROW OLDER	HAND IT OUT	HARSH NOTE
GROW PEARS	HAND OF GOD	HARSH TONE
GROW STALE	HAND ROUND	HARSH WORD
GROW TIRED	HANDS DOWN	HAVE A BALL
GROW WEARY	HAND'S TURN	HAVE A BASH
GUARD DUTY	HAND TOWEL	HAVE A BATH
GUARD ROOM	HANDY ANDY	HAVE A BITE
GUARD'S TIE	HANG ABOUT	HAVE A CARE
GUARD'S VAN	HANG HEAVY	HAVE A CASE
GUESS WHEN	HANGING ON	HAVE A CHAT
GUEST ROOM	HANG IT ALL	HAVE A COLD
GUEST STAR	HANG ROUND	HAVE A DATE
GUIDE BOOK	HANSOM CAB	HAVE A GAME
GUILTY ACT	HAPPY DAYS	HAVE A HOPE
GUILTY MAN	HAPPY GIRL	HAVE A LARK
GUINEA HEN	HAPPY HOME	HAVE A LOOK
GUM ARABIC	HAPPY IDEA	HAVE A MEAL
GUN BATTLE	HAPPY LIFE	HAVE AN EGG
GUN TURRET	HAPPY MEAN	HAVE A PLAN
GUY FAWKES	HAPPY OMEN	HAVE A REST
GYPSY BAND	HAPPY PAIR	HAVE A SALE
	HAPPY TRIO	HAVE A SEAT
	HARD APORT	HAVE A SHOT
H—9	HARD CATCH	HAVE A STAB
HAIL A TAXI	HARD CLIMB	HAVE A TRIM
HAIR CREAM	HARD COURT	HAVE A WISH
HAIR SHIRT	HARD FACTS	HAVE FAITH
HAIR STYLE	HARD FIGHT	HAVE IT OUT
HAIR TONIC	HARD FRANC	HAVE LUNCH
HALF A LOAF	HARD FROST	HAVE MERCY
HALF AN EYE	HARD FRUIT	HAVE ROOTS
HALF A PINT	HARD GOING	HAVE SENSE

HAVE TASTE	HIGH FEVER	HOLD UNDER
HAVE VIEWS	HIGH GRADE	HOLD WATER
HAVE WORDS	HIGH HEELS	HOLE IN ONE
HAVING FUN	HIGH HOPES	HOLLOW OUT
HAZEL EYES	HIGH HORSE	HOLLY BUSH
HEAD FIRST	HIGH JINKS	HOLY BIBLE
HEADS I WIN	HIGH LEVEL	HOLY GHOST
HEAD TO TOE	HIGH MARKS	HOLY GRAIL
HEAP ABUSE	HIGH PITCH	HOLY MOSES
HEAVE AWAY	HIGH PLANE	HOLY PLACE
HEAVE COAL	HIGH PRICE	HOLY SMOKE
HEAVY BLOW	HIGH SCORE	HOLY WATER
HEAVY COLD	HIGH SPEED	HOME AGAIN
HEAVY COST	HIGH SPOTS	HOME FIRES
HEAVY FALL	HIGH STOOL	HOME FLEET
HEAVY FINE	HIGH TABLE	HOME FRONT
HEAVY GUNS	HIGH TOWER	HOME GROWN
HEAVY HAND	HIGH VALUE	HOME GUARD
HEAVY LIDS	HIGH VOICE	HOME JAMES
HEAVY LOAD	HIGH WAGES	HOME LOVER
HEAVY LOSS	HIGH WATER	HOMELY WIT
HEAVY MEAL	HIGH WORDS	HOME MATCH
HEAVY MIST	HILL TRIBE	HOME OF MAN
HEAVY ODDS	HIRE A MAID	HOME TRADE
HEAVY POLL	HIRED HAND	HOME TRUTH
HEAVY POST	HIRED HELP	HONEST MAN
HEAVY RAIN	HIRED THUG	HOOT OF JOY
HEAVY SEAS	HIS HONOUR	HOPE CHEST
HEAVY SNOW	HIT AND RUN	HOP GARDEN
HEAVY TASK	HITCH HIKE	HOP PICKER
HEAVY TYPE	HIT FOR SIX	HORSE FAIR
HEAVY WIND	HIT NUMBER	HORSE RACE
HEAVY WORK	HIT OR MISS	HORSE SHOW
HELL TO PAY	HIT PARADE	HOT AS HELL
HELP ALONG	HIT THE HAY	HOTEL BILL
HELPED OUT	HIT WICKET	HOTEL ROOM
HEM STITCH	HIT WILDLY	HOT NUMBER
HENRY FORD	HOG THE LOT	HOT POTATO
HENRY HALL	HOI POLLOI	HOT SHOWER
HERE BELOW	HOIST SAIL	HOT SPRING
HERNE HILL	HOLD ALOFT	HOT SUMMER
HEROIC AGE	HOLD ALOOF	HOT TEMPER
HEY PRESTO	HOLD A SALE	HOUND DOWN
HIGH ABOVE	HOLD AT BAY	HOUSE BOAT
HIGH ALTAR	HOLD CHEAP	HOUSE FULL
HIGH BIRTH	HOLD COURT	HOUSE NAME
HIGH BOOTS	HOLD FORTH	HOUSE RENT
HIGH CHAIR	HOLD HANDS	HOUSE ROOM
HIGH COURT	HOLDING ON	HOW ABSURD!
HIGH DUTCH	HOLD STILL	HOW AND WHY
HIGHER PAY	HOLD TIGHT	HOW ARE YOU?

HOW GOES IT?	IN A BUNKER	INDIAN TEA
HUDSON BAY	IN A CANTER	IN DISGUST
HUE AND CRY	IN A CIRCLE	IN DISPUTE
HUM AND HAW	IN A CLINCH	IN DRY DOCK
HUMAN LIFE	IN A CORNER	IN DUE TIME
HUMAN RACE	IN A CRISIS	IN EARNEST
HUMAN SOUL	IN ADVANCE	IN ECHELON
HUMBLE PIE	IN A FRENZY	IN ENGLAND
HUNGRY MAN	IN A GROOVE	IN ENGLISH
HUNTED AIR	IN A HUDDLE	INERT MASS
HURL ABUSE	IN A MINUTE	IN FASHION
HURRIED UP	IN A MOMENT	IN FETTERS
HURRY AWAY	IN A MUDDLE	IN FRONT OF
HURRY BACK	IN ANY CASE	IN FULL CRY
HURRY DOWN	IN A PICKLE	IN GENERAL
HURRY HOME	IN ARREARS	IN GERMANY
HURRY OVER	IN A SCRAPE	IN GLASGOW
HURST PARK	IN A SECOND	INGLE NOOK
HURT PRIDE	IN A STUPOR	IN HARBOUR
HUSH MONEY	IN A TANGLE	IN HARMONY
	IN A TEMPER	IN HARNESS
I—9	IN A TRANCE	IN HOLLAND
ICE CORNET	IN AUSTRIA	IN HUNGARY
ICED DRINK	IN A VACUUM	IN INFANCY
ICED WATER	IN BAD FORM	IN IRELAND
ICE HOCKEY	IN BAD PART	IN ITALIAN
ICY MANNER	IN BELGIUM	IN ITALICS
ICY REMARK	IN BETWEEN	IN JANUARY
IDA LUPINO	IN BILLETS	INK BOTTLE
IDEAL GIFT	IN BLOSSOM	IN KEEPING
IDEAL HOME	IN BORSTAL	INK ERASER
IDEAL TIME	IN CARDIFF	INLAND SEA
IDEAL TYPE	IN CIRCLES	INNER EDGE
IDEAL WIFE	IN CIVVIES	INNER ROOM
IDLE BOAST	INCOME TAX	INNER SELF
IDLE FANCY	IN COMFORT	INNER TUBE
IDLE HANDS	IN COMMAND	IN NEUTRAL
IDLE HOURS	IN COMPANY	IN NEW YORK
IDLE STORY	IN CONCERT	IN NO DOUBT
IDLE TEARS	IN CONTACT	IN OCTOBER
IFS AND ANS	IN CONTROL	IN ONE MOVE
ILL AT EASE	IN COPPERS	IN ONE WORD
ILL CHANCE	IN COSTUME	IN OUTLINE
ILL EFFECT	IN COUNCIL	IN PASSING
ILL FAVOUR	IN CUSTODY	IN POVERTY
ILL HEALTH	IN DEFAULT	IN PRIVATE
ILL HUMOUR	IN DEFENCE	IN PROFILE
ILL REPORT	IN DENMARK	IN PROTEST
ILL REPUTE	IN DESPAIR	IN PURSUIT
IN A BAD WAY	IN DIALECT	IN REALITY
IN A BIG WAY	INDIAN INK	IN RESERVE

IN RESPECT	IN THE MOOD	IRON CROSS
IN RETREAT	IN THE MOON	IRONED OUT
IN REVERSE	IN THE NAVY	IRON FRAME
IN RUMANIA	IN THE NECK	IRON GUARD
IN RUSSIAN	IN THE NEST	IRON HORSE
IN SERVICE	IN THE NEWS	IRON NERVE
IN SESSION	IN THE NUDE	IRON TONIC
INSIDE JOB	IN THE OPEN	IRON WORKS
INSIDE OUT	IN THE OVEN	ISLE OF ELY
IN SILENCE	IN THE PACK	ISLE OF MAN
IN SLAVERY	IN THE PARK	IT'S A CINCH
IN SOCIETY	IN THE PAST	IVORY GATE
IN SOME WAY	IN THE PINK	
IN SPANISH	IN THE POST	J—9
IN SUPPORT	IN THE RAIN	JACK BENNY
IN TATTERS	IN THE REAR	JACK FROST
INTER ALIA	IN THE RING	JACK HOBBS
IN THE ALPS	IN THE ROAD	JACK JONES
IN THE AREA	IN THE SAFE	JACK KETCH
IN THE ARMY	IN THE SNOW	JACK PAYNE
IN THE BAND	IN THE SOUP	JACK SPRAT
IN THE BANK	IN THE SWIM	JACK TRAIN
IN THE BATH	IN THE TEAM	JADE GREEN
IN THE BUSH	IN THE TILL	JAMES BOND
IN THE CART	IN THE TOWN	JAMES DEAN
IN THE CITY	IN THE VEIN	JAMES WATT
IN THE COLD	IN THE WAKE	JAM SPONGE
IN THE DARK	IN THE WARS	JANE WYMAN
IN THE DOCK	IN THE WASH	JAY WALKER
IN THE DUSK	IN THE WEST	JELLY BABY
IN THE EAST	IN THE WIND	JENNY LIND
IN THE FACE	INTO FOCUS	JENNY WREN
IN THE FALL	IN TOP FORM	JERSEY COW
IN THE FILE	IN TOP GEAR	JET ENGINE
IN THE FIRE	IN TORMENT	JET FLIGHT
IN THE FOLD	INTO TOUCH	JEWEL CASE
IN THE FRAY	IN TRAFFIC	JOAN OF ARC
IN THE GODS	IN TRANSIT	JOAN REGAN
IN THE HOLD	IN TRIUMPH	JOB OF WORK
IN THE HOME	IN TROUBLE	JOE MILLER
IN THE KNOW	IN UNIFORM	JO GRIMOND
IN THE LAKE	INVOKE AID	JOHN ADAMS
IN THE LEAD	IN WAITING	JOHN BLUNT
IN THE LIFT	IN WRITING	JOHN BROWN
IN THE LOFT	IONIAN SEA	JOHN CABOT
IN THE MAIL	IPSO FACTO	JOHN KEATS
IN THE MAIN	IRISH BULL	JOHN MILLS
IN THE MASS	IRISH EYES	JOHN SMITH
IN THE MIND	IRISH FLAG	JOHN WAYNE
IN THE MINE	IRISH PEER	JOIN HANDS
IN THE MODE	IRISH STEW	JOIN ISSUE

JOINT HEIR
JOINT WILL
JOLLY GOOD
JOLLY TIME
JOLLY WELL
JOT IT DOWN
JUDAS KISS
JUDAS TREE
JUDGE'S CAP
JUDGE WELL
JUG OF MILK
JUMP ABOUT
JUMP AHEAD
JUMP CLEAR
JUNE BRIDE
JUNGLE LAW
JUST A DROP
JUST CAUSE
JUST CLAIM
JUST FANCY
JUST PRICE
JUST RIGHT
JUST THINK

K—9
KATHIE KAY
KEEN FIGHT
KEEN FROST
KEEN MATCH
KEEN PRICE
KEEN SIGHT
KEEP A DATE
KEEP AHEAD
KEEP ALIVE
KEEP APART
KEEP ASIDE
KEEP AT BAY
KEEP CLEAR
KEEP CLOSE
KEEP COUNT
KEEP FAITH
KEEP FRESH
KEEP GOING
KEEP GUARD
KEEP HOUSE
KEEP ON ICE
KEEP ORDER
KEEP QUIET
KEEP SCORE
KEEP SHORT
KEEP SOBER

KEEP STILL
KEEP STOCK
KEEP UNDER
KEEP VIGIL
KEEP WATCH
KEG BITTER
KELLY'S EYE
KEPT AT BAY
KEPT ON ICE
KEPT WOMAN
KERRY BLUE
KEW BRIDGE
KEW PALACE
KEY MOMENT
KEY WORKER
KICKED OFF
KICKED OUT
KID GLOVES
KIEL CANAL
KIND HEART
KINDLY ACT
KIND WORDS
KING CAROL
KING COBRA
KING DAVID
KING HENRY
KING MIDAS
KING PRIAM
KING'S HEAD
KING'S LYNN
KING'S PAWN
KING'S ROAD
KING'S ROOK
KING STORK
KIRBY GRIP
KISS HANDS
KNEEL DOWN
KNEES BEND
KNOCK COLD
KNOCK DOWN
KNOCKED UP
KNOCK HARD
KNOCK ONCE
KNOCK OVER
KNOW AGAIN
KNOW NO LAW
KOREAN WAR
KUBLA KHAN

L—9
LABOUR DAY

LACK DRIVE
LADIES' BAR
LADIES' DAY
LADIES' MAN
LADY'S MAID
LAG BEHIND
LAGER BEER
LA GUARDIA
LAID WASTE
LAKE HURON
LAKE POETS
LAMB'S WOOL
LAMP SHADE
LAND A BLOW
LAND AGENT
LAND AHEAD
LAND FORCE
LAND OF NOD
LAND ROVER
LAND SPEED
LAP RECORD
LARGE AREA
LARGE ARMY
LARGE BEER
LARGE BILL
LARGE CAST
LARGE CITY
LARGE FLAT
LARGE HEAD
LARGE LOAF
LARGE PORT
LARGE ROOM
LARGE SIZE
LARGE TOWN
LARGE TYPE
LARK ABOUT
LASER BEAM
LASHED OUT
LAS PALMAS
LAST APRIL
LAST CRUMB
LAST DANCE
LAST DITCH
LAST DREGS
LAST DRINK
LAST EVENT
LAST FLING
LAST HOURS
LAST LAUGH
LAST NIGHT
LAST MAN IN

LAST MARCH	LAW REFORM	LETTER BOX
LAST MATCH	LAW REPORT	LETTING UP
LAST MONTH	LAW SCHOOL	LET US PRAY
LAST NIGHT	LAZY BONES	LEVEL BEST
LAST OF ALL	LEAD OXIDE	LEYDEN JAR
LAST OFFER	LEAF MOULD	LIBEL CASE
LAST OF SIX	LEAN YEARS	LIBEL SUIT
LAST OF TEN	LEASE LEND	LIE ASLEEP
LAST ORDER	LEAST SAID	LIE AT REST
LAST PENNY	LEAVE A GAP	LIE DIRECT
LAST PLACE	LEAVE A TIP	LIE FALLOW
LAST RITES	LEAVE HOME	LIE HIDDEN
LAST ROUND	LEAVE OPEN	LIE IN WAIT
LAST SCENE	LEAVE OVER	LIFE CLASS
LAST SHIFT	LEAVE ROOM	LIFE CYCLE
LAST STAGE	LEAVE WORD	LIFE FORCE
LAST STAND	LEAVE WORK	LIFE STORY
LAST STRAW	LE BOURGET	LIFE STUDY
LAST TANGO	LED ASTRAY	LIFE'S WORK
LAST THING	LEFT ALONE	LIFT A HAND
LAST THROW	LEFT FLANK	LIGHT BLUE
LAST TRAIN	LEFT TO DIE	LIGHT BULB
LAST TRUMP	LEFT TO ROT	LIGHT DIET
LAST VERSE	LEFT WHEEL	LIGHT MEAL
LAST VISIT	LEGAL CODE	LIGHT RAIN
LAST WALTZ	LEGAL FARE	LIGHT SIDE
LAST WORDS	LEGAL HEIR	LIGHTS OUT
LATE CROPS	LEGAL MIND	LIGHT SUIT
LATE ENTRY	LEGAL TERM	LIGHT TANK
LATE EXTRA	LEGER LINE	LIGHT UPON
LATE FROST	LEG GLANCE	LIGHT WAVE
LATE HOURS	LEG OF LAMB	LIGHT WINE
LATE NIGHT	LEG OF PORK	LIGHT WORK
LATER DATE	LEGS APART	LIGHT YEAR
LATE RISER	LEG THEORY	LIKE A BIRD
LATE SHIFT	LEIGH HUNT	LIKE A BOMB
LATE STAGE	LEMON CURD	LIKE A CORK
LATE START	LEMON PEEL	LIKE A DUCK
LATIN CRIB	LEMON SOLE	LIKE A FOOL
LATIN RACE	LENA HORNE	LIKE A KING
LATTER END	LEND A HAND	LIKE A LAMB
LAUGH AWAY	LEND AN EAR	LIKE A LION
LAUGH DOWN	LEND MONEY	LIKE A MULE
LAUGH LINE	LEN HUTTON	LIKE A SHOT
LAUGH OVER	LESSON ONE	LIKELY LAD
LAUNCH OUT	LESSON SIX	LIKE MAGIC
LAVA BREAD	LESSON TEN	LIKE MUSIC
LAWFUL ACT	LESSON TWO	LIKE SMOKE
LAWFUL AGE	LESS SPEED	LIKE WATER
LAWN MOWER	LET HER RIP	LILAC TIME
LAW OFFICE	LE TOUQUET	LILAC TREE

LIME GREEN	LONG DRIVE	LORD DERBY
LIME GROVE	LONG GRASS	LORD MAYOR
LIME JUICE	LONG HOURS	LOSE A LIMB
LION'S CAGE	LONG LEASE	LOSE AN EYE
LION'S MANE	LONG MARCH	LOSE CASTE
LION'S SKIN	LONG NIGHT	LOSE COUNT
LION'S TAIL	LONG PANTS	LOSE FAITH
LION TAMER	LONG PURSE	LOSE HEART
LIP READER	LONG QUEUE	LOSE MONEY
LIQUID AIR	LONG RANGE	LOSER PAYS
LIQUOR LAW	LONG REACH	LOSE TOUCH
LIST PRICE	LONG REIGN	LOSE TRACK
LITTER BIN	LONG SIEGE	LOSING BET
LITTER BUG	LONG SIGHT	LOSING RUN
LITTLE BIT	LONG SINCE	LOST AT SEA
LITTLE BOY	LONG SKIRT	LOST CAUSE
LITTLE DOG	LONG SLEEP	LOST CHORD
LITTLE MAN	LONG SPELL	LOST COUNT
LITTLE ONE	LONG STAGE	LOST HABIT
LITTLE TOE	LONG STORY	LOST SCENT
LITTLE WAY	LONG TRAIN	LOST SHEEP
LIVE AGAIN	LONG TRIAL	LOST SKILL
LIVE ALONE	LONG VISIT	LOT OF GOOD
LIVE APART	LONG VOWEL	LOTS OF FUN
LIVE ISSUE	LONG WHIST	LOUD KNOCK
LIVE ON AIR	LOOK A FOOL	LOUD LAUGH
LIVE OR DIE	LOOK AFTER	LOUD MUSIC
LIVE ROUGH	LOOK AHEAD	LOUD NOISE
LIVING LIE	LOOK ALIVE	LOUD PEDAL
LOADED GUN	LOOK A MESS	LOUD SOUND
LOAD OF HAY	LOOK BLACK	LOUD VOICE
LOAF SUGAR	LOOK BLANK	LOUNGE BAR
LOATH TO GO	LOOKED FOR	LOVE APPLE
LOCAL CALL	LOOK FRESH	LOVE CHILD
LOCAL NAME	LOOK GRAVE	LOVED ONES
LOCAL NEWS	LOOKING UP	LOVE FORTY
LOCAL TIME	LOOK NIPPY	LOVELY DAY
LOCAL VETO	LOOK RIGHT	LOVE LYRIC
LOCKED OUT	LOOK ROUND	LOVE MATCH
LOFTY AIMS	LOOK SEEDY	LOVE MY DOG
LOG OF WOOD	LOOK SHARP	LOVE OF WAR
LONDON BUS	LOOK SILLY	LOVE STORY
LONDON ZOO	LOOK SMALL	LOVE TOKEN
LONG AFTER	LOOK SMART	LOVING CUP
LONG BEACH	LOOK THERE	LOW BRIDGE
LONG BEARD	LOOM LARGE	LOW CHURCH
LONG CHALK	LOOSE BALL	LOW COMEDY
LONG DELAY	LOOSE CASH	LOW DEGREE
LONG DOZEN	LOOSE TALK	LOWER CASE
LONG DRESS	LOOSE TILE	LOWER DECK
LONG DRINK	LORD BYRON	LOWER DOWN

LOWER FORM	MAIL TRAIN	MAKE NOTES
LOWER LIFE	MAIN FORCE	MAKE OR MAR
LOWER LIMB	MAIN ISSUE	MAKE PEACE
LOWER PART	MAIN POINT	MAKE PLAIN
LOW FELLOW	MAIN THEME	MAKE PLANS
LOW GERMAN	MAIN THING	MAKE READY
LOW GROUND	MAJOR DOMO	MAKE SENSE
LOW INCOME	MAJOR PART	MAKE TERMS
LOW IN TONE	MAJOR POET	MAKE TIGHT
LOW NUMBER	MAJOR ROAD	MAKE-UP MAN
LOW PERSON	MAJOR SNAG	MAKE-UP SET
LOW RELIEF	MAJOR SUIT	MAKE VALID
LOW RESORT	MAJOR WORK	MAKE WHOLE
LOW RETURN	MAKE A BACK	MAKE WORSE
LOW SALARY	MAKE A BOOK	MAKING HAY
LOW STAKES	MAKE A CAKE	MALE CHOIR
LOW STATUS	MAKE A CALL	MALE NURSE
LUCID MIND	MAKE A COPY	MALE SCREW
LUCKY DRAW	MAKE A DATE	MALE VOICE
LUCKY FIND	MAKE A DEAL	MAN AND BOY
LUCKY GIRL	MAKE A FACE	MAN FRIDAY
LUCKY MOVE	MAKE A FIRE	MAN OF IRON
LUCKY OMEN	MAKE A FUSS	MAN OF KENT
LUCKY SHOT	MAKE A HOLE	MAN OF MARK
LUCKY STAR	MAKE A JOKE	MAN OF NOTE
LUMP SUGAR	MAKE A KILL	MAN OF RANK
LUNACY ACT	MAKE A LIST	MANOR FARM
LUNAR YEAR	MAKE A LOSS	MANOR PARK
LUNCH DATE	MAKE A MESS	MANY A SLIP
LUNCH HOUR	MAKE A MOVE	MANY A TIME
LUNCH TIME	MAKE A NOTE	MANY HANDS
LURID PAST	MAKE A PASS	MANY TIMES
LYING DOWN	MAKE A PILE	MANY WORDS
LYME REGIS	MAKE A PLAN	MANY YEARS
LYRIC POEM	MAKE A RING	MAPLE LEAF
LYRIC POET	MAKE A SHOW	MAPLE TREE
	MAKE A SIGN	MAP OF ROME
	MAKE A SLIP	MAPPED OUT
M—9	MAKE A STIR	MARCH AWAY
MADE OF TIN	MAKE A TART	MARCH HARE
MADE READY	MAKE A WILL	MARCH PAST
MAD HATTER	MAKE A WISH	MARCH WIND
MAD SCHEME	MAKE CLEAR	MARCO POLO
MAGGIE MAY	MAKE FACES	MARDI GRAS
MAGIC LAMP	MAKE FUN OF	MARE'S NEST
MAGIC RING	MAKE HASTE	MARIA MONK
MAGIC SIGN	MAKE KNOWN	MARKED MAN
MAGIC WAND	MAKE LEGAL	MARKET DAY
MAGIC WORD	MAKE MERRY	MARK TWAIN
MAIDA VALE	MAKE MONEY	MARRY WELL
MAIL ORDER	MAKE MUSIC	MASKED MAN
MAIL PLANE		

MASS MEDIA	MINK STOLE	MOVIE STAR
MASTER KEY	MINOR PART	MOWED DOWN
MASTER SPY	MINOR POET	MRS. BEATON
MATCH PLAY	MINOR ROAD	MRS GRUNDY
MATE IN ONE	MINOR ROLE	MR. SPEAKER
MATE IN TWO	MINOR SUIT	MUCH ALIKE
MATT MONRO	MINT JULEP	MUCH LATER
MAX ADRIAN	MINT SAUCE	MUCH MOVED
MAX MILLER	MINUS SIGN	MUCH NOISE
MEANS TEST	MINUTE MAN	MUCH SPACE
MEAN TO SAY	MISSED OUT	MUCH WORSE
MEANT WELL	MISS WORLD	MUFFIN MAN
MEASLY LOT	MIX A DRINK	MUFFLED UP
MEAT JELLY	MIXED NUTS	MUG OF BEER
MEAT PASTE	MOCK TRIAL	MUM AND DAD
MEDAL PLAY	MODEL FARM	MUSIC CASE
MEDIUM DRY	MODEL GIRL	MUSIC HALL
MEIN KAMPF	MODERN ART	MUSIC ROOM
MEL FERRER	MONEY DOWN	MUTINY ACT
MEN AT WORK	MONIED MAN	MUTTON FAT
MEND A FUSE	MONKEY NUT	MUTUAL AID
MENTAL AGE	MONT BLANC	MUTUAL AIM
MERCY SEAT	MOON ABOUT	MY DARLING
MERE TRUTH	MOON RIVER	MY DEAR SIR
MERE WORDS	MOOT POINT	MY HUSBAND
MERRY QUIP	MORAL CODE	MY OPINION
MERRY TUNE	MORAL EVIL	
MESS ABOUT	MORAL TONE	**N—9**
METAL DISC	MORE HASTE	NAKED CITY
METAL RING	MORE LIGHT	NAKED LADY
METAL TUBE	MORE MONEY	NANNY GOAT
METRIC TON	MORE SCOPE	NARROW WIN
MID-DAY SUN	MORSE CODE	NASTY BLOW
MIDDLE AGE	MORTAL SIN	NASTY MESS
MIDDLE WAY	MOSAIC LAW	NASTY TYPE
MIGHTY FEW	MOSS GREEN	NASTY WORD
MIGHTY MAN	MOST NOBLE	NATIVE WIT
MILD STEEL	MOST OF ALL	NAVAL BASE
MILES AWAY	MOTHER WIT	NAVAL RANK
MILK CHURN	MOTOR RACE	NAVAL TYPE
MILK DRINK	MOTOR ROAD	NAZI PARTY
MILK FLOAT	MOTOR SHOW	NEARLY ALL
MILK PUNCH	MOTOR TOUR	NEAR SIGHT
MILK ROUND	MOUNTED UP	NEAR THING
MILK SHAKE	MOUNT ETNA	NEAT DRINK
MILK STOUT	MOUTH WASH	NEAT TRICK
MILK TEETH	MOVE ABOUT	NEEDS MUST
MILL ABOUT	MOVE ALONG	NEON LIGHT
MILLS BOMB	MOVE APART	NET AMOUNT
MINE SHAFT	MOVE HOUSE	NET LOSSES
MINI SKIRT	MOVE ROUND	NET PROFIT

NET RESULT	NIGHT BELL	NO PARKING
NET RETURN	NIGHT CLUB	NO QUARTER
NEVER A ONE	NIGHT DUTY	NO REGRETS
NEVER FEAR	NIGHT LIFE	NORTH CAPE
NEVER MIND	NIGHT SPOT	NORTH POLE
NEVER MORE	NIGHT WORK	NORTH SIDE
NEVER REST	NILE DELTA	NORTH STAR
NEVER SEEN	NILE GREEN	NORTH WIND
NEVER STOP	NINE CARAT	NORTH ZONE
NEVER VARY	NINE DOZEN	NOSMO KING
NEW BARNET	NINE GROSS	NO SMOKING
NEW BONNET	NINE HOLES	NO SPIRITS
NEW CUSTOM	NINE HOURS	NO STRINGS
NEW DEALER	NINE LIVES	NOT AT HOME
NEW ENERGY	NINE MILES	NOT FAR OFF
NEW FOREST	NINE MUSES	NOT GUILTY
NEW FRIEND	NINE OR TEN	NOTHING ON
NEW GROUND	NINE PARTS	NOT HUNGRY
NEW GUINEA	NINE SCORE	NOT IN TIME
NEW JERSEY	NINE TIMES	NOT LATELY
NEW MASTER	NINE TO ONE	NOT LIKELY
NEW MEMBER	NINE WEEKS	NOT PROVEN
NEW METHOD	NINE YEARS	NOTRE DAME
NEW MEXICO	NINTH HOLE	NO TROUBLE
NEW PLANET	NINTH PART	NOT SO GOOD
NEW POLICY	NINTH TIME	NOT STRONG
NEW POTATO	NISSEN HUT	NOT TOO BAD
NEW READER	NOBLE LADY	NOT UP TO IT
NEW RECORD	NOBLE LINE	NOT WANTED
NEW REGIME	NOBLE LORD	NOVEL ITEM
NEW ROMNEY	NOBLE PART	NO WAITING
NEW SCHOOL	NOBLE PILE	NO WARNING
NEW SERIES	NO CHICKEN	NUMBER ONE
NEWS FLASH	NO COMMENT	NUMBER SIX
NEWS SHEET	NOD ASSENT	NUMBER TEN
NEW STREET	NO DEFENCE	NUMBER TWO
NEWS VALUE	NO EFFECTS	NUTS IN MAY
NEW YORKER	NO FISHING	O—9
NEXT APRIL	NO FLOWERS	OAST HOUSE
NEXT ISSUE	NO FOOLING	OBJET D'ART
NEXT MAN IN	NO FURTHER	OCEAN LANE
NEXT MARCH	NO GROUNDS	OCEAN WAVE
NEXT MONTH	NO HAWKERS	OCTANE GAS
NEXT OF KIN	NO INKLING	ODD CHOICE
NEXT STAGE	NOISES OFF	ODD CORNER
NEXT TRAIN	NO KIDDING	ODD COUPLE
NEXT WORLD	NO MANNERS	ODD JOB MAN
NICE POINT	NO MEANING	ODD MAN OUT
NICE SLEEP	NO MISTAKE	ODD MOMENT
NICE TASTE	NO MODESTY	ODD NUMBER
NICE TO SEE	NO ONE ELSE	ODD OR EVEN

ODD PERSON	OLD STREET	ON IMPULSE
OFF CENTRE	OLIVE TREE	ONION SKIN
OFF CHANCE	ON ACCOUNT	ONION SOUP
OFF COLOUR	ON A CHARGE	ONLY CHILD
OFF COURSE	ON A PICNIC	ONLY HUMAN
OFFICE BOY	ON ARRIVAL	ON MY RIGHT
OFFICE CAT	ON A STRING	ON ONE SIDE
OFF MOMENT	ON A TANDEM	ON ONE'S OWN
OFF SEASON	ON AVERAGE	ON ONE'S WAY
OFF TARGET	ON BALANCE	ON PURPOSE
OFF THE AIR	ONCE AGAIN	ON RATIONS
OFF THE MAP	ONCE A WEEK	ON RUNNERS
OFF THE PEG	ONCE A YEAR	ON SUNDAYS
OFF THE SET	ONCE ROUND	ON THE BALL
OF NO AVAIL	ON DEPOSIT	ON THE BEAM
OF NO WORTH	ON DISPLAY	ON THE BEAT
OF ONE MIND	ON DRAUGHT	ON THE BOIL
OF THAT ILK	ON DRY LAND	ON THE BONE
OIL COOKER	ONE ACROSS	ON THE CHIN
OILED SILK	ONE AND ALL	ON THE DOLE
OIL HEATER	ONE AND ONE	ON THE EDGE
OIL TANKER	ONE AND SIX	ON THE FARM
OIL TYCOON	ONE AND TEN	ON THE FIRE
OLD AND NEW	ONE AND TWO	ON THE FLAT
OLD AS ADAM	ONE BETTER	ON THE HEAD
OLD AS TIME	ONE DEGREE	ON THE HOOF
OLD BAILEY	ONE DOLLAR	ON THE HOUR
OLD BRANDY	ONE EIGHTH	ON THE HUNT
OLD BUFFER	ONE FOR ALL	ON THE JURY
OLD CODGER	ONE FOURTH	ON THE LAKE
OLD COUPLE	ONE GALLON	ON THE LAND
OLD CROCKS	ONE GUINEA	ON THE LEAD
OLD CUSTOM	ONE IN FIVE	ON THE LEFT
OLD EMPIRE	ONE IN FOUR	ON THE LINE
OLDEN DAYS	ONE IN NINE	ON THE LIST
OLD FAGGOT	ONE LENGTH	ON THE MAKE
OLD FAMILY	ONE-MAN DOG	ON THE MARK
OLD FELLOW	ONE MINUTE	ON THE MEND
OLD FOSSIL	ONE MOMENT	ON THE MENU
OLD FRIEND	ONE O'CLOCK	ON THE MOON
OLD MASTER	ONE OCTAVE	ON THE MOVE
OLD METHOD	ONE OF MANY	ON THE NAIL
OLD PEOPLE	ONE SECOND	ON THE NOSE
OLD RECORD	ONE'S EQUAL	ON THE PIER
OLD REEKIE	ONE STRIPE	ON THE RACK
OLD RÉGIME	ONE STROKE	ON THE RISE
OLD ROWLEY	ONE TO COME	ON THE ROAD
OLD SAYING	ONE TOO FEW	ON THE ROOF
OLD SCHOOL	ONE WICKET	ON THE SIDE
OLD SCORES	ON HALF PAY	ON THE SPOT
OLD STAGER	ON HOLIDAY	ON THE TOTE

ON THE TOWN	OUT OF DATE	PANT AFTER
ON THE TROT	OUT OF DEBT	PAPAL BULL
ON THE TURF	OUT OF FORM	PAPER BACK
ON THE TURN	OUT OF GEAR	PAPER BILL
ON THE WALL	OUT OF HAND	PAPER CLIP
ON THE WANE	OUT OF LINE	PAPER DOLL
ON THE WING	OUT OF LOVE	PAPER GAME
ON THIN ICE	OUT OF LUCK	PAPER MILL
ON TUESDAY	OUT OF MIND	PAPER OVER
OPEN A SHOP	OUT OF PAIN	PAPER RACK
OPEN COURT	OUT OF PITY	PAPER WORK
OPEN DRAIN	OUT OF PLAY	PARCEL OUT
OPEN EVENT	OUT OF STEP	PARIAH DOG
OPEN FIELD	OUT OF TIME	PARI PASSU
OPEN GRATE	OUT OF TOWN	PARIS GOWN
OPEN GRAVE	OUT OF TRIM	PARK BENCH
OPEN HEART	OUT OF TRUE	PARKED CAR
OPEN HOUSE	OUT OF TUNE	PARK ROYAL
OPEN MATCH	OUT OF TURN	PARTY GAME
OPEN MOUTH	OUT OF WORK	PARTY LINE
OPEN ORDER	OUT ON BAIL	PARTY MOOD
OPEN PORES	OUT WITH IT	PARTY RULE
OPEN PURSE	OUT YONDER	PARTY WALL
OPEN SHIRT	OVER AGAIN	PARTY WHIP
OPEN SKIES	OVER FORTY	PAS DE DEUX
OPEN SPACE	OVER PROOF	PAS DU TOUT
OPEN TO ALL	OVER THERE	PASS ALONG
OPEN WOUND	OVER TO YOU	PASSED OFF
ORANGE GIN	OWEN NARES	PASSED OUT
ORANGE PIP	OWEN TUDOR	PASSING BY
ORDER ARMS	OWN A HOUSE	PASSING ON
ORDER BOOK	OXFORD DON	PASS ROUND
ORDER FORM	OYSTER BAR	PAST GLORY
ORGAN LOFT	OYSTER BED	PAST SHAME
ORGAN STOP		PAST TENSE
ORLOP DECK	P—9	PATCHED UP
ORRIS ROOT	PACKED OUT	PATCH IT UP
OTHER DAYS	PADDED OUT	PATNA RICE
OTHER HALF	PAGE EIGHT	PATROL CAR
OTHER SELF	PAGE PROOF	PAUL JONES
OTHER SIDE	PAGE SEVEN	PAVED ROAD
OUR CHOICE	PAGE THREE	PAVED WALK
OUR FATHER	PAINT OVER	PAWN'S MOVE
OUT AND OUT	PAIRED OFF	PAY A VISIT
OUT AT HEEL	PALE BROWN	PAY DOUBLE
OUTER EDGE	PALE GREEN	PAY HOMAGE
OUTER SKIN	PALE HANDS	PAY IN FULL
OUTER TUBE	PALM BEACH	PAYING OUT
OUT FOR TEA	PALMY DAYS	PAY IN KIND
OUT OF A JOB	PANAMA HAT	PAY OFFICE
OUT OF BOND	PANEL GAME	PAY ON CALL

PAY ONE OUT	PIGEON PIE	PLAYED OUT
PAY PACKET	PIGGY BANK	PLAY FALSE
PAY RANSOM	PIG MARKET	PLAY GAMES
PEACE PACT	PILAU RICE	PLAY HAVOC
PEACH TREE	PILLAR BOX	PLAY POKER
PEAKED CAP	PILOT FISH	PLAY ROUGH
PEARL BUCK	PINE AFTER	PLAY SHARP
PEAR MELBA	PINK ICING	PLAY TO WIN
PEGGED OUT	PINK PEARL	PLAY WHIST
PENAL CODE	PIN-UP GIRL	PLEASE SIR
PENAL LAWS	PIOUS DUTY	PLOD ALONG
PENAL WORK	PIOUS HOPE	PLUGGED IN
PEN AND INK	PIPE DREAM	PLUMP DOWN
PEN FRIEND	PIPE MAJOR	PLUS FOURS
PENNY BANK	PIPE MUSIC	PLY A TRADE
PENNY POST	PIPING HOT	POETIC ART
PENNY WISE	PISTON ROD	POINT DUTY
PEPPER POT	PITCH DARK	POISON GAS
PEP UP PILL	PITCHED IN	POISON IVY
PER CAPITA	PITCH INTO	POISON PEN
PER CENTUM	PITCH UPON	POKE FUN AT
PER CONTRA	PIT PONIES	POKER DICE
PERRY COMO	PIT STALLS	POKER FACE
PETAL SOFT	PIT WORKER	POKER HAND
PETER COOK	PIXIE RING	POLA NEGRI
PETER WEST	PLACE A BET	POLAR BEAR
PETIT FOUR	PLACE KICK	POLE VAULT
PET NOTION	PLACE NAME	POLICE BOX
PETROL CAN	PLAIN CAKE	POLICE CAR
PETROL TAX	PLAIN COOK	POLICE DOG
PET THEORY	PLAIN FACT	POLISH OFF
PETTY CASH	PLAIN FOOD	POLITE ACT
PETTY JURY	PLAIN JANE	POLO MATCH
PEWTER POT	PLAIN WORK	POODLE CUT
PHONE CALL	PLAN AHEAD	POOK'S HILL
PHONEY WAR	PLANE TREE	POOR CATCH
PIANO DUET	PLANT LIFE	POOR CHILD
PIANO LEGS	PLATE RACK	POOR CLASS
PIANO SOLO	PLAY ABOUT	POOR DEVIL
PICK A LOCK	PLAY A CARD	POOR GRADE
PICK A TEAM	PLAY A FISH	POOR GUIDE
PICKED MAN	PLAY A JOKE	POOR HOUSE
PICKED OFF	PLAY AN ACE	POOR JUDGE
PICKED OUT	PLAY A NOTE	POOR LIGHT
PICK FRUIT	PLAY A PART	POOR MARKS
PICK HOLES	PLAY BINGO	POOR MATCH
PICKING UP	PLAY BOWLS	POOR SCORE
PICK OAKUM	PLAY BY EAR	POOR SPORT
PIECE RATE	PLAY CARDS	POOR START
PIED PIPER	PLAY CHESS	POOR STUFF
PIER GLASS	PLAY DARTS	POOR TABLE

POOR TASTE
POOR THING
POOR THROW
POOR VALUE
POOR VOICE
POOR WOMAN
POOR YIELD
POP NUMBER
POPPED OFF
POP RECORD
POP SINGER
PORT LIGHT
POST EARLY
POT THE RED
POUND AWAY
POUND NOTE
POUR FORTH
POWDER KEG
POWER DIVE
POWER UNIT
PRAY ALOUD
PRESS BACK
PRESS CLUB
PRESS DATE
PRESS DOWN
PRESSED ON
PRESS GANG
PRESS HARD
PRESS HOME
PRESS LAWS
PRESS ROOM
PRESS SEAT
PRESS SHOW
PRETTY BAD
PRETTY BIG
PRICE LIST
PRICE RING
PRIME BEEF
PRIME COST
PRISON VAN
PRIVY SEAL
PRIZE BULL
PRIZE CREW
PRIZE LIST
PRIZE POEM
PRIZE RING
PROOF COPY
PRO PATRIA
PROPER DAY
PROPER MAN
PROPER WAY

PROPPED UP
PROSE POEM
PROUD STEP
PROVE TRUE
PRUNE AWAY
PUBLIC BAR
PUBLIC EYE
PUFFED OUT
PULL A FACE
PULL AHEAD
PULL APART
PULL ASIDE
PULLED OFF
PULLED OUT
PULL FACES
PULL IT OFF
PULL IT OUT
PULL ROUND
PULL TIGHT
PULL WIRES
PUNCH BOWL
PUNCH LINE
PUNIC WARS
PUPPY LOVE
PURE SPITE
PURE WATER
PURE WHITE
PURE WOMAN
PUSH ASIDE
PUSHED OFF
PUSHED OUT
PUT ACROSS
PUT AT EASE
PUT IN GAOL
PUT IN GEAR
PUT IN HAND
PUT IN JAIL
PUT IN MIND
PUT IN QUOD
PUT IT DOWN
PUT IT OVER
PUT ON AIRS
PUT ON OATH
PUT ON SALE
PUT ON SHOW
PUT ON SIDE
PUT ON TAPE
PUT PAID TO
PUT TO ROUT
PUT TO WORK
PUT UP BAIL

PUT UP WITH
PUZZLE OUT

Q—9

QUEEN ANNE
QUEEN BESS
QUEEN MARY
QUEER BIRD
QUEER CARD
QUEER COVE
QUEER FISH
QUEUE HERE
QUICK FIRE
QUICK SALE
QUICK STEP
QUICK TIME
QUICK WITS
QUICK WORK
QUIET LIFE
QUIET READ
QUIET TIME
QUIET TONE
QUITE A FEW
QUITE FULL
QUITE GOOD
QUITE NEAR
QUITE NICE
QUITE SURE
QUITE WELL

R—9

RABBIT PIE
RACE AHEAD
RACE RIOTS
RACE TRACK
RACING CAR
RACING MAN
RACING SET
RACING TIP
RACY STYLE
RADIO MAST
RADIO PLAY
RADIO STAR
RADIO WAVE
RAIN BLOWS
RAIN CLOUD
RAIN GAUGE
RAIN WATER
RAISE CAIN
RAISE HELL

RALPH LYNN	RED INDIAN	RIGHT NAME
RAPID FIRE	RED LETTER	RIGHT NOTE
RAPID RATE	RED MENACE	RIGHT ROAD
RAREE SHOW	RED MULLET	RIGHT RULE
RARE EVENT	RED PENCIL	RIGHT SIDE
RARE STAMP	RED PEPPER	RIGHT SIZE
RARE STEAK	RED PLANET	RIGHT TIME
RARE TREAT	RED RIBAND	RIGHT TURN
RATE OF PAY	RED RIBBON	RIGHT VIEW
RAT POISON	RED SETTER	RIGHT WING
RATTLE OFF	RED SQUARE	RIGHT WORD
RAVEN HAIR	RED SPIDER	RING A BELL
RAVING MAD	REED ORGAN	RING AGAIN
RAW CARROT	REELED OFF	RING A PEAL
RAW COTTON	REFUSE BIN	RING CRAFT
RAW SPIRIT	RELAY RACE	RING FALSE
RAW TOMATO	RELIEF BUS	RING FENCE
RAY OF HOPE	RELIEF MAP	RING ROUND
REACH HOME	RENT A FLAT	RIN TIN TIN
REACH LAND	REPAIR JOB	RIO GRANDE
READ A BOOK	REPLY PAID	RIOT SQUAD
READ ALOUD	REP PLAYER	RIPE FRUIT
READ IN BED	RESCUE BID	RISE ABOVE
READ MORSE	RHINE WINE	RISE EARLY
READ MUSIC	RIB OF BEEF	RISING AIR
READ VERSE	RICE PAPER	RISING MAN
READY CASH	RICH UNCLE	RISING SUN
READY TO GO	RICH WIDOW	RITUAL ACT
REAL CREAM	RICH WOMAN	RIVAL FIRM
REAL DOUBT	RIDE IT OUT	RIVER AVON
REAL SPORT	RIDE ROUGH	RIVER BANK
REAL THING	RIDING CAP	RIVER BOAT
REAL TONIC	RIDING KIT	RIVER FISH
REAL TRUTH	RIFLE FIRE	RIVER NILE
REAL WORLD	RIFLE SHOT	RIVER STYX
REAR LIGHT	RIGHT AWAY	RIVER TEST
REAR WHEEL	RIGHT BACK	RIVER TRIP
REASON WHY	RIGHT BANK	ROAD AGENT
REBEL ARMY	RIGHT CARD	ROAD BLOCK
RECORD BID	RIGHT DOWN	ROAD BOARD
RECORD RUN	RIGHT FACE!	ROAD DRILL
RECORD SUM	RIGHT FOOT	ROAD METAL
RED CARPET	RIGHT FORM	ROAD SENSE
RED CHEEKS	RIGHT HALF	ROAD TO RIO
RED CHEESE	RIGHT HAND	ROAD WORKS
RED CIRCLE	RIGHT HOOK	ROAST BEEF
RED COTTON	RIGHT IDEA	ROAST DUCK
RED DRAGON	RIGHT LINE	ROAST LAMB
RED DUSTER	RIGHT MIND	ROAST MEAT
RED ENSIGN	RIGHT MOOD	ROAST PORK
RED GROUSE	RIGHT MOVE	ROAST VEAL

ROBIN HOOD	ROUND OATH	RUSH ABOUT
ROCK 'N' ROLL	ROUND POND	RUSH ORDER
ROCK PLANT	ROUND SHOT	RUS IN URBE
ROD OF IRON	ROUND TOUR	RYE WHISKY
ROLL ALONG	ROUND TRIP	
ROLLING UP	ROUTED OUT	
ROLL OF FAT	ROVING EYE	**S—9**
ROMAN BATH	ROWAN TREE	SABLE COAT
ROMAN CAMF	ROWING MAN	SACRED COW
ROMAN NOSE	ROYAL ARMS	SAD ENDING
ROMAN ORGY	ROYAL BLUE	SAD PLIGHT
ROMAN POET	ROYAL DUKE	SAFE CATCH
ROMAN ROAD	ROYAL LINE	SAFE HANDS
ROMAN TYPE	ROYAL MAIL	SAFE PLACE
ROMAN WALL	ROYAL MILE	SAFEST WAY
ROMANY RYE	ROYAL MINT	SAFETY NET
ROOK RIFLE	ROYAL NAVY	SAGE GREEN
ROOK'S MOVE	ROYAL PARK	SAIL ALONG
ROOK'S NEST	ROYAL ROAD	SAIL FORTH
ROOK'S PAWN	ROYAL ROBE	SAILOR BOY
ROOM TO LET	ROYAL SCOT	SAILOR HAT
ROOT CAUSE	ROYAL SEAT	SAIL ROUND
ROOTED OUT	ROYAL SHOW	SAINT IVES
ROPE ONE IN	ROYAL TOUR	SAINT JOAN
ROPE TRICK	ROY CASTLE	SAINT JOHN
ROSE MARIE	ROY ROGERS	SAINT PAUL
ROSE PETAL	RUBBED OUT	SAINT'S DAY
ROSE WATER	RUB GENTLY	SALAD BOWL
ROSS ON WYE	RUDE WORDS	SALAD DAYS
ROTTEN EGG	RUE THE DAY	SALE PRICE
ROTTEN ROW	RUGBY BALL	SALES TALK
ROUGH CAST	RUGBY TEAM	SALLY LUNN
ROUGH COAT	RUINED MAN	SALOON BAR
ROUGH COPY	RULE OF LAW	SALOON CAR
ROUGH EDGE	RUM AND PEP	SALT FLATS
ROUGHED IT	RUM BOTTLE	SALT SPOON
ROUGH GAME	RUMP STEAK	SALT WATER
ROUGH IDEA	RUM RATION	SAM BROWNE
ROUGH LUCK	RUM RUNNER	SAME AGAIN
ROUGH PLAN	RUN ACROSS	SAME STAMP
ROUGH PLAY	RUN A HORSE	SAME TO YOU
ROUGH ROAD	RUN AROUND	SAM WELLER
ROUGH SKIN	RUN ASHORE	SANDY SOIL
ROUGH TIME	RUN IT FINE	SAN MARINO
ROUGH TYPE	RUNNING IN	SANS SOUCI
ROUGH WORK	RUNNING ON	SANTA CRUZ
ROUND FACE	RUN OF LUCK	SARAH GAMP
ROUND GAME	RUN SECOND	SAVAGE DOG
ROUND HAND	RUN TOO FAR	SAVE MONEY
ROUND HEAD	RUN TO SEED	SAVE SPACE
ROUND HOLE	RURAL DEAN	SAVILE ROW

SAW THE AIR	SEE NO EVIL	SHADY SIDE
SAX ROHMER	SEE REASON	SHADY TREE
SAY CHEESE	SEE THINGS	SHAGGY DOG
SAY LITTLE	SEIZE UPON	SHAKE A LEG
SAY NO MORE	SELECT FEW	SHAKE DOWN
SAY PLEASE	SELL BADLY	SHAKY HAND
SCALE DOWN	SELL SHORT	SHAM FIGHT
SCAPA FLOW	SELL SPACE	SHAM SLEEP
SCENT GAME	SEND A CHIT	SHANGRI LA
SCHOOL AGE	SEND A WIRE	SHAPE WELL
SCHOOL CAP	SEND FORTH	SHARP BEND
SCHOOL TIE	SENIOR BOY	SHARP BLOW
SCORE A TRY	SENIOR MAN	SHARP EDGE
SCORE CARD	SENNA PODS	SHARP EYES
SCOTCH EGG	SERGE SUIT	SHARP FALL
SCOTCH FIR	SERVE TIME	SHARP NOTE
SCOTS PINE	SERVE WELL	SHARP PAIN
SCRAPE OFF	SET ADRIFT	SHARP RISE
SCRAP IRON	SET ALIGHT	SHARP TURN
SCREAM OUT	SET AT EASE	SHARP WITS
SCREW DOWN	SET AT ODDS	SHARP WORK
SCRUM HALF	SET AT REST	SHED A TEAR
SEA BATTLE	SET A WATCH	SHED BLOOD
SEA BOTTOM	SET COURSE	SHED LIGHT
SEA BREEZE	SET EYES ON	SHEEP FARM
SEALED OFF	SET FIRE TO	SHEER DROP
SEAMY SIDE	SET IN HAND	SHEER FUNK
SEARCH FEE	SET MOVING	SHEER LUCK
SEARCH FOR	SET ON EDGE	SHEER SILK
SEARCH OUT	SET ON FIRE	SHEET IRON
SEA SHANTY	SET ON FOOT	SHELL PEAS
SEA TRAVEL	SET PHRASE	SHIP'S BELL
SEA URCHIN	SET SPEECH	SHIP'S BOAT
SEA VOYAGE	SET SQUARE	SHIP'S GUNS
SECOND ACT	SET THEM UP	SHOCK WAVE
SECOND CUP	SETTING IN	SHOE BRUSH
SECOND DAY	SETTING UP	SHOOT DOWN
SECOND ROW	SETTLED IN	SHOP FLOOR
SECOND SET	SETTLED UP	SHOP FRONT
SECOND TEE	SET TO WORK	SHOP HOURS
SECOND TRY	SET UP SHOP	SHOP TO LET
SECRET ART	SEVEN AGES	SHORN LAMB
SECURE JOB	SEVEN DAYS	SHORT HAIR
SEE A GHOST	SEVEN DEEP	SHORT HEAD
SEE DOUBLE	SEVEN FEET	SHORT HOLE
SEED PEARL	SEVEN QUID	SHORT LIFE
SEEING RED	SEVEN SEAS	SHORT LIST
SEEK A CLUE	SEX APPEAL	SHORT NOTE
SEEK AFTER	SEX SYMBOL	SHORT ODDS
SEEK PEACE	SHADY DEAL	SHORT POEM
SEEK SCOPE	SHADY NOOK	SHORT PUTT

SHORT READ	SIMON PURE	SLEEP WELL
SHORT REST	SIMPLE SUM	SLEEPY AIR
SHORT SLIP	SIMPLY FAB	SLIDE BACK
SHORT SPAN	SING A SONG	SLIDE DOWN
SHORT STAY	SINGLE BED	SLIM WAIST
SHORT STEP	SINGLE MAN	SLINK AWAY
SHORT TAIL	SINGLE OUT	SLINK PAST
SHORT TERM	SING SMALL	SLIPPED IN
SHORT TIME	SINK A PUTT	SLIPPED UP
SHORT VIEW	SINK A WELL	SLIT SKIRT
SHORT WALK	SIREN SONG	SLOP BASIN
SHORT WAVE	SIREN SUIT	SLOPE ARMS
SHORT WORD	SIT AT HOME	SLOPE DOWN
SHORT WORK	SITTING UP	SLOPPY JOE
SHOUT DOWN	SIT UP LATE	SLOUCH HAT
SHOVEL HAT	SIX AND ONE	SLOW DEATH
SHOVE PAST	SIX AND SIX	SLOW MARCH
SHOW CAUSE	SIX AND TEN	SLOW MATCH
SHOWED OFF	SIX AND TWO	SLOW MUSIC
SHOWED OUT	SIX A PENNY	SLOW PULSE
SHOW FIGHT	SIX HEARTS	SLOW START
SHOW MERCY	SIX MONTHS	SLOW TEMPO
SHOW ONE IN	SIX O'CLOCK	SLOW TRAIN
SHOW PIECE	SIX OUNCES	SLOW WALTZ
SHOW PLACE	SIX POINTS	SLY AS A FOX
SHOW ROUND	SIX POUNDS	SLY CORNER
SHOW SIGNS	SIX SPADES	SLY HUMOUR
SHOW STYLE	SIXTH FORM	SMALL ARMS
SHRIEK OUT	SIXTH HOLE	SMALL BEER
SHRILL CRY	SIXTH PART	SMALL BORE
SHRIVEL UP	SIXTH RACE	SMALL COAL
SHUT TIGHT	SIXTH TIME	SMALL COIN
SICK LEAVE	SIX TO FOUR	SMALL DEBT
SICKLY HUE	SIX TRICKS	SMALL DOOR
SIDE ISSUE	SIX WHEELS	SMALL FEET
SIGHT GAME	SIZE EIGHT	SMALL FLAT
SIGHT LAND	SIZE SEVEN	SMALL GAME
SIGNAL BOX	SIZE THREE	SMALL HEAD
SIGN A PACT	SKATE OVER	SMALL HOLE
SIGN BELOW	SKETCH MAP	SMALL ITEM
SIGNED OFF	SKETCH OUT	SMALL LOAF
SILK PURSE	SKIM ALONG	SMALL LOAN
SILK SCARF	SKIN DIVER	SMALL MIND
SILK SOCKS	SKIP A MEAL	SMALL PART
SILLY FOOL	SLACK ROPE	SMALL PORT
SILLY TALK	SLACK TIME	SMALL RISK
SILVER CUP	SLANG WORD	SMALL ROOM
SILVER FIR	SLATE CLUB	SMALL SIZE
SILVER FOX	SLAVE AWAY	SMALL SLAM
SILVER SEA	SLAVE CAMP	SMALL SPOT
SILVER URN	SLEEP ON IT	SMALL TALK

SMALL TOWN
SMALL TWIG
SMALL TYPE
SMART ALEC
SMARTEN UP
SMART GIRL
SMART PACE
SMART SUIT
SMART WALK
SMELL A RAT
SMOKE A LOT
SMOKE BOMB
SMOKED EEL
SMOKED HAM
SMOKE RING
SMOKY CITY
SMOKY FIRE
SMOKY ROOM
SMOOTH OUT
SMOOTH SEA
SMUGGLE IN
SNAIL PACE
SNAKE BITE
SNAPPED UP
SNEAK AWAY
SNEAK PAST
SNOB VALUE
SNOW QUEEN
SNOW SCENE
SNOW STORM
SNOW WHITE
SNUGGLE UP
SOAP OPERA
SOAR ABOVE
SOBER DOWN
SOBER FACT
SOB SISTER
SOCIAL WAR
SODA WATER
SOFT DRINK
SOFT FRUIT
SOFT GOING
SOFT GOODS
SOFT HEART
SOFT LIGHT
SOFT MUSIC
SOFT PEDAL
SOFT THING
SOFT TOUCH
SOFT VOICE
SOFT WATER

SOFT WORDS
SO IT SEEMS
SOLAR TIME
SOLAR YEAR
SOLDIER ON
SOLE AGENT
SOLEMN VOW
SOLE OWNER
SO LET IT BE
SOLE TRUST
SOLID BALL
SOLID BODY
SOLID FOOD
SOLID FUEL
SOLID GOLD
SOLID MASS
SOLID MEAL
SOLID TYRE
SOLID VOTE
SOLO DANCE
SOLO WHIST
SOME HOPES
SONG CYCLE
SONG TITLE
SON OF A GUN
SOON AFTER
SORE PLACE
SORE POINT
SORE TRIAL
SO TO SPEAK
SOTTO VOCE
SOUL OF WIT
SOUND BODY
SOUND MIND
SOUND TYPE
SOUND WAVE
SOUP LADLE
SOUP PLATE
SOUP SPOON
SOUR CREAM
SOUR TASTE
SOUTH BANK
SOUTH POLE
SOUTH SEAS
SOUTH WIND
SOUTH ZONE
SPACE RACE
SPACE SHIP
SPACE SUIT
SPARE CASH
SPARE COPY

SPARE PART
SPARE ROOM
SPARE TIME
SPARE TYRE
SPARKS FLY
SPEAK WELL
SPEECH DAY
SPEEDED UP
SPEED IT UP
SPEED KING
SPEND TIME
SPILL OVER
SPILL SALT
SPILT MILK
SPIN A COIN
SPIN A DISC
SPIN A YARN
SPIN DRIER
SPIN ROUND
SPIT IT OUT
SPLIT OPEN
SPLIT PEAS
SPLIT VOTE
SPONGE BAG
SPONGE OUT
SPORTS CAR
SPORTS DAY
SPORTS FAN
SPOT CHECK
SPOT DANCE
SPOT OF INK
SPOT PRIZE
SPOT TO EAT
SPREAD OUT
SPRING OUT
SPUN GLASS
SQUARE JAW
SQUARE LEG
SQUARE OFF
SQUARE ONE
SQUARE PEG
SQUAT DOWN
SQUEEZE IN
STABLE BOY
STAFF FUND
STAFF ROOM
STAFF WORK
STAGE DOOR
STAGE NAME
STAGE PLAY
STAGE SHOW

STAGGER IN	STEEL MILL	STRAW POLL
STAG PARTY	STEEL TAPE	STRAW VOTE
STALE CAKE	STEEP HILL	STRAY AWAY
STALE JOKE	STEP ASIDE	STREAK OUT
STALE LOAF	STEP DANCE	STREAM OUT
STALE NEWS	STEP SHORT	STREET MAP
STAMP DOWN	STICK AT IT	STRETCH UP
STAMP DUTY	STICK 'EM UP	STRIDE OFF
STAND AWAY	STICK FAST	STRIDE OUT
STAND BACK	STICK IT ON	STRIKE OFF
STAND BAIL	STICK TO IT	STRIKE OIL
STAND DOWN	STICKY END	STRIKE OUT
STAND EASY	STIFF GALE	STRIKE PAY
STAND FAST	STIFF NECK	STRING BAG
STAND FIRM	STIFF TEST	STRING OUT
STAND HIGH	STILL LIFE	STRIP BARE
STAND IDLE	STILL MORE	STRIP CLUB
STAND OVER	STILL OPEN	STRONG ALE
ST. ANDREWS	STILL ROOM	STRONG ARM
STAND UP TO	STILL WINE	STRONG BOX
STAR ACTOR	STINK BOMB	STRONG MAN
STARE DOWN	STIRRED UP	STRONG TEA
STAR PUPIL	ST. MATTHEW	STRUCK OFF
STARRY SKY	ST. MICHAEL	STRUCK OUT
STAR SHELL	STOCK FARM	STRUNG OUT
START A ROW	STOCK LIST	STUD HORSE
START A WAR	STOCK PART	STUDIO ONE
START BACK	STOCK PILE	STUD POKER
STARTED UP	STOCK SIZE	STUDY FORM
START TO GO	STOKE CITY	STUDY HARD
START WITH	STOLE AWAY	SUB JUDICE
START WORK	STONE COLD	SUDDEN END
STARVE OUT	STONE DEAD	SUDDEN FIT
STATE FAIR	STONE DEAF	SUEZ CANAL
STATE FARM	STONE WALL	SUGAR BEET
STATUS QUO	STOOP DOWN	SUGAR CANE
STAY ALIVE	STOP A BLOW	SUGAR PLUM
STAY AWAKE	STOP A LEAK	SUIT AT LAW
STAYED OUT	STOP AND GO	SULTRY AIR
STAYED PUT	STOP IN BED	SUMMING UP
STAY IN BED	STOPPED UP	SUN BONNET
STAY STILL	STOP PRESS	SUNDAY TEA
ST. BERNARD	STOP SHORT	SUN HELMET
STEAL AWAY	STOP THIEF!	SUNK FENCE
STEAL PAST	STOP VALVE	SUN LOUNGE
STEAL UP ON	STORE AWAY	SUNNY SIDE
STEAM BATH	STORM CONE	SUN VALLEY
STEAM IRON	STORMY SEA	SUN YAT-SEN
STEAM OPEN	ST. PANCRAS	SUPPOSE SO
STEEL BAND	ST. PATRICK	SURE THING
STEEL BILL	STRAP DOWN	SURE TO WIN

M.C.D.—4

SURVEY MAP	TAKE A NOTE	TALL STORY
SUSAN SHAW	TAKE APART	TALL WOMAN
SWAGGER IN	TAKE A PEEP	TANK CORPS
SWALLOW UP	TAKE A PILL	TAR BARREL
SWARM OVER	TAKE A REST	TAROT CARD
SWEAR BY IT	TAKE A RISK	TASK FORCE
SWEAR WORD	TAKE A SEAT	TASMAN SEA
SWEEP AWAY	TAKE A SNAP	TAWNY PORT
SWEEP DOWN	TAKE A TAXI	TAX DEMAND
SWEEP PAST	TAKE A TEST	TAX FIDDLE
SWEET CORN	TAKE A TOSS	TAX REBATE
SWEET DISH	TAKE A TRAM	TAX RELIEF
SWEET NELL	TAKE A TRIP	TAY BRIDGE
SWEET PEAS	TAKE A TURN	TEA FOR TWO
SWEET SHOP	TAKE A VIEW	TEA GARDEN
SWEET SONG	TAKE A VOTE	TEA KETTLE
SWEET WINE	TAKE A WALK	TEA LEAVES
SWELL IDEA	TAKE A WIFE	TEAR ABOUT
SWELL TIME	TAKE COVER	TEAR ALONG
SWEPT AWAY	TAKE DRUGS	TEAR APART
SWING BACK	TAKE HEART	TEA RATION
SWING HIGH	TAKE IN TOW	TEAR IN TWO
SWISS ALPS	TAKE ISSUE	TEDDY BEAR
SWISS CITY	TAKE LEAVE	TEDDY GIRL
SWISS NAVY	TAKE LUNCH	TELL NO LIE
SWISS ROLL	TAKE MY TIP	TELL NO ONE
SWITCH OFF	TAKEN DOWN	TELL TALES
SWOOP DOWN	TAKE NOTES	TEMPLE BAR
	TAKE ON OIL	TEMPT FATE
T—9	TAKE PAINS	TEN AND ONE
TAB HUNTER	TAKE PLACE	TEN AND SIX
TABLE BIRD	TAKE PRIDE	TEN AND TEN
TABLE FISH	TAKE RISKS	TEN AND TWO
TABLE SALT	TAKE ROOMS	TEN A PENNY
TABLE TALK	TAKE SHAPE	TENDER AGE
TABLE WINE	TAKE SIDES	TEN MONTHS
TAKE ABACK	TAKE SNUFF	TENNIS ACE
TAKE A BATH	TAKE STEPS	TENNIS NET
TAKE A CARD	TAKE STOCK	TEN O'CLOCK
TAKE A CASE	TAKE TURNS	TENOR CLEF
TAKE A COPY	TAKE UP ART	TENOR DRUM
TAKE A CURE	TAKING OFF	TENOR OBOE
TAKE A DROP	TAKING OUT	TEN OUNCES
TAKE A FALL	TALE OF WOE	TEN POINTS
TAKE AFTER	TALK ABOUT	TEN POUNDS
TAKE A HAND	TALKED BIG	TEN ROUNDS
TAKE A HINT	TALKED OUT	TENTH HOLE
TAKE A LOOK	TALK ROUND	TENTH PART
TAKE A MEAL	TALK SENSE	TENTH TIME
TAKE AMISS	TALK TRIPE	TEST MATCH
TAKE AN ELL	**TALL ORDER**	TEST PAPER

TEST PIECE	THE LIZARD	THE TEMPLE
TEST PILOT	THE LOSERS	THE THAMES
TEXAS CITY	THE LOUVRE	THE TICKET
THAT'S THAT	THE MAQUIS	THE TIVOLI
THE ALBANY	THE MASSES	THE UMPIRE
THE ALBION	THE MASTER	THE UNSEEN
THE ALLIES	THE MEDWAY	THE WAY OUT
THE AMAZON	THEME SONG	THE WINNER
THE ARMADA	THE METHOD	THE WINTER
THE AUTUMN	THE MIKADO	THEY'RE OFF!
THE AZORES	THE MINUET	THICK HAIR
THE BALTIC	THE MORGUE	THICK HEAD
THE BIG TOP	THE MOVIES	THICK MIST
THE BOARDS	THE OCCULT	THICK SKIN
THE BOTTOM	THE OLD VIC	THICK SNOW
THE BOUNTY	THE OLD WAY	THICK SOUP
THE BOURSE	THE ORIENT	THICK WIRE
THE BOWERY	THE PAPERS	THIN BLOOD
THE BROADS	THE PEOPLE	THINK BACK
THE BUDGET	THE PLAGUE	THINK BEST
THE CINEMA	THE PLOUGH	THINK FAST
THE CLERGY	THE POLICE	THINK HARD
THE CREEPS	THE PUBLIC	THINK LONG
THE CRIMEA	THE QUEENS	THINK OVER
THE DALEKS	THE RABBLE	THIN ON TOP
THE DANUBE	THE RED SEA	THIN SHELL
THE DELUGE	THE RINGER	THIN SLICE
THE DESERT	THE RIVALS	THIN TWINE
THE EMPIRE	THE ROCKET	THIRD FORM
THE FALLEN	THE RUBBER	THIRD GEAR
THE FINISH	THE SCOTCH	THIRD HAND
THE FLICKS	THE SCRIPT	THIRD HEAT
THE FLOODS	THESE DAYS	THIRD HOLE
THE FRENCH	THE SENATE	THIRD JUMP
THE FUHRER	THE SEVERN	THIRD LINE
THE FUTURE	THE SHAKES	THIRD PART
THE GANGES	THE SHIRES	THIRD RACE
THE GENTRY	THE SIGHTS	THIRD RATE
THE GOSPEL	THE SOLENT	THIRD TEAM
THE GRACES	THE SPHINX	THIRD TERM
THE GUARDS	THE SPLITS	THIRD TEST
THE HILTON	THE SPOILS	THIRD TIME
THE ICE AGE	THE SPRING	THIRD WEEK
THE JET AGE	THE SQUIRE	THIRD YEAR
THE JUNGLE	THE STATES	THIRST FOR
THE KAISER	THE STITCH	THIRTY ALL
THE LANCET	THE STOCKS	THIS EARTH
THE LATEST	THE STONES	THIS MONTH
THE LATTER	THE STRAND	THIS WAY IN
THE LEVANT	THE SUMMER	THIS WAY UP
THE LIVING	THE TATLER	THORPE BAY

THRASH OUT	TIPPED OFF	TOTE PRICE
THREE ACES	TIPSY CAKE	TO THE BONE
THREE ACTS	TIP-UP SEAT	TO THE BRIM
THREE DAYS	TIRED EYES	TO THE EAST
THREE DEEP	TIRING JOB	TO THE FORE
THREE EGGS	TIT FOR TAT	TO THE FULL
THREE FEET	TITHE BARN	TO THE GOOD
THREE LAPS	TITIAN RED	TO THE HILT
THREE PIPS	TITLE DEED	TO THE LAST
THREE QUID	TITLE PAGE	TO THE LEFT
THREE SETS	TITLE ROLE	TO THE LIFE
THREE STAR	TITO GOBBI	TO THE MOON
THREE TENS	TO A DEGREE	TO THE WEST
THROW A FIT	TOAST RACK	TO THIS DAY
THROW AWAY	TO BE BRIEF	TOUCH DOWN
THROW BACK	TODAY WEEK	TOUCHED UP
THROW DOWN	TODDLE OFF	TOUCH UPON
THROWN OUT	TOGGED OUT	TOUCH WOOD
THROW OPEN	TOILET SET	TOUGHEN UP
THROW OVER	TOKEN VOTE	TOUGH LUCK
TICKED OFF	TO LEEWARD	TOUGH MEAT
TIC-TAC MAN	TOMMY FARR	TOUGH SKIN
TIDAL FLOW	TOM PEARSE	TOUGH SPOT
TIDAL RACE	TOM SAWYER	TOWER HILL
TIDAL WAVE	TON OF COAL	TOWER OVER
TIED HOUSE	TON OF COKE	TOWN CLERK
TIE IN A BOW	TON OF LEAD	TOWN CRIER
TIGER HUNT	TON OF SALT	TOWN HOUSE
TIGER LILY	TON WEIGHT	TOWN MOUSE
TIGER MOTH	TOOK PLACE	TOY POODLE
TIGHTEN UP	TOOL CHEST	TRACE BACK
TIGHT GRIP	TOO LITTLE	TRACK DOWN
TIGHT HAND	TO ONE SIDE	TRACK SUIT
TIGHT REIN	TOO STRONG	TRADE BOOM
TIGHT SPOT	TOP DRAWER	TRADE FAIR
TIME BEING	TOP PEOPLE	TRADE MARK
TIME CHECK	TOP SECRET	TRADE NAME
TIME FLIES	TOP STOREY	TRADE WIND
TIME LIMIT	TOP TO TAIL	TRAIL ARMS
TIME OF DAY	TOP TWENTY	TRAIL BOSS
TIME OF WAR	TOP WEIGHT	TRAIN FARE
TIME STUDY	TORCH SONG	TRAIN LOAD
TIME TAKEN	TORY PARTY	TRAM DEPOT
TIME TO EAT	TOSS ABOUT	TRAMPLE ON
TIME TO PAY	TOSS A COIN	TRAP THREE
TINDER BOX	TOSS ASIDE	TREAD DOWN
TIN HELMET	TOSS FOR IT	TREE HOUSE
TIN LIZZIE	TOSSING UP	TREE STUMP
TIN OF SOUP	TOTAL COST	TRIAL GAME
TIN OPENER	TOTAL LOSS	TRIAL JURY
TIP AND RUN	TOTEM POLE	TRIAL SPIN

TRIAL TRIP	TURN GREEN	**U—9**
TRIBAL LAW	TURNING IN	UGLY AS SIN
TRIBAL WAR	TURNING UP	UGLY CROWD
TRICKY BIT	TURN IT OFF	UNCLE TOBY
TRICKY JOB	TURN LOOSE	UNDER A BAN
TRIED HARD	TURN NASTY	UNDER ARMS
TRIED IT ON	TURN RIGHT	UNDER FIRE
TRILBY HAT	TURN ROUND	UNDER OATH
TRIM WAIST	TURN TO ICE	UNDER SAIL
TRIPPED UP	TURN WHITE	UNDER SEAL
TROJAN WAR	TWEED SUIT	UNHEARD OF
TROT ALONG	TWELVE MEN	UNHOLY JOY
TROT IT OUT	TWICE A DAY	UNHOLY ROW
TRUDGE OFF	TWICE FIVE	UNION CARD
TRUE STORY	TWICE FOUR	UNION FLAG
TRUE VALUE	TWICE NINE	UNION JACK
TRUE WORTH	TWICE OVER	UNIT TRUST
TRUMP CARD	TWICE TOLD	UP AGAINST
TRUNK CALL	TWIGGED IT	UP AND AT 'EM
TRUNK LINE	TWIN GIRLS	UP AND AWAY
TRUNK ROAD	TWIN SCREW	UP AND DOWN
TRUSSED UP	TWIN SOULS	UP AND OVER
TRUST DEED	TWO AND ONE	UP COUNTRY
TRUST FUND	TWO AND SIX	UP FOR SALE
TRUTH DRUG	TWO AND TEN	UPPER CASE
TRUTH GAME	TWO AND TWO	UPPER DECK
TRY HARDER	TWO A PENNY	UPPER FORM
TRY IN VAIN	TWO COPIES	UPPER HAND
TRY TO STOP	TWO FIFTHS	UPPER LIMB
TSETSE FLY	TWO FOR ONE	UPPER PART
TUBAL CAIN	TWO FOR TEA	UP THE HILL
TUBE TRAIN	TWO HALVES	UP THE LINE
TUCK ONE IN	TWO HEARTS	UP THE POLE
TUCK ONE UP	TWO LOAVES	UP THE WALL
TUDOR ROSE	TWO MONTHS	UP TO SNUFF
TULIP TREE	TWO NINTHS	URCHIN CUT
TULSE HILL	TWO O'CLOCK	URIAH HEEP
TUMBLE OFF	TWO OUNCES	URSA MAJOR
TUMBLE OUT	TWO POINTS	URSA MINOR
TUMMY ACHE	TWO POUNDS	USE AS A PEG
TUNNY FISH	TWO QUARTS	USUAL TEXT
TUN OF BEER	TWO ROUNDS	UTTER LOSS
TUN OF WINE	TWO SPADES	UTTER RUIN
TURFED OUT	TWO STOOLS	
TURK'S HEAD	TWO STRAWS	**V—9**
TURN ABOUT	TWO THIRDS	VACANT LOT
TURN AGAIN	TWO TO COME	VADE MECUM
TURN A HAIR	TWO TRICKS	VAGUE HOPE
TURN ASIDE	TWO VERSES	VAGUE IDEA
TURNED OFF	TWO VOICES	VAIN ABUSE
TURNED OUT	TWO WHEELS	VAIN BOAST

VAIN GLORY	WAIT THERE	WATER POLO
VANITY BAG	WAKE EARLY	WATER RATE
VAST FRAME	WAKES WEEK	WATER TANK
VAULT OVER	WALK ABOUT	WAVE ASIDE
VEER RIGHT	WALKED OFF	WAVE A WAND
VEER ROUND	WALKED OUT	WAX CANDLE
VENIAL SIN	WALKER CUP	WAX EFFIGY
VERSE FORM	WALK ON AIR	WAX FIGURE
VERS LIBRE	WALK OUT ON	WAX STRONG
VERY IMAGE	WALTZ HOME	WAY BEHIND
VERY LIGHT	WALTZ KING	WAY OF LIFE
VERY OFTEN	WALTZ TIME	WEAK CHEST
VERY QUICK	WALTZ TUNE	WEAKER SEX
VERY STEEP	WANDER OFF	WEAK HEART
VERY SWEET	WANDER OUT	WEAK POINT
VEX A SAINT	WANTED MAN	WEAK STATE
VICE SQUAD	WAR DAMAGE	WEAK STYLE
VICE VERSA	WAR EFFORT	WEAK THING
VICKI BAUM	WAR GRAVES	WEAK VOICE
VIC OLIVER	WAR HEROES	WEAK WOMAN
VILLA PARK	WAR LEADER	WEALTH TAX
VIN DU PAYS	WARM HEART	WEAR A HALO
VINGT ET UN	WARM NIGHT	WEAR A MASK
VIOLIN BOW	WARM PLACE	WEAR BLACK
VISUAL AID	WARM SPELL	WEAVE A WEB
VITAL PART	WAR MUSEUM	WEB OF LIES
VITAL ROLE	WARM WATER	WEEDED OUT
VIVE LE ROI	WARNED OFF	WEIGH DOWN
VIVID BLUE	WAR OFFICE	WEIGHED IN
VOID SPACE	WAR ON WANT	WELCOME IN
VOLTE FACE	WAR POLICY	WELL AGAIN
VOLUME ONE	WAR RECORD	WELL AHEAD
VOLUME SIX	WAR VICTIM	WELL AIRED
VOLUME TEN	WAR WORKER	WELL BEGUN
VOLUME TWO	WASH CLEAN	WELL BELOW
VOTING AGE	WASHED OUT	WELL OILED
VOTING DAY	WASPS' NEST	WELL SET UP
VOX HUMANA	WASP STING	WELL SPENT
VOX POPULI	WASP WAIST	WELL TAPED
	WASTE AWAY	WELSH BARD
	WASTE FOOD	WELSH HARP
W—9	WASTE LAND	WENT AHEAD
WAGE CLAIM	WASTE TIME	WENT BELOW
WAGE PAUSE	WATCH OVER	WENT FORTH
WAGES BILL	WATER BABY	WENT ROUND
WAGE SCALE	WATER DOWN	WENT TO BED
WAGE SLAVE	WATER FOWL	WENT TO POT
WAIST HIGH	WATER HOLE	WENT TO SEA
WAIT ABOUT	WATER JUMP	WENT TO WAR
WAIT FOR IT!	WATER LILY	WENT UNDER
WAIT FOR ME!	WATER MAIN	WENT WRONG
WAIT TABLE		

WEST COAST	WIDE FIELD	WORD MAGIC
WEST FRONT	WIDE GUESS	WORK BENCH
WEST POINT	WIDE RANGE	WORKED OUT
WEST WALES	WIDE SCOPE	WORKER BEE
WET SEASON	WIDE SWEEP	WORK IT OUT
WET SPONGE	WIDE WORLD	WORK LOOSE
WET WICKET	WIGAN PIER	WORK OF ART
WHALE MEAT	WILD BEAST	WORK PARTY
WHAT A LARK!	WILD GOOSE	WORKS BAND
WHAT A LIFE!	WILD GRASS	WORK STUDY
WHAT A PITY!	WILD GUESS	WORK TABLE
WHAT'S WHAT	WILD HORSE	WORLD BANK
WHEAT GERM	WILD NIGHT	WORLD FAIR
WHEEL AWAY	WILD PARTY	WORLD'S END
WHERE IS IT?	WILD STATE	WORLD TOUR
WHIP ROUND	WILD THYME	WORSE LUCK
WHISK AWAY	WILL POWER	WORST PART
WHITE BEAR	WILL TO WIN	WORST TEAM
WHITE CITY	WIN A FIGHT	WORTH A LOT
WHITE FISH	WIN A MATCH	WORTH A TRY
WHITE FLAG	WIN A POINT	WORTHY AIM
WHITE GOLD	WIN A PRIZE	WRAPPED UP
WHITE HAIR	WIND GAUGE	WRAP ROUND
WHITE HEAT	WINDING UP	WRENCH OUT
WHITE HOPE	WIND SCALE	WRITE BACK
WHITE KING	WINDY SIDE	WRITE DOWN
WHITE LADY	WIN EASILY	WRITE HOME
WHITE LEAD	WINE GLASS	WRITE WELL
WHITE LINE	WINE PARTY	WRONG DATE
WHITE LOAF	WIN FAVOUR	WRONG DOOR
WHITE MARK	WINGED ANT	WRONG IDEA
WHITE MEAT	WINKLE OUT	WRONG MOVE
WHITE MICE	WIN OR LOSE	WRONG NAME
WHITE NILE	WIN RENOWN	WRONG RATE
WHITE NOTE	WIN THE CUP	WRONG ROAD
WHITE PAWN	WIN THE DAY	WRONG SIDE
WHITE PINE	WIPE CLEAN	WRONG STEP
WHITE PORT	WIRE FENCE	WRONG TIME
WHITE RACE	WISE WOMAN	WRONG TURN
WHITE ROOK	WITCH HUNT	WRONG VIEW
WHITE ROSE	WITH A BANG	WRONG WORD
WHITE SALE	WITH A WILL	WROUGHT UP
WHITE SPOT	WITH SKILL	WYATT EARP
WHITE STAR	WITH SUGAR	WYE VALLEY
WHITE WINE	WOMAN'S MAN	
WHOLE SKIN	WOMEN'S LIB	**Y—9**
WICKED LIE	WONDER WHY	YACHT CLUB
WICKED ONE	WOODEN BOX	YACHT RACE
WIDE APART	WOODEN LEG	YARD OF ALE
WIDE AWAKE	WOOD GREEN	YEA AND NAY
WIDE BERTH	WOOD NYMPH	YELLOW DOG

YELLOW SEA	ACT OF UNION	ALL OF A HEAP
YES PLEASE	ACT THE FOOL	ALL OF A KIND
YET TO COME	ACT THE GOAT	ALL PARTIES
YORKED OUT	ACT THE HERO	ALL PRESENT
YOUNG BIRD	ACT THE HOST	ALL SET TO GO
YOUNG GIRL	ACT THE PART	ALL THE BEST
YOUNG FOLK	ACUTE ANGLE	ALL THE LUCK
YOUNG IDEA	ADAM AND EVE	ALL THE MORE
YOUNG LADY	ADAM'S APPLE	ALL THE RAGE
YOUNG LOVE	ADD A CLAUSE	ALL THE REST
YOUNG THUG	ADDIS ABABA	ALL THE SAME
YOUR FAULT	ADELE LEIGH	ALL THE TIME
YOUR GRACE	ADOLF HITLER	ALL THE YEAR
YOUR SHARE	ADOPTED SON	ALL THROUGH
YOUTH CLUB	ADVICE NOTE	ALL-TIME LOW
	ADVISE WELL	ALL TOO SOON
Z—9	AERIAL VIEW	ALL TOO WELL
ZOO INMATE	AFRICA STAR	ALMOND CAKE
ZUYDER ZEE	AFTER A TIME	ALMOND TREE
	AFTER DEATH	ALMOST DEAD
A—10	AFTER HOURS	ALMOST FULL
ABE LINCOLN	AFTER LUNCH	ALMOST OVER
A BIT PAST IT	AFTER TODAY	ALPACA COAT
ABJECT FEAR	A GREAT DEAL	ALPINE CLUB
ABLE FELLOW	A GREAT MANY	ALPINE RACE
ABLE SEAMAN	AID AND ABET	ALTAR CLOTH
ABLE TO COPE	AIM TOO HIGH	AMBER LIGHT
ABOARD SHIP	AIR DEFENCE	AMBLE ALONG
ABOVE BOARD	AIR DISPLAY	AMEN CORNER
ABOVE IT ALL	AIR FREIGHT	AMPLE CAUSE
ABOVE PRICE	AIR HOSTESS	AMPLE MEANS
ABOVE WATER	AIR MARSHAL	AMPLE SCOPE
ABRUPT EXIT	AIR SERVICE	AMY JOHNSON
ACE OF CLUBS	AIR WARFARE	AND ALL THAT
ACE SERVICE	ALARM CLOCK	AND SO FORTH
ACETIC ACID	ALBERT HALL	AND SO TO BED
ACHING FEET	ALF'S BUTTON	AND THE LIKE
ACHING VOID	ALL BUT A FEW	AND THE REST
ACID REMARK	ALL COLOURS	ANGEL CHILD
ACID TONGUE	ALL CORRECT	ANGLED SHOT
ACT AS AGENT	ALL DAY LONG	ANGORA GOAT
ACT AS COACH	ALL FORLORN	ANGORA WOOL
ACT AS GUIDE	ALL FOR LOVE	ANGRY SCENE
ACTIVE LIFE	ALL HALLOWS	ANGRY WORDS
ACTIVE LIST	ALL HAYWIRE	ANILINE DYE
ACTIVE MIND	ALL IN A HEAP	ANIMAL FARM
ACTIVE PART	ALL IN ORDER	ANIMAL FOOD
ACT OF FAITH	ALL KEYED UP	ANIMAL GRAB
ACT OF FOLLY	ALL MIXED UP	ANIMAL LIFE
ACT OF GRACE	ALL MOD CONS	ANKLE SOCKS
ACT OF MERCY	ALL OF A GLOW	ANNABEL LEE
ACT OF PIETY		

ANNA NEAGLE
ANNE BOLEYN
ANNO DOMINI
ANNUAL RENT
ANOTHER DAY
ANOTHER WAY
ANSWER BACK
ANY OLD IRON
ANY OLD TIME
APPLE GREEN
APPLE SAUCE
APPLIED ART
APRICOT JAM
APRON STAGE
APT ANALOGY
APT SCHOLAR
AQUA FORTIS
ARABIAN SEA
ARAB LEAGUE
ARABLE FARM
ARAB LEGION
ARABLE LAND
ARAB STATES
ARCHED BACK
ARENA STAGE
ARMED FORCE
ARMED GUARD
ARMED TRUCE
ARMS AKIMBO
ARM'S LENGTH
ARMY DOCTOR
ARMY ORDERS
ARRIVE LATE
ART GALLERY
ARTHUR RANK
ART STUDENT
ART SUBJECT
ART THEATRE
AS ARRANGED
ASCOT HEATH
ASCOT RACES
AS INTENDED
ASK A FAVOUR
ASK FOR HELP
ASK FOR MORE
ASK FOR TIME
ASK TOO MUCH
AS MAN TO MAN
AS PER USUAL
AS PROMISED
ASTON VILLA

ASTRAL BODY
AT ALL COSTS
AT ALL HOURS
AT ALL TIMES
AT ANY PRICE
AT A PREMIUM
AT A STRETCH
AT A TANGENT
AT A VENTURE
AT DAYBREAK
AT DAYLIGHT
AT FULL TIDE
AT GUN-POINT
AT HALF-MAST
AT ITS WORST
AT LONG LAST
ATOMIC BOMB
ATOMIC PILE
AT ONE'S BEST
AT ONE SCOOP
AT ONE'S DOOR
AT ONE'S EASE
AT ONE'S FEET
AT ONE'S POST
AT ONE'S SIDE
AT SEA LEVEL
ATTEND MASS
AT THE ALTAR
AT THE DERBY
AT THE FRONT
AT THE LOCAL
AT THE OPERA
AT THE READY
AT THE SLOPE
AT THE WHEEL
AT THE WORST
AT VARIANCE
AT WHAT TIME?
AUBURN HAIR
AULD REEKIE
AU PAIR GIRL
AUTUMN WIND
AVA GARDNER
AVANT GARDE
AVERAGE AGE
AVERAGE MAN
AVERAGE OUT
AVID DESIRE
AWAIT TRIAL
AWFUL SIGHT
AWKWARD AGE

AXE TO GRIND
AXLE GREASE

B—10
BABE IN ARMS
BABE UNBORN
BABY FARMER
BABY'S DUMMY
BABY SITTER
BACK A HORSE
BACK A LOSER
BACK GARDEN
BACK IN TIME
BACK MARKER
BACK NUMBER
BACK RASHER
BACK STAIRS
BACK STITCH
BACK STREET
BACK STROKE
BACK TO BACK
BACK TO BASE
BACK TO WORK
BACON CURER
BAD ACCOUNT
BAD ACTRESS
BAD BARGAIN
BAD CLIMATE
BAD COMPANY
BAD CONDUCT
BAD DICTION
BAD EXAMPLE
BAD FORTUNE
BAD GRAMMAR
BAD HARVEST
BAD HUSBAND
BAD LEARNER
BAD LOOKOUT
BAD MANAGER
BAD MANNERS
BAD MISTAKE
BAD OUTLOOK
BAD QUALITY
BAD SERVANT
BAD SERVICE
BAD SOCIETY
BAD TACTICS
BAD THEATRE
BAD WEATHER
BAD WRITING
BAG OF BONES

BAG OF FLOUR	BEAT HOLLOW	BEST SELLER
BAG OF NAILS	BEAT THE AIR	BEST SILVER
BAGS OF TIME	BEAUTY SHOP	BEST WAY OUT
BAITED TRAP	BEAUTY SPOT	BEST WISHES
BAKED APPLE	BE CHAIRMAN	BE SUPERIOR
BAKED BEANS	BECKY SHARP	BE TOO SMART
BAKER'S SHOP	BECOME LESS	BETTE DAVIS
BALAAM'S ASS	BECOME SANE	BETTER DAYS
BALANCE DUE	BEDDED DOWN	BETTER DEAD
BALLET SHOE	BED OF NAILS	BETTER HALF
BALL OF FIRE	BED OF ROSES	BETTER HOLE
BALL OF WOOL	BEEF CATTLE	BETTER IDEA
BALTIC PORT	BEER BARREL	BETTER SELF
BANANA BOAT	BEER BOTTLE	BETTER SORT
BANANA SKIN	BEER CELLAR	BETTING ACT
BAND LEADER	BEER GARDEN	BETTING MAN
BAND OF HOPE	BEFORE DAWN	BEYOND HOPE
BAND OF IRON	BEFORE DUSK	BE YOURSELF
BANDY WORDS	BEFORE LONG	BIBLE CLASS
BANK RAIDER	BEFORE NOON	BID AGAINST
BANK ROBBER	BEFORE TIME	BIG BAD WOLF
BANK TO BANK	BEG A FAVOUR	BIG BROTHER
BANK VAULTS	BEG FOR MORE	BIGGER SIZE
BANNED BOOK	BEG FOR TIME	BIGGIN HILL
BANTAM COCK	BEGGAR MAID	BIG HELPING
BAN THE BOMB	BEGIN AGAIN	BIG SUCCESS
BARBARY APE	BEHAVE WELL	BIG SWINDLE
BARBED WIRE	BEHIND BARS	BIJOU VILLA
BARD OF AVON	BEHIND TIME	BILL AND COO
BARE BOARDS	BE INFERIOR	BILL BENBOW
BARE CHANCE	BELL THE CAT	BILL OF FARE
BARELY PASS	BELOW DECKS	BILL OF SALE
BARLEY WINE	BELTED EARL	BING CROSBY
BAR PARLOUR	BE MERCIFUL	BINGO NIGHT
BARREN LAND	BE MISTAKEN	BIRD IN HAND
BASE MOTIVE	BENDED KNEE	BIRD OF PREY
BASIC TRUTH	BENEATH ONE	BISCUIT BOX
BAT AND BALL	BENT DOUBLE	BISCUIT TIN
BATH OLIVER	BEN TRAVERS	BISHOP'S HAT
BATTEN DOWN	BE PREPARED	BITE THE LIP
BATTER DOWN	BERLIN WALL	BITING WIND
BATTERY HEN	BE SENSIBLE	BIT OF A MESS
BAWDY HOUSE	BE SOCIABLE	BIT OF FLUFF
BEACH GAMES	BEST BITTER	BITTER BEER
BEACHY HEAD	BEST CHANCE	BITTER BLOW
BEACON FIRE	BEST EFFORT	BITTER PILL
BEAK STREET	BEST FRIEND	BITTER RICE
BEAR GARDEN	BEST OF FIVE	BLACK ANGUS
BEAR IN MIND	BEST OF PALS	BLACK ARROW
BEAR MALICE	BEST PEOPLE	BLACK AS INK
BEAR WITH ME	BEST POLICY	BLACK AS JET

BLACK BEARD	BLOOD SERUM	BOOT POLISH
BLACK BEAST	BLOOD SPORT	BORED STIFF
BLACK BOOKS	BLOODY MARY	BORING WORK
BLACK BOOTS	BLOTTED OUT	BORN LEADER
BLACK BREAD	BLOW BY BLOW	BORN TO RULE
BLACK CLOUD	BLOW ME DOWN	BORSTAL BOY
BLACK DEATH	BLUE AND RED	BOSTON REEL
BLACK DRESS	BLUE CHEESE	BO TO A GOOSE
BLACKED OUT	BLUE DANUBE	BOTTLED ALE
BLACK FRIAR	BLUE DEVILS	BOTTOM GEAR
BLACK HEART	BLUE ENSIGN	BOTTOM RUNG
BLACK HORSE	BLUE GROTTO	BOUGHT OVER
BLACK LACES	BLUE LAGOON	BOULDER DAM
BLACK LOOKS	BLUE MONDAY	BOUNCE BACK
BLACK MAGIC	BLUE MURDER	BOUND TO WIN
BLACK MARIA	BLUE PENCIL	BOWIE KNIFE
BLACK PAINT	BLUE RIBAND	BOWL A BREAK
BLACK PAPER	BLUE RIBBON	BOWLED OVER
BLACK PATCH	BLUE STREAK	BOWL OF RICE
BLACK PIECE	BLUNT WORDS	BOWL OF SOUP
BLACK QUEEN	BOAT RACING	BOW THE KNEE
BLACK SHEEP	BOBBED HAIR	BOX BARRAGE
BLACK SHIRT	BOBBY HOWES	BOXING RING
BLACK SHOES	BODILY HARM	BOX OF DATES
BLACK SOCKS	BODILY PAIN	BOX OF PILLS
BLACK WATCH	BODY SWERVE	BOY AND GIRL
BLACK WIDOW	BOGGED DOWN	BOYS IN BLUE
BLANK PAPER	BOILED BEEF	BRACING AIR
BLANK SHEET	BOILED FISH	BRAIN CHILD
BLANK SPACE	BOILED RICE	BRAIN DRAIN
BLANK STARE	BOILER ROOM	BRAIN FEVER
BLANK VERSE	BOILER SUIT	BRAIN STORM
BLASTED OAK	BOILING HOT	BRANCH LINE
BLAZE A PATH	BOILING OIL	BRASS PLATE
BLAZING SUN	BOLD DESIGN	BRASS TACKS
BLEAK HOUSE	BOLD RELIEF	BRAVE FRONT
BLEED WHITE	BOLD STROKE	BRAVE IT OUT
BLEW THE LOT	BOMBAY DUCK	BREAD FRUIT
BLIND ALLEY	BOMB CRATER	BREAD ROUND
BLIND DRUNK	BOMB DAMAGE	BREAD SAUCE
BLIND FAITH	BONDED DEBT	BREAK A BONE
BLIND GUESS	BOND STREET	BREAK A DATE
BLITZ KRIEG	BONE TO PICK	BREAK A FALL
BLOCK OF ICE	BONUS ISSUE	BREAK AN ARM
BLONDE HAIR	BOOBY PRIZE	BREAK BREAD
BLOOD COUNT	BOOK A TABLE	BREAK COVER
BLOOD DONOR	BOOK CRITIC	BREAK FAITH
BLOOD GROUP	BOOKING FEE	BREAK FORTH
BLOOD HORSE	BOOK OF FATE	BREAK IN TWO
BLOOD MONEY	BOOK REVIEW	BREAK IT OFF
BLOOD ROYAL	BOOK RIGHTS	BREAK LOOSE

BREAK OF DAY	BROWN SHOES	C—10
BREAK RANKS	BROWN STONE	CABIN TRUNK
BREAK SHORT	BROWN STUDY	CADET CORPS
BREATHE OUT	BROWN SUGAR	CADET FORCE
BRER RABBIT	BRUSH ASIDE	CADGE A LIFT
BRETT YOUNG	BRUTE FORCE	CAFÉ AU LAIT
BRIDAL GOWN	BUBBLE BATH	CAKE OF SOAP
BRIDAL VEIL	BUBBLE OVER	CALL A TRUCE
BRIDGE A GAP	BUCKET SEAT	CALL BY NAME
BRIDGE CLUB	BUCKET SHOP	CALLED AWAY
BRIDGE HAND	BUCK RABBIT	CALL IT A DAY
BRIDGE OVER	BULK BUYING	CALL OF DUTY
BRIDGE ROLL	BULLET HEAD	CALL SPADES
BRIDLE PATH	BULLET HOLE	CALL TO ARMS
BRIDLE REIN	BULL MARKET	CALL TO MIND
BRIEF VISIT	BUMPER CROP	CALL TRUMPS
BRIGHT BLUE	BUMPING CAR	CAMDEN TOWN
BRIGHT EYES	BUMP SUPPER	CAME IN LAST
BRIGHT IDEA	BURNE JONES	CAME IN VIEW
BRIGHT SIDE	BURNT AMBER	CAMEL CORPS
BRIGHT SPOT	BURNT BLACK	CAMEL'S HUMP
BRIGHT STAR	BURNT TOAST	CAMEL'S MILK
BRING ABOUT	BURST FORTH	CAMEL TRAIN
BRING A CASE	BUSHEY PARK	CAMPING OUT
BRING A SUIT	BUS SHELTER	CANDY FLOSS
BRING FORTH	BUS STATION	CANNED BEER
BRING ROUND	BUSY AS A BEE	CANNED FOOD
BRING TO BAY	BUSY PERSON	CANNEL COAL
BRISK TRADE	BUSY STREET	CANNON BALL
BROAD ACRES	BUSY WORKER	CAP AND GOWN
BROAD ARROW	BUTTER DISH	CAPE COLONY
BROAD BEANS	BUTTONED UP	CAPER SAUCE
BROAD GAUGE	BUY AND SELL	CARBON COPY
BROKEN BACK	BUY BRITISH	CARD PLAYER
BROKEN BONE	BY ACCIDENT	CAREER GIRL
BROKEN DOWN	BY ALL MEANS	CARGO SPACE
BROKEN HOME	BY AND LARGE	CAR LICENCE
BROKEN LINE	BY ANY MEANS	CAROLE CARR
BROKEN NECK	BY CONTRAST	CARRIED OFF
BROKEN NOSE	BY DAYLIGHT	CARRIER BAG
BROKEN REED	BY GASLIGHT	CARRY COALS
BROKEN WORD	BYGONE DAYS	CARRY IT OFF
BROKER'S MAN	BY INSTINCT	CARSON CITY
BROUGHT LOW	BY SNATCHES	CART GREASE
BROWN BOOTS	BY SURPRISE	CASE A JOINT
BROWN BREAD	BY THE CLOCK	CASE OF WINE
BROWNED OFF	BY THE DOZEN	CASE RECORD
BROWN LACES	BY THE RIVER	CASHEW NUTS
BROWN PAINT	BY TRANSFER	CASH IN HAND
BROWN PAPER	BY YOURSELF	CASK OF WINE
BROWN SHIRT		CASPIAN SEA

CAST A CLOUT
CAST ANCHOR
CAST A SPELL
CASTING OFF
CASUAL WARD
CASUS BELLI
CAT BURGLAR
CATCH A BALL
CATCH A COLD
CATCH A CRAB
CATCH A TRAM
CATCHY TUNE
CATHODE RAY
CATO STREET
CAT'S CRADLE
CATTLE FARM
CATTLE FOOD
CATTLE SHOW
CAUGHT COLD
CAUGHT FIRE
CAUSE ALARM
CAUSE A RIOT
CAUSE A STIR
CAUSTIC WIT
CAXTON HALL
CELERY SALT
CENTRE HALF
CERTAIN DAY
CHAIN SMOKE
CHAIN STORE
CHAIR COVER
CHANCE SHOT
CHANGE ENDS
CHANGE GEAR
CHANGE OVER
CHANGE STEP
CHAPEL FOLK
CHAPTER ONE
CHAPTER SIX
CHAPTER TWO
CHARGE HAND
CHEAP MONEY
CHEAP PAPER
CHEAP SKATE
CHEAT DEATH
CHECK POINT
CHEESE DISH
CHEESED OFF
CHEESE RIND
CHEESE ROLL
CHELSEA BUN

CHELSEA SET
CHEQUE BOOK
CHERRY LIPS
CHERRY RIPE
CHERRY TART
CHERRY TREE
CHESS BOARD
CHESS MATCH
CHESS PIECE
CHEST OF TEA
CHEVY CHASE
CHEWING GUM
CHEW THE CUD
CHEW THE FAT
CHEW THE RAG
CHEYNE WALK
CHICKEN RUN
CHIEF CLERK
CHIEF POINT
CHIEF SCOUT
CHILD BRIDE
CHILD'S PLAY
CHILLY ROOM
CHIMNEY TOP
CHINA PLATE
CHINESE BOX
CHIPPING IN
CHORUS GIRL
CHOSEN RACE
CHURCH ARMY
CHURCH DOOR
CHURN IT OUT
CIDER APPLE
CIGAR SMOKE
CIGAR STORE
CILLA BLACK
CINQUE PORT
CIRCUS RING
CITRIC ACID
CITY CENTRE
CITY EDITOR
CITY FATHER
CITY LIGHTS
CITY LIMITS
CITY OF BATH
CITY OFFICE
CITY POLICE
CITY STREET
CITY TEMPLE
CITY WORKER
CIVIC CROWN

CIVIC PRIDE
CIVIL COURT
CIVIL STATE
CIVIL WRONG
CLAP EYES ON
CLAP HOLD OF
CLAP ON SAIL
CLARK GABLE
CLASP HANDS
CLASSY DAME
CLAY PIGEON
CLEAN BREAK
CLEANED OUT
CLEAN FIGHT
CLEAN HABIT
CLEAN HANDS
CLEAN LINEN
CLEAN LIVER
CLEAN SHAVE
CLEAN SHEET
CLEAN SLATE
CLEAN SWEEP
CLEAN TOWEL
CLEAN WATER
CLEAR AS DAY
CLEAR AS MUD
CLEAR FIELD
CLEAR IMAGE
CLEAR LIGHT
CLEAR PRINT
CLEAR ROUND
CLEAR SPACE
CLEAR STYLE
CLEAR VOICE
CLEAR WATER
CLEFT STICK
CLEVER DICK
CLEVER IDEA
CLEVER MOVE
CLEVER SAVE
CLIMB A HILL
CLIMB A TREE
CLOCK TOWER
CLOSED BOOK
CLOSED DOOR
CLOSED MIND
CLOSED SHOP
CLOSE GRIPS
CLOSE MATCH
CLOSE OF DAY
CLOSE ORDER

CLOSE SHAVE
CLOSE STUDY
CLOSE THING
CLOSE WATCH
CLOSING BID
CLOVE HITCH
CLOVEN FOOT
CLOVEN HOOF
CLOVER LEAF
CLUB MEMBER
CLUMSY HAND
COACH PARTY
COAL CELLAR
COARSE FISH
COARSE JOKE
COARSE MIND
COAST ALONG
COAT OF ARMS
COAT OF MAIL
COAT POCKET
COBALT BLUE
COBALT BOMB
COCK A SNOOK
COCONUT OIL
COCONUT SHY
CODDLED EGG
COFFEE BEAN
COFFEE ROOM
COFFIN NAIL
COIL MAGNET
COLD BUFFET
COLD REASON
COLD REGION
COLD SEASON
COLD SHOWER
COLD TONGUE
COLD TURKEY
COLD WINTER
COLE PORTER
COLLEGE BOY
COLLEGE RAG
COLOUR FILM
COLOUR TONE
COME ACROSS
COME ADRIFT
COME AND SEE
COME AROUND
COME ASHORE
COME AT ONCE
COME CLOSER
COMEDY HOUR

COME HITHER
COME IN LAST
COME INSIDE
COME NEARER
COME SECOND
COME TO BITS
COME TO HAND
COME TO HARM
COME TO HEEL
COME TO KNOW
COME TO LIFE
COME TO PASS
COME TO REST
COME TO STAY
COME UNDONE
COMIC OPERA
COMIC PAPER
COMIC STRIP
COMIC VERSE
COMMON BOND
COMMON COLD
COMMON FORM
COMMON FUND
COMMON GOOD
COMMON HERD
COMMON JEST
COMMON LAND
COMMON NAME
COMMON NOUN
COMMON ROOM
COMMON SALT
COMMON SEAL
COMMON SORT
COMMON TALK
COMMON TASK
COMMON TIME
COMMON TYPE
COMPANY LAW
COMPANY TAX
CONAN DOYLE
CONTACT MAN
CONTOUR MAP
COOKED MEAT
COPPER BELT
COPPER COIN
COPPER MINE
COPPER WIRE
COPYING INK
COPY TYPIST
COR ANGLAIS
CORDON BLEU

CORK JACKET
CORNED BEEF
CORNER FLAG
CORNER KICK
CORNER POST
CORNER SEAT
CORNER SHOP
CORNER SITE
CORNET SOLO
COS LETTUCE
COSMIC RAYS
COSTA BRAVA
COSY CORNER
COTTAGE PIE
COTTON MILL
COTTON REEL
COTTON YARN
COUNTED OUT
COUNT HANDS
COUNT HEADS
COUNT ME OUT
COUNTRY INN
COUNTRY PUB
COUNT SHEEP
COUNTY CORK
COUNTY DOWN
COUNTY HALL
COUNTY MAYO
COUNTY TOWN
COUP DE MAIN
COURT DRESS
COURT OF LAW
COURT ORDER
COURT SCENE
COURT USHER
COVER DRIVE
COVERED WAY
COVER POINT
COWBOY SUIT
COW PARSLEY
COX'S ORANGE
CRACK A CRIB
CRACK A JOKE
CRACKED EGG
CRADLE SONG
CRAWL ABOUT
CREDIT CARD
CREDIT NOTE
CREDIT SIDE
CRÊPE PAPER
CRÊPE SOLES

CRICKET BAT
CRICKET CAP
CRIMEAN WAR
CRIME STORY
CROOKED MAN
CROSS IT OFF
CROSS IT OUT
CROSS PATHS
CROSS WORDS
CROUCH DOWN
CROWDED OUT
CROWD ROUND
CROWD SCENE
CROWN AGENT
CROWN DERBY
CROWN GLASS
CROWN LEASE
CROWN PIECE
CRUDE FACTS
CRUDE FORCE
CRUDE METAL
CRUEL SHAME
CRUSTY LOAF
CRUSTY PORT
CRY FOR HELP
CRY OF AGONY
CRY OUT LOUD
CRYSTAL SET
CRY TOO SOON
CUCKOO PINT
CUNARD LINE
CUP AND BALL
CUPID'S DART
CUP OF COCOA
CUP OF WATER
CUP WINNERS
CURATE'S EGG
CURED BACON
CURL THE LIP
CURRANT BUN
CURRENT HIT
CURTAIN OFF
CURTAIN ROD
CURT ANSWER
CURVED LINE
CURZON LINE
CUSTARD PIE
CUT A FIGURE
CUT ASUNDER
CUT A TUNNEL
CUT CORNERS

CUT FLOWERS
CUT FOR DEAL
CUT IT SHORT
CUT THE CAKE
CUT THE COST
CUT THE KNOT
CUT THE TAPE
CUT THROUGH
CUTTING OUT
CUTTLE FISH
CUT UP ROUGH
CYCLE RALLY

D—10
DAB OF PAINT
DAILY BREAD
DAILY DOZEN
DAILY EVENT
DAILY GRIND
DAILY HABIT
DAILY PAPER
DAILY PRESS
DAILY ROUND
DAINTY DISH
DAIRY CREAM
DAIRY FRESH
DAISY CHAIN
DAMASK ROSE
DAMP COURSE
DANCE MUSIC
DANCING MAN
DANGER LINE
DANGER LIST
DANISH BLUE
DARK CLOUDS
DARK COLOUR
DARK CORNER
DARK PURPLE
DARK SECRET
DARTS BOARD
DARTS MATCH
DASH OF SODA
DAS KAPITAL
DATIVE CASE
DAVID FROST
DAVID NIVEN
DAVID NIXON
DAWN ATTACK
DAWN CHORUS
DAWN OF HOPE
DAWN OF LIFE

DAWN OF LOVE
DAWN PATROL
DAY DREAMER
DAY NURSERY
DAY OF GRACE
DAYS GONE BY
DAYS OF YORE
DAYS TO COME
DAY TRIPPER
DEAD CENTRE
DEADEN PAIN
DEAD GROUND
DEAD LETTER
DEADLY BLOW
DEADLY DULL
DEAD MATTER
DEAD ON TIME
DEAD SEASON
DEAD SECRET
DEAD WEIGHT
DEAL GENTLY
DEALT A BLOW
DEAN MARTIN
DEAR BRUTUS
DEAR FRIEND
DEAR READER
DEATH HOUSE
DEATH KNELL
DEATH SCENE
DEATH'S DOOR
DEATH'S HEAD
DEBIT ENTRY
DECENT TYPE
DECK QUOITS
DECK TENNIS
DECLARE OFF
DECLARE WAR
DECREE NISI
DEEP BREATH
DEEPEST DYE
DEEP FREEZE
DEEP IN DEBT
DEEP LITTER
DEEPLY HURT
DEEP PURPLE
DEEP REGRET
DEEP SECRET
DEEP SORROW
DEEP WATERS
DEEP YELLOW
DEER FOREST

DELFT CHINA	DIZZY SPELL	DOUBLE BASS
DEL SHANNON	DIZZY WHIRL	DOUBLE BLUE
DEMAND NOTE	DO A BAD TURN	DOUBLE CHIN
DEMON RUMMY	DO A STRETCH	DOUBLE DATE
DEN OF LIONS	DO AWAY WITH	DOUBLE FIVE
DENSE CROWD	DO BUSINESS	DOUBLE FOUR
DENY ACCESS	DOCK LABOUR	DOUBLE LIFE
DEODAR TREE	DOCK MASTER	DOUBLE LOCK
DERBY CHINA	DOCTOR FELL	DOUBLE NINE
DERBY HORSE	DOCTOR'S FEE	DOUBLE ROOM
DERBY SWEEP	DOG BISCUIT	DOUBLE STAR
DERNIER CRI	DOG EATS DOG	DOUBLE TAKE
DESERT SONG	DOGGER BANK	DOUBLE TALK
DEUCES WILD	DOG LICENCE	DOUBLE TIME
DEVIL'S DYKE	DOG'S CHANCE	DOUBLING UP
DEVIL'S LUCK	DOG'S DINNER	DOUBLY SURE
DEVIL TO PAY	DOG TRAINER	DOUGLAS FIR
DICK BARTON	DOING RIGHT	DO VIOLENCE
DICK TURPIN	DOING WRONG	DOWER HOUSE
DIE FOR LOVE	DO IN THE EYE	DOWN AND OUT
DIE OF GRIEF	DO IT AT ONCE	DOWN AT HEEL
DIE OF SHOCK	DO LIKEWISE	DOWN THE PIT
DIEPPE RAID	DOLLAR AREA	D'OYLE CARTE
DIESEL FUEL	DOLLAR BILL	DRAKE'S DRUM
DIG A TRENCH	DOLL'S HOUSE	DRAUGHT ALE
DIG FOR GOLD	DONALD DUCK	DRAW A BLANK
DILLY DALLY	DON BRADMAN	DRAW A PRIZE
DINAH SHORE	DONE BY HAND	DRAW BREATH
DINE AT HOME	DONEGAL BAY	DRAWING INK
DINING CLUB	DONKEY WORK	DRAW IT FINE
DINING HALL	DO NOT TOUCH!	DRAW IT MILD
DINING ROOM	DON QUIXOTE	DRAWN MATCH
DINNER BELL	DON'T BE RUDE!	DRAWN SWORD
DINNER GONG	DO ONE PROUD	DRAW ONE OUT
DINNER HOUR	DO ONE'S BEST	DRAW STUMPS
DINNER SUIT	DO ONE'S DUTY	DRAW SWORDS
DINNER TIME	DO ONE'S HAIR	DR. BARNARDO
DIP THE FLAG	DOOR HANDLE	DREAM HOUSE
DIRECT LINE	DOOR TO DOOR	DREAM WORLD
DIRTY HABIT	DO OVERTIME	DREAMY EYES
DIRTY LINEN	DOPE ADDICT	DREAMY LOOK
DIRTY MONEY	DOPE PEDLAR	DRESS SENSE
DIRTY STORY	DORIAN GRAY	DRESS SHIRT
DIRTY TRICK	DOROTHY BAG	DRIED FRUIT
DIRTY WATER	DO THE HALLS	DRIFT ALONG
DISC JOCKEY	DO THE TANGO	DRIFT APART
DISC BRAKES	DO THE TRICK	DRINK MONEY
DISPEL FEAR	DO THE TWIST	DRINK VODKA
DIVINE KING	DOTTED LINE	DRINK WATER
DIVING BIRD	DOTTED NOTE	DRIVEN SNOW
DIZZY ROUND	DOUBLE BACK	DROP A BRICK

DROP A CATCH	**E—10**	EDAM CHEESE
DROP ANCHOR	EACH AND ALL	EDISON BELL
DROP ASTERN	EACH TO EACH	EDMUNDO ROS
DROP BEHIND	EACH-WAY BET	EDWARD LEAR
DROP BY DROP	EAGLE'S NEST	EDWIN DROOD
DROP OF RAIN	EARL'S COURT	EFFECTS MAN
DROPPED OFF	EARLY DOORS	EGG CUSTARD
DROPPED OUT	EARLY HOURS	EGG ON CHIPS
DROP THE HEM	EARLY LUNCH	EGG ON TOAST
DROWNED OUT	EARLY NIGHT	EGG SHAMPOO
DROWNED RAT	EARLY RISER	EIGHT BELLS
DRUG ADDICT	EARLY STAGE	EIGHT DOZEN
DRUMMED OUT	EARLY START	EIGHT DRAWS
DRUMMER BOY	EARLY TO BED	EIGHT GROSS
DRY AS A BONE	EARLY TRAIN	EIGHTH ARMY
DRY BATTERY	EARLY TUDOR	EIGHTH HOLE
DRY CANTEEN	EARLY VISIT	EIGHT HOURS
DRY CLIMATE	EARLY WORKS	EIGHTH PART
DRY MARTINI	EARTHA KITT	EIGHTH RACE
DRY MEASURE	EAR TRUMPET	EIGHTH TIME
DRY ONESELF	EASILY DONE	EIGHT MILES
DRY SHAMPOO	EAST AFRICA	EIGHT PARTS
DRY THE EYES	EAST ANGLIA	EIGHT PINTS
DRY WEATHER	EAST BERLIN	EIGHT SCORE
DUEL OF WITS	EASTER TERM	EIGHTS WEEK
DUE RESPECT	EASTER TIME	EIGHT TIMES
DUFFEL COAT	EASTER WEEK	EIGHT TO ONE
DUKE OF KENT	EAST INDIAN	EIGHT WEEKS
DUKE OF YORK	EAST INDIES	EIGHTY DAYS
DULCE DOMUM	EAST IS EAST	EIGHT YEARS
DULL COLOUR	EAST LONDON	ELEVEN DAYS
DULL MOMENT	EAST OF SUEZ	ELEVEN FEET
DUMB ANIMAL	EAST RIDING	ELEVEN PLUS
DUMB BLONDE	EAST TO WEST	ELEVEN QUID
DUMB CRAMBO	EASY ACCESS	ELINOR GLYN
DUMB WAITER	EASY DOES IT	ELLEN TERRY
DUMMY WHIST	EASY GALLOP	EMERY CLOTH
DUNDEE CAKE	EASY IN MIND	EMERY PAPER
DUSKY BRIDE	EASY MANNER	EMPIRE GOWN
DUSTBIN LID	EASY MARKET	EMPTY BOAST
DUST JACKET	EASY STAGES	EMPTY CHAIR
DUST TO DUST	EASY STREET	EMPTY CURSE
DUTCH BULBS	EASY TARGET	EMPTY GLASS
DUTCH PARTY	EASY TO COPY	EMPTY HOUSE
DUTCH TREAT	EASY VIRTUE	EMPTY PURSE
DUTCH UNCLE	EASY WAY OUT	EMPTY SHELL
DUTY ROSTER	EASY WICKET	EMPTY SOUND
DWARF BEANS	EASY WINNER	EMPTY SPACE
DWARF PLANT	EAT ONE'S HAT	EMPTY TRUCK
DYING CAUSE	EBB AND FLOW	EMPTY WORDS
DYING WORDS	ECCLES CAKE	END IN SMOKE

END PRODUCT
ENEMY AGENT
ENEMY ALIEN
ENEMY FLEET
ENEMY LINES
ENGAGE A CAB
ENGINE ROOM
ENJOY PEACE
ENOCH ARDEN
ENOUGH ROOM
ENOUGH SAID
ENOUGH TIME
ENOUGH TO DO
ENTICE AWAY
ENTRY MONEY
EPIC POETRY
EPSOM DOWNS
EPSOM RACES
EPSOM SALTS
EQUAL PARTS
EQUAL SHARE
EQUALS SIGN
EQUAL TERMS
EQUAL VALUE
ERIC AMBLER
ERIC BARKER
ERIC COATES
ERRING WIFE
ERROL FLYNN
ESCORT DUTY
ESTATE DUTY
ETHEL M. DELL
ETON COLLAR
ETON JACKET
EUSTON ROAD
EVE BOSWELL
EVELYN LAYE
EVEN CHANCE
EVEN HIGHER
EVEN NUMBER
EVEN TEMPER
EVER SO MANY
EVER SO MUCH
EVERY MONTH
EVERY OTHER
EVERY WOMAN
EVIL GENIUS
EVIL INTENT
EVIL SPIRIT
EVIL TEMPER
EXACT IMAGE

EXACT SENSE
EXCESS FARE
EXCISE BILL
EXCISE DUTY
EX DIVIDEND
EXETER CITY
EXIT PERMIT
EXPERT SHOT
EXPORT ONLY
EXPRESS FEE
EXTRA COVER
EXTRA MONEY
EXTRA POWER
EYES OF BLUE
EYE WITNESS

F—10
FACE DANGER
FACE DEFEAT
FACE POWDER
FACE TO FACE
FACE UP TO IT
FACTORY ACT
FADED YOUTH
FAIL TO COME
FAIL TO MEET
FAIL TO MOVE
FAIL TO OBEY
FAINT HEART
FAINT LIGHT
FAINT SOUND
FAIR AMOUNT
FAIR CHANCE
FAIR ENOUGH
FAIR EXCUSE
FAIR INCOME
FAIRLY GOOD
FAIRLY WARM
FAIRLY WELL
FAIR OF FACE
FAIR REPORT
FAIR SAMPLE
FAIR SHARES
FAIR TACKLE
FAIRY QUEEN
FAIRY STORY
FAIRY WORLD
FALL ASLEEP
FALL ASTERN
FALL BEHIND
FALLEN IDOL

FALL FOUL OF
FALLING OFF
FALL IN LINE
FALL IN LOVE
FALL IN WITH
FALL OF SNOW
FALL OF TROY
FALLOW DEER
FALLOW LAND
FALL SILENT
FALL TO BITS
FALSE ALARM
FALSE ALIBI
FALSE BEARD
FALSE CLAIM
FALSE CREED
FALSE FRONT
FALSE HOPES
FALSE IMAGE
FALSE LIGHT
FALSE LOGIC
FALSE PRIDE
FALSE SCENT
FALSE SHAME
FALSE START
FALSE TEETH
FAMILY FEUD
FAMILY FIRM
FAMILY LIFE
FAMILY NAME
FAMILY SEAT
FAMILY TIES
FAMILY TREE
FAMOUS DEED
FAMOUS NAME
FAMOUS WORK
FANCY DRESS
FANCY GOODS
FANCY PRICE
FANCY SOCKS
FANNY ADAMS
FAN THE FIRE
FAR AND AWAY
FAR AND NEAR
FAR AND WIDE
FAR BETWEEN
FAR COUNTRY
FARM ANIMAL
FARM BUTTER
FARMER'S BOY
FARM WORKER

FAR-OFF LAND	FIELD EVENT	FIND FAVOUR
FAR THE BEST	FIELD SPORT	FIND GUILTY
FAR TOO MANY	FIERY CROSS	FIND RELIEF
FAR TOO MUCH	FIERY STEED	FIND THE WAY
FAST ASLEEP	FIESTA TIME	FINE CHANCE
FAST BOWLER	FIFTEEN ALL	FINE FELLOW
FAST COLOUR	FIFTEEN MEN	FINE FETTLE
FAST READER	FIFTH FLOOR	FINE FIGURE
FAST WICKET	FIFTH GREEN	FINE PERSON
FAST WORKER	FIFTH OF MAY	FINE SHOWER
FATAL CAUSE	FIFTH PLACE	FINEST HOUR
FATAL CRASH	FIFTH ROUND	FINE VELLUM
FATAL ERROR	FIFTY MILES	FINE WRITER
FATAL WOUND	FIFTY TIMES	FINGER WAVE
FAT AND LEAN	FIFTY TO ONE	FINISH LAST
FATHER'S DAY	FIFTY YEARS	FINITE VERB
FATHER TIME	FIGHT A DUEL	FIRE A SALVO
FATS WALLER	FIGHT FOR IT	FIRE BUCKET
FATTED CALF	FIGHT IT OUT	FIRE ESCAPE
FAY COMPTON	FIGHT SHY OF	FIRE POLICY
FEARFUL DIN	FILE A CLAIM	FIRE SCREEN
FEATHER BED	FILIAL DUTY	FIRING LINE
FEATHER BOA	FILL IN TIME	FIRM ADVICE
FEAT OF ARMS	FILL THE AIR	FIRM BELIEF
FEEBLE JOKE	FILL THE GAP	FIRM DEMAND
FEEBLE MIND	FILM ADDICT	FIRM DENIAL
FEED THE CAT	FILM CENSOR	FIRM FRIEND
FEED THE DOG	FILM COLONY	FIRM GROUND
FEEL AT EASE	FILM CRITIC	FIRST BATCH
FEEL AT HOME	FILM OF DUST	FIRST BLOOD
FEEL BETTER	FILM REVIEW	FIRST BLUSH
FEEL CHILLY	FILM RIGHTS	FIRST CAUSE
FEEL DEEPLY	FILM STUDIO	FIRST CHILD
FEEL GROGGY	FILTHY TALK	FIRST CLAIM
FEEL HUNGRY	FINAL CAUSE	FIRST CLASS
FEELING ILL	FINAL CLAIM	FIRST DANCE
FEELING SAD	FINAL COUNT	FIRST DRAFT
FEEL NO PITY	FINAL EVENT	FIRST ENTRY
FEEL RELIEF	FINAL FLING	FIRST EVENT
FEEL SECURE	FINAL ISSUE	FIRST FLOOR
FEEL SLEEPY	FINAL OFFER	FIRST FLUSH
FEEL UNWELL	FINAL POINT	FIRST GREEN
FEEL UP TO IT	FINAL PROOF	FIRST HOUSE
FEET OF CLAY	FINAL SCENE	FIRST ISSUE
FELL INTENT	FINAL SCORE	FIRST LIGHT
FENCE ROUND	FINAL STAGE	FIRST MAN IN
FEN COUNTRY	FINAL TERMS	FIRST MATCH
FETTER LANE	FINAL TOUCH	FIRST NIGHT
FEUDAL LORD	FINANCE ACT	FIRST NOVEL
FEVER PITCH	FIND A BASIS	FIRST OF ALL
FIBRE GLASS	FIND A PLACE	FIRST OF MAY

FIRST PLACE	FIVE TO FOUR	FOGGY NIGHT
FIRST PRIZE	FIVE TRICKS	FOG WARNING
FIRST PROOF	FIXED ABODE	FOLDED ARMS
FIRST ROUND	FIXED IDEAS	FOLK DANCER
FIRST SHIFT	FIXED POINT	FOLK SINGER
FIRST SIGHT	FIXED PRICE	FOLLOW SUIT
FIRST STAGE	FIXED SMILE	FOND BELIEF
FIRST STEPS	FIXED STARS	FOND PARENT
FIRST TEETH	FIX THE DATE	FOOD PARCEL
FIRST THING	FIX THE TIME	FOOD SUPPLY
FIRST THROW	FLAG WAVING	FOOD TABLET
FIRST TO ACT	FLAMING RED	FOOL AROUND
FIRST VERSE	FLASH POINT	FOOT BY FOOT
FIRST WATCH	FLAT DENIAL	FOR A CHANGE
FIRST WATER	FLAT GROUND	FOR ALL THAT
FIRST WOMAN	FLAT IN TOWN	FOR ALL TIME
FIRTH OF TAY	FLAT RACING	FOR A SEASON
FISH COURSE	FLAT SEASON	FORCE A DRAW
FISH DINNER	FLATTEN OUT	FORCE APART
FISH FINGER	FLAXEN HAIR	FORCED LOAN
FISHING NET	FLEA CIRCUS	FORCED SALE
FISH KETTLE	FLESH WOUND	FORCE OF LAW
FISH MARKET	FLIGHT DECK	FOR CERTAIN
FISH SUPPER	FLING ABOUT	FOR CHARITY
FISHY STORY	FLING ASIDE	FORE AND AFT
FIT AND WELL	FLINT GLASS	FOREIGN LAW
FIT OF ANGER	FLOAT ABOUT	FOREST FIRE
FIT OF BLUES	FLOAT A LOAN	FOREST HILL
FIT THE BILL	FLOAT ON AIR	FOREST LAND
FIT TO BURST	FLOODED OUT	FOREST TREE
FIT TO PLEAD	FLOOD GATES	FOR EXAMPLE
FIVE AND ONE	FLOOD LEVEL	FORGE AHEAD
FIVE AND SIX	FLOOD WATER	FORGED NOTE
FIVE AND TEN	FLOOR SPACE	FORK SUPPER
FIVE AND TWO	FLOUNCE OUT	FORMAL CALL
FIVE A PENNY	FLOWER SHOW	FORM A QUEUE
FIVE FIFTHS	FLOWER VASE	FORMER DAYS
FIVE HEARTS	FLUID OUNCE	FORMER LAND
FIVE MONTHS	FLY FOR HELP	FORM MASTER
FIVE NINTHS	FLYING BOAT	FOR NOTHING
FIVE O'CLOCK	FLYING BOMB	FOR THE BEST
FIVE OUNCES	FLYING CLUB	FOR TWO PINS
FIVE POINTS	FLYING FISH	FORTY MILES
FIVE POUNDS	FLYING HIGH	FORTY TIMES
FIVE QUARTS	FLYING JUMP	FORTY WINKS
FIVE ROUNDS	FLYING KICK	FORTY YEARS
FIVES COURT	FLYING LEAP	FOSTER HOPE
FIVE SENSES	FLYING SHOT	FOUL MANNER
FIVE SIXTHS	FLY THE FLAG	FOUL MOTIVE
FIVE SPADES	FOAM RUBBER	FOUL STROKE
FIVE STONES	FOCAL POINT	FOUL TEMPER

FOUR-ALE BAR	FREE OF COST	FRUGAL MEAL
FOUR AND SIX	FREE OF DEBT	FRUIT DRINK
FOUR AND TEN	FREE OF DUTY	FRUIT JELLY
FOUR AND TWO	FREE ON RAIL	FRUIT JUICE
FOUR A PENNY	FREE PARDON	FRUIT LOLLY
FOUR BY FOUR	FREE SAMPLE	FRUIT SALAD
FOUR EIGHTS	FREE SPEECH	FUEL CRISIS
FOUR FIFTHS	FREE TICKET	FULL BELIEF
FOUR HEARTS	FREEZE HARD	FULL BOTTLE
FOUR IN HAND	FREEZE ON TO	FULL CHORUS
FOUR KNAVES	FREEZE OVER	FULL CIRCLE
FOUR MONTHS	FRENCH ALPS	FULL EXTENT
FOUR NINTHS	FRENCH BEAN	FULL FIGURE
FOUR O'CLOCK	FRENCH BRED	FULL GALLOP
FOUR OR FIVE	FRENCH HORN	FULL GROWTH
FOUR OUNCES	FRENCH LOAF	FULL IMPORT
FOUR POINTS	FRENCH PORT	FULL LENGTH
FOUR POUNDS	FRENCH ROLL	FULL OF HATE
FOUR QUARTS	FRENCH WINE	FULL OF HOPE
FOUR QUEENS	FRESH BLOOD	FULL OF LIFE
FOUR SEVENS	FRESH BREAD	FULL OF LOVE
FOUR SPADES	FRESH CREAM	FULL OF NEWS
FOURTH FORM	FRESH FRUIT	FULL OF ZEAL
FOURTH HAND	FRESH HOPES	FULL OF ZEST
FOURTH HOLE	FRESH LIGHT	FULL PARDON
FOURTH PART	FRESH PAINT	FULL REPORT
FOURTH RACE	FRESH SLANT	FULL SISTER
FOUR THREES	FRESH SPURT	FULL VOLUME
FOURTH TEST	FRESH START	FULLY ARMED
FOURTH TIME	FRESH WATER	FULLY AWARE
FOUR TRICKS	FRESH WOUND	FULLY WOUND
FOUR WHEELS	FRIED BACON	FUNDED DEBT
FOX HUNTING	FRIED BREAD	FUNNY STORY
FOX TERRIER	FRIGID TONE	FUNNY THING
FRANZ KAFKA	FRIGID ZONE	FUSSY STYLE
FRANZ LEHAR	FROM ABROAD	
FRANZ LISZT	FROM BEHIND	
FRAYED EDGE	FROM MEMORY	G—10
FRED ARCHER	FROM THE AIR	GAIETY GIRL
FRED WINTER	FROM THE TOP	GAIN ACCESS
FREE ACCESS	FRONT BENCH	GAIN CREDIT
FREE ACTION	FRONT COVER	GAIN FAVOUR
FREE ADVICE	FRONT TEETH	GAIN GROUND
FREE CHOICE	FRONT TOOTH	GAIN HEIGHT
FREE CHURCH	FRONT WHEEL	GAIN THE DAY
FREE DRINKS	FROZEN FISH	GAIN WEIGHT
FREE FOR ALL	FROZEN FOOD	GALLANT ACT
FREE FRENCH	FROZEN OVER	GALLUP POLL
FREE LABOUR	FROZEN PEAS	GAMBLE AWAY
FREE LIVING	FROZEN SNOW	GAME AND SET
FREE MARKET	FRUGAL DIET	GAME OF DICE

GAME WARDEN	GET EXCITED	GIVE GROUND
GAMING LAWS	GET HITCHED	GIVE IT A TRY
GARAGE HAND	GET IN A MESS	GIVEN A LIFT
GARBAGE MAN	GET IN TOUCH	GIVEN LEAVE
GARDEN CITY	GET MARRIED	GIVE NOTICE
GARDEN FETE	GET NOWHERE	GIVE ORDERS
GARDEN FLAT	GET RATTLED	GIVE PRAISE
GARDEN GATE	GET SPLICED	GIVE RISE TO
GARDEN HOSE	GET STARTED	GIVE THANKS
GARDEN PATH	GET THE BIRD	GIVE THE CUE
GARDEN PEAS	GET THE BOOT	GIVE TONGUE
GARDEN PEST	GET THE FEEL	GIVE UP HOPE
GARDEN SEAT	GET THE HUMP	GIVE UP WORK
GARDEN WALL	GET THE PUSH	GLANCE BACK
GARLIC SALT	GET THE SACK	GLANCE DOWN
GARY COOPER	GET THROUGH	GLANCE OVER
GAS CHAMBER	GETTING HOT	GLASS BEADS
GAS COMPANY	GETTING OFF	GLASS COACH
GAS COUNCIL	GETTING OLD	GLASS OF ALE
GAS LIGHTER	GETTING OUT	GLASS PRISM
GAS ONESELF	GET TO GRIPS	GLASSY LOOK
GAS TURBINE	GET UP EARLY	GLAZED EYES
GAS WARFARE	GET UP STEAM	GLAZED LOOK
GATHER FOOD	GET WEAVING	GLEE SINGER
GATHER WOOL	GHOST STORY	GLIB TONGUE
GATLING GUN	GHOST TRAIN	GLOVE MONEY
GAVE GROUND	GIANT CRANE	GO ALL FUNNY
GAVE NOTICE	GIANT PANDA	GO A LONG WAY
GAVE VENT TO	GIDDY LIMIT	GO BACKWARD
GAY COLOURS	GIDDY SPELL	GO BANKRUPT
GAY COMPANY	GIFT COUPON	GOBI DESERT
GAY GORDONS	GIFT OF LIFE	GO CRACKERS
GEISHA GIRL	GIFT PARCEL	GOD OF MERCY
GENE PITNEY	GILDED CAGE	GO DOWNHILL
GENERAL LEE	GIN AND LIME	GO DOWN WELL
GENERAL RUN	GINGER BEER	GOD WILLING
GENE TUNNEY	GINGER WINE	GO FOR A BLOW
GENIAL HOST	GIPSY DANCE	GO FOR A RIDE
GENTLE BLOW	GIPSY QUEEN	GO FOR A SAIL
GENTLE HEAT	GIRL FRIEND	GO FOR A SPIN
GENTLE PUSH	GIVE A CATCH	GO FOR A SWIM
GEORGE SAND	GIVE ADVICE	GO FOR A TRIP
GERMAN BAND	GIVE A LEG UP	GO FOR A WALK
GERMAN MARK	GIVE AN INCH	GO GINGERLY
GET A LIVING	GIVE A PARTY	GO IN AND OUT
GET A LOOK IN	GIVE A SHOUT	GO IN AND WIN
GET A MOVE ON	GIVE BATTLE	GO IN EASILY
GET A WICKET	GIVE BY WILL	GOING BADLY
GET DRESSED	GIVE COLOUR	GOING CHEAP
GET ELECTED	GIVE CREDIT	GOING FORTH
GET ENGAGED	GIVE FREELY	GOING ROUND

GOING SOUTH
GOING UNDER
GOLDEN CALF
GOLDEN DAYS
GOLDEN DISC
GOLDEN GATE
GOLDEN GIRL
GOLDEN HAIR
GOLDEN HIND
GOLDEN HORN
GOLDEN HOUR
GOLDEN MEAN
GOLDEN MILE
GOLDEN RAIN
GOLDEN RULE
GOLD NUGGET
GOLD SHARES
GOLD STRIKE
GOLD THREAD
GOLF COURSE
GOLF STROKE
GONE TO SEED
GOOD ACCORD
GOOD ADVICE
GOOD AND ALL
GOOD AND BAD
GOOD AS GOLD
GOOD BRAINS
GOOD CARVER
GOOD CELLAR
GOOD CHANCE
GOOD CINEMA
GOOD DINNER
GOOD DRIVER
GOOD EATING
GOOD EFFECT
GOOD EFFORT
GOOD ENDING
GOOD ENOUGH
GOOD EXCUSE
GOOD FAMILY
GOOD FARMER
GOOD FELLOW
GOOD FIGURE
GOOD FOR ONE
GOOD FOR YOU
GOOD FRIDAY
GOOD FRIEND
GOOD GRACES
GOOD GROUND
GOOD HABITS

GOOD HEALTH
GOOD HIDING
GOOD HUMOUR
GOOD INCOME
GOOD INTENT
GOOD JUMPER
GOOD LENGTH
GOOD LIVING
GOOD MARGIN
GOOD MARKET
GOOD MEMORY
GOOD MORALS
GOOD MORROW
GOOD NATURE
GOOD NOTICE
GOOD NUMBER
GOOD PEOPLE
GOOD PLAYER
GOOD POLICY
GOOD REASON
GOOD RECORD
GOOD REPORT
GOOD REPUTE
GOOD RESULT
GOOD RETURN
GOOD SAILOR
GOOD SEAMAN
GOOD SECOND
GOOD SELLER
GOOD SERMON
GOOD SPEECH
GOOD STAYER
GOOD STRAIN
GOODS TRAIN
GOOD STROKE
GOOD SUPPLY
GOODS WAGON
GOOD TEMPER
GOOD TENANT
GOOD TIMING
GOOD TIPPER
GOOD TO HEAR
GOOD TO KNOW
GOOD WICKET
GOOD WISHES
GOOD WORKER
GO ON A BLIND
GO ON A SPREE
GO ON STRIKE
GO ON TIPTOE
GO ON WHEELS

GO OVERSEAS
GO SCOT-FREE
GO SHOOTING
GO SHOPPING
GO SLUMMING
GO STRAIGHT
GO SWIMMING
GO THE LIMIT
GOTHIC ARCH
GO TO BLAZES!
GO TO CHURCH
GO TOGETHER
GO TO GROUND
GO TO HEAVEN
GO TO MARKET
GO TO PIECES
GO TO PRISON
GO TO SCHOOL
GO TO THE BAD
GO TO THE BAR
GO TO THE TOP
GO TO THE ZOO
GOT THE SACK
GO UPSTAIRS
GRACE KELLY
GRAND CANAL
GRAND CROSS
GRAND DUCHY
GRAND HOTEL
GRAND LODGE
GRAND MARCH
GRAND OPERA
GRAND PIANO
GRAND SCALE
GRAND STAND
GRAND STYLE
GRAND TOTAL
GRANNY KNOT
GRANT A LOAN
GRANT A WISH
GRAPE JUICE
GRAPHIC ART
GRASS COURT
GRASS SKIRT
GRASS SNAKE
GRASS VERGE
GRASS WIDOW
GRASSY BANK
GRAVE DOUBT
GRAVE FEARS
GRAVEL PATH

GRAVELY ILL	GROUND ARMS	HALF A POUND
GRAVE WORDS	GROUND BAIT	HALF A SCORE
GRAY'S ELEGY	GROUND CORN	HALF A SHAKE
GREASY POLE	GROUND CREW	HALF ASLEEP
GREASY ROAD	GROUND DOWN	HALF AS MUCH
GREAT ASSET	GROUND PLAN	HALF BOTTLE
GREAT CATCH	GROUND RENT	HALF DOLLAR
GREAT GROSS	GROUND RICE	HALF LENGTH
GREAT HEART	GROUP OF SIX	HALF OF MILD
GREAT HOPES	GROUP OF TEN	HALF SHARES
GREAT JUDGE	GROUSE MOOR	HALF STEWED
GREAT LAKES	GROW A BEARD	HALF VOLLEY
GREAT MERIT	GROW APPLES	HALF YEARLY
GREAT MINDS	GROW BETTER	HALL OF FAME
GREAT MOGUL	GROW BIGGER	HALL PORTER
GREAT NIECE	GROWING BOY	HAM AND EGGS
GREAT POWER	GROWING OLD	HAMMER AWAY
GREAT SAINT	GROW LARGER	HAMMER DOWN
GREAT SHOCK	GROW LONGER	HAMMER HOME
GREAT SPEED	GROWN WOMAN	HAMMER TOES
GREAT TREAT	GROW TALLER	HAND IN HAND
GREAT UNCLE	GRUB STREET	HAND IT OVER
GREAT VALUE	GRUFF VOICE	HAND LOTION
GREAT WHEEL	GUESS AGAIN	HAND OF TIME
GREAT WOMAN	GUESS RIGHT	HAND SIGNAL
GRECIAN URN	GUESS WRONG	HAND TO HAND
GREEK CROSS	GUEST HOUSE	HANG AROUND
GREEK DRAMA	GUEST NIGHT	HANG BEHIND
GREEK VERSE	GUEST TOWEL	HAPPY BREED
GREEN BAIZE	GUILTY LOOK	HAPPY CHILD
GREEN CLOTH	GUILTY MIND	HAPPY EVENT
GREEN FIELD	GUINEA FOWL	HAPPY KNACK
GREEN FLASH	GUITAR SOLO	HAPPY WOMAN
GREEN GRASS	GULF OF ADEN	HARBOUR BAR
GREEN LIGHT	GULF OF SUEZ	HARD AS IRON
GREEN PAINT	GULF STREAM	HARD AS TEAK
GREEN SALAD	GUN LICENCE	HARD ASTERN
GREEN STAMP	GUST OF WIND	HARD AT WORK
GREEN STUFF		HARD CENTRE
GREEN TABLE	H—10	HARD CHEESE
GRETA GARBO	HACKNEY CAB	HARD GROUND
GREY FRIARS	HACK WRITER	HARD HITTER
GREY FUTURE	HAIR LOTION	HARD KERNEL
GREY MATTER	HALF A CROWN	HARD KNOCKS
GREY STREAK	HALF A DOZEN	HARD LABOUR
GREY TOPPER	HALF A GLASS	HARD LESSON
GRID SYSTEM	HALF A GROSS	HARD LIQUOR
GRILLED HAM	HALF A JIFFY	HARDLY EVER
GRIP OF IRON	HALF AN ACRE	HARD MASTER
GROSS ERROR	HALF AN HOUR	HARD NATURE
GROSS VALUE	HALF AN INCH	HARD PENCIL

HARD RIDING	HEAR NO EVIL	HIGHER RANK
HARD SCHOOL	HEART OF OAK	HIGH ESTEEM
HARD TO BEAR	HEART'S EASE	HIGH FAVOUR
HARD TO HOLD	HEARTY MEAL	HIGH FIGURE
HARD TO TAKE	HEAR VOICES	HIGH FLYING
HARD WINTER	HEAT STROKE	HIGH GERMAN
HARD WORKER	HEAVE A SIGH	HIGH GROUND
HARPOON GUN	HEAVY CHILL	HIGH IDEALS
HARRY WORTH	HEAVY CLOUD	HIGH INCOME
HARSH SOUND	HEAVY FRANC	HIGH LIVING
HARSH VOICE	HEAVY GOING	HIGHLY PAID
HASTY WORDS	HEAVY HEART	HIGH MORALE
HATCH AN EGG	HEAVY METAL	HIGH NUMBER
HATCH A PLOT	HEAVY NIGHT	HIGH OCTANE
HAVE A CHAIR	HEAVY SLEEP	HIGH OFFICE
HAVE A CRACK	HEAVY STORM	HIGH PLACES
HAVE A DRINK	HEAVY STUFF	HIGH POLISH
HAVE A FIGHT	HEAVY STYLE	HIGH PRAISE
HAVE A FLING	HEAVY SWELL	HIGH PRIEST
HAVE A GUESS	HEAVY TOUCH	HIGH REGARD
HAVE A HEART	HEAVY TREAD	HIGH RELIEF
HAVE A HUNCH	HEAVY WATER	HIGH REPUTE
HAVE AN IDEA	HECTIC TIME	HIGH SALARY
HAVE A PARTY	HEDY LAMARR	HIGH SCHOOL
HAVE A SMOKE	HEEL AND TOE	HIGH STAKES
HAVE A SNACK	HELEN WILLS	HIGH STATUS
HAVE BRAINS	HELLO DOLLY	HIGH STREET
HAVE DINNER	HELL'S BELLS	HIGH SUMMER
HAVE DOUBTS	HENNA RINSE	HILARY TERM
HAVE EFFECT	HENRY FONDA	HINDER PART
HAVE FAULTS	HENRY JAMES	HIS AND HERS
HAVE IN HAND	HENRY MOORE	HIS MAJESTY
HAVE IN MIND	HENRY TUDOR	HIS WORSHIP
HAVE IN VIEW	HERB GARDEN	HIT AND MISS
HAVE NO FEAR	HERD OF DEER	HIT THE MARK
HAVE NO HOPE	HERE AND NOW	HIT THE POST
HAVE NO VOTE	HERE YOU ARE	HOBBY HORSE
HAVE QUALMS	HER MAJESTY	HOCKEY BALL
HEAD HUNTER	HERMIT CRAB	HOCKEY CLUB
HEAD KEEPER	HEROIC DEED	HOCKEY TEAM
HEAD OFFICE	HEROIC POEM	HOCUS POCUS
HEAD OF HAIR	HERR HITLER	HOLD A PARTY
HEAD TO FOOT	HIDDEN HAND	HOLD NO HOPE
HEAD TO TAIL	HIGH AND DRY	HOLD OFFICE
HEAD WAITER	HIGH AND LOW	HOLD THE KEY
HEAD WARDER	HIGH CASTLE	HOLIDAY PAY
HEADY DRINK	HIGH CHURCH	HOLLOW TREE
HEALING ART	HIGH COLLAR	HOLY FATHER
HEALTH CURE	HIGH COLOUR	HOLY GROUND
HEAP OF WORK	HIGH COMEDY	HOLY ISLAND
HEARING AID	HIGH DEGREE	HOLY OFFICE

HOLY ORDERS
HOLY SPIRIT
HOLY TEMPLE
HOLY TERROR
HOME AND DRY
HOME CIRCLE
HOME COUNTY
HOME FORCES
HOME FOR TEA
HOME GROUND
HOME MARKET
HOME OFFICE
HOME TRUTHS
HOME WATERS
HONEST FACE
HONEST FOLK
HONEST JOHN
HONEST LOOK
HONEST TOIL
HONEST WORK
HONOURS MAN
HOOK AND EYE
HOOKED NOSE
HOPPING MAD
HORNED MOON
HORNED TOAD
HORROR FILM
HORSE LAUGH
HORSE OPERA
HORSE SENSE
HORSE THIEF
HOSTILE ACT
HOT AND COLD
HOT AS HADES
HOT CLIMATE
HOT COCKLES
HOTEL STAFF
HOTEL SUITE
HOT PURSUIT
HOT WEATHER
HOUR BY HOUR
HOUR OF DOOM
HOUR OF NEED
HOURS ON END
HOUSE AGENT
HOUSE GUEST
HOUSE OF GOD
HOUSE ORGAN
HOUSE PARTY
HOUSE RULES
HOUSE TO LET

HOUSING ACT
HOVER ABOUT
HOW DARE YOU!
HOW DO YOU DO?
HOW ON EARTH
HUGE PROFIT
HUG ONESELF
HUG THE LAND
HUMAN BEING
HUMAN CHAIN
HUMAN ERROR
HUMAN FRAME
HUMAN SKILL
HUMAN VOICE
HUMBLE FARE
HUMBLE FOLK
HUMBLE HOME
HUMMING TOP
HUNDRED MEN
HUNGRY LOOK
HUNTING DOG
HUNTING KIT
HUNT THE FOX
HURDLE RACE
HURRY ALONG
HURRY FORTH
HUSKY VOICE
HYBRID RACE
HYMN OF HATE
I—10
ICED COFFEE
ICE SKATING
ICING SUGAR
ICY COLD DAY
ICY SURFACE
IDEAL PLACE
IDEAL WOMAN
IDLE GOSSIP
IDLE MOMENT
IDLE RUMOUR
IDLE THREAT
IF POSSIBLE
ILKLEY MOOR
ILL CONTENT
ILLEGAL ACT
ILL FEELING
ILL FORTUNE
ILL MANNERS
IMPORT DUTY
IMPOSE A BAN
IMPOSE UPON

IN A BAD MOOD
IN ABEYANCE
IN ADDITION
IN A DECLINE
IN A DILEMMA
IN A DRAUGHT
IN A FAIR WAY
IN A FASHION
IN A FERMENT
IN A FLUTTER
IN A GOOD WAY
IN ALLIANCE
IN AN ASYLUM
IN AN UPROAR
IN ANY EVENT
IN A PASSION
IN A TANTRUM
IN AT THE END
IN A TURMOIL
IN A WHISPER
IN BAD ODOUR
IN BAD SHAPE
IN BAD TASTE
IN BARRACKS
IN BOOK FORM
IN BRACKETS
IN BUSINESS
IN CHAMBERS
IN CHANCERY
INCH BY INCH
IN CONFLICT
IN CONTEMPT
IN CONTRAST
IN DARKNESS
IN DARTMOOR
IN DAYLIGHT
IN DECEMBER
IN DEFIANCE
INDEX TABLE
INDIAN ARMY
INDIAN CLUB
INDIAN CORN
INDIAN FILE
INDIAN HEMP
INDIAN MEAL
INDIA PAPER
INDIGO BLUE
IN DISARRAY
IN DISGRACE
IN DISGUISE
IN DISORDER

IN DISTRESS
INDOOR GAME
IN EVERY WAY
IN EVIDENCE
IN EXCHANGE
IN EXTREMIS
IN FAVOUR OF
IN FEBRUARY
IN FULL SAIL
IN FULL VIEW
IN GOOD FORM
IN GOOD PART
IN GOOD TIME
IN GOOD TRIM
IN HOSPITAL
IN HOT BLOOD
IN HOT WATER
INIGO JONES
IN JEOPARDY
INJURY TIME
INLAND PORT
INLAND TOWN
INLET VALVE
IN LONGHAND
IN LOW WATER
IN MANY WAYS
IN MEMORIAM
IN MOURNING
IN NAME ONLY
INNER HOUSE
INNER LIGHT
INNER VOICE
IN NOVEMBER
IN OFF WHITE
IN ONE PIECE
IN ONE'S CUPS
IN ONE SENSE
IN ONE'S HEAD
IN ONE'S MIND
IN ONE'S ROOM
IN PAKISTAN
IN PARADISE
IN PARALLEL
IN POLITICS
IN PORTUGAL
IN POSITION
IN PRACTICE
IN PROGRESS
IN PROSPECT
IN QUESTION
IN REAL LIFE

IN RESPONSE
IN ROTATION
INS AND OUTS
INSANE IDEA
IN SCOTLAND
IN SEQUENCE
INSIDE EDGE
INSIDE LEFT
INSIDE SEAT
IN SLOW TIME
IN SOMERSET
IN SOME WAYS
IN STERLING
IN STITCHES
IN SUSPENSE
IN SYMPATHY
INTENT LOOK
IN THE ATTIC
IN THE BLOOD
IN THE CHAIR
IN THE CHOIR
IN THE CLEAR
IN THE DERBY
IN THE DITCH
IN THE DOUGH
IN THE DRINK
IN THE DUMPS
IN THE EVENT
IN THE FIELD
IN THE FILES
IN THE FINAL
IN THE FLESH
IN THE FRONT
IN THE GRAVE
IN THE HOUSE
IN THE INDEX
IN THE KITTY
IN THE LIGHT
IN THE LOCAL
IN THE LURCH
IN THE MONEY
IN THE NIGHT
IN THE NORTH
IN THE OCEAN
IN THE PAPER
IN THE PRESS
IN THE QUEUE
IN THE RANKS
IN THE RIGHT
IN THE RIVER
IN THE ROUGH

IN THE ROUND
IN THE SCRUM
IN THE SHADE
IN THE SLIPS
IN THE SLUMS
IN THE SOUTH
IN THE STAND
IN THE STARS
IN THE STUDY
IN THE SWING
IN THE TOWER
IN THE TRADE
IN THE TRAIN
IN THE VOGUE
IN THE WATER
IN THE WILDS
IN THE WINGS
IN THE WOODS
IN THE WORLD
IN THE WRONG
INTO BATTLE
IN TRAINING
IN TWO MINDS
IN TWO TICKS
INVALID OUT
IN WHISPERS
IRISH LINEN
IRISH SWEEP
IRISH TWEED
IRON RATION
ISLAND RACE
ISLE OF BUTE
ISLE OF DOGS
ISLE OF ELBA
ISLE OF MULL
ISLE OF SARK
ISLE OF SKYE
ISSUE A WRIT
ISSUE FORTH
ITALIAN CUT
ITALIC TYPE
IT'S A WANGLE
IVORY BLACK
IVORY COAST
IVORY PAINT
IVORY TOWER

J—10
JACK ARCHER
JACK HORNER
JACK HYLTON

JACK LONDON	JUST FOR NOW	KING EDWARD
JACK SPRATT	JUST IN CASE	KING GEORGE
JACK WARNER	JUST IN TIME	KING HAROLD
JAGGED EDGE	JUST REWARD	KING OF ARMS
JAMAICA INN		KING'S BENCH
JAMAICA RUM	**K—10**	KING'S COURT
JAMES AGATE	KANSAS CITY	KING'S CROSS
JAMES JOYCE	KATHY KIRBY	KING'S PRIZE
JAMES MASON	KAY HAMMOND	KING'S SCOUT
JAM SESSION	KAY KENDALL	KING WILLOW
JANE AUSTEN	KEEN GLANCE	KINKY BOOTS
JAR OF HONEY	KEEN MEMBER	KISS CANNON
JOCKEY CLUB	KEEP A DIARY	KISS ME KATE
JOCKEY'S CAP	KEEP AFLOAT	KISS OF LIFE
JOE BECKETT	KEEPING FIT	KISS THE ROD
JOHN ARLOTT	KEEP IN HAND	KITCHEN BOY
JOHN BRIGHT	KEEP IN MIND	KITH AND KIN
JOHN BUCHAN	KEEP IN PAWN	KNIFE WOUND
JOHN BUNYAN	KEEP IN PLAY	KNOCK ABOUT
JOHN CALVIN	KEEP IN STEP	KNOCKED OUT
JOHN DRYDEN	KEEP IN TUNE	KNOT OF HAIR
JOHN GILPIN	KEEP IN VIEW	KNOW BETTER
JOHN LENNON	KEEP IT DARK	KNOW THE LAW
JOHN MILTON	KEEP MOVING	KNOW THE WAY
JOHN O'GAUNT	KEEP POSTED	KU KLUX KLAN
JOHN RUSKIN	KEEP SECRET	
JOHN WESLEY	KEEP SILENT	**L—10**
JOIN BATTLE	KEEP STEADY	LABOUR CAMP
JOIN FORCES	KEEP TABS ON	LABOUR CLUB
JOINT OWNER	KEEP TRYING	LABOUR POOL
JOINT STOCK	KEEP WICKET	LABOUR VOTE
JOLLY ROGER	KEIR HARDIE	LACE STITCH
JOSE FERRER	KENNEL CLUB	LACK BRAINS
JO STAFFORD	KENNEL MAID	LACK FINISH
JOYS OF LIFE	KENNY BAKER	LACK OF FOOD
JUDO EXPERT	KENNY LYNCH	LACK OF FORM
JUDO LESSON	KENTISH COB	LACK OF NEWS
JUGGED HARE	KENTISH MAN	LACK OF TIME
JULES VERNE	KETTLE DRUM	LACK OF ZEAL
JUMBLE SALE	KEW GARDENS	LACK SPIRIT
JUMP A CLAIM	KEY WITNESS	LADIES' MAID
JUMP FOR JOY	KICK UP A ROW	LADY BE GOOD
JUMP THE GUN	KID BROTHER	LADY DOCKER
JUNGLE BOOK	KIDNEY BEAN	LADY DOCTOR
JUNIOR MISS	KID ONESELF	LADY GODIVA
JURY SYSTEM	KILL OR CURE	LA GIOCONDA
JUST AN IDEA	KIND HEARTS	LAID TO REST
JUST AS WELL	KIND PERSON	LAKE GENEVA
JUST BEFORE	KING ALFRED	LAKE LUGANO
JUST ENOUGH	KING ARTHUR	LAKE SCHOOL
JUST FOR FUN	KING CANUTE	LAMB CUTLET

LAMB'S TALES
LAME EXCUSE
LAND AGENCY
LAND AND SEA
LAND FORCES
LAND IN GAOL
LAND OF SONG
LAND REFORM
LAND TENURE
LAND TRAVEL
LARA'S THEME
LARCENY ACT
LARGE CROWD
LARGE DRINK
LARGE FLEET
LARGE HOUSE
LARGE ORDER
LARGE PARTY
LARGE PIECE
LARGE POWER
LARGE PRINT
LARGE SCALE
LARGE SPACE
LARGE STAFF
LARGE STOCK
LARGE STONE
LARGE VODKA
LARGE WAIST
LARRY ADLER
LAST AUTUMN
LAST BREATH
LAST BUT ONE
LAST BUT TWO
LAST CHANCE
LAST COURSE
LAST DEMAND
LAST EASTER
LAST FRIDAY
LAST GLANCE
LAST IN LINE
LAST LESSON
LAST LETTER
LAST MAN OUT
LAST MINUTE
LAST MOMENT
LAST MONDAY
LAST OF FIVE
LAST OF FOUR
LAST OF NINE
LAST ORDERS
LAST PERSON

LAST REFUGE
LAST RESORT
LAST RUBBER
LAST SEASON
LAST SERIES
LAST SPRING
LAST STROKE
LAST SUMMER
LAST SUNDAY
LAST SUPPER
LAST TO COME
LAST VOLUME
LAST WINTER
LATE AUTUMN
LATE DINNER
LATE FOR TEA
LATE GOTHIC
LATE IN LIFE
LATENT HEAT
LATE SPRING
LATEST NEWS
LATEST WORD
LATE SUMMER
LATE SUPPER
LATIN PROSE
LATIN VERSE
LA TRAVIATA
LATTER HALF
LAUGH IT OFF
LAVISH CARE
LAWFUL WIFE
LAWN TENNIS
LAW OFFICER
LAW OF LIBEL
LAW SOCIETY
LAW STUDENT
LAWYER'S FEE
LAY A COURSE
LAY BROTHER
LAY CLAIM TO
LAY HANDS ON
LAY IN DRINK
LAY IN RUINS
LAY IN STOCK
LAY SIEGE TO
LAY THE DUST
LAY THE FIRE
LAY THE ODDS
LAZY PERSON
LEAD A PARTY
LEAD ASTRAY

LEAD A TRUMP
LEADED TYPE
LEADEN FEET
LEADER PAGE
LEADING MAN
LEAD PENCIL
LEAD THE WAY
LEAD TRUMPS
LEAD WEIGHT
LEAP FOR JOY
LEARNED MAN
LEARN MUSIC
LEARN TO FLY
LEAST OF ALL
LEATHER BAG
LEAVE ALONE
LEAVE A MARK
LEAVE A NOTE
LEAVE A WILL
LEAVE EARLY
LED TO AGREE
LEFT BEHIND
LEFT INSIDE
LEFT WINGER
LEGAL CLAIM
LEGAL COSTS
LEGAL FORCE
LEGAL ISSUE
LEGAL LIGHT
LEGAL OWNER
LEGAL RIGHT
LEGAL TITLE
LEGAL TRIAL
LEGS ELEVEN
LEMON DRINK
LEMON JUICE
LEND COLOUR
LEND WEIGHT
LENIN'S TOMB
LENTIL SOUP
LESSER EVIL
LESSON FIVE
LESSON FOUR
LESSON NINE
LETHAL DOSE
LET IT SLIDE
LET IT STAND
LET ONE KNOW
LET'S FACE IT
LETTER CARD
LETTER CASE

LETTER FILE	LIQUID FIRE	LOCAL PAPER
LETTER POST	LIQUID FOOD	LOCAL RATES
LETTER RATE	LIQUID FUEL	LOCAL TRAIN
LETTING OFF	LIQUID MEAL	LOCAL VICAR
LETTING OUT	LIQUOR LAWS	LOCH LOMOND
LEVEL SCORE	LITTER LOUT	LOCK AND KEY
LIE DORMANT	LITTLE BEAR	LOCKED DOOR
LIE IN RUINS	LITTLE BIRD	LOCK OF HAIR
LIE IN STATE	LITTLE DROP	LOCK-UP SHOP
LIFE MEMBER	LITTLE FISH	LONDON AREA
LIFE OF EASE	LITTLE FOLK	LONDON TOWN
LIFE POLICY	LITTLE GAIN	LONDON WALL
LIFE'S BLOOD	LITTLE GIRL	LONELY LIFE
LIFE TO COME	LITTLE GOOD	LONE RANGER
LIGHT A FIRE	LITTLE HOPE	LONG CAREER
LIGHT A PIPE	LITTLE JOHN	LONG CREDIT
LIGHT AS AIR	LITTLE LAMB	LONG CRUISE
LIGHT AS DAY	LITTLE LESS	LONG ENOUGH
LIGHT BLUES	LITTLE MARY	LONGER ODDS
LIGHT BROWN	LITTLE MORE	LONGEST DAY
LIGHT GREEN	LITTLE NELL	LONGEST WAY
LIGHT HEART	LITTLE ROCK	LONG FLIGHT
LIGHT LUNCH	LITTLE ROOM	LONG ISLAND
LIGHT MUSIC	LITTLE SHIP	LONG LADDER
LIGHT OF DAY	LITTLE SLAM	LONG LETTER
LIGHT OPERA	LITTLE TIME	LONG MEMORY
LIGHT SLEEP	LITTLE USED	LONG PERIOD
LIGHT SNACK	LIVE ABROAD	LONG PLAYER
LIGHT TOUCH	LIVE AFLOAT	LONG SPEECH
LIGHT TREAD	LIVE AT EASE	LONG TUNNEL
LIGHT VERSE	LIVE IN DIGS	LONG VISION
LIKE A CHARM	LIVE IN FEAR	LONG VOYAGE
LIKE A FLASH	LIVE IN HOPE	LONG WINTER
LIKE A THIEF	LIVE IN WANT	LOOK AGHAST
LIKELY SPOT	LIVE IT DOWN	LOOK AROUND
LIKELY TALE	LIVELY MIND	LOOK AT LIFE
LIME STREET	LIVELY TUNE	LOOK A TREAT
LIMPET MINE	LIVE UP TO IT	LOOK A WRECK
LINDEN TREE	LIVING ROOM	LOOK DOWN ON
LINEN CHEST	LIVING SOUL	LOOK GUILTY
LINE OF DUTY	LIVING WAGE	LOOK INSIDE
LINE OF FIRE	LLOYDS BANK	LOOK INTO IT
LINE OF LIFE	LLOYDS LIST	LOOK IN VAIN
LINE OF TYPE	LOADED DICE	LOOK LIVELY
LINSEED OIL	LOADING BAY	LOOK-OUT MAN
LIONEL BART	LOAD OF COAL	LOOK SLIPPY
LION'S MOUTH	LOAD OF COKE	LOOK YONDER
LION'S SHARE	LOAD OF JUNK	LOOSE COVER
LIP READING	LOBSTER POT	LOOSE LIVER
LIP SERVICE	LOCAL BOARD	LOOSE STATE
LIQUID DIET	LOCAL IDIOM	LOOSE TOOTH

LOOSE WOMAN
LORD ATTLEE
LORD CURZON
LORD HAW-HAW
LORD HELP US!
LORD LISTER
LORD NELSON
LORD'S TABLE
LORD WARDEN
LORNA DOONE
LOS ANGELES
LOSE A TRICK
LOSE COLOUR
LOSE CREDIT
LOSE FAVOUR
LOSE GROUND
LOSE HEIGHT
LOSE NO TIME
LOSE THE DAY
LOSE THE WAY
LOSE WEIGHT
LOSING GAME
LOSING HAND
LOSING SIDE
LOSING TEAM
LOSING TOSS
LOSS OF FACE
LOSS OF HOPE
LOSS OF LIFE
LOSS OF TIME
LOST BATTLE
LOST CHANCE
LOST LABOUR
LOST LEADER
LOST TO VIEW
LOST TRIBES
LOTS OF LUCK
LOTS OF ROOM
LOTS OF TIME
LOUD CHEERS
LOUD COLOUR
LOUD OUTCRY
LOUD PRAISE
LOUD REPORT
LOUIS SEIZE
LOUNGE SUIT
LOVE AFFAIR
LOVE DEARLY
LOVE EMBLEM
LOVE LETTER
LOVELY GRUB

LOVELY TIME
LOVE OF LIFE
LOVE POTION
LOVERS' KNOT
LOVERS' LANE
LOVERS' LEAP
LOVERS' TIFF
LOVERS' VOWS
LOVE THIRTY
LOVING CARE
LOW CEILING
LOW COMPANY
LOW CONTENT
LOW CUNNING
LOW DENSITY
LOWER A FLAG
LOWER CLASS
LOWER FARES
LOWER HOUSE
LOWER LIMIT
LOWER PITCH
LOWER RANKS
LOWER SIXTH
LOWER WAGES
LOWER WORLD
LOW IN PRICE
LOW OPINION
LOW QUALITY
LOW SPIRITS
LOW STATION
LOW STATURE
LOW TENSION
LUCID STYLE
LUCKY BREAK
LUCKY CHARM
LUCKY GUESS
LUCKY PATCH
LUCKY PENNY
LUCKY STARS
LUCKY START
LUGGAGE VAN
LUMP OF CLAY
LUMP OF LEAD
LUNAR MONTH
LUNCH BREAK
LUNCH SCORE
LUPINO LANE
LURID LIGHT
LURID STYLE
LUTINE BELL
LUXURY FLAT

LYING KNAVE
LYRIC DRAMA
LYRIC VERSE

M—10
MACHINE AGE
MADE BY HAND
MADE FAMOUS
MADE TO LAST
MADE-UP DISH
MADE USEFUL
MAD WITH JOY
MAGIC FLUTE
MAGIC POWER
MAGIC RITES
MAGIC SPELL
MAGIC SWORD
MAGIC TOUCH
MAGIC TRICK
MAGIC WORDS
MAGIC WORLD
MAGNA CARTA
MAGNUM OPUS
MAIDEN AUNT
MAIDEN LANE
MAIDEN NAME
MAIDEN OVER
MAID MARIAN
MAILED FIST
MAIL PACKET
MAIN ARTERY
MAIN CHANCE
MAIN CHARGE
MAIN CLAUSE
MAIN COURSE
MAIN OFFICE
MAIN REASON
MAIN SOURCE
MAIN STREAM
MAIN STREET
MAIN SWITCH
MAJOR CHORD
MAJOR ISSUE
MAJOR SCALE
MAJOR THIRD
MAKE A BREAK
MAKE A CATCH
MAKE A CLAIM
MAKE A GUESS
MAKE A JOINT

MAKE A MATCH	MARCH TO WAR	MEET THE BUS
MAKE AMENDS	MARCH WINDS	MEET THE EYE
MAKE AN EXIT	MARIA BUENO	MELBA TOAST
MAKE A NOISE	MARIE CURIE	MELTING POT
MAKE A POINT	MARIE LLOYD	MELT THE ICE
MAKE A SCENE	MARIO LANZA	MEMORY LANE
MAKE A STAND	MARK ANTONY	MEMORY TEST
MAKE A START	MARKET HALL	MENIAL WORK
MAKE BETTER	MARKET TOWN	MENTAL CASE
MAKE EYES AT	MARKING INK	MENTAL HOME
MAKE GAME OF	MARK OF CAIN	MENTAL PAIN
MAKE IT A DAY	MARK WYNTER	MENTAL TEST
MAKE NO SIGN	MARRIED MAN	MENTAL WARD
MAKE PASSES	MARRY YOUNG	MERE NOTION
MAKE PUBLIC	MARTIAL LAW	MERE NOVICE
MAKE SPARKS	MARY MARTIN	MERINO WOOL
MAKE THE BED	MARY STUART	MERRY DANCE
MAKE THE TEA	MASKED BALL	MERRY HEART
MAKE TRACKS	MASS APPEAL	MERRY MONTH
MAKE-UP ROOM	MASS ATTACK	MERRY PRANK
MAKE UP TIME	MASS MARKET	MERRY WIDOW
MALE CHORUS	MASS MURDER	MERRY WIVES
MALE DANCER	MASTER MIND	MERSEY BEAT
MALTED MILK	MASTER PLAN	MESS JACKET
MALT LIQUOR	MASTER RACE	METAL PLATE
MAN AND WIFE	MATCH POINT	MEXICO CITY
MAN OF DEEDS	MATCH TRICK	MIAMI BEACH
MAN OF IDEAS	MATINÉE HAT	MICE AND MEN
MAN OF MONEY	MATING CALL	MICKEY FINN
MAN OF MOODS	MATT DILLON	MICK JAGGER
MAN OF PARTS	MATTED HAIR	MIDAS TOUCH
MAN OF PEACE	MATURE MIND	MIDDAY MEAL
MAN OF STEEL	MAXIM GORKY	MIDDLE AGES
MAN OF STRAW	MAY BLOSSOM	MIDDLE DECK
MAN OF TASTE	MAY FLOWERS	MIDDLE EAST
MAN ON TRIAL	MAY MORNING	MIDDLE LIFE
MANOR HOUSE	MEADOW LAND	MIDDLE PART
MAN OR MOUSE?	MEAGRE DIET	MIDDLE ROAD
MAN'S ESTATE	MEAL TICKET	MIDDLE TERM
MAN THE GUNS	MEAN NO HARM	MIDDLE WEST
MAN TO WATCH	MEAN STREAK	MIGHTY ATOM
MANUAL WORK	MEASURE OUT	MIGHTY DEEP
MANY THANKS	MEAT COURSE	MIGHTY FINE
MAO-TSE TUNG	MEAT MARKET	MILD ANSWER
MAPLE SUGAR	MEAT RATION	MILD AS MILK
MAPLE SYRUP	MEDICAL ART	MILD REBUKE
MAP OF SPAIN	MEDICAL MAN	MILD SPOKEN
MAP READING	MEDIUM DONE	MILD WINTER
MARBLE ARCH	MEDIUM RARE	MILES APART
MARCEL WAVE	MEDIUM SIZE	MILK BOTTLE
MARCH FORTH	MEDIUM WAVE	MILL AROUND

MILLED EDGE
MINCED MEAT
MINCED OATH
MINCE WORDS
MINERAL OIL
MINER'S LAMP
MINOR CANON
MINOR CHORD
MINOR POINT
MINOR SCALE
MINOR THIRD
MINUS THREE
MINUTE BOOK
MINUTE HAND
MIRACLE MAN
MISERLY PAY
MISS A CATCH
MISS A TRICK
MISS MUFFET
MISS POINTS
MISS THE BUS
MIXED BLOOD
MIXED BREED
MIXED BUNCH
MIXED DRINK
MIXED GRILL
MIXED HERBS
MIXED PARTY
MIXED TRAIN
MIXED-UP KID
MOBILE UNIT
MOCK TURTLE
MODEL DRESS
MODEL PLANE
MODEL TRAIN
MODEL YACHT
MODE OF LIFE
MODERN GIRL
MODERN MISS
MOIST SUGAR
MONEYED MAN
MONEY ORDER
MONEY PRIZE
MONEY TALKS
MONKEY SUIT
MONK'S HABIT
MONTE CARLO
MONTEGO BAY
MONTE VIDEO
MOON AROUND
MOORING FEE

MORAL BLAME
MORAL FIBRE
MORAL ISSUE
MORAL LAPSE
MORAL POWER
MORAL RIGHT
MORAL SENSE
MORAY FIRTH
MORBID FEAR
MORDANT WIT
MORE OR LESS
MORE TO COME
MORNING SUN
MORNING TEA
MORTAL BLOW
MORTAL COIL
MORTAL FEAR
MORTAL SPAN
MOSAIC WORK
MOSS STITCH
MOST LIKELY
MOST PEOPLE
MOTHER LOVE
MOTHER'S BOY
MOTHER'S DAY
MOTHER SHIP
MOTOR COACH
MOTOR RALLY
MOUNT GUARD
MOUNT KENYA
MOUNT SINAI
MOUTH ORGAN
MOVE ACROSS
MOVE IN A RUT
MOVE SLOWLY
MOVE TROOPS
MOVING BELT
MOVING PART
MOW THE LAWN
MR. MICAWBER
MRS. SQUEERS
MR. UNIVERSE
MUCH BETTER
MUCH SORROW
MUDDY BOOTS
MUDDY WATER
MUFFIN BELL
MULLED WINE
MUMBO JUMBO
MURDER CASE
MUSICAL BOX

MUSICAL EAR
MUSIC LOVER
MUSIC STAND
MUSIC STOOL
MUSKET FIRE
MUSTARD GAS
MUSTARD POT
MUTE APPEAL
MUTTON CHOP
MUTUAL LOVE
MY CUP OF TEA
MY DEAR CHAP
MY FAIR LADY
MY GOODNESS!
MY HEARTIES
MY OLD DUTCH
MY OLD WOMAN
MYSTERY MAN

N—10
NAIL POLISH
NAKED FACTS
NAKED FLAME
NAKED LIGHT
NAKED STEEL
NAKED SWORD
NAKED TRUTH
NAME THE DAY
NARROW DOWN
NARROW MIND
NARROW MISS
NARROW PATH
NARROW ROAD
NARROW VIEW
NASAL ORGAN
NASAL TWANG
NASTY HABIT
NASTY KNOCK
NASTY SHOCK
NASTY SPILL
NASTY TASTE
NASTY TRICK
NATIVE LAND
NATIVE RACE
NATIVE SOIL
NATURAL GAS
NATURAL KEY
NATURAL LAW
NATURAL WIT
NATURE CURE
NAUGHTY BOY

NAUTCH GIRL	NEW RECRUIT	NIP ON AHEAD
NAVAL CADET	NEW RESOLVE	NITRIC ACID
NAVAL CRAFT	NEWS AGENCY	NO APPETITE
NAVAL POWER	NEWS CINEMA	NOBEL PRIZE
NAVAL STORE	NEWS EDITOR	NOBLE BIRTH
NAVY LEAGUE	NEWS LETTER	NOBLE BLOOD
NAZI RÉGIME	NEW SPEAKER	NOBLE HOUSE
NEAR AND FAR	NEWS REPORT	NOBODY ELSE
NEAR AT HAND	NEW UNIFORM	NO DECISION
NEAR ENOUGH	NEW VERSION	NO DISTANCE
NEAR FRIEND	NEW ZEALAND	NOD THE HEAD
NEAR FUTURE	NEXT AUTUMN	NOEL COWARD
NEARLY OVER	NEXT BUT ONE	NO ENTRANCE
NEAR THE END	NEXT BUT TWO	NO FRICTION
NEAR THE SEA	NEXT DOOR TO	NO HARM DONE
NEAR THE TOP	NEXT FRIDAY	NO INTEREST
NEAT AS A PIN	NEXT IN LINE	NO LEFT TURN
NEAT FIGURE	NEXT MONDAY	NO LOVE LOST
NEAT SCOTCH	NEXT PERSON	NO MAN'S LAND
NEAT STROKE	NEXT PLEASE	NOM DE PLUME
NEAT WHISKY	NEXT SEASON	NO MEAN CITY
NECK OF LAMB	NEXT SPRING	NOMINAL FEE
NECK OF LAND	NEXT SUMMER	NOMINAL SUM
NEEDLE'S EYE	NEXT SUNDAY	NONE OF THAT!
NEGRO MUSIC	NEXT TO COME	NO NONSENSE
NELSON EDDY	NEXT VICTIM	NON-STOP RUN
NERVE TONIC	NEXT WINTER	NOODLE SOUP
NERVOUS TIC	NICE ENOUGH	NOONDAY SUN
NESTLE DOWN	NICE PEOPLE	NO PATIENCE
NEVER AGAIN	NICE TO KNOW	NO RESPONSE
NEVER LEARN	NICKEL COIN	NORMAL LIFE
NEVER NEVER	NICK OF TIME	NORMAL LOAD
NEVER WAVER	NIGHT FROST	NORMAL PACE
NEVER WORRY	NIGHT NURSE	NORTH COAST
NEVER WRONG	NIGHT SHIFT	NORTH DEVON
NEVIL SHUTE	NIGHT TRAIN	NORTH DOWNS
NEW ADDRESS	NIGHT WATCH	NORTH WALES
NEW ARRIVAL	NINE AND ONE	NOSE TO TAIL
NEW CHAPTER	NINE AND SIX	NO SHORTAGE
NEW CLOTHES	NINE AND TEN	NO SOLUTION
NEW COINAGE	NINE AND TWO	NO STANDING
NEW COLLEGE	NINE MONTHS	NO STRANGER
NEW CONVERT	NINE O'CLOCK	NO SUCH LUCK
NEW EDITION	NINE OUNCES	NOSY PARKER
NEW ENGLAND	NINE POINTS	NOT A CHANCE
NEW FASHION	NINE POUNDS	NOT CRICKET
NEW HORIZON	NINE TENTHS	NOTE OF HAND
NEW-LAID EGG	NINTH GREEN	NOT FAR AWAY
NEW-MOWN HAY	NINTH OF MAY	NOT FOR SALE
NEW ORLEANS	NINTH PLACE	NO THANK YOU
NEW PROCESS	NINTH ROUND	NOTHING NEW

NOT JUST NOW
NOT LONG AGO
NOT ONE OF US
NOT PRESENT
NOT SO DUSTY
NOT THE SAME
NOT THE TYPE
NOT TO WORRY
NOT VISIBLE
NOT WORKING
NOT WORTH IT
NOVA SCOTIA
NOVEL TITLE
NOW AND THEN
NO WEAKNESS
NOW OR NEVER
NUCLEAR WAR
NUDE FIGURE
NUDIST CAMP
NUDIST CLUB
NUMBER FIVE
NUMBER FOUR
NUMBER NINE
NUT AND BOLT
NUTS AND MAY
NUTTY SLACK

O—10
OBEY ORDERS
OCEAN LINER
OCEAN WAVES
ODD AND EVEN
OEDIPUS REX
OF A PATTERN
OFF BALANCE
OFFER TO PAY
OFFICE DESK
OFFICE GIRL
OFFICE SAFE
OFFICE WORK
OFF LICENCE
OFF ONE'S NUT
OFFSIDE LAW
OFF THE BEAM
OFF THE CUFF
OFF THE CUSH
OFF THE HOOK
OFF THE LAND
OFF THE MARK
OFF THE MENU

OFF THE REEL
OIL COMPANY
OLD AND MILD
OLD AND TRUE
OLD BRIGADE
OLD CLOTHES
OLD COUNTRY
OLD EDITION
OLD ENGLAND
OLD ENGLISH
OLDEN TIMES
OLD ETONIAN
OLD OAK TREE
OLD PALS ACT
OLD ROUTINE
OLD SO-AND-SO
OLD SOLDIER
OLD VERSION
OLD VETERAN
OLD WARRIOR
OLD WINDBAG
OLD YEAR OUT
OLIVE GREEN
OLIVE GROVE
OL' MAN RIVER
ON A CRUSADE
ON ALL FOURS
ON ALL HANDS
ON ALL SIDES
ON APPROVAL
ON BAD TERMS
ON BUSINESS
ONCE A MONTH
ONCE BITTEN
ONCE IN A WAY
ON CRUTCHES
ON DELIVERY
ON EACH SIDE
ONE-ACT PLAY
ONE AND FIVE
ONE AND FOUR
ONE AND NINE
ONE AND ONLY
ONE ANOTHER
ONE AT A TIME
ONE BILLION
ONE DIAMOND
ONE FINE DAY
ONE FURLONG
ONE HUNDRED
ONE IN EIGHT

ONE IN SEVEN
ONE IN THREE
ONE-MAN BAND
ONE MILLION
ONE NO-TRUMP
ONE PER CENT
ONE QUARTER
ONE SEVENTH
ONE'S OWN WAY
ONE SQUARED
ONE SWALLOW
ONE TOO MANY
ONE TWELFTH
ONE WAY ONLY
ON FURLOUGH
ONION SAUCE
ON LOCATION
ONLY CHANCE
ONLY CHOICE
ON MORTGAGE
ON MY HONOUR
ON OCCASION
ON ONE'S BACK
ON ONE'S FEET
ON ONE'S LEGS
ON ONE'S TOES
ON SATURDAY
ON SCHEDULE
ON SENTRY-GO
ON THE ALERT
ON THE BEACH
ON THE BENCH
ON THE BIBLE
ON THE BOARD
ON THE BOOKS
ON THE BOOZE
ON THE BRAIN
ON THE BRINK
ON THE CARDS
ON THE CHEAP
ON THE CLOCK
ON THE CLYDE
ON THE COAST
ON THE CREST
ON THE CROSS
ON THE FENCE
ON THE FILES
ON THE FLANK
ON THE FLOOR
ON THE GREEN
ON THE HALLS

ON THE HOUSE	OPEN MARKET	OUT OF REACH
ON THE LATCH	OPEN PRISON	OUT OF SCALE
ON THE LEVEL	OPEN REVOLT	OUT OF SHAPE
ON THE LINKS	OPEN SEASON	OUT OF SIGHT
ON THE LOOSE	OPEN SECRET	OUT OF SORTS
ON THE MARCH	OPEN SESAME	OUT OF SPITE
ON THE PANEL	OPEN TO VIEW	OUT OF STOCK
ON THE PHONE	OPEN WINDOW	OUT OF TOUCH
ON THE PROWL	OPERA GLASS	OUT OF WATER
ON THE QUIET	OPERA HOUSE	OUT ON A LIMB
ON THE RADIO	OPERA MUSIC	OUT PATIENT
ON THE RAILS	OPIUM EATER	OUTWARD EYE
ON THE RHINE	OPIUM HABIT	OVER AND OUT
ON THE RIGHT	OPIUM POPPY	OVER EXPOSE
ON THE RIVER	OPTIC NERVE	OVER POLITE
ON THE ROCKS	ORANGE PEEL	OVER THE AIR
ON THE SANDS	ORANGE TREE	OVER THE BAR
ON THE SCENT	ORANGE WINE	OVER THE SEA
ON THE SHELF	ORDER A MEAL	OVER THE TOP
ON THE SLANT	ORDER PAPER	OVER THE WAY
ON THE SLATE	ORGAN MUSIC	OWE LOYALTY
ON THE SOMME	ORIENT LINE	OWNER'S RISK
ON THE SPREE	ORION'S BELT	OX-EYE DAISY
ON THE STAFF	OSCAR AWARD	OXFORD BAGS
ON THE STAGE	OSCAR WILDE	OXFORD BLUE
ON THE STAND	OSTRICH EGG	OXTAIL SOUP
ON THE TABLE	OTHER RANKS	OXYGEN MASK
ON THE TELLY	OTHER WORLD	OXYGEN TENT
ON THE TILES	OUIJA BOARD	P—10
ON THE TRACK	OUR BETTERS	PACK ANIMAL
ON THE TRAIL	OUR VERSION	PACK A PUNCH
ON THE VERGE	OUT AND HOME	PACK OF LIES
ON THE WAGON	OUT AT ELBOW	PADDED CELL
ON THE WATCH	OUTER COVER	PADDY FIELD
ON THE WATER	OUTER SPACE	PAGE ELEVEN
ON THE WAY IN	OUTER WORLD	PAGE TWELVE
ON THE WAY UP	OUT IN FORCE	PAID A VISIT
ON THE WHOLE	OUT IN FRONT	PAIL OF MILK
ON THIS SIDE	OUT OF COURT	PAINED LOOK
ON THURSDAY	OUT OF DOORS	PAIR OF ACES
ON VACATION	OUT OF FOCUS	PAIR OF OARS
OPEN ARREST	OUT OF FUNDS	PAIR OF TENS
OPEN BREACH	OUT OF HOURS	PAIR OF TWOS
OPEN CHEQUE	OUT OF JOINT	PALE AND WAN
OPEN CREDIT	OUT OF MONEY	PALE YELLOW
OPEN DRAWER	OUT OF MY WAY	PALM SUNDAY
OPEN GROUND	OUT OF ORBIT	PANCAKE DAY
OPEN HEARTH	OUT OF ORDER	PAPAL COURT
OPENING BID	OUT OF PLACE	PAPER CHAIN
OPENING DAY	OUT OF PRINT	PAPER MONEY
OPEN LETTER	OUT OF RANGE	PAPER ROUND

PARCEL POST	PEACE TERMS	PIER MASTER
PAR CONTEST	PEACH MELBA	PIGEON POST
PARENT BIRD	PEAK PERIOD	PIG IN A POKE
PARENTS' DAY	PEARL DIVER	PILOT LIGHT
PARENT SHIP	PEARLY KING	PINE FOREST
PARENT TREE	PEAS IN A POD	PINK RIBBON
PARI MUTUEL	PEA-SOUP FOG	PINNED DOWN
PARISH PUMP	PECKHAM RYE	PINT OF BEER
PARK AVENUE	PECK OF DIRT	PINT OF MILD
PARKING BAY	PEDDLE DOPE	PINT OF MILK
PARKING FEE	PEEPING TOM	PIOUS HOPES
PARKING LOT	PEGGED DOWN	PIOUS TRUTH
PART BY PART	PEGGY MOUNT	PIPED MUSIC
PARTED LIPS	PENALTY BOX	PIPES OF PAN
PARTY DRESS	PENCIL CASE	PIRATE FLAG
PARTY FROCK	PENNY BLACK	PIRATE SHIP
PARTY FUNDS	PENNY PIECE	PISTOL SHOT
PARTY PIECE	PENNY PLAIN	PITCH A TENT
PARTY TRICK	PENNY STAMP	PITCH A YARN
PASS FRIEND	PENSION OFF	PITCH BLACK
PASSING FAD	PEPPER MILL	PITH HELMET
PASS MUSTER	PEPYS' DIARY	PLACED LAST
PASS ORDERS	PERFECT FIT	PLACE MONEY
PASS THE CAN	PERIOD PLAY	PLACE ON END
PASS THE HAT	PERRY MASON	PLAGUE SPOT
PAST BELIEF	PERSIAN CAT	PLAIN FACTS
PAST CARING	PERSIAN MAT	PLAIN FOLLY
PAST MASTER	PERSIAN RUG	PLAIN PAPER
PAST RECORD	PETE MURRAY	PLAIN SKIRT
PASTRY CHEF	PETER FINCH	PLAIN SOCKS
PASTRY COOK	PETER PIPER	PLAIN TERMS
PATH OF DUTY	PETER SCOTT	PLAIN TO SEE
PATROL DUTY	PETIT POINT	PLAIN TRUTH
PAUL DOMBEY	PETITS POIS	PLAIN WORDS
PAUL REVERE	PETROL DUMP	PLANE CRASH
PAUL TEMPLE	PETROL PUMP	PLANT A TREE
PAVE THE WAY	PETROL TANK	PLASTIC ART
PAWN TICKET	PETTY CRIME	PLASTIC BAG
PAY A REWARD	PETTY THEFT	PLASTIC MAC
PAY AS YOU GO	PETTY THIEF	PLASTIC TOY
PAY CORKAGE	PHIL ARCHER	PLAT DU JOUR
PAY DAMAGES	PHIL HARRIS	PLATE GLASS
PAYING GAME	PHRASE BOOK	PLAY A CHORD
PAY-OFF LINE	PIANO STOOL	PLAY A SCALE
PAY ONE'S WAY	PIANO TUNER	PLAY AT HOME
PAY ON SIGHT	PICK A FIGHT	PLAY A TRICK
PAY THE BILL	PICK FAULTS	PLAY A WALTZ
PAY THE RENT	PICK STRAWS	PLAY BO-PEEP
PAY TRIBUTE	PICK UP NEWS	PLAY BRIDGE
PEACE OFFER	PICTURE HAT	PLAY HAMLET
PEACE PARTY	PIED-À-TERRE	PLAY HOCKEY

PLAY HOOKEY	POOR SAILOR	PRETTY FAIR
PLAY IT COOL	POOR SECOND	PRETTY GIRL
PLAY POSSUM	POOR SERMON	PRETTY GOOD
PLAY PRANKS	POOR STAYER	PRETTY MESS
PLAY RUGGER	POOR WRETCH	PRETTY PASS
PLAY SCALES	POOR YORICK	PRETTY POLL
PLAY SOCCER	POPLAR TREE	PRETTY SURE
PLAY SQUASH	POPULAR AIR	PRETTY TUNE
PLAY STREET	PORK FILLET	PRETTY WELL
PLAY TENNIS	PORK-PIE HAT	PRICE INDEX
PLAY THE MAN	PORT ARTHUR	PRICE LABEL
PLAY THE WAG	PORT DARWIN	PRICE LEVEL
PLAY TRICKS	PORT ENGINE	PRIMA DONNA
PLAY TRUANT	PORTION OUT	PRIMA FACIE
PLAY TRUMPS	PORT NELSON	PRIME CAUSE
PLENTY MORE	PORT OF CALL	PRIME MOVER
PLENTY TO DO	PORT TALBOT	PRINCE IGOR
PLOT OF LAND	POSTAL RATE	PRINT DRESS
PLOUGH BACK	POST MORTEM	PRIOR CLAIM
PLOVER'S EGG	POST OFFICE	PRISON BARS
PLUCKY CHAP	POTATO PEEL	PRISON CAMP
PLUMB CRAZY	POT HUNTING	PRISON CELL
PLY FOR HIRE	POT OF HONEY	PRISON DIET
POACHED EGG	POT OF MONEY	PRISON FARE
POCKET COMB	POT OF PAINT	PRISON GATE
POETIC VEIN	POTTED MEAT	PRISON YARD
POINT BLANK	POTTER'S BAR	PRIVATE BAR
POINT OF LAW	POT THE BLUE	PRIVATE BUS
POKER PARTY	POT THE PINK	PRIVATE CAR
POLES APART	POUNCE UPON	PRIVATE EYE
POLE TO POLE	POUND OF TEA	PRIVATE LAW
POLICE BALL	POULTRY RUN	PRIVATE WAR
POLICE RAID	POURING WET	PRIVATE WAY
POLICE TRAP	POWDER BLUE	PRIVY PURSE
POLLING DAY	POWDER BOWL	PRIZE COURT
POLO GROUND	POWDER PUFF	PRIZE ENTRY
POLO PLAYER	POWDER ROOM	PRIZE ESSAY
POMPOUS ASS	POWER HOUSE	PRIZE FIGHT
PONDER'S END	POWER PLANT	PRIZE IDIOT
POOR BEGGAR	POWER POINT	PRIZE MONEY
POOR CHANCE	POWER PRESS	PROFITS TAX
POOR CHOICE	PRAIRIE DOG	PROMPT BOOK
POOR EXCUSE	PRAWN CURRY	PROPER CARE
POOR FELLOW	PRAWN SALAD	PROPER MIND
POOR GROUND	PRAYER BOOK	PROPER NAME
POOR HEALTH	PREP. SCHOOL	PROPER NOUN
POOR PEOPLE	PRESENT DAY	PROPER TIME
POOR PLAYER	PRESS AGENT	PROSE WORKS
POOR RELIEF	PRESS AHEAD	PRO TEMPORE
POOR RESULT	PRESS BARON	PROUD BOAST
POOR RETURN	PRETTY FACE	PROUD FLESH

PROUD HEART
PROUD SIGHT
PROVEN FACT
PROWL ABOUT
PRYING EYES
PSYCHIC BID
PUBLIC GOOD
PUBLIC LIFE
PUBLIC PARK
PUBLIC PATH
PUBLIC ROAD
PUBLIC ROOM
PUBLIC SALE
PUBLIC WEAL
PUERTO RICO
PUFF OF WIND
PUFF PASTRY
PULLMAN CAR
PUNCH DRUNK
PUPPET SHOW
PURE ACCENT
PURE CHANCE
PURE COLOUR
PURE REASON
PURE SILVER
PURSED LIPS
PUSH AROUND
PUSH TOO FAR
PUT AND TAKE
PUT AN END TO
PUT A STOP TO
PUT ASUNDER
PUT FORWARD
PUT IN A BOOK
PUT IN A CELL
PUT IN A WORD
PUT IN FRONT
PUT IN IRONS
PUT IN ORDER
PUT IN POWER
PUT IN RHYME
PUT IN VERSE
PUT IN WORDS
PUT ON AN ACT
PUT ON A SHOW
PUT ON BLACK
PUT ON BOARD
PUT ONE OVER
PUT ONE WISE
PUT ON FLESH
PUT ON SPEED

PUT ON TRIAL
PUT THE SHOT
PUT THROUGH
PUTTING OFF
PUTTING OUT
PUT TO DEATH
PUT TO MUSIC
PUT TO SHAME
PUT TO SLEEP
PUTTY MEDAL
PUT UP A SHOW
PUT UP A SIGN
PUZZLED AIR
PUZZLE OVER

Q—10
QUACK, QUACK
QUAI D'ORSAY
QUAINT IDEA
QUAKER GIRL
QUARTER DAY
QUEEN'S HALL
QUEEN'S HEAD
QUEEN'S PAWN
QUEEN'S ROOK
QUEER SOUND
QUICK LUNCH
QUICK MARCH
QUICK TEMPO
QUICK TRICK
QUID PRO QUO
QUIET START
QUITE CLEAR
QUITE CLOSE
QUITE EMPTY
QUITE HAPPY
QUITE RIGHT
QUITE STILL
QUITE WRONG
QUIT OFFICE
QUIZ MASTER

R—10
RABBIT SKIN
RACE HATRED
RACING CARD
RACING FORM
RACING NEWS
RACING TOUT
RADIATE JOY
RADIO DRAMA

RADIO TIMES
RADIUM BOMB
RAGGED EDGE
RAILWAY ACT
RAISE A DUST
RAISE A HAND
RAISE A LOAN
RAISE ALOFT
RAISE MONEY
RAISE STEAM
RAISE TAXES
RALLY ROUND
RANCH HOUSE
RANDOM SHOT
RAPID PULSE
RARE CHANCE
RARING TO GO
RASH BELIEF
RATHER COOL
RATHER FLAT
RATHER GOOD
RATHER LATE
RATION BOOK
RATION CARD
RATTLE AWAY
RAW RECRUIT
RAY CHARLES
RAYNES PARK
RAY OF LIGHT
RAZOR BLADE
RAZOR'S EDGE
RAZOR SHARP
RAZOR STROP
READ A STORY
READ DEEPLY
READY FOR IT
READY MONEY
READY REPLY
READY TO CRY
READY TO DIE
READY TO EAT
REAL DANGER
REAL ESTATE
REAL FRIEND
REALLY MEAN
REAL MADRID
REAL OBJECT
REAL PERSON
REAL SCHOOL
REAL TENNIS
REAR WINDOW

RECENT DATE	RICHARD ROE	RIVER TRENT
RECENT PAST	RICH PEOPLE	RIVER TROUT
RECIPE BOOK	RICH REWARD	RIVER TWEED
RECORD CROP	RICH SOURCE	ROAD SAFETY
RECORD GATE	RICH SUPPLY	ROAD TO FAME
RECORD ROOM	RIDING COAT	ROAD TO HELL
RECORD SALE	RIDING CROP	ROAD TO RUIN
RECORD SHOP	RIDING HIGH	ROAD-UP SIGN
RECORD TIME	RIDING SEAT	ROAST ALIVE
RED ADMIRAL	RIDING WHIP	ROBBER BAND
RED AS A ROSE	RIFLE CORPS	ROBERT ADAM
RED BALLOON	RIFLE RANGE	ROBERT PEEL
RED BIRETTA	RIGHT ABOUT	ROBIN ADAIR
RED CABBAGE	RIGHT AHEAD	ROB THE TILL
RED CURRANT	RIGHT ANGLE	ROCK BOTTOM
RED FLANNEL	RIGHT DRESS	ROCKET BASE
RED HERRING	RIGHT FLANK	ROCKET SITE
RED PIGMENT	RIGHT LINES	ROCK GARDEN
RED, RED ROSE	RIGHT OF WAY	ROCK HUDSON
REFINED OIL	RIGHT ON TOP	ROCK OF AGES
REFORM BILL	RIGHT PLACE	ROCKS AHEAD
REFORM CLUB	RIGHT ROUND	ROCK SALMON
REFUSE BAIL	RIGHT ROYAL	ROCKY COAST
REFUSE DUMP	RIGHT THING	ROD AND LINE
REFUSE TO GO	RIGHT TOTAL	ROGER BACON
RELIEF FUND	RIGHT TRACK	ROLLED GOLD
REMAIN CALM	RIGHT TRAIL	ROLLED OATS
REMAIN DUMB	RIGHT WAY UP	ROLLS OF FAT
REMAND HOME	RIGHT WHEEL	ROMAN EAGLE
REMOTE AGES	RIGHT WOMAN	ROMAN FORUM
REMOVAL MAN	RING FINGER	ROMAN RUINS
REMOVAL VAN	RING MASTER	ROMAN TUNIC
RENEW A BOOK	RINGO STARR	ROMAN VILLA
RENT A HOUSE	RIPEN EARLY	ROMPER SUIT
REPAY A LOAN	RIPE OLD AGE	ROOF GARDEN
REPORT BACK	RIPE TOMATO	ROOM NUMBER
REPORT SICK	RISE HIGHER	ROOM TO MOVE
RESCUE SHIP	RISE IN ARMS	ROOM TO TURN
RESCUE TEAM	RISING COST	ROPE A STEER
RESCUE WORK	RISING TIDE	ROPE LADDER
REST AWHILE	RIVAL CAMPS	ROSE COLOUR
REST CENTRE	RIVAL CAUSE	ROSE GARDEN
REST PERIOD	RIVAL CLAIM	ROSY CHEEKS
RETAIL SHOP	RIVER BASIN	ROTARY CLUB
RETIRED PAY	RIVER CLYDE	ROTTEN HAND
RETIRE HURT	RIVER CRAFT	ROTTEN IDEA
RETURN FARE	RIVER LEVEL	ROTTEN LUCK
RETURN GAME	RIVER MOUTH	ROUGH CIDER
RETURN HALF	RIVER PLATE	ROUGH DRAFT
RETURN HOME	RIVER RHINE	ROUGH GOING
REVIEW COPY	RIVER RHONE	ROUGH GUESS

ROUGH GUIDE	RUDE PERSON	SAD TIDINGS
ROUGH HANDS	RUDE REMARK	SAFE IN PORT
ROUGH HOUSE	RUDOLF HESS	SAFE METHOD
ROUGH NIGHT	RUGBY FIELD	SAFE POLICY
ROUGH STATE	RUGBY MATCH	SAFE REFUGE
ROUGH STONE	RUGBY PITCH	SAFETY BELT
ROUGH STUFF	RUGBY SCRUM	SAFETY LAMP
ROUGH TRACK	RUGBY TRIAL	SAIL A YACHT
ROUGH USAGE	RUGBY UNION	SAILING AID
ROUGH WATER	RUGGER BLUE	SAILOR SUIT
ROUGH WORDS	RUM AND LIME	SAINT LOUIS
ROUND ABOUT	RUN ABREAST	SAINT PETER
ROUND DANCE	RUN AGAINST	SALAD CREAM
ROUND DOZEN	RUN AGROUND	SALE OF WORK
ROUND GUESS	RUN A MINUTE	SALES STAFF
ROUND ROBIN	RUN AT A LOSS	SALLY FORTH
ROUND SCORE	RUN ERRANDS	SALMON PINK
ROUND TABLE	RUN FOR HELP	SALT CELLAR
ROUND TERMS	RUN FOR PORT	SALTED AWAY
ROUND TOWER	RUN IN PAIRS	SALTED BEEF
ROUTE MARCH	RUN LIKE MAD	SALT OF LIFE
ROWING BLUE	RUNNER BEAN	SAM GOLDWYN
ROWING BOAT	RUNNING OUT	SAMPLE BOOK
ROWING CLUB	RUN THE RISK	SAND CASTLE
ROW OF BEANS	RUN THE SHOW	SANDIE SHAW
ROW OF TREES	RUN THROUGH	SANDS OF DEE
ROW UPON ROW	RUN TO EARTH	SANDY BEACH
ROYAL ASCOT	RUN TO WASTE	SANE ENOUGH
ROYAL BARGE	RUN UP A BILL	SANTA CLAUS
ROYAL BIRTH	RURAL SCENE	SANTA LUCIA
ROYAL BLOOD	RUSS CONWAY	SARAH MILES
ROYAL FLUSH	RUSSIAN EGG	SARDINE TIN
ROYAL HOUSE	RUSSIAN TEA	SATIN DRESS
ROYAL LODGE	RUSTIC ARCH	SAUCER EYES
ROYAL SCOTS	RUSTIC SEAT	SAVAGE BLOW
ROYAL SUITE	RUSTIC WORK	SAVAGE CLUB
ROYAL TRAIN		SAVAGE RACE
ROYAL VISIT		SAVE A TRICK
ROYAL YACHT		SAVE LABOUR
ROY EMERSON		SAVE THE DAY
ROY ORBISON	**S—10**	SAVING GAME
RUB AGAINST	SABBATH DAY	SAVOY HOTEL
RUBBER BALL	SABLE STOLE	SAY A PRAYER
RUBBER BAND	SACK OF COAL	SAY GOOD-BYE
RUBBER HOSE	SACK OF COKE	SAY NOTHING
RUBBER SOLE	SACK OF CORN	SAY THE WORD
RUBBER TUBE	SACK THE LOT	SCALDED CAT
RUBBER TYRE	SACRED BOOK	SCALE MODEL
RUBY MURRAY	SACRED RITE	SCAMPER OFF
RUDE ANSWER	SACRED WRIT	SCARLET HAT
RUDE HEALTH	SAD OUTLOOK	SCARS OF WAR

SCENE THREE	SECOND HOME	SEND A CABLE
SCENT SPRAY	SECOND JUMP	SEND BY HAND
SCHOOL BELL	SECOND LEAD	SEND BY POST
SCHOOL BOOK	SECOND LINE	SEND FLYING
SCHOOL DAYS	SECOND MATE	SENIOR GIRL
SCHOOL FEES	SECOND NAME	SENSE ORGAN
SCHOOL SONG	SECOND PART	SENT FLYING
SCHOOL TERM	SECOND POST	SENTRY DUTY
SCHOOL YEAR	SECOND RACE	SERENE LOOK
SCORE A BULL	SECOND RANK	SERIOUS AIR
SCORE A DUCK	SECOND SELF	SERVE A MEAL
SCORE A GOAL	SECOND SLIP	SERVE AN ACE
SCOTCH KALE	SECONDS OUT	SERVE A WRIT
SCOTCH MIST	SECOND TEAM	SERVE BADLY
SCOTCH PINE	SECOND TERM	SERVING MAN
SCOTCH REEL	SECOND TEST	SET A COURSE
SCOTS GREYS	SECOND TIME	SET AGAINST
SCOUT ROUND	SECOND WEEK	SET AT LARGE
SCRAPE AWAY	SECOND WIFE	SET FORMULA
SCRAPE HOME	SECOND WIND	SET IN ORDER
SCRAP METAL	SECOND YEAR	SET IN PLACE
SCRAP PAPER	SECRET CODE	SET OF BELLS
SCRATCH MAN	SECRET DOOR	SET OF CHESS
SCRATCH OUT	SECRET FILE	SET OF CLUBS
SCREECH OWL	SECRET PACT	SET OF DARTS
SCREEN IDOL	SECRET SIGN	SET OF EIGHT
SCREEN TEST	SECRET VICE	SET OF RULES
SCREW LOOSE	SECRET VOTE	SET OF SEVEN
SCRIP ISSUE	SEDAN CHAIR	SET OF STUDS
SCUTTLE OFF	SEE ABOUT IT	SET OF TEETH
SEA ANEMONE	SEE A DOCTOR	SET OF THREE
SEA BATHING	SEE A LAWYER	SET OF TOOLS
SEA CAPTAIN	SEE CLEARLY	SET PROBLEM
SEALED BOOK	SEEING LIFE	SET PURPOSE
SEALED LIPS	SEEK ACCORD	SET STORE BY
SEA MONSTER	SEEK ADVICE	SET THE PACE
SEAN O'CASEY	SEEK OFFICE	SETTING OFF
SEA OF FACES	SEEK REFUGE	SETTING OUT
SEA PASSAGE	SEEK SAFETY	SETTING SUN
SEA SERPENT	SEE NOTHING	SETTLE DOWN
SECOND BELL	SEE ONE'S WAY	SET TO MUSIC
SECOND BEST	SEE SERVICE	SET UP HOUSE
SECOND COAT	SEE THE JOKE	SEVEN A SIDE
SECOND COPY	SEE THROUGH	SEVEN CLUBS
SECOND CROP	SEE VISIONS	SEVEN DIALS
SECOND FORM	SEIZE POWER	SEVEN DOZEN
SECOND GEAR	SELECT CLUB	SEVEN GROSS
SECOND HALF	SELL AN IDEA	SEVEN HOURS
SECOND HAND	SELL IN BULK	SEVEN KINGS
SECOND HEAT	SELL SHARES	SEVEN MILES
SECOND HOLE	SELSEY BILL	SEVEN PARTS

SEVEN PINTS	SHOE A HORSE	SHUT UP SHOP
SEVEN SCORE	SHOE POLISH	SIAMESE CAT
SEVEN STARS	SHOOT AHEAD	SICK AS A DOG
SEVENTH DAY	SHOOT A LINE	SICK HUMOUR
SEVENTH ROW	SHOOT FORTH	SICKLY LOOK
SEVENTH TEE	SHOOT IT OUT	SICK OF WORK
SEVEN TIMES	SHOP WINDOW	SICK PARADE
SEVEN TO ONE	SHORE LEAVE	SICK PERSON
SEVEN VEILS	SHORT BURST	SIDE BY SIDE
SEVEN WEEKS	SHORT DRINK	SIDE EFFECT
SEVEN YEARS	SHORT DRIVE	SIDE OF BEEF
SEVERE BLOW	SHORT HAIRS	SIDE POCKET
SEVERE LOOK	SHORT HOURS	SIDE STAKES
SEVERE LOSS	SHORT LEASE	SIDE STREET
SEVERE PAIN	SHORT LEAVE	SIDE TO SIDE
SEVERE TEST	SHORT PANTS	SIDE WINDOW
SEVERN BORE	SHORT PRICE	SIDLE ALONG
SEWAGE FARM	SHORT QUEUE	SIGH DEEPLY
SHABBY DEAL	SHORT RANGE	SIGH NO MORE
SHADY PLACE	SHORT SIGHT	SIGNAL LAMP
SHADY TRICK	SHORT SKIRT	SIGNED COPY
SHAKE HANDS	SHORT SLEEP	SIGNET RING
SHAKE IT OFF	SHORT SOCKS	SIGN MANUAL
SHALLOW END	SHORT SPELL	SIGN OF LIFE
SHANK'S PONY	SHORT STAGE	SILENT FILM
SHANTY TOWN	SHORT STORY	SILKEN HAIR
SHAPE BADLY	SHORT VISIT	SILKEN HOSE
SHARE A FLAT	SHOT AT DAWN	SILK FABRIC
SHARE A TAXI	SHOVE ASIDE	SILK GLOVES
SHARP FROST	SHOW A LIGHT	SILK SQUARES
SHARP KNIFE	SHOWER BATH	SILLY BILLY
SHARP POINT	SHOW FAVOUR	SILLY DEVIL
SHARP TASTE	SHOW NO PITY	SILLY GOOSE
SHARP TWIST	SHOW NO SIGN	SILLY IDIOT
SHARP VOICE	SHOW SPIRIT	SILLY MID-ON
SHARP WORDS	SHOW TALENT	SILLY POINT
SHED A LIGHT	SHOW THE WAY	SILVER BAND
SHEEP'S EYES	SHOW UP WELL	SILVER COIN
SHEER FLUKE	SHOW VALOUR	SILVER DISC
SHEER FOLLY	SHREWD BLOW	SILVER FOIL
SHEER FORCE	SHREWD FACE	SILVER HAIR
SHEER WASTE	SHREWD IDEA	SILVER MINE
SHEET GLASS	SHREWD MOVE	SILVER RING
SHEET METAL	SHREWD TURN	SILVER STAR
SHEET MUSIC	SHRILL NOTE	SILVER TRAY
SHEET OF ICE	SHRILL TONE	SILVER WIRE
SHIFT ABOUT	SHRINK AWAY	SIMMER DOWN
SHINE FORTH	SHRINK BACK	SIMNEL CAKE
SHIN OF BEEF	SHUFFLE OFF	SIMON PETER
SHIP'S CARGO	SHUFFLE OUT	SIMPLE DIET
SHIRE HORSE	SHUTTING UP	SIMPLE FARE

SIMPLE IDEA	SIZE ELEVEN	SMALL WOMAN
SIMPLE LIFE	SIZE OF TYPE	SMALL WORLD
SIMPLE MIND	SIZE TWELVE	SMART HOUSE
SIMPLE PAST	SKETCH BOOK	SMART WOMAN
SIMPLE SOUL	SKIPPED OFF	SMILE AGAIN
SINE QUA NON	SKIPPED OUT	SMITH MINOR
SING A DIRGE	SKIRT ROUND	SMOKE A PIPE
SING FOR JOY	SKITTLE OUT	SMOKED FISH
SING IN TUNE	SLACKEN OFF	SMOKING CAP
SINGLE BLOW	SLACK WATER	SMOKING HOT
SINGLE FARE	SLAP-UP MEAL	SMOOTH AWAY
SINGLE FILE	SLATE LOOSE	SMOOTH CHIN
SINGLE LIFE	SLAVE DANCE	SMOOTH DOWN
SINGLE LINE	SLAVE STATE	SMOOTH FACE
SINGLE MIND	SLAVE TRADE	SMOOTH HAIR
SINGLE NOTE	SLEEP IT OFF	SMOOTH OVER
SINGLE ROOM	SLEEP ROUGH	SMOOTH SKIN
SINGLE VOTE	SLEEP TIGHT	SMUGGLE OUT
SINK A SHAFT	SLEIGH RIDE	SNAIL'S PACE
SINK OR SWIM	SLICED LOAF	SNAP ANSWER
SIRE AND DAM	SLICK CHICK	SNAP INTO IT
SIR GALAHAD	SLIDE VALVE	SNATCH AWAY
SIR OR MADAM	SLIGHT BLOW	SNEAK ABOUT
SISTER SHIP	SLIGHT COLD	SNEAK ROUND
SIT AND FUME	SLIM CHANCE	SNEAK THIEF
SITTING OUT	SLIM FIGURE	SNOW AND ICE
SIX BILLION	SLIM VOLUME	SNOW MAIDEN
SIX COURSES	SLIP OF A BOY	SNOWY WHITE
SIX DEGREES	SLIPPED OFF	SOAKING WET
SIX DOLLARS	SLIPPED OUT	SOAP BUBBLE
SIX FATHOMS	SLOW BOWLER	SOAP FLAKES
SIX GALLONS	SLOW GROWTH	SOAP POWDER
SIX HUNDRED	SLOW MOTION	SOAP RATION
SIX MINUTES	SLOW POISON	SOAPY WATER
SIX OCTAVES	SLOW WICKET	SOBER TRUTH
SIX OF CLUBS	SMALL BLAME	SOCCER TEAM
SIX OR SEVEN	SMALL BUILD	SOCIAL CLUB
SIX PER CENT	SMALL CHILD	SOCIAL EVIL
SIX SHOOTER	SMALL CRAFT	SOCIAL ILLS
SIX SQUARED	SMALL CROWD	SOCIAL LIFE
SIX STROKES	SMALL HOPES	SOCIAL RANK
SIXTH FLOOR	SMALL HOURS	SOCIAL RUIN
SIXTH GREEN	SMALL HOUSE	SOCIAL WORK
SIXTH OF MAY	SMALL MEANS	SODIUM LAMP
SIXTH PLACE	SMALL ORDER	SOFT ANSWER
SIXTH ROUND	SMALL PIECE	SOFT AS SILK
SIXTH SENSE	SMALL PRINT	SOFT AS SOAP
SIXTY MILES	SMALL SCALE	SOFT CENTRE
SIXTY TIMES	SMALL THING	SOFT COLLAR
SIXTY YEARS	SMALL VOICE	SOFT COLOUR
SIX WICKETS	SMALL WAIST	SOFT GROUND

SOFT NUMBER	SPARE WHEEL	SQUARE MEAL
SOFT PALATE	SPEAK ALOUD	SQUARE MILE
SOFT PENCIL	SPEAK DUTCH	SQUARE ROOT
SOFT TONGUE	SPEAK WELSH	SQUARE SAIL
SOFT WICKET	SPECIAL BUS	SQUARE UP TO
SOHO SQUARE	SPECIAL DAY	SQUARE YARD
SOLAR MONTH	SPEED FIEND	SQUEEZE DRY
SOLEMN FACE	SPEED GAUGE	SQUEEZE OUT
SOLEMN LOOK	SPEED LIMIT	STABLE DOOR
SOLEMN OATH	SPEED TRIAL	STABLE MATE
SOLE RIGHTS	SPELL IT OUT	STACK OF HAY
SOLE TRADER	SPEND MONEY	STAFF NURSE
SOLID BUILD	SPENT FORCE	STAG BEETLE
SOLID FACTS	SPICED WINE	STAGE FEVER
SOLID IVORY	SPICY STORY	STAGGER OFF
SOLID SENSE	SPIDER'S WEB	STAGGER OUT
SOLID WATER	SPIKE JONES	STAKE MONEY
SOLO EFFORT	SPILL BLOOD	STALE BREAD
SOLO FLIGHT	SPINAL CORD	STAMP ALBUM
SON AND HEIR	SPIN BOWLER	STAND ABOUT
SONG OF LOVE	SPIRAL DOWN	STAND ALONE
SONG WRITER	SPIRIT AWAY	STAND ALOOF
SONJA HENIE	SPIRIT LAMP	STAND APART
SONNIE HALE	SPLIT HAIRS	STAND ASIDE
SOON ENOUGH	SPLIT IN TWO	STAND AT BAY
SOOTH TO SAY	SPODE CHINA	STAND CLEAR
SORDID GAIN	SPOKEN WORD	STAND ERECT
SORE THROAT	SPONGE CAKE	STAND FOR IT
SORRY SIGHT	SPONGE DOWN	STAND GUARD
SORRY STATE	SPORTS CLUB	STAND IN AWE
SORRY TO SAY	SPORTS COAT	STANDING BY
SOUND BASIS	SPORTS PAGE	STANDING UP
SOUND RADIO	SPOTTED DOG	STAND ON END
SOUND SENSE	SPREAD FEAR	STAND READY
SOUND SLEEP	SPREAD SAIL	STAND STILL
SOUND TRACK	SPRING AWAY	STAND TO WIN
SOUND VIEWS	SPRING BACK	STAND TREAT
SOUND WAVES	SPRING DOWN	STAND TRIAL
SOUP COURSE	SPRING OPEN	STAND UP FOR
SOUP TICKET	SPRING OVER	STAPLE DIET
SOUR GRAPES	SPRING SALE	STARK NAKED
SOUR NATURE	SPRING SONG	STARLIT SKY
SOUTH COAST	SPRING TIDE	STAR OF HOPE
SOUTH DEVON	SPUN SILVER	STAR PLAYER
SOUTH DOWNS	SQUAD DRILL	START A FIRE
SOUTH WALES	SQUARE CHIN	START AGAIN
SOW THE SEED	SQUARE DEAL	START A RIOT
SPACE PROBE	SQUARE FOOT	START YOUNG
SPANISH FLY	SQUARE GAME	STATE A CASE
SPAN OF LIFE	SQUARE HOLE	STATE COACH
SPARE FRAME	SQUARE INCH	STATED TIME

STATE GRANT	STICKY MESS	STRICT DIET
STATE NURSE	STIFF CLIMB	STRICT TIME
STATE OF WAR	STIFF DRINK	STRIKE BACK
STATE TRIAL	STIFF FENCE	STRIKE CAMP
STATE VISIT	STIFF PRICE	STRIKE DOWN
STATUTE LAW	STILL OWING	STRIKE DUMB
STAY AT HOME	STILL THERE	STRIKE GOLD
STAY BEHIND	STILL WATER	STRIKE HARD
STAY IN A RUT	STIRRUP CUP	STRIKE HOME
STAY INSIDE	STIR THE POT	STRIKE SAIL
STAY UP LATE	STITCHED UP	STRING BAND
ST. DUNSTAN'S	ST. LAWRENCE	STRING TRIO
STEADY BEAM	ST. LUKE'S DAY	STRING VEST
STEADY FLOW	STOCK REPLY	STRIP POKER
STEADY HAND	STOCK STILL	STRIP TEASE
STEADY PACE	STODGY FOOD	STROKE PLAY
STEADY RAIN	STOKE POGES	STRONG BREW
STEADY SALE	STOLE A KISS	STRONG CASE
STEADY WIND	STONE STEPS	STRONG GRIP
STEAK HOUSE	STONE WALLS	STRONG HAND
STEAL A KISS	STONY BROKE	STRONG HEAD
STEAL ALONG	STONY HEART	STRONG LINE
STEALING BY	STONY STARE	STRONG MEAT
STEALING UP	STOOD TRIAL	STRONG MIND
STEAM NAVVY	STOP AT HOME	STRONG PULL
STEAM ORGAN	STOP A TOOTH	STRONG ROOM
STEAM POWER	STOP AT WILL	STRONG SIDE
STEAM RADIO	STOP CRYING	STRONG SUIT
STEAM TRAIN	STOP FOR TEA	STRONG WILL
STEAM YACHT	STOP IN TIME	STRONG WIND
STEEL WORKS	STOPPED ONE	STRUCK DOWN
STEELY LOOK	STOPPED OUT	STRUCK DUMB
STEEP CLIMB	STOP THE BUS	STRUGGLE BY
STEEP PRICE	STOP THE GAP	STRUGGLE ON
STEER CLEAR	STOP THE ROT	ST. STEPHEN'S
STEP ASHORE	STORE OF WIT	STUDIO FLAT
STEP BY STEP	STORK'S NEST	STUDY MUSIC
STEP INSIDE	STORMY LIFE	STUFFED OWL
STEP LIVELY	STOUT HEART	STUFFY ROOM
STEPPED OUT	STOUT WOMAN	STUMP ALONG
STERN CHASE	STRAIGHT BY	STUMPED OUT
STERN TRUTH	STRAIGHT IN	STUMPY TAIL
STERN WORDS	STRAIGHT ON	STURDY LEGS
STEWED BEEF	STRAIGHT UP	SUCH IS LIFE
STEWED EELS	STRANGE MAN	SUCKING PIG
STEWED LAMB	STREAK AWAY	SUDDEN BANG
STEWED MEAT	STREAK PAST	SUDDEN BLOW
STICK IT OUT	STREET ARAB	SUDDEN FEAR
STICK TIGHT	STREET DOOR	SUDDEN HUSH
STICK UP FOR	STREET LAMP	SUDDEN STOP
STICKY BOMB	STRETCH OUT	SUEDE SHOES

SUFFER LOSS	SWING ALONG	TAKE ORDERS
SUFFER PAIN	SWING FOR IT	TAKE PITY ON
SUGAR CANDY	SWING MUSIC	TAKE POISON
SUGAR DADDY	SWING ROUND	TAKE REFUGE
SUMMER CAMP	SWISS GUARD	TAKE THE AIR
SUMMER HEAT	SWISS WATCH	TAKE THE CUP
SUMMER RAIN	SWITCH BACK	TAKE THE RAP
SUMMER SALE	SWITCH OVER	TAKE TO ARMS
SUMMER TERM	SWORD DANCE	TAKE TO TASK
SUMMER TIME	SWORN ENEMY	TAKE UP ARMS
SUM OF MONEY		TAKE UP TIME
SUN AND MOON		TAKING WAYS
SUNDAY BEST	**T—10**	TALENT SHOW
SUNDAY SUIT	TABLE D'HÔTE	TALE OF A TUB
SUN GLASSES	TABLE KNIFE	TALK AWHILE
SUNKEN REEF	TABLE LINEN	TALK IT OVER
SUNNY SMILE	TABLE MONEY	TALK TURKEY
SUNNY SOUTH	TABLE WATER	TALLEST BOY
SUN-RAY LAMP	TAKE A BRIEF	TALLEST MAN
SUNSET GLOW	TAKE A CHAIR	TAME AFFAIR
SUPERB VIEW	TAKE ACTION	TAME ANIMAL
SUPPER TIME	TAKE A DEKKO	TANGLED WEB
SUPPLY BASE	TAKE ADVICE	TAP LIGHTLY
SUPPLY SHIP	TAKE AN OATH	TAP THE LINE
SURE AS FATE	TAKE A PHOTO	TAP THE WIRE
SURE ENOUGH	TAKE A PUNCH	TARGET AREA
SURE GROUND	TAKE A SHARE	TARGET DATE
SURGE AHEAD	TAKE A SNACK	TARGET SHIP
SURPLUS FAT	TAKE AS READ	TARIFF WALL
SWAGGER OUT	TAKE A STAND	TARTAN KILT
SWAN OF AVON	TAKE A TITLE	TART ANSWER
SWEARING IN	TAKE A TRAIN	TASK IN HAND
SWEAT BLOOD	TAKE CHARGE	TASTE BLOOD
SWEAT IT OUT	TAKE CREDIT	TASTY SNACK
SWEEP ALONG	TAKE EFFECT	TATTOO MARK
SWEEP ASIDE	TAKE FLIGHT	TAUT NERVES
SWEEP CLEAN	TAKE FRIGHT	TAX EVASION
SWEET DRINK	TAKE IN HAND	TAXI DRIVER
SWEET HERBS	TAKE IN SAIL	T-BONE STEAK
SWEET MUSIC	TAKE IN VAIN	TEACH CLASS
SWEET SLEEP	TAKE IT BACK	TEACH MUSIC
SWEET SMELL	TAKE IT EASY	TEA CLIPPER
SWEET SMILE	TAKE IT HARD	TEA DRINKER
SWEET SOUND	TAKE KINDLY	TEAM OF FOUR
SWEET SYRUP	TAKE MY HAND	TEAM SPIRIT
SWEET TOOTH	TAKE MY WORD	TEA PLANTER
SWEET VOICE	TAKEN ABACK	TEAR IN HALF
SWEET WORDS	TAKE NO PART	TEAR TO BITS
SWERVE PAST	TAKE NOTICE	TEA SERVICE
SWIM ACROSS	TAKE OFFICE	TEENY WEENY
SWINE FEVER	TAKE ON A JOB	TELL A STORY

TELLING OFF	THE BALKANS	THE MAESTRO
TEN AND FIVE	THE BEATLES	THE MARINES
TEN AND FOUR	THE BEST MAN	THE MAZURKA
TEN AND NINE	THE BIG FIVE	THEME MUSIC
TEN BILLION	THE BOER WAR	THE MENDIPS
TEN DEGREES	THE BRAVEST	THE MESSIAH
TENDER CARE	THE BRONTËS	THE MILITIA
TENDER LOVE	THE CABINET	THE MIXTURE
TENDER MEAT	THE CAPITAL	THE NEEDFUL
TENDER SPOT	THE CHANNEL	THE NEEDLES
TEN DOLLARS	THE COLD WAR	THE NEW LOOK
TEN FATHOMS	THE COMMONS	THE ODYSSEY
TEN GALLONS	THE CRITICS	THE OLD ADAM
TEN GUINEAS	THE CURRAGH	THE OLD FIRM
TEN MILLION	THE CUSTOMS	THE ORKNEYS
TEN MINUTES	THÉ DANSANT	THE PEERAGE
TENNIS BALL	THE DEAD SEA	THE PLANETS
TENNIS CLUB	THE DEEP END	THE PRELUDE
TENNIS STAR	THE DYNASTS	THE PREMIER
TEN OF CLUBS	THE EAST END	THE QUAKERS
TENOR VOICE	THE ENGLISH	THE QUALITY
TEN PAST ONE	THE ETERNAL	THE RED ARMY
TEN PAST SIX	THE EVIL EYE	THE RED FLAG
TEN PAST TWO	THE EVIL ONE	THE REGENCY
TEN PER CENT	THE EXPERTS	THE RENT ACT
TEN SECONDS	THE FAIR SEX	THERE THERE!
TEN SQUARED	THE FAR EAST	THE REVENGE
TENTH GREEN	THE FIDGETS	THE RIOT ACT
TENTH OF MAY	THE FIFTIES	THE RIVIERA
TENTH PLACE	THE FORTIES	THE ROCKERS
TENTH ROUND	THE GALLERY	THE ROCKIES
TEN TO EIGHT	THE GALLOWS	THE SABBATH
TEN TO SEVEN	THE GESTAPO	THE SAME KEY
TEN TO THREE	THE GIGGLES	THE SAPPERS
TEN WICKETS	THE GLAD EYE	THE SEASONS
TEPID WATER	THE GORBALS	THE SEEKERS
TERRA COTTA	THE GUNNERS	THE SHADOWS
TERRA FIRMA	THE HARD WAY	THE SHIVERS
TEST FLIGHT	THE HEIRESS	THE SIXTIES
TEST OF TIME	THE HERMITS	THE SPEAKER
TEST RESULT	THE HOLLIES	THE STARTER
TEST WICKET	THE HORRORS	THE STEPPES
THE ACCUSED	THE JACKPOT	THE ST. LEGER
THE AMAZONS	THE JONESES	THE SUBURBS
THE ANIMALS	THE KNOW-HOW	THE TAIL-END
THE ARCHERS	THE KREMLIN	THE TEMPEST
THE ARSENAL	THE LANCERS	THE THEATRE
THEATRE BAR	THE LAST BUS	THE THINKER
THEATRE FAN	THE LAST LAP	THE THIN MAN
THE BACKING	THE LINCOLN	THE TITANIC
THE BAHAMAS	THE LOW-DOWN	THE TROPICS

THE TWELFTH	THORNY PATH	TIE THE KNOT
THE UNITIES	THREE BALLS	TIGHT DRESS
THE UNKNOWN	THREE BEARS	TIGHT GRASP
THE VATICAN	THREE BRACE	TIGHT PLACE
THE VICTORY	THREE CARDS	TIGHT SKIRT
THE VIKINGS	THREE CLUBS	TILLER GIRL
THE WEATHER	THREE DARTS	TIMBER TREE
THE WEST END	THREE DOZEN	TIME A PUNCH
THE WILLIES	THREE DRAWS	TIME ENOUGH
THICK SKULL	THREE FATES	TIME FACTOR
THICK SLICE	THREE FIVES	TIME FOR BED
THICK TWINE	THREE FOURS	TIME FOR TEA
THIN EXCUSE	THREE GROSS	TIME IN HAND
THING OR TWO	THREE HOLES	TIMELY EXIT
THINK ABOUT	THREE HOURS	TIMELY WORD
THINK AGAIN	THREE IN ONE	TIME OF LIFE
THINK AHEAD	THREE JACKS	TIME OF YEAR
THINK ALIKE	THREE KINGS	TIME, PLEASE
THINK ALOUD	THREE LUMPS	TIME SIGNAL
THINK IT OUT	THREE MILES	TIME TO COME
THINK TWICE	THREE NINES	TIME TO KILL
THINNED OUT	THREE PAIRS	TIME TO LOSE
THIN STRING	THREE PARTS	TIME TO STOP
THIRD CHILD	THREE PINTS	TINKER BELL
THIRD CLASS	THREE PUTTS	TINKER WITH
THIRD FLOOR	THREE SCORE	TINNED CRAB
THIRD GREEN	THREE SIDES	TINNED FISH
THIRD MONTH	THREE SIXES	TINNED FOOD
THIRD OF MAY	THREE STARS	TINNED MEAT
THIRD PARTY	THREE TIMES	TINNED MILK
THIRD PLACE	THREE TO ONE	TINNED SOUP
THIRD POWER	THREE WEEKS	TINNY NOISE
THIRD PRIZE	THREE YEARS	TINNY SOUND
THIRD REICH	THRIFT CLUB	TIN OF BEANS
THIRD ROUND	THROW ABOUT	TIN OF COCOA
THIRD STAGE	THROW A KISS	TIN OF FRUIT
THIRD VERSE	THROW ASIDE	TIN OF PAINT
THIRTY DAYS	THRUST DOWN	TIN SOLDIER
THIRTY LOVE	THRUST HOME	TIN WHISTLE
THIS FRIDAY	THRUST OPEN	TIP A WINNER
THIS MONDAY	THRUST PAST	TIP THE WINK
THIS OR THAT	THUMB A LIFT	TITIAN HAIR
THIS SEASON	THUMB A RIDE	TITLED RANK
THIS SIDE UP	THUMB INDEX	TITLE FIGHT
THIS SPRING	THUMBS DOWN	TITUS OATES
THIS SUMMER	TIDAL BASIN	TOBACCO ROW
THIS SUNDAY	TIDAL RIVER	TODAY'S DATE
THIS WAY OUT	TIDY INCOME	TOE THE LINE
THIS WINTER	TIE IN KNOTS	TOE THE MARK
THOMAS GRAY	TIE-ON LABEL	TOILET SOAP
THOMAS HOOD	TIES OF RACE	TOKEN MONEY

TOLL BRIDGE	TRADE UNION	TRUSS OF HAY
TOMATO SOUP	TRAFFIC COP	TRUSTEE ACT
TOM BOWLING	TRAFFIC JAM	TRUST HOUSE
TONIC SOLFA	TRAGIC MASK	TRY A NEW WAY
TONIC WATER	TRAGIC MUSE	TRYING TIME
TONS OF LOVE	TRAGIC NEWS	TUDOR HOUSE
TONS OF TIME	TRAGIC TALE	TUDOR KINGS
TONY CURTIS	TRAIN CRASH	TUDOR STYLE
TONY WELLER	TRAINED EYE	TUFT OF HAIR
TOO FAR GONE	TRAINED MAN	TUMBLE DOWN
TOOL SETTER	TRAIN FERRY	TUMBLE OVER
TO ONE'S FACE	TRAIN SMASH	TUNING FORK
TOOTING BEC	TRAM DRIVER	TUNNEL INTO
TOP AND TAIL	TRAMPLED ON	TURKEY TROT
TOP BILLING	TRAM TICKET	TURN ADRIFT
TOP HONOURS	TRAPEZE ACT	TURN AROUND
TOPPLE DOWN	TRAVEL BOOK	TURN COLOUR
TOPPLE OVER	TREAD ON AIR	TURN IT DOWN
TOP QUALITY	TREAD WATER	TURN OF DUTY
TOP THE BILL	TREAT BADLY	TURN THE KEY
TORRID ZONE	TREATY PORT	TURN TO DUST
TORY LEADER	TREBLE CLEF	TURN TO GOLD
TOTAL BLANK	TREE DOCTOR	TURN TURTLE
TOTAL WRECK	TREE OF LIFE	TURN YELLOW
TO THE ALTAR	TRENCH COAT	TURTLE DOVE
TO THE NORTH	TRENCH FEET	TURTLE SOUP
TO THE POINT	TRIAL MATCH	TWELFTH DAY
TO THE RIGHT	TRIAL SCENE	TWELFTH MAN
TO THE SOUTH	TRICK OR TWO	TWELFTH ROW
TOUCH AND GO	TRIFLE WITH	TWELVE DAYS
TOUCH JUDGE	TRIGGER OFF	TWELVE FEET
TOUCH LUCKY	TRIM ANKLES	TWELVE QUID
TOUGH BREAK	TRIM FIGURE	TWENTY QUID
TOUGH FIGHT	TRIP ABROAD	TWICE A WEEK
TOUR AROUND	TRIPLE STAR	TWICE A YEAR
TOURING CAR	TRIPLE TIME	TWICE DAILY
TOUR OF DUTY	TRIP TO TOWN	TWICE EIGHT
TO WINDWARD	TROLLEY BUS	TWICE ROUND
TOWN CENTRE	TROOP TRAIN	TWICE SEVEN
TOWN SQUARE	TROTTED OFF	TWICE THREE
TOY SOLDIER	TROTTED OUT	TWINE ROUND
TOY SPANIEL	TROY WEIGHT	TWIN SISTER
TOY TERRIER	TRUDGE PAST	TWIRL ROUND
TRACKER DOG	TRUE CHARGE	TWIST ABOUT
TRACK EVENT	TRUE FRIEND	TWIST MY ARM
TRADE CYCLE	TRUE REPORT	TWIST ROUND
TRADE PAPER	TRUE SAMPLE	TWO AND FIVE
TRADE PRICE	TRUE TO FORM	TWO AND FOUR
TRADER HORN	TRUE TO LIFE	TWO AND NINE
TRADE ROUTE	TRUE TO TYPE	TWO AT A TIME
TRADE TERMS	TRULY RURAL	TWO BILLION

TWO COLOURS	UNPAID BILL	VAL PARNELL
TWO COURSES	UNSOLD BOOK	VAMPIRE BAT
TWO DEGREES	UNTIDY MIND	VANESSA LEE
TWO DOLLARS	UNTIE A KNOT	VANILLA ICE
TWO FATHOMS	UP A GUM TREE	VANITY CASE
TWO GALLONS	UP ALL NIGHT	VANITY FAIR
TWO GUINEAS	UP AND ABOUT	VANTAGE OUT
TWO HUNDRED	UP AND DOING	VAPOUR BATH
TWO LENGTHS	UP AT OXFORD	VARIETY ACT
TWO MASTERS	UP FOR TRIAL	VAST EXTENT
TWO MILLION	UPHILL TASK	VAST PLAINS
TWO MINUTES	UPHILL WALK	VEAL AND HAM
TWO OCTAVES	UPHILL WORK	VEAL CUTLET
TWO OF A KIND	UP IN A PLANE	VENTURE OUT
TWO OF CLUBS	UP IN THE AIR	VERY HUNGRY
TWO OR THREE	UP IN THE SKY	VERY LIKELY
TWO PER CENT	UPON MY SOUL	VERY LITTLE
TWO RASHERS	UPON MY WORD	VERY NEARLY
TWO SECONDS	UPPER BERTH	VERY SELDOM
TWO SQUARED	UPPER CLASS	VETERAN CAR
TWO STRIPES	UPPER CRUST	VICHY WATER
TWO STROKES	UPPER HOUSE	VICIOUS LIE
TWO WICKETS	UPPER LIMIT	VICTOR HUGO
TYBURN TREE	UPPER SIXTH	VICTORY DAY
TYPING POOL	UPPER STORY	VILE BODIES
	UPRIGHT MAN	VILLAGE INN
U—10	UPSIDE DOWN	VINE GROWER
UGLY RUMOUR	UP THE AISLE	VINTAGE CAR
UGLY SISTER	UP THE CREEK	VIOLENT END
UGLY THREAT	UP THE RIVER	VIOLIN CASE
ULTRA VIRES	UP THE SPOUT	VIOLIN SOLO
UNCLE REMUS	UP TO A POINT	VIRGIN CLAY
UNCUT PAGES	UP TO NO GOOD	VIRGIN LAND
UNCUT STONE	UP TO SAMPLE	VIRGIN MARY
UNDER A TREE	UP TO THE HUB	VIRGIN SOIL
UNDER COVER	USE FINESSE	VITAL ERROR
UNDER GLASS	USEFUL HINT	VITAL FLAME
UNDER PROOF	USE THE POST	VITAL FORCE
UNDER STEAM	USUAL THING	VITAL POINT
UNDER TRIAL	UTTERLY BAD	VITAL POWER
UNDER WATER	UTTER TRIPE	VITAL SPARK
UNDUE HASTE		VITAL WOUND
UNION BOARD	**V—10**	VIVID GREEN
UNION CHIEF	VACANT LOOK	VOCAL CORDS
UNION RULES	VACANT POST	VOCAL GROUP
UNIQUE CASE	VACUUM PUMP	VOCAL MUSIC
UNIT OF HEAT	VAIN EFFORT	VOCAL ORGAN
UNIT OF TIME	VAIN PERSON	VOLLEY BALL
UNIT OF WORK	VAIN REGRET	VOTE LABOUR
UNKIND DEED	VALE AND LEA	VOTING LIST
UNKIND WORD	VALID POINT	VOUCH FOR IT

VOWEL SOUND
VULGAR HERD

W—10
WADE ACROSS
WADING BIRD
WAD OF MONEY
WAD OF NOTES
WAGE FREEZE
WAGE PACKET
WAGES CLERK
WAGES OF SIN
WAGON TRAIN
WAG THE HEAD
WAIT AND SEE
WAIT AROUND
WAIT AWHILE
WALK ACROSS
WALK AROUND
WALK BEHIND
WALK IN FEAR
WALK OF LIFE
WALK SLOWLY
WALK SOFTLY
WALL OF FIRE
WALL STREET
WALNUT TREE
WALT DISNEY
WALTZ MUSIC
WALTZ ROUND
WANDER AWAY
WANING MOON
WANT OF CARE
WANT OF LOVE
WANT OF ZEAL
WARD SISTER
WAR FOOTING
WAR MEMOIRS
WARM FRIEND
WARMING PAN
WARNING CRY
WAR OF WORDS
WARPED MIND
WAR SAVINGS
WASH AND DRY
WASHING DAY
WASP'S STING
WASTE MONEY
WASTE PAPER
WASTE WORDS
WATCH CHAIN

WATCHED POT
WATCH FOR IT
WATER BOARD
WATER LEVEL
WATER MELON
WATER MUSIC
WATER NYMPH
WATER ON TAP
WATER POWER
WATER'S EDGE
WATER TOWER
WAVE LENGTH
WAX AND WANE
WAXED PAPER
WAXING MOON
WAY IN FRONT
WAY OFF BEAM
WAYSIDE INN
WAY THROUGH
WEAK EXCUSE
WEAK STROKE
WEAK WILLED
WEALTHY MAN
WEARY WORLD
WEATHER EYE
WEATHER MAP
WEBBED FEET
WEDDED PAIR
WEDDED WIFE
WEDDING DAY
WEED KILLER
WEEK BY WEEK
WEEKLY RENT
WEEKLY WAGE
WEEP FOR JOY
WEEP NO MORE
WEIGH HEAVY
WEIGHING IN
WELCOME END
WELL BEATEN
WELL BEHIND
WELL CAUGHT
WELL ENOUGH
WELL I NEVER!
WELL IN HAND
WELL OF LIFE
WELL PLACED
WELL PLAYED
WELLS FARGO
WELL VERSED
WELSH CORGI

WELSH WALES
WENT AROUND
WENT DIRECT
WENT TO TOWN
WEST AFRICA
WEST BERLIN
WEST INDIAN
WEST INDIES
WEST IS WEST
WEST LONDON
WEST RIDING
WESTWARD HO!
WET BATTERY
WET BLANKET
WET CANTEEN
WET CLOTHES
WET SHAMPOO
WET THROUGH
WET WEATHER
WHAT AM I BID?
WHAT A NERVE!
WHAT A SHAME!
WHAT GOES ON?
WHAT'S YOURS?
WHEAT FIELD
WHEEL ABOUT
WHEEL ROUND
WHELK STALL
WHIFF OF AIR
WHIPPED OFF
WHIRL ROUND
WHIST DRIVE
WHISTLE FOR
WHITE BREAD
WHITE CARGO
WHITE CHALK
WHITE FRIAR
WHITE FROST
WHITE HORSE
WHITE HOUSE
WHITE LIGHT
WHITE MAGIC
WHITE METAL
WHITE MOUSE
WHITE PAINT
WHITE PAPER
WHITE PIECE
WHITE QUEEN
WHITE SAUCE
WHITE SHEET
WHITE SHIRT

WHITE SLAVE
WHITE SUGAR
WHITE TRASH
WHIT MONDAY
WHIT SUNDAY
WHOLE TRUTH
WHOLE WORLD
WICKED DEED
WICKED WAYS
WIDE APPEAL
WIDE CHOICE
WIDE CIRCLE
WIDELY HELD
WIDE MARGIN
WIDE SCREEN
WIDE VISION
WIDOW'S MITE
WIDOW'S PEAK
WIDOW WOMAN
WIELD POWER
WIFE BEATER
WIG AND GOWN
WILD ANIMAL
WILD CHEERS
WILD CHERRY
WILD FLOWER
WILD HORSES
WILD SCHEME
WILL OF IRON
WILLOW TREE
WILL TO LIVE
WILLY NILLY
WILY PERSON
WIN A RUBBER
WIN BY A GOAL
WIN BY A HEAD
WIN BY A NECK
WINDOW PANE
WINE BIBBER
WINE BOTTLE
WINE CELLAR
WINE TASTER
WINE TAVERN
WINE WAITER
WIN FREEDOM
WIN HONOURS
WINNING BET
WINNING HIT
WINNING RUN
WINNING TRY
WIN ON MERIT

WINTER COAT
WINTER FEED
WINTER SALE
WINTER TIME
WINTER WEAR
WIN THE GAME
WIN THE RACE
WIN THE TOSS
WIN THROUGH
WIRE BASKET
WIRE PUZZLE
WISE CHOICE
WISE OLD OWL
WISH IN VAIN
WISH UNDONE
WITCH HAZEL
WITH A SMILE
WITHER AWAY
WITHIN CALL
WITHIN HAIL
WITHOUT END
WITH REGRET
WITNESS BOX
WIZARD OF OZ
WOMAN HATER
WOMAN'S HOUR
WOMAN'S WORK
WOMEN'S ARMY
WOMEN'S PAGE
WOMEN'S WEAR
WON BY A HEAD
WON BY A NECK
WONDER DRUG
WOODEN CLUB
WOODEN SEAT
WOODEN SHOE
WOOD STREET
WOOLLY HAIR
WORD MAKING
WORD OF A LIE
WORD PUZZLE
WORD SQUARE
WORKING DAY
WORKING MAN
WORK IN HAND
WORK IN VAIN
WORK ON HAND
WORK PERMIT
WORK TO RULE
WORK UNDONE
WORLD ATLAS

WORLD COURT
WORLD POWER
WORLD TITLE
WORLD TRADE
WORRIED MAN
WORST OF ALL
WORST TASTE
WORTH WHILE
WOUNDED MAN
WREAK HAVOC
WRIGGLE OUT
WRITE A BOOK
WRITE ABOUT
WRITE AGAIN
WRITE A NOTE
WRITE A POEM
WRITE A SONG
WRITE BADLY
WRITE BOOKS
WRITE IN INK
WRITE IT OFF
WRITE MUSIC
WRITE NOTES
WRITE PLAYS
WRITE VERSE
WRITING INK
WRITTEN LAW
WRONG LINES
WRONG PLACE
WRONG TOTAL
WRONG TRACK
WRONG WOMAN

X—10
X-RAY CAMERA

Y—10
YARD BY YARD
YEAR BY YEAR
YEARLY RENT
YEAR TO YEAR
YELLOW BOOK
YELLOW CARD
YELLOW FLAG
YELLOW JACK
YELLOW RACE
YELLOW ROSE
YELLOW STAR
YIELD CROPS
YIELD FRUIT
YOUNG BLOOD
YOUNG CHILD

YOUNGER SON
YOUNG IDEAS
YOUNG WOMAN
YOUR CHOICE
YOUR HONOUR
YOURS TRULY
YOU'VE HAD IT
YUL BRYNNER

Z—10
ZIG-ZAG LINE
ZOO ANIMALS

A—11
AARON'S BEARD
ABANDON HOPE
ABANDON SHIP
ABIDE WITH ME
ABLE TO SPEAK
ABODE OF LOVE
ABOVE GROUND
ABOVE NORMAL
ABOVE RUBIES
ABOVE THE LAW
ABSTRACT ART
ACCENT GRAVE
ACCOUNT BOOK
ACCOUNT PAID
ACE OF HEARTS
ACE OF SPADES
ACE OF TRUMPS
ACHING HEART
ACHING TOOTH
ACT AS A BRAKE
ACT IN UNISON
ACTIVE VOICE
ACT OF HOMAGE
ACT ON ADVICE
ACT TOGETHER
ACUTE ACCENT
ACUTE ATTACK
ADD A CODICIL
ADDRESS BOOK
ADDRESS CARD
ADEQUATE SUM
AD INFINITUM
ADMIT BEARER
ADMIT DEFEAT
ADOLF HITLER
ADOPTION ACT
ADRIATIC SEA

ADVANCE BASE
ADVANCE COPY
ADVANCED AGE
ADVANCE DATE
ADVANCE FATE
AEOLIAN HARP
AFFECTED AIR
AFGHAN HOUND
AFRICA HOUSE
AFTER A WHILE
AFTER CHURCH
AFTER DINNER
AFTER SCHOOL
AFTER SUNSET
AFTER SUPPER
AFTER THE WAR
AGAINST TIME
AGE OF WISDOM
AGES AND AGES
AGONY COLUMN
AHEAD OF TIME
AID TO BEAUTY
AID TO MEMORY
AIM STRAIGHT
AIM TO PLEASE
AIR MINISTER
AIR MINISTRY
AIR TERMINAL
AIR TERMINUS
ALAMODE BEEF
ALARM SIGNAL
ALDGATE PUMP
ALFRED MARKS
ALFRED NOYES
ALISTAIR SIM
ALIVE OR DEAD
ALL COCK-EYED
ALL CREATION
ALL FALL DOWN
ALL FOOL'S DAY
ALL FOR MONEY
ALL GOES WELL
ALL HOPE GONE
ALL IN FAVOUR
ALL OF A PIECE
ALL OF A SHAKE
ALL ONE CAN DO
ALLOT SHARES
ALL-OUT DRIVE
ALLOW CREDIT
ALL QUARTERS

ALL SOULS' DAY
ALL STANDING
ALL-STAR CAST
ALL STRAIGHT
ALL THAT JAZZ
ALL THE SIGNS
ALL THE VOGUE
ALL THE WHILE
ALL THE WORLD
ALL TOGETHER
ALL TOGGED UP
ALL TO PIECES
ALL VERY FINE
ALL VERY WELL
ALL WASHED-UP
ALL WEEK LONG
ALMIGHTY GOD
ALMOND PASTE
ALMOST THERE
ALONE I DID IT
ALPINE GUIDE
ALSATIAN DOG
ALTER COURSE
AMATEUR SIDE
AMATEUR TEAM
AMERICAN BAR
AMERICAN WAR
AMERICA'S CUP
AMOS AND ANDY
AMOUR PROPRE
AN APPLE A DAY
ANCIENT CITY
ANCIENT ROME
ANDY STEWART
ANGELIC HOST
ANGELIC LOOK
ANGLING CLUB
ANIMAL TAMER
ANIMAL WORLD
ANISEED BALL
ANITA EKBERG
ANNA LUCASTA
ANNA PAVLOVA
ANNE SHELTON
ANN HATHAWAY
ANNIE BESANT
ANNIE LAURIE
ANNIE OAKLEY
ANN SHERIDAN
ANNUAL EVENT
ANNUAL LEAVE

ANNUAL TREAT
ANN VERONICA
ANOTHER TIME
ANTHONY EDEN
ANTHONY HOPE
ANTIQUE SHOP
ANTI-TANK GUN
ANVIL CHORUS
ANXIOUS TIME
APACHE DANCE
APPEAL COURT
APPEAL JUDGE
APPLE-PIE BED
APRIL SHOWER
ARCTIC OCEAN
ARE YOU READY?
ARMED ATTACK
ARMED BANDIT
ARMED COMBAT
ARMED ESCORT
ARMED FORCES
ARM OF THE LAW
ARM OF THE SEA
ARMOURED CAR
ARMOUR PLATE
ARMS AND LEGS
ARMS COUNCIL
ARMS STRETCH
ARMS TRAFFIC
ARMY BLANKET
ARMY CANTEEN
ARMY OFFICER
ARMY RESERVE
ARMY SURPLUS
AROMATIC GUM
ARRIVE EARLY
ARSENE LUPIN
ART DIRECTOR
ARTEMUS WARD
ARTFUL DODGE
ARTHUR ASKEY
ARTHUR'S SEAT
ARTS COUNCIL
ARTS THEATRE
ASCOT STAKES
AS DRY AS DUST
AS EASY AS PIE
AS GOOD AS NEW
ASK FOR A RISE
ASK FOR MERCY
ASK FOR TERMS

ASK THE PRICE
AS MUCH AGAIN
AS NICE AS PIE
ASSES' BRIDGE
ASSUME A RÔLE
ASSUMED NAME
A STAR IS BORN
ASTRAL PLANE
AS UGLY AS SIN
AS YOU LIKE IT
AT A DISCOUNT
AT A DISTANCE
AT ALL EVENTS
AT ALL POINTS
AT A LOOSE END
AT ATTENTION
AT CAMBRIDGE
AT FIRST HAND
AT FULL SPEED
AT GREAT RISK
AT HALF PRICE
A THING OR TWO
ATHOLE BROSE
AT INTERVALS
ATOMIC CLOCK
ATOMIC POWER
AT ONE'S ELBOW
AT ONE'S HEELS
AT ONE'S PERIL
AT ONE'S WORST
ATTACHÉ CASE
AT THE BOTTOM
AT THE CINEMA
AT THE CIRCUS
AT THE DOUBLE
AT THE FINISH
AT THE MOMENT
AT THE SUMMIT
AT THE TILLER
AT THE WICKET
AT THE ZENITH
AT WHAT PLACE?
AT WHICH TIME?
AUCTION ROOM
AUCTION SALE
AUTHOR'S NOTE
AUTUMN TINTS
AVERAGE HAND
AVERAGE TYPE
AVERAGE WAGE
AVERTED EYES

AVOCADO PEAR
AVOID DEFEAT
AWAY WITH YOU!
AWKWARD TIME
AYES AND NOES

B—11
BABY BUNTING
BABY CLOTHES
BACK A WINNER
BACK HEAVILY
BACK PAYMENT
BACK-ROOM BOY
BACK TO FRONT
BACKWARD BOY
BACON AND EGG
BACON SLICER
BAD BUSINESS
BADEN POWELL
BAD EYESIGHT
BAD FEELINGS
BAD FOR TRADE
BADGE OF RANK
BAD JUDGMENT
BAD LANGUAGE
BAD LIKENESS
BADLY PLACED
BADLY SHAKEN
BADLY WANTED
BAD PRACTICE
BAD TEACHING
BAG OF CRISPS
BAG OF NERVES
BAG OF SWEETS
BAG OF TRICKS
BAGS OF MONEY
BAIT THE TRAP
BAKED POTATO
BAKER'S DOZEN
BAKER STREET
BALCONY SEAT
BALD AS A COOT
BALLOT PAPER
BANANA SPLIT
BANBURY CAKE
BANG THE DOOR
BANK ACCOUNT
BANK BALANCE
BANK CHARGES
BANK DEPOSIT
BANK HOLIDAY

BANK MANAGER	BEAT THE BAND	BEST REGARDS
BANK THE FIRE	BEAT THE BANK	BETTER BY FAR
BARBED ARROW	BEAT THE BOOK	BETTER TERMS
BARBED SHAFT	BEAT THE DRUM	BETTER TIMES
BARBED WORDS	BEAU BRUMMEL	BETTER VALUE
BARBER'S POLE	BEAU SABREUR	BETTER WAGES
BARBER'S SHOP	BEAUTY QUEEN	BETTING SHOP
BARE MIDRIFF	BEAUTY SALON	BETTING SLIP
BARE MINIMUM	BEAUTY SLEEP	BETTY GRABLE
BARGAIN SALE	BEBE DANIELS	BETTY HUTTON
BARKING DOGS	BECK AND CALL	BETTY MARTIN
BARLEY SUGAR	BECOME AWARE	BETWEEN MAID
BARLEY WATER	BECOME SOLID	BEYOND A JOKE
BARNARD'S INN	BED AND BOARD	BEYOND DOUBT
BARON OF BEEF	BE DIFFERENT	BEYOND PRICE
BARON'S COURT	BED OF THE SEA	BICYCLE BELL
BARRACK ROOM	BED OF THORNS	BID DEFIANCE
BARREL ORGAN	BEDSIDE LAMP	BID FAREWELL
BARREN HEATH	BEEF EXTRACT	BIG BUSINESS
BARREN WASTE	BEER SHAMPOO	BIG TURNOVER
BARRIER REEF	BEER TANKARD	BILLIARD CUE
BAR SINISTER	BEES' WEDDING	BILL OF COSTS
BASIC RIGHTS	BEFORE LUNCH	BILLY BUNTER
BASKET CHAIR	BEG FOR MERCY	BILLY COTTON
BAT AN EYELID	BEGGING BOWL	BILLY THE KID
BATED BREATH	BEGIN TO PALL	BILLY WALKER
BATHING POOL	BEG TO DIFFER	BIRD FANCIER
BATTING SIDE	BEHAVE BADLY	BIRD WATCHER
BATTLE ABBEY	BELGIAN PORT	BISHOP'S MOVE
BATTLE ARRAY	BELGIAN TOWN	BISHOP'S PAWN
BATTLE DRESS	BELINDA FAIR	BITE ONE'S LIP
BATTLE ORDER	BELLY DANCER	BITE THE DUST
BATTLE ROYAL	BELOW GROUND	BITTER ALOES
BATTLE SCENE	BELOW STAIRS	BITTER ENEMY
BAY OF BENGAL	BELT OF TREES	BITTER GRIEF
BAY OF BISCAY	BEND FORWARD	BITTER LEMON
BAY OF NAPLES	BEND THE KNEE	BITTER SWEET
BEAM OF LIGHT	BEND THE MIND	BITTER TASTE
BEAR A GRUDGE	BENGAL LIGHT	BITTER TEARS
BEAR BAITING	BENGAL TIGER	BITTER WORDS
BEARDED LADY	BE OF SERVICE	BLACK AND TAN
BEARER BONDS	BE REALISTIC	BLACK AS COAL
BEAR ILL-WILL	BERNARD SHAW	BLACK AS SOOT
BEARING REIN	BERNESE ALPS	BLACK BEAUTY
BEARSKIN RUG	BEST CIRCLES	BLACK BEETLE
BEAR THE COST	BEST CLOTHES	BLACK BISHOP
BEAR THE NAME	BEST EDITION	BLACK BOTTOM
BEAR WITNESS	BEST OF TASTE	BLACK CASTLE
BEAST OF PREY	BEST OF TERMS	BLACK COFFEE
BEAT A TATTOO	BEST OF THREE	BLACK COTTON
BEATEN TRACK	BEST QUALITY	BLACK FRIARS

BLACK FRIDAY
BLACK FOREST
BLACK GRAPES
BLACK KNIGHT
BLACK LETTER
BLACK MARKET
BLACK MONDAY
BLACK PEPPER
BLACK PRINCE
BLACK SQUARE
BLACK TO MOVE
BLACK TO PLAY
BLACK VELVET
BLANK CHEQUE
BLANKET BATH
BLAZE A TRAIL
BLAZING FIRE
BLESS MY SOUL!
BLESS THE DAY
BLIND AS A BAT
BLIND CHANCE
BLIND CORNER
BLIND FLYING
BLOCK LETTER
BLOCK OF WOOD
BLOCK THE WAY
BLOOD ORANGE
BLOOD STREAM
BLOOD VESSEL
BLOODY TOWER
BLOSSOM TIME
BLOW BUBBLES
BLOW FOR BLOW
BLOW ME TIGHT!
BLOW ONE'S TOP
BLOW SKY-HIGH
BLOW THE FIRE
BLOW THE GAFF
BLUE-COAT BOY
BLUE-EYED BOY
BLUE FOR A BOY
BLUE HORIZON
BLUNT REMARK
BLUSH UNSEEN
BOARD SCHOOL
BOATING SONG
BOB CRATCHIT
BODY AND SOUL
BODY POLITIC
BOGNOR REGIS
BOILED BACON

BOILED SHIRT
BOILED SWEET
BOLD AS A LION
BOLD AS BRASS
BOLD ATTEMPT
BOLD OUTLINE
BOLT THE DOOR
BOLT UPRIGHT
BOMBER PILOT
BOMB SHELTER
BOND OF UNION
BONNE BOUCHE
BONNY DUNDEE
BOOKING HALL
BOOK OF VERSE
BOOK OF WORDS
BOOK VOUCHER
BORACIC ACID
BORN ACTRESS
BORN AND BRED
BORROW A BOOK
BORROW MONEY
BOSOM FRIEND
BOSS THE SHOW
BOSTON BEANS
BOTTLED BEER
BOTTLE GREEN
BOTTLE OF GIN
BOTTLE OF INK
BOTTLE OF RUM
BOTTLE PARTY
BOTTOM LAYER
BOTTOM MARKS
BOTTOM TEETH
BOUND TO LOSE
BOW AND ARROW
BOWL A YORKER
BOWL OF FRUIT
BOWL OF PUNCH
BOXING BOOTH
BOXING GLOVE
BOXING MATCH
BOX OF BRICKS
BOX OF CIGARS
BOX OF PAINTS
BOX OF TRICKS
BOY NEXT DOOR
BOYS' BRIGADE
BRACE AND BIT
BRACING WIND
BRAIN DAMAGE

BRAIN INJURY
BRAINS TRUST
BRAISED BEEF
BRANDY GLASS
BRASS MONKEY
BRASSY VOICE
BRAVE EFFORT
BRAVE PERSON
BRAZEN IT OUT
BREAD AND JAM
BREAD OF LIFE
BREAD RATION
BREAD STREET
BREAD WINNER
BREAK A HABIT
BREAK BOUNDS
BREAK FOR TEA
BREAK GROUND
BREAK STONES
BREAK THE ICE
BREAK THE LAW
BREATHE FIRE
BREATHE HARD
BREATH OF AIR
BREEZE BLOCK
BRENNER PASS
BREWER'S DRAY
BRIAN INGLIS
BRIDAL MARCH
BRIDAL PARTY
BRIDAL SUITE
BRIDAL TRAIN
BRIDGE DRIVE
BRIDGE FIEND
BRIDGE PARTY
BRIDGE TABLE
BRIDLE STRAP
BRIEF MOMENT
BRIEF SKETCH
BRIGHT CHILD
BRIGHT GREEN
BRIGHT LIGHT
BRIGHT PUPIL
BRIGHT SPARK
BRING TO BEAR
BRING TO BOOK
BRING TO HEEL
BRING TO LIFE
BRING TO MIND
BRING TO PASS
BRING TO REST

BRING TO RUIN	BUNDLE OF FUN	CAKES AND ALE
BRISTOL CITY	BUNNY RABBIT	CALCUTTA CUP
BRISTOL MILK	BURGLAR BILL	CALL FOR HELP
BRITISH ARMY	BURIAL AT SEA	CALLING CARD
BRITISH CAMP	BURIAL PLACE	CALL IT QUITS
BRITISH FLAG	BURIED ALIVE	CALL ME MADAM
BRITISH LION	BURIED AT SEA	CALLOW YOUTH
BRITISH MADE	BURNING BUSH	CALL THE ROLL
BRITISH NAVY	BURNT ALMOND	CALL THE TIME
BRITISH RAIL	BURNT EFFIGY	CALL THE TUNE
BRITISH RULE	BURN TO ASHES	CALL TO A HALT
BRITISH WARM	BURNT SIENNA	CALL TO ORDER
BRITISH ZONE	BURST OF FIRE	CALM WEATHER
BROAD ACCENT	BURY ONESELF	CALYPSO BAND
BROAD COMEDY	BUSHEY HEATH	CAME FORWARD
BROAD SCOTCH	BUSINESS END	CAMOMILE TEA
BROADSIDE ON	BUSINESS MAN	CAMPING SITE
BROAD STREET	BUS TERMINUS	CANADA HOUSE
BROGUE SHOES	BUT ME NO BUTS	CANCEL LEAVE
BROKE GROUND	BUTTER BEANS	CANDIED PEEL
BROKEN ANKLE	BUYING PRICE	CANDY KISSES
BROKEN BONES	BUYING SPREE	CANDY STRIPE
BROKEN GLASS	BUY ON CREDIT	CANINE TOOTH
BROKEN HEART	BUY OUTRIGHT	CANNED BEANS
BRONZED SKIN	BY AUTHORITY	CANNED FRUIT
BRONZE MEDAL	BY FAIR MEANS	CANNED GOODS
BROTHER LOVE	BYGONE TIMES	CANNED MUSIC
BROTH OF A BOY	BY LAMPLIGHT	CANNING TOWN
BROUGHT HOME	BY MAIN FORCE	CAN OF PETROL
BROWN BOMBER	BY MESSENGER	CAP AND BELLS
BROWN RIBBON	BY MISCHANCE	CAPITAL CITY
BROWN SHERRY	BY MOONLIGHT	CAPITAL FUND
BRUNO WALTER	BY THAT MEANS	CAPITAL GAIN
BUDDING POET	BY THIS TOKEN	CAPITAL IDEA
BUD FLANAGAN	BY TRADITION	CAPITAL LEVY
BUENOS AIRES	BY YOUR LEAVE	CAPITAL SHIP
BUFFALO BILL		CAPTAIN AHAB
BUFFER STATE	**C—11**	CAPTAIN COOK
BUILD A HOUSE	CABARET STAR	CAPTAIN HOOK
BUILT ON SAND	CABBAGE LEAF	CAPTAIN KIDD
BUILT TO LAST	CABBAGE MOTH	CAPTAIN WEBB
BUILT-UP AREA	CABBAGE ROSE	CARAVAN SITE
BULGING EYES	CABINET SIZE	CARAWAY SEED
BULL AND BUSH	CABIN WINDOW	CARBON PAPER
BULL AT A GATE	CABLE STITCH	CARDIGAN BAY
BULL BAITING	CAESAR'S WIFE	CARDINAL RED
BULLET WOUND	CAFÉ DE PARIS	CARDINAL SIN
BULL TERRIER	CAFÉ SOCIETY	CAREER WOMAN
BULLY FOR YOU!	CAGED ANIMAL	CARGO VESSEL
BUMPING RACE	CAIN AND ABEL	CAR INDUSTRY
BUNCH OF KEYS	CAKE MIXTURE	CARLTON CLUB

CARMEN JONES
CAROL SINGER
CARRION CROW
CARRY ACROSS
CARRY A TORCH
CARRY THE CAN
CARRY THE DAY
CARRY TOO FAR
CARRY WEIGHT
CASE HISTORY
CASE IN POINT
CASH ACCOUNT
CASH A CHEQUE
CASH BETTING
CASH CHEMIST
CASH PAYMENT
CASSIUS CLAY
CAST A GLANCE
CAST AN EYE ON
CAST A SHADOW
CASTILE SOAP
CASTING VOTE
CASTOR SUGAR
CASUAL VISIT
CAT AND MOUSE
CATCH A CHILL
CATCH ALIGHT
CATCH A PLANE
CATCH A THIEF
CATCH A TRAIN
CATCH PHRASE
CATCH THE EYE
CATHODE RAYS
CATS AND DOGS
CATS' CONCERT
CAT'S WHISKER
CATTLE RANCH
CATTLE THIEF
CATTY REMARK
CAUSE DAMAGE
CAUSTIC SODA
CAVALRY UNIT
CAVE DRAWING
CAVE DWELLER
CEASE TO LIVE
CECIL BEATON
CECIL RHODES
CELLAR STEPS
CELLO PLAYER
CELTIC CROSS
CEMENT MIXER

CENTRAL ASIA
CENTRAL HALL
CENTRAL IDEA
CENTRAL LINE
CENTRAL PARK
CENTRE COURT
CENTRE PARTY
CEREAL PLANT
CERTAIN CURE
CERTAIN HOPE
CHAFING DISH
CHAIN LETTER
CHAIN SMOKER
CHAIN STITCH
CHALK CLIFFS
CHALK GARDEN
CHANCERY INN
CHANGE A NOTE
CHANGE BUSES
CHANGE HANDS
CHANGE OF AIR
CHANGE ROUND
CHANGE SEATS
CHANGE SIDES
CHAPEL ROYAL
CHAPTER FIVE
CHAPTER FOUR
CHARGE EXTRA
CHARGE SHEET
CHARIOT RACE
CHARITY BALL
CHARLES LAMB
CHARMED LIFE
CHARM SCHOOL
CHEAP AS DIRT
CHEAP LABOUR
CHEAP REMARK
CHEAP RETURN
CHEAP THRILL
CHEAP TICKET
CHEEK BY JOWL
CHEEKY DEVIL
CHEER LEADER
CHEESE SALAD
CHEESE STRAW
CHEMIN DE FER
CHEMMY PARTY
CHERRY STONE
CHESHIRE CAT
CHESS PLAYER
CHEVAL GLASS

CHICKEN COOP
CHICKEN FARM
CHICKEN FEED
CHICKEN SOUP
CHIEF PRIEST
CHIEF STOKER
CHILD LABOUR
CHILLED BEEF
CHINA ORANGE
CHINESE FOOD
CHINESE JUNK
CHINESE MEAL
CHIT OF A GIRL
CHOICE OF TWO
CHOIR MASTER
CHOOSE A WIFE
CHOOSE SIDES
CHU CHIN CHOW
CHURCH BELLS
CHURCH CHOIR
CHURCH HOUSE
CHURCH LANDS
CHURCH MOUSE
CHURCH MUSIC
CHURCH ORGAN
CHURCH SPIRE
CHURCH TOWER
CINDER TRACK
CINEMA QUEUE
CINEMA USHER
CINEMA WORLD
CINQUE PORTS
CIRCLE ROUND
CIRCULAR SAW
CIRCUS RIDER
CITIZEN KANE
CITRUS FRUIT
CITY COMPANY
CITY COUNCIL
CITY FATHERS
CIVIC CENTRE
CIVIC RIGHTS
CIVIL ACTION
CIVIL ANSWER
CIVIL RIGHTS
CIVIL TONGUE
CIVVY STREET
CLAIM TO FAME
CLAIM TO KNOW
CLAIRE BLOOM
CLAM CHOWDER

CLAP IN IRONS	COARSE GRAIN	COME OUT BEST
CLARET GLASS	COARSE GRASS	COME OUTSIDE
CLARION CALL	COARSE VOICE	COME THIS WAY
CLASH OF ARMS	COASTAL ROAD	COME THROUGH
CLASS HATRED	COAT OF PAINT	COME TO A HALT
CLASSIC RACE	COAT THE PILL	COME TO A HEAD
CLASS SYMBOL	COAXING WAYS	COME TO AN END
CLAUDE DUVAL	COCK AND BULL	COME TO A STOP
CLEAN BOWLED	COCK ONE'S EYE	COME TO BLOWS
CLEAN BREAST	COCK SPARROW	COME TO EARTH
CLEAN COLLAR	COCKTAIL BAR	COME TO GRIEF
CLEAN FORGOT	COCOA BUTTER	COME TO GRIPS
CLEAN RECORD	COCOANUT OIL	COME TO LIGHT
CLEAR A HEDGE	COCONUT PALM	COME TO ORDER
CLEARLY SEEN	CODE MESSAGE	COME TO POWER
CLEAR OF DEBT	COD-LIVER OIL	COME TO TERMS
CLEAR PROFIT	COFFEE BEANS	COME UNSTUCK
CLEAR THE AIR	COFFEE BREAK	COME WHAT MAY
CLEAR THE WAY	COFFEE CREAM	COMIC RELIEF
CLEFT PALATE	COFFEE HOUSE	COMME IL FAUT
CLEVER DODGE	COFFEE SPOON	COMMON CAUSE
CLEVER STUFF	COFFEE STALL	COMMON CHORD
CLEVER TRICK	COFFEE TABLE	COMMON ENEMY
CLINCH A DEAL	COIN A PHRASE	COMMON FAULT
CLOSE ARREST	COLD AS DEATH	COMMON FRONT
CLOSE AT HAND	COLD CLIMATE	COMMON PLEAS
CLOSE BEHIND	COLD COMFORT	COMMON PURSE
CLOSE COMBAT	COLD DRAUGHT	COMMON SENSE
CLOSED DOORS	COLD SHIVERS	COMMON STOCK
CLOSED PURSE	COLD STORAGE	COMMON THIEF
CLOSE FINISH	COLD WEATHER	COMMON TO ALL
CLOSE FRIEND	COLD WELCOME	COMMON TOUCH
CLOSE OF PLAY	COLLECT DUST	COMMON USAGE
CLOSE SEASON	COLLEGE GIRL	COMPLETE ASS
CLOSE SECOND	COLNEY HATCH	COMPLETE SET
CLOSE SECRET	COLOMBO PLAN	COMPOST HEAP
CLOSE THE GAP	COLONIAL WAR	COMPUTER AGE
CLOSING DATE	COLOUR BLIND	CONCERT HALL
CLOSING TIME	COLOUR CHART	CONEY ISLAND
CLOTHES LINE	COLOURED MAN	CONSTANT USE
CLOTH OF GOLD	COLOUR PHOTO	CONTACT LENS
CLOT OF BLOOD	COLOUR PLATE	CONTACT MINE
CLOUD OF DUST	COME A PURLER	CONTOUR LINE
CLUB COLOURS	COME BETWEEN	CONTRACT OUT
CLUB STEWARD	COME FORWARD	CONTROL ROOM
CLUB TO DEATH	COME IN FIRST	CONVERT A TRY
CLUMSY STYLE	COME IN FRONT	COOKERY BOOK
COACHING INN	COME IN HANDY	COOK GENERAL
COAL SCUTTLE	COMELY WENCH	COOL AND CALM
COALS OF FIRE	COME OFF BEST	COOL HUNDRED
COARSE CLOTH	COME OFF WELL	COPPER BEECH

COPPER'S NARK
CORAL ISLAND
CORDON ROUGE
CORFE CASTLE
CORNERED RAT
CORNER TABLE
CORN IN EGYPT
CORN PLASTER
CORPS D'ÉLITE
CORRECT TIME
COSTUME BALL
COSTUME PLAY
COTTAGE LOAF
COTTON CLOTH
COTTON DRESS
COTTON FIELD
COTTON FROCK
COTTON GOODS
COTTON PLANT
COTTON SOCKS
COTTON WASTE
COUNCIL FLAT
COUNTER HAND
COUNTRY CLUB
COUNTRY CODE
COUNTRY FOLK
COUNTRY LANE
COUNTRY LIFE
COUNTRY SEAT
COUNTRY TOWN
COUNTRY WALK
COUNTY CLARE
COUNTY COURT
COUNTY MATCH
COUP DE GRÂCE
COURT DEFEAT
COURT JESTER
COVER A STORY
COVER CHARGE
COVER GROUND
COWSLIP WINE
CRACK OF DAWN
CRACK OF DOOM
CRACK PLAYER
CRACK TROOPS
CRANE DRIVER
CRASH COURSE
CRASH HELMET
CRAZY NOTION
CRAZY PAVING
CREAM CHEESE

CREAMED RICE
CREATE A NEED
CREATE A RÔLE
CREATE A STIR
CREATE HAVOC
CREDIT ENTRY
CREDIT TERMS
CREDIT TITLE
CRÊPE RUBBER
CRICKET BALL
CRICKET CLUB
CRICKET TEAM
CRIMINAL LAW
CRIMSON LAKE
CRITICAL AGE
CROCK OF GOLD
CROOKED DEAL
CROOKED PATH
CROP FAILURE
CROPPED HAIR
CROQUET BALL
CROQUET CLUB
CROQUET HOOP
CROQUET LAWN
CROSSBOW MAN
CROSS STITCH
CROSS SWORDS
CROSS THE BAR
CROSS THE SEA
CROWDED HOUR
CROWDED ROOM
CROWN A TOOTH
CROWN COLONY
CROWNED HEAD
CROWN JEWELS
CROWN OFFICE
CROWN PRINCE
CRUCIAL TEST
CRUEL TYRANT
CRUMBLE AWAY
CRY FOR MERCY
CRYING SHAME
CRYPTIC CLUE
CRYSTAL BALL
CUB REPORTER
CUCKOO CLOCK
CULINARY ART
CUPID'S ARROW
CUP OF COFFEE
CUP OF POISON
CUP OF SORROW

CUPPED HANDS
CURDLED MILK
CURE OF SOULS
CURLING CLUB
CURLING IRON
CURL OF SMOKE
CURL ONE'S LIP
CURRANT CAKE
CURRANT LOAF
CURRENT DATE
CURRENT NEWS
CURRENT WEEK
CURRENT YEAR
CURRY FAVOUR
CURRY POWDER
CURSE OF CAIN
CURTAIN CALL
CUSTARD TART
CUSTOM HOUSE
CUSTOMS DUTY
CUT A LECTURE
CUT AND DRIED
CUT-AWAY COAT
CUT BOTH WAYS
CUT IN SALARY
CUT OFF SHORT
CUT OF HIS JIB
CUT ONE'S HAIR
CUT THE CARDS
CUT THE GRASS
CUT THE SCENE
CUTTING EDGE
CUTTING WIND
CUT TO PIECES
CYCLE TO WORK
CYCLING CLUB

D—11

DAILY MARKET
DAILY MIRROR
DAILY RECORD
DAILY REPORT
DAILY SKETCH
DAILY WORKER
DAIRY CATTLE
DAME FORTUNE
DAMON RUNYON
DANA ANDREWS
DANCE A TANGO
DANCE A WALTZ
DANCE FOR JOY

DANCING BEAR	DEATH COLUMN	DIE OF HUNGER
DANCING GIRL	DEATHLY HUSH	DIESEL TRAIN
DANGER MONEY	DEATHLY PALE	DIET OF WORMS
DANGER POINT	DEATH NOTICE	DIG AND DELVE
DANIEL DEFOE	DEATH RATTLE	DINNER DANCE
DANISH BACON	DEBORAH KERR	DINNER PARTY
DARK CLOTHES	DEB'S DELIGHT	DINNER WAGON
DARKEST HOUR	DECK OF CARDS	DIRECT ROUTE
DARK GLASSES	DEED OF MERCY	DIRECT STYLE
DARK LANTERN	DEEP BLUE SEA	DIRE STRAITS
DART FORWARD	DEEP CONCERN	DIRK BOGARDE
DARTING PAIN	DEEP FEELING	DISMAL JIMMY
DARTS PLAYER	DEEP IN A BOOK	DISPATCH BOX
DASHED HOPES	DEEP INSIGHT	DISPLAY CARD
DASH FORWARD	DEEP MYSTERY	DISTAFF SIDE
DASH THROUGH	DEEP REMORSE	DISTANT PAST
DATE OF BIRTH	DEEP THINKER	DISTANT VIEW
DATE OF DEATH	DEEP THOUGHT	DISUSED WELL
DAVID JACOBS	DEFENCE WORK	DIVIDE BY SIX
DAWN GODDESS	DEFERRED PAY	DIVIDE BY TEN
DAY AFTER DAY	DEFY THE WHIP	DIVIDE BY TWO
DAY AND NIGHT	DELIVERY MAN	DIVINE BEING
DAY IN, DAY OUT	DELLA ROBBIA	DIVINE GRACE
DAY LABOURER	DE-LUXE MODEL	DIVINE RIGHT
DAY OF PRAYER	DEMON BARBER	DIVINING ROD
DAYS AND DAYS	DEMON BOWLER	DIVISION ONE
DAY'S JOURNEY	DENIS NORDEN	DIVISION SUM
DAYS OF GRACE	DENMARK HILL	DIVISION TWO
DAZZLING WIT	DENNIS NOBLE	DIVORCE CASE
DEAD AGAINST	DENSE FOREST	DIVORCE LAWS
DEAD AND GONE	DENTAL CHAIR	DIVORCE SUIT
DEAD AS A DODO	DE PROFUNDIS	DIZZY HEIGHT
DEAD CERTAIN	DEPTH CHARGE	DO A GOOD TURN
DEAD EARNEST	DERBY COUNTY	DO ALL ONE CAN
DEADEN SOUND	DERBY STAKES	DO A MISCHIEF
DEAD FAILURE	DERBY WINNER	DO A WAR-DANCE
DEAD FLOWERS	DESERT SANDS	DOCTOR OF LAW
DEADLY CRIME	DESERT WASTE	DOFF ONE'S HAT
DEADLY ENEMY	DESERVE WELL	DOING NICELY
DEADLY PERIL	DEVIL OF A JOB	DO IT IN STYLE
DEADLY RIVAL	DEVIL'S ELBOW	DOLEFUL LOOK
DEAD OF NIGHT	DEVOTED WIFE	DOLEFUL TALE
DEAD OR ALIVE	DIAMOND MINE	DOLLY VARDEN
DEAD SILENCE	DIAMOND RING	DO ME A FAVOUR
DEAD TO SHAME	DICK BENTLEY	DOMESTIC PET
DEAF AND DUMB	DICK VAN DYKE	DONALD PEERS
DEAF AS A POST	DO THE TWIST	DONE TO A TURN
DEAF TO MUSIC	DIE BY INCHES	DONE TO DEATH
DEAR BELOVED	DIE FIGHTING	DOOMED TO DIE
DEAR OCTOPUS	DIE LIKE A DOG	DO ONE'S WORST
DEAR OLD PALS	DIE OF FRIGHT	DO REVERENCE

DORIC COLUMN
DORIS ARCHER
DOT AND CARRY
DO THE ROUNDS
DO THE SPLITS
DOUBLE BLANK
DOUBLE CROSS
DOUBLE DOORS
DOUBLE DUMMY
DOUBLE DUTCH
DOUBLE EAGLE
DOUBLE EIGHT
DOUBLE ENTRY
DOUBLE EVENT
DOUBLE FAULT
DOUBLE FIRST
DOUBLE MARCH
DOUBLE SEVEN
DOUBLE SHARE
DOUBLE SHIFT
DOUBLE THREE
DOUBLE TRACK
DOVE OF PEACE
DOVER CASTLE
DOVER PATROL
DOWN AT HEART
DOWN IN PRICE
DOWN PAYMENT
DOWN THE AGES
DOWN THE HILL
DOWN THE LINE
DOWN THE MINE
DOWN THE ROAD
DOWN THE SINK
DOWN THE WELL
DOWN TO EARTH
DOWN YOUR WAY
DRAMA CRITIC
DRAMA SCHOOL
DRAMATIC ART
DRAUGHT BEER
DRAW A CIRCLE
DRAW A SALARY
DRAWING ROOM
DRAW RATIONS
DRAW THE CORK
DRAW THE LINE
DRAW TO AN END
DRAW TO SCALE
DRAW UP A PLAN
DREAM DREAMS

DREAMY MUSIC
DRESS CIRCLE
DRESSED CRAB
DRESS TO KILL
DREYFUS CASE
DRINK ADDICT
DRINK A PINTA
DRINK A TOAST
DRINKING DEN
DRIPPING WET
DRIVE AROUND
DRIVE INSANE
DRIVE ONE MAD
DRIVE SLOWLY
DRIVING RAIN
DRIVING TEST
DROP A CURTSY
DROP A LETTER
DROP AN AITCH
DROP A REMARK
DROP A SITTER
DROP A STITCH
DROP IN PRICE
DROP ME A LINE
DROP OF BLOOD
DROP OF WATER
DROPPED GOAL
DROP THE MASK
DROP TOO MUCH
DROWNING MAN
DRUG TRAFFIC
DRUNKEN ORGY
DRY AS A STICK
DRY CLEANERS
DRY CLEANING
DRY ONE'S EYES
DUAL CONTROL
DUAL PURPOSE
DUCHESSE SET
DUCK-EGG BLUE
DULCET TONES
DULL READING
DULL SCHOLAR
DULL WEATHER
DUMB CHARADE
DUMB DESPAIR
DUMB FRIENDS
DURANCE VILE
DUSTY MILLER
DUTCH CHEESE
DUTCH SCHOOL

DUTCH TULIPS
DUTY OFFICER
DWINDLE AWAY
DYE ONE'S HAIR
DYING BREATH
DYING EMBERS
DYING TO KNOW
DYLAN THOMAS

E—11
EAGER BEAVER
EAR FOR MUSIC
EARL MARSHAL
EARL OF ARRAN
EARLY AUTUMN
EARLY CHURCH
EARLY GOTHIC
EARLY IN LIFE
EARLY RISING
EARLY SPRING
EARLY SUMMER
EARLY TO RISE
EARN A LIVING
EARTH'S CRUST
EARTH TREMOR
EASE THE PAIN
EASILY MOVED
EAST AND WEST
EAST GERMANY
EAST LOTHIAN
EASY PROBLEM
EASY TO GRASP
EASY VICTORY
EAT AND DRINK
EAT AND SLEEP
EATING HOUSE
EAT LIKE A PIG
EAT ONE'S FILL
ECONOMIC AID
ECONOMY SIZE
EDDIE FISHER
EDGE ONE'S WAY
EDGWARE ROAD
EDIBLE FUNGI
EDITH CAVELL
EDMUND BURKE
EDUCATED MAN
EDWARD HEATH
EDWARD MY SON
EGG AND BACON
EGG AND CHIPS

EGG SANDWICH
EIFFEL TOWER
EIGHT AND ONE
EIGHT AND SIX
EIGHT AND TEN
EIGHT AND TWO
EIGHTH FLOOR
EIGHTH GREEN
EIGHTH MONTH
EIGHTH OF MAY
EIGHTH PLACE
EIGHTH ROUND
EIGHT MONTHS
EIGHT NINTHS
EIGHT O'CLOCK
EIGHT OR NINE
EIGHT OUNCES
EIGHT POINTS
EIGHT POUNDS
EIGHT ROUNDS
EIGHTY MILES
EIGHTY TIMES
EIGHTY YEARS
EILEEN JOYCE
ELASTIC BAND
ELBOW GREASE
ELDERS FIRST
ELDER SISTER
ELDEST CHILD
ELECTION DAY
ELECTRIC EEL
ELECTRIC EYE
ELECTRIC FAN
ELECTRIC RAY
ELECTRIC VAN·
ELEPHANT BOY
ELEPHANT GUN
ELEVEN A SIDE
ELEVEN DOZEN
ELEVEN GROSS
ELEVEN HOURS
ELEVEN MILES
ELEVEN PARTS
ELEVEN SCORE
ELEVENTH DAY
ELEVENTH ROW
ELEVEN TIMES
ELEVEN WEEKS
ELLIS ISLAND
EMERALD ISLE
EMERALD RING

EMPIRE STYLE
EMPIRE TRADE
EMPTY BOTTLE
EMPTY LARDER
EMPTY POCKET
EMPTY STREET
EMPTY THE BAG
EMPTY THREAT
EMPTY WALLET
ENA SHARPLES
EN CASSEROLE
ENDLESS BAND
ENDLESS BELT
ENDLESS TIME
END OF THE DAY
END OF THE WAR
END ONE'S DAYS
END ONE'S LIFE
ENEMY ACTION
ENEMY PATROL
ENEMY TROOPS
ENEMY VESSEL
ENGAGED TONE
ENGINE HOUSE
ENGINE POWER
ENGLISH HORN
ENGLISH POET
ENGLISH PORT
ENGLISH ROSE
ENLARGE UPON
ENLISTED MAN
ENOCH POWELL
ENTER A PHASE
ENTER A STAGE
ENTRANCE FEE
EQUAL CHANCE
EQUAL HEIGHT
EQUAL RIGHTS
EQUAL SHARES
EQUAL WEIGHT
ERECT FIGURE
ERIC PORTMAN
ERMINE STOLE
ERNEST BEVIN
ESCAPE DEATH
ESCAPE HATCH
ESCAPE ROUTE
ESCAPING GAS
ESTATE AGENT
ETERNAL CITY
ETERNAL HOME

ETERNAL LIFE
ETERNAL REST
ETHEL MERMAN
ETON COLLEGE
EVADE THE LAW
EVELYN WAUGH
EVENING MEAL
EVENING NEWS
EVENING STAR
EVER AND A DAY
EVER AND ANON
EVER AND EVER
EVERY EXCUSE
EVERY MINUTE
EVERY VIRTUE
EVIL CONDUCT
EVIL THOUGHT
EXACT AMOUNT
EXALTED RANK
EXEUNT OMNES
EXHAUST PIPE
EXPLAIN AWAY
EXPORT DRIVE
EXPORT ORDER
EXPORT TRADE
EXPRESS LIFT
EXPRESS POST
EXTRA CHARGE
EXTRA STRONG
EXTREME CASE
EXTREME EDGE
EXTREME PAIN
EYE FOR AN EYE
EYES AND EARS

F—11

FACE MASSAGE
FACE REALITY
FACE THE ODDS
FACE UPWARDS
FACTORY ACTS
FACTORY BAND
FACTORY HAND
FACTS OF LIFE
FADED BEAUTY
FADING HOPES
FADING LIGHT
FAIL THE TEST
FAIL TO AGREE
FAIL TO REPLY
FAIL TO SCORE

FAINT EFFORT
FAINTING FIT
FAINT PRAISE
FAIR COMMENT
FAIR FORTUNE
FAIR HEARING
FAIRLY CLOSE
FAIR WARNING
FAIR WEATHER
FAIRY CIRCLE
FAIRY LIGHTS
FAITH HEALER
FALL ASUNDER
FALLEN ANGEL
FALL IN DROPS
FALLING STAR
FALL IN PLACE
FALL IN PRICE
FALL IN RUINS
FALL IN VALUE
FALL THROUGH
FALL TO EARTH
FALSE BOTTOM
FALSE CHARGE
FALSE COLOUR
FALSE FRIEND
FALSE REPORT
FALSE RUMOUR
FALSE VALUES
FALSE VANITY
FAMILY ALBUM
FAMILY BIBLE
FAMILY CARES
FAMILY CREST
FAMILY HOTEL
FAMILY MOTTO
FAMILY PARTY
FAMILY PRIDE
FAMILY TREAT
FAMILY VAULT
FAMINE PRICE
FAMOUS WOMEN
FAN THE FLAME
FAR-AWAY LOOK
FAR DISTANCE
FARES PLEASE
FAR FROM HERE
FAR FROM HOME
FARMER GILES
FARMER'S WIFE
FARMING TYPE

FARM MANAGER
FARM PRODUCE
FASHION SHOW
FAST BOWLING
FAST COLOURS
FAST FRIENDS
FATAL ATTACK
FATAL INJURY
FATA MORGANA
FAT AS BUTTER
FATHER BROWN
FATHER IMAGE
FATHERLY EYE
FATIGUE DUTY
FATTY TISSUE
FEARFUL BORE
FEARFUL ODDS
FEAR OF DEATH
FEAR TO TREAD
FEATURE FILM
FEEBLE BRAIN
FEEBLE GRASP
FEEDING TIME
FEEL CERTAIN
FEEL NO SHAME
FEEL NOTHING
FEEL ONE'S WAY
FEEL PECKISH
FEEL REMORSE
FEEL STRANGE
FEEL THE COLD
FEEL THE HEAT
FEEL THE URGE
FEEL THE WIND
FELIX AYLMER
FELIX THE CAT
FELL THROUGH
FEMALE SCREW
FEMALE VOICE
FEMME FATALE
FEN DISTRICT
FERTILE LAND
FERTILE MIND
FERTILE SOIL
FERVENT HOPE
FESTIVE MOOD
FEVERED BROW
FIDDLE ABOUT
FIDEL CASTRO
FIELD EVENTS
FIELD OF CORN

FIELD OF PLAY
FIELD OF VIEW
FIELD SPORTS
FIERCE GLARE
FIERY DRAGON
FIERY ORDEAL
FIERY SPEECH
FIERY SPIRIT
FIERY TEMPER
FIFTEEN LOVE
FIFTH AVENUE
FIFTH COLUMN
FIFTH LETTER
FIFTH OF JULY
FIFTH OF JUNE
FIFTH STOREY
FIFTH VOLUME
FIGHT FOR AIR
FIGHTING FIT
FIGHTING MAD
FIGHTING MAN
FIGURE EIGHT
FIGURE IT OUT
FIGURE OF FUN
FIJI ISLANDS
FILING CLERK
FILL AN ORDER
FILLET STEAK
FILL THE BILL
FILL THE TILL
FILM ACTRESS
FILM COMPANY
FILTHY LUCRE
FINAL ANSWER
FINAL CHOICE
FINAL CLAUSE
FINAL DEFEAT
FINAL DEMAND
FINAL NOTICE
FINAL REPORT
FINAL RESULT
FINAL SPEECH
FINAL STROKE
FINANCE BILL
FIND A REFUGE
FIND A REMEDY
FIND A WAY OUT
FIND FREEDOM
FIND ONESELF
FIND ONE'S WAY
FIND SHELTER

FIND THE LADY
FIND THE TIME
FINE FLAVOUR
FINE RAIMENT
FINE SOLDIER
FINE TEXTURE
FINE WEATHER
FINE WRITING
FINGAL'S CAVE
FINISH EARLY
FINISH FIRST
FINNISH BATH
FIRE AND FURY
FIRE A SALUTE
FIRE A VOLLEY
FIRE BRIGADE
FIRE CURTAIN
FIRE SERVICE
FIRE STATION
FIRING PARTY
FIRING SQUAD
FIRM AS A ROCK
FIRM BACKING
FIRM CONTROL
FIRM FRIENDS
FIRM PROMISE
FIRM RESOLVE
FIRST CHARGE
FIRST CHOICE
FIRST COURSE
FIRST COUSIN
FIRST DEGREE
FIRST ELEVEN
FIRST FIDDLE
FIRST FINGER
FIRST FLIGHT
FIRST FRUITS
FIRST GLANCE
FIRST IN LINE
FIRST LEADER
FIRST LEAGUE
FIRST LESSON
FIRST LETTER
FIRST MAN OUT
FIRST OF JULY
FIRST OF JUNE
FIRST PERSON
FIRST REMOVE
FIRST RUBBER
FIRST SEASON
FIRST SERIES

FIRST SERVED
FIRST SINGLE
FIRST SKETCH
FIRST STOREY
FIRST STRING
FIRST STROKE
FIRST TO COME
FIRST TO LAND
FIRST TO LAST
FIRST VIOLIN
FIRST VOLUME
FIRST WICKET
FISHER OF MEN
FISH FINGERS
FISHING BIRD
FISHING BOAT
FISHING LINE
FIT FOR A KING
FIT OF ENERGY
FIT OF NERVES
FIT OF TEMPER
FIT OF TERROR
FITTING ROOM
FITTING SHOP
FITTING TIME
FIT TO BE SEEN
FIVE AND FIVE
FIVE AND FOUR
FIVE AND NINE
FIVE AT A TIME
FIVE-BAR GATE
FIVE COURSES
FIVE-DAY WEEK
FIVE DOLLARS
FIVE EIGHTHS
FIVE FATHOMS
FIVE FINGERS
FIVE GALLONS
FIVE GUINEAS
FIVE HUNDRED
FIVE MINUTES
FIVE OCTAVES
FIVE OF CLUBS
FIVE PER CENT
FIVE SQUARED
FIVE STROKES
FIVE WICKETS
FIX BAYONETS
FIXED AMOUNT
FIXED ASSETS
FIXED BELIEF

FIXED CHARGE
FIXED INCOME
FIXED SALARY
FIX THE PRICE
FIX THE TERMS
FIXTURE LIST
FLAG CAPTAIN
FLAG OFFICER
FLAG OF TRUCE
FLAKY PASTRY
FLAME COLOUR
FLAMING JUNE
FLANK ATTACK
FLASH A SMILE
FLASK OF WINE
FLAT FOR SALE
FLAT HUNTING
FLAT REFUSAL
FLAT SURFACE
FLEET AIR-ARM
FLEET OF CABS
FLEET OF CARS
FLEET OF FOOT
FLEET PRISON
FLEET STREET
FLESH COLOUR
FLESH TIGHTS
FLIMSY PAPER
FLOATING RIB
FLOOD DAMAGE
FLOOR POLISH
FLORAL DANCE
FLORA ROBSON
FLORID STYLE
FLOWING BOWL
FLOWING HAND
FLOWING TIDE
FLOW OF WORDS
FLOW THROUGH
FLOW TOWARDS
FLUID INTAKE
FLUSH OF DAWN
FLUSH OF HOPE
FLUTTER DOWN
FLY AWAY PAUL
FLYING CORPS
FLYING FIELD
FLYING SPEED
FLYING SQUAD
FLYING START
FLYING VISIT

FOLDED HANDS	FORWARD LINE	FREE LIBRARY
FOLK DANCING	FORWARD MOVE	FREE ON BOARD
FOLLOW AFTER	FORWARD PLAY	FREE ONESELF
FOLLOW A PLAN	FOSTER CHILD	FREE PARKING
FOND EMBRACE	FOUL JOURNEY	FREE PASSAGE
FONDEST LOVE	FOUL THE LINE	FREE SERVICE
FOND OF A DRAM	FOUL WEATHER	FREE SPENDER
FOND REGARDS	FOUND A PARTY	FREE THINKER
FOOD COUNTER	FOUNDERS' DAY	FREE THOUGHT
FOOD SUBSIDY	FOUND GUILTY	FREE TO SPEAK
FOOLISH IDEA	FOUNTAIN PEN	FREE TRIBUTE
FOOLISH TALK	FOUR AND FIVE	FRENCH BEANS
FOOL'S ERRAND	FOUR AND FOUR	FRENCH BREAD
FOOLS RUSH IN	FOUR AND NINE	FRENCH CHALK
FOOTBALL FAN	FOUR AT A TIME	FRENCH COAST
FOOT THE BILL	FOUR CORNERS	FRENCH FARCE
FOR ALL TO SEE	FOUR COURSES	FRENCH FRANC
FOR A PURPOSE	FOUR-DAY WEEK	FRENCH FRIED
FORCE A WAY IN	FOUR DEGREES	FRENCH LEAVE
FORCED ENTRY	FOUR DOLLARS	FRENCH MONEY
FORCED LAUGH	FOUR FATHOMS	FRENCH NOVEL
FORCED MARCH	FOUR FIGURES	FRENCH SALON
FORCED SMILE	FOUR GALLONS	FRESH BREEZE
FORCE OF ARMS	FOUR GUINEAS	FRESH BUTTER
FOR DEAR LIFE	FOUR HUNDRED	FRESH FIELDS
FOREIGN BODY	FOUR JUST MEN	FRESH GROUND
FOREIGN COIN	FOUR MINUTES	FRESH SALMON
FOREIGN FILM	FOUR OCTAVES	FRESH TROOPS
FOREIGN LAND	FOUR OF CLUBS	FRET AND FUME
FOREIGN NAME	FOUR PER CENT	FRIDAY NIGHT
FOREIGN NEWS	FOUR SEASONS	FRIED ONIONS
FOREIGN RULE	FOUR SQUARED	FRIENDLY ACT
FOREIGN SOIL	FOUR STROKES	FRIENDLY TIP
FOREIGN TOUR	FOURTH FLOOR	FRIEND OF MAN
FOR INSTANCE	FOURTH GREEN	FRIEND OR FOE
FORLORN HOPE	FOURTH OF MAY	FRIGHTEN OFF
FORMAL DRESS	FOURTH PLACE	FRITTER AWAY
FORMAL OFFER	FOURTH ROUND	FROM SCRATCH
FORMAL VISIT	FOUR WICKETS	FROM THE EAST
FORM AN IMAGE	FOX AND GEESE	FROM THE WEST
FORMER PUPIL	FRAME OF MIND	FROM THE WOOD
FORMER TIMES	FRANK AVOWAL	FROM WITHOUT
FOR PLEASURE	FRANK IFIELD	FRONT GARDEN
FOR SOME TIME	FRANTIC PACE	FRONT LIGHTS
FORSYTE SAGA	FRANTIC RUSH	FRONT WINDOW
FORTH BRIDGE	FRED ASTAIRE	FROSTED LENS
FOR THE NONCE	FREE AND EASY	FROSTY SMILE
FOR THE WORSE	FREE AS A BIRD	FROZEN NORTH
FORT WILLIAM	FREE CITIZEN	FROZEN PIPES
FORTY NIGHTS	FREE COUNTRY	FROZEN SOLID
FORTY THIRTY	FREE ECONOMY	FROZEN STIFF

FROZEN WATER
FRUIT MARKET
FRUITY VOICE
FULL ACCOUNT
FULL ADDRESS
FULL APOLOGY
FULL AS AN EGG
FULL BROTHER
FULL CONSENT
FULL DETAILS
FULL ENQUIRY
FULL FLAVOUR
FULL GENERAL
FULL MEASURE
FULL OF BEANS
FULL OF FIGHT
FULL OF GRACE
FULL OF HOLES
FULL OF IDEAS
FULL OF MIRTH
FULL OF PRIDE
FULL REGALIA
FULL SERVICE
FULL SUPPORT
FULL-TIME JOB
FULLY BOOKED
FULLY RIGGED
FUN AND GAMES
FUNERAL HYMN
FUNERAL PACE
FUNERAL PILE
FUNERAL PYRE
FUNERAL SONG
FUNNY AFFAIR
FUNNY PERSON
FURIOUS PACE
FUTURE HOPES
FUTURE PLANS
FUTURE STATE
FUTURE TENSE

G—11
GAIN CONTROL
GAIN IN VALUE
GAIN THE LEAD
GALA EVENING
GALE WARNING
GALLERY SEAT
GALLEY PROOF
GALLEY SLAVE
GALLON OF OIL

GAMBLING DEN
GAME CHICKEN
GAME LICENCE
GAME OF BOWLS
GAME OF CARDS
GAME OF CHESS
GAME OF SKILL
GAME OF WHIST
GAME RESERVE
GAMES MASTER
GAMING HOUSE
GAMING TABLE
GAMMON STEAK
GANG ROBBERY
GANG WARFARE
GARDEN CHAIR
GARDEN FENCE
GARDEN PARTY
GARDEN TOOLS
GARRICK CLUB
GATHER ROSES
GATHER ROUND
GATHER SPEED
GAY BACHELOR
GAY DECEIVER
GAY LOTHARIO
GAY NINETIES
GENERAL IDEA
GENERAL LEVY
GENERAL POST
GENERAL RATE
GENERAL VIEW
GENERIC NAME
GENEROUS ACT
GENEVA CROSS
GENTLE BIRTH
GENTLE SLOPE
GENTLE TOUCH
GENTLE VOICE
GENUINE CASE
GEORGE BROWN
GEORGE CROSS
GEORGE ELIOT
GEORGE MEDAL
GEORGE ROBEY
GERMAN MONEY
GERM CARRIER
GERM WARFARE
GET A BAD NAME
GET A DIVORCE
GET A MENTION

GET AN ENCORE
GET A RECEIPT
GET CRACKING
GET DOWN TO IT
GET EVEN WITH
GET IN THE WAY
GET INTO A ROW
GET INTO A RUT
GET INTO DEBT
GET ONE'S GOAT
GET ONE'S WISH
GET ON WITH IT
GET OUT OF BED
GET SUNBURNT
GET THE FACTS
GET THE KNACK
GET THE POINT
GET THE TASTE
GETTING WARM
GETTING WELL
GET TOGETHER
GET TO THE TOP
GET UNDER WAY
GET WELL SOON
GET WISE TO IT
GHASTLY MESS
GHASTLY PALE
GHOST WRITER
GIANT KILLER
GIANT OF A MAN
GIFT OF MONEY
GIFT VOUCHER
GILDED YOUTH
GILD THE LILY
GILD THE PILL
GIN AND LEMON
GIN AND TONIC
GINGER GROUP
GIRLS' SCHOOL
GIRL STUDENT
GIVE AND TAKE
GIVE AN ORDER
GIVE A REASON
GIVE A RULING
GIVE IT A MISS
GIVE IT A NAME
GIVE IT A REST
GIVE LESSONS
GIVEN PERIOD
GIVEN THE TIP
GIVE OFFENCE

GIVE QUARTER	GOLDEN EAGLE	GOOD OFFICES
GIVE SUPPORT	GOLDEN GATES	GOOD OLD DAYS
GIVE THE SACK	GOLDEN GOOSE	GOOD OLD TIME
GIVE THE WORD	GOLDEN SANDS	GOOD OPENING
GIVE TROUBLE	GOLDEN SYRUP	GOOD OPINION
GIVE WARNING	GOLDEN TOUCH	GOOD QUALITY
GLAD TIDINGS	GOLD FILLING	GOOD READING
GLAMOUR GIRL	GOLD RESERVE	GOOD SCHOLAR
GLANCE ASIDE	GO LIKE A BOMB	GOOD SEND OFF
GLANCE TO LEG	GONE FOR EVER	GOOD SERVANT
GLASS HOUSES	GONE FOR GOOD	GOOD SERVICE
GLASS OF BEER	GONE TO EARTH	GOOD SOCIETY
GLASS OF MILK	GONE TO GLORY	GOOD SOLDIER
GLASS OF PORT	GONE TO LUNCH	GOOD SPENDER
GLASS OF WINE	GONE TO WASTE	GOOD SPIRITS
GLASS VESSEL	GOOD ACCOUNT	GOOD SWIMMER
GLASSY STARE	GOOD ACTRESS	GOOD TEMPLAR
GLEAM OF HOPE	GOOD ADDRESS	GOOD THEATRE
GLEEFUL MOOD	GOOD AND EVIL	GOOD TIDINGS
GLEEFUL NEWS	GOOD AS A PLAY	GOOD WEATHER
GLEE SINGERS	GOOD AT HEART	GOOD WORKMAN
GLIB SPEAKER	GOOD BARGAIN	GOOD WRITE-UP
GLIDER PILOT	GOOD BEARING	GO ON A PICNIC
GLYNIS JOHNS	GOOD BEATING	GO ONE BETTER
GLORIOUS DAY	GOOD CITIZEN	GO ON FOR EVER
GLORIOUS FUN	GOOD COMPANY	GO ON HOLIDAY
GLORIOUS ROW	GOOD CONDUCT	GO ON THE DOLE
GLOSSY PAINT	GOOD COUNSEL	GO OUT TO WORK
GNAWING PAIN	GOOD DEFENCE	GO OVER THERE
GO-AHEAD SIGN	GOOD DICTION	GORDIAN KNOT
GO ALL THE WAY	GOOD EVENING	GORDON RIOTS
GO BACKWARDS	GOOD EXAMPLE	GORGON'S HEAD
GO BY DEFAULT	GOOD FEEDING	GOSPEL TRUTH
GO BY THE BOOK	GOOD FEELING	GO THE ROUNDS
GODFREY WINN	GOOD FICTION	GOTHIC STYLE
GOD OF THE SEA	GOOD FORTUNE	GO THROUGH IT
GOG AND MAGOG	GOOD FRIENDS	GO TO BED LATE
GO GREAT GUNS	GOOD GRAMMAR	GO TO HALIFAX
GOING STEADY	GOOD GROUNDS	GO TO JERICHO
GOING STRONG	GOOD HARMONY	GO TO PARTIES
GO IN PURSUIT	GOOD HARVEST	GO TO THE DOGS
GO INTO EXILE	GOOD HEARING	GO TO THE FAIR
GO INTO ORBIT	GOOD HEAVENS	GO TO THE MOON
GOLD BULLION	GOOD HUNTING	GO TO THE WALL
GOLD COINAGE	GOOD HUSBAND	GO TO THE WARS
GOLD DEPOSIT	GOOD INNINGS	GOT UP TO KILL
GOLDEN APPLE	GOOD IN PARTS	GO UP IN SMOKE
GOLDEN ARROW	GOOD MANAGER	GRAIN OF GOLD
GOLDEN BOUGH	GOOD MANNERS	GRAIN OF SALT
GOLDEN BROWN	GOOD MEASURE	GRAIN OF SAND
GOLDEN DREAM	GOOD MORNING	GRAND CANYON

GRAND CIRCLE
GRAND FELLOW
GRAND FINALE
GRAND MANNER
GRAND MASTER
GRAND OLD MAN
GRAND REVIEW
GRAND VIZIER
GRANITE CITY
GRANT ACCESS
GRANT ASYLUM
GRANT A TRUCE
GRAPHIC ARTS
GRAVE ACCENT
GRAVE AFFAIR
GRAVE CHARGE
GRAVE CRISIS
GRAVE DOUBTS
GRAVE MATTER
GRAVEN IMAGE
GRAVE SPEECH
GREASE PAINT
GREAT AMOUNT
GREAT BEAUTY
GREAT BURDEN
GREAT CAESAR
GREAT CHANCE
GREAT CHANGE
GREAT CIRCLE
GREAT DAMAGE
GREAT DANCER
GREAT DANGER
GREAT DARING
GREAT DETAIL
GREAT DIVIDE
GREAT DOINGS
GREAT EFFORT
GREATER GOOD
GREATER PART
GREAT FAVOUR
GREAT FRIEND
GREAT HEALER
GREAT HEIGHT
GREAT HONOUR
GREAT IMPORT
GREAT NEPHEW
GREAT NUMBER
GREAT PLAGUE
GREAT PLAYER
GREAT REGRET
GREAT RELIEF

GREAT SNAKES
GREAT SORROW
GREAT STRAIN
GREAT STRESS
GREAT TALKER
GREAT THINGS
GREAT UNPAID
GREAT WEALTH
GREAT WEIGHT
GRECIAN BEND
GRECIAN KNOT
GRECIAN NOSE
GREEK CHURCH
GREEK COMEDY
GREEK LEGEND
GREEK STATUE
GREEN BOTTLE
GREEN CHEESE
GREEN FIELDS
GREEN GABLES
GREEN GINGER
GREEN PEPPER
GREEN RIBBON
GREER GARSON
GREGORY PECK
GRESHAM'S LAW
GRETNA GREEN
GRILLED CHOP
GRILLED FISH
GRILLED SOLE
GRIM COURAGE
GRIM OUTLOOK
GRIM PASTIME
GRIND TO BITS
GRIP OF STEEL
GRIZZLY BEAR
GROCER'S SHOP
GROSS AMOUNT
GROSS INCOME
GROSS PROFIT
GROSS RETURN
GROSS WEIGHT
GROUND FLOOR
GROUND FROST
GROUND GLASS
GROUND LEVEL
GROUND SPEED
GROUND STAFF
GROUND SWELL
GROUND TO AIR
GROUP OF FIVE

GROUP OF FOUR
GROUP OF NINE
GROUSE MOORS
GROWING GIRL
GROW SHORTER
GROW SMALLER
GROW UPWARDS
GROW YOUNGER
GUAVA CHEESE
GUERILLA WAR
GUEST ARTIST
GUIDING HAND
GUIDING STAR
GUILTY PARTY
GUILTY WOMAN
GULF OF GENOA
GUMMED LABEL
GUSTAV HOLST
GUTTER PRESS

H—II
HACKNEY WICK
HAGGARD LOOK
HAIRPIN BEND
HALCYON DAYS
HALF A BOTTLE
HALF A DOLLAR
HALF A GALLON
HALF A GUINEA
HALF A LEAGUE
HALF A LENGTH
HALF A MINUTE
HALF A MOMENT
HALF AND HALF
HALF AN OUNCE
HALF A SECOND
HALF BROTHER
HALF HOLIDAY
HALF THE TIME
HALTING GAIT
HAMMER IT OUT
HAMMER THROW
HAM OMELETTE
HAMPTON WICK
HAM SANDWICH
HAND AND FOOT
HAND GRENADE
HAND IN GLOVE
HAND OF CARDS
HAND OF DEATH
HANDSOME BOY

HANDSOME MAN	HAVE A HAIR-DO	HEAVE A BRICK
HANDSOME SUM	HAVE A LIKING	HEAVY AS LEAD
HANDSOME TIP	HAVE AND HOLD	HEAVY BOMBER
HANDS ON HIPS	HAVE AN EYE ON	HEAVY BURDEN
HAND TO MOUTH	HAVE AN EYE TO	HEAVY EATING
HANG-DOG LOOK	HAVE ANOTHER	HEAVY FATHER
HANGING BILL	HAVE A PICNIC	HEAVY HUMOUR
HANG ONESELF	HAVE A POLICY	HEAVY OBJECT
HANG THE HEAD	HAVE A SECRET	HEAVY SHOWER
HANG UP TO DRY	HAVE A SHOWER	HEAVY SMOKER
HANKER AFTER	HAVE A SNOOZE	HEAVY WEIGHT
HAPPY AND GAY	HAVE A SQUINT	HECTIC FLUSH
HAPPY CHANCE	HAVE A STROKE	HEDDA GABLER
HAPPY COUPLE	HAVE A THEORY	HELD CAPTIVE
HAPPY DREAMS	HAVE A THIRST	HELD HOSTAGE
HAPPY ENDING	HAVE COMPANY	HELD IN CHECK
HAPPY FAMILY	HAVE COURAGE	HELD IN TRUST
HAPPY MEDIUM	HAVE IN STORE	HELEN JACOBS
HAPPY VALLEY	HAVE NO DOUBT	HELEN OF TROY
HARBOUR A SPY	HAVEN OF REST	HELL ON EARTH
HARBOUR DUES	HAVE NO MERCY	HELPING HAND
HARD AND FAST	HAVE NO VOICE	HENRIK IBSEN
HARD AS NAILS	HAVE ONE'S DAY	HENRY COOPER
HARD AS STEEL	HAVE ONE'S SAY	HENRY COTTON
HARD BARGAIN	HAVE ONE'S WAY	HENRY ESMOND
HARD CONTEST	HAVE REGRETS	HENRY IRVING
HARD DRINKER	HAVE THE URGE	HERALDIC ART
HARD DRIVING	HAVE THE VOTE	HERD OF GOATS
HARD MEASURE	HAVE TROUBLE	HER HIGHNESS
HARD PRESSED	HAYLEY MILLS	HER LADYSHIP
HARD PUT TO IT	HEAD AND TAIL	HEROIC VERSE
HARD SURFACE	HEAD TEACHER	HERO WORSHIP
HARD TO CATCH	HEAD THE LIST	HERRING GULL
HARD TO GRASP	HEALING GIFT	HERRING POND
HARDY ANNUAL	HEAL THE SICK	HIDDEN FIRES
HARICOT BEAN	HEALTHY FEAR	HIDDEN MERIT
HAROLD LLOYD	HEALTHY MIND	HIDDEN PANEL
HARRIS TWEED	HEAPED PLATE	HIDE AND SEEK
HARRY LAUDER	HEAPS OF TIME	HIDING PLACE
HARRY TRUMAN	HEAR NOTHING	HIGH ACCOUNT
HARVEST HOME	HEART ATTACK	HIGH CALLING
HARVEST MOON	HEAR THE CALL	HIGH CEILING
HARVEST TIME	HEART OF GOLD	HIGH CIRCLES
HASTY GLANCE	HEART'S BLOOD	HIGH COMMAND
HASTY TEMPER	HEARTS OF OAK	HIGH CONTENT
HATCHET FACE	HEARTY CHEER	HIGH COURAGE
HATEFUL TASK	HEARTY EATER	HIGH DENSITY
HAUNT OF VICE	HEARTY LAUGH	HIGH DUDGEON
HAVANA CIGAR	HEARTY SMACK	HIGHER CLASS
HAVE A CHOICE	HEAT BARRIER	HIGHER FARES
HAVE A FRIGHT	HEATED WORDS	HIGHER LEVEL

HIGHER POWER
HIGHER WAGES
HIGH FEATHER
HIGH FINANCE
HIGH HOLBORN
HIGH MOTIVES
HIGH OLD TIME
HIGH OPINION
HIGH QUALITY
HIGH RESOLVE
HIGH SHERIFF
HIGH SOCIETY
HIGH SPIRITS
HIGH STATION
HIGH TENSION
HIGH TRAGEDY
HIGH TREASON
HIGH VOLTAGE
HIGHWAY CODE
HIGH-WIRE ACT
HIGH WYCOMBE
HILL AND DALE
HILL COUNTRY
HILTON HOTEL
HINDLE WAKES
HIP AND THIGH
HIPS AND HAWS
HIS EMINENCE
HIS HIGHNESS
HIS LORDSHIP
HISTORY BOOK
HITHER GREEN
HITLER YOUTH
HIT THE TRAIL
H.M.S. PINAFORE
HOARD WEALTH
HOARSE COUGH
HOARSE LAUGH
HOARSE VOICE
HOBBLE SKIRT
HOCKEY MATCH
HOCKEY STICK
HOLD CLASSES
HOLD IN CHECK
HOLD IN LEASH
HOLD IN TRUST
HOLD ONE'S JAW
HOLD ONE'S OWN
HOLD ON TIGHT
HOLD OUT HOPE
HOLD THE BABY

HOLD THE FORT
HOLD THE LEAD
HOLD THE LINE
HOLD THE ROAD
HOLD TO SCORN
HOLIDAY CAMP
HOLIDAY HOME
HOLIDAY MOOD
HOLIDAY SNAP
HOLIDAY TASK
HOLIDAY TIME
HOLIDAY WEAR
HOLLAND PARK
HOLLAND'S GIN
HOLLOW LAUGH
HOLLOW SOUND
HOLLOW TOOTH
HOLLOW TRUCE
HOLLOW TRUTH
HOLLOW VOICE
HOLY TRINITY
HOLY UNCTION
HOLY WEDLOCK
HOME AFFAIRS
HOME AND AWAY
HOME CIRCUIT
HOME COOKING
HOME COUNTRY
HOME FOR GOOD
HOME-MADE JAM
HOME ON LEAVE
HOME SERVICE
HOME STRETCH
HOMO SAPIENS
HONEST DOUBT
HONEST INJUN
HONEST MONEY
HONEST PENNY
HONEST TRUTH
HONEST WOMAN
HONITON LACE
HONOUR A BILL
HONOUR BOUND
HONOURED SIR
HONOURS EASY
HONOURS EVEN
HONOURS LIST
HOPE AND PRAY
HOPE DIAMOND
HOPEFUL SIGN
HORNED VIPER

HORNET'S NEST
HORROR COMIC
HORS D'OEUVRE
HORSE DEALER
HORSE DOCTOR
HORSE GUARDS
HORSE MARINE
HORSE PISTOL
HORSE RACING
HORSE'S MOUTH
HOSPITAL BED
HOSTILE ARMY
HOSTILE VOTE
HOT AS PEPPER
HOT CHESTNUT
HOT-CROSS BUN
HOT-DOG STAND
HOTEL ANNEXE
HOTEL KEEPER
HOTEL LOUNGE
HOTEL PORTER
HOT-WATER TAP
HOUND'S TOOTH
HOURLY VIGIL
HOUR OF TRIAL
HOURS OF WORK
HOUSE ARREST
HOUSE HUNTER
HOUSE MARTIN
HOUSE MASTER
HOUSE MOTHER
HOUSE NUMBER
HOUSE OF CALL
HOUSE OF KEYS
HOUSE OF REST
HOUSE OF YORK
HOUSE ON FIRE
HOVER AROUND
HOWLING WIND
HUDSON RIVER
HUGE EXPENSE
HUGE SUCCESS
HUGHIE GREEN
HUG THE COAST
HUG THE SHORE
HUMAN DYNAMO
HUMAN EFFORT
HUMAN FAMILY
HUMAN NATURE
HUMAN RIGHTS
HUMBLE BIRTH

HUMBLE HEART	IN AN INSTANT	IN FULL SPATE
HUMBLE STOCK	IN A NUTSHELL	IN FULL SWING
HUMMING BIRD	IN A QUANDARY	IN GOOD FAITH
HUMS AND HAWS	IN A REAL MESS	IN GOOD HANDS
HUNDRED DAYS	IN A SMALL WAY	IN GOOD HEART
HUNGER MARCH	IN AT THE KILL	IN GOOD ODOUR
HUNK OF BREAD	IN AUSTRALIA	IN GOOD SHAPE
HUNT BIG GAME	IN AUTHORITY	IN GOOD TASTE
HUNTER'S MOON	IN BAD REPAIR	IN GOOD VOICE
HUNT FOR A JOB	IN CAPTIVITY	IN GRATITUDE
HUNTING CROP	IN CHARACTER	IN GREAT FORM
HUNTING HORN	IN COLD BLOOD	IN HYSTERICS
HUNTING PACK	IN COLLISION	IN IGNORANCE
HUNTING PINK	IN COLLUSION	INITIAL MOVE
HUNTING SONG	IN COMMITTEE	INJURED BACK
HUNT IN PAIRS	IN CONDITION	INJURED LOOK
HUNT THE HARE	IN CONFUSION	IN LOW RELIEF
HURRIED MEAL	INCUR LOSSES	IN MINIATURE
HUSBAND TO BE	IN DAYS OF OLD	INMOST BEING
HUSHED TONES	IN DEEP WATER	IN MY OPINION
HUSH-HUSH JOB	IN DETENTION	INNER CIRCLE
	INDEX FINGER	INNER MARGIN
I—II	INDEX NUMBER	INNER TEMPLE
IAIN MACLEOD	INDIAN BRAVE	INNOCENT MAN
IDEAL SCHEME	INDIAN CHIEF	IN NO RESPECT
IDES OF MARCH	INDIAN CURRY	INNS OF COURT
IDLE DISPLAY	INDIAN OCEAN	IN ONE'S HEART
IDLE THOUGHT	INDIAN SQUAW	IN ONE'S POWER
IF YOU PLEASE	INDIAN TRIBE	IN ONE'S PRIME
IGNEOUS ROCK	INDIA OFFICE	IN ONE'S SHELL
IGNITION KEY	INDIA RUBBER	IN ONE'S SLEEP
IGNORANT MAN	INDIRECT TAX	IN ONE'S TEENS
ILE DE FRANCE	INDOOR GAMES	IN OPEN COURT
I'LL BE HANGED!	IN DREAMLAND	IN OPERATION
ILLICIT LOVE	IN DUE COURSE	IN PANTOMIME
IL PENSEROSO	IN DUE SEASON	IN PRINCIPLE
IL TROVATORE	IN DUPLICATE	IN PROFUSION
I'M A DUTCHMAN!	IN DUTY BOUND	IN PURGATORY
IMPOSE A DUTY	IN ECSTASIES	IN READINESS
IMPROPER USE	IN EDINBURGH	IN REBELLION
IN A BAD STATE	IN EVERY PORT	IN REPERTORY
IN A FEW WORDS	IN EXISTENCE	IN RESIDENCE
IN A FLAT SPIN	IN FACSIMILE	IN SAFE HANDS
IN A GOOD MOOD	IN FINE STYLE	IN SECLUSION
IN AGREEMENT	IN FOR A PENNY	INSECT WORLD
IN A HAYSTACK	IN FOR A POUND	IN SEPTEMBER
IN ALL EVENTS	IN FOR A STORM	IN SHORTHAND
IN A LOW VOICE	IN FORMATION	INSIDE RIGHT
IN A MINORITY	INFRA-RED RAY	INSIDE STORY
IN AND AROUND	IN FULL BLAST	INSIDE TRACK
INANE REMARK	IN FULL BLOOM	INSTANT CURE

M.C.D.—7

INTENSE COLD	IN THE VALLEY	JAMES BRIDIE
INTENSE HEAT	IN THE WAKE OF	JAMES CAGNEY
IN THAT PLACE	IN THE WINDOW	JAMESON RAID
IN THE CELLAR	IN THE WINTER	JAM SANDWICH
IN THE CENTRE	IN THE ZENITH	JAM TOMORROW
IN THE CHARTS	IN THIS PLACE	JANE SEYMOUR
IN THE CHORUS	INTO THE BLUE	JAPANESE ART
IN THE CHURCH	INTO THE WIND	JARRING NOTE
IN THE CINEMA	INTO THIN AIR	JAUNTING CAR
IN THE CIRCLE	IN TWO SHAKES	JAWS OF DEATH
IN THE CLOUDS	INVALID DIET	JAZZ SESSION
IN THE CORNER	INVERT SUGAR	JEALOUS WIFE
IN THE CRADLE	IN WHICH CASE	JEAN BOROTRA
IN THE DEPTHS	IONIC COLUMN	JEAN COCTEAU
IN THE DESERT	IRISH BROGUE	JEAN SIMMONS
IN THE FAMILY	IRISH GUARDS	JELLIED EELS
IN THE FIELDS	IRISH SETTER	JET AIRCRAFT
IN THE FINISH	IRISH WHISKY	JINGLE BELLS
IN THE FOREST	IRMA LA DOUCE	JOAN HAMMOND
IN THE FRIDGE	IRON CURTAIN	JOHN GIELGUD
IN THE FUTURE	IRON FILINGS	JOHN GREGSON
IN THE GARAGE	IRON FOUNDRY	JOHN HALIFAX
IN THE GARDEN	IRON PYRITES	JOHN OF GAUNT
IN THE GROOVE	IRON RATIONS	JOHN O'GROATS
IN THE GROUND	IRONY OF FATE	JOHN O'LONDON
IN THE GUARDS	ISAAC NEWTON	JOHN OSBORNE
IN THE GUTTER	ISAAC PITMAN	JOIE DE VIVRE
IN THE JUNGLE	ISLE OF ARRAN	JOINT ACTION
IN THE LOCK-UP	ISLE OF CAPRI	JOINT APPEAL
IN THE MAKING	ISLE OF WIGHT	JOINT EFFORT
IN THE MARGIN	ISSUE SHARES	JOIN THE ARMY
IN THE MARKET	ITALIA CONTI	JOIN THE NAVY
IN THE MIDDLE	ITALIAN ALPS	JOINT OF BEEF
IN THE MIRROR	ITALIAN WINE	JOINT OF LAMB
IN THE MORGUE	ITCHING PALM	JOINT OF PORK
IN THE NAME OF	IT'S A FAIR COP	JOINT OF VEAL
IN THE OFFICE	IT STRIKES ME	JOINT TENANT
IN THE OFFING	IVOR NOVELLO	JOKING APART
IN THE PAPERS	IVORY CASTLE	JOLLY HUNGRY
IN THE PLURAL	IZAAK WALTON	JOSEPH'S COAT
IN THE PULPIT		JOURNEY'S END
IN THE PURPLE	**J—11**	JUBILEE YEAR
IN THE SADDLE	JACK AND JILL	JUDGMENT DAY
IN THE SEASON	JACK DEMPSEY	JUDY GARLAND
IN THE SECRET	JACK HAWKINS	JUGULAR VEIN
IN THE SPRING	JACK HULBERT	JUKE-BOX JURY
IN THE STALLS	JACKIE TRENT	JULIE ROGERS
IN THE STOCKS	JACK JACKSON	JUMPING BEAN
IN THE STREET	JACK JOHNSON	JUMPING JACK
IN THE STUDIO	JACK OF CLUBS	JUNE WEDDING
IN THE THROES	JAFFA ORANGE	JUNGLE FEVER

JUNGLE GREEN
JUNGLE JUICE
JUNIPER TREE
JURY SERVICE
JUST A CHANCE
JUST A LITTLE
JUST A MINUTE
JUST A MOMENT
JUST A SECOND
JUST DESERTS
JUST FOR ONCE
JUST IMAGINE
JUST MARRIED
JUST PERFECT
JUST THE SAME
JUST THE TIME
JUST VISIBLE
JUST WILLIAM

K—11
KEEN BARGAIN
KEEN CONTEST
KEEN HEARING
KEEN STUDENT
KEEP ABREAST
KEEP AN EYE ON
KEEP A RECORD
KEEP A SECRET
KEEP COMPANY
KEEP COUNSEL
KEEP IN CHECK
KEEP IN SIGHT
KEEP IN STOCK
KEEP IN STORE
KEEP IN TOUCH
KEEP IT GOING
KEEP ONE'S JOB
KEEP OUT OF IT
KEEP RIGHT ON
KEEP SMILING
KEEP THE CASH
KEEP TRACK OF
KEEP WAITING
KELLOGG PACT
KEMPTON PARK
KENNETH MORE
KENSAL GREEN
KENTISH TOWN
KEY INDUSTRY
KEY POSITION
KEY QUESTION

KHAKI SHORTS
KICK AGAINST
KICK UP A DUST
KICK UP A FUSS
KIDNEY BEANS
KILKENNY CAT
KILLER WHALE
KILLING PACE
KILL ONESELF
KIND FRIENDS
KIND GESTURE
KINDRED SOUL
KIND REGARDS
KIND THOUGHT
KIND WELCOME
KING CHARLES
KINGDOM COME
KING EMPEROR
KING OF BIRDS
KING OF CLUBS
KING OF KINGS
KING PENGUIN
KING RICHARD
KING'S BISHOP
KING'S BOUNTY
KING'S COLOUR
KING'S FLIGHT
KING'S KNIGHT
KING SOLOMON
KING'S RANSOM
KING WILLIAM
KIRK DOUGLAS
KISSING GAME
KISSING GATE
KISS ME, HARDY
KISS OF JUDAS
KISS OF PEACE
KISS THE BOOK
KISS THE DUST
KITCHEN FIRE
KITCHEN HAND
KITCHEN MAID
KITCHEN SINK
KITCHEN UNIT
KNIGHT'S MOVE
KNIGHT'S PAWN
KNIT THE BROW
KNITTING BEE
KNOCK AROUND
KNOCK IT BACK
KNOCK ON WOOD

KNOTTY POINT
KNOW A LITTLE
KNOW BY HEART
KNOW BY SIGHT
KNOWING LOOK
KNOW ONE'S JOB
KNOW ONE'S WAY
KNOW THE FORM
KNOW THYSELF
KNOW TOO MUCH
KNUCKLE DOWN
KUALA LUMPUR

L—11
LABOUR FORCE
LABOUR PARTY
LABRADOR DOG
LACK COURAGE
LACK OF DRIVE
LACK OF FAITH
LACK OF FLAIR
LACK OF MONEY
LACK OF POWER
LACK OF SCOPE
LACK OF SENSE
LACK OF SHAPE
LACK OF SLEEP
LACK OF TASTE
LACK SPARKLE
LADIES FIRST
LADIES' NIGHT
LA DOLCE VITA
LADY ALMONER
LADY BARNETT
LADY MACBETH
LADY MACDUFF
LADY'S FINGER
LADY TEACHER
LAKE LUCERNE
LAKE ONTARIO
LAKE SUCCESS
LAMBETH WALK
LANDING GEAR
LAND MEASURE
LAND OF ROSES
LANKY FIGURE
LANTERN JAWS
LAPIS LAZULI
LAP OF LUXURY
LAPSE OF TIME
LARGE AMOUNT

LARGE AS LIFE	LATEST STYLE	LEAVE A TRAIL
LARGE BRANDY	LATEST THING	LEAVE BEHIND
LARGE CIRCLE	LATIN CHURCH	LEAVE FALLOW
LARGE FAMILY	LATIN LESSON	LEAVE IT OPEN
LARGE INCOME	LATIN MASTER	LEAVE IT TO ME
LARGE NUMBER	LATIN PRIMER	LEAVE NO HOPE
LARGE PROFIT	LAUGHING GAS	LEAVE SCHOOL
LARGE SALARY	LAUNDRY BILL	LEAVE UNDONE
LARGE SCOTCH	LAUNDRY MAID	LEAVE UNSAID
LARGE SCREEN	LAUREL CROWN	LECTURE HALL
LARGE SHERRY	LAW AND ORDER	LECTURE TOUR
LARGE SUPPLY	LAWFUL ORDER	LEDGER CLERK
LARGE VESSEL	LAW MERCHANT	LEFT HANGING
LARGE VOLUME	LAW OF NATURE	LEFT LUGGAGE
LARGE WHISKY	LAW OF THE SEA	LEFT OUTSIDE
LASH OF A WHIP	LAY ABOUT ONE	LEGAL ACTION
LAST ADDRESS	LAY IN AMBUSH	LEGAL ADVICE
LAST ARRIVAL	LAY IN A STOCK	LEGAL BATTLE
LAST ATTEMPT	LAY OUT MONEY	LEGAL ENTITY
LAST BASTION	LAY PREACHER	LEGAL JARGON
LAST CENTURY	LAY THE CLOTH	LEGAL REMEDY
LAST CHAPTER	LAY THE GHOST	LEGAL RULING
LAST EDITION	LAY THE TABLE	LEGAL TENDER
LAST EVENING	LAZY HOLIDAY	LEG OF MUTTON
LAST FOR EVER	LEADEN HOURS	LEISURE TIME
LAST HONOURS	LEADING CASE	LEMON BARLEY
LAST INNINGS	LEADING EDGE	LEMON SQUASH
LAST JANUARY	LEADING LADY	LEMON YELLOW
LAST JOURNEY	LEADING NOTE	LEND SUPPORT
LAST OF EIGHT	LEADING PART	LEON TROTSKY
LAST OF SEVEN	LEADING RÔLE	LESLIE CARON
LAST OF THREE	LEADING WREN	LESS AND LESS
LAST OUTPOST	LEAGUE MATCH	LESSER BREED
LAST QUARTER	LEAN AGAINST	LESSON EIGHT
LAST TO LEAVE	LEAN AS A RAKE	LESSON SEVEN
LAST TRIBUTE	LEAN FORWARD	LESSON THREE
LAST TUESDAY	LEAN TOWARDS	LESS TROUBLE
LAST VESTIGE	LEARN A HABIT	LET A MAN DOWN
LATE ARRIVAL	LEARN A TRADE	LET IN THE SUN
LATE AT NIGHT	LEARN TO HATE	LET OFF STEAM
LATE EDITION	LEARN TO LOVE	LEVEL FLIGHT
LATE EVENING	LEARN TO PLAY	LEVEL TEMPER
LATE FOR WORK	LEARN TO READ	LIBEL ACTION
LATE HARVEST	LEARN TO RIDE	LIBERAL ARTS
LATE HUSBAND	LEARN TO WALK	LIBERAL VIEW
LATE STARTER	LEARN WISDOM	LIBERTY BOAT
LATEST CRAZE	LEATHER BELT	LIBERTY HALL
LATEST ISSUE	LEATHER COAT	LIBERTY SHIP
LATEST MODEL	LEATHER LANE	LIBRARY BOOK
LATEST SCORE	LEATHER SOLE	LIBRARY LIST
LATEST SHADE	LEAVE A SPACE	LICK OF PAINT

LICK THE DUST	LIMITED TIME	LOCAL CUSTOM
LIE AT ANCHOR	LIMPID STYLE	LOCAL GOSSIP
LIE DETECTOR	LINCOLN CITY	LOCAL OPTION
LIE END TO END	LINCOLN'S INN	LOCAL TALENT
LIE IN AMBUSH	LINE DRAWING	LOCK THE DOOR
LIE IN PRISON	LINEN DRAPER	LOCUM TENENS
LIE ON VELVET	LINE OF MARCH	LOGICAL MIND
LIE PARALLEL	LINE OF SIGHT	LOGICAL STEP
LIFE HISTORY	LION RAMPANT	LONDON CRIES
LIFE OF BLISS	LISLE THREAD	LONDON DOCKS
LIFE OF CRIME	LIST OF ITEMS	LONDON PRIDE
LIFE OR DEATH	LIST OF NAMES	LONDON STAGE
LIFE PARTNER	LITERARY MAN	LONDON STONE
LIFE PEERAGE	LITERARY SET	LONG ACCOUNT
LIFE SAVINGS	LITMUS PAPER	LONG CLOTHES
LIFT A FINGER	LITTLE ANGEL	LONG DROUGHT
LIFT THE ROOF	LITTLE DEVIL	LONG HOLIDAY
LIFT THE VEIL	LITTLE KNOWN	LONG INNINGS
LIGHT A MATCH	LITTLE SPACE	LONG JOURNEY
LIGHT BOMBER	LITTLE THING	LONG, LONG AGO
LIGHT BREEZE	LITTLE TO SAY	LONG MEASURE
LIGHT COLOUR	LITTLE WHILE	LONG SERVICE
LIGHT COMEDY	LITTLE WOMAN	LONG SESSION
LIGHT DUTIES	LITTLE WOMEN	LONG STRETCH
LIGHTER FUEL	LITTLE VALUE	LONG STRIDES
LIGHTER VEIN	LIVE FOR EVER	LONG TIME AGO
LIGHT OF FOOT	LIVE IN DREAD	LONG WEEK-END
LIGHT RELIEF	LIVE IN PEACE	LOOK A FRIGHT
LIGHT REMARK	LIVE IN STYLE	LOOK ASKANCE
LIGHT THE GAS	LIVELONG DAY	LOOK DAGGERS
LIGHT THE WAY	LIVELY DANCE	LOOK FOOLISH
LIGHT VESSEL	LIVELY PARTY	LOOK FOR DIGS
LIGHT WEIGHT	LIVELY PITCH	LOOK FORWARD
LIGHT YELLOW	LIVE ON BOARD	LOOK FOR WORK
LIKE A MASTER	LIVE THEATRE	LOOK GHASTLY
LIKE AN ARROW	LIVE THROUGH	LOOK LIKE NEW
LIKE AN IDIOT	LIVING BEING	LOOK-OUT POST
LIKE A PARROT	LIVING DEATH	LOOK OUTSIDE
LIKE A STATUE	LIVING IMAGE	LOOK PLEASED
LIKE A STREAK	LIVING PROOF	LOOK THE PART
LIKE A TROJAN	LIVING SPACE	LOOK THROUGH
LIKE FOR LIKE	LIVING THING	LOOK VOLUMES
LIKE IT OR NOT	LIZARD POINT	LOOP THE LOOP
LIKELY STORY	LLOYD GEORGE	LOOSE CHANGE
LIKE THE IDEA	LOAD OF STRAW	LOOSE LIVING
LIKE THE WIND	LOAD OF TRIPE	LOOSE MORALS
LILAC DOMINO	LOAF OF BREAD	LOOSE THREAD
LILLI PALMER	LO AND BEHOLD	LORD BALDWIN
LILY LANGTRY	LOAN OF MONEY	LORD BOOTHBY
LILI MARLENE	LOCAL BRANCH	LORD PROVOST
LIMB OF SATAN	LOCAL COLOUR	LORD RUSSELL

LORDS' DEBATE
LORD'S PRAYER
LORD'S SUPPER
LORRY DRIVER
LOSE A CHANCE
LOSE CONTROL
LOSE COURAGE
LOSE FRIENDS
LOSE ONE'S ALL
LOSE ONESELF
LOSE ONE'S WAY
LOSE SIGHT OF
LOSE THE GAME
LOSE THE LEAD
LOSE THE RACE
LOSE THE TOSS
LOSE THE VOTE
LOSS OF BLOOD
LOSS OF FAITH
LOSS OF MONEY
LOSS OF NERVE
LOSS OF SIGHT
LOSS OF SMELL
LOSS OF SOUND
LOSS OF TOUCH
LOSS OF VALUE
LOSS OF VOICE
LOST HORIZON
LOST TO SHAME
LOST TO SIGHT
LOST WEEK-END
LOTS AND LOTS
LOTS OF MONEY
LOUD AND LONG
LOUD PROTEST
LOUD SPEAKER
LOUIS QUINZE
LOUIS TREIZE
LOUNGE ABOUT
LOVE AND HATE
LOVE FIFTEEN
LOVE IS BLIND
LOVELY MONEY
LOVELY NIGHT
LOVELY SIGHT
LOVE OF MONEY
LOVE OF ORDER
LOVE OF TRUTH
LOVE OR MONEY
LOVE PHILTRE
LOVING WORDS

LOW ALTITUDE
LOW COMEDIAN
LOWER ANIMAL
LOWER SCHOOL
LOW ESTIMATE
LOW FOREHEAD
LOW LATITUDE
LOW POSITION
LOW PRESSURE
LOW RAINFALL
LOW STANDARD
LOYAL FRIEND
L-SHAPED ROOM
LUCID MOMENT
LUCILLE BALL
LUCKY BEGGAR
LUCKY CHANCE
LUCKY ESCAPE
LUCKY FELLOW
LUCKY MASCOT
LUCKY MOMENT
LUCKY NUMBER
LUCKY RASCAL
LUCKY STREAK
LUCKY STRIKE
LUCKY STROKE
LUCKY WINNER
LUDGATE HILL
LUGGAGE RACK
LULL TO SLEEP
LUMP OF SUGAR
LUNCHEON CAR
LUNDY ISLAND
LUXURY FOODS
LUXURY GOODS
LUXURY HOTEL
LUXURY PRICE
LYRIC POETRY

M—11

MACASSAR OIL
MACHINE HAND
MACHINE SHOP
MACHINE TOOL
MACKEREL SKY
MADE A KNIGHT
MADE A MEMBER
MADE IN ITALY
MADE IN JAPAN
MADE IN SPAIN
MADEIRA CAKE

MADEIRA WINE
MADE OF MONEY
MADE OF STRAW
MADE TO ORDER
MADE WELCOME
MADONNA LILY
MADRAS CURRY
MAD SCRAMBLE
MAD WITH RAGE
MAGIC CARPET
MAGIC CIRCLE
MAGIC MIRROR
MAGIC MOMENT
MAGIC POTION
MAGIC RECIPE
MAGIC REMEDY
MAGIC SQUARE
MAGINOT LINE
MAGNUM BONUM
MAILING LIST
MAIL SERVICE
MAIN ELEMENT
MAIN FEATURE
MAIN MEANING
MAIN PROBLEM
MAIN PURPOSE
MAIN STATION
MAJOR CRISIS
MAJOR PLANET
MAKE A CHANGE
MAKE A CHOICE
MAKE A CORNER
MAKE A DETOUR
MAKE A FOOL OF
MAKE A LIVING
MAKE AND MEND
MAKE AN ENTRY
MAKE AN ERROR
MAKE AN OFFER
MAKE A PACKET
MAKE A PROFIT
MAKE A RECORD
MAKE A REMARK
MAKE A REPORT
MAKE A SEARCH
MAKE A SIGNAL
MAKE A SPEECH
MAKE A SPLASH
MAKE BELIEVE
MAKE CERTAIN
MAKE CHANGES

MAKE CONTACT	MAN OF REPUTE	MAX BEERBOHM
MAKE DEMANDS	MAN ON THE JOB	MAX BYGRAVES
MAKE ENEMIES	MAN PROPOSES	MAY THE FIFTH
MAKE EXCUSES	MANSARD ROOF	MAY THE FIRST
MAKE FRIENDS	MAN THE PUMPS	MAY THE NINTH
MAKE HEADWAY	MAN THE WALLS	MAY THE SIXTH
MAKE HISTORY	MAP OF EUROPE	MAY THE TENTH
MAKE INROADS	MAP OF FRANCE	ME AND MY GIRL
MAKE IT CLEAR	MAP OF GREECE	MEANING LOOK
MAKE IT PLAIN	MAP OF LONDON	MEAN NOTHING
MAKE IT STICK	MAP OF NORWAY	MEASURE TIME
MAKE LIGHTER	MAP OF SWEDEN	MEAT EXTRACT
MAKE LIGHT OF	MARBLE HALLS	MEDAL RIBBON
MAKE MUCH ADO	MARCH IN STEP	MEDICAL BOOK
MAKE NO NOISE	MARCH OF TIME	MEDICAL CARE
MAKE NO SOUND	MARIA CALLAS	MEDICAL CASE
MAKE OBVIOUS	MARIE STOPES	MEDICAL TEST
MAKE ONE'S BED	MARINE CORPS	MEDICAL WARD
MAKE ONE'S BOW	MARINE STORE	MEDICINE HAT
MAKE ONE'S WAY	MARITIME LAW	MEDICINE MAN
MAKE OR BREAK	MARKED CARDS	MEDIUM BUILD
MAKE SMALLER	MARKET OVERT	MEEK AND MILD
MAKES NO ODDS	MARKET PLACE	MEET HALFWAY
MAKE SPORT OF	MARKET PRICE	MEET ONE'S END
MAKE THE FIRE	MARKET RASEN	MEET THE BILL
MAKE THE PACE	MARKET TREND	MEGATON BOMB
MAKE TROUBLE	MARKET VALUE	MELODY MAKER
MAKE WELCOME	MARKET WOMAN	MELTING MOOD
MAKE WHOOPEE	MARK MY WORDS	MELT IN TEARS
MALACCA CANE	MARK THE SPOT	MEMBERS ONLY
MALAY STATES	MARRIAGE TIE	MEMORIAL DAY
MALE DESCENT	MARRIED LIFE	MENAI STRAIT
MALMSEY WINE	MARRIED NAME	MEN AND WOMEN
MALT VINEGAR	MARRON GLACÉ	MENDIP HILLS
MAN AND WOMAN	MARRYING MAN	MENTAL ERROR
MAN AT THE TOP	MARSHAL FOCH	MENTAL GRASP
MAN BITES DOG	MARSHAL TITO	MENTAL IMAGE
MANFRED MANN	MARSTON MOOR	MENTAL LAPSE
MAN FROM MARS	MARTIAL RACE	MENTALLY ILL
MANICURE SET	MARTIN'S BANK	MENTAL POWER
MAN IN CHARGE	MASONIC HALL	MENTAL SHOCK
MAN IN OFFICE	MASSED BANDS	MENTAL STATE
MANLY FIGURE	MASS EMOTION	MERE FEELING
MANLY SPIRIT	MASSIVE ROCK	MERE NOTHING
MAN OF ACTION	MASS MEETING	MERLE OBERON
MAN OF GENIUS	MATE IN THREE	MERRY ANDREW
MAN OF HONOUR	MATERIAL AID	MERSEY DOCKS
MAN OF METTLE	MATINEE IDOL	MERSEY SOUND
MAN OF MUSCLE	MATT SURFACE	MERVYN JOHNS
MAN OF PRAYER	MATURE YEARS	METAL POLISH
MAN OF RENOWN	MAUNDY MONEY	METHOD ACTOR

MEWS COTTAGE	MOB HYSTERIA	MORTISE LOCK
MICKEY MOUSE	MOB VIOLENCE	MOSAIC FLOOR
MIDDLE CLASS	MOCKING BIRD	MOSELLE WINE
MIDDLE POINT	MOCK MODESTY	MOSQUITO NET
MIDDLE STUMP	MODERN BLOCK	MOTHER CAREY
MIDDLE WATCH	MODERN DANCE	MOTHER EARTH
MIDLAND BANK	MODERN DRESS	MOTHER GOOSE
MIDLAND TOWN	MODERN HOUSE	MOTHER'S HELP
MIDNIGHT OIL	MODERN IDEAS	MOTHER'S MILK
MIDNIGHT SUN	MODERN IDIOM	MOTHER'S RUIN
MIGHT AS WELL	MODERN LATIN	MOTION STUDY
MILD CLIMATE	MODERN MUSIC	MOTIVE FORCE
MILD FLUTTER	MODERN NOVEL	MOTIVE POWER
MILD REPROOF	MODERN STYLE	MOTLEY CROWD
MILD WEATHER	MODERN TIMES	MOTOR LAUNCH
MILE A MINUTE	MODERN TREND	MOTOR RACING
MILE END ROAD	MODERN USAGE	MOTOR TRIALS
MILITARY AID	MODERN YOUTH	MOULIN ROUGE
MILITARY LAW	MODEST HOPES	MOUNT A HORSE
MILITARY MAN	MODEST MEANS	MOUNTAIN AIR
MILKING TIME	MOIRA LISTER	MOUNTAIN ASH
MILK PUDDING	MOLLY MALONE	MOUNTAIN DEW
MINCING LANE	MONDAY NIGHT	MOUNTAIN TOP
MIND THE BABY	MONEY FOR JAM	MOUNT ARARAT
MIND THE STEP	MONEY MARKET	MOUNT VERNON
MINERAL VEIN	MONEY MATTER	MOUTH HONOUR
MINIMUM WAGE	MONEY SPIDER	MOVABLE TYPE
MINOR DETAIL	MONEY'S WORTH	MOVE FORWARD
MINOR INJURY	MONEY TO BURN	MOVE QUICKLY
MINOR MATTER	MONKEY ABOUT	MOVE TO ANGER
MINOR PLANET	MONTE CRISTO	MOVE TO TEARS
MINSTREL BOY	MONTHLY RENT	MOVE TOWARDS
MINT FLAVOUR	MONTH'S LEAVE	MOVING FORCE
MINT OF MONEY	MOON GODDESS	MOVING SCENE
MINUTE STEAK	MOP ONE'S BROW	MOVING STORY
MINUTE WALTZ	MORAL APATHY	MOVING WORDS
MIRACLE DRUG	MORAL DEFECT	MOW THE GRASS
MIRACLE PLAY	MORAL EFFECT	MRS. MALAPROP
MISS A CHANCE	MORAL IMPACT	MUCH MARRIED
MISS A SITTER	MORE AND MORE	MUCH OBLIGED
MISSED CATCH	MORE THAN ONE	MUCH THE SAME
MISS ENGLAND	MORNING CALL	MUCH TROUBLE
MISSING HEIR	MORNING COAT	MUCH WENLOCK
MISSING LINK	MORNING POST	MUFFLED DRUM
MISS NOTHING	MORNING STAR	MUM'S THE WORD
MISS ONE'S WAY	MORRIS DANCE	MURDER TRIAL
MISS THE BOAT	MORTAL AGONY	MURKY DEPTHS
MISS THE MARK	MORTAL ENEMY	MUSCOVY DUCK
MISS THE POST	MORTALLY ILL	MUSEUM PIECE
MISTER RIGHT	MORTAL PERIL	MUSICAL NOTE
MIXED SCHOOL	MORTAL WOUND	MUSICAL SHOW

MUSICAL TRIO
MUSICAL WORK
MUSIC CRITIC
MUSIC LESSON
MUSIC MASTER
MUSTARD BATH
MUSTARD SEED
MUSWELL HILL
MUTTON CURRY
MUTUAL TERMS
MYSTERY BOAT
MYSTERY PLAY
MYSTERY SHIP
MYSTERY TOUR
MYSTERY TRIP
MYSTIC RITES

N—11
NAGGING PAIN
NAGGING WIFE
NAIL VARNISH
NAME NO NAMES
NAOMI JACOBS
NARROW GAUGE
NARROW SHAVE
NARROW TRAIL
NASAL ACCENT
NASTY PEOPLE
NASTY TEMPER
NASTY TUMBLE
NATIVE CHIEF
NATIVE DRESS
NATIVE HEATH
NATIVE STATE
NATIVE TRIBE
NAT KING COLE
NATURAL BENT
NATURAL GIFT
NATURAL LIFE
NATURE LOVER
NATURE STUDY
NAUGHTY GIRL
NAUGHTY WORD
NAVAL BATTLE
NAVAL RATING
NAVAL STORES
NAVEL ORANGE
NAZI GERMANY
NEAR AND DEAR
NEAR FAILURE
NEARLY READY

NEARLY THERE
NEAR ONE'S END
NEAR PERFECT
NEAR THE BONE
NEAR THE EDGE
NEAR THE MARK
NEAR THE WIND
NEAT AND TIDY
NEAT AND TRIM
NECK AND CROP
NECK AND NECK
NEEDLE MATCH
NEEDLE POINT
NEGRO MELODY
NELSON TOUCH
NE PLUS ULTRA
NERVE CENTRE
NETBALL TEAM
NET CURTAINS
NETHER LIMBS
NETHER WORLD
NET PRACTICE
NET RECEIPTS
NEUTRAL TINT
NEUTRAL ZONE
NEVER BEFORE
NEVER ENDING
NEVER FORGET
NEVER ON TIME
NEVER SAY DIE
NEW APPROACH
NEW ATLANTIS
NEW-BORN BABE
NEW-BORN BABY
NEW BRIGHTON
NEWGATE GAOL
NEW HEBRIDES
NEW POTATOES
NEW PROSPECT
NEWS CAPTION
NEWS IN BRIEF
NEWS SUMMARY
NEWTON ABBOT
NEW TO THE JOB
NEW YEAR'S DAY
NEW YEAR'S EVE
NEW YORK CITY
NEXT CENTURY
NEXT CHAPTER
NEXT IN ORDER
NEXT JANUARY

NEXT OCTOBER
NEXT STATION
NEXT TUESDAY
NICE AND EVEN
NICE MANNERS
NICE PICTURE
NIGHT AND DAY
NIGHT ATTIRE
NIGHT CURFEW
NIGHT EDITOR
NIGHT FLIGHT
NIGHT FLYING
NIGHT PATROL
NIGHT PORTER
NIGHT SCHOOL
NIGHT SISTER
NIGHT WORKER
NINE AND FIVE
NINE AND FOUR
NINE AND NINE
NINE DEGREES
NINE DOLLARS
NINE FATHOMS
NINE GALLONS
NINE GUINEAS
NINE HUNDRED
NINE MINUTES
NINE OF CLUBS
NINE PER CENT
NINE SQUARED
NINETY MILES
NINETY TIMES
NINETY YEARS
NINE WICKETS
NINTH LETTER
NINTH OF JULY
NINTH OF JUNE
NINTH STOREY
NINTH VOLUME
NIP IN THE AIR
NIP IN THE BUD
NIP OF BRANDY
NIP OF WHISKY
NO ADMISSION
NO AUTHORITY
NOBBY CLARKE
NOBLE EFFORT
NOBLE FAMILY
NOBLE FIGURE
NOBLE NATURE
NOBLE SAVAGE

NOBLE STRAIN
NOBODY'S FOOL
NO CIRCULARS
NOD ONE'S HEAD
NO EXCEPTION
NO GENTLEMAN
NOGGIN OF ALE
NO GREAT LOSS
NO HOPE AT ALL
NO ILLUSIONS
NOISE ABROAD
NOMADIC RACE
NOM DE GUERRE
NOMINAL HEAD
NOMINAL LIST
NOMINAL RATE
NOMINAL RENT
NONE SO BLIND
NONE THE LESS
NONE TOO WARM
NO, NO, NANETTE
NON-STOP SHOW
NO OBJECTION
NO QUESTIONS
NORFOLK SUIT
NO RIGHT TURN
NORMAL SIGHT
NORMAL STATE
NORMAN STYLE
NORTH AFRICA
NORTH BORNEO
NORTH DAKOTA
NORTH ISLAND
NORTH LONDON
NORTH RIDING
NOSE FOR NEWS
NOSEY PARKER
NOT A BIT OF IT
NOT ALL THERE
NOT A RED CENT
NOT FAR WRONG
NOTHING LEFT
NOTHING LIKE
NOTHING MUCH
NOTHING TO DO
NOTHING TO IT
NOTICE BOARD
NOT MUCH GOOD
NOT-OUT SCORE
NO-TRUMP HAND
NOT SPEAKING

NOT THE THING
NOTTING HILL
NOTTS COUNTY
NOTTS FOREST
NOT UP-TO-DATE
NOT UP TO MUCH
NOT VERY MANY
NOT VERY MUCH
NOT VERY WELL
NOT YOUR TYPE
NO VACANCIES
NOW AND AGAIN
NOWHERE NEAR
NOWHERE TO GO
NUCLEAR BOMB
NULL AND VOID
NUMBER EIGHT
NUMBER PLATE
NUMBER SEVEN
NUMBER THREE
NUPTIAL VOWS
NURSE CAVELL
NURSERY GAME
NURSERY MAID
NURSERY TALE
NURSING HOME

O—11

OAK-APPLE DAY
OBITER DICTA
OBLIQUE LINE
OBTUSE ANGLE
OCEAN TRAVEL
ODDLY ENOUGH
ODDS AGAINST
ODDS AND ENDS
OFFER ADVICE
OFFER A PRICE
OFFER NO HOPE
OFFICE BLOCK
OFFICE CLOCK
OFFICE HOURS
OFFICE PARTY
OFFICE STAFF
OFFICE STOOL
OFFICE SWEEP
OFF ONE'S BEAT
OFF ONE'S FEED
OFF ONE'S FOOD
OFF ONE'S HEAD
OFF-SIDE RULE

OFF THE BOOZE
OFF THE COAST
OFF THE GREEN
OFF THE LEASH
OFF THE POINT
OFF THE RAILS
OFF THE SCENT
OFF THE STAGE
OFF THE TRACK
OF GOOD STOCK
OF ILL REPUTE
OF LATE YEARS
OF NO ACCOUNT
OIL AND WATER
OIL OF CLOVES
OIL PAINTING
OIL REFINERY
OLD AND TRIED
OLD CUSTOMER
OLDER SISTER
OLD FAITHFUL
OLD GREY MARE
OLD KENT ROAD
OLD KING COLE
OLD MAN RIVER
OLD MEMORIES
OLD OAK CHEST
OLD OFFENDER
OLD OLD STORY
OLD POTATOES
OLD TRAFFORD
OLD WAR-HORSE
OLIVE BRANCH
OLIVER LODGE
OLIVER TWIST
OMAR KHAYYAM
OMNIBUS BOOK
ON ALL POINTS
ON AN AVERAGE
ON A PEDESTAL
ON A PITTANCE
ON AUTHORITY
ON BOARD SHIP
ON BOTH SIDES
ONCE OR TWICE
ONCE REMOVED
ONE AND A HALF
ONE AND EIGHT
ONE AND SEVEN
ONE AND THREE
ON EASY TERMS

ONE ELEVENTH
ONE FARTHING
ONE GOOD TURN
ONE IN THE EYE
ONE IN TWELVE
ONE-MAN REVUE
ONE MAN'S MEAT
ONE MEAT BALL
ONE'S BETTERS
ONE SHILLING
ONE'S HOSTESS
ONE SPOONFUL
ONE'S VERY OWN
ONE SYLLABLE
ONE THOUSAND
ON EVERY SIDE
ON GOOD TERMS
ON HORSEBACK
ONION SELLER
ONLY THE BEST
ON NO ACCOUNT
ON ONE'S GUARD
ON ONE'S HANDS
ON ONE'S KNEES
ON ONE'S PLATE
ON ONE'S RIGHT
ON POINT DUTY
ON PRINCIPLE
ON PROBATION
ON THE AGENDA
ON THE ATTACK
ON THE BOARDS
ON THE BOTTLE
ON THE BRIDGE
ON THE CARPET
ON THE COMMON
ON THE CORNER
ON THE COURSE
ON THE DANUBE
ON THE FIDDLE
ON THE FRINGE
ON THE GROUND
ON THE INSIDE
ON THE MARKET
ON THE MORROW
ON THE PARISH
ON THE RAZZLE
ON THE RECORD
ON THE SCALES
ON THE SCREEN
ON THE SQUARE

ON THE STAIRS
ON THE STOCKS
ON THE SWINGS
ON THE TARGET
ON THE THAMES
ON THE THRONE
ON THE WAGGON
ON THE WAY OUT
ON TWO WHEELS
ONUS OF PROOF
ONWARD MARCH
ON WEDNESDAY
OPAQUE GLASS
OPEN ACCOUNT
OPEN-AIR LIFE
OPEN-AIR TYPE
OPEN AND SHUT
OPEN CIRCUIT
OPEN COUNTRY
OPENING MOVE
OPENING TIME
OPEN MEETING
OPEN OUTWARD
OPEN QUARREL
OPEN RUPTURE
OPEN SCANDAL
OPEN THE BALL
OPEN THE CASE
OPEN THE DOOR
OPEN THE EYES
OPEN THE GATE
OPEN THE SAFE
OPEN THIS END
OPEN TO DOUBT
OPEN TO ERROR
OPEN TO OFFER
OPEN VERDICT
OPEN WARFARE
OPERA BOUFFE
OPERA SINGER
OPINION POLL
OPIUM ADDICT
OPIUM SMOKER
OPPOSITE SEX
OPPOSITE WAY
ORANGE DRINK
ORANGE GROVE
ORANGE JUICE
ORCHID HOUSE
ORDER DINNER
ORDERLY DUTY

ORDERLY ROOM
ORDER TO VIEW
ORDINARY MAN
ORDNANCE MAP
ORGANIC LIFE
ORIEL WINDOW
ORIENTAL ART
ORIGINAL SIN
ORNATE STYLE
ORPHAN CHILD
ORSON WELLES
ORTHODOX JEW
OSTRICH FARM
OTHER PEOPLE
OUT AND ABOUT
OUT COURTING
OUTDOOR GAME
OUTDOOR LIFE
OUTER CIRCLE
OUTER OFFICE
OUTER TEMPLE
OUT FOR A DUCK
OUT FOR BLOOD
OUT FOR KICKS
OUT OF ACTION
OUT OF BOUNDS
OUT OF BREATH
OUT OF DANGER
OUT OF FAVOUR
OUT OF HUMOUR
OUT OF OFFICE
OUT OF PETROL
OUT OF POCKET
OUT OF REPAIR
OUT OF SCHOOL
OUT OF SEASON
OUT OF THE ARK
OUT OF THE BAG
OUT OF THE CUP
OUT OF THE SKY
OUT OF THE SUN
OUT OF THE WAY
OUT ON STRIKE
OUTRIGHT WIN
OUTSIDE EDGE
OUTSIDE HELP
OUTSIDE LEFT
OUTSIDE WORK
OUTWARD SELF
OUTWARD SHOW
OVER AGAINST

OVER AND OVER
OVER ANXIOUS
OVERCAST SKY
OVER SHE GOES
OVER THE EDGE
OVER THE HILL
OVER THE LINE
OVER THE MARK
OVER THE MOON
OVER THE ODDS
OVER THE ROAD
OVER THE SIDE
OVER THE WALL
OVERTIME PAY
OWNER DRIVER
OWN FREE WILL
OXFORD COACH
OXFORD GROUP
OXFORD SHOES
OXFORD UNION
OYSTER SHELL

P—II
PABLO CASALS
PACE THE DECK
PACKAGE DEAL
PACKED HOUSE
PACKED LUNCH
PACKET OF TEN
PACK OF CARDS
PACK OF FOOLS
PACK UP AND GO
PAGAN PEOPLE
PAGE HEADING
PAID SERVANT
PAID TRIBUTE
PAIL OF WATER
PAINFUL TASK
PAINTED LADY
PAINTED SHIP
PAINTED VEIL
PAINT IN OILS
PAIR OF BOOTS
PAIR OF CLOGS
PAIR OF CUFFS
PAIR OF DUCKS
PAIR OF FIVES
PAIR OF FOURS
PAIR OF HANDS
PAIR OF HORNS

PAIR OF JACKS
PAIR OF KINGS
PAIR OF LACES
PAIR OF NINES
PAIR OF PANTS
PAIR OF PUMPS
PAIR OF SHOES
PAIR OF SIXES
PAIR OF SOCKS
PAIR OF SPATS
PAIR OF SPURS
PAIR OF STAYS
PAIR OF STEPS
PAIR OF TONGS
PALACE GUARD
PALAIS GLIDE
PALE AS DEATH
PAMPAS GRASS
PANAMA CANAL
PANCAKE RACE
PANDIT NEHRU
PANDORA'S BOX
PANEL DOCTOR
PANE OF GLASS
PAPER PROFIT
PAPIER MÂCHÉ
PARAFFIN OIL
PARISH CLERK
PARISH VICAR
PARLOUR GAME
PARLOUR MAID
PARSNIP WINE
PARSON'S NOSE
PART COMPANY
PART FRIENDS
PARTING GIFT
PARTING SHOT
PART PAYMENT
PART-TIME JOB
PARTY LEADER
PARTY MEMBER
PARTY SLOGAN
PARTY SPIRIT
PARTY SYSTEM
PAS DE CALAIS
PASS A REMARK
PASSING RICH
PASSING SHOW
PASSING WHIM
PASSING WORD
PASSION PLAY

PASSION WEEK
PASSIVE ROLE
PASS THE BALL
PASS THE BUCK
PASS THE PORT
PASS THE SALT
PASS THE TEST
PASS THE TIME
PASS THIS WAY
PASS THROUGH
PAST AND GONE
PASTEL SHADE
PAST HISTORY
PAST THE POST
PATH TO GLORY
PAT OF BUTTER
PATROL PLANE
PATRON OF ART
PATRON SAINT
PATTERN SHOP
PAUL ROBESON
PAX VOBISCUM
PAY A FORFEIT
PAY AND A HALF
PAY A PENALTY
PAY A PREMIUM
PAY BY CHEQUE
PAY CASH DOWN
PAY INCREASE
PAYING GUEST
PAY INTEREST
PAY ON DEMAND
PAY ON THE DOT
PAY THE COSTS
PAY THE DEVIL
PAY THE PIPER
PAY THE PRICE
PAY THE SCORE
PAY THE TABLE
PAY UP OR ELSE!
PEACEFUL END
PEACE OF MIND
PEACE PLEDGE
PEACE SPEECH
PEACE TREATY
PEACH BRANDY
PEACOCK BLUE
PEAL OF BELLS
PEARL BAILEY
PEARL BARLEY
PEARL BUTTON

PEARLY GATES	PICK THE LOCK	PLAY FORWARD
PEARLY QUEEN	PICK UP SPEED	PLAYING CARD
PEBBLE BEACH	PICNIC PARTY	PLAY MARBLES
PEBBLY BEACH	PICTURE BOOK	PLAY ON WORDS
PELTING RAIN	PIECE OF CAKE	PLAY PONTOON
PENAL COLONY	PIECE OF LAND	PLAY THE BALL
PENAL REFORM	PIECE OF LUCK	PLAY THE FOOL
PENAL SYSTEM	PIECE OF NEWS	PLAY THE GAME
PENALTY AREA	PIE IN THE SKY	PLAY THE HARP
PENALTY GOAL	PIERCED EARS	PLAY THE HERO
PENALTY KICK	PIGEON'S MILK	PLAY THE HOST
PENALTY LINE	PILE OF CHIPS	PLAY THE LEAD
PENALTY SPOT	PILE OF MONEY	PLEAD GUILTY
PEN AND PAPER	PILLION RIDE	PLEASANT DAY
PENNY POINTS	PILLION SEAT	PLEASURE MAD
PENSION FUND	PILLOW FIGHT	PLENTY TO EAT
PENSIVE MOOD	PILOT ENGINE	PLOT A COURSE
PERFECT CASE	PILOT SCHEME	PLUMB WICKET
PERFECT CURE	PILOT VESSEL	PLUM PUDDING
PERFECT FOOL	PILSEN LAGER	PLUS OR MINUS
PERFECT LADY	PILTDOWN MAN	PLYMOUTH HOE
PERFECT TRIM	PINCH OF SALT	POCKET GUIDE
PERIOD DRESS	PINT MEASURE	POCKET MONEY
PERIOD HOUSE	PINT OF CIDER	POCKET VENUS
PERIOD PIECE	PINT OF STOUT	POETIC STYLE
PERSIAN GULF	PINT TANKARD	POETS' CORNER
PERSIAN LAMB	PIPE CLEANER	POINT A MORAL
PERSONAL LAW	PIPE OF PEACE	POINTED CLUE
PET AVERSION	PIPE ON BOARD	POINT OF TIME
PETER DAWSON	PIPE TOBACCO	POINT OF VIEW
PETER GRIMES	PIRATE RADIO	POINT THE WAY
PETER O'TOOLE	PITHY REMARK	POKER PLAYER
PETER'S PENCE	PITHY SAYING	POKER SCHOOL
PETER WIMSEY	PLACE OF CALL	POKE THE FIRE
PETROL FUMES	PLACE OF REST	POLAR CIRCLE
PETTY TYRANT	PLAIN ANSWER	POLAR LIGHTS
PETULA CLARK	PLAIN FIGURE	POLAR REGION
PEWTER PLATE	PLAIN LIVING	POLE VAULTER
PHANTOM SHIP	PLAIN PEOPLE	POLICE COURT
PHOENIX PARK	PLAIN SPEECH	POLICE FORCE
PHONE NUMBER	PLAIN STUPID	POLICE STATE
PHOTO FINISH	PLASTER CAST	POLO SWEATER
PIANO LESSON	PLASTIC BOMB	PONY AND TRAP
PIANO PLAYER	PLATE ARMOUR	PONY EXPRESS
PICK A WINNER	PLAY AGAINST	POOLS COUPON
PICKET FENCE	PLAY-BOY TYPE	POOR CALIBRE
PICK FLOWERS	PLAY COWBOYS	POOR COMPANY
PICK HOLES IN	PLAY CRICKET	POOR HARVEST
PICK ONE'S WAY	PLAYER PIANO	POOR LOOK-OUT
PICK POCKETS	PLAY FOR LOVE	POOR OLD SOUL
PICK THE BEST	PLAY FOR TIME	POOR OPINION

POOR OUTLOOK
POOR QUALITY
POOR SOLDIER
POOR SWIMMER
POOR VINTAGE
POPULAR HERO
POPULAR NAME
POPULAR PLAY
POPULAR SONG
POPULAR TUNE
POPULAR WILL
PORK BUTCHER
PORTLAND BAY
PORT OF ENTRY
PORT OF SPAIN
PORT THE HELM
POSTAGE FREE
POSTAGE PAID
POST A LETTER
POSTAL ORDER
POSTAL UNION
POSTERN GATE
POTATO CHIPS
POTATO CRISP
POTATO SALAD
POT OF COFFEE
POTS AND PANS
POTS OF MONEY
POTTED PLANT
POTTER ABOUT
POTTER'S CLAY
POT THE BLACK
POTTING SHED
POULTRY FARM
POURING RAIN
POWER OF GOOD
PRACTICE RUN
PRACTISE LAW
PRAED STREET
PRAIRIE FIRE
PRAIRIE WOLF
PRANCE ABOUT
PRAY FOR RAIN
PRECISE TIME
PREMIUM BOND
PRESENT ARMS
PRESENT TIME
PRESS A CLAIM
PRESSED BEEF
PRESS NOTICE
PRESS OFFICE

PRESS ONWARD
PRESS TICKET
PRESTER JOHN
PRETTY AWFUL
PRETTY DANCE
PRETTY PENNY
PRETTY POLLY
PRETTY SCENE
PRETTY SMART
PRE-WAR PRICE
PREY TO FEARS
PRICE OF FAME
PRICE TICKET
PRICKLY HEAT
PRICKLY PEAR
PRIDE AND JOY
PRIDE OF RANK
PRIEST'S HOLE
PRIME FACTOR
PRIME NUMBER
PRIME OF LIFE
PRIMROSE DAY
PRIMUS STOVE
PRINCESS IDA
PRINTED PAGE
PRINTED WORD
PRINTER'S INK
PRINTER'S PIE
PRINTING INK
PRISON BREAK
PRISON GATES
PRISON GUARD
PRISON HOUSE
PRISON WALLS
PRIVATE BANK
PRIVATE BILL
PRIVATE HELL
PRIVATE LIFE
PRIVATE LINE
PRIVATE MASS
PRIVATE PATH
PRIVATE ROAD
PRIVATE ROOM
PRIVATE SALE
PRIVATE TALK
PRIVATE VIEW
PRIVATE WARD
PRIVET HEDGE
PRIZE CATTLE
PROBATE DUTY
PROBE DEEPLY

PROBLEM PLAY
PRODIGAL SON
PROM CONCERT
PROMISE WELL
PROMPT REPLY
PROOF READER
PROOF SPIRIT
PROPER PLACE
PROPER PRIDE
PROPER SENSE
PROPERTY TAX
PROS AND CONS
PROSE POETRY
PROTEIN DIET
PROUD FATHER
PROVE GUILTY
PRUSSIC ACID
PUBLIC ALARM
PUBLIC BATHS
PUBLIC ENEMY
PUBLIC FUNDS
PUBLIC HOUSE
PUBLIC IMAGE
PUBLIC MONEY
PUBLIC PURSE
PUBLIC TASTE
PUBLIC WORKS
PUBLIC WRONG
PUDDING FACE
PUDDING LANE
PUFF AND BLOW
PUFF OF SMOKE
PULL ASUNDER
PULL ONE'S LEG
PULL STRINGS
PULL THROUGH
PULL UP SHORT
PUMICE STONE
PUPPET STATE
PURCHASE TAX
PURE ALCOHOL
PURE ENGLISH
PURE FICTION
PURE IN HEART
PURE MOTIVES
PURE SCIENCE
PURL OR PLAIN
PURPLE HEART
PURPLE PATCH
PURSE OF GOLD
PUSH AND PULL

PUSH FORWARD
PUSH THROUGH
PUSS IN BOOTS
PUT A SPOKE IN
PUT IN A CLAIM
PUT IN CHARGE
PUT IN DANGER
PUT IN LIGHTS
PUT IN MOTION
PUT IN OFFICE
PUT IN PRISON
PUT IN THE WAY
PUT INTO CODE
PUT INTO TYPE
PUT IT MILDLY
PUT ON A SPURT
PUT ON A STUNT
PUT ONE'S CASE
PUT ON PAROLE
PUT ON RECORD
PUT ON THE MAP
PUT ON WEIGHT
PUT OUT TO SEA
PUT STRAIGHT
PUT THE LID ON
PUT TO FLIGHT
PUT TOGETHER
PUT TO RANSOM
PUT TO RIGHTS
PUTT THE SHOT
PUT UP A BLACK
PUT UP A BLUFF
PUT-UP AFFAIR
PUT UP A FIGHT
PUT WISE TO IT
PUZZLE IT OUT
PYJAMA PARTY

Q—11
QUACK DOCTOR
QUACK REMEDY
QUART BOTTLE
QUARTER DECK
QUARTER LEFT
QUARTER MILE
QUART OF BEER
QUARTO PAPER
QUEEN MOTHER
QUEEN SALOTE
QUEEN'S BENCH
QUEEN'S COURT

QUEER PERSON
QUEER STREET
QUICK ANSWER
QUICK FREEZE
QUICK GLANCE
QUICK GROWTH
QUICK PROFIT
QUICK RETURN
QUICK TEMPER
QUICK TONGUE
QUICK WORKER
QUIET DREAMS
QUIETEN DOWN
QUIET PLEASE!
QUITE AT HOME
QUITE ENOUGH
QUITE LIKELY
QUIT THE RING
QUOTED PRICE

R—11
RABBIT PUNCH
RABBIT'S FOOT
RACE HISTORY
RACE MEETING
RACE PROBLEM
RACE SUICIDE
RACIAL PRIDE
RACING EIGHT
RACING MODEL
RACING SLANG
RACING WORLD
RACING YACHT
RACK AND RUIN
RACY FLAVOUR
RADAR SCREEN
RADIANT HEAT
RADIATE LOVE
RADICAL CURE
RADICAL IDEA
RADICAL SIGN
RADIO BEACON
RADIO SIGNAL
RAGGED ROBIN
RAGTIME ARMY
RAGTIME BAND
RAILWAY ARCH
RAILWAY LINE
RAINBOW'S END
RAIN OF BLOWS
RAIN OR SHINE

RAINY SEASON
RAISE A CHEER
RAISE A LAUGH
RAISE A STORM
RAISED VOICE
RAISE MORALE
RAISE ON HIGH
RAISE PRICES
RAISE THE BID
RAISE THE HEM
RAISON D'ÊTRE
RALLY AROUND
RALLYING CRY
RAMBLER ROSE
RANGING SHOT
RANK AND FILE
RANSOM MONEY
RANT AND RAVE
RAPID CHANGE
RAPID EFFECT
RAPID GLANCE
RAPID GROWTH
RAPID MOTION
RAPID SPEECH
RARE EXAMPLE
RARE QUALITY
RASH PROMISE
RATTLE ALONG
RAW MATERIAL
REACH BOTTOM
REACH SAFETY
REACH THE END
REACH THE TOP
READ A SPEECH
READING DESK
READING GAOL
READING LAMP
READING LIST
READING ROOM
READ THE WILL
READ THROUGH
READY ACCESS
READY ANSWER
READY ENOUGH
READY FOR BED
READY FOR USE
READY RETORT
READY TO DROP
READY TO HAND
READY TONGUE
READY TO WEAR

READY WORKER
REAM OF PAPER
REAP A PROFIT
REAPING HOOK
REAR ADMIRAL
REBECCA WEST
REBEL ATTACK
REBEL LEADER
RECEIPT BOOK
RECEIVE NEWS
RECENT ISSUE
RECENT TIMES
RECORD ALBUM
RECORD CROWD
RECORD ENTRY
RECORD SCORE
RECORD TOKEN
RED AND BLACK
RED AND GREEN
RED AND WHITE
RED BURGUNDY
RED-HOT COALS
RED-HOT POKER
RED MAHOGANY
RED, RED ROBIN
RED SQUIRREL
RED TRIANGLE
REDUCED FARE
REDUCED RATE
REDUCE SPEED
REFINED GOLD
REFLEX LIGHT
REFUGEE CAMP
REFUSE A GIFT
REFUSE TO ACT
REFUSE TO MIX
REFUSE TO PAY
REGATTA WEEK
REGENCY BUCK
REGENT'S PARK
REGULAR ARMY
REGULAR HERO
REGULAR LIFE
REGULAR VERB
REGULAR WORK
RELEASE DATE
RELIEF FORCE
RELIEF PARTY
REMAIN ALOOF
REMAIN AWAKE
REMNANT SALE

REMOTE CAUSE
RENEW A LEASE
RENEWED HOPE
RENTAL VALUE
RENT ASUNDER
RENT CONTROL
REPORT STAGE
REQUEST ITEM
REQUEST NOTE
REQUEST STOP
REQUIEM MASS
RESCUE FORCE
RESCUE PARTY
RESCUE SQUAD
RESERVE FUND
RESERVE TEAM
REST ASSURED
REST CONTENT
REST IN PEACE
RETAIL PRICE
RETAIL TRADE
RETIRED LIFE
RETIRED LIST
RETIRE TO BED
RETIRING AGE
RETURN A BLOW
RETURN FIGHT
RETURN MATCH
RETURN VISIT
REVERSE GEAR
REVERSE SIDE
REVISED COPY
REX HARRISON
RHODE ISLAND
RHUBARB TART
RHYMED VERSE
RICE PUDDING
RICH HARVEST
RICH HUSBAND
RICH IN IDEAS
RIDE A TANDEM
RIDING BOOTS
RIDING HABIT
RIGGED TRIAL
RIGHT AMOUNT
RIGHT ANSWER
RIGHT AS RAIN
RIGHT A WRONG
RIGHT INSIDE
RIGHT MOMENT
RIGHT NUMBER

RIGHT PEOPLE
RIGHT SIDE UP
RIGHTS OF MAN
RIGHT TO VOTE
RIGHT WINGER
RIGHT YOU ARE
RIGOR MORTIS
RINGING TONE
RING OF ROSES
RING OF TRUTH
RING THE BELL
RIOT OF SOUND
RISE AGAINST
RISE AND FALL
RISE IN PRICE
RISE TO A PEAK
RISE TO POWER
RISE TO SPEAK
RISING COSTS
RISING SALES
RITUAL DANCE
RIVER DANUBE
RIVER GANGES
RIVER JORDAN
RIVER LAUNCH
RIVER MEDWAY
RIVER MERSEY
RIVER OF LAVA
RIVER PATROL
RIVER POLICE
RIVER SEVERN
RIVER THAMES
RIVER TRAVEL
ROAD HAULAGE
ROAD REPAIRS
ROADSIDE INN
ROAD SURFACE
ROAD SWEEPER
ROAD TRAFFIC
ROARING FIRE
ROAR OF ANGER
ROASTING HOT
ROAST MUTTON
ROAST POTATO
ROAST TURKEY
ROBBER BARON
ROBE OF STATE
ROBERT BRUCE
ROBERT BURNS
ROBERT CLIVE
ROBERT DONAT

ROCK AND ROLL
ROCKET RANGE
ROCK THE BOAT
ROCK TO SLEEP
ROD IN PICKLE
ROES ON TOAST
ROLLER BLIND
ROLLER TOWEL
ROLLING GAIT
ROLLING HOME
ROLLING ROAD
ROLL INTO ONE
ROLL OF DRUMS
ROLL OF PAPER
ROLL THE LAWN
ROLL-TOP DESK
ROMAN CANDLE
ROMAN CHURCH
ROMAN EMPIRE
ROMANTIC ART
ROMNEY MARSH
ROOKERY NOOK
ROOM SERVICE
ROSES ARE RED
ROSY OUTLOOK
ROSY PICTURE
ROTARY PRESS
ROTARY VALVE
ROTTEN APPLE
ROUGE ET NOIR
ROUGH GROUND
ROUGH MANNER
ROUGH SCHEME
ROUGH SKETCH
ROUGH TONGUE
ROUND CHEEKS
ROUND FIGURE
ROUND LETTER
ROUND NUMBER
ROUND OBJECT
ROUND OF BEEF
ROUND OF FIRE
ROUND OF GOLF
ROUSING SONG
ROW OF HOUSES
ROW OF MEDALS
ROWS AND ROWS
ROWTON HOUSE
ROYAL ASSENT
ROYAL CIRCLE
ROYAL FAMILY

ROYAL MARINE
ROYAL OCTAVO
ROYAL PALACE
ROYAL PARDON
ROYAL PURPLE
ROYAL SALUTE
RUBBER GLOVE
RUBBER HEELS
RUBBER PLANT
RUBBER SOLES
RUBBER STAMP
RUBBISH DUMP
RUBBISH HEAP
RUB TOGETHER
RUBY WEDDING
RUDDY CHEEKS
RUDE GESTURE
RUGBY LEAGUE
RUGBY SCHOOL
RUGBY TACKLE
RUGGER FIELD
RUGGER MATCH
RUGGER PITCH
RUGGER SCRUM
RUINED HOUSE
RUIN ONESELF
RULE OF FORCE
RULE OF MIGHT
RULE OF THREE
RULE OF THUMB
RULING CLASS
RULING PARTY
RULING POWER
RULING PRICE
RUM CUSTOMER
RUMMAGE SALE
RUMOUR HAS IT
RUN A MAN DOWN
RUN AN ERRAND
RUN FOR COVER
RUN FOR MAYOR
RUN INTO DEBT
RUN INTO FORM
RUN INTO PORT
RUN MESSAGES
RUNNER BEANS
RUNNING AMOK
RUNNING COLD
RUNNING COST
RUNNING DOWN
RUNNING FIRE

RUNNING JUMP
RUNNING KNOT
RUNNING OVER
RUNNING RIOT
RUNNING WILD
RUN PARALLEL
RUN SMOOTHLY
RUN STRAIGHT
RUN TOGETHER
RUN UP A SCORE
RUSH FORWARD
RUSH THROUGH
RUSSIAN BATH
RUSSIAN EGGS

S—11

SABRINA FAIR
SACK OF FLOUR
SACRED HEART
SACRED MUSIC
SACRED TRUST
SAD FAREWELL
SADLY MISSED
SAD TO RELATE
SAFE AND SURE
SAFE AND WELL
SAFE BREAKER
SAFE COMPANY
SAFE CONDUCT
SAFE CUSTODY
SAFE DEPOSIT
SAFE JOURNEY
SAFE KEEPING
SAFE LANDING
SAFE RETREAT
SAFETY CATCH
SAFETY FIRST
SAFETY MATCH
SAFETY RAZOR
SAFETY STRAP
SAFETY VALVE
SAFFRON CAKE
SAGO PUDDING
SAILING BOAT
SAILING CLUB
SAILING DATE
SAILING SHIP
SAILING TIME
SAILOR'S HOME
SAILOR'S KNOT
SAINT GEORGE

SAINT HELENA	SCOUT AROUND	SEEK A WAY OUT
SAINT HELIER	SCOUT MASTER	SEE NEXT WEEK
SALMON STEAK	SCRAP DEALER	SEE STRAIGHT
SALMON TROUT	SCRAPE ALONG	SEE THE LIGHT
SAL VOLATILE	SCRAPPY MEAL	SEE THE POINT
SAME FOOTING	SCRATCH CREW	SEE THE TRUTH
SAME MEANING	SCRATCH RACE	SEE THE WORLD
SAME OLD GAME	SCRATCH SIDE	SEETHING MOB
SAME PATTERN	SCRATCH TEAM	SELF CONTROL
SAMUEL PEPYS	SCRATCHY PEN	SELF-MADE MAN
SANCHO PANZA	SEA ELEPHANT	SELL AT A LOSS
SANDOWN PARK	SEA FRONTAGE	SELLING LINE
SANDS OF TIME	SEAM BOWLING	SELLING RACE
SANDWICH BAR	SEARCH PARTY	SELL THE PASS
SAPPHIRE SEA	SEASIDE TOWN	SELL TICKETS
SATANIC HOST	SEAT OF KINGS	SENATE HOUSE
SATIN FINISH	SEAT OF POWER	SEND A LETTER
SATIN STITCH	SEAT ONESELF	SEND AN ORDER
SAUCEPAN LID	SECOND CHILD	SEND A SIGNAL
SAUDI ARABIA	SECOND CLASS	SEND FOR A CAB
SAUSAGE MEAT	SECOND EVENT	SEND FOR HELP
SAUSAGE ROLL	SECOND FLOOR	SEND PACKING
SAVAGE BEAST	SECOND FRONT	SEND TO SLEEP
SAVAGE BRUTE	SECOND GRADE	SENILE DECAY
SAVAGE SCENE	SECOND GREEN	SENIOR PUPIL
SAVAGE TRIBE	SECOND HOUSE	SENSE OF DUTY
SAVE NOTHING	SECOND JOINT	SENSE OF LOSS
SAVE ONESELF	SECOND MONTH	SENSE OF PAIN
SAVE THE MARK	SECOND OF MAY	SENSIBLE BOY
SAVING GRACE	SECOND PARTY	SENSIBLE MAN
SAVINGS BANK	SECOND PLACE	SENT HAYWIRE
SAVOIR FAIRE	SECOND PRIZE	SENT PACKING
SAVOURY DISH	SECOND ROUND	SERIAL STORY
SCALDED MILK	SECOND SHIFT	SERIOUS BOOK
SCARED STIFF	SECOND SIGHT	SERIOUS LOOK
SCENT BOTTLE	SECONDS LATE	SERIOUS LOSS
SCENT DANGER	SECOND STAGE	SERIOUS MIND
SCENTED SOAP	SECOND TEETH	SERIOUS MOOD
SCILLY ISLES	SECOND VERSE	SERIOUS PLAY
SCHOOL BADGE	SECOND YOUTH	SERIOUS STEP
SCHOOL BOARD	SECRET AGENT	SERIOUS TALK
SCHOOL HOURS	SECRET ENEMY	SERIOUS VEIN
SCHOOL HOUSE	SECRET HAUNT	SERIOUS VIEW
SCHOOL OF ART	SECRET PLACE	SERVANT GIRL
SCHOOL TREAT	SECURED LOAN	SERVE A FAULT
SCORE A POINT	SECURE GRASP	SERVE NOTICE
SCORE FREELY	SEE A DENTIST	SERVICE FLAT
SCORE SLOWLY	SEE DAYLIGHT	SERVICE ROAD
SCOTCH BROTH	SEED OF DOUBT	SERVICE ROOM
SCOTS ACCENT	SEE EYE TO EYE	SERVING TIME
SCOTS GUARDS	SEE FAIR PLAY	SET AN AMBUSH

SET AND MATCH	SHARP CORNER	SHORT NOTICE
SET A PROBLEM	SHARP LESSON	SHORT OF CASH
SET AT NAUGHT	SHARP REBUFF	SHORT OF FOOD
SET IN MOTION	SHARP TEMPER	SHORT OF TIME
SET MOVEMENT	SHARP TONGUE	SHORT OF WORK
SET OF CHAIRS	SHARP TWINGE	SHORT PERIOD
SET OF STAMPS	SHAVEN CROWN	SHORT SHRIFT
SET ONE RIGHT	SHAVING SOAP	SHORT SPEECH
SET QUESTION	SHEAF OF CORN	SHORT STROLL
SET STANDARD	SHED THE LOAD	SHORT SUPPLY
SET STRAIGHT	SHEEP FARMER	SHORT TEMPER
SET THE ALARM	SHEER LUNACY	SHORT VOYAGE
SET THE FIELD	SHEER MURDER	SHORT WAY OFF
SET THE SCENE	SHEET ANCHOR	SHORT WEIGHT
SETTING FREE	SHEET COPPER	SHOT THROUGH
SETTLING DAY	SHERRY GLASS	SHOUT FOR JOY
SET TO RIGHTS	SHERRY PARTY	SHOUT HURRAH
SET UP A CLAIM	SHIFT WORKER	SHOW A PROFIT
SET UP IN TYPE	SHILLING TIP	SHOW COURAGE
SEVEN AND ONE	SHINING HOUR	SHOW FEELING
SEVEN AND SIX	SHIP OF STATE	SHOW NO FIGHT
SEVEN AND TEN	SHIP'S COURSE	SHOW NO MERCY
SEVEN AND TWO	SHIP'S DOCTOR	SHOW OF FORCE
SEVEN DWARFS	SHIP'S MASTER	SHOW OF HANDS
SEVEN HEARTS	SHIP'S PAPERS	SHOW ONE'S AGE
SEVEN MONTHS	SHIP'S PURSER	SHOW ONESELF
SEVEN NINTHS	SHIP'S STOKER	SHOW PROMISE
SEVEN O'CLOCK	SHOAL OF FISH	SHOW PROWESS
SEVEN OUNCES	SHOCK OF HAIR	SHOW RESPECT
SEVEN POINTS	SHOCK TROOPS	SHOW RESULTS
SEVEN POUNDS	SHODDY GOODS	SHOW THE FLAG
SEVEN SPADES	SHOE LEATHER	SHOW UP AGAIN
SEVEN TENTHS	SHOOTING BOX	SHOW WILLING
SEVENTH HOLE	SHOOTING WAR	SHREWD GUESS
SEVENTH PART	SHOOT TO KILL	SHRILL SOUND
SEVENTH RACE	SHOP COUNTER	SHRILL VOICE
SEVENTH TIME	SHOP DOORWAY	SHUN COMPANY
SEVEN TO FOUR	SHOP FOR SALE	SHUT THE DOOR
SEVERE FROST	SHOPPING BAG	SHUT THE GATE
SEVERE SHOCK	SHOP STEWARD	SIAMESE TWIN
SEVERE STYLE	SHORT AND FAT	SICK AT HEART
SEWING CLASS	SHORT ANSWER	SICK BENEFIT
SEXTON BLAKE	SHORTEN SAIL	SICKLY SMILE
SHABBY TRICK	SHORTEST BOY	SICK TO DEATH
SHAGGY BEARD	SHORTEST DAY	SIDE AGAINST
SHALLOW DISH	SHORTEST MAN	SIDE OF BACON
SHALLOW MIND	SHORTEST WAY	SIDE TURNING
SHAM ILLNESS	SHORT JACKET	SIDNEY JAMES
SHANKS'S PONY	SHORT LESSON	SIEGE OF TROY
SHARP ANSWER	SHORT LETTER	SIERRA LEONE
SHARP ATTACK	SHORT MEMORY	SIGNAL CORPS

SIGNAL LIGHT	SITTING DUCK	SLICE OF MEAT
SIGNS OF WEAR	SITTING ROOM	SLIDING DOOR
SILAS MARNER	SITTING SHOT	SLIDING ROOF
SILENT MIRTH	SIX AND A HALF	SLIDING SEAT
SILENT NIGHT	SIX AND EIGHT	SLIGHT DOUBT
SILLY ANSWER	SIX AND SEVEN	SLIGHT PAUSE
SILLY DONKEY	SIX AND THREE	SLIPPED DISC
SILLY DUFFER	SIX DIAMONDS	SLIPPER BATH
SILLY PERSON	SIX FEET TALL	SLIP OF A GIRL
SILLY REMARK	SIX FURLONGS	SLIP OF PAPER
SILLY SEASON	SIX NO-TRUMPS	SLIP THROUGH
SILVER BIRCH	SIX OF HEARTS	SLOPING DESK
SILVER MEDAL	SIX OF SPADES	SLOPING EDGE
SILVER MONEY	SIX OF TRUMPS	SLOPING FACE
SILVER PAPER	SIXPENNY TIP	SLOPING ROOF
SILVER PLATE	SIX SEVENTHS	SLOPING TYPE
SILVER SPOON	SIXTH LETTER	SLOPPY SMILE
SILVERY MOON	SIXTH OF JULY	SLOT MACHINE
SILVERY TONE	SIXTH OF JUNE	SLOUCH ALONG
SIMNEL BREAD	SIX THOUSAND	SLOW AND SURE
SIMPLE HEART	SIXTH STOREY	SLOW BOWLING
SIMPLE SIMON	SIXTH VOLUME	SLOW BUT SURE
SIMPLE SOUND	SKATING RINK	SLOW DECLINE
SIMPLE STYLE	SKEIN OF WOOL	SLOW DEGREES
SIMPLE TASTE	SKELETON KEY	SLOW FOXTROT
SIMPLE TRUTH	SKETCHY MEAL	SLOW PROCESS
SIMPLON PASS	SKILLED WORK	SLOW STARTER
SIMPLY AWFUL	SKIMMED MILK	SLOW TO ANGER
SINEWS OF WAR	SKIM THROUGH	SLOW TO LEARN
SINGING BIRD	SKIN AND BONE	SLUM DWELLER
SINGING FOOL	SKIN DISEASE	SMALL AMOUNT
SINGLE BERTH	SKIN MASSAGE	SMALL BITTER
SINGLE ENTRY	SKYE TERRIER	SMALL CHANCE
SINGLE HEART	SLAB OF STONE	SMALL CHANGE
SINGLE PIECE	SLACK MARKET	SMALL CHARGE
SINGLE STATE	SLACK SEASON	SMALL CIRCLE
SINGLE TRACK	SLADE SCHOOL	SMALL FAMILY
SINGLE VOICE	SLAM THE DOOR	SMALL FARMER
SINGLE WOMAN	SLATE PENCIL	SMALL INCOME
SINKING FAST	SLAVE LABOUR	SMALL LETTER
SINKING FUND	SLAVE MARKET	SMALL MATTER
SINKING SHIP	SLAVE TO DUTY	SMALL NUMBER
SINK THE BOAT	SLEEP DOUBLE	SMALL PROFIT
SIP OF BRANDY	SLEEPING BAG	SMALL SALARY
SIR JOHN HUNT	SLEEPING CAR	SMALL SCOTCH
SIR LANCELOT	SLEEPING DOG	SMALL SHERRY
SISTER SHIPS	SLEIGH BELLS	SMALL VESSEL
SISTER SUSIE	SLENDER HOPE	SMALL WHISKY
SIT-DOWN MEAL	SLICED BREAD	SMART DEVICE
SITTING BULL	SLICE OF CAKE	SMART PEOPLE
SITTING DOWN	SLICE OF LUCK	SMART PERSON

SMART RETORT	SOLID GROUND	SPEAK FREELY
SMART SAYING	SOLID MATTER	SPEAK FRENCH
SMART TALKER	SOLID SILVER	SPEAK GERMAN
SMELL DANGER	SOLITARY MAN	SPEAK NO EVIL
SMILE PLEASE	SOLWAY FIRTH	SPEAK OPENLY
SMOKE A CIGAR	SOMEONE ELSE	SPEAK POLISH
SMOKED GLASS	SOME TIME AGO	SPEAK SLOWLY
SMOKED TROUT	SONG CONTEST	SPEAK SOFTLY
SMOKE SCREEN	SONG OF SONGS	SPECIAL CASE
SMOKE SIGNAL	SONG RECITAL	SPECIAL DIET
SMOKING ROOM	SONNY LISTON	SPECIAL DUTY
SMOOTH AS ICE	SOPHIA LOREN	SPECIAL GIFT
SMOOTH WATER	SORDID STORY	SPECIAL JURY
SNAKE POISON	SORELY TRIED	SPECIAL LINE
SNAKES ALIVE!	SORE PRESSED	SPECIAL NOTE
SNAP OUT OF IT	SORE SUBJECT	SPECK OF DUST
SNATCH A KISS	SORRY FIGURE	SPEED MANIAC
SNOWED UNDER	SORRY PLIGHT	SPEED RECORD
SNOW LEOPARD	SOUND ADVICE	SPEED TRIALS
SOB BITTERLY	SOUND ASLEEP	SPELL DANGER
SOBER COLOUR	SOUND CREDIT	SPELLING BEE
SOBER PERSON	SOUND IN MIND	SPELL OF DUTY
SOCCER MATCH	SOUND PLAYER	SPELL OF WORK
SOCIAL CLASS	SOUND POLICY	SPEND FREELY
SOCIAL GROUP	SOUND REASON	SPICE OF LIFE
SOCIAL PARTY	SOUP KITCHEN	SPIKED SHOES
SOCIAL ROUND	SOUTH AFRICA	SPINNING TOP
SOCIAL SCALE	SOUTH BY EAST	SPIRIT LEVEL
SOCIAL WHIRL	SOUTH BY WEST	SPLIT SECOND
SOCIETY LADY	SOUTH DAKOTA	SPOILS OF WAR
SOCIETY NEWS	SOUTH EALING	SPOILT CHILD
SOCIETY PAGE	SOUTH HARROW	SPOIL THE FUN
SODA AND MILK	SOUTH LONDON	SPORTING DOG
SO FAR, SO GOOD	SOUTH MOLTON	SPORTING GUN
SOFT AND RIPE	SOUTH RIDING	SPORTING MAN
SOFT OUTLINE	SOVIET UNION	SPORTS ARENA
SOILED GOODS	SPACE FLIGHT	SPORTS MODEL
SOILED LINEN	SPACE OF TIME	SPORTS SHIRT
SOIL EROSION	SPACE TRAVEL	SPOTTED DICK
SOLAR PLEXUS	SPADE GUINEA	SPOT THE BALL
SOLAR SYSTEM	SPANISH GOLD	SPREAD GLOOM
SOLD FOR A PUP	SPANISH MAIN	SPRING A LEAK
SOLDIER KING	SPANISH TOWN	SPRING APART
SOLDIER'S KIT	SPANISH WINE	SPRING A TRAP
SOLDIER'S PAY	SPARE A PENNY	SPRING FEVER
SOLE AND HEEL	SPARE THE ROD	SPRING ONION
SOLE COMFORT	SPARK OF LIFE	SPRING VALVE
SOLEMN MUSIC	SPARTAN FARE	SPRING WATER
SOLEMN TRUTH	SPARTAN LIFE	SPROUT WINGS
SOLE SUPPORT	SPATE OF NEWS	SQUARE DANCE
SOLID FIGURE	SPEAK FIRMLY	SQUARE WORLD

SQUASH COURT	ST. AUGUSTINE	STOCK LETTER
SQUEEZE PLAY	STAY INDOORS	STOCK MARKET
SQUIRE'S LADY	STAY IN SIGHT	STOCK PHRASE
STACK OF COAL	STAY NEUTRAL	STOLE A MARCH
STACK OF WORK	STAY OUTSIDE	STOLEN FRUIT
STAFF OF LIFE	STAY THE PACE	STOLEN GOODS
STAGE EFFECT	STAY TOO LONG	STONE QUARRY
STAGE FRIGHT	ST. DAVID'S DAY	STONE'S THROW
STAGE MAKE-UP	STEADY FLAME	STONY GROUND
STAGE PLAYER	STEADY LIGHT	STOP A BULLET
STAGE STRUCK	STEADY PULSE	STOP BURNING
STAIR CARPET	STEADY TREND	STOP OUTSIDE
STAKE A CLAIM	STEAL A MARCH	STOP PAYMENT
STALK ABROAD	STEAMED FISH	STOP SMOKING
STALKY AND CO.	STEAM ENGINE	STOP TALKING
STAMP DEALER	STEAMING HOT	STOP TEASING
STAND A DRINK	STEAM LAUNCH	STOP THE FLOW
STAND AGHAST	STEEL GIRDER	STOP TO THINK
STANDARD ONE	STEEL HELMET	STOP WORKING
STAND A ROUND	ST. ELMO'S FIRE	STORE OF NUTS
STAND AROUND	STEM THE TIDE	STORM CENTRE
STAND AT EASE	STEM TO STERN	STORM CLOUDS
STAND IN FEAR	STEP FORWARD	STORM SIGNAL
STAND IN LINE	STEP OUTSIDE	STORM TROOPS
STAND IN NEED	STEP THIS WAY	STORMY NIGHT
STAND OR FALL	STERILE LAND	STORMY SCENE
STAND SQUARE	STERN REBUKE	STORY WRITER
STAND TO GAIN	STEWED FRUIT	STOUT CORTEZ
STAND TO LOSE	STEWED PEARS	STOUT EFFORT
STAR CHAMBER	STICK IN A RUT	STOUT FELLOW
STARCHY FOOD	STICK OF ROCK	STRAIGHT BAT
STAR CLUSTER	STICKY LABEL	STRAIGHT HIT
STAR OF DAVID	STICKY PAPER	STRAIGHT MAN
STAR OF INDIA	STICKY STUFF	STRAIGHT OFF
STAR QUALITY	STIFF BREEZE	STRAIGHT OUT
STARRY NIGHT	STIFF COLOUR	STRAIGHT RUN
STAR STUDDED	STIFLE A YAWN	STRAIGHT SET
START A FIGHT	STILL HOPING	STRAIGHT TIP
START AFRESH	STILL TO COME	STRAIGHT WIN
STARTER'S GUN	STILL TONGUE	STRANGE LAND
START SAVING	STILL WATERS	STRAY BULLET
STATE A CLAIM	STILL WITH IT	STRAY REMARK
STATED TERMS	STIR A FINGER	STREAM FORTH
STATELY HOME	STIR ONE'S TEA	STREET CRIES
STATE OF FLUX	STIRRUP PUMP	STREET LEVEL
STATE OF MIND	STIR THE FIRE	STREET OF INK
STATE PRISON	ST. JOHN'S WOOD	STREET SCENE
STATE SCHOOL	ST. MARGARET'S	STRICT ORDER
STATE SECRET	STOCK ANSWER	STRICT TEMPO
STATUTE BOOK	STOCK EXCUSE	STRICT TRUTH
STATUTE MILE	STOCK IN HAND	STRIDE ALONG

STRIKE A BLOW
STRIKE A NOTE
STRIKE A POSE
STRIKE BLIND
STRIKE LUCKY
STRING ALONG
STRING BEANS
STRING MUSIC
STRIP OF LAND
STRIVE AFTER
STRONG DRINK
STRONG FAITH
STRONG LIGHT
STRONG POINT
STRONG PULSE
STRONG SMELL
STRONG TASTE
STRONG VIEWS
STRONG VOICE
STRONG WORDS
STUB ONE'S TOE
STUDENT BODY
STUDENT DAYS
STUDENTS' RAG
STUDIO COUCH
STUFFED BIRD
STUFFED FOWL
STUFF IT AWAY
STUMBLE OVER
STUMBLE UPON
STUMP ORATOR
STUNT FLYING
STURDY FRAME
STURDY LIMBS
ST. VALENTINE
SUAVE MANNER
SUBLIME LIFE
SUCH AND SUCH
SUDDEN BREAK
SUDDEN DEATH
SUDDEN SHOCK
SUE FOR LIBEL
SUE FOR PEACE
SUET PUDDING
SUFFER A BLOW
SUFFER A LOSS
SUICIDE CLUB
SUICIDE NOTE
SUICIDE PACT
SUIT OF CARDS
SUMMER DRESS

SUMMIT LEVEL
SUMMIT TALKS
SUM OF THINGS
SUNDAY HOURS
SUNDAY JOINT
SUNDAY LUNCH
SUNDAY NIGHT
SUNDAY PAPER
SUNDAY TIMES
SUNDRY ITEMS
SUNK IN GLOOM
SUNNY SIDE UP
SUNSET STRIP
SUPERIOR AIR
SUPPER PARTY
SUPPER TABLE
SUPPORT LIFE
SUPPLY DEPOT
SUPREME GOOD
SURE FOOTING
SURFACE AREA
SURFACE MAIL
SURPLUS CASH
SURREY HILLS
SUSSEX DOWNS
SWALLOW DIVE
SWANEE RIVER
SWANSEA TOWN
SWARM OF ANTS
SWARM OF BEES
SWEAR AN OATH
SWEAR ON OATH
SWEDISH BATH
SWEENEY TODD
SWEET AND LOW
SWEET AS A NUT
SWEET DREAMS
SWEET NATURE
SWEET PICKLE
SWEET POTATO
SWEET SHERRY
SWEET TEMPER
SWEET THINGS
SWELLED HEAD
SWIFT GLANCE
SWIFT OF FOOT
SWISS CANTON
SWISS CHALET
SWISS CHEESE
SWISS GUARDS
SWISS RESORT

SWIVEL CHAIR
SWOLLEN HEAD
SWORD IN HAND
SWORD THRUST
SYDNEY SMITH
SYRUP OF FIGS

T—11
TABLE FOR TWO
TABLE TENNIS
TACTICAL WAR
TAINTED GOLD
TAKE A CENSUS
TAKE A CHANCE
TAKE A CORNER
TAKE A COURSE
TAKE A CRUISE
TAKE A DEGREE
TAKE A GANDER
TAKE A HEADER
TAKE A LETTER
TAKE AN OFFER
TAKE A NUMBER
TAKE A PLEDGE
TAKE A POWDER
TAKE A STROLL
TAKE A TICKET
TAKE A TUMBLE
TAKE A WICKET
TAKE BY FORCE
TAKE BY STORM
TAKE CAPTIVE
TAKE CHANCES
TAKE COMFORT
TAKE COMMAND
TAKE COUNSEL
TAKE COURAGE
TAKE LESSONS
TAKE LIGHTLY
TAKE NO RISKS
TAKE OFFENCE
TAKE ON BOARD
TAKE ONE'S CUE
TAKE ON TRUST
TAKE ON WATER
TAKE-OVER BID
TAKE POT-LUCK
TAKE SHELTER
TAKE STOCK OF
TAKE THE BAIT
TAKE THE CAKE

TAKE THE HELM	TEA INTERVAL	TEST CRICKET
TAKE THE HINT	TEAM CAPTAIN	TESTING TIME
TAKE THE LEAD	TEA MERCHANT	TEST OF SKILL
TAKE THE LIFT	TEAM OF MULES	THAMES BASIN
TAKE THE OATH	TEAM SUPPORT	THANK HEAVEN!
TAKE THE VEIL	TEAR ASUNDER	THAT IS TO SAY
TAKE THOUGHT	TEARS OF PITY	THAT'S THE WAY
TAKE TIME OFF	TEARS OF RAGE	THAT'S TORN IT
TAKE TO COURT	TEA STRAINER	THE ALMIGHTY
TAKE TO DRINK	TEA WITH MILK	THE ALPHABET
TAKE TO HEART	TEDIOUS TASK	THE ATLANTIC
TAKE TOO MUCH	TEDIOUS WORK	THEATRE BILL
TAKE TROUBLE	TEEMING RAIN	THEATRE CLUB
TAKE UMBRAGE	TEEN-AGE CLUB	THEATRE LAND
TAKE UP A CASE	TEETH ON EDGE	THEATRE SEAT
TAKE WARNING	TELEGRAM BOY	THEATRE SHOW
TALENT MONEY	TELL AGAINST	THE AVENGERS
TALENT SCOUT	TELL NO TALES	THE BARBICAN
TALKING BIRD	TELL THE TALE	THE BASTILLE
TALKING DOLL	TELL THE TIME	THE BEREAVED
TALK OUT TIME	TEMPLE BELLS	THE BEST PART
TALK RUBBISH	TEMPUS FUGIT	THE BIG HOUSE
TALK TOO MUCH	TEN AND A HALF	THE BISMARCK
TALK TREASON	TEN AND EIGHT	THE BITER BIT
TALK TWADDLE	TEN AND SEVEN	THE BLUE LAMP
TALL AND SLIM	TEN AND THREE	THE BOAT RACE
TALLEST GIRL	TENDER HEART	THE CANARIES
TAMMANY HALL	TENDER MERCY	THE CENOTAPH
TAM O'SHANTER	TENDER STEAK	THE CHAMPION
TANK WARFARE	TENDER YEARS	THE CHEVIOTS
TAPE MACHINE	TEND THE SICK	THE CLASSICS
TAP ONE'S FEET	TENNIS COURT	THE COLONIES
TAP ONE'S FOOT	TENNIS DRESS	THE CONQUEST
TAP THE WIRES	TENNIS ELBOW	THE CREATION
TARRY AWHILE	TENNIS MATCH	THE CRUEL SEA
TARTAN PLAID	TEN OF HEARTS	THE CRUSADES
TARTAN SHIRT	TEN OF SPADES	THE DAY AFTER
TARTAN SKIRT	TEN OF TRUMPS	THE EIGHTIES
TARTAN SOCKS	TEN OR ELEVEN	THE ELEMENTS
TASTY MORSEL	TENSE MOMENT	THE FAITHFUL
TATE GALLERY	TENTH LETTER	THE FINE ARTS
TAX INCREASE	TENTH OF JULY	THE FIRST TWO
TEA AND CAKES	TENTH OF JUNE	THE FUGITIVE
TEA AND TOAST	TEN THOUSAND	THE GAME IS UP
TEA CANISTER	TENTH STOREY	THE GREATEST
TEACHER'S PET	TENTH VOLUME	THE GREAT WAR
TEACH SCHOOL	TERM OF ABUSE	THE GREEN MAN
TEACH TO READ	TERM OF YEARS	THE GOLD RUSH
TEACH TO RIDE	TERRY THOMAS	THE GOOD BOOK
TEACH TO SWIM	TERSE SPEECH	THE HAVE-NOTS
TEA FOR THREE	TESSIE O'SHEA	THE HEBRIDES

THE HIGH SEAS
THE HOLY CITY
THE HOLY LAND
THE HUNT IS UP
THE HUSTINGS
THE INFINITE
THE INKSPOTS
THE INNER MAN
THE INNOCENT
THE INTERIOR
THE JUNGFRAU
THE KATTEGAT
THE KING AND I
THE LAST GASP
THE LAST PAGE
THE LAST POST
THE LAST WORD
THE LIBERALS
THE LISTENER
THE LOVED ONE
THE LOWLANDS
THE LUCY SHOW
THE LUDDITES
THE MAJORITY
THE MARATHON
THE MIDLANDS
THE MILKY WAY
THE MIND'S EYE
THE MINISTRY
THE MINORITY
THE MOHICANS
THE MONUMENT
THE MOUNTIES
THE NAKED EYE
THE NEAR EAST
THE NEW WORLD
THE NINETIES
THE OBSERVER
THE OCCIDENT
THE OLD FOLKS
THE OLD GUARD
THE OLD WORLD
THE ONCE-OVER
THE OPEN ROAD
THE OTHER DAY
THE OTHER MAN
THE OTHER ONE
THE OTHER WAY
THE PANTHEON
THE PENNINES
THE PENTAGON

M.C.D.—8

THE PROPHETS
THE PYRAMIDS
THE PYRENEES
THE REVEREND
THERMAL UNIT
THE SERVICES
THE SKIN GAME
THE SORBONNE
THESPIAN ART
THE SQUEAKER
THE SUPREMES
THE TAJ MAHAL
THE TALISMAN
THE THIRD MAN
THE THIRTIES
THE TWENTIES
THE TREASURY
THE UNIVERSE
THE VERY FACT
THE VERY SAME
THE VERY SPOT
THE WALL GAME
THE WAXWORKS
THE WELL-TO-DO
THE WHOLE HOG
THE WHOLE LOT
THE WILD DUCK
THE WOOLSACK
THICK SPEECH
THICK STRING
THIEF OF TIME
THIN AS A LATH
THIN AS A RAKE
THINKING CAP
THINK IT OVER
THINK MUCH OF
THINK WELL OF
THIN RED LINE
THIRD CHOICE
THIRD COURSE
THIRD DEGREE
THIRD ESTATE
THIRD FINGER
THIRD LEAGUE
THIRD LESSON
THIRD LETTER
THIRD OF JULY
THIRD OF JUNE
THIRD PERSON
THIRD SEASON
THIRD STOREY

THIRD STROKE
THIRD VOLUME
THIRST AFTER
THIRSTY WORK
THIRTY FORTY
THIRTY MILES
THIRTY TIMES
THIRTY YEARS
THIS AND THAT
THIS CENTURY
THIS DAY WEEK
THIS ENGLAND
THIS INSTANT
THIS MORNING
THIS TUESDAY
THOMAS HARDY
THRASH IT OUT
THREAD BEADS
THREAT OF WAR
THREE AND ONE
THREE AND SIX
THREE AND TEN
THREE AND TWO
THREE A PENNY
THREE CHEERS
THREE COPIES
THREE DECKER
THREE EIGHTS
THREE FIFTHS
THREE GRACES
THREE HEARTS
THREE KNAVES
THREE MONTHS
THREE O'CLOCK
THREE OR FOUR
THREE OUNCES
THREE POINTS
THREE POUNDS
THREE QUARTS
THREE QUEENS
THREE SEVENS
THREE SPADES
THREE TENTHS
THREE THREES
THREE TRICKS.
THREE WHEELS
THREE WISHES
THREE VERSES
THRESH ABOUT
THROUGH ROAD
THROUGH TRIP

THROW A LIGHT
THROW A PARTY
THROW A PUNCH
THROW STONES
THRUST ASIDE
THUMPING LIE
TICKLED PINK
TICKLE TROUT
TICKLISH JOB
TIDAL WATERS
TIDE ONE OVER
TIED COTTAGE
TIED IN A KNOT
TIES OF BLOOD
TIGHT CORNER
TILL THE SOIL
TIMBER TRADE
TIME AND TIDE
TIME ELEMENT
TIME IS MONEY
TIME MACHINE
TIME OF NIGHT
TIMES CHANGE
TIMES SQUARE
TIME TO GET UP
TIME TO LEAVE
TIME TO SPARE
TIME TO START
TIME TO THINK
TIME TO WASTE
TINKER'S CUSS
TINKER'S DAMN
TINNED BEANS
TINNED FRUIT
TINNED GOODS
TINNED MUSIC
TINNED PEARS
TIN OF POLISH
TIN OF SALMON
TIN PAN ALLEY
TIN SOLDIERS
TIP THE SCALE
TIRED OF LIFE
TISSUE PAPER
TITLE HOLDER
TOAST MASTER
TOBACCO ROAD
TOBOGGAN RUN
TODDLE ALONG
TOFFEE APPLE
TOILET WATER

TOKEN OF LOVE
TOLL THE BELL
TOMATO JUICE
TOMATO SAUCE
TOMMY ATKINS
TOMMY COOPER
TOMMY DORSEY
TOMMY STEELE
TOMMY TUCKER
TONE CONTROL
TONE OF VOICE
TON OF BRICKS
TO NO PURPOSE
TONS AND TONS
TONS OF MONEY
TONY HANCOCK
TOO FAMILIAR
TOO MUCH ROOM
TOP-BACK ROOM
TOPICAL NEWS
TOP SERGEANT
TOP TO BOTTOM
TORCH SINGER
TORPEDO BOAT
TORPEDO TUBE
TOSS AND TURN
TOTAL AMOUNT
TOTAL CHANGE
TOTAL DEFEAT
TOTAL NUMBER
TOTAL OUTPUT
TO THE BOTTOM
TO THE LETTER
TO THE MINUTE
TO THE RESCUE
TO THE TUNE OF
TO THE UTMOST
TOTTER ABOUT
TOUCH BOTTOM
TOUCH GROUND
TOUCH TYPING
TOUCH TYPIST
TOUGH AS TEAK
TOUR DE FORCE
TOUSLED HAIR
TOUT DE SUITE
TOUT LE MONDE
TOWER BRIDGE
TOWER OF PISA
TOWN AND GOWN
TOWN COUNCIL

TOWN DWELLER
TRADE SECRET
TRADING POST
TRAFFIC LANE
TRAGIC EVENT
TRAGIC IRONY
TRAGIC SCENE
TRAIL BEHIND
TRAIL BLAZER
TRAIL DRIVER
TRAIL OF DUST
TRAIL OF SAND
TRAINED BAND
TRAMPLE DOWN
TRANSFER FEE
TRAVEL ABOUT
TRAVEL AGENT
TRAVEL ALONG
TRAVEL LIGHT
TREACLE TART
TREAD SOFTLY
TREAD WARILY
TREE DWELLER
TREE SURGERY
TRENCH FEVER
TRENT BRIDGE
TRIAL BY JURY
TRIAL FLIGHT
TRIAL PERIOD
TRIAL STAKES
TRICK RIDING
TRIED BY JURY
TRIM THE HAIR
TRIM THE LAMP
TRIM THE WICK
TRINITY HALL
TRINITY TERM
TRIPLE CROWN
TRIPLE EVENT
TRIP LIGHTLY
TRITE REMARK
TRIUMPH OVER
TRIVIAL LOSS
TROJAN HORSE
TROPICAL KIT
TROPICAL SEA
TROPICAL SUN
TROUBLE FREE
TROUBLE SPOT
TROUT STREAM
TRUCK DRIVER

TRUDGE ALONG	TWELVE YEARS	UNBROKEN RUN
TRUE ACCOUNT	TWENTY MILES	UNCALLED FOR
TRUE COLOURS	TWENTY TIMES	UNDER A CLOUD
TRUE EQUINOX	TWENTY TO ONE	UNDER A CURSE
TRUE PICTURE	TWENTY WEEKS	UNDER ARREST
TRUE READING	TWICE A MONTH	UNDER A SPELL
TRUE TO SCALE	TWICE AS MUCH	UNDER CANVAS
TRULY SPOKEN	TWICE AS NICE	UNDER DURESS
TRUMPET CALL	TWICE ELEVEN	UNDER NOTICE
TRUNDLE DOWN	TWICE THE MAN	UNDER ORDERS
TRUST TO LUCK	TWICE TWELVE	UNDER PAROLE
TRUSTY STEED	TWICE WEEKLY	UNDER REPAIR
TRUSTY SWORD	TWICE YEARLY	UNDER REVIEW
TRUTH TO TELL	TWIN BROTHER	UNDER STRAIN
TRYING TIMES	TWIN SISTERS	UNDER STRESS
TRY ONE'S BEST	TWIST AROUND	UNDER THE MAT
TRY ONE'S HAND	TWIST THE ARM	UNDER THE SEA
TRY ONE'S LUCK	TWO AND A HALF	UNDER THE SUN
TRY TO BE FAIR	TWO AND EIGHT	UNDER WEIGHT
TRY TO PLEASE	TWO AND SEVEN	UNDYING LOVE
TRY, TRY AGAIN	TWO AND THREE	UNEASY TRUCE
TUBE STATION	TWO DIAMONDS	UNFAIR MEANS
TUDOR PERIOD	TWO EXTREMES	UNFAIR PRICE
TUESDAY WEEK	TWO-FEET TALL	UNFIT FOR USE
TUFT OF GRASS	TWO-FOOT RULE	UNFOLD A TALE
TUITION FEES	TWO FURLONGS	UNHOLY NOISE
TURKISH BATH	TWO HUSBANDS	UNIFORM HEAT
TURN AGAINST	TWO NO-TRUMPS	UNIFORM SIZE
TURN CRIMSON	TWO OF A TRADE	UNION LEADER
TURN HOSTILE	TWO OF SPADES	UNITED FRONT
TURN OF SPEED	TWO OF TRUMPS	UNITED PRESS
TURN OUT WELL	TWO'S COMPANY	UNIT OF SOUND
TURN THE PAGE	TWO SEVENTHS	UNLAWFUL ACT
TURN THE TIDE	TWO THOUSAND	UNLICKED CUB
TURN TO ASHES	TYPE A LETTER	UNLUCKY STAR
TURN TO STONE	TYPICAL CASE	UNSHED TEARS
TURN TRAITOR	TYPING ERROR	UNSOUND MIND
TURN UPWARDS	TYPING SPEED	UNTIMELY END
TWEED JACKET	TYPISTS' POOL	UNUSUAL NAME
TWELFTH HOLE	TYROLEAN HAT	UP AGAINST IT
TWELFTH HOUR		UP AND COMING
TWELFTH PART	**U—11**	UP FOR THE CUP
TWELVE DOZEN	UGLY RUFFIAN	UP FOR THE DAY
TWELVE GROSS	UGLY SISTERS	UPHILL CLIMB
TWELVE HOURS	UGLY THOUGHT	UPHILL FIGHT
TWELVE MILES	UGLY WEATHER	UP ON A CHARGE
TWELVE PARTS	ULTIMATE END	UPPER CIRCLE
TWELVE PENCE	ULTIMA THULE	UPPER SCHOOL
TWELVE SCORE	ULTRA VIOLET	UPPER STOREY
TWELVE TIMES	UMBRELLA MAN	UPRIGHT POST
TWELVE WEEKS	UNABLE TO PAY	UPS AND DOWNS

UP THE REBELS!
UP THE STAIRS
UP THE STREET
UP THE THAMES
UP TO SCRATCH
UP TO THE EARS
UP TO THE EYES
UP TO THE HILT
UP TO THE MARK
UP TO THE NECK
UPWARD TREND
URSULA BLOOM
USELESS WORD
USE ONE'S EARS
USE ONE'S HEAD
USE ONE'S LOAF
USE ONE'S WITS
USE THE KNIFE
USE THE 'PHONE
USE THE PRESS
USE VIOLENCE
USUAL CUSTOM
UTMOST SPEED
UTTER BUNKUM
UTTER COWARD
UTTER DEFEAT
UTTER MISERY

V—11
VACANT HOUSE
VACANT STARE
VACUUM BRAKE
VACUUM FLASK
VAGRANCY ACT
VAIN ATTEMPT
VAL DOONICAN
VALE OF TEARS
VALID REASON
VALLEY FORGE
VANITY TABLE
VAPOUR TRAIL
VARIETY SHOW
VAST ACREAGE
VAST EXPANSE
VAST EXPENSE
VATICAN CITY
VAULTED ROOF
VELVET GLOVE
VELVET TREAD
VENETIAN RED
VENUS DI MILO

VERY PLEASED
VERY SPECIAL
VERY STRANGE
VERY WELL OFF
VERY WORRIED
VESTA TILLEY
V FOR VICTORY
VICAR OF BRAY
VICTORIA DAY
VICTORY ROLL
VICTORY SIGN
VIENNA WOODS
VILLAGE FÉTE
VILLAGE HALL
VILLAGE LIFE
VILLAGE POND
VILLAGE PUMP
VILLAGE SHOP
VILLAGE TALK
VILLAGE TEAM
VINTAGE PORT
VINTAGE WINE
VINTAGE YEAR
VIOLENT BLOW
VIOLENT RAGE
VIRGIN BIRTH
VIRGIN QUEEN
VIRILE STYLE
VISITING DAY
VITAL ENERGY
VITAMIN PILL
VIVID COLOUR
VIVID YELLOW
VIVIEN LEIGH
VOCAL CHORDS
VOCAL EFFORT
VOCAL NUMBER
VOCAL ORGANS
VOCAL TALENT
VOICE OF DOOM
VOID OF SENSE
VOLATILE OIL
VOLATILE WIT
VOLCANIC ASH
VOLUME THREE
VOTE AGAINST
VOTE BY PROXY
VOTE LIBERAL
VOTE TO ORDER
VOTING PAPER

W—11
WADDLE ALONG
WADE THROUGH
WAG ONE'S HEAD
WAGON WHEELS
WAILING WALL
WAIT A MINUTE
WAIT A MOMENT
WAIT A SECOND
WAIT AT TABLE
WAITING GAME
WAITING LIST
WAITING ROOM
WAKE THE DEAD
WAKE UP EARLY
WAKING DREAM
WAKING HOURS
WALK IN FRONT
WALKING PACE
WALKING RACE
WALKING TOUR
WALK OFF WITH
WALK OUT WITH
WALK QUICKLY
WALK TOWARDS
WALK UPRIGHT
WALL OF DEATH
WALL OF FLAME
WALLOW IN MUD
WALTER MITTY
WALTER SCOTT
WALT WHITMAN
WANDER ABOUT
WANDER ALONG
WANING LIGHT
WANT OF FAITH
WAR AND PEACE
WAR CRIMINAL
WARD OF COURT
WARD ORDERLY
WARM AS TOAST
WARM CLIMATE
WARM CLOTHES
WARM COUNTRY
WAR MEASURES
WAR MEMORIAL
WAR MINISTER
WARM WEATHER
WARM WELCOME
WAR NEUROSES
WARNING LOOK

WARNING NOTE
WARNING SHOT
WARNING SIGN
WAR OF NERVES
WARP AND WEFT
WARP AND WOOF
WASHING SOAP
WASHING SODA
WASTE GROUND
WASTE NO TIME
WASTE OF TIME
WATCHFUL EYE
WATCH POCKET
WATCH POINTS
WATER BABIES
WATER COLOUR
WATERED SILK
WATERLOO CUP
WATER OF LIFE
WATER PISTOL
WATER SKIING
WATER SPORTS
WATER SUPPLY
WATER TRAVEL
WATER VAPOUR
WATERY GRAVE
WAVE GOODBYE
WEAK AS WATER
WEAKEST LINK
WEAK LOOKING
WEAK SERVICE
WEAK STOMACH
WEALD OF KENT
WEAR AND TEAR
WEARY WILLIE
WEATHER SHIP
WEATHER SIDE
WEAVE A SPELL
WEAVE SPELLS
WEB OF DECEIT
WEDDED BLISS
WEDDING CAKE
WEDDING CARD
WEDDING HYMN
WEDDING RING
WEDDING VOWS
WEEKLY PAPER
WEEK'S NOTICE
WEIGH ANCHOR
WEIRD SISTER
WELCOME GIFT

WELCOME HOME
WELCOME SIGN
WELFARE WORK
WELL AND GOOD
WELL CONTENT
WELL GROOMED
WELL IN FRONT
WELL MATCHED
WELL OUT OF IT
WELL-READ MAN
WELL-TO-DO MAN
WELL WORTH IT
WELL WRITTEN
WELSH ACCENT
WELSH BORDER
WELSH COLLIE
WELSH GUARDS
WELSH LEGEND
WELSH RABBIT
WELSH WIZARD
WEND ONE'S WAY
WENDY HILLER
WENT FLAT OUT
WEST AFRICAN
WEST BY NORTH
WEST BY SOUTH
WEST CENTRAL
WEST COUNTRY
WESTERN ROLE
WESTERN ROLL
WEST GERMANY
WET ONE'S LIPS
WHACKING LIE
WHAT A RELIEF!
WHAT HAVE YOU
WHAT'S MY LINE?
WHAT YOU WILL
WHEEL OF LIFE
WHEN PIGS FLY
WHIPPING BOY
WHISTLE AWAY
WHISTLE STOP
WHITE AS MILK
WHITE AS SNOW
WHITE BISHOP
WHITE CASTLE
WHITE CIRCLE
WHITE CLIFFS
WHITE COFFEE
WHITE COLLAR
WHITE COTTON

WHITE ENSIGN
WHITE FRIARS
WHITE HORSES
WHITE KNIGHT
WHITE PEPPER
WHITE POWDER
WHITE RABBIT
WHITE RIBBON
WHITE RUSSIA
WHITE SQUARE
WHITE TO MOVE
WHITE TO PLAY
WHITSUN WEEK
WHITTLE AWAY
WHITTLE DOWN
WHO GOES HOME?
WHOLE NUMBER
WICKED FAIRY
WICKED UNCLE
WICKED WITCH
WICKED WORLD
WICKER CHAIR
WIDEN THE GAP
WIDE READING
WIDE VARIETY
WIDOW'S CRUSE
WIDOW'S WEEDS
WIELD THE BAT
WIGHTMAN CUP
WILD COUNTRY
WILD DELIGHT
WILD FLOWERS
WILFUL WASTE
WILLIAM PEAR
WILLIAM PENN
WILLIAM PITT
WILLIAM TELL
WILLING HAND
WILLING HELP
WILL OF ALLAH
WIN A FORTUNE
WINDING ROAD
WIND ONE'S WAY
WINDY CORNER
WINE AND DINE
WINE HARVEST
WINE VINEGAR
WINGED HORSE
WINGED WORDS
WING FORWARD
WING ONE'S WAY

WINK OF SLEEP
WINNING CARD
WINNING GAME
WINNING GOAL
WINNING HAND
WINNING LEAD
WINNING LINE
WINNING MOVE
WINNING POST
WINNING SHOT
WINNING SIDE
WINNING TEAM
WINNING TOSS
WINNING WAYS
WIN ON POINTS
WIN OUTRIGHT
WINSOME WAYS
WINSON GREEN
WINTER SLEEP
WINTER WHEAT
WIN THE FIGHT
WIN THE MATCH
WIN THE POOLS
WIN THE TITLE
WIN THE TRICK
WINTRY SMILE
WIPE THE EYES
WIRELESS SET
WISDOM TOOTH
WISE AS AN OWL
WISE AS SOLON
WISE COUNSEL
WISE OLD BIRD
WISHING WELL
WITCH DOCTOR
WITCHES' BREW
WITCH'S SPELL
WITH ABANDON
WITH HONOURS
WITHIN AN ACE
WITHIN DOORS
WITHIN RANGE
WITHIN REACH
WITHIN SIGHT
WITH KNOBS ON
WITH MEANING
WITHOUT BIAS
WITHOUT FAIL
WITHOUT HOPE
WITHOUT LOSS
WITHOUT PEER

WITHOUT PITY
WITH RESERVE
WITH RESPECT
WITH THE TIDE
WITH THE WIND
WITTY REMARK
WITTY RETORT
WITTY SPEECH
WIZARD PRANG
WOBURN ABBEY
WOLF WHISTLE
WOMAN DOCTOR
WOMAN DRIVER
WOMAN'S WORLD
WOMEN POLICE
WOMEN'S GUILD
WOOD ALCOHOL
WOODEN FRAME
WOODEN HORSE
WOODEN SPOON
WOOL SHEARER
WORD FOR WORD
WORD OF MOUTH
WORD PERFECT
WORD PICTURE
WORDS FAIL ME!
WORK AGAINST
WORK AND PLAY
WORK AS A TEAM
WORKING LIFE
WORKING WEEK
WORKS OUTING
WORK TO DEATH
WORK WONDERS
WORLD BEATER
WORLD CRUISE
WORLD EVENTS
WORLDLY WISE
WORLD RECORD
WORLDS APART
WORLD TO COME
WORLD-WAR ONE
WORLD-WAR TWO
WORM ONE'S WAY
WORRIED LOOK
WORSE TO COME
WORTH SEEING
WORTHY CAUSE
WRAPPED LOAF
WRESTLE WITH
WRETCHED MAN

WRINGING WET
WRITE A LYRIC
WRITE A NOVEL
WRITE A STORY
WRITE IT DOWN
WRITE POETRY
WRITING DESK
WRITING ROOM
WRITTEN WORD
WRONG ANSWER
WRONG CHANGE
WRONG COURSE
WRONG MOMENT
WRONG NUMBER
WRONG PERSON
WRONG TICKET
WROUGHT IRON

Y—11
YACHTING CAP
YACHT RACING
YARD MEASURE
YEAR AND A DAY
YEAR OF GRACE
YEARS GONE BY
YEARS TO COME
YELLOW FEVER
YELLOW METAL
YELLOW OCHRE
YELLOW PAINT
YELLOW PERIL
YELLOW PRESS
YELLOW RIVER
YELLOW SANDS
YELLOW SPOTS
YIELD A POINT
YOLK OF AN EGG
YORK MINSTER
YOU AND YOURS
YOUNG AND OLD
YOUNGEST BOY
YOUNGEST SON
YOUNG MONKEY
YOUNG PEOPLE
YOUNG PERSON
YOUNG RASCAL
YOUR MAJESTY
YOUR OPINION
YOURS ALWAYS
YOUR VERSION
YOUR VERY OWN

YOUR WORSHIP
YOUTH CENTRE
YOUTH HOSTEL
YOUTH LEADER

A—12
ABBEY THEATRE
ABILITY TO MIX
ABJECT SPIRIT
ABLATIVE CASE
ABOUT AVERAGE
ABOVE AVERAGE
ABOVE THE LINE
ABRUPT MANNER
ABSOLUTE COLD
ABSOLUTE FACT
ABSOLUTE FOOL
ABSOLUTE RULE
ABSOLUTE ZERO
ABSTRACT IDEA
ABSTRACT NOUN
ABSTRACT TERM
ABSURD MANNER
ABUSE THE MIND
ACADEMY AWARD
ACCEPT ADVICE
ACCEPT DEFEAT
ACCEPT IN TOTO
ACCEPT OFFICE
ACCIDENT SPOT
ACE IN THE HOLE
ACHILLES' HEEL
ACROSS THE SKY
ACROSS THE WAY
ACT FOOLISHLY
ACT IN CONCERT
ACTION SCHOOL
ACTIVE MEMBER
ACT LIKE A FOOL
ACT LIKE MAGIC
ACT OF CHARITY
ACT OF COURAGE
ACT OF TREASON
ACT OF WORSHIP
ACT OF IMPULSE
ACTOR MANAGER
ADAGIO DANCER
ADD A FEW WORDS
ADDER'S TONGUE
ADDITION SIGN

ADD TO THE LIST
ADELINA PATTI
ADHESIVE TAPE
ADJUTANT BIRD
ADMIT NOTHING
ADMIT ONE'S AGE
ADMITTED FACT
ADMITTED FREE
ADOPTED CHILD
ADVANCED IDEA
ADVANCE GUARD
ADVANCE PARTY
AERATED WATER
AERIAL SURVEY
AESOP'S FABLES
AFFECTED AIRS
A FINE ROMANCE
AFRICAN QUEEN
AFTERNOON NAP
AFTERNOON TEA
AFTER SUNDOWN
AFTER THE BALL
AFTER THE FACT
AFTER THE RAIN
AGE OF CONSENT
AGREED RESULT
AGREE TO TERMS
AIM AT THE MOON
AIR COMMODORE
AIR-FORCE BLUE
AIR OF MYSTERY
AIR OF TRIUMPH
AIR ONE'S VIEWS
AIR PASSENGER
AIR PERSONNEL
AIR-SEA RESCUE
AIR TRANSPORT
AIR TRAVELLER
ALADDIN'S CAVE
ALADDIN'S LAMP
ALAN MELVILLE
ALAS AND ALACK!
ALBERT BRIDGE
ALBERT FINNEY
ALDOUS HUXLEY
ALEC GUINNESS
ALEXANDRA DAY
ALFRESCO MEAL
ALGERIAN WINE
ALICE SPRINGS
ALIEN ELEMENT

ALIGN ONESELF
ALL AND SUNDRY
ALL ATTENTION
ALL BY ONESELF
ALLIED FORCES
ALLIED TROOPS
ALL IN THE GAME
ALL IN THE MIND
ALL IS NOT LOST
ALL MOONSHINE
ALL MY OWN WORK
ALL NIGHT LONG
ALL OF A DITHER
ALL OF A QUIVER
ALL OF A SUDDEN
ALL OF THE TIME
ALL ON ONE SIDE
ALL ON ONE'S OWN
ALL OR NOTHING
ALLOTTED SPAN
ALLOTTED TASK
ALLOW TO STAND
ALL SAINTS' DAY
ALL STEAMED UP
ALL THE BETTER
ALL THE FAMILY
ALL THE OTHERS
ALL TO PLAY FOR
ALL TO THE GOOD
ALMOND TOFFEE
A LONG TIME AGO
ALPACA JACKET
ALPHA TO OMEGA
ALPINE FLOWER
ALPINE GARDEN
ALTER THE CASE
AMATEUR ACTOR
AMATEUR BOXER
AMATEUR STAGE
AMERICAN FILM
AMERICAN FLAG
AMERICAN NAVY
A MILE A MINUTE
AMONG FRIENDS
AMOROUS DITTY
AMUSE ONESELF
ANCHOVY PASTE
ANCHOVY SAUCE
ANCIENT HOUSE
ANCIENT ROMAN
ANCIENT RUINS

ANCIENT TIMES
ANCIENT WORLD
ANEURIN BEVAN
ANGELIC SMILE
ANGEL OF DEATH
ANGEL OF MERCY
ANGELS OF MONS
ANGORA RABBIT
ANGRY SILENCE
ANIMAL DOCTOR
ANNA KARENINA
ANNE HATHAWAY
ANNE OF CLEVES
ANNUAL AFFAIR
ANNUAL BUDGET
ANNUAL DINNER
ANNUAL OUTING
ANNUAL REPORT
ANNUAL RETURN
ANOTHER GUESS
ANOTHER STORY
ANOTHER THING
ANY QUESTIONS
ANYTHING GOES
APOSTLE SPOON
APPEAL TO ARMS
APPLE BLOSSOM
APPLE FRITTER
APPLE HARVEST
APPLE OF SODOM
APPLE ORCHARD
APPLY FOR A JOB
APPLY FOR BAIL
APPLY ONESELF
APPLY THE MIND
APPROACH ROAD
APPROACH SHOT
APPROVED LIST
APRIL IN PARIS
APRIL SHOWERS
APRON STRINGS
APTITUDE TEST
APT QUOTATION
AQUATIC PLANT
AQUATIC SPORT
AQUILINE NOSE
ARCH CRIMINAL
ARCH OF HEAVEN
ARCH ONE'S BACK
ARCTIC CIRCLE
ARCTIC REGION

ARCTIC WINTER
ARDENT SPIRIT
ARGUE THE CASE
ARGUE THE TOSS
ARMED ROBBERY
ARMISTICE DAY
ARMY CHAPLAIN
ARMY EXERCISE
ARMY GRATUITY
ARMY PAY CORPS
ARMY QUARTERS
ARNOLD WESKER
ARRANGE A DATE
ARRESTER GEAR
ARRIVE ON TIME
ART CRITICISM
ARTERIAL ROAD
ARTESIAN WELL
ARTFUL DODGER
ARTHUR MILLER
ARTISTIC WORK
ARTIST'S MODEL
ARTIST'S PROOF
ART OF DEFENCE
ART OF HEALING
ART TREASURES
ASBESTOS SUIT
AS BLACK AS INK
AS BUSY AS A BEE
ASCENSION DAY
AS CLEAR AS DAY
AS CLEAR AS MUD
ASCOT GOLD CUP
AS GOOD AS DEAD
AS GOOD AS EVER
AS GOOD AS GOLD
ASHES TO ASHES
ASH WEDNESDAY
ASK A QUESTION
ASK FOR ADVICE
ASK FOR CREDIT
ASK ME ANOTHER
ASK NO FAVOURS
ASK QUESTIONS
AS LIGHT AS AIR
AS MUCH AS EVER
ASSEMBLY HALL
ASSEMBLY LINE
ASSEMBLY ROOM
ASSUMED TITLE
AS SURE AS EGGS

AS SURE AS FATE
AS SWEET AS PIE
AS UNDERSTOOD
AT A LATER DATE
AT ALL HAZARDS
AT ARM'S LENGTH
AT CLOSE GRIPS
AT DEATH'S DOOR
AT FIRST SIGHT
AT FULL GALLOP
AT FULL LENGTH
ATHLETE'S FOOT
ATLANTIC CITY
ATOMIC ENERGY
ATOMIC NUMBER
ATOMIC THEORY
ATOMIC WEIGHT
AT SECOND-HAND
AT SOME LENGTH
ATTAR OF ROSES
ATTEND CHURCH
AT THE LAUNDRY
AT THE SEASIDE
AT THE STATION
AT THE THEATRE
AT THE WEIGH-IN
AT WHICH PLACE
AUCTION ROOMS
AULD LANG SYNE
AUSTIN FRIARS
AUTUMN CROCUS
AUTUMN LEAVES
AVERAGE CHILD
AVERAGE SPEED
AVERAGE WOMAN
AWAIT PAYMENT
AWAKE THE DEAD
AWAY DULL CARE!
AWAY FROM HOME
AWFUL SILENCE
AWKWARD SQUAD

B—12
BABY CARRIAGE
BABY SNATCHER
BACHELOR FLAT
BACHELOR GIRL
BACK AND FORTH
BACK AND FRONT
BACK ENTRANCE

BACK OF BEYOND
BACK-ROOM BOYS
BACK THE FIELD
BACK TO MOTHER
BACK TO NATURE
BACK TO NORMAL
BACKWARD STEP
BACON AND EGGS
BAD BEGINNING
BAD BEHAVIOUR
BAD CHARACTER
BAD CONDUCTOR
BAD DIGESTION
BAD ELOCUTION
BADGE OF MERIT
BAD HALFPENNY
BAD HOUSEWIFE
BAD INFLUENCE
BADLY BEHAVED
BADLY DAMAGED
BADLY WOUNDED
BAD NEIGHBOUR
BAD OF ITS KIND
BAD QUALITIES
BAD REPORTING
BAD TREATMENT
BAG OF TOFFEES
BAILEY BRIDGE
BAKED CUSTARD
BAKEWELL TART
BAKING POWDER
BALANCED DIET
BALANCED MIND
BALANCE SHEET
BALANCE WHEEL
BALANCING ACT
BALCONY SCENE
BALKAN STATES
BALLAD SINGER
BALL AND CHAIN
BALL BEARINGS
BALLET DANCER
BALLET MASTER
BALLET SCHOOL
BALL OF STRING
BALL OF THREAD
BALL-POINT PEN
BALM OF GILEAD
BALTIC STATES
BAMBOO SHOOTS
BANBURY CROSS

BAND OF HEROES
BAND TOGETHER
BANG IN THE EYE
BANG ONE'S HEAD
BANKER'S DRAFT
BANKER'S ORDER
BANKING HOURS
BANK INTEREST
BARBARA KELLY
BARBARY COAST
BARBARY SHEEP
BARBER'S CHAIR
BARCLAY'S BANK
BARE CUPBOARD
BAREFACED LIE
BARE MAJORITY
BARE ONE'S HEAD
BARGAIN PRICE
BARKING CREEK
BARNABY RUDGE
BARNACLE BILL
BARNES BRIDGE
BARNES COMMON
BARNYARD FOWL
BAROQUE STYLE
BARRED WINDOW
BARREL OF BEER
BARS AND BOLTS
BASEBALL TEAM
BASEMENT FLAT
BASIC ENGLISH
BASK IN THE SUN
BASS CLARINET
BATCH OF BREAD
BATHING BEACH
BATTERING RAM
BATTING ORDER
BATTLE OF LIFE
BATTLE OF WITS
BAY AT THE MOON
BAYONET DRILL
BEACH PYJAMAS
BEAMING SMILE
BEANS ON TOAST
BEARDED WOMAN
BEAR DOWN UPON
BEARD THE LION
BEARER CHEQUE
BEAR THE BLAME
BEAR THE BRUNT
BEAT A RETREAT

BEATEN HOLLOW
BEATING HEART
BEAT THE CLOCK
BEAT THE COUNT
BEAUTY OF MIND
BECHER'S BROOK
BECOME PUBLIC
BECOME SILENT
BED OF NETTLES
BED-TIME STORY
BEEF SANDWICH
BEEF SAUSAGES
BEFORE CHRIST
BEFORE DINNER
BEFORE SUPPER
BEFORE THE WAR
BEG FOR CRUMBS
BEGGAR'S OPERA
BEHIND THE BAR
BELGIAN CONGO
BELOVED ENEMY
BELOW AVERAGE
BELOW THE BELT
BELOW THE KNEE
BELOW THE LINE
BELOW THE MARK
BENARES BRASS
BEND BACKWARD
BEND SINISTER
BEND THE ELBOW
BEND THE RULES
BENEFIT MATCH
BENEFIT NIGHT
BENIGN MANNER
BENNY GOODMAN
BE OFF WITH YOU!
BEREFT OF LIFE
BERING STRAIT
BERNARD MILES
BERTRAM MILLS
BESETTING SIN
BESIDE THE SEA
BEST OF THE LOT
BEST ONE CAN DO
BETHNAL GREEN
BET ON THE SIDE
BETRAY A TRUST
BETTER CHOICE
BETTER THINGS
BETTING HOUSE
BETWEEN MEALS

BETWEEN TIMES	BLACK CLOTHES	BOLT ONE'S FOOD
BEVERLY HILLS	BLACK COUNTRY	BOMB DISPOSAL
BEXHILL ON SEA	BLACK DESPAIR	BONFIRE NIGHT
BEYOND A DOUBT	BLACK LOOK-OUT	BONNY WEE LASS
BEYOND BELIEF	BLACK OR WHITE	BOOK A PASSAGE
BEYOND BOUNDS	BLACK OUTLOOK	BOOK A SLEEPER
BEYOND REASON	BLACK PUDDING	BOOKING CLERK
BEYOND RECALL	BLADE OF GRASS	BOOK LEARNING
BEYOND REPAIR	BLARNEY STONE	BOOK OF PSALMS
BEYOND THE LAW	BLASTED HEATH	BOOK OF STAMPS
BIB AND TUCKER	BLAST FURNACE	BOOK OF WISDOM
BIBLE SOCIETY	BLAZE OF GLORY	BORDER BALLAD
BIBLE THUMPER	BLAZE OF LIGHT	BORED TO DEATH
BICYCLE CHAIN	BLEACHED HAIR	BORED TO TEARS
BICYCLE THIEF	BLEAK OUTLOOK	BORIS KARLOFF
BIDE ONE'S TIME	BLEED TO DEATH	BORN IN A TRUNK
BIG AND LITTLE	BLESSED STATE	BORN OPTIMIST
BIG HINDRANCE	BLIND BARGAIN	BORROW A FIVER
BIG OFFENSIVE	BLIND IMPULSE	BORROW A POUND
BILLIARD BALL	BLITHE SPIRIT	BORROWED TIME
BILLIARD HALL	BLOATER PASTE	BOSOM FRIENDS
BILLIARD REST	BLOCK LETTERS	BOTH ENDS MEET
BILLIARD ROOM	BLOCK OF FLATS	BOTH TOGETHER
BILL OF HEALTH	BLOCK OF STONE	BOTTLED CIDER
BILL OF LADING	BLONDE-HAIRED	BOTTLED FRUIT
BILL OF RIGHTS	BLOOD AND IRON	BOTTLE OF BEER
BILLYCOCK HAT	BLOOD AND SAND	BOTTLE OF HOCK
BIRDCAGE WALK	BLOOD BROTHER	BOTTLE OF MILK
BIRD'S-EYE VIEW	BLOOD DISEASE	BOTTLE OF PORT
BIRD WATCHING	BLOOM OF YOUTH	BOTTLE OF WINE
BIRTH CONTROL	BLOSSOM FORTH	BOTTLE OPENER
BIRTHDAY CAKE	BLOW A WHISTLE	BOTTOM DOLLAR
BIRTHDAY CARD	BLOWN SKY-HIGH	BOTTOM DRAWER
BIRTHDAY GIFT	BLOW OFF STEAM	BOTTOM WEIGHT
BIRTHDAY SUIT	BLOW TO PIECES	BOULTER'S LOCK
BISHOP'S APRON	BLUE AS THE SKY	BOUNCING BABY
BISHOP'S MITRE	BLUE-BLACK INK	BOUNDARY LINE
BITE ONE'S LIPS	BLUE STOCKING	BOUND EDITION
BITE THE THUMB	BLUE WITH COLD	BOW AND SCRAPE
BIT OF AN UPSET	BLUFF KING HAL	BOWLING ALLEY
BIT OF SCANDAL	BOARD MEETING	BOWLING GREEN
BIT OF TROUBLE	BOARD OF TRADE	BOXING GLOVES
BITTERLY COLD	BOB MONKHOUSE	BOX OF MATCHES
BITTER MEMORY	BOB UP AND DOWN	BOX ON THE EARS
BITTER ORANGE	BODY OF TROOPS	BOY ARTIFICER
BITTER STRIFE	BODY SNATCHER	BOY MEETS GIRL
BITTER TONGUE	BOHEMIAN GIRL	BRACE OF BIRDS
BLACK AND BLUE	BOILED SWEETS	BRACE ONESELF
BLACK AND TANS	BOILING POINT	BRAIN SURGEON
BLACK AS NIGHT	BOILING WATER	BRAIN SURGERY
BLACK AS PITCH	BOIL WITH RAGE	BRAIN WASHING

BRAISED STEAK
BRAMBLE JELLY
BRANCH MEMBER
BRANCH OFFICE
BRANDED GOODS
BRANDING IRON
BRANDY BOTTLE
BRANDY BUTTER
BRASS SECTION
BRAVE AS A LION
BRAVE ATTEMPT
BRAVE WARRIOR
BREAD AND MILK
BREAD AND WINE
BREAD PUDDING
BREAK A RECORD
BREAK CONTACT
BREAKFAST CUP
BREAK NO BONES
BREAK RECORDS
BREAK SURFACE
BREAK THE BANK
BREAK THE NEWS
BREAK THE RULE
BREAK THE SEAL
BREAK THROUGH
BREAST POCKET
BREAST STROKE
BREATHE AGAIN
BREATH OF LIFE
BREECHES BUOY
BREEZY MANNER
BRICK BY BRICK
BRIDGE LESSON
BRIDGE PLAYER
BRIDGE THE GAP
BRIEF OUTLINE
BRIEF SUMMARY
BRIGADE MAJOR
BRIGHT COLOUR
BRIGHT LIGHTS
BRIGHTON ROCK
BRIGHT PERIOD
BRIGHT PURPLE
BRIGHT YELLOW
BRILLIANT WIT
BRING A CHARGE
BRING COMFORT
BRING FORWARD
BRING THROUGH
BRING TO A HEAD

BRING TO AN END
BRING TO LIGHT
BRING TO TERMS
BRING TO TRIAL
BRISTOL BOARD
BRISTOL CREAM
BRITISH ISLES
BROAD OUTLINE
BROAD OUTLOOK
BROKEN ACCENT
BROKEN GROUND
BROKEN THREAD
BROKEN VOYAGE
BROKEN WINDOW
BROOK NO DELAY
BROUGHT FORTH
BROWN AND MILD
BROWN WINDSOR
BRUCE FORSYTH
BRUIN THE BEAR
BRUSH AGAINST
BRUSH AND COMB
BRUSSELS LACE
BUCKING HORSE
BUDDHIST MONK
BUDDING ACTOR
BUDDING YOUTH
BUDGET SPEECH
BUGLE-CALL RAG
BUILD A BRIDGE
BUILDER'S MATE
BUILDING LAND
BUILDING PLOT
BUILDING SITE
BUILT OF STONE
BUILT ON A ROCK
BULBOUS PLANT
BULLDOG BREED
BULL ELEPHANT
BUNCH OF ROSES
BUNDLE OF RAGS
BUNSEN BURNER
BURGLAR ALARM
BURIAL GROUND
BURMA CHEROOT
BURNHAM SCALE
BURNING FEVER
BURNING GLASS
BURNING SHAME
BURNING TORCH
BURNT ALMONDS

BURNT FINGERS
BURNT TO ASHES
BURN WITH LOVE
BURST OF ANGER
BURST OF SOUND
BURST OF SPEED
BURY ONE'S HEAD
BUS CONDUCTOR
BUSINESS DEAL
BUSINESS LIFE
BUSINESS TRIP
BUSTER KEATON
BUTCHER'S SHOP
BUTTERED ROLL
BUTTERFLY NET
BUYER'S MARKET
BY A LONG CHALK
BY COMPARISON
BY EASY STAGES
BY FAR THE BEST
BY PERSUASION
BY THE SEASIDE
BY THE WAYSIDE
BY WAY OF A JOKE

C—12
CABBAGE PATCH
CABIN CRUISER
CABINET MAKER
CABIN STEWARD
CABLE RAILWAY
CABLE'S LENGTH
CAFÉ CHANTANT
CAIRN TERRIER
CAKED WITH MUD
CALABASH PIPE
CALAMITY JANE
CALENDAR YEAR
CALL A MEETING
CALL FOR ORDER
CALL INTO PLAY
CALL IT SQUARE
CALL OF THE SEA
CALL THE BANNS
CALL TO PRAYER
CALL TO THE BAR
CALYPSO MUSIC
CAMP FOLLOWER
CANARY YELLOW
CANDID CAMERA
CANDID CRITIC

CANDID FRIEND
CANDLE GREASE
CANNON FODDER
CANNON STREET
CANON COLLINS
CANVEY ISLAND
CAPABLE HANDS
CAPE PROVINCE
CAPITAL ASSET
CAPITAL CRIME
CAPITAL GAINS
CAPITAL GOODS
CAPTAIN BLOOD
CAPTAIN SCOTT
CARAFE OF WINE
CARAWAY SEEDS
CARBOLIC ACID
CARBOLIC SOAP
CARDBOARD BOX
CARDINAL'S HAT
CAREFREE MIND
CAREFUL STUDY
CARELESS TALK
CARIBBEAN SEA
CARNEGIE HALL
CARNIVAL TIME
CARNIVAL WEEK
CARPET KNIGHT
CARRIAGE PAID
CARRY A REPORT
CARRY FORWARD
CARRY ONE'S BAT
CARRY THROUGH
CARTE BLANCHE
CARVING KNIFE
CASE OF MURDER
CASE OF SCOTCH
CASE OF WHISKY
CASE THE JOINT
CASE TO ANSWER
CASH AND CARRY
CASH CUSTOMER
CASH ON DEMAND
CASH REGISTER
CAST AWAY FEAR
CAST-IRON CASE
CAST ONE'S VOTE
CAST THE BLAME
CASUAL GLANCE
CASUAL LABOUR
CASUAL MANNER

CASUAL REMARK
CASUALTY LIST
CASUALTY WARD
CASUAL WORKER
CAT AND FIDDLE
CATCH A TARTAR
CATCH BENDING
CATCH NAPPING
CATCH SIGHT OF
CATCH THE POST
CATCH THE TUBE
CAT'S WHISKERS
CATTLE DEALER
CATTLE MARKET
CAUSE CÉLÈBRE
CAUSE OF DELAY
CAUSE OFFENCE
CAUSE TROUBLE
CAUTION MONEY
CAUTIOUS MOVE
CAUTIOUS TYPE
CAVALRY HORSE
CAVALRY TWILL
CAVEAT EMPTOR
CEASE TO EXIST
CEILING PRICE
CEMENT A UNION
CENTURIES OLD
CERTAIN DEATH
CERTAIN ISSUE
CERTAINLY NOT
CERTAIN PLACE
C'EST LA GUERRE
CHAISE LONGUE
CHALLENGE CUP
CHAMBER MUSIC
CHAMPAGNE CUP
CHANCE REMARK
CHANCERY LANE
CHANGE COLOUR
CHANGE COURSE
CHANGE HORSES
CHANGE OF DIET
CHANGE OF FACE
CHANGE OF LUCK
CHANGE OF MIND
CHANGE OF MOOD
CHANGE PLACES
CHANGE TRAINS
CHANGING ROOM
CHAOTIC STATE

CHAPTER HOUSE
CHAPTER THREE
CHARING CROSS
CHARITY MATCH
CHARLES BOYER
CHARLES PEACE
CHARLES READE
CHARLES'S WAIN
CHARLEY'S AUNT
CHARLIE DRAKE
CHARNEL HOUSE
CHARTER PARTY
CHARTER PLANE
CHASE SHADOWS
CHEAP-DAY FARE
CHEAP EDITION
CHEAP SUCCESS
CHEAP TWISTER
CHEAT AT CARDS
CHECK THE TILL
CHEDDAR GORGE
CHEEK TO CHEEK
CHEEKY MONKEY
CHEERFUL FIRE
CHEERFUL MOOD
CHEERY MANNER
CHEESE STRAWS
CHELSEA CHINA
CHEMICAL FUEL
CHEMICAL TEST
CHEMISTRY SET
CHEMIST'S SHOP
CHERISH HOPES
CHERRY BRANDY
CHESS OPENING
CHESS PROBLEM
CHESTNUT TREE
CHEVIOT HILLS
CHICKEN CURRY
CHICKEN LIVER
CHIEF CASHIER
CHIEF JUSTICE
CHIEF MOURNER
CHIEF OFFICER
CHIEF OF STAFF
CHIEF SKIPPER
CHIEF STEWARD
CHIEF SUSPECT
CHIEF WITNESS
CHILDE HAROLD
CHILDISH WAYS

CHILD PRODIGY
CHILDREN'S TOY
CHILD WELFARE
CHILLI PEPPER
CHILLY MANNER
CHIMNEY SWEEP
CHINA CABINET
CHINESE WHITE
CHOCOLATE BAR
CHOCOLATE BOX
CHOCOLATE EGG
CHOICE MORSEL
CHOOSE FREELY
CHOP AND CHIPS
CHOSEN CAREER
CHOSEN PEOPLE
CHRISTIAN ERA
CHRISTMAS BOX
CHRISTMAS DAY
CHRISTMAS EVE
CHROME YELLOW
CHUBBY CHEEKS
CHURCH BAZAAR
CHURCH LIVING
CHURCH MEMBER
CHURCH OF ROME
CHURCH PARADE
CHURCH SCHOOL
CIGARETTE ASH
CIGARETTE END
CIGARETTE TIN
CINEMA SCREEN
CINEMA STUDIO
CIRCLE AROUND
CIRCUIT COURT
CIRCUIT JUDGE
CIRCULAR TOUR
CITY ALDERMAN
CITY BOUNDARY
CITY MERCHANT
CITY OF LONDON
CIVIC WELCOME
CIVIL DEFENCE
CIVILIAN LIFE
CIVILIZED MAN
CIVIL LIBERTY
CIVIL SERVANT
CIVIL SERVICE
CLAIM A REWARD
CLAIM DAMAGES
CLAP THE HANDS

CLASH OF STEEL
CLASH OF VIEWS
CLASPED HANDS
CLASSICAL AGE
CLASSICAL ART
CLASSIC STYLE
CLASS WARFARE
CLEAN LICENCE
CLEAR AS A BELL
CLEAR OUTLINE
CLEAR PASSAGE
CLEAR THE PATH
CLEAR THE ROAD
CLEAR THE ROOM
CLEAR THOUGHT
CLEAR WARNING
CLEAR WEATHER
CLENCHED FIST
CLERICAL GARB
CLERICAL GREY
CLERICAL WORK
CLERK OF WORKS
CLEVER MANNER
CLEVER SPEECH
CLEVER STROKE
CLIFFORD'S INN
CLIFF RAILWAY
CLIFF RICHARD
CLIMB TO POWER
CLINGING VINE
CLING LIKE IVY
CLINK GLASSES
CLIPPED HEDGE
CLIP THE WINGS
CLIVE OF INDIA
CLOCK WATCHER
CLOCKWORK TOY
CLOSE BARGAIN
CLOSE CONTACT
CLOSE CONTEST
CLOSED CIRCLE
CLOSED DRAWER
CLOSE HARMONY
CLOSE TEXTURE
CLOSE THE DOOR
CLOSE THE EYES
CLOSE THE GATE
CLOSE TO DEATH
CLOSING PRICE
CLOSING WORDS
CLOTHES BRUSH

CLOTHES HORSE
CLOTHES SENSE
CLOTHING CLUB
CLOTTED CREAM
CLOUD EFFECTS
CLOUDLESS SKY
CLOUD OF SMOKE
CLOUD OF STEAM
CLUB OFFICIAL
CLUB SANDWICH
CLUB TOGETHER
CLUMP OF TREES
CLUTCH OF EGGS
COACH AND FOUR
COACH AND PAIR
COACHING DAYS
COACH STATION
COAL INDUSTRY
COAL MERCHANT
COAL SHORTAGE
COARSE FABRIC
COARSE MANNER
COASTAL TRADE
COAST TO COAST
COAT AND SKIRT
CODE NAPOLEON
CODE OF HONOUR
COILED SPRING
COLD AS MARBLE
COLD COMPRESS
COLD SHOULDER
COLD-WATER TAP
COLIN COWDREY
COLLAR AND TIE
COLLECT TAXES
COLOGNE WATER
COLONEL BLIMP
COLONEL BOGEY
COLONIAL LIFE
COLOURED BIRD
COLOUR SCHEME
COMBAT TROOPS
COMB ONE'S HAIR
COME A CROPPER
COME AND GET IT
COME DOWN A PEG
COME IN SECOND
COME IN TO LAND
COME INTO LINE
COME INTO PLAY
COME INTO VIEW

COME IN USEFUL	CONCERT GRAND	COULD BE WORSE
COME IT STRONG	CONCERT PARTY	COUNCIL HOUSE
COME OUT ON TOP	CONCERT PITCH	COUNCIL OF WAR
COME OVER HERE	CONCRETE FACT	COUNT DRACULA
COME TO A CLOSE	CONCRETE PATH	COUNTER CLAIM
COME TO A POINT	CONCRETE POST	COUNTRY DANCE
COME TOGETHER	CONDEMNED MAN	COUNTRY HOUSE
COME TO NAUGHT	CONFUSED MIND	COUNTRY MOUSE
COME TO NO GOOD	CONIC SECTION	COUNT THE COST
COME TO NO HARM	CONSOLE TABLE	COUNT THE DAYS
COME TO PIECES	CONTENTED MAN	COUNT THE RISK
COME TO THE END	CONTOUR LINES	COUNT UP TO TEN
COME UP FOR AIR	CONTROL PANEL	COUNTY ANTRIM
COME UPSTAIRS	CONTROL TOWER	COUNTY FAMILY
COME UP TRUMPS	CONVEX MIRROR	COUNTY SCHOOL
COMIC SECTION	CONVEYOR BELT	COUPE JACQUES
COMING EVENTS	CONVICTED MAN	COURSE OF DUTY
COMMANDO RAID	COOKERY CLASS	COURSE OF LIFE
COMMANDO UNIT	COOKING APPLE	COURSE OF LOVE
COMMIT A CRIME	COOK THE BOOKS	COURSE OF TIME
COMMIT BIGAMY	COOK UP A STORY	COURSE OF WORK
COMMIT MURDER	COOL CUSTOMER	COURSE RECORD
COMMITTEE MAN	COOLING AGENT	COURTEOUS ACT
COMMON ACCENT	COOLING PLANT	COURTESY CALL
COMMON AS DIRT	COOL JUDGMENT	COURT MARTIAL
COMMON CENTRE	COOL THOUSAND	COURT OFFICER
COMMON FACTOR	COPIOUS NOTES	COURT PLASTER
COMMON FRIEND	COPPER KETTLE	COURT SUMMONS
COMMON GENDER	COPYRIGHT ACT	COUSIN GERMAN
COMMON GOSSIP	CORDIAL SMILE	COVENT GARDEN
COMMON GROUND	CORNET PLAYER	COVENTRY CITY
COMMON HATRED	CORN EXCHANGE	COVERED COURT
COMMON LAWYER	CORN IN ISRAEL	COVERED DRAIN
COMMON MARKET	CORNISH CREAM	COVERED WAGON
COMMON ORIGIN	CORNISH PASTY	COVER THE COST
COMMON PEOPLE	CORN MERCHANT	COVER THE LOSS
COMMON PERSON	CORN ON THE COB	CRACK A BOTTLE
COMMON PRAYER	CORONER'S JURY	CRACKED VOICE
COMMON PRISON	CORRECT DRESS	CRACKING PACE
COMMON SAYING	CORRECT STYLE	CRACKING SHOW
COMMON SPEECH	CORRECT THING	CRACK-POT IDEA
COMMUNAL FARM	COSSACK DANCE	CRACK THE WHIP
COMPANIES ACT	COST ACCOUNTS	CRAFTY FELLOW
COMPANION WAY	COST OF LIVING	CRAIG DOUGLAS
COMPARE NOTES	COST OF UPKEEP	CRAMPED STYLE
COMPASS POINT	COST THE EARTH	CRASHING BORE
COMPLETE LIST	COSTUME PIECE	CRASH LANDING
COMPOSE MUSIC	COTTAGE PIANO	CRAVEN SPIRIT
COMPOS MENTIS	COTTON GLOVES	CREAM CRACKER
COMPOUND TIME	COTTON THREAD	CREAM SHAMPOO
CONCEITED PUP	COUGH MIXTURE	CREATE A SCENE

CREATIVE MIND
CREATIVE MOOD
CREATIVE URGE
CREATIVE WORK
CREDIT TITLES
CRÊPE DE CHINE
CRÊPE SUZETTE
CRESCENT MOON
CRICKET EXTRA
CRICKET MATCH
CRICKET PITCH
CRICKET SCORE
CRICKET STUMP
CRIMINAL CASE
CRIMINAL CODE
CRIMINAL SUIT
CRIMINAL TYPE
CRIPPLING TAX
CRITICAL TIME
CROMWELL ROAD
CROSSED LINES
CROSSED WIRES
CROSS OF DAVID
CROSS SECTION
CROSS THE LINE
CROSS THE ROAD
CROSSWORD FAN
CROWNED HEADS
CROWN WITNESS
CRUDE MANNERS
CRUDE METHODS
CRUISE AROUND
CRUSHING BLOW
CRUST OF BREAD
CRY LIKE A BABY
CRY OF DESPAIR
CRY ONE'S WARES
CRYPTIC SMILE
CRYSTAL CLEAR
CRYSTAL GLASS
CUBIC CONTENT
CULINARY HERB
CULLODEN MOOR
CUP AND SAUCER
CUPBOARD LOVE
CUP FINALISTS
CURDS AND WHEY
CURIOUS SIGHT
CURIOUS SOUND
CURIOUS THING
CURL OF THE LIP

CURL UP AND DIE
CURRANT BREAD
CURRENCY NOTE
CURRENT CRAZE
CURRENT ISSUE
CURRENT MONTH
CURRENT OF AIR
CURRENT PRICE
CURRENT TIMES
CURRENT TREND
CURRY AND RICE
CURTIS REPORT
CURVE INWARDS
CUSHION COVER
CUSHION OF AIR
CUSTOM DUTIES
CUSTOMS UNION
CUT AND THRUST
CUT FOR TRUMPS
CUT OFF THE GAS
CUT OF ONE'S JIB
CUT ONE'S NAILS
CUT ONE'S TEETH
CUT THE CACKLE
CUTTING TEETH
CUTTING WORDS
CUT TO RIBBONS
CUT TO THE BONE
CYNICAL SMILE
CZAR OF RUSSIA

D—12
DAGGERS DRAWN
DAILY EXPRESS
DAILY ROUTINE
DAILY SERVICE
DAINTY HABITS
DAINTY PALATE
DAIRY FARMING
DAIRY PRODUCE
DALMATIAN DOG
DAMAGED GOODS
DAME MYRA HESS
DANCE HOSTESS
DANCE OF DEATH
DANCE ROUTINE
DANCE SESSION
DANDY DINMONT
DANGEROUS JOB
DANGEROUS MAN
DANGER SIGNAL

DANISH BUTTER
DANISH PASTRY
DANSE MACABRE
DARBY AND JOAN
DARKENED MIND
DARK THOUGHTS
DASH TO PIECES
DAVID GARRICK
DAVID KOSSOFF
DAYLIGHT RAID
DAY OF LEISURE
DAY OF WORSHIP
DEAD AS MUTTON
DEAD LANGUAGE
DEADLY COMBAT
DEADLY POISON
DEADLY SECRET
DEADLY WEAPON
DEAD MAN'S HAND
DEAD-SEA FRUIT
DEAD STRAIGHT
DEAFENING ROW
DEAF TO REASON
DEAL THE CARDS
DEAR DEPARTED
DEAREST HEART
DEAR OLD THING
DEARTH OF FOOD
DEATH CHAMBER
DEATH PENALTY
DEATH WARRANT
DEBATING HALL
DEBIT BALANCE
DEBT OF HONOUR
DECIDING VOTE
DECIMAL POINT
DEEP FEELINGS
DEEP INTEREST
DEEP-LAID PLOT
DEEP MOURNING
DEEP-SEA DIVER
DEEP THOUGHTS
DEFENCE BONDS
DEFENCE MEDAL
DEFINITE TIME
DEJECTED LOOK
DELICATE HINT
DELIVERY DATE
DELIVERY NOTE
DEMAND RANSOM
DEMON FOR WORK

DENIS COMPTON
DEN OF THIEVES
DEPUTY LEADER
DESCENT OF MAN
DESERT ISLAND
DESERVE A RISE
DESIGN CENTRE
DESK CALENDAR
DESPATCH CASE
DESPERATE BID
DESPERATE DAN
DESPERATE MAN
DESSERT KNIFE
DESSERT SPOON
DETACHED MIND
DETACHED VIEW
DETAILED PLAN
DEVIL MAY CARE
DEVIL OF A MESS
DEVIL OF A TIME
DEVIL'S ISLAND
DEVIL'S TATTOO
DEVIL WORSHIP
DEVIOUS MEANS
DEVIOUS PATHS
DEVOID OF FEAR
DEVON VIOLETS
DIAGONAL LINE
DIALLING TONE
DIAMOND CLASP
DIAMOND TIARA
DIANA'S TEMPLE
DICTATE TERMS
DIE IN HARNESS
DIE IN ONE'S BED
DIESEL ENGINE
DIFFICULT JOB
DIFFICULT SUM
DIFFUSED HEAT
DIG IN THE RIBS
DIG ONESELF IN
DIG ONE'S GRAVE
DIG UP THE PAST
DINING SALOON
DIN IN THE EARS
DIRECT ACTION
DIRECT COURSE
DIRECT METHOD
DIRECT OBJECT
DIRECT SPEECH
DIRE DISTRESS

DIRTY WEATHER
DISASTER AREA
DISCOVERY BAY
DISHONEST ACT
DISPATCH CASE
DISPENSE WITH
DISTRICT BANK
DISTRICT LINE
DIVE FOR COVER
DIVIDE BY FIVE
DIVIDE BY FOUR
DIVIDE BY NINE
DIVIDED SKIRT
DIVIDING LINE
DIVIDING WALL
DIVINE COMEDY
DIVINE NATURE
DIVINE RIGHTS
DIVISION BELL
DIVISION SIGN
DIVORCE COURT
DIZZY FEELING
DIZZY HEIGHTS
DO A HAND'S TURN
DO AS ONE'S TOLD
DO AS OTHERS DO
DO AS ROME DOES
DOCK LABOURER
DOCTOR FOSTER
DOCTOR JEKYLL
DOCTOR WATSON
DOG IN A MANGER
DO IT YOURSELF
DOMBEY AND SON
DOMESDAY BOOK
DOMESTIC HELP
DOMINANT FACT
DONALD WOLFIT
DONEGAL TWEED
DONKEY ENGINE
DONKEY'S YEARS
DO NO MAN WRONG
DO NOT DISTURB
DOOMSDAY BOOK
DO ONE A FAVOUR
DO ONE'S UTMOST
DORMER WINDOW
DOROTHY TUTIN
DORSET SQUARE
DOSE OF PHYSIC
DO THE HONOURS

DO THE NEEDFUL
DO THE WASHING
DOUBLE BARREL
DOUBLE BRANDY
DOUBLE ELEVEN
DOUBLE FLOWER
DOUBLE SCOTCH
DOUBLES MATCH
DOUBLE THE BID
DOUBLE TWELVE
DOUBLE TWENTY
DOUBLE VISION
DOUBLE WHISKY
DOUGHTY DEEDS
DOWN PLATFORM
DOWNRIGHT LIE
DOWN THE AISLE
DOWN THE DRAIN
DOWN THE FIELD
DOWN THE HATCH
DOWN THE RIVER
DOWN THE SPOUT
DOWN THE YEARS
DOWNWARD BEND
DOWNWARD PATH
DOZEN OYSTERS
DRAGGING FEET
DRAG ONE'S FEET
DRAGON'S BLOOD
DRAGON'S TEETH
DRAMATIC FORM
DRAMATIC POEM
DRAMATIC POET
DRAPERY STORE
DRAUGHT CIDER
DRAUGHT HORSE
DRAUGHT STOUT
DRAW A MEANING
DRAW A PENSION
DRAW A PICTURE
DRAWING PAPER
DRAW INTEREST
DRAWN TO SCALE
DRAW THE BLIND
DRAW THE MORAL
DRAW THE SWORD
DRAW THE TEETH
DRAW TO A CLOSE
DRAW TOGETHER
DREADFUL BORE
DREADFUL PAIN

DREAD SUMMONS
DREAM OF YOUTH
DRESDEN CHINA
DRESS CLOTHES
DRESSED IN RED
DRESSING CASE
DRESSING DOWN
DRESSING GOWN
DRESSING ROOM
DRESS THE PART
DRESS UNIFORM
DRINK HEAVILY
DRINKING BOUT
DRINKING CLUB
DRINKING ORGY
DRINKING SONG
DRINKING TIME
DRINK OF WATER
DRIVE FORWARD
DRIVE THROUGH
DRIVE TO DRINK
DRIVING FORCE
DROP A CLANGER
DROP A CURTSEY
DROP OF BRANDY
DROP OF SCOTCH
DROP OF WHISKY
DROPPED CATCH
DROP THE PILOT
DROWN ONESELF
DRUNK AS A LORD
DRUNKEN BRAWL
DUCKING STOOL
DUCK ONE'S HEAD
DUCK'S DISEASE
DUE DEFERENCE
DULL MONOTONY
DUMB CHARADES
DUMB CREATURE
DUM-DUM BULLET
DUNMOW FLITCH
DUPLICATE KEY
DURING THE DAY
DURING THE WAR
DUST AND ASHES
DUTCH AUCTION
DUTCH COMFORT
DUTCH COURAGE
DUTCH GUILDER
DYERS' COMPANY
DYNAMIC FORCE

E—12
EALING COMMON
EAR AND THROAT
EARLY CLOSING
EARLY EDITION
EARLY ENGLISH
EARLY MORNING
EARLY WARNING
EARNED INCOME
EARNEST MONEY
EARN ONE'S KEEP
EASE ONE'S MIND
EASILY SOLVED
EAST CHINA SEA
EASTER BONNET
EASTER ISLAND
EASTERLY GALE
EASTER MONDAY
EASTER PARADE
EASTER RISING
EASTER SUNDAY
EASY ON THE EYE
EASY PAYMENTS
EASY SOLUTION
EASY TO PLEASE
EAT HUMBLE-PIE
EATING HABITS
EAT ONE'S WORDS
EAT SPARINGLY
EAU DE COLOGNE
ECONOMY DRIVE
EDGAR WALLACE
EDGE OF BEYOND
EDIBLE FUNGUS
EDITH SITWELL
EDWARD GIBBON
EEL-PIE ISLAND
EFFORT OF WILL
EGGS AND BACON
EGYPTIAN GODS
EIGHT AND FIVE
EIGHT AND FOUR
EIGHT AND NINE
EIGHT DEGREES
EIGHT DOLLARS
EIGHT FATHOMS
EIGHT GALLONS
EIGHT GUINEAS
EIGHTH LETTER
EIGHTH OF JULY
EIGHTH OF JUNE

EIGHTH STOREY
EIGHT HUNDRED
EIGHTH VOLUME
EIGHT MINUTES
EIGHT OF CLUBS
EIGHT PER CENT
EIGHT SQUARED
EIGHT WICKETS
ELBOW ONE'S WAY
ELDER BROTHER
ELDEST SISTER
ELECTION DATE
ELECTION YEAR
ELECTRIC BELL
ELECTRIC BLUE
ELECTRIC BULB
ELECTRIC FIRE
ELECTRIC HARE
ELECTRIC HORN
ELECTRIC IRON
ELECTRIC LAMP
ELECTRIC OVEN
ELECTRIC PLUG
ELECTRIC WIRE
ELEGANT LINES
ELEVEN AND ONE
ELEVEN AND SIX
ELEVEN AND TEN
ELEVEN AND TWO
ELEVEN MONTHS
ELEVEN O'CLOCK
ELEVEN OUNCES
ELEVEN POINTS
ELEVENTH HOLE
ELEVENTH HOUR
ELGIN MARBLES
ELIXIR OF LIFE
ELVIS PRESLEY
ELY CATHEDRAL
EMERALD GREEN
EMPEROR WALTZ
EMPTY FEELING
EMPTY STOMACH
EMPTY VESSELS
END IN FAILURE
ENDLESS CHAIN
ENDLESS WORRY
END OF CHAPTER
END OF THE LINE
END OF THE ROAD
END OF THE WEEK

END OF THE YEAR
ENDURING FAME
ENDURING LOVE
ENFIELD RIFLE
ENGAGED IN WAR
ENGINE DRIVER
ENGLISH MONEY
ENGLISH VERSE
ENJOY ONESELF
ENORMOUS MEAL
ENQUIRE AFTER
ENQUIRY AGENT
ENRICO CARUSO
ENTERIC FEVER
ENTRANCE FREE
ENTRANCE HALL
EPPING FOREST
EQUAL CONTEST
EQUAL THE BEST
ERIC ROBINSON
ERMINE COLLAR
ERUDITE STYLE
ESCAPE CLAUSE
ESCAPE NOTICE
ESCORT VESSEL
ESSAYS OF ELIA
ESSENTIAL OIL
ESTEEM HIGHLY
ETERNAL YOUTH
ETERNITY RING
ETON WALL-GAME
EUGENE O'NEILL
EUROPEAN CITY
EVENING CLASS
EVENING DRESS
EVENING PAPER
EVEN TEMPERED
EVE OF THE POLL
EVER AND AGAIN
EVER-OPEN DOOR
EVER SO LITTLE
EVERY FEW DAYS
EVERY MAN JACK
EVERY MORNING
EVERY QUARTER
EVERY SO OFTEN
EVERY TUESDAY
EVIL SPEAKING
EVIL THOUGHTS
EVOKE THE PAST
EXACT ACCOUNT

EXACTLY RIGHT
EXACT MEANING
EXACT SCIENCE
EXALTED STYLE
EXCEL ONESELF
EXCESS PROFIT
EXCESS WEIGHT
EXCHANGE RATE
EXCITING BOOK
EXCITING NEWS
EXCITING PLAY
EXERCISE BOOK
EXERT ONESELF
EXHAUST VALVE
EXPANSE OF SEA
EXPANSE OF SKY
EXPERT ADVICE
EXPLODED IDEA
EXPORT MARKET
EXPOSED NERVE
EXPRESS GRIEF
EXPRESS SPEED
EXPRESS TRAIN
EX-SERVICE MAN
EXTEND CREDIT
EXTENDED PLAY
EXTERIOR WALL
EXTRA EDITION
EXTRA SPECIAL
EXTREMES MEET
EXTREME VIEWS
EXTREME YOUTH
EYE FOR BEAUTY
EYE FOR COLOUR
EYE OF A NEEDLE
EYES OF THE LAW
EYE ON THE BALL

F—12

FABLED ANIMAL
FABULOUS SIZE
FACE BOTH WAYS
FACE DISGRACE
FACE THE ENEMY
FACE THE FACTS
FACE THE FRONT
FACE THE ISSUE
FACE THE MUSIC
FACE THE TRUTH
FACT AND FANCY
FAERIE QUEENE

FAILING LIGHT
FAILING SIGHT
FAIL IN HEALTH
FAIL TO APPEAR
FAIL TO FINISH
FAINT ATTEMPT
FAIR DECISION
FAIR EXCHANGE
FAIR PROSPECT
FAIR QUESTION
FAIR TO MEDIUM
FAIT ACCOMPLI
FAITHFUL COPY
FALL BACK UPON
FALL BY THE WAY
FALLEN ARCHES
FALL HEADLONG
FALL IN BATTLE
FALLING SALES
FALLING TEARS
FALL IN PRICE
FALL INTO LINE
FALL INTO RUIN
FALL OF FRANCE
FALL TO PIECES
FALSE ACCOUNT
FALSE ADDRESS
FALSE COLOURS
FALSE ECONOMY
FALSE HORIZON
FALSE MODESTY
FALSE PICTURE
FALSE PROPHET
FALSE VERDICT
FALSE WITNESS
FALSE WORSHIP
FAMILIAR FACE
FAMILIAR RING
FAMILY AFFAIR
FAMILY CIRCLE
FAMILY DOCTOR
FAMILY FRIEND
FAMILY JEWELS
FAMILY LAWYER
FAMILY MATTER
FAMINE RELIEF
FANCY ONESELF
FAN THE EMBERS
FAN THE FLAMES
FAR DIFFERENT
FARE THEE WELL

FAREWELL SONG
FARMHOUSE TEA
FARMING STOCK
FARM LABOURER
FAROE ISLANDS
FASCIST PARTY
FASHION HOUSE
FASHION MODEL
FASHION PLATE
FAST AND LOOSE
FAST THINKING
FATAL BLUNDER
FATAL DISEASE
FATAL MISTAKE
FATHER AND SON
FATHER FIGURE
FATHER THAMES
FATIGUE PARTY
FAT LOT OF GOOD
FAT OF THE LAND
FATUOUS SMILE
FAULTY SWITCH
FEAR EXPOSURE
FEAR THE WORST
FEAT OF MEMORY
FEATURE STORY
FEDERAL AGENT
FEDERAL COURT
FEDERAL STATE
FEDERAL UNION
FEEBLE ATTACK
FEEBLE EFFORT
FEEBLE EXCUSE
FEEBLE SPEECH
FEED THE BRUTE
FEEL DOUBTFUL
FEEL GRATEFUL
FEEL HELPLESS
FEEL HOMESICK
FEEL ONE'S FEET
FEEL STRONGLY
FEEL SUPERIOR
FEEL SYMPATHY
FEEL THE PANGS
FEEL THE PINCH
FEET FOREMOST
FELL HEADLONG
FELLOW MEMBER
FERTILE BRAIN
FESTIVAL HALL
FESTIVE BOARD

FEUDAL SYSTEM
FEUDAL TENURE
FEVERISH COLD
FIELDING SIDE
FIELD KITCHEN
FIELD MARSHAL
FIELD OFFICER
FIELD OF STUDY
FIELD OF WHEAT
FIERCE ATTACK
FIERCE HATRED
FIERCE TEMPER
FIERY FURNACE
FIFTEEN FORTY
FIFTEEN MILES
FIFTH CENTURY
FIFTH OF APRIL
FIFTH OF MARCH
FIFTY DOLLARS
FIFTY GUINEAS
FIFTY PER CENT
FIGHT AGAINST
FIGHTER PILOT
FIGHTER PLANE
FIGHTING COCK
FIGHTING TALK
FIGHTING TRIM
FIGHT ONE'S WAY
FIGURE SKATER
FILING SYSTEM
FILL A VACANCY
FILM DIRECTOR
FILM FESTIVAL
FILM INDUSTRY
FILM MAGAZINE
FILM PREMIERE
FILM PRODUCER
FINAL ACCOUNT
FINAL ATTEMPT
FINAL CURTAIN
FINAL EDITION
FINAL EPISODE
FINAL OPINION
FINAL OUTCOME
FINAL PAYMENT
FINAL PROCESS
FINAL VICTORY
FINAL WARNING
FINANCIAL AID
FIND A FORMULA
FIND A HUSBAND

FIND AN OUTLET
FIND NO FAVOUR
FIND ONE'S FEET
FIND ONE'S LEGS
FIND PLEASURE
FIND THE CAUSE
FIND THE MONEY
FIND THE PLACE
FINE AND DANDY
FINE AND LARGE
FINE FEATHERS
FINE FEATURES
FINE GOINGS-ON
FINE PROSPECT
FINER FEELING
FINE SPECIMEN
FINISHED WORK
FINISH SECOND
FINISH THE JOB
FINSBURY PARK
FIRE AND SWORD
FIRE AND WATER
FIRE AT RANDOM
FIREMAN'S LIFT
FIRE OF LONDON
FIRE PRACTICE
FIRESIDE CHAT
FIRESIDE TALK
FIRM DECISION
FIRM FOOTHOLD
FIRMLY ROOTED
FIRM MEASURES
FIRM PRESSURE
FIRM PROPOSAL
FIRST-AID POST
FIRST AND LAST
FIRST ARRIVAL
FIRST ATTEMPT
FIRST CENTURY
FIRST CHAPTER
FIRST EDITION
FIRST FOOTING
FIRST INNINGS
FIRST OF APRIL
FIRST OFFENCE
FIRST OFFICER
FIRST OF MARCH
FIRST PAYMENT
FIRST QUARTER
FIRST READING
FIRST REFUSAL

FIRST RESERVE
FIRST SEA-LORD
FIRST SERVICE
FIRST SESSION
FIRST THOUGHT
FIRST TIME OUT
FIRST TO LEAVE
FIRST TURNING
FIRST-YEAR MAN
FIRTH OF CLYDE
FIRTH OF FORTH
FISH AND CHIPS
FISH FOR TROUT
FISHING FLEET
FISHING SMACK
FISHING SPEAR
FIT AND PROPER
FIT AS A FIDDLE
FITFUL BREEZE
FIT OF MADNESS
FITTED CARPET
FIVE AND A HALF
FIVE AND EIGHT
FIVE AND SEVEN
FIVE AND THREE
FIVE-DAY MATCH
FIVE DIAMONDS
FIVE FEET TALL
FIVE FURLONGS
FIVE-LINE WHIP
FIVE NO-TRUMPS
FIVE OF HEARTS
FIVE OF SPADES
FIVE OF TRUMPS
FIVE SEVENTHS
FIVE THOUSAND
FIVE-YEAR PLAN
FIXED CAPITAL
FIXED PAYMENT
FIXED PURPOSE
FIXED ROUTINE
FLAGON OF WINE
FLAMING HEART
FLASHING EYES
FLASH OF LIGHT
FLEECY CLOUDS
FLEET OF SHIPS
FLEET OF TAXIS
FLIGHT NUMBER
FLIGHT OF TIME
FLIMSY EXCUSE

FLOATING DEBT
FLOATING DOCK
FLOATING FUND
FLOATING MINE
FLOATING VOTE
FLOCK OF BIRDS
FLOCK OF GEESE
FLOCK OF GOATS
FLOCK OF SHEEP
FLODDEN FIELD
FLOOD OF TEARS
FLOOD OF WATER
FLOOD OF WORDS
FLOOR SERVICE
FLOUNCE ABOUT
FLOWERED SILK
FLOWER GARDEN
FLOWER MARKET
FLOWER-POT MEN
FLOWER SELLER
FLOWERY STYLE
FLOWING LOCKS
FLOWING WATER
FLUENT FRENCH
FLUID MEASURE
FLURRY OF SNOW
FLUSH OF YOUTH
FLUTED COLUMN
FLY AWAY PETER
FLYING BEETLE
FLYING CARPET
FLYING CIRCUS
FLYING COLUMN
FLYING DOCTOR
FLYING GROUND
FLYING SAUCER
FLYING TACKLE
FLY INTO A RAGE
FOAM MATTRESS
FOGGY WEATHER
FOLDING CHAIR
FOLDING DOORS
FOLDING STOOL
FOLD ONE'S ARMS
FOLLOW ADVICE
FOLLOW MY LEAD
FOLLOW THE SEA
FOND OF A GLASS
FOOD AND DRINK
FOOD SHORTAGE
FOOD SUPPLIES

FOOT AND MOUTH
FOOTBALL CLUB
FOOTBALL POOL
FOOTBALL TEAM
FOOTPLATE MAN
FOOT REGIMENT
FOR A LIFETIME
FOR AMUSEMENT
FOR A RAINY DAY
FORCE AN ENTRY
FORCE AN ISSUE
FORCED GAIETY
FORCED LABOUR
FORCE MAJEURE
FORCE OF HABIT
FORCE ONE'S WAY
FORCE THE PACE
FOREIGN AGENT
FOREIGN LANDS
FOREIGN MONEY
FOREIGN PARTS
FOREIGN STAMP
FOREIGN TRADE
FOREST OF DEAN
FOREST RANGER
FOREVER AMBER
FOR GALLANTRY
FORGE A CHEQUE
FORGE ONE'S WAY
FORK OUT MONEY
FORMAL GARDEN
FORMAL SPEECH
FORMER FRIEND
FOR PITY'S SAKE
FOR THE BETTER
FOR THE MOMENT
FOR THE RECORD
FORTY FIFTEEN
FORTY PER CENT
FORTY THIEVES
FORWARD DRIVE
FORWARD MARCH
FORWARD PUPIL
FOSTER FATHER
FOSTER MOTHER
FOSTER PARENT
FOSTER SISTER
FOUL LANGUAGE
FOUND MISSING
FOUND WANTING
FOUR AND A HALF

FOUR AND EIGHT
FOUR AND SEVEN
FOUR AND THREE
FOUR DIAMONDS
FOUR FEATHERS
FOUR FEET TALL
FOUR FREEDOMS
FOUR FURLONGS
FOUR HORSEMEN
FOUR NO-TRUMPS
FOUR OF HEARTS
FOUR OF SPADES
FOUR OF TRUMPS
FOURPENNY ONE
FOUR QUARTERS
FOUR SEVENTHS
FOURTEEN DAYS
FOURTH ESTATE
FOURTH FINGER
FOURTH LEAGUE
FOURTH LETTER
FOURTH OF JULY
FOURTH OF JUNE
FOUR THOUSAND
FOURTH SEASON
FOURTH STOREY
FOURTH VOLUME
FOX AND HOUNDS
FRACTURED ARM
FRACTURED LEG
FRAGRANT WEED
FRANCIS BACON
FRANCIS DRAKE
FRANK COUSINS
FRANK SINATRA
FRANTIC HASTE
FRAYED NERVES
FREDDIE MILLS
FREE AS THE AIR
FREE DELIVERY
FREE FROM CARE
FREE FROM DEBT
FREE FROM PAIN
FREE FROM RAIN
FREE FROM VICE
FREE FROM WANT
FREE MOVEMENT
FREE OF CHARGE
FREE QUARTERS
FREE THINKING
FREE TO CHOOSE

FREEZING COLD
FREIGHT TRAIN
FRENCH ACCENT
FRENCH CUSTOM
FRENCH GUINEA
FRENCH LESSON
FRENCH MASTER
FRENCH PASTRY
FRENCH POLISH
FRENCH POODLE
FRENCH WINDOW
FRENZIED RAGE
FRESH ADVANCE
FRESH AS PAINT
FRESH CHAPTER
FRESH COURAGE
FRESH FLOWERS
FRESH HERRING
FRESH OUTLOOK
FRIAR'S BALSAM
FRIDAY'S CHILD
FRIEND INDEED
FRIEND IN NEED
FRIENDLY CHAT
FRIENDLY FACE
FRIENDLY HAND
FRIENDLY WORD
FRIGHTEN AWAY
FROM ALL SIDES
FROM DAY TO DAY
FROM END TO END
FROM THE FIRST
FROM THE NORTH
FROM THE SOUTH
FROM THE START
FROM TOP TO TOE
FRONT AND BACK
FRONTIER ZONE
FRONT PARLOUR
FROSTED GLASS
FROZEN ASSETS
FRUIT MACHINE
FUEL MERCHANT
FULHAM PALACE
FULL CAPACITY
FULL COVERAGE
FULL DAYLIGHT
FULLER'S EARTH
FULL MATURITY
FULL OF ACTION
FULL OF ENERGY

FULL OF HORROR
FULL OF SORROW
FULL OF SPIRIT
FULL PRESSURE
FULLY DRESSED
FULLY ENGAGED
FULLY SECURED
FUME WITH RAGE
FUND OF HUMOUR
FUNERAL MARCH
FUNERAL RITES
FUNNY FEELING
FUN OF THE FAIR
FUR-LINED COAT
FURNITURE VAN
FURNIVAL'S INN
FURTHER DELAY
FURTHER PLANS
FUTILE EFFORT
FUTURE EVENTS

G—12
GAIN A FOOTING
GAIN A HEARING
GAIN A VICTORY
GAIN CURRENCY
GAIN ONE'S ENDS
GAIN PRESTIGE
GAIN STRENGTH
GALA OCCASION
GALLON OF BEER
GALLON OF MILK
GAMBLING DEBT
GAMBLING GAME
GAMBLING HELL
GAME AND MATCH
GAME OF CHANCE
GAME OF TENNIS
GAME PRESERVE
GAMING TABLES
GAMMON RASHER
GARBLED STORY
GARDEN OF EDEN
GARDEN ROLLER
GARDEN SUBURB
GARDEN TROWEL
GARRISON TOWN
GARTER STITCH
GAS POISONING
GATE-LEG TABLE
GENERAL ALARM

GENERAL ALERT	GIPSY CARAVAN	GLOBE THEATRE
GENERAL BOOTH	GIRLS AND BOYS	GLOOMY ASPECT
GENERAL GRANT	GIVE A CONCERT	GLORIOUS MESS
GENERAL ISSUE	GIVE A LECTURE	GLORIOUS TIME
GENERAL SMUTS	GIVE AN ENCORE	GLORIOUS VIEW
GENERAL STAFF	GIVE A PRESENT	GLOWING TERMS
GENERAL STALL	GIVE A RECEIPT	GO AND EAT COKE
GENERAL TERMS	GIVE A SUMMARY	GO BACK IN TIME
GENERAL TREND	GIVE AUDIENCE	GO BACK TO WORK
GENERAL USAGE	GIVE EVIDENCE	GO BY THE BOARD
GENERAL VOICE	GIVE FIRST-AID	GOD BE WITH YOU
GENERAL WOLFE	GIVE HIM SOCKS	GO DOWNSTAIRS
GENITIVE CASE	GIVE IN CHARGE	GO FIFTY-FIFTY
GENTLE BREEZE	GIVE IT A TWIST	GO FOR A BURTON
GENTLEMAN JIM	GIVE IT THE GUN	GO FOR A CRUISE
GENTLE NATURE	GIVE JUDGMENT	GO FOR A STROLL
GENTLE READER	GIVEN A CHANCE	GO FOR A VOYAGE
GENTLE REBUKE	GIVEN A PARDON	GO FOR NOTHING
GENTLY DOES IT!	GIVEN THE BIRD	GO HOT AND COLD
GEORGE BORROW	GIVEN THE BOOT	GOING BEGGING
GEORGE ORWELL	GIVEN THE CANE	GOING CONCERN
GEORGE ROMNEY	GIVEN THE PUSH	GO INTO DETAIL
GERMAN LESSON	GIVEN THE SACK	GO INTO HIDING
GERMAN SCHOOL	GIVEN THE SLIP	GOLD BRACELET
GERMAN SILVER	GIVEN THE VOTE	GOLDEN FLEECE
GERM OF AN IDEA	GIVE ONE A LIFT	GOLDEN GLOVES
GET CLEAN AWAY	GIVE ONE'S BEST	GOLDEN NUMBER
GET CLEAR AWAY	GIVE ONE'S LIFE	GOLDEN REMEDY
GET INTO A MESS	GIVE ONE'S VOTE	GOLDEN SQUARE
GET NO SUPPORT	GIVE ONE'S WORD	GOLDEN SUNSET
GET ONE'S CARDS	GIVE PLEASURE	GOLDERS GREEN
GET ONE'S EYE IN	GIVE SECURITY	GOLDFISH BOWL
GET OUT OF HAND	GIVE THE ALARM	GOLDFISH POND
GET PLASTERED	GIVE THE FACTS	GOLD MERCHANT
GET PROMOTION	GIVE THE ORDER	GOLD RESERVE
GET TECHNICAL	GIVE UP EATING	GOLD STANDARD
GET THE CREDIT	GIVE UP OFFICE	GOLF CHAMPION
GET THE NEEDLE	GIVE UP TRYING	GONE IN A FLASH
GET THE STITCH	GLADSTONE BAG	GONE TO GROUND
GET THE WIND UP	GLADYS COOPER	GOOD AND READY
GET WELL-OILED	GLANCING BLOW	GOOD APPETITE
GIANT DESPAIR	GLARING ERROR	GOOD ARGUMENT
GIANT'S STRIDE	GLASS FACTORY	GOOD BREEDING
GIDDY FEELING	GLASS OF STOUT	GOOD BUSINESS
GIDDY HEIGHTS	GLASS OF WATER	GOOD CLEAN FUN
GIFT OF THE GAB	GLASS SLIPPER	GOOD CROSSING
GIN AND FRENCH	GLASS STOPPER	GOOD DAY'S WORK
GIN AND ORANGE	GLASS TANKARD	GOOD DELIVERY
GINGER BRANDY	GLASS TOO MUCH	GOOD EYESIGHT
GINGER ROGERS	GLASS TUMBLER	GOOD FEATURES
GINGHAM FROCK	GLEAM OF LIGHT	GOOD FOR TRADE

GOOD GRACIOUS
GOOD JUDGMENT
GOOD LIKENESS
GOOD LINGUIST
GOOD LISTENER
GOOD MATERIAL
GOOD OLD TIMES
GOOD PHYSIQUE
GOOD POSITION
GOOD PRACTICE
GOOD PROGRESS
GOOD QUARTERS
GOOD QUESTION
GOOD RECOVERY
GOOD RIDDANCE
GOOD ROUND SUM
GOOD SHEPHERD
GOOD SHOOTING
GOOD SMACKING
GOOD SPANKING
GOODS STATION
GOOD TEMPLARS
GOOD THINKING
GOOD THRILLER
GOOD-TIME GIRL
GOOD WATCH-DOG
GOODWIN SANDS
GOODWOOD PARK
GO ON ALL FOURS
GO ON AN ERRAND
GO ON AS BEFORE
GO ONE'S OWN WAY
GO ON THE SPREE
GO ON THE STAGE
GOOSE PIMPLES
GO OVER THE TOP
GORGEOUS TIME
GO-SLOW POLICY
GO-SLOW STRIKE
GOSSIP COLUMN
GOSSIP WRITER
GO SWIMMINGLY
GO THE SAME WAY
GOTHIC SCRIPT
GO TO A WEDDING
GO TO EXTREMES
GO TO HOSPITAL
GO TO ONE'S HEAD
GO TO THE DEVIL
GO TO THE FRONT
GO TO THE OPERA

GO TO THE POLLS
GO TO THE RACES
GO UP IN FLAMES
GO WITH A SWING
GRACE DARLING
GRACEFUL EXIT
GRACIE FIELDS
GRACIOUS LADY
GRAHAM GREENE
GRAIN HARVEST
GRAIN OF SENSE
GRAIN OF TRUTH
GRAND CENTRAL
GRAND DUCHESS
GRAND FEELING
GRAND GUIGNOL
GRAND LARCENY
GRAND MISTAKE
GRAND OPENING
GRAND SEND-OFF
GRAPE HARVEST
GRASS WIDOWER
GRATED CHEESE
GRATING LAUGH
GRATING VOICE
GRAVE MISTAKE
GRAVE OFFENCE
GRAVE SCANDAL
GREAT BRAVERY
GREAT BRITAIN
GREAT COMFORT
GREAT COMPANY
GREAT EASTERN
GREAT EXPENSE
GREAT FORTUNE
GREAT FRIENDS
GREAT MALVERN
GREAT PAINTER
GREAT RESPECT
GREAT SECRECY
GREAT SOLDIER
GREAT SUCCESS
GREAT TRAGEDY
GREAT TRIUMPH
GREAT URGENCY
GREAT VARIETY
GREAT VICTORY
GRECIAN STYLE
GREEK PROFILE
GREEK SCHOLAR
GREEK THEATRE

GREEK TRAGEDY
GREEK VERSION
GREEN FINGERS
GREEN HOWARDS
GREEN IN MY EYE
GREEN WITH AGE
GREY EMINENCE
GREY SQUIRREL
GRIEVOUS PAIN
GRILLED BACON
GRILLED STEAK
GRILLED TROUT
GRIM BUSINESS
GRIM LAUGHTER
GRIND ONE'S AXE
GRIPPING TALE
GRIT THE TEETH
GROCERY CHAIN
GROCERY STORE
GROPE ONE'S WAY
GROSS BLUNDER
GROSS NEGLECT
GROSS RETURNS
GROSS TONNAGE
GROUND GINGER
GROUND TO DUST
GROUP CAPTAIN
GROUP OF EIGHT
GROUP OF SEVEN
GROUP OF THREE
GROUP THERAPY
GROUSE SEASON
GROW ANIMATED
GROWING CHILD
GROWING PAINS
GROWING THING
GROW POTATOES
GROW RADISHES
GROW TOGETHER
GRUDGING HAND
GUARD AGAINST
GUARDED REPLY
GUERRILLA WAR
GUESSING GAME
GUIDING LIGHT
GUILT COMPLEX
GUILTY PERSON
GUILTY SECRET
GUITAR PLAYER
GUITAR STRING
GULF OF MEXICO

GUNSHOT WOUND
GUY MANNERING
GUYS AND DOLLS
GUY'S HOSPITAL

H—12
HABEAS CORPUS
HABIT FORMING
HABITUAL LIAR
HACKING COUGH
HACK TO PIECES
HADRIAN'S WALL
HAIR MATTRESS
HAIR OF THE DOG
HAIR RESTORER
HAIR'S BREADTH
HALF DISTANCE
HALF MEASURES
HALF MOURNING
HALF OF BITTER
HALF-SEAS OVER
HALF-WAY HOUSE
HALLEY'S COMET
HALL OF MEMORY
HALTING PLACE
HAM AND TONGUE
HAMBURG STEAK
HAMPTON COURT
HANDEL'S LARGO
HANDFUL OF MEN
HANDICAP RACE
HAND OVER FIST
HAND OVER HAND
HANDS AND FEET
HAND'S BREADTH
HANGING JUDGE
HANGMAN'S ROPE
HANG ONE'S HEAD
HANG TOGETHER
HANS ANDERSEN
HAPPY AS A KING
HAPPY AS A LARK
HAPPY HOLIDAY
HAPPY LANDING
HAPPY NEW YEAR
HAPPY OUTCOME
HAPPY RELEASE
HAPPY RETURNS
HAPPY THOUGHT
HAPPY WARRIOR
HARBOUR LIGHT

HARD CURRENCY
HARD DRINKING
HARD FEELINGS
HARD MATTRESS
HARD MEASURES
HARD QUESTION
HARD SHOULDER
HARD STRUGGLE
HARD SWEARING
HARD THINKING
HARD THOUGHTS
HARD TO COME BY
HARD TO FATHOM
HARD TO HANDLE
HARD TO PLEASE
HARD TRAINING
HARE AND HOUND
HARICOT BEANS
HARLEY STREET
HARMLESS DRUG
HAROLD PINTER
HAROLD WILSON
HARRY CORBETT
HARRY SECOMBE
HARVEST MOUSE
HARVEST QUEEN
HASTY PUDDING
HASTY RETREAT
HATTON GARDEN
HAUNTED HOUSE
HAUTE COUTURE
HAVE A FLUTTER
HAVE A PURPOSE
HAVE A RELAPSE
HAVE A VACANCY
HAVE FEELINGS
HAVE NO ANSWER
HAVE NO CHOICE
HAVE NO DOUBTS
HAVE NO OPTION
HAVE ONE'S WILL
HAVE PATIENCE
HAVE PRIORITY
HAVE SCRUPLES
HAVE THE FACTS
HAVE THE FLOOR
HAVE THE KNACK
HAVE THE LAUGH
HAVE THE MEANS
HAVE THE POWER
HAZARD A GUESS

HEAD FOREMOST
HEAD GARDENER
HEAD IN THE AIR
HEADLINE NEWS
HEAD MISTRESS
HEAD OF CATTLE
HEAD OUT TO SEA
HEAD SHRINKER
HEADS OR TAILS
HEAD THE QUEUE
HEADY MIXTURE
HEADY PERFUME
HEALING CREAM
HEALING POWER
HEALING TOUCH
HEALTH CENTRE
HEALTH RESORT
HEALTHY STATE
HEAP OF STONES
HEAPS OF MONEY
HEAR A PIN DROP
HEAR IN CAMERA
HEART AND HAND
HEART AND SOUL
HEART DISEASE
HEART FAILURE
HEAR THE TRUTH
HEART OF FLINT
HEART OF STONE
HEART'S DESIRE
HEART SURGERY
HEART TO HEART
HEART TROUBLE
HEARTY ASSENT
HEATING AGENT
HEAT OF BATTLE
HEAT OF THE DAY
HEAT OF THE SUN
HEAVE IN SIGHT
HEAVEN FORBID!
HEAVENLY BODY
HEAVENLY CITY
HEAVENLY HOST
HEAVENS ABOVE!
HEAVY AT HEART
HEAVY BIDDING
HEAVY BRIGADE
HEAVY DRINKER
HEAVY PENALTY
HEAVY SLEEPER
HEAVY TRAFFIC

HEAVY VEHICLE
HEAVY WEATHER
HEDGE SPARROW
HEIGHT OF FAME
HEINOUS CRIME
HEIR APPARENT
HELD IN COMMON
HELD TO RANSOM
HELEN SHAPIRO
HELL LET LOOSE
HELL OF A NOISE
HELP YOURSELF
HENRY PURCELL
HERBAL REMEDY
HERD INSTINCT
HERD OF CATTLE
HERD TOGETHER
HERE AND THERE
HEROIC POETRY
HERO OF THE DAY
HERO'S WELCOME
HEWERS OF WOOD
HIDDEN DANGER
HIDDEN DEPTHS
HIDDEN MENACE
HIDDEN TALENT
HIDDEN WEALTH
HIDE ONE'S FACE
HIDE ONE'S HEAD
HIDEOUS CRIME
HIDEOUS NOISE
HIDE THE TRUTH
HIGH ALTITUDE
HIGH BUILDING
HIGH DIVIDEND
HIGHER DEGREE
HIGHER ORDERS
HIGH ESTIMATE
HIGHEST POINT
HIGHEST SCORE
HIGH FIDELITY
HIGHGATE HILL
HIGH INTEREST
HIGH IN THE AIR
HIGHLAND CLAN
HIGHLAND REEL
HIGH LATITUDE
HIGHLY AMUSED
HIGHLY STRUNG
HIGHLY VALUED
HIGH MOUNTAIN

HIGH OFFICIAL
HIGH POSITION
HIGH PRESSURE
HIGH RAINFALL
HIGH STANDARD
HIGH STANDING
HIGH VELOCITY
HILLY COUNTRY
HIP- HIP HURRAH!
HIRED SERVANT
HIRE PURCHASE
HIS REVERENCE
HIT A BOUNDARY
HITCHING POST
HIT ON THE HEAD
HIT THE BOTTLE
HIT THE STUMPS
HIT THE TARGET
HOARY WITH AGE
HOCKEY PLAYER
HOIST THE FLAG
HOIST THE SAIL
HOLD A MEETING
HOLD DOWN A JOB
HOLD IN COMMON
HOLD IN ESTEEM
HOLD IN HORROR
HOLD IN PLEDGE
HOLD ONE'S LEAD
HOLD OUT A HAND
HOLD OUT HOPES
HOLD THE CARDS
HOLD THE FIELD
HOLD THE REINS
HOLD THE STAGE
HOLD TOGETHER
HOLD TO RANSOM
HOLIDAY HAUNT
HOLIDAY MONEY
HOLLAND HOUSE
HOLLOW CHEEKS
HOLLOW SPHERE
HOLLOW SQUARE
HOLLOW THREAT
HOLLOW VESSEL
HOLY ALLIANCE
HOLY MACKEREL
HOLY OF HOLIES
HOME COMFORTS
HOME COUNTIES
HOME FROM HOME

HOME INDUSTRY
HOMELY PERSON
HOME-MADE CAKE
HOME PRODUCTS
HOMING PIGEON
HONEST FELLOW
HONEST LABOUR
HONEST LIVING
HONEYED WORDS
HONORARY RANK
HONOUR BRIGHT
HONOURED NAME
HONOURS OF WAR
HOODED TERROR
HOOKS AND EYES
HOPE DEFERRED
HOPELESS CASE
HOPELESS LOSS
HOPELESS MESS
HOPELESS TASK
HORN OF PLENTY
HORRIBLE BORE
HORS DE COMBAT
HORSE AND CART
HORSE AND TRAP
HORSE BLANKET
HORSE DEALING
HORSE MARINES
HORSE SOLDIER
HORSE TRAINER
HOSPITAL CASE
HOSPITAL SHIP
HOSPITAL WARD
HOSTILE CROWD
HOSTILE FORCE
HOSTILE PRESS
HOT AND STRONG
HOTBED OF VICE
HOT CHESTNUTS
HOT CHOCOLATE
HOT CROSS-BUNS
HOTEL OMNIBUS
HOT FAVOURITE
HOT GOSPELLER
HOT-WATER PIPE
HOUND TO DEATH
HOURLY CHIMES
HOUR OF DANGER
HOUR OF THE DAY
HOUSE AND HOME
HOUSE BREAKER

HOUSE COLOURS
HOUSE FOR SALE
HOUSEHOLD GOD
HOUSE OF CARDS
HOUSE OF LORDS
HOUSE OF PEERS
HOUSE OF TUDOR
HOUSE OF USHER
HOUSE PAINTER
HOUSE SPARROW
HOUSE SURGEON
HOUSE TO HOUSE
HOUSE WARMING
HOUSEY HOUSEY
HOW'S THE ENEMY?
HUMAN AFFAIRS
HUMANE KILLER
HUMAN ELEMENT
HUMAN FAILING
HUMAN FRAILTY
HUMAN REMAINS
HUMAN SPECIES
HUMBLE ORIGIN
HUMBLE PERSON
HUMMING SOUND
HUMOROUS VEIN
HUMPTY DUMPTY
HUNDRED A YEAR
HUNDRED LINES
HUNDRED MILES
HUNDRED TO ONE
HUNDRED YARDS
HUNDRED YEARS
HUNGER STRIKE
HUNK OF CHEESE
HUNTING FIELD
HUNTING LODGE
HUNTING SPEAR
HUNTSMAN'S CRY
HURL DEFIANCE
HURRIED VISIT
HURT FEELINGS
HYDRAULIC RAM
HYDROGEN BOMB
HYMN OF PRAISE

I—12
ICE-CREAM SODA
ICY RECEPTION
IDEAL HUSBAND
IDENTITY CARD

IDENTITY DISC
IDLE THOUGHTS
IF THE CAP FITS
IGNEOUS ROCKS
ILLEGAL ENTRY
ILLICIT GAINS
ILLICIT MEANS
ILLICIT STILL
ILL-TIMED JEST
IMMORTAL FAME
IMMORTAL NAME
IMMORTAL POET
IMMORTAL SOUL
IMPERIAL PINT
IMPERIAL RULE
IMPLIED TRUTH
IMPROPER WORD
IN A BAD TEMPER
IN A COLD SWEAT
IN A DEAD FAINT
IN A GOOD LIGHT
IN ALL HONESTY
IN A LOUD VOICE
IN AN ACCIDENT
IN AN ARMCHAIR
IN APPEARANCE
IN A SHORT TIME
IN ATTENDANCE
IN AT THE DEATH
IN CASE OF NEED
INCHCAPE ROCK
INCHES TALLER
INCOMING TIDE
IN CONCLUSION
IN CONFERENCE
IN CONFIDENCE
INCREASED PAY
IN DEEP WATERS
INDELIBLE INK
INDIAN MILLET
INDIAN MUTINY
INDIAN SUMMER
IN DIFFICULTY
INDIRECT HINT
INDOOR AERIAL
INDOOR SPORTS
IN EMPLOYMENT
INFANT IN ARMS
INFANTRY UNIT
INFANT SCHOOL
INFERIOR RANK

IN FINE FETTLE
INFINITE TIME
INFRA-RED LAMP
INFRA-RED RAYS
IN FULL FLIGHT
IN GOOD HEALTH
IN GOOD REPAIR
IN GOOD SUPPLY
IN HIGH FAVOUR
IN HIGH RELIEF
IN HOLY ORDERS
IN HOT PURSUIT
INITIAL STAGE
INJURED PARTY
INJURED PRIDE
IN LEAGUE WITH
IN LIKE MANNER
IN LOVE AND WAR
IN LOW SPIRITS
IN MODERATION
IN NEED OF HELP
INNER CABINET
INNER SANCTUM
IN NO FIT STATE
IN OCCUPATION
IN ONE RESPECT
IN ONE'S FAVOUR
IN ONE'S HEYDAY
IN ONE'S OLD AGE
IN ONE'S SENSES
IN ONE'S STRIDE
IN OPPOSITION
IN OTHER WORDS
IN OUR OPINION
IN PARTICULAR
IN POOR HEALTH
IN POSSESSION
IN PROCESSION
IN PROPORTION
IN QUARANTINE
IN RECORD TIME
IN RETIREMENT
IN RETROSPECT
INSANE ASYLUM
INSECURE HOLD
IN SETTLEMENT
IN SILHOUETTE
IN SINGLE FILE
IN SLOW MOTION
IN SUBJECTION
IN SUCCESSION

INTEGRAL PART
INTEREST FREE
INTEREST RATE
INTERIOR WALL
IN TERMS OF LAW
IN THE BALANCE
IN THE BALCONY
IN THE BEDROOM
IN THE CABINET
IN THE CAPITAL
IN THE COUNTRY
IN THE CRYSTAL
IN THE DAYTIME
IN THE DEEP END
IN THE EVENING
IN THE EXTREME
IN THE FASHION
IN THE GALLERY
IN THE HONOURS
IN THE INTERIM
IN THE KITCHEN
IN THE LIBRARY
IN THE LONG RUN
IN THE MORNING
IN THE NURSERY
IN THE OLD DAYS
IN THE OPEN AIR
IN THE PADDOCK
IN THE PARLOUR
IN THE PEERAGE
IN THE PICTURE
IN THE PRESENT
IN THE RUNNING
IN THE SHADOWS
IN THE SUBURBS
IN THE THEATRE
IN THE TROPICS
IN THE VERY ACT
IN THE VILLAGE
IN THE YEAR ONE
IN TRIPLICATE
IN UNDERTONES
IN UTMOST NEED
INVALID CHAIR
INVERSE ORDER
INVERSE RATIO
INVERTED SNOB
INVERTED TURN
INVISIBLE INK
INVISIBLE MAN
INVOICE CLERK

IN YUGOSLAVIA
IRISH COLLEEN
IRISH TERRIER
IRISH WHISKEY
IRON AND STEEL
IRONING BOARD
IRVING BERLIN
ISLAND OF CUBA
ISLE OF CYPRUS
ISLE OF THANET
ISOLATED CASE
ISSUE A THREAT
ITALIAN MONEY
IT ALL DEPENDS
IT'S AN ILL WIND
IT'S A PLEASURE

J—12
JACKET POTATO
JACKIE COOGAN
JACK IN OFFICE
JACK OF HEARTS
JACK OF SPADES
JACK OF TRUMPS
JACK ROBINSON
JACK SHEPPARD
JACOB'S LADDER
JADE NECKLACE
JAMES BOSWELL
JAMES STEWART
JAMES THURBER
JANETTE SCOTT
JANUARY SALES
JAUNDICED EYE
JAZZ FESTIVAL
JEAN METCALFE
JE NE SAIS QUOI
JERMYN STREET
JIG-SAW PUZZLE
JIMMY DURANTE
JIMMY EDWARDS
JIMMY WHEELER
JIM THE PENMAN
JOAN CRAWFORD
JOG THE MEMORY
JOHN CLEMENTS
JOHNNY MATHIS
JOHN TRAVOLTA
JOIN IN THE FUN
JOIN ONE'S SHIP
JOINT ACCOUNT

JOINT CONCERN
JOIN THE CHOIR
JOIN THE DANCE
JOIN THE ENEMY
JOIN THE PARTY
JOIN THE QUEUE
JOIN THE RANKS
JOINT HOLDING
JOIN TOGETHER
JOINT TENANCY
JOINT TRUSTEE
JOKING MATTER
JOLLY JACK TAR
JOLLY SWAGMAN
JONATHAN WILD
JORDAN ALMOND
JOSEPH CONRAD
JOSEPH COTTON
JOSEPH STALIN
JUDGE AND JURY
JUDGMENT SEAT
JULIAN HUXLEY
JULIE ANDREWS
JULIENNE SOUP
JULIUS CAESAR
JULY THE FIFTH
JULY THE FIRST
JULY THE NINTH
JULY THE SIXTH
JULY THE TENTH
JULY THE THIRD
JUMP THE QUEUE
JUMP THE RAILS
JUNE THE FIFTH
JUNE THE FIRST
JUNE THE NINTH
JUNE THE SIXTH
JUNE THE TENTH
JUNE THE THIRD
JUNIOR SCHOOL
JUNIOR TYPIST
JUST AS YOU SAY
JUST FOR SPITE
JUST THE THING
JUST THIS ONCE
JUVENILE LEAD

K—12
KEEN APPETITE
KEEN AS A RAZOR
KEEN INTEREST

KEEN PLEASURE	KNIFE AND FORK	LADY JANE GREY
KEEP ACCOUNTS	KNIFE GRINDER	LADY MARGARET
KEEP A LOOK-OUT	KNIGHT ERRANT	LADY MAYORESS
KEEP A PROMISE	KNIGHTLY DEED	LADY NICOTINE
KEEP CHEERFUL	KNIT A SWEATER	LADY'S BICYCLE
KEEP-FIT CLASS	KNIT ONE'S BROW	LADY SUPERIOR
KEEP GOOD TIME	KNIT THE BROWS	LAGER AND LIME
KEEP GUESSING	KNIT TOGETHER	LAISSEZ FAIRE
KEEP IN PRISON	KNOCK AGAINST	LAKE DISTRICT
KEEP IN PURDAH	KNOCK OFF WORK	LAKE MAGGIORE
KEEP IN REPAIR	KNOCK-OUT BLOW	LAKE MICHIGAN
KEEP ONE'S FEET	KNOW FOR A FACT	LAKE SUPERIOR
KEEP ONE'S HEAD	KNOW FULL WELL	LAKE VICTORIA
KEEP ONE'S SEAT	KNOW NO BETTER	LAKE WINNIPEG
KEEP ONE'S WORD	KNOW NO BOUNDS	LAMBENT LIGHT
KEEP ON TRYING	KNOW ONE'S DUTY	LAMB SANDWICH
KEEP PRISONER	KNOW THE DRILL	LANDED ESTATE
KEEP THE BOOKS	KNOW THE FACTS	LANDED GENTRY
KEEP THE PEACE	KNOW THE ROPES	LANDING CRAFT
KEEP THE SCORE	KNOW THE SCORE	LANDING PARTY
KEEP TOGETHER	KNOW THE TRUTH	LANDING PLACE
KEEP UP-TO-DATE	KNOW THE WORST	LANDING STRIP
KENNETH HORNE	KNOW WHAT TO DO	LAND OF DREAMS
KEPT ON A LEASH	KNUCKLE UNDER	LAND OF PLENTY
KETTLE OF FISH	KNUR AND SPELL	LAND SURVEYOR
KEY OF THE DOOR		LAND TRANSFER
KEY SIGNATURE	**L—12**	LANTERN SLIDE
KEYSTONE COPS	LABOURED JOKE	LAP OF THE GODS
KEY TO THE SAFE	LABOUR IN VAIN	LARGE ACCOUNT
KHAKI UNIFORM	LABOUR LEADER	LARGE EXPANSE
KILL BY INCHES	LABOUR MARKET	LARGE HELPING
KILL OUTRIGHT	LABOUR OFFICE	LARGE PORTION
KINDLING WOOD	LABOUR OF LOVE	LARGE SECTION
KING AND QUEEN	LABOUR POLICY	LARGE VARIETY
KING OF BEASTS	LACE CURTAINS	LASH THE WAVES
KING OF FRANCE	LACKING MONEY	LAST BUT THREE
KING OF HEARTS	LACKING POINT	LAST DELIVERY
KING OF SPADES	LACKING POISE	LAST ELECTION
KING OF TRUMPS	LACKING PROOF	LAST FRONTIER
KING'S COLLEGE	LACKING SENSE	LASTING PEACE
KING'S COUNSEL	LACK INTEREST	LAST JUDGMENT
KING'S ENGLISH	LACK OF BRAINS	LAST RESOURCE
KING'S HIGHWAY	LACK OF FINISH	LAST SATURDAY
KING'S PROCTOR	LACK OF POLISH	LAST SYLLABLE
KITCHEN CHAIR	LACK OF PROFIT	LAST THURSDAY
KITCHEN RANGE	LACK OF REASON	LAST TO ARRIVE
KITCHEN STOVE	LACK OF SPIRIT	LATE IN THE DAY
KITCHEN TABLE	LACK OF WISDOM	LATE LAMENTED
KNACKER'S YARD	LACROSSE TEAM	LATE MARRIAGE
KNAVE OF CLUBS	LADDER OF FAME	LATENT ENERGY
KNEE BREECHES	LADY HAMILTON	LATENT TALENT

LATEST REPORT
LATIN AMERICA
LATIN GRAMMAR
LATIN QUARTER
LATIN TEACHER
LAUGH OUT LOUD
LAUGH TO SCORN
LAUNCHING PAD
LAUREL WREATH
LAVENDER HILL
LAVISH PRAISE
LAW OF ENGLAND
LAW OF GRAVITY
LAW OF THE LAND
LAWS OF MOTION
LAWYER'S BRIEF
LAY A FINGER ON
LAY DOWN A PLAN
LAYER ON LAYER
LAY IT ON THICK
LEAD A GAY LIFE
LEADER WRITER
LEADING ACTOR
LEADING LIGHT
LEAD IN PRAYER
LEAD THE DANCE
LEAD THE FIELD
LEANING TOWER
LEAP IN THE AIR
LEARN A LESSON
LEARN BY HEART
LEARNED JUDGE
LEARN TO DRIVE
LEARN TO RELAX
LEARN TO WRITE
LEATHER GOODS
LEATHER STRAP
LEAVE A LEGACY
LEAVE IT ALONE
LEAVE NO DOUBT
LEAVE NO TRACE
LEAVE NO WISER
LEAVE OFF WORK
LEAVE THE ARMY
LEAVE THE NAVY
LEAVE THE NEST
LEAVE THE ROOM
LED ONE A DANCE
LED TO BELIEVE
LEFT AND RIGHT
LEFT-HAND BEND

LEFT-HAND SIDE
LEFT-HAND TURN
LEFT IN THE AIR
LEFT NO CHOICE
LEFT SHOULDER
LEFT STANDING
LEFT TO CHANCE
LEGAL ADVISER
LEGAL CUSTODY
LEGAL DEFENCE
LEGAL FICTION
LEGAL JOURNAL
LEGAL OPINION
LEGAL PROCESS
LEGAL VERDICT
LEGS TOGETHER
LEG TO STAND ON
LEISURE HOURS
LEMON PUDDING
LENGTH OF TIME
LESSON ELEVEN
LESSON TWELVE
LESS THAN COST
LETHAL WEAPON
LET ONESELF GO
LET OUT ON HIRE
LETTER OPENER
LETTER WRITER
LET THINGS RIP
LET WELL ALONE
LEVEL PEGGING
LEVEL STRETCH
LEWIS CARROLL
LEYTON ORIENT
LIBERAL DONOR
LIBERAL PARTY
LIBERAL SHARE
LIBERTY HORSE
LIBYAN DESERT
LICENSING ACT
LICENSING LAW
LICK ONE'S LIPS
LIE OF THE LAND
LIE PROSTRATE
LIFE AND DEATH
LIFE IMMORTAL
LIFE INSTINCT
LIFE INTEREST
LIFE IN THE RAW
LIFE OF LUXURY
LIFE SENTENCE

LIFT ONE'S HAND
LIFT THE ELBOW
LIGHT A CANDLE
LIGHT AND AIRY
LIGHT AND DARK
LIGHT BRIGADE
LIGHT CAVALRY
LIGHT CRUISER
LIGHT DRAGOON
LIGHTED TORCH
LIGHT FINGERS
LIGHTNING ROD
LIGHT OF HEART
LIGHT RAILWAY
LIGHT READING
LIGHT SLEEPER
LIGHT THE LAMP
LIGHT TRAFFIC
LIGHT VEHICLE
LIKE HOT CAKES
LIKE OLD BOOTS
LIKE SARDINES
LIKE THE DEVIL
LIKE UNTO LIKE
LIKE WILDFIRE
LILY OF LAGUNA
LIMB FROM LIMB
LIMB OF THE LAW
LIMITED MEANS
LIMITED SCOPE
LIMITED SCORE
LIMITED SPACE
LINCOLN GREEN
LINE OF ACTION
LINE OF BATTLE
LINE OF FLIGHT
LINE REGIMENT
LINE UPON LINE
LINGUA FRANCA
LINK TOGETHER
LIQUEUR GLASS
LIQUID ASSETS
LIQUID MAKE-UP
LIST OF VOTERS
LITERAL ERROR
LITERAL TRUTH
LITERARY AIMS
LITERARY CLUB
LITERARY FAME
LITERARY HACK
LITERARY LION

LITERARY PAGE	LONG AND OFTEN	LOSE THE ASHES
LITERARY STAR	LONG CORRIDOR	LOSE THE MATCH
LITERARY WORK	LONG DISTANCE	LOSE THE SCENT
LITTER BASKET	LONG DIVISION	LOSING BATTLE
LITTLE CHANCE	LONG DRAWN-OUT	LOSING HAZARD
LITTLE CHANGE	LONGEST NIGHT	LOSING TICKET
LITTLE DEMAND	LONG EXPECTED	LOSS OF CUSTOM
LITTLE DORRIT	LONG FAREWELL	LOSS OF ENERGY
LITTLE ENOUGH	LONG-FELT WANT	LOSS OF HEALTH
LITTLE FINGER	LONG FOR PEACE	LOSS OF HONOUR
LITTLE HITLER	LONG SENTENCE	LOSS OF MEMORY
LITTLE MONKEY	LONG STANDING	LOSS OF MORALE
LITTLE PEOPLE	LONG-TERM LOAN	LOSS OF PROFIT
LITTLE SISTER	LONG-TERM VIEW	LOSS OF REASON
LITTLE SQUIRT	LONG TROUSERS	LOSS OF SPEECH
LITTLE TERROR	LONG VACATION	LOSS OF VISION
LITTLE THANKS	LONG WAY ROUND	LOSS OF WEIGHT
LITTLE THINGS	LONSDALE BELT	LOST AND FOUND
LITTLE TIN GOD	LOOK BOTH WAYS	LOST ELECTION
LITTLE WONDER	LOOK DOWNCAST	LOST FOR A WORD
LIVE AND LEARN	LOOK DOWN UPON	LOST FOR WORDS
LIVE FOR KICKS	LOOK ONE'S BEST	LOST IN WONDER
LIVE FOR TODAY	LOOK PECULIAR	LOST PROPERTY
LIVE IN A DREAM	LOOK PLEASANT	LOTUS BLOSSOM
LIVE IN CLOVER	LOOK SHEEPISH	LOUD AND CLEAR
LIVE IN LUXURY	LOOK SIDEWAYS	LOUD APPLAUSE
LIVELY DEBATE	LOOK SUPERIOR	LOUD LAUGHTER
LIVE ON CREDIT	LOOSE CLOTHES	LOUIS GOLDING
LIVE ONE'S LIFE	LOOSE CONDUCT	LOUIS PASTEUR
LIVER SAUSAGE	LOOSE GARMENT	LOUNGE LIZARD
LIVERY STABLE	LORD ADVOCATE	LOVE INTEREST
LIVE TOGETHER	LORD ALMIGHTY	LOVELY FIGURE
LIVING MATTER	LORD LEIGHTON	LOVE OF NATURE
LIVING MEMORY	LORD MACAULAY	LOVING COUPLE
LIVING TISSUE	LORD OF APPEAL	LOW CHURCHMAN
LOAD SHEDDING	LORD TENNYSON	LOW CONDITION
LOBSTER PATTY	LORETTA YOUNG	LOW COUNTRIES
LOBSTER SALAD	LOSE BUSINESS	LOW-DOWN TRICK
LOCAL AFFAIRS	LOSE INTEREST	LOWER ANIMALS
LOCAL DIALECT	LOSE MOMENTUM	LOWER BRACKET
LOCAL FEELING	LOSE ONE'S FORM	LOWER CHAMBER
LOCALISED WAR	LOSE ONE'S GRIP	LOWER CLASSES
LOCK-UP GARAGE	LOSE ONE'S HAIR	LOWER ONESELF
LODGING HOUSE	LOSE ONE'S HEAD	LOWER REGIONS
LOGICAL ERROR	LOSE ONE'S LIFE	LOWER THE FLAG
LOGICAL ORDER	LOSE ONE'S SEAT	LOWEST BIDDER
LONDON BRIDGE	LOSE ONE'S WIFE	LOWEST DEPTHS
LONDON EDITOR	LOSE ONE'S WITS	LOW FREQUENCY
LONDON LIGHTS	LOSE PATIENCE	LOW VALUATION
LONDON SEASON	LOSE PRESTIGE	LOW WATER MARK
LONG ANCESTRY	LOSE STRENGTH	LOYAL CITIZEN

LOYAL SUBJECT
LOYAL SUPPORT
LUCIFER MATCH
LUCKY AT CARDS
LUCKY VENTURE
LUGGAGE LABEL
LULWORTH COVE
LUMBER JACKET
LUMP TOGETHER
LUSH PASTURES
LUST FOR POWER
LUXURIOUS BED
LUXURY CRUISE
LYRIC THEATRE

M—12
MACHINE TOOLS
MAD AS A HATTER
MADDING CROWD
MADE IN FRANCE
MADE IN HEAVEN
MAGIC FORMULA
MAGIC LANTERN
MAGNETIC FISH
MAGNETIC MINE
MAGNETIC POLE
MAGNETIC TAPE
MAIDEN FLIGHT
MAIDEN SPEECH
MAIDEN STAKES
MAIDEN VOYAGE
MAID OF HONOUR
MAIN BUSINESS
MAIN DRAINAGE
MAIN ENTRANCE
MAIN INDUSTRY
MAIN QUESTION
MAIN SEQUENCE
MAÎTRE D'HÔTEL
MAJOR BARBARA
MAJOR EDITION
MAJOR GENERAL
MAJORITY RULE
MAJORITY VOTE
MAJOR PREMISE
MAJOR PROPHET
MAJOR TRAGEDY
MAKE A BARGAIN
MAKE A BEE-LINE
MAKE A BEQUEST
MAKE A BONFIRE

MAKE ABSOLUTE
MAKE A CENTURY
MAKE A CIRCUIT
MAKE A CURTSEY
MAKE A DEAD SET
MAKE ADVANCES
MAKE A FAUX PAS
MAKE A FORTUNE
MAKE A GESTURE
MAKE A GET-AWAY
MAKE A HUNDRED
MAKE A LANDING
MAKE A LONG ARM
MAKE A MISTAKE
MAKE AN APPEAL
MAKE AN ARREST
MAKE AN EFFORT
MAKE AN ESCAPE
MAKE A NEW WILL
MAKE A PRESENT
MAKE A PROMISE
MAKE A PROTEST
MAKE A REQUEST
MAKE BAD BLOOD
MAKE BANKRUPT
MAKE ENDS MEET
MAKE IT SNAPPY
MAKE MISCHIEF
MAKE NO PROFIT
MAKE ONE'S EXIT
MAKE ONE SIT UP
MAKE ONE'S MARK
MAKE ONE'S PILE
MAKE ONE'S WILL
MAKE OUT A CASE
MAKE PROGRESS
MAKE SPEECHES
MAKE THE GRADE
MAKE-UP ARTIST
MAKE UP LEEWAY
MALAY STRAITS
MALTESE CROSS
MALVERN HILLS
MAN ABOUT TOWN
MAN AT THE HELM
MANDERIN DUCK
MANGO CHUTNEY
MANILLA PAPER
MAN IN THE DOCK
MAN IN THE MOON
MAN-MADE FIBRE

MAN OF DESTINY
MAN OF FASHION
MAN OF FORTUNE
MAN OF HIS WORD
MAN OF LEISURE
MAN OF LETTERS
MAN OF MYSTERY
MAN OF SCIENCE
MAN OF THE HOUR
MAN ON THE MOON
MAN ON THE SPOT
MAN OVERBOARD
MANSION HOUSE
MAN THE BREACH
MAN-TO-MAN TALK
MANUAL LABOUR
MANUAL WORKER
MANY A LONG DAY
MANY RESPECTS
MANY YEARS AGO
MAP OF AUSTRIA
MAP OF BELGIUM
MAP OF DENMARK
MAP OF ENGLAND
MAP OF GERMANY
MAP OF HOLLAND
MAP OF IRELAND
MARATHON RACE
MARCHING SONG
MARGINAL LAND
MARGINAL NOTE
MARGINAL SEAT
MARIE CELESTE
MARIE CORELLI
MARIE TEMPEST
MARIE THERESA
MARINE ANIMAL
MARINE ENGINE
MARINE GROWTH
MARINE PARADE
MARINE STORES
MARITIME ALPS
MARIUS GORING
MARKED MANNER
MARKET GARDEN
MARKET SQUARE
MARKET STREET
MARKET TRENDS
MARK OF ESTEEM
MARK OF GENIUS
MARK THE CARDS

MARK THE SCORE
MARLEY'S GHOST
MARLON BRANDO
MARMALADE CAT
MARRIAGE KNOT
MARRIAGE RATE
MARRIAGE TIES
MARRIAGE VOWS
MARRIED BLISS
MARRIED WOMAN
MARRY BY PROXY
MARRY IN HASTE
MARSHALL PLAN
MARTIAL MUSIC
MARTIN LUTHER
MARX BROTHERS
MARY OF ARGYLL
MARY PICKFORD
MASONIC LODGE
MASSED CHOIRS
MASSES OF FOOD
MASS HYSTERIA
MASS MOVEMENT
MASS MURDERER
MASS OF NERVES
MASTER AND MAN
MASTER CUTLER
MASTER GUNNER
MASTER OF ARTS
MASTER SPIRIT
MASTER STROKE
MASTER TAILOR
MATCHING PAIR
MATERIAL GAIN
MATERNAL LOVE
MATING SEASON
MATTER IN HAND
MATTER OF FACT
MAXIMUM PRICE
MAXIMUM SPEED
MAYPOLE DANCE
MAY THE EIGHTH
MAY THE FOURTH
MAY THE SECOND
MEAN BUSINESS
MEAN MISCHIEF
MEANS TO AN END
MEASURED MILE
MEAT AND DRINK
MEAT SANDWICH
MEDICAL BOARD

MEDICAL CHECK
MEDICAL STAFF
MEDICINE BALL
MEDIUM HEIGHT
MEDIUM SHERRY
MEET BY CHANCE
MEETING HOUSE
MEETING PLACE
MEETING POINT
MEET IN SECRET
MEET ONE'S FATE
MEET THE PLANE
MEET THE TRAIN
MELTED BUTTER
MELTED CHEESE
MELTING POINT
MELT THE HEART
MEMORIAL HALL
MEND ONE'S WAYS
MEN OF HARLECH
MENTAL ASYLUM
MENTAL EFFORT
MENTAL ENERGY
MENTAL HEALTH
MENTALLY SICK
MENTAL STRAIN
MENTAL STRESS
MERCHANT BANK
MERCHANT NAVY
MERCHANT SHIP
MERCY KILLING
MERE FLEA-BITE
MERE PITTANCE
MERRY MONARCH
MERRY OLD SOUL
MERSEY TUNNEL
MESSENGER BOY
METAL FATIGUE
METEOR SHOWER
METHOD ACTING
METRICAL UNIT
METRIC SYSTEM
MEZZO SOPRANO
MICHAEL ARLEN
MICHAEL ASPEL
MICHAEL CAINE
MICKEY ROONEY
MIDDLE AND LEG
MIDDLE COURSE
MIDDLE FINGER
MIDDLE TEMPLE

MIDDLE WICKET
MIDNIGHT BLUE
MIDNIGHT HOUR
MIDNIGHT MASS
MIDNIGHT SWIM
MIDSUMMER DAY
MIGHT AND MAIN
MIGHT IS RIGHT
MIGHTY EFFORT
MIGHTY HUNTER
MILES PER HOUR
MILE UPON MILE
MILFORD HAVEN
MILITARY BAND
MILITARY BASE
MILITARY BODY
MILITARY CAMP
MILITARY DUTY
MILITARY LIFE
MILITARY PACE
MILITARY RANK
MILITARY TYPE
MILITARY UNIT
MILK AND A DASH
MILK AND HONEY
MILK AND SUGAR
MILK AND WATER
MILKING STOOL
MILK SHORTAGE
MILLION YEARS
MINCE MATTERS
MINCING STEPS
MIND HOW YOU GO!
MIND YOUR HEAD!
MIND YOUR STEP!
MINERAL SALTS
MINERAL WATER
MINERAL WORLD
MINIATURE DOG
MINING EXPERT
MINING RIGHTS
MINOR AILMENT
MINORITY RULE
MINORITY VOTE
MINOR PREMISE
MINOR PROPHET
MINOR SET-BACK
MINOR TRAGEDY
MINSTREL SHOW
MISPLACED WIT
MISSED CHANCE

MISSING PIECE
MISS THE PLANE
MISS THE POINT
MISS THE TRAIN
MISS UNIVERSE
MISTAKEN IDEA
MISTRESS FORD
MIXED BATHING
MIXED COMPANY
MIXED DOUBLES
MIXED FARMING
MIXED MOTIVES
MIXED PICKLES
MIX IN SOCIETY
MOATED GRANGE
MOBILE COLUMN
MODEL HUSBAND
MODEL PATIENT
MODEL RAILWAY
MODE OF LIVING
MODERATE RENT
MODERN SCHOOL
MODEST INCOME
MODEST PERSON
MODUS VIVENDI
MOIRA SHEARER
MOLL FLANDERS
MOMENT OF TIME
MONASTIC LIFE
MONASTIC VOWS
MONDAY'S CHILD
MONETARY HELP
MONETARY UNIT
MONEYED CLASS
MONEY MATTERS
MONEY TO SPARE
MONKEY GLANDS
MONKEY JACKET
MONKEY PUZZLE
MONKEY TRICKS
MONTH BY MONTH
MONTHLY VISIT
MONTH'S NOTICE
MOOR OF VENICE
MOOT QUESTION
MORAL CONDUCT
MORAL COURAGE
MORALITY PLAY
MORALLY BOUND
MORAL SCIENCE
MORAL STAMINA

MORAL SUPPORT
MORAL VICTORY
MORE'S THE PITY
MORE THAN EVER
MORE THAN ONCE
MORMON CHURCH
MORNING AFTER
MORNING DRESS
MORNING GLORY
MORNING PAPER
MORRIS DANCER
MORTAL COMBAT
MORTAL TERROR
MORTE D'ARTHUR
MORTGAGE DEED
MOSQUITO BITE
MOST EXCITING
MOST GRACIOUS
MOST OF THE DAY
MOST REVEREND
MOTE IN THE EYE
MOTHER AND SON
MOTHER CHURCH
MOTHER GRUNDY
MOTHERLY LOVE
MOTHER NATURE
MOTHER OF MINE
MOTHERS' UNION
MOTHER TONGUE
MOTOR BICYCLE
MOTOR CRUISER
MOTORING CLUB
MOTOR LICENCE
MOTOR SCOOTER
MOTOR VEHICLE
MOUNTAIN GOAT
MOUNTAIN LAKE
MOUNTAIN PASS
MOUNTAIN PEAK
MOUNTAIN TARN
MOUNT A LADDER
MOUNT EVEREST
MOUNT OF VENUS
MOUNT OLYMPUS
MOUNT PEGASUS
MOURA LYMPANY
MOUSTACHE CUP
MOUTH TO MOUTH
MOVABLE FEAST
MOVED TO TEARS
MOVE SIDEWAYS

MOVING APPEAL
MOVING FINGER
MOVING SPEECH
MOVING SPIRIT
MOVING TARGET
MUCH IMPROVED
MUCH IN DEMAND
MUCH MISTAKEN
MUD IN YOUR EYE
MUFFLED DRUMS
MUFFLED TONES
MUFFLED VOICE
MUGGY WEATHER
MULBERRY BUSH
MULBERRY TREE
MULTIPLE SHOP
MULTIPLE STAR
MUNICH CRISIS
MUNICIPAL LAW
MURDER CHARGE
MURDER VICTIM
MURDER WEAPON
MURIEL PAVLOW
MUSCATEL WINE
MUSHROOM SOUP
MUSICAL PIECE
MUSICAL SCALE
MUSICAL SCORE
MUSICAL SOUND
MUSICAL VOICE
MUSIC AT NIGHT
MUSIC LICENCE
MUSIC TEACHER
MUTED STRINGS
MUTTON CUTLET
MUTUAL FRIEND
MUTUAL HATRED
MUTUAL PROFIT
MUTUAL REGARD
MY BLUE HEAVEN
MY DEAR FELLOW
MY DEAR WATSON
MY GOOD FRIEND
MYSTERY STORY

N—12
NAIL POLISHER
NAIL SCISSORS
NAKED REALITY
NAME IN LIGHTS
NARROW DEFEAT

NARROW ESCAPE	NEAR RELATION	NICKEL SILVER
NARROW GROOVE	NEAR RELATIVE	NIGEL PATRICK
NARROW MARGIN	NEAR THE COAST	NIGGLING PAIN
NARROW SQUEAK	NEAR THE SHORE	NIGHT CLASSES
NARROW STREET	NEAR THE TRUTH	NIGHT CLOTHES
NARROW THE GAP	NECKING PARTY	NIGHT DRIVING
NARROW TUNNEL	NECK OF MUTTON	NIGHT FIGHTER
NATIONAL BANK	NEEDLESS RISK	NIGHT NURSERY
NATIONAL DEBT	NEGATIVE POLE	NIGHT OF BLISS
NATIONAL DISH	NEGATIVE SIGN	NIGHT PROWLER
NATIONAL FLAG	NEGATIVE VOTE	NINE AND A HALF
NATIONAL GAME	NEON LIGHTING	NINE AND EIGHT
NATIONAL GRID	NERVE ONESELF	NINE AND SEVEN
NATIONAL HERO	NERVOUS STATE	NINE AND THREE
NATIONAL PARK	NERVOUS WRECK	NINE OF HEARTS
NATIONAL POLL	NEST OF TABLES	NINE OF SPADES
NATIONAL ROAD	NEUTER GENDER	NINE OF TRUMPS
NATIONAL STUD	NEUTRAL POWER	NINE OUT OF TEN
NATION IN ARMS	NEUTRAL STATE	NINE THOUSAND
NATIVE CUSTOM	NEVER DESPAIR	NINTH CENTURY
NATIVE TONGUE	NEVER GO WRONG	NINTH OF APRIL
NATIVE TROOPS	NEVER THE SAME	NINTH OF MARCH
NATIVITY PLAY	NEVER TOO LATE	NITROUS OXIDE
NATURAL BREAK	NEVER YOU MIND!	NO ADMITTANCE
NATURAL CHARM	NEW AMSTERDAM	NO BED OF ROSES
NATURAL CHILD	NEW BRUNSWICK	NOBLE BEARING
NATURAL COVER	NEW DEPARTURE	NOBLE DESCENT
NATURAL DEATH	NEW ENGLANDER	NOBLE EDIFICE
NATURAL ENEMY	NEW HAMPSHIRE	NOBLE GESTURE
NATURAL FIBRE	NEW INVENTION	NOBLE MANNERS
NATURAL ORDER	NEW JERUSALEM	NOBODY'S CHILD
NATURAL PRIDE	NEWLY MARRIED	NOBODY'S FAULT
NATURAL SCALE	NEW PARAGRAPH	NO-CLAIM BONUS
NATURAL STATE	NEWS BULLETIN	NO COMPARISON
NAUGHTY CHILD	NEWS OF THE DAY	NO DIFFERENCE
NAUTICAL FLAG	NEW STATESMAN	NO DOUBT AT ALL
NAUTICAL LIFE	NEW TECHNIQUE	NO EARTHLY USE
NAUTICAL MILE	NEW TESTAMENT	NO END OF MONEY
NAUTICAL ROLL	NEW YORK STATE	NO FIXED ABODE
NAVAL ATTACHE	NEW ZEALANDER	NO FLIES ON HIM
NAVAL BRIGADE	NEXT ELECTION	NO IMPORTANCE
NAVAL COLLEGE	NEXT QUESTION	NOLENS VOLENS
NAVAL COMMAND	NEXT SATURDAY	NOMINAL POWER
NAVAL OFFICER	NEXT THURSDAY	NOMINAL PRICE
NAVAL RESERVE	NIAGARA FALLS	NOMINAL RULER
NAVAL SERVICE	NICE AND HANDY	NOMINAL VALUE
NAVAL STATION	NICE AND SWEET	NONE THE WISER
NAVAL TACTICS	NICE AND TIGHT	NONE THE WORSE
NAVAL UNIFORM	NICE BUSINESS	NONE WHATEVER
NAVAL WARFARE	NICELY PLACED	NON-STOP REVUE
NEAR DISTANCE	NICE QUESTION	NON-STOP TRAIN

NO PREFERENCE	OCEAN TRAFFIC	OMINOUS CLOUD
NORMAN WISDOM	ODDS AND EVENS	OMISSION MARK
NORTH AMERICA	ODD SENSATION	OMIT NO DETAIL
NORTH BRITAIN	ODDS-ON CHANCE	ON A GOOD THING
NORTH COUNTRY	OF EVIL REPUTE	ON A LEVEL WITH
NORTHERN LINE	OFFER A CHOICE	ON AN EVEN KEEL
NORTH GERMANY	OFFER A REWARD	ON A STRETCHER
NORTH SHIELDS	OFFER FOR SALE	ONCE AND AGAIN
NORTH TO SOUTH	OFFERTORY BOX	ONCE IN A WHILE
NOTABLE POINT	OFF HIS OWN BAT	ONCE TOO OFTEN
NOTARY PUBLIC	OFF HIS ROCKER	ON COMMISSION
NOT A STITCH ON	OFFICER CADET	ONE AND A PENNY
NOTHING AMISS	OFFICERS' MESS	ONE AND ELEVEN
NOTHING AT ALL	OFFICIAL COPY	ONE AND TWENTY
NOTHING DOING	OFFICIAL DUTY	ONE-DAY STRIKE
NOTHING FOR IT	OFFICIAL FORM	ONE FELL SWOOP
NOTHING KNOWN	OFFICIAL LIST	ONE FOR HIS NOB
NOTHING TO ADD	OFFICIAL VIEW	ONE FOR THE POT
NOTHING TO EAT	OFF LIKE A SHOT	ONE-HORSE SHOW
NOTHING TO PAY	OFF ONE'S CHUMP	ONE-HORSE TOWN
NOTHING TO SAY	OFF ONE'S GUARD	ONE JUMP AHEAD
NOTICE TO QUIT	OFF ONE'S HANDS	ONE-LEGGED MAN
NO TIME TO LOSE	OFF THE COURSE	ONE LONG DREAM
NOT IN KEEPING	OFF THE RECORD	ONE MOVE AHEAD
NOT IN THE MOOD	OFF THE SCREEN	ONE OF THE BEST
NOT WORTH A RAP	OF GREAT WORTH	ONE OF THE GANG
NOUVEAU RICHE	OF MICE AND MEN	ONE OF THE LADS
NOVEMBER DAYS	OIL OF JUNIPER	ON EQUAL TERMS
NUDIST COLONY	OIL OF VITRIOL	ONE'S FAIR NAME
NUMBER ELEVEN	OIL THE WHEELS	ONE-SIDED VIEW
NUMBER-ONE MAN	OKLAHOMA CITY	ONE-TRACK MIND
NUMBER, PLEASE	OLD AS HISTORY	ONE-WAY STREET
NUMBER TWELVE	OLD BATTLE-AXE	ON FIRM GROUND
NUMBER TWENTY	OLDER BROTHER	ON FOUR WHEELS
NUMB WITH COLD	OLD FAVOURITE	ONLY DAUGHTER
NURSERY CLASS	OLD FOLKS' HOME	ON ONE'S HONOUR
NURSERY RHYME	OLD FOR HIS AGE	ON ONE'S METTLE
NURSERY STORY	OLD GENTLEMAN	ON ONE'S UPPERS
NURSING STAFF	OLD HARROVIAN	ON REFLECTION
NUT CHOCOLATE	OLD HUNDREDTH	ON SAFE GROUND
NUTMEG GRATER	OLD MAN'S BEARD	ON SENTRY DUTY
NUTS AND BOLTS	OLD MORTALITY	ON SUFFERANCE
	OLD PRETENDER	ON TELEVISION
O—12	OLD SCHOOL TIE	ON THE AVERAGE
OBITER DICTUM	OLD SHOULDERS	ON THE CEILING
OBJECT LESSON	OLD TESTAMENT	ON THE COUNCIL
OBJECT OF PITY	OLD-TIME DANCE	ON THE COUNTER
OBLIQUE ANGLE	OLD-TIME WALTZ	ON THE DECLINE
OBSTACLE RACE	OLD WIVES' TALE	ON THE DEFENCE
OCCULT POWERS	OLYMPIC GAMES	ON THE FAIRWAY
OCEANS OF TIME	OLYMPIC MEDAL	ON THE FAR SIDE

ON THE HORIZON
ON THE LEE-SIDE
ON THE LOOK-OUT
ON THE OFF-SIDE
ON THE ONE HAND
ON THE OUTSIDE
ON THE PAY-ROLL
ON THE QUI VIVE
ON THE RAMPAGE
ON THE REBOUND
ON THE RETREAT
ON THE SURFACE
ON THE TERRACE
ON THE TOP RUNG
ON THE TOW-PATH
ON THE UP-AND-UP
ON THE UPGRADE
ON THE WARPATH
ON THE WAY DOWN
ON WITH THE JOB
OPEN ALL NIGHT
OPEN CARRIAGE
OPEN CHAMPION
OPEN CONFLICT
OPENING NIGHT
OPENING SCENE
OPENING WORDS
OPEN ONE'S EYES
OPEN OUTWARDS
OPEN QUESTION
OPEN SANDWICH
OPEN TO ATTACK
OPEN TO CHANCE
OPEN TO CHOICE
OPERA COMIQUE
OPERA GLASSES
OPERATIC ARIA
OPERATIC STAR
OPIUM TRAFFIC
OPPOSING SIDE
OPPOSING TEAM
OPPOSITE CAMP
OPPOSITE ENDS
OPPOSITE SIDE
OPTICAL GLASS
ORANGE PIPPIN
ORANGE SQUASH
ORDEAL BY FIRE
ORDER IN COURT
ORDER OF MERIT
ORDINARY FARE

ORGAN BUILDER
ORGAN GRINDER
ORGAN OF SIGHT
ORGAN RECITAL
ORIEL COLLEGE
ORIGINAL COPY
ORIGINAL COST
ORIGINAL IDEA
ORIGINAL PLAN
OSBORNE HOUSE
OTHER EXTREME
OUNCE OF FLESH
OUNCE OF SENSE
OUNCE OF SNUFF
OUR ANCESTORS
OUTDATED WORD
OUTDOOR GAMES
OUTDOOR SPORT
OUTDOOR STAFF
OUTER GARMENT
OUT FIRST BALL
OUT FOR A SPREE
OUT FOR SCALPS
OUTGOING SHIP
OUTGOING TIDE
OUT IN THE COLD
OUT IN THE OPEN
OUT OF BALANCE
OUT OF COMPANY
OUT OF CONCEIT
OUT OF CONTEXT
OUT OF CONTROL
OUT OF EARSHOT
OUT OF FASHION
OUT OF HARMONY
OUT OF HARNESS
OUT OF HEARING
OUT OF KEEPING
OUT OF ONE'S WAY
OUT OF SERVICE
OUT OF SPIRITS
OUT OF THE BLUE
OUT OF THE RACE
OUT OF THE ROAD
OUT OF THE ROOM
OUT OF THE WIND
OUT OF THE WOOD
OUT OF TROUBLE
OUT OF UNIFORM
OUTRIGHT GIFT
OUTSIDE COURT

OUTSIDE PRICE
OUTSIDE RIGHT
OUTWARD BOUND
OUTWARD SIGNS
OVER AND ABOVE
OVERDO THINGS
OVERNIGHT BAG
OVER ONE'S HEAD
OVER THE COALS
OVER THE HILLS
OVER THE LIMIT
OVER THE VERGE
OVER THE WATER
OVER THE WAVES
OVER THE WORST
OVER THE YEARS
OWE OBEDIENCE
OXFORD ACCENT
OXFORD CIRCUS
OXFORD STREET

P—12
PABLO PICASSO
PACIFIC OCEAN
PACKET OF PINS
PACK OF HOUNDS
PACK OF WOLVES
PACK ONE'S BAGS
PADDLING POOL
PAGE OF HONOUR
PAID-UP MEMBER
PAINFUL SIGHT
PAINTED IMAGE
PAINTED OCEAN
PAINTED WOMAN
PAINTING BOOK
PAINT THE LILY
PAINT THE WALL
PAIR OF BRACES
PAIR OF EIGHTS
PAIR OF GLOVES
PAIR OF HORSES
PAIR OF KNAVES
PAIR OF PLIERS
PAIR OF QUEENS
PAIR OF SCALES
PAIR OF SEVENS
PAIR OF SHEARS
PAIR OF SHORTS
PAIR OF SKATES
PAIR OF SLACKS

PAIR OF THREES
PAIR OF TIGHTS
PAIR OF TRUNKS
PAISLEY SCARF
PAISLEY SHAWL
PALE AS A GHOST
PALETTE KNIFE
PALMERS GREEN
PAPER PATTERN
PAPER THE ROOM
PAPER THE WALL
PAPER WEDDING
PARADE GROUND
PARADISE LOST
PARAFFIN LAMP
PARALLEL BARS
PARISH CHURCH
PARISH PRIEST
PARISH RELIEF
PARISH SCHOOL
PARKING METER
PARKING PLACE
PARKING SPACE
PARLOUR TRICK
PARLOUS STATE
PARMA VIOLETS
PARQUET FLOOR
PARSLEY SAUCE
PART EXCHANGE
PARTHIAN SHOT
PARTIAL TRUTH
PARTING GUEST
PARTING WORDS
PART OF SPEECH
PART OF THE ACT
PART OF THE WAY
PART ONE'S HAIR
PART-TIME WORK
PARTY IN POWER
PARTY MANNERS
PASSAGE MONEY
PASSING FANCY
PASSING PHASE
PASSION FRUIT
PASSIVE VOICE
PASS JUDGMENT
PASS SENTENCE
PASS THE CRUET
PASS THE SAUCE
PAST MIDNIGHT
PAST ONE'S BEST

PASTORAL POEM
PATENT OFFICE
PATENT REMEDY
PATENT RIGHTS
PATERNAL LOVE
PATERNAL ROOF
PATIENT AS JOB
PAT ON THE BACK
PAT ON THE HEAD
PATROL LEADER
PATTERN MAKER
PAUPER'S GRAVE
PAW THE GROUND
PAY A DIVIDEND
PAY AS YOU EARN
PAY AS YOU WEAR
PAY ATTENTION
PAY DIVIDENDS
PAY IN ADVANCE
PAYING-IN BOOK
PAYING-IN SLIP
PAY ONE'S DEBTS
PAY ONE'S SHARE
PAY ON THE NAIL
PEACE ON EARTH
PEACH BLOSSOM
PEACOCK'S TAIL
PEAK DISTRICT
PEANUT BUTTER
PEARL FISHING
PEARL HARBOUR
PEASE PUDDING
PEDIGREE HERD
PELT WITH RAIN
PEN AND PENCIL
PENCIL SKETCH
PENNY FOR THEM
PENNY WHISTLE
PEOPLE'S PARTY
PEPPER'S GHOST
PERFECT FIFTH
PERFECT IMAGE
PERFECT MATCH
PERFECT ORDER
PERFECT PEACE
PERFECT SIGHT
PERFECT STYLE
PERFECT TENSE
PERFECT WRECK
PERMANENT JOB
PERMANENT WAY

PERMIT TO LAND
PERSONA GRATA
PERSONAL CALL
PERSONAL GAIN
PERSONAL LOAN
PERSONAL NOTE
PERSON OF NOTE
PETER AND PAUL
PETER CUSHING
PETER SELLERS
PETER USTINOV
PET GRIEVANCE
PETROL ENGINE
PETROL RATION
PETTING PARTY
PETTY DETAILS
PETTY LARCENY
PETTY OFFICER
PETTY TREASON
PHARAOH'S TOMB
PHILIP HARBEN
PHONE CHARGES
PHYSICAL PAIN
PIANO RECITAL
PICK A QUARREL
PICKED TROOPS
PICKLED ONION
PICK OUT A TUNE
PICK TO PIECES
PICNIC BASKET
PICNIC HAMPER
PICTORIAL ART
PICTURE FRAME
PICTURE HOUSE
PICTURE PAPER
PICTURE STORY
PIECE BY PIECE
PIECE OF BREAD
PIECE OF CHALK
PIECE OF MUSIC
PIECE OF PAPER
PIERCED HEART
PIERCING LOOK
PIERCING NOTE
PIG'S TROTTERS
PILE UP A SCORE
PILLAR-BOX RED
PILLAR OF SALT
PILLAR TO POST
PILLION RIDER
PILOT OFFICER

PINCH OF SNUFF
PING-PONG BALL
PINK AND WHITE
PINK ELEPHANT
PINK FOR A GIRL
PIN ONE'S FAITH
PIN ONE'S HOPES
PINT OF BITTER
PINT OF WALLOP
PIONEER CORPS
PITCH AND TOSS
PLACE AN ORDER
PLACE BETTING
PLACE IN ORDER
PLACE OF BIRTH
PLACE OF EXILE
PLAIN AND PURL
PLAIN CLOTHES
PLAIN COOKING
PLAIN DEALING
PLAIN ENGLISH
PLAIN SAILING
PLAINTIVE CRY
PLAIN WRAPPER
PLANE SPOTTER
PLAN OF ACTION
PLAN OF ATTACK
PLANT ONESELF
PLASTER SAINT
PLATES OF MEAT
PLATINUM RING
PLATONIC LOVE
PLAY CHARADES
PLAY DOMINOES
PLAY DRAUGHTS
PLAY FOOTBALL
PLAY FOR A DRAW
PLAY FORFEITS
PLAY FOR MONEY
PLAYING CARDS
PLAYING FIELD
PLAY LEAP-FROG
PLAY OLD HARRY
PLAY ONE FALSE
PLAY ONE'S PART
PLAY OPPOSITE
PLAY ROULETTE
PLAY SKITTLES
PLAY THE BANJO
PLAY THE CLOWN
PLAY THE DEUCE

PLAY THE DEVIL
PLAY THE FIELD
PLAY THE HALLS
PLAY THE ORGAN
PLAY THE PIANO
PLAY WITH FIRE
PLEAD POVERTY
PLEA FOR MERCY
PLEA FOR PEACE
PLEA OF GUILTY
PLEASANT NEWS
PLEASANT TIME
PLEASANT TRIP
PLEASANT WEEK
PLEASURE BOAT
PLEASURE TRIP
PLEATED DRESS
PLEATED SKIRT
PLENTY IN HAND
PLENTY OF GUTS
PLENTY OF ROOM
PLENTY OF ROPE
PLENTY OF TIME
PLIGHTED WORD
PLIMSOLL LINE
PLIMSOLL MARK
PLOUGHED LAND
PLOUGH MONDAY
PLUCK A PIGEON
PLUMBER'S MATE
PLUS AND MINUS
PLYMOUTH ROCK
POETIC FRENZY
POET LAUREATE
POINT AT ISSUE
POINT BY POINT
POINT OF ISSUE
POINT OF ORDER
POINTS SYSTEM
POINT TO POINT
POISONED DART
POKE IN THE EYE
POKER SESSION
POLAR REGIONS
POLES ASUNDER
POLICE ACTION
POLICE CORDON
POLICE ESCORT
POLICE MATTER
POLICE PATROL
POLICE PERMIT

POLITE PHRASE
POLITICAL MAP
POLITICAL SET
POLLING BOOTH
POLYTHENE BAG
PONS ASINORUM
POOL OF LABOUR
POOL OF LONDON
POOR ARGUMENT
POOR CREATURE
POOR DELIVERY
POOR FEATURES
POOR IN SPIRIT
POOR LINGUIST
POOR PHYSIQUE
POOR PROSPECT
POOR RELATION
POOR RELATIVE
POOR SPECIMEN
POPULAR BRAND
POPULAR FANCY
POPULAR FRONT
POPULAR MUSIC
POPULAR NOVEL
POPULAR PRESS
POPULAR PRICE
POPULAR SPORT
PORGY AND BESS
PORK AND BEANS
PORK SAUSAGES
PORT ADELAIDE
PORT AND LEMON
PORTER'S LODGE
PORTLAND BILL
PORTLAND BOWL
PORTLAND VASE
PORTLY FIGURE
PORT OF LONDON
PORT SUNLIGHT
POSE A PROBLEM
POSITIVE POLE
POSITIVE SIGN
POSSIBLE NEED
POSTAGE STAMP
POSTED ABROAD
POST MERIDIAN
POST OF HONOUR
POST-WAR WORLD
POTATO CRISPS
POTATO FAMINE
POTTER'S WHEEL

POULTRY HOUSE
POUND FOOLISH
POUND OF FLESH
POUND OF SUGAR
POUND THE BEAT
POUR WITH RAIN
POUTER PIGEON
POWDER MONKEY
POWER OF SIGHT
POWER STATION
POWERS THAT BE
PRACTICE GAME
PRACTISED EYE
PRAY FOR MERCY
PRAY FOR PEACE
PRECIOUS BANE
PRECIOUS LAMB
PREEN ONESELF
PREMIUM BONDS
PREMIUM OFFER
PREPARE A CASE
PREPARE A MEAL
PREPARED TEXT
PRESENT TENSE
PRESS COUNCIL
PRESS CUTTING
PRESSED STEEL
PRESS FORWARD
PRESS GALLERY
PRESS HAND-OUT
PRESSING NEED
PRESS OFFICER
PRESS ONWARDS
PRESS THE BELL
PRESSURE PUMP
PRETTY ACTIVE
PRETTY PICKLE
PRETTY SPEECH
PRETTY USEFUL
PRICE CONTROL
PRICE OF MONEY
PRICKLY PLANT
PRIDE OF LIONS
PRIDE OF PLACE
PRIDE ONESELF
PRIMITIVE ART
PRIMITIVE MAN
PRIMO CARNERA
PRIMROSE HILL
PRIMROSE PATH
PRINCE ALBERT

PRINCE EDWARD
PRINCE GEORGE
PRINCE PHILIP
PRINCE REGENT
PRINCE RUPERT
PRINCESS ANNE
PRINCIPAL BOY
PRINTED SHEET
PRINTER'S COPY
PRISON RECORD
PRISON REFORM
PRISON WARDEN
PRISON WARDER
PRIVATE BEACH
PRIVATE CLASS
PRIVATE FIGHT
PRIVATE HOTEL
PRIVATE HOUSE
PRIVATE LIVES
PRIVATE MEANS
PRIVATE PARTY
PRIVATE TUTOR
PRIVATE VISIT
PRIVATE WORLD
PRIVATE WRONG
PRIVY COUNCIL
PRIZE EDITION
PROBATE COURT
PROBLEM CHILD
PROFIT MARGIN
PROFIT MOTIVE
PROMISED LAND
PROMISE TO PAY
PROMPT ACTION
PROMPT ANSWER
PROMPT CORNER
PROOF OF GUILT
PROPER COURSE
PROPER PERSON
PROPERTY DEAL
PROPHET OF WOE
PROTEST MARCH
PROTOTYPE CAR
PROUD AS PUNCH
PROUD PRESTON
PROVEN GUILTY
PROVE THE RULE
PROVIDE LUNCH
PRUNING KNIFE
PRUSSIAN BLUE
PSYCHIC FORCE

PUBLIC AFFAIR
PUBLIC APATHY
PUBLIC DEMAND
PUBLIC FIGURE
PUBLIC HEALTH
PUBLIC NOTICE
PUBLIC OFFICE
PUBLIC ORATOR
PUBLIC OUTCRY
PUBLIC POLICY
PUBLIC SCHOOL
PUBLIC SPEECH
PUBLIC SPIRIT
PUDDING BASIN
PUFFING BILLY
PUFFIN ISLAND
PULL A FAST ONE
PULLING POWER
PULL THE WIRES
PULL TOGETHER
PULL TO PIECES
PULP MAGAZINE
PUNCH AND JUDY
PUPIL TEACHER
PURE NONSENSE
PURL AND PLAIN
PURSE THE LIPS
PURSUE A THEME
PURSUIT PLANE
PUSH ONE'S LUCK
PUT AN END TO IT
PUT A QUESTION
PUT A SOCK IN IT
PUT A STOP TO IT
PUT IN ITALICS
PUT IN SPLINTS
PUT IN THE DOCK
PUT INTO FORCE
PUT INTO RHYME
PUT INTO SHAPE
PUT INTO WORDS
PUT IN WRITING
PUT IT BLUNTLY
PUTNEY BRIDGE
PUTNEY COMMON
PUT ONE ACROSS
PUT ONE'S OAR IN
PUT ON ONE SIDE
PUT ON THE LIST
PUT ON THE RACK
PUT OUT OF GEAR

PUT THE CAT OUT
PUT THE WIND UP
PUTTING GREEN
PUT TO AUCTION
PUT TO GOOD USE
PUT TO THE RACK
PUT TO THE TEST
PUT TO THE VOTE
PUT TO TORTURE
PUT UP FOR SALE

Q—12
QUARTER FINAL
QUARTER RIGHT
QUARTER TO ONE
QUARTER TO SIX
QUARTER TO TEN
QUARTER TO TWO
QUART MEASURE
QUEEN CONSORT
QUEEN OF CLUBS
QUEEN OF SHEBA
QUEEN OF TONGA
QUEEN'S BISHOP
QUEEN'S BOUNTY
QUEEN'S COLOUR
QUEEN'S FLIGHT
QUEEN'S GAMBIT
QUEEN'S KNIGHT
QUEEN'S SPEECH
QUEEN TITANIA
QUEER FEELING
QUESTION MARK
QUESTION TIME
QUEUE JUMPING
QUICK JOURNEY
QUICK RETURNS
QUIET WEDDING
QUIET WEEK-END
QUITE CERTAIN
QUITE CORRECT
QUITE IN ORDER
QUIT ONE'S POST
QUIT THE SCENE
QUIT THE STAGE
QUOTE THE ODDS

R—12
RABBIT WARREN
RACE OF GIANTS
RACIAL HATRED

RACING DRIVER
RACING JARGON
RACING SEASON
RACING STABLE
RADAR STATION
RADIANT SMILE
RADICAL ERROR
RADIO AMATEUR
RADIO LICENCE
RADIO MESSAGE
RADIO NETWORK
RADIO STATION
RAFFLE TICKET
RAGING TEMPER
RAGLAN SLEEVE
RAGS AND BONES
RAGS TO RICHES
RAIDING PARTY
RAILWAY HOTEL
RAILWAY LINES
RAILWAY TRAIN
RAILWAY TRUCK
RAINBOW TROUT
RAINY CLIMATE
RAINY WEATHER
RAISE A FAMILY
RAISED VOICES
RAISE ONE'S HAT
RAISE THE ANTE
RAISE THE DEAD
RAISE THE DUST
RAISE THE FARE
RAISE THE RENT
RAISE THE ROOF
RAISE THE WIND
RAKE TOGETHER
RAMBLING ROSE
RANDOM EFFORT
RANDOM SAMPLE
RANK OUTSIDER
RAPID DECLINE
RAPID SPEAKER
RAPID STRIDES
RAPID TRANSIT
RAPIER THRUST
RASPBERRY JAM
RASPING VOICE
RATABLE VALUE
RATHER LITTLE
RATHER POORLY
RAVEN TRESSES

RAY ELLINGTON
RAY OF COMFORT
REACH FORWARD
REACT AGAINST
REACT SHARPLY
READ AND WRITE
READING GLASS
READ ONE'S HAND
READ ONE'S PALM
READ THE CARDS
READ THE SIGNS
READ THE STARS
READY CONSENT
READY FOR WEAR
READY TO BURST
READY TO LEARN
READY TO LEAVE
READY TO START
REALM OF PLUTO
REAL PRESENCE
REAL PROPERTY
REAL SECURITY
REAR ENTRANCE
REAR ONE'S HEAD
RECALL TO LIFE
RECALL TO MIND
RECEIVING END
RECEIVING SET
RECENT EVENTS
RECITE POETRY
RECORD OFFICE
RECORD OUTPUT
RECORD PLAYER
RED AND YELLOW
RED CORPUSCLE
RED FOR DANGER
RED IN THE FACE
RED-LETTER DAY
RED STOCKINGS
REDUCED FARES
REDUCED PRICE
REDUCED SPEED
REDUCE IN RANK
REDUCE TO PULP
REDUCE TO SIZE
RED WITH ANGER
REEFER JACKET
REEL OF COTTON
REFINED SUGAR
REFINED TASTE
REFLEX ACTION

REFORM SCHOOL	RESERVED SEAT	RINGING SOUND
REFUSE CREDIT	RESERVE PRICE	RINGING TONES
REFUSE OFFICE	RESERVE STOCK	RING IN THE NEW
REFUSE TO MEET	RESIDE ABROAD	RINGSIDE SEAT
REFUSE TO MOVE	RESORT TO ARMS	RIO DE JANEIRO
REFUSE TO PLAY	RESTING ACTOR	RIOT OF COLOUR
REFUSE TO SIGN	RESTING PLACE	RIPE TOMATOES
REFUSE TO VOTE	REST OF THE DAY	RIP VAN WINKLE
REFUSE TO WORK	REST ONE'S CASE	RISE AND SHINE
REGAL BEARING	REST ONE'S EYES	RISE IN REVOLT
REGENCY HOUSE	RESTORE ORDER	RISE TO THE FLY
REGENCY STYLE	RETAIL DEALER	RISE TO THE TOP
REGENT'S CANAL	RETAINING FEE	RISING GROUND
REGENT STREET	RETURN A VISIT	RISING PRICES
REGIONAL NEWS	RETURN OF POST	RISK ONE'S LIFE
REGULAR BRICK	RETURN TICKET	RISK ONE'S NECK
REGULAR DEMON	RETURN TO BASE	RIVAL COMPANY
REGULAR HABIT	RETURN TO PORT	RIVER OF BLOOD
REGULAR HOURS	RETURN VOYAGE	RIVER SHANNON
REGULAR MEALS	REVERSE ORDER	RIVER STEAMER
REGULAR ORDER	REVERT TO TYPE	RIVER TRAFFIC
REIGN SUPREME	REVOLVER SHOT	ROAD ACCIDENT
REITH LECTURE	RHESUS MONKEY	ROAD JUNCTION
RELEVANT FACT	RHYMING SLANG	ROADSIDE CAFÉ
RELIEF WORKER	RICHARD CONTE	ROAR FOR MERCY
RELIGIOUS WAR	RICHMOND HILL	ROARING TRADE
REMAIN AT HOME	RICHMOND PARK	ROAR WITH PAIN
REMAIN BEHIND	RICH RELATION	ROAR WITH RAGE
REMAIN SEATED	RICH RELATIVE	ROAST CHICKEN
REMAIN SILENT	RIDE AT ANCHOR	ROASTED ALIVE
REMAIN SINGLE	RIDE BARE-BACK	ROBE OF HONOUR
REMOTE CHANCE	RIDE FOR A FALL	ROBERT BEATTY
REMOTE FUTURE	RIDE FULL TILT	ROBERT GRAVES
REMOTE OBJECT	RIDER HAGGARD	ROBERT MORLEY
REMOVE BODILY	RIDE THE STORM	ROBERT NEWTON
REMOVE ERRORS	RIDE TO HOUNDS	ROBERT TAYLOR
RENDER THANKS	RIDING LESSON	ROBUST HEALTH
REND THE SKIES	RIDING MASTER	ROCKING HORSE
RENÉE HOUSTON	RIDING SCHOOL	ROGATION DAYS
RENT A CARAVAN	RIDING STABLE	ROGATION WEEK
RENT A COTTAGE	RIFLE BRIGADE	ROLLER SKATES
RENT TRIBUNAL	RIGHT AND LEFT	ROLLING STOCK
REPAIR OUTFIT	RIGHTFUL HEIR	ROLLING STONE
REPEAT ACTION	RIGHT-HAND MAN	ROLL OF HONOUR
REPORTED CASE	RIGHT OF ENTRY	ROLL ONE'S EYES
REPTILE HOUSE	RIGHT OR WRONG	ROMAN EMPEROR
REPUTED OWNER	RIGHT OUTSIDE	ROMAN FIGURES
RESCUE WORKER	RIGHT QUALITY	ROMAN HISTORY
RESEARCH TEAM	RIGHT THROUGH	ROMAN HOLIDAY
RESEARCH WORK	RIG THE MARKET	ROMAN LETTERS
RESERVED LIST	RINGING LAUGH	ROMAN NUMBERS

ROMAN REMAINS
ROMAN SOLDIER
ROMANTIC FOOL
ROMANTIC GIRL
ROMANTIC IDEA
RONALD COLMAN
RONALD SHINER
RONNIE HILTON
ROOM AT THE TOP
ROOM FOR DOUBT
ROOM THIRTEEN
ROOM TO EXPAND
ROPE OF ONIONS
ROPE OF PEARLS
ROSE AND CROWN
ROSE-HIP SYRUP
ROSE OF TRALEE
ROSE TO THE TOP
ROSETTA STONE
ROSY PROSPECT
ROTARY ACTION
ROTTEN BRANCH
ROUGH COUNTRY
ROUGH DIAMOND
ROUGH DRAWING
ROUGH JUSTICE
ROUGH MANNERS
ROUGH PASSAGE
ROUGH PICTURE
ROUGH SURFACE
ROUGH TEXTURE
ROUGH WEATHER
ROUND BY ROUND
ROUND FIGURES
ROUND OF CALLS
ROUND OF TOAST
ROUND THE BACK
ROUND THE BEND
ROUND THE CAPE
ROUND THE EDGE
ROUND THE FIRE
ROUND THE MOON
ROUND THE TOWN
ROUSE ONESELF
ROUSING CHEER
ROUTINE CHECK
ROVING REPORT
ROW OF BUTTONS
ROYAL ACADEMY
ROYAL ARSENAL
ROYAL BANQUET

ROYAL CHARTER
ROYAL CIRCLES
ROYAL COMMAND
ROYAL CONSENT
ROYAL DYNASTY
ROYAL HUNT CUP
ROYAL MARINES
ROYAL SOCIETY
ROYAL WARRANT
ROYAL WEDDING
ROYAL WELCOME
RUBBER CHEQUE
RUBBER DINGHY
RUBBER GLOVES
RUB ONE'S HANDS
RUB SHOULDERS
RUDE REMINDER
RUGBY COLOURS
RUGGER GROUND
RUGGER PLAYER
RUINED CASTLE
RUINOUS FOLLY
RULE OF TERROR
RULE THE ROOST
RUMOURS OF WAR
RUN-AWAY HORSE
RUN-AWAY MATCH
RUN AWAY TO SEA
RUN-AWAY TRAIN
RUN FOR OFFICE
RUN FOR SAFETY
RUN LIKE A DEER
RUN LIKE A HARE
RUNNING COSTS
RUNNING FIGHT
RUNNING FLUSH
RUNNING TITLE
RUNNING TRACK
RUNNING WATER
RUN OF BAD LUCK
RUN OF THE MILL
RUN ON THE BANK
RUPERT BROOKE
RUSH HEADLONG
RUSHING WATER
RUSSIAN BOOTS
RUSSIAN DANCE
RUSSIAN NOVEL
RUSSIAN SALAD
RUSSIAN VODKA
RUSTIC BRIDGE

S—12
SACRED NUMBER
SACRED PLEDGE
SADDLE OF LAMB
SADLER'S WELLS
SAD SPECTACLE
SAFE AND SOUND
SAFE AS HOUSES
SAFE CROSSING
SAFE DISTANCE
SAFETY DEVICE
SAFETY FACTOR
SAGE AND ONION
SAHARA DESERT
SAILING BARGE
SAINT BERNARD
SAINT PANCRAS
SAINT PATRICK
SAINT SWITHIN
SALE OR RETURN
SALES FIGURES
SALES MANAGER
SALIENT ANGLE
SALIENT POINT
SALOON PRICES
SALTED ALMOND
SALTED BUTTER
SALT LAKE CITY
SALUTING BASE
SALVADOR DALI
SALVAGE CORPS
SALVAGE MONEY
SAMPLE BOTTLE
SAMUEL BUTLER
SAN FRANCISCO
SAN SEBASTIAN
SAPPHIRE RING
SARACEN'S HEAD
SARDONIC GRIN
SATAN'S PALACE
SATURDAY CLUB
SAUCE TARTARE
SAVAGE ATTACK
SAVAGE TEMPER
SAVE ONE'S FACE
SAVE ONE'S LIFE
SAVE ONE'S NECK
SAVE ONE'S SKIN
SAVE OUR SOULS
SAVING CLAUSE
SAVING FACTOR

SAVINGS STAMP
SAVOY CABBAGE
SAY A FEW WORDS
SAY A GOOD WORD
SAY A MOUTHFUL
SAY ONE'S PIECE
SAY SOMETHING
SCALE DRAWING
SCALLOP SHELL
SCARLET FEVER
SCARLET WOMAN
SCENE OF CHAOS
SCENE STEALER
SCENTED PAPER
SCEPTRED ISLE
SCHOLAR GIPSY
SCHOOL BLAZER
SCHOOL FRIEND
SCHOOL MATRON
SCHOOL OUTING
SCHOOL REPORT
SCHOOL SPORTS
SCOOP THE POOL
SCORCHING HOT
SCORE A SINGLE
SCORE THROUGH
SCOTCH BONNET
SCOTCH HUMOUR
SCOTCH WHISKY
SCOTLAND YARD
SCOTTISH PEER
SCOTTISH REEL
SCOUT'S HONOUR
SCRAMBLED EGG
SCRAP OF PAPER
SCRIPT WRITER
SCROLL OF FAME
SCULLERY MAID
SEAFARING MAN
SEAL A BARGAIN
SEALED ORDERS
SEAL OF OFFICE
SEALSKIN COAT
SEA OF GALILEE
SEA OF MARMORA
SEA OF TROUBLE
SEARCH IN VAIN
SEASONAL WIND
SEASON TICKET
SEAT OF HONOUR
SEBASTIAN COE

SECLUDED SPOT
SECOND CHANCE
SECOND CHOICE
SECOND COURSE
SECOND COUSIN
SECOND DANIEL
SECOND DEGREE
SECOND ELEVEN
SECOND FIDDLE
SECOND FINGER
SECOND GLANCE
SECOND LEAGUE
SECOND LESSON
SECOND LETTER
SECOND NATURE
SECOND OF JULY
SECOND OF JUNE
SECOND PERSON
SECOND RUBBER
SECOND SEASON
SECOND SERIES
SECOND STOREY
SECOND STRING
SECOND TO NONE
SECOND VIOLIN
SECOND VOLUME
SECRET BALLOT
SECRET DRAWER
SECRET ERRAND
SECRET PAPERS
SECRET POLICE
SECRET TREATY
SECRET WEAPON
SECURE FUTURE
SECURE OLD-AGE
SECURITY LEAK
SECURITY RISK
SEE AT A GLANCE
SEEDED PLAYER
SEED MERCHANT
SEEDS OF DECAY
SEEDS OF DOUBT
SEE IN THE DARK
SEE IT THROUGH
SEEK A FORMULA
SEEK A FORTUNE
SEEK AN EFFECT
SEEK A QUARREL
SEEK GUIDANCE
SEESAW MOTION
SEE THE SIGHTS

SEETHING MASS
SELL FOR A SONG
SELLING PLATE
SELLING PRICE
SELL ON CREDIT
SELL ONE'S SOUL
SELL THE DUMMY
SEND A MESSAGE
SEND TO PRISON
SENIOR BRANCH
SENIOR MASTER
SENIOR MEMBER
SENIOR PURSER
SENIOR SCHOOL
SENSE OF GUILT
SENSE OF SHAME
SENSE OF SIGHT
SENSE OF SMELL
SENSE OF TASTE
SENSE OF TOUCH
SENSE OF WRONG
SENSIBLE GIRL
SENSITIVE EAR
SENT TO BLAZES
SENT TO SCHOOL
SEPARATE WAYS
SERENE NATURE
SERENE TEMPER
SERIAL NUMBER
SERIAL RIGHTS
SERIOUSLY ILL
SERIOUS MUSIC
SERIOUS OFFER
SERIOUS RIVAL
SERIOUS WOUND
SERRIED RANKS
SERVANT CLASS
SERVANTS' HALL
SERVE AT TABLE
SERVE ITS TURN
SERVICE CHIEF
SERVICE DEPOT
SERVICE DRESS
SERVICE OF GOD
SERVICE RIFLE
SERVING HATCH
SET AN EXAMPLE
SET A STANDARD
SET AT LIBERTY
SET BY THE EARS
SET OF LANCERS

SET ONE AT EASE	SHAH OF PERSIA	SHORN OF GLORY
SET ONE'S TEETH	SHAKE THE HEAD	SHORT ACCOUNT
SET PROGRAMME	SHALLOW GRAVE	SHORT CIRCUIT
SETTLE A SCORE	SHALLOW WATER	SHORT COMMONS
SETTLE IN TOWN	SHAMELESS LIE	SHORTER HOURS
SETTLE THE DAY	SHARE CAPITAL	SHORTEST GIRL
SEVEN AND FIVE	SHARE THE LOAD	SHORT EXTRACT
SEVEN AND FOUR	SHARE THE LOOT	SHORT JOURNEY
SEVEN AND NINE	SHARP LOOK-OUT	SHORTLY AFTER
SEVEN COURSES	SHARP OUTLINE	SHORT MEASURE
SEVEN DEGREES	SHARP REPROOF	SHORT OF FUNDS
SEVEN DOLLARS	SHAVING BRUSH	SHORT OF MONEY
SEVEN EIGHTHS	SHAVING STICK	SHORT OF SPACE
SEVEN FATHOMS	SHEEPISH GRIN	SHORT OF STAFF
SEVEN GALLONS	SHEEPISH LOOK	SHORT OF WORDS
SEVEN GUINEAS	SHEEP'S TONGUE	SHORT PASSAGE
SEVEN HUNDRED	SHEER TORTURE	SHORT ROMANCE
SEVEN LEAGUES	SHEET OF FLAME	SHORT SESSION
SEVEN MINUTES	SHEET OF GLASS	SHORT SUMMARY
SEVEN OCTAVES	SHEET OF PAPER	SHORT TENANCY
SEVEN OF CLUBS	SHEET OF WATER	SHORT TIME AGO
SEVEN OR EIGHT	SHEIK OF ARABY	SHORT VERSION
SEVEN PER CENT	SHELLING PEAS	SHOT AND SHELL
SEVEN SISTERS	SHEPHERD'S PIE	SHOT IN THE ARM
SEVEN SQUARED	SHERRY TRIFLE	SHOT ONE'S BOLT
SEVENTH FLOOR	SHETLAND PONY	SHOT TO PIECES
SEVENTH GREEN	SHINING LIGHT	SHOULDER ARMS
SEVENTH OF MAY	SHINING WHITE	SHOUT FOR HELP
SEVENTH PLACE	SHIPPING LANE	SHOUT THE ODDS
SEVENTH ROUND	SHIPPING LINE	SHOVE HA'PENNY
SEVENTY MILES	SHIP'S BISCUIT	SHOW APTITUDE
SEVENTY TIMES	SHIP'S CAPTAIN	SHOW BUSINESS
SEVENTY YEARS	SHIP'S COMPANY	SHOWER OF RAIN
SEVEN VIRTUES	SHIP'S COMPASS	SHOW INTEREST
SEVEN WICKETS	SHIP'S STEWARD	SHOWN THE DOOR
SEVEN WISE MEN	SHIRLEY EATON	SHOW OF REASON
SEVEN WONDERS	SHIRT SLEEVES	SHOW ONE ROUND
SEVERAL TIMES	SHIVERING FIT	SHOW ONE'S FACE
SEVERE ATTACK	SHOCKING COLD	SHOW ONE'S HAND
SEVERE CRITIC	SHOCKING PINK	SHOW PRUDENCE
SEVERE MASTER	SHOCK TACTICS	SHRIMPING NET
SEVERE STRAIN	SHOCK THERAPY	SHUFFLE ALONG
SEVERE WINTER	SHOE REPAIRER	SHUT OFF STEAM
SEVERN BRIDGE	SHOE-SHINE BOY	SHUT ONE'S EYES
SEVERN TUNNEL	SHOOTER'S HILL	SHUT YOUR TRAP!
SEWING CIRCLE	SHOOTING PAIN	SIAMESE TWINS
SEW ON A BUTTON	SHOOTING STAR	SICK AND TIRED
SHADE OF DOUBT	SHOOT ONESELF	SICK OF TRYING
SHADOW BOXING	SHOOT THE MOON	SIDE ENTRANCE
SHADY RETREAT	SHOPPING LIST	SIDE MOVEMENT
SHAFT OF LIGHT	SHORE TO SHORE	SIDE OF MUTTON

SIDNEY STREET	SIXTEEN MILES	SLOW PROGRESS
SIEGE OF PARIS	SIXTH CENTURY	SLOW PUNCTURE
SIERRA NEVADA	SIXTH OF APRIL	SLUM PROPERTY
SIGH OF RELIEF	SIXTH OF MARCH	SMALL ACCOUNT
SIGHTING SHOT	SIXTY MINUTES	SMALL COMFORT
SIGMUND FREUD	SIXTY PER CENT	SMALL FORTUNE
SIGNAL DEFEAT	SIXTY SECONDS	SMALL HELPING
SIGNAL REWARD	SKEIN OF GEESE	SMALL HOLDING
SIGN LANGUAGE	SKELETON CREW	SMALL LETTERS
SIGN OF DANGER	SKIFFLE GROUP	SMALL MEASURE
SIGN ONE'S NAME	SKIN AND BONES	SMALL MERCIES
SILENT LETTER	SKIN GRAFTING	SMALL PORTION
SILENT PRAYER	SKITTLE ALLEY	SMALL PURPOSE
SILK STOCKING	SKYE BOAT-SONG	SMALL SAVINGS
SILLY SUFFOLK	SLACKEN SPEED	SMALL WRITING
SILVER DOLLAR	SLAP IN THE EYE	SMART CLOTHES
SILVER LINING	SLAVE TO DRINK	SMART DEALING
SILVER SALVER	SLAVE TRAFFIC	SMART OFFICER
SILVER SCREEN	SLEEPING DOGS	SMART SERVANT
SILVER STREAK	SLEEPING LION	SMART TURN-OUT
SILVER TEA-POT	SLEEPING PILL	SMASH AND GRAB
SILVER THREAD	SLEEP SOUNDLY	SMASHING BLOW
SIMON TEMPLAR	SLEEP SWEETLY	SMELL SWEETLY
SIMPLE ANSWER	SLENDER HOPES	SMILE SWEETLY
SIMPLE ATTIRE	SLENDER MEANS	SMOKE A LITTLE
SIMPLE BEAUTY	SLENDER PURSE	SMOKED SALMON
SIMPLE DEVICE	SLENDER WAIST	SMOKED TONGUE
SIMPLE EFFORT	SLICE OF BREAD	SMOKER'S COUGH
SIMPLE MATTER	SLICE OF LEMON	SMOKER'S HEART
SIMPLE PERSON	SLICE OF TOAST	SMOKE TOO MUCH
SIMPLE REMEDY	SLICE THE BALL	SMOOTH TEMPER
SINGING VOICE	SLIDING PANEL	SMOOTH THE WAY
SING IN UNISON	SLIDING SCALE	SMOOTH TONGUE
SINGLE COMBAT	SLIGHT CHANCE	SNACK COUNTER
SINGLE HANDED	SLIGHT CHANGE	SNAKE CHARMER
SINGLE NUMBER	SLIGHT DAMAGE	SNAP AND SNARL
SINGLE PERSON	SLIGHT FIGURE	SNAP DECISION
SINGLE SCOTCH	SLIGHT INJURY	SNAP JUDGMENT
SINGLES MATCH	SLIGHTLY DEAF	SNOW CRYSTALS
SINGLE TICKET	SLIMMING DIET	SOAP AND WATER
SINGLE WHISKY	SLIP AND SLIDE	SOBER THOUGHT
SINISTER MOVE	SLIP OF A THING	SOCIAL CENTRE
SIR HENRY WOOD	SLIP OF THE PEN	SOCIAL CIRCLE
SIR JOHN MOORE	SLIP THE CABLE	SOCIAL CREDIT
SIR TOBY BELCH	SLIP UP ON A JOB	SOCIAL MISFIT
SIT AT THE BACK	SLITHER ALONG	SOCIAL SEASON
SIT IN COUNCIL	SLOANE SQUARE	SOCIAL STATUS
SIX FEET UNDER	SLOANE STREET	SOCIAL SURVEY
SIX OF THE BEST	SLOPING SIDES	SOCIAL UNREST
SIXPENCE EACH	SLOW MOVEMENT	SOCIAL WORKER
SIX SHILLINGS	SLOW OF SPEECH	SOCIETY WOMAN

SOCK IN THE EYE	SPANISH TANGO	SPLIT THE VOTE
SODA FOUNTAIN	SPANKING PACE	SPOILED CHILD
SOFT AS BUTTER	SPARE A COPPER	SPORTING LIFE
SOFT AS VELVET	SPARE BEDROOM	SPORTING NEWS
SOFT CURRENCY	SPARE NO PAINS	SPORT OF KINGS
SOFT HANDLING	SPARE-TIME JOB	SPORT ONE'S OAK
SOFT NOTHINGS	SPARKING PLUG	SPORTS EDITOR
SOLAR ECLIPSE	SPARKLING WIT	SPORTS GROUND
SOLEMN THREAT	SPARTAN BREED	SPORTS JACKET
SOLE SURVIVOR	SPATE OF WORDS	SPORTS MASTER
SOLID CITIZEN	SPEAK CLEARLY	SPORTS REPORT
SOLITARY LIFE	SPEAK ENGLISH	SPORTS TROPHY
SOLITARY WALK	SPEAKING PART	SPOT AND PLAIN
SOLOMON'S SEAL	SPEAKING TUBE	SPOT OF BOTHER
SOMETHING NEW	SPEAK ITALIAN	SPOT OF WHISKY
SOMETHING OLD	SPEAK PLAINLY	SPREAD ABROAD
SOME TIME BACK	SPEAK RAPIDLY	SPREAD CANVAS
SON ET LUMIÈRE	SPEAK RUSSIAN	SPRING BUDGET
SONG AND DANCE	SPEAK SPANISH	SPRING GREENS
SONG OF A SHIRT	SPEAK VOLUMES	SPRING ONIONS
SONG OF PRAISE	SPECIAL AGENT	SPRING SEASON
SONIC BARRIER	SPECIAL CHARM	SPRING TO MIND
SON OF THE SOIL	SPECIAL ISSUE	SPURN AN OFFER
SONS OF BELIAL	SPECIAL NURSE	SQUARE NUMBER
SOPRANO VOICE	SPECIAL OFFER	STACK OF CHIPS
SORE DISTRESS	SPECIAL POINT	STACK OF STRAW
SORRY OUTCOME	SPECIAL PRICE	STACK THE DECK
SOUL OF HONOUR	SPECIAL TERMS	STAFF CAPTAIN
SOUND AND FURY	SPECIAL TRAIN	STAFF COLLEGE
SOUND AS A BELL	SPECIAL TREAT	STAFF OFFICER
SOUND BACKING	SPECIFIC HEAT	STAFF PROBLEM
SOUND BARRIER	SPECIMEN COPY	STAGE A STRIKE
SOUND EFFECTS	SPECIMEN PAGE	STAGE BY STAGE
SOUND OF MUSIC	SPEECH DEFECT	STAGE EFFECTS
SOUND SLEEPER	SPEED OF LIGHT	STAGE MANAGER
SOUND TACTICS	SPEED OF SOUND	STAGE VILLAIN
SOUP OF THE DAY	SPEEDY ANSWER	STAGE WHISPER
SOUTH AFRICAN	SPELLING GAME	STAINED GLASS
SOUTH AMERICA	SPENCER TRACY	STALL FOR TIME
SOUTHEND PIER	SPEND A PACKET	STAMP AUCTION
SOUTHERN AREA	SPICK AND SPAN	STAMP MACHINE
SOUTH PACIFIC	SPIDER AND FLY	STAMP OF TRUTH
SOUTH SHIELDS	SPIKE THE GUNS	STAND ABASHED
SOVIET RUSSIA	SPILL THE MILK	STAND ACCUSED
SPACE FICTION	SPILL THE SALT	STAND A CHANCE
SPACE STATION	SPINAL COLUMN	STAND AGAINST
SPACE TO BUILD	SPIN LIKE A TOP	STAND AND WAIT
SPADE AND FORK	SPIN THE WHEEL	STANDARD LAMP
SPANISH DANCE	SPIRIT OF EVIL	STANDARD RATE
SPANISH MONEY	SPLENDID TIME	STANDARD ROSE
SPANISH ONION	SPLIT THE ATOM	STANDARD SIZE

STANDARD TIME
STANDARD WORK
STAND BETWEEN
STAND IN FRONT
STANDING ARMY
STANDING JOKE
STANDING ONLY
STANDING ROOM
ST. ANDREW'S DAY
STAND THE PACE
STAND THE TEST
STAND-UP FIGHT
STAND UPRIGHT
STAND WAITING
STANLEY BLACK
ST. ANNE'S ON SEA
STARK MADNESS
STARK REALITY
STARLIT NIGHT
STAR MATERIAL
STARRING ROLE
STARTING GATE
STARTING POST
START PACKING
START TALKING
START TO CHEER
START TOO LATE
START TOO SOON
STARVE A FEVER
STATE CONTROL
STATED PERIOD
STATE FUNERAL
STATE LIBRARY
STATE LOTTERY
STATE OF BLISS
STATE OF GRACE
STATE OF PEACE
STATE OF SIEGE
STATE PENSION
STATE SCHOLAR
STATE SUBSIDY
STATION HOTEL
STATION WAGON
STATUE OF EROS
STATUS SYMBOL
STAYING POWER
STAY ONE'S HAND
STAY THE NIGHT
STAY TO DINNER
STAY TO THE END
ST. BERNARD DOG

STEADY DEMAND
STEADY INCOME
STEAK TARTARE
STEAL THE SHOW
STEALTHY STEP
STEAM TURBINE
STEAM WHISTLE
STEERING GEAR
STEP BACKWARD
STEP ON THE GAS
STERLING AREA
STERN REALITY
STEWED APPLES
STEWED PRUNES
ST. GEORGE'S DAY
STICK NO BILLS
STICK OF BOMBS
STICK OF CHALK
STICK OR TWIST
STICK TO PROSE
STICKY TOFFEE
STICKY WICKET
STIFF PENALTY
STILETTO HEEL
STINGING BLOW
STINGING PAIN
STIRLING MOSS
STIRRING GAME
STIRRING NEWS
STIRRING TALE
STIR THE BLOOD
STIR UP STRIFE
STITCH IN TIME
ST. JAMES'S PARK
ST. LOUIS BLUES
ST. MARYLEBONE
STOCK COMPANY
STOCK EXAMPLE
STOCKING FEET
STOCK IN TRADE
STOKE THE FIRE
STOLEN KISSES
STONE OF SCONE
STONE TO DEATH
STOOD THE TEST
STOOGE AROUND
STOP AND START
STOP DRINKING
STOP FIGHTING
STOP-GO POLICY
STOP LAUGHING

STOP ONE'S EARS
STOP SWANKING
STOP THE CLOCK
STOP THE FIGHT
STOP THE NIGHT
STOP WORRYING
STORAGE SPACE
STORM BREWING
STORM OF ABUSE
STORM TROOPER
STORM WARNING
STORMY CAREER
STORMY DEBATE
STORMY PETREL
STORMY TEMPER
STOUT AND MILD
STOUT OF HEART
STOVEPIPE HAT
ST. PETERSBURG
STRAIGHT AWAY
STRAIGHT BACK
STRAIGHT DEAL
STRAIGHT DOWN
STRAIGHT DROP
STRAIGHTEN UP
STRAIGHT FACE
STRAIGHT HAIR
STRAIGHT HOME
STRAIGHT LEFT
STRAIGHT LINE
STRAIGHT NOSE
STRAIGHT PART
STRAIGHT PLAY
STRAIGHT ROAD
STRAIGHT SETS
STRAIGHT SHOT
STRAIGHT TALK
STRAIN A POINT
STRAIT JACKET
STRAND OF HAIR
STRANGE FACES
STRANGE PLACE
STRANGE TO SAY
STRANGE WOMAN
STRAPPING LAD
STREAK OF LUCK
STREAKY BACON
STREAM OF CARS
STREET ARTIST
STREET CORNER
STREET MARKET

STREETS AHEAD	STUPID ANSWER	SURGICAL CASE
STREET SELLER	STUPID FELLOW	SURGICAL WARD
STREET SINGER	STYGIAN SHORE	SURPLUS FLESH
STREET TRADER	SUBDUED LIGHT	SURPLUS GOODS
STREET URCHIN	SUBMARINE PEN	SURPLUS STOCK
STREET VENDOR	SUBTLE CHANGE	SURPRISE MOVE
STRETCH NYLON	SUCCESS STORY	SUSAN HAYWARD
STRETCH TIGHT	SUCK AN ORANGE	SUSAN MAUGHAN
STRICTLY TRUE	SUDDEN ATTACK	SUSTAIN A LOSS
STRICT ORDERS	SUDDEN CHANGE	SWALLOW WHOLE
STRIFE AND WOE	SUDDEN MOTION	SWARM OF FLIES
STRIKE A CHORD	SUDDEN STRAIN	SWARM OF GNATS
STRIKE ACTION	SUDDEN TWITCH	SWARM UP A ROPE
STRIKE A LIGHT	SUFFER DEFEAT	SWAY TO AND FRO
STRIKE A MATCH	SUFFOLK PUNCH	SWEAR FALSELY
STRIKE BOTTOM	SUGAR CONTENT	SWEDISH DRILL
STRIKE IT RICH	SUGAR IS SWEET	SWEEP THE DECK
STRIKE ME DEAD!	SUGAR REFINER	SWEEP THROUGH
STRIKE ME PINK!	SUGAR THE PILL	SWEET ADELINE
STRIKE TERROR	SUICIDAL IDEA	SWEET AND SOUR
STRIKE THE EYE	SUITE OF ROOMS	SWEET AS HONEY
STRIKE WEAPON	SUIT OF ARMOUR	SWEET AS SUGAR
STRING OF LIES	SUIT YOURSELF	SWEET CONTENT
STRIP CARTOON	SULTAN'S HAREM	SWEET MARTINI
STRIP OF PAPER	SULTAN'S WIVES	SWEET PICKLES
STRIP OF WATER	SUMMARY COURT	SWEET REVENGE
STRIVE IN VAIN	SUMMER MONTHS	SWEET SIXTEEN
STROKE OF LUCK	SUMMER RESORT	SWEET SUCCESS
STROKE OF WORK	SUMMER SCHOOL	SWEET THOUGHT
STROKE THE CAT	SUMMER SEASON	SWEET VIOLETS
STROKE THE DOG	SUNDAY DINNER	SWEET WILLIAM
STRONG-ARM MAN	SUNDAY'S CHILD	SWIFT CURRENT
STRONG AS AN OX	SUNDAY SCHOOL	SWIFT TO ANGER
STRONG COLOUR	SUNKEN CHEEKS	SWIMMING BATH
STRONG DEMAND	SUNKEN GARDEN	SWIMMING CLUB
STRONG DENIAL	SUNNY WEATHER	SWIMMING GALA
STRONG DESIRE	SUNSHINE ROOF	SWIMMING POOL
STRONGLY MADE	SUN-TAN LOTION	SWIM UP-STREAM
STRONG NERVES	SUPERB FIGURE	SWING THE LEAD
STRONG THIRST	SUPERB FINISH	SWISS COTTAGE
STRONG WHISKY	SUPERIOR AIRS	SWOLLEN RIVER
STRUGGLE HARD	SUPERIOR RANK	SWORD OF STATE
STUDENT OF LAW	SUPERIOR TYPE	SWORN ENEMIES
STUDY CLOSELY	SUPPORT A WIFE	SYCAMORE TREE
STUFFED HEART	SUPREME BEING	SYDNEY BRIDGE
STUFFED OLIVE	SUPREME COURT	SYDNEY CARTON
STUFFED SHIRT	SUPREME ISSUE	
STUFF ONESELF	SUPREME POWER	
STUMBLE ALONG	SURE TO PLEASE	**T—12**
STUMP ORATORY	SURGE FORWARD	TABLE A MOTION
STUNNING BLOW	SURGERY HOURS	TABLE MANNERS

TABLET OF SOAP	TAKE UP A STAND	TEMPTING BAIT
TAIL OF THE EYE	TAKE UP OFFICE	TENANT FARMER
TAILORED SUIT	TALCUM POWDER	TEN-GALLON HAT
TAILOR'S DUMMY	TALE OF A SHIRT	TENNIS LESSON
TAILOR'S GOOSE	TALK AT LENGTH	TENNIS PLAYER
TAILS YOU LOSE!	TALK AT RANDOM	TENNIS RACKET
TAINTED GOODS	TALK BUSINESS	TEN-POUND NOTE
TAINTED MONEY	TALKING POINT	TEN SHILLINGS
TAKE A BEATING	TALK NONSENSE	TENTH CENTURY
TAKE A HOLIDAY	TALK OF ANGELS	TENTH OF APRIL
TAKE A LIBERTY	TALK POLITICS	TENTH OF MARCH
TAKE A LOOK-SEE	TALK STRAIGHT	TERMINAL HOME
TAKE A PENALTY	TALK TO NOBODY	TERM OF OFFICE
TAKE A POT-SHOT	TALLEST WOMAN	TERRACED ROOF
TAKE A PRIDE IN	TALLOW CANDLE	TERRIBLE TIME
TAKE A READING	TANGLED SKEIN	TEST-TUBE BABY
TAKE DELIVERY	TANKARD OF ALE	TEXAS RANGERS
TAKE DOWN A PEG	TANK REGIMENT	THAMES DITTON
TAKE EXERCISE	TAP AT THE DOOR	THAMES TUNNEL
TAKE FOR A RIDE	TAPE RECORDER	THAMES VALLEY
TAKE GOOD CARE	TAP ON THE HEAD	THATCHED ROOF
TAKE IT FROM ME	TAP THE BARREL	THE ACROPOLIS
TAKE MEASURES	TARIFF REFORM	THE ADMIRALTY
TAKE MY ADVICE	TASTE OF HONEY	THE ALCHEMIST
TAKE NO DENIAL	TASTES DIFFER	THE ALL-BLACKS
TAKE NO NOTICE	TAX COLLECTOR	THE ANTARCTIC
TAKE ON A PILOT	TAX INSPECTOR	THE ANTIPODES
TAKE ONE'S EASE	TEACH SKATING	THE APPLE-CART
TAKE ONE'S HOOK	TEAM OF HORSES	THE ARCADIANS
TAKE ONE'S NAME	TEARING HURRY	THE ARGENTINE
TAKE ONE'S PICK	TEAR ONE'S HAIR	THE ARGONAUTS
TAKE ONE'S TIME	TEARS OF GRIEF	THEATRE OF WAR
TAKE ONE'S TURN	TEAR TO PIECES	THEATRE QUEUE
TAKE ONE'S WORD	TEAR TO SHREDS	THEATRE ROYAL
TAKE PLEASURE	TEA WITH LEMON	THEATRE USHER
TAKE PRISONER	TEEM WITH RAIN	THEATRE WORLD
TAKE THE BLAME	TEEN-AGE DREAM	THE BACHELORS
TAKE THE CHAIR	TEEN-AGE YEARS	THE BIG DIPPER
TAKE THE COUNT	TEENY-BOPPERS	THE BITTER END
TAKE THE FIELD	TELEGRAPH BOY	THE BLUE ANGEL
TAKE THE FLOOR	TELEPHONE BOX	THE BOSPHORUS
TAKE THE MICKY	TELL A WHOPPER	THE BOY FRIEND
TAKE THE POINT	TELL EVERYONE	THE CATACOMBS
TAKE THE PRIZE	TELL FORTUNES	THE CATECHISM
TAKE THE REINS	TELL ME A STORY	THE CHILTERNS
TAKE THE STAGE	TELL-TALE SIGN	THE COMMON MAN
TAKE THE STAND	TELL THE TRUTH	THE CONQUEROR
TAKE THE TRICK	TELL THE WORLD	THE CONTINENT
TAKE TO FLIGHT	TEMPLE OF FAME	THE COTSWOLDS
TAKE TO PIECES	TEMPORARY JOB	THE CRUSADERS
TAKE TO THE AIR	TEMPT FORTUNE	THE DARK BLUES

THE DAY BEFORE
THE DEEP SOUTH
THE DEFENDERS
THE DEVIL'S OWN
THE DIE IS CAST
THE DOLOMITES
THE DONE THING
THE DOVER ROAD
THE FALL OF MAN
THE FAVOURITE
THE FIVE TOWNS
THE FOLLOWING
THE FOUR WINDS
THE GENTLE SEX
THE GRAMPIANS
THE GUILDHALL
THE HAPPY MEAN
THE HAYMARKET
THE HEREAFTER
THE HERMITAGE
THE HIGHLANDS
THE HIMALAYAS
THE IMMORTALS
THE IRONSIDES
THE IVY LEAGUE
THE LAST DITCH
THE LAST LAUGH
THE LAST STRAW
THE LAST TRUMP
THE LIMELIGHT
THE LISTENERS
THE LOST CHORD
THE MAD HATTER
THE MAYFLOWER
THE MORSE CODE
THE MOUSETRAP
THEN AND THERE
THE NEW FOREST
THE NORTH-EAST
THE NORTH-WEST
THE OLD BAILEY
THE OLD ONE-TWO
THE OLD SCHOOL
THE OTHER SIDE
THE OUTSKIRTS
THE PALLADIUM
THE PARTHENON
THE PIPER'S SON
THE POLONAISE
THE POTTERIES
THE PROVINCES

THE REAL THING
THERE AND BACK
THERE AND THEN
THE REICHSTAG
THE REMAINDER
THERE'S THE RUB
THERMOS FLASK
THE SAME THING
THE SEAMY SIDE
THE SEARCHERS
THE SEVEN SEAS
THE SEVENTIES
THE SOUTH-EAST
THE SOUTH-WEST
THE SPECTATOR
THE STORY GOES
THE THING TO DO
THE TRUTH GAME
THE UPPER HAND
THE VERY DEVIL
THE VERY IMAGE
THE VERY PLACE
THE VERY THING
THE WEAKER SEX
THE WHOLE TIME
THE WILL TO WIN
THE WOMENFOLK
THE WORM TURNS
THE WORST OF IT
THE YARDBIRDS
THE YOUNG IDEA
THICK AND FAST
THICK AND THIN
THICK GLASSES
THIEVES' SLANG
THIN AS A WAFER
THIN DISGUISE
THINGS CHANGE
THINGS TO COME
THINK ABOUT IT
THIN MATERIAL
THIRD CENTURY
THIRD CHANNEL
THIRD CHAPTER
THIRD EDITION
THIRD OF APRIL
THIRD OFFICER
THIRD OF MARCH
THIRD QUARTER
THIRD READING
THIRTEEN DAYS

THIS ABOVE ALL
THIS SATURDAY
THIS THURSDAY
THIS VERY ROOM
THOMAS ARNOLD
THOMAS EDISON
THOMAS WOLSEY
THOSE AGAINST
THREAD OF LIFE
THREAT OF RAIN
THREE-ACT PLAY
THREE AND FIVE
THREE AND FOUR
THREE AND NINE
THREE AT A TIME
THREE BY THREE
THREE COLOURS
THREE COURSES
THREE-DAY WEEK
THREE DEGREES
THREE DOLLARS
THREE EIGHTHS
THREE FATHOMS
THREE FIGURES
THREE GALLONS
THREE GUESSES
THREE GUINEAS
THREE HUNDRED
THREE LENGTHS
THREE MILLION
THREE MINUTES
THREE OCTAVES
THREE OF A KIND
THREE OF CLUBS
THREE PER CENT
THREE-PLY WOOD
THREE-PLY WOOL
THREE RASHERS
THREE'S A CROWD
THREE SISTERS
THREE SQUARED
THREE STOOGES
THREE STRIPES
THREE STROKES
THREE UNITIES
THREE WICKETS
THREE WISE MEN
THREE WITCHES
THROATY LAUGH
THROTTLE DOWN
THROUGH COACH

THROUGH TRAIN
THROW A GLANCE
THROW A SWITCH
THYROID GLAND
TICKET HOLDER
TICKET OFFICE
TICKET POCKET
TIDE OF EVENTS
TIE ONE'S HANDS
TIGHT AS A LORD
TIGHT BANDAGE
TIGHT SQUEEZE
TILL ALL HOURS
TILL DOOMSDAY
TILL NEXT TIME
TILTING MATCH
TIMBERED ROOF
TIME AND AGAIN
TIME AND A HALF
TIME AND MONEY
TIME AND PLACE
TIME AND SPACE
TIME EXPOSURE
TIME FOR LUNCH
TIMELY ADVICE
TIME SCHEDULE
TIME TO FINISH
TIME TO GO HOME
TIME WILL TELL
TINKER'S CURSE
TINNED SALMON
TINTERN ABBEY
TIP THE SCALES
TIP THE WINNER
TIRED OF IT ALL
TIRED TO DEATH
TISSUE OF LIES
TITLED PEOPLE
TITLED PERSON
TITTLE TATTLE
TO ALL INTENTS
TOASTING FORK
TOBACCO JUICE
TOBACCO PLANT
TOBACCO POUCH
TOBACCO SMOKE
TOBACCO STAIN
TO ERR IS HUMAN
TOKEN GESTURE
TOKEN PAYMENT
TOMATO CATSUP

TOM COURTENAY
TOMMY HANDLEY
TOMMY TRINDER
TONGUE OF LAND
TOO HOT TO HOLD
TOOK A DIM VIEW
TOOLS OF TRADE
TOO MANY COOKS
TO ONE'S CREDIT
TOOTH AND CLAW
TOOTH AND NAIL
TOOT ONE'S HORN
TOPLESS DRESS
TOP OF THE BILL
TOP OF THE FORM
TOP OF THE HILL
TOP OF THE MILK
TOP OF THE POLL
TOP OF THE POPS
TOP OF THE TREE
TOREADOR SONG
TORN TO SHREDS
TORY MAJORITY
TORY MINORITY
TOSS A PANCAKE
TOSS FOR SIDES
TOSS ONE'S HEAD
TOSS THE CABER
TOTAL ECLIPSE
TO THE GALLOWS
TO THE LAST MAN
TOTTER AROUND
TOUCH OF FROST
TOUCH ONE'S CAP
TOUCHY PERSON
TOUGH AS NAILS
TOUGH AS STEEL
TOUR DE FRANCE
TOURIST CLASS
TOURIST TRADE
TOUT ENSEMBLE
TOWERING RAGE
TOWER OF BABEL
TOWN PLANNING
TOWN SURVEYOR
TRACER BULLET
TRACING PAPER
TRADE FIGURES
TRADE JOURNAL
TRADE RETURNS
TRADE SURPLUS

TRADING HOUSE
TRADING STAMP
TRAFFIC LIGHT
TRAFFIC RULES
TRAFFORD PARK
TRAGIC ENDING
TRAGIC LOVERS
TRAILING EDGE
TRAINED NURSE
TRAINED VOICE
TRAINING SHIP
TRAIN JOURNEY
TRAIN OF IDEAS
TRAIN ROBBERY
TRAIN SERVICE
TRAIN SPOTTER
TRAIN THE MIND
TRAITOR'S GATE
TRAMP STEAMER
TRANQUIL MIND
TRAPPIST MONK
TRAVEL ABROAD
TRAVEL AGENCY
TRAVEL AROUND
TRAVEL BUREAU
TRAVEL BY LAND
TRAVEL BY TUBE
TREAD LIGHTLY
TREASURE HUNT
TREASURY BILL
TREASURY NOTE
TREAT IN STORE
TREAT LIGHTLY
TREAT ROUGHLY
TREATY OF ROME
TREBLE CHANCE
TRENCHANT WIT
TRENCH MORTAR
TRESPASS UPON
TRESTLE TABLE
TREVOR HOWARD
TRIAL BALANCE
TRIAL IN COURT
TRIBAL CUSTOM
TRIBAL SYSTEM
TRICK CYCLIST
TRIED IN COURT
TRIFLING TALK
TRIGGER HAPPY
TRIM THE SAILS
TRINITY HOUSE

TRIPE DRESSER
TRIVIAL ROUND
TROMBONE SOLO
TROOP CARRIER
TROPHY HUNTER
TROPICAL BIRD
TROPICAL FISH
TROPICAL HEAT
TROPICAL MOON
TROPICAL SUIT
TROPICAL WIND
TROTTING PACE
TROUBLE AHEAD
TROUBLED MIND
TROUSER PRESS
TROUT FISHING
TRUE BELIEVER
TRUE FEELINGS
TRUE TO NATURE
TRUE TO THE END
TRUMPET BLAST
TRUNDLE ALONG
TRUSS OF STRAW
TRUST COMPANY
TRUSTEE STOCK
TRUSTY FRIEND
TRUTH WILL OUT
TRYING PERSON
TRY ONE'S SKILL
TSAR OF RUSSIA
TUBELESS TYRE
TUESDAY NIGHT
TUGBOAT ANNIE
TUNES OF GLORY
TUNNEL OF LOVE
TURKISH TOWEL
TURN A DEAF EAR
TURNED-UP NOSE
TURNHAM GREEN
TURNING POINT
TURN INTO CASH
TURN OF EVENTS
TURN OF PHRASE
TURN OF SPEECH
TURN ONE'S BACK
TURN ONE'S HEAD
TURN ON THE GAS
TURN ON THE TAP
TURN THE PAGES
TURN THE SCALE
TURN THE SCREW

TURN THE TAP ON
TURN UP TRUMPS
TWELFTH GREEN
TWELFTH NIGHT
TWELFTH OF MAY
TWELFTH PLACE
TWELFTH ROUND
TWELVE AND ONE
TWELVE AND SIX
TWELVE AND TEN
TWELVE AND TWO
TWELVE MONTHS
TWELVE O'CLOCK
TWELVE OUNCES
TWELVE POINTS
TWELVE POUNDS
TWELVE TRICKS
TWENTY POINTS
TWENTY POUNDS
TWICE AS HEAVY
TWICE AS QUICK
TWICE MONTHLY
TWICE NIGHTLY
TWICE REMOVED
TWICE THE SIZE
TWIN BROTHERS
TWIN CHILDREN
TWINGE OF PAIN
TWIST AND BUST
TWIST AND TURN
TWIST ONE'S ARM
TWO AND ELEVEN
TWO IN THE BUSH
TWO-SEATER CAR
TWO SHILLINGS
TWO SIXPENCES
TWO-SPEED GEAR
TWO SYLLABLES
TWO-WAY STREET
TYPHOID FEVER
TYPING LESSON
TYPIST'S ERROR
TYRE PRESSURE

U—12

UGLY CUSTOMER
UGLY DUCKLING
UMBRELLA BIRD
UMPTEEN TIMES
UNABLE TO COPE

UNABLE TO HELP
UNABLE TO MOVE
UNBROKEN LINE
UNCERTAIN JOY
UNCUT DIAMOND
UNDER A BUSHEL
UNDER A LADDER
UNDER AND OVER
UNDER A STRAIN
UNDER CONTROL
UNDER ENQUIRY
UNDER HATCHES
UNDER LICENCE
UNDER ONE ROOF
UNDER ONE'S HAT
UNDER PROTEST
UNDER SHERIFF
UNDER TENSION
UNDER THE HEEL
UNDER THE LASH
UNDER THE ROSE
UNDER THE SKIN
UNDER THE WING
UNEVEN CHANCE
UNFAIR CHOICE
UNFIT FOR WORK
UNHAPPY TIMES
UNIFORM SPEED
UNION MEETING
UNITED ACTION
UNITED EFFORT
UNITED STATES
UNIT OF ENERGY
UNIT OF LENGTH
UNKINDEST CUT
UNKNOWN THING
UNLUCKY PATCH
UNMARRIED MAN
UNPAID LABOUR
UNPAID WORKER
UNTIE THE KNOT
UNTIMELY JEST
UNTOLD WEALTH
UNUSUAL TWIST
UNWORTHY PART
UNWRITTEN LAW
UP FOR AUCTION
UP IN A BALLOON
UP IN THE HILLS
UP ONE'S SLEEVE
UP ONE'S STREET

UPON MY HONOUR
UPPER CHAMBER
UPPER CIRCLES
UPPER CLASSES
UPPER REGIONS
UPRIGHT GRAND
UPRIGHT PIANO
UPSTAIRS ROOM
UP THE CHIMNEY
UP TO MISCHIEF
UP TO ONE'S EYES
UP TO ONE'S NECK
UP TO STANDARD
UP TO STRENGTH
UP TO THE NINES
UP TO THE WAIST
UPWARD GLANCE
UPWARD MOTION
UPWARD STROKE
UP WITH THE SUN
URGENT DEMAND
URGENT MATTER
USEFUL ADVICE
USE OF KITCHEN
USE ONE'S BRAIN
USE ONE'S HANDS
UTMOST EXTENT
UTTER FAILURE
UTTER POVERTY
UTTER RUBBISH
UTTER SILENCE
UTTER THREATS

V—12

VACANT OFFICE
VALE OF SORROW
VALET SERVICE
VALIANT HEART
VALUED ADVICE
VALUED FRIEND
VANDYKE BEARD
VANTAGE POINT
VARIABLE GEAR
VARIETY HOUSE
VARIETY STAGE
VARIOUS TYPES
VARSITY MATCH
VAST QUANTITY
VEGETABLE DYE
VEGETABLE OIL

VEILED THREAT
VENETIAN LACE
VENI, VIDI, VICI
VENTURE FORTH
VENTURE TO SAY
VERBAL ATTACK
VERNAL SEASON
VERONICA LAKE
VERTICAL LINE
VERY REVEREND
VERY TOUCHING
VESTED RIGHTS
VIALS OF WRATH
VICE-LIKE GRIP
VICTIM OF FATE
VICTORIA LINE
VICTORIAN AGE
VICTORIAN ERA
VICTORIA PLUM
VICTORY AT SEA
VICTORY BONDS
VICTORY MARCH
VICTORY MEDAL
VILLAGE GREEN
VILLAGE IDIOT
VIM AND VIGOUR
VINCENT PRICE
VIN ORDINAIRE
VIOLENT DEATH
VIOLENT STORM
VIOLENT UPSET
VIOLET CARSON
VIOLIN PLAYER
VIOLIN STRING
VIRGIN FOREST
VIRGINIA MAYO
VIRGINIA REEL
VIRULENT TONE
VISIBLE MEANS
VISIT FRIENDS
VISITING CARD
VISITING TEAM
VISITING TIME
VISITORS' BOOK
VISIT THE SICK
VITAL CONCERN
VIVE LA FRANCE
VIVID PICTURE
VOCATIVE CASE
VODKA AND LIME
VOLCANIC ROCK

VOLGA BOATMAN
VOLUME OF FIRE
VOODOO DOCTOR
VOODOO PRIEST
VOTE IN FAVOUR
VOTE OF THANKS
VOW OF SILENCE
VULGAR TASTES

W—12

WAGE INCREASE
WAG OF THE HEAD
WAG THE FINGER
WAITING WOMAN
WAIT ONE'S TURN
WALK GINGERLY
WALKING MATCH
WALK ON STILTS
WALK ON TIPTOE
WALK SIDEWAYS
WALK STRAIGHT
WALK THE EARTH
WALK THE PLANK
WALK TOGETHER
WALK WITH EASE
WALLED GARDEN
WANDERING JEW
WAND OF OFFICE
WANTED PERSON
WARLIKE TRIBE
WARM THE BLOOD
WARM THE HEART
WARNING LIGHT
WARNING SOUND
WARNING VOICE
WAR TO END WARS
WASH AND DRY UP
WASHED ASHORE
WASH ONE'S FACE
WASH ONE'S HAIR
WASTED EFFORT
WASTED LABOUR
WASTE NOTHING
WASTE NO WORDS
WASTE OF MONEY
WASTE PRODUCT
WATCH AND PRAY
WATCH AND WAIT
WATCH CLOSELY
WATCH REPAIRS
WATER BISCUIT

WATER COLOURS	WELL AND TRULY	WILBUR WRIGHT
WATER DIVINER	WELL DESERVED	WILD APPLAUSE
WATER HYDRANT	WELL DISPOSED	WILD CREATURE
WATERING CART	WELL IN POCKET	WILD HYACINTH
WATER SPANIEL	WELL-MADE SUIT	WILD LAUGHTER
WAVE FAREWELL	WELL REPORTED	WILD-WEST SHOW
WAXWORKS SHOW	WELL TAILORED	WILFUL DAMAGE
WAYNE FONTANA	WELL-TIMED ACT	WILFUL MURDER
WAYS AND MEANS	WELSH COSTUME	WILLIAM BLAKE
WAYWARD CHILD	WELSH DRESSER	WILLIAM BOOTH
WEAK APPROACH	WELSH RAREBIT	WILLIAM RUFUS
WEAK ARGUMENT	WEST BROMWICH	WILLING HANDS
WEAKER VESSEL	WEST-END STAGE	WILLING HEART
WEAKEST POINT	WESTERLY WIND	WILLING HORSE
WEAK SOLUTION	WESTERN FRONT	WILLING PARTY
WEALTHY WIDOW	WESTERN ISLES	WILLING SLAVE
WEAPONS OF WAR	WESTERN UNION	WILLING VOTER
WEAR BLINKERS	WESTERN WORLD	WILL OF HEAVEN
WEAR MOURNING	WEST VIRGINIA	WILL O' THE WISP
WEAR THE CLOTH	WET TO THE SKIN	WILTON CARPET
WEAR THE CROWN	WHALE OF A TIME	WIN BY A LENGTH
WEATHER CHART	WHAT'S COOKING?	WINDING TRAIL
WEATHER GAUGE	WHAT'S THE GAME?	WINDMILL GIRL
WEATHER GLASS	WHAT'S THE ODDS?	WIND OF CHANGE
WEB OF CUNNING	WHAT THE DEUCE?	WINDOW SCREEN
WEDDED COUPLE	WHEN AND WHERE?	WINDSOR CHAIR
WEDDING BELLS	WHERE AND WHEN?	WIND THE CLOCK
WEDDING DRESS	WHETHER OR NOT	WINDY WEATHER
WEDDING FEAST	WHET THE KNIFE	WINE AND WOMEN
WEDDING GROUP	WHICH IS WHICH?	WINE IMPORTER
WEDDING GUEST	WHIFF OF SMOKE	WINE MERCHANT
WEDDING MARCH	WHILE YOU WAIT	WINGED INSECT
WEDDING RITES	WHIPPED CREAM	WIN HANDS DOWN
WEDGWOOD BLUE	WHIPPING POST	WIN IN A CANTER
WEEK-END LEAVE	WHIPSNADE ZOO	WINNING HORSE
WEEK-END PARTY	WHISKY GALORE	WINNING SCORE
WEEKLY COLUMN	WHISTLE FOR IT	WINNING SMILE
WEEKLY MARKET	WHITE CABBAGE	WIN ONE'S SPURS
WEEKLY REPORT	WHITE FEATHER	WINSOME SMILE
WEEKLY SALARY	WHITE HEATHER	WINTER ABROAD
WEEP WITH RAGE	WHITE OF AN EGG	WINTER GARDEN
WEIGH HEAVILY	WHITE RUSSIAN	WINTER RESORT
WEIGH ONESELF	WHITE WEDDING	WINTER SEASON
WEIGHT FOR AGE	WHITHER BOUND?	WINTER SPORTS
WEIRD SISTERS	WHO GOES THERE?	WIN THE BATTLE
WELCOME EVENT	WICKED TYRANT	WIN THE RUBBER
WELCOME GUEST	WICKER BASKET	WIPE ONE'S EYES
WELCOME SIGHT	WICKET KEEPER	WIPE ONE'S FEET
WELD TOGETHER	WIDE CURRENCY	WIPE THE FLOOR
WELFARE STATE	WIDELY SPACED	WISE DECISION
WELL ADVANCED	WIDOW TWANKEY	WIT AND WISDOM

WITCHING HOUR
WITCH OF ENDOR
WITH ALL HASTE
WITH ALL SPEED
WITH AN ACCENT
WITH A PURPOSE
WITH IMPUNITY
WITHIN BOUNDS
WITHIN LIMITS
WITHIN RADIUS
WITHIN REASON
WITH INTEREST
WITHIN THE LAW
WITH ONE VOICE
WITH OPEN ARMS
WITH OPEN EYES
WITHOUT A BEAN
WITHOUT A CARE
WITHOUT A CENT
WITHOUT A HOPE
WITHOUT A WORD
WITHOUT CAUSE
WITHOUT DELAY
WITHOUT DOUBT
WITHOUT FAULT
WITHOUT LIMIT
WITHOUT PRICE
WITHOUT STINT
WITHOUT SUGAR
WITH PLEASURE
WITH THIS RING
WOMAN IN WHITE
WOMAN'S HONOUR
WOMAN STUDENT
WOMAN TO WOMAN
WOMEN'S RIGHTS
WON BY A STREET
WON IN A CANTER
WOODEN BUCKET
WOOD SHAVINGS
WOOLLEN SOCKS
WOOL MERCHANT
WORD IN SEASON

WORD IN THE EAR
WORD OF ADVICE
WORD OF HONOUR
WORDS OF CHEER
WORDY WARFARE
WORKABLE PLAN
WORK FOR PEACE
WORKING CLASS
WORKING HOURS
WORKING MODEL
WORKING ORDER
WORKING PARTY
WORKING WIVES
WORKING WOMAN
WORK MIRACLES
WORK OFF STEAM
WORK ONE'S WILL
WORK OVERTIME
WORKS CANTEEN
WORKS COUNCIL
WORKS MANAGER
WORK TOGETHER
WORLDLY GOODS
WORLD OF SPORT
WORLD OF TODAY
WORM'S EYE VIEW
WORRIED FROWN
WORRYING TIME
WORRY TO DEATH
WORSE FOR WEAR
WORTH A PACKET
WORTH NOTHING
WORTHY OF NOTE
WOULD YOU MIND?
WOUNDED PRIDE
WRACK AND RUIN
WRETCHED DIGS
WRITE A CHEQUE
WRITE A LETTER
WRITE AN ESSAY
WRITE A REPORT
WRITE A SONNET
WRITER'S CRAMP

WRITHE IN PAIN
WRITING PAPER
WRITING TABLE
WRITTEN MUSIC
WRITTEN ORDER
WRITTEN REPLY
WRITTEN TERMS
WRONG ADDRESS
WRONG MEANING
WRONG SIDE OUT
WRONG SOCIETY
WRONG TURNING
WRONG VERDICT

Y—12
YACHTING CLUB
YANKEE DOODLE
YARD AND A HALF
YEARLY SALARY
YEARS OF STUDY
YELLOW BASKET
YELLOW COLOUR
YELLOW FLOWER
YELLOW RIBBON
YELLOW STREAK
YELL WITH PAIN
YOUNG AT HEART
YOUNG ENGLAND
YOUNGEST GIRL
YOUNG HOPEFUL
YOUNG IN HEART
YOUNG WOODLEY
YOUR EMINENCE
YOUR HIGHNESS
YOUR LADYSHIP
YOUR LORDSHIP
YOUR OWN FAULT
YOURS IN HASTE

Z—12
ZACHARY SCOTT
ZIGZAG COURSE

A—13
ABERDEEN ANGUS
ABIDE BY THE LAW
ABJECT APOLOGY
ABJECT POVERTY
ABJECT SLAVERY
ABOUT ONE'S EARS
ABOVE ONE'S HEAD
ABOVE REPROACH
ABOVE SEA-LEVEL
ABOVE STRENGTH
ABRAHAM'S BOSOM
ABRUPT DESCENT
ABSENCE OF MIND
ABSENT FRIENDS
ABSOLUTE POWER
ABSOLUTE PROOF
ABSOLUTE RULER
ABSOLUTE TRUST
ABSTRACT TERMS
ABUSIVE SPEECH
ABYSSINIAN CAT
ACADEMIC DRESS
ACADEMIC TITLE
ACCEPT AN OFFER
ACCEPTED TRUTH
ACCEPT PAYMENT
ACCIDENT PRONE
ACCORDION BAND
ACCOUNTS CLERK
ACCUSED PERSON
ACCUSE FALSELY
ACE OF DIAMONDS
ACHES AND PAINS
ACQUIRED SKILL
ACQUIRED TASTE
ACQUIT ONESELF
ACROSS AND DOWN
ACROSS COUNTRY
ACROSS THE ROAD
ACT AS CHAIRMAN
ACT FOR THE BEST
ACTING CAPTAIN
ACTING MANAGER
ACTION PAINTER
ACTION PICTURE
ACTIVE PARTNER
ACTIVE SERVICE
ACTIVE VOLCANO
ACT LIKE A CHARM
ACT LIKE A TONIC

ACT OF COURTESY
ACT OF HUMANITY
ACT OF KINDNESS
ACT OF VIOLENCE
ACUTE DISTRESS
ADAM FIREPLACE
ADDED PLEASURE
ADDED STRENGTH
ADDING MACHINE
ADEQUATE CAUSE
A DEUCE OF A MESS
ADIPOSE TISSUE
ADJUST THE TYPE
ADMIRAL NELSON
ADMIRALTY ARCH
ADMISSION CARD
ADMISSION FREE
ADMITTED GUILT
ADVANCED LEVEL
ADVANCED PUPIL
ADVANCE NOTICE
ADVISE AGAINST
ADVISORY BOARD
AERIAL RAILWAY
AERIAL TORPEDO
AERIAL WARFARE
AFFECTED STYLE
AFFECTED VOICE
AFFORDING HOPE
AFRAID TO SPEAK
AFTER A FASHION
AFTER MIDNIGHT
AFTERNOON POST
AFTERNOON REST
AFTER THE EVENT
AFTER THE STORM
AGAIN AND AGAIN
AGAINST THE LAW
AGE OF CHIVALRY
AGREE TO DIFFER
AIR A GRIEVANCE
AIR-FORCE CROSS
AIR OF APPROVAL
AIR ON A G STRING
AIR OPERATIONS
AIRPORT LOUNGE
AIR-RAID WARDEN
AIRS AND GRACES
ALEXANDER POPE
ALEXANDRA PARK
ALFRED DREYFUS

ALICE BLUE GOWN
ALL CHANGE HERE
ALL-DAY SESSION
ALLEGED MOTIVE
ALLEGED REASON
ALL FOR NOTHING
ALL FOR THE BEST
ALL FOR THE GOOD
ALL HALLOWS' EVE
ALLIED ADVANCE
ALLIED LANDING
ALLIGATOR PEAR
ALLIGATOR SKIN .
ALL IN A FLUSTER
ALL IN GOOD TIME
ALL IN ONE PIECE
ALL-IN WRESTLER
ALL OF A TREMBLE
ALL OF A TWITTER
ALL THE ANSWERS
ALL THE WINNERS
ALL-TIME RECORD
ALLUVIAL PLAIN
ALMOND BLOSSOM
ALONG THE COAST
A LONG WAY AFTER
A LONG WAY AHEAD
ALPHA AND OMEGA
ALPINE CLIMBER
ALTER THE RULES
ALTOGETHER BAD
ALWAYS ON THE GO
AMATEUR BOXING
AMATEUR GOLFER
AMATEUR PLAYER
AMATEUR SLEUTH
AMATEUR STATUS
AMATEUR TALENT
AMERICAN CLOTH
AMERICAN EAGLE
AMERICAN NEGRO
AMERICAN ORGAN
AMERICAN SLANG
AMOROUS GLANCE
AMUSEMENT PARK
ANATOLE FRANCE
ANCESTRAL HALL
ANCESTRAL HOME
ANCIENT BRITON
ANCIENT GREECE
ANCIENT GRUDGE

ANCIENT LIGHTS
ANCIENT WISDOM
ANDREW JACKSON
ANGELIC VOICES
ANGEL PAVEMENT
ANGRY YOUNG MAN
ANGUISH OF MIND
ANGULAR FIGURE
ANIMAL KINGDOM
ANIMAL RESERVE
ANIMAL SPIRITS
ANIMAL TRAINER
ANIMATED SMILE
ANNOTATED TEXT
ANNUAL ECLIPSE
ANNUAL FIXTURE
ANNUAL HOLIDAY
ANNUAL MEETING
ANNUAL PAYMENT
ANNUAL PREMIUM
ANOINT WITH OIL
ANONYMOUS GIFT
ANOTHER CHANCE
ANOTHER MATTER
ANOTHER PLEASE
ANSWER THE BELL
ANSWER THE HELM
ANTHONY NEWLEY
ANTHONY QUAYLE
ANTHROPOID APE
ANTIQUE DEALER
ANTONY ADVERSE
ANXIOUS MOMENT
ANYBODY'S GUESS
APPEAL FOR HELP
APPEALING LOOK
APPEAR IN COURT
APPLE DUMPLING
APPLE FRITTERS
APPLE OF THE EYE
APPLE-PIE ORDER
APPLE TURNOVER
APPLY FOR A LOAN
APPLY FOR LEAVE
APPLY PRESSURE
APPLY THE BRAKE
APPLY THE MATCH
APOLLO THEATRE
APOSTLES' CREED
APPOINTED TIME
APRICOT BRANDY

APRIL FOOL'S DAY
APRIL THE FIFTH
APRIL THE FIRST
APRIL THE NINTH
APRIL THE SIXTH
APRIL THE TENTH
APRIL THE THIRD
ARABIAN DESERT
ARABIAN NIGHTS
ARC DE TRIOMPHE
ARCHIE ANDREWS
ARCTIC REGIONS
ARDENT ADMIRER
ARDENT SPIRITS
ARGUE THE POINT
ARMAMENTS RACE
ARMED CONFLICT
ARMS AND THE MAN
ARMS PROGRAMME
ARMY COMMANDER
ARMY ESTIMATES
ARMY EXERCISES
ARMY PAY-OFFICE
ARNOLD BENNETT
AROUND THE TOWN
ARRANGE A MATCH
ARREARS OF WORK
ART COLLECTION
ART DEPARTMENT
ART EXHIBITION
ARTHUR ENGLISH
ARTICLED CLERK
ARTICLES OF WAR
ARTIFICIAL ARM
ARTIFICIAL FLY
ARTIFICIAL LEG
ARTILLERY FIRE
ARTISTIC VALUE
ARTISTS' COLONY
ARTISTS' RIFLES
ARTIST'S STUDIO
ART OF SPEAKING
ARTS AND CRAFTS
AS BLIND AS A BAT
AS BOLD AS BRASS
AS DARK AS NIGHT
AS DARK AS PITCH
AS FAR AS IT GOES
AS FULL AS AN EGG
AS GOOD AS A PLAY
AS HARD AS NAILS

ASHDOWN FOREST
AS HEAVY AS LEAD
ASK A POLICEMAN
ASK FOR NOTHING
ASK FOR TROUBLE
ASK PERMISSION
AS LARGE AS LIFE
AS LIKELY AS NOT
AS LONG AS MY ARM
AS PALE AS DEATH
ASPARAGUS TIPS
AS RIGHT AS RAIN
ASSEMBLY ROOMS
ASSERT ONESELF
ASSUME AN ALIAS
ASSUME COMMAND
AS SURE AS CAN BE
AS SWEET AS A NUT
AS THIN AS A LATH
A STITCH IN TIME
AS TRUE AS STEEL
AS WARM AS TOAST
AS WEAK AS WATER
ATALANTA'S RACE
AT AN ADVANTAGE
AT A STANDSTILL
AT FULL STRETCH
AT GREAT LENGTH
ATHLETE'S HEART
ATHLETIC COACH
ATLANTIC LINER
ATLANTIC OCEAN
AT LOGGERHEADS
ATOMIC FISSION
ATOMIC REACTOR
ATOMIC WARFARE
ATOMIC WARHEAD
AT ONE'S LEISURE
AT ONE'S OWN RISK
AT ONE'S WITS' END
AT RIGHT-ANGLES
AT SHORT NOTICE
ATTEND COLLEGE
AT THE CONTROLS
AT THE DENTIST'S
AT THE LAST GASP
AT THE RINGSIDE
AT THE SAME TIME
AT THE WAXWORKS
ATTORNEY AT LAW
ATTRACT NOTICE

AT YOUR SERVICE
AUCTION BRIDGE
AUDITORY NERVE
AUDREY HEPBURN
AUGEAN STABLES
AUTHENTIC WORK
AUTOMATIC LIFT
AUTOMATIC LOCK
AUTUMN COLOURS
AUXILIARY VERB
AVENGING ANGEL
AVENUE OF TREES
AVERAGE AMOUNT
AVERAGE FIGURE
AVERAGE HEIGHT
AVERAGE PERSON
AVERAGE WEIGHT
AVERT ONE'S EYES
AVOID THE ISSUE
AWAY FROM IT ALL
AWKWARD PERSON

B—13
BABBLING BROOK
BACHELOR OF LAW
BACK-HAND DRIVE
BACK IN HARNESS
BACK IN THE FOLD
BACK OF THE HAND
BACK OF THE HEAD
BACK OF THE NECK
BACK ONE'S FANCY
BACK THE WINNER
BACK TO THE LAND
BACK TO THE WALL
BACKWARD CHILD
BACON SANDWICH
BAD COMPLEXION
BAD CONNECTION
BAD CONSCIENCE
BADGE OF OFFICE
BAD IMPRESSION
BADLY HAMMERED
BADLY REPORTED
BAD MANAGEMENT
BAD REPUTATION
BAD UPBRINGING
BAG AND BAGGAGE
BAGGY TROUSERS
BALANCE IN HAND
BALD ADMISSION

BALD STATEMENT
BALL AND SOCKET
BALLET DANCING
BALLOON ASCENT
BALLY NUISANCE
BAMBOO CURTAIN
BAND OF OUTLAWS
BAND OF ROBBERS
BANG ON THE HEAD
BANKER'S CREDIT
BANK MESSENGER
BANK OF ENGLAND
BANK OF IRELAND
BANK OVERDRAFT
BANKRUPT STOCK
BANKS AND BRAES
BANK STATEMENT
BAPTISMAL NAME
BAPTISM OF FIRE
BAPTIST CHURCH
BARBARA MULLEN
BARBECUE PARTY
BARBER SURGEON
BARCELONA NUTS
BARE-BACK RIDER
BARE EXISTENCE
BARE-FACED LIAR
BARE ONE'S TEETH
BARGAIN HUNTER
BARK AT THE MOON
BARK ONE'S SHINS
BAR OF THE HOUSE
BARRISTER'S WIG
BARTERED BRIDE
BASHFUL MANNER
BASIC INSTINCT
BASQUE COUNTRY
BASSO PROFUNDO
BATHED IN TEARS
BATHING BEAUTY
BATHING TRUNKS
BATTER PUDDING
BATTERSEA PARK
BATTERY OF GUNS
BATTLE CRUISER
BATTLE HONOURS
BATTLE OF WORDS
BAYONET CHARGE
BAYSWATER ROAD
BEANS AND BACON
BEAR THE BURDEN

BEAST OF BELSEN
BEAST OF BURDEN
BEAT ALL-COMERS
BEATLES' RECORD
BEAT ONE HOLLOW
BEAT THE BOUNDS
BEAT THE RECORD
BEAUFORT SCALE
BEAUTIFUL FACE
BEAUTIFUL VIEW
BEAUTY CONTEST
BEAUTY CULTURE
BEAUTY PARLOUR
BECOME A MARTYR
BECOME A MEMBER
BECOME A NEW MAN
BECOME ENGAGED
BECOME EXTINCT
BECOME FRIENDS
BE CONSPICUOUS
BEDSIDE MANNER
BEETLING BROWS
BEFORE THE DAWN
BEFORE THE FACT
BEFORE THE MAST
BEFORE THE WIND
BEG FOR FAVOURS
BEGGING LETTER
BEGINNER'S LUCK
BEGIN TO WEAKEN
BEG PERMISSION
BEHAVE ONESELF
BEHIND THE LINE
BEHIND THE VEIL
BE IN DISFAVOUR
BE IN THE SADDLE
BELATED EFFORT
BELISHA BEACON
BELLES LETTRES
BELONGING TO ME
BELONGING TO US
BELOVED OBJECT
BELOW FREEZING
BELOW SEA-LEVEL
BELOW STANDARD
BELOW STRENGTH
BE MY VALENTINE
BEND BACKWARDS
BEND IN THE ROAD
BENEATH NOTICE
BENEATH THE SUN

BE OF GOOD CHEER
BE OF GOOD HEART
BERNARD BRADEN
BESIDE ONESELF
BESIDE THE MARK
BESSEMER STEEL
BEST BEHAVIOUR
BEST END OF NECK
BESTIR ONESELF
BEST OF A BAD JOB
BEST OF FRIENDS
BEST OF ITS KIND
BEST OF MOTIVES
BEST THING TO DO
BETTER ONESELF
BETTER OR WORSE
BEYOND ALL HELP
BEYOND COMPARE
BEYOND CONTROL
BEYOND DISPUTE
BEYOND MEASURE
BEYOND ONE'S KEN
BEYOND THE PALE
BEYOND THE VEIL
BICYCLE RACING
BID FOR FREEDOM
BIG-GAME HUNTER
BIG WHITE CHIEF
BILLIARD TABLE
BIRD IN THE HAND
BIRD OF ILL OMEN
BIRD OF PASSAGE
BIRD ON THE WING
BIRD SANCTUARY
BIRD'S-NEST SOUP
BIRDS OF THE AIR
BIRTHDAY PARTY
BIRTHDAY TREAT
BISCUIT BARREL
BITE ONE'S NAILS
BITE ONE'S THUMB
BITING SARCASM
BIT OF A MYSTERY
BIT OF NONSENSE
BITS AND PIECES
BITTER DRAUGHT
BITTER FLAVOUR
BITTER QUARREL
BITTER REMORSE
BLACK AND WHITE
BLACK AS A SWEEP

BLACK DIAMONDS
BLACKPOOL ROCK
BLANKET FINISH
BLANKET OF SNOW
BLANKET STITCH
BLAZE OF COLOUR
BLAZE THE TRAIL
BLAZING TEMPER
BLEEDING HEART
BLESS THE BRIDE
BLIGHTED HOPES
BLINDING LIGHT
BLINDING STORM
BLIND IN ONE EYE
BLINDMAN'S BUFF
BLISSFUL STATE
BLOCK CAPITALS
BLOOD BROTHERS
BLOOD PRESSURE
BLOOD RELATION
BLOODSHOT EYES
BLOODY ASSIZES
BLOTTING PAPER
BLOW GREAT GUNS
BLUE IN THE FACE
BLUNT QUESTION
BLUSH FOR SHAME
BLUSHING BRIDE
BOARDING HOUSE
BOARDING PARTY
BOB'S YOUR UNCLE
BODY CORPORATE
BODY OF OPINION
BOHEMIAN GLASS
BOLSHOI BALLET
BOMBER COMMAND
BONY STRUCTURE
BOOKING OFFICE
BOOK OF GENESIS
BOOK OF THE FILM
BOOK OF THE PLAY
BOOK OF THE YEAR
BOOK OF TICKETS
BOOK ONE'S BERTH
BOOMING MARKET
BOON COMPANION
BOOSTER ROCKET
BOOT AND SADDLE
BORDER BALLADS
BORDER COUNTRY
BORN IN WEDLOCK

BORN ORGANISER
BORN YESTERDAY
BORROWED MONEY
BORSTAL SYSTEM
BOSTON TERRIER
BOSTON TWO-STEP
BOTTLED SWEETS
BOTTLE OF SCENT
BOTTLE OF STOUT
BOTTLE OF WATER
BOTTOMLESS PIT
BOUGHT AND SOLD
BOUNDARY FENCE
BOUNDARY STONE
BOUNDLESS DEEP
BOWLER'S WICKET
BOWLING CREASE
BOW TO THE STORM
BOX OF BISCUITS
BOX OF CRACKERS
BOX THE COMPASS
BRACE OF SHAKES
BRANCH LIBRARY
BRANCH MEETING
BRANCH OFFICER
BRANDY AND SODA
BRASS BEDSTEAD
BRASS FARTHING
BRAVE NEW WORLD
BREACH OF FAITH
BREACH OF TRUST
BREAD AND WATER
BREAD OF HEAVEN
BREAD POULTICE
BREAD SHORTAGE
BREADTH OF MIND
BREADTH OF VIEW
BREAK A JOURNEY
BREAK A PROMISE
BREAKDOWN GANG
BREAKERS AHEAD
BREAKFAST DISH
BREAKFAST FOOD
BREAKFAST TIME
BREAKING POINT
BREAK INTO A RUN
BREAK INTO SONG
BREAK IT GENTLY
BREAK OFF SHORT
BREAK ONE'S BACK
BREAK ONE'S DUCK

BREAK ONE'S FAST
BREAK ONE'S NECK
BREAK ONE'S WORD
BREAK THE PEACE
BREAK THE RULES
BREAK THE SPELL
BREAK TO PIECES
BREAST THE TAPE
BREATHE FREELY
BREATHING ROOM
BREATHING TUBE
BRED IN THE BONE
BRIDE AND GROOM
BRIDGE BUILDER
BRIDGE OF BOATS
BRIDGE OF SIGHS
BRIDGE PROBLEM
BRIEF INTERVAL
BRIGHTON BEACH
BRIGHTON BELLE
BRIGHTON RACES
BRILLIANT IDEA
BRILLIANT MIND
BRING AN ACTION
BRING INTO LINE
BRING INTO PLAY
BRING TO A CLOSE
BRING TOGETHER
BRING UP TO DATE
BRISKET OF BEEF
BRISK MOVEMENT
BRISTOL ROVERS
BRITISH COLONY
BRITISH CONSUL
BRITISH EMPIRE
BRITISH GUIANA
BRITISH LEGION
BRITISH MUSEUM
BRITISH PUBLIC
BROAD DAYLIGHT
BROKEN ENGLISH
BROKEN PROMISE
BROKEN ROMANCE
BROKEN SILENCE
BROOK NO DENIAL
BROTHERLY LOVE
BROUGHT TO BOOK
BROWN AS A BERRY
BRUSH ONE'S HAIR
BRUSQUE MANNER
BRUTE STRENGTH

BUBONIC PLAGUE
BUCKET OF WATER
BUDDING AUTHOR
BUDDING GENIUS
BUDGET SURPLUS
BUFF ORPINGTON
BUILDING BLOCK
BULLS AND BEARS
BUMPER HARVEST
BUNCH OF GRAPES
BURDEN OF GUILT
BURDEN OF POWER
BURDEN OF PROOF
BURIAL CUSTOMS
BURIAL SERVICE
BURKE'S PEERAGE
BURLESQUE SHOW
BURNING DESIRE
BURNING THIRST
BURN ONE'S BOATS
BURN ONE'S MONEY
BURN TO A CINDER
BURNT OFFERING
BURN WITH ANGER
BURSTING POINT
BURST OF ENERGY
BURST THE BONDS
BURTON ON TRENT
BUSH TELEGRAPH
BUSINESS HOURS
BUSINESS HOUSE
BUSINESS LUNCH
BUSINESS TERMS
BUSINESS WOMAN
BUSINESS WORLD
BUTLER'S PANTRY
BUTTERED TOAST
BUTTERFLY KISS
BUTTON YOUR LIP
BY ALL ACCOUNTS
BY APPOINTMENT
BY ARRANGEMENT
BY CANDLELIGHT
BY INSTALMENTS
BY THE ROADSIDE
BY UNDERGROUND
BY WORD OF MOUTH

C—13
CABINET MEMBER
CALCULATED LIE

CALENDAR MONTH
CALL FOR TRUMPS
CALL INTO BEING
CALL OF THE WILD
CALL ONE'S BLUFF
CALL THE POLICE
CALL TO ACCOUNT
CALL TO WITNESS
CAMBRIDGE BLUE
CAMEL-HAIR COAT
CAMERA OBSCURA
CAMPAIGN MEDAL
CAMPING GROUND
CANARY ISLANDS
CANDID OPINION
CANNIBAL TRIBE
CAPACITY CROWD
CAPACITY HOUSE
CAPE CANAVERAL
CAPITAL CHARGE
CAPITAL FELLOW
CAPITAL LETTER
CAPITAL MURDER
CAP OF DARKNESS
CAPTAIN CUTTLE
CAPTAIN KETTLE
CAPTAIN'S TABLE
CARAFE OF WATER
CARBON DIOXIDE
CARDINAL POINT
CAREER OF CRIME
CAREFUL DRIVER
CARNEGIE TRUST
CARNIVAL QUEEN
CARPET CLEANER
CARPET SWEEPER
CARRIER PIGEON
CARRY THE BLAME
CARRY THE TORCH
CARRY TO EXCESS
CARTRIDGE CASE
CARVE ONE'S NAME
CARVE THE JOINT
CASH IN ADVANCE
CASH IN THE BANK
CASHMERE SHAWL
CASH ON THE NAIL
CASSE NOISETTE
CAST IN ONE'S LOT
CAST-IRON ALIBI
CASTLE IN SPAIN

CASUAL CLOTHES
CASUAL MEETING
CASUAL VISITOR
CAT-AND-DOG LIFE
CATCH A GLIMPSE
CATCH AT STRAWS
CATCH UNAWARES
CATERING CORPS
CATHEDRAL CITY
CATHEDRAL TOWN
CATHERINE PARR
CATHOLIC FAITH
CAT O' NINE TAILS
CATTLE BREEDER
CATTLE FARMING
CAUGHT BENDING
CAUGHT IN A TRAP
CAUGHT NAPPING
CAUSE A FLUTTER
CAUSE FOR ALARM
CAUSE OF INJURY
CAUSTIC REMARK
CAVALRY CHARGE
CAVALRY SCHOOL
CAVALRY TROOPS
CAYENNE PEPPER
CELEBRATED MAN
CELESTIAL BODY
CELESTIAL CITY
CELESTIAL POLE
CEMENT MIXTURE
CENTRAL AFRICA
CENTRAL EUROPE
CENTRAL FIGURE
CENTRAL LONDON
CENTRAL OFFICE
CENTRE FORWARD
CENTRE OF TRADE
CERTAIN EXTENT
CERTAIN PERSON
CERTIFIED MILK
CHAIN OF EVENTS
CHAIN OF OFFICE
CHAIN REACTION
CHALLENGE FATE
CHAMP AT THE BIT
CHAMPION BOXER
CHANCE MEETING
CHANCE ONE'S ARM
CHANGE A CHEQUE
CHANGED PERSON

CHANGE OF FRONT
CHANGE OF HEART
CHANGE OF PLACE
CHANGE OF SCENE
CHANGE OF VENUE
CHANGING ROOMS
CHANGING VOICE
CHANNEL BRIDGE
CHANNEL TUNNEL
CHARACTER PART
CHARGE ACCOUNT
CHARGE TOO MUCH
CHARITY BAZAAR
CHARLES DARWIN
CHARLES WESLEY
CHARLOT'S REVUE
CHARM BRACELET
CHARMED CIRCLE
CHARM OF MANNER
CHARTER FLIGHT
CHASE ONE'S TAIL
CHEAP AND NASTY
CHECK THE SPEED
CHEDDAR CHEESE
CHEERFUL GIVER
CHEERFUL SIGHT
CHEESE AND WINE
CHEESE BISCUIT
CHEF DE CUISINE
CHELSEA BRIDGE
CHELTENHAM SPA
CHEMICAL AGENT
CHERISH AN IDEA
CHERRY BLOSSOM
CHERRY ORCHARD
CHESS CHAMPION
CHEST EXPANDER
CHESTNUT BROWN
CHESTNUT HORSE
CHICKEN FARMER
CHIEF ARMOURER
CHIEF ENGINEER
CHIEF OF POLICE
CHILDHOOD DAYS
CHILDISH PRANK
CHILD OF NATURE
CHILDREN'S BOOK
CHILDREN'S GAME
CHILDREN'S HOME
CHILDREN'S HOUR
CHILLY WELCOME

CHILTERN HILLS
CHIMNEY CORNER
CHIMNEY-POT HAT
CHINESE PUZZLE
CHOCOLATE DROP
CHOICE OF WORDS
CHOIR PRACTICE
CHOP AND CHANGE
CHOPPING BLOCK
CHORAL CONCERT
CHORAL SERVICE
CHORAL SOCIETY
CHORUS OF ABUSE
CHRIS CHATAWAY
CHRISTIAN NAME
CHRISTMAS CAKE
CHRISTMAS CARD
CHRISTMAS FAIR
CHRISTMAS GIFT
CHRISTMAS ROSE
CHRISTMAS TREE
CHURCHILL TANK
CHURCH OFFICER
CHURCH SERVICE
CHURCH STEEPLE
CHURCH WEDDING
CIGARETTE CARD
CIGARETTE CASE
CIGARETTE GIRL
CIRCLE OF LIGHT
CIRCUS MANAGER
CITY OF THE DEAD
CIVIL AVIATION
CIVIL ENGINEER
CIVILIAN DRESS
CIVIL MARRIAGE
CIVIL QUESTION
CLAIM THE CROWN
CLAPHAM COMMON
CLAP OF THUNDER
CLAP ONE'S HANDS
CLAP ON THE BACK
CLARENCE HOUSE
CLASSIC REMARK
CLASS STRUGGLE
CLEAN THE SLATE
CLEARANCE SALE
CLEARING HOUSE
CLEAR SPEAKING
CLEAR THE COURT
CLEAR THE DECKS

CLEAR THE TABLE
CLEAR THINKING
CLEMENT ATTLEE
CLENCHED TEETH
CLERICAL BLACK
CLERICAL DRESS
CLERICAL ERROR
CLERICAL STAFF
CLIFFS OF DOVER
CLIMBING IRONS
CLIMBING PLANT
CLIMBING SHRUB
CLIMB LIKE A CAT
CLINCH THE DEAL
CLING TOGETHER
CLIP ONE'S WINGS
CLIP ONE'S WORDS
CLIPPED SPEECH
CLOSED CHAPTER
CLOSED CIRCUIT
CLOSE FIGHTING
CLOSELY ALLIED
CLOSE ONE'S EYES
CLOSE PRISONER
CLOSE QUARTERS
CLOSE RELATIVE
CLOSE SECURITY
CLOSE THE RANKS
CLOSE TOGETHER
CLOSE TO NATURE
CLOSING SEASON
CLOSING SPEECH
CLOSING STAGES
CLOTHES BASKET
CLOTHING TRADE
CLOUD THE ISSUE
COARSE FISHING
COASTAL RESORT
COASTAL WATERS
COAST DOWNHILL
COBBLED STREET
COCKER SPANIEL
COCKNEY ACCENT
COCK OF THE WALK
COCKTAIL DRESS
COCKTAIL PARTY
COCKTAIL STICK
CODE OF CONDUCT
COFFEE ESSENCE
COFFEE GROUNDS
COFFEE PLANTER

COLD AS CHARITY
COLD COLLATION
COLD IN THE HEAD
COLD RECEPTION
COLD-WATER CURE
COLLECTION BOX
COLLECT STAMPS
COLLEGE OF ARMS
COLONIAL HOUSE
COLONIAL STYLE
COLOURED CHALK
COLOURED SLIDE
COLOURED WATER
COLOUR PROBLEM
COLUMN OF ROUTE
COLUMN OF SMOKE
COMBINED FORCE
COMBINE FORCES
COME ALONGSIDE
COME AWAY EMPTY
COME BACK AGAIN
COME DOWN HEADS
COME DOWN TAILS
COMEDY ACTRESS
COMEDY THEATRE
COME IN CONTACT
COME INTO BEING
COME INTO FORCE
COME INTO MONEY
COME INTO SIGHT
COME OUT EASILY
COME OVER QUEER
COME TO A BAD END
COME TO A CLIMAX
COME TO A CRISIS
COME TO NOTHING
COME TO ONESELF
COME TO THE BALL
COME TO THE FAIR
COME TO THE FORE
COME UNDER FIRE
COME UNINVITED
COME UP FOR MORE
COME UP SMILING
COMING SHORTLY
COMMERCIAL ART
COMMERCIAL LAW
COMMIT A FELONY
COMMIT AN ERROR
COMMIT ONESELF
COMMIT PERJURY

COMMIT SUICIDE
COMMITTEE ROOM
COMMIT TO PAPER
COMMON ASSAULT
COMMON CARRIER
COMMON CONSENT
COMMON FEATURE
COMMON GROUNDS
COMMON HONESTY
COMMON MEASURE
COMMON MISTAKE
COMMON PATTERN
COMMON PURPOSE
COMMON SOLDIER
COMMUNION WINE
COMMUNIST BLOC
COMPANY LAWYER
COMPANY MERGER
COMPANY REPORT
COMPASS NEEDLE
COMPLAINT BOOK
COMPLETE WORKS
COMPLEX SYSTEM
COMPONENT PART
COMPOSING ROOM
COMPRESSED AIR
COMRADE IN ARMS
CONCEDE A POINT
CONCERT ARTIST
CONCRETE MIXER
CONCRETE OFFER
CONDEMNED CELL
CONDENSED FORM
CONDENSED MILK
CONDUCTED TOUR
CONFIDENCE MAN
CONFINED PLACE
CONFINED SPACE
CONFINED TO BED
CONFIRMED CASE
CONFIRMED LIAR
CONGRESS MEDAL
CONGRESS PARTY
CONISTON WATER
CONNECTING ROD
CONNIE FRANCIS
CONSCRIPT ARMY
CONSTANT LOSER
CONSTANT NYMPH
CONSUL GENERAL
CONSUMER GOODS

CONTACT LENSES
CONTENTED MIND
CONTENT TO REST
CONTINUITY MAN
CONTRITE HEART
CONTROL CENTRE
CONTROL PRICES
CONVENT SCHOOL
COOKERY LESSON
COOKING MEDIUM
COOKING SHERRY
COOK ONE'S GOOSE
COOLING BREEZE
COOL ONE'S HEELS
COOL RECEPTION
COPPER COINAGE
CORAL NECKLACE
CORONATION CUP
CORONER'S COURT
CORPORATE BODY
CORPS DE BALLET
CORPUS CHRISTI
CORPUS DELICTI
CORRECT ACCENT
CORRECT ANSWER
CORRECT SPEECH
CORRIDOR TRAIN
COSTLY FAILURE
COSTLY VENTURE
COTSWOLD HILLS
COTSWOLD STONE
COTTAGE CHEESE
COTTON PLANTER
COULD BE BETTER
COULEUR DE ROSE
COUNCIL ESTATE
COUNCIL SCHOOL
COUNTING HOUSE
COUNTRY COUSIN
COUNTRY CUSTOM
COUNTRY SQUIRE
COUNT THE HOURS
COUNTY BOROUGH
COUNTY COUNCIL
COUNTY CRICKET
COURSE BETTING
COURSE OF STUDY
COURT CIRCULAR
COURT DISASTER
COURTESY TITLE
COURT INTRIGUE

COURT OF APPEAL
COURT OF RECORD
COURT REPORTER
COVERED MARKET
COWARD AT HEART
CRABBED OLD AGE
CRACK REGIMENT
CRAFTSMAN'S JOB
CRAVEN COTTAGE
CRAZY PAVEMENT
CREAM OF TARTAR
CREATE A RUMPUS
CREATE A VACUUM
CREATE DISCORD
CREATE TROUBLE
CREDIT ACCOUNT
CREDIT BALANCE
CREDIT COMPANY
CREDIT SQUEEZE
CREEPING JENNY
CRÊME DE MENTHE
CRIBBAGE BOARD
CRICKET ELEVEN
CRICKET GROUND
CRICKET SEASON
CRICKET UMPIRE
CRICK ONE'S NECK
CRIME REPORTER
CRIMINAL CLASS
CRIMINAL COURT
CRIMINAL ERROR
CRIMINAL TRIAL
CRIMINAL WORLD
CRIPPLING BLOW
CRITICAL ANGLE
CRITICALLY ILL
CRITICAL POWER
CRITICAL STAGE
CROCHET NEEDLE
CROIX DE GUERRE
CROQUET MALLET
CROSSED CHEQUE
CROSSED IN LOVE
CROSS EXAMINED
CROSS ONE'S MIND
CROSS ONE'S PALM
CROSS ONE'S PATH
CROSS PURPOSES
CROSS THE FLOOR
CROSS THE OCEAN
CROWDED CANVAS

CROWDED STREET
CROWD OF PEOPLE
CROWD TOGETHER
CROWN COLONIES
CROWNING GLORY
CROWNING MERCY
CROWN OF THORNS
CROWN PRINCESS
CROWN PROPERTY
CRUCIAL MOMENT
CRUCIAL PERIOD
CRUDE ESTIMATE
CRUISING SPEED
CRUSHING REPLY
CRUSH TO PIECES
CRY BLUE MURDER
CRY FOR NOTHING
CRY FOR THE MOON
CRY LIKE A CHILD
CRY OF DERISION
CRYPTIC REMARK
CRYSTAL GAZING
CRYSTAL PALACE
CUBIC CAPACITY
CUBIC CONTENTS
CUCUMBER FRAME
CUDDLE UP CLOSE
CULTIVATED MAN
CUNNING FELLOW
CUP THAT CHEERS
CURIOSITY SHOP
CURIOUS DESIGN
CURIOUS EFFECT
CURIOUS TO KNOW
CURRENT ASSETS
CURRENT BELIEF
CURRENT EVENTS
CURRENT NUMBER
CURRENT REPORT
CURRENT RUMOUR
CURRENT SERIES
CURSE AND SWEAR
CURSORY GLANCE
CURTAIN OF FIRE
CURTAIN RAISER
CUT DOWN TO SIZE
CUT OFF A CORNER
CUT ONE'S LOSSES
CUT ONE'S THROAT
CUT THE PAINTER
CUTTING REMARK

CUTTING RETORT
CUT TO THE QUICK
CYCLE OF EVENTS
CYCLE OF THE SUN
CYRIL FLETCHER

D—13
DADDY AND MUMMY
DADDY LONG-LEGS
DAILY DELIVERY
DAILY PRACTICE
DAILY PURSUITS
DAME CLARA BUTT
DAME COMMANDER
DAMP THE ARDOUR
DANCE THE POLKA
DANCE THE TANGO
DANCE WITH RAGE
DANCING LESSON
DANCING MASTER
DANCING SCHOOL
DANDELION WINE
DANDIE DINMONT
DANGEROUS BEND
DANGEROUS DRUG
DANGEROUS GAME
DANGEROUS LEAK
DANTE'S INFERNO
DARE-DEVIL TYPE
DARING ATTEMPT
DARK CONTINENT
DARKEST AFRICA
DARNING NEEDLE
DASH ONE'S HOPES
DAUGHTER OF EVE
DAUNTLESS HERO
DAWN OF A NEW ERA
DAY OF JUDGMENT
DAY OF MOURNING
DAYS AND NIGHTS
DAYS OF THE WEEK
DAY TO REMEMBER
DAZZLING SMILE
DEAD AND BURIED
DEAD AS THE DODO
DEAD CERTAINTY
DEADLY SILENCE
DEAD MAN'S CHEST
DEAD MEN'S SHOES
DEAD RECKONING

DEARLY BELOVED
DEATH AND GLORY
DEATH-BED SCENE
DEATH BY INCHES
DEATH REGISTER
DEATH SENTENCE
DEATH STRUGGLE
DEBATING POINT
DEBT COLLECTOR
DEBTORS' PRISON
DECIDE AGAINST
DECIDUOUS TREE
DECIMAL SYSTEM
DECLINE OF LIFE
DECORATIVE ART
DEDICATED LIFE
DEED OF RELEASE
DEEP ANTIPATHY
DEEP BREATHING
DEEP GRATITUDE
DEEP IN THOUGHT
DEEPLY TOUCHED
DEEP-SEA DIVING
DEFEND ONESELF
DEFINITE PROOF
DEFRAY THE COST
DEFY AUTHORITY
DEGREE OF SKILL
DEIGN TO NOTICE
DELAYED ACTION
DELIBERATE LIE
DELICATE CHILD
DELICATE POINT
DELICATE SHADE
DELICATE STAGE
DELICATE TOUCH
DELIGHT THE EAR
DELPHIC ORACLE
DELUDE ONESELF
DE LUXE EDITION
DEMAND JUSTICE
DEMAND PAYMENT
DEMERARA SUGAR
DEMON PATIENCE
DEN OF INIQUITY
DENTAL SURGEON
DENTAL SURGERY
DENTIST'S CHAIR
DENTIST'S DRILL
DENY THE CHARGE
DEPARTED GLORY

DEPRESSED AREA
DEPRIVE OF LIFE
DEPTH OF WINTER
DEPUTY PREMIER
DEPUTY SHERIFF
DESERT WARFARE
DESERVE NOTICE
DESERVING CASE
DESERVING POOR
DESIRED EFFECT
DESIRED OBJECT
DESOLATE SCENE
DESPATCH CLERK
DESPATCH RIDER
DESPERATE MOVE
DESPERATE RUSH
DETACHED HOUSE
DETECTIVE WORK
DEUCE OF HEARTS
DEVILISH FUNNY
DEVIL'S KITCHEN
DEVIL'S OWN LUCK
DEVIOUS MANNER
DEVOID OF SENSE
DEVOID OF TRUTH
DEVOUT ADMIRER
DIAGONAL LINES
DIAL THE POLICE
DIAMOND BROOCH
DIAMOND CUTTER
DIAMOND SCULLS
DIATONIC SCALE
DICE WITH DEATH
DIE AT ONE'S POST
DIE FLEDERMAUS
DIE OF EXPOSURE
DIE OF LAUGHING
DIFFERENT KIND
DIFFERENT TUNE
DIFFERENT VIEW
DIFFICULT CASE
DIFFICULT TASK
DIFFUSED LIGHT
DIGESTIVE PILL
DIG FOR VICTORY
DIG IN ONE'S TOES
DIGNIFIED EXIT
DIG ONE'S TOES IN
DING-DONG FIGHT
DINNER AT EIGHT
DINNER SERVICE

DIONNE WARWICK
DIPLOMATIC BAG
DIRECT CONTACT
DIRECT CURRENT
DIRECT DESCENT
DIRECTION POST
DIRE NECESSITY
DISCOUNT HOUSE
DISMAL FAILURE
DISOBEY ORDERS
DISPATCH RIDER
DISPUTED POINT
DISTANT COUSIN
DISTANT FUTURE
DISTANT OBJECT
DISTRICT COURT
DISTRICT NURSE
DISTURBED MIND
DIVIDE AND RULE
DIVIDE BY EIGHT
DIVIDE BY SEVEN
DIVIDE BY THREE
DIVIDED WE FALL
DIVINE JUSTICE
DIVINE SERVICE
DIVISION LOBBY
DIVISION THREE
DIVORCE DECREE
DO AS YOU PLEASE
DOCTOR FAUSTUS
DOCTOR JOHNSON
DOCTOR KILDARE
DOCTOR OF MUSIC
DOCTOR'S ORDERS
DOCTOR THE WINE
DODGE IN AND OUT
DODGE THE ISSUE
DOLL'S HOSPITAL
DOLPHIN SQUARE
DOME OF ST. PAUL'S
DOMESTIC BLISS
DONE FOR EFFECT
DON'T BELIEVE IT
DON'T FENCE ME IN
DON'T MENTION IT
DO ONESELF WELL
DOOR TO SUCCESS
DORMITORY AREA
DORMITORY TOWN
DOROTHY LAMOUR
DOROTHY SAYERS

DOTING HUSBAND
DOTS AND DASHES
DOUBLE BASSOON
DOUBLE DEALING
DOUBLE FIFTEEN
DOUBLE FIGURES
DOUBLE GLOSTER
DOUBLE HARNESS
DOUBLE HELPING
DOUBLE MEANING
DOUBLE OR QUITS
DOUBLE PORTION
DOUBLE SIXTEEN
DOUBLE TROUBLE
DOUBLE WEDDING
DOUBTFUL POINT
DOUBTFUL REPLY
DOWNING STREET
DOWN ON THE FARM
DOWNRIGHT LIAR
DOWN THE COURSE
DOWN THE STAIRS
DOWN THE STRAND
DOWN THE STREET
DOWN THE THAMES
DOWN TO BEDROCK
DOWNWARD CURVE
DOWNWARD SLOPE
DOWNWARD TREND
DRAB EXISTENCE
DRAGOON GUARDS
DRAINING BOARD
DRAIN THE DREGS
DRAMA FESTIVAL
DRAMATIC SCENE
DRASTIC REMEDY
DRAW A PARALLEL
DRAW ATTENTION
DRAW A VEIL OVER
DRAWING MASTER
DRAWN FROM LIFE
DRAW ONE'S SCREW
DRAW ONE'S SWORD
DRAW THE BLINDS
DREADED MOMENT
DREADFUL SIGHT
DREADFUL STORY
DREADFUL VOICE
DREAM SEQUENCE
DREARY OUTLOOK
DRENCHING RAIN

DRESS DESIGNER
DRESSED TO KILL
DRESSING TABLE
DRESS MATERIAL
DRESS OPTIONAL
DRIBS AND DRABS
DRILL SERGEANT
DRINKING GLASS
DRINKING PARTY
DRINKING STRAW
DRINKING WATER
DRINK ONE'S FILL
DRINK TO EXCESS
DRIVE A BARGAIN
DRIVE HEADLONG
DRIVE-IN CINEMA
DRIVEN TO DRINK
DRIVE WITH CARE
DRIVING LESSON
DRIVING MIRROR
DRIVING SCHOOL
DROP OF QUININE
DROP ONE'S GUARD
DROP ONE'S VOICE
DROPPED STITCH
DRUM-HEAD COURT
DRUNKEN SAILOR
DRUNKEN STUPOR
DRYING MACHINE
DUAL OWNERSHIP
DUBIOUS MANNER
DUCHESS OF KENT
DUELLING SWORD
DUE REFLECTION
DUKE ELLINGTON
DUKE OF BEDFORD
DUKE OF NORFOLK
DUKE OF WINDSOR
DULL AND DREARY
DULLING EFFECT
DUMB INSOLENCE
DUODENAL ULCER
DURING REPAIRS
DUSTING POWDER
DWELLING HOUSE
DYED IN THE WOOL
DYNAMIC ENERGY

E—13
EACH-WAY DOUBLE
EACH-WAY TREBLE

EAGER TO PLEASE
EAMONN ANDREWS
EARL OF WARWICK
EARLY DECISION
EARN A DIVIDEND
EARNEST DESIRE
EARTHLY THINGS
EASE THE BURDEN
EASILY AROUSED
EASILY MANAGED
EASILY PLEASED
EASTERN BAZAAR
EASTERN CHURCH
EAST GRINSTEAD
EAT LIKE A HORSE
EAT WITH RELISH
ECLIPSE STAKES
ECONOMIC VALUE
EDGAR ALLAN POE
EDIFYING STORY
EDINBURGH ROCK
EDITION DE LUXE
EDITORIAL DESK
EDITOR IN CHIEF
EDMUND SPENSER
EDWARDIAN DAYS
EFFACE ONESELF
EGGSHELL CHINA
EGYPTIAN MUMMY
EIGHT AND A HALF
EIGHT AND EIGHT
EIGHT AND SEVEN
EIGHT AND THREE
EIGHT-DAY CLOCK
EIGHTEEN CARAT
EIGHTEEN HOLES
EIGHTEEN MILES
EIGHTEEN PENCE
EIGHT FURLONGS
EIGHTH CENTURY
EIGHTH OF APRIL
EIGHTH OF MARCH
EIGHT OF HEARTS
EIGHT OF SPADES
EIGHT OF TRUMPS
EIGHTSOME REEL
EIGHT THOUSAND
EIGHTY PER CENT
EJECTION ORDER
ELABORATE MEAL
ELECTION AGENT

ELECTION FEVER
ELECTION NIGHT
ELECTORAL ROLL
ELECTRIC CABLE
ELECTRIC CHAIR
ELECTRIC CLOCK
ELECTRIC DRILL
ELECTRIC FENCE
ELECTRIC LIGHT
ELECTRIC METER
ELECTRIC MIXER
ELECTRIC MOTOR
ELECTRIC ORGAN
ELECTRIC PIANO
ELECTRIC POWER
ELECTRIC RAZOR
ELECTRIC SHOCK
ELECTRIC STORM
ELECTRIC STOVE
ELECTRIC TORCH
ELECTRIC TRAIN
ELEMENT OF RISK
ELEPHANT'S TUSK
ELEVEN AND FIVE
ELEVEN AND FOUR
ELEVEN AND NINE
ELEVEN GUINEAS
ELEVEN MINUTES
ELEVEN PER CENT
ELEVENTH GREEN
ELEVENTH OF MAY
ELEVENTH PLACE
ELEVENTH ROUND
ELUSIVE PERSON
ELY CULBERTSON
ELYSIAN FIELDS
EMERGENCY CALL
EMERGENCY EXIT
EMERGENCY STOP
EMERGENCY WARD
EMINENTLY FAIR
EMOTIONAL LIFE
EMPIRE BUILDER
EMPTY PROMISES
EMULSION PAINT
END IN DISASTER
ENDLESS EFFORT
END OF THE MONTH
END OF THE STORY
END OF THE WORLD
END UP IN PRISON

ENDURANCE TEST
ENDURE FOR EVER
ENEMY AIRCRAFT
ENFORCE THE LAW
ENGAGED COUPLE
ENGAGED SIGNAL
ENGAGING SMILE
ENGINE FAILURE
ENGINE TROUBLE
ENGLISH GARDEN
ENGLISH LESSON
ENGLISH MASTER
ENGLISH SETTER
ENJOY IMMUNITY
ENJOY IMPUNITY
ENLARGED HEART
ENORMOUS SALES
ENOUGH'S ENOUGH
ENQUIRING MIND
ENTER A PROTEST
ENTER THE LISTS
ENTRANCE MONEY
EQUABLE TEMPER
EQUAL DIVISION
EQUAL QUANTITY
ERECT A BARRIER
ERIC LINKLATER
ERNEST MARPLES
ERRAND OF MERCY
ESCAPE ME NEVER
ESCORT CARRIER
ESPRIT DE CORPS
ESSENTIAL PART
ESTIMATED COST
ESTIMATED TIME
ETON AND HARROW
EUCALYPTUS OIL
EUSTON STATION
EVADE THE ISSUE
EVASION OF DUTY
EVASIVE ACTION
EVASIVE ANSWER
EVENING PRAYER
EVENING STROLL
EVEN THINGS OUT
EVERGREEN TREE
EVERY FEW HOURS
EVERY FEW YEARS
EVERY OTHER DAY
EVERY SATURDAY
EVERY THURSDAY

EVIL INFLUENCE
EXACT LIKENESS
EXALTED PERSON
EXCELLENT SHOT
EXCESS BAGGAGE
EXCESSIVE ZEAL
EXCESS LUGGAGE
EXCESS PROFITS
EXCHANGE BLOWS
EXCHANGE CARDS
EXCHANGE IDEAS
EXCHANGE SHOTS
EXCHANGE VALUE
EXCHANGE VIEWS
EXCHANGE WORDS
EXCHEQUER BOND
EXCISE OFFICER
EXCITING MATCH
EXCITING SCENE
EXCLUSIVE CLUB
EXCURSION RATE
EXCUSE-ME DANCE
EXCUSE ONESELF
EXECUTIVE BODY
EXEMPLI GRATIA
EXERCISE A PULL
EXERCISE POWER
EXERT PRESSURE
EXORBITANT FEE
EXPECTANT HEIR
EXPECTED THING
EXPECT TOO MUCH
EXPENSIVE ITEM
EXPENSIVE LINE
EXPERT OPINION
EXPERT TUITION
EXPERT WITNESS
EXPLOSION SHOT
EXPOSED TO VIEW
EXPRESS DESIRE
EXPRESS LETTER
EXPRESS REGRET
EXTENSIVE VIEW
EXTERIOR ANGLE
EXTINCT ANIMAL
EXTRACT A TOOTH
EXTRACT OF BEEF
EXTREME HATRED
EXTREMELY NICE
EXTREME OLD AGE
EYEBROW PENCIL

EYELASH CURLER
EYELESS IN GAZA
EYES LIKE A HAWK
EYES LIKE STARS
EYE TO BUSINESS
F—13
FABIAN SOCIETY
FABULOUS BEAST
FABULOUS STORY
FACE DOWNWARDS
FACED WITH RUIN
FACE HEAVY ODDS
FACIAL MASSAGE
FACT OR FICTION
FACTORY HOOTER
FACULTY MEMBER
FACULTY OF ARTS
FAEROE ISLANDS
FAILING HEALTH
FAIL MISERABLY
FAIL TO CONNECT
FAINT WITH FEAR
FAIR AND SQUARE
FAIR APPRAISAL
FAIR CONDITION
FAIRLY CERTAIN
FAIRLY CONTENT
FAIRLY WELL OFF
FAIRLY WRITTEN
FAIR RECEPTION
FAIR TREATMENT
FAIRY PRINCESS
FAKE JEWELLERY
FALL FROM GRACE
FALLING LEAVES
FALLING PRICES
FALLING VALUES
FALL INTO A RAGE
FALL INTO A TRAP
FALL INTO ERROR
FALL INTO PLACE
FALL OF JERICHO
FALL OUT OF LOVE
FALL OVERBOARD
FALL PROSTRATE
FALSE CLAIMANT
FALSE EVIDENCE
FALSE OPTIMISM
FALSE POSITION
FALSE TEACHING
FALSETTO VOICE

FAMILIAR FACES
FAMILIAR SIGHT
FAMILIAR STYLE
FAMILIAR TERMS
FAMILIAR VOICE
FAMILY BUTCHER
FAMILY CONCERN
FAMILY FAILING
FAMILY MATTERS
FAMILY PRAYERS
FAMILY QUARREL
FAMILY REUNION
FAMILY WELFARE
FAR-AWAY PLACES
FAREWELL PARTY
FARM BUILDINGS
FARTHEST POINT
FASCIST REGIME
FASHION PARADE
FATAL ACCIDENT
FATAL CASUALTY
FATAL DECISION
FATHER NEPTUNE
FATHER WILLIAM
FAVOURITE TUNE
FAVOUR ONE SIDE
FEAR OF HEIGHTS
FEAR OF THE DARK
FEAST OF REASON
FEAST ONE'S EYES
FEATHER DUSTER
FEATHER PILLOW
FEATHER STITCH
FEATURE EDITOR
FED AND WATERED
FEDERAL STATES
FED TO THE TEETH
FEEBLE ATTEMPT
FEEBLE GESTURE
FEEDING BOTTLE
FEED THE FLAMES
FEEL EXHAUSTED
FEEL MORTIFIED
FEEL NO EMOTION
FEEL ONE'S PULSE
FEIGN SICKNESS
FELLOW CITIZEN
FELLOW FEELING
FELLOW SOLDIER
FEMALE WARRIOR
FEMININE CHARM

FEMININE LOGIC
FEMININE WILES
FENCING LESSON
FENCING MASTER
FENCING SCHOOL
FERTILE GROUND
FERTILE REGION
FERVENT DESIRE
FESTIVE SEASON
FESTIVE SPIRIT
FETCH AND CARRY
FEVER HOSPITAL
FEVERISH HASTE
FEVERISH STATE
FICTION WRITER
FIDDLERS THREE
FIELD DRESSING
FIELD HOSPITAL
FIELD OF ACTION
FIELD OF BATTLE
FIELD OF HONOUR
FIELD OF VISION
FIFTEEN AND SIX
FIFTEEN AND TEN
FIFTEEN AND TWO
FIFTEEN ROUNDS
FIFTEEN THIRTY
FIFTEENTH HOLE
FIFTH DIVIDEND
FIFTH OF AUGUST
FIFTH SYMPHONY
FIFTY THOUSAND
FIGHTER PATROL
FIGHTING DRUNK
FIGHT PROMOTER
FIGURE OF EIGHT
FIGURE SKATING
FILING CABINET
FILLET OF STEAK
FILL ONE'S GLASS
FILM PROJECTOR
FILTER THROUGH
FINAL DECISION
FINAL DIVIDEND
FINAL ESTIMATE
FINAL JUDGMENT
FINAL MOVEMENT
FINANCIAL NEWS
FINANCIAL PAGE
FINANCIAL RUIN
FINANCIAL YEAR

FIND A FOOTHOLD
FIND A LOOP-HOLE
FIND A SOLUTION
FIND ONE'S LEVEL
FIND ONE'S MATCH
FIND SALVATION
FIND THE NEEDLE
FIND THE REMEDY
FINE CHARACTER
FINE GENTLEMAN
FINER FEELINGS
FINE SELECTION
FINE SITUATION
FINE TOOTH-COMB
FINGER OF SCORN
FINISHING POST
FINISH THE RACE
FINNAN HADDOCK
FINNEGAN'S WAKE
FIRE A QUESTION
FIRE INSURANCE
FIREWORK PARTY
FIRM FAVOURITE
FIRM HANDSHAKE
FIRM PRINCIPLE
FIRM TREATMENT
FIRST-AID CLASS
FIRST BIRTHDAY
FIRST DELIVERY
FIRST DIVIDEND
FIRST DIVISION
FIRST LANGUAGE
FIRST OF AUGUST
FIRST OFFENDER
FIRST OF THE FEW
FIRST QUESTION
FIRST SYMPHONY
FIRST THOUGHTS
FIRST TO ARRIVE
FIRST WORLD WAR
FISHING RIGHTS
FISHING SEASON
FISHING TACKLE
FISHY BUSINESS
FIT FOR NOTHING
FIT FOR THE GODS
FITFUL SLUMBER
FIT LIKE A GLOVE
FIT OF COUGHING
FIT OF LAUGHTER
FIT OF THE BLUES

FIT OF THE SULKS
FITS AND STARTS
FIVE AND A PENNY
FIVE AND ELEVEN
FIVE-O'CLOCK TEA
FIVE-POUND NOTE
FIVE SHILLINGS
FIXED DOMICILE
FIXED INTERVAL
FLANDERS POPPY
FLANK MOVEMENT
FLASHING SMILE
FLASH IN THE PAN
FLASH OF GENIUS
FLAT OF THE HAND
FLEA IN ONE'S EAR
FLEMISH SCHOOL
FLESH AND BLOOD
FLICKER OF HOPE
FLIGHT OF FANCY
FLIGHT OF STEPS
FLITCH OF BACON
FLOAT A COMPANY
FLOATING VOTER
FLOCK TOGETHER
FLOODS OF TEARS
FLORA AND FAUNA
FLORAL PATTERN
FLORAL TRIBUTE
FLOUR AND WATER
FLOWERING TREE
FLOWER OF YOUTH
FLOWERY SPEECH
FLOW LIKE WATER
FLOW OF SPIRITS
FLOW OF TRAFFIC
FLUSHED CHEEKS
FLYING COLOURS
FLYING MACHINE
FLYING OFFICER
FLYING TRAPEZE
FLY THE COUNTRY
FOLD ONE'S HANDS
FOLIES BERGÈRE
FOLLOWING WIND
FOLLOW ROUTINE
FOLLOW THE BAND
FOLLOW THE FLAG
FOLLOW THE HERD
FOLLOW THE HUNT
FOLLOW THE ROAD

FOLLOW THROUGH
FOND OF COMFORT
FOND OF DISPLAY
FOOD AND WARMTH
FOOD FOR FISHES
FOOD OF THE GODS
FOOD POISONING
FOOLISH ACTION
FOOLISH FELLOW
FOOLISH PERSON
FOOLISH VIRGIN
FOOLSCAP PAPER
FOOL'S PARADISE
FOOTBALL FIELD
FOOTBALL MATCH
FOOTBALL PITCH
FOOTBALL POOLS
FOR AND AGAINST
FORBIDDEN GAME
FORBIDDEN TREE
FORCE A PASSAGE
FORCED LANDING
FORCED SAVINGS
FORCE ONE'S HAND
FORCE THE ISSUE
FORCIBLE ENTRY
FOREHAND DRIVE
FOREIGN ACCENT
FOREIGN EDITOR
FOREIGN FIELDS
FOREIGN LEGION
FOREIGN MARKET
FOREIGN OFFICE
FOREIGN ORIGIN
FOREIGN POLICY
FOREIGN SHORES
FOREIGN TONGUE
FOREIGN TRAVEL
FOREST OF ARDEN
FOREST OF MASTS
FORGET ONESELF
FOR GOOD AND ALL
FORK LIGHTNING
FORMAL PROTEST
FORMAL REQUEST
FORM AN OPINION
FOR MERCY'S SAKE
FORMER STUDENT
FORM OF ADDRESS
FORM OF WORSHIP
FOR THE PRESENT

FORTIFIED POST
FORTIFIED TOWN
FORTIFIED WINE
FORTUNE HUNTER
FORTUNES OF WAR
FORTUNE'S WHEEL
FORTUNE TELLER
FORTY-HOUR WEEK
FORTY THOUSAND
FOSTER BROTHER
FOUNDED ON FACT
FOUNDER MEMBER
FOUNT OF HONOUR
FOUNT OF WISDOM
FOUR AND A PENNY
FOUR AND TWENTY
FOUR FARTHINGS
FOUR-POSTER BED
FOUR SHILLINGS
FOUR SYLLABLES
FOURTEEN MILES
FOURTH CENTURY
FOURTH OF APRIL
FOURTH OFFICER
FOURTH OF MARCH
FOWLS OF THE AIR
FRAGRANT SMELL
FRAME A PICTURE
FRANKIE HOWERD
FRANTIC APPEAL
FRATERNITY PIN
FREAK OF NATURE
FREE ADMISSION
FREE AS THE WIND
FREE FROM BLAME
FREE FROM ERROR
FREE FROM FAULT
FREE FROM GUILE
FREE FROM GUILT
FREEHOLD HOUSE
FREE RENDERING
FREE TO CONFESS
FREE-TRADE AREA
FREEZE TO DEATH
FREEZING AGENT
FREEZING POINT
FREIGHT CHARGE
FRENCH ACADEMY
FRENCH CRICKET
FRENCH CUISINE
FRENCH GRAMMAR

FRENCH MUSTARD
FRENCH PERFUME
FRENCH TEACHER
FRENCH WINDOWS
FREQUENCY BAND
FRESH-AIR FIEND
FRESH APPROACH
FRESH AS A DAISY
FRESH EVIDENCE
FRESH OUTBREAK
FRICTION MATCH
FRIDAY EVENING
FRIDAY MORNING
FRIED POTATOES
FRIED TOMATOES
FRIEND AT COURT
FRIEND IN COURT
FRIENDLY MATCH
FRIENDLY TERMS
FRIENDLY TOUCH
FRIEND'S FRIEND
FRIGHTFUL TIME
FRINGE BENEFIT
FRITZ KREISLER
FROM A DISTANCE
FROM ONE'S HEART
FROM THE BOTTOM
FROM THE CRADLE
FROM THE OUTSET
FRONTAL ATTACK
FRONT ENTRANCE
FRONTIER GUARD
FRONT-PAGE NEWS
FRONT POSITION
FROSTY WEATHER
FROSTY WELCOME
FROZEN BALANCE
FROZEN TO DEATH
FRUIT AND CREAM
FRUITLESS TASK
FRUIT MERCHANT
FRYING TONIGHT
FULL ASSURANCE
FULL IN THE FACE
FULL OF COURAGE
FULL OF MEANING
FULL OF PROMISE
FULL OF REGRETS
FULL OF THE NEWS
FULL OWNERSHIP
FULL PROGRAMME

FULL TO THE BRIM
FULL TREATMENT
FULLY EQUIPPED
FULLY LICENSED
FULLY OCCUPIED
FULLY RESTORED
FUMBLE THE BALL
FUME WITH ANGER
FUNERAL SERMON
FUNNY BUSINESS
FUNNY PECULIAR
FUR AND FEATHER
FURIOUS TEMPER
FURNISHED FLAT
FURNISHED ROOM
FURTHER NOTICE
FURTHEST POINT
FUSS AND BOTHER
FUTILE ATTEMPT
FUTILE PURSUIT
FUTURE HUSBAND
FUTURE OUTLOOK
FUTURE PERFECT

G—13
GADARENE SWINE
GAGGLE OF GEESE
GAIETY THEATRE
GAIN ADMISSION
GAIN SUPREMACY
GALE-FORCE WIND
GALLANT MEMBER
GAMES MISTRESS
GAME TO THE LAST
GANG OF THIEVES
GANGWAY PLEASE
GARBLED REPORT
GARDENING CLUB
GARDEN OF WEEDS
GARDEN PRODUCE
GARDEN SYRINGE
GARLIC SAUSAGE
GASP FOR BREATH
GATHER FLOWERS
GAY YOUNG THING
GENERAL CUSTER
GENERAL DEALER
GENERAL EXODUS
GENERAL FRANCO
GENERAL GORDON
GENERAL MARKET

GENERAL PARDON
GENERAL PUBLIC
GENERAL READER
GENERAL STORES
GENERAL STRIKE
GENERAL SURVEY
GENEROUS GIVER
GENEROUS OFFER
GENEROUS SHARE
GENEROUS TERMS
GENIUS WILL OUT
GENTLE AS A LAMB
GENTLE BEARING
GENTLE MANNERS
GENTLE REPROOF
GENUINE REGARD
GEORGE GISSING
GEORGE SANDERS
GEORGIAN HOUSE
GERMAN MEASLES
GERMAN SAUSAGE
GET AT THE FACTS
GET AT THE TRUTH
GET AWAY WITH IT
GET IN ON THE ACT
GET IT STRAIGHT
GET OFF LIGHTLY
GET ONE'S HAND IN
GET ONE'S OWN WAY
GET ON TOGETHER
GET OUT OF SIGHT
GET THE GIGGLES
GET THE MESSAGE
GET THERE FIRST
GETTING ON A BIT
GETTING STONED
GET TO ONE'S FEET
GET TO WINDWARD
GIACONDA SMILE
GIFT OF TONGUES
GIN AND BITTERS
GIN AND ITALIAN
GIPSY'S WARNING
GIRTON COLLEGE
GIUSEPPE VERDI
GIVE A DOG A BONE
GIVE A FIRM DATE
GIVE AN ACCOUNT
GIVE AN EXAMPLE
GIVE AN OPINION
GIVE-AWAY PRICE

GIVE COMMUNION
GIVE IT A CHANCE
GIVEN A NEW LOOK
GIVEN IN CHARGE
GIVE NO QUARTER
GIVE NO TROUBLE
GIVEN THE STRAP
GIVEN THE WORKS
GIVEN TO EXCESS
GIVE ONESELF UP
GIVE ONE THE LIE
GIVE ONE THE PIP
GIVE THE SIGNAL
GIVE UP ALL HOPE
GIVE UP SMOKING
GIVE UP THE IDEA
GIVE UTTERANCE
GLACIAL PERIOD
GLAD OF A CHANCE
GLASS AND CHINA
GLASS MOUNTAIN
GLASS OF SHERRY
GLASS OF WHISKY
GLASS WITH CARE
GLASSY SURFACE
GLEAM OF HUMOUR
GLIMMER OF HOPE
GLOATING SMILE
GLOOMY OUTLOOK
GLOOMY PICTURE
GLORIA SWANSON
GLORIOUS DEVON
GLORIOUS MUSIC
GLORIOUS REIGN
GLORIOUS YEARS
GLOWING CHEEKS
GLOWING EMBERS
GLOWING REPORT
GLOW WITH PRIDE
GNASH THE TEETH
GO AS YOU PLEASE
GODDESS OF LOVE
GOD OF LAUGHTER
GO FOR A JOURNEY
GOING FOR A SONG
GOING STRAIGHT
GO INTO A TRANCE
GO INTO DETAILS
GOLD AND SILVER
GOLDEN HAMSTER
GOLDEN JUBILEE

GOLDEN TRESSES
GOLDEN WEDDING
GOLD MEDALLIST
GO LIKE THE WIND
GONE TO THE DOGS
GOOD ACOUSTICS
GOOD AFTERNOON
GOOD AND PROPER
GOOD AT FIGURES
GOOD BEGINNING
GOOD BEHAVIOUR
GOOD BREAKFAST
GOOD CHARACTER
GOOD CONDITION
GOOD CONDUCTOR
GOOD DIGESTION
GOOD FOR A LAUGH
GOOD GROUNDING
GOOD HOUSEWIFE
GOOD HUSBANDRY
GOOD INFLUENCE
GOOD NEIGHBOUR
GOOD PROSPECTS
GOOD QUEEN BESS
GOOD RECEPTION
GOOD SAMARITAN
GOOD SELECTION
GOOD SPORTSMAN
GOOD TALKING-TO
GOOD THRASHING
GOOD WALLOPING
GOODWOOD RACES
GOODY TWO-SHOES
GO OFF ONE'S HEAD
GO ON THE PARISH
GO THE WHOLE HOG
GO TO THE BOTTOM
GO TO THE CINEMA
GO TO THE CIRCUS
GO TO THE MOVIES
GO TO THE OFFICE
GO TO THE RESCUE
GO UNDERGROUND
GOVERNING BODY
GO WITH THE TIDE
GRADUAL CHANGE
GRAIN OF POWDER
GRAMMAR SCHOOL
GRAND ALLIANCE
GRAND ENTRANCE
GRAND FUNCTION

GRAND JUNCTION
GRAND NATIONAL
GRAND STRATEGY
GRANT A DIVORCE
GRANT A REQUEST
GRANT IMMUNITY
GRAPES OF WRATH
GRAPPLING IRON
GRASP AT A STRAW
GRASP OF DETAIL
GRATEFUL HEART
GRATE ON THE EAR
GRAVE DECISION
GRAVE THOUGHTS
GREASE THE PALM
GREAT DISTANCE
GREATER LONDON
GREAT IN NUMBER
GREAT INTEREST
GREAT KINDNESS
GREATLY MISSED
GREAT MAJORITY
GREAT OCCASION
GREAT PATIENCE
GREAT PLEASURE
GREAT QUANTITY
GREAT SALT LAKE
GREAT STRENGTH
GREAT THOUGHTS
GREAT UNWASHED
GREAT WEST ROAD
GREAT WHITE WAY
GREAT YARMOUTH
GREEK ALPHABET
GREEK LANGUAGE
GREEN FRACTURE
GREEN PASTURES
GREENWICH TIME
GREEN WITH ENVY
GREENWOOD TREE
GREETINGS CARD
GREYHOUND RACE
GRILLED CUTLET
GRIN AND BEAR IT
GRIND INTO DUST
GRIND THE TEETH
GRIND TO POWDER
GRIP LIKE A VICE
GRIPPING STORY
GRIT ONE'S TEETH
GROANING BOARD

GROAN INWARDLY
GROSS RECEIPTS
GROUP ACTIVITY
GROW BEAUTIFUL
GROW DESPERATE
GROW DOWNWARDS
GRUELLING HEAT
GRUELLING PACE
GRUELLING RACE
GRUELLING TIME
GRUYÈRE CHEESE
GUARDED REMARK
GUARDIAN ANGEL
GUARD OF HONOUR
GUARDS' OFFICER
GUERRILLA BAND
GUEST OF HONOUR
GUIDED MISSILE
GUILTY FEELING
GUNNERY SCHOOL
GUNPOWDER PLOT
GUSHING LETTER
GUTTERAL VOICE
GYPSY'S WARNING

H—13
HACKING JACKET
HAILE SELASSIE
HAIL OF BULLETS
HAIR OF THE HEAD
HALE AND HEARTY
HALF A FARTHING
HALF SOVEREIGN
HALF THE BATTLE
HALF THE NUMBER
HALF-TIME SCORE
HALL OF JUSTICE
HALL OF MIRRORS
HALLOWED PLACE
HALTING SPEECH
HALVE THE MATCH
HAMILTON HOUSE
HANDLE ROUGHLY
HAND OF BANANAS
HAND OUT ADVICE
HANDSOME OFFER
HANDSOME STYLE
HANDSOME THING
HANG BY A THREAD
HANGING GARDEN
HANGING MATTER

HANG ONE'S HAT UP	HAVELOCK ELLIS
HANG UP ONE'S HAT	HAVEN OF REFUGE
HANNEN SWAFFER	HAVE NO REGRETS
HANOVER SQUARE	HAVE NO SECRETS
HAPPILY IN LOVE	HAVE NO TROUBLE
HAPPY ACCIDENT	HAVE ONE'S FLING
HAPPY BIRTHDAY	HAVE ONE'S WHACK
HAPPY FAMILIES	HAVE THE ANSWER
HAPPY MARRIAGE	HAVE THE HONOUR
HAPPY MEMORIES	HAVE THE OPTION
HAPPY WANDERER	HAVE THE WIND UP
HARBOUR LIGHTS	HAYLING ISLAND
HARBOUR MASTER	HAYWARDS HEATH
HARD-BOILED EGG	HEADLONG SPEED
HARDEN ONESELF	HEAD OF THE FORM
HARD-LUCK STORY	HEAD OF THE POLL
HARD NECESSITY	HEAD OVER HEELS
HARD OF HEARING	HEADS TOGETHER
HARD TO BELIEVE	HEALING SPIRIT
HARD TO IMAGINE	HEAL THE BREACH
HARD TO SATISFY	HEALTH OFFICER
HARD TO SWALLOW	HEALTH SERVICE
HARDWARE STORE	HEALTH VISITOR
HARE AND HOUNDS	HEALTHY COLOUR
HARMONIC SCALE	HEAPS OF PEOPLE
HARROWING TALE	HEAR BOTH SIDES
HARROWING TIME	HEARD IN CAMERA
HARRY THE HORSE	HEARTH AND HOME
HARSH CONTRAST	HEART OF HEARTS
HARSH DECISION	HEART OF MARBLE
HARSH SENTENCE	HEART'S CONTENT
HARVEST SUNDAY	HEARTY DISLIKE
HARVEST SUPPER	HEARTY WELCOME
HASTEN ONE'S END	HEATED DISPUTE
HASTY DECISION	HEATED QUARREL
HATEFUL OBJECT	HEATH ROBINSON
HATFIELD HOUSE	HEAT TREATMENT
HATTER'S CASTLE	HEAVEN HELP HIM!
HATTIE JACQUES	HEAVENLY CHOIR
HAVE A BAD NIGHT	HEAVENLY TWINS
HAVE A BREATHER	HEAVEN ON EARTH
HAVE A GOOD MIND	HEAVILY LOADED
HAVE A GOOD TALK	HEAVY DOWNPOUR
HAVE A GOOD TIME	HEAVY EXPENSES
HAVE A MANICURE	HEAVY HYDROGEN
HAVE AN ADDRESS	HEAVY INDUSTRY
HAVE A TOOTH OUT	HEAVY MATERIAL
HAVE A WALK-OVER	HEAVY SENTENCE
HAVE DELUSIONS	HEIGHT OF FOLLY
HAVE HALF A MIND	HELD FOR RANSOM
HAVE HYSTERICS	HELL UPON EARTH

HELPFUL ADVICE
HENLEY REGATTA
HENRY FIELDING
HENRY THE FIFTH
HENRY THE FIRST
HENRY THE SIXTH
HENRY THE THIRD
HERALDIC SWORD
HERCULEAN TASK
HERCULE POIROT
HER EXCELLENCY
HEROIC COUPLET
HEW OUT A CAREER
HIDDEN MEANING
HIDDEN RESERVE
HIGH AND MIGHTY
HIGH BIRTH-RATE
HIGH CHARACTER
HIGH CHURCHMAN
HIGH COLOURING
HIGH ENDEAVOUR
HIGHER BRACKET
HIGHEST BIDDER
HIGH EXPLOSIVE
HIGH FREQUENCY
HIGHLAND CHIEF
HIGHLAND DANCE
HIGHLAND DRESS
HIGHLAND FLING
HIGHLAND GAMES
HIGHLY PLEASED
HIGH VALUATION
HIGH-WATER MARK
HIGHWAY PATROL
HIGHWAY ROBBER
HIKING HOLIDAY
HILAIRE BELLOC
HINDU RELIGION
HIRED ASSASSIN
HIS EXCELLENCY
HISTORIC SCENE
HISTORIC TENSE
HISTORY LESSON
HISTORY MASTER
HISTRIONIC ART
HIT THE JACKPOT
HIT THE UPRIGHT
HOBSON'S CHOICE
HOLD AN INQUEST
HOLD AN INQUIRY
HOLD AN OPINION

HOLD IN BONDAGE
HOLD IN RESPECT
HOLD ONE GUILTY
HOLD ONE'S PEACE
HOLD THAT TIGER!
HOLD THE RECORD
HOLD THE RUDDER
HOLD THE SCALES
HOLD THE STAKES
HOLE AND CORNER
HOLE IN THE ROAD
HOLIDAY CHALET
HOLIDAY COURSE
HOLIDAY RESORT
HOLIDAY SEASON
HOLIDAY SPIRIT
HOLLOW FEELING
HOLLOW MOCKERY
HOLLOW VICTORY
HOLLYWOOD BOWL
HOLY COMMUNION
HOLY INNOCENTS
HOLY MATRIMONY
HOME ECONOMICS
HOME FOR THE DAY
HOME INTERESTS
HOME-MADE BREAD
HOME PROGRAMME
HOMERIC BATTLE
HOME SECRETARY
HOME SWEET HOME
HOMEWARD BOUND
HONEST ATTEMPT
HONEST DEALING
HONEYDEW MELON
HONOR BLACKMAN
HONOURABLE MAN
HONOUR AND OBEY
HONOURED GUEST
HONOURS DEGREE
HOOK OF HOLLAND
HOPE AND BELIEF
HOPELESS STATE
HORACE WALPOLE
HORATIO NELSON
HORRIBLE CRIME
HORRIBLE NOISE
HORRIBLE SIGHT
HORSE AND GROOM
HORSE CHESTNUT
HORSESHOE BEND

HOSPITAL NURSE
HOSPITAL TRAIN
HOSTILE ATTACK
HOSTILE CRITIC
HOSTILE MANNER
HOST OF FRIENDS
HOT-HOUSE PLANT
HOT ON THE SCENT
HOT ON THE TRAIL
HOUR AFTER HOUR
HOURLY SERVICE
HOUR OF TRIUMPH
HOURS AND HOURS
HOUSEHOLD GODS
HOUSEHOLD HINT
HOUSEHOLD LOAF
HOUSEHOLD WORD
HOUSE MAGAZINE
HOUSE OF BRICKS
HOUSE OF ORANGE
HOUSE OF PRAYER
HOUSE OF REFUGE
HOUSE ON WHEELS
HOUSE PROPERTY
HOUSING ESTATE
HUB OF INDUSTRY
HUGH GAITSKELL
HUMAN ACTIVITY
HUMAN CREATURE
HUMAN DOCUMENT
HUMANE SOCIETY
HUMAN INTEREST
HUMAN PROGRESS
HUMAN TRIANGLE
HUMAN WEAKNESS
HUMBLE ADMIRER
HUMBLE APOLOGY
HUMBLE OPINION
HUMBLE REQUEST
HUMBLE SERVANT
HUMBLE STATION
HUMPBACK WHALE
HUNDRED AND ONE
HUNDRED POUNDS
HUNGER MARCHER
HUNGRY FORTIES
HUNTING SEASON
HURRICANE LAMP
HURRIED GLANCE
HURRIED SPEECH
HURT ONE'S PRIDE

HYDRAULIC JACK
HYDRAULIC LIFT

I—13
IAN CARMICHAEL
ICE-CREAM WAFER
IDEALLY SUITED
IDENTICAL TWIN
IF YOU DON'T MIND!
ILL MANAGEMENT
IMAGINARY LINE
IMITATION WARE
IMPENDING DOOM
IMPERIAL CROWN
IMPERIAL EAGLE
IMPERIAL GUARD
IMPERIAL TOKAY
IMPLICIT FAITH
IMPORTANT POST
IMPUDENT ROGUE
IN A CLEFT STICK
IN A GENERAL WAY
IN A GOOD TEMPER
IN ALL FAIRNESS
IN ALL RESPECTS
IN ALL WEATHERS
IN AN AMBULANCE
IN AN EMERGENCY
IN AN UNDERTONE
IN A SORRY STATE
IN A STILL VOICE
IN A STRANGE WAY
IN AT THE FINISH
INBORN ABILITY
INCENSE BURNER
IN CIRCULATION
INCLINED PLANE
IN COLD STORAGE
INCOME BRACKET
INCOMES POLICY
INCOME-TAX FORM
IN COMPETITION
IN CONFINEMENT
IN CONSEQUENCE
IN CONVULSIONS
INCREASED WAGE
INCREASE OF PAY
INCUR A PENALTY
IN DEAD EARNEST
INDECENT HASTE
IN DESPERATION

INDIAN CHUTNEY
INDIRECT ROUTE
IN DIRE TROUBLE
INDOOR SERVANT
IN EVERY DETAIL
INFANT BAPTISM
INFANT PRODIGY
INFERIOR GOODS
IN FINE FEATHER
INFINITE SPACE
INFLATED IDEAS
INFLATED PRICE
IN FOR A STRETCH
INFORM AGAINST
INFORMAL DRESS
INFORMAL PARTY
IN FORMER TIMES
IN FULL FEATHER
IN FULL MEASURE
IN FULL RETREAT
IN GREAT DEMAND
INGRID BERGMAN
IN HIGH FEATHER
IN HONOUR BOUND
IN IMAGINATION
INITIAL LETTER
INITIAL OUTLAY
INITIAL STAGES
INITIATION FEE
INK ERADICATOR
INLAND REVENUE
IN LIQUIDATION
IN MORTAL PERIL
INNATE ABILITY
INNER CONFLICT
INNER HEBRIDES
INNOCENT PARTY
IN ONE'S ELEMENT
IN ONE SENTENCE
IN ONE'S OWN NAME
IN PARTNERSHIP
IN PERSPECTIVE
IN POINT OF FACT
IN PREPARATION
IN QUEER STREET
INQUIRING MIND
INQUIRY OFFICE
IN SAFE KEEPING
IN SCANDINAVIA
IN SELF-DEFENCE
INSERT A NOTICE

IN SHORT SUPPLY
INSIDE FORWARD
IN SIGHT OF LAND
IN SO MANY WORDS
IN SOME MEASURE
INSPECTION PIT
INSPIRED GUESS
INSPIRED WORDS
INSTANT COFFEE
INSULAR HABITS
INSURANCE CARD
INSURANCE RISK
INSURED PERSON
IN SWITZERLAND
INTEREST RATES
INTERIM PERIOD
INTERIM REPORT
INTERVAL MUSIC
IN THE ABSTRACT
IN THE AIR FORCE
IN THE AUDIENCE
IN THE BASEMENT
IN THE BUSINESS
IN THE CORRIDOR
IN THE DARKNESS
IN THE DAYLIGHT
IN THE DISTANCE
IN THE DISTRICT
IN THE DOG-HOUSE
IN THE DOLDRUMS
IN THE FOUNTAIN
IN THE GLOAMING
IN THE INTERIOR
IN THE INTERVAL
IN THE LION'S DEN
IN THE MAJORITY
IN THE MEANTIME
IN THE MIND'S EYE
IN THE MINORITY
IN THE NEGATIVE
IN THE ORIGINAL
IN THE PAVILION
IN THE SAME BOAT
IN THE SAME CAMP
IN THE SERVICES
IN THE SINGULAR
IN THE STIRRUPS
IN THE STRAIGHT
IN THE SUNSHINE
IN THE TREASURY
IN THE TRENCHES

IN THE TWILIGHT
IN THE USUAL WAY
IN THE VANGUARD
IN THE VICINITY
IN THE WRONG BOX
INTIMATE REVUE
INTIMATE STYLE
INTIMATE TERMS
IN TIMES OF YORE
INTO THE BREACH
IN TOWN TONIGHT
IN TREPIDATION
IN VARIOUS WAYS
INVERNESS CAPE
INVERTED ORDER
INVERTED PLEAT
IN VINO VERITAS
INVITE TENDERS
INVOLVED STYLE
IRISH BAGPIPES
IRISH LANGUAGE
IRISH REGIMENT
IRREGULAR VERB
ISLE OF SHEPPEY
ISLES OF GREECE
ISOBEL BARNETT
ISOLATION WARD
ISSUE A COMMAND
ISSUE A SUMMONS
ISSUED CAPITAL
ITALIAN LESSON
IT'S NOT CRICKET
IVORY CHESSMAN

J—13
JACK THE RIPPER
JACOBEAN STYLE
JAUNDICED VIEW
JEKYLL AND HYDE
JENNIFER JONES
JET PROPULSION
JEWELLER'S SHOP
JOAN GREENWOOD
JOB'S COMFORTER
JOG ONE'S MEMORY
JOHANN STRAUSS
JOHN CONSTABLE
JOHN MASEFIELD
JOIN THE ANGELS
JOIN THE FORCES
JOINT PARTNERS

JOLLY GOOD CHAP
JONATHAN SWIFT
JORDAN ALMONDS
JOSEPH ADDISON
JOYCE GRENFELL
JUDAS ISCARIOT
JUDGE ADVOCATE
JUDGE JEFFREYS
JUDICIAL COURT
JULIA LOCKWOOD
JULY THE EIGHTH
JULY THE FOURTH
JULY THE SECOND
JUMP AT AN OFFER
JUMPING SEASON
JUMP OVERBOARD
JUMP THE COURSE
JUNE THE EIGHTH
JUNE THE FOURTH
JUNE THE SECOND
JUNGLE WARFARE
JUNIOR COUNSEL
JUNIOR PARTNER
JUNIOR SERVICE
JUST A FEW LINES
JUST AS YOU LIKE
JUST PUBLISHED
JUST-SO STORIES
JUVENILE COURT

K—13
KAISER WILHELM
KEEN AS MUSTARD
KEEP AN ACCOUNT
KEEP GOOD HOURS
KEEP IN CUSTODY
KEEP IN THE DARK
KEEP LATE HOURS
KEEP ONE'S END UP
KEEP ONE'S EYE IN
KEEP ONE'S HAT ON
KEEP ONE'S PLACE
KEEP ON THE BEAM
KEEP OPEN HOUSE
KEEP THE CHANGE
KEEP TO ONESELF
KEEP TO THE LEFT
KEEP UP THE PACE
KEEP YOUR SEATS
KENTUCKY DERBY
KEPT IN RESERVE

KEPT IN THE DARK
KEPT ON THE TROT
KEY TO A MYSTERY
KICK INTO TOUCH
KICK ONE'S HEELS
KICK THE BUCKET
KICK UP A SHINDY
KILL THE RUMOUR
KINDRED SPIRIT
KING OF DENMARK
KING OF ENGLAND
KING'S BIRTHDAY
KING'S CHAMPION
KING'S EVIDENCE
KING'S RHAPSODY
KISS AND CUDDLE
KISS AND MAKE UP
KISSING COUSIN
KISS IN THE RING
KISS THE GROUND
KITCHEN GARDEN
KIT INSPECTION
KNAVE OF HEARTS
KNAVE OF SPADES
KNAVE OF TRUMPS
KNAVISH TRICKS
KNEW IN ADVANCE
KNIT ONE'S BROWS
KNOCK-DOWN BLOW
KNOCK-OUT DROPS
KNOCK SIDEWAYS
KNOCK SPOTS OFF
KNOTTY PROBLEM
KNOW BACKWARDS
KNOWING FELLOW
KNOWING PERSON
KNOW ONE'S PLACE
KNOW WHAT'S WHAT

L—13
LA BELLE FRANCE
LABOUR TROUBLE
LABOUR VICTORY
LABURNUM GROVE
LACE INSERTION
LACK OF CANDOUR
LACK OF CAUTION
LACK OF FEELING
LACK OF HARMONY
LACK OF MEANING
LACK OF RESPECT

LACK OF WARNING
LADIES' GALLERY
LADS AND LASSES
LADY BOUNTIFUL
LADY COMPANION
LADY IN WAITING
LADY OF LEISURE
LADY OF QUALITY
LADY OF SHALOTT
LADY OF THE LAKE
LADY OF THE LAMP
LADY PRINCIPAL
LAKE CONSTANCE
LAKE ULLSWATER
LAMBETH BRIDGE
LAMBETH PALACE
LAMBING SEASON
LANCE PERCIVAL
LANDING GROUND
LAND IN THE SOUP
LAND-LOCKED SEA
LAND OF PROMISE
LAND OF THE FREE
LAND ON THE MOON
LANE OF TRAFFIC
LAPSE OF MEMORY
LAPSUS LINGUAE
LARGE AND SMALL
LARGE AUDIENCE
LARGE MAJORITY
LARGE MINORITY
LARGE PRACTICE
LARGE QUANTITY
LARGE-SCALE MAP
LAST CHRISTMAS
LAST EXTREMITY
LAST HANDSHAKE
LAST OF THE LINE
LAST WEDNESDAY
LATE AFTERNOON
LATE BREAKFAST
LATE FOR DINNER
LATE FOR SCHOOL
LATE-NIGHT NEWS
LATENT ABILITY
LATEST FASHION
LATIN AMERICA
LATIN LANGUAGE
LATTICE WINDOW
LAUGH AT DANGER
LAUGHING HYENA

LAUGHING STOCK
LAUGHING WATER
LAUGH OUTRIGHT
LAUNCHING SITE
LAUNDRY BASKET
LAVENDER WATER
LAWFUL WEDLOCK
LAW OF AVERAGES
LAW OF CONTRACT
LAY BY THE HEELS
LAY DOWN THE LAW
LAY IN THE GRAVE
LEAD A DOG'S LIFE
LEAD BY THE HAND
LEAD BY THE NOSE
LEADING DANCER
LEADING SEAMAN
LEADING STOKER
LEAD ONE A DANCE
LEAD ONE ASTRAY
LEAD POISONING
LEAGUE CRICKET
LEAGUE OF PEACE
LEAMINGTON SPA
LEAN BACKWARDS
LEAP IN THE DARK
LEARNED FRIEND
LEARNER DRIVER
LEARN THE ROPES
LEARN THE TRUTH
LEATHER GLOVES
LEATHER JACKET
LEAVE A FORTUNE
LEAVE A MESSAGE
LEAVE HALF-DONE
LEAVE HOSPITAL
LEAVE IN THE AIR
LEAVE NO CHOICE
LEAVE NO OPTION
LEAVE ONE'S CARD
LEAVE STANDING
LEAVE THE STAGE
LEAVE TO APPEAL
LED TO THE ALTAR
LEFT AT THE POST
LEFT-HAND DRIVE
LEFT-HAND SCREW
LEFT TO ONESELF
LEGAL CURRENCY
LEGAL DOCUMENT
LEGAL EVIDENCE

LEGAL GUARDIAN
LEGAL LANGUAGE
LEGAL POSITION
LEGAL SENTENCE
LEMON MERINGUE
LEMON SQUEEZER
LEOPARD'S SPOTS
LES MISERABLES
LESTER PIGGOTT
LET GO THE REINS
LETHAL CHAMBER
LET IN DAYLIGHT
LET OUT A SECRET
LETTER PERFECT
LETTERS OF FIRE
LETTERS OF GOLD
LETTERS PATENT
LET THINGS SLIP
LEVEL CROSSING
LIABLE TO ERROR
LIBERAL LEADER
LIBERAL MINDED
LIBERAL POLICY
LIBRARY TICKET
LICENCE HOLDER
LICENCE TO KILL
LICENSED TRADE
LICENSING LAWS
LICK INTO SHAPE
LICK ONE'S CHOPS
LIE ON ONE'S BACK
LIFE ASSURANCE
LIFEBOAT DRILL
LIFE HEREAFTER
LIFE INSURANCE
LIFELONG ENEMY
LIFELONG HABIT
LIFE OF LEISURE
LIFETIME'S WORK
LIFT ATTENDANT
LIGHT AND SHADE
LIGHT AS A FAIRY
LIGHT COMEDIAN
LIGHT FINGERED
LIGHT INDUSTRY
LIGHT INFANTRY
LIGHTNING MOVE
LIGHT OF MY EYES!
LIGHT OF MY LIFE!
LIGHT OF NATURE
LIGHT SENTENCE

LIGHT THE STOVE
LIGHT TRAINING
LIKE A BAD PENNY
LIKE CLOCKWORK
LIKE GRIM DEATH
LIKE LIGHTNING
LIKE MEETS LIKE
LIKE ONE O'CLOCK
LIMITED AMOUNT
LIMITED APPEAL
LIMITED CHOICE
LIMITED NUMBER
LIMITED PERIOD
LIMITED SEASON
LIMITED SUPPLY
LIMP HANDSHAKE
LINEAR MEASURE
LINE OF ADVANCE
LINE OF CONDUCT
LINE OF COUNTRY
LINE OF DEFENCE
LINE OF RETREAT
LINE OF THOUGHT
LINGERING LOOK
LINGERING NOTE
LIQUEUR BRANDY
LIQUEUR WHISKY
LIQUID MEASURE
LIQUID SHAMPOO
LISTENING POST
LIST OF RUNNERS
LITERARY AGENT
LITERARY STYLE
LITERARY THEFT
LITERARY WORKS
LITERARY WORLD
LITTLE AND GOOD
LITTLE BOY BLUE
LITTLE BUT GOOD
LITTLE COMFORT
LITTLE SIR ECHO
LITTLE THEATRE
LITTLE TO SPARE
LITTLE TROUBLE
LIVE BROADCAST
LIVE CARTRIDGE
LIVE FOR THE DAY
LIVE IN COMFORT
LIVE IN HARMONY
LIVE IN HISTORY
LIVE IN POVERTY

LIVE IN SQUALOR
LIVE IN THE PAST
LIVE LIKE A LORD
LIVEN THINGS UP
LIVE ON NOTHING
LIVE PROGRAMME
LIVER AND BACON
LIVE RECORDING
LIVERY COMPANY
LIVERY SERVANT
LIVID WITH RAGE
LIVING THEATRE
LOAD OF RUBBISH
LOAD OF TROUBLE
LOCAL CURRENCY
LOCAL LANDMARK
LOCAL PREACHER
LODGE AN APPEAL
LOFTY AMBITION
LOFTY CONTEMPT
LOFTY THOUGHTS
LOGICAL ACTION
LOGICAL RESULT
LOMBARD STREET
LONDON AIRPORT
LONDON GAZETTE
LONDON SPECIAL
LONE-STAR STATE
LONG PARAGRAPH
LONG TIME NO SEE!
LONG WAY BEHIND
LONG WAY TO FALL
LONNIE DONEGAN
LOOK DANGEROUS
LOOK DIFFERENT
LOOK IMPORTANT
LOOK IN THE FACE
LOOK OVER THERE
LOOK SURPRISED
LOOK UP AND DOWN
LOOSE THINKING
LORD AND MASTER
LORD KITCHENER
LORDLY GESTURE
LORD MAYOR'S DAY
LORD PRESIDENT
LORD PRIVY SEAL
LORD PROTECTOR
LORDS TEMPORAL
LOSE COHERENCE
LOSE HANDS DOWN

LOSE ONE'S FAITH
LOSE ONE'S HEART
LOSE ONE'S LOOKS
LOSE ONE'S MONEY
LOSE ONE'S NERVE
LOSE ONE'S PLACE
LOSE ONE'S SHIRT
LOSE ONE'S SIGHT
LOSE ONE'S STAKE
LOSE ONE'S VOICE
LOSE THE BATTLE
LOSE THE RUBBER
LOSE THE THREAD
LOSS OF BALANCE
LOSS OF CONTROL
LOSS OF FORTUNE
LOSS OF FREEDOM
LOST IN THOUGHT
LOST IN TRANSIT
LOTS OF FRIENDS
LOTTERY TICKET
LOUD EXPLOSION
LOUIS QUATORZE
LOVE AND KISSES
LOVE OF COUNTRY
LOVE OF THE GAME
LOVE ONE'S ENEMY
LOVE ON THE DOLE
LOVING GESTURE
LOWER AND LOWER
LOWER ONE'S FLAG
LOWER REGISTER
LOWER THE LIGHT
LOWER THE PRICE
LOWLAND SCOTCH
LOW VISIBILITY
LOYAL DEVOTION
LOYALIST CAUSE
LUCID ARGUMENT
LUCID INTERVAL
LUCK OF THE DRAW
LUCK OF THE GAME
LUCKY SIXPENCE
LUCKY TALISMAN
LUCRATIVE DEAL
LUDGATE CIRCUS
LUKEWARM WATER
LUMINOUS PAINT
LUNATIC ASYLUM
LUNATIC FRINGE
LUNCHEON PARTY

LUNCHEON TABLE
LUXURIOUS FOOD
LUXURY HOLIDAY
LYCEUM THEATRE
LYRICAL POETRY
LYRICAL PRAISE

M—13
MACHINE MINDER
MADAME TUSSAUD
MADE IN ENGLAND
MADE IN GERMANY
MADE IN IRELAND
MAD ENTERPRISE
MADE THE WEIGHT
MADE TO MEASURE
MADISON SQUARE
MAGAZINE RIFLE
MAGAZINE STORY
MAGNETIC FIELD
MAGNETIC NORTH
MAGNETIC POLES
MAGNETIC STORM
MAIDEN CENTURY
MAID OF ALL WORK
MAID OF ORLEANS
MAIDS OF HONOUR
MAIMED FOR LIFE
MAIN CHARACTER
MAJOR DISASTER
MAJOR INCIDENT
MAJOR INTERVAL
MAKE A COME-BACK
MAKE A CONQUEST
MAKE A CROSSING
MAKE A DECISION
MAKE A GOOD WIFE
MAKE ALLOWANCE
MAKE A LONG NOSE
MAKE A MESS OF IT
MAKE AN ATTEMPT
MAKE AN OPENING
MAKE A PROPOSAL
MAKE DO AND MEND
MAKE ECONOMIES
MAKE INQUIRIES
MAKE MINCEMEAT
MAKE MINE MUSIC
MAKE NO DEMANDS
MAKE NO MISTAKE
MAKE OBEISANCE

MAKE ONE'S DEBUT
MAKE ONE'S PEACE
MAKE ONE'S POINT
MAKE OVERTURES
MAKE PROVISION
MAKE REDUNDANT
MAKE SHORT WORK
MAKE THE ASCENT
MAKE THE EFFORT
MAKE THE FUR FLY
MAKE THiNGS HUM
MALADIE DU PAYS
MALTESE FALCON
MANAGING CLERK
MAN AT THE WHEEL
MAN OF BREEDING
MAN OF BUSINESS
MAN OF DECISION
MAN OF EMINENCE
MAN OF FEW WORDS
MAN OF LEARNING
MAN OF PROPERTY
MAN OF THE WORLD
MANSFIELD PARK
MAP OF SCOTLAND
MAP OF THE WORLD
MARCH OF EVENTS
MARCH THE FIFTH
MARCH THE FIRST
MARCH THE NINTH
MARCH THE SIXTH
MARCH THE TENTH
MARCH THE THIRD
MARGARET SMITH
MARGIN OF ERROR
MARGIN OF PROOF
MARGOT FONTEYN
MARILYN MONROE
MARINE COMPASS
MARINE OFFICER
MARITIME TRADE
MARKET DRAYTON
MARK OF RESPECT
MARRIAGE BANNS
MARRIAGE BELLS
MARRIAGE FEAST
MARRIAGE LINES
MARRIAGE RITES
MARRIED COUPLE
MARRY A FORTUNE
MARTELLO TOWER

MARTIAL SPIRIT
MARY MAGDALENE
MASS EXECUTION
MASS FORMATION
MASTER BUILDER
MASTER MARINER
MASTER'S TICKET
MATCH-BOX LABEL
MATCH ONE'S WITS
MATERIAL ISSUE
MATERIAL POINT
MATERIAL SENSE
MATERNITY WARD
MATINÉE JACKET
MATTHEW ARNOLD
MATURE THOUGHT
MAXIMUM AMOUNT
MAXIMUM CHARGE
MAXIMUM GROWTH
MAXIMUM POINTS
MAY.THE SEVENTH
MAY THE TWELFTH
MEALS ON WHEELS
MEANS OF ACCESS
MEANS OF ASCENT
MEANS OF ESCAPE
MEANS OF SAFETY
MEASURED TREAD
MEASURE OF LAND
MEASURE SWORDS
MEASURING TAPE
MEAT AND TWO VEG
MECHANICAL AID
MECHANICAL MAN
MEDAL OF HONOUR
MEDICAL ADVICE
MEDICAL SCHOOL
MEDICINAL BATH
MEDICINE CHEST
MEDICINE GLASS
MEDIUM QUALITY
MEET ONE'S MAKER
MEET ONE'S MATCH
MELTON MOWBRAY
MEMORIAL STONE
MEND A PUNCTURE
MENTAL BALANCE
MENTAL CALIBRE
MENTAL CRUELTY
MENTAL DISEASE
MENTAL FATIGUE

MENTAL HYGIENE
MENTAL ILLNESS
MENTALLY ALERT
MENTALLY BLIND
MENTALLY SOUND
MENTAL PATIENT
MENTAL PICTURE
MENTAL PROCESS
MENTAL RESERVE
MENTAL THERAPY
MENTAL TORMENT
MENTAL TORTURE
MENTAL TROUBLE
MERCANTILE LAW
MERCENARY ARMY
MERCI BEAUCOUP
MERE BAGATELLE
MERE EXISTENCE
MERMAID TAVERN
MERRIE ENGLAND
MERTHYR TYDFIL
MERTON COLLEGE
MESS OF POTTAGE
MESSY BUSINESS
METALLIC SOUND
METAL MERCHANT
METRIC MEASURE
MICHAELMAS DAY
MICK THE MILLER
MIDDLE-AGED MAN
MIDDLE CLASSES
MIDDLE ENGLISH
MIDLAND ACCENT
MIDLAND COUNTY
MIDSUMMER'S DAY
MILD AND BITTER
MILD EXPLETIVE
MILE AFTER MILE
MILES AND MILES
MILITARY CLOAK
MILITARY CROSS
MILITARY DRESS
MILITARY FORCE
MILITARY MARCH
MILITARY MEDAL
MILITARY MUSIC
MILITARY STAFF
MILITARY STORE
MILK CHOCOLATE
MILLING THRONG
MIND OF ONE'S OWN

MINERAL SPRING
MINIMUM AMOUNT
MINIMUM CHARGE
MINISTER OF WAR
MINOR COUNTIES
MINOR INCIDENT
MINOR INTERVAL
MINT CONDITION
MINUS QUANTITY
MIRACLE WORKER
MISCHIEF AFOOT
MISSING PERSON
MISSPENT YOUTH
MISS PINKERTON
MISS THE TARGET
MIXED BLESSING
MIXED FEELINGS
MIXED FOURSOME
MIXED MARRIAGE
MIXED METAPHOR
MOBILE CANTEEN
MOBILE LIBRARY
MOBILE WARFARE
MODELLING CLAY
MODE OF ADDRESS
MODERATE MEANS
MODERATE PRICE
MODERATE SKILL
MODERATE SPEED
MODERN COSTUME
MODERN ENGLISH
MODERN FASHION
MODERN HISTORY
MODERN METHODS
MODERN OUTLOOK
MODERN PAINTER
MODERN SETTING
MODERN SOCIETY
MODERN WARFARE
MODEST DEMANDS
MODEST FORTUNE
MODEST REQUEST
MODUS OPERANDI
MOMENT OF TRUTH
MONASTIC ORDER
MONDAY EVENING
MONDAY MORNING
MONETARY VALUE
MONEY IN THE BAG
MONEY TROUBLES
MONOTONOUS JOB

MONTHLY REPORT
MONTHLY SALARY
MOONLESS NIGHT
MOONLIGHT FLIT
MORAL CONFLICT
MORAL PRESSURE
MORAL STRENGTH
MORAL TRAINING
MORAL WEAKNESS
MORBID CRAVING
MORE THAN A JOKE
MORNING COFFEE
MORNING PRAYER
MORTALITY RATE
MORTAL REMAINS
MOST DESIRABLE
MOST EXCELLENT
MOTH-BALL FLEET
MOTHER COUNTRY
MOTHER HUBBARD
MOTHER OF PEARL
MOTHER SHIPTON
MOTION PICTURE
MOTOR MECHANIC
MOUNTAIN CHAIN
MOUNTAIN RANGE
MOUNTAIN SHEEP
MOUNTAIN SLOPE
MOUNTAIN TRAIL
MOUNTED POLICE
MOUNTED TROOPS
MOUNTING ANGER
MOUNT OF OLIVES
MOUNT PLEASANT
MOVE IN SOCIETY
MOVE MOUNTAINS
MOVING ACCOUNT
MOVING PICTURE
MOWING MACHINE
MUCH REGRETTED
MUDDLE THROUGH
MULTIPLE STORE
MULTIPLY BY SIX
MULTIPLY BY TEN
MULTIPLY BY TWO
MULTUM IN PARVO
MUMMY AND DADDY
MUNICIPAL BANK
MUNICIPAL PARK
MURAL PAINTING
MURDER MYSTERY

MURDER WILL OUT
MUSE OF DANCING
MUSE OF HISTORY
MUSICAL CHAIRS
MUSICAL COMEDY
MUSICAL STRESS
MUSIC FESTIVAL
MUSIC-HALL JOKE
MUSIC-HALL STAR
MUSIC-HALL TURN
MUSIC MISTRESS
MUSTARD PICKLE
MUSTARD YELLOW
MUTUAL BENEFIT
MUTUAL CONSENT
MUTUAL DISLIKE
MUTUAL FRIENDS
MUTUAL RESPECT
MYSTERY OF LIFE
MYSTERY WRITER
MYTHICAL BEING

N—13
NAGGING TONGUE
NAME ONE'S PRICE
NARRATIVE POEM
NARROW OUTLOOK
NARROW PASSAGE
NARROW VICTORY
NASTY BUSINESS
NATIONAL DANCE
NATIONAL DRESS
NATIONAL DRINK
NATIONAL GUARD
NATIONAL PRIDE
NATIONAL SPORT
NATIONAL TRUST
NATIONAL UNITY
NATIVE COSTUME
NATIVE QUARTER
NATURAL BEAUTY
NATURAL CAUSES
NATURAL COLOUR
NATURAL COURSE
NATURAL HAZARD
NATURAL SYSTEM
NATURAL TALENT
NATURAL WEALTH
NATURE RESERVE
NATURE WORSHIP
NAVAL BARRACKS

NAVAL EXPLOITS
NAVAL HOSPITAL
NEAPOLITAN ICE
NEAR NEIGHBOUR
NEAR ONE'S HEART
NEAR THE GROUND
NEAR THE WICKET
NEAT AS A NEW PIN
NECESSARY EVIL
NECK OR NOTHING
NEEDLESS TO SAY
NEGATIVE REPLY
NELLIE WALLACE
NELSON'S COLUMN
NERVE HOSPITAL
NERVES OF STEEL
NERVOUS ENERGY
NERVOUS SYSTEM
NERVOUS TWITCH
NESTING SEASON
NEST OF HORNETS
NETHER REGIONS
NEUTRAL COLOUR
NEUTRAL CORNER
NEUTRAL GROUND
NEVER LOOK BACK
NEVER ON SUNDAY
NEW BOND STREET
NEW EXPERIMENT
NEW FOUNDATION
NEWGATE PRISON
NEW IMPRESSION
NEW REGULATION
NEW RESOLUTION
NEW SOUTH WALES
NEWSPAPER FILE
NEWSPAPER RACK
NEXT BEST THING
NEXT CHRISTMAS
NEXT GENTLEMAN
NEXT ON THE LIST
NEXT TO NOTHING
NEXT WEDNESDAY
NICE AND TENDER
NICKEL COINAGE
NIGHTLY VISITS
NIGHT MUST FALL
NIGHT OF TERROR
NIGHT WATCHMAN
NIMBLE FINGERS
NINE AND A PENNY

NINE AND ELEVEN
NINE SHILLINGS
NINETEEN MILES
NINETY PER CENT
NINTH OF AUGUST
NINTH SYMPHONY
NO ALTERNATIVE
NOBLE AMBITION
NOBODY ON EARTH
NO BONES BROKEN
NO EXPECTATION
NO EXTRA CHARGE
NO GREAT SHAKES
NO HIDING PLACE
NO HOLDS BARRED
NOMINAL CHARGE
NOMINATION DAY
NONSENSE RHYME
NONSENSE VERSE
NON-STOP TALKER
NO OIL PAINTING
NOOK AND CRANNY
NORFOLK BROADS
NORFOLK JACKET
NORMAL SERVICE
NORMAN ENGLISH
NORMAN VAUGHAN
NORTH AMERICAN
NORTH AND SOUTH
NORTH ATLANTIC
NORTH CAROLINA
NORTH-EAST WIND
NOTABLE SPEECH
NOTE OF CENSURE
NOTE OF TRIUMPH
NOTE OF WARNING
NOT GOOD ENOUGH
NOTHING LIKE IT
NOTHING TO COME
NOTHING TO GAIN
NOTHING TO GO ON
NOTHING TO LOSE
NOT IMPOSSIBLE
NOT IN LUCK'S WAY
NOT IN THE LEAST
NOT LONG TO WAIT
NOT MY CUP OF TEA
NOT NEGOTIABLE
NOT ON YOUR LIFE
NUCLEAR ENERGY
NUISANCE VALUE

NUMBER ENGAGED
NUMERICAL LIST
NURSERY GARDEN
NURSERY SCHOOL
NURSERY SLOPES
NURSING SISTER

O—13
OBEY AN IMPULSE
OBJECTIVE CASE
OBJECT OF MIRTH
OBJECT OF PRIDE
OBJECT OF SCORN
OBLIGE A FRIEND
OBSCURE MOTIVE
OBSERVER CORPS
OCCUPY THE MIND
OCEANS OF MONEY
OFF AT A TANGENT
OFFER AN EXCUSE
OFF-HAND MANNER
OFFICE CLEANER
OFFICE MANAGER
OFFICE OF WORKS
OFFICE ROUTINE
OFFICIAL REPLY
OFF ONE'S OWN BAT
OFF ONE'S ROCKER
OFF-SEASON RATE
OFF THE DEEP END
OFF THE FAIRWAY
OFF THE SUBJECT
OF LITTLE WORTH
OIL AND VINEGAR
OLD-AGE PENSION
OLD AS THE HILLS
OLD CAMPAIGNER
OLD-CLOTHES MAN
OLD CROCKS' RACE
OLDER AND WISER
OLDER THAN TIME
OLD FATHER TIME
OLD FOUNDATION
OLD IN THE TOOTH
OLD TRADITIONS
OLD WIVES' TALES
OLYMPIC RECORD
OMNIBUS VOLUME
ON A BROOMSTICK
ON A GRAND SCALE
ON A LARGE SCALE

ON A SHOE-STRING
ON A SMALL SCALE
ON BENDED KNEES
ONCE AND FOR ALL
ONCE UPON A TIME
ONE AND THE SAME
ONE FOR THE ROAD
ONE IN A HUNDRED
ONE IN A MILLION
ONE OF THE CROWD
ONE OR THE OTHER
ONE'S PROSPECTS
ONE'S RELATIVES
ONE-WAY TRAFFIC
ONE WICKET DOWN
ON HER BEAM ENDS
ON ITS LAST LEGS
ONLY EXCEPTION
ON ONE'S OWN FEET
ON PAIN OF DEATH
ON TENTER-HOOKS
ON THE CONTRARY
ON THE DOOR-STEP
ON THE FACE OF IT
ON THE FIRST LAP
ON THE FRONTIER
ON THE HIGH SEAS
ON THE INCREASE
ON THE LEFT SIDE
ON THE LONG SIDE
ON THE NEAR-SIDE
ON THE PAVEMENT
ON THE PLATFORM
ON THE PREMISES
ON THE ROOF-TOPS
ON THE SAFE SIDE
ON THE SCAFFOLD
ON THE SCROUNGE
ON THE SICK LIST
ON THE STRENGTH
ON THE WIRELESS
ON WINGS OF SONG
OPEN A CAMPAIGN
OPEN-AIR MARKET
OPEN AN ACCOUNT
OPEN CONSONANT
OPENED IN ERROR
OPEN HOSTILITY
OPENING GAMBIT
OPENING SPEECH
OPEN ONE'S HEART

OPEN ONE'S MOUTH
OPEN ONE'S PURSE
OPEN REBELLION
OPEN THE DEBATE
OPEN THE DRAWER
OPEN THE WINDOW
OPERATION ROOM
OPERATIVE WORD
OPPOSITE CAMPS
OPPOSITE POLES
OPPOSITE SIDES
OPPOSITE VIEWS
OPTICAL DEVICE
ORANGE BITTERS
ORANGE BLOSSOM
ORANGE FLAVOUR
ORB AND SCEPTRE
ORDEAL BY WATER
ORDER A RETREAT
ORDERLY MANNER
ORDER OF BATTLE
ORDER OF THE DAY
ORDINAL NUMBER
ORDINARY SHARE
ORDINARY STOCK
ORDNANCE CORPS
ORGANIC CHANGE
ORGANIC MATTER
ORGAN OF SPEECH
ORGAN OF VISION
ORIGINAL MODEL
ORKNEY ISLANDS
OSBERT SITWELL
OTHER WAY ROUND
OTTOMAN EMPIRE
OUT AT THE ELBOW
OUTBOARD MOTOR
OUTBREAK OF WAR
OUTDOOR RELIEF
OUTDOOR SPORTS
OUTER DARKNESS
OUTER HEBRIDES
OUT FOR THRILLS
OUT-HEROD HEROD
OUT LIKE A LIGHT
OUT OF BUSINESS
OUT-OF-DATE IDEA
OUT OF HARM'S WAY
OUT OF INTEREST
OUT OF KINDNESS
OUT OF MISCHIEF

OUT OF MOURNING
OUT OF ONE'S HEAD
OUT OF ONE'S MIND
OUT OF PATIENCE
OUT OF POSITION
OUT OF PRACTICE
OUT OF SYMPATHY
OUT OF TRAINING
OUT ON ONE'S FEET
OUTSIDE CHANCE
OUTSIDE THE LAW
OVER-ALL LENGTH
OVERHEAD CABLE
OVERHEAD WIRES
OVERLAND ROUTE
OVERLAND TRAIN
OVERNIGHT CASE
OVERSEAS TRADE
OVER THE BORDER
OVER THE STICKS
OVER THE WICKET
OVER TWENTY-ONE
OWNER OCCUPIER
OXFORD COLLEGE
OXFORD ENGLISH

P—13
PACE UP AND DOWN
PACIFIC ISLAND
PACKET OF SEEDS
PACK OF THIEVES
PAGAN FESTIVAL
PAGAN LOVE SONG
PAID BY THE HOUR
PAIN IN THE NECK
PAINT A PICTURE
PAINT ONE'S FACE
PAIR OF BELLOWS
PAIR OF GARTERS
PAIR OF GLASSES
PAIR OF KIPPERS
PAIR OF PINCERS
PAIR OF PYJAMAS
PAIR OF SANDALS
PALACE THEATRE
PALAIS DE DANSE
PALE AS A CORPSE
PALE IMITATION
PALE WITH ANGER
PAMELA FRANKAU
PANDA CROSSING

PANELLED WALLS
PANEL OF JUDGES
PANG OF REMORSE
PANGS OF HUNGER
PANIC MEASURES
PANTOMIME DAME
PAPER-BACK BOOK
PAPER CLIPPING
PAPER CURRENCY
PAPER SHORTAGE
PAPER THE WALLS
PARACHUTE JUMP
PARAFFIN STOVE
PARALLEL LINES
PAR EXCELLENCE
PARIS AND HELEN
PARIS CREATION
PARIS FASHIONS
PARISH COUNCIL
PARK ATTENDANT
PARKINSON'S LAW
PAR OF EXCHANGE
PARROT FASHION
PART AND PARCEL
PARTIAL CHANGE
PARTIAL EXCUSE
PARTLY COVERED
PART OF HISTORY
PART OF THE PLAN
PART OF THE TIME
PARTY OFFICIAL
PARTY POLITICS
PASSAGE OF ARMS
PASSAGE OF TIME
PASS AND REPASS
PASS AN OPINION
PASSENGER LIST
PASSENGER SHIP
PASSING GLANCE
PASSING REMARK
PASSION FLOWER
PASSION SUNDAY
PASS THE BUTTER
PASS THE PEPPER
PASS UNNOTICED
PAST BEHAVIOUR
PAST ENDURANCE
PAST ONE'S PRIME
PATENT LEATHER
PATENT PENDING
PATENT SWINDLE

PATHETIC SIGHT
PATIENCE OF JOB
PATRIOTIC SONG
PAUL McCARTNEY
PAVED WITH GOLD
PAWN IN THE GAME
PAX BRITANNICA
PAY BY THE PIECE
PAY LIP-SERVICE
PAYMENT IN KIND
PAYMENT IN LIEU
PAY THE PENALTY
PEACE AND QUIET
PEACE OFFERING
PEAK OF SUCCESS
PEAL OF THUNDER
PEARL NECKLACE
PEBBLE GLASSES
PECULIAR SMELL
PECUNIARY LOSS
PEGGY ASHCROFT
PENALTY CLAUSE
PENCIL DRAWING
PENDULUM CLOCK
PENINSULAR WAR
PENNY DREADFUL
PENNY FARTHING
PENSION SCHEME
PEOPLE AT LARGE
PEPPER AND SALT
PERCUSSION CAP
PERFECT CIRCLE
PERFECT FOURTH
PERFECT FRIGHT
PERFECT NUMBER
PERFECT RHYTHM
PERFECT SCREAM
PERFECT SQUARE
PERFECT TIMING
PERFECT WICKET
PERFORM A STUNT
PERIOD COSTUME
PERISHING COLD
PERKIN WARBECK
PERMANENT HOME
PERMANENT PASS
PERMANENT POST
PERMANENT WAVE
PERSIAN CARPET
PERSIAN GARDEN
PERSIAN MARKET

PERSONAL ABUSE
PERSONAL CHARM
PERSONAL CLAIM
PERSONAL GUEST
PERSONAL PRIDE
PERSONAL STYLE
PERSONAL TOUCH
PETER CAVANAGH
PETER THE GREAT
PETIT DÉJEUNER
PETROL LIGHTER
PETROL STATION
PETTICOAT LANE
PETTY OFFICIAL
PETTY SESSIONS
PEWTER TANKARD
PHANTOM FIGURE
PHYSICAL FORCE
PHYSICAL JERKS
PHYSICALLY FIT
PHYSICAL POWER
PHYSICAL WRECK
PHYSICS MASTER
PIANO CONCERTO
PIANO EXERCISE
PICK AND CHOOSE
PICK AND SHOVEL
PICKLED WALNUT
PICK OF THE POPS
PICK ONE'S WORDS
PICK THE WINNER
PICK UP A LIVING
PICTS AND SCOTS
PICTURE PALACE
PIDGIN ENGLISH
PIECE OF ADVICE
PIECE OF STRING
PIECES OF EIGHT
PIECE TOGETHER
PIG AND WHISTLE
PIGEON FANCIER
PILE OF RUBBISH
PILOT'S LICENCE
PILTDOWN SKULL
PING-PONG TABLE
PINK ELEPHANTS
PINKY AND PERKY
PIN-STRIPE SUIT
PIONEER SPIRIT
PIOUS THOUGHTS
PIPE OF TOBACCO

PISTACHIO NUTS
PISTOLS FOR TWO
PITCH DARKNESS
PITCHED BATTLE
PITCH ONE'S TENT
PITH AND MARROW
PLACE END TO END
PLACE IN THE SUN
PLACE OF HONOUR
PLACE OF REFUGE
PLACE ON RECORD
PLAIN ENVELOPE
PLAIN FEATURES
PLAIN LANGUAGE
PLAIN QUESTION
PLAIN SPEAKING
PLAUSIBLE TALE
PLAY A LONE HAND
PLAY FOR SAFETY
PLAY HARD TO GET
PLAYING TRICKS
PLAY ONE'S CARDS
PLAY THE DESPOT
PLAY THE FIDDLE
PLAY THE GUITAR
PLAY THE MARKET
PLAY THE MARTYR
PLAY THE TYRANT
PLAY THE VIOLIN
PLAY THE WANTON
PLAY UPON WORDS
PLEAD FOR MERCY
PLEAD INNOCENT
PLEAD THE CAUSE
PLEA OF ABSENCE
PLEASED TO COME
PLEASE ONESELF
PLEDGE ONESELF
PLENTIFUL FARE
PLENTY OF MONEY
PLENTY TO SPARE
PLOUGH A FURROW
PLOUGHED FIELD
PLOUGH THE LAND
PLUCKED PIGEON
PLUMB NONSENSE
PLYMOUTH SOUND
PNEUMATIC TYRE
POCKET BOROUGH
POCKET EDITION
POETICAL WORKS

POETIC JUSTICE
POETIC LICENCE
POETRY READING
POINTED REMARK
POINTED SAYING
POINT FOR POINT
POINT IN COMMON
POINT IN FAVOUR
POINT OF HONOUR
POINT OF THE JAW
POISONED ARROW
POISON THE MIND
POLAR EXPLORER
POLICEMAN'S LOT
POLICE MESSAGE
POLICE OFFICER
POLICE STATION
POLICE WHISTLE
POLISHED ACTOR
POLISHED STYLE
POLITE FICTION
POLITE FORMULA
POLITE REFUSAL
POLITE SOCIETY
POLITE WELCOME
POLITICAL BLOC
POLITICAL NEWS
POLITICAL UNIT
POLITICAL VIEW
POMERANIAN DOG
PONTIUS PILATE
PONTOON BRIDGE
POOL RESOURCES
POOR BUT HONEST
POOR CONDITION
POOR IN QUALITY
POORLY DRESSED
POOR PERFORMER
POOR PROSPECTS
POOR RECEPTION
POPPING CREASE
POPULAR BALLAD
POPULAR CHOICE
POPULAR DECREE
POPULAR DEMAND
POPULAR ESTEEM
POPULAR FIGURE
POPULAR PEOPLE
POPULAR PRICES
POPULAR RESORT
POPULAR SINGER

POPULATED AREA
PORTABLE RADIO
PORT ELIZABETH
PORTLAND STONE
POSE A QUESTION
POSITIVE PROOF
POSTAL ADDRESS
POSTAL SERVICE
POSTED MISSING
POSTER COLOURS
POSTE RESTANTE
POSTMAN'S KNOCK
POST-OFFICE RED
POST-WAR CREDIT
POTTED SHRIMPS
POULTRY FARMER
POUND OF APPLES
POUND OF BUTTER
POUND STERLING
POUR OUT THE TEA
POWDER AND SHOT
POWDER COMPACT
POWDER SHAMPOO
POWER AND GLORY
POWERFUL VOICE
POWER OF SPEECH
POWER OF THE LAW
POWER POLITICS
PRACTICAL JOKE
PRACTICAL MIND
PRACTICAL TEST
PRACTICE MATCH
PRACTICE ROUND
PRACTISED HAND
PRACTISED LIAR
PRAIRIE OYSTER
PRAWN COCKTAIL
PRAYER MEETING
PRAYING MANTIS
PRECIOUS METAL
PRECIOUS STONE
PRECIOUS WORDS
PRECISE MOMENT
PRECISION TOOL
PREFER A CHARGE
PREPARE A DRINK
PREPARE FOR WAR
PRESENT EVENTS
PRESENT MOMENT
PRESS CAMPAIGN
PRESS CUTTINGS

PRESSED FLOWER
PRESSED TONGUE
PRESS EXCHANGE
PRESS FASTENER
PRESSING CLAIM
PRESS ONE'S SUIT
PRESSURE GAUGE
PRESSURE GROUP
PRETTY PICTURE
PREY ON THE MIND
PRICE INCREASE
PRIM AND PROPER
PRIMARY COLOUR
PRIMARY SCHOOL
PRIME MINISTER
PRIMEVAL CHAOS
PRIMITIVE FORM
PRINCE CHARLES
PRINCE CONSORT
PRINCE OF PEACE
PRINCE OF WALES
PRINCESS DRESS
PRINCESS ROYAL
PRINCE'S STREET
PRINCE WILLIAM
PRINCIPAL FOOD
PRINCIPAL PART
PRINCIPAL TOWN
PRINTED LETTER
PRINTED MATTER
PRINTER'S DEVIL
PRINTER'S ERROR
PRINTING PRESS
PRINTING WORKS
PRISONER OF WAR
PRISONER'S BASE
PRISON VISITOR
PRIVATE AFFAIR
PRIVATE INCOME
PRIVATE LESSON
PRIVATE LETTER
PRIVATE MATTER
PRIVATE MEMBER
PRIVATE OFFICE
PRIVATE PERSON
PRIVATE REASON
PRIVATE SCHOOL
PRIVATE SOURCE
PRIZE SPECIMEN
PROBABLE ERROR
PROCESSED FOOD

PROCESS OF TIME
PRODUCER GOODS
PROFANE PERSON
PROFIT AND LOSS
PROFIT SHARING
PROFOUND SLEEP
PROFUSE THANKS
PROGRESS CHART
PROLONGED NOTE
PROMENADE DECK
PROMISING IDEA
PROMPT PAYMENT
PROMPT SERVICE
PROOF POSITIVE
PROPER CHARLEY
PROPERTY OWNER
PROPOSE A TOAST
PROSAIC PERSON
PROSPEROUS MAN
PROVE ONE'S CASE
PROVIDE AN HEIR
PROVING GROUND
PUBLIC ADDRESS
PUBLIC AFFAIRS
PUBLIC ANALYST
PUBLIC COMMENT
PUBLIC COMPANY
PUBLIC GALLERY
PUBLIC HANGING
PUBLIC HIGHWAY
PUBLIC HOLIDAY
PUBLIC INQUIRY
PUBLIC LECTURE
PUBLIC LIBRARY
PUBLIC MEETING
PUBLIC OPINION
PUBLIC OUTRAGE
PUBLIC PROTEST
PUBLIC RECORDS
PUBLIC SCANDAL
PUBLIC SERVANT
PUBLIC SERVICE
PUBLIC SPEAKER
PUBLIC TRUSTEE
PUBLIC UTILITY
PUBLIC VEHICLE
PUBLIC WARNING
PUBLIC WORSHIP
PUBLISHED WORK
PULITZER PRIZE
PULL A LONG FACE

PULL INTO SHAPE
PULL NO PUNCHES
PUNCTURED TYRE
PUNISHING WORK
PUPPET THEATRE
PURCHASE MONEY
PURCHASE PRICE
PURE AND SIMPLE
PURE IN THOUGHT
PURE MISCHANCE
PURE PREJUDICE
PURPLE AND GOLD
PURPLE EMPEROR
PURPLE HEATHER
PURPLE PASSAGE
PURSE ONE'S LIPS
PURSER'S OFFICE
PUSH-BUTTON WAR
PUSHED FOR TIME
PUSH TO THE WALL
PUT IN FOR A RISE
PUT IN JEOPARDY
PUT IN THE KITTY
PUT IN THE SHADE
PUT IN THE WRONG
PUT ONE'S BACK UP
PUT ONESELF OUT
PUT ONE'S FEET UP
PUT ONE'S HAIR UP
PUT ON PRESSURE
PUT ON THE BRAKE
PUT ON THE LIGHT
PUT ON THE SCREW
PUT ON THE STAGE
PUT OUT A FEELER
PUT OUT FEELERS
PUT OUT OF COURT
PUT OUT OF JOINT
PUT OUT OF SIGHT
PUT OUT TO GRASS
PUT PEN TO PAPER
PUT THE BRAKE ON
PUT THE CAP ON IT
PUT THE LID ON IT
PUT TO THE BLUSH
PUT TO THE PROOF
PUT TO THE SWORD
PUT UP THE BANNS
PUT UP THE MONEY
PUT UP THE PRICE

Q—13
QUADRUPLE TIME
QUALITY STREET
QUANTUM THEORY
QUARTER BOTTLE
QUARTERLY RENT
QUARTER TO FIVE
QUARTER TO FOUR
QUARTER TO NINE
QUEEN CAROLINE
QUEEN OF HEARTS
QUEEN OF SPADES
QUEEN OF THE MAY
QUEEN OF TRUMPS
QUEEN'S COLLEGE
QUEEN'S COUNSEL
QUEEN'S ENGLISH
QUEEN'S HIGHWAY
QUEEN'S PROCTOR
QUEEN VICTORIA
QUEER CUSTOMER
QUEER GOINGS-ON
QUEER THE PITCH
QUICK AS A FLASH
QUICK MOVEMENT
QUICK RECOVERY
QUICK-SET HEDGE
QUICK THINKING
QUICK TURNOVER
QUIET AS A MOUSE
QUITE POSITIVE
QUITE POSSIBLE
QUITE THE THING
QUIZ PROGRAMME
QUOTATION MARK

R—13
RACE PREJUDICE
RACING CIRCUIT
RACING TIPSTER
RACING TRAINER
RACK ONE'S BRAIN
RADIANT ENERGY
RADIATION BELT
RADICAL CHANGE
RADICAL REFORM
RADIO OPERATOR
RADIO RECEIVER
RAG-AND-BONE MAN
RAGING TEMPEST
RAGING TORRENT

RAID THE LARDER
RAILWAY BRIDGE
RAILWAY ENGINE
RAILWAY SHARES
RAILWAY SIDING
RAILWAY SIGNAL
RAILWAY SYSTEM
RAILWAY TICKET
RAILWAY TUNNEL
RAISE A BARRIER
RAISE CHICKENS
RAISED GLASSES
RAISE ONE'S EYES
RAISE ONE'S HAND
RAISE THE ALARM
RAISE THE FUNDS
RAISE THE MONEY
RAISE THE PRICE
RAISE THE SIEGE
RAISE THE TEMPO
RAISE THE VOICE
RAKE'S PROGRESS.
RAKE UP THE PAST
RALLYING POINT
RALPH WIGHTMAN
RANGE OF CHOICE
RANGE OF COLOUR
RAPE OF THE LOCK
RAPID PROGRESS
RAPID TURNOVER
RAPT ATTENTION
RASH BEHAVIOUR
RASHER OF BACON
RASH STATEMENT
RASPBERRY CANE
RATEABLE VALUE
RATE COLLECTOR
RATE FOR THE JOB
RATES AND TAXES
RATIONAL DRESS
RAVAGES OF TIME
RAVENOUS BEAST
RAVING LUNATIC
RAYMOND BAXTER
RAYMOND MASSEY
RAY OF SUNSHINE
REACH A NEW HIGH
REACH A VERDICT
REACH MATURITY
REACH ONE'S GOAL
REACH THE LIMIT

REACT IN FAVOUR
READER'S DIGEST
READ FOR THE BAR
READING MATTER
READING PUBLIC
READ THE FUTURE
READ THE LESSON
READY-MADE SUIT
READY RECKONER
READY RESPONSE
READY, STEADY, GO!
READY TO ATTACK
READY TO POUNCE
READY TO SPRING
REAL-LIFE STORY
REALMS OF FANCY
REAP THE FRUITS
REAP THE REWARD
RECEIPT IN FULL
RECEIVE NOTICE
RECEIVE ORDERS
RECENT ARRIVAL
RECEPTION DESK
RECEPTION ROOM
RECEPTIVE MIND
RECKLESS SPEED
RECKLESS YOUTH
RECLAIMED LAND
RECORD ATTEMPT
RECORD BREAKER
RECORD COUNTER
RECORDED MUSIC
RECORD ROUND-UP
RECORD SESSION
RED AS A LOBSTER
RED-CROSS NURSE
REDEEM A PLEDGE
RED RAG TO A BULL
RED RIDING HOOD
RED SEALING-WAX
RED SKY AT NIGHT
REDUCE TO ASHES
REDUCE TO SCALE
REDUCE TO TEARS
REDUCING AGENT
REDUCING PILLS
REFERENCE BOOK
REFER TO DRAWER
REFINED ACCENT
REFINED PALATE
REFUSE A CHANCE

REFUSE AN OFFER
REFUSE PAYMENT
REFUSE THE BAIT
REFUSE TO SPEAK
REGAIN COMMAND
REGAIN CONTROL
REGAIN THE LEAD
REGENCY STRIPE
REGRET THE LOSS
REGULAR FORCES
REGULAR HABITS
REGULAR INCOME
REGULAR PEOPLE
REGULAR READER
REGULAR SALARY
REGULAR STAGES
REGULAR TROOPS
REGULAR VISITS
REHEARSAL ROOM
REIGNING QUEEN
REIGN OF TERROR
REJECTION SLIP
RELATIVE MERIT
RELATIVE PROOF
RELATIVE VALUE
RELATIVE WORTH
RELAXED THROAT
RELEASE ON BAIL
REMAIN AT PEACE
REMAIN HOPEFUL
REMAIN NEUTRAL
REMAIN PASSIVE
REMAIN THE SAME
REMAIN UPRIGHT
REMAIN VISIBLE
REMARKABLE BOY
REMARKABLE MAN
REMITTANCE MAN
REMOTE CONTROL
REMOTE VILLAGE
REMOVE ONE'S HAT
RENEWED ENERGY
RENEW ONE'S VOWS
RENT COLLECTOR
RENT IN ADVANCE
REPEAT A SIGNAL
REPEAT ONESELF
REPEL AN ATTACK
REPETITIVE JOB
REPLY BY RETURN
REPORT FOR DUTY

REPUBLICAN ERA
RESERVED TABLE
RESERVE ELEVEN
RESIGN ONESELF
RESPECT THE LAW
RESTAURANT CAR
RESTIVE NATURE
RESTLESS NIGHT
REST ONE'S BONES
RESTORE TO LIFE
REST SATISFIED
RETAIL TRADING
RETAINING WALL
RETARDED BRAIN
RETARDED CHILD
RETIRED PEOPLE
RETROUSSÉ NOSE
RETURN A FAVOUR
RETURN A PROFIT
RETURN JOURNEY
RETURN SERVICE
RETURN TO EARTH
REVENUE CUTTER
REVERSE MOTION
REVOLT AGAINST
REVOLVING DOOR
REWARD OFFERED
REYNARD THE FOX
RHODES SCHOLAR
RHONDDA VALLEY
RHYMED COUPLET
RIBSTON PIPPIN
RICEYMAN STEPS
RICHARD BURTON
RICHARD HEARNE
RICHARD TAUBER
RICHARD WAGNER
RICH AS CROESUS
RICHMOND GREEN
RICH OFFERINGS
RIDE A TRICYCLE
RIDE POST-HASTE
RIDE ROUGH-SHOD
RIDE THE WINNER
RIFLE PRACTICE
RIFT IN THE LUTE
RIGHT AND WRONG
RIGHT APPROACH
RIGHT AT THE END
RIGHT DECISION
RIGHT-DOWN LIAR

RIGHTFUL OWNER
RIGHTFUL SHARE
RIGHT-HAND BEND
RIGHT-HAND SIDE
RIGHT-HAND TURN
RIGHT OF ACCESS
RIGHT OF APPEAL
RIGHT OF CHOICE
RIGHT OF SEARCH
RIGHT ON THE DOT
RIGHT OPPOSITE
RIGHT REVEREND
RIGHT SHOULDER
RIGHT TO THE END
RIGHT TO THE TOP
RIGHT UP TO DATE
RING OUT THE OLD
RIOT OF EMOTION
RIOTOUS LIVING
RISE IN DISGUST
RISE OF THE TIDE
RISE TO THE BAIT
RISING SPIRITS
RISK ONE'S MONEY
RISKY BUSINESS
RITUAL KILLING
RIVAL BUSINESS
RIVER CROSSING
RIVERSIDE WALK
ROAD DIVERSION
ROAD TO SUCCESS
ROAD TRANSPORT
ROAST CHESTNUT
ROAST POTATOES
ROBBINS REPORT
ROBERT BRIDGES
ROBERT MITCHUM
ROBERTSON HARE
ROBERT SOUTHEY
ROCKET WARFARE
ROCK THE CRADLE
ROGUE ELEPHANT
ROGUES' GALLERY
ROLL AND BUTTER
ROLLED INTO ONE
ROLLER COASTER
ROLLING IN CASH
ROLLING STONES
ROLL IN THE DUST
ROMAN ALPHABET
ROMAN CATHOLIC

ROMAN NUMERALS
ROMANTIC NOVEL
ROMANTIC SCENE
ROMANTIC STORY
ROMNEY MARSHES
RONALD CHESNEY
ROOM TO BREATHE
ROOM WITH A VIEW
ROOT AND BRANCH
ROOTED DISLIKE
ROOT OF ALL EVIL
ROOT VEGETABLE
ROPE AND PULLEY
ROTATE THE CROP
ROTTEN BOROUGH
ROUGH AND READY
ROUGH CROSSING
ROUGH CUSTOMER
ROUGH ESTIMATE
ROUGH EXTERIOR
ROUGH HANDLING
ROUGH QUARTERS
ROULETTE TABLE
ROULETTE WHEEL
ROUND-ABOUT WAY
ROUND AND ABOUT
ROUND AND ROUND
ROUNDLY ABUSED
ROUND OF DRINKS
ROUND OF GAIETY
ROUND OF VISITS
ROUND THE BLOCK
ROUND THE CLOCK
ROUND THE EARTH
ROUND THE HOUSE
ROUND THE TABLE
ROUND THE WAIST
ROUND THE WORLD
ROUSING CHEERS
ROUSING CHORUS
ROUSING SERMON
ROUTINE DUTIES
ROUTINE MATTER
ROYAL AERO CLUB
ROYAL AIR FORCE
ROYAL EXCHANGE
ROYAL FUNCTION
ROYAL HIGHNESS
ROYAL·HOSPITAL
ROYAL MARRIAGE
ROYAL OCCASION

ROYAL STANDARD
RUBBER PLANTER
RUB OF THE GREEN
RUDE AWAKENING
RUGBY FOOTBALL
RUGGED COUNTRY
RUINED FOR LIFE
RUINOUS CHARGE
RULE BRITANNIA
RULE OF THE ROAD
RULING CLASSES
RULING PASSION
RUN FOR SHELTER
RUN IN THE BLOOD
RUN INTO DANGER
RUN LIKE BLAZES
RUNNING BATTLE
RUNNING BUFFET
RUNNING STREAM
RUN OF THE GREEN
RUN OF THE HOUSE
RUN ON SMOOTHLY
RUN ON THE ROCKS
RUN OUT OF FUNDS
RUN OUT OF MONEY
RUN OUT OF STEAM
RUN OUT OF WORDS
RUN THINGS FINE
RURAL DISTRICT
RURAL INDUSTRY
RUSHING STREAM
RUSH INTO PRINT
RUSSELL SQUARE
RUSSIAN BALLET
RUSSIAN LESSON

S—13
SACRED EDIFICE
SAFE ANCHORAGE
SAFETY CURTAIN
SAFETY HARNESS
SAFETY MEASURE
SAFFRON WALDEN
SAGE AND ONIONS
SAILING MASTER
SAILING ORDERS
SAILING VESSEL
SAINT AUGUSTUS
SAINT LAWRENCE
SAINT NICHOLAS
SALAD DRESSING

SALARIED CLASS
SALE BY AUCTION
SALMON FISHING
SALT AND PEPPER
SALT-WATER FISH
SALUTE THE FLAG
SALVATION ARMY
SAMUEL JOHNSON
SAND IN THE EYES
SARATOGA TRUNK
SATELLITE TOWN
SATURDAY NIGHT
SAUCE PIQUANTE
SAUTÉ POTATOES
SAVE ONE'S BACON
SAY BO TO A GOOSE
SCALDING TEARS
SCARCITY VALUE
SCARED TO DEATH
SCARLET RUNNER
SCARLETT O'HARA
SCENE OF STRIFE
SCENIC RAILWAY
SCHOOL EDITION
SCHOOL HOLIDAY
SCHOOL OF MUSIC
SCHOOL PREFECT
SCHOOL UNIFORM
SCIENCE MASTER
SCIENCE MUSEUM
SCIENTIFIC AGE
SCILLY ISLANDS
SCORCHED EARTH
SCORE A CENTURY
SCORE A SUCCESS
SCORING STROKE
SCOTCH AND SODA
SCOTCH TERRIER
SCRAMBLED EGGS
SCRAPE A LIVING
SCRAPE THROUGH
SCRAP MERCHANT
SCRATCH PLAYER
SCRATCH RUNNER
SCREEN VERSION
SCRIBBLED NOTE
SCRIPT WRITING
SEALED VERDICT
SEAL OF SECRECY
SEA OF TROUBLES
SEA OPERATIONS

SEARCHING LOOK
SEARCH WARRANT
SEASIDE RESORT
SEAT OF JUSTICE
SECOND ATTEMPT
SECOND CENTURY
SECOND CHAMBER
SECOND CHAPTER
SECOND EDITION
SECOND FEATURE
SECOND-HAND CAR
SECOND HELPING
SECOND HUSBAND
SECOND INNINGS
SECOND OF APRIL
SECOND OFFENCE
SECOND OFFICER
SECOND OF MARCH
SECOND OPINION
SECOND QUARTER
SECOND READING
SECOND SERVICE
SECOND TURNING
SECRET ARRIVAL
SECRETARY BIRD
SECRET FORMULA
SECRET INQUIRY
SECRET MEETING
SECRET PASSAGE
SECRET PROCESS
SECRET SERVICE
SECRET SESSION
SECRET SOCIETY
SECRET THOUGHT
SECRET WRITING
SECURE FOOTING
SECURITY CHECK
SEDENTARY LIFE
SEE FOR ONESELF
SEE HOW THEY RUN
SEEK ADVENTURE
SEEK A SOLUTION
SEEMLY CONDUCT
SEE ONE THROUGH
SEE THINGS DONE
SEIZE THE CROWN
SELECT CIRCLES
SELECT COMPANY
SELECTION LIST
SELFISH MOTIVE
SELL AT A PROFIT

SELL BY AUCTION
SELLER'S MARKET
SEMPER FIDELIS
SEND A POSTCARD
SEND A REMINDER
SEND A TELEGRAM
SEND TO JERICHO
SENIOR PARTNER
SENIOR SERVICE
SENSELESS TALK
SENSE OF DANGER
SENSE OF HUMOUR
SENSE OF INJURY
SENSE OF RELIEF
SENSE OF TIMING
SENSE OF VALUES
SENSIBLE CHILD
SENSIBLE WOMAN
SEPARATE COVER
SEPARATE ROOMS
SEPTEMBER MORN
SEPTEMBER TIDE
SERGEANT MAJOR
SERGEANTS' MESS
SERIOUS CHARGE
SERIOUS DAMAGE
SERIOUS DANGER
SERIOUS DEFEAT
SERIOUS INJURY
SERIOUS MATTER
SERIOUS PERSON
SERPENT'S TOOTH
SERVE A PURPOSE
SERVE AS A MODEL
SERVE ONE RIGHT
SERVE ONE'S TIME
SERVE ONE'S TURN
SERVE THE DEVIL
SERVE UP DINNER
SERVICE CHARGE
SERVIETTE RING
SET A NEW RECORD
SET AT DEFIANCE
SET AT VARIANCE
SET ONE'S SIGHTS
SET THE FASHION
SETTING LOTION
SETTLEMENT DAY
SEVEN AND A HALF
SEVEN AND EIGHT
SEVEN AND SEVEN

SEVEN AND THREE	SHELTERED SPOT
SEVEN DIAMONDS	SHEPHERD'S BUSH
SEVEN FURLONGS	SHEPTON MALLET
SEVEN NO-TRUMPS	SHERATON TABLE
SEVEN OF HEARTS	SHERIFF'S POSSE
SEVEN OF SPADES	SHERRY COBBLER
SEVEN OF TRUMPS	SHETLAND ISLES
SEVEN SLEEPERS	SHIFTING SANDS
SEVENTH HEAVEN	SHIFTING SCENE
SEVENTH LETTER	SHIFT THE BLAME
SEVENTH OF JULY	SHIFT THE SCENE
SEVENTH OF JUNE	SHILLING PIECE
SEVEN THOUSAND	SHILLING STAMP
SEVENTH STOREY	SHINING ARMOUR
SEVENTH VOLUME	SHINING KNIGHT
SEVEN-YEAR ITCH	SHIP IN A BOTTLE
SEVEN YEARS OLD	SHIP OF THE LINE
SEVEN YEARS' WAR	SHIPPING AGENT
SEVERE ILLNESS	SHIPPING CLERK
SEVERE WEATHER	SHIPPING ORDER
SEVILLE ORANGE	SHIP'S CHANDLER
SEWING MACHINE	SHIP'S CORPORAL
SHADES OF NIGHT	SHIP'S REGISTER
SHADOW CABINET	SHIRLEY BASSEY
SHADOW FACTORY	SHIRLEY TEMPLE
SHADOW OF DEATH	SHOCK ABSORBER
SHADOW OF DOUBT	SHOCKING STATE
SHADY BUSINESS	SHOOTING BRAKE
SHAKE ONE'S FIST	SHOOTING MATCH
SHAKE ONE'S HEAD	SHOOTING PAINS
SHAKE WITH COLD	SHOOTING PARTY
SHAKE WITH FEAR	SHOOTING RANGE
SHALLOW STREAM	SHOOT STRAIGHT
SHALLOW VESSEL	SHOOT THE WORKS
SHAME THE DEVIL	SHOP ASSISTANT
SHAMPOO AND SET	SHOP DETECTIVE
SHAPELY FIGURE	SHOPPING SPREE
SHARE EXPENSES	SHORT AND SWEET
SHARE THE BLAME	SHORT DISTANCE
SHARP AS A KNIFE	SHORTEST NIGHT
SHARP AS A RAZOR	SHORTEST ROUTE
SHARP FEATURES	SHORTEST WOMAN
SHARP PRACTICE	SHORTHAND NOTE
SHARP'S THE WORD	SHORTLY BEFORE
SHAVING SALOON	SHORT OF BREATH
SHED LIGHT UPON	SHORT OF CHANGE
SHEEP AND GOATS	SHORT OF SPEECH
SHEEPSKIN COAT	SHORT OF TALENT
SHEER NONSENSE	SHORT SENTENCE
SHELTERED LIFE	SHORT SYNOPSIS
SHELTERED SIDE	SHORT-TERM LOAN

SHORT TROUSERS
SHORT VACATION
SHOT IN THE BACK
SHOT IN THE DARK
SHOULDER STRAP
SHOUTING MATCH
SHOW ANIMOSITY
SHOW DEFERENCE
SHOW FORESIGHT
SHOW NO REMORSE
SHOW NO RESPECT
SHOW ONE'S CARDS
SHOW ONE'S PACES
SHOW ONE'S TEETH
SHOW RESTRAINT
SHREDDED WHEAT
SHROPSHIRE LAD
SHROVE TUESDAY
SHUT YOUR MOUTH
SICK OF WAITING
SICK UNTO DEATH
SIDE ELEVATION
SIEGFRIED LINE
SIGNAL EXAMPLE
SIGNAL FAILURE
SIGNAL SUCCESS
SIGNAL VICTORY
SIGNATURE TUNE
SIGNED ARTICLE
SIGNIFY ASSENT
SIGNIFY LITTLE
SIGN OF EMOTION
SIGN OF FATIGUE
SIGN OF SUCCESS
SIGN THE PLEDGE
SILENT CONSENT
SILENT PARTNER
SILENT PROTEST
SILENT SERVICE
SILK STOCKINGS
SILLY QUESTION
SILLY SYMPHONY
SILVER AND GOLD
SILVER COINAGE
SILVER JUBILEE
SILVER PLATTER
SILVER TANKARD
SILVER THIMBLE
SILVER THREADS
SILVER WEDDING
SIMON STYLITES

SIMPLE PROBLEM
SIMPLE REQUEST
SIMPLY FURIOUS
SIMPLY KILLING
SINCERELY FELT
SINGING MASTER
SING IN HARMONY
SINGLE ARTICLE
SINGLE PURPOSE
SINGLE THOUGHT
SINGLETON LEAD
SING LIKE A BIRD
SING LIKE A LARK
SING ME TO SLEEP
SING-SONG VOICE
SING THE CHORUS
SIR DON BRADMAN
SIRLOIN OF BEEF
SIR ROBERT PEEL
SISTER OF MERCY
SISTINE CHAPEL
SIT-DOWN STRIKE
SIT IN CONCLAVE
SIT IN JUDGMENT
SIT IN THE FRONT
SIT ON ONE'S TAIL
SIT ON THE FENCE
SIT ON THE FLOOR
SITTING PRETTY
SITTING TARGET
SITTING TENANT
SIX O'CLOCK NEWS
SIX OF DIAMONDS
SIXPENNY PIECE
SIXPENNY STAMP
SIXTEEN AND SIX
SIXTEEN AND TEN
SIXTEEN AND TWO
SIXTEEN OUNCES
SIXTEENTH HOLE
SIXTH OF AUGUST
SIXTH SYMPHONY
SIXTY THOUSAND
SKELETON STAFF
SKETCHES BY BOZ
SKI-ING HOLIDAY
SKILLED LABOUR
SKILLED WORKER
SKINFUL OF WINE
SKIN TREATMENT
SKITTLES MATCH

SLANDER ACTION	SMUGGLED GOODS
SLANGING MATCH	SNOOKER PLAYER
SLAP AND TICKLE	SNOWBALL FIGHT
SLAP IN THE FACE	SOAP-BOX ORATOR
SLAP ON THE BACK	SOARING PRICES
SLEEPING PILLS	SOBER AS A JUDGE
SLEEP LIKE A LOG	SOBER ESTIMATE
SLEEP LIKE A TOP	SOBER THOUGHTS
SLEIGHT OF HAND	SOCIAL CIRCLES
SLENDER CHANCE	SOCIAL CLIMBER
SLENDER INCOME	SOCIAL DEMANDS
SLICK OPERATOR	SOCIAL EVENING
SLIGHTLY BUILT	SOCIAL MACHINE
SLIGHT QUARREL	SOCIAL OUTCAST
SLING ONE'S HOOK	SOCIAL PROBLEM
SLIP INTO PLACE	SOCIAL RE-UNION
SLIPPERY SLOPE	SOCIAL SCIENCE
SLIP THE COLLAR	SOCIAL SERVICE
SLOPING GROUND	SOCIAL SUCCESS
SLOW AND STEADY	SOCIAL WELFARE
SLUM CLEARANCE	SOCIETY COLUMN
SMACK ONE'S LIPS	SOCIETY GOSSIP
SMALL ADDITION	SOCIETY PEOPLE
SMALL BUSINESS	SOFTEN THE BLOW
SMALL CAPITALS	SOFT IN THE HEAD
SMALL DIVIDEND	SOIL ONE'S HANDS
SMALL INVESTOR	SOLDIERS THREE
SMALL MAJORITY	SOLDIER'S TUNIC
SMALL OFFERING	SOLEMN PROMISE
SMALL POTATOES	SOLEMN SILENCE
SMALL PRACTICE	SOLEMN WARNING
SMALL QUANTITY	SOLE OWNERSHIP
SMART TROUSERS	SOLICIT ORDERS
SMASH TO PIECES	SOLITAIRE RING
SMEAR CAMPAIGN	SOLOMON GRUNDY
SMELLING SALTS	SOLVE A PROBLEM
SMOKED HADDOCK	SOME OF THE TIME
SMOKED SAUSAGE	SOME OTHER TIME
SMOKE-FREE ZONE	SOMERSET HOUSE
SMOKELESS FUEL	SOMETHING DONE
SMOKELESS ZONE	SOMETHING ELSE
SMOKER'S THROAT	SOMETHING LIKE
SMOKING JACKET	SOMETHING NICE
SMOOTH AS GLASS	SOMETHING OVER
SMOOTHING IRON	SOMETHING TO DO
SMOOTH JOURNEY	SOME TIME LATER
SMOOTH MANNERS	SOMEWHERE ELSE
SMOOTH PASSAGE	SONG OF SOLOMON
SMOOTH SAILING	SONG OF THE FLEA
SMOOTH SURFACE	SONG OF TRIUMPH
SMOOTH TEXTURE	SON OF A SEA COOK

SONS AND LOVERS
SOONER OR LATER
SOONEST MENDED
SOON FORGOTTEN
SOOTHING MUSIC
SOOTHING SYRUP
SOOTHING TOUCH
SOOTHING WORDS
SOP TO CERBERUS
SORRY BUSINESS
SORTING OFFICE
SORT THINGS OUT
SOUND A FANFARE
SOUND ARGUMENT
SOUND CURRENCY
SOUND DETECTOR
SOUND DOCTRINE
SOUNDING BOARD
SOUNDING BRASS
SOUND JUDGMENT
SOUND MATERIAL
SOUND ONE'S HORN
SOUND THE ALARM
SOURCE OF LIGHT
SOURCE OF POWER
SOURCE OF PRIDE
SOUR SUBSTANCE
SOUSED HERRING
SOUTH CAROLINA
SOUTH CHINA SEA
SOUTH-EAST WIND
SOUTHERN CROSS
SOUTHERN STATE
SOUTH OF FRANCE
SPANISH ARMADA
SPANISH GUITAR
SPANISH LESSON
SPANISH ONIONS
SPARE A THOUGHT
SPARE NO EFFORT
SPARKLING WINE
SPARK OF GENIUS
SPARTAN REGIME
SPEAK AT LENGTH
SPEAKER'S NOTES
SPEAKING TERMS
SPEAKING VOICE
SPEAK ONE'S MIND
SPEAK THE TRUTH
SPECIAL BRANCH
SPECIAL FAVOUR

SPECIAL FRIEND
SPECIAL NUMBER
SPECIAL PRAYER
SPECIAL SCHOOL
SPECIFIED DOSE
SPECK OF COLOUR
SPECTACLE CASE
SPEECH THERAPY
SPEED MERCHANT
SPEEDWAY TRACK
SPELL DISASTER
SPEND A FORTUNE
SPENDING MONEY
SPENDING POWER
SPENDING SPREE
SPIKE MILLIGAN
SPIKE ONE'S GUNS
SPILL THE BEANS
SPINNING JENNY
SPINNING WHEEL
SPIN OF THE COIN
SPIRITED REPLY
SPIRIT OF YOUTH
SPIRITUAL LIFE
SPIRITUAL PEER
SPIRITUAL SELF
SPIRITUAL SONG
SPIRIT WRITING
SPIT AND POLISH
SPITEFUL WOMAN
SPITTING IMAGE
SPLINTER GROUP
SPLINTER PARTY
SPLIT DECISION
SPLITTING HEAD
SPOILT DARLING
SPOIL THE CHILD
SPORTING EVENT
SPORTING GOODS
SPORTING OFFER
SPORTING PRESS
SPORTING PRINT
SPORTING RIFLE
SPORTING WORLD
SPORTS EDITION
SPORTS STADIUM
SPOT OF TROUBLE
SPOT THE WINNER
SPRAINED ANKLE
SPREAD A RUMOUR
SPREAD THE LOAD

SPREAD THE NEWS
SPRING BALANCE
SPRING BLOSSOM
SPRING CHICKEN
SPRING FLOWERS
SPRING MADNESS
SPRING MEETING
SPRING THE TRAP
SPRING THROUGH
SPY OUT THE LAND
SQUARE BASHING
SQUARE MEASURE
SQUASH RACKETS
SQUIRE OF DAMES
STAB IN THE BACK
STACK THE CARDS
STAFF ENTRANCE
STAFF OF OFFICE
STAFF PROBLEMS
STAFF SERGEANT
STAGGERING SUM
STAKE ONE'S LIFE
STAMP OF GENIUS
STAND AND FIGHT
STAND AND STARE
STANDARD BREAD
STANDARD GAUGE
STANDARD MODEL
STANDARD PRICE
STANDARD USAGE
STANDING ORDER
STANDING START
STAND IN THE WAY
STAND ON TIPTOE
STAND OPPOSITE
STAND OUT A MILE
STAND PREPARED
STAND TOGETHER
STAND TO REASON
STANLEY LUPINO
STAR AND GARTER
STARBOARD BEAM
STARBOARD SIDE
STAR OF THE SHOW
STAR PERFORMER
START A QUARREL
STARTING POINT
STARTING PRICE
START LAUGHING
STARTLING NEWS
STAR TREATMENT

START THINKING
START TO FINISH
START TOGETHER
STATE BOUNDARY
STATE CARRIAGE
STATE CRIMINAL
STATE FUNCTION
STATE MONOPOLY
STATE OCCASION
STATE OF FRENZY
STATE OF NATURE
STATE OF REASON
STATE OF UNREST
STATE ONE'S CASE
STATE PRISONER
STATE RELIGION
STATIC WARFARE
STATION IN LIFE
STATION MASTER
STATUTORY MILE
STAY OVERNIGHT
STAY THE COURSE
STAY UNMARRIED
ST. BARTHOLOMEW
ST. BERNARD PASS
ST. CRISPIN'S DAY
STEADY ADVANCE
STEADY AS A ROCK
STEAK AND CHIPS
STEAL A MARCH ON
STEEL INDUSTRY
STEERAGE CLASS
STEERING WHEEL
STEP OUT OF LINE
STEPTOE AND SON
STERLING WORTH
STERN MEASURES
STEVE DONOGHUE
STICKING POINT
STICK IN THE MUD
STICK LIKE GLUE
STICK OF CELERY
STICK OUT A MILE
STICK TOGETHER
STICKY PROBLEM
STIFF AND STARK
STIFF AS A BOARD
STIFF AS A POKER
STIFF SENTENCE
STIFF UPPER-LIP
STILETTO HEELS

STILL LEMONADE
STILTON CHEESE
STIR IN THE WIND
STIRRING MUSIC
STIRRING TIMES
STIR THE EMBERS
STIR UP TROUBLE
STOCK EXCHANGE
STOCK QUESTION
STOLEN ARTICLE
STOLE THE TARTS
STOMACH POWDER
STONE THE CROWS!
STOP AT NOTHING
STOP BREATHING
STOPPING PLACE
STOPPING TRAIN
STOP-PRESS NEWS
STORMY MEETING
STORMY PASSAGE
STORMY SESSION
STORMY WEATHER
ST. PATRICK'S DAY
ST. PAUL'S SCHOOL
STRAIGHT ACTOR
STRAIGHT AHEAD
STRAIGHT ANGLE
STRAIGHT DRAMA
STRAIGHT DRIVE
STRAIGHTEN OUT
STRAIGHT FIGHT
STRAIGHT FLUSH
STRAIGHT RIGHT
STRAIN AT A GNAT
STRAIN ONESELF
STRAIN THE EYES
STRAIT OF DOVER
STRANGE DEVICE
STRANGE GROUND
STRANGE MANNER
STRAPPING GIRL
STRAWBERRY BED
STRAWBERRY ICE
STRAWBERRY JAM
STRAWBERRY TEA
STRAW MATTRESS
STRAY CUSTOMER
STRAY FROM HOME
STREAK OF LIGHT
STREAMING COLD
STREAM OF BLOOD

STREAM OF LIGHT
STREAM OF TEARS
STREAM OF WATER
STREET BETTING
STREET CLOTHES
STRESS THE FACT
STRETCH A POINT
STRETCHER CASE
STRETCH OF LAND
STRETCH OF ROAD
STRICT INQUIRY
STRICTLY LEGAL
STRICT PARENTS
STRIKE IT LUCKY
STRIKE THE BALL
STRIKE THE FLAG
STRIKE THE HOUR
STRIKE UP A TUNE
STRIKING CLOCK
STRIKING FORCE
STRING OF BEADS
STRING OF NAMES
STRING OF OATHS
STRING QUARTET
STRIP LIGHTING
STRONG AS A LION
STRONG BACKING
STRONG CURRENT
STRONG DEFENCE
STRONG DISLIKE
STRONG EMOTION
STRONG FEELING
STRONG GROUNDS
STRONG PROTEST
STRONG REQUEST
STRONG STOMACH
STRONG SUPPORT
STRONG SWIMMER
STRUGGLE ALONG
ST. SWITHIN'S DAY
STUDENT PRINCE
STUDY ALL SIDES
STUDY MEDICINE
STUDY THE FACTS
STUDY THE PLANS
STUDY THE STARS
STUFFED MARROW
STUFFED OLIVES
STUFFED TURKEY
STUMBLE ACROSS
STUNG TO ACTION

STUNTED GROWTH
ST. VITUS'S DANCE
SUBJECT MATTER
SUBJECT TO DUTY
SUB-MACHINE GUN
SUBMARINE BASE
SUBMARINE CREW
SUBMIT A REPORT
SUBURBAN HOUSE
SUBURBAN VILLA
SUCCESSFUL MAN
SUCCESS SYMBOL
SUCK ONE'S THUMB
SUDDEN DISLIKE
SUDDEN IMPULSE
SUDDEN THOUGHT
SUE FOR DAMAGES
SUE FOR DIVORCE
SUFFER A STROKE
SUFFER DAMAGES
SUFFERING CATS!
SUFFER TORMENT
SUGAR AND SPICE
SUGARED ALMOND
SUGARLESS DIET
SUGAR REFINERY
SUGGESTION BOX
SUICIDAL MANIA
SUITABLE MATCH
SUIT OF CLOTHES
SULPHURIC ACID
SULTAN'S PALACE
SUMMER HOLIDAY
SUMMER MADNESS
SUMMER SESSION
SUMMER VISITOR
SUMMIT MEETING
SUNBURN LOTION
SUNDAY CLOSING
SUNDAY CLOTHES
SUNDAY EVENING
SUNDAY MORNING
SUNDAY SERVICE
SUN-DRIED BRICK
SUNK IN DESPAIR
SUPERIOR BEING
SUPERIOR COURT
SUPERIOR FORCE
SUPREME SOVIET
SURE OF ONESELF
SURE OF SUCCESS

SURFACE RAIDER
SURGEON'S KNIFE
SURGICAL KNIFE
SURPLUS ENERGY
SURPRISE PARTY
SURPRISE VISIT
SURTAX BRACKET
SUSPECT A TRICK
SUSPENDER BELT
SUSTAINED NOTE
SWANEE WHISTLE
SWAP AND CHANGE
SWAY IN THE WIND
SWEATED LABOUR
SWEEPING CLAIM
SWEEPING GAINS
SWEEP THE BOARD
SWEEP THE FLOOR
SWEET CHESTNUT
SWEET LAVENDER
SWEET NOTHINGS
SWEET SURPRISE
SWEET THOUGHTS
SWEET TO THE EAR
SWELLING SAILS
SWELL THE RANKS
SWELTERING SUN
SWIM LIKE A FISH
SWIMMING MATCH
SWING ONE'S ARMS
SWORN EVIDENCE
SYDNEY HARBOUR
SYMPHONIC POEM

T—13
TABLEAU VIVANT
TABLE DELICACY
TABLE MOUNTAIN
TAKE A BACK SEAT
TAKE A BREATHER
TAKE ADVANTAGE
TAKE A FIRM HOLD
TAKE A HIGH TONE
TAKE A LONG TIME
TAKE AN AVERAGE
TAKE A SHORT CUT
TAKE A SNAPSHOT
TAKE BY THE HAND
TAKE DICTATION
TAKE EXCEPTION
TAKE FOR GOSPEL

TAKE GREAT CARE
TAKE IN BAD PART
TAKE IN LODGERS
TAKE IN WASHING
TAKE IT IN TURNS
TAKE IT TO COURT
TAKE IT TO HEART
TAKE LIBERTIES
TAKEN AT RANDOM
TAKEN DOWN A PEG
TAKEN FOR A RIDE
TAKE NO CHANCES
TAKE NO REFUSAL
TAKEN PRISONER
TAKEN UNAWARES
TAKE OFF WEIGHT
TAKE ONE'S FANCY
TAKE ONE'S LEAVE
TAKE ONE'S PLACE
TAKE ONE'S PULSE
TAKE ONE'S STAND
TAKE OUT TRUMPS
TAKE SANCTUARY
TAKE SERIOUSLY
TAKE SHORTHAND
TAKE SOUNDINGS
TAKE THE CREDIT
TAKE THE DAY OFF
TAKE THE MICKEY
TAKE THE PLEDGE
TAKE THE PLUNGE
TAKE THE SALUTE
TAKE THE STRAIN
TAKE THE TILLER
TAKE THE WATERS
TAKE TO ONE'S BED
TAKE TO THE ROAD
TALENT CONTEST
TALENT SPOTTER
TALK FOR EFFECT
TALK GIBBERISH
TALKING PARROT
TALK IN RIDDLES
TALK LIKE A FOOL
TALK OF THE TOWN
TALK OUT OF TURN
TALK PRIVATELY
TALK TO ONESELF
TANGIBLE ASSET
TANKARD OF BEER
TANKARD OF MILD

TAN THE HIDE OFF
TAPE RECORDING
TAP ONE'S CLARET
TAR AND FEATHER
TASTE FOR MUSIC
TAUGHT A LESSON
TAURUS THE BULL
TAWNY COLOURED
TAXABLE INCOME
TAX CONCESSION
TAX ONE'S MEMORY
TEACHING STAFF
TEACH SWIMMING
TEAM OF EXPERTS
TEA PLANTATION
TEAR OFF A STRIP
TEARS OF SORROW
TEAR TO RIBBONS
TEAR UP THE ROAD
TECHNICAL TERM
TELEGRAPH LINE
TELEGRAPH POLE
TELEGRAPH POST
TELEGRAPH WIRE
TELEPHONE BILL
TELEPHONE BOOK
TELEPHONE CALL
TELEPHONE LINE
TELEPHOTO LENS
TELEVISION FAN
TELEVISION SET
TELL A GOOD TALE
TELL A GOOD YARN
TELL AN UNTRUTH
TELL AT A GLANCE
TELLING EFFECT
TELL ME ANOTHER
TELL ONE'S BEADS
TEMPERATE ZONE
TEMPER THE WIND
TEMPLE OF DIANA
TEMPORAL POWER
TEMPORARY HOME
TEMPORARY LEAD
TEMPORARY LOAN
TEMPORARY RANK
TEMPORARY STOP
TEMPTING OFFER
TEMPT THE DEVIL
TENANT FOR LIFE
TEN CIGARETTES

TENDER FEELING
TENDER MERCIES
TENDER PASSION
TEN-DOLLAR BILL
TENEMENT HOUSE
TEN OF DIAMONDS
TENOR CLARINET
TENPENNY STAMP
TENPIN BOWLING
TENTH OF AUGUST
TEPID RESPONSE
TERMINAL POINT
TERRIBLE CHILD
TERRIBLE HAVOC
TERRIBLE TWINS
TERRIFIC STORM
TERRORIST ARMY
TERRORIST BAND
TEST-BAN TREATY
TEST CRICKETER
THANE OF CAWDOR
THANK GOODNESS!
THANKLESS TASK
THE ABDICATION
THEATRE CRITIC
THEATRE SISTER
THEATRE TICKET
THE BARBARIANS
THE BEST OF LUCK
THE BEST PEOPLE
THE BIG BAD WOLF
THE BLUE DANUBE
THE CHALLENGER
THE CHARLESTON
THE COLLECTION
THE COMMON HERD
THE DEEPEST DYE
THE DEUCE TO PAY
THE DEVIL TO PAY
THE DIRECT ROAD
THE DOLL'S HOUSE
THE EISTEDDFOD
THE EMBANKMENT
THE FIRST TRAIN
THE FIRST WATER
THE FOOTLIGHTS
THE GIDDY LIMIT
THE GOLDEN RULE
THE GONDOLIERS
THE GOVERNMENT
THE GUILLOTINE

M.C.D.—13

THE HONOURABLE
THE INS AND OUTS
THE ISRAELITES
THE JOY STRINGS
THE KERRY DANCE
THE LAST SUPPER
THE LAW IS AN ASS
THE LIBERATION
THE LIGHT BLUES
THE MAGIC FLUTE
THE MAIN CHANCE
THE MATTERHORN
THE MERRY WIDOW
THE METROPOLIS
THE MILLENNIUM
THE MOODY BLUES
THE NOES HAVE IT
THE NORTH DOWNS
THE OLD BRIGADE
THE OLD COUNTRY
THE OPPOSITION
THE OTHER WOMAN
THE OTHER WORLD
THE QUAKER GIRL
THE RESISTANCE
THE ROUNDHEADS
THE SAME ANSWER
THE SCOTS GREYS
THE SECOND-RATE
THE SERPENTINE
THE SHALLOW END
THE SIMPLE LIFE
THE SMALL HOURS
THE SNOW MAIDEN
THE SOUTH DOWNS
THE SPOKEN WORD
THE THREE BEARS
THE TIME IS RIPE
THE UNDERWORLD
THE UNEMPLOYED
THE UNEXPECTED
THE UNFORESEEN
THE VANQUISHED
THE VIGILANTES
THE WATER-WAGON
THE WHITE HOUSE
THE WHOLE TRUTH
THE WHOLE WORLD
THE WILDERNESS
THE WILL TO LIVE
THE WINSLOW BOY

THE WIZARD OF OZ
THICK WITH DUST
THIEF OF BAGDAD
THING OF BEAUTY
THINK BETTER OF
THINK LITTLE OF
THINK STRAIGHT
THINK THE WORST
THIRD DIVIDEND
THIRD DIVISION
THIRD ENGINEER
THIRD OF AUGUST
THIRD SYMPHONY
THIRTEEN HOURS
THIRTEEN MILES
THIRTEEN TIMES
THIRTEEN WEEKS
THIRTEEN YEARS
THIRTY FIFTEEN
THIRTY GUINEAS
THIRTY MINUTES
THIRTY-ONE DAYS
THIRTY PER CENT
THIRTY SECONDS
THIS LITTLE PIG
THIS WEDNESDAY
THOMAS À BECKET
THOMAS BEECHAM
THOMAS CARLYLE
THORNY PROBLEM
THORNY SUBJECT
THOROUGH ROGUE
THOSE IN FAVOUR
THOUSAND MILES
THOUSAND YEARS
THREAD A NEEDLE
THREAD ONE'S WAY
THREE AND A HALF
THREE AND EIGHT
THREE AND SEVEN
THREE AND THREE
THREE BAGS FULL
THREE-DAY MATCH
THREE DIAMONDS
THREE FEET TALL
THREE-FOOT RULE
THREE FURLONGS
THREE-LINE WHIP
THREE NO-TRUMPS
THREE OF HEARTS
THREE OF SPADES

THREE OF TRUMPS
THREEPENNY BIT
THREE QUARTERS
THREE SEVENTHS
THREE THOUSAND
THRICE BLESSED
THROES OF AGONY
THROUGH A STRAW
THROW A LIGHT ON
THROW IN THE AIR
THUMB ONE'S NOSE
THUMP THE TABLE
THURSDAY NIGHT
TICHBORNE CASE
TICKET MACHINE
TICKET OF LEAVE
TICKETS PLEASE
TIDAL MOVEMENT
TIDE OF AFFAIRS
TIED UP IN KNOTS
TIE WITH STRING
TILT AT THE RING
TILT THE SCALES
TIME AFTER TIME
TIME AND MOTION
TIME FOR DINNER
TIME FOR SUPPER
TIMELY RETREAT
TIMELY WARNING
TIME MARCHES ON
TIME OF ARRIVAL
TIME OUT OF MIND
TIMES OF STRESS
TIME TO REFLECT
TIMID AS A MOUSE
TIMON OF ATHENS
TINNED PEACHES
TIN OF SARDINES
TIP-AND-RUN RAID
TIP ONE THE WINK
TIPPED THE WINK
TIRED OF LIVING
TIRESOME CHORE
TITLE OF HONOUR
TOAD IN THE HOLE
TO A HIGH DEGREE
TOASTED CHEESE
TO BE CONTINUED
TO BE OR NOT TO BE
TOGETHER AGAIN
TOKEN OF ESTEEM

TOLL OF THE ROAD
TOMATO KETCHUP
TOMORROW NIGHT
TOMORROW WE DIE
TONGUE IN CHEEK
TONGUE OF FLAME
TONGUE TWISTER
TONGUE WAGGING
TOO GOOD BY HALF
TOO GOOD TO LAST
TOO LITTLE ROOM
TOO MUCH PEPPER
TOOTING COMMON
TOO WEAK TO RISE
TOP OF THE CLASS
TOP OF THE SCALE
TOP OF THE TABLE
TOP-SECRET FILE
TORE OFF A STRIP
TORRENT OF RAIN
TO SOME PURPOSE
TOSTI'S "GOODBYE"
TOTAL DARKNESS
TO THE BACKBONE
TOUCHING SCENE
TOUCH-OF COLOUR
TOUCH OF GARLIC
TOUCH OF GENIUS
TOUCH OF NATURE
TOUCH OF THE SUN
TOUCH ONE'S TOES
TOUCH ON THE RAW
TOUCH THE HEART
TOUGH CUSTOMER
TOURIST AGENCY
TOURIST CENTRE
TOURIST SEASON
TOURIST TICKET
TOURIST TROPHY
TOUR OF BRITAIN
TOUT FOR CUSTOM
TOWER OF LONDON
TOWN AND AROUND
TOY WITH AN IDEA
TRACTOR DRIVER
TRADE DISCOUNT
TRADE ENTRANCE
TRADE MAGAZINE
TRADE UNIONIST
TRADING CENTRE
TRADING ESTATE

TRADING VESSEL
TRAFFIC ISLAND
TRAFFIC LIGHTS
TRAFFIC SIGNAL
TRAFFIC WARDEN
TRAIL ONE'S COAT
TRAINED SINGER
TRAIN OF CAMELS
TRAIN OF EVENTS
TRAIN SPOTTING
TRAIN TERMINUS
TRAITOR'S DEATH
TRAM CONDUCTOR
TRANQUIL SCENE
TRANSISTOR SET
TRANSPORT CAFÉ
TRAPEZE ARTIST
TRAVEL BY TRAIN
TRAVELLER'S JOY
TRAVEL LIGHTLY
TREACLE TOFFEE
TREAD THE STAGE
TREASURE CHEST
TREASURE HOUSE
TREASURE TRAIL
TREASURE TROVE
TREASURY BENCH
TREASURY BILLS
TREASURY BONDS
TREAT LIKE DIRT
TREAT WITH CARE
TREE OF LIBERTY
TREMENDOUS JOB
TRENCH WARFARE
TREND OF EVENTS
TRIAL AND ERROR
TRIAL MARRIAGE
TRIBAL WARFARE
TRICK QUESTION
TRICKY PROBLEM
TRIFLING ERROR
TRIGGER FINGER
TRILLING SOUND
TRINITY CHURCH
TRIUMPHAL ARCH
TRIVIAL MATTER
TROPICAL FRUIT
TROPICAL PLANT
TROPICAL STORM
TROTTING RACES
TROUSER BUTTON

TRUE CRITERION
TRUE STATEMENT
TRUE TO HIS SALT
TRUE TO ONESELF
TRUE TO THE LAST
TRUE UNTO DEATH
TRULY GRATEFUL
TRULY GREAT MAN
TRUMPET PLAYER
TRUST ACCOUNTS
TRUST TO CHANCE
TRUSTY SERVANT
TRYING JOURNEY
TRYSTING PLACE
TRYSTING POINT
TUBE OF MUSTARD
TUESDAY'S CHILD
TUNNEL THROUGH
TURKISH COFFEE
TURN A BLIND EYE
TURN CLOCKWISE
TURN DOWNWARDS
TURNED TO STONE
TURNING WICKET
TURN INSIDE OUT
TURN INTO MONEY
TURN OFF THE GAS
TURN OFF THE TAP
TURN OF THE CARD
TURN OF THE TIDE
TURN ON THE HEAT
TURN THE CORNER
TURN THE HEAT ON
TURN THE TABLES
TURN TO ACCOUNT
TURN TO THE LEFT
TURQUOISE BLUE
TWEED TROUSERS
TWELFTH LETTER
TWELFTH OF JULY
TWELFTH OF JUNE
TWELVE AND FIVE
TWELVE AND FOUR
TWELVE AND NINE
TWELVE DOLLARS
TWELVE GOOD MEN
TWELVE GUINEAS
TWELVE MINUTES
TWELVE PER CENT
TWELVE SQUARED
TWENTY DOLLARS

TWENTY GUINEAS
TWENTY MINUTES
TWENTY-ONE DAYS
TWENTY PER CENT
TWICE-TOLD TALE
TWILIGHT SLEEP
TWINKLING EYES
TWINKLING FEET
TWINKLING STAR
TWIST AND SHAKE
TWIST AND TWIRL
TWISTED NATURE
TWIST THE WORDS
TWO-EDGED SWORD
TWO-LETTER WORD
TWO-MASTED SHIP
TWO OF DIAMONDS
TWOPENNY STAMP
TWOS AND THREES
TWO-TIERED CAKE
TWO-WAY STRETCH
TWO-WAY TRAFFIC

U—I3
UGLY SITUATION
ULTERIOR PLANS
ULTIMATE CAUSE
UMBRELLA STAND
UNABLE TO PLEAD
UNANIMOUS VOTE
UNARMED COMBAT
UNATTACHED MAN
UNBOLT THE DOOR
UNBOUNDED LOVE
UNBROKEN FRONT
UNBROKEN HORSE
UNCROWNED KING
UNDATED CHEQUE
UNDECLARED WAR
UNDER CONTRACT
UNDER-COVER MAN
UNDER MILK WOOD
UNDER ONE'S NOSE
UNDER ONE'S SKIN
UNDER ONE'S WING
UNDER PRESSURE
UNDER SENTENCE
UNDER STRENGTH
UNDER THE KNIFE
UNDER THE TABLE
UNDER THE THUMB

UNDER TRAINING
UNDER TWO FLAGS
UNDUE PRESSURE
UNEASY FEELING
UNEVEN CONTEST
UNEVEN SURFACE
UNFAIR PICTURE
UNFAIR VERDICT
UNFRIENDLY ACT
UNFURL THE FLAG
UNGUARDED HOUR
UNHAPPY REMARK
UNIFORM WEIGHT
UNIONIST PARTY
UNION JACK CLUB
UNITED IN DEATH
UNITED KINGDOM
UNITED NATIONS
UNITED WE STAND
UNIT OF CURRENT
UNIVERSAL AUNT
UNIVERSAL BUTT
UNIVERSITY RAG
UNKIND THOUGHT
UNKNOWN ORIGIN
UNKNOWN PERSON
UNLAWFUL ENTRY
UNLOCK THE DOOR
UNLUCKY CHOICE
UNLUCKY COLOUR
UNLUCKY IN LOVE
UNLUCKY NUMBER
UNLUCKY PERSON
UNPAID SERVANT
UNSECURED DEBT
UNSECURED LOAN
UNSEEN DANGERS
UNSKILLED WORK
UNSOLVED CRIME
UNTIMELY DEATH
UNTOLD NUMBERS
UNVEIL A STATUE
UNWANTED CHILD
UNWORTHY CAUSE
UP AT CAMBRIDGE
UP BOYS AND AT 'EM
UP IN THE CLOUDS
UP IN THE SADDLE
UPPER REGISTER
UPRIGHT FELLOW
UPRIGHT FIGURE

UPRIGHT PERSON
UP THE MOUNTAIN
UP TO HIS TRICKS
UP TO SOMETHING
UP TO THE ELBOWS
UP TO THE MINUTE
UPTURNED GLASS
UP WITH THE DAWN
UP WITH THE LARK
URBAN DISTRICT
USEFUL PURPOSE
USEFUL STAND-BY
USE OF BATHROOM
USE ONE'S BRAINS
USUAL CHANNELS
USUAL QUESTION
UTTER CONTEMPT
UTTER DEVOTION
UTTER NONSENSE

V—13
VACUUM CLEANER
VALENTINE CARD
VALENTINE'S DAY
VALE OF EVESHAM
VALIANT EFFORT
VALID ARGUMENT
VALID CONTRACT
VALLEY OF DEATH
VALUE FOR MONEY
VALUE ONE'S LIFE
VALUE RECEIVED
VANTAGE GROUND
VARIABLE WINDS
VARICOSE VEINS
VARIETY ARTIST
VARNISHING DAY
VAUDEVILLE ACT
VAULTING HORSE
VAULT OF HEAVEN
VEAL AND HAM PIE
VEER TO THE LEFT
VEGETABLE DIET
VEGETABLE DISH
VEGETABLE LIFE
VEGETABLE SOUP
VENERABLE BEDE
VENETIAN BLIND
VENETIAN GLASS
VENOMOUS SNAKE
VERBAL QUIBBLE

VERNAL EQUINOX
VERSATILE MIND
VERTICAL PLANE
VERY DIFFERENT
VESSEL OF WRATH
VETERAN TROOPS
VEXED IN SPIRIT
VEXED QUESTION
VICIOUS CIRCLE
VICIOUS GOSSIP
VICTOR HERBERT
VICTORIA CROSS
VICTORIA FALLS
VICTORIAN DAYS
VICTORY PARADE
VIENNESE GLASS
VIENNESE WALTZ
VILLAGE BEAUTY
VILLAGE CHURCH
VILLAGE GOSSIP
VILLAGE SCHOOL
VILLAGE SMITHY
VILLAGE SQUIRE
VILLAGE STREET
VINEGARY SMILE
VIOLATE THE LAW
VIOLENT ATTACK
VIOLENT CHANGE
VIOLENT EFFORT
VIOLENT NATURE
VIOLENT SPEECH
VIOLENT TEMPER
VIOLIN RECITAL
VIRGINIA STOCK
VIRGINIA WATER
VIRGINIA WOOLF
VIRGIN ISLANDS
VIRULENT ABUSE
VISIBLE EFFECT
VISITING HOURS
VISITING TERMS
VITAL QUESTION
VITAMIN TABLET
VOICE OF REASON
VOICE TRAINING
VOID OF FEELING
VOLLEY OF ABUSE
VOLUME CONTROL
VOLUME OF SMOKE
VOLUNTARY ARMY
VOLUNTARY GIFT

VOLUNTARY WORK
VOLUNTEER ARMY
VOTED A FAILURE
VOTE OF CENSURE
VOTES FOR WOMEN
VULGAR DISPLAY

W—13

WAG ONE'S FINGER
WAIT FOR ORDERS
WAIT PATIENTLY
WALK BACKWARDS
WALKING-ON PART
WALK INTO A TRAP
WALK THE BOARDS
WALK UP AND DOWN
WALLOW IN MONEY
WALLS HAVE EARS
WALTER PIDGEON
WALTER RALEIGH
WANDERING MIND
WANTED ON BOARD
WANT OF COURAGE
WANT OF THOUGHT
WAR DEPARTMENT
WARDOUR STREET
WARLIKE HABITS
WARLIKE MANNER
WARLIKE PEOPLE
WARM RECEPTION
WARNING NOTICE
WARNING SIGNAL
WAR TO THE DEATH
WAR TO THE KNIFE
WASHING POWDER
WASH ONE'S HANDS
WASH THE DISHES
WASPISH NATURE
WASTE OF BREATH
WATCH AND CHAIN
WATCH EXPENSES
WATCHING BRIEF
WATCH ONE'S STEP
WATCH THE BIRDY
WATCH THE CLOCK
WATERING PLACE
WATER SHORTAGE
WATER SOFTENER
WATLING STREET
WAVE OF FEELING

WAVE OF THE HAND
WAY OF ALL FLESH
WAY OF THE CROSS
WAY OF THE WORLD
WAY OF THINKING
WAYSIDE TAVERN
WAY TO THE STARS
WEAK AS A KITTEN
WEAK CHARACTER
WEAK IN THE HEAD
WEAK ON HIS PINS
WEATHER BUREAU
WEATHER EXPERT
WEATHER REPORT
WEB OF INTRIGUE
WEDGWOOD CHINA
WEDNESDAY WEEK
WEED THE GARDEN
WEEK AFTER NEXT
WEEK AFTER WEEK
WEEK IN, WEEK OUT
WEEKLY ACCOUNT
WEEKLY PAYMENT
WEEK OF SUNDAYS
WEEKS AND WEEKS
WEEPING WILLOW
WEIGH THINGS UP
WEIGHTY MATTER
WELCOME RELIEF
WELFARE CENTRE
WELFARE WORKER
WELL-AIMED SHOT
WELL BROUGHT UP
WELL-KNIT FRAME
WELL PRESERVED
WELL-SPENT LIFE
WELL THOUGHT OF
WELL TO THE FORE
WELL TURNED OUT
WELSH REGIMENT
WENT LIKE A BOMB
WENT TO THE DOGS
WESTERLY WINDS
WESTERN CHURCH
WESTERN DESERT
WESTERN EUROPE
WESTERN POWERS
WEST HAM UNITED
WEST OF ENGLAND
WEST SIDE STORY
WHAT DO YOU KNOW?

WHATEVER YOU DO
WHIRLING ROUND
WHISKY AND SODA
WHISPER SOFTLY
WHITE AS A GHOST
WHITE AS A SHEET
WHITE AS MARBLE
WHITE ELEPHANT
WHITE FLANNELS
WHITE HORSE INN
WHITE OF THE EYE
WHITE SAPPHIRE
WHOLE OF THE DAY
WHOLESOME FOOD
WHOOPING COUGH
WIDE INTERESTS
WIDE KNOWLEDGE
WIDE OF THE MARK
WIDE PUBLICITY
WIDOW'S PENSION
WIELD THE BATON
WILD AND WOOLLY
WILD-CAT STRIKE
WILDEST DREAMS
WILFUL SILENCE
WILLIAM CAXTON
WILLIAM COWPER
WILLIAM MORRIS
WILLIAM WALTON
WILLING HELPER
WILLING WORKER
WILL OF ONE'S OWN
WILLOW PATTERN
WILLOWY FIGURE
WIMPOLE STREET
WINDING COURSE
WINDING STAIRS
WINDOW CLEANER
WINDOW DRESSER
WINDOW SHOPPER
WINDSOR CASTLE
WINED AND DINED
WIN FIRST PRIZE
WING COMMANDER
WINGED MONSTER
WINGED VICTORY
WINNIE THE POOH
WINNING COUPON
WINNING DOUBLE
WINNING HAZARD
WINNING NUMBER

WINNING STREAK
WINNING STROKE
WINNING TICKET
WINNING TREBLE
WINTER GARDENS
WINTER HOLIDAY
WINTER SESSION
WINTER VISITOR
WINTER WEATHER
WIN THE JACKPOT
WINTRY WEATHER
WIPE OFF THE MAP
WIPE ONE'S HANDS
WIRED FOR SOUND
WIRELESS WAVES
WISE AS SOLOMON
WISH OTHERWISE
WITH A BAD GRACE
WITH A FLOURISH
WITH A HIGH HAND
WITH AUTHORITY
WITH BOTH HANDS
WITH CERTAINTY
WITHERING LOOK
WITHIN EARSHOT
WITHIN HEARING
WITHIN MEASURE
WITH ONE ACCORD
WITHOUT A DOUBT
WITHOUT A HITCH
WITHOUT A RIVAL
WITHOUT CHARGE
WITHOUT MALICE
WITHOUT NOTICE
WITHOUT NUMBER
WITHOUT REASON
WITHOUT REGARD
WITHOUT REMARK
WITHOUT WARMTH
WITHOUT WEIGHT
WITH RESTRAINT
WITH THE LID OFF
WITH THE STREAM
WOLF AT THE DOOR
WOLF IN THE FOLD
WONDERFUL NEWS
WOOD ENGRAVING
WOOLLEN GLOVES
WORD IN ONE'S EAR
WORD OF COMFORT
WORD OF COMMAND

WORD OF WARNING
WORDS AND MUSIC
WORDS OF WISDOM
WORD TO THE WISE
WORDY ARGUMENT
WORK LIKE MAGIC
WORKMEN'S TRAIN
WORK OF FICTION
WORK ONE'S WAY UP
WORK THE ORACLE
WORK UP A LATHER
WORK WITH A WILL
WORLD CHAMPION
WORLDLY WISDOM
WORLD OF NATURE
WORLD PREMIÈRE
WORLD-WIDE FAME
WORM ONE'S WAY IN
WORN TO A SHADOW
WORSE AND WORSE
WORSE THAN EVER
WORST POSSIBLE
WORTH A FORTUNE
WORTH A MILLION
WORTHLESS JUNK
WORTH MILLIONS
WORTH ONE'S SALT
WORTH VISITING
WRAPPING PAPER
WRITE AT LENGTH
WRITE IN PENCIL
WRITE ONE'S NAME
WRITHE IN AGONY
WRITTEN ANSWER
WRITTEN MATTER
WRITTEN PERMIT
WRITTEN SPEECH
WRONG APPROACH
WRONG DECISION
WRONG TENDENCY

X—13
X-RAY APPARATUS

Y—13
YARDS AND YARDS
YEAR AFTER YEAR
YEAR IN, YEAR OUT
YEHUDI MENUHIN
YELLOW BUNTING
YELLOW WAGTAIL

YELLOW WITH AGE
YEOMAN SERVICE
YORKSHIRE POST
YOUNG CHILDREN
YOUNGER SISTER
YOUNGEST CHILD
YOUNG HOOLIGAN
YOUR NUMBER'S UP
YOUTH MOVEMENT

Z—13
ZEBRA CROSSING

A—14
A BOOK AT BEDTIME
ABOVE CRITICISM
ABOVE SUSPICION
ABOVE THE GROUND
A BOW AT A VENTURE
ABRAHAM LINCOLN
ABRUPT ENTRANCE
ABSOLUTE DECREE
ABSOLUTE MASTER
ABSOLUTE PIFFLE
ABSTRACT DESIGN
ABSTRACT NUMBER
ABUSE ONE'S POWER
ACADEMIC DEGREE
ACADEMIC MANNER
ACCESSIBLE SPOT
ACCIDENT POLICY
ACCORDING TO LAW
ACCORDION PLEAT
ACCUSATIVE CASE
ACCUSING FINGER
ACHIEVE ONE'S AIM
ACHIEVE VICTORY
ACHILLES' TENDON
ACROSS THE OCEAN
ACROSS THE RIVER
ACT ACCORDINGLY
ACT AS A LANDMARK
ACT AS GUARANTOR
ACT IMMEDIATELY
ACT IN GOOD FAITH
ACTION FOR LIBEL
ACTION PAINTING
ACTION STATIONS
ACTIVE INTEREST
ACTIVE STRENGTH
ACT THE BUSYBODY

ADDRESS THE BALL
ADDRESS UNKNOWN
ADD TO ONE'S GRIEF
ADELPHI TERRACE
ADELPHI THEATRE
ADEQUATE AMOUNT
ADEQUATE INCOME
ADEQUATE REASON
ADJUST THE HANDS
ADMIRALTY CHART
ADMIRALTY HOUSE
ADMIT THE CHARGE
ADOPTION PAPERS
ADVANCE BOOKING
ADVANCING YEARS
ADVENTURE STORY
ADVERSE BALANCE
AESTHETIC SENSE
AESTHETIC TASTE
AFFAIRE DE COEUR
AFFAIR OF HONOUR
AFFAIRS OF STATE
AFFECTED MANNER
AFFECTED SPEECH
AFFILIATED BODY
AFTER BREAKFAST
AFTER CHRISTMAS
AFTER-DINNER NAP
AFTER LIGHTS-OUT
AFTER THE DELUGE
AGAINST ALL ODDS
AGAINST THE ODDS
AGAINST THE TIDE
AGAINST THE WIND
AGATHA CHRISTIE
AGE OF IGNORANCE
AGE OF INNOCENCE
AGREE IN MEANING
AIM AT THE TARGET
AIRBORNE FORCES
AIRBORNE TROOPS
AIRING CUPBOARD
AIR OF GRIEVANCE
AIR ONE'S OPINION
AIR PHOTOGRAPHY
AIR-RAID SHELTER
AIR-RAID WARNING
AIR VICE-MARSHAL
ALBERT EINSTEIN
ALBERT MEMORIAL
ALCOCK AND BROWN

ALCOHOLIC DRINK
ALDWYCH THEATRE
ALEXANDRE DUMAS
ALFRED TENNYSON
ALFRED THE GREAT
ALL GUNS BLAZING
ALL HANDS ON DECK
ALLIED LANDINGS
ALL IN A DAY'S WORK
ALL-IN WRESTLING
ALL KINDS OF WAYS
ALLOTTED SPHERE
ALL OVER THE SHOP
ALL-ROUND PLAYER
ALL THE KING'S MEN
ALL WELL AND GOOD
ALMIGHTY DOLLAR
ALPES MARITIMES
ALSACE LORRAINE
AMATEUR COMPANY
AMERICAN ACCENT
AMERICAN INDIAN
AMERICAN LEGION
AMERICAN PATROL
AMERICAN SCHOOL
AMERICAN TROOPS
AMMUNITION DUMP
AMONGST FRIENDS
ANCIENT BRITAIN
ANCIENT HISTORY
ANCIENT LINEAGE
ANCIENT MARINER
ANDAMAN ISLANDS
ANDREW CARNEGIE
ANGINA PECTORIS
ANGLICAN CHURCH
ANIMAL CRACKERS
ANNUAL TURNOVER
ANNUS MIRABILIS
ANONYMOUS DONOR
ANOTHER OPINION
ANOTHER VERSION
ANSWER ONE'S NAME
ANTARCTIC OCEAN
ANY SUGGESTIONS?
ANYTHING TO COME
APARTMENT HOUSE
APARTMENT TO LET
APPEAL FOR FUNDS
APPEAL FOR MERCY
APPEAL TO REASON

APPEAR IN PUBLIC
APPLE CHARLOTTE
APPLE OF DISCORD
APPLE OF ONE'S EYE
APPLES AND PEARS
APPLIED PHYSICS
APPLIED SCIENCE
APPLY THE BRAKES
APPROVED SCHOOL
APRIL THE EIGHTH
APRIL THE FOURTH
APRIL THE SECOND
ARABIC NUMERALS
ARBITER OF TASTE
ARMCHAIR CRITIC
ARMS OF MORPHEUS
ARMY CADET FORCE
ARMY MANOEUVRES
AROUND THE WORLD
ARRANT NONSENSE
ARROGANT MANNER
ART FOR ART'S SAKE
ARTFUL CUSTOMER
ARTICLE OF FAITH
ARTIFICIAL HAND
ARTIFICIAL LAKE
ARTIFICIAL LIMB
ARTIFICIAL POND
ARTIFICIAL SILK
ARTISTIC EFFECT
ARTISTIC EFFORT
ART OF REASONING
AS A GENERAL RULE
AS BLACK AS NIGHT
AS BRAVE AS A LION
ASCENDING ORDER
ASCENDING SCALE
AS DEAD AS MUTTON
AS DRUNK AS A LORD
AS FAST AS YOU CAN
AS FIT AS A FIDDLE
AS FRESH AS PAINT
AS GOOD AS A FEAST
AS GREEN AS GRASS
AS HARD AS A STONE
ASK FORGIVENESS
AS MAD AS A HATTER
AS PALE AS A GHOST
AS PLAIN AS PLAIN
AS SAFE AS HOUSES
ASSENTING PARTY

AS SMART AS PAINT
ASSOCIATION CUP
AS SOFT AS BUTTER
AS SOFT AS VELVET
AS SOUND AS A BELL
AS SWEET AS SUGAR
AS THE CASE MAY BE
AS THE CROW FLIES
AS TIGHT AS A DRUM
AT DAGGERS DRAWN
ATHLETIC GROUND
ATHLETIC SPORTS
ATLANTIC FLIGHT
ATLANTIC ROLLER
ATLAS MOUNTAINS
AT ONE FELL SWOOP
AT ONE'S DISPOSAL
A TOWN LIKE ALICE
ATTACKING FIELD
ATTACK OF NERVES
ATTEMPT TOO MUCH
AT THE RIGHT TIME
AT THE THRESHOLD
AT THIS JUNCTURE
ATTITUDE OF MIND
AUF WIEDERSEHEN
AUGUST THE FIFTH
AUGUST THE FIRST
AUGUST THE NINTH
AUGUST THE SIXTH
AUGUST THE TENTH
AUGUST THE THIRD
AUGUSTUS CAESAR
AURORA BOREALIS
AUSTRALIA HOUSE
AUSTRALIAN BUSH
AUTOGRAPH ALBUM
AUTOMATIC RIFLE
AUTOMOBILE CLUB
AVERAGE ABILITY
AVIATION SPIRIT
AVOID A DECISION
AVOID BLOODSHED
AWKWARD SILENCE

B—14
BABES IN THE WOOD
BACHELOR OF ARTS
BACK-SEAT DRIVER
BACKS TO THE WALL
BACKWARD GLANCE

BACONIAN THEORY
BAD CIRCULATION
BAD FOR BUSINESS
BAD HANDWRITING
BAD HOUSEKEEPER
BADMINTON COURT
BAD VENTILATION
BAGATELLE TABLE
BALANCED BUDGET
BALANCE OF POWER
BALANCE OF TRADE
BALANCING TRICK
BALL AT ONE'S FEET
BALLET MISTRESS
BALLIOL COLLEGE
BALL OF THE THUMB
BALLOON BARRAGE
BALMORAL CASTLE
BALTIC EXCHANGE
BANANA FRITTERS
BANDED TOGETHER
BAND OF BROTHERS
BAND OF PILGRIMS
BANE OF ONE'S LIFE
BANGERS AND MASH
BANKING ACCOUNT
BANK OF SCOTLAND
BANNER HEADLINE
BANQUETING HALL
BARE-BACK RIDING
BARE ESSENTIALS
BARELY POSSIBLE
BARGAIN COUNTER
BARKIS IS WILLIN'
BAR OF CHOCOLATE
BARRAGE BALLOON
BAR THE ENTRANCE
BASIC SUBSTANCE
BASKET-BALL TEAM
BATHING COSTUME
BATHING MACHINE
BATHROOM SCALES
BATTING AVERAGE
BATTLE OF NASEBY
BATTLE STATIONS
BAYEUX TAPESTRY
BEACH INSPECTOR
BE-ALL AND END-ALL
BEAR ALLEGIANCE
BEAT GENERATION
BEAT ONE'S BRAINS

BEAT ONE'S BREAST
BEAT THE BIG DRUM
BEAT TO A FRAZZLE
BEAUTIFUL VOICE
BEAUTIFUL WOMAN
BECOME A CITIZEN
BECOME AIRBORNE
BECOME A PATIENT
BECOME CHAMPION
BEDROOM SLIPPER
BEDSIDE READING
BED-SITTING ROOM
BEFORE AND AFTER
BEFORE AND SINCE
BEFORE DAYLIGHT
BEFORE MIDNIGHT
BEFORE ONE'S EYES
BEFORE ONE'S TIME
BEFORE THE JUDGE
BEG FORGIVENESS
BEG THE QUESTION
BEHIND ONE'S BACK
BEHIND SCHEDULE
BEHIND THE CLOCK
BEHIND THE TIMES
BEHIND THE WHEEL
BELGRAVE SQUARE
BELIEVE IT OR NOT
BELLE OF NEW YORK
BELLE OF THE BALL
BELOW THE GROUND
BENCH OF BISHOPS
BENEATH ACCOUNT
BENEFIT SOCIETY
BENEVOLENT FUND
BEREFT OF REASON
BERKELEY SQUARE
BERLIN QUESTION
BESEECHING LOOK
BESIDE THE POINT
BEST DRESSED MAN
BEST INTENTIONS
BEST LEG FORWARD
BEST OF THE BUNCH
BETSEY TROTWOOD
BETTER FEELINGS
BETTER THAN EVER
BETTER THAN MOST
BETTER THOUGHTS
BETWEEN FRIENDS
BETWEEN THE EYES

BEWARE OF THE DOG
BEYOND ALL DOUBT
BEYOND HUMAN AID
BEYOND REPROACH
BEYOND THE GRAVE
BEYOND THE LIMIT
BID GOOD MORNING
BIFOCAL GLASSES
BIG-GAME HUNTING
BIGGEST PORTION
BIJOU RESIDENCE
BILLIARD MARKER
BILLIARD PLAYER
BILLIARD SALOON
BILL OF EXCHANGE
BIRD OF PARADISE
BIRTH OF A NATION
BISHOP AUCKLAND
BITE ONE'S TONGUE
BIT OF A COME-DOWN
BIT OF A NUISANCE
BITTER FEELINGS
BITTER MEMORIES
BITTER STRUGGLE
BITTER THOUGHTS
BITUMINOUS COAL
BLACK AS THUNDER
BLACK-EYED SUSIE
BLACK IN THE FACE
BLACKPOOL TOWER
BLACK STOCKINGS
BLANK CARTRIDGE
BLASTING POWDER
BLAZING INFERNO
BLEACHING AGENT
BLENHEIM ORANGE
BLENHEIM PALACE
BLESS THIS HOUSE
BLIND IGNORANCE
BLIND REASONING
BLOCK AND TACKLE
BLOCK OF OFFICES
BLOOD POISONING
BLOUSE AND SKIRT
BLOW EVERYTHING
BLOW HOT AND COLD
BLOWING BUBBLES
BLOW SMOKE-RINGS
BLOW THE EXPENSE
BLOW THE MAN DOWN
BLUE-COAT SCHOOL

BLUE SPECTACLES
BLUNT STATEMENT
BOA CONSTRICTOR
BOARDING SCHOOL
BOARD OF CONTROL
BOARD OF INQUIRY
BOARD RESIDENCE
BODILY MOVEMENT
BODILY STRENGTH
BODILY WEAKNESS
BODY OF SOLDIERS
BOILED POTATOES
BOLD EXPERIMENT
BONNIE SCOTLAND
BOOK DEPARTMENT
BOOK OF NONSENSE
BOOK OF PROVERBS
BOOK OF THE MONTH
BOOK PRODUCTION
BOOMING ECONOMY
BOON COMPANIONS
BORDERLINE CASE
BORDER MINSTREL
BORDER REGIMENT
BORDER SKIRMISH
BOROUGH COUNCIL
BORROWED PLUMES
BOSTON CRACKERS
BOSTON TEA PARTY
BOTTLE OF BRANDY
BOTTLE OF BUBBLY
BOTTLE OF CLARET
BOTTLE OF SCOTCH
BOTTLE OF SWEETS
BOTTLE OF WHISKY
BOTTOM OF THE BAG
BOTTOM OF THE SEA
BOUGHT FOR A SONG
BOUT OF SICKNESS
BOWLING AVERAGE
BOWL OF CHERRIES
BOXER REBELLION
BOYS WILL BE BOYS
BRACING CLIMATE
BRADSHAW'S GUIDE
BREACH OF ORDERS
BREAD AND BUTTER
BREAD AND CHEESE
BREAD AND SCRAPE
BREADFRUIT TREE
BREAKFAST IN BED

BREAKFAST TABLE
BREAKNECK SPEED
BREAK NEW GROUND
BREAK ONE'S HEART
BREAK THE CORDON
BREAK THE RECORD
BREAK THE THREAD
BREAST THE WAVES
BREATHE HEAVILY
BREATHE REVENGE
BREATHING SPACE
BREATH OF SEA AIR
BREATH OF SPRING
BREEDING GROUND
BREWERS' COMPANY
BRIEF ENCOUNTER
BRIEF INTERLUDE
BRIGHT AND EARLY
BRIGHT AS SILVER
BRIGHT PROSPECT
BRIGHT'S DISEASE
BRIGITTE BARDOT
BRIMFUL OF IDEAS
BRING GOOD CHEER
BRING IN A PROFIT
BRING INTO BEING
BRING INTO FOCUS
BRING TO ACCOUNT
BRING TO JUSTICE
BRING TO THE BOIL
BRING TO THE FORE
BRING UP THE REAR
BRISTOL CHANNEL
BRISTOL FASHION
BRITANNIA METAL
BRITISH COUNCIL
BRITISH EMBASSY
BRITISH SUBJECT
BRITTLE AS GLASS
BROAD IN THE BEAM
BROAD SHOULDERS
BROADWAY MELODY
BROKEN CONTRACT
BROKEN MARRIAGE
BROKE THE WICKET
BROKE TO THE WIDE
BRONCHIAL TUBES
BROOKLYN BRIDGE
BROOK NO REFUSAL
BROTHER OFFICER
BROTHERS IN ARMS

BROUGHT TO LIGHT
BRUSH ONE'S TEETH
BRUSSELS CARPET
BUBBLING STREAM
BUCKET AND SPADE
BUILDING BRICKS
BULLDOG COURAGE
BULLET-PROOF CAR
BUMP OF LOCALITY
BUNCH OF BANANAS
BUNCH OF FLOWERS
BUNDLE OF NERVES
BURIED TREASURE
BURN AT THE STAKE
BURNHAM BEECHES
BURNISHED BRASS
BURNT SACRIFICE
BURNT TO A CINDER
BURST INTO FLAME
BURST INTO TEARS
BURST ONE'S BONDS
BURST THE BUBBLE
BURY ONE'S TALENT
BURY THE HATCHET
BUS CONDUCTRESS
BUSINESS CAREER
BUSINESS LETTER
BUSINESS MATTER
BUSINESS ON HAND
BUSINESS TYCOON
BUSMAN'S HOLIDAY
BUTTONS AND BOWS
BUY A PIG IN A POKE
BY A LONG STRETCH
BY PRESCRIPTION
BY THE SAME TOKEN

C—14
CABBAGE LETTUCE
CABINET MEETING
CABINET PUDDING
CAGE ME A PEACOCK
CALAMINE LOTION
CALCIUM CARBIDE
CALCULATED ODDS
CALCULATED RISK
CALF'S-FOOT JELLY
CALLED TO THE BAR
CALL FOR A REPORT
CALLING ALL CARS
CALL IN QUESTION

CALL OFF THE DOGS
CALM REFLECTION
CAMBRIDGE COACH
CAMP COMMANDANT
CAMPHORATED OIL
CAMPING HOLIDAY
CANADIAN POLICE
CANNING FACTORY
CANTERBURY BELL
CANTERBURY LAMB
CAPABLE OF PROOF
CAPE OF GOOD HOPE
CAPITAL OFFENCE
CAPITAL OF ITALY
CAPITAL OF SPAIN
CAPTAIN BOYCOTT
CAPTIVE BALLOON
CARAVAN HOLIDAY
CARBON MONOXIDE
CARDEW ROBINSON
CARDIAC DISEASE
CARDINAL NEWMAN
CARDINAL NUMBER
CARDINAL POINTS
CARDINAL VIRTUE
CARDINAL WOLSEY
CAREFUL THOUGHT
CARMELITE ORDER
CARPET SLIPPERS
CARRY ONE'S POINT
CARTRIDGE PAPER
CASEMENT WINDOW
CASH ON DELIVERY
CAST ASPERSIONS
CAST INTO PRISON
CAST-IRON EXCUSE
CASTLE IN THE AIR
CASTLES IN SPAIN
CAST SHEEP'S EYES
CASUAL LABOURER
CASUAL OBSERVER
CATCH ONE'S DEATH
CATCH RED-HANDED
CATCH THE BREATH
CATHEDRAL CLOSE
CATHERINE BOYLE
CATHERINE WHEEL
CATHODE-RAY TUBE
CAT ON HOT BRICKS
CAT OUT OF THE BAG
CAUGHT IN A STORM

CAUGHT IN THE ACT
CAUGHT ON THE HOP
CAUGHT STEALING
CAUGHT UNAWARES
CAULIFLOWER EAR
CAUSE AND EFFECT
CAUSE A STOPPAGE
CAUSE CONFUSION
CAUSE FOR REGRET
CAUTIONARY TALE
CAVALRY OFFICER
CELESTIAL BLISS
CELESTIAL GLOBE
CENTRAL AMERICA
CENTRAL HEATING
CENTRAL STATION
CERTAIN VICTORY
CHAINED TO A DESK
CHAIN OF COMMAND
CHAIN OF THOUGHT
CHAIR THE WINNER
CHALK AND CHEESE
CHALLENGE ROUND
CHAMPAGNE GLASS
CHAMPAGNE LUNCH
CHAMPION GOLFER
CHAMPION JOCKEY
CHANCERY OFFICE
CHANGE OF BELIEF
CHANGE OF COURSE
CHANGE ONE'S LUCK
CHANGE ONE'S MIND
CHANGE ONE'S NAME
CHANGE ONE'S TUNE
CHANGE ONE'S WAYS
CHANGE PARTNERS
CHANGE THE ORDER
CHANGE THE VENUE
CHANNEL ISLANDS
CHANNEL STEAMER
CHANNEL SWIMMER
CHAPTER HEADING
CHARACTER ACTOR
CHARACTER STUDY
CHARCOAL BURNER
CHARGE THE EARTH
CHARITABLE DEED
CHARITABLE GIFT
CHARITY MEETING
CHARLES CHAPLIN
CHARLES DICKENS

CHARLES GARVICE
CHARLIE CHESTER
CHARLOTTE RUSSE
CHARMING FELLOW
CHARMING MANNER
CHARRED REMAINS
CHASE ME CHARLIE
CHEAP EXCURSION
CHECKING SYSTEM
CHEER TO THE ECHO
CHEESE SANDWICH
CHEMICAL CHANGE
CHEMICAL ENERGY
CHEMISTRY CLASS
CHESHIRE CHEESE
CHESTNUT SUNDAY
CHEST OF DRAWERS
CHEST PROTECTOR
CHEWING TOBACCO
CHICKEN IN ASPIC
CHIEF CONSTABLE
CHIEF EXECUTIVE
CHIEF INSPECTOR
CHILD ALLOWANCE
CHILD OF FORTUNE
CHILDREN'S NURSE
CHILDREN'S PARTY
CHILDREN'S STORY
CHINESE CRACKER
CHINESE LANTERN
CHINESE LAUNDRY
CHINESE TORTURE
CHIPPING BARNET
CHIPPING NORTON
CHOCOLATE CREAM
CHOCOLATE WAFER
CHOPPED PARSLEY
CHRISTMAS BONUS
CHRISTMAS CAROL
CHRISTMAS CHEER
CHRISTMAS DAISY
CHRISTMAS PARTY
CHRISTOPHER FRY
CHROMATIC SCALE
CHRONIC INVALID
CHUCK OVERBOARD
CHUCK UP ONE'S JOB
CHURCH ASSEMBLY
CHURCH DOCTRINE
CHURCH MILITANT
CHURCH PROPERTY

CIGARETTE PAPER
CIRCLE THE EARTH
CIRCULAR COURSE
CIRCULAR LETTER
CIRCULAR TICKET
CITY MAGISTRATE
CIVILIZED WORLD
CIVIL LIBERTIES
CLAIM ATTENTION
CLAIM THE REWARD
CLAP INTO PRISON
CLARENDON PRESS
CLASH OF CYMBALS
CLASS CONSCIOUS
CLASSICAL LATIN
CLASSICAL MUSIC
CLASSICAL TASTE
CLASSIC EXAMPLE
CLASSIC QUALITY
CLASSICS MASTER
CLASS PREJUDICE
CLEAN AS A NEW PIN
CLEAN ONE'S TEETH
CLEANSING CREAM
CLEAN THE SILVER
CLEAR AS CRYSTAL
CLEAR STATEMENT
CLEAR THE GROUND
CLEAR THE THROAT
CLEMENT WEATHER
CLERICAL COLLAR
CLERICAL DUTIES
CLERICAL WORKER
CLICK ONE'S HEELS
CLIMB A MOUNTAIN
CLIMBING PRICES
CLOAK AND DAGGER
CLOCKWORK TRAIN
CLOISTERED LIFE
CLOSE AN ACCOUNT
CLOSE ATTENTION
CLOSELY GUARDED
CLOSE ONE'S MOUTH
CLOSE PROXIMITY
CLOSE THE WINDOW
CLOSE TO THE WIND
CLOTHING COUPON
CLOUD FORMATION
CLOUT ON THE HEAD
CLUB MEMBERSHIP
CLUBS ARE TRUMPS

CLUSTER OF STARS
CLUTCH AT STRAWS
COACH AND HORSES
COALING STATION
COARSE LANGUAGE
COASTAL BATTERY
COASTAL COMMAND
COASTAL EROSION
COCK OF THE NORTH
COCKTAIL SHAKER
COFFEE STRAINER
COHERENT MANNER
COIN OF THE REALM
COLLAR ATTACHED
COLLECTED POEMS
COLLECTIVE FARM
COLLECTIVE NOUN
COLLECT ONESELF
COLLECTOR'S ITEM
COLLEGE PUDDING
COLLEGE STUDENT
COLONIAL OFFICE
COLONIAL SYSTEM
COLORADO BEETLE
COLOUR QUESTION
COLOUR SERGEANT
COMBINED EFFORT
COME BACK TO ERIN
COME DOWNSTAIRS
COMEDY OF ERRORS
COME FACE TO FACE
COME FROM BEHIND
COME FULL CIRCLE
COME-HITHER LOOK
COME INTO FAVOUR
COME ON THE SCENE
COME ROUND AGAIN
COME SECOND BEST
COME TO A DEAD-END
COME TO THE FRONT
COME TO THE POINT
COMFORTABLY OFF
COMIC INTERLUDE
COMING OF ARTHUR
COMING-OUT PARTY
COMMANDING LEAD
COMMAND OF WORDS
COMMAND RESPECT
COMMAND SILENCE
COMMAND SUPPORT
COMMERCIAL ROOM

COMMIT A FAUX PAS
COMMIT FOR TRIAL
COMMIT HARA-KIRI
COMMITTEE STAGE
COMMIT TO MEMORY
COMMIT TO PRISON
COMMON ANCESTOR
COMMON COURTESY
COMMON CURRENCY
COMMON ENTRANCE
COMMON FRONTIER
COMMON HUMANITY
COMMON INFORMER
COMMON INTEREST
COMMON MULTIPLE
COMMON NUISANCE
COMMON OR GARDEN
COMMON PARLANCE
COMMON PRACTICE
COMMON PROPERTY
COMMON SERJEANT
COMMUNION BREAD
COMMUNION TABLE
COMMUNIST PARTY
COMMUNITY CHEST
COMPANION PIECE
COMPANY MANNERS
COMPANY MATTERS
COMPANY MEETING
COMPANY OFFICER
COMPASS BEARING
COMPASS READING
COMPLEAT ANGLER
COMPLETE ANSWER
COMPLETE CHANGE
COMPLETE FIASCO
COMPONENT PARTS
COMPOSED MANNER
COMPOSE ONESELF
COMPULSORY LOAN
COMRADES IN ARMS
CONCEALED DRIVE
CONCERT PIANIST
CONDEMN TO DEATH
CONDUCT A SEARCH
CONFER A BENEFIT
CONFERENCE ROOM
CONFIRMED ENEMY
CONFIRMED HABIT
CONIFEROUS TREE
CONJUGAL RIGHTS

CONJURING TRICK
CONQUERING HERO
CONSIGN TO EARTH
CONSTANT READER
CONSTANT STRAIN
CONSTANT SUPPLY
CONSULTING ROOM
CONSUMER DEMAND
CONTAIN ONESELF
CONTINUITY GIRL
CONTRACT BRIDGE
CONTRARY ADVICE
CONTROLLED RENT
CONTROL ONESELF
CONVERSION LOAN
CONVEY A MEANING
COOKING UTENSIL
COPPER SULPHATE
COPS AND ROBBERS
COPYHOLD ESTATE
CORDIAL WELCOME
CORNFLOWER BLUE
CORNISH RIVIERA
CORPORATION TAX
CORRUGATED IRON
COTTON EXCHANGE
COTTON INDUSTRY
COUNCIL CHAMBER
COUNCIL MEETING
COUNCIL OF STATE
COUNTLESS TIMES
COUNT ONE'S BEADS
COUNT ONE'S MONEY
COUNTRY BUMPKIN
COUNTRY COTTAGE
COUNTRY RETREAT
COUNTY PALATINE
COURSE OF ACTION
COURSE OF EVENTS
COURTING COUPLE
COURT OF INQUIRY
COURT OF JUSTICE
COURT PROCEDURE
COVERED WITH ICE
COVERING LETTER
CRACK OF THE WHIP
CRADLE SNATCHER
CRAMP ONE'S STYLE
CRANBERRY SAUCE
CRASH ONE'S GEARS
CRASS IGNORANCE

CRASS STUPIDITY
CREAM OF SOCIETY
CREATE AN EFFECT
CREATE AN UPROAR
CREATE A SCANDAL
CREATIVE ARTIST
CREATIVE GENIUS
CREATIVE WORKER
CREATIVE WRITER
CREDIT CUSTOMER
CREDIT TRANSFER
CRÈME DE LA CRÈME
CREST OF THE WAVE
CRICKET FIXTURE
CRICKET RESULTS
CRIME DETECTION
CRIME DOESN'T PAY
CRIME OF PASSION
CRIME PASSIONEL
CRIMINAL CHARGE
CRIMINAL LAWYER
CRIMINAL RECORD
CRINOLINE DRESS
CRITICAL MOMENT
CRITICAL PERIOD
CROCODILE TEARS
CROOK THE FINGER
CROSSED FINGERS
CROSS ONE'S HEART
CROSS REFERENCE
CROSS THE BORDER
CROSS THE BRIDGE
CROSS THE STREET
CROWN AND ANCHOR
CROWNING STROKE
CROWN OF THE HEAD
CROWN OF THE ROAD
CRUMBLING POWER
CRUMB OF COMFORT
CRUSHING DEFEAT
CRUSHING REMARK
CRUSHING RETORT
CRY ONE'S EYES OUT
CULTIVATED LAND
CULTIVATED MIND
CULTURAL CENTRE
CUP FINAL TICKET
CUP OF HAPPINESS
CURB ONE'S TEMPER
CURDLE THE BLOOD
CURIOUS MIXTURE

CURRANT PUDDING
CURRENT ACCOUNT
CURRENT AFFAIRS
CURRENT EDITION
CURRENT FASHION
CURRENT OPINION
CURRIED CHICKEN
CURTAIN LECTURE
CURTAIN OF SMOKE
CUSTOM AND USAGE
CUSTOMS BARRIER
CUSTOMS OFFICER
CUT A FINE FIGURE
CUT A POOR FIGURE
CUT FOR PARTNERS
CUTLERS' COMPANY
CUT OFF ONE'S NOSE
CUT OFF THE JOINT
CUT-THROAT PRICE
CUT-THROAT RAZOR

D—14
DAILY ENDEAVOUR
DAILY HAPPENING
DAILY NEWSPAPER
DAILY TELEGRAPH
DAILY TRAVELLER
DAMAGING REPORT
DAME EDITH EVANS
DAME ELLEN TERRY
DANCE PROGRAMME
DANCING ACADEMY
DANCING DERVISH
DANCING LICENCE
DANCING PARTNER
DANGEROUSLY ILL
DARING YOUNG MAN
DARK COMPLEXION
DARKEN ONE'S DOOR
DAVID TOMLINSON
DAVID WHITFIELD
DAY IN AND DAY OUT
DAYLIGHT SAVING
DAY OF ATONEMENT
DAY OF RECKONING
DAZZLING BEAUTY
DEAD MAN'S HANDLE
DEAD TO THE WORLD
DEAL A DEATH BLOW
DEAN AND CHAPTER
DEAR AT THE PRICE

DEATH BY BURNING
DEATHLY SILENCE
DEBASED COINAGE
DEBATABLE POINT
DEBIT AND CREDIT
DECEIVE ONESELF
DECENT INTERVAL
DECENTLY HOUSED
DECIDING FACTOR
DECIMAL COINAGE
DECISIVE FACTOR
DECLINE AND FALL
DECLINE IN VALUE
DECLINE TO STAND
DECLINING YEARS
DECREE ABSOLUTE
DEEP DEPRESSION
DEEPLY AFFECTED
DEEPLY OFFENDED
DEEP REFLECTION
DEEP-SEA FISHING
DEFEAT THE ENEMY
DEFENCE COUNSEL
DEFENCE IN DEPTH
DEFENCE MEASURE
DEFENCE WITNESS
DEFERRED SHARES
DEFINITE FIGURE
DEFRAY EXPENSES
DEGREES OF FROST
DELAYING ACTION
DELICATE HEALTH
DELICIOUS TASTE
DELIVER A SERMON
DELIVER A SPEECH
DEMAND A HEARING
DEMAND A RE-COUNT
DEMAND ENTRANCE
DEMAND SECURITY
DENTAL PRACTICE
DEPARTED SPIRIT
DEPART FROM LIFE
DEPARTING GUEST
DEPOSIT ACCOUNT
DEPRESSED CLASS
DEPRESSING NEWS
DEPRIVED PERSON
DEPTH OF FEELING
DEPTHS OF MISERY
DEPUTY CHAIRMAN
DERBY FAVOURITE

DERELICT VESSEL
DEROGATORY TERM
DESERT ONE'S POST
DESIRABLE THING
DESPATCH BY MAIL
DESPERATE STATE
DETACHED MANNER
DETAILED REPORT
DETECTIVE NOVEL
DETECTIVE STORY
DETENTION ORDER
DEVELOP THE MIND
DEVIL INCARNATE
DEVIL OF A TEMPER
DEVIL'S ADVOCATE
DEVIL'S DISCIPLE
DEVOTED ADMIRER
DEVOTED HUSBAND
DEVOTION TO DUTY
DIAMOND JUBILEE
DIAMOND WEDDING
DIARY OF A NOBODY
DICTATE A LETTER
DICTATION SPEED
DICTIONARY WORD
DIE IN ONE'S SHOES
DIEU ET MON DROIT
DIFFERENT ANGLE
DIFFICULT CATCH
DIFFICULT CLIMB
DIG IN ONE'S HEELS
DIGNIFIED STYLE
DIG ONE'S SPURS IN
DIMINUTIVE SIZE
DING-DONG BATTLE
DINNER AND DANCE
DINNER IS SERVED
DIPLOMATIC BODY
DIPLOMATIC MOVE
DIRECT APPROACH
DIRECT EVIDENCE
DIRECT OPPOSITE
DIRECT QUESTION
DIRECT TAXATION
DISABLED PERSON
DISCHARGE A DEBT
DISCORDANT NOTE
DISCOUNT BROKER
DISGUISED VOICE
DISORDERED MIND
DISTILLED WATER

DISTORTED IMAGE
DISTRESSED AREA
DISTRESS SIGNAL
DISTURBED NIGHT
DISTURBED SLEEP
DIVIDE BY ELEVEN
DIVIDE BY TWELVE
DIVIDED LOYALTY
DIVIDE THE HOUSE
DIVISION OF WORK
DIVORCED PERSON
DOCTOR BARNARDO
DOCTORS' COMMONS
DOCTOR'S DILEMMA
DOCTOR'S MANDATE
DODGE THE COLUMN
DOG IN THE MANGER
DOLL'S FURNITURE
DOMESTIC ANIMAL
DOMESTIC DRUDGE
DOMESTIC POLICY
DOMINION STATUS
DONALD CAMPBELL
DONKEY SERENADE
DO ONESELF PROUD
DOROTHY PERKINS
DOSE OF MEDICINE
DOT AND CARRY ONE
DOUBLE EIGHTEEN
DOUBLE ENTENDRE
DOUBLE EXPOSURE
DOUBLE FOURTEEN
DOUBLE NEGATIVE
DOUBLE NINETEEN
DOUBLE STANDARD
DOUBLE STOPPING
DOUBLET AND HOSE
DOUBLE THIRTEEN
DOUBTFUL FUTURE
DOUBTFUL ORIGIN
DOUBTFUL TEMPER
DOUBTING THOMAS
DOUGHTY WARRIOR
DOWAGER DUCHESS
DOWN IN THE DUMPS
DOWN IN THE MOUTH
DOWN IN THE WORLD
DOWN LAMBETH WAY
DOWN MEMORY LANE
DOWN ON ONE'S LUCK
DOWNSTAIRS ROOM

DOWN THE CHIMNEY
DOWNWARD MOTION
DOWNWARD STROKE
DOZENS OF PEOPLE
DRAIN ONE'S GLASS
DRAMATIC CRITIC
DRAMATIC EFFECT
DRAMATIC FINISH
DRAPERS' COMPANY
DRAWERS OF WATER
DRAW FIRST BLOOD
DRAW THE CURTAIN
DRAW THE LONG-BOW
DRAW THE RATIONS
DREAMING SPIRES
DREGS OF SOCIETY
DRESSED IN BLACK
DRESSED OVER ALL
DRESS FOR DINNER
DRESS REHEARSAL
DRINKING HABITS
DRINKING TROUGH
DRINKING VESSEL
DRINK LIKE A FISH
DRIVE CAREFULLY
DRIVE TO DESPAIR
DRIVE TO THE WALL
DRIVING LICENCE
DROP FROM THE SKY
DROP IN THE OCEAN
DROP OFF TO SLEEP
DROP THE SUBJECT
DROWNED IN TEARS
DUBIOUS COMPANY
DUBLIN BAY PRAWN
DUCKS AND DRAKES
DUELLING PISTOL
DUEL TO THE DEATH
DUKE OF BURGUNDY
DUKE OF CLARENCE
DUKE OF CORNWALL
DUPLICATE SHEET
DURATION OF LIFE
DURING THE NIGHT
DUTY-FREE DRINKS
DWELL ON THE PAST
DYING FOR A DRINK

E—14
EACH FOR HIMSELF
EARL OF HAREWOOD
EARLY BREAKFAST
EARLY VICTORIAN
EARN ONE'S LIVING
EARTH SATELLITE
EAR TO THE GROUND
EASE OF HANDLING
EASTER HOLIDAYS
EASTER OFFERING
EASTER VACATION
EASY COME, EASY GO
EASY CONSCIENCE
EASY IN ONE'S MIND
EAT ONE'S HEAD OFF
ECONOMIC CRISIS
ECONOMY OF WORDS
EDITORIAL CHAIR
EDITORIAL STAFF
EDUCATE THE MIND
EDUCATIONAL TOY
EDWARDIAN HOUSE
EFFICIENCY TEST
EIGHT AND A PENNY
EIGHT AND ELEVEN
EIGHTEEN AND SIX
EIGHTEEN AND TEN
EIGHTEEN AND TWO
EIGHTEENTH HOLE
EIGHTH OF AUGUST
EIGHTH SYMPHONY
EIGHT SHILLINGS
EIGHTY THOUSAND
ELABORATE STYLE
ELDERBERRY WINE
ELDER STATESMAN
ELDEST DAUGHTER
ELECTION RESULT
ELECTRICAL UNIT
ELECTRIC CHARGE
ELECTRIC COOKER
ELECTRIC GUITAR
ELECTRIC HEATER
ELECTRICITY CUT
ELECTRIC KETTLE
ELECTRIC SHAVER
ELECTRIC WASHER
ELEMENTARY RULE
ELEMENT OF DOUBT
ELEMENT OF TRUTH

ELEPHANT'S TRUNK
ELEVEN OR TWELVE
ELEVENTH LETTER
ELEVENTH OF JULY
ELEVENTH OF JUNE
ELEVEN THOUSAND
ELICIT THE TRUTH
ELIZABETHAN AGE
ELIZABETHAN ERA
ELIZA DOOLITTLE
ELLA FITZGERALD
ELOCUTION CLASS
ELOQUENT TONGUE
EMINENT SOLDIER
EMINENT SPEAKER
EMOTIONAL WRECK
EMPEROR OF JAPAN
EMPHATIC DENIAL
EMPIRE LOYALIST
EMPTY OF MEANING
EMPTY PLEASURES
ENCLOSE A CHEQUE
ENDEARING SMILE
ENDLESS PROBLEM
ENDLESS TROUBLE
END OF ALL THINGS
END OF THE MATTER
END OF THE STREET
ENDS OF THE EARTH
ENDURE TO THE END
ENEMY OF FREEDOM
ENEMY OF MANKIND
ENEMY TERRITORY
ENFANT TERRIBLE
ENGAGED IN TRADE
ENGAGEMENT RING
ENGAGE THE ENEMY
ENGAGING MANNER
ENGLISH BY BIRTH
ENGLISH CHANNEL
ENGLISH GRAMMAR
ENGLISH HISTORY
ENGLISH MUSTARD
ENGLISH TEACHER
ENIGMATIC SMILE
ENJOY ILL HEALTH
ENLARGE THE MIND
ENLIGHTENED AGE
ENORMOUS NUMBER
ENTERTAIN A HOPE
ENTER THE CHURCH

M.C.D.—14

ENTRECOTE STEAK
EQUABLE CLIMATE
EQUALLY DIVIDED
EQUAL THE RECORD
ERRATIC CONDUCT
ESCAPED CONVICT
ESPRESSO COFFEE
ETHEREAL BEAUTY
EUCALYPTUS TREE
EVADE DETECTION
EVAPORATED MILK
EVENING CLOTHES
EVENING SERVICE
EVERGREEN PLANT
EVERGREEN SHRUB
EVERY BIT AS MUCH
EVERY INCH A KING
EVERY SECOND DAY
EVERYTHING GOES
EVIDENCE ON OATH
EVIL REPUTATION
EXACTING MASTER
EXCEED THE LIMIT
EXCELLENT MARKS
EXCHANGE OF VOWS
EXCHANGE VISITS
EXCITABLE STATE
EXCURSION TRAIN
EXECUTION BLOCK
EXECUTIVE SUITE
EXERT AUTHORITY
EXHIBIT FEELING
EXPANSIVE SMILE
EXPENSE ACCOUNT
EXPLAIN ONESELF
EXPLODED BELIEF
EXPORT MERCHANT
EXPOSE TO DANGER
EXPRESS COMMAND
EXPRESS ONESELF
EXPRESS PURPOSE
EXPRESS REGRETS
EXPURGATED BOOK
EXQUISITE TASTE
EXTENDED CREDIT
EXTENSIVE FIELD
EXTENSIVE SALES
EXTINCT VOLCANO
EXTREME DISLIKE
EXTREME PENALTY
EXTREME POVERTY

EXTREME UNCTION
EYE FOR BUSINESS

F—14
FABULOUS WEALTH
FABULOUS WRITER
FACE OF THE GLOBE
FACE UP TO THINGS
FACT AND FICTION
FACTORY CHIMNEY
FACTS OF THE CASE
FAIL IN ONE'S DUTY
FAIL TO INTEREST
FAIR COMPARISON
FAIR COMPLEXION
FAIR TO MIDDLING
FAIR TO MODERATE
FAIRY GODMOTHER
FAITHFUL FRIEND
FAITHFUL REPORT
FAITHFUL SPOUSE
FALL DOWNSTAIRS
FALL INTO DISUSE
FALL ON EVIL DAYS
FALL ON ONE'S FEET
FALSE COLOURING
FALSE EYELASHES
FALSELY ACCUSED
FALSE MOUSTACHE
FALSE PRETENCES
FALSE REASONING
FALSE STATEMENT
FALTERING STEPS
FALTERING VOICE
FAME AND FORTUNE
FAMILIAR MANNER
FAMILIAR SPIRIT
FAMILY BUSINESS
FAMILY HEIRLOOM
FAMILY LIKENESS
FAMILY PORTRAIT
FAMILY RETAINER
FAMILY SKELETON
FANCY-DRESS BALL
FAREWELL SPEECH
FAREWELL TO ARMS
FAR-FLUNG EMPIRE
FARMING SUBSIDY
FAST AND FURIOUS
FATALLY WOUNDED

FATHER SUPERIOR
FAT-STOCK PRICES
FATUOUS ATTEMPT
FAVOURABLE WIND
FAVOURED PERSON
FAVOURITE PIECE
FEARLESS HITTER
FEAST OF STEPHEN
FEAT OF STRENGTH
FEATURE PICTURE
FEATURES EDITOR
FEDERAL COUNCIL
FEEL THE BENEFIT
FEEL THE DRAUGHT
FELLOW COMMONER
FELLOW CREATURE
FEMININE APPEAL
FEMININE GENDER
FEMME DE CHAMBRE
FEND FOR ONESELF
FEVERISH DESIRE
FICTITIOUS NAME
FIELD AMBULANCE
FIELD ARTILLERY
FIELD OF INQUIRY
FIELD TELEGRAPH
FIFTEEN AND FIVE
FIFTEEN AND FOUR
FIFTEEN AND NINE
FIFTEEN PER CENT
FIFTEENTH GREEN
FIFTEENTH OF MAY
FIFTEENTH ROUND
FIFTH COLUMNIST
FIFTH OF JANUARY
FIFTH OF OCTOBER
FIFTY-ONE AND SIX
FIFTY-SIX AND SIX
FIFTY-TWO AND SIX
FIGHTER COMMAND
FIGHTING CHANCE
FIGHTING SPIRIT
FIGHT TO A FINISH
FIGURE OF SPEECH
FILLETED PLAICE
FILLING STATION
FILL THE VACANCY
FILL UP THE RANKS
FILL WITH DISMAY
FILTHY LANGUAGE
FINAL INTENTION

FINAL RECKONING
FINANCIAL TIMES
FINANCIAL WORRY
FIND A PUBLISHER
FINDERS, KEEPERS
FIND THE MEANING
FINGER IN THE PIE
FINGERS AND TOES
FINGER'S BREADTH
FINIAN'S RAINBOW
FINISHING TOUCH
FINISH STRONGLY
FINITE QUANTITY
FIRE A BROADSIDE
FIRE DEPARTMENT
FIREMAN'S HELMET
FIREMAN'S LADDER
FIRE PROTECTION
FIRM CONVICTION
FIRM FOUNDATION
FIRM GOVERNMENT
FIRM IMPRESSION
FIRM MANAGEMENT
FIRM OPPOSITION
FIRST AND SECOND
FIRST-BORN CHILD
FIRST CHRISTMAS
FIRST-CLASS FARE
FIRST-CLASS IDEA
FIRST-CLASS SHOT
FIRST CONDITION
FIRST-FLOOR FLAT
FIRST INTENTION
FIRST MAGNITUDE
FIRST OF JANUARY
FIRST OF OCTOBER
FIRST ON THE LIST
FIRST PRINCIPLE
FIRST-RATE ACTOR
FIRST SECRETARY
FIRST TIME LUCKY
FIRST TIME ROUND
FIRST VIOLINIST
FISHERMAN'S YARN
FISHING LICENCE
FISHING VILLAGE ,
FISH OUT OF WATER
FIT OF GIDDINESS
FIT THE OCCASION
FIVE-BARRED GATE
FIVE-DOLLAR BILL

FIVE OF DIAMONDS
FIVEPENNY STAMP
FIXED ALLOWANCE
FLAG LIEUTENANT
FLAG OF DISTRESS
FLASHING STREAM
FLAT AS A PANCAKE
FLAT ON ONE'S BACK
FLAT ON ONE'S FACE
FLATTER ONESELF
FLEE THE COUNTRY
FLEETING GLANCE
FLIGHT OF STAIRS
FLIGHT SERGEANT
FLIPPANT SPEECH
FLOATING BRIDGE
FLOATING KIDNEY
FLOATING PALACE
FLOCK OF PIGEONS
FLOG A DEAD HORSE
FLOOD WITH LIGHT
FLOWERING PLANT
FLOWERING SHRUB
FLUSH OF TRIUMPH
FLUSH WITH ANGER
FLUSH WITH MONEY
FLY FOR ONE'S LIFE
FLYING BEDSTEAD
FLYING BUTTRESS
FLYING DUTCHMAN
FLYING FORTRESS
FLYING SCOTSMAN
FLYING SQUIRREL
FLY INTO A TEMPER
FLY TO THE RESCUE
FLY-WEIGHT TITLE
FOAM AT THE MOUTH
FOLD UP ONE'S TENT
FOLLOW A CALLING
FOLLOW A PATTERN
FOLLOW MY LEADER
FOLLOW ONE'S NOSE
FOLLOW THE CROWD
FOLLOW THE SCENT
FOLLOW THE TRAIL
FOOD CONTROLLER
FOOD FOR THE GODS
FOOD FOR THE MIND
FOOD FOR THOUGHT
FOOD PRODUCTION

FOOTBALL COUPON
FOOTBALL GROUND
FOOTBALL LEAGUE
FOOTBALL PLAYER
FOOTBALL SEASON
FOR ALL THE WORLD
FORBIDDEN FRUIT
FORBID THE BANNS
FORCED MARRIAGE
FORCE OF GRAVITY
FORCIBLE DEMAND
FOREIGN AFFAIRS
FOREIGN CAPITAL
FOREIGN COUNTRY
FOREIGN SERVICE
FOREIGN STATION
FOR EVER AND A DAY
FOR EVER AND EVER
FOR HEAVEN'S SAKE!
FOR LOVE OR MONEY
FORMAL APPROACH
FORMAL OCCASION
FORMAL SANCTION
FORM AN ESTIMATE
FORMATIVE YEARS
FORMIDABLE TASK
FOR THE DURATION
FOR THE LAST TIME
FOR THE LIFE OF ME
FOR THE MOST PART
FORTUNATE EVENT
FOR WANT OF A NAIL
FOSTER DAUGHTER
FOUNDER'S SHARES
FOUR-DOOR SALOON
FOUR-LEAF CLOVER
FOUR LETTER WORD
FOUR-MASTED SHIP
FOUR-MILE RADIUS
FOUR-MINUTE MILE
FOUR OF DIAMONDS
FOURPENNY STAMP
FOURTEEN OUNCES
FOURTEEN POUNDS
FOURTEENTH HOLE
FOURTH DIVIDEND
FOURTH DIVISION
FOURTH OF AUGUST
FOURTH SYMPHONY
FRACTIONAL PART

FRAGRANT MEMORY
FRAIL STRUCTURE
FRANKIE VAUGHAN
FRANK STATEMENT
FREEDOM FROM WAR
FREE ENTERPRISE
FREE FROM DANGER
FREEMASONS' HALL
FREE OF INTEREST
FREEZING MANNER
FRENCH CANADIAN
FRENCH DRESSING
FRENCH LANGUAGE
FRENCH POLISHER
FRENCH VERMOUTH
FRESHWATER FISH
FREUDIAN SCHOOL
FRIENDLY ACTION
FRIENDLY CRITIC
FRIENDLY DEBATE
FRIENDLY NATION
FRIGHTFUL SIGHT
FROM BAD TO WORSE
FROM BANK TO BANK
FROM EAST TO WEST
FROM HAND TO HAND
FROM HEAD TO FOOT
FROM SIDE TO SIDE
FROM THE CONTEXT
FROM TIME TO TIME
FROM WALL TO WALL
FRONT ELEVATION
FRONT-PAGE STORY
FROTH AND BUBBLE
FROZEN SHOULDER
FULFIL A PROMISE
FULHAM BROADWAY
FULL COMPLEMENT
FULL DIRECTIONS
FULL EMPLOYMENT
FULL MEMBERSHIP
FULL OF INTEREST
FULL OF MISCHIEF
FULL OF NONSENSE
FULL OF VITALITY
FULL-SCALE MODEL
FULL SETTLEMENT
FULL SPEED AHEAD
FULL STEAM AHEAD
FULL TO CAPACITY

FULLY CONSCIOUS
FULLY DEVELOPED
FULLY FASHIONED
FULLY FURNISHED
FUNERAL ORATION
FUNERAL PARLOUR
FUNNY PROGRAMME
FUR-LINED GLOVES
FURNISHED HOUSE
FURNISH SUPPORT
FURNITURE STORE
FURTHER DETAILS
FURTHER OUTLOOK

G—14

GAIN ADMITTANCE
GAIN CONFIDENCE
GAIN EXPERIENCE
GAIN POSSESSION
GAINS AND LOSSES
GAIN THE MASTERY
GAIN THE VICTORY
GALLANT COMPANY
GALLANT SOLDIER
GALLOPING MAJOR
GALVANIZED IRON
GAMBLING CHANCE
GAME OF DRAUGHTS
GAME OF SKITTLES
GARBLED VERSION
GARGANTUAN MEAL
GARLAND OF ROSES
GATHERING STORM
GATHER MOMENTUM
GATHER STRENGTH
GATHER TOGETHER
GATWICK AIRPORT
GENERAL AMNESTY
GENERAL BENEFIT
GENERAL CONSENT
GENERAL COUNCIL
GENERAL MANAGER
GENERAL MEETING
GENERAL OFFICER
GENERAL OUTLINE
GENERAL OUTLOOK
GENERAL POVERTY
GENERAL RELEASE
GENERAL ROUTINE
GENERAL SERVANT

GENERAL SERVICE
GENERAL SURGEON
GENERAL SURGERY
GENERAL WARRANT
GENEROUS AMOUNT
GENEROUS NATURE
GENEROUS PRAISE
GENEROUS SPIRIT
GENIE OF THE LAMP
GENTLE BREEDING
GENTLE HANDLING
GENTLEMAN CROOK
GENTLEMAN'S CODE
GENTLEMAN USHER
GENTLE REMINDER
GENUINE ARTICLE
GENUINE EXAMPLE
GENUINE RESPECT
GEORGE BRADSHAW
GEORGE GERSHWIN
GEORGE HARRISON
GEORGE MEREDITH
GEORGE MITCHELL
GEORGES SIMENON
GERMAN LANGUAGE
GET AN EXTENSION
GET INTO TROUBLE
GET IT IN THE NECK
GET OFF SCOT-FREE
GET ONE'S DESERTS
GET ONE'S FEET WET
GET ONE'S OWN BACK
GET OUT OF THE WAY
GET THE BEST OF IT
GET THE BETTER OF
GET THE BREEZE UP
GET THE HANG OF IT
GET THE WHIP-HAND
GHASTLY MISTAKE
GHOST OF A CHANCE
GIANT REFRESHED
GIANT'S CAUSEWAY
GIFTED COMPOSER
GILBERT HARDING
GIMCRACK STAKES
GINGERBREAD MAN
GIRD UP THE LOINS
GIRL IN A MILLION
GIVE A MAN HIS DUE
GIVE AN INSTANCE
GIVE ASSISTANCE

GIVE ASSURANCES
GIVE FULL CREDIT
GIVE GENEROUSLY
GIVE IN MARRIAGE
GIVE IT A THOUGHT
GIVEN A REPRIEVE
GIVE ONE A ROCKET
GIVE ONE HIS HEAD
GIVE ONE'S ASSENT
GIVE ONE THE BIRD
GIVE ONE THE PUSH
GIVE ONE THE SLIP
GIVE PERMISSION
GIVE THE GLAD EYE
GIVE TO THE WORLD
GIVE UP DRINKING
GIVE UP ONE'S SEAT
GIVE UP THE GHOST
GLAMOROUS NIGHT
GLARING MISTAKE
GLASGOW RANGERS
GLEAMING ARMOUR
GLOBE ARTICHOKE
GLOOMY FORECAST
GLOOMY PROSPECT
GLORIOUS MUDDLE
GLORIOUS SUNSET
GLOSSY MAGAZINE
GLOWING ACCOUNT
GLOWING COLOURS
GLOW WITH HEALTH
GLUTTON FOR FOOD
GLUTTON FOR WORK
GNASH ONE'S TEETH
GO DOWN FIGHTING
GOD SAVE THE KING!
GOD'S OWN COUNTRY
GOING! GOING! GONE!
GOING GREAT GUNS
GOING TO THE DOGS
GO INTO HOSPITAL
GO INTO MOURNING
GO INTO RAPTURES
GOLDEN PHEASANT
GOLDEN TREASURY
GOLDSMITHS' HALL
GOLF TOURNAMENT
GO LIKE HOT CAKES
GONE BY THE BOARD
GONE FOR A BURTON
GOOD BACKGROUND

GOOD-BYE MR. CHIPS
GOOD COMPANIONS
GOOD COMPARISON
GOOD COMPLEXION
GOOD CONSCIENCE
GOOD DISCIPLINE
GOOD FELLOWSHIP
GOOD FOR NOTHING
GOOD FOR THE SOUL
GOOD FOUNDATION
GOOD IMPRESSION
GOOD INTENTIONS
GOOD INVESTMENT
GOOD LITERATURE
GOOD MANAGEMENT
GOOD NEIGHBOURS
GOOD REPUTATION
GOOD RESOLUTION
GOODS IN TRANSIT
GOOD TIME-KEEPER
GOOD UPBRINGING
GO OFF LIKE A BOMB
GO OFF THE HANDLE
GOOSEBERRY BUSH
GOOSEBERRY FOOL
GO OUT OF ONE'S WAY
GORDON RICHARDS
GO TO ANY LENGTHS
GO TO CONFESSION
GO TO THE COUNTRY
GO TO THE SEASIDE
GO TO THE THEATRE
GO UP IN THE WORLD
GOVERNMENT LOAN
GOVERNMENT POST
GOVERNMENT WHIP
GO WEST, YOUNG MAN
GO WITH THE TIMES
GRACE AND FAVOUR
GRACIOUS LIVING
GRADUAL DECLINE
GRADUATED SCALE
GRAIN OF COMFORT
GRAIN OF MUSTARD
GRAND COMMITTEE
GRAND CONDITION
GRANDSTAND VIEW
GRAPHIC ACCOUNT
GRAPHIC DRAWING
GRASP THE NETTLE
GRAVE ADMISSION

GRAVE SITUATION
GRAVE STATEMENT
GRAVE SUSPICION
GRAVEYARD COUGH
GREASE ONE'S PALM
GREAT BED OF WARE
GREAT IGNORANCE
GREAT INJUSTICE
GREAT IN STATURE
GREAT NORTH ROAD
GREAT RECEPTION
GREAT SACRIFICE
GREAT SCOUNDREL
GREAT STATESMAN
GREAT VARIATION
GRECIAN PROFILE
GREEN LINE COACH
GREEN VEGETABLE
GRENADIER GUARD
GREYHOUND DERBY
GREYHOUND TRACK
GRIND ONE'S TEETH
GRIST TO THE MILL
GROCER'S COMPANY
GROPE IN THE DARK
GROSS INJUSTICE
GROSVENOR HOUSE
GROUND LANDLORD
GROUNDLESS FEAR
GROUSE SHOOTING
GROWING ANXIETY
GROW UP TOGETHER
GROW VEGETABLES
GRUB STREET HACK
GRUDGING PRAISE
GUERRILLA CHIEF
GUERRILLA FORCE
GUESS THE ANSWER
GUEST CELEBRITY
GUIDED BY REASON
GUILTY OF MURDER
GUN EMPLACEMENT
GURKHA REGIMENT
GUTTURAL ACCENT
GUTTURAL SPEECH

H—14
HACKNEY MARSHES
HALF A SOVEREIGN
HALF-DAY HOLIDAY
HALF-MOON STREET

HALFPENNY STAMP
HALF-SPOKEN WORD
HALLÉ ORCHESTRA
HALLOWEEN PARTY
HALT FOR A MOMENT
HAMMER AND TONGS
HAMPSTEAD HEATH
HAND EMBROIDERY
HANDLE TENDERLY
HANDLE WITH CARE
HAND ON THE TORCH
HANDSOME MARGIN
HANDSOME PROFIT
HANGING GARDENS
HANG OUT A SIGNAL
HANG THE EXPENSE
HAPPILY MARRIED
HAPPY CHILDHOOD
HAPPY CHRISTMAS
HARBOUR REVENGE
HARD DISCIPLINE
HARDENED SINNER
HARDLY ANYTHING
HARDLY CREDIBLE
HARD NUT TO CRACK
HARD TASKMASTER
HARD TO CONVINCE
HARD TO DESCRIBE
HARRY BELAFONTE
HARSH TREATMENT
HAUNTING MELODY
HAVE A GOOD NIGHT
HAVE A SUSPICION
HAVE COMPASSION
HAVE CONFIDENCE
HAVE IT BOTH WAYS
HAVE MISGIVINGS
HAVE NO SCRUPLES
HAVE ONE'S DOUBTS
HAVE ONE'S OWN WAY
HAVE THE COURAGE
HAVE THE KNOW-HOW
HEAD ABOVE WATER
HEADACHE POWDER
HEAD FOR FIGURES
HEAD FOR HEIGHTS
HEADLONG FLIGHT
HEAD OF THE HOUSE
HEAD OF THE RIVER
HEAD OF THE TABLE
HEALTHY OUTLOOK

HEALTHY RESPECT
HEART CONDITION
HEART OF ENGLAND
HEARTY APPETITE
HEARTY APPROVAL
HEARTY LAUGHTER
HEATED ARGUMENT
HEATHER MIXTURE
HEAVEN AND EARTH
HEAVIER THAN AIR
HEAVY ARTILLERY
HEAVY TRANSPORT
HEAVY WITH SLEEP
HEEL OF ACHILLES
HEIGHT OF GENIUS
HEIGHT OF SUMMER
HEIR TO A FORTUNE
HELD IN CONTEMPT
HELL-FIRE CORNER
HELL FOR LEATHER
HELL HATH NO FURY
HELPLESS VICTIM
HELP ONE ANOTHER
HEMEL HEMPSTEAD
HENLEY ON THAMES
HENRY KISSINGER
HENRY THE EIGHTH
HENRY THE FOURTH
HENRY THE SECOND
HERALDIC COLOUR
HERALDIC DEVICE
HERALDIC SHIELD
HERALD'S COLLEGE
HERBERT SPENCER
HEREFORD CASTLE
HERO AND LEANDER
HIDDEN TREASURE
HIGH AS A STEEPLE
HIGH CASUALTIES
HIGH CHANCELLOR
HIGH COMMISSION
HIGH COURT JUDGE
HIGH IN THE SCALE
HIGHLAND CATTLE
HIGH-LEVEL TALKS
HIGHLY EDUCATED
HIGHLY ESTEEMED
HIGHLY ORIGINAL
HIGHLY POLISHED
HIGHLY POSSIBLE
HIGHLY SEASONED

HIGH PERCENTAGE
HIGHWAY ROBBERY
HIP MEASUREMENT
HISTORICAL PLAY
HISTORICAL WORK
HISTORIC MOMENT
HISTORY TEACHER
HIT OVER THE HEAD
HIVE OF ACTIVITY
HIVE OF INDUSTRY
HOB-NAILED BOOTS
HOLD AN ARGUMENT
HOLD AN ELECTION
HOLD EVERYTHING
HOLD IN ABEYANCE
HOLD IN CONTEMPT
HOLDING COMPANY
HOLDING QUALITY
HOLD IN SUSPENSE
HOLD ONE'S BREATH
HOLD ONE'S GROUND
HOLD ONE'S HEAD UP
HOLD ONE'S HORSES
HOLD ONE'S TONGUE
HOLD UP ONE'S HEAD
HOLIDAY TRAFFIC
HOLIDAY WITH PAY
HOLIER THAN THOU
HOLLOWAY PRISON
HOLLOW LAUGHTER
HOLLOW PRETENCE
HOME DEPARTMENT
HOMELESS PERSON
HOME ON THE RANGE
HOMES FOR HEROES
HONEYMOON HOTEL
HONORARY DEGREE
HONORARY FELLOW
HONORARY MEMBER
HONORARY STATUS
HONOUR AND GLORY
HOPE AND BELIEVE
HOPE FOR THE BEST
HOPELESS MISFIT
HOP, SKIP AND JUMP
HORIZONTAL BARS
HORIZONTAL LINE
HORSE AND HOUNDS
HORSE ARTILLERY
HORSE OF THE YEAR
HOSPITAL ANNEXE

HOSPITAL MATRON
HOSPITAL SUNDAY
HOSTILE COUNTRY
HOSTILE VERDICT
HOSTILE WITNESS
HOT-AIR MERCHANT
HOT AND BOTHERED
HOTEL DETECTIVE
HOTLY CONTESTED
HOT ON ONE'S HEELS
HOT ON ONE'S TRAIL
HOT-WATER BOTTLE
HOT-WATER SUPPLY
HOT-WATER SYSTEM
HOUSE DECORATOR
HOUSE DETECTIVE
HOUSEHOLD GOODS
HOUSEHOLD LINEN
HOUSEHOLD STAFF
HOUSEMAID'S KNEE
HOUSE OF COMMONS
HOUSE OF HANOVER
HOUSE OF ONE'S OWN
HOUSE OF THE LORD
HOUSE OF WINDSOR
HOUSE OF WORSHIP
HOUSE PHYSICIAN
HOUSING PROBLEM
HOUSING PROJECT
HOWLING DERVISH
HOWLING SUCCESS
HOW THE LAND LIES
HUMAN ENDEAVOUR
HUMAN RELATIONS
HUMAN SACRIFICE
HUMAN SUFFERING
HUMBLE DWELLING
HUMBLE PETITION
HUMPBACK BRIDGE
HUMPHREY BOGART
HUNDRED DOLLARS
HUNDRED GUINEAS
HUNDRED PER CENT
HUNT HIGH AND LOW
HUNT THE SLIPPER
HUNT THE THIMBLE
HURT EXPRESSION
HUSBAND AND WIFE
HYDE PARK CORNER
HYDE PARK ORATOR
HYDRAULIC POWER

HYDRAULIC PRESS
HYPHENATED WORD
HYPNOTIC TRANCE

I—14
ICE-CREAM CORNET
ICE-CREAM SUNDAE
IDEAL COMPANION
IDENTICAL TWINS
IDENTITY PARADE
IGNOMINIOUS END
IGNORANT MASSES
IGNORANT PERSON
ILLEGAL TRAFFIC
ILL-GOTTEN GAINS
ILL-TIMED REMARK
IMAGINARY POINT
IMMEDIATE REPLY
IMMEMORIAL ELMS
IMMINENT DANGER
IMMORAL CONDUCT
IMMOVABLE FEAST
IMPART MOMENTUM
IMPENDING STORM
IMPERATIVE MOOD
IMPERFECT RHYME
IMPERFECT TENSE
IMPERIAL BALLET
IMPERIAL GALLON
IMPERIAL PURPLE
IMPERIAL WEIGHT
IMPLACABLE MOOD
IMPLIED CONSENT
IMPORTANT EVENT
IMPOSING FIGURE
IMPOSSIBLE TASK
IMPROPER PERSON
IMPROVE MATTERS
IMPROVE ONESELF
IMPUDENT CHARGE
IMPUDENT SPEECH
IMPURE THOUGHTS
IN A LITTLE WHILE
IN ALL INNOCENCE
IN A MORTAL HURRY
IN ANCIENT TIMES
IN ANOTHER CLASS
IN ANTICIPATION
IN A STATE OF FLUX
INCENDIARY BOMB
IN CERTAIN CASES

INCLINE ONE'S EAR
INCLUSIVE TERMS
INCOMING TENANT
IN COURSE OF TIME
INCREASED FARES
INCREASED SPEED
IN DEEP MOURNING
INDEFINITE TIME
INDEPENDENT AIR
INDIAN ELEPHANT
INDICATIVE MOOD
IN DIFFICULTIES
INDIRECT EFFECT
INDIRECT METHOD
INDIRECT OBJECT
INDIRECT SPEECH
INDUSTRIAL AREA
INDUSTRAIL ARTS
IN EVERY QUARTER
IN EVERY RESPECT
INEXORABLE FATE
INFERIOR NATURE
INFERIOR STATUS
INFINITE NUMBER
INFORMAL SPEECH
INFRINGE THE LAW
INGRAINED HABIT
INITIAL ATTEMPT
INITIAL EXPENSE
INITIATIVE TEST
INJURED HUSBAND
INLAND WATERWAY
IN LOCO PARENTIS
INMOST THOUGHTS
INNERMOST BEING
INNER SANCTUARY
INNINGS VICTORY
INNOCENT ABROAD
INNOCENT REMARK
INNOCENT VICTIM
INNS OF CHANCERY
IN ONE'S BORN DAYS
IN ONE'S MIND'S EYE
IN ONE'S OWN LIGHT
IN ONE'S OWN RIGHT
IN ORDER OF MERIT
IN RELATIONSHIP
IN ROUND NUMBERS
INSIDE POSITION
IN SOUTH AMERICA
INSPIRE RESPECT

INSTANT DISLIKE
INSULATED CABLE
INSULTING WORDS
INSULT TO INJURY
INSURANCE AGENT
INSURANCE CLAIM
INTENSE DISLIKE
INTENSE FEELING
INTENSE LONGING
INTENSIVE STUDY
INTERESTED LOOK
INTERNAL STRIFE
INTERNMENT CAMP
INTERVAL OF TIME
IN THE AFTERNOON
IN THE AGGREGATE
IN THE ASCENDANT
IN THE BEGINNING
IN THE FIRM'S TIME
IN THE FOREFRONT
IN THE HEADLINES
IN THE LIMELIGHT
IN THE MEANWHILE
IN THE MOONLIGHT
IN THE MOUNTAINS
IN THE NEWSPAPER
IN THE NEXT WORLD
IN THE ORCHESTRA
IN THE PROVINCES
IN THE PUBLIC EYE
IN THE SAME CLASS
IN THE THICK OF IT
INTIMATE CIRCLE
INTIMATE FRIEND
INTO A COCKED HAT
INTO THE BARGAIN
INTRINSIC VALUE
INTRINSIC WORTH
INTRODUCE A BILL
INVARIABLE RULE
INVENT AN EXCUSE
INVERTED COMMAS
INVETERATE LIAR
INVINCIBLE ARMY
INVITE A QUARREL
INVITE RIDICULE
IRISH FREE STATE
IRISH PEASANTRY
IRONS IN THE FIRE
IRREGULAR UNION
ISLAND IN THE SUN

ISLAND PARADISE
IT'S A SMALL WORLD

J—14

JACK OF DIAMONDS
JACOBITE RISING
JAYNE MANSFIELD
JEALOUS HUSBAND
JESSIE MATTHEWS
JIMMINY CRICKET
JOAN SUTHERLAND
JOBS FOR THE BOYS
JOHN BARLEYCORN
JOHN BROWN'S BODY
JOHN DRINKWATER
JOHN GALSWORTHY
JOHN LOGIE BAIRD
JOHN THE BAPTIST
JOIN IN MARRIAGE
JOINT COMMITTEE
JOIN THE COLOURS
JOIN THE RAT-RACE
JOINT LIABILITY
JOINT OWNERSHIP
JOINT-STOCK BANK
JOSHUA REYNOLDS
JUDE THE OBSCURE
JUDICIAL MANNER
JUDICIAL MURDER
JUDICIAL NOTICE
JULIAN CALENDAR
JULY THE SEVENTH
JULY THE TWELFTH
JUMPING CRACKER
JUNE THE SEVENTH
JUNE THE TWELFTH
JUNIOR REPORTER
JUPITER PLUVIUS

K—14

KEEP A GOOD TABLE
KEEP A TIGHT REIN
KEEP EARLY HOURS
KEEP IN SUSPENSE
KEEP IN THE SHADE
KEEP ONE'S CHIN UP
KEEP ONE'S FIGURE
KEEP ONE'S HAIR ON
KEEP ONE'S HAND IN
KEEP ONE'S SENSES
KEEP ONE'S TEMPER

KEEP OUT OF SIGHT
KEEP STRAIGHT ON
KEEP THE COLD OUT
KEEP TO THE RIGHT
KEEP TO THE RULES
KEEP UNDER COVER
KEEP WELL IN HAND
KENSINGTON GORE
KEPT IN HIS PLACE
KEYSTONE COMEDY
KIDNEY AND BACON
KIDNEY POTATOES
KILLED IN ACTION
KINDLY INTEREST
KING AND COUNTRY
KING ARTHUR'S MEN
KING OF DIAMONDS
KING'S MESSENGER
KITCHEN CABINET
KITCHEN DRESSER
KITCHEN UTENSIL
KNIGHT IN ARMOUR
KNIGHTS OF MALTA
KNITTING NEEDLE
KNIVES AND FORKS
KNOCK-ABOUT TURN
KNOCK AT THE DOOR
KNOCK-DOWN PRICE
KNOCK INTO SHAPE
KNOCK ON THE DOOR
KNOCK ON THE HEAD
KNOW A MOVE OR TWO
KNOW BY INSTINCT
KNOW FOR CERTAIN
KNOWLEDGE OF LAW
KNOWN CHARACTER
KNOW ONE'S ONIONS
KNOW WHEN TO STOP

L—14
LABOUR EXCHANGE
LABOUR MAJORITY
LABOUR MINORITY
LABOUR MOVEMENT
LABOUR THE POINT
LACK OF EVIDENCE
LACK OF FRICTION
LACK OF INTEREST
LACK OF JUDGMENT
LACK OF PRACTICE
LACK OF STRENGTH

LACK OF SYMPATHY
LACK OF TRAINING
LACRIMA CHRISTI
LADY CHATTERLEY
LADY OF THE HOUSE
LADY OF THE MANOR
LADY WINDERMERE
LAID BY THE HEELS
LAID ON THE SHELF
LAKE WINDERMERE
LAME CONCLUSION
LANCASTER HOUSE
LAND COMMISSION
LANDED INTEREST
LANDED PROPERTY
LAND OF NO RETURN
LAND ON ONE'S FEET
LANGUAGE MASTER
LANTERN LECTURE
LARGE OVERDRAFT
LARGER THAN LIFE
LASSIES AND LADS
LAST APPEARANCE
LAST CONNECTION
LAST GENERATION
LASTING BENEFIT
LASTING QUALITY
LASTING SUCCESS
LAST INSTALMENT
LAST IN THE QUEUE
LATE NIGHT FINAL
LATEST BULLETIN
LATH AND PLASTER
LATTER-DAY SAINT
LAUGHING MATTER
LAUNCH AN ATTACK
LAUNCHING STAGE
LAUREL AND HARDY
LAURENCE HARVEY
LAURENCE STERNE
LAW ENFORCEMENT
LAWFUL OCCASION
LAW OF THE JUNGLE
LAY DOWN A CELLAR
LAY ON TRANSPORT
LEADING ACTRESS
LEADING ARTICLE
LEADING CITIZEN
LEADING COUNSEL
LEADING STRINGS
LEAD THE FASHION

LEAD TO THE ALTAR
LEAGUE FOOTBALL
LEAPS AND BOUNDS
LEARNED COUNSEL
LEARNED SOCIETY
LEASEHOLD HOUSE
LEAVE A LOOPHOLE
LEAVE DESTITUTE
LEAVE NO ADDRESS
LEAVE OF ABSENCE
LEAVE SENSELESS
LEAVE THE GROUND
LEAVE WELL ALONE
LEDA AND THE SWAN
LEEWARD ISLANDS
LEFT HIGH AND DRY
LEFT IN THE LURCH
LEFT SPEECHLESS
LEFT UNFINISHED
LEGAL AUTHORITY
LEGAL CHICANERY
LEGAL ETIQUETTE
LEGAL FORMALITY
LEGAL LIABILITY
LEGALLY BINDING
LEGAL OWNERSHIP
LEGAL PROCEDURE
LEGION OF HONOUR
LEMONADE POWDER
LEMONADE SHANDY
LENDING LIBRARY
LEND ME YOUR EARS
LESLIE MITCHELL
LET DOWN LIGHTLY
LET DOWN THE SIDE
LET OR HINDRANCE
LETTER OF ADVICE
LETTER OF CREDIT
LETTER OF THE LAW
LET THE SIDE DOWN
LET THINGS SLIDE
LETTRE DE CACHET
LIAISON OFFICER
LIBERAL HELPING
LIBRARY EDITION
LICK ONE'S WOUNDS
LICK THE PLATTER
LIFE EXPECTANCY
LIFELONG FRIEND
LIFE OF PLEASURE
LIFE WITH FATHER

LIFT UP ONE'S HEAD
LIGHT AND BITTER
LIGHT ARTILLERY
LIGHT BREAKFAST
LIGHTEN THE LOAD
LIGHTER THAN AIR
LIGHT FANTASTIC
LIGHTING-UP TIME
LIGHTNING FLASH
LIGHTNING SPEED
LIGHT PROGRAMME
LIGHTS OF LONDON
LIGHT TRANSPORT
LIKE A BOMBSHELL
LIKE A MILLSTONE
LILY-WHITE HANDS
LIMITED COMPANY
LIMITED EDITION
LIMITING FACTOR
LINE OF APPROACH
LINE OF BUSINESS
LINGERING DEATH
LINK IN THE CHAIN
LION OF THE NORTH
LISLE STOCKINGS
LISTEN TO REASON
LIST OF CONTENTS
LITERAL ACCOUNT
LITERAL MEANING
LITERARY CRITIC
LITERARY DIGEST
LITERARY EDITOR
LITERARY OUTPUT
LITTLE AND OFTEN
LITTLE BROWN JUG
LITTLE BY LITTLE
LITTLE CHILDREN
LITTLE CORPORAL
LITTLE DISTANCE
LITTLE IN COMMON
LITTLE INTEREST
LITTLE LEARNING
LITTLE PITCHERS
LITTLE PROGRESS
LITTLE RESPONSE
LITTLE STRANGER
LIVE A CLEAN LIFE
LIVE AMMUNITION
LIVE AND LET LIVE
LIVE ON ONE'S WITS
LIVER AND ONIONS

LIVE TO A HUNDRED
LIVING LANGUAGE
LIVING QUARTERS
LIVING REMINDER
LIVING STANDARD
LLOYD'S REGISTER
LOADED QUESTION
LOAD ON ONE'S MIND
LOAD WITH CHAINS
LOCAL AUTHORITY
LOCAL NEWSPAPER
LOFTY AMBITIONS
LOGICAL CONDUCT
LOGICAL PROCESS
LONDONDERRY AIR
LONDON HOSPITAL
LONDON REGIMENT
LONDON RHAPSODY
LONDON SCOTTISH
LONDON TERMINUS
LONG ENGAGEMENT
LONGHAND WRITER
LONG IN THE TOOTH
LONG JOHN SILVER
LONG-LOST FRIEND
LONG PARLIAMENT
LONG-TERM POLICY
LOOK FOR TROUBLE
LOOK IN THE GLASS
LOOK ON ALL SIDES
LOOK PROSPEROUS
LOOK TO THE FRONT
LOOSE BEHAVIOUR
LOOSE RENDERING
LORD CHANCELLOR
LORD LIEUTENANT
LORD MAYOR'S SHOW
LORD OF CREATION
LORD OF THE ISLES
LORD OF THE MANOR
LORD PALMERSTON
LORDS AND LADIES
LORDS SPIRITUAL
LORD'S TAVERNERS
LOSE CONFIDENCE
LOSE ONE'S MEMORY
LOSE ONE'S REASON
LOSE ONE'S TEMPER
LOSE ONE'S TICKET
LOSE ONE'S TONGUE
LOSS OF APPETITE

LOSS OF INTEREST
LOSS OF PRESTIGE
LOSS OF STRENGTH
LOST TO THE WORLD
LOT TO ANSWER FOR
LOUIS ARMSTRONG
LOVE IN A COTTAGE
LOVE IN IDLENESS
LOVELY TO LOOK AT
LOVE OF PLEASURE
LOVING KINDNESS
LOWER ONE'S VOICE
LOW TEMPERATURE
LOYAL SUPPORTER
LUBRICATING OIL
LUCK OF THE DEVIL
LUCK OF THE IRISH
LUCREZIA BORGIA
LUNATIC AT LARGE
LUNCHEON BASKET
LUNCH-TIME SCORE
LYON KING OF ARMS
LYTTON STRACHEY
M—14
MACARONI CHEESE
MACHINE-GUN POST
MADAM BUTTERFLY
MADAM POMPADOUR
MADE FOR THE PART
MAGNETIC NEEDLE
MAGNOLIA STREET
MAIL VAN ROBBERY
MAIN ATTRACTION
MAIN INGREDIENT
MAINTENANCE MAN
MAJOR OPERATION
MAJOR ROAD AHEAD
MAKE A BEGINNING
MAKE A BIG SPLASH
MAKE A BOLT FOR IT
MAKE A COMPLAINT
MAKE A DISCOVERY
MAKE A GOOD GUESS
MAKE A GOOD SCORE
MAKE A GOOD START
MAKE ALLOWANCES
MAKE AN ENTRANCE
MAKE AN ESTIMATE
MAKE A NIGHT OF IT
MAKE A REFERENCE
MAKE A STATEMENT

MAKE DELIVERIES
MAKE EXCEPTIONS
MAKE FEW DEMANDS
MAKE FOR THE DOOR
MAKE NO PROGRESS
MAKE PROVISIONS
MAKE REPARATION
MAKE RINGS ROUND
MAKE SACRIFICES
MAKE THE RUNNING
MAKE THINGS EASY
MAKE UP A QUARREL
MAKE UP ONE'S MIND
MALCOLM SARGENT
MALE VOICE CHOIR
MANAGING EDITOR
MAN AND SUPERMAN
MANCHESTER CITY
MANDARIN ORANGE
MAN-EATING SHARK
MAN IN THE STREET
MAN OF CHARACTER
MAN OF INFLUENCE
MAN OF MANY PARTS
MAN OF SUBSTANCE
MAN OF THE MOMENT
MAN OF THE PEOPLE
MAN ON HORSEBACK
MAN'S BEST FRIEND
MAN THE DEFENCES
MANUAL LABOURER
MAPPIN TERRACES
MARATHON RUNNER
MARCHING ORDERS
MARCH THE EIGHTH
MARCH THE FOURTH
MARCH THE SECOND
MARCUS ANTONIUS
MARCUS AURELIUS
MARGIN OF ERROR
MARGIN OF PROFIT
MARGIN OF SAFETY
MARINE ENGINEER
MARITIME NATION
MARKED TENDENCY
MARKET GARDENER
MARKETING BOARD
MARKET RESEARCH
MARK OF APPROVAL
MARK OF THE BEAST
MARK OUT A COURSE

MARRIAGE BROKER
MARRIAGE BUREAU
MARRIAGE MARKET
MARSUPIAL POUCH
MASHED POTATOES
MASS PRODUCTION
MASTERMAN READY
MASTER OF HOUNDS
MATCH FOR ANYONE
MATERIAL WEALTH
MATRON OF HONOUR
MATTER OF CHOICE
MATTER OF COURSE
MATTER OF RECORD
MATTER OF REGRET
MATTERS OF STATE
MAUNDY THURSDAY
MAY THE ELEVENTH
MEANS OF SUPPORT
MECHANISED ARMY
MEDICAL ADVISER
MEDICAL COLLEGE
MEDICAL HISTORY
MEDICAL OFFICER
MEDICAL SCIENCE
MEDICAL STUDENT
MEDICINAL VALUE
MEDICINE BOTTLE
MEERSCHAUM PIPE
MELT IN THE MOUTH
MEMBER OF THE BAR
MEMBERSHIP CARD
MENDICANT ORDER
MENTAL ATTITUDE
MENTAL CAPACITY
MENTAL CONFLICT
MENTAL DISORDER
MENTAL EXERCISE
MENTAL HOSPITAL
MENTAL SICKNESS
MENTAL STIMULUS
MENTAL STRUGGLE
MENTAL WEAKNESS
MERCHANT BANKER
MERCHANT PRINCE
MERCHANT SEAMAN
MERCHANT TAILOR
MERCHANT VESSEL
MERMAID THEATRE
MERRY AND BRIGHT
MERRY CHRISTMAS

METEORIC SHOWER	MONOTONOUS LIFE
MEZZANINE FLOOR	MONROE DOCTRINE
MICHAEL BENTINE	MONSTROUS CRIME
MICHAEL FARADAY	MONTHLY ACCOUNT
MICHAELMAS TERM	MONTHLY PAYMENT
MICHAEL WILDING	MONTH OF SUNDAYS
MIDDLE DISTANCE	MONUMENTAL WORK
MIDDLE OF THE DAY	MOONLIGHT NIGHT
MIDDLE REGISTER	MORAL BLACKMAIL
MIDNIGHT REVELS	MORAL CERTAINTY
MIDSHIPMAN EASY	MORAL CHARACTER
MIDSUMMER NIGHT	MORAL COWARDICE
MILD PUNISHMENT	MORAL IGNORANCE
MILITARY ATTACK	MORAL NECESSITY
MILITARY CAREER	MORAL PRINCIPLE
MILITARY ESCORT	MORAL TURPITUDE
MILITARY GENIUS	MORE THAN A MATCH
MILITARY PARADE	MORE THAN ENOUGH
MILITARY POLICE	MORE TO THE POINT
MILITARY SCHOOL	MORNING SERVICE
MILITARY SPIRIT	MOROCCO LEATHER
MILITARY TATTOO	MOST HONOURABLE
MILK OF MAGNESIA	MOST OF THE NIGHT
MILLION DOLLARS	MOTHER AND CHILD
MILL ON THE FLOSS	MOTHER'S DARLING
MIND OVER MATTER	MOTHERS' MEETING
MINERAL DEPOSIT	MOTHER SUPERIOR
MINERAL KINGDOM	MOTLEY ASSEMBLY
MINESTRONE SOUP	MOTOR AMBULANCE
MINING ENGINEER	MOTOR TRANSPORT
MINISTRY OF FOOD	MOUNTAIN RESORT
MINOR OPERATION	MOUNTING DANGER
MISSIONARY WORK	MOUNT THE THRONE
MISTER MICAWBER	MOVE TO LAUGHTER
MISTLETOE BOUGH	MOVING PAVEMENT
MNEMONIC DEVICE	MUCH IN EVIDENCE
MOBILE FEATURES	MUCH-MARRIED MAN
MOCK TURTLE SOUP	MULTIPLY BY FIVE
MODEL AEROPLANE	MULTIPLY BY FOUR
MODEL BEHAVIOUR	MULTIPLY BY NINE
MODEL HOUSEHOLD	MUNITIONS OF WAR
MODERATE DEGREE	MURDER MOST FOUL
MODERATE HEALTH	MUSCULAR ENERGY
MODERATE HEIGHT	MUSEUM SPECIMEN
MODERATE INCOME	MUSHROOM GROWTH
MODERATE WEIGHT	MUSHROOM SUBURB
MODERN BUILDING	MUSICAL ABILITY
MODERN LANGUAGE	MUSICAL EVENING
MODS AND ROCKERS	MUSICAL GLASSES
MONEY IN THE BANK	MUSICAL MOMENTS
MONKEY BUSINESS	MUSICAL PRODIGY

MUSICAL QUALITY
MUSIC PUBLISHER
MUSTARD PLASTER
MUTE ADMIRATION
MUTUAL GOODWILL
MUTUAL SYMPATHY
MUZZLE VELOCITY
MY LADY NICOTINE

N—14
NAME AND ADDRESS
NAMELESS TERROR
NAME YOUR POISON
NAMING CEREMONY
NAPOLEON BRANDY
NAPOLEONIC CODE
NAPOLEONIC WARS
NARRATIVE VERSE
NARROW INTERVAL
NARROW MAJORITY
NASTY BIT OF WORK
NATIONAL ANTHEM
NATIONAL CREDIT
NATIONAL CRISIS
NATIONAL DEVICE
NATIONAL EMBLEM
NATIONAL FIGURE
NATIONAL HEALTH
NATIONAL INCOME
NATIONAL SPIRIT
NATIONAL STATUS
NATIONAL WEALTH
NATIONAL WINNER
NATION-WIDE HUNT
NATIVE COMPOUND
NATIVE LANGUAGE
NATIVE QUARTERS
NATURAL HARBOUR
NATURAL HISTORY
NATURAL IMPULSE
NATURAL PROCESS
NATURAL SCIENCE
NAVAL ARCHITECT
NAVAL EXERCISES
NAVAL OPERATION
NAVIGABLE RIVER
NEANDERTHAL MAN
NEAR NEIGHBOURS
NEAR THE KNUCKLE
NEAT AS A BANDBOX
NEEDLES AND PINS

NE'ER CAST A CLOUT
NEGATIVE ACTION
NEGATIVE ANSWER
NEGATIVE RESULT
NEGRO SPIRITUAL
NERVOUS TENSION
NETHER GARMENTS
NEUTRAL COUNTRY
NEVER-NEVER LAND
NEVER SATISFIED
NEW CONSIGNMENT
NEW-FANGLED IDEA
NEW LAMPS FOR OLD
NEW LEASE OF LIFE
NEWS OF THE WORLD
NEWSPAPER WORLD
NEXT BEST FRIEND
NEXT GENERATION
NICE DIFFERENCE
NICELY BALANCED
NICE PERCEPTION
NIGGER MINSTREL
NIGHT BLINDNESS
NIGHT-CLUB QUEEN
NIL DESPERANDUM
NINE DAYS' WONDER
NINE MEN'S MORRIS
NINE O'CLOCK NEWS
NINE OF DIAMONDS
NINEPENNY STAMP
NINETEEN AND SIX
NINETEEN AND TEN
NINETEEN AND TWO
NINETEENTH HOLE
NINETEEN TWENTY
NINETY THOUSAND
NINTH OF JANUARY
NINTH OF OCTOBER
NIPPED IN THE BUD
NOBLESSE OBLIGE
NOBODY'S DARLING
NO END OF A FELLOW
NO FIXED ADDRESS
NO HALF MEASURES
NOISE ABATEMENT
NO JOKING MATTER
NOMINAL CAPITAL
NOMINAL DAMAGES
NOMINATIVE CASE
NORMAL SOLUTION
NORMAN CONQUEST

NO ROOM AT THE INN
NO ROOM FOR DOUBT
NORTH AUSTRALIA
NORTHERN ACCENT
NORTHERN LIGHTS
NORTH OF ENGLAND
NORTH OF THE WASH
NORTHWARD BOUND
NOSE OUT OF JOINT
NO STOMACH FOR IT
NOTHING DAUNTED
NOTHING TO OFFER
NOTHING TO SPARE
NOTHING VENTURE
NO THOROUGHFARE
NO TROUBLE AT ALL
NOUN OF ASSEMBLY
NOVEL SITUATION
NO VISIBLE MEANS
NUCLEAR FISSION
NUCLEAR PHYSICS
NUCLEAR REACTOR
NUCLEAR WARFARE
NUMBER THIRTEEN
NUMERICAL ORDER
NURSERY CANNONS
NURSING SERVICE
NUTS AND RAISINS
NYLON STOCKINGS

O—14
OBITUARY NOTICE
OBJECT OF TERROR
OBSCURE PROBLEM
OBSERVATION CAR
OCCASIONAL SHOT
OCCUPYING FORCE
OCEAN GREYHOUND
OCTAVIUS CAESAR
OEDIPUS COMPLEX
OFFER AN OPINION
OFFICE BUILDING
OFFICE OF PROFIT
OFFICER OF STATE
OFFICERS AND MEN
OFFICIAL CENSUS
OFFICIAL NOTICE
OFFICIAL REPORT
OFFICIAL SECRET
OFFICIAL SOURCE
OFFICIAL STRIKE

OFF LIKE A STREAK
OFFSET PRINTING
OFF THE PREMISES
OFF WITH THE HEAD
OF HUMAN BONDAGE
OLD BOYS' REUNION
OLD CLOTHES SHOP
OLD FOLKS AT HOME
OLD MAN OF THE SEA
OLD MOTHER RILEY
OLD PEOPLE'S HOME
OLD-TIME DANCING
OLD-WORLD GARDEN
OLIVER CROMWELL
OMNIBUS EDITION
ON A HEROIC SCALE
ON A HIGHER PLANE
ONE AND A QUARTER
ONE AND SIXPENCE
ONE AND TENPENCE
ONE AND TWOPENCE
ONE-ARMED BANDIT
ONE CLAIM TO FAME
ONE CROWDED HOUR
ONE FINE MORNING
ONE IN A THOUSAND
ONE-MAN BUSINESS
ONE NIGHT OF LOVE
ONE OF THE FAMILY
ONE OF THE PEOPLE
ONE OF THESE DAYS
ONE THAT GOT AWAY
ONLY TOO PLEASED
ON ONE CONDITION
ON ONE'S BEAM-ENDS
ON ONE'S DEATH-BED
ON ONE'S HIND LEGS
ON ONE'S LAST LEGS
ON ONE'S OWN TERMS
ON PLEASURE BENT
ON PUBLIC GROUND
ON SHORT RATIONS
ON SUBSCRIPTION
ON THE BAND-WAGON
ON THE CONTINENT
ON THE DEBIT SIDE
ON THE DEFENSIVE
ON THE DOWNGRADE
ON THE HOME FRONT
ON THE LARGE SIZE
ON THE OFF CHANCE

ON THE OFFENSIVE
ON THE OTHER HAND
ON THE OTHER SIDE
ON THE OUTSKIRTS
ON THE PROMENADE
ON THE RIGHT SIDE
ON THE SHADY SIDE
ON THE SHORT LIST
ON THE SHORT SIDE
ON THE SMALL SIDE
ON THE SUNNY SIDE
ON THE TELEPHONE
ON THE THRESHOLD
ON THE TIGHT SIDE
ON THE TOUCH-LINE
ON THE WRONG FOOT
ON THE WRONG SIDE
ON THE WRONG TRACK
ON TO A GOOD THING
ON WITH THE DANCE
OPEN-AIR CONCERT
OPEN-AIR SERVICE
OPEN-AIR SPEAKER
OPEN-AIR THEATRE
OPEN-CAST MINING
OPEN CONFESSION
OPEN DISCUSSION
OPEN-DOOR POLICY
OPENING BATSMAN
OPEN PARLIAMENT
OPEN THE BIDDING
OPEN THE INNINGS
OPEN THE SLUICES
OPEN TO ARGUMENT
OPEN TO QUESTION
OPEN TOURNAMENT
OPERATING TABLE
OPERATIONS ROOM
OPPOSITE NUMBER
OPPOSITION WHIP
ORCHESTRA STALL
ORDER IN ADVANCE
ORDER IN COUNCIL
ORDERLY CONDUCT
ORDERLY OFFICER
ORDER OF THE BATH
ORDER OF THE BOOT
ORDINARY SEAMAN
ORDINARY SHARES
ORDNANCE SURVEY
ORGANIC DISEASE

ORGANISED GAMES
ORNAMENTAL POND
ORNAMENTAL TREE
ORTHODOX CHURCH
OSTRICH FEATHER
OTHER FISH TO FRY
OUNCE OF TOBACCO
OUT-AND-OUT ROGUE
OUTDOOR MEETING
OUTDOOR SERVANT
OUT FOR THE COUNT
OUTGOING TENANT
OUT OF CHARACTER
OUT OF CONDITION
OUT OF CURIOSITY
OUT OF ONE'S DEPTH
OUT OF ONE'S SHELL
OUT OF THE COMMON
OUT OF THE GUTTER
OUT OF THIS WORLD
OUTSIDE ONE'S KEN
OUTSIDE OPINION
OVERCOME BY FEAR
OVERDUE ACCOUNT
OVER THE COUNTER
OVER THE RAINBOW
OXFORD MOVEMENT
OXYGEN CYLINDER

P—14
PACKET OF CRISPS
PACKET OF TWENTY
PACKING STATION
PACK OF NONSENSE
PACK ONE'S TRUNKS
PAGES OF HISTORY
PAINT AND POWDER
PAINT A PORTRAIT
PAIR OF BREECHES
PAIR OF CALIPERS
PAIR OF CLIPPERS
PAIR OF CRUTCHES
PAIR OF SCISSORS
PAIR OF SLIPPERS
PAIR OF TROUSERS
PAIR OF TWEEZERS
PALM OF ONE'S HAND
PANCAKE LANDING
PANCAKE TUESDAY
PANGS OF REMORSE
PANTOMIME QUEEN

PANZER DIVISION
PARADISE FOR TWO
PARALLEL COURSE
PARCHMENT PAPER
PARISH MAGAZINE
PARISH REGISTER
PARKING PROBLEM
PARLIAMENT HILL
PARMESAN CHEESE
PAROXYSM OF RAGE
PARTIAL CONSENT
PARTIAL ECLIPSE
PARTIAL SUCCESS
PARTING PRESENT
PARTISAN SPIRIT
PARTNER IN CRIME
PARTY MACHINERY
PARTY PROGRAMME
PASS DOWN THE CAR
PASSENGER PLANE
PASSENGER TRAIN
PASSING THOUGHT
PASSIONATE PLEA
PASS THE MUSTARD
PAST AND PRESENT
PAST EXPERIENCE
PASTORAL LETTER
PAST PARTICIPLE
PAST REDEMPTION
PATCHWORK QUILT
PATÉ DE FOIE GRAS
PATENT MEDICINE
PATERNOSTER ROW
PAUSE FOR A WHILE
PAUSE FOR BREATH
PAVEMENT ARTIST
PAVING MATERIAL
PAYABLE AT SIGHT
PAY A COMPLIMENT
PAY NO ATTENTION
PEACE AND PLENTY
PEACEFUL ENDING
PEACE IN OUR TIME
PEAL OF LAUGHTER
PEARLS OF WISDOM
PECULIAR PEOPLE
PECULIAR PERSON
PEDIGREE CATTLE
PEER OF THE REALM
PEG-TOP TROUSERS
PENAL SERVITUDE

PENCIL AND PAPER
PENNY FOR THE GUY
PENNY IN THE SLOT
PENSIONABLE AGE
PEPPERCORN RENT
PERCUSSION BAND
PERFECT DARLING
PERFECT EXAMPLE
PERFECT SETTING
PERFECT SILENCE
PERFORMING BEAR
PERFORMING FLEA
PERFORMING SEAL
PERPETUAL BLISS
PERPETUAL WORRY
PERSONAL APPEAL
PERSONAL COLUMN
PERSONAL ESTATE
PERSONAL ESTEEM
PERSONAL FACTOR
PERSONAL FAVOUR
PERSONAL LETTER
PERSONAL MATTER
PERSONAL REMARK
PERSON IN CHARGE
PERSON OF REPUTE
PERSONS UNKNOWN
PERSON TO PERSON
PERTINENT REPLY
PETER AND GORDON
PETER THE HERMIT
PETROLEUM JELLY
PETROL SHORTAGE
PETTY GRIEVANCE
PHOTOGRAPH WELL
PHRASE AND FABLE
PHYSICAL BEAUTY
PHYSICAL ENERGY
PICCADILLY LINE
PICKLED CABBAGE
PICKLED HERRING
PICK OF THE BUNCH
PICK UP A FEW TIPS
PICK UP STRENGTH
PICKWICK PAPERS
PICTURE GALLERY
PICTURE OF GLOOM
PICTURE WRITING
PIERCE THE HEART
PIERCING GLANCE
PIETRO ANNIGONI

PILE ON THE AGONY
PILGRIM FATHERS
PILLAR OF THE LAW
PILLAR OF WISDOM
PILOTLESS PLANE
PINCER MOVEMENT
PINCH AND SCRAPE
PINEAPPLE JUICE
PINNACLE OF FAME
PINS AND NEEDLES
PITCH OVERBOARD
PLACE IN HISTORY
PLACE OF ONE'S OWN
PLACE OF WORSHIP
PLAGUE OF LONDON
PLAICE AND CHIPS
PLAIN AND SIMPLE
PLAIN CHOCOLATE
PLAIN STATEMENT
PLANETARY ORBIT
PLANNED ECONOMY
PLANNING OFFICE
PLAN OF CAMPAIGN
PLANTATION SONG
PLASTER OF PARIS
PLASTIC SURGEON
PLASTIC SURGERY
PLATFORM ORATOR
PLATFORM TICKET
PLATINUM BLONDE
PLAUSIBLE ROGUE
PLAY AT SOLDIERS
PLAY FOR ENGLAND
PLAY GOOSEBERRY
PLAY THE TRAITOR
PLAY THE VILLAIN
PLAY TO THE CROWD
PLEAD IGNORANCE
PLEAD NOT GUILTY
PLEAD ONE'S CAUSE
PLEASANT DREAMS
PLEASANT MANNER
PLEASANT PEOPLE
PLEASED AS PUNCH
PLEASE TURN OVER
PLEASURE CRUISE
PLEASURE GROUND
PLEASURE LAUNCH
PLEASURE SEEKER
PLEDGE ONE'S WORD
PLOT ONE'S COURSE

M.C.D.—15

PLOUGHING MATCH
PLOUGH THE WAVES
PLUCK UP COURAGE
PLUMB THE DEPTHS
PLUNGED IN GRIEF
PLUNGE INTO DEBT
PNEUMATIC BRAKE
PNEUMATIC DRILL
POCKET AN INSULT
POET AND PEASANT
POETRY IN MOTION
POINT OF CONTACT
POINT OUT THE WAY
POINT WELL TAKEN
POISED TO STRIKE
POISONOUS PLANT
POKE ONE'S NOSE IN
POLARIZED GLASS
POLICEMAN'S BEAT
POLICE SERGEANT
POLISH CORRIDOR
POLISH OFF A MEAL
POLITICAL AGENT
POLITICAL EXILE
POLITICAL PARTY
POLITICAL SPIRIT
POLLING STATION
PONTEFRACT CAKE
POOR MAN'S FRIEND
POOR MAN'S LAWYER
POOR VISIBILITY
POOR VOCABULARY
POPPA PICCOLINO
POP THE QUESTION
POPULAR CONCERT
POPULAR EDITION
POPULAR OPINION
POPULAR REQUEST
POPULAR SCIENCE
POPULAR VERDICT
PORTLAND CEMENT
PORTRAIT ARTIST
POSITIVE ACTION
POSITIVE CHARGE
POSITIVE COLOUR
POSITIVE DEGREE
POSITIVE MENACE
POSSESSIVE CASE
POSSESSIVE LOVE
POSTAL DELIVERY
POSTAL DISTRICT

POSTHUMOUS FAME
POST-WAR CREDITS
POWDER AND PAINT
POWDER MAGAZINE
POWERFUL SPEECH
PRACTICAL JOKER
PRACTISE DECEIT
PRECIOUS LITTLE
PRE-NATAL CLINIC
PREPARE A BUDGET
PREPARED SPEECH
PREPARE ONESELF
PRESCRIBED TEXT
PRESENCE OF MIND
PRESENT A CHEQUE
PRESENT ADDRESS
PRESENT COMPANY
PRESERVED FRUIT
PRESIDENT ELECT
PRESIDING JUDGE
PRESSED FOR TIME
PRESS FOR ACTION
PRESSING DANGER
PRESSING DUTIES
PRESS THE BUTTON
PRESSURE COOKER
PRESSURE OF WORK
PREVAILING WIND
PREY ON ONE'S MIND
PRICE OF SILENCE
PRICE REDUCTION
PRICKLY FEELING
PRIMA BALLERINA
PRIMARY MEANING
PRIME CONDITION
PRIMEVAL FOREST
PRIMITIVE TRIBE
PRIMROSE LEAGUE
PRIMROSE YELLOW
PRINCE CHARMING
PRINCE OF ORANGE
PRINCE OF ROGUES
PRISON CHAPLAIN
PRISON GOVERNOR
PRISON SENTENCE
PRIVATE ADDRESS
PRIVATE CITIZEN
PRIVATE COMPANY
PRIVATE HEARING
PRIVATE OPINION
PRIVATE SOCIETY

PRIVATE SOLDIER
PRIVATE TEACHER
PRIVATE TUITION
PRIZE-GIVING DAY
PROBABLE WINNER
PRO BONO PUBLICO
PRODUCE RESULTS
PRODUCTION LINE
PROFITABLE DEAL
PROFITLESS TASK
PROFOUND EFFECT
PROFOUND SECRET
PROGRAMME MUSIC
PROGRESS OF TIME
PROGRESS REPORT
PROHIBITION ERA
PROLIFIC WRITER
PROMISING PUPIL
PROMISING START
PROMISSORY NOTE
PROMPT DECISION
PROMPT DELIVERY
PROOF OF POSTING
PROPER FRACTION
PROPOSE A MOTION
PROPOSED ACTION
PROSCENIUM ARCH
PROSPEROUS YEAR
PROTECTED STATE
PROTEST AGAINST
PROTEST MEETING
PROTEST TOO MUCH
PROVE EXPENSIVE
PROVEN INNOCENT
PROVE ONE'S POINT
PROVIDE HEATING
PROVOST MARSHAL
PUBLIC APPLAUSE
PUBLIC DISGRACE
PUBLIC ENTRANCE
PUBLIC EXPOSURE
PUBLIC FOOTPATH
PUBLIC INTEREST
PUBLICITY AGENT
PUBLIC NUISANCE
PUBLIC PROPERTY
PUBLIC SPIRITED
PUBLISHER'S NOTE
PULL ONE'S WEIGHT
PULL THE STRINGS
PULL THE TRIGGER

PUMPING STATION
PUNCH ON THE HEAD
PUNCH ON THE NOSE
PUNITIVE ACTION
PURE CONJECTURE
PURSUIT OF POWER
PUSHED FOR MONEY
PUSH OUT THE BOAT
PUSH THE BOAT OUT
PUT IN A BAD LIGHT
PUT IN A GOOD WORD
PUT IN ONE'S PLACE
PUT IN THE MIDDLE
PUT IN THE STOCKS
PUT IT IN WRITING
PUT IT TO THE VOTE
PUT NEW LIFE INTO
PUT OFF THE SCENT
PUT ON A BOLD FACE
PUT ON A PEDESTAL
PUT ONE'S SPOKE IN
PUT ON THE AGENDA
PUT ON THE MARKET
PUT ON THE SCALES
PUT OUT OF ACTION
PUT OUT THE LIGHT
PUT THE CLOCKS ON
PUT THE HELM DOWN
PUT THE KETTLE ON
PUT THE KIBOSH ON
PUT THE QUESTION
PUT THINGS RIGHT
PUT UNDER ARREST
PUT UP A GOOD SHOW
PUT UP A STRUGGLE
PYRRHIC VICTORY

Q—14
QUALITY OF MERCY
QUARTER OF A YARD
QUARTER PAST ONE
QUARTER PAST SIX
QUARTER PAST TEN
QUARTER PAST TWO
QUARTER TO EIGHT
QUARTER TO SEVEN
QUARTER TO THREE
QUEEN ANNE HOUSE
QUEEN ANNE'S GATE
QUEEN ANNE STYLE
QUEEN CHARLOTTE

QUEEN ELIZABETH
QUEEN OF ENGLAND
QUEEN'S BIRTHDAY
QUEEN'S EVIDENCE
QUEEN'S PLEASURE
QUEEN'S SHILLING
QUEEN'S SUBJECTS
QUEER IN THE HEAD
QUEER ONE'S PITCH
QUEER SITUATION
QUESTION MASTER
QUESTION OF TIME
QUICK AS THOUGHT
QUICK-FIRING GUN
QUICK LOOK ROUND
QUICK ON THE DRAW
QUICK VENGEANCE
QUITE A STRANGER
QUITE DIFFERENT
QUIVER AND SHAKE
QUIVER WITH RAGE
QUOTATION MARKS

R—14
RACING CALENDAR
RACKED WITH PAIN
RADICAL OUTLOOK
RADIO ANNOUNCER
RADIO ASTRONOMY
RADIO FREQUENCY
RADIO PROGRAMME
RADIO TELEGRAPH
RADIO TELEPHONE
RADIO TELESCOPE
RADIO THERAPIST
RAGS AND TATTERS
RAILWAY COMPANY
RAILWAY CUTTING
RAILWAY JOURNEY
RAILWAY SLEEPER
RAILWAY STATION
RAILWAY VIADUCT
RAILWAY WARRANT
RAIN IN TORRENTS
RAISE A MEMORIAL
RAISE A QUESTION
RAISED EYEBROWS
RAISED PLATFORM
RAISE ONE'S GLASS
RAISE ONE'S HOPES
RAISE ONE'S VOICE

RAISE THE SIGHTS
RAKE IN THE MONEY
RAKE OUT THE FIRE
RANGE OF MEANING
RAPID PROMOTION
RAPT EXPRESSION
RARE ATMOSPHERE
RARE OCCURRENCE
RASH ASSUMPTION
RATE OF EXCHANGE
RATE OF INTEREST
RATE OF PROGRESS
RATTLE THE SABRE
RAVENOUS HUNGER
REACH A DECISION
REACH AGREEMENT
REACH FOR THE SKY
REACH THE DEPTHS
REACH THE ZENITH
READING GLASSES
READ MEN'S HEARTS
READ THE MINUTES
READ THE RIOT ACT
REALLY AND TRULY
REAPING MACHINE
REAP THE BENEFIT
REAP THE HARVEST
REAR-VIEW MIRROR
REAR-VIEW WINDOW
REASONABLE TIME
RECEIVE A LEGACY
RECEIVE A LETTER
RECEIVE QUARTER
RECEIVING ORDER
RECEPTION CLERK
RECKLESS DRIVER
RECKLESS GAMBLE
RECORDING ANGEL
RECORD TURNOVER
RECOVER ONESELF
RECREATION ROOM
REDUCE IN NUMBER
REDUCE TO POWDER
REED INSTRUMENT
REFECTORY TABLE
REFINED SOCIETY
REFLECTED GLORY
REFLECTED IMAGE
REFLECTIVE MOOD
REFORMED CHURCH
REFRESHMENT BAR

REFRESH ONESELF
REFUGEE PROBLEM
REFUSE A HEARING
REFUSE DISPOSAL
REGAL SPLENDOUR
REGIMENTAL BAND
REGISTERED MAIL
REGISTERED POST
REGISTRY OFFICE
REGULAR BEDTIME
REGULAR SERVICE
REGULAR SOLDIER
REGULATION SIZE
REIGNING BEAUTY
REIGNING FAMILY
RELATIVE CLAUSE
RELATIVE VALUES
RELIC OF THE PAST
RELIEVING FORCE
RELIGIOUS FAITH
RELIGIOUS HOUSE
RELIGIOUS MANIA
RELIGIOUS ORDER
RELIGIOUS RITES
RELIGIOUS TRACT
REMAINS OF A MEAL
REMARKABLE GIRL
REMEMBRANCE DAY
REMOTE ANCESTOR
REMOVE FRICTION
RENDER A SERVICE
RENEW ONE'S YOUTH
RENEW THE ATTACK
REPAIRING LEASE
REPEATING RIFLE
REPEATING WATCH
REPORTED SPEECH
REPORT PROGRESS
REPRESS THE NEWS
REPUBLICAN VOTE
REPULSIVE FORCE
RESEARCH WORKER
RESERVE ACCOUNT
RESIDENT ABROAD
RESISTANCE COIL
RESISTANCE UNIT
RESPECT ONESELF
RESPONSIBLE MAN
RESTLESS NATURE
REST ON ONE'S OARS
RESTORE HARMONY

RESTORE TO POWER
RESTRICTED AREA
RETAILER OF NEWS
RETAINING FORCE
RETROGRADE STEP
RETURN A VERDICT
RETURN TO HEALTH
RETURN TO NORMAL
RETURN TO SENDER
REVENGE IS SWEET
REVENGE ONESELF
REVENUE OFFICER
REVERSIBLE COAT
REVERT TO NORMAL
REVISED EDITION
REVISED VERSION
REVOLVING DOORS
REVOLVING STAGE
RHAPSODY IN BLUE
RHEUMATIC FEVER
RHINOCEROS HIDE
RHODE ISLAND RED
RHYME NOR REASON
RHYMING COUPLET
RICHARD MURDOCH
RICHARD STRAUSS
RICH IN VITAMINS
RICHMOND BRIDGE
RICH VOCABULARY
RIDE A COCK-HORSE
RIDE SIDE-SADDLE
RIDING BREECHES
RIGHT ABOUT FACE
RIGHT ABOUT TURN
RIGHT AND PROPER
RIGHT AS A TRIVET
RIGHT DIRECTION
RIGHT FIRST TIME
RIGHT FROM WRONG
RIGHT-HAND DRIVE
RING IN ONE'S EARS
RING THE CHANGES
RIPE EXPERIENCE
RISE IN THE WORLD
RISE TO ONE'S FEET
RISK EVERYTHING
RITUAL PRACTICE
ROAD TO THE ISLES
ROAD TRAFFIC ACT
ROARING FORTIES
ROARING SUCCESS

ROAR OF LAUGHTER
ROBERT BROWNING
ROBERT CUMMINGS
ROBERT HELPMANN
ROBERT THE BRUCE
ROBIN REDBREAST
ROBINSON CRUSOE
ROCKY MOUNTAINS
RODENT OPERATOR
ROD FOR ONE'S BACK
ROD, POLE OR PERCH
ROGER BANNISTER
ROLL A CIGARETTE
ROLLED UMBRELLA
ROLLING COUNTRY
ROLLING EXPANSE
ROLLING IN MONEY
ROMANTIC AFFAIR
ROMANTIC COMEDY
ROMEO AND JULIET
ROOF OF THE MOUTH
ROOF OF THE WORLD
ROOM FOR DISPUTE
ROSES ALL THE WAY
ROSES OF PICARDY
ROUGH AND TUMBLE
ROUGH TREATMENT
ROUND SHOULDERS
ROUND THE CORNER
ROUND THE HOUSES
ROUND THE WICKET
ROUSE CURIOSITY
ROUTE NATIONALE
ROVING REPORTER
ROW OVER NOTHING
ROYAL ARTILLERY
ROYAL AUTHORITY
ROYAL ENCLOSURE
ROYAL ENGINEERS
ROYAL FUSILIERS
ROYAL HOUSEHOLD
ROYAL RECEPTION
ROYAL RESIDENCE
ROYAL TANK CORPS
RUBBER OF BRIDGE
RUB THE WRONG WAY
RUDYARD KIPLING
RUGGED FEATURES
RUINOUS EXPENSE
RULE ABSOLUTELY
RULE OUT OF ORDER

RULES OF CRICKET
RULES OF THE GAME
RUMP PARLIAMENT
RUNAWAY VICTORY
RUN FOR DEAR LIFE
RUN FOR ONE'S LIFE
RUN INTO TROUBLE
RUN LIKE A RABBIT
RUN LIKE THE WIND
RUNNING ACCOUNT
RUNNING REMARKS
RUNNING REPAIRS
RUN OF THE MARKET
RUN OUT OF PETROL
RUN THE GAUNTLET
RUN UP AN ACCOUNT
RUN WITH THE HARE
RUN WITH THE PACK
RUSH-HOUR TRAVEL
RUSH INTO THINGS
RUSH ONE'S FENCES
RUSSIAN LEATHER
RUSTLE OF SPRING

S—14
SACK OF POTATOES
SACRED PRECINCT
SACRED WRITINGS
SADDER AND WISER
SADDLE OF MUTTON
SAFETY MEASURES
SAGE REFLECTION
SALIENT FEATURE
SALINE SOLUTION
SALISBURY PLAIN
SALT OF THE EARTH
SALUTARY LESSON
SAMUEL PICKWICK
SAMUEL PLIMSOLL
SARAH BERNHARDT
SARTOR RESARTUS
SATANIC MAJESTY
SATELLITE STATE
SATURDAY'S CHILD
SAUSAGE AND MASH
SAVELOY SAUSAGE
SAVE ONE'S BREATH
SAVINGS ACCOUNT
SAY GOOD-MORNING
SAYING AND DOING
SAY ONE'S PRAYERS

SCALE OF CHARGES
SCALP TREATMENT
SCATTER THE SEED
SCENARIO WRITER
SCHEME OF THINGS
SCHOLASTIC POST
SCHOOL BUILDING
SCHOOL GOVERNOR
SCHOOL HOLIDAYS
SCHOOL MAGAZINE
SCHOOL OF WHALES
SCIENCE FICTION
SCIENTIFIC GAME
SCOBIE BREASLEY
SCORE A BULL'S EYE
SCOTCH AND WATER
SCOTCH THE SNAKE
SCOTCH WOODCOCK
SCOTS FUSILIERS
SCOTTISH CHURCH
SCOTTISH LEAGUE
SCOTTISH OFFICE
SCRAPE TOGETHER
SCRATCH A LIVING
SCREAMING FARCE
SCROLL OF HONOUR
SCRUBBING BRUSH
SCRUPULOUS CARE
SCUM OF THE EARTH
SEA-GOING VESSEL
SEALED ENVELOPE
SEAL OF APPROVAL
SEARCH FOR TRUTH
SEASIDE HOLIDAY
SEASONABLE GIFT
SEASONABLE TIME
SEASONED TIMBER
SEAT IN THE LORDS
SEAT OF LEARNING
SEAT ON THE BENCH
SEAT ON THE BOARD
SECLUDED CORNER
SECOND DIVIDEND
SECOND DIVISION
SECOND ENGINEER
SECOND-HAND BOOK
SECOND-HAND SHOP
SECOND INTERVAL
SECOND MARRIAGE
SECOND OF AUGUST
SECOND-RATE MIND

SECOND SYMPHONY	SETTLE ACCOUNTS
SECOND THOUGHTS	SETTLE A QUARREL
SECOND WORLD WAR	SETTLED PURPOSE
SECRET INTRIGUE	SETTLED WEATHER
SECURE A VICTORY	SETTLE ONE'S HASH
SECURE FOOTHOLD	SEVEN AGES OF MAN
SECURE POSITION	SEVENTEEN MILES
SECURITY POLICE	SEVENTH CENTURY
SEE JUSTICE DONE	SEVENTH OF APRIL
SEE WHAT HAPPENS	SEVENTH OF MARCH
SEIDLITZ POWDER	SEVENTY PER CENT
SEIZE THE CHANCE	SEVERE SENTENCE
SELECTION BOARD	SHADOW MINISTER
SELF-SERVICE BAR	SHADOW OF A DOUBT
SEMI-FINAL MATCH	SHADY CHARACTER
SEMI-FINAL ROUND	SHAGGY-DOG STORY
SEND A MESSENGER	SHAKE BEFORE USE
SEND IN ONE'S CARD	SHAKE LIKE A LEAF
SEND ONE PACKING	SHAKE OF THE HEAD
SEND TO THE STAKE	SHAKE THE BOTTLE
SENIOR REGIMENT	SHAKE UP AND DOWN
SENIOR WRANGLER	SHALLOW PRETEXT
SENSELESS ORDER	SHANNON AIRPORT
SENSE OF BALANCE	SHARE THE SPOILS
SENSE OF DECENCY	SHARP AS A NEEDLE
SENSE OF HEARING	SHARP ENCOUNTER
SENSE OF LOYALTY	SHARPEN THE WITS
SENSE OF PURPOSE	SHARP REJOINDER
SENSITIVE PAPER	SHARPS AND FLATS
SENSITIVE PLANT	SHATTERING BLOW
SENTIMENTAL BOY	SHEEPDOG TRIALS
SENT TO COVENTRY	SHEEP'S CLOTHING
SEPARATE TABLES	SHEET LIGHTNING
SERENE HIGHNESS	SHEFFIELD PLATE
SERIES OF EVENTS	SHEFFIELD STEEL
SERIOUS ATTEMPT	SHEPHERD MARKET
SERIOUS ILLNESS	SHEPHERD'S CROOK
SERIOUS MISTAKE	SHEPHERD'S PURSE
SERIOUS OFFENCE	SHERLOCK HOLMES
SERIOUS STUDENT	SHERWOOD FOREST
SERIOUS SUBJECT	SHILLING A POUND
SERIOUS THOUGHT	SHINING EXAMPLE
SERIOUS TROUBLE	SHIP IN DISTRESS
SERVANT PROBLEM	SHIPPING CENTRE
SERVE A SENTENCE	SHIPPING OFFICE
SERVES ONE RIGHT	SHIP'S CARPENTER
SERVICE STATION	SHIVER AND SHAKE
SET A BAD EXAMPLE	SHOCKED SILENCE
SET ARRANGEMENT	SHOCKING TEMPER
SET OF GOLF-CLUBS	SHOCK TREATMENT
SET THINGS RIGHT	SHOOTING RIGHTS

SHOOTING SEASON
SHOOTING TROPHY
SHOOT THE RAPIDS
SHOPPING ARCADE
SHOPPING BASKET
SHOPPING CENTRE
SHORT AND STOCKY
SHORTHAND SPEED
SHORT OF CAPITAL
SHORT PARAGRAPH
SHORT STATEMENT
SHOT-GUN WEDDING
SHOULDER OF LAMB
SHOULDER OF VEAL
SHOW A BOLD FRONT
SHOW COMPASSION
SHOW MODERATION
SHOW OF STRENGTH
SHOW OF SYMPATHY
SHOW ONE'S TICKET
SHOW ONE THE DOOR
SHOW RELUCTANCE
SHOW REPENTANCE
SHREWD OBSERVER
SHRIMP COCKTAIL
SHUTTLE SERVICE
SICKENING SIGHT
SIEGE OF LUCKNOW
SIGH WITH RELIEF
SIGMUND ROMBERG
SIGNALS OFFICER
SIGN OF GOOD LUCK
SIGN OF STRENGTH
SIGN OF THE CROSS
SIGN OF THE TIMES
SIGN OF WEAKNESS
SILENCE IN COURT
SILENCE REIGNED
SILENT REPROACH
SILKS AND SATINS
SILVANA MANGANO
SILVER BRACELET
SILVER STANDARD
SIMPLE ADDITION
SIMPLE EQUATION
SIMPLE FRACTION
SIMPLE FRACTURE
SIMPLE INTEREST
SIMPLE SENTENCE
SIMPLE SOLUTION

SIMPLY FABULOUS
SIMPLY STARVING
SINCERE APOLOGY
SINGLE INSTANCE
SINGULAR NUMBER
SINKING FEELING
SINK LIKE A STONE
SINK OF INIQUITY
SINS OF OMISSION
SINS OF THE FLESH
SIR ADRIAN BOULT
SIR EDWARD ELGAR
SIR HENRY IRVING
SIR HUGH WALPOLE
SIR ISAAC NEWTON
SIR ISAAC PITMAN
SIR JAMES BARRIE
SIR JOHN GIELGUD
SIR WALTER SCOTT
SIT ON THE GROUND
SIT ON THE THRONE
SIXES AND SEVENS
SIX FEET OF EARTH
SIXTEEN AND FIVE
SIXTEEN AND FOUR
SIXTEEN AND NINE
SIXTEEN PER CENT
SIXTEENTH GREEN
SIXTEENTH OF MAY
SIXTH OF JANUARY
SIXTH OF OCTOBER
SIXTY-SIX AND SIX
SIXTY-TWO AND SIX
SIX WICKETS DOWN
SKATE ON THIN ICE
SKILLED WORKMAN
SKITTLES PLAYER
SLASHING ATTACK
SLAVE OF FASHION
SLAVE OF THE LAMP
SLAVE TO FASHION
SLEEPING BEAUTY
SLEEPING TABLET
SLEEPLESS NIGHT
SLEEP LIKE A BABY
SLEEP OF THE JUST
SLEEPY SICKNESS
SLIP ONE'S MEMORY
SLOW-MOTION FILM
SLOW PROCESSION

SLUGS AND SNAILS
SLUM POPULATION
SMALL-BORE RIFLE
SMALL OF THE BACK
SMALL REDUCTION
SMALL-TIME CROOK
SMART INVENTION
SMASHING DEFEAT
SMELL OF BURNING
SMILING THROUGH
SMOKE-ROOM STORY
SMOKING CONCERT
SMOOTH AS MARBLE
SMOOTH AS VELVET
SMOOTH CROSSING
SMOOTH ONE'S PATH
SNATCH A VERDICT
SNIP OFF THE ENDS
SOBERLY DRESSED
SOCIAL ACTIVITY
SOCIAL CLIMBING
SOCIAL DEMOCRAT
SOCIAL INFERIOR
SOCIAL PLANNING
SOCIAL POSITION
SOCIAL REGISTER
SOCIAL SECURITY
SOCIAL STANDING
SOCIAL SUPERIOR
SOCIETY ISLANDS
SOCIETY WEDDING
SODIUM CHLORIDE
SOFT FURNISHING
SOFT-SHOE DANCER
SOLDIER'S CHORUS
SOLE BONNE FEMME
SOLED AND HEELED
SOLEMN ENTREATY
SOLEMNLY AFFIRM
SOLEMN OCCASION
SOLE POSSESSION
SOLE PROPRIETOR
SOLID SUBSTANCE
SOLOMON ISLANDS
SOLVE THE RIDDLE
SOME DAY OR OTHER
SOMETHING EXTRA
SOMETHING FISHY
SOMETHING TO SAY
SOMEWHERE ABOUT

SO MUCH THE WORSE
SONG OF THE SHIRT
SONGS OF SOLOMON
SORE AFFLICTION
SOUND CHARACTER
SOUND EDUCATION
SOUND PRINCIPLE
SOUND REASONING
SOUND RECORDING
SOUND THE CHARGE
SOURCE OF DANGER
SOUR EXPRESSION
SOUSED MACKEREL
SOUTH AUSTRALIA
SOUTHERN ACCENT
SOUTHERN ASPECT
SOUTHERN REGION
SOUTHERN STATES
SOUTH OF ENGLAND
SOUTH SEA BUBBLE
SOVEREIGN POWER
SOVEREIGN STATE
SPACE PROGRAMME
SPACE TRAVELLER
SPARE NO EXPENSE
SPARING OF WORDS
SPEAKERS' CORNER
SPEAK ESPERANTO
SPEAK IN EARNEST
SPEAK IN RIDDLES
SPEAK OUT OF TURN
SPEAK THE TONGUE
SPECIAL DAMAGES
SPECIAL EDITION
SPECIAL FEATURE
SPECIAL LICENCE
SPECIAL MENTION
SPECIAL MISSION
SPECIAL REQUEST
SPECIAL SERVICE
SPECIAL TROUBLE
SPECIAL VERDICT
SPECIFIC ANSWER
SPECIFIC OBJECT
SPECIFIC REMEDY
SPEECH TRAINING
SPEED OF THOUGHT
SPEED THE PLOUGH
SPEEDWAY RACING
SPEEDY RECOVERY

SPELLING LESSON
SPENT CARTRIDGE
SPINNING MOTION
SPIRITED ATTACK
SPIRIT OF THE AGE
SPIRIT OF THE LAW
SPIRITS OF SALTS
SPIRITUAL NEEDS
SPIRITUAL POWER
SPLENDID CHANCE
SPLIT ONE'S SIDES
SPOIL FOR A FIGHT
SPOIL THE EFFECT
SPOIL THE MARKET
SPOKEN LANGUAGE
SPOKEN LIKE A MAN
SPORTING CHANCE
SPORTING FINISH
SPORTS PAVILION
SPORTS REPORTER
SPRAY OF FLOWERS
SPREAD MISCHIEF
SPRIG OF HEATHER
SPRINGHEEL JACK
SPRING IN THE AIR
SPRING MATTRESS
SQUADRON LEADER
SQUARE ACCOUNTS
SQUARE BRACKETS
SQUASH RACQUETS
STAGE A COMEBACK
STAGE CARPENTER
STAGE DIRECTION
STAGGERED HOURS
STAGGERING BLOW
STAINLESS STEEL
STAKE ONE'S CLAIM
STAMFORD BRIDGE
STAMP COLLECTOR
STAMPING GROUND
STANDARD WEIGHT
STAND CONDEMNED
STAND CONVICTED
STAND CORRECTED
STANDING CUSTOM
STANDING ORDERS
STAND IN THE DOCK
ST. ANDREW'S CROSS
STANDS TO REASON
STAND THE RACKET
STAND THE STRAIN

STANLEY BALDWIN
STAPLE INDUSTRY
STAR ATTRACTION
STARBOARD WATCH
STARE IN THE FACE
STARTER'S ORDERS
STARTING HANDLE
STARTING PISTOL
START SOMETHING
START TO QUARREL
STARVATION DIET
STARVATION WAGE
STATE DOCUMENTS
STATE OF AFFAIRS
STATE OF DENMARK
STATE OWNERSHIP
STATIONERS' HALL
STAY-AT-HOME TYPE
STAY ON THE SHELF
ST. CLEMENT DANES
STEADY INCREASE
STEADY PROGRESS
STEAK AND KIDNEY
STEAK AND ONIONS
STEEL ENGRAVING
STEEL ONE'S HEART
STEEPED IN CRIME
STEERING COLUMN
STEM THE CURRENT
STEPHEN LEACOCK
STEPHEN SPENDER
STEP ON THE JUICE
STEP UP THE SPEED
STERLING SILVER
STEWART GRANGER
ST. GEORGE'S CROSS
STICK AT NOTHING
STICK OF RHUBARB
STICKS OUT A MILE
STICK UP A NOTICE
STIFF AS A RAMROD
STILL-LIFE STUDY
STINGING NETTLE
STING IN THE TAIL
STIRLING CASTLE
STIR ONE'S STUMPS
STIRRING SPEECH
ST. JAMES'S PALACE
ST. JAMES'S STREET
STOCK-CAR RACING
STOCK CHARACTER

STOCKINGED FEET
STOCKTON ON TEES
STOKE NEWINGTON
STOKE THE BOILER
STOLEN PROPERTY
STOMACH TROUBLE
STONE-COLD SOBER
STOOP TO CONQUER
STORAGE BATTERY
STORE DETECTIVE
STORM IN A TEA-CUP
STORMY EXCHANGE
STRADDLE A HORSE
STRAIGHT ANSWER
STRAIGHT AS A DIE
STRAIGHT COMEDY
STRAIN AT THE BIT
STRAINED MUSCLE
STRAIN ONE'S EYES
STRAIN THE TRUTH
STRAITS OF DOVER
STRAND OF COTTON
STRANGE BUT TRUE
STRANGE DESTINY
STRANGE FEELING
STRANGE REQUEST
STRATEGIC SKILL
STRAWBERRY FAIR
STRAWBERRY HILL
STRAWBERRY MARK
STRAWBERRY ROAN
STRAW IN THE WIND
STREAK OF HUMOUR
STREAM-LINED CAR
STREET FIGHTING
STREET LIGHTING
STREET MUSICIAN
STRENGTH OF MIND
STRENGTH OF WILL
STRETCH OF WATER
STRICTLY HONEST
STRICT TRAINING
STRIKE A BALANCE
STRIKE A BARGAIN
STRIKE A NEW NOTE
STRIKE ONE'S FLAG
STRIKE WITH FEAR
STRIKING EFFECT
STRING OF HORSES
STRING OF ONIONS
STRING OF PEARLS

STRING TOGETHER
STRIP FOR ACTION
STRIP-TEASE SHOW
STRIVE FOR GLORY
STROKE OF GENIUS
STROKE OF THE PEN
STRONG ARGUMENT
STRONG AS A HORSE
STRONG FEELINGS
STRONG IN THE ARM
STRONG LANGUAGE
STRONGLY WORDED
STRONG MEASURES
STRONG POSITION
STRONG RIGHT ARM
STRONG SOLUTION
STUBBORN FELLOW
STUDIO AUDIENCE
STUDIO PORTRAIT
STUMBLING BLOCK
STUPID QUESTION
STYLISH FASHION
SUBMERGED TENTH
SUBMIT TO DEFEAT
SUBSTANTIAL SUM
SUCCESSFUL PLAY
SUDDEN DOWNPOUR
SUDDEN MOVEMENT
SUDDEN PROGRESS
SUGAR-PLUM FAIRY
SUITABLE TENANT
SUMMARY JUSTICE
SUMMER HOLIDAYS
SUMMER VACATION
SUMPTUOUS FEAST
SUNK IN OBLIVION
SUPERIOR PERSON
SUPPORT A FAMILY
SUPPORTERS' CLUB
SUPPORTING CAST
SUPPORTING FILM
SUPPORTING PART
SUPPORTING ROLE
SUPREME COMMAND
SUPREME CONTROL
SUPREME COUNCIL
SURFACE TENSION
SURGICAL SPIRIT
SURPRISE ATTACK
SURPRISE PACKET
SURRENDER VALUE

SUSPEND PAYMENT
SUSPICIOUS MIND
SUZANNE LENGLEN
SWAGGER CLOTHES
SWALLOW THE BAIT
SWALLOW THE PILL
SWARM OF INSECTS
SWARTHY SKINNED
SWEAR TO SECRECY
SWEEPING ACTION
SWEEPING GLANCE
SWEEPING REMARK
SWEEP THE BOARDS
SWEET AND TWENTY
SWEET SEVENTEEN
SWEETS OF OFFICE
SWEET SUBSTANCE
SWEET SURRENDER
SWELL WITH PRIDE
SWELTERING HEAT
SWIFT AS AN ARROW
SWIMMING LESSON
SWIMMING TRUNKS
SWIM THE CHANNEL
SWORD SWALLOWER
SWORN STATEMENT
SWORN TO SECRECY
SYBIL THORNDIKE

T—14
TABLE OF WEIGHTS
TACTICAL WEAPON
TAILOR-MADE SUIT
TAKE AN INTEREST
TAKE A RISE OUT OF
TAKE BY SURPRISE
TAKE FIRST PRIZE
TAKE FOR GRANTED
TAKE IN GOOD PART
TAKE IN MARRIAGE
TAKE IT FROM HERE
TAKE NO INTEREST
TAKE ONE'S CHANCE
TAKE ONE'S CHOICE
TAKE ONESELF OFF
TAKE ONE'S FENCES
TAKE ONE'S HAT OFF
TAKE OUT A PATENT
TAKE OUT A POLICY
TAKE POSSESSION
TAKE PRECEDENCE

TAKE THE BISCUIT
TAKE THE EDGE OFF
TAKE THE GILT OFF
TAKE THE LIBERTY
TAKE THE TROUBLE
TAKE THINGS EASY
TAKE TO THE BOATS
TAKE TO THE HILLS
TAKE TO THE WATER
TAKE TO THE WOODS
TAKE UP AN OPTION
TAKE UP THE SLACK
TALK IN A WHISPER
TALKING PICTURE
TALK OF THE DEVIL
TANGIBLE OBJECT
TANGLED THREADS
TANNED BY THE SUN
TAPIOCA PUDDING
TAP OUT A MESSAGE
TARGET PRACTICE
TARPAULIN SHEET
TARTAN TROUSERS
TASTE OF THE WHIP
TAXED TO THE HILT
TEA AND BISCUITS
TEA AND SYMPATHY
TEAR OFF THE MASK
TECHNICAL HITCH
TECHNICAL SKILL
TEETH OF THE WIND
TELEGRAPH WIRES
TELEPHONE KIOSK
TELEPHONE WIRES
TELESCOPIC LENS
TELESCOPIC VIEW
TELEVISION MAST
TELEVISION PLAY
TELEVISION STAR
TELL A TALL STORY
TELL EVERYTHING
TEMPLE OF APOLLO
TEMPORARY ABODE
TEMPORARY LEASE
TEMPORARY VISIT
TEN AND A QUARTER
TEN AND SIXPENCE
TEN AND TENPENCE
TEN AND TWOPENCE
TENDER FEELINGS
TEN-MINUTE ALIBI

TENSE SITUATION	THE PHILLIPINES
TENTH OF JANUARY	THE PLANEMAKERS
TENTH OF OCTOBER	THE PLANETARIUM
TERM OF CONTEMPT	THE POLICE FORCE
TERMS OF THE WILL	THE POLYTECHNIC
TERRIBLE ORDEAL	THE REFORMATION
TERRIBLE WRENCH	THE RENAISSANCE
TESTIFY AGAINST	THE RESTORATION
TEST OF STRENGTH	THE SEVEN DWARFS
THANKLESS CHILD	THE SHINING HOUR
THANKS A MILLION	THE SINGING FOOL
THANKS VERY MUCH	THE STAR CHAMBER
THAT CERTAIN AGE	THE TIME MACHINE
THAT'S THE TICKET	THE UNCONSCIOUS
THEATRICAL STAR	THE UNDERGROUND
THE AUTHORITIES	THE UNDERSIGNED
THE BEE'S WEDDING	THE VICAR OF BRAY
THE BEST CIRCLES	THE WATER BABIES
THE BLACK FOREST	THE WHEREWITHAL
THE BLACK PRINCE	THE WINTER'S TALE
THE CESAREWITCH	THE WORST IS OVER
THE COMMON TOUCH	THICK AS THIEVES
THE CORINTHIANS	THICK OF THE FRAY
THE CRUCIFIXION	THIEVES' KITCHEN
THE DARDANELLES	THIEVING MAGPIE
THE END OF THE DAY	THINK CAREFULLY
THE ETERNAL CITY	THINK OF ANOTHER
THE EXACT AMOUNT	THINK OF A NUMBER
THE EXTREMITIES	THINK OF THE PAST
THE FIRST CUCKOO	THINK THINGS OUT
THE FIRST PERSON	THIRD DIMENSION
THE FLINTSTONES	THIRD-FLOOR BACK
THE FORSYTE SAGA	THIRD OF JANUARY
THE FOUR JUST MEN	THIRD OF OCTOBER
THE GOLDEN BOUGH	THIRD-PARTY RISK
THE GOOD OLD DAYS	THIRD PROGRAMME
THE GRAND MANNER	THIRD TIME LUCKY
THE GRAND OLD MAN	THIRST FOR BLOOD
THE GREAT DIVIDE	THIRTEEN AND SIX
THE HIGHWAY CODE	THIRTEEN AND TEN
THE INQUISITION	THIRTEEN AND TWO
THEIR MAJESTIES	THIRTEEN MONTHS
THE JUNGLE BOOKS	THIRTEEN OUNCES
THE LILAC DOMINO	THIRTEENTH HOLE
THE LORD'S PRAYER	THIRTEEN TRICKS
THE LOTUS-EATERS	THIRTIETH OF MAY
THE MINSTREL BOY	THIRTY THOUSAND
THE NELSON TOUCH	THIRTY YEARS' WAR
THE NETHERLANDS	THIS HAPPY BREED
THE OLD GREY MARE	THIS IS YOUR LIFE
THE OLD OAK CHEST	THOMAS SHERATON

THORN IN THE SIDE
THOROUGH SEARCH
THOUGHTFUL MOOD
THOUSAND AND ONE
THOUSAND POUNDS
THREADING BEADS
THREAD TOGETHER
THREATEN DANGER
THREE AND A PENNY
THREE AND ELEVEN
THREE BLIND MICE
THREE-BOTTLE MAN
THREE-CARD TRICK
THREE FARTHINGS
THREE MEN IN A TUB
THREE-MILE LIMIT
THREE-PIECE SUIT
THREE SHILLINGS
THREE-SPEED GEAR
THREE SYLLABLES
THRILLER WRITER
THROAT PASTILLE
THROATY CHUCKLE
THROUGH THE AGES
THROUGH THE MILL
THROUGH THE NOSE
THROUGH THE POST
THROUGH THE TOWN
THROW IN ONE'S LOT
THROW LIGHT UPON
THROW OF THE DICE
THROW OVERBOARD
THROW THE HAMMER
THROW TO THE DOGS
THURSDAY ISLAND
THURSDAY'S CHILD
TICKLED TO DEATH
TICKLISH MATTER
TIMBER MERCHANT
TIME FOR THOUGHT
TIME IMMEMORIAL
TIMELY REMINDER
TIME OF ONE'S LIFE
TIME WITHOUT END
TIN OF PILCHARDS
TIP OF THE TONGUE
TIRELESS WORKER
TOAD OF TOAD HALL
TO A GREAT EXTENT
TO A LARGE DEGREE
TO A LARGE EXTENT

TOASTED TEA-CAKE
TOAST OF THE TOWN
TOBACCO AUCTION
TOBACCO LICENCE
TOBACCO PLANTER
TOIL AND TROUBLE
TOKEN OF RESPECT
TOOTH FOR A TOOTH
TOP-HAT AND TAILS
TOPICAL SUBJECT
TOP OF ONE'S VOICE
TOP OF THE CHARTS
TOP OF THE LADDER
TOP OF THE LEAGUE
TORRENTIAL RAIN
TORRENT OF ABUSE
TORTURE CHAMBER
TORTURED BY FEAR
TOTAL ABSTAINER
TOTAL IGNORANCE
TOTAL IMMERSION
TO THE BITTER END
TO THE END OF TIME
TOUCH A SOFT SPOT
TOUGH AS LEATHER
TOURING COMPANY
TOUR THE COUNTRY
TOWN AND COUNTRY
TOWN COUNCILLOR
TRACKED VEHICLE
TRACTION ENGINE
TRADE REFERENCE
TRADING STATION
TRAFFIC CONTROL
TRAFFIC DENSITY
TRAFFIC PROBLEM
TRAINED SOLDIER
TRAINING GROUND
TRAINING SCHOOL
TRAIN OF THOUGHT
TRANSFER BY DEED
TRANSITIVE VERB
TRANSPORT HOUSE
TRANSPORT PLANE
TRAVEL BROCHURE
TRAVELLER'S REST
TRAVELLER'S TALE
TRAVELLING TIME
TRAVEL THE WORLD
TREACLE PUDDING
TREAD THE BOARDS

TREAD UNDERFOOT
TREASURE ISLAND
TREMBLE TO THINK
TREMBLING HANDS
TREMBLING VOICE
TRIANGULAR DUEL
TRICKLE OF BLOOD
TRICKLE OF WATER
TRICK OF FORTUNE
TRICKY BUSINESS
TRICKY QUESTION
TRIED FOR MURDER
TRIFLING AMOUNT
TRIFLING CHARGE
TRIFLING MATTER
TRIFLING ,REMARK
TRINITY COLLEGE
TRIPE AND ONIONS
TRIPLE ALLIANCE
TRISTRAM SHANDY
TRIUMPHAL CROWN
TROOP MOVEMENTS
TROOP THE COLOUR
TROPIC OF CANCER
TROUBLE BREWING
TROUBLED WATERS
TROUBLE IN STORE
TROUPE OF ACTORS
TROUSERS POCKET
TRUE CONFESSION
TRUMPED-UP STORY
TRUNDLE THEM OUT
TRY AND TRY AGAIN
TRY ONE'S FORTUNE
TRY ONE'S HARDEST
TUESDAY EVENING
TUESDAY MORNING
TUMBLER OF WATER
TUNBRIDGE WELLS
TURF ACCOUNTANT
TURKISH DELIGHT
TURKISH TOBACCO
TURN AT THE WHEEL
TURN DOWN THE BED
TURN DOWN THE GAS
TURN EVERY STONE
TURN OFF THE HEAT
TURN OF THE SCREW
TURN OF THE WHEEL
TURN ON ONE'S HEEL
TURN ON THE LIGHT

TURN OUT TO GRASS
TURN RIGHT ROUND
TURN TOPSYTURVY
TURN TO THE RIGHT
TURN UP ONE'S NOSE
TURN UPSIDE DOWN
TWELFTH CENTURY
TWELFTH OF APRIL
TWELFTH OF MARCH
TWELVE AND A HALF
TWELVE AND EIGHT
TWELVE AND SEVEN
TWELVE AND THREE
TWELVE APOSTLES
TWELVE THOUSAND
TWENTIETH OF MAY
TWENTY THOUSAND
TWICE THE WEIGHT
TWIST OF TOBACCO
TWISTS AND TURNS
TWITTER OF BIRDS
TWO AND A QUARTER
TWO AND SIXPENCE
TWO AND TENPENCE
TWO AND TWOPENCE
TWO-HANDED SWORD
TWO-HEADED EAGLE
TWO WICKETS DOWN
TYPICAL EXAMPLE

U—14
ULTERIOR MOTIVE
ULTERIOR OBJECT
ULTIMATE RESULT
ULTRA-VIOLET RAY
UNABLE TO CHOOSE
UNACCOUNTED FOR
UNBALANCED MIND
UNBOSOM ONESELF
UNBROKEN SPIRIT
UNCIVILIZED MAN
UNCLE TOM'S CABIN
UNDER A HANDICAP
UNDER AN EMBARGO
UNDER CROSS-FIRE
UNDER DETENTION
UNDERGO REPAIRS
UNDER GUARANTEE
UNDER ONE'S THUMB
UNDER RESTRAINT
UNDER SUSPICION

UNDER THE BONNET
UNDER THE CARPET
UNDER THE DOCTOR
UNDER THE GROUND
UNDER THE HAMMER
UNDER THE HARROW
UNDER TREATMENT
UNDER TWENTY-ONE
UNDRESS UNIFORM
UNDUE INFLUENCE
UNEARNED INCOME
UNEASY PROGRESS
UNFAMILIAR WORD
UNIFORM PATTERN
UNINVITED GUEST
UNIQUE OCCASION
UNITED SERVICES
UNIVERSAL AGENT
UNIVERSAL AUNTS
UNIVERSAL JOINT
UNIVERSAL PEACE
UNIVERSITY TERM
UNIVERSITY TOWN
UNIVERSITY VOTE
UNKNOWN COUNTRY
UNKNOWN ELEMENT
UNKNOWN SOLDIER
UNKNOWN WARRIOR
UNLIMITED SCOPE
UNLIMITED SPACE
UNMARRIED WOMAN
UNOCCUPIED FLAT
UNPLEASANT DUTY
UNPLOUGHED LAND
UNREQUITED LOVE
UNSALTED BUTTER
UNSETTLING NEWS
UNSUITABLE TIME
UNTER DEN LINDEN
UNWELCOME GUEST
UPHILL STRUGGLE
UPON REFLECTION
UPRIGHT POSTURE
USUAL SIGNATURE
USURP THE THRONE

V—14
VACATE ONE'S SEAT
VAGRANCY CHARGE
VAGUE SUSPICION
VAIN AS A PEACOCK

VALET DE CHAMBRE
VALID OBJECTION
VALSE DES FLEURS
VANILLA FLAVOUR
VANISHING CREAM
VANISHING POINT
VANISHING TRICK
VARIABLE TEMPER
VARIETY THEATRE
VARIOUS COLOURS
VARIOUS REASONS
VARNISH REMOVER
VARYING SUCCESS
VAST DIFFERENCE
VAST EXPERIENCE
VATICAN COUNCIL
VAUDEVILLE SHOW
VEER TO THE RIGHT
VEGETABLE CURRY
VEGETABLE FIBRE
VEGETABLE SALAD
VEGETABLE WORLD
VEGETARIAN DIET
VEGETARIAN DISH
VEGETARIAN MEAL
VENDING MACHINE
VENERABLE BEARD
VENERABLE RUINS
VENETIAN CARPET
VENETIAN SCHOOL
VENETIAN WINDOW
VENUS AND ADONIS
VERBAL ARGUMENT
VERBAL CONTRACT
VERBAL EVIDENCE
VERBATIM REPORT
VERIFY THE FACTS
VERSATILE ACTOR
VERTICAL FLIGHT
VESTED INTEREST
VETERAN SERVICE
VICTIM OF CHANGE
VICTORIA PALACE
VICTORIA REGINA
VIEW WITH FAVOUR
VIOLENT QUARREL
VIOLENT TEMPEST
VIOLETS ARE BLUE
VIOLIN CONCERTO
VISIBLE EXPORTS
VISIBLE HORIZON

VITAL PRINCIPLE
VOICE AN OPINION
VOLATILE LIQUID
VOLUNTEER CORPS
VOTING STRENGTH
VULGAR FRACTION
VULGAR LANGUAGE
VULGAR PARLANCE
VULNERABLE SPOT

W—14
WAG A FOREFINGER
WAGGING TONGUES
WAIFS AND STRAYS
WAIT TILL THE END
WAKE WITH A START
WALKING HOLIDAY
WALKING LIBRARY
WALK INTO A PUNCH
WALK INTO DANGER
WALLOW IN LUXURY
WALLS OF JERICHO
WALPURGIS NIGHT
WALTER DE LA MARE
WALTZ COTILLION
WANTED BY THE LAW
WANT FOR NOTHING
WANT OF ALACRITY
WANT OF PRACTICE
WANT OF SYMMETRY
WARD IN CHANCERY
WARD OF THE COURT
WARDROBE DEALER
WARM FRIENDSHIP
WARM TO ONE'S WORK
WARNER BROTHERS
WARNING EXAMPLE
WAR OF ATTRITION
WAR OF EXPANSION
WARRANT OFFICER
WARREN HASTINGS
WARSAW CONCERTO
WARS OF THE ROSES
WARWICK DEEPING
WASH AND BRUSH-UP
WASH DIRTY LINEN
WASHING MACHINE
WASHINGTON POST
WASTE ONE'S WORDS
WATCH CAREFULLY
WATCH COMMITTEE

WATCH THE BIRDIE
WATERLOO BRIDGE
WATER ON THE KNEE
WATER THE GARDEN
WATER THE HORSES
WATER THE WICKET
WAVE OF VIOLENCE
WAVERLEY NOVELS
WEAK AT THE KNEES
WE ARE NOT AMUSED
WEARING APPAREL
WEATHER BALLOON
WEATHER OUTLOOK
WEATHER PROPHET
WEATHER STATION
WEDDING MORNING
WEDDING PRESENT
WEDDING SERVICE
WEDNESDAY NIGHT
WEEK-END VISITOR
WEEKLY MAGAZINE
WEEK'S GOOD CAUSE
WEIGH ONE'S WORDS
WEIGHTY PROBLEM
WELFARE OFFICER
WELL ACQUAINTED
WELL-CHOSEN WORD
WELL-EARNED REST
WELLINGTON BOOT
WELL-READ PERSON
WELL-WORN PHRASE
WELL WORTH WHILE
WELSH MOUNTAINS
WEMBLEY STADIUM
WENT WITH A SWING
WESTERN GERMANY
WEST HARTLEPOOL
WET ONE'S WHISTLE
WHAT DO YOU THINK?
WHAT IN THE WORLD?
WHAT OF THE CLOCK?
WHAT OF THE NIGHT?
WHAT'S THE DAMAGE?
WHAT'S THE MATTER?
WHAT THE DICKENS!
WHEELED TRAFFIC
WHEEL OF FORTUNE
WHICH WAY TO TURN
WHIGS AND TORIES
WHITE CHRISTMAS
WHITE CORPUSCLE

WHITE IN THE FACE
WHITE MAN'S GRAVE
WHITER THAN SNOW
WHITSUN HOLIDAY
WHOLE-MEAL BREAD
WHOLESALE PRICE
WIDDICOMBE FAIR
WIDELY BELIEVED
WIDEN THE BREACH
WIDE OF THE TRUTH
WIDE-OPEN SPACES
WIDE VOCABULARY
WIELD THE WILLOW
WIFE IN NAME ONLY
WILD ACCUSATION
WILD ENTHUSIASM
WILD EXCITEMENT
WILD-GOOSE CHASE
WILFRED PICKLES
WILLIAM AND MARY
WILLIAM HOGARTH
WILLING AND ABLE
WIN BY A KNOCK-OUT
WIND INSTRUMENT
WINDOW CURTAINS
WINDOW DRESSING
WINDOW ENVELOPE
WINDOW SHOPPING
WIND UP A COMPANY
WINE BY THE GLASS
WINIFRED ATWELL
WINNER TAKES ALL
WIN SECOND PRIZE
WINTER CLOTHING
WINTER PLANTING
WINTER QUARTERS
WINTER WOOLLIES
WISE AS A SERPENT
WITH A GOOD GRACE
WITH ALL MY HEART
WITH A VENGEANCE
WITHHOLD ASSENT
WITHOUT BLEMISH
WITHOUT CEASING
WITHOUT CONTEXT
WITHOUT MEASURE
WITHOUT PURPOSE
WITHOUT REMORSE
WITHOUT RESERVE
WITHOUT RESPECT
WITHOUT STRINGS

WITHOUT WARNING
WITH PERMISSION
WITH THE COLOURS
WITH THE CURRENT
WOMAN OF FASHION
WOMEN'S LAND ARMY
WOMEN'S QUARTERS
WOMEN'S SUFFRAGE
WONDERFUL SIGHT
WONDERFUL WORLD
WOOLLEN SWEATER
WOOLLY THINKING
WORCESTER SAUCE
WORKING CAPITAL
WORKING CLOTHES
WORKING FOREMAN
WORKING HOLIDAY
WORK IN PROGRESS
WORK LIKE A CHARM
WORK LIKE A HORSE
WORK LIKE A NAVVY
WORK LIKE BLAZES
WORK ONE'S TICKET
WORK TO SCHEDULE
WORLDLY AFFAIRS
WORLD OF FASHION
WORLD OF MEANING
WORLD OF ONE'S OWN
WORLD OF REALITY
WORLD SITUATION
WORMWOOD SCRUBS
WORN TO A FRAZZLE
WORTH A BOB OR TWO
WORTH IMITATING
WORTH ONE'S WHILE
WORTHY CHAMPION
WORTHY OF ESTEEM
WORTHY OF PRAISE
WORTHY OF REMARK
WRAPPED IN GLOOM
WRATH OF THE GODS
WREAK VENGEANCE
WRESTLING MATCH
WRIGHT BROTHERS
WRING ONE'S HANDS
WRITTEN APOLOGY
WRITTEN CONSENT
WRITTEN IN VERSE
WRITTEN MESSAGE
WRONG DIRECTION
WRONGFUL ARREST

Y—14
YACHTING CENTRE
YELLOWISH BROWN
YELLOW JAUNDICE
YELLOW SAPPHIRE
YORKSHIRE DALES
YORKSHIRE MOORS
YOUNG AND TENDER
YOUNGER BROTHER
YOUNGEST SISTER
YOUNG LOCHINVAR
YOUNG MAN'S FANCY
YOUNG PRETENDER
YOUNG SHOULDERS
YOU'RE TELLING ME!
YOUR EXCELLENCY
YOURS SINCERELY
YOU SHOULD WORRY!

A—15
ABANDON ONE'S POST
ABERDEEN TERRIER
ABLAZE WITH LIGHT
ABODE OF WARRIORS
ABOVE EVERYTHING
ABOVE THE AVERAGE
ABOVE THE SURFACE
ABOVE THE WEATHER
ABRIDGED VERSION
ABRUPT DEPARTURE
ABSOLUTE MINIMUM
ABSOLUTE MONARCH
ABSTRACT PAINTER
ABSTRACT SCIENCE
ABUNDANCE OF FOOD
ABUSE OF LANGUAGE
ACADEMIC CIRCLES
ACCEPT A PROPOSAL
ACCEPTED MEANING
ACCEPTED VERSION
ACCIDENTAL DEATH
ACCIDENT OF BIRTH
ACCORDING TO PLAN
ACCOUNT RENDERED
ACCREDITED AGENT
A CHRISTMAS CAROL
ACQUISITIVE MIND
ACROSS THE STREET
ACTIVE SUPPORTER
ACT OF AGGRESSION
ACT OF DEDICATION

ACT OF FRIENDSHIP
ACT OF PARLIAMENT
ACT OF PROVIDENCE
ACT OF SETTLEMENT
ACT THE GIDDY GOAT
ADDED ATTRACTION
ADDISON'S DISEASE
ADD TO ONE'S INCHES
ADHESIVE PLASTER
ADJUTANT GENERAL
ADMIT EVERYTHING
ADOPTION SOCIETY
A DROP IN THE OCEAN
ADVANCED BOOKING
ADVANCED IN YEARS
ADVANCED STUDENT
ADVANCED STUDIES
ADVANCED THINKER
ADVERTISING SITE
AEROPLANE TRIALS
AFFLUENT SOCIETY
AFRAID OF COMPANY
AFTER MY OWN HEART
AFTERNOON SIESTA
AGAINST ONE'S WILL
AGAINST THE CLOCK
AGAINST THE GRAIN
AGAINST THE RULES
AGE OF AUTOMATION
AGE OF DISCRETION
AGING POPULATION
AGREE BEFOREHAND
AGREE ON A VERDICT
AGREE TO DISAGREE
AHEAD OF SCHEDULE
AIDER AND ABETTER
AIMLESS ACTIVITY
AIR CHIEF MARSHAL
AIR CONDITIONING
AIRCRAFT CARRIER
AIREDALE TERRIER
AIR FORCE OFFICER
AIR FORCE RESERVE
AIR MINISTRY ROOF
AIR OF DETACHMENT
ALBERT CHEVALIER
ALDERSHOT TATTOO
ALEXANDRA PALACE
ALFRED HITCHCOCK
ALIMENTARY CANAL
A LITTLE LEARNING

ALIVE AND KICKING
ALL ALONG THE LINE
ALL FOUR QUARTERS
ALL MANNER OF WAYS
ALL-NIGHT SESSION
ALL-NIGHT SITTING
ALLOTMENT HOLDER
ALL OVER THE PLACE
ALL PASSION SPENT
ALL PULL TOGETHER
ALL-ROUND ABILITY
ALL-ROUND ATHLETE
ALL THE TRIMMINGS
ALL THE WORLD OVER
ALL THE YEAR ROUND
ALONE IN THE WORLD
ALTERNATIVE PLAN
ALTERNATIVE VOTE
AMATEUR CHAMPION
AMATEUR FOOTBALL
AMBIGUOUS SAYING
AMBITIOUS SCHEME
AMBULANCE DRIVER
AMERICAN EMBASSY
AMERICAN IN PARIS
AMMUNITION BOOTS
AMUSEMENT ARCADE
ANCIENT LANGUAGE
ANCIENT MONUMENT
ANCIENT PEDIGREE
ANDERSON SHELTER
AND SO SAY ALL OF US
ANGULAR VELOCITY
ANIMAL MAGNETISM
ANIMATED CARTOON
ANIMATED GESTURE
ANNIE GET YOUR GUN
ANNIVERSARY DATE
ANNOUNCE ONESELF
ANONYMOUS LETTER
ANOTHER CUP OF TEA
ANTARCTIC CIRCLE
ANTE-NATAL CLINIC
ANTE POST BETTING
ANTHONY TROLLOPE
ANTI-AIRCRAFT GUN
ANTIQUE MERCHANT
ANXIETY NEUROSIS
ANXIOUS TO PLEASE
ANY PORT IN A STORM
APPEALING GLANCE

APPEALING MANNER
APPLICATION FORM
APPLIED RESEARCH
APPLY THE CLOSURE
APPROACH MANHOOD
APPROXIMATE COST
APRIL THE SEVENTH
APRIL THE TWELFTH
ARMED NEUTRALITY
ARMED TO THE TEETH
AROUND THE CORNER
ARRIVAL PLATFORM
ARTICLES FOR SALE
ARTICLES OF FAITH
ARTIFICIAL FIBRE
ARTIFICIAL LIGHT
ARTIFICIAL SMILE
ARTIFICIAL STONE
ARTIFICIAL TEETH
ART OF MANAGEMENT
AS A MATTER OF FACT
AS AN ALTERNATIVE
ASCEND THE THRONE
ASCENSION ISLAND
AS FAR AS POSSIBLE
AS FAR AS YOU CAN GO
AS FRESH AS A DAISY
AS GENTLE AS A LAMB
AS GOOD AS ONE GETS
AS HARD AS GRANITE
AS KEEN AS MUSTARD
ASK FOR ONE'S CARDS
AS LIKE AS TWO PEAS
AS LONG AS YOU LIKE
AS NEAT AS A NEW PIN
AS OLD AS THE HILLS
AS QUIET AS A MOUSE
AS RICH AS CROESUS
ASSISTANT MASTER
ASSISTED PASSAGE
ASSOCIATED IDEAS
ASSORTED TOFFEES
AS STIFF AS A POKER
ASSUME A DISGUISE
AS THE SAYING GOES
ASTRAL INFLUENCE
ASTRONOMER ROYAL
A STUDY IN SCARLET
AS WHITE AS A SHEET
AT A DISADVANTAGE
AT A LOSS FOR WORDS

AT CLOSE QUARTERS
AT CROSS PURPOSES
ATLANTIC CHARTER
ATOMIC SUBMARINE
ATTEMPTED MURDER
AT THE CROSS-ROADS
AT THE DROP OF A HAT
ATTORNEY GENERAL
AT TRINITY CHURCH
AUGUST THE EIGHTH
AUGUST THE FOURTH
AUGUST THE SECOND
AUSTERITY BUDGET
AUTOGRAPH HUNTER
AUTOMATIC CHANGE
AUTOMATIC PISTOL
AUTUMNAL EQUINOX
AUXILIARY FORCES
AUXILIARY TROOPS
AVERAGE SPECIMEN
AWKWARD CUSTOMER
AWKWARD POSITION
AWKWARD QUESTION

B—15
BABY-FACED NELSON
BACHELOR OF MUSIC
BACHELOR'S BUTTON
BACKGROUND MUSIC
BACK OF THE BEYOND
BACKSTAGE NERVES
BACKWARD PEOPLES
BALACLAVA HELMET
BALANCE THE BOOKS
BALLROOM DANCING
BANKRUPTCY COURT
BANKS OF THE CLYDE
BANNER HEADLINES
BANNS OF MARRIAGE
BARBARA STANWYCK
BARBER OF SEVILLE
BARE POSSIBILITY
BARE SUBSISTENCE
BARGAIN BASEMENT
BARNUM AND BAILEY
BARON MUNCHAUSEN
BARRISTER'S CLERK
BARROW IN FURNESS
BARTHOLOMEW FAIR
BASIC INGREDIENT
BATCH OF RECRUITS

BATS IN THE BELFRY
BATTERSEA BRIDGE
BATTLE OF BRITAIN
BATTLE OF FLOWERS
BATTLE OF JUTLAND
BATTLE OF THE NILE
BAYONET PRACTICE
BEAST OF THE FIELD
BEATEN ON THE POST
BEAUTIFUL FIGURE
BEAUTY TREATMENT
BEAUTY UNADORNED
BECOME ENAMOURED
BECOME INVISIBLE
BED AND BREAKFAST
BEE IN ONE'S BONNET
BEER AND SKITTLES
BEFORE BREAKFAST
BEFORE THE FINISH
BEGINNERS, PLEASE
BEGINNING AND END
BEGIN THE BEGUINE
BEHAVE NATURALLY
BEHIND THE SCENES
BEHIND THE STUMPS
BELLOW LIKE A BULL
BELONG TO THE PAST
BELOW THE AVERAGE
BELOW THE HORIZON
BELOW THE SURFACE
BENEATH CONTEMPT
BENEFIT OF CLERGY
BENITO MUSSOLINI
BENJAMIN BRITTEN
BERNE CONVENTION
BERNESE OBERLAND
BERTRAND RUSSELL
BESSEMER PROCESS
BEST FOOT FORWARD
BEST OF ALL WORLDS
BET ON A CERTAINTY
BETRAY THE SECRET
BETTER AND BETTER
BETTER RELATIONS
BETWEEN THE LINES
BETWEEN TWO FIRES
BETWEEN YOU AND ME
BEVERIDGE REPORT
BEVERLEY NICHOLS
BEVERLEY SISTERS
BEWARE OF THE BULL

BEYOND ALL BOUNDS
BEYOND CRITICISM
BEYOND ONE'S DEPTH
BEYOND ONE'S GRASP
BEYOND ONE'S MEANS
BEYOND ONE'S PRIME
BEYOND ONE'S REACH
BEYOND THE FRINGE
BIGGER AND BETTER
BIGGER AND BIGGER
BILLIARDS PLAYER
BINDING CONTRACT
BIRDS OF A FEATHER
BIRTHDAY HONOURS
BIRTHDAY PRESENT
BIRTH OF THE BLUES
BITE ONE'S HEAD OFF
BLACK AS MIDNIGHT
BLACK AS THE DEVIL
BLACKBURN ROVERS
BLACK-COAT WORKER
BLACKMAIL LETTER
BLACKWALL TUNNEL
BLACKWATER FEVER
BLEACHING POWDER
BLISSFULLY HAPPY
BLOOD AND THUNDER
BLOOMSBURY GROUP
BLOW HOT; BLOW COLD
BLOW TO ONE'S PRIDE
BLUES IN THE NIGHT
BLUNT INSTRUMENT
BLUSHING HONOURS
BOARD AND LODGING
BOARDING OFFICER
BODLEIAN LIBRARY
BODY-LINE BOWLING
BODY OF KNOWLEDGE
BODY TEMPERATURE
BOLD IMAGINATION
BOLTED AND BARRED
BOLT FROM THE BLUE
BONDED WAREHOUSE
BOOKMAKER'S CLERK
BOOK OF REFERENCE
BORN IN THE PURPLE
BORROWING POWERS
BOTANICAL GARDEN
BOTTLE OF PERFUME
BOTTLE OF VINEGAR
BOTTOMLESS PURSE

BOTTOM OF THE FORM
BOTTOM OF THE HILL
BOTTOM OF THE POLL
BOTTOM THE WEAVER
BOWL AT THE STUMPS
BOWLED BY A YORKER
BOWLING ANALYSIS
BOW-STREET RUNNER
BOX OF CHOCOLATES
BRASS INSTRUMENT
BRAVE ALL HAZARDS
BREACH OF PROMISE
BREAD OF IDLENESS
BREAKFAST CEREAL
BREAKING OF BREAD
BREAK ON THE WHEEL
BREAK THE BAD NEWS
BREAK THE SILENCE
BREAST OF CHICKEN
BREATHE ONE'S LAST
BREATHLESS HURRY
BREATH OF SCANDAL
BRICKS AND MORTAR
BRIDES IN THE BATH
BRIDGE OF THE NOSE
BRIGADE OF GUARDS
BRIGADIER GERARD
BRIGHT AND BREEZY
BRIGHT AS A BUTTON
BRIGHT AS A NEW PIN
BRIGHTON AND HOVE
BRIGHT PROSPECTS
BRIGHT YOUNGSTER
BRILLIANT SUNSET
BRING IN A VERDICT
BRING IN NEW BLOOD
BRING TO FRUITION
BRISTLE WITH RAGE
BRITISH COLUMBIA
BRITISH HONDURAS
BRITISH PASSPORT
BRITISH RAILWAYS
BROAD-BRIMMED HAT
BROADEN ONE'S MIND
BROADLY SPEAKING
BRONZE MEDALLIST
BROTHER JONATHAN
BROTHER OFFICERS
BROWN AS MAHOGANY
BRUSSELS SPROUTS
BUBBLE AND SQUEAK

BUDDING CHAMPION
BUDGET ESTIMATES
BUILDING SOCIETY
BULLDOG DRUMMOND
BULLET-PROOF VEST
BULL'S-EYE LANTERN
BUMP OF KNOWLEDGE
BURIAL OF THE DEAD
BURLINGTON HOUSE
BURNHAM ON CROUCH
BURNING QUESTION
BURN ONE'S BRIDGES
BURN ONE'S FINGERS
BURNT AT THE STAKE
BURNT TO A FRAZZLE
BURST AT THE SEAMS
BURST INTO FLAMES
BURST INTO FLOWER
BURST OF APPLAUSE
BURST OF LAUGHTER
BUSINESS ADDRESS
BUSINESS AFFAIRS
BUSINESS AS USUAL
BUSINESS CIRCLES
BUSINESS COLLEGE
BUSINESS CONTACT
BUSINESS FOOTING
BUSINESS MANAGER
BUSINESS MEETING
BUSINESS METHODS
BUSINESS ROUTINE
BUSINESS VENTURE
BUTTERFLY COLLAR
BUTTERFLY STROKE
BUTTON MUSHROOMS
BY FITS AND STARTS
BY HOOK OR BY CROOK
BY THE SHORT HAIRS
BYZANTINE EMPIRE
BYZANTINE SCHOOL

C—15
CABINET MINISTER
CALCIUM CHLORIDE
CALCULATING MIND
CALEDONIAN CANAL
CALL AN AMBULANCE
CALL ATTENTION TO
CALL IN THE DOCTOR
CALL IN THE POLICE
CALL NO MAN MASTER

CALL TO SURRENDER
CALM AS A MILL-POND
CAMBERWELL GREEN
CAMBRIDGE CIRCUS
CAMEMBERT CHEESE
CAME TO THE THRONE
CANADIAN PACIFIC
CANDLEWICK COVER
CANTERBURY BELLS
CANTERBURY TALES
CAPABILITY BROWN
CAPITAL GAINS TAX
CAPITAL OF FRANCE
CAPITAL OF NORWAY
CAPITAL OF SWEDEN
CAPITAL SENTENCE
CARDIFF ARMS PARK
CARDINAL NUMBERS
CARDINAL VIRTUES
CARDS ON THE TABLE
CARELESS DRIVING
CARELESS RAPTURE
CARES OF THE WORLD
CARPENTER'S BENCH
CARRIAGE AND PAIR
CARRIAGE FORWARD
CARRY CONVICTION
CARRY OUT ONE'S BAT
CARRY THE CAN BACK
CASH IN ONE'S CHIPS
CASH TRANSACTION
CASTING DIRECTOR
CASTLES IN THE AIR
CASTOR AND POLLUX
CASUAL REFERENCE
CASUALTY STATION
CAT AND THE FIDDLE
CATCH AS CATCH CAN
CATCH BY THE HEELS
CATCH ONE NAPPING
CATCH ONE'S BREATH
CATERING OFFICER
CATHEDRAL SQUARE
CAUGHT AMIDSHIPS
CAUGHT AND BOWLED
CAUGHT RED-HANDED
CAUSE A SENSATION
CAVALRY REGIMENT
CEASELESS ENERGY
CEDARS OF LEBANON
CELESTIAL SPHERE

CELLULOID COLLAR
CELLULOID EMPIRE
CENTRAL POSITION
CENTRE OF GRAVITY
CERTAIN EVIDENCE
CERTAIN QUANTITY
CERTIFIED INSANE
CHAMPAGNE BOTTLE
CHAMPAGNE SUPPER
CHANCE DISCOVERY
CHANCE ENCOUNTER
CHANCE OF SUCCESS
CHANGE DIRECTION
CHANGE OF ADDRESS
CHANGE OF CLIMATE
CHANGE OF CLOTHES
CHANGE OF COSTUME
CHANGE OF FORTUNE
CHANGE OF OPINION
CHANGE OF PURPOSE
CHANGE OF SCENERY
CHANGE OF TACTICS
CHANGE ONE'S IDEAS
CHANNEL CROSSING
CHANTREY BEQUEST
CHAPTER AND VERSE
CHARACTER SKETCH
CHARCOAL DRAWING
CHARGE TOO LITTLE
CHARITABLE CAUSE
CHARLES KINGSLEY
CHARLES LAUGHTON
CHARLES THE FIRST
CHARLOTTE BRONTË
CHATSWORTH HOUSE
CHEAP AT THE PRICE
CHEAP RESTAURANT
CHEAT THE GALLOWS
CHECK ONE'S COURSE
CHECK THE RECORDS
CHEERFUL CONSENT
CHEERFUL OLD SOUL
CHELSEA ARTS BALL
CHELSEA BARRACKS
CHEMICAL FORMULA
CHEMICAL PROCESS
CHEMICAL WARFARE
CHEQUERED CAREER
CHERCHEZ LA FEMME
CHESS TOURNAMENT
CHICKEN MARYLAND

CHICKEN SANDWICH
CHIEF MAGISTRATE
CHILDHOOD FRIEND
CHILDISH ATTEMPT
CHILD PSYCHOLOGY
CHILDREN'S ANNUAL
CHILDREN'S CORNER
CHILLED WITH FEAR
CHILLY RECEPTION
CHIPPED POTATOES
CHOCOLATE ÉCLAIR
CHOCOLATE FINGER
CHOCOLATE SUNDAE
CHOICE OF COLOURS
CHOICE OF WEAPONS
CHOOSE ONE'S WORDS
CHRISTMAS ANNUAL
CHRISTMAS DINNER
CHRISTMAS ISLAND
CHRISTMAS SEASON
CHRISTMAS SPIRIT
CHRISTOPHER WREN
CHRIST'S HOSPITAL
CHURCH OF ENGLAND
CIGARETTE COUPON
CIGARETTE HOLDER
CINDERELLA DANCE
CIRCLE OF FRIENDS
CITY AND SUBURBAN
CITY CORPORATION
CIVILIAN CLOTHES
CLAIMS OF SOCIETY
CLAIM THE VICTORY
CLAPHAM JUNCTION
CLASHING COLOURS
CLASH OF OPINIONS
CLASSICAL BALLET
CLASSICAL WRITER
CLASSIC FEATURES
CLASSICS SCHOLAR
CLEAN AS A WHISTLE
CLEANING UTENSIL
CLEAN THE WINDOWS
CLEAR AS DAYLIGHT
CLEAR CONSCIENCE
CLEAR IN ONE'S MIND
CLEAR ONE'S THROAT
CLEAR REFLECTION
CLENCH ONE'S FISTS
CLENCH ONE'S TEETH
CLERK OF THE COURT

CLERK OF THE HOUSE
CLERK OF THE WORKS
CLEVER DECEPTION
CLIFF MICHELMORE
CLING LIKE THE IVY
CLINICAL LECTURE
CLINICAL SURGERY
CLOAK-ROOM TICKET
CLOSE AS AN OYSTER
CLOSE COMPANIONS
CLOSE FRIENDSHIP
CLOSER AND CLOSER
CLOSE TO THE SHORE
CLOSING-DOWN SALE
CLOTHING COUPONS
CLOUD-CUCKOO LAND
COACHING STATION
COCKPIT OF EUROPE
COCKTAIL CABINET
CODE OF BEHAVIOUR
COLD AS CHRISTMAS
COLD COMFORT FARM
COLDSTREAM GUARD
COLERIDGE TAYLOR
COLLAPSIBLE BOAT
COLLECT EVIDENCE
COLLECTING POINT
COLLECTION PLATE
COLLECT MATERIAL
COLLECT ONE'S WITS
COLLECTOR'S PIECE
COLLIERY MANAGER
COLLISION COURSE
COLORADO SPRINGS
COLOUR BLINDNESS
COLOURFUL BORDER
COLOURING MATTER
COLOURLESS FLUID
COLOUR PREJUDICE
COMBINATION LOCK
COME DOWN TO EARTH
COME HOME TO ROOST
COME IN LIKE A LION
COME INTO CONTACT
COME INTO ONE'S OWN
COME INTO THE OPEN
COME OUT ON STRIKE
COME TO A DEAD STOP
COME TO A DECISION
COME TO A FULL STOP
COME TO ATTENTION

COME TO THE RESCUE
COME TO THINK OF IT
COME UP TO SCRATCH
COMFORTABLE SEAT
COMFORTING WORDS
COMMANDING VOICE
COMMERCIAL HOTEL
COMMERCIAL VALUE
COMMISSION AGENT
COMMIT AN OFFENCE
COMMIT TO WRITING
COMMON AGREEMENT
COMMON COMPLAINT
COMMON KNOWLEDGE
COMMON OWNERSHIP
COMMUNAL FEEDING
COMMUNAL KITCHEN
COMMUNITY CENTRE
COMPANION IN ARMS
COMPANION LADDER
COMPANION VOLUME
COMPANY DIRECTOR
COMPANY PROMOTER
COMPLETE ABANDON
COMPLETE CONTROL
COMPLETE DEBACLE
COMPLETE EDITION
COMPLETE FAILURE
COMPLETE SWINDLE
COMPLETE VICTORY
COMPLETE WASH-OUT
COMPLEX SENTENCE
COMPOUND A FELONY
COMPULSORY GAMES
CONCERTED ACTION
CONCERTED EFFORT
CONCERT PLATFORM
CONCLUSIVE PROOF
CONDITIONAL MOOD
CONDITION POWDER
CONFERENCE TABLE
CONFESS THE TRUTH
CONFIDENCE TRICK
CONFUSE THE ISSUE
CONGENITAL IDIOT
CONSCIENCE MONEY
CONSCIOUS HUMOUR
CONSENTING PARTY
CONSIDERABLE SUM
CONSIGNMENT NOTE
CONSOLATION RACE

CONSTANT ANXIETY
CONSTANT CHATTER
CONSULAR SERVICE
CONSUMMATE SKILL
CONTEMPT OF COURT
CONTINENTAL TIME
CONTROLLED PRICE
CONVENIENT PLACE
CONVERSION TABLE
CONVIVIAL PERSON
COOKING UTENSILS
COOK THE ACCOUNTS
COOL AS A CUCUMBER
CORDIAL GREETING
CORNER THE MARKET
CORONATION COACH
CORONATION ROBES
CORONATION STONE
CORONER'S INQUEST
CORONER'S VERDICT
CORRECTED PROOFS
CORRECT ESTIMATE
CORRUGATED PAPER
COTTAGE BY THE SEA
COTTAGE HOSPITAL
COTTAGE INDUSTRY
COUNCIL OF ELDERS
COUNCIL OF EUROPE
COUNSEL'S OPINION
COUNTERFEIT COIN
COUNTER IRRITANT
COUNT FOR NOTHING
COUNT ONE'S CHANGE
COUNTRY OF ORIGIN
COUNT THE MINUTES
COUNT THE TAKINGS
COUNTY CRICKETER
COURT DRESSMAKER
COURT OF JUDGMENT
COVER MUCH GROUND
COVER ONE'S TRACKS
CRADLE OF THE DEEP
CRAMPED QUARTERS
CRAZY MIXED-UP KID
CREAMED POTATOES
CREASE RESISTANT
CREATE AN OPENING
CREATE A NUISANCE
CREATE A STOPPAGE
CREATIVE WRITING
CREATURE COMFORT

CREATURE OF HABIT
CREDULOUS PERSON
CREEPING BARRAGE
CREMORNE GARDENS
CRICKET PAVILION
CRIMINAL AT LARGE
CRIMINAL CLASSES
CRIMINAL LUNATIC
CRIMINAL NEGLECT
CRIMINAL OFFENCE
CRIPPLED FOR LIFE
CRITICAL OPINION
CROOKED SIXPENCE
CROSS-COUNTRY RUN
CROSSING THE LINE
CROSS THE CHANNEL
CROSS THE RUBICON
CROSSWORD PUZZLE
CROWD PSYCHOLOGY
CRUCIAL QUESTION
CRUSADING SPIRIT
CRUSHING VICTORY
CRUX OF THE MATTER
CUCKOO IN THE NEST
CUDGEL ONE'S BRAIN
CULTIVATE A HABIT
CULTIVATED PEARL
CULTIVATED TASTE
CUP OF BITTERNESS
CURRENT EXPENSES
CURSE OF SCOTLAND
CURTAIN MATERIAL
CUSTOMS OFFICIAL
CUT AND COME AGAIN
CUT A SORRY FIGURE
CUT DOWN EXPENSES
CUT ONESELF LOOSE

D—15
DAILY OCCURRENCE
DAME LAURA KNIGHT
DAME NELLIE MELBA
DAMNING EVIDENCE
DAMON AND PYTHIAS
DAMPENED SPIRITS
DANCE ATTENDANCE
DANCE OF THE HOURS
DANCING MISTRESS
DANGEROUS CORNER
DANGEROUS PERSON
DANGEROUS VOYAGE

DANGEROUS WEAPON
DASH TO THE GROUND
DAVID AND GOLIATH
DAVY JONES' LOCKER
DAYLIGHT ROBBERY
DAY OF ABSTINENCE
DAY OF LIBERATION
DEAD AS A DOORNAIL
DEAD ON THE TARGET
DEAFENING CHEERS
DEAF TO ALL ADVICE
DEAL DESTRUCTION
DEAR LITTLE THING
DEATH BY DROWNING
DEATH ON THE ROADS
DEBT OF GRATITUDE
DECEIVED HUSBAND
DECIMAL FRACTION
DECISIVE VICTORY
DECLARED MISSING
DECLARE ONE'S LOVE
DECREE OF NULLITY
DEFECTIVE MEMORY
DEFECTIVE VISION
DEFENCE MINISTER
DEFENSIVE BATTLE
DEFENSIVE WEAPON
DEFERRED PAYMENT
DEFINITE ARTICLE
DELAYED REACTION
DELAYING TACTICS
DELICATE BALANCE
DELIRIUM TREMENS
DELIVERED BY HAND
DELIVER JUDGMENT
DELIVER THE GOODS
DEMAND AND SUPPLY
DEMAND ATTENTION
DEMENTIA PRAECOX
DEMOCRATIC PARTY
DEMOLITION SQUAD
DENIAL OF JUSTICE
DENTAL TREATMENT
DEPARTMENT STORE
DEPARTURE LOUNGE
DEPTHS OF DESPAIR
DESCENDING ORDER
DESCRIBE A CIRCLE
DESERTED VILLAGE
DESIGN FOR LIVING
DESIGNING FEMALE

DESIRABLE OBJECT
DESOLATE COUNTRY
DESPERATE PLIGHT
DESPERATE REMEDY
DETACHED OPINION
DETAILED ACCOUNT
DETENTION CENTRE
DETERRENT EFFECT
DEVALUE THE POUND
DEVELOPMENT AREA
DEVILLED KIDNEYS
DEVIL'S COMPANION
DEVIL'S PUNCH BOWL
DEVONSHIRE CREAM
DEVONSHIRE HOUSE
DIAMOND MERCHANT
DIAMOND NECKLACE
DIAMOND SMUGGLER
DICKIE HENDERSON
DICKIE VALENTINE
DICK WHITTINGTON
DIE IN THE ATTEMPT
DIE WITH LAUGHTER
DIFFERENT TASTES
DIFFICULT CHOICE
DIFFICULT MATTER
DIFFICULT PERSON
DIFFIDENT MANNER
DIG ONE'S OWN GRAVE
DINING-ROOM TABLE
DIPLOMATIC AGENT
DIPLOMATIC CORPS
DIPLOMATIC STAFF
DIRECT INFLUENCE
DIRECTION FINDER
DIRECTOR GENERAL
DIRT-TRACK RACING
DISAPPEARING ACT
DISARMAMENT PLAN
DISCARDED CUSTOM
DISCHARGE PAPERS
DISGUISE ONESELF
DISLOCATED ELBOW
DISORDERED BRAIN
DISORDERLY HOUSE
DISPENSE CHARITY
DISPENSE JUSTICE
DISPLACED PERSON
DISPOSABLE GOODS
DISPUTE THE FACTS
DISTANT LIKENESS

DISTANT PROSPECT
DISTANT RELATIVE
DISTINCTIVE NOTE
DISTORT THE TRUTH
DISTRESSING NEWS
DISTRESS WARRANT
DISTRICT OFFICER
DISTRICT RAILWAY
DISTRICT VISITOR
DISTURB THE PEACE
DIVIDEND WARRANT
DIVINE MESSENGER
DIVINITY STUDENT
DO A ROARING TRADE
DO AS THE ROMANS DO
DOCTOR OF SCIENCE
DOCUMENTARY FILM
DOG WITH TWO TAILS
DO-IT-YOURSELF FAN
DO-IT-YOURSELF KIT
DOLLAR RESOURCES
DOLLARS AND CENTS
DOMESTIC AFFAIRS
DOMESTIC ECONOMY
DOMESTIC OFFICES
DOMESTIC PROBLEM
DOMESTIC SCIENCE
DOMESTIC SERVANT
DOMESTIC SERVICE
DONE IN COLD BLOOD
DO ONE'S LEVEL BEST
DORA COPPERFIELD
DORCHESTER HOTEL
DORMITORY SUBURB
DO THE CHARLESTON
DO THE CIVIL THING
DO THE IMPOSSIBLE
DO THE RIGHT THING
DO THE WRONG THING
DO THINGS IN STYLE
DOUBLE ADVANTAGE
DOUBLE INDEMNITY
DOUBLE OR NOTHING
DOUBLE-QUICK TIME
DOUBLE SEVENTEEN
DOUBLE THE STAKES
DOUBLE WHITE LINE
DOUBLE YOUR MONEY
DOUBTFUL STARTER
DOWN IN THE DEPTHS
DOWN IN THE VALLEY

DOWN THE MOUNTAIN
DOWN THE STRAIGHT
DOWN TO THE GROUND
DOZENS AND DOZENS
DRAIN TO THE DREGS
DRAMATIC GESTURE
DRAMATIC SETTING
DRAMATIC SOCIETY
DRASTIC MEASURES
DRAW A COMPARISON
DRAW A DEEP BREATH
DRAW AN INFERENCE
DRAW A RED HERRING
DRAW CONCLUSIONS
DRAW IN ONE'S HORNS
DRAW INSPIRATION
DRAW ONE'S PENSION
DRAW THE CURTAINS
DREAMER OF DREAMS
DRESSING STATION
DRILLING MACHINE
DRILL INSTRUCTOR
DRINK ONE'S HEALTH
DRINK ON THE HOUSE
DRIVEN TO THE WALL
DRIVE RECKLESSLY
DROOPING SPIRITS
DROP IN THE BUCKET
DROP OF GOOD STUFF
DROP OVER THE SIDE
DRUG ON THE MARKET
DRUM AND FIFE BAND
DRUMHEAD SERVICE
DUAL CARRIAGE-WAY
DUAL PERSONALITY
DUBIOUS BLESSING
DUBLIN BAY PRAWNS
DUCHY OF CORNWALL
DUELLING PISTOLS
DUKE OF EDINBURGH
DUKE OF LANCASTER

E—15
EAGER FOR THE FRAY
EARLY-CLOSING DAY
EARLY-MORNING TEA
EARNING CAPACITY
EARTHLY PARADISE
EASTERN COUNTIES
EASTERN QUESTION
EASY-PACED WICKET

EAT ONE'S HEART OUT
EBENEZER SCROOGE
ECLIPSE OF THE SUN
ECONOMIC WARFARE
EDINBURGH CASTLE
EDITORIAL COLUMN
EDITOR'S DECISION
EDMUND HOCKRIDGE
EDWARD THE FOURTH
EDWARD THE SECOND
EGG-AND-SPOON RACE
EIGHTEEN AND FIVE
EIGHTEEN AND FOUR
EIGHTEEN AND NINE
EIGHTEEN HUNDRED
EIGHTEEN PER CENT
EIGHTEENTH GREEN
EIGHTEENTH OF MAY
EIGHTH OF JANUARY
EIGHTH OF OCTOBER
EIGHT O'CLOCK NEWS
EIGHT OF DIAMONDS
EIGHTPENNY STAMP
EIGHTY-ONE AND SIX
EIGHTY-SIX AND SIX
EIGHTY-TWO AND SIX
ELABORATE DESIGN
ELABORATE DETAIL
ELECTION ADDRESS
ELECTION RESULTS
ELECTORAL DEFEAT
ELECTORAL SYSTEM
ELECTRICAL FAULT
ELECTRIC BATTERY
ELECTRIC BLANKET
ELECTRIC CIRCUIT
ELECTRIC CURRENT
ELECTRIC FURNACE
ELECTRICITY BILL
ELECTRIC MACHINE
ELECTRIC RAILWAY
ELECTRIC TOASTER
ELECTRONIC BRAIN
ELEVATED RAILWAY
ELEVEN AND A PENNY
ELEVEN AND ELEVEN
ELEVEN SHILLINGS
ELEVENTH CENTURY
ELEVENTH OF APRIL
ELEVENTH OF MARCH
ELIZABETH TAYLOR

ELOCUTION LESSON
EMANUEL SHINWELL
EMERALD BRACELET
EMERALD NECKLACE
EMERGENCY POWERS
EMERGENCY RATION
EMOTIONAL RELIEF
ENCASED IN ARMOUR
ENDEAVOUR TO HELP
ENDLESS ARGUMENT
ENDLESS ATTEMPTS
END OF ONE'S TETHER
END OF THE CENTURY
END OF THE CHAPTER
END OF THE JOURNEY
ENDOWMENT POLICY
ENEMY OF PROGRESS
ENERGETIC PERSON
ENGAGEMENT DIARY
ENGINEER A STRIKE
ENGLAND AND WALES
ENGLISH LANGUAGE
ENGLISHMAN'S HOME
ENJOY GOOD HEALTH
ENJOY POOR HEALTH
ENTENTE CORDIALE
ENTER PARLIAMENT
EPICUREAN TASTES
EPSOM RACECOURSE
EQUESTRIAN SKILL
ERNEST HEMINGWAY
ERRONEOUS BELIEF
ERROR OF JUDGMENT
ERROR OF OMISSION
ESCAPED PRISONER
ESCAPE MECHANISM
ESPOUSE THE CAUSE
ESSENTIAL CLAUSE
ESTABLISH A CLAIM
ETERNAL TRIANGLE
ETON BOATING-SONG
EVENING STANDARD
EVEN MONEY CHANCE
EVERLASTING FAME
EVERY MOTHER'S SON
EVERY NOW AND THEN
EVERYONE'S FRIEND
EVIDENCE IN COURT
EXAGGERATED IDEA
EXALTED POSITION
EXAMINATION HALL

EXCELLENT CHANCE
EXCELLENT REASON
EXCELLENT RESULT
EXCEPTIONAL WORD
EXCESSIVE CHARGE
EXCESSIVE WEIGHT
EXCHANGE AND MART
EXCHANGE CONTROL
EXCHANGE GLANCES
EXCHANGE LETTERS
EXCHANGE OF VIEWS
EXCHANGE SIGNALS
EXCLAMATION MARK
EXCLUSIVE REPORT
EXCLUSIVE RIGHTS
EXCURSION TICKET
EXERCISE CONTROL
EXERCISE THE MIND
EXERCISE THE VETO
EXHAUSTION POINT
EXORBITANT PRICE
EXPANDING BULLET
EXPECT OTHERWISE
EXPENSE NO OBJECT
EXPENSIVE TASTES
EXPERT KNOWLEDGE
EXPLODE WITH RAGE
EXPLOSIVE CHARGE
EXPLOSIVE DEVICE
EXPORT AND IMPORT
EXPOSED POSITION
EXPOSED TO DANGER
EXPRESS CONTEMPT
EXPRESS DELIVERY
EXPRESSIVE SMILE
EXQUISITE CHOICE
EXTENSION OF TIME
EXTORTIONATE FEE
EXTREME KINDNESS
EXTREME MEASURES
EXTREME PATIENCE
EYEBROW TWEEZERS

F—15
FACE LIKE A FIDDLE
FACE THE OTHER WAY
FACE THE PROSPECT
FACT OF THE MATTER
FACTS AND FIGURES
FADED REPUTATION
FAIR MAID OF PERTH

FAIR MEANS OR FOUL
FAIR WEAR AND TEAR
FAITHFUL ACCOUNT
FAITHFUL PROMISE
FAITHFUL SERVANT
FALKLAND ISLANDS
FALL ON HARD TIMES
FALL TO THE GROUND
FALSE ACCUSATION
FALSE APPEARANCE
FALSE CONCEPTION
FALSE IMPRESSION
FALSE REPUTATION
FAMILY ALLOWANCE
FAMILY GATHERING
FAMILY LOYALTIES
FAMILY SOLICITOR
FAMOUS LAST WORDS
FANCY-DRESS DANCE
FANNY BY GASLIGHT
FAN-TAILED PIGEON
FAREWELL ADDRESS
FAR FROM THE TRUTH
FARMING ACCOUNTS
FARTHING DAMAGES
FASHIONABLE AREA
FASTER THAN SOUND
FATAL ATTRACTION
FATHER AND MOTHER
FATHER CHRISTMAS
FATHER CONFESSOR
FATHERLESS CHILD
FAVOURABLE ISSUE
FAVOURABLE REPLY
FAVOURABLE START
FAVOURABLE TERMS
FEAR FOR ONE'S LIFE
FEAST FOR THE GODS
FEATHERED FRIEND
FEATHER ONE'S NEST
FEDERAL REPUBLIC
FEEBLE IMITATION
FEEL COMFORTABLE
FEEL IN ONE'S BONES
FEET ON THE GROUND
FELLOWSHIP HOUSE
FELLOW TRAVELLER
FEMININE PRONOUN
FENCED ENCLOSURE
FENCHURCH STREET
FESTIVAL GARDENS

FESTIVE OCCASION
FIELD OF ACTIVITY
FIELD PUNISHMENT
FIFTEEN AND A HALF
FIFTEEN AND EIGHT
FIFTEEN AND SEVEN
FIFTEEN AND THREE
FIFTEENTH LETTER
FIFTEENTH OF JULY
FIFTEENTH OF JUNE
FIFTEEN THOUSAND
FIFTH OF DECEMBER
FIFTH OF FEBRUARY
FIFTH OF NOVEMBER
FIFTY-FIVE AND SIX
FIFTY-NINE AND SIX
FIGHT FOR FREEDOM
FIGHT LIKE DEVILS
FIGHT TO THE DEATH
FIGURATIVE SENSE
FILL IN THE CRACKS
FILTH AND SQUALOR
FINANCE MINISTER
FINANCIAL CRISIS
FINANCIAL WIZARD
FINDING'S KEEPING
FINE OPPORTUNITY
FINISHED PRODUCT
FINISHING SCHOOL
FINISHING STROKE
FIREWORK DISPLAY
FIRST-AID STATION
FIRST APPEARANCE
FIRST BEGINNINGS
FIRST-CLASS HOTEL
FIRST-CLASS MATCH
FIRST-FLOOR FRONT
FIRST IMPORTANCE
FIRST IMPRESSION
FIRST INSTALMENT
FIRST INTENTIONS
FIRST IN THE FIELD
FIRST IN THE QUEUE
FIRST LIEUTENANT
FIRST OCCURRENCE
FIRST OF DECEMBER
FIRST OF FEBRUARY
FIRST OF NOVEMBER
FIRST PORT OF CALL
FIRST PRINCIPLES
FIRST-RATE ACTING

FIRST WICKET DOWN
FISH AND CHIP SHOP
FISHING INDUSTRY
FISHMONGERS' HALL
FIT OF GENEROSITY
FIT OF THE VAPOURS
FIVE AND A QUARTER
FIVE AND SIXPENCE
FIVE AND TENPENCE
FIVE AND TWOPENCE
FIVE WICKETS DOWN
FIXED IMPRESSION
FLAGGING SPIRITS
FLAMBOROUGH HEAD
FLAMING NUISANCE
FLANNEL TROUSERS
FLAWLESS DIAMOND
FLAWLESS MANNERS
FLEETING GLIMPSE
FLEET OPERATIONS
FLEMISH LANGUAGE
FLICK OF THE WRIST
FLING INTO PRISON
FLIRT WITH THE LAW
FLOATING CAPITAL
FLOOR OF THE HOUSE
FLOURISHING TIME
FLOWER OF THE ARMY
FLY INTO A PASSION
FLY OFF THE HANDLE
FOLLOW PRECEDENT
FOLLOW THE HOUNDS
FOLLOW THE PLOUGH
FOND OF THE BOTTLE
FOOL OF THE FAMILY
FOOTBALL RESULTS
FOOT OF THE LADDER
FOR ALL ONE'S WORTH
FOR A YEAR AND A DAY
FORBIDDEN GROUND
FORCE AN ENTRANCE
FORCE THE BIDDING
FORCIBLE FEEDING
FOREIGN CURRENCY
FOREIGN EXCHANGE
FOREIGN LANGUAGE
FOREIGN MINISTER
FORENSIC CHEMIST
FORFEIT ONE'S BAIL
FORGED SIGNATURE
FORGET ONE'S PIECE

FORGIVING NATURE
FOR GOODNESS' SAKE!
FORGOTTEN CUSTOM
FORKED LIGHTNING
FORM A GOVERNMENT
FORMAL AGREEMENT
FORMAL COMPLAINT
FORMAL STATEMENT
FOR MANY A LONG DAY
FOR OLD TIMES' SAKE
FOR THE FIRST TIME
FOR THE THIRD TIME
FOR THE TIME BEING
FORTY-EIGHT HOURS
FORTY-FIVE AND SIX
FORTY-FOUR AND SIX
FORTY-NINE AND SIX
FORTY-NINTH STATE
FORWARDING AGENT
FORWARD MOVEMENT
FOR WHAT IT'S WORTH
FOSTER AN OPINION
FOUNDATION CREAM
FOUNDATION STONE
FOUNTAIN OF YOUTH
FOUR AND A QUARTER
FOUR AND-SIXPENCE
FOUR AND TWOPENCE
FOURTEEN AND FIVE
FOURTEEN AND FOUR
FOURTEEN AND NINE
FOURTEEN PER CENT
FOURTEENTH GREEN
FOURTEENTH OF MAY
FOURTH DIMENSION
FOURTH OF JANUARY
FOURTH OF OCTOBER
FOUR WICKETS DOWN
FRAGRANT PERFUME
FRANCIS OF ASSISI
FRANCO-GERMAN WAR
FRANKLY SPEAKING
FREDERICK DELIUS
FREE ASSOCIATION
FREEDOM FROM FEAR
FREEDOM FROM WANT
FREEDOM OF ACCESS
FREEDOM OF ACTION
FREEDOM OF CHOICE
FREEDOM OF SPEECH
FREEDOM OF THE AIR

FREE FROM SLAVERY
FREEHAND DRAWING
FREELANCE WRITER
FREE OF INCOME-TAX
FREE TRANSLATION
FREEZE ONE'S BLOOD
FREEZING MIXTURE
FRENCH BREAKFAST
FRENCH DICTATION
FRENCH GRAND PRIX
FRENCH PEASANTRY
FRENCH SUBTITLES
FRENZIED EFFORTS
FREQUENT VISITOR
FRESH COMPLEXION
FRICASSEE OF VEAL
FRICTIONAL FORCE
FRIDAY AFTERNOON
FRIENDLY FEELING
FRIENDLY FOOTING
FRIENDLY GESTURE
FRIENDLY ISLANDS
FRIENDLY RIVALRY
FRIENDLY SOCIETY
FRIGHTENED CHILD
FROG IN THE THROAT
FROM ALL QUARTERS
FROM FIRST TO LAST
FROM HAND TO MOUTH
FROM LEFT TO RIGHT
FROM OBSERVATION
FROM STEM TO STERN
FROM THE ROOF-TOPS
FROM TOP TO BOTTOM
FRONT-LINE TROOPS
FROTH AT THE MOUTH
FRUITFUL SESSION
FRUITLESS SEARCH
FRUITS OF VICTORY
FUEL TO THE FLAMES
FULL-BOTTOMED WIG
FULL-DRESS DEBATE
FULL EXPLANATION
FULL OF INCIDENTS
FULL OF SURPRISES
FULL SPEED ASTERN
FULLY GUARANTEED
FUND OF KNOWLEDGE
FUNERAL CEREMONY
FUNERAL DIRECTOR
FURNISH EVIDENCE

FURNITURE POLISH
FUTURE EXISTENCE
FUTURE REFERENCE

G—15
GAIN A REPUTATION
GAIN INFORMATION
GAIN ONE'S FREEDOM
GALA PERFORMANCE
GALL AND WORMWOOD
GAME FOR ANYTHING
GAME, SET AND MATCH
GARDEN OF ENGLAND
GARGANTUAN FEAST
GATE-LEGGED TABLE
GATHERING CLOUDS
GATHERING STICKS
GENERAL ASSEMBLY
GENERAL DE GAULLE
GENERAL DELIVERY
GENERAL ELECTION
GENERAL FACTOTUM
GENERAL HOSPITAL
GENERAL INTEREST
GENERAL LAUGHTER
GENERAL OVERHAUL
GENERAL PRACTICE
GENERATING PLANT
GENEROUS GESTURE
GENEROUS HELPING
GENEROUS MEASURE
GENTLEMAN FARMER
GEOFFREY CHAUCER
GEOGRAPHY LESSON
GEORGE THE FOURTH
GET CONFIDENTIAL
GET DOWN TO THE JOB
GET INTO HOT WATER
GET INTO MISCHIEF
GET ONE'S MONKEY UP
GET ON ONE'S NERVES
GET ON SWIMMINGLY
GET ON WITH THE JOB
GET OUT OF THE ROAD
GET OUT OF TROUBLE
GET THE ADVANTAGE
GET THE UPPER HAND
GET THE WORST OF IT
GET UP TO MISCHIEF
GET YOUR SKATES ON
GHOSTS OF THE PAST

GIFT FROM THE GODS
GIN AND ANGOSTURA
GIRD UP ONE'S LOINS
GIRLISH LAUGHTER
GIST OF THE MATTER
GIVE A LEATHERING
GIVE FULL DETAILS
GIVE IN THE MIDDLE
GIVE ONE A BAD TIME
GIVE ONE'S CONSENT
GIVE ONESELF AIRS
GIVE ONESELF AWAY
GIVE ONE THE WORKS
GIVE PARTICULARS
GIVE THE ALL-CLEAR
GIVE THE GAME AWAY
GIVE THE PASSWORD
GIVE THE SHOW AWAY
GIVE UP THE SPONGE
GLITTERING PRIZE
GLOBE ARTICHOKES
GLOOMY COMPANION
GLORIOUS HOLIDAY
GLORIOUSLY DRUNK
GLORIOUS TWELFTH
GLORIOUS VICTORY
GLUT ON THE MARKET
GO A LONG WAY ROUND
GO BY UNDERGROUND
GODDESS OF WISDOM
GOD-FORSAKEN HOLE
GOD SAVE THE QUEEN
GO IN FOR LUXURIES
GO INTO ECSTASIES
GOLDEN HANDSHAKE
GOLDEN RETRIEVER
GOLDEN SOVEREIGN
GONE WITH THE WIND
GOOD CIRCULATION
GOOD CITIZENSHIP
GOOD CONNECTIONS
GOOD DAY'S JOURNEY
GOOD ENOUGH TO EAT
GOOD HANDWRITING
GOOD HOUSEKEEPER
GOODNESS OF HEART
GOOD RESOLUTIONS
GOOD VENTILATION
GO OFF AT A TANGENT
GO OFF THE DEEP END
GO OUT OF BUSINESS

GO OVER THE GROUND
GORGEOUS WEATHER
GO THE LONGEST WAY
GO THROUGH WITH IT
GO TO MUCH TROUBLE
GO TO THE SCAFFOLD
GOVERNMENT GRANT
GOVERNMENT HOUSE
GOVERNOR GENERAL
GO WITHOUT SAYING
GO WITH THE STREAM
GRACE BEFORE MEAT
GRACEFUL GESTURE
GRADUAL PROGRESS
GRAMOPHONE MUSIC
GRAND INQUISITOR
GRANDIOSE MANNER
GRAND UNION CANAL
GRANT ABSOLUTION
GRANULATED SUGAR
GRAPEFRUIT JUICE
GRAVE MISGIVINGS
GREASE THE WHEELS
GREAT ASSISTANCE
GREATEST RESPECT
GREAT EXCITEMENT
GREAT EXHIBITION
GREAT IMPORTANCE
GREATLY ESTEEMED
GREATLY INDEBTED
GREATLY SUPERIOR
GREAT MISFORTUNE
GREAT POPULARITY
GREEK MEETS GREEK
GREEK RESTAURANT
GREEN CHARTREUSE
GREENHOUSE PLANT
GRENADIER GUARDS
GREYHOUND RACING
GRIEVOUS MISTAKE
GRILLED SAUSAGES
GRILLED TOMATOES
GRIST FOR THE MILL
GROCERY BUSINESS
GROSS NEGLIGENCE
GROSVENOR SQUARE
GROUND-FLOOR FLAT
GROUND-NUT SCHEME
GROW INDIFFERENT
GUARDED LANGUAGE
GUESS ONE'S WEIGHT

GUILTY BEHAVIOUR
GUILTY BUT INSANE
GUNNER'S DAUGHTER
GUNNERY PRACTICE
GUY DE MAUPASSANT

H—I5
HACKNEY CARRIAGE
HACKNEYED PHRASE
HACKNEYED SAYING
HAGUE CONVENTION
HAIL AND FAREWELL
HAILING DISTANCE
HALF AS MUCH AGAIN
HALF-TERM HOLIDAY
HALF THE DISTANCE
HALIBUT-LIVER OIL
HAMMER AND SICKLE
HANDFUL OF SILVER
HANDSOME APOLOGY
HANDSOME FORTUNE
HANDSOME PRESENT
HAND-TO-HAND FIGHT
HANGED BY THE NECK
HANGING ORNAMENT
HANG OUT THE FLAGS
HANG UP A STOCKING
HANSEL AND GRETEL
HAPPY AS A SANDBOY
HAPPY IN ONE'S WORK
HARBOUR FEELINGS
HARBOUR OF REFUGE
HARD AND FAST RULE
HARDEN ONE'S HEART
HARDNESS OF HEART
HARE AND TORTOISE
HARMLESS LUNATIC
HAROLD MACMILLAN
HARP ON ONE STRING
HARROW ON THE HILL
HARVEST FESTIVAL
HAUL DOWN THE FLAG
HAUNCH OF VENISON
HAUNTING REFRAIN
HAVE A BONE TO PICK
HAVE AN INTERVIEW
HAVE A SWEET TOOTH
HAVE ONE'S REVENGE
HAVE THE BEST OF IT
HAVE THE LAST WORD

HAVE THE PLEASURE
HAVE THE WHIP-HAND
HAVE WHAT IT TAKES
HAZARD AN OPINION
HEAD IN THE CLOUDS
HEAD OF THE FAMILY
HEAD OF THE SCHOOL
HEAD-ON COLLISION
HEALING OINTMENT
HEALTH AND WEALTH
HEALTH INSURANCE
HEALTHY APPETITE
HEALTHY EXERCISE
HEAP COALS OF FIRE
HEARSAY EVIDENCE
HEARTBREAK HOUSE
HEARTLESS MANNER
HEARTS ARE TRUMPS
HEARTY BREAKFAST
HEARTY GREETINGS
HEAT OF THE MOMENT
HEAVEN BE PRAISED
HEAVY CASUALTIES
HEAVY PUNISHMENT
HEIGHT OF FASHION
HEIR PRESUMPTIVE
HEIR TO THE THRONE
HENRY THE SEVENTH
HERBACEOUS PLANT
HERBERT MORRISON
HEREDITARY TITLE
HEREWARD THE WAKE
HERMIONE GINGOLD
HEROIC QUALITIES
HERRING INDUSTRY
HESITATION WALTZ
HIDE UNDERGROUND
HIGHER AND HIGHER
HIGHER CRITICISM
HIGHER EDUCATION
HIGHLAND COSTUME
HIGHLY COMMENDED
HIGHLY CONNECTED
HIGHLY DANGEROUS
HIGHLY DELIGHTED
HIGHLY EFFICIENT
HIGHLY QUALIFIED
HIGH TEMPERATURE
HIPPOCRATIC OATH
HIS MASTER'S VOICE
HISTORICAL NOVEL

HISTORIC PRESENT
HIT BELOW THE BELT
HIT THE HEADLINES
HIT THE HIGH SPOTS
HOLD ONE TO RANSOM
HOLD OUT ONE'S HAND
HOLD THE BEST HAND
HOLD UP YOUR HANDS
HOLE IN THE CORNER
HOLE IN THE GROUND
HOLES AND CORNERS
HOLIDAY BY THE SEA
HOLY ROMAN EMPIRE
HOME CONSUMPTION
HOMERIC LAUGHTER
HOMEWARD JOURNEY
HOME WITH THE MILK
HOMICIDAL MANIAC
HONEYMOON COUPLE
HONEYSUCKLE ROSE
HONOURS OF BATTLE
HOPE AGAINST HOPE
HOPELESS FAILURE
HORIZONTAL PLANE
HORNS OF A DILEMMA
HORRIBLE WEATHER
HORSE-SHOE MAGNET
HOSPITAL ALMONER
HOSPITAL GROUNDS
HOSPITAL SURGEON
HOSTILE EVIDENCE
HOTEL PROPRIETOR
HOT FROM THE PRESS
HOURS OF BUSINESS
HOURS OF IDLENESS
HOUSEHOLD CHORES
HOUSEHOLD DRUDGE
HOUSEHOLD TROOPS
HOUSING MINISTER
HOUSING SHORTAGE
HOVER ON THE BRINK
HOW GOES THE ENEMY?
HUCKLEBERRY FINN
HUDDLED TOGETHER
HUMAN EXPERIENCE
HUMANLY POSSIBLE
HUMANLY SPEAKING
HUMID ATMOSPHERE
HUNDRED THOUSAND
HUNDRED YEARS WAR
HUNGER AND THIRST

HUNGRY AS A HUNTER
HUSH-HUSH SUBJECT

I—15
ICE-CREAM PARLOUR
ICE-CREAM SELLERS
ICE HOCKEY PLAYER
IDEAL SUGGESTION
IDLEWILD AIRPORT
ILLUSTRATED WORK
ILLUSTRIOUS PAST
IMITATION PEARLS
IMMACULATE STYLE
IMMEDIATE ACTION
IMMERSED IN STUDY
IMMERSION HEATER
IMMORTAL DREAMER
IMMOVABLE OBJECT
IMPENDING DANGER
IMPERIAL COLLEGE
IMPERIAL MEASURE
IMPLORING GLANCE
IMPORTANT MATTER
IMPORTANT PERSON
IMPOSSIBLE STORY
IMPRESSIVE SCENE
IMPROBABLE STORY
IMPROVED VERSION
IMPROVE IN HEALTH
IMPROVE ON NATURE
IMPULSIVE NATURE
IN A LESSER DEGREE
IN ALL CONSCIENCE
IN ALL DIRECTIONS
IN ALL LIKELIHOOD
INANIMATE MATTER
IN APPLE-PIE ORDER
IN A STRAIGHT LINE
INAUGURAL SPEECH
IN BLACK AND WHITE
INCIDENTAL MUSIC
INCLINE ONE'S HEAD
INCLUSIVE CHARGE
INCOME-TAX DEMAND
INCOME-TAX REBATE
INCOME-TAX RELIEF
INCOME-TAX RETURN
IN CONSIDERATION
INCREASED DEMAND
INDELIBLE PENCIL
INDEPENDENCE DAY

INDIAN ROPE-TRICK
INDIA-RUBBER BALL
INDIA-RUBBER BAND
INDIRECT CURRENT
INDIVIDUAL STYLE
INDOOR FIREWORKS
INDULGENT PARENT
INDUSTRIAL PLANT
IN EXTREME DANGER
INFAMOUS CONDUCT
INFANT MORTALITY
INFANTRY SOLDIER
INFERIOR ARTICLE
INFERIOR NUMBERS
INFERIOR QUALITY
INFERIOR VERSION
INFERNAL MACHINE
INFERNAL REGIONS
INFIRM OF PURPOSE
INFORMATION DESK
INFORMATION ROOM
INFORMED OPINION
IN FULL AGREEMENT
INGENIOUS DEVICE
INGENIOUS EXCUSE
INIQUITOUS PRICE
INITIAL EXPENSES
INJURED INNOCENT
IN JUXTAPOSITION
INNINGS DECLARED
INNOCENTS ABROAD
IN ONE'S RIGHT MIND
INORDINATE PRIDE
INORGANIC MATTER
IN SEARCH OF TRUTH
INSECURE FOOTING
IN SHARP CONTRAST
INSPECTOR FRENCH
INSTANT RESPONSE
INSTRUMENT BOARD
INSTRUMENT PANEL
INSUPERABLE ODDS
INSURANCE BROKER
INSURANCE OFFICE
INSURANCE POLICY
INTELLIGENT FOLK
INTELLIGENT TALK
INTERESTED PARTY
INTERIM DIVIDEND
INTERNAL AFFAIRS
IN THE ACCUSATIVE

IN THE ALTOGETHER
IN THE BACKGROUND
IN THE FIRST PLACE
IN THE FOREGROUND
IN THE LABORATORY
IN THE LAST RESORT
IN THE LIGHT OF DAY
IN THE LION'S MOUTH
IN THE MANNER BORN
IN THE MELTING-POT
IN THE MIDDLE EAST
IN THE NEAR FUTURE
IN THE NICK OF TIME
IN THE RIGHT PLACE
IN THE SAME BREATH
IN THE SHOP-WINDOW
IN THE SMALL HOURS
IN THE VERNACULAR
IN THE WILDERNESS
IN THE WITNESS-BOX
IN THE WRONG PLACE
INVALID CARRIAGE
INVENTIVE GENIUS
INVESTMENT TRUST
INVEST WITH POWER
INVISIBLE EXPORT
INVISIBLE IMPORT
INVITATION WALTZ
INVITED AUDIENCE
IRISH SWEEPSTAKE
IRREGULAR TROOPS
IRREPARABLE HARM
IRREPARABLE LOSS
ISLAND CONTINENT
ISSUE A CHALLENGE
ITALIAN VERMOUTH
IT'S THAT MAN AGAIN
IVAN THE TERRIBLE

J—15
JACK OF ALL TRADES
JANUARY THE FIFTH
JANUARY THE FIRST
JANUARY THE NINTH
JANUARY THE SIXTH
JANUARY THE TENTH
JANUARY THE THIRD
JERRY-BUILT HOUSE
JEWEL AND WARRISS
JOBBING GARDENER
JOCKEY FOR PLACES

JOIN IN THE CHORUS
JOINT GOVERNMENT
JOIN THE MAJORITY
JOINT OPERATIONS
JOINT POSSESSION
JOLLY GOOD FELLOW
JUDGE FOR ONESELF
JUDGMENT OF PARIS
JUDGMENT SUMMONS
JUICE OF THE GRAPE
JULY THE ELEVENTH
JUMPING-OFF PLACE
JUNE THE ELEVENTH
JUNIOR BARRISTER
JUPITER SYMPHONY
JUST ABOUT ENOUGH

K—15
KATHLEEN FERRIER
KEEN COMPETITION
KEENLY CONTESTED
KEEP AT A DISTANCE
KEEPER OF THE KEYS
KEEP IN CAPTIVITY
KEEP IN IGNORANCE
KEEP NOTHING BACK
KEEP OFF THE GRASS
KEEP ONE GUESSING
KEEP ONE'S BALANCE
KEEP ONE'S COUNSEL
KEEP ONE'S PROMISE
KEEP ONE'S SHIRT ON
KEEP ON THE COURSE
KEEP OUT OF THE WAY
KEEP THE DOOR OPEN
KEEP THINGS GOING
KEEP TO THE MIDDLE
KEEP UNDER ARREST
KENNETH MCKELLAR
KERB-SIDE PARKING
KEY TO THE MYSTERY
KICK UP ONE'S HEELS
KID-GLOVE METHODS
KIDNEYS AND BACON
KINDLE OF KITTENS
KINDNESS OF HEART
KINGDOM OF HEAVEN
KING OF THE BEASTS
KING OF THE CASTLE
KING OF THE FOREST
KING OF THE JUNGLE

KITTEN ON THE KEYS
KNAVE OF DIAMONDS
KNIGHT COMMANDER
KNIGHT OF THE BATH
KNIGHT OF THE ROAD
KNIGHTS TEMPLARS
KNITTING MACHINE
KNITTING PATTERN
KNOW A THING OR TWO
KNOW ONE'S OWN MIND

L—15
LABOUR CANDIDATE
LABOUR RELATIONS
LABOUR SUPPORTER
LACK OF EDUCATION
LACK OF KNOWLEDGE
LACK OF WILL POWER
LADDER OF SUCCESS
LADIES' COMPANION
LADIES IN WAITING
LAND OF MY FATHERS
LAND OF THE LIVING
LANDSCAPE ARTIST
LANGUAGE BARRIER
LANGUAGE PROBLEM
LANGUAGE TEACHER
LARGE PERCENTAGE
LARGE POPULATION
LAST BUT NOT LEAST
LASTING MONUMENT
LAST PERFORMANCE
LATEST INVENTION
LATEST QUOTATION
LAUGH AND GROW FAT
LAUGHING JACKASS
LAUGH LIKE A DRAIN
LAUGH LIKE A HYENA
LAUGH OUT OF COURT
LAUGHTER IN COURT
LAURENCE OLIVIER
LAVENDER HILL MOB
LAY DOWN ONE'S ARMS
LAY DOWN ONE'S LIFE
LEAD A DOUBLE LIFE
LEAD A MERRY DANCE
LEADER OF FASHION
LEADER OF SOCIETY
LEADER OF THE BAND
LEADING BUSINESS
LEADING NOVELIST

LEADING QUESTION
LEADING THE FIELD
LEAGUE OF NATIONS
LEAP OVER THE MOON
LEARN ONE'S LESSON
LEATHER INDUSTRY
LEAVE FOOTPRINTS
LEAVE IN SUSPENSE
LEAVE IN THE LURCH
LEAVE IT TO CHANCE
LEAVE NOTHING OUT
LEAVE THE COUNTRY
LEAVE UNFINISHED
LEGAL DEPARTMENT
LEGAL PROFESSION
LEGAL SEPARATION
LEGAL SETTLEMENT
LEG BEFORE WICKET
LEGISLATIVE BODY
LEGITIMATE CLAIM
LEGITIMATE DRAMA
LEGITIMATE STAGE
LEGUMINOUS PLANT
LEICESTER SQUARE
LEIGHTON BUZZARD
LEISURED CLASSES
LEMON CHEESE-CAKE
LENGTH OF SERVICE
LENGTHY ARGUMENT
LENGTHY BUSINESS
LENIENT SENTENCE
LEONARDO DA VINCI
LESSEN THE STRAIN
LESS THAN THE DUST
LET DOWN ONE'S HAIR
LET ONE'S HAIR DOWN
LETTER OF REQUEST
LET THERE BE LIGHT!
LETTRES DE CACHET
LIBERAL MAJORITY
LIBERAL MINORITY
LICENCE ENDORSED
LICK AND A PROMISE
LICK ONE'S FINGERS
LIE IN ONE'S THROAT
LIE LIKE A TROOPER
LIFE-BOAT STATION
LIFT THE RECEIVER
LIFT UP ONE'S VOICE
LIFT UP YOUR HEART
LIGHT AS A FEATHER

LIGHT LITERATURE
LIGHT MACHINE-GUN
LIGHTNING SKETCH
LIGHTNING STRIKE
LIGHT OF THE WORLD
LIGHT PUNISHMENT
LIKE A DROWNED RAT
LIKE A DUTCH UNCLE
LIKE A HOUSE AFIRE
LIKE QUICKSILVER
LILY OF THE VALLEY
LINCOLN HANDICAP
LINCOLN MEMORIAL
LINE OF DIRECTION
LINE ONE'S POCKETS
LINK WITH THE PAST
LIQUID RESOURCES
LIST TO STARBOARD
LITERARY CIRCLES
LITERARY FORGERY
LITERARY OUTLINE
LITERARY SUBJECT
LITTLE ENGLANDER
LITTLE GENTLEMAN
LITTLE KNOWLEDGE
LITTLE MISS FIX-IT
LITTLE OR NOTHING
LITTLE WOODEN HUT
LIVE DANGEROUSLY
LIVE IN A SMALL WAY
LIVE IN SECLUSION
LIVE LIKE A PAUPER
LIVERPOOL STREET
LIVING TESTIMONY
LOADED WITH MONEY
LOAD OFF ONE'S MIND
LOAVES AND FISHES
LOCAL GOVERNMENT
LOCAL INHABITANT
LOCH NESS MONSTER
LOCKED AND BOLTED
LODGE A COMPLAINT
LOGICAL ARGUMENT
LOGICAL SEQUENCE
LONDON ALLOWANCE
LONDON TRANSPORT
LONG ARM OF THE LAW
LONGEST WAY ROUND
LONG LIVE THE KING!
LONG-TERM SOLDIER
LONG-WINDED STORY

LOOK BACK IN ANGER
LOOK FOR A WELCOME
LOOK FOR SYMPATHY
LOOK THE OTHER WAY
LOOK TO THE FUTURE
LORD CHAMBERLAIN
LORD HIGH ADMIRAL
LORD HIGH STEWARD
LORD MAYOR'S COACH
LORDS AND COMMONS
LORDS OF CREATION
LOSE COUNTENANCE
LOSE ONE'S BALANCE
LOSE ONE'S FOOTING
LOSE ONE'S HUSBAND
LOSE ONE'S STRIPES
LOSE ON THE SWINGS
LOSE THE ELECTION
LOST OPPORTUNITY
LOVE ME, LOVE MY DOG
LOVE OF ADVENTURE
LOVER AND HIS LASS
LOWER ONE'S SIGHTS
LOW SUBSCRIPTION
LUKEWARM SUPPORT
LUMP IN THE THROAT
LUNCHEON SAUSAGE
LUNCHEON VOUCHER
LUTON GIRLS' CHOIR
LUXURIANT GROWTH

M—15
MAD AS A MARCH HARE
MAGAZINE ARTICLE
MAGAZINE SECTION
MAGIC INSTRUMENT
MAGNETIC COMPASS
MAGNIFYING GLASS
MAGNIFYING POWER
MAIN CLAIM TO FAME
MAIN LINE STATION
MAJESTY OF THE LAW
MAJORITY VERDICT
MAKE A COLLECTION
MAKE A CONFESSION
MAKE A FRESH START
MAKE ALTERATIONS
MAKE AN ASSERTION
MAKE AN EXCEPTION
MAKE APPLICATION
MAKE A PREDICTION

MAKE A RESOLUTION
MAKE A SUGGESTION
MAKE COMPARISONS
MAKE CONCESSIONS
MAKE CORRECTIONS
MAKE ONE'S FORTUNE
MAKE REPARATIONS
MAKE RESTITUTION
MAKE SHORT WORK OF
MAKE THE BEST OF IT
MAKE THE MOST OF IT
MAKE THINGS CLEAR
MAKE THINGS WORSE
MALE SUPERIORITY
MALIGNANT GROWTH
MALIGN INFLUENCE
MALVERN FESTIVAL
MANIC DEPRESSION
MANILLA ENVELOPE
MAN IN POSSESSION
MANNEQUIN PARADE
MAN OF EXPERIENCE
MANY-HEADED BEAST
MARCH OF PROGRESS
MARCH THE SEVENTH
MARCH THE TWELFTH
MARGINAL COMMENT
MARIE ANTOINETTE
MARINE INSURANCE
MARINER'S COMPASS
MARK OF AUTHORITY
MARK THE OCCASION
MARLENE DIETRICH
MARRIAGEABLE AGE
MARRIAGE ADVISER
MARRIAGE BY PROXY
MARRIAGE LICENCE
MARRIAGE PARTNER
MARRIAGE PORTION
MARRIAGE SERVICE
MARRIED QUARTERS
MARSHALLING YARD
MARY'S LITTLE LAMB
MASCULINE GENDER
MASQUERADE DRESS
MASS INFORMATION
MASS OBSERVATION
MASTER CARPENTER
MASTER CRAFTSMAN
MASTER OF SCIENCE
MATERIAL BENEFIT

MATERIAL SUCCESS
MATERIAL WITNESS
MATERNAL FEELING
MATTER OF OPINION
MAXIMUM PRESSURE
MAY THE FIFTEENTH
MAY THE SIXTEENTH
MAY THE THIRTIETH
MAY THE TWENTIETH
MEANS OF APPROACH
MEAN WHAT ONE SAYS
MEASURE OF LENGTH
MECHANICAL MEANS
MECHANICAL POWER
MEMBER OF SOCIETY
MEMBER OF THE CAST
MEMORIAL SERVICE
MENTAL AGITATION
MENTAL BREAKDOWN
MENTAL DEFECTIVE
MENTAL FACULTIES
MENTAL TELEPATHY
MENTAL TREATMENT
MERCENARY TROOPS
MERCHANT SERVICE
MERE COINCIDENCE
MERRY AS A CRICKET
MERRY MONTH OF MAY
MESSAGE RECEIVED
METHOD OF WORKING
MEXICAN HAIRLESS
MICHAEL FLANDERS
MICHAEL HOLLIDAY
MICHAELMAS DAISY
MICHAELMAS GOOSE
MICHAEL REDGRAVE
MIDDLE-AGE SPREAD
MIDDLE OF THE ROAD
MIDDLE OF THE ROOM
MIDLAND COUNTIES
MIDNIGHT MATINEE
MILITARY ACADEMY
MILITARY BEARING
MILITARY COLLEGE
MILITARY COLOURS
MILITARY FUNERAL
MILITARY HISTORY
MILITARY HONOURS
MILITARY MISSION
MILITARY SERVICE
MILITARY STATION

MILITARY TACTICS
MILITARY TRIBUNE
MILITARY TWO-STEP
MILITATE AGAINST
MILLICENT MARTIN
MILLIONAIRE'S ROW
MIND ONE'S MANNERS
MIND THE WET PAINT
MINIATURE POODLE
MINISTER OF POWER
MINISTER OF STATE
MINISTER OF WORKS
MINISTRY OF POWER
MINISTRY OF STATE
MINISTRY OF WORKS
MIRROR OF FASHION
MISERABLE SINNER
MISS ONE'S FOOTING
MISTRESS QUICKLY
MIXTURE AS BEFORE
MODEL OF INDUSTRY
MODE OF BEHAVIOUR
MODERATE DEMANDS
MODERATE DRINKER
MODERATE SUCCESS
MODEST BEHAVIOUR
MOLOTOV COCKTAIL
MOMENT OF MADNESS
MONASTERY GARDEN
MONDAY AFTERNOON
MONEY FOR NOTHING
MONEY FOR OLD ROPE
MONEY MAKES MONEY
MONTE CARLO RALLY
MONTH AFTER MONTH
MONTHLY MAGAZINE
MONTHLY PAYMENTS
MONTHS AND MONTHS
MONTHS OF THE YEAR
MONUMENTAL MASON
MOON AND SIXPENCE
MOONLIGHT SONATA
MORAL INJUNCTION
MORAL OBLIGATION
MORAL PHILOSOPHY
MORAL REARMAMENT
MORAL STANDPOINT
MORBID CURIOSITY
MORE THAN WELCOME
MORRISON SHELTER
MOST INTERESTING

MOST RESPECTABLE
MOTHER AND FATHER
MOTHERING SUNDAY
MOTHERLESS CHILD
MOTIVATING FORCE
MOTLEY GATHERING
MOTORING OFFENCE
MOUNTAIN OF FLESH
MOUNTAINOUS AREA
MOUNTAIN RAILWAY
MOUNTAIN TORRENT
MOUTH OF THE RIVER
MOVING SPECTACLE
MOVING STAIRCASE
MUCH OF A MUCHNESS
MUCH SOUGHT AFTER
MULBERRY HARBOUR
MULTIPLY BY EIGHT
MULTIPLY BY SEVEN
MULTIPLY BY THREE
MUNICH AGREEMENT
MURAL DECORATION
MURDEROUS WEAPON
MUSICAL DIRECTOR
MUSICAL FESTIVAL
MUSICAL INTERVAL
MUSIC-HALL ARTIST
MUSIC HATH CHARMS
MUSTARD AND CRESS
MUSTER UP COURAGE
MUTUAL AFFECTION
MUTUAL AGREEMENT
MUTUAL HOSTILITY
MUTUAL INSURANCE
MUTUAL SUSPICION
MY LEARNED FRIEND
MYTHOLOGICAL AGE

N—15
NATIONAL COLOURS
NATIONAL COSTUME
NATIONAL DEFENCE
NATIONAL GALLERY
NATIONAL HOLIDAY
NATIONAL LIBERAL
NATIONAL LIBRARY
NATIONAL LOTTERY
NATIONAL SAVINGS
NATIONAL SERVICE
NATIONAL SOCIETY
NATIONAL THEATRE

NATURAL APTITUDE
NATURAL CAPACITY
NATURAL INSTINCT
NAUGHTY NINETIES
NAVAL ENGAGEMENT
NAVAL OPERATIONS
NAVAL TOURNAMENT
NAVIGATION LIGHT
NEARER AND NEARER
NEAREST RELATIVE
NEAT AS NINEPENCE
NEAT BUT NOT GAUDY
NEAT HANDWRITING
NEAT PIECE OF WORK
NECK-AND-NECK RACE
NECTAR OF THE GODS
NEEDLE AND COTTON
NEEDLE AND THREAD
NEGATIVE REQUEST
NEGLECT ONE'S DUTY
NEGOTIABLE BONDS
NERVOUS DISORDER
NEVER A CROSS WORD
NEVER-ENDING TASK
NEW ACQUAINTANCE
NEWCASTLE ON TYNE
NEWCASTLE UNITED
NEW ENGLISH BIBLE
NEWFOUNDLAND DOG
NEWGATE CALENDAR
NEWS COMMENTATOR
NEW SCOTLAND YARD
NEWS FROM NOWHERE
NEWSPAPER REPORT
NEWSPAPER SELLER
NIBBLE AT THE BAIT
NICE DISTINCTION
NICE LITTLE THING
NIGGER MINSTRELS
NIGHT AFTER NIGHT
NIGHT ON THE TILES
NIGHT STARVATION
NINE AND A QUARTER
NINE AND SIXPENCE
NINE AND TENPENCE
NINE AND TWOPENCE
NINETEEN AND FIVE
NINETEEN AND FOUR
NINETEEN AND NINE
NINETEEN PER CENT
NINETEENTH OF MAY

NINETY-ONE AND SIX
NINE WICKETS DOWN
NINTH OF DECEMBER
NINTH OF FEBRUARY
NINTH OF NOVEMBER
NOBEL PEACE PRIZE
NOBLE SENTIMENTS
NOBODY'S BUSINESS
NO CONCERN OF MINE
NO DISTANCE AT ALL
NOISY NEIGHBOURS
NOMINATION PAPER
NON COMPOS MENTIS
NONE BUT THE BRAVE
NORFOLK DUMPLING
NORMAL BEHAVIOUR
NORMAL PROCEDURE
NORTHERN IRELAND
NORTH OF THE RIVER
NORTH OF THE TWEED
NO STONE UNTURNED
NOT A LIVING THING
NOTHING IN COMMON
NOT IN THE RUNNING
NOT OUT OF THE WOOD
NOT STRONG ENOUGH
NOTTING HILL GATE
NOVEL EXPERIENCE
NUCLEAR REACTION
NUFFIELD COLLEGE
NUREMBERG TRIALS
NURSE A GRIEVANCE
NURSE AN AMBITION
NURSERY HANDICAP
NUTCRACKER SUITE

O—15
OBEDIENT SERVANT
OBEY REGULATIONS
OBJECT OF CHARITY
OBJECT OF DISLIKE
OBJECT OF WORSHIP
OBLIQUE QUESTION
OBSERVATION POST
OCCASIONAL TABLE
OCCUPYING TENANT
OCTOBER THE FIFTH
OCTOBER THE FIRST
OCTOBER THE NINTH
OCTOBER THE SIXTH
OCTOBER THE TENTH

OCTOBER THE THIRD
ODDS-ON FAVOURITE
ODOUR OF SANCTITY
OFFENSIVE MANNER
OFFENSIVE REMARK
OFFENSIVE WEAPON
OFFER IN EXCHANGE
OFFICER IN CHARGE
OFFICER MATERIAL
OFFICER OF THE DAY
OFFICIAL INQUIRY
OFFICIAL JOURNAL
OFFICIOUS PERSON
OFF TO A FINE START
OFF TO A GOOD START
OF THE FIRST WATER
OLD ACQUAINTANCE
OLD-AGE PENSIONER
OLD AS METHUSELAH
OLD CONTEMPTIBLE
OLDER GENERATION
OLD FATHER THAMES
OLIVER GOLDSMITH
OMNIA VINCIT AMOR
ON ACTIVE SERVICE
ONCE IN A BLUE MOON
ONCE IN A LIFETIME
ONE AFTER ANOTHER
ONE AND FIVEPENCE
ONE AND FOURPENCE
ONE AND NINEPENCE
ONE MAN WENT TO MOW
ONE OF THE COMPANY
ONE OVER THE EIGHT
ONE STAGE AT A TIME
ONE THING AT A TIME
ONE WAY OR ANOTHER
ON HANDS AND KNEES
ON ONE'S HIGH HORSE
ON SPEAKING TERMS
ON THE BORDERLINE
ON THE BRADEN BEAT
ON THE BRIGHT SIDE
ON THE CREDIT SIDE
ON THE DOTTED LINE
ON THE RIGHT LINES
ON THE RIGHT SCENT
ON THE RIGHT TRACK
ON THE ROAD TO RUIN
ON THE WATER-WAGON
ON THE WRONG LINES

ON THE WRONG SCENT
ON THE WRONG TRACK
ON TOP OF THE WORLD
ON VISITING TERMS
ON WITH THE MOTLEY
OPEN-AND-SHUT CASE
OPEN COMPETITION
OPEN HOSTILITIES
OPENING CEREMONY
OPENING SENTENCE
OPEN SCHOLARSHIP
OPEN THE QUESTION
OPEN THE THROTTLE
OPEN TO CRITICISM
OPEN TO OBJECTION
OPEN TO SUSPICION
OPEN TO THE PUBLIC
OPPORTUNE MOMENT
OPPORTUNE REMARK
OPPOSING COUNSEL
OPPOSITE EXTREME
OPPOSITE MEANING
OPPOSITE PARTIES
OPPOSITION BENCH
OPPOSITION PARTY
OPTICAL ILLUSION
ORAL EXAMINATION
ORANGE FREE STATE
ORANGE MARMALADE
ORCHESTRAL MUSIC
ORCHESTRA STALLS
ORDERLY CORPORAL
ORDERLY SERGEANT
ORDNANCE OFFICER
ORGANISED LABOUR
ORIENTAL SCHOLAR
ORIGINAL MEANING
ORIGIN OF SPECIES
ORNAMENTAL PLANT
OUNCE OF PRACTICE
OUR MUTUAL FRIEND
OUTDOOR CLOTHING
OUTDOOR EXERCISE
OUT OF COMMISSION
OUT OF EMPLOYMENT
OUT OF HIS ELEMENT
OUT OF ONE'S SENSES
OUT OF PROPORTION
OUT OF THE COUNTRY
OUT OF THE PICTURE
OUT OF THE RUNNING

OUT-OF-THE-WAY SPOT
OUTRIGHT SCANDAL
OUTSIDE INTEREST
OUTSTANDING DEBT
OVER AND DONE WITH
OVERCOME BY GRIEF
OVERFLOW MEETING
OVERHEAD CHARGES
OVERHEAD RAILWAY
OVERSTEP THE MARK
OVER THE BASE-LINE

P—15
PADDINGTON GREEN
PAINT THE TOWN RED
PAIR OF CALLIPERS
PAIR OF COMPASSES
PAIR OF DUMB-BELLS
PAIR OF STOCKINGS
PALACE OF SOVIETS
PALAEOLITHIC AGE
PARACHUTE TROOPS
PARAGON OF VIRTUE
PARENTAL CONSENT
PARENTAL CONTROL
PARKHURST PRISON
PARTIAL LIKENESS
PARTNERS IN CRIME
PARTY CONFERENCE
PASS ALONG PLEASE
PASS A RESOLUTION
PASS AWAY THE TIME
PASSIVE INTEREST
PASSIVE RESISTER
PASS ROUND THE HAT
PASS THE HAT ROUND
PASS WITH HONOURS
PASTEURIZED MILK
PATCH UP A QUARREL
PATENTLY OBVIOUS
PATERNAL FEELING
PATRICK CAMPBELL
PATRON OF THE ARTS
PATTERN OF VIRTUE
PAUSE FOR A MOMENT
PAWNBROKER'S SIGN
PAYABLE ON DEMAND
PAY COMPENSATION
PAY OFF OLD SCORES
PAY ONE'S RESPECTS
PEACE AT ANY PRICE

PEACE CONFERENCE
PEACE WITH HONOUR
PEACHES AND CREAM
PECULIAR FLAVOUR
PENAL SETTLEMENT
PENCIL SHARPENER
PENNY IN THE POUND
PEOPLE IN GENERAL
PEOPLE OF FASHION
PEOPLE OF QUALITY
PER ARDUA AD ASTRA
PERCENTAGE BASIS
PEREGRINE FALCON
PERFECT CREATURE
PERFECT INTERVAL
PERFECT LIKENESS
PERFECTLY HONEST
PERFECT NONSENSE
PERFECT NUISANCE
PERFECT STRANGER
PERFECT TREASURE
PERFORMING FLEAS
PERILOUS VENTURE
PERIOD FURNITURE
PERISHABLE GOODS
PERMANENT RECORD
PERPETUAL MOTION
PERSONAL ACCOUNT
PERSONAL AFFRONT
PERSONAL BENEFIT
PERSONAL EFFECTS
PERSONALITY CULT
PERSONAL OPINION
PERSONAL PRONOUN
PERSONAL REASONS
PERSONAL SERVICE
PERSONA NON GRATA
PERTINENT REMARK
PESTLE AND MORTAR
PETER AND THE WOLF
PETER THE PAINTER
PETITION OF RIGHT
PETRIFIED FOREST
PETROL RATIONING
PHOTOGRAPH ALBUM
PHYSICAL CRAVING
PHYSICAL CULTURE
PHYSICAL FATIGUE
PHYSICAL SCIENCE
PICK UP THE PIECES
PICK UP THE THREAD

PICTURE OF HEALTH
PICTURE OF MISERY
PICTURE POSTCARD
PIECE OF EVIDENCE
PIECE OF GOOD NEWS
PIECE OF NONSENSE
PIECE OF ONE'S MIND
PILLAR OF SOCIETY
PINCHED WITH COLD
PINK OF CONDITION
PIOUS SENTIMENTS
PIPPED AT THE POST
PIT OF THE STOMACH
PLACE OF BUSINESS
PLAGUE OF LOCUSTS
PLAIN-CLOTHES MAN
PLANETARY SYSTEM
PLANNING OFFICER
PLAY A DOUBLE GAME
PLAY A LOSING GAME
PLAY CAT AND MOUSE
PLAYERS' ENTRANCE
PLAY FIRST FIDDLE
PLAY HIDE-AND-SEEK
PLAY ONE'S OWN HAND
PLAY THE BAGPIPES
PLAY THE INFORMER
PLAY THE PARASITE
PLAYTHING OF FATE
PLAY TIDDLYWINKS
PLEASANT EVENING
PLEASANT FLAVOUR
PLEASURE GARDENS
PLEASURE GROUNDS
PLEASURE STEAMER
PLIGHT ONE'S TROTH
PLOUGH THE FIELDS
PLUM IN ONE'S MOUTH
PLYMOUTH BROTHER
PLYMOUTH HARBOUR
POCKET ONE'S PRIDE
POETICAL JUSTICE
POINT-BLANK RANGE
POINTED REMINDER
POINTLESS REMARK
POINT OF NO RETURN
POLAR EXPEDITION
POLICE CONSTABLE
POLICE INSPECTOR
POLISHED MANNERS
POLITICAL ASYLUM

POLITICAL CAREER
POLITICAL EVENTS
POLITICAL OFFICE
POLITICAL RIGHTS
POLITICAL SPEECH
POLITICAL THEORY
POLITICAL WEAPON
POLITICAL WRITER
POMP AND CEREMONY
POOR CIRCULATION
POOR CONSOLATION
POOR VENTILATION
POPEYE THE SAILOR
POPULAR LANGUAGE
PORTMANTEAU WORD
PORTRAIT GALLERY
PORTRAIT OF A LADY
PORTRAIT PAINTER
POSITION OF POWER
POSITION OF TRUST
POSITIVE ELEMENT
POST-DATED CHEQUE
POST-OFFICE GUIDE
POTENTIAL DANGER
POTENTIAL ENERGY
POWER OF ATTORNEY
POWER OF JUDGMENT
POWER OF RECOVERY
POWER OF THE PRESS
PRACTICAL RESULT
PRACTISE SORCERY
PRAIRIE SCHOONER
PRAYER FOR THE DAY
PREACH THE GOSPEL
PREACH TO THE WISE
PRECARIOUS STATE
PREFECT OF POLICE
PREFERENCE SHARE
PREFERRED SHARES
PRELIMINARY HEAT
PRELIMINARY STEP
PREMEDITATED ACT
PRE-PAID TELEGRAM
PREPARED TO FIGHT
PRESERVED GINGER
PRESERVING SUGAR
PRESIDENT NASSER
PRESS CONFERENCE
PRESSED FOR FUNDS
PRESSED FOR MONEY
PRESSED FOR SPACE

PRESS FOR PAYMENT
PRESS THE TRIGGER
PRESTON NORTH END
PRETTY MUCH ALIKE
PREVAILING TASTE
PREVAILING WINDS
PREVIOUS OFFENCE
PRICE ON ONE'S HEAD
PRICE REGULATION
PRICK ONE'S EARS UP
PRICK UP ONE'S EARS
PRIMARY ELECTION
PRIMITIVE COLOUR
PRINCE OF DENMARK
PRINCIPAL CLAUSE
PRINCIPAL PERSON
PRIOR CONDITIONS
PRIOR ENGAGEMENT
PRISONER OF STATE
PRISONER OF ZENDA
PRISONER'S FRIEND
PRIVATE CARRIAGE
PRIVATE CHANNELS
PRIVATE DEVOTION
PRIVATE HOSPITAL
PRIVATE LANGUAGE
PRIVATE PRACTICE
PRIVATE PROPERTY
PRIVATE QUARTERS
PRIVATE TEACHING
PRIVILEGED CLASS
PRIVY COUNCILLOR
PROBABLE STARTER
PROCESSED CHEESE
PRODIGAL'S RETURN
PROFESSED BELIEF
PROFESSIONAL AIR
PROFESSIONAL FEE
PROFESSIONAL MAN
PROFOUND THINKER
PROFOUND THOUGHT
PROGRAMME PARADE
PROGRAMME SELLER
PROHIBITION DAYS
PROHIBITION ZONE
PROLONG THE AGONY
PRONOUNCE GUILTY
PROOF OF PURCHASE
PROPERLY DRESSED
PROPER TREATMENT
PROPOSE MARRIAGE

PROSPECTIVE WIFE
PROUD AS A PEACOCK
PROVE ACCEPTABLE
PROVIDE THE MEANS
PROVINCIAL PAPER
PRUNES AND PRISMS
PUBLIC CHARACTER
PUBLIC DECEPTION
PUBLIC EDUCATION
PUBLIC ENCLOSURE
PUBLIC EXECUTION
PUBLIC KNOWLEDGE
PUBLIC MANIFESTO
PUBLIC OWNERSHIP
PUBLIC RELATIONS
PUBLIC-SCHOOL BOY
PUBLIC TRANSPORT
PUBLISH THE BANNS
PULL FOR THE SHORE
PULL ONE'S PUNCHES
PULL OUT THE STOPS
PULL-UP FOR CARMEN
PULL UP ONE'S SOCKS
PUNCTUATION MARK
PURCHASING POWER
PURE COINCIDENCE
PURELY AND SIMPLY
PURE MATHEMATICS
PURR WITH CONTENT
PURSUE AN INQUIRY
PURSUE THE MATTER
PUSS IN THE CORNER
PUT AN END TO IT ALL
PUT BACK THE CLOCK
PUT IN A WORD OR TWO
PUT IN POSSESSION
PUT IN QUARANTINE
PUT IN THE PICTURE
PUT INTO PRACTICE
PUT IT ANOTHER WAY
PUT IT ON THE SHELF
PUT ONE'S FOOT DOWN
PUT ONE'S FOOT IN IT
PUT ONE'S NAME DOWN
PUT ON ONE'S ARMOUR
PUT THE CLOCK BACK
PUTTING IT MILDLY
PUT UP A GOOD FIGHT
PUT UP FOR AUCTION

Q—15
QUALIFIED PERSON
QUARTERLY REVIEW
QUARTER OF AN HOUR
QUARTER OF A POUND
QUARTER PAST FIVE
QUARTER PAST FOUR
QUARTER PAST NINE
QUARTER SESSIONS
QUARTER TO ELEVEN
QUARTER TO TWELVE
QUEEN OF DIAMONDS
QUEEN OF THE SOUTH
QUEEN'S MESSENGER
QUICKEN THE PULSE
QUICK OFF THE MARK
QUICK SUCCESSION
QUIET AS THE GRAVE
QUIET RESENTMENT
QUITE A CHARACTER
QUITE DELIGHTFUL
QUITE THE REVERSE
QUOTE FROM MEMORY

R—15
RACE AGAINST TIME
RACIAL TOLERANCE
RACING CERTAINTY
RACKING HEADACHE
RADIO-ACTIVE ZONE
RADIO ASTRONOMER
RADIO JOURNALISM
RAILWAY ACCIDENT
RAILWAY CARRIAGE
RAILWAY JUNCTION
RAILWAY TERMINUS
RAIN CATS AND DOGS
RAIN STOPPED PLAY
RAISE A HUE AND CRY
RAISE OBJECTIONS
RAISE ONE'S SIGHTS
RAISE THE CURTAIN
RAISE THE SUBJECT
RAISE VEGETABLES
RALPH RICHARDSON
RAMSAY MACDONALD
RAPID SUCCESSION
RATTLING SUCCESS
RAZE TO THE GROUND
REACH FOR THE MOON
REACH PERFECTION

REACH ROCK-BOTTOM
READY AND WILLING
READY-BUILT HOUSE
READY FOR THE FRAY
READY-MADE EXCUSE
REARGUARD ACTION
REASONABLE DOUBT
REASONABLE OFFER
REASONABLE TERMS
RECENT DISCOVERY
RECEPTION CENTRE
RECKLESS EXPENSE
RECKLESS SPENDER
RECORDING STUDIO
RECOVER LOST TIME
RECOVER ONE'S MIND
RECOVER THE ASHES
RECRUITING DRIVE
RED-CURRANT JELLY
REDUCE TO NOTHING
REDUCE TO POVERTY
REDUCE TO SILENCE
RED, WHITE AND BLUE
REFILL ONE'S GLASS
REFLECTED VISION
REFRESHER COURSE
REFRESHMENT ROOM
REFRESHMENT TENT
REFUSE COLLECTOR
REGIMENTAL BADGE
REGIMENTAL MARCH
REGIMENTAL STAFF
REGIMENT OF WOMEN
REGISTRATION FEE
REGULAR CUSTOMER
REGULAR EXERCISE
REGULAR FEATURES
REGULAR PRACTICE
REGULATION DRESS
REGULATION SPEED
REIGNING MONARCH
RELATIVE DENSITY
RELATIVELY QUIET
RELATIVE PRONOUN
RELAXING CLIMATE
RELEASE ONE'S HOLD
RELIABLE QUALITY
RELIABLE SERVICE
RELIGIOUS BELIEF
RELIGIOUS MANIAC
REMARKABLE CHILD

REMARKABLE SIGHT
REMARKABLE VOICE
REMARKABLE WOMAN
REMEMBER NOTHING
REMOVE ALL TRACES
REMOVE MOUNTAINS
REMOVE THE TRACES
RENDER AN ACCOUNT
RENDER NECESSARY
RENT RESTRICTION
RE-OPEN OLD WOUNDS
REPAIRING CLAUSE
REPAIR THE DAMAGE
REPENT AT LEISURE
REPUBLICAN PARTY
REPULSE AN ATTACK
RESEARCH CHEMIST
RESERVE OF ENERGY
RESERVE STRENGTH
RESIDENTIAL AREA
RESIDENT SURGEON
RESTORATION FUND
RESTORATION PLAY
RESTORE TO HEALTH
RESTORE TO REASON
RESTORE TO SANITY
RESTRAINING HAND
RESTRICT IMPORTS
RESURRECTION DAY
RETORT COURTEOUS
RETURN IN TRIUMPH
RETURN TO SERVICE
RETURN TO THE PAST
REVERSION TO TYPE
RICHARD DIMBLEBY
RICHARD THE THIRD
RICHLY FURNISHED
RIDE A BROOMSTICK
RIDE A HOBBY-HORSE
RIDE OUT THE STORM
RIGHT DOWN THE CAR
RIGHT HONOURABLE
RIGHT OFF THE REEL
RIGHT OF PURCHASE
RIGHTS AND WRONGS
RIGHT TO THE POINT
RIGHT WAVELENGTH
RIGID DISCIPLINE
RINGING APPLAUSE
RIPE FOR MISCHIEF
RISE FROM THE DEAD

RISE WITH THE LARK
RITUAL FIRE-DANCE
ROARING TWENTIES
ROARS OF LAUGHTER
ROBBED OF FREEDOM
ROBIN GOODFELLOW
ROB WITH VIOLENCE
ROCK-BOTTOM PRICE
ROCK OF GIBRALTAR
ROGER DE COVERLEY
ROGET'S THESAURUS
ROLL OF WALLPAPER
ROLY-POLY PUDDING
ROMULUS AND REMUS
ROOM TEMPERATURE
ROOM TO SWING A CAT
ROOTED OBJECTION
ROOTED TO THE SPOT
ROOT OF THE MATTER
ROSS AND CROMARTY
ROTATION OF CROPS
ROTTEN AT THE CORE
ROTTEN TO THE CORE
ROUGHLY SPEAKING
ROUNDABOUT ROUTE
ROUND OF APPLAUSE
ROUND OF PLEASURE
ROYAL ALBERT HALL
ROYAL AND ANCIENT
ROYAL COMMISSION
ROYAL OPERA HOUSE
ROYAL TOURNAMENT
RUBBER TRUNCHEON
RUDDY COMPLEXION
RUDE FOREFATHERS
RUFFLED FEATHERS
RUFFLED FEELINGS
RUIN ONE'S CHANCES
RULES OF FOOTBALL
RUN A TEMPERATURE
RUN-AWAY MARRIAGE
RUN FOR ONE'S MONEY
RUN FOR PRESIDENT
RUN LIKE WILD-FIRE
RURAL POPULATION
RUSSIAN LANGUAGE
RUSSIAN ROULETTE

S—15
SAFETY IN NUMBERS

SAIL INTO THE WIND
SAIL NEAR THE WIND
SAILOR'S HORNPIPE
SAINT GEORGE'S DAY
SAINT MARYLEBONE
SALES RESISTANCE
SALLY IN OUR ALLEY
SALMON AND SHRIMP
SAMSON AGONISTES
SANDWICH ISLANDS
SARATOGA SPRINGS
SARDINE SANDWICH
SARDINES ON TOAST
SATURATION POINT
SATURDAY EVENING
SATURDAY MORNING
SAUSAGE AND CHIPS
SAUSAGES AND MASH
SAVAGE CRITICISM
SAVE APPEARANCES
SAVINGS MOVEMENT
SAVOURY OMELETTE
SAY THE MAGIC WORD
SAY WITH EMPHASIS
SCALENE TRIANGLE
SCALES OF JUSTICE
SCALE THE HEIGHTS
SCENE OF THE CRIME
SCHEDULED FLIGHT
SCHNEIDER TROPHY
SCHOLASTIC AGENT
SCHOOLBOY HOWLER
SCHOOL INSPECTOR
SCHOOL OF DANCING
SCHOOL OF THOUGHT
SCIENTIFIC BOXER
SCIENTIFIC WORLD
SCOTTISH TERRIER
SCOTTISH THISTLE
SCRAPE THE BARREL
SCRATCH OF THE PEN
SCRATCH ONE'S HEAD
SCRIBBLING BLOCK
SCRIMP AND SCRAPE
SCRIPTURE LESSON
SCRUFF OF THE NECK
SEA ISLAND COTTON
SEARCHING GLANCE
SEARCH ONE'S HEART
SEASIDE LANDLADY
SEATING CAPACITY

SEAWORTHY VESSEL
SECONDARY COLOUR
SECONDARY MATTER
SECONDARY MODERN
SECONDARY SCHOOL
SECOND-BEST THING
SECOND CHILDHOOD
SECOND FAVOURITE
SECOND-HAND GOODS
SECOND IN COMMAND
SECOND INTENTION
SECOND OF JANUARY
SECOND OF OCTOBER
SECOND-RATE HOTEL
SECOND TIME ROUND
SECRET ANIMOSITY
SECRET COURTSHIP
SECRET INFLUENCE
SECRET STAIRCASE
SECURITY COUNCIL
SECURITY MEASURE
SECURITY OFFICER
SEEDS OF MISTRUST
SEEK A COMPROMISE
SEEK INFORMATION
SEEK ONE'S FORTUNE
SEE NAPLES AND DIE
SEE ONE'S WAY CLEAR
SEE THE FUNNY SIDE
SEE WHAT YOU CAN DO
SELECT COMMITTEE
SELF-EDUCATED MAN
SELF-IMPOSED TASK
SELF-SERVICE SHOP
SELL INTO SLAVERY
SELL ONE'S COUNTRY
SEMOLINA PUDDING
SEND AN ULTIMATUM
SEND ROUND THE HAT
SEND THE CAP ROUND
SEND TO THE BOTTOM
SENIOR BARRISTER
SENIORES PRIORES
SENSATIONAL NEWS
SENSATION MONGER
SENSE OF DISTANCE
SENSE OF PLEASURE
SENSE OF SECURITY
SENSITIVE MARKET
SENSITIVE NATURE
SENSUAL PLEASURE

M.C.D.—17

SENTENCE OF DEATH
SENTENCE TO DEATH
SENTIMENTAL GIRL
SEPARATION ORDER
SERIOUS ACCIDENT
SERIOUS LANGUAGE
SERIOUS QUESTION
SERMONS IN STONES
SERVANT QUESTION
SERVED WITH A WRIT
SERVE TWO MASTERS
SERVICE INCLUDED
SERVICE REVOLVER
SESAME AND LILIES
SET A GOOD EXAMPLE
SET A LOW STANDARD
SET OF FALSE TEETH
SET OF QUADRILLES
SETTLE AN ACCOUNT
SETTLE OLD SCORES
SETTLE THE MATTER
SET UP IN BUSINESS
SEVEN DEADLY SINS
SEVEN OF DIAMONDS
SEVENPENNY STAMP
SEVENTEEN AND SIX
SEVENTEEN AND TWO
SEVENTEENTH HOLE
SEVENTH OF AUGUST
SEVENTH SYMPHONY
SEVEN TIMES SEVEN
SEVENTY THOUSAND
SEVERE THRASHING
SHABBY GENTILITY
SHABBY TREATMENT
SHADY REPUTATION
SHAKE LIKE A JELLY
SHAKEN TO THE CORE
SHALLOW ARGUMENT
SHARPEN ONE'S WITS
SHARP IMPRESSION
SHEATHE THE SWORD
SHEEPSKIN JACKET
SHEER PERFECTION
SHEFFIELD UNITED
SHETLAND ISLANDS
SHIFT FOR ONESELF
SHIFT ONE'S GROUND
SHIP OF THE DESERT
SHIPPING COMPANY
SHIPPING MAGNATE

SHIP'S COMPLEMENT
SHIVER ME TIMBERS
SHOCKING SCANDAL
SHOCKING WEATHER
SHOOTING GALLERY
SHORTHAND TYPIST
SHORTHAND WRITER
SHORT OF PRACTICE
SHORT-TERM POLICY
SHOTGUN MARRIAGE
SHOT IN THE LOCKER
SHOUT OF LAUGHTER
SHOW DISCOURTESY
SHOW FAVOURITISM
SHOW INGRATITUDE
SHOW ONE'S COLOURS
SHOW TO ADVANTAGE
SHRED OF EVIDENCE
SHRINKING VIOLET
SHUFFLE THE CARDS
SICKNESS BENEFIT
SIEGE OF MAFEKING
SIGHT FOR THE GODS
SIGHT-SEEING TOUR
SIGN OF THE ZODIAC
SIGN THE REGISTER
SILENCE IS GOLDEN
SILENT AS THE TOMB
SILVER MEDALLIST
SIMPLE PLEASURES
SIMPLY AND SOLELY
SINCE THE YEAR DOT
SING ANOTHER SONG
SING ANOTHER TUNE
SINK ONE'S CAPITAL
SINK TO ONE'S KNEES
SINK TO THE BOTTOM
SIN OF COMMISSION
SIR EDWARD GERMAN
SIR FRANCIS DRAKE
SIR JOHN FALSTAFF
SISTER OF CHARITY
SITUATION VACANT
SITUATION WANTED
SIX AND FIVEPENCE
SIX AND FOURPENCE
SIX AND NINEPENCE
SIXTEEN AND A HALF
SIXTEEN AND EIGHT
SIXTEEN AND SEVEN
SIXTEEN AND THREE

SIXTEENTH LETTER
SIXTEENTH OF JULY
SIXTEENTH OF JUNE
SIXTEEN THOUSAND
SIXTH OF DECEMBER
SIXTH OF FEBRUARY
SIXTH OF NOVEMBER
SIXTY-FIVE AND SIX
SIXTY-FOUR AND SIX
SKELETON SERVICE
SKIM THE ROOF-TOPS
SKIN OF ONE'S TEETH
SKIP OUT OF THE WAY
SLAB OF CHOCOLATE
SLACKEN ONE'S PACE
SLAKE ONE'S THIRST
SLANG EXPRESSION
SLAPSTICK COMEDY
SLEEPING DRAUGHT
SLEEPING PARTNER
SLEEVELESS DRESS
SLIGHT VARIATION
SLINGS AND ARROWS
SLIP OF THE TONGUE
SLIPPERY AS AN EEL
SLIPPERY SURFACE
SLOUGH OF DESPOND
SLOW BOAT TO CHINA
SLOW IN THE UPTAKE
SLOWLY AND SURELY
SLOWLY BUT SURELY
SMALL PERCENTAGE
SMELTING FURNACE
SMOKE A CIGARETTE
SMOKY ATMOSPHERE
SNAKE IN THE GRASS
SNAP ONE'S FINGERS
SNAP ONE'S NOSE OFF
SOAKED TO THE SKIN
SOARING AMBITION
SOARING THOUGHTS
SOBERING THOUGHT
SOB ONE'S HEART OUT
SOCIAL GATHERING
SOCIAL INSURANCE
SOCIAL OSTRACISM
SODA-WATER SYPHON
SODIUM CARBONATE
SOFT-NOSED BULLET
SOFT-SHOE SHUFFLE
SOLD INTO SLAVERY

SOLICITOR'S CLERK
SOLID FOUNDATION
SOLO PERFORMANCE
SOMEBODY OR OTHER
SOME CONSOLATION
SOMERSET MAUGHAM
SOMETHING IN HAND
SOMETHING ROTTEN
SOMETHING TO COME
SOMETHING TO GO ON
SOME TIME OR OTHER
SOMEWHERE AROUND
SO MUCH THE BETTER
SORRY FOR ONESELF
SOUND EXPRESSION
SOUND INVESTMENT
SOUND OF BOW BELLS
SOUND THE KEYNOTE
SOUND THE RETREAT
SOURCE OF TROUBLE
SOUTH AFRICAN WAR
SOUTHERN RAILWAY
SOUTH KENSINGTON
SOUTH OF THE RIVER
SOUTH OF THE TWEED
SOUTH SEA ISLANDS
SOVEREIGN REMEDY
SOW ONE'S WILD OATS
SPADES ARE TRUMPS
SPANISH BURGUNDY
SPANISH CHESTNUT
SPANISH LANGUAGE
SPARRING PARTNER
SPEAK FOR ONESELF
SPEAK IN A WHISPER
SPEAK OF THE DEVIL
SPECIAL DELIVERY
SPECIAL OCCASION
SPECIAL PLEADING
SPECIFIC GRAVITY
SPEED-BOAT RACING
SPEEDY VENGEANCE
SPELLING MISTAKE
SPINAL COMPLAINT
SPIRAL STAIRCASE
SPIRITED DISPLAY
SPLASH ONE'S MONEY
SPLENDID VICTORY
SPLENDID WEATHER
SPLIT INFINITIVE
SPOIL EVERYTHING

SPOIL ONE'S RECORD
SPOILS OF VICTORY
SPORTING CONDUCT
SPORTING FIXTURE
SPORTING GESTURE
SPORTS ANNOUNCER
SPORTS EQUIPMENT
SPOT ADVERTISING
SPOTLESSLY CLEAN
SPRAY OF DIAMONDS
SPREAD ONE'S WINGS
SPREAD THE GOSPEL
SPRING A SURPRISE
SPRINGER SPANIEL
SPUR OF THE MOMENT
SQUARE THE CIRCLE
SQUATTER'S RIGHTS
SQUATTING RIGHTS
SQUEEZED TO DEATH
STABLE COMPANION
STAGE DIRECTIONS
STAGE-DOOR JOHNNY
STAKE EVERYTHING
STAMP COLLECTING
STAMP COLLECTION
STAMP OF APPROVAL
STAND AND DELIVER
STANDARD EDITION
STANDARD ENGLISH
STANDARD PRODUCT
STAND BARE-HEADED
STAND IN FULL VIEW
STANDING OVATION
STAND IN THE LIGHT
STAND IN THE QUEUE
STAND NO NONSENSE
STAND ON CEREMONY
STAND ONE'S GROUND
STAND ON ONE'S HEAD
STAND ON ONE'S TOES
STAND STOCK-STILL
STANLEY HOLLOWAY
STANLEY MATTHEWS
STARK, STARING MAD
STAR OF BETHLEHEM
STARS AND STRIPES
START AN ARGUMENT
STARVED WITH COLD
STATE APARTMENTS
STATE ASSISTANCE
STATE DEPARTMENT

STATE ENTERPRISE
STATELESS PERSON
STATEMENT OF FACT
STATEMENT ON OATH
STATE OF COLLAPSE
STATE OF CONFLICT
STATE OF DISORDER
STATE OF EQUALITY
STATE OF SOBRIETY
STATION APPROACH
STATUE OF LIBERTY
STAY OF EXECUTION
STAY UNDERGROUND
STAY WHERE YOU ARE
STEALER OF HEARTS
STEAL THE THUNDER
STENTORIAN VOICE
STICKING PLASTER
STICK LIKE A LEECH
STICK OF DYNAMITE
STICKS AND STONES
STICK THE SPURS IN
STICK TO ONE'S GUNS
STICK TO ONE'S LAST
STICK TO THE FACTS
STICK TO THE POINT
STICK TO THE RULES
STICK TO THE TRUTH
STICKY SITUATION
STILL AS THE GRAVE
STILL OF THE NIGHT
STILL, SMALL VOICE
STIR THE PORRIDGE
STIR UP THE EMBERS
ST. MARTIN'S SUMMER
ST. MICHAEL'S MOUNT
STOCKS AND SHARES
STOCKTAKING SALE
STOMACH DISORDER
STOOD UP STRAIGHT
STOP ME AND BUY ONE!
STOPPED THE FIGHT
STOP THE BLEEDING
STOP WHERE YOU ARE
STORM OF APPLAUSE
STRAIGHT ACTRESS
STRAIGHT BOURBON
STRAIGHT DEALING
STRAIGHT IN FRONT
STRAIGHT STRETCH
STRAIN ONE'S LUNGS

STRAIN THE NERVES
STRANGE GOINGS-ON
STRANGE TO RELATE
STRAPPING FELLOW
STRATFORD ON AVON
STRAWS IN THE WIND
STREAM OF THOUGHT
STREAM OF TRAFFIC
STREET DIRECTORY
STRENUOUS EFFORT
STRESS AND STRAIN
STRETCHER BEARER
STRETCH ONE'S LEGS
STRICKEN IN YEARS
STRICTLY NEUTRAL
STRICTLY PRIVATE
STRIKE A BAD PATCH
STRIKE AN AVERAGE
STRIKE A RICH VEIN
STRIKE UP THE BAND
STRIKING SUCCESS
STRING ORCHESTRA
STRING QUARTETTE
STRINGS ATTACHED
STRIVE FOR EFFECT
STROLLING PLAYER
STRONG INFLUENCE
STRONG OBJECTION
STRONG, SILENT MAN
STRONG SITUATION
STRONG WILL POWER
STRUGGLE FOR LIFE
STRUGGLE THROUGH
STUBBORN AS A MULE
STUNT ONE'S GROWTH
ST. VALENTINE'S DAY
STYGIAN DARKNESS
SUBJUNCTIVE MOOD
SUBMARINE CHASER
SUBMIT A QUESTION
SUBSTANTIAL MEAL
SUBURBAN STATION
SUCCESS ALL ROUND
SUCH SWEET SORROW
SUDDEN DEPARTURE
SUFFER IN SILENCE
SUGAR PLANTATION
SUITABLE PARTNER
SUITED TO THE PART
SUIT THE OCCASION
SUM AND SUBSTANCE

SUMMER LIGHTNING
SUMMER RESIDENCE
SUMMON UP COURAGE
SUNDAY AFTERNOON
SUNDAY NEWSPAPER
SUNDAY TELEGRAPH
SUN, MOON AND STARS
SUPERIOR NUMBERS
SUPERIOR OFFICER
SUPERIOR QUALITY
SUPERSONIC SPEED
SUPPLY AND DEMAND
SUPREME CONTEMPT
SURE OF ONE'S FACTS
SURPRISE IN STORE
SURPRISE VISITOR
SURPRISING THING
SUSPECTED PERSON
SUSPECT FOUL PLAY
SUSPEND SENTENCE
SUSPENSE ACCOUNT
SUSTAINED ACTION
SUSTAINED EFFORT
SUSTAIN INJURIES
SWALLOW AN INSULT
SWALLOW-TAIL COAT
SWEAR ALLEGIANCE
SWEAR ON THE BIBLE
SWEAT OF ONE'S BROW
SWEEPING CHANGES
SWEEPING REFORMS
SWEEPING SUCCESS
SWEEPING VICTORY
SWEEP THE CHIMNEY
SWEET FANNY ADAMS
SWEET SIMPLICITY
SWEET TO THE TASTE
SWIM FOR THE SHORE
SWIMMING COSTUME
SWIM WITH THE TIDE
SWORD OF DAMOCLES
SYDNEY WOODERSON
SYLVIA PANKHURST
SYMBOL OF JUSTICE
SYMPHONY CONCERT
SYNTHETIC RUBBER
SYSTEMATIC STUDY

T—15
TABLEAUX VIVANTS
TABLE DECORATION

TABLE OF CONTENTS
TABLES AND CHAIRS
TAILOR AND CUTTER
TAKE A COLLECTION
TAKE A DEEP BREATH
TAKE A FLYING LEAP
TAKE A PHOTOGRAPH
TAKE A RESOLUTION
TAKE A SECOND LOOK
TAKE A STRONG LINE
TAKE FRENCH LEAVE
TAKE INTO ACCOUNT
TAKE INTO CUSTODY
TAKE IT LYING DOWN
TAKE IT ON THE CHIN
TAKE IT OR LEAVE IT
TAKEN AT THE FLOOD
TAKE ONE'S COAT OFF
TAKE ONE'S MEASURE
TAKE PRECAUTIONS
TAKE THE BLOOM OFF
TAKE THE CHILL OFF
TAKE THE LONG VIEW
TAKE THE SEA ROUTE
TAKE THE SHILLING
TAKE TO ONE'S HEELS
TAKE TO THE BOTTLE
TAKE UP THE THREAD
TALE OF TWO CITIES
TALES OF HOFFMANN
TANGERINE ORANGE
TANKARD OF BITTER
TAPERED TROUSERS
TASTE OF THE STRAP
TATTENHAM CORNER
TATTERED AND TORN
TEAR ONE'S CLOTHES
TEAR ONESELF AWAY
TEARS OF LAUGHTER
TECHNICAL SCHOOL
TELEGRAPH OFFICE
TELEPHONE NUMBER
TELEPHONE SYSTEM
TELESCOPIC SIGHT
TELEVISION TABLE
TELL IT NOT IN GATH
TELL ONE'S FORTUNE
TEMPERANCE HOTEL
TEMPORARY RELIEF
TEMPT PROVIDENCE
TENACIOUS MEMORY

TEN AND FIVEPENCE
TEN AND FOURPENCE
TEN AND NINEPENCE
TEN COMMANDMENTS
TENSE ATMOSPHERE
TEN-SHILLING NOTE
TENTH OF DECEMBER
TENTH OF FEBRUARY
TENTH OF NOVEMBER
TERENCE RATTIGAN
TERM OF REFERENCE
TERRIBLE TRAGEDY
TERRIBLE WEATHER
TERRIFIC SERVICE
TERRITORIAL ARMY
TEST OF ENDURANCE
THANKSGIVING DAY
THATCHED COTTAGE
THE AMOROUS PRAWN
THE ANCIENT WORLD
THE ARTFUL DODGER
THE BACK OF BEYOND
THE BARON KNIGHTS
THE BEGGAR'S OPERA
THE BLACK COUNTRY
THE BOHEMIAN GIRL
THE CAT AND FIDDLE
THE COAST IS CLEAR
THE COMMON MARKET
THE COMMON PEOPLE
THE COMMONWEALTH
THE COST OF LIVING
THE DANCING YEARS
THE DEMON ALCOHOL
THE DESCENT OF MAN
THE DEVIL YOU KNOW
THE ELEVENTH HOUR
THE EMPEROR JONES
THE END OF THE ROAD
THE FIRST SWALLOW
THE FOUR FEATHERS
THE FOURTH ESTATE
THE FOURTH OF JULY
THE GARDEN OF EDEN
THE GOLDEN FLEECE
THE HAPPY WARRIOR
THE HOUSE OF USHER
THE INVISIBLE MAN
THE KING'S ENGLISH
THE LAP OF THE GODS
THE LAST MINSTREL

THE LATE-LAMENTED
THE LONDON SEASON
THE LONG VACATION
THE LOW COUNTRIES
THE MAN IN THE MOON
THE MARSEILLAISE
THE MERRY MONARCH
THE MORNING AFTER
THE NAME'S THE SAME
THE OLD PRETENDER
THE PLOT THICKENS
THE POTTER'S WHEEL
THE POWERS THAT BE
THE PRETTY THINGS
THE PRIMROSE PATH
THE PROMISED LAND
THE QUEEN OF SHEBA
THE ROYAL SOCIETY
THE SHOW MUST GO ON
THE SKY'S THE LIMIT
THE SOUND OF MUSIC
THE SUBCONSCIOUS
THE SUN NEVER SETS
THE SUPERNATURAL
THE THANKSGIVING
THE THREE ESTATES
THE TIME WILL COME
THE UNTOUCHABLES
THE VERY REVEREND
THE WOMAN IN WHITE
THE WORLD AT LARGE
THE WORSE FOR WEAR
THIEF IN THE NIGHT
THINK BETTER OF IT
THINK THINGS OVER
THINLY SCATTERED
THIN ON THE GROUND
THIRD OF DECEMBER
THIRD OF FEBRUARY
THIRD OF NOVEMBER
THIRTEEN AND FIVE
THIRTEEN AND FOUR
THIRTEEN AND NINE
THIRTEEN AT TABLE
THIRTEEN MINUTES
THIRTEEN OF A SUIT
THIRTEEN PER CENT
THIRTEENTH GREEN
THIRTEENTH OF MAY
THIRTIETH OF JULY
THIRTIETH OF JUNE

THIRTY-NINE STEPS
THIRTY-ONE AND SIX
THIRTY-SIX AND SIX
THIRTY-TWO AND SIX
THIS YEAR OF GRACE
THORN IN ONE'S SIDE
THORN IN THE FLESH
THOUSAND GUINEAS
THREATENING LOOK
THREE BRASS BALLS
THREE-LEGGED RACE
THREE-LETTER WORD
THREE LITTLE PIGS
THREE-MASTED SHIP
THREE MEN IN A BOAT
THREE MUSKETEERS
THREE OF DIAMONDS
THREEPENNY OPERA
THREEPENNY PIECE
THREEPENNY STAMP
THREE-PIECE SUITE
THREE-TIERED CAKE
THREE TIMES THREE
THRILLED WITH JOY
THRILLING CLIMAX
THROUGH CARRIAGE
THROUGH THE NIGHT
THROUGH THE YEARS
THROW IN ONE'S HAND
THROW IN THE TOWEL
THROW OFF THE YOKE
THROW OUT A FEELER
THROW TO THE WINDS
THUMBNAIL SKETCH
THURSDAY EVENING
THURSDAY MORNING
TICKET COLLECTOR
TICKET INSPECTOR
TICKLE ONE'S FANCY
TICKLE THE PALATE
TICKLISH PROBLEM
TIED HAND AND FOOT
TIES OF AFFECTION
TIGHTEN ONE'S BELT
TIGHTEN ONE'S GRIP
TIGHT-ROPE WALKER
TILLER OF THE SOIL
TILL WE MEET AGAIN
TIME OF DEPARTURE
TIME ON ONE'S HANDS
TIP OF ONE'S TONGUE

TIPPED CIGARETTE
TITANIC STRENGTH
TITUS ANDRONICUS
TO HAVE AND TO HOLD
TO LITTLE PURPOSE
TOMATOES ON TOAST
TOM, DICK AND HARRY
TOMORROW EVENING
TOMORROW MORNING
TOM, THE PIPER'S SON
TONSORIAL ARTIST
TOO CLEVER BY HALF
TOO FULL FOR WORDS
TOO GOOD TO BE TRUE
TOOK THE LONG VIEW
TOOLS OF THE TRADE
TOOTHSOME MORSEL
TOPICAL ALLUSION
TOPICAL INTEREST
TOP-LEVEL MEETING
TOP OF THE MORNING
TOSSING THE CABER
TOTAL ABSTINENCE
TOTAL CASUALTIES
TO THE FULL EXTENT
TO THE MANNER BORN
TOUCH ROCK-BOTTOM
TOUGH ASSIGNMENT
TOUGH NUT TO CRACK
TOURIST INDUSTRY
TOWERING PASSION
TOWER OF STRENGTH
TRADE COMMISSION
TRADE DELEGATION
TRADE SUPPLEMENT
TRADITIONAL FARE
TRADITIONAL JAZZ
TRAFALGAR SQUARE
TRAFFIC MOVEMENT
TRAIN CONNECTION
TRAINING COLLEGE
TRAIN OF THOUGHTS
TRANSFER A PLAYER
TRANSPORT SYSTEM
TRAVEL INCOGNITO
TRAVEL IN COMFORT
TRAVELLER'S TALES
TRAVELLING CLOCK
TRAVELLING CRANE
TREASURED MEMORY
TREATED LIKE DIRT

TREATY OF LOCARNO
TREE OF KNOWLEDGE
TREMBLE WITH FEAR
TREMBLING POPLAR
TREND OF THE TIMES
TRESPASS AGAINST
TRIAL OF STRENGTH
TRICK OF THE TRADE
TRICKY SITUATION
TRIUMPHANT SMILE
TROOP OF SOLDIERS
TROUBLE-FREE MIND
TRUE TO THE LETTER
TRUMPED-UP CHARGE
TRY ANYTHING ONCE
TRY ONE'S PATIENCE
TRY ONE'S STRENGTH
TURN A SOMERSAULT
TURN A WILLING EAR
TURN FOR THE WORSE
TURN IN ONE'S GRAVE
TURN OFF THE LIGHT
TURN OUT A FAILURE
TURN OUT THE GUARD
TURN OUT THE LIGHT
TURN THE LIGHT OFF
TURN UP THE VOLUME
TWELFTH OF AUGUST
TWELVE AND A PENNY
TWELVE AND ELEVEN
TWELVE DISCIPLES
TWELVE-MILE LIMIT
TWELVE SHILLINGS
TWENTIETH LETTER
TWENTIETH OF JULY
TWENTIETH OF JUNE
TWENTY-FOUR HOURS
TWENTY-ONE AND SIX
TWENTY QUESTIONS
TWENTY SHILLINGS
TWENTY-SIX AND SIX
TWENTY-TWO AND SIX
TWIST OF THE WRIST
TWO AND FIVEPENCE
TWO AND FOURPENCE
TWO AND NINEPENCE
TWO-FISTED ATTACK
TWO OF EVERYTHING
TWO-STROKE ENGINE

U—15
ULTRA-VIOLET RAYS
UMPIRE'S DECISION
UNANIMOUS CHOICE
UNBRIDLED TONGUE
UNCIVILIZED RACE
UNDENIABLE TRUTH
UNDER A FALSE NAME
UNDERARM BOWLING
UNDER CLOSE GUARD
UNDER COMPLEMENT
UNDER COMPULSION
UNDER CORRECTION
UNDER-COVER AGENT
UNDER DISCIPLINE
UNDER DISCUSSION
UNDER LOCK AND KEY
UNDER OBLIGATION
UNDER ONE'S BREATH
UNDER-SEA WARFARE
UNDER THE COUNTER
UNDER THE SURFACE
UNDER THE WEATHER
UNDERWATER CRAFT
UNDESERVING CASE
UNEMPLOYMENT PAY
UNEQUAL STRUGGLE
UNEXPECTED EVENT
UNEXPECTED VISIT
UNFAIR ADVANTAGE
UNFAIR TREATMENT
UNFEELING PERSON
UNFINISHED STATE
UNFOUNDED REPORT
UNFROCKED PRIEST
UNFURNISHED FLAT
UNFURNISHED ROOM
UNGUARDED MINUTE
UNGUARDED MOMENT
UNGUARDED REMARK
UNHAPPY MEMORIES
UNION IS STRENGTH
UNITED PROVINCES
UNIVERSAL REMEDY
UNIVERSITY GRANT
UNKIND CRITICISM
UNKNOWN QUANTITY
UNLEAVENED BREAD
UNLUCKY THIRTEEN
UNMARRIED MOTHER
UNPAID SECRETARY

UNPUBLISHED WORK
UNSKILLED LABOUR
UNSOLVED MYSTERY
UNTOUCHED BY HAND
UNTROUBLED SLEEP
UNTRUE STATEMENT
UNVARNISHED TALE
UP BEFORE THE BEAK
UP GUARDS AND AT 'EM!
UPRIGHT CARRIAGE
UPRIGHT POSITION
UP THE GARDEN PATH
UP TO THE EYEBROWS
URBAN POPULATION
UTTER A FALSEHOOD
UTTER STARVATION

V—15
VACCINATION MARK
VAIN EXPECTATION
VANCOUVER ISLAND
VANILLA ICE-CREAM
VARSITY BOAT-RACE
VAST IMPROVEMENT
VAUGHAN WILLIAMS
VAUXHALL GARDENS
VEGETABLE GARDEN
VEGETABLE MARKET
VEGETABLE MARROW
VENERABLE PRIEST
VENGEANCE IS MINE
VERBAL AGREEMENT
VERBAL CRITICISM
VETO THE PROPOSAL
VICHY GOVERNMENT
VICTORIA STATION
VICTORY IN THE AIR
VIOLATE THE TERMS
VIOLENT CONTRAST
VIOLENT EXERCISE
VIOLENT OUTBURST
VIOLENT REACTION
VIOLENT STRUGGLE
VIRGINIA CREEPER
VIRGINIA TOBACCO
VIRGIN TERRITORY
VISIBLE DISTANCE
VISION OF DELIGHT
VITAL STATISTICS
VOICE PRODUCTION
VOLLEY OF THUNDER

VOLUNTARY SCHOOL
VULNERABLE POINT

W—15
WADDLE LIKE A DUCK
WAISTCOAT POCKET
WAITING FOR GODOT
WALKING DISTANCE
WALK INTO TROUBLE
WALL OF MOUNTAINS
WALRUS MOUSTACHE
WALTZING MATILDA
WANDERING WILLIE
WANTED FOR MURDER
WAR PREPARATIONS
WASHED OVERBOARD
WASTE NOT, WANT NOT
WASTE ONE'S BREATH
WATCH ON THE RHINE
WATCH WITH MOTHER
WATERLOO STATION
WATER ON THE BRAIN
WATERTIGHT ALIBI
WEALTH OF NATIONS
WEAR THE BREECHES
WEAR THE TROUSERS
WEATHER FORECAST
WEATHER THE STORM
WEDDING CEREMONY
WEDNESDAY'S CHILD
WEEK-END SHOPPING
WEEKLY NEWSPAPER
WEIGHING MACHINE
WEIGHT OF NUMBERS
WEIGHT OF OPINION
WEIGHTY ARGUMENT
WELCOME STRANGER
WELLINGTON BOOTS
WELL-MEANING TYPE
WELL REPRESENTED
WENT LIKE THE WIND
WESTERN ALLIANCE
WESTMINSTER BANK
WESTMINSTER HALL
WET THE BABY'S HEAD
WHATEVER HAPPENS
WHAT'S THE VERDICT?
WHERE THERE'S LIFE
WHET THE APPETITE
WHIFF OF FRESH AIR
WHILE THERE'S LIFE

WHIRLING DERVISH
WHISPER TOGETHER
WHISTLE-STOP TOUR
WHISTLING KETTLE
WHITED SEPULCHRE
WHITEHALL PALACE
WHITE MAN'S BURDEN
WHITER THAN WHITE
WHITES OF THE EYES
WHITSUN VACATION
WHOLESALE DEALER
WHOLESALE MURDER
WHOM THE GODS LOVE
WIELD THE SCEPTRE
WIENER SCHNITZEL
WIFE AND CHILDREN
WILD IMAGINATION
WILL AND BEQUEATH
WILLIAM CONGREVE
WILLIAM OF ORANGE
WILLIAM THE FIRST
WILLIAM THE THIRD
WILLING TO PLEASE
WILL SHAKESPEARE
WIMBLEDON COMMON
WIN BY A SHORT HEAD
WINCHESTER RIFLE
WINDMILL THEATRE
WINDSCREEN WIPER
WINDWARD ISLANDS
WINE BY THE BARREL
WINES AND SPIRITS
WINNING POSITION
WINNING SEQUENCE
WINTER SPORTSMAN
WIN THE LAST ROUND
WIRELESS LICENCE
WIRELESS MESSAGE
WIRELESS STATION
WISDOM OF SOLOMON
WISE MEN OF GOTHAM
WISHFUL THINKING
WISH YOU WERE HERE
WITCHES' CAULDRON
WITH A DIFFERENCE
WITH A LITTLE LUCK
WITH COMPLIMENTS
WITHERING GLANCE
WITHHOLD PAYMENT
WITHIN EASY REACH
WITHIN ONE'S GRASP

WITHOUT AN EFFORT
WITHOUT A PURPOSE
WITHOUT A SCRATCH
WITHOUT CEREMONY
WITHOUT INCIDENT
WITHOUT INTEREST
WITHOUT PARALLEL
WITHOUT THINKING
WOMAN OF FEW WORDS
WOMAN OF THE WORLD
WOMAN'S INTUITION
WOMAN'S PRIVILEGE
WOMEN'S INSTITUTE
WOODCUTTERS' BALL
WOODEN PARTITION
WOOLLEN INDUSTRY
WOOLWICH ARSENAL
WORK AGAINST TIME
WORKERS' PLAYTIME
WORKING MAJORITY
WORKING-MAN'S CLUB
WORK LIKE A NIGGER
WORK LIKE A TROJAN
WORK OF REFERENCE
WORK ONE'S PASSAGE
WORK UNDERGROUND
WORLD GOVERNMENT
WORLD OF COMMERCE
WORLD OF LEARNING
WORLD WITHOUT END
WORTHY ADVERSARY

WOUNDED FEELINGS
WRESTLING SCHOOL
WRETCHED WEATHER
WRINKLED WITH AGE
WRITING MATERIAL
WRITTEN CONTRACT
WRITTEN EVIDENCE
WRITTEN LANGUAGE
WRONG ASSUMPTION
WRONG IMPRESSION
WRONG WAVE-LENGTH
WROUGHT-IRON GATE

X—15
XMAS DECORATIONS

Y—15
YELLOWSTONE PARK
YELL WITH DELIGHT
YEOMEN OF ENGLAND
YESTERDAY'S PAPER
YIELD GRACEFULLY
YIELD TO PRESSURE
YORKSHIRE RELISH
YOU NEVER CAN TELL
YOUNG AND HEALTHY
YOUNGER DAUGHTER
YOUNGEST BROTHER
YOURS FAITHFULLY
YOURS OBEDIENTLY
YOUTH-CLUB LEADER

WORDS

A—3	B—3	CAW	DUD	FEN
ABC	BAA	CHA	DUE	FEW
ACE	BAD	CID	DUG	FEY
ACT	BAG	COB	DUN	FEZ
ADD	BAH	COD	DUO	FIB
ADO	BAN	COG	DYE	FIE
AFT	BAR	COL		FIG
AGA	BAT	CON	E—3	FIN
AGE	BAY	COO	EAR	FIR
AGO	BBC	COP	EAT	FIT
AHA	BED	COS	EAU	FIX
AID	BEE	COT	EBB	FLU
AIL	BEG	COW	EEL	FLY
AIM	BEN	COX	E'EN	FOB
AIN	BET	COY	E'ER	FOE
AIR	BEY	CRY	EFT	FOG
AIT	BIB	CUB	EGG	FOP
ALB	BID	CUD	EGO	FOR
ALE	BIG	CUE	EKE	FOX
ALL	BIN	CUP	ELF	FRO
ALP	BIS	CUR	ELI	FRY
ALT	BIT	CUT	ELK	FUG
AMP	BOA	CWT	ELL	FUN
ANA	BOB		ELM	FUR
AND	BOG	D—3	ELY	
ANN	BOO	DAB	EMU	
ANT	BOW	DAD	END	
ANY	BOX	DAM	EON	
APE	BOY	DAN	ERA	G—3
APT	BOZ	DAW	ERE	GAB
ARC	BUD	DAY	ERG	GAD
ARE	BUG	DEB	ERR	GAG
ARK	BUM	DEE	ESS	GAL
ARM	BUN	DEN	ETC	GAP
ART	BUS	DEW	EVE	GAR
ASH	BUT	DIB	EWE	GAS
ASK	BUY	DID	EYE	GAT
ASP	BYE	DIE		GAY
ASS		DIG		GEE
ATE		DIM	F—3	GEM
AUK		DIN	FAD	GEN
AVA	C—3	DIP	FAG	GET
AVE	CAB	DOE	FAN	GIB
AWA	CAD	DOG	FAR	GIE
AWE	CAM	DOH	FAT	GIG
AWL	CAN	DON	FAY	GIN
AWN	CAP	DOT	FEB	GNU
AXE	CAR	DRY	FED	GOB
AYE	CAT	DUB	FEE	GOD

GOG	IMP	LAY	MUG	ORC
GOT	INK	LBW	MUM	ORE
GUM	INN	LEA		ORT
GUN	ION	LED	**N—3**	OUR
GUT	I.O.U.	LEE	NAB	OUT
GUY	IRE	LEG	NAG	OVA
GYM	IRK	LEI	NAP	OWE
GYP	ISM	LEO	NAY	OWL
	ITS	LET	N.C.O.	OWN
H—3	IVY	LEW	NEB	
HAD		LEX	NEE	**P—3**
HAG	**J—3**	LIB	NEO	PAD
HAH	JAB	LID	NET	PAH
HAM	JAG	LIE	NEW	PAL
HAP	JAM	LIP	N!B	PAM
HAS	JAP	LIT	NIL	PAN
HAT	JAR	LOB	NIP	PAP
HAW	JAW	LOG	NIT	PAR
HAY	JAY	LOO	NIX	PAS
HEM	JET	LOP	NOB	PAT
HEN	JEW	LOT	NOD	PAW
HEP	JIB	LOW	NOG	PAX
HER	JIG	LSD	NOR	PAY
HEW	JOB	LUD	NOT	PEA
HEY	JOE	LUG	NOW	PEG
HID	JOG	LYE	NUB	PEN
HIE	JOT		NUN	PEP
HIM	JOY	**M—3**	NUT	PER
HIP	JUG	MAB	NYE	PET
HIS	JUT	MAC		PEW
HIT		MAD	**O—3**	PIE
HOB	**K—3**	MAN	OAF	PIG
HOD	KAY	MAP	OAK	PIN
HOE	KEG	MAR	OAR	PIP
HOG	KEN	MAT	OAT	PIT
HOP	KEY	MAW	OBI	PLY
HOT	KID	MAX	OCH	POD
HOW	KIM	MAY	ODD	POE
HUB	KIN	MEN	ODE	POM
HUE	KIP	MET	O'ER	POP
HUG	KIT	MEW	OFF	POT
HUM		MID	OFT	POW
HUN	**L—3**	MIX	OHM	PRO
HUT	LAC	MOA	OHO	PRY
	LAD	MOB	OIL	PUB
I—3	LAG	MOO	OLD	PUG
IAN	LAM	MOP	ONE	PUN
ICE	LAP	MOT	OOF	PUP
ICY	LAR	MOW	OPE	PUS
ILK	LAW	MRS	OPT	PUT
ILL	LAX	MUD	ORB	PYX

R—3	SEC	TED	VIZ	**A—4**
RAG	SEE	TEE	VOW	ABBE
RAJ	SEN	TEG		ABED
RAM	SET	TEN	**W—3**	ABET
RAN	SEW	THE	WAD	ABLE
RAP	SEX	THO'	WAG	ABUT
RAS	SHE	THY	WAN	ACER
RAT	SHY	TIC	WAR	ACHE
RAW	SIC	TIE	WAS	ACID
RAY	SIN	TIN	WAT	ACME
RED	SIP	TIP	WAX	ACNE
REF	SIR	TIS	WAY	ACRE
REP	SIS	TIT	WEB	ADAM
RET	SIT	TOD	WED	ADIT
REV	SIX	TOE	WEE	ADZE
REX	SKI	TOG	WEN	AFAR
RIB	SKY	TOM	WET	AGED
RID	SLY	TON	WHO	AGOG
RIG	SOB	TOO	WHY	AGUE
RIM	SOD	TOP	WIG	AHEM
RIO	SOL	TOR	WIN	AHOY
RIP	SON	TOT	WIT	AIDA
ROB	SOP	TOW	WOE	AIDE
ROC	SOS	TOY	WON	AIRY
ROD	SOT	TRY	WOO	AJAR
ROE	SOU	TUB	WOT	AKIN
ROM	SOW	TUG	WOW	ALAR
RON	SOX	TUN	WRY	ALAS
ROT	SOY	TUP	WYE	ALEE
ROW	SPA	TUT		ALGA
ROY	SPY	TWA	**Y—3**	ALLY
RUB	STY	TWO	YAH	ALMA
RUE	SUB		YAK	ALMS
RUG	SUE	**U—3**	YAM	ALOE
RUM	SUM	UGH	YAP	ALPS
RUN	SUN	ULT	YAW	ALSO
RUT	SUP	UNA	YEA	ALTO
RYE		UNO	YEN	ALUM
	T—3	URE	YEP	AMBO
S—3	TAB	URN	YES	AMEN
SAC	TAG	USE	YET	AMID
SAD	TAJ	UVA	YEW	AMMO
SAG	TAN		YON	AMOK
SAL	TAP	**V—3**	YOU	AMYL
SAM	TAR	V.A.D.		ANEW
SAP	TAT	VAN	**Z—3**	ANIL
SAT	TAU	VAT	ZED	ANNA
SAW	TAW	VET	ZIP	ANON
SAX	TAX	VEX	ZOO	ANTE
SAY	TEA	VIA		APED
SEA	TEC	VIE		APEX
		VIM		

APSE	BANG	BIRD	BRER	CASH
AQUA	BANK	BITE	BREW	CASK
ARAB	BANT	BLAB	BRIE	CAST
ARCH	BARB	BLED	BRIG	CAVE
AREA	BARD	BLEW	BRIM	CAVY
ARIA	BARE	BLOB	BRIO	CEDE
ARID	BARK	BLOC	BROW	CELL
ARIL	BARM	BLOT	BUCK	CELT
ARMS	BARN	BLOW	BUDE	CENT
ARMY	BART	BLUB	BUFF	CERE
ARTS	BASE	BLUE	BUHL	CERT
ARTY	BASH	BLUR	BULB	CHAP
ARUM	BASK	BOAR	BULK	CHAR
ASHY	BASS	BOAT	BULL	CHAT
ASIA	BAST	BODE	BUMP	CHEF
ASTI	BATH	BODY	BUNG	CHEW
ATOM	BAWD	BOER	BUNK	CHIC
ATOP	BAWL	BOGY	BUOY	CHIN
AUNT	BAYS	BOIL	BURN	CHIP
AURA	BEAD	BOKO	BURR	CHIT
AUTO	BEAK	BOLD	BURY	CHOP
AVER	BEAM	BOLE	BUSH	CHOW
AVID	BEAN	BOLL	BUSS	CHUB
AVON	BEAR	BOLT	BUST	CHUG
AVOW	BEAT	BOMB	BUSY	CHUM
AWAY	BEAU	BOND	BUTT	CITE
AWED	BECK	BONE	BUZZ	CITY
AWRY	BEDE	BONY	BYRE	CLAD
AXED	BEEF	BOOB		CLAM
AXIL	BEEN	BOOK	**C—4**	CLAN
AXIS	BEER	BOOM	CADE	CLAP
AXLE	BEET	BOON	CADI	CLAW
AYAH	BELL	BOOR	CAFÉ	CLAY
B—4	BELT	BOOT	CAGE	CLEF
BAAL	BEND	BORE	CAIN	CLIO
BAAS	BENT	BORN	CAKE	CLIP
BABA	BERG	BOSH	CAKY	CLOD
BABE	BEST	BOSS	CALF	CLOG
BABU	BETA	BOTH	CALL	CLOT
BABY	BEVY	BOUT	CALM	CLOY
BACK	BIAS	BOWL	CAME	CLUB
BADE	BIDE	BOWS	CAMP	CLUE
BAIL	BIER	BRAD	CANE	COAL
BAIT	BIFF	BRAE	CANT	COAT
BAKE	BIKE	BRAG	CAPE	COAX
BALD	BILE	BRAN	CARD	COCA
BALE	BILK	BRAT	CARE	COCK
BALL	BILL	BRAW	CARL	COCO
BALM	BIND	BRAY	CARP	CODA
BAND	BINE	BRED	CART	CODE
BANE	BING	BREN	CASE	COIF

COIL	CURL	DESK	DRAM	EDAM
COIN	CURT	DEWY	DRAT	EDDA
COIR	CUSP	DHOW	DRAW	EDDY
COKE	CUTE	DIAL	DRAY	EDEN
COLD	CYST	DICE	DREE	EDGE
COLE	CZAR	DICK	DREY	EDGY
COLT		DIDO	DREW	EDIT
COMA	D—4	DIED	DRIP	EGAD
COMB	DACE	DIET	DROP	EIRE
COME	DADO	DIGS	DRUB	ELAN
CONE	DAFT	DIKE	DRUG	ELIA
CONK	DAGO	DILL	DRUM	ELMO
CONS	DAIL	DIME	DUAL	ELSE
COOK	DAIS	DINE	DUCE	ELUL
COOL	DALE	DING	DUCK	EMIR
COON	DALI	DINT	DUCT	EMIT
COOP	DAME	DIRE	DUDE	ENOW
COOT	DAMN	DIRK	DUDS	ENSA
COPE	DAMP	DIRT	DUEL	ENVY
COPT	DANE	DISC	DUET	EPEE
COPY	DANK	DISH	DUFF	EPIC
CORD	DARE	DISK	DUKE	ERGO
CORE	DARK	DISS	DUKW	ERIC
CORK	DARN	DIVA	DULL	ERIN
CORM	DART	DIVE	DULY	ERNE
CORN	DASH	DOCK	DUMA	EROS
COSH	DATA	DODO	DUMB	ERSE
COST	DATE	DOER	DUMP	ERST
COSY	DAUB	DOFF	DUNE	ESPY
COTE	DAVY	DOGE	DUNG	ETCH
COUP	DAWN	DOLE	DUNK	ETNA
COVE	DAZE	DOLL	DUPE	ETON
COWL	D-DAY	DOLT	DUSE	ETUI
CRAB	DEAD	DOME	DUSK	EVEN
CRAG	DEAF	DONE	DUST	EVER
CRAM	DEAL	DOOM	DUTY	EVIL
CRAN	DEAN	DOOR	DYAK	EWER
CRAW	DEAR	DOPE	DYED	EXAM
CREW	DEBT	DORA	DYER	EXIT
CRIB	DECK	DORY	DYKE	EXON
CROP	DEED	DOSE		EYED
CROW	DEEM	DOSS	E—4	EYOT
CRUX	DEEP	DOTE	EACH	EYRE
CUBE	DEER	DOTH	EARL	EYRY
CUFF	DEFT	DOUR	EARN	
CULL	DEFY	DOVE	EASE	F—4
CULM	DELL	DOWN	EAST	FACE
CULT	DEMY	DOZE	EASY	FACT
CURB	DENE	DOZY	EBON	FADE
CURD	DENT	DRAB	ECHO	FAIL
CURE	DENY	DRAG	ECRU	FAIN

FAIR	FLEX	GAIT	GOLF	HARM
FAKE	FLIP	GALA	GONE	HARP
FALL	FLIT	GALE	GONG	HART
FAME	FLOE	GALL	GOOD	HASH
FANG	FLOG	GAME	GOOF	HASP
FARE	FLOP	GAMP	GORE	HATE
FARM	FLOW	GANG	GORY	HATH
FARO	FLUE	GAOL	GOSH	HAUL
FASH	FLUX	GAPE	GOTH	HAVE
FAST	FOAL	GARB	GOUT	HAWK
FATE	FOAM	GASH	GOWN	HAZE
FAUN	FOIL	GASP	GRAB	HAZY
FAWN	FOLD	GATE	GRAF	HEAD
FEAR	FOLK	GAUD	GRAM	HEAL
FEAT	FOND	GAUL	GRAY	HEAP
FEED	FONT	GAVE	GREW	HEAR
FEEL	FOOD	GAWK	GREY	HEAT
FEET	FOOL	GAZE	GRID	HEBE
FELL	FOOT	GEAR	GRIM	HEED
FELT	FORD	GENT	GRIN	HEEL
FEND	FORE	GERM	GRIP	HEIR
FERN	FORK	GEUM	GRIT	HELD
FETE	FORM	GIBE	GROG	HELL
FEUD	FORT	GIFT	GROW	HELM
FIAT	FOUL	GILD	GRUB	HELP
FIFE	FOUR	GILL	GULF	HEMP
FILE	FOWL	GILT	GULL	HERB
FILL	FOXY	GIMP	GULP	HERD
FILM	FRAU	GIRD	GUSH	HERE
FIND	FRAY	GIRL	GUST	HERN
FINE	FREE	GIRT	GYVE	HERO
FINN	FRET	GIST		HERR
FIRE	FROG	GIVE	H—4	HERS
FIRM	FROM	GLAD	HACK	HEWN
FISH	FUEL	GLEE	HAFT	HICK
FIST	FULL	GLEN	HA-HA	HIDE
FIVE	FUME	GLIB	HAIL	HIED
FIZZ	FUMY	GLIM	HAIR	HIGH
FLAG	FUND	GLOW	HAKE	HIKE
FLAK	FUNK	GLUE	HALE	HILL
FLAM	FURL	GLUM	HALF	HILT
FLAN	FURY	GLUT	HALL	HIND
FLAP	FUSE	G-MAN	HALO	HINT
FLAT	FUSS	GNAT	HALT	HIRE
FLAW	FUZZ	GNAW	HAME	HISS
FLAX		GOAD	HAND	HIST
FLAY	G—4	GOAL	HANG	HIVE
FLEA	GAEL	GOAT	HANK	HOAR
FLED	GAFF	GOBY	HARD	HOAX
FLEE	GAGE	GODS	HARE	HOBO
FLEW	GAIN	GOLD	HARK	HOCK

HOED	IMPI	KEEL	LANA	LILT
HOLD	INCA	KEEN	LAND	LILY
HOLE	INCH	KEEP	LANE	LIMB
HOLM	INKY	KELP	LANK	LIME
HOLT	INTO	KEMP	LAPP	LIMN
HOLY	IOTA	KENT	LARD	LIMP
HOME	IRAN	KEPI	LARK	LIMY
HOMY	IRIS	KEPT	LASH	LINE
HONE	IRON	KERB	LASS	LING
HONK	ISIS	KHAN	LAST	LINK
HOOD	ISLE	KICK	LATE	LINO
HOOF	ITCH	KILL	LATH	LINT
HOOK	ITEM	KILN	LAUD	LION
HOOP		KILO	LAVA	LIRA
HOOT	**J—4**	KILT	LAVE	LIRE
HOPE	JACK	KIND	LAWN	LISP
HOPS	JADE	KINE	LAZE	LIST
HORN	JAIL	KING	LAZY	LIVE
HOSE	JAMB	KINK	LEAD	LOAD
HOST	JANE	KIRK	LEAF	LOAF
HOUR	JAPE	KISS	LEAK	LOAM
HOVE	JAZZ	KITE	LEAL	LOAN
HOWL	JEAN	KITH	LEAN	LOBE
HUED	JEEP	KIWI	LEAP	LOCH
HUFF	JEER	KNAP	LEAR	LOCK
HUGE	JEHU	KNEE	LEDA	LODE
HULA	JERK	KNEW	LEEK	LOFT
HULK	JEST	KNIT	LEER	LOIN
HULL	JIFF	KNOB	LEES	LOLL
HUMP	JILL	KNOT	LEET	LONE
HUNG	JILT	KNOW	LEFT	LONG
HUNK	JINX	KNUR	LEND	LOOK
HUNT	JOCK	KRIS	LENO	LOOM
HURL	JOEY	KUDU	LENS	LOON
HURT	JOHN	KURD	LENT	LOOP
HUSH	JOKE	KYLE	LESS	LOOS
HUSK	JOLT		LEST	LOOT
HYMN	JOSS	**L—4**	LETT	LOPE
HYPO	JOVE	LACE	LEVY	LORD
	JOWL	LACK	LEWD	LORE
	JUDO	LADE	LIAR	LORN
I—4	JUDY	LADY	LICE	LORY
IBEX	JU-JU	LAIC	LICK	LOSE
IBIS	JUMP	LAID	LIDO	LOSS
ICED	JUNE	LAIN	LIED	LOST
ICON	JUNK	LAIR	LIEF	LOTH
IDEA	JUNO	LAKE	LIEN	LOUD
IDES	JURY	LAMA	LIEU	LOUR
IDLE	JUST	LAMB	LIFE	LOUT
IDLY		LAME	LIFT	LOVE
IDOL	**K—4**	LAMP	LIKE	LUCK
IMAM	KALE			

LUDO	MEET	MOTE	NOEL	OUSE
LUFF	MELT	MOTH	NOLL	OUST
LUGE	MEMO	MOUE	NONE	OVAL
LULL	MEND	MOVE	NOOK	OVEN
LUMP	MENU	MOWN	NOON	OVER
LUNG	MERE	MUCH	NORM	OVUM
LURE	MESH	MUCK	NOSE	OWED
LURK	MESS	MUFF	NOSY	OXEN
LUSH	METE	MULE	NOTE	OYES
LUST	MEWS	MULL	NOUN	OYEZ
LUTE	MICA	MURK	NOUS	
LYNX	MICE	MUSE	NOVA	**P—4**
LYON	MIEN	MUSH	NOWT	PACE
LYRE	MIKE	MUSK	NUDE	PACK
	MILD	MUST	NULL	PACT
	MILE	MUTE	NUMB	PAGE
M—4	MILK	MUTT		PAID
MACE	MILL	MYTH	**O—4**	PAIL
MADE	MIME		OAKS	PAIN
MAGI	MIND	**N—4**	OAST	PAIR
MAID	MINE	NAIL	OATH	PALE
MAIL	MING	NAME	OBEY	PALI
MAIM	MINI	NAPE	OBIT	PALL
MAIN	MINK	NARD	OBOE	PALM
MAKE	MINT	NARK	ODDS	PANE
MALE	MINX	NAVE	ODIN	PANG
MALL	MIRE	NAVY	OGEE	PANT
MALT	MIRY	NAZE	OGLE	PAPA
MAMA	MISS	NAZI	OGPU	PARA
MANE	MIST	NEAP	OGRE	PARD
MANX	MITE	NEAR	OILY	PARE
MANY	MITT	NEAT	OKAY	PARK
MARE	MOAN	NECK	OLIO	PARR
MARK	MOAT	NEED	OMAR	PART
MARL	MOCK	NEEP	OMEN	PASS
MARS	MODE	NE'ER	OMIT	PAST
MART	MODS	NEON	ONCE	PATE
MASH	MOKE	NERO	ONER	PATH
MASK	MOLE	NESS	ONLY	PAUL
MASS	MOLL	NEST	ONUS	PAVE
MAST	MONK	NETT	ONYX	PAWL
MATE	MOOD	NEWS	OOZE	PAWN
MAUD	MOON	NEWT	OPAL	PAYE
MAUL	MOOR	NEXT	OPEN	PEAK
MAZE	MOOT	NIBS	OPUS	PEAL
MEAD	MOPE	NICE	ORAL	PEAR
MEAL	MOPS	NICK	ORFE	PEAT
MEAN	MORE	NIGH	ORGY	PECK
MEAT	MORN	NINE	OTIC	PEEK
MEED	MOSS	NISI	OUCH	PEEL
MEEK	MOST	NODE	OURS	PEEP

PEER	PONY	QUIN	RIFE	RUMP
PEKE	POOH	QUIP	RIFF	RUNE
PELF	POOL	QUIT	RIFT	RUNG
PELT	POOP	QUIZ	RIGA	RUNT
PENT	POOR	QUOD	RILE	RUSE
PEON	POPE		RILL	RUSH
PERI	PORE	**R—4**	RIME	RUSK
PERK	PORK	RACE	RIND	RUSS
PERM	PORT	RACK	RING	RUST
PERT	POSE	RACY	RINK	RUTH
PESO	POSH	RAFT	RIOT	RYOT
PEST	POST	RAGE	RIPE	
PHEW	POSY	RAID	RISE	**S—4**
PHIZ	POUR	RAIL	RISK	SACK
PHUT	POUT	RAIN	RITE	SAFE
PICA	PRAM	RAKE	RIVE	SAGA
PICE	PRAY	RALE	ROAD	SAGE
PICK	PREP	RAMP	ROAM	SAGO
PICT	PREY	RAND	ROAN	SAID
PIED	PRIG	RANI	ROAR	SAIL
PIER	PRIM	RANK	ROBE	SAKE
PIKE	PROA	RANT	ROCK	SAKI
PILE	PROD	RAPE	RODE	SALE
PILL	PROM	RAPT	ROLE	SALT
PINE	PROP	RARE	ROLL	SAME
PING	PROS	RASH	ROME	SAND
PINK	PROW	RASP	ROMP	SANE
PINT	PROX	RATE	ROOD	SANG
PIPE	PUCE	RAVE	ROOF	SANK
PISH	PUCK	RAZE	ROOK	SANS
PITH	PUFF	READ	ROOM	SARD
PITY	PULL	REAL	ROOT	SARI
PLAN	PULP	REAM	ROPE	SARK
PLAY	PUMA	REAP	ROPY	SASH
PLEA	PUMP	REAR	ROSE	SATE
PLOD	PUNK	REDE	ROSS	SAUL
PLOP	PUNT	REED	ROSY	SAVE
PLOT	PUNY	REEF	ROTA	SAWN
PLOY	PUPA	REEK	ROTE	SAXE
PLUG	PURE	REEL	ROUE	SCAB
PLUM	PURL	REIN	ROUP	SCAN
PLUS	PURR	REIS	ROUT	SCAR
POEM	PUSH	RELY	ROVE	SCOT
POET	PUSS	REND	RUBY	SCOW
POKE	PUTT	RENT	RUCK	SCUD
POKY	PYRE	REST	RUDD	SCUM
POLE		RHEA	RUDE	SCUT
POLL	**Q—4**	RICE	RUED	SEAL
POLO	QUAD	RICH	RUFF	SEAM
POMP	QUAY	RICK	RUIN	SEAN
POND	QUID	RIDE	RULE	SEAR

SEAT	SIZE	SOIL	SUDS	TAXI
SECT	SKEP	SOKE	SUED	TEAK
SEED	SKEW	SOLA	SUET	TEAL
SEEK	SKID	SOLD	SUEZ	TEAM
SEEM	SKIM	SOLE	SUIT	TEAR
SEEN	SKIN	SOLO	SULK	TEAT
SEEP	SKIP	SOME	SUMP	TEED
SEER	SKIT	SONG	SUNG	TEEM
SELF	SKUA	SOON	SUNK	TELL
SELL	SKYE	SOOT	SURE	TEND
SEMI	SLAB	SORE	SURF	TENT
SEND	SLAG	SORT	SWAB	TERM
SENT	SLAM	SO-SO	SWAG	TERN
SEPT	SLAP	SOUL	SWAM	TEST
SERB	SLAT	SOUP	SWAN	THAI
SERE	SLAV	SOUR	SWAP	THAN
SERF	SLAY	SOWN	SWAT	THAT
SETT	SLED	SOYA	SWAY	THAW
SEWN	SLEW	SPAM	SWIG	THEE
SHAD	SLID	SPAN	SWIM	THEM
SHAG	SLIM	SPAR	SWOP	THEN
SHAH	SLIP	SPAT	SWOT	THEY
SHAW	SLIT	SPEC	SWUM	THIN
SHED	SLOE	SPED	SYCE	THIS
SHEW	SLOG	SPIN		THOR
SHIM	SLOP	SPIT	T—4	THOU
SHIN	SLOT	SPIV	TACK	THRO
SHIP	SLOW	SPOT	TACT	THUD
SHOD	SLUG	SPRY	TAEL	THUG
SHOE	SLUM	SPUD	TAFT	THUS
SHOO	SLUR	SPUN	TAIL	TICK
SHOP	SLUT	SPUR	TAKE	TIDE
SHOT	SMEE	STAB	TALC	TIDY
SHOW	SMEW	STAG	TALE	TIED
SHUN	SMUG	STAR	TALK	TIER
SHUT	SMUT	STAY	TALL	TIFF
SICK	SNAG	STEM	TAME	TIKE
SIDE	SNAP	STEN	TAMP	TILE
SIFT	SNIP	STEP	TANG	TILL
SIGH	SNOB	STET	TANK	TILT
SIGN	SNOW	STEW	TAPE	TIME
SIKH	SNUB	STIR	TARA	TINE
SILK	SNUG	STOP	TARE	TING
SILL	SOAK	STOW	TARN	TINT
SILO	SOAP	STUB	TARO	TINY
SILT	SOAR	STUD	TART	TIRE
SINE	SOCK	STUN	TASK	TOAD
SING	SODA	STYE	TASS	TOBY
SINK	SOFA	STYX	TA-TA	TO-DO
SIRE	SOFT	SUCH	TATE	TOED
SITE	SOHO	SUCK	TAUT	TOFF

TOGA	'TWAS	VISA	WEND	WOVE
TOGS	TWIG	VIVA	WENT	WRAP
TOIL	TWIN	VIVE	WEPT	WREN
TOLD	TWIT	VOCE	WERE	WRIT
TOLL	TYKE	VOID	WERT	
TOMB	TYNE	VOLE	WEST	**X—4**
TOME	TYPE	VOLT	WHAT	XMAS
TONE	TYRE	VOTE	WHEN	X-RAY
TONY	TYRO		WHET	
TOOK		**W—4**	WHEW	**Y—4**
TOOL	**U—4**	WADE	WHEY	YANK
TOOT	UGLY	WADI	WHIG	YARD
TOPE	ULNA	WAFT	WHIM	YARN
TORE	UNCO	WAGE	WHIN	YAWL
TORN	UNDO	WAIF	WHIP	YAWN
TORT	UNIT	WAIL	WHIT	YAWS
TORY	UNTO	WAIN	WHOA	YEAH
TOSH	UPAS	WAIT	WHOM	YEAR
TOSS	UPON	WAKE	WICK	YELL
TOTE	URDU	WALE	WIDE	YELP
TOUR	URGE	WALK	WIFE	YETI
TOUT	URSA	WALL	WILD	YOGA
TOWN	USED	WALT	WILE	YOGI
TRAM	USER	WAND	WILL	YO-HO
TRAP		WANE	WILT	YOKE
TRAY	**V—4**	WANT	WILY	YOLK
TREE	VAIN	WARD	WIND	YORE
TREK	VALE	WARE	WINE	YOUR
TRET	VAMP	WARM	WING	YOWL
TREY	VANE	WARN	WINK	YO-YO
TRIM	VARY	WARP	WIPE	YULE
TRIO	VASE	WART	WIRE	
TRIP	VAST	WARY	WIRY	**Z—4**
TROD	VEAL	WASH	WISE	ZANY
TROT	VEER	WASP	WISH	ZEAL
TROY	VEIL	WATT	WISP	ZEBU
TRUE	VEIN	WAVE	WITH	ZERO
TRUG	VEND	WAVY	WOAD	ZEST
TSAR	VENT	WAXY	WOLD	ZETA
TUBA	VERB	WEAK	WOLF	ZEUS
TUBE	VERT	WEAL	WOMB	ZINC
TUCK	VERY	WEAN	WONT	ZING
TUFT	VEST	WEAR	WOOD	ZION
TUNA	VETO	WEED	WOOF	ZONE
TUNE	VICE	WEEK	WOOL	ZOOM
TURF	VIDE	WEEP	WORD	ZULU
TURK	VIED	WEFT	WORE	
TURN	VIEW	WEIR	WORK	**A—5**
TUSH	VILE	WELD	WORM	ABACK
TUSK	VINE	WELL	WORN	ABAFT
TUTU	VIOL	WELT	WORT	ABASE
				ABASH

ABATE	AGLOW	AMPLE	ASDIC	BACON
ABBEY	AGONE	AMPLY	ASHEN	BADGE
ABBOT	AGONY	AMUCK	ASHES	BADLY
ABEAM	AGREE	AMUSE	ASHET	BAGGY
ABELE	AHEAD	ANENT	ASIAN	BAIRN
ABHOR	AHEAP	ANGEL	ASIDE	BAIZE
ABIDE	AIDED	ANGER	ASKED	BAKED
ABIES	AILED	ANGLE	ASKEW	BAKER
ABLER	AIMED	ANGRY	ASPEN	BALED
ABODE	AIRED	ANISE	ASPIC	BALER
ABOIL	AISLE	ANKLE	ASSAY	BALMY
ABOUT	AITCH	ANNEX	ASSES	BALSA
ABOVE	AKELE	ANNOY	ASSET	BAMBI
ABUSE	ALACK	ANNUL	ASTER	BANAL
ABYSS	ALARM	ANODE	ASTIR	BANDY
ACHED	ALBUM	ANONA	ASTON	BANJO
ACORD	ALDER	ANTIC	ATILT	BANNS
ACRID	ALERT	ANVIL	ATLAS	BANTU
ACTED	ALGAE	ANZAC	ATOLL	BARED
ACTON	ALIAS	AORTA	ATONE	BARGE
ACTOR	ALIBI	APACE	ATTAR	BARMY
ACUTE	ALIEN	APART	ATTIC	BARON
ADAGE	ALIGN	APHIS	AUDIT	BARRY
ADAPT	ALIKE	APING	AUGER	BASAL
ADDED	ALIVE	APISH	AUGHT	BASED
ADDER	ALLAH	APORT	AUGUR	BASIC
ADDLE	ALLAY	APPAL	AUNTY	BASIL
ADEPT	ALLEY	APPLE	AURAL	BASIN
ADIEU	ALL-IN	APPLY	AVAIL	BASIS
ADMIT	ALLOT	APRIL	AVAST	BASSO
ADMIX	ALLOW	APRON	AVENS	BASTE
ADOBE	ALLOY	APTLY	AVERT	BATCH
ADOPT	ALOFT	ARABY	AVIAN	BATED
ADORE	ALONE	ARECA	AVION	BATHE
ADORN	ALONG	ARENA	AVOID	BATON
ADSUM	ALOOF	ARGON	AWAIT	BATTY
ADULT	ALOUD	ARGOT	AWAKE	BAULK
AEGIS	ALPHA	ARGUE	AWARD	BAWDY
AERIE	ALTAR	ARGUS	AWARE	BAYED
AESOP	ALTER	ARIEL	AWASH	BEACH
AFFIX	AMASS	ARIES	AWFUL	BEADS
AFIRE	AMAZE	ARISE	AWING	BEADY
AFOOT	AMBER	ARMED	AWOKE	BE-ALL
AFTER	AMBIT	AROMA	AXIAL	BEANO
AGAIN	AMBLE	AROSE	AXIOM	BEARD
AGAPE	AMEER	ARRAS	AZTEC	BEAST
AGATE	AMEND	ARRAY	AZURE	BEDEW
AGAVE	AMISS	ARROW		BEECH
AGENT	AMITY	ARSON	**B—5**	BEEFY
AGILE	AMONG	ARYAN	BABEL	BEERY
AGLEY	AMOUR	ASCOT	BACCY	BEFIT

BEFOG	BLAST	BORAX	BROIL	CABLE
BEGAD	BLAZE	BORED	BROKE	CACAO
BEGAN	BLEAK	BORER	BRONX	CACHE
BEGAT	BLEAR	BORNE	BROOD	CADDY
BEGET	BLEAT	BORON	BROOK	CADET
BEGIN	BLEED	BOSOM	BROOM	CADGE
BEGOT	BLEND	BOSSY	BROSE	CADRE
BEGUM	BLESS	BOSUN	BROTH	CAGED
BEGUN	BLEST	BOTCH	BROWN	CAGEY
BEIGE	BLIMP	BOUGH	BRUIN	CAIRN
BEING	BLIND	BOUND	BRUNT	CAKED
BELAY	BLINK	BOWED	BRUSH	CAMEL
BELCH	BLISS	BOWEL	BRUTE	CAMEO
BELIE	BLOCK	BOWER	BUDDY	CANAL
BELLE	BLOKE	BOWIE	BUDGE	CANDY
BELOW	BLOND	BOWLS	BUFFS	CANED
BENCH	BLOOD	BOXED	BUGGY	CANNA
BERET	BLOOM	BOXER	BUGLE	CANNY
BERRY	BLOWN	BOYER	BUILD	CANOE
BERTH	BLOWY	BRACE	BUILT	CANON
BERYL	BLUED	BRACT	BULGE	CANTO
BESET	BLUER	BRAID	BULGY	CAPER
BESOM	BLUES	BRAIN	BULKY	CAPON
BESOT	BLUEY	BRAKE	BULLY	CARAT
BETEL	BLUFF	BRAND	BUMPY	CARED
BETTY	BLUNT	BRASH	BUNCE	CARET
BEVEL	BLURB	BRASS	BUNCH	CARGO
BHANG	BLURT	BRAVE	BUNNY	CARIB
BIBLE	BLUSH	BRAVO	BUNTY	CAROB
BIDDY	BOARD	BRAWL	BURGH	CAROL
BIDET	BOAST	BRAWN	BURKE	CARRY
BIGHT	BOBBY	BRAZE	BURLY	CARTE
BIGOT	BOCHE	BREAD	BURNT	CARVE
BIJOU	BODED	BREAK	BURRO	CASED
BILGE	BODGE	BREAM	BURST	CASTE
BILLY	BOGEY	BREED	BUSBY	CATCH
BINGE	BOGGY	BREVE	BUSES	CATER
BINGO	BOGIE	BRIAR	BUSHY	CATTY
BIPED	BOGUS	BRIBE	BUTTS	CAULK
BIRCH	BOHEA	BRICK	BUTTY	CAUSE
BIRTH	BOLAS	BRIDE	BUXOM	CAVIL
BISON	BONED	BRIEF	BUYER	CAWED
BITCH	BONES	BRIER	BWANA	CEASE
BITER	BONNE	BRILL	BY-LAW	CEDAR
BLACK	BONUS	BRINE	BY-WAY	CEDED
BLADE	BOOBY	BRING		CELLO
BLAME	BOOED	BRINK	C—5	CERES
BLAND	BOOST	BRINY	CABAL	CHAFE
BLANK	BOOTH	BRISK	CABBY	CHAFF
BLARE	BOOTS	BROAD	CABER	CHAIN
BLASE	BOOTY	BROCK	CABIN	CHAIR

CHALK	CITED	COMET	CRAZY	CURRY
CHAMP	CIVET	COMIC	CREAK	CURSE
CHANT	CIVIC	COMMA	CREAM	CURVE
CHAOS	CIVIL	COMPO	CREDO	CUSHY
CHAPS	CIVVY	CONCH	CREED	CUTER
CHARD	CLACK	CONEY	CREEK	CUTTY
CHARM	CLAIM	CONGA	CREEL	CYCLE
CHART	CLAMP	CONGE	CREEP	CYDER
CHARY	CLAMS	CONGO	CREPE	CYNIC
CHASE	CLANG	CONIC	CREPT	CZECH
CHASM	CLANK	COOED	CRESS	
CHEAP	CLARE	COOMB	CREST	D—5
CHEAT	CLASH	CO-OPT	CREWE	DADDY
CHECK	CLASP	COPAL	CRICK	DAILY
CHEEK	CLASS	COPED	CRIED	DAIRY
CHEEP	CLEAN	COPER	CRIER	DAISY
CHEER	CLEAR	COPRA	CRIES	DALAI
CHESS	CLEAT	COPSE	CRIME	DALLY
CHEST	CLEEK	CORAL	CRIMP	DAMON
CHICK	CLEFT	CORGI	CRISP	DANCE
CHIDE	CLERK	CORNY	CROAK	DANDY
CHIEF	CLICK	CORPS	CROCK	DARBY
CHILD	CLIFF	COSTS	CROFT	DARED
CHILI	CLIMB	COUGH	CRONE	DATED
CHILL	CLIME	COULD	CRONY	DATUM
CHIME	CLING	COUNT	CROOK	DAUNT
CHINA	CLINK	COUPE	CROON	DAVIT
CHINE	CLOAK	COURT	CRORE	DAZED
CHINK	CLOCK	COVER	CROSS	DEALT
CHIPS	CLOSE	COVET	CROUP	DEATH
CHIRP	CLOTH	COVEY	CROWD	DEBAR
CHIVE	CLOUD	COWED	CROWN	DEBIT
CHOCK	CLOUT	COWER	CRUDE	DEBUT
CHOIR	CLOVE	COWRY	CRUEL	DECAY
CHOKE	CLOWN	COYLY	CRUET	DECOR
CHOPS	CLUCK	COYPU	CRUMB	DECOY
CHORD	CLUMP	COZEN	CRUMP	DECRY
CHORE	CLUNG	CRACK	CRUSE	DEFER
CHOSE	CLUNK	CRAFT	CRUSH	DEIFY
CHUCK	CLUNY	CRAIG	CRUST	DEIGN
CHUMP	COACH	CRAKE	CRYPT	DEITY
CHUNK	COAST	CRAMP	CUBAN	DEKKO
CHURL	COATI	CRANE	CUBED	DELAY
CHURN	COBRA	CRANK	CUBIC	DELFT
CHUTE	COCKY	CRAPE	CUBIT	DELTA
CIDER	COCOA	CRASH	CUPID	DELVE
CIGAR	CODED	CRASS	CURED	DEMOB
CINCH	CODEX	CRATE	CURER	DEMON
CIRCA	COLIC	CRAVE	CURIE	DEMUR
CIRCE	COLIN	CRAWL	CURIO	DENIM
CISSY	COLON	CRAZE	CURLY	DENSE

DEPOT	DOSED	DUCAL	ELFIN	EVENT
DEPTH	DOTED	DUCAT	ELGIN	EVERT
DERBY	DOTTY	DUCHY	ELIDE	EVERY
DETER	DOUBT	DULLY	ELITE	EVICT
DEUCE	DOUGH	DUMMY	ELOPE	EVOKE
DEVIL	DOUSE	DUMPS	ELUDE	EXACT
DHOBI	DOVER	DUMPY	ELVER	EXALT
DHOTI	DOWDY	DUNCE	EMBED	EXCEL
DIANA	DOWEL	DUPED	EMBER	EXEAT
DIARY	DOWER	DUSKY	EMEER	EXERT
DICED	DOWNY	DUSTY	EMEND	EXILE
DICKY	DOWRY	DUTCH	EMERY	EXIST
DICTA	DOYEN	DUVET	EMMET	EXPEL
DIGIT	DOZED	DWARF	EMPTY	EXTOL
DIMLY	DOZEN	DWELL	ENACT	EXTRA
DINAR	DRAFT	DWELT	ENDED	EXUDE
DINED	DRAIN	DYING	END-ON	EXULT
DINER	DRAKE		ENDOR	EYING
DINGO	DRAMA	E—5	ENDOW	EYRIE
DINGY	DRANK	EAGER	ENEMY	
DINKY	DRAPE	EAGLE	ENJOY	
DIODE	DRAWL	EAGRE	ENNUI	F—5
DIRGE	DRAWN	EARED	ENROL	FABLE
DIRTY	DREAD	EARLY	ENSUE	FACED
DITCH	DREAM	EARTH	ENTER	FACET
DITTO	DREAR	EASED	ENTRY	FADDY
DITTY	DREGS	EASEL	ENVOI	FAGIN
DIVAN	DRESS	EATEN	ENVOY	FAINT
DIVED	DRIED	EAVES	EPHOD	FAIRY
DIVER	DRIER	EBBED	EPOCH	FAITH
DIVES	DRIFT	EBONY	EPSOM	FAKED
DIVOT	DRILL	ECLAT	EQUAL	FAKIR
DIXIE	DRILY	EDGED	EQUIP	FALSE
DODGE	DRINK	EDICT	ERASE	FAMED
DODGY	DRIVE	EDIFY	ERATO	FANCY
DOGGO	DROIT	EDUCE	ERECT	FARAD
DOGGY	DROLL	EERIE	ERICA	FARED
DOGMA	DROME	EGGED	ERODE	FARCE
DOILY	DRONE	EGRET	ERRED	FATAL
DOING	DROOL	EIDER	ERROR	FATED
DOLCE	DROOP	EIGHT	ERUPT	FATES
DOLED	DROPS	EJECT	ESSAY	FATLY
DOLLY	DROSS	EKING	ESTER	FATTY
DOMED	DROVE	ELAND	ESTOP	FAULT
DONAH	DROWN	ELATE	ETHER	FAUNA
DONAT	DRUID	ELBOW	ETHIC	FAUST
DONNA	DRUNK	ELDER	ETHOS	FEAST
DONOR	DRUPE	ELECT	ETHYL	FED-UP
DOPED	DRYAD	ELEGY	ETUDE	FEIGN
DORIC	DRYER	ELEMI	EVADE	FEINT
DORMY	DRYLY	ELEVE	EVENS	FELIX

FELON	FLIER	FREAK	GAUZE	GOLLY
FEMUR	FLIES	FREED	GAUZY	GONER
FENCE	FLING	FREER	GAVEL	GOODS
FERNY	FLINT	FRESH	GAWKY	GOODY
FERRY	FLIRT	FRIAR	GAYER	GOOSE
FETCH	FLOAT	FRIED	GAZED	GORED
FETED	FLOCK	FRILL	GECKO	GORGE
FEVER	FLONG	FRISK	GEESE	GORSE
FEWER	FLOOD	FRITZ	GELID	GOUDA
FIBRE	FLOOR	FRIZZ	GENET	GOUGE
FICHU	FLORA	FROCK	GENIE	GOURD
FIELD	FLOSS	FROND	GENOA	GOUTY
FIEND	FLOUR	FRONT	GENRE	GRACE
FIERY	FLOUT	FROST	GENUS	GRADE
FIFTH	FLOWN	FROTH	GET-UP	GRAFT
FIFTY	FLUFF	FROWN	GHOST	GRAIL
FIGHT	FLUID	FROZE	GHOUL	GRAIN
FILCH	FLUKE	FRUIT	GIANT	GRAND
FILED	FLUKY	FRUMP	GIBED	GRANT
FILLY	FLUNG	FRYER	GIBUS	GRAPE
FILMY	FLUSH	FUDGE	GIDDY	GRAPH
FILTH	FLUTE	FUGUE	GIGOT	GRASP
FINAL	FLYER	FULLY	GIPSY	GRASS
FINCH	FOAMY	FUNGI	GIRTH	GRATE
FINED	FOCAL	FUNKY	GIVEN	GRAVE
FINER	FOCUS	FUNNY	GIVER	GRAVY
FINIS	FOGEY	FURRY	GIVES	GRAZE
FIORD	FOGGY	FURZE	GLACE	GREAT
FIRED	FOIST	FUSED	GLADE	GREBE
FIRST	FOLIO	FUSEE	GLAND	GREED
FIRTH	FOLLY	FUSIL	GLARE	GREEK
FISHY	FORAY	FUSSY	GLASS	GREEN
FITCH	FORBY	FUSTY	GLAZE	GREET
FITLY	FORCE	FUZZY	GLEAM	GREYS
FIVER	FORGE		GLEAN	GRIEF
FIVES	FORGO	**G—5**	GLEBE	GRILL
FIXED	FORME	GABLE	GLIDE	GRIME
FJORD	FORTE	GAFFE	GLINT	GRIMY
FLAIL	FORTH	GAILY	GLOAT	GRIND
FLAIR	FORTY	GALOP	GLOBE	GRIPE
FLAKE	FORUM	GAMED	GLOOM	GRIST
FLAKY	FOSSE	GAMIN	GLORY	GRITS
FLAME	FOUND	GAMMA	GLOSS	GROAN
FLANK	FOUNT	GAMUT	GLOVE	GROAT
FLARE	FOXED	GAPED	GLUED	GROCK
FLASH	FOYER	GARTH	GLUEY	GROIN
FLASK	FRAIL	GASSY	GNARL	GROOM
FLECK	FRAME	GATED	GNASH	GROPE
FLEET	FRANC	GAUDY	GNOME	GROSS
FLESH	FRANK	GAUGE	GODLY	GROUP
FLICK	FRAUD	GAUNT	GOING	GROUT

GROVE	HAVEN	HORDE	IMPLY	JETTY
GROWL	HAVER	HORNY	INANE	JEWEL
GROWN	HAVOC	HORSE	INAPT	JEWRY
GRUEL	HAWSE	HORSY	INCOG	JIBED
GRUFF	HAZEL	HOTEL	INCUR	JIFFY
GRUNT	HEADS	HOTLY	INDEX	JIMMY
GUANO	HEADY	HOUND	INEPT	JINGO
GUARD	HEARD	HOURI	INERT	JINKS
GUAVA	HEART	HOUSE	INFER	JOINT
GUESS	HEATH	HOVEL	INFIX	JOIST
GUEST	HEDGE	HOVER	INGLE	JOKED
GUIDE	HEFTY	HOWDY	INGOT	JOKER
GUILD	HEIGH	HUBBY	INKED	JOLLY
GUILE	HELIX	HUFFY	IN-LAW	JONAH
GUISE	HELLO	HULLO	INLAY	JOUST
GULCH	HELOT	HUMAN	INLET	JUDAS
GULES	HE-MAN	HUMID	INNER	JUDGE
GULLY	HENCE	HUMPH	INPUT	JUICE
GUNNY	HENNA	HUMUS	INSET	JUICY
GUSTO	HENRY	HUNCH	INTER	JULEP
GUSTY	HEROD	HUNKS	INURE	JUMBO
GUTTA	HERON	HURRY	IONIC	JUMPY
GUTTY	HEWED	HUSKY	IRAQI	JUNTA
GUYED	HEWER	HUSSY	IRATE	JUROR
GYPSY	HIKED	HUTCH	IRENE	
GYVES	HIKER	HYDRA	IRISH	**K—5**
	HILLY	HYDRO	IRKED	KAPOK
H—5	HINDI	HYENA	IRONS	KAYAK
HABIT	HINDU	HYRAX	IRONY	KEDGE
HADES	HINGE	HYTHE	ISLAM	KEEPS
HADJI	HINNY		ISLET	KETCH
HAIRY	HIPPO	**I—5**	ISSUE	KEYED
HALLO	HIRED	ICENI	ITCHY	KHAKI
HALMA	HIRER	ICHOR	IVIED	KIDDY
HALVE	HITCH	ICIER	IVORY	KINGS
HANDY	HIVED	ICILY	IXION	KINKY
HANKY	HIVES	ICING		KIOSK
HAPLY	HOARD	IDEAL	**J—5**	KITTY
HAPPY	HOARY	IDIOM	JABOT	KLOOF
HARDY	HOBBY	IDIOT	JADED	KNACK
HARED	HOCUS	IDLED	JAMES	KNARL
HAREM	HODGE	IDLER	JAMMY	KNAVE
HARPY	HOIST	IDRIS	JAPAN	KNEAD
HARRY	HOLLY	IDYLL	JAUNT	KNEED
HARSH	HOMER	IGLOO	JAWED	KNEEL
HASTE	HONED	ILIAD	JEANS	KNELL
HASTY	HONEY	ILIUM	JELLY	KNELT
HATCH	HOOCH	IMAGE	JEMMY	KNIFE
HATED	HOOEY	IMAGO	JENNY	KNOCK
HAULM	HOPED	IMBUE	JERKY	KNOLL
HAUNT	HOPPY	IMPEL	JERRY	KNOUT

KNOWN	LEASH	LOCAL	MADGE	MECCA
KNURL	LEAST	LOCUM	MADLY	MEDAL
KOALA	LEAVE	LODGE	MAFIA	MEDIA
KOPJE	LEDGE	LOFTY	MAGIC	MEDOC
KORAN	LEECH	LOGAN	MAGOG	MELEE
KRAAL	LEERY	LOGIC	MAHDI	MELON
KRAIT	LEGAL	LOLLY	MAIZE	MERCY
KRONE	LEGER	LOOFA	MAJOR	MERGE
KUDOS	LEGGY	LOONY	MAKER	MERIT
KUKRI	LEMON	LOOPY	MALAY	MERLE
KULAK	LEMUR	LOOSE	MALTY	MERRY
KVASS	LENTO	LOPED	MAMBA	MESSY
	LEPER	LORDS	MAMMA	METAL
L—5	LETHE	LORIS	MAMMY	METED
LABEL	LET-UP	LORRY	MANED	METER
LACED	LEVEE	LOSER	MANET	METRE
LADEN	LEVEL	LOTTO	MANGE	MEWED
LADLE	LEVER	LOTUS	MANGO	MEZZO
LAGER	LEWIS	LOUGH	MANGY	MIAOW
LAIRD	LIANA	LOUIS	MANIA	MICKY
LAITY	LIBEL	LOUSE	MANLY	MIDAS
LAKER	LIBRA	LOUSY	MANNA	MIDDY
LAMED	LICIT	LOVAT	MANOR	MIDGE
LANCE	LIEGE	LOVED	MANSE	MID-ON
LANKY	LIFER	LOVER	MAORI	MIDST
LAPEL	LIGHT	LOWER	MAPLE	MIGHT
LAPSE	LIKED	LOWLY	MARCH	MILCH
LARCH	LIKEN	LOYAL	MARGE	MILER
LARDY	LILAC	LUCID	MARRY	MILKY
LARGE	LIMBO	LUCKY	MARSH	MIMED
LARGO	LIMIT	LUCRE	MASAI	MIMIC
LARRY	LINED	LUGER	MASHY	MINCE
LARVA	LINEN	LUMPY	MASON	MINED
LASSO	LINER	LUNAR	MASSA	MINER
LATCH	LINGO	LUNCH	MASSE	MINIM
LATER	LINKS	LUNGE	MATCH	MINOR
LATEX	LISLE	LUPIN	MATED	MINUS
LATHE	LISTS	LURCH	MATER	MIRTH
LATIN	LITHE	LURED	MATEY	MISER
LAUGH	LITHO	LURID	MATIN	MISSY
LAURA	LITRE	LUSTY	MAUVE	MISTY
LAVED	LIVED	LYCEE	MAVIS	MITRE
LAXLY	LIVEN	LYING	MAWKY	MIXED
LAY-BY	LIVER	LYMPH	MAXIM	MIXER
LAYER	LIVID	LYNCH	MAYBE	MIX-UP
LAZED	LLAMA	LYRIC	MAYOR	MOCHA
LEACH	LLANO		MEALY	MODEL
LEAFY	LOACH	M—5	MEANS	MODUS
LEANT	LOAMY	MACAW	MEANT	MOGUL
LEARN	LOATH	MACON	MEATH	MOIRE
LEASE	LOBBY	MADAM	MEATY	MOIST

MOLAR	MUSTY	NIZAM	OKAPI	OXLIP
MOLLY	MUTED	NOBBY	OLDEN	OZONE
MOLTO	MUZZY	NOBEL	OLDER	
MONDE	MYNAH	NOBLE	OLEIC	P—5
MONEY	MYOPE	NOBLY	OLIVE	PACED
MONTE	MYRRH	NODAL	OMAHA	PACER
MONTH	N—5	NODDY	OMBRE	PADDY
MOOCH	NABOB	NOHOW	OMEGA	PADRE
MOODY	NACRE	NOISE	ONION	PAEAN
MOOED	NADIR	NOISY	ONSET	PAGAN
MOONY	NAIAD	NOMAD	OOMPH	PAGED
MOOSE	NAIVE	NONCE	OOZED	PAINT
MOPED	NAKED	NONET	OPERA	PALED
MORAL	NAMED	NOOSE	OPINE	PALMY
MORAY	NANNY	NORMA	OPIUM	PALSY
MORON	NAPOO	NORSE	OPTED	PANDA
MORSE	NAPPY	NORTH	OPTIC	PANED
MOSES	NASAL	NOSED	ORANG	PANEL
MOSSY	NASTY	NOSEY	ORATE	PANIC
MOTET	NATAL	NOTCH	ORBED	PANSY
MOTIF	NATTY	NOTED	ORBIT	PANTS
MOTOR	NAVAL	NOVEL	ORDER	PAPAL
MOTTO	NAVEL	NOYAU	OREAD	PAPAW
MOULD	NAVVY	NUDGE	ORGAN	PAPER
MOULT	NAWAB	NURSE	ORIEL	PAPPY.
MOUND	NAZIS	NUTTY	ORION	PARCH
MOUNT	NEDDY	NYLON	ORLON	PARED
MOURN	NEEDS		ORLOP	PARKY
MOUSE	NEEDY	O—5	ORMER	PARRY
MOUSY	NEGRO	OAKEN	ORRIS	PARSE
MOUTH	NEGUS	OAKUM	OSIER	PARTS
MOVED	NEIGH	OARED	OTHER	PARTY
MOVER	NERVE	OASIS	OTTER	PASHA
MOVIE	NERVY	OATEN	OUGHT	PASSE
MOWED	NEVER	OBEAH	OUIJA	PASTE
MOWER	NEWEL	OBESE	OUNCE	PASTY
MUCKY	NEWLY	OCCUR	OUSEL	PATCH
MUCUS	NEWSY	OCEAN	OUTDO	PATEN
MUDDY	NEXUS	OCHRE	OUTER	PATER
MUFTI	NICER	OCTET	OUTRE	PATIO
MUGGY	NICHE	ODDLY	OVATE	PATLY
MULCH	NIECE	ODEON	OVERT	PATTY
MULCT	NIFTY	ODIUM	OVINE	PAUSE
MUMMY	NIGHT	ODOUR	OVOID	PAVAN
MUMPS	NIHIL	OFFAL	OVULE	PAVED
MUNCH	NINNY	OFFER	OWING	PAWED
MURAL	NINON	OFLAG	OWLET	PAWKY
MURKY	NINTH	OFTEN	OWNED	PAYEE
MUSED	NIOBE	OGIVE	OWNER	PAYER
MUSHY	NIPPY	OGLED	OX-EYE	PEACE
MUSIC	NITRE	OILED	OXIDE	PEACH

PEAKY	PLAIN	PRIDE	QUAIL	RASED
PEARL	PLAIT	PRIED	QUAKE	RATED
PEASE	PLANE	PRIMA	QUAKY	RATEL
PEATY	PLANK	PRIME	QUALM	RATIO
PECAN	PLANT	PRIMO	QUANT	RATTY
PEDAL	PLATE	PRINK	QUART	RAVED
PEGGY	PLATO	PRINT	QUASH	RAVEL
PEKOE	PLAZA	PRIOR	QUASI	RAVEN
PENAL	PLEAD	PRISE	QUEEN	RAWLY
PENCE	PLEAT	PRISM	QUEER	RAYON
PENNY	PLEBS	PRIVY	QUELL	RAZED
PEONY	PLIED	PRIZE	QUERY	RAZOR
PERCH	PLUCK	PROBE	QUEST	REACH
PERDU	PLUMB	PROEM	QUEUE	REACT
PERIL	PLUME	PRONE	QUICK	READY
PERKY	PLUMP	PRONG	QUIET	REALM
PERRY	PLUSH	PROOF	QUIFF	RE-ARM
PESKY	POACH	PROPS	QUILL	REBEL
PETAL	PODGE	PROSE	QUILT	REBID
PETER	PODGY	PROSY	QUINS	REBUS
PETIT	POESY	PROUD	QUIRE	REBUT
PEWIT	POILU	PROVE	QUIRK	RECCE
PHASE	POINT	PROWL	QUITE	RECTO
PHIAL	POISE	PROXY	QUITS	RECUR
PHLOX	POKED	PRUDE	QUOIN	REDAN
PHONE	POKER	PRUNE	QUOIT	REDLY
PHOTO	POLAR	PSALM	QUOTA	RE-DYE
PIANO	POLIO	PUFFY	QUOTE	REEDY
PICOT	POLKA	PUKKA	QUOTH	REEVE
PIECE	POLLY	PULED		REFER
PIETY	POPPY	PULPY	R—5	REFIT
PIGMY	PORCH	PULSE	RABBI	REFIX
PILAU	PORED	PUNCH	RABID	REGAL
PILAW	PORKY	PUNIC	RACED	REICH
PILED	POSED	PUPIL	RACER	REIGN
PILOT	POSER	PUPPY	RADAR	REINS
PINED	POSSE	PUREE	RADII	RELAX
PINKY	POTTO	PURER	RADIO	RELAY
PINNY	POTTY	PURGE	RADIX	RELET
PIN-UP	POUCH	PURSE	RAGED	RELIC
PIOUS	POULT	PUSSY	RAINY	RELIT
PIPED	POUND	PUTTY	RAISE	REMIT
PIPER	POWER	PUT-UP	RAJAH	RENAL
PIPIT	PRANG	PYGMY	RAKED	RENEW
PIQUE	PRANK	PYLON	RALLY	RENTE
PITCH	PRATE	PYRUS	RANCH	REPAY
PITHY	PRAWN		RANEE	REPEL
PIVOT	PREEN	Q—5	RANGE	REPLY
PIXIE	PRESS	QUACK	RANGY	REPOT
PLACE	PRICE	QUADS	RAPID	RESET
PLAID	PRICK	QUAFF	RARER	RESIN

RESOW	ROUSE	SAPID	SCRUB	SHEET
RETCH	ROUTE	SAPOR	SCRUM	SHEIK
RETRY	ROVED	SAPPY	SCUFF	SHELF
REVEL	ROVER	SATAN	SCULL	SHELL
REVUE	ROWAN	SATED	SCURF	SHEWN
RHEUM	ROWDY	SATIN	SEAMY	SHIED
RHINE	ROWED	SATYR	SEDAN	SHIFT
RHINO	ROWEL	SAUCE	SEDGE	SHINE
RHOMB	ROWER	SAUCY	SEEDY	SHINY
RHYME	ROYAL	SAUNA	SEINE	SHIRE
RIANT	RUCHE	SAUTE	SEIZE	SHIRK
RIBES	RUDDY	SAVED	SENNA	SHIRT
RIDER	RUDER	SAVER	SENSE	SHOAL
RIDGE	RUGBY	SAVOY	SEPAL	SHOCK
RIFLE	RUING	SAVVY	SEPIA	SHONE
RIGHT	RULED	SAWED	SEPOY	SHOOK
RIGID	RULER	SAXON	SERAI	SHOOT
RIGOR	RUMBA	SAY-SO	SERGE	SHORE
RILED	RUMMY	SCALA	SERIF	SHORN
RIMED	RUNIC	SCALD	SERUM	SHORT
RINSE	RUN-IN	SCALE	SERVE	SHOUT
RIPEN	RUNNY	SCALP	SETAE	SHOVE
RIPER	RUPEE	SCALY	SET-TO	SHOWN
RIPON	RURAL	SCAMP	SET-UP	SHOWY
RISEN	RUSTY	SCANT	SEVEN	SHRED
RISER	RUTTY	SCARE	SEVER	SHREW
RISKY		SCARF	SEWER	SHRUB
RIVAL	S—5	SCARP	SHACK	SHRUG
RIVEN	SABLE	SCENA	SHADE	SHUCK
RIVER	SABOT	SCENE	SHADY	SHUNT
RIVET	SABRE	SCENT	SHAFT	SHYLY
ROACH	SADLY	SCION	SHAKE	SIBYL
ROAST	SAFER	SCOFF	SHAKO	SIDED
ROBED	SAGAN	SCOLD	SHAKY	SIDLE
ROBIN	SAHIB	SCONE	SHALE	SIEGE
ROBOT	SAINT	SCOOP	SHALL	SIEVE
ROCKY	SAITH	SCOOT	SHALT	SIGHT
RODEO	SALAD	SCOPE	SHAME	SIGMA
ROGER	SALIC	SCORE	SHANK	SILKY
ROGUE	SALIX	SCORN	SHAPE	SILLY
ROMAN	SALLY	SCOTS	SHARD	SINCE
ROMEO	SALMI	SCOUR	SHARE	SINEW
RONDO	SALON	SCOUT	SHARK	SINGE
ROOMY	SALTS	SCOWL	SHARP	SINUS
ROOST	SALTY	SCRAG	SHAVE	SIOUX
ROPED	SALVE	SCRAM	SHAWL	SIRED
ROSIN	SALVO	SCRAP	SHEAF	SIREN
ROTOR	SAMBA	SCREE	SHEAR	SISAL
ROUGE	SAMMY	SCREW	SHEEN	SISSY
ROUGH	SANDY	SCRIM	SHEEP	SIXTH
ROUND	SANER	SCRIP	SHEER	SIXTY

SIZED	SMELT	SOUPY	SPRAY	STOCK
SKATE	SMILE	SOUSE	SPREE	STOEP
SKEAN	SMIRK	SOUTH	SPRIG	STOIC
SKEIN	SMITE	SOWAR	SPRIT	STOKE
SKIED	SMITH	SOWED	SPUME	STOLE
SKIER	SMOCK	SOWER	SPURN	STOMA
SKIFF	SMOKE	SPACE	SPURT	STONE
SKILL	SMOKY	SPADE	SQUAB	STONY
SKIMP	SMOTE	SPAHI	SQUAD	STOOD
SKINK	SNACK	SPAKE	SQUAT	STOOK
SKIRL	SNAIL	SPANK	SQUAW	STOOL
SKIRT	SNAKE	SPARE	SQUIB	STOOP
SKULK	SNAKY	SPARK	SQUID	STORE
SKULL	SNARE	SPASM	STACK	STORK
SKUNK	SNARL	SPATE	STAFF	STORM
SLACK	SNATH	SPAWN	STAGE	STORY
SLADE	SNEAD	SPEAK	STAGY	STOUP
SLAIN	SNEAK	SPEAR	STAID	STOUR
SLAKE	SNEER	SPECK	STAIN	STOUT
SLANG	SNICK	SPECS	STAIR	STOVE
SLANT	SNIDE	SPEED	STAKE	STRAD
SLASH	SNIFF	SPELL	STALE	STRAP
SLATE	SNIPE	SPELT	STALK	STRAW
SLATY	SNOEK	SPEND	STALL	STRAY
SLAVE	SNOOD	SPERM	STAMP	STREW
SLEEK	SNOOP	SPICE	STAND	STRIP
SLEEP	SNORE	SPICK	STANK	STROP
SLEET	SNORT	SPICY	STARE	STRUM
SLEPT	SNOUT	SPIED	STARK	STRUT
SLICE	SNOWY	SPIKE	START	STUCK
SLICK	SNUFF	SPIKY	STATE	STUDY
SLIDE	SOAPY	SPILL	STAVE	STUFF
SLIME	SOBER	SPILT	STEAD	STUMP
SLIMY	SOGGY	SPINE	STEAK	STUNG
SLING	SOLAR	SPINY	STEAL	STUNK
SLINK	SOLDO	SPIRE	STEAM	STUNT
SLOOP	SOLED	SPITE	STEED	STYLE
SLOPE	SOL-FA	SPLAY	STEEL	STYLO
SLOSH	SOLID	SPLIT SPLAT	STEEP	SUAVE
SLOTH	SOLUS	SPODE	STEER	SUEDE
SLUMP	SOLVE	SPOIL	STEIN	SUETY
SLUNG	SONIC	SPOKE	STERN	SUGAR
SLUNK	SONNY	SPOOF	STICK	SUING
SLUSH	SOOTH	SPOOK	STIFF	SUITE
SLYLY	SOOTY	SPOOL	STILE	SULKS
SMACK	SOPPY	SPOON	STILL	SULKY
SMALL	SORBO	SPOOR	STILT	SULLY
SMART	SORER	SPORE	STING	SUNNY
SMASH	SORRY	SPORT	STINK	SUN-UP
SMEAR	SOUGH	SPOUT	STINT	SUPER
SMELL	SOUND	SPRAT	STOAT	SURER

SURGE	TAMIL	THING	TOPER	TRUMP
SURLY	TAMMY	THINK	TOPIC	TRUNK
SWAIN	TANGO	THIRD	TOQUE	TRUSS
SWALE	TANGY	THOLE	TORCH	TRUST
SWAMP	TANSY	THONG	TORSO	TRUTH
SWANK	TAPED	THORN	TOTAL	TRY-ON
SWARD	TAPER	THOSE	TOTEM	TRYST
SWARF	TAPIR	THREE	TOTED	TUBBY
SWARM	TARDY	THREW	TOUCH	TUBED
SWATS	TAROT	THROB	TOUGH	TUBER
SWEAR	TARRY	THROE	TOWED	TUDOR
SWEAT	TASTE	THROW	TOWEL	TULIP
SWEDE	TATTY	THUMB	TOWER	TULLE
SWEEP	TAUNT	THUMP	TOWNY	TUNED
SWEET	TAWNY	THYME	TOXIC	TUNER
SWELL	TAXED	TIARA	TOXIN	TUNIS
SWEPT	TEACH	TIBET	TOYED	TUNNY
SWIFT	TEASE	TIBIA	TRACE	TURFY
SWILL	TEDDY	TIDAL	TRACK	TURPS
SWINE	TEENS	TIDED	TRACT	TUTOR
SWING	TEENY	TIGER	TRADE	TUTTI
SWIPE	TEETH	TIGHT	TRAIL	TWAIN
SWIRL	TEHEE	TILED	TRAIN	TWANG
SWISH	TEMPO	TILER	TRAMP	TWEAK
SWISS	TEMPT	TILTH	TRASH	TWEED
SWOON	TENCH	TIMED	TRAWL	TWEEN
SWOOP	TENET	TIMID	TREAD	TWERP
SWORD	TENON	TIMON	TREAT	TWICE
SWORE	TENOR	TINED	TREED	TWILL
SWORN	TENSE	TINGE	TREND	TWINE
SWUNG	TENTH	TINNY	TRESS	TWINS
SYLPH	TEPEE	TIPSY	TREWS	TWIRL
SYNOD	TEPID	TIRED	TRIAL	TWIST
SYRUP	TEPOR	TITAN	TRIBE	TWITE
	TERRA	TITHE	TRICE	TWIXT
T—5	TERRY	TITLE	TRICK	TYING
TABBY	TERSE	TIZZY	TRIED	TYPED
TABLE	TESTY	TOADY	TRIER	
TABOO	THANE	TOAST	TRILL	U—5
TACIT	THANK	TO-DAY	TRIPE	U-BOAT
TACKY	THEFT	TODDY	TRITE	UDDER
TAFFY	THEIR	TOKAY	TROLL	UHLAN
TAILS	THEME	TOKEN	TRONC	UKASE
TAINT	THERE	TOMMY	TROOP	ULCER
TAKEN	THERM	TONAL	TROTH	ULNAR
TAKER	THESE	TONED	TROUT	ULTRA
TALES	THETA	TONGA	TROVE	UMBEL
TALLY	THICK	TONIC	TRUCE	UMBER
TALON	THIEF	TOOTH	TRUCK	UMBRA
TAMED	THIGH	TOPAZ	TRUER	UNAPT
TAMER	THINE	TOPEE	TRULY	UNARM

UNBAR	VANED	VOWEL	WHERE	WORST
UNBID	VAPID	VYING	WHICH	WORTH
UNCLE	VASTY		WHIFF	WOULD
UNCUT	VAULT	**W—5**	WHILE	WOUND
UNDER	VAUNT	WADED	WHINE	WOVEN
UNDID	VELDT	WADER	WHIRL	WRACK
UNDUE	VENAL	WAFER	WHISK	WRATH
UNFED	VENOM	WAGED	WHIST	WREAK
UNFIT	VENUE	WAGER	WHITE	WRECK
UNFIX	VENUS	WAGES	WHIZZ	WREST
UNIFY	VERGE	WAGON	WHOLE	WRING
UNION	VERSE	WAIST	WHOOP	WRIST
UNITE	VERSO	WAITS	WHORL	WRITE
UNITY	VERST	WAIVE	WHOSE	WRONG
UNLED	VERVE	WAKEN	WHOSO	WROTE
UNLET	VESPA	WALTZ	WIDEN	WRUNG
UNMAN	VESTA	WANED	WIDER	WRYLY
UNPEG	VETCH	WANLY	WIDOW	
UNPEN	VEXED	WARES	WIDTH	
UNPIN	VIAND	WASHY	WIELD	**X—5**
UNSET	VICAR	WASTE	WIGHT	XEBEC
UNTIE	VIGIL	WATCH	WILLY	X-RAYS
UNTIL	VILER	WATER	WINCE	
UNWED	VILLA	WAVED	WINCH	
UP-END	VIOLA	WAVER	WINDY	**Y—5**
UPPER	VIPER	WAXED	WINED	YACHT
UPSET	VIRGO	WAXEN	WIPED	YAHOO
URBAN	VIRTU	WEALD	WIPER	YAWED
URGED	VIRUS	WEARY	WIRED	YEARN
URIAL	VISIT	WEAVE	WISER	YEAST
USAGE	VISOR	WEDGE	WISPY	YIELD
USHER	VISTA	WEEDS	WITCH	YODEL
USING	VITAL	WEEDY	WITHY	YOKED
USUAL	VIVAT	WEEPY	WITTY	YOKEL
USURP	VIVID	WEIGH	WIVES	YOUNG
USURY	VIZOR	WEIRD	WODEN	YOURS
UTTER	VOCAL	WELSH	WOMAN	YOUTH
UVULA	VODKA	WENCH	WOMEN	YUCCA
	VOGUE	WHACK	WOODY	
V—5	VOICE	WHALE	WOOED	
VAGUE	VOILE	WHANG	WOOER	**Z—5**
VALET	VOMIT	WHARF	WORDY	ZEBRA
VALID	VOTED	WHEAT	WORLD	ZEBUS
VALSE	VOTER	WHEEL	WORMY	ZINCO
VALUE	VOUCH	WHELK	WORRY	ZONAL
VALVE	VOWED	WHELP	WORSE	ZONED

A—6	ADMIRE	ALLIED	APLOMB
ABACUS	ADONIS	ALLIES	APPEAL
ABASED	ADORED	ALL-OUT	APPEAR
ABATED	ADRIFT	ALLUDE	APPEND
ABBESS	ADROIT	ALLURE	ARABIC
ABDUCT	ADVENT	ALMOND	ARABIS
ABIDED	ADVERT	ALMOST	ARABLE
ABJECT	ADVICE	ALPACA	ARBOUR
ABJURE	ADVISE	ALPINE	ARCADE
ABLAZE	AENEID	ALPINI	ARCADY
ABLEST	AERATE	ALUMNA	ARCHED
ABLOOM	AERIAL	ALUMNI	ARCHER
ABOARD	AFFAIR	ALWAYS	ARCHLY
ABOUND	AFFECT	AMAZED	ARCING
ABRADE	AFFIRM	AMAZON	ARCTIC
ABROAD	AFFORD	AMBLED	ARDENT
ABRUPT	AFFRAY	AMBLER	ARDOUR
ABSENT	AFGHAN	AMBUSH	ARGALI
ABSORB	AFLAME	AMOEBA	ARGENT
ABSURD	AFLOAT	AMORAL	ARGOSY
ABUSED	AFRAID	AMOUNT	ARGUED
ACACIA	AFRESH	AMPERE	ARIGHT
ACCEDE	AGARIC	AMPLER	ARISEN
ACCENT	AGEING	AMULET	ARMADA
ACCEPT	AGENCY	AMUSED	ARMIES
ACCESS	AGENDA	ANCHOR	ARMING
ACCORD	AGHAST	ANCONA	ARMLET
ACCOST	AGNATE	ANGINA	ARMOUR
ACCRUE	AGOING	ANGLED	ARMPIT
ACCUSE	AGOUTI	ANGLER	ARNICA
ACETIC	AGREED	ANGOLA	AROUND
ACHING	AIDING	ANGORA	AROUSE
ACIDIC	AILING	ANIMAL	ARRACK
ACK-ACK	AIMING	ANIMUS	ARRANT
ACQUIT	AIR-BED	ANKLET	ARREAR
ACROSS	AIR-GUN	ANNALS	ARREST
ACTING	AIRILY	ANNEAL	ARRIVE
ACTION	AIRING	ANNEXE	ARTERY
ACTIVE	AIRMAN	ANNUAL	ARTFUL
ACTUAL	AIR-SAC	ANOINT	ARTIST
ACUITY	AIRWAY	ANONYM	ASCEND
ACUMEN	AKIMBO	ANSWER	ASCENT
ADAGIO	ALARUM	ANTHEM	ASHAKE
ADDICT	ALBEIT	ANTHER	ASHLAR
ADDING	ALBERT	ANTLER	ASHORE
ADDLED	ALBINO	ANYHOW	ASH-PAN
ADDUCE	ALBION	ANYWAY	ASH-PIT
ADHERE	ALCOVE	APACHE	ASKANT
ADJOIN	ALIGHT	APATHY	ASKARI
ADJURE	ALKALI	APIARY	ASKING
ADJUST	ALLEGE	APIECE	ASLANT

ASLEEP	AWAKEN	BANYAN	BAYARD
ASPECT	AWEIGH	BANZAI	BAYEUX
ASPIRE	AWHEEL	BAOBAB	BAYING
ASSAIL	AWHILE	BARBED	BAZAAR
ASSENT	AWNING	BARBEL	BEACHY
ASSERT	AYE-AYE	BARBER	BEACON
ASSESS	AZALEA	BARDIC	BEADED
ASSIGN		BARELY	BEADLE
ASSIST	B—6	BAREST	BEAGLE
ASSIZE	BAAING	BARGED	BEAKER
ASSORT	BABBLE	BARGEE	BEAMED
ASSUME	BABOON	BARING	BEARER
ASSURE	BACKED	BARIUM	BEATEN
ASTERN	BACKER	BARKED	BEATER
ASTHMA	BADGER	BARKER	BEAUNE
ASTRAL	BAFFLE	BARKIS	BEAUTY
ASTRAY	BAGFUL	BARLEY	BEAVER
ASTUTE	BAGGED	BARMAN	BECALM
ASYLUM	BAGMAN	BARNEY	BECAME
ATHENE	BAGNIO	BARONY	BECKET
AT-HOME	BAILED	BARQUE	BECKON
ATKINS	BAILEY	BARRED	BECOME
ATOMIC	BAILIE	BARREL	BEDAUB
ATONED	BAITED	BARREN	BED-BUG
ATTACH	BAKERY	BARROW	BEDDED
ATTACK	BAKING	BARSAC	BEDDER
ATTAIN	BALAAM	BARTER	BEDECK
ATTEND	BALDER	BARTON	BEDLAM
ATTEST	BALDLY	BASALT	BEETLE
ATTIRE	BALEEN	BASELY	BEFALL
ATTUNE	BALING	BASHED	BEFORE
AUBURN	BALKAN	BASING	BEFOUL
AUGURY	BALKED	BASKED	BEGGAR
AUGUST	BALLAD	BASKET	BEGGED
AUNTIE	BALLET	BASQUE	BEGONE
AURIST	BALLOT	BASSET	BEHALF
AURORA	BALSAM	BASTED	BEHAVE
AUSSIE	BALTIC	BATEAU	BEHEAD
AUSTER	BAMBOO	BATHED	BEHELD
AUSTIN	BANANA	BATHER	BEHEST
AUTHOR	BANDED	BATHOS	BEHIND
AUTUMN	BANDIT	BATMAN	BEHOLD
AVAUNT	BANGED	BATTED	BELDAM
AVENGE	BANGLE	BATTEN	BELFRY
AVENUE	BANISH	BATTER	BELIAL
AVERSE	BANKED	BATTLE	BELIED
AVIARY	BANKER	BAUBLE	BELIEF
AVIDLY	BANNED	BAWBEE	BELLOW
AVOCET	BANNER	BAWLED	BELONG
AVOWAL	BANTAM	BAWLEY	BELTED
AVOWED	BANTER	BAXTER	BEMOAN

BEMUSE	BITING	BOOING	BREACH
BENDER	BITTEN	BOOKED	BREAST
BENGAL	BITTER	BOOKIE	BREATH
BENIGN	BLAMED	BOOMED	BREECH
BENNET	BLANCH	BOOTED	BREEKS
BENUMB	BLARED	BOOTEE	BREEZE
BENZOL	BLAZED	BO-PEEP	BREEZY
BERATE	BLAZER	BORAGE	BRETON
BERBER	BLEACH	BORDER	BREVET
BEREFT	BLEARY	BOREAS	BREWED
BERLIN	BLENNY	BORING	BREWER
BERTHA	BLIGHT	BORROW	BRIBED
BESIDE	BLITHE	BORZOI	BRIDAL
BESTED	BLONDE	BOSCHE	BRIDGE
BESTIR	BLOODY	BOSSED	BRIDLE
BESTOW	BLOTCH	BOSTON	BRIGHT
BETAKE	BLOTTO	BOTANY	BRITON
BETHEL	BLOUSE	BOTHER	BROACH
BETIDE	BLOWED	BOTHIE	BROADS
BETONY	BLOWER	BOTTLE	BROGAN
BETRAY	BLOWZY	BOTTOM	BROGUE
BETTED	BLUEST	BOUFFE	BROKEN
BETTER	BLUING	BOUGHT	BROKER
BETTOR	BLUISH	BOUNCE	BROLLY
BEWAIL	BOATER	BOUNTY	BRONCO
BEWARE	BOBBED	BOURSE	BRONZE
BEYOND	BOBBIN	BOVINE	BROOCH
BIASED	BOBBLE	BOWERY	BROODY
BIBBER	BODEGA	BOWING	BROUGH
BICEPS	BODGER	BOWLED	BROWSE
BICKER	BODICE	BOWLER	BRUISE
BIDDER	BODILY	BOWMAN	BRUTAL
BIDING	BODING	BOW-SAW	BRUTUS
BIFFED	BODKIN	BOW-TIE	BRYONY
BIGAMY	BOFFIN	BOW-WOW	BUBBLE
BIG-END	BOGGLE	BOXING	BUBBLY
BIGGER	BOG-OAK	BOYISH	BUCKED
BIG-WIG	BOILED	BRACED	BUCKET
BIKING	BOILER	BRACER	BUCKLE
BILKED	BOLDER	BRAHMA	BUDDED
BILKER	BOLDLY	BRAINY	BUDDHA
BILLED	BOLERO	BRAISE	BUDGET
BILLET	BOLTED	BRAKED	BUFFED
BILLIE	BOMBED	BRANCH	BUFFER
BILLOW	BON-BON	BRANDY	BUFFET
BINDER	BONDED	BRASSY	BUGLER
BIRDIE	BONING	BRAVED	BULGAR
BISECT	BONNET	BRAVER	BULGED
BISHOP	BONNIE	BRAWNY	BULKED
BISLEY	BOODLE	BRAZED	BULLET
BISTRO	BOOHOO	BRAZEN	BUMPED

BUMPER	CABMAN	CANUCK	CAVERN
BUNDLE	CACHED	CANVAS	CAVIAR
BUNGED	CACHET	CANYON	CAVIES
BUNGLE	CACHOU	CAPFUL	CAVING
BUNION	CACKLE	CAPPED	CAVITY
BUNKED	CACTUS	CAPTOR	CAVORT
BUNKER	CADDIE	CARAFE	CAXTON
BUNKUM	CADDIS	CARBON	CAYMAN
BUNSEN	CADGED	CARBOY	CAYUSE
BUNTER	CADGER	CARDED	CEASED
BUOYED	CAESAR	CAREEN	CEDING
BURBLE	CAGING	CAREER	CELERY
BURDEN	CAHOOT	CARESS	CELLAR
BUREAU	CAIMAN	CARFAX	CELTIC
BURGEE	CAIQUE	CARIES	CEMENT
BURGLE	CAJOLE	CARMAN	CENSER
BURIAL	CAKING	CARMEN	CENSOR
BURIED	CALICO	CARNAL	CENSUS
BURMAN	CALIPH	CARNET	CENTRE
BURNED	CALLED	CARPED	CEREAL
BURNER	CALLER	CARPEL	CERISE
BURNET	CALLOW	CARPET	CHAFED
BURRED	CALMED	CARROT	CHAFER
BURROW	CALMLY	CARTED	CHAISE
BURSAR	CALVED	CARTEL	CHALET
BURTON	CAMBER	CARTER	CHALKY
BUSHEL	CAMERA	CARTON	CHANCE
BUSIED	CAMLET	CARVED	CHANCY
BUSILY	CAMPED	CARVER	CHANGE
BUSKER	CAMPER	CASHED	CHANTY
BUSMEN	CAMPUS	CASHEW	CHAPEL
BUSTED	CANAPE	CASING	CHAPPY
BUSTER	CANARD	CASINO	CHARGE
BUSTLE	CANARY	CASKET	CHARON
BUTANE	CANCAN	CASQUE	CHASED
BUTLER	CANCEL	CASSIA	CHASER
BUTTED	CANCER	CASTLE	CHASSE
BUTTER	CANDID	CASTOR	CHASTE
BUTTON	CANDLE	CASUAL	CHATTY
BUYING	CANINE	CATCHY	CHEEKY
BUZZED	CANING	CATGUT	CHEERY
BUZZER	CANKER	CATHAY	CHEESE
BYE-BYE	CANNED	CATKIN	CHEESY
BYGONE	CANNON	CATNIP	CHEQUE
BY-PASS	CANNOT	CATSUP	CHERRY
BY-PLAY	CANOPY	CATTLE	CHERUB
BY-ROAD	CANTAB	CAUCUS	CHESTY
BY-WORD	CANTED	CAUDAL	CHEVAL
	CANTER	CAUGHT	CHEWED
C—6	CANTON	CAUSED	CHILDE
CABLED	CANTOR	CAVEAT	CHILLI

CHILLY	CLICHE	COLDER	COQUET
CHIMED	CLIENT	COLDLY	CORBEL
CHINTZ	CLIMAX	COLLIE	CORDED
CHIPPY	CLINCH	COLLOP	CORDON
CHIRPY	CLINIC	COLONY	CORKED
CHISEL	CLIQUE	COLOUR	CORKER
CHITTY	CLOCHE	COLUMN	CORNEA
CHOICE	CLOSED	COMBAT	CORNED
CHOKED	CLOSER	COMBED	CORNER
CHOKER	CLOSET	COMBER	CORNET
CHOLER	CLOTHE	COMEDY	CORONA
CHOOSE	CLOUDY	COMELY	CORPSE
CHOOSY	CLOVEN	COMFIT	CORPUS
CHOPIN	CLOVER	COMING	CORRAL
CHOPPY	CLOYED	COMMIT	CORSET
CHORAL	CLUMSY	COMMON	CORTES
CHORUS	CLUTCH	COMPEL	COSHED
CHOSEN	COARSE	COMPLY	COSIER
CHOUGH	COATED	CONCHY	COSILY
CHROME	COATEE	CONCUR	COSINE
CHUBBY	COAXED	CONNED	COSMIC
CHUKKA	COAXER	CONDOR	COSMOS
CHUMMY	COBALT	CONFAB	COSSET
CHURCH	COBBLE	CONFER	COSTER
CICADA	COBNUT	CONGEE	COSTLY
CICELY	COBURG	CONGER	COTTAR
CICERO	COBWEB	CONKED	COTTER
CINDER	COCKED	CONKER	COTTON
CINEMA	COCKER	CONSUL	COUGAR
CINQUE	COCKLE	CONTRA	COUPLE
CIPHER	COCOON	CONVEX	COUPON
CIRCLE	CODDED	CONVEY	COURSE
CIRCUS	CODDLE	CONVOY	COUSIN
CIRRUS	CODGER	COOEED	COVERT
CITING	CODIFY	COOING	COWARD
CITRIC	CODING	COOKED	COW-BOY
CITRON	CODLIN	COOKER	COWING
CITRUS	COERCE	COOKIE	COWLED
CIVICS	COEVAL	COOLED	COW-MAN
CLAMMY	COFFEE	COOLER	COWRIE
CLARET	COFFER	COOLIE	COYOTE
CLASSY	COFFIN	COOLLY	CRABBY
CLAUSE	COGENT	COOPED	CRADLE
CLAWED	COGNAC	COOPER	CRAFTY
CLAYEY	CO-HEIR	COPECK	CRAGGY
CLEAVE	COHERE	COPIED	CRAMBO
CLENCH	COHORT	COPIER	CRANED
CLERGY	COILED	COPING	CRANKY
CLERIC	COINED	COPPED	CRANNY
CLEVER	COINER	COPPER	CRATED
CLEVIS	COKING	COPTIC	CRATER

CRAVAT	CURLEW	DARKER	DEFECT
CRAVED	CURSED	DARKLY	DEFEND
CRAVEN	CURTLY	DARNED	DEFIED
CRAYON	CURTSY	DARNEL	DEFILE
CRAZED	CURVED	DARNER	DEFINE
CREAMY	CUSTOM	DARTED	DEFORM
CREASE	CUTEST	DASHED	DEFRAY
CREATE	CUTLER	DATING	DEFTLY
CRECHE	CUTLET	DATIVE	DEFUSE
CREDIT	CUT-OFF	DAUBED	DEGREE
CREEPY	CUT-OUT	DAVITS	DE-ICER
CREOLE	CUTTER	DAWDLE	DEJECT
CRESTA	CUTTLE	DAWNED	DELETE
CRETIN	CYCLED	DAY-BED	DELUDE
CREWEL	CYGNET	DAY-FLY	DELUGE
CRIKEY	CYMBAL	DAZING	DEMAND
CRINGE	CYMRIC	DAZZLE	DEMEAN
CRISES	CYPHER	DEACON	DEMISE
CRISIS	CYPRUS	DEADEN	DEMODE
CRISPY		DEADLY	DEMOTE
CRITIC	D—6	DEAFEN	DEMURE
CROCUS	DABBED	DEAFLY	DENIAL
CROTCH	DABBLE	DEALER	DENIED
CROUCH	DACOIT	DEARER	DENIER
CROWED	DAFTLY	DEARIE	DENOTE
CRUDER	DAGGER	DEARLY	DENSER
CRUISE	DAHLIA	DEARTH	DENTAL
CRUMBY	DAINTY	DEBASE	DENUDE
CRUNCH	DAMAGE	DEBATE	DEODAR
CRUSTY	DAMASK	DEBRIS	DEPART
CRUTCH	DAMMED	DEBTOR	DEPEND
CRYING	DAMNED	DEBUNK	DEPICT
CUBISM	DAMPED	DECADE	DEPLOY
CUBIST	DAMPEN	DECAMP	DEPORT
CUCKOO	DAMPER	DECANT	DEPOSE
CUDDLE	DAMPLY	DECEIT	DEPUTE
CUDGEL	DAMSEL	DECENT	DEPUTY
CULLED	DAMSON	DECIDE	DERAIL
CUPFUL	DANCED	DECKED	DERATE
CUPOLA	DANCER	DECKLE	DERIDE
CUPPED	DANDER	DECODE	DERIVE
CUP-TIE	DANDLE	DECREE	DERMAL
CURACY	DANGER	DEDUCE	DERMIS
CURARE	DANGLE	DEDUCT	DESCRY
CURATE	DANIEL	DEEMED	DESERT
CURBED	DANISH	DEEPEN	DESIGN
CURDLE	DAPHNE	DEEPER	DESIRE
CURFEW	DAPPER	DEEPLY	DESIST
CURING	DAPPLE	DEFACE	DESPOT
CURLED	DARING	DEFAME	DETACH
CURLER	DARKEN	DEFEAT	DETAIL

DETAIN	DISBAR	DOTARD	DULLED
DETECT	DISBUD	DOTING	DULLER
DETEST	DISCUS	DOTTED	DUMBLY
DETOUR	DISHED	DOTTLE	DUMDUM
DETUNE	DISMAL	DOUANE	DUMPED
DEUCED	DISMAY	DOUBLE	DUNLIN
DEVICE	DISOWN	DOUCHE	DUNNED
DEVISE	DISPEL	DOUGHY	DUPING
DEVOID	DISTIL	DOURLY	DURBAR
DEVOTE	DISUSE	DOUSED	DURESS
DEVOUR	DITHER	DOWNED	DURHAM
DEVOUT	DIVERS	DOWSED	DURING
DEWLAP	DIVERT	DOWSER	DUSTER
DEXTER	DIVEST	DOYLEY	DUYKER
DIADEM	DIVIDE	DOZING	DYEING
DIAPER	DIVINE	DRACHM	DYNAMO
DIATOM	DIVING	DRAGON	DYNAST
DIBBED	DOBBIN	DRAPED	
DIBBER	DOCILE	DRAPER	E—6
DIBBLE	DOCKED	DRAWER	EAGLET
DICING	DOCKER	DREAMT	EAR-CAP
DICKER	DOCKET	DREAMY	EARFUL
DICKEY	DOCTOR	DREARY	EARNED
DICTUM	DODDER	DREDGE	EARTHY
DIDDLE	DODGED	DRENCH	EARWIG
DIESEL	DODGER	DRESSY	EASIER
DIETED	DOFFED	DRIEST	EASILY
DIFFER	DOGATE	DRIVEL	EASING
DIGEST	DOG-FOX	DRIVEN	EASTER
DIGGER	DOGGED	DRIVER	EATING
DIK-DIK	DOINGS	DRONED	EBBING
DIKING	DOLING	DROPSY	ECARTE
DILATE	DOLLAR	DROVER	ECHOED
DILUTE	DOLLED	DROWSY	ECLAIR
DIMITY	DOLLOP	DRUDGE	ECZEMA
DIMMED	DOLMEN	DRY-BOB	EDDIED
DIMMER	DOLOUR	DRY-FLY	EDGING
DIMPLE	DOMAIN	DRYING	EDIBLE
DIMPLY	DOMINO	DRYISH	EDITED
DINGHY	DONATE	DRY-ROT	EDITOR
DINGLE	DONJON	DUBBED	EDUCED
DINING	DONKEY	DUBBIN	EERILY
DINKUM	DOODLE	DUCKED	EFFACE
DINNED	DOOMED	DUENNA	EFFECT
DINNER	DOPING	DUFFEL	EFFETE
DIPOLE	DORCAS	DUFFER	EFFIGY
DIPPED	DORIAN	DUFFLE	EFFLUX
DIPPER	DORMER	DUGONG	EFFORT
DIRECT	DORSAL	DUGOUT	EGG-CUP
DIREST	DOSAGE	DUIKER	EGGING
DISARM	DOTAGE	DULCET	EGG-NOG

EGOISM	ENMESH	ETHNIC	FACILE
EGOIST	ENMITY	EUCHRE	FACING
EGRESS	ENNEAD	EUCLID	FACTOR
EIFFEL	ENOUGH	EULOGY	FADING
EIGHTH	ENRAGE	EUNUCH	FAERIE
EIGHTY	ENRICH	EUREKA	FAG-END
EITHER	ENROBE	EUSTON	FAGGED
ELAINE	ENSIGN	EVADED	FAGGOT
ELAPSE	ENSUED	EVENER	FAILED
ELATED	ENSURE	EVENLY	FAIRER
ELDEST	ENTAIL	EVILLY	FAIRLY
ELEVEN	ENTICE	EVINCE	FAKING
ELFISH	ENTIRE	EVOLVE	FALCON
ELICIT	ENTITY	EXCEED	FALLAL
ELIXIR	ENTOMB	EXCEPT	FALLEN
ELOPED	ENTRAP	EXCESS	FALLOW
ELUDED	ENTREE	EXCISE	FALSER
ELVISH	ENVIED	EXCITE	FALTER
ELYSEE	ENWRAP	EXCUSE	FAMILY
EMBALM	ENZYME	EXEMPT	FAMINE
EMBARK	EOCENE	EXEUNT	FAMISH
EMBLEM	EOLITH	EXHALE	FAMOUS
EMBODY	EQUATE	EXHORT	FANGED
EMBOSS	EQUINE	EXHUME	FANNED
EMBRYO	EQUITY	EXILED	FAN-TAN
EMERGE	ERASED	EXODUS	FARINA
EMETIC	ERASER	EXOTIC	FARING
EMIGRE	EREBUS	EXPAND	FARMED
EMPIRE	ERENOW	EXPECT	FARMER
EMPLOY	ERMINE	EXPEND	FARROW
ENABLE	ERODED	EXPERT	FASCIA
ENAMEL	EROTIC	EXPIRE	FASTED
ENCAGE	ERRAND	EXPIRY	FASTEN
ENCAMP	ERRANT	EXPORT	FASTER
ENCASE	ERRATA	EXPOSE	FATHER
ENCASH	ERRING	EXTANT	FATHOM
ENCORE	ERSATZ	EXTEND	FATTED
END-ALL	ESCAPE	EXTENT	FATTEN
ENDEAR	ESCHEW	EXTORT	FATTER
ENDING	ESCORT	EXUDED	FAUCET
ENDIVE	ESCUDO	EYEFUL	FAULTY
ENDURE	ESKIMO	EYEING	FAVOUR
ENERGY	ESPIAL	EYELET	FAWNED
ENFOLD	ESPIED	EYELID	FEALTY
ENGAGE	ESPRIT		FEARED
ENGINE	ESSENE	F—6	FEDORA
ENGULF	ESTATE	FABIAN	FEEBLE
ENIGMA	ESTEEM	FABLED	FEEBLY
ENJOIN	ETCHED	FABRIC	FEEDER
ENLACE	ETCHER	FACADE	FEELER
ENLIST	ETHICS	FACIAL	FELINE

FELLAH	FINGER	FLOPPY	FORKED
FELLED	FINIAL	FLORAL	FORMAL
FELLER	FINING	FLORET	FORMAT
FELLOE	FINISH	FLORID	FORMED
FELLOW	FINITE	FLORIN	FORMER
FELONY	FINNAN	FLOSSY	FORMIC
FELTED	FINNED	FLOURY	FOSSIL
FEMALE	FIRING	FLOWER	FOSTER
FENCED	FIRKIN	FLUENT	FOUGHT
FENCER	FIRMED	FLUFFY	FOULED
FENDED	FIRMLY	FLUKED	FOULLY
FENDER	FISCAL	FLUNKY	FOURTH
FENIAN	FISHED	FLURRY	FOWLER
FENNEL	FISHER	FLUTED	FOXILY
FERRER	FISHES	FLUXED	FOXING
FERRET	FISTED	FLYING	FRACAS
FERVID	FISTIC	FLY-NET	FRAMED
FESCUE	FITFUL	FOALED	FRAPPE
FESTAL	FITTED	FOAMED	FRAYED
FESTER	FITTER	FOBBED	FREELY
FETISH	FIXING	FO'C'SLE	FREEZE
FETTER	FIXITY	FODDER	FRENCH
FETTLE	FIZZED	FOEMAN	FRENZY
FEUDAL	FIZZER	FOETID	FRESCO
FEWEST	FIZZLE	FOGGED	FRIARY
FIACRE	FLABBY	FOIBLE	FRIDAY
FIANCE	FLAGON	FOILED	FRIDGE
FIASCO	FLAKED	FOKKER	FRIEND
FIBBED	FLAMED	FOLDED	FRIEZE
FIBBER	FLANGE	FOLDER	FRIGHT
FIBULA	FLANKS	FOLLOW	FRIGID
FICKLE	FLARED	FOMENT	FRINGE
FIDDLE	FLASHY	FONDER	FRISKY
FIDGET	FLATLY	FONDLE	FROGGY
FIERCE	FLATTY	FONDLY	FROLIC
FIGARO	FLAUNT	FOOLED	FROSTY
FIGURE	FLAVIN	FOOTED	FROTHY
FILIAL	FLAXEN	FOOTER	FROWSY
FILING	FLAYED	FOOTLE	FROZEN
FILLED	FLEDGE	FOOZLE	FRUGAL
FILLER	FLEECE	FORAGE	FRUITY
FILLET	FLEECY	FORBID	FRUMPY
FILLIP	FLESHY	FORBYE	FUDDLE
FILMED	FLEXED	FORCED	FUDGED
FILTER	FLEXOR	FORDED	FULFIL
FILTHY	FLICKS	FOREGO	FULHAM
FINALE	FLIGHT	FOREST	FULLER
FINDER	FLIMSY	FORGED	FULMAR
FINELY	FLINCH	FORGER	FUMBLE
FINERY	FLINTY	FORGET	FUNDED
FINEST	FLITCH	FORGOT	FUNGUS

FUNKED	GARCON	GIFTED	GOLFER
FUNNEL	GARDEN	GIGGLE	GONGED
FURIES	GARGLE	GIGOLO	GOODLY
FURLED	GARISH	GILDED	GOOGLY
FURORE	GARLIC	GILDER	GOPHER
FURROW	GARNER	GILLIE	GORGED
FUSING	GARNET	GILPIN	GORGET
FUSION	GARRET	GIMBAL	GORGIO
FUSSED	GARTER	GIMLET	GORGON
FUTILE	GAS-BAG	GINGER	GORING
FUTURE	GASCON	GIRDED	GOSHEN
	GASHED	GIRDER	GOSPEL
G—6	GASKET	GIRDLE	GOSSIP
GABBLE	GAS-MAN	GITANA	GOTHIC
GABLED	GASPED	GIVING	GOUGED
GADDED	GASPER	GLADLY	GOVERN
GADFLY	GASSED	GLANCE	GOWNED
GADGET	GATEAU	GLARED	GRACED
GAELIC	GATHER	GLASSY	GRACES
GAFFED	GATING	GLAZED	GRADED
GAFFER	GAUCHE	GLAZER	GRAINS
GAGGED	GAUCHO	GLIBLY	GRAMME
GAGGLE	GAUGED	GLIDED	GRANGE
GAIETY	GAYEST	GLIDER	GRANNY
GAINED	GAZEBO	GLOBAL	GRASSY
GAITER	GAZING	GLOOMY	GRATER
GALAXY	GEARED	GLORIA	GRATIS
GALLEY	GEEZER	GLOSSY	GRAVEL
GALLIC	GEIGER	GLOVED	GRAVEN
GALLON	GEISHA	GLOVER	GRAVER
GALLOP	GEMINI	GLOWED	GRAVES
GALLUP	GENDER	GLOWER	GRAZED
GALOOT	GENERA	GLUING	GREASE
GALORE	GENEVA	GLUMLY	GREASY
GALOSH	GENIAL	GNAWED	GREATS
GAMBIT	GENIUS	GNOMON	GREECE
GAMBLE	GENTLE	GOADED	GREEDY
GAMBOL	GENTLY	GOATEE	GREENS
GAMELY	GENTRY	GO-BANG	GRETNA
GAMING	GEORGE	GOBBET	GRIEVE
GAMMER	GERMAN	GOBBLE	GRILLE
GAMMON	GERUND	GOBLET	GRILSE
GANDER	GEW-GAW	GOBLIN	GRIMED
GANGER	GEYSER	GO-CART	GRIMLY
GANNET	GHARRY	GO-DOWN	GRINGO
GANTRY	GHETTO	GODSON	GRIPED
GAOLED	GIBBER	GODWIT	GRIPPE
GAOLER	GIBBET	GOFFER	GRISLY
GAPING	GIBBON	GOGGLE	GRITTY
GARAGE	GIBING	GOITRE	GROATS
GARBLE	GIBLET	GOLDEN	GROCER

GROGGY	HALLOW	HEADER	HICCUP
GROOVE	HALOED	HEALED	HIDDEN
GROPED	HALTED	HEALER	HIDING
GROTTO	HALTER	HEALTH	HIEING
GROUND	HALVED	HEAPED	HIGHER
GROUSE	HAMLET	HEARER	HIGHLY
GROVEL	HAMMAM	HEARSE	HIKING
GROWER	HAMMER	HEARTH	HILARY
GROWTH	HAMPER	HEARTY	HINDER
GROYNE	HANDED	HEATED	HINDOO
GRUBBY	HANDLE	HEATER	HINGED
GRUDGE	HANGAR	HEAVED	HINTED
GRUMPY	HANGED	HEAVEN	HIPPED
GRUNDY	HANGER	HEBREW	HIRING
GUFFAW	HANKER	HECATE	HISSED
GUIDED	HANSEL	HECKLE	HITHER
GUIDER	HANSOM	HECTIC	HITTER
GUIDON	HAPPEN	HECTOR	HOARSE
GUILTY	HARASS	HEDGED	HOAXED
GUINEA	HARDEN	HEEDED	HOAXER
GUITAR	HARDER	HEE-HAW	HOBBLE
GULLED	HARDLY	HEELED	HOBNOB
GULLET	HARD-UP	HEIFER	HOCKEY
GULLEY	HARING	HEIGHT	HOEING
GULPED	HARKED	HELIUM	HOGGET
GUMMED	HARKEN	HELMET	HOLDER
GUN-MAN	HARLOT	HELPED	HOLD-UP
GUN-MEN	HARMED	HELPER	HOLIER
GUNNEL	HARPED	HEMMED	HOLILY
GUNNER	HARRIS	HEMPEN	HOLLOW
GUN-SHY	HARROW	HERALD	HOMAGE
GURGLE	HASTEN	HERBAL	HOMELY
GURKHA	HAT-BOX	HERDED	HOMILY
GURNET	HATING	HEREAT	HOMING
GUSHED	HAT-PEG	HEREBY	HONEST
GUSHER	HAT-PIN	HEREIN	HONING
GUSSET	HATRED	HEREOF	HONKED
GUTTED	HATTED	HEREON	HONOUR
GUTTER	HATTER	HERESY	HOODED
GUZZLE	HAULED	HERETO	HOODIE
GYBING	HAUNCH	HERMES	HOODOO
GYPSUM	HAVANA	HERMIT	HOOFED
GYRATE	HAVING	HERNIA	HOOKAH
	HAWHAW	HEROIC	HOOKED
H—6	HAWKED	HEROIN	HOOKER
HACKED	HAWKER	HERPES	HOOPED
HACKLE	HAWSER	HERREN	HOOPER
HAGGIS	HAY-BOX	HETMAN	HOOP-LA
HAGGLE	HAZARD	HEWING	HOOPOE
HAILED	HAZILY	HEYDAY	HOOTED
HALLOA	HEADED	HIATUS	HOOTER

HOPING	**I—6**	INDUCT	INWARD
HOPPED	IAMBIC	INFAMY	IODINE
HOPPER	IBERIA	INFANT	IONIAN
HORNED	IBIDEM	INFECT	IRITIS
HORNER	ICARUS	INFEST	IRKING
HORNET	ICE-AGE	INFIRM	IRONED
HORRID	ICE-AXE	INFLOW	IRONER
HORROR	ICE-CAP	INFLUX	IRONIC
HOSIER	ICE-MAN	INFORM	ISABEL
HOSTEL	ICE-SAW	INFUSE	ISLAND
HOT-BED	ICICLE	INHALE	ISOBAR
HOT-DOG	ICIEST	INHERE	ISRAEL
HOT-POT	IDIOCY	INJECT	ISSUED
HOTTER	IDLING	INJURE	ISSUER
HOURLY	IGNITE	INJURY	ITALIC
HOUSED	IGNORE	INK-BAG	ITCHED
HOWDAH	IGUANA	INKING	ITSELF
HOWLED	ILLUDE	INK-POT	**J—6**
HOWLER	ILLUME	INK-SAC	JABBED
HOYDEN	IMBIBE	INLAID	JABBER
HUBBUB	IMBUED	INLAND	JACKAL
HUDDLE	IMMUNE	INMATE	JACKED
HUFFED	IMMURE	INMOST	JACKET
HUGELY	IMPACT	INNATE	JAGGED
HUMANE	IMPAIR	INROAD	JAGUAR
HUMBLE	IMPALA	INRUSH	JAILED
HUMBLY	IMPALE	INSANE	JAILER
HUMBUG	IMPART	INSECT	JAMMED
HUMMED	IMPEDE	INSERT	JANGLE
HUMOUR	IMPEND	INSIDE	JARGON
HUMPED	IMPISH	INSIST	JARRED
HUNGER	IMPORT	INSOLE	JASPER
HUNGRY	IMPOSE	INSPAN	JAUNTY
HUNTED	IMPOST	INSTAL	JAWING
HUNTER	IMPUGN	INSTEP	JAZZED
HURDLE	IMPURE	INSTIL	JEERED
HURLED	IMPUTE	INSULT	JENNET
HURRAH	INBORN	INSURE	JERBOA
HURTLE	INBRED	INTACT	JERKED
HUSHED	INCHED	INTAKE	JERKIN
HUSKED	INCISE	INTEND	JERSEY
HUSSAR	INCITE	INTENT	JESTED
HUSSIF	INCOME	INTERN	JESTER
HUSTLE	INDEED	INTONE	JESUIT
HUTTED	INDENT	INURED	JETSAM
HYBRID	INDIAN	INVADE	JEWESS
HYMNAL	INDICT	INVENT	JEWISH
HYPHEN	INDIGO	INVERT	JIBBED
HYSSOP	INDITE	INVEST	JIGGED
	INDOOR	INVITE	JIGGLE
	INDUCE	INVOKE	JIG-SAW

JILTED	KENNEL	LACTIC	LAXITY
JINGLE	KERNEL	LADDER	LAYING
JOBBER	KERSEY	LADDIE	LAYMAN
JOB-LOT	KETTLE	LADING	LAY-OUT
JOCKEY	KEY-MEN	LADLED	LAZIER
JOCOSE	KIBOSH	LAGGED	LAZILY
JOCUND	KICKED	LAGOON	LAZING
JOGGED	KICKER	LAID-UP	LAZULI
JOHNNY	KIDDED	LAMBED	LEADED
JOINED	KIDDER	LAMELY	LEADEN
JOINER	KIDNAP	LAMENT	LEADER
JOKING	KIDNEY	LAMINA	LEAD-IN
JOLTED	KILLED	LAMING	LEAFED
JORDAN	KILLER	LAMMAS	LEAGUE
JOSEPH	KILTED	LAMMED	LEAKED
JOSSER	KILTIE	LANCED	LEANED
JOSTLE	KIMONO	LANCER	LEANER
JOTTED	KINDER	LANCET	LEAN-TO
JOVIAL	KINDLE	LANDAU	LEAPED
JOYFUL	KINDLY	LANDED	LEASED
JOYOUS	KINEMA	LAPDOG	LEAVEN
JUDAIC	KINGLY	LAPFUL	LEAVER
JUDGED	KINKED	LAPPED	LEDGER
JUGFUL	KIPPER	LAPSED	LEERED
JUGGED	KIRSCH	LARDED	LEEWAY
JUGGLE	KIRTLE	LARDER	LEGACY
JUJUBE	KISMET	LARGER	LEGATE
JULIAN	KISSED	LARIAT	LEGATO
JUMBLE	KISSER	LARRUP	LEG-BYE
JUMPED	KIT-BAG	LARVAE	LEGEND
JUMPER	KITSCH	LARVAL	LEGGED
JUNGLE	KITTEN	LARYNX	LEGION
JUNIOR	KLAXON	LASCAR	LEGIST
JUNIUS	KNIFED	LASHED	LEGUME
JUNKER	KNIGHT	LASSIE	LENDER
JUNKET	KNOBBY	LASTED	LENGTH
JURIST	KNOTTY	LASTLY	LENTEN
JUSTER	KOODOO	LATEEN	LENTIL
JUSTLY	KOREAN	LATELY	LESION
JUTTED	KOSHER	LATENT	LESSEE
	KOW-TOW	LATEST	LESSEN
K—6	KULTUR	LATHER	LESSER
KAFFIR	KUMMEL	LATTER	LESSON
KAISER		LAUDED	LESSOR
KANAKA	L—6	LAUDER	LETHAL
KAOLIN	LAAGER	LAUNCH	LET-OFF
KEELED	LABIAL	LAUREL	LETTER
KEENED	LABOUR	LAVING	LEVANT
KEENER	LACING	LAVISH	LEVITE
KEENLY	LACKED	LAWFUL	LEVITY
KEEPER	LACKEY	LAWYER	LEWDLY

LEYDEN	LOAFED	LUGGER	MANFUL
LIABLE	LOAFER	LULLED	MANGER
LIAISE	LOANED	LUMBAR	MANGLE
LIBYAN	LOATHE	LUMBER	MANIAC
LICHEN	LOBATE	LUMPED	MANIOC
LICKED	LOBBED	LUNACY	MANNED
LIDDED	LOCALE	LUNATE	MANNER
LIEDER	LOCATE	LUNGED	MANTEL
LIFTED	LOCKED	LUPINE	MANTIS
LIFTER	LOCKER	LURING	MANTLE
LIGNUM	LOCKET	LURKED	MANTUA
LIKELY	LOCK-UP	LUSTED	MANUAL
LIKING	LOCUST	LUSTRE	MANURE
LIMBED	LODGED	LUTINE	MAOIST
LIMBER	LODGER	LUXURY	MAPPED
LIMING	LOFTED	LYCEUM	MAQUIS
LIMPED	LOGGED		MARAUD
LIMPET	LOGGIA	M—6	MARBLE
LIMPID	LOG-HUT	MACRON	MARCEL
LINAGE	LOGMAN	MADCAP	MARGIN
LINDEN	LOITER	MADDEN	MARIAN
LINEAL	LOLLED	MADDER	MARINE
LINEAR	LOLLOP	MADMAN	MARKED
LINE-UP	LONELY	MADRAS	MARKER
LINGER	LONGER	MAENAD	MARKET
LINING	LOOFAH	MAGGOT	MARMOT
LINKED	LOOKED	MAGNET	MAROON
LINNET	LOOKER	MAGNUM	MARQUE
LINTEL	LOOMED	MAGPIE	MARRED
LIONEL	LOOPED	MAGYAR	MARRON
LIPPED	LOOPER	MAHOUT	MARROW
LIQUID	LOOSEN	MAIDEN	MARSHY
LIQUOR	LOOTED	MAIGRE	MARTEN
LISBON	LOOTER	MAILED	MARTIN
LISPED	LOPING	MAIMED	MARTYR
LISSOM	LOPPED	MAINLY	MARVEL
LISTED	LORDED	MAKE-UP	MASCOT
LISTEN	LORDLY	MAKING	MASHED
LISTER	LOSING	MALADY	MASHER
LITANY	LOTION	MALAGA	MASHIE
LITCHI	LOUDER	MALICE	MASKED
LITMUS	LOUDLY	MALIGN	MASKER
LITTER	LOUNGE	MALLET	MASQUE
LITTLE	LOUVRE	MALLOW	MASSED
LIVELY	LOVELY	MALTED	MASSIF
LIVERY	LOVING	MAMMAL	MASTED
LIVING	LOWEST	MAMMON	MASTER
LIZARD	LOWING	MANAGE	MASTIC
LLOYD'S	LUBBER	MANANA	MATING
LOADED	LUFFED	MANCHU	MATINS
LOADER	LUGGED	MANEGE	MATRIX

MATRON	MERLIN	MINOAN	MONODY
MATTED	MERMAN	MINTED	MOOING
MATTER	MESHED	MINUET	MOONED
MATURE	MESSED	MINUTE	MOONER
MAULED	METEOR	MIRAGE	MOOTED
MAUNDY	METHOD	MIRING	MOOTER
MAUSER	METHYL	MIRROR	MOPING
MAY-BUG	METIER	MISCUE	MOPISH
MAY-DAY	METING	MISERE	MOPPED
MAY-FLY	METRIC	MISERY	MOPPET
MAYHAP	METTLE	MISFIT	MORALE
MAYHEM	MEWING	MISHAP	MORASS
MEADOW	MIASMA	MISLAY	MORBID
MEAGRE	MICKLE	MISLED	MORGUE
MEALIE	MICRON	MISSAL	MORMON
MEANLY	MID-AIR	MISSED	MOROSE
MEASLY	MIDDAY	MISSEL	MORRIS
MEDDLE	MIDDEN	MISSIS	MORROW
MEDIAL	MIDDLE	MISTER	MORSEL
MEDIAN	MIDGET	MISUSE	MORTAL
MEDICO	MID-OFF	MITRAL	MORTAR
MEDIUM	MID-RfB	MITRED	MOSAIC
MEDLAR	MIDWAY	MITTEN	MOSLEM
MEDLEY	MIGHTY	MIXING	MOSQUE
MEDUSA	MIGNON	MIZZEN	MOSTLY
MEEKER	MIKADO	MOANED	MOTHER
MEEKLY	MILADY	MOATED	MOTION
MEETLY	MILDEN	MOBBED	MOTIVE
MEGILP	MILDER	MOBCAP	MOTLEY
MEGOHM	MILDEW	MOBILE	MOTTLE
MEGRIM	MILDLY	MOB-LAW	MOULDY
MELLOW	MILIEU	MOCKED	MOUNTY
MELODY	MILKED	MOCKER	MOUSER
MELTED	MILKEN	MODENA	MOUSSE
MELTER	MILKER	MODERN	MOUTHY
MELTON	MILLED	MODEST	MOVIES
MEMBER	MILLER	MODIFY	MOVING
MEMOIR	MILLET	MODISH	MOWING
MEMORY	MILORD	MODULE	MUCKED
MENACE	MIMING	MOHAIR	MUCKER
MENAGE	MIMOSA	MOHAWK	MUCKLE
MENDED	MINCED	MOIETY	MUCOUS
MENDER	MINCER	MOLOCH	MUDDLE
MENIAL	MINDED	MOLEST	MUD-PIE
MENTAL	MINDER	MOLTEN	MUFFED
MENTOR	MINGLE	MOMENT	MUFFIN
MERCER	MINIFY	MONDAY	MUFFLE
MERELY	MINING	MONGOL	MUGGED
MERGED	MINION	MONIED	MULISH
MERGER	MINNIE	MONIES	MULLED
MERINO	MINNOW	MONKEY	MULLET

MUMBLE	NEARER	NODDLE	OARAGE
MUMMER	NEARLY	NODOSE	OARING
MURDER	NEATLY	NODULE	OBELUS
MURMUR	NEBULA	NOGGIN	OBERON
MURPHY	NECKED	NONAGE	OBEYED
MUSCAT	NECTAR	NONARY	OBEYER
MUSCLE	NEED-BE	NON-COM	OBITER
MUSEUM	NEEDED	NON-EGO	OBJECT
MUSING	NEEDER	NOODLE	OBLATE
MUSKET	NEEDLE	NOOSED	OBLIGE
MUSLIM	NEEDLY	NORDIC	OBLONG
MUSLIN	NEGATE	NORMAL	OBOIST
MUSSED	NEPHEW	NORMAN	OBSESS
MUSSEL	NEREID	NORROY	OBTAIN
MUSTER	NERVED	NO-SIDE	OBTUSE
MUTATE	NESTED	NOSING	OBVERT
MUTELY	NESTLE	NOTARY	OCCULT
MUTING	NESTOR	NOTICE	OCCUPY
MUTINY	NETHER	NOTIFY	OCELOT
MUTISM	NETTED	NOTING	O'CLOCK
MUTTER	NETTLE	NOTION	OCTANE
MUTTON	NEUTER	NOUGAT	OCTANT
MUTUAL	NEWISH	NOUGHT	OCTAVE
MUZZLE	NIBBED	NOVENA	OCTAVO
MYOPIA	NIBBLE	NOVICE	OCULAR
MYOPIC	NICELY	NOWAYS	ODDITY
MYRIAD	NICENE	NOWISE	ODIOUS
MYRTLE	NICEST	NOZZLE	OEDEMA
MYSELF	NICETY	NUANCE	OFFEND
MYSTIC	NICHED	NUBIAN	OFFICE
	NICKED	NUBILE	OFFING
N—6	NICKEL	NUCLEI	OFFISH
NAGGED	NICKER	NUDELY	OFFSET
NAGGER	NIGGER	NUDGED	OGLING
NAILED	NIGGLE	NUDISM	OGRESS
NAILER	NIMBLE	NUDIST	OIL-CAN
NAMELY	NIMBLY	NUDITY	OIL-GAS
NAMING	NIMBUS	NUGGET	OILING
NAPERY	NIMROD	NUMBED	OIL-MAN
NAPKIN	NINETY	NUMBER	OIL-NUT
NAPPED	NIPPED	NUNCIO	OLDEST
NARROW	NIPPER	NURSED	OLDISH
NATANT	NIPPLE	NURSER	OLIVER
NATION	NITRIC	NUTANT	OLIVET
NATIVE	NITWIT	NUTMEG	OMELET
NATTER	NO-BALL	NUT-OIL	OMENED
NATURE	NOBBLE	NUTRIA	OMNIUM
NAUGHT	NOBLER	NUZZLE	ONAGER
NAUSEA	NOBODY		ONCOST
NEAPED	NODDED	**O—6**	ONE-MAN
NEARBY	NODDER	OAFISH	ONE-WAY

ONFLOW	OUTFIT	PALTRY	PATCHY
ONIONY	OUTFLY	PAMPAS	PATENT
ONRUSH	OUTING	PAMPER	PATHIC
ONWARD	OUTLAW	PANADA	PATHOS
OODLES	OUTLAY	PANAMA	PATINA
OOLITE	OUTLET	PANDER	PATOIS
OOZING	OUTPUT	PANDIT	PATROL
OPAQUE	OUTRUN	PANFUL	PATRON
OPENED	OUTSET	PANNED	PATTED
OPENER	OUTWIT	PANTED	PATTEN
OPENLY	OVALLY	PANTER	PATTER
OPIATE	OVERDO	PANTRY	PAUNCH
OPINED	OWLERY	PANZER	PAUPER
OPPOSE	OWLISH	PAPACY	PAUSED
OPPUGN	OWNING	PAPERY	PAUSER
OPTICS	OXALIC	PAPISH	PAVAGE
OPTIME	OX-EYED	PAPISM	PAVANE
OPTING	OXFORD	PAPIST	PAVING
OPTION	OXLIKE	PAPUAN	PAWING
ORACLE	OXTAIL	PARADE	PAWNED
ORALLY	OXYGEN	PARCEL	PAWNEE
ORANGE	OYSTER	PARDON	PAWNER
ORATED		PAREIL	PAWPAW
ORATOR	P—6	PARENT	PAY-DAY
ORCHID	PACIFY	PARGET	PAYING
ORDAIN	PACING	PARIAH	PAY-OFF
ORDEAL	PACKED	PARING	PEACHY
ORDURE	PACKER	PARISH	PEAHEN
ORGASM	PACKET	PARITY	PEAKED
ORGIES	PADDED	PARKED	PEALED
ORIENT	PADDER	PARKER	PEA-NUT
ORIGAN	PADDLE	PARKIN	PEA-POD
ORIGIN	PADUAN	PARLEY	PEARLY
ORIOLE	PAGING	PARODY	PEBBLE
ORISON	PAGODA	PAROLE	PEBBLY
ORMULU	PAINED	PARROT	PECKED
ORNATE	PAIRED	PARSED	PECKER
ORPHAN	PALACE	PARSEE	PECTEN
ORPHIC	PALATE	PARSON	PECTIC
OSIRIS	PALELY	PARTED	PECTIN
OSMIUM	PALING	PARTER	PEDANT
OSPREY	PALISH	PARTLY	PEDATE
OSSIFY	PALLAS	PASSED	PEDDLE
OSTEND	PALLED	PASSEE	PEDLAR
OSTLER	PALLET	PASSER	PEELED
OTIOSE	PALLID	PASSIM	PEELER
OUSTED	PALLOR	PASTED	PEEPED
OUSTER	PALMAR	PASTEL	PEEPER
OUTBID	PALMED	PASTIL	PEERER
OUTCRY	PALMER	PASTOR	PEEVED
OUTDID	PALTER	PASTRY	PEEWIT

PEGGED	PICKLE	PLACER	POISON
PEG-LEG	PICK-UP	PLACET	POKING
PEG-TOP	PICNIC	PLACID	POLICE
PELLET	PICRIC	PLAGUE	POLICY
PELMET	PIDGIN	PLAGUY	POLING
PELOTA	PIECED	PLAICE	POLISH
PELVIC	PIECER	PLAINT	POLITE
PELVIS	PIEDOG	PLANED	POLITY
PENCIL	PIEMAN	PLANER	POLLED
PENMAN	PIERCE	PLANET	POLLEN
PENNED	PIFFLE	PLAQUE	POLLUX
PENNON	PIGEON	PLASHY	POLONY
PENTAD	PIGNUT	PLASMA	POMACE
PENT-UP	PIG-STY	PLATAN	POMADE
PEÑULT	PILAFF	PLATED	POMMEL
PENURY	PILFER	PLATEN	POMONA
PEOPLE	PILING	PLATER	POM-POM
PEPPER	PILLAR	PLAYED	POMPON
PEPSIN	PILLAU	PLAYER	PONDER
PEPTIC	PILLED	PLEACH	POODLE
PERIOD	PILLOW	PLEASE	POOLED
PERISH	PILULE	PLEDGE	POOPED
PERKED	PIMPLE	PLEIAD	POORER
PERMIT	PIMPLY	PLENTY	POORLY
PERSON	PINCER	PLENUM	POPERY
PERTLY '	PINDAR	PLEURA	POPGUN
PERUKE	PINEAL	PLEXUS	POPISH
PERUSE	PINGED	PLIANT	POPLAR
PESETA	PINING	PLIERS	POPLIN
PESTER	PINION	PLIGHT	POPPED
PESTLE	PINKED	PLINTH	POPPER
PETARD	PINNED	PLOUGH	POPPET
PETITE	PIPING	PLOVER	PORING
PETREL	PIPKIN	PLUCKY	PORKER
PETROL	PIPPED	PLUG-IN	PORKET
PETTED	PIPPIN	PLUMED	POROUS
PEWTER	PIQUED	PLUMPY	PORTAL
PHAROS	PIQUET	PLUNGE	PORTER
PHENOL	PIRACY	PLURAL	PORTLY
PHLEGM	PIRATE	PLUSHY	POSEUR
PHOBIA	PISCES	PLYERS	POSING
PHOEBE	PISTIL	PLYING	POSSET
PHONED	PISTOL	POCKED	POSSUM
PHONEY	PISTON	POCKET	POSTAL
PHONIC	PITCHY	PODDED	POSTED
PHRASE	PITIED	PODIUM	POSTER
PHYSIC	PITIER	POETIC	POTASH
PIAZZA	PITMAN	POETRY	POTATO
PICKED	PITSAW	POGROM	POTBOY
PICKER	PITTED	POISED	POTEEN
PICKET	PLACED	POISER	POTENT

POTHER	PROPEL	PURITY	RABBLE
POTION	PROPER	PURLED	RABIES
POT-LID	PROSED	PURLER	RACIAL
POTMAN	PROSER	PURPLE	RACILY
POTTED	PROSIT	PURRED	RACING
POTTER	PROTON	PURSED	RACKED
POUDRE	PROVED	PURSER	RACKER
POUFFE	PROVEN	PURSUE	RACKET
POUNCE	PROVER	PURVEY	RACOON
POURED	PRUNED	PUSHED	RADIAL
POURER	PRYING	PUSHER	RADIAN
POUTED	PSEUDO	PUTRID	RADISH
POUTER	PSYCHE	PUTSCH	RADIUM
POWDER	PUBLIC	PUTTED	RADIUS
POW-POW	PUCKER	PUTTEE	RAFFIA
PRAISE	PUDDLE	PUTTER	RAFFLE
PRANCE	PUFFED	PUZZLE	RAFTER
PRATED	PUFFIN	PYEDOG	RAGGED
PRATER	PUG-DOG	PYEMIA	RAGING
PRAYED	PUISNE	PYEMIC	RAGLAN
PRAYER	PUKKHA	PYOSIS	RAGMAN
PREACH	PULING	PYRENE	RAGOUT
PRECIS	PULLED	PYRITE	RAG-TAG
PREFAB	PULLER	PYTHON	RAIDED
PREFER	PULLET		RAIDER
PREFIX	PULLEY	Q—6	RAILED
PREPAY	PULPED	QUAGGA	RAILER
PRESTO	PULPIT	QUAGGY	RAINED
PRETOR	PULQUE	QUAINT	RAISED
PRETTY	PULSED	QUAKED	RAISER
PRE-WAR	PUMICE	QUAKER	RAISIN
PREYED	PUMMEL	QUARRY	RAJPUT
PREYER	PUMPED	QUARTO	RAKERY
PRICED	PUMPER	QUARTZ	RAKING
PRIDED	PUNCHY	QUAVER	RAKISH
PRIEST	PUNDIT	QUAYED	RAMBLE
PRIMAL	PUNIER	QUEASY	RAMIFY
PRIMER	PUNISH	QUENCH	RAMMED
PRIMLY	PUNNET	QUEUED	RAMMER
PRIMUS	PUNTED	QUINCE	RAMPED
PRINCE	PUNTER	QUINSY	RAMROD
PRIORY	PUPPED	QUINZE	RANCHO
PRISED	PUPPET	QUIRED	RANCID
PRISMY	PURDAH	QUIRKY	RANDOM
PRISON	PURELY	QUIVER	RANGED
PRIVET	PUREST	QUORUM	RANGER
PRIZED	PURGED	QUOTED	RANKER
PROFIT	PURGER		RANKLE
PROLIX	PURIFY	R—6	RANKLY
PROMPT	PURISM	RABBIN	RANSOM
PRONTO	PURIST	RABBIT	RANTED

RANTER	REBURY	REGAIN	RENTES
RAPHIA	RECALL	REGALE	RE-OPEN
RAPIER	RECANT	REGARD	REPACK
RAPINE	RECAST	REGENT	REPAID
RAPING	RECEDE	REGILD	REPAIR
RAPPED	RECENT	REGIME	REPASS
RAPPER	RECESS	REGINA	REPAST
RAREFY	RECIPE	REGION	REPEAL
RARELY	RECITE	REGIUS	REPEAT
RAREST	RECKED	REGIVE	REPENT
RARITY	RECKON	REGLOW	REPINE
RASCAL	RECOAL	REGNAL	REPLAY
RASHER	RECOCT	REGNUM	REPORT
RASHLY	RECOIL	REGRET	REPOSE
RASING	RECOIN	REHANG	REPPED
RASPED	RECORD	REHASH	REPUGN
RASPER	RECOUP	REHEAR	REPUTE
RASURE	RECTOR	REHEAT	REREAD
RATHER	RECUSE	REINED	RESAIL
RATIFY	REDACT	REJECT	RESALE
RATING	REDCAP	REJOIN	RESCUE
RATION	REDDEN	RELAID	RESEAT
RATTAN	REDEEM	RELATE	RESECT
RAT-TAT	RED-EYE	RELENT	RESELL
RATTED	RED-GUM	RELICT	RESEND
RATTER	RED-HOT	RELIED	RESENT
RATTLE	RED-OAK	RELIEF	RESHIP
RAVAGE	REDRAW	RELIER	RESIDE
RAVINE	REDUCE	RELISH	RESIGN
RAVING	REDUIT	RELIVE	RESINY
RAVISH	RE-DYED	RELOAD	RESIST
RAWISH	RE-ECHO	RELUME	RESOLD
RAZING	REEDED	REMADE	RESORB
READER	REEFED	REMAIN	RESORT
REALLY	REEFER	REMAKE	RESOWN
REALTY	REEKED	REMAND	RESTED
REAMED	REELED	REMARK	RESULT
REAMER	REELER	REMAST	RESUME
REAPED	REFILL	REMEDY	RETAIL
REAPER	REFINE	REMIND	RETAIN
REARED	REFLEX	REMISE	RETAKE
REARER	REFLOW	REMISS	RETARD
REASON	REFLUX	REMOTE	RETINA
REAVOW	REFOLD	REMOVE	RETIRE
REBATE	REFOOT	RENAME	RETOLD
REBECK	REFORM	RENDER	RETOOK
REBIND	REFUEL	RENNET	RETORT
REBOIL	REFUGE	RENOWN	RETRIM
REBORN	REFUND	RENTAL	RETYRE
REBUFF	REFUSE	RENTED	REUTER
REBUKE	REFUTE	RENTER	REVAMP

REVEAL	RIPEST	ROSIER	RUSHER
REVERE	RIPPED	ROSILY	RUSSET
REVERS	RIPPER	ROSINY	RUSSIA
REVERT	RIPPLE	ROSTER	RUSTED
REVIEW	RIPPLY	ROTARY	RUSTIC
REVILE	RIPSAW	ROTATE	RUSTLE
REVIVE	RISING	ROT-GUT	RUTTED
REVOKE	RISKED	ROTTED	
REVOLT	RISKER	ROTTEN	S—6
REVVED	RISQUE	ROTTER	SABLED
REWARD	RITUAL	ROTUND	SACHET
REWOOD	RIVAGE	ROUBLE	SACKED
REWORD	RIVING	ROUGED	SACKER
RHESUS	ROAMED	ROUMAN	SACRED
RHEUMY	ROAMER	ROUSED	SADDEN
RHYMED	ROARED	ROUSER	SADDLE
RHYMER	ROARER	ROUTED	SADISM
RHYTHM	ROBBED	ROUTER	SAFARI
RIALTO	ROBBER	ROVING	SAFELY
RIBALD	ROBING	ROWING	SAFEST
RIBAND	ROBUST	RUBATO	SAFETY
RIBBED	ROCKED	RUBBED	SAGELY
RIBBON	ROCKER	RUBBER	SAGEST
RICHER	ROCKET	RUBBLE	SAGGED
RICHES	ROCOCO	RUBBLY	SAHARA
RICHLY	RODENT	RUBIED	SAILED
RICKED	ROILED	RUBRIC	SAILER
RIDDEN	ROLAND	RUCKLE	SAILOR
RIDDLE	ROLLED	RUDDER	SALAAM
RIDGED	ROLLER	RUDELY	SALAME
RIDING	ROMAIC	RUDEST	SALARY
RIFFLE	ROMANY	RUEFUL	SALINE
RIFLED	ROMIST	RUFFED	SALIVA
RIFLER	ROMPED	RUFFLE	SALLOW
RIFTED	ROMPER	RUFOUS	SALMON
RIGGED	RONDEL	RUGATE	SALOON
RIGGER	ROOFED	RUGGED	SALTED
RIGOUR	ROOFER	RUGGER	SALTER
RIG-OUT	ROOKED	RUGOSE	SALTLY
RILING	ROOKER	RUINED	SALUKI
RILLED	ROOKIE	RUINER	SALUTE
RILLET	ROOMED	RULING	SALVED
RIMMED	ROOMER	RUMBLE	SALVER
RIMMER	ROOTED	RUMOUR	SALVIA
RINDED	ROOTER	RUMPLE	SAMELY
RINGER	ROOTLE	RUMPUS	SAMIAN
RINSED	ROPERY	RUNLET	SAMITE
RINSER	ROPING	RUNNEL	SAMLET
RIOTED	ROSARY	RUNNER	SAMOAN
RIOTER	ROSERY	RUNWAY	SAMPAN
RIPELY	ROSIED	RUSHED	SAMPLE

SANDAL	SCORER	SEEING	SEWING
SANDED	SCOTCH	SEEKER	SEXTAN
SANELY	SCOTIA	SEEMED	SEXTET
SANEST	SCRAPE	SEEMER	SEXTON
SANIFY	SCRAWL	SEEMLY	SEXUAL
SANITY	SCREAM	SEEPED	SHABBY
SAPPED	SCREED	SEE-SAW	SHADED
SAPPER	SCREEN	SEETHE	SHADOW
SAPPHO	SCREWY	SEISED	SHAGGY
SARONG	SCRIBE	SEISIN	SHAKEN
SASHES	SCRIMP	SEIZED	SHAKER
SATEEN	SCRIPT	SEIZIN	SHAMED
SATING	SCROLL	SEIZOR	SHANTY
SATINY	SCRUFF	SELDOM	SHAPED
SATIRE	SCULPT	SELECT	SHAPER
SATRAP	SCUMMY	SELENE	SHARED
SATURN	SCURFY	SELLER	SHARER
SAUCED	SCURRY	SELVES	SHAVED
SAUCER	SCURVY	SENATE	SHAVER
SAVAGE	SCUTUM	SENDER	SHEARS
SAVANT	SCYLLA	SENILE	SHEATH
SAVING	SCYTHE	SENIOR	SHEIKH
SAVORY	SEA-COB	SENORA	SHEKEL
SAVOUR	SEA-COW	SENSED	SHELLY
SAVVEY	SEA-DOG	SENTRY	SHELVE
SAW-FLY	SEA-FOX	SEPSIS	SHELVY
SAWING	SEA-GOD	SEPTET	SHERRY
SAW-PIT	SEA-HOG	SEPTIC	SHIELD
SAW-SET	SEALED	SEPTUM	SHIFTY
SAWYER	SEALER	SEQUEL	SHIMMY
SAXONY	SEAMAN	SEQUIN	SHINDY
SAYING	SEAMED	SERAPH	SHINER
SCABBY	SEAMER	SEREIN	SHINTO
SCALED	SEA-MEW	SERENE	SHIRES
SCALER	SEANCE	SERIAL	SHIRTY
SCALES	SEARCH	SERIES	SHIVER
SCAMPI	SEARED	SERMON	SHOALY
SCANTY	SEASON	SEROUS	SHODDY
SCARAB	SEATED	SERVED	SHOOED
SCARCE	SEA-WAY	SERVER	SHOPPY
SCARED	SECANT	SESAME	SHORED
SCATHE	SECEDE	SESTET	SHORER
SCATTY	SECOND	SET-OFF	SHORTS
SCENIC	SECRET	SETOSE	SHOULD
SCHEME	SECTOR	SET-OUT	SHOVED
SCHISM	SECUND	SETTEE	SHOVEL
SCHOOL	SECURE	SETTER	SHOVER
SCILLA	SEDATE	SETTLE	SHOWER
SCONCE	SEDUCE	SEVERE	SHRANK
SCORCH	SEEDED	SEVRES	SHREWD
SCORED	SEEDER	SEWAGE	SHRIEK

SHRIFT	SINGLE	SLITHY	SNOBBY
SHRIKE	SINGLY	SLIVER	SNOOZE
SHRILL	SINKER	SLOGAN	SNORED
SHRIMP	SINNER	SLOPED	SNORER
SHRINE	SIPHON	SLOPPY	SNOTTY
SHRINK	SIPPED	SLOUCH	SNOUTY
SHRIVE	SIPPER	SLOUGH	SNOWED
SHROUD	SIPPET	SLOVAK	SNUBBY
SHROVE	SIRDAR	SLOVEN	SNUDGE
SHRUNK	SIRING	SLOWER	SNUFFY
SHUCKS	SIRIUS	SLOWLY	SNUGLY
SHYING	SIRRAH	SLUDGE	SOAKED
SICKER	SISKIN	SLUDGY	SOAKER
SICKEN	SISTER	SLUICE	SOAPED
SICKLE	SITTER	SLUING	SOARED
SICKLY	SIZING	SLUMPY	SOBBED
SIDING	SIZZLE	SLURRY	SOCAGE
SIDLED	SKATED	SLUSHY	SOCCER
SIENNA	SKATER	SLYEST	SOCIAL
SIERRA	SKERRY	SMALLS	SOCKED
SIESTA	SKETCH	SMARMY	SOCKET
SIFTED	SKEWER	SMARTY	SODDEN
SIFTER	SKILLY	SMEARY	SODIUM
SIGHED	SKIMPY	SMELLY	SO-EVER
SIGHER	SKINNY	SMILAX	SOFISM
SIGNAL	SKYISH	SMILED	SOFTEN
SIGNED	SLABBY	SMILER	SOFTER
SIGNER	SLAKED	SMIRCH	SOFTLY
SIGNET	SLANGY	SMITER	SOILED
SIGNOR	SLAP-UP	SMITHY	SOIREE
SILAGE	SLATED	SMOKED	SOLACE
SILENT	SLATER	SMOKER	SOLDER
SILICA	SLAVED	SMOOTH	SOLELY
SILKEN	SLAVER	SMOUCH	SOLEMN
SILLER	SLAVEY	SMUDGE	SO-LONG
SILTED	SLAVIC	SMUDGY	SOLVED
SILVAN	SLAYER	SMUGLY	SOLVER
SILVER	SLEAZY	SMUTCH	SOMBRE
SIMIAL	SLEDGE	SMUTTY	SONANT
SIMIAN	SLEEPY	SNAGGY	SONATA
SIMILE	SLEETY	SNAKED	SONNET
SIMMER	SLEEVE	SNAPPY	SOONER
SIMNEL	SLEIGH	SNARED	SOOTHE
SIMONY	SLEUTH	SNARER	SOPPED
SIMPER	SLEWED	SNATCH	SOPPER
SIMPLE	SLICED	SNEEZE	SORBET
SIMPLY	SLICER	SNIFFY	SORDID
SINEWY	SLIDER	SNIPER	SORELY
SINFUL	SLIGHT	SNIPPY	SOREST
SINGED	SLINKY	SNITCH	SORREL
SINGER	SLIPPY	SNIVEL	SORROW

SORTED	SPOUSE	STATUE	STRESS
SORTER	SPRAIN	STATUS	STREWN
SORTIE	SPRANG	STAVED	STRIAE
SOUGHT	SPRAWL	STAVES	STRICT
SOURCE	SPREAD	STAYED	STRIDE
SOURER	SPRENT	STAYER	STRIFE
SOURLY	SPRING	STAY-IN	STRIKE
SOUSED	SPRINT	STEADY	STRING
SOVIET	SPRITE	STEAMY	STRIPE
SOWING	SPROUT	STEELY	STRIVE
SOZZLE	SPRUCE	STENCH	STRODE
SPACED	SPRUNG	STEPPE	STROKE
SPACER	SPRYER	STEREO	STROLL
SPADED	SPUNKY	STEWED	STRONG
SPADIX	SPURGE	STICKY	STROVE
SPARED	SPURRY	STIFLE	STRUCK
SPARER	SPYING	STIGMA	STRUNG
SPARES	SPYISM	STILLY	STUBBY
SPARKS	SQUALL	STINGO	STUCCO
SPARRY	SQUARE	STINGY	STUDIO
SPARSE	SQUASH	STITCH	STUFFY
SPAVIN	SQUAWK	STOCKY	STUMER
SPECIE	SQUEAK	STODGE	STUMPS
SPECKY	SQUEAL	STODGY	STUMPY
SPEECH	SQUILL	STOKED	STUPID
SPEEDY	SQUINT	STOKER	STUPOR
SPENCE	SQUIRE	STOLEN	STURDY
SPHERE	SQUIRM	STOLID	STYLAR
SPHINX	SQUIRT	STONED	STYLED
SPICED	STABLE	STONER	STYLET
SPIDER	STABLY	STOOGE	STYLUS
SPIGOT	STAGED	STORED	STYMIE
SPIKED	STAGER	STORER	STYRAX
SPINAL	STAGEY	STORES	SUABLE
SPINED	STAKED	STOREY	SUBDUE
SPINET	STALAG	STORMY	SUBITO
SPINNY	STALER	STOVED	SUBLET
SPIRAL	STALKY	STOVER	SUBMIT
SPIRED	STAMEN	STOWED	SUBORN
SPIRIT	STANCE	STOWER	SUBTIL
SPITED	STANCH	STRAFE	SUBTLE
SPLASH	STANZA	STRAIN	SUBTLY
SPLEEN	STAPLE	STRAIT	SUBURB
SPLICE	STARCH	STRAKE	SUBWAY
SPLINE	STARED	STRAND	SUCKED
SPOKEN	STARER	STRASS	SUCKER
SPONGE	STARRY	STRATA	SUCKLE
SPONGY	STARVE	STRAWY	SUDDEN
SPOOKY	STATED	STREAK	SUEING
SPOONY	STATER	STREAM	SUFFER
SPOTTY	STATIC	STREET	SUFFIX

SUGARY	SWERVE	TANGLE	TEASER
SUITED	SWINGE	TANGLY	TEA-SET
SUITOR	SWIPED	TANKED	TEA-URN
SUIVEZ	SWIPES	TANKER	TEDIUM
SULKED	SWITCH	TANNED	TEEING
SULLEN	SWIVEL	TANNER	TEEMED
SULTAN	SYLVAN	TANNIC	TEETER
SULTRY	SYMBOL	TANNIN	TEETHE
SUMMED	SYNDIC	TANNOY	TELLER
SUMMER	SYNTAX	TAOISM	TEMPER
SUMMIT	SYPHON	TAOIST	TEMPLE
SUMMON	SYRIAC	TAPING	TENACE
SUNBOW	SYRIAN	TAPPED	TENANT
SUNDAE	SYRINX	TAPPER	TENDED
SUNDAY	SYRUPY	TAPPET	TENDER
SUNDER	SYSTEM	TARGET	TENDON
SUN-DEW		TARIFF	TENNER
SUN-DOG		TARMAC	TENNIS
SUNDRY	T—6	TARPON	TENSED
SUN-GOD	TABARD	TARSAL	TENSER
SUN-HAT	TABBED	TARSIA	TENTED
SUNKEN	TABLED	TARSUS	TENTER
SUNLIT	TABLET	TARTAN	TENURE
SUNNED	TABOUR	TARTAR	TENUTO
SUNSET	TACKED	TARTLY	TEPEFY
SUN-TAN	TACKER	TASKED	TERCET
SUPERB	TACKLE	TASKER	TERMED
SUPINE	TACTIC	TASSEL	TERMLY
SUPPED	TAGGED	TASTED	TERROR
SUPPER	TAGGER	TASTER	TESTED
SUPPLE	TAG-RAG	TATLER	TESTER
SUPPLY	TAILED	TATTED	TETCHY
SURELY	TAILOR	TATTER	TETHER
SUREST	TAKE-IN	TATTLE	TETRAD
SURETY	TAKING	TATTOO	TEUTON
SURGED	TALBOT	TAUGHT	THALER
SURREY	TALCKY	TAURUS	THALIA
SURTAX	TALENT	TAUTEN	THANKS
SURVEY	TALKED	TAUTER	THATCH
SUTLER	TALKER	TAVERN	THAWED
SUTTEE	TALLER	TAWDRY	THEBAN
SUTURE	TALLOW	TAWING	THEIRS
SVELTE	TALMUD	TAXIED	THEISM
SWAMPY	TAMELY	TAXING	THEIST
SWANKY	TAMEST	TCHICK	THENAR
SWARDY	TAMPED	TEA-CUP	THENCE
SWARMY	TAMPER	TEAMED	THEORY
SWATCH	TAMPON	TEA-POT	THESIS
SWATHE	TAM-TAM	TEARER	THETIS
SWAYED	TANDEM	TEASED	THEWED
SWEATY	TANGED	TEASEL	THIEVE

THINLY	TIMELY	TONGUE	TRASHY
THIRST	TIMING	TONING	TRAUMA
THIRTY	TIMIST	TONISH	TRAVEL
THORNY	TINDER	TONSIL	TREATY
THORPE	TINGED	TOOLED	TREBLE
THOUGH	TINGLE	TOOTED	TREMOR
THRALL	TINIER	TOOTER	TRENCH
THRASH	TINKER	TOOTHY	TRENDY
THREAD	TINKLE	TOOTLE	TREPAN
THREAT	TINMAN	TOO-TOO	TREPID
THRESH	TINNED	TOP-DOG	TRIBAL
THRICE	TINNER	TOP-HAT	TRICAR
THRIFT	TIN-POT	TOPMAN	TRICKY
THRILL	TINSEL	TOPPED	TRICOT
THRIVE	TINTED	TOPPER	TRIFID
THROAT	TINTER	TOPPLE	TRIFLE
THRONE	TIP-CAT	TORERO	TRILBY
THRONG	TIP-OFF	TORPID	TRIMLY
THROVE	TIPPED	TORPOR	TRINAL
THROWN	TIPPET	TORQUE	TRIODE
THRUSH	TIPPLE	TORRID	TRIPLE
THRUST	TIP-TOE	TOSSED	TRIPLY
THWACK	TIP-TOP	TOSSER	TRIPOD
THWART	TIRADE	TOSS-UP	TRIPOS
THYMOL	TIRING	TOTING	TRISTE
THYMUS	TISANE	TOTTED	TRITON
TIBIAL	TISSUE	TOTTER	TRIUNE
TICKED	TIT-BIT	TOUCAN	TRIVET
TICKER	TITHED	TOUCHY	TROIKA
TICKET	TITLED	TOUPEE	TROJAN
TICKLE	TITTER	TOURED	TROLLY
TICKLY	TITTUP	TOUSLE	TROPHY
TIC-TAC	TOCSIN	TOUTED	TROPIC
TIDIED	TODDLE	TOUTER	TROPPO
TIDIER	TOE-CAP	TOWAGE	TROUGH
TIDILY	TOEING	TOWARD	TROUPE
TIEING	TOFFEE	TOWERY	TROWEL
TIE-PIN	TOGGED	TOWING	TRUANT
TIERCE	TOGGLE	TOWSER	TRUDGE
TIE-WIG	TOILED	TOY-BOX	TRUEST
TIFFIN	TOILER	TOYING	TRUISM
TIGHTS	TOILET	TOYISH	TRUSTY
TILERY	TOLEDO	TOY-MAN	TRYING
TILING	TOLLED	TRACED	TRY-OUT
TILLED	TOLLER	TRACER	TSETSE
TILLER	TOMATO	TRADED	TUBAGE
TILTED	TOMBED	TRADER	TUBBED
TILTER	TOMBOY	TRAGIC	TUBING
TIMBAL	TOM-CAT	TRANCE	TUCKED
TIMBER	TOM-TIT	TRAPES	TUCKER
TIMBRE	TOMTOM	TRAPPY	TUFFET

TUFTED	TYRIAN	UNGIRT	UNSEAT
TUGGED		UNGLUE	UNSEEN
TUGGER	U—6	UNGOWN	UNSENT
TUMBLE	UBIETY	UNGUAL	UNSEWN
TUMOUR	UGLIER	UNHAND	UNSHED
TUMULI	UGLIFY	UNHANG	UNSHOD
TUMULT	UGLILY	UNHASP	UNSHOT
TUNDRA	ULLAGE	UNHEWN	UNSHUT
TUNE-IN	ULSTER	UNHOLY	UNSOLD
TUNING	ULTIMO	UNHOOK	UNSOWN
TUNNED	UMBRAL	UNHUNG	UNSPIN
TUNNEL	UMLAUT	UNHURT	UNSTOP
TUPPED	UMPIRE	UNIPED	UNSUNG
TURBAN	UNABLE	UNIQUE	UNSURE
TURBID	UNAWED	UNISON	UNTACK
TURBOT	UNBEND	UNITED	UNTAME
TUREEN	UNBENT	UNITER	UNTIDY
TURFED	UNBIND	UNJUST	UNTIED
TURGID	UNBOLT	UNKEPT	UNTOLD
TURKEY	UNBORN	UNKIND	UNTORN
TURNED	UNBRED	UNKNOT	UNTROD
TURNER	UNCAGE	UNLACE	UNTRUE
TURNIP	UNCASE	UNLAID	UNTUCK
TURN-UP	UNCATE	UNLASH	UNTUNE
TURRET	UNCIAL	UNLENT	UNUSED
TURTLE	UNCLAD	UNLESS	UNVEIL
TUSCAN	UNCLOG	UNLIKE	UNWARY
TUSKED	UNCOIL	UNLOAD	UNWELL
TUSKER	UNCORD	UNLOCK	UNWEPT
TUSSLE	UNCORK	UNMADE	UNWIND
TU-WHIT	UNCURL	UNMAKE	UNWIRE
TU-WHOO	UNDATE	UNMASK	UNWISE
TUXEDO	UNDIES	UNOWED	UNWORN
TWEENY	UNDINE	UNPACK	UNWRAP
TWELVE	UNDOCK	UNPAID	UNYOKE
TWENTY	UNDOER	UNPICK	UPBEAR
TWIGGY	UNDONE	UNPROP	UPCAST
TWINED	UNDULY	UNREAD	UPHILL
TWINER	UNEASE	UNREAL	UPHOLD
TWINGE	UNEASY	UNREST	UPKEEP
TWITCH	UNEVEN	UNRIPE	UPLAND
TWO-PLY	UNFAIR	UNROBE	UPLEAN
T'WOULD	UNFEED	UNROLL	UPLIFT
TWO-WAY	UNFELT	UNROOF	UP-LINE
TYBURN	UNFOLD	UNROOT	UPMOST
TYCOON	UNFREE	UNROPE	UPPING
TYPHUS	UNFURL	UNRULY	UPPISH
TYPIFY	UNGEAR	UNSAFE	UPRISE
TYPING	UNGILD	UNSAID	UPROAR
TYPIST	UNGILT	UNSEAL	UPROOT
TYRANT	UNGIRD	UNSEAM	UPRUSH

UPSHOT	VECTOR	VINERY	WAITED
UPSIDE	VEERED	VINOUS	WAITER
UPTAKE	VEILED	VINTED	WAIVED
UPTURN	VEINED	VINTRY	WAIVER
UPWARD	VELLUM	VIOLET	WAKING
URAEUS	VELOCE	VIOLIN	WALKED
URANIA	VELOUR	VIRAGO	WALKER
URANIC	VELVET	VIRGIN	WALLAH
URANUS	VENDED	VIRILE	WALLED
URBANE	VENDEE	VIROUS	WALLER
URCHIN	VENDER	VIRTUE	WALLET
URGENT	VENDOR	VISAGE	WALLOP
URGING	VENDUE	VISCID	WALLOW
URSINE	VENEER	VISHNU	WALNUT
USABLE	VENERY	VIZIER	WALRUS
USANCE	VENIAL	VISION	WAMBLE
USEFUL	VENITE	VISUAL	WAMPUM
USURER	VENTED	VITALS	WANDER
UTERUS	VERBAL	VIVACE	WANGLE
UTMOST	VERGED	VIVIFY	WANING
UTOPIA	VERGER	VIZARD	WANTED
UVULAR	VERIFY	VOICED	WANTER
V—6	VERILY	VOIDED	WANTON
VACANT	VERITY	VOIDER	WARBLE
VACATE	VERMIN	VOLANT	WAR-CRY
VACUUM	VERNAL	VOLLEY	WARDED
VAGARY	VERSED	VOLUME	WARDEN
VAGUER	VERSER	VOODOO	WARDER
VAINER	VERSUS	VORTEX	WARIER
VAINLY	VERTEX	VOTARY	WARILY
VALISE	VERVET	VOTING	WARMER
VALLEY	VESPER	VOTIVE	WARMLY
VALLUM	VESSEL	VOWING	WARMTH
VALOUR	VESTAL	VOYAGE	WARNED
VALUED	VESTED	VULCAN	WARPED
VALUER	VESTRY	VULGAR	WARREN
VALVED	VETOED		WASHED
VAMPED	VETTED	W—6	WASHER
VAMPER	VEXING	WADDED	WASH-UP
VANDAL	VIABLE	WADDLE	WASTED
VANISH	VIANDS	WADING	WASTER
VANITY	VICTIM	WAFERY	WATERY
VAN-MAN	VICTOR	WAFFLE	WATTLE
VAPOUR	VICUNA	WAFTED	WAVING
VARIED	VIEWED	WAFTER	WAX-END
VARIER	VIEWER	WAGGED	WAXIER
VARLET	VIGOUR	WAGGLE	WAXING
VASSAL	VIKING	WAGGON	WAYLAY
VASTER	VILELY	WAGING	WEAKEN
VASTLY	VILEST	WAILED	WEAKER
VAULTY	VILIFY	WAILER	WEAKLY

WEALTH	WIDELY	WOMBAT	YOICKS
WEANED	WIDEST	WONDER	YOKING
WEAPON	WIELDY	WONTED	YOLKED
WEARER	WIFELY	WOODED	YONDER
WEASEL	WIGEON	WOODEN	YORKER
WEAVER	WIGGED	WOOING	YOWLED
WEAZEN	WIGGLE	WOOLLY	
WEBBED	WIGWAM	WORDED	Z—6
WEB-EYE	WILDER	WORKED	ZEALOT
WEDDED	WILDLY	WORKER	ZENANA
WEDGED	WILFUL	WORMED	ZENITH
WEEDED	WILIER	WORSEN	ZEPHYR
WEEDER	WILILY	WORTHY	ZIG-ZAG
WEEKLY	WILLED	WOUNDY	ZILLAH
WEEPER	WILLER	WRAITH	ZINNIA
WEEVER	WILLOW	WREATH	ZIPPED
WEEVIL	WILTED	WRENCH	ZIRCON
WEIGHT	WIMPLE	WRETCH	ZITHER
WELDED	WINCED	WRIGHT	ZODIAC
WELDER	WINCER	WRITER	ZONATE
WELKIN	WINCEY	WRITHE	
WELLED	WINDED	WYVERN	A—7
WELTED	WINDER		ABANDON
WELTER	WINDLE	X—6	ABASHED
WENDED	WINDOW	XANADU	ABASING
WET-BOB	WIND-UP	XERXES	ABATING
WETHER	WINGED	X-RAYED	ABDOMEN
WETTER	WINGER		ABETTED
WHALER	WINKED	Y—6	ABETTER
WHEEZE	WINKER	YAMMER	ABIDING
WHEEZY	WINKLE	YANKED	ABIGAIL
WHENCE	WINNER	YANKEE	ABILITY
WHERRY	WINNOW	YAPPED	ABJURED
WHILED	WINTRY	YAPPER	ABJURER
WHILES	WIPING	YARNED	ABOLISH
WHILOM	WIRING	YARROW	ABRADED
WHILST	WIZARD	YAWING	ABREAST
WHIMSY	WISDOM	YAWLED	ABRIDGE
WHINED	WISELY	YAWNED	ABROACH
WHINER	WISEST	YCLEPT	ABSCESS
WHINNY	WISHED	YEANED	ABSCOND
WHIPPY	WISHER	YEARLY	ABSENCE
WHISKY	WISTLY	YEASTY	ABSINTH
WHITEN	WITHAL	YELLED	ABSOLVE
WHITER	WITHER	YELLOW	ABSTAIN
WHITES	WITHIN	YELPED	ABUSING
WHOLLY	WITTED	YELPER	ABUSIVE
WHOMSO	WOBBLE	YEOMAN	ABUTTAL
WICKED	WOBBLY	YES-MAN	ABUTTED
WICKER	WOEFUL	YESTER	ABYSMAL
WICKET	WOLVES	YOGISM	ABYSSAL

ACADEMY	ADORNED	A-LA-MORT	AMMETER
ACCEDED	ADRENAL	ALARMED	AMMONAL
ACCLAIM	ADULATE	ALASKAN	AMMONIA
ACCOUNT	ADVANCE	ALBUMEN	AMNESIA
ACCRETE	ADVERSE	ALCALDE	AMNESTY
ACCRUED	ADVISED	ALCHEMY	AMONGST
ACCUSED	ADVISOR	ALCOHOL	AMORIST
ACCUSER	AEOLIAN	ALEMBIC	AMOROUS
ACETATE	AERATED	ALENGTH	AMPHORA
ACETIFY	AERATOR	ALERTLY	AMPLEST
ACETONE	AEROBUS	ALFALFA	AMPLIFY
ACHATES	AFFABLE	ALGEBRA	AMPOULE
ACHERON	AFFABLY	ALIDADE	AMPULLA
ACHIEVE	AFFINED	ALIGNED	AMUSING
ACIDIFY	AFFIXED	ALIMENT	AMUSIVE
ACIDITY	AFFLICT	ALIMONY	AMYLOID
ACK-EMMA	AFFRONT	ALIQUOT	ANAEMIA
ACOLYTE	AFRICAN	ALLAYED	ANAEMIC
ACONITE	AGAINST	ALLEGED	ANAGRAM
ACQUIRE	AGELESS	ALLEGRO	ANALOGY
ACREAGE	AGELONG	ALLERGY	ANALYSE
ACROBAT	AGENDUM	ALLOWED	ANALYST
ACTABLE	AGGRESS	ALLOYED	ANARCHY
ACTRESS	AGILELY	ALLUDED	ANATOMY
ACTUARY	AGILITY	ALLURED	ANCHOVY
ACTUATE	AGITATE	ALLUVIA	ANCIENT
ACUSHLA	AGITATO	ALLYING	ANDANTE
ACUTELY	AGNOMEN	ALMANAC	ANDIRON
ADAMANT	AGONIZE	ALMONER	ANEMONE
ADAPTED	AGROUND	ALMONRY	ANEROID
ADAPTER	AIDLESS	ALMSMAN	ANEURIN
ADDENDA	AILERON	ALREADY	ANGELIC
ADDRESS	AILMENT	ALSATIA	ANGELUS
ADDUCED	AIMLESS	ALTERED	ANGERED
ADDUCER	AIR-BASE	ALTHAEA	ANGEVIN
ADELPHI	AIR-BATH	ALUMNUS	ANGLICE
ADENOID	AIR-CELL	ALYSSUM	ANGLING
ADHERED	AIR-HOLE	AMALGAM	ANGRILY
ADHERER	AIRLESS	AMASSED	ANGUINE
ADIPOSE	AIRLIFT	AMATEUR	ANGUISH
ADJOURN	AIR-LINE	AMATIVE	ANGULAR
ADJUDGE	AIR-LOCK	AMATORY	ANILINE
ADJUNCT	AIR-MAIL	AMAZING	ANILITY
ADJURED	AIR-PORT	AMBAGES	ANIMATE
ADJURER	AIR-PUMP	AMBIENT	ANIMISM
ADMIRAL	AIR-RAID	AMBLING	ANIMIST
ADMIRED	AIR-SHIP	AMENDED	ANISEED
ADMIRER	AIR-TRAP	AMENITY	ANNATES
ADONAIS	AIR-WAYS	AMERCED	ANNEXED
ADOPTED	ALADDIN	AMIABLE	ANNOYED
ADORING	A-LA-MODE	AMIABLY	ANNUITY

ANNULAR	ARBUTUS	ASSAGAI	AVARICE
ANNULET	ARCADED	ASSAULT	AVENGED
ANODYNE	ARCADIA	ASSAYED	AVENGER
ANOMALY	ARCANUM	ASSAYER	AVERAGE
ANOSMIA	ARCHAIC	ASSEGAI	AVERRED
ANOTHER	ARCHERY	ASSUAGE	AVERTED
ANTACID	ARCHING	ASSUMED	AVIATOR
ANT-BEAR	ARCHWAY	ASSURED	AVIDITY
ANTENNA	ARC-LAMP	ASSURER	AVOCADO
ANT-HILL	ARDENCY	ASTATIC	AVOIDED
ANTHONY	ARDUOUS	ASTOUND	AVOWING
ANTHRAX	ARENOSE	ASTRIDE	AWAITED
ANTIQUE	ARIDITY	ASUNDER	AWAKING
ANTI-RED	ARIGHTS	ATAVISM	AWARDED
ANTI-LIKE	ARIPPLE	ATELIER	AWESOME
ANT-LION	ARISING	ATHEISM	AWFULLY
ANTONYM	ARMHOLE	ATHEIST	AWKWARD
ANXIETY	ARMIGER	ATHIRST	AWNLESS
ANXIOUS	ARMLESS	ATHLETE	AXIALLY
ANYBODY	ARMOIRE	ATHWART	AXLE-BOX
ANYWISE	ARMOURY	ATOMIST	AXLE-PIN
APANAGE	AROUSAL	ATOMIZE	AXOLOTL
APELIKE	AROUSED	ATONING	
APHASIA	ARRAIGN	ATROPHY	B—7
APHONIA	ARRANGE	ATTABOY	BABBLED
APISHLY	ARRAYED	ATTACHE	BABBLER
APOCOPE	ARRIVAL	ATTEMPT	BABYISH
APOGEAN	ARSENAL	ATTIRED	BABYISM
APOLOGY	ARSENIC	ATTRACT	BABYLON
APOSTLE	ARTICLE	ATTUNED	BACCHIC
APPAREL	ARTISAN	AUBERGE	BACCHUS
APPEASE	ARTISTE	AUCTION	BACILLI
APPLAUD	ARTLESS	AUDIBLE	BACKEND
APPLIED	ASCETIC	AUDIBLY	BACKING
APPOINT	ASCRIBE	AUDITED	BACK-LOG
APPRISE	ASEPSIS	AUDITOR	BADNESS
APPRIZE	ASEPTIC	AUGMENT	BAFFLED
APPROVE	ASEXUAL	AUGURED	BAFFLER
APRICOT	ASHAMED	AURALLY	BAGGAGE
APRONED	ASHIVER	AUREATE	BAGGING
APROPOS	ASH-TRAY	AUREOLA	BAGPIPE
APSIDAL	ASIATIC	AUREOLE	BAILAGE
APTNESS	ASININE	AURICLE	BAILIFF
AQUARIA	ASKANCE	AUROCHS	BAILING
AQUATIC	ASPERSE	AUSTERE	BAITING
AQUEOUS	ASPHALT	AUSTRAL	BALANCE
ARABIAN	ASPIRED	AUTOBUS	BALCONY
ARABIST	ASPIRIN	AUTOCAR	BALDEST
ARACHIS	ASPRAWL	AUTONYM	BALDISH
ARAMAIC	ASPROUT	AUTOPSY	BALDRIC
ARBITER	ASQUINT	AVAILED	BALEFUL

BALKING	BATH-BUN	BEGONIA	BESPEAK
BALLAST	BATHING	BEGORED	BESPOKE
BALL-BOY	BATSMAN	BEGRIME	BESTIAL
BALLOON	BATTELS	BEGUILE	BESTILL
BALMILY	BATTERY	BEGUINE	BESTING
BALMING	BATTING	BEHAVED	BEST-MAN
BAMBINO	BATTLED	BEHOVED	BESTREW
BANBURY	BATTLER	BEJEWEL	BETAKEN
BANDAGE	BAULKED	BEKNOWN	BETHINK
BANDANA	BAUXITE	BELACED	BETHUMB
BANDBOX	BAWDILY	BELATED	BETHUMP
BANDEAU	BAWLING	BELAYED	BETIDED
BANDIED	BAYONET	BELCHED	BETIMES
BANDING	BAY-TREE	BELCHER	BETITLE
BAND-SAW	BAYWOOD	BELGIAN	BETOKEN
BANEFUL	BEACHED	BELIEVE	BETROTH
BANGING	BEADING	BELL-HOP	BETTING
BANKING	BEAMING	BELLIED	BETWEEN
BANNING	BEARDED	BELLING	BETWIXT
BANNOCK	BEARING	BELL-MAN	BEWITCH
BANQUET	BEARISH	BELLOWS	BEZIQUE
BANSHEE	BEAR-PIT	BELOVED	BIASING
BANTING	BEASTLY	BELTING	BIAXIAL
BAPTISM	BEATIFY	BELYING	BICYCLE
BAPTIST	BEATING	BEMAZED	BIDDING
BAPTIZE	BECAUSE	BEMIRED	BIFOCAL
BARBARY	BECLOUD	BEMUSED	BIGGEST
BARBATE	BEDDING	BENCHER	BIGGISH
BARDISM	BEDEVIL	BENDING	BIGOTED
BARGAIN	BEDEWED	BENEATH	BIGOTRY
BARGING	BED-GOWN	BENEFIT	BILGING
BARKING	BED-MATE	BENGALI	BILIOUS
BARMAID	BEDOUIN	BENISON	BILKING
BARMIER	BED-POST	BENZENE	BILLING
BARNABY	BED-REST	BENZOIN	BILLION
BARN-OWL	BED-ROCK	BEPAINT	BILLOWY
BARONET	BEDROOM	BEQUEST	BILTONG
BAROQUE	BEDSIDE	BERATED	BINDING
BARRACK	BED-SORE	BEREAVE	BIOLOGY
BARRAGE	BED-TICK	BERHYME	BIOTICS
BARRIER	BEDTIME	BERRIED	BIPEDAL
BARRING	BEDWARF	BERSERK	BIPLANE
BASENJI	BEEF-TEA	BERTHED	BIRCHED
BASHFUL	BEE-HIVE	BESEECH	BIRDMAN
BASHING	BEE-LINE	BESHAME	BIRETTA
BASILIC	BEE-MOTH	BESHONE	BISCUIT
BASKING	BEESWAX	BESHREW	BISMUTH
BASSOON	BEETLED	BESIDES	BITTERN
BASTARD	BEGGARY	BESIEGE	BITUMEN
BASTING	BEGGING	BESMEAR	BIVALVE
BASTION	BEGLOOM	BESMOKE	BIVOUAC

BIZARRE	BLUCHER	BOOKLET	BRAMBLY
BLABBED	BLUE-CAP	BOOKMAN	BRANCHY
BLABBER	BLUEING	BOOMING	BRANDED
BLACKED	BLUFFED	BOORISH	BRASSIE
BLACKEN	BLUFFER	BOOSTED	BRAVADO
BLACKER	BLUFFLY	BOOSTER	BRAVELY
BLACKLY	BLUNDER	BOOT-LEG	BRAVERY
BLADDER	BLUNGER	BOOZING	BRAVEST
BLAMING	BLUNTED	BORACIC	BRAVING
BLANDLY	BLUNTER	BOREDOM	BRAVURA
BLANKET	BLUNTLY	BOROUGH	BRAWLED
BLANKLY	BLURRED	BORSTAL	BRAWLER
BLARING	BLURTED	BOSOMED	BRAYING
BLARNEY	BLUSHED	BOSSING	BRAZIER
BLASTED	BLUSTER	BOSWELL	BRAZING
BLASTER	BOARDED	BOTANIC	BREADTH
BLATANT	BOARDER	BOTCHED	BREAKER
BLATHER	BOARISH	BOTCHER	BREATHE
BLATTER	BOASTED	BOTTLED	BREEDER
BLAZING	BOASTER	BOTTLER	BREVITY
BLEAKER	BOAT-CAR	BOUDOIR	BREWERY
BLEAKLY	BOAT-FLY	BOULDER	BREWING
BLEATED	BOATFUL	BOULTER	BRIBERY
BLEMISH	BOATING	BOUNCED	BRIBING
BLENDED	BOATMAN	BOUNCER	BRICKED
BLENDER	BOBADIL	BOUNDED	BRIDGED
BLESSED	BOBBING	BOUNDEN	BRIDLED
BLETHER	BOBBISH	BOUNDER	BRIDLER
BLIGHTY	BOB-SLED	BOUQUET	BRIEFED
BLINDED	BOB-STAY	BOURBON	BRIEFER
BLINDER	BOBTAIL	BOWLESS	BRIEFLY
BLINDLY	BODEFUL	BOWLINE	BRIGADE
BLINKED	BOGGLED	BOWLING	BRIGAND
BLISTER	BOILING	BOW-SHOT	BRIMFUL
BLOATED	BOLDEST	BOX-CALF	BRIMMED
BLOATER	BOLLARD	BOX-COAT	BRIMMER
BLOCKED	BOLLING	BOX-IRON	BRINDLE
BLONDIN	BOLOGNA	BOX-KITE	BRINISH
BLOODED	BOLSTER	BOX-WOOD	BRIOCHE
BLOOMED	BOLTING	BOYCOTT	BRISKER
BLOOMER	BOMBARD	BOYHOOD	BRISKET
BLOSSOM	BOMBAST	BRACING	BRISKLY
BLOTCHY	BOMBING	BRACKEN	BRISTLE
BLOTTED	BONANZA	BRACKET	BRISTLY
BLOTTER	BONDAGE	BRAGGED	BRISTOL
BLOWFLY	BONDING	BRAIDED	BRITISH
BLOW-GUN	BONDMAN	BRAILLE	BRITTLE
BLOWING	BONFIRE	BRAINED	BROADEN
BLOW-OUT	BONNILY	BRAISED	BROADER
BLOWZED	BOOKING	BRAKING	BROADLY
BLUBBER	BOOKISH	BRAMBLE	BROCADE

BROILED	BULRUSH	BUZZARD	CALYPSO
BROILER	BULWARK	BUZZING	CAMBIUM
BROKAGE	BUMMALO	BUZZ-SAW	CAMBRIC
BROKING	BUMPING	BY-AND-BY	CAMELOT
BROMIDE	BUMPKIN	BYRONIC	CAMORRA
BRONZED	BUNCHED		CAMPHOR
BROODED	BUNDLED		CAMPING
BROOKED	BUNGLED	C—7	CAMPION
BROTHER	BUNGLER	CABARET	CANDIED
BROUGHT	BUNKING	CABBAGE	CANDOUR
BROWNED	BUNTING	CABBALA	CANASTA
BROWNER	BUOYAGE	CAB-FARE	CANNERY
BROWNIE	BUOYANT	CABINED	CANNING
BROWSED	BUOYING	CABINET	CANTATA
BRUISED	BURDOCK	CABLING	CANTEEN
BRUISER	BURETTE	CABOOSE	CANTING
BRUMOUS	BURGEON	CAB-RANK	CANVASS
BRUSHED	BURGESS	CA'CANNY	CAPABLE
BRUSQUE	BURGHAL	CACKLED	CAPABLY
BRUTIFY	BURGHER	CACKLER	CAP-A-PIE
BRUTISH	BURGLAR	CADDISH	CAPELIN
BRUTISM	BURGLED	CADENCE	CAPERED
BUBBLED	BURLIER	CADENCY	CAPERER
BUBONIC	BURLING	CADENZA	CAPITAL
BUCKING	BURMESE	CADGING	CAPITAN
BUCKISH	BURNING	CAESURA	CAPITOL
BUCKISM	BURNISH	CAFFEIN	CAPORAL
BUCKLED	BURNOUS	CAITIFF	CAPPING
BUCKLER	BURRING	CAJOLED	CAPRICE
BUCKRAM	BURSARY	CAJOLER	CAPRINE
BUCKSAW	BURTHEN	CALCIFY	CAPROIC
BUCOLIC	BURYING	CALCINE	CAPSIZE
BUDDING	BUSH-CAT	CALCIUM	CAPSTAN
BUDGING	BUSHIDO	CALDRON	CAPSULE
BUDLESS	BUSHMAN	CALENDS	CAPTAIN
BUFFALO	BUSKING	CALIBAN	CAPTION
BUFFING	BUS-STOP	CALIBRE	CAPTIVE
BUFFOON	BUSTARD	CALIPER	CAPTURE
BUGBEAR	BUSTLED	CALKING	CAPULET
BUILT-UP	BUSTLER	CALL-BOY	CARAMEL
BULBOUS	BUSYING	CALLING	CARAVAN
BULGING	BUTCHER	CALLOUS	CARAVEL
BULKIER	BUTLERY	CALMING	CARAWAY
BULKING	BUTMENT	CALOMEL	CARBIDE
BULLACE	BUTT-END	CALORIC	CARBINE
BULL-DOG	BUTTERY	CALORIE	CARCASE
BULLIED	BUTTING	CALTROP	CARDIAC
BULLING	BUTTOCK	CALUMET	CARDING
BULLION	BUTTONS	CALUMNY	CARDOON
BULLOCK	BUXOMLY	CALVARY	CAREFUL
BULL-PUP	BUYABLE	CALVING	CARIBOU

CARIOUS	CAVE-MAN	CHARING	CHILLED
CARKING	CAVIARE	CHARIOT	CHILLER
CARLINE	CAYENNE	CHARITY	CHIMNEY
CARMINE	CEASING	CHARLEY	CHINDIT
CARNAGE	CEDARED	CHARMED	CHINESE
CAROTID	CEDILLA	CHARMER	CHINKED
CAROUSE	CEILING	CHARNEL	CHIP-HAT
CARPING	CELLIST	CHARRED	CHIPPED
CARRIED	CENSING	CHARTED	CHIPPER
CARRIER	CENSURE	CHARTER	CHIRPED
CARRION	CENTAUR	CHASING	CHIRPER
CARROTY	CENTAVO	CHASSIS	CHIRRED
CARTAGE	CENTIME	CHASTEN	CHIRRUP
CARTING	CENTRAL	CHATEAU	CHITTER
CARTOON	CENTRED	CHATTED	CHLORAL
CARVING	CENTURY	CHATTEL	CHLORIC
CASCADE	CERAMIC	CHATTER	CHOIRED
CASCARA	CERTAIN	CHEAPEN	CHOKING
CASE-LAW	CERTIFY	CHEAPER	CHOLERA
CASEMAN	CESSION	CHEAPLY	CHOOSER
CASHIER	CESS-PIT	CHEATED	CHOPPED
CASHING	CHABLIS	CHEATER	CHOPPER
CASSAVA	CHAFFED	CHECKED	CHORALE
CASSOCK	CHAFFER	CHECKER	CHORTLE
CASTING	CHAFING	CHEDDAR	CHOWDER
CASTLED	CHAGRIN	CHEEKED	CHRONIC
CAST-OFF	CHAINED	CHEEPED	CHUCKED
CASUIST	CHAIRED	CHEERED	CHUCKLE
CATALAN	CHALDEE	CHEERIO	CHUMMED
CATARRH	CHALICE	CHEETAH	CHURCHY
CAT-CALL	CHALLIS	CHELSEA	CHURNED
CATCHER	CHAMBER	CHEMISE	CHURRED
CATCHUP	CHAMOIS	CHEMIST	CINDERY
CATERAN	CHAMPED	CHEQUER	CIRCEAN
CATERED	CHANCED	CHERISH	CIRCLED
CATERER	CHANCEL	CHEROOT	CIRCLET
CAT-EYED	CHANGED	CHERVIL	CIRCUIT
CAT-FISH	CHANGER	CHESTED	CISTERN
CATHEAD	CHANNEL	CHEVIOT	CITABLE
CATHODE	CHANTED	CHEVRON	CITADEL
CAT-LIKE	CHANTER	CHEWING	CITIZEN
CAT-MINT	CHANTRY	CHIANTI	CITRATE
CAT'S-EYE	CHAOTIC	CHICANE	CITRINE
CAT'S-PAW	CHAPLET	CHICKEN	CIVILLY
CATTISH	CHAPMAN	CHICORY	CIVVIES
CAUDATE	CHAPPED	CHIDING	CLACKED
CAULKED	CHAPTER	CHIEFLY	CLAIMED
CAUSING	CHARADE	CHIFFON	CLAIMER
CAUSTIC	CHARGED	CHIGNON	CLAMANT
CAUTION	CHARGER	CHILEAN	CLAMBER
CAVALRY	CHARILY	CHILIAD	CLAMMED

CLAMOUR	CLOSING	CODFISH	COMPLEX
CLAMPED	CLOSURE	CODICIL	COMPORT
CLAMPER	CLOTHED	CODLING	COMPOSE
CLANGED	CLOTTED	COERCED	COMPOST
CLANKED	CLOUDED	COEXIST	COMPOTE
CLAP-NET	CLOUTED	COGENCY	COMPUTE
CLAPPED	CLOWNED	COGNATE	COMRADE
CLAPPER	CLUBBED	COHABIT	CONCAVE
CLARIFY	CLUBBER	COHERED	CONCEAL
CLARION	CLUB-LAW	COHERER	CONCEDE
CLARITY	CLUB-MAN	COIFFED	CONCEIT
CLASHED	CLUCKED	COILING	CONCEPT
CLASPED	CLUMBER	COINAGE	CONCERN
CLASPER	CLUMPED	COINING	CONCERT
CLASSED	CLUSTER	COJUROR	CONCISE
CLASSIC	CLUTTER	COLDEST	CONCOCT
CLATTER	COACHED	COLDISH	CONCORD
CLAVIER	COACTED	COLICKY	CONCUSS
CLAWING	COAGENT	COLITIS	CONDEMN
CLAYING	COAL-BED	COLLATE	CONDIGN
CLAYISH	COAL-BOX	COLLECT	CONDOLE
CLAY-PIT	COAL-GAS	COLLEEN	CONDONE
CLEANED	COALING	COLLEGE	CONDUCE
CLEANER	COALMAN	COLLIDE	CONDUCT
CLEANLY	COAL-PIT	COLLIER	CONDUIT
CLEANSE	COAL-TAR	COLLOID	CONFECT
CLEAN-UP	COAL-TIT	COLLUDE	CONFESS
CLEARED	COARSEN	COLONEL	CONFEST
CLEARER	COARSER	COLOURS	CONFIDE
CLEARLY	COASTAL	COLTISH	CONFINE
CLEAVED	COASTED	COMBINE	CONFIRM
CLEAVER	COASTER	COMBING	CONFLUX
CLEMENT	COATING	COMFORT	CONFORM
CLEMMED	CO-AXIAL	COMICAL	CONFUSE
CLICKED	COAXING	COMMAND	CONFUTE
CLIMATE	COBBING	COMMEND	CONGEAL
CLIMBED	COBBLED	COMMENT	CONGEST
CLIMBER	COBBLER	COMMERE	CONICAL
CLINKED	COCAINE	COMMODE	CONIFER
CLIPPED	COCKADE	COMMONS	CONJOIN
CLIPPER	COCKEYE	COMMUNE	CONJURE
CLIPPIE	COCKING	COMMUTE	CONJURY
CLOAKED	COCKLED	COMPACT	CONNATE
CLOBBER	COCKLER	COMPANY	CONNECT
CLOCKED	COCKNEY	COMPARE	CONNING
CLOCKER	COCKPIT	COMPART	CONNIVE
CLOGGED	COCO-NUT	COMPASS	CONNOTE
CLOGGER	COCOTTE	COMPEER	CONQUER
CLOSELY	CODDING	COMPERE	CONSENT
CLOSEST	CODDLED	COMPETE	CONSIGN
CLOSE-UP	CODEINE	COMPILE	CONSIST

CONSOLE	COROLLA	COWLING	CRINGED
CONSOLS	CORONER	COWSLIP	CRINGER
CONSORT	CORONET	COXCOMB	CRINKLE
CONSULT	CORRECT	COYNESS	CRINOID
CONSUME	CORRODE	COZENED	CRIPPLE
CONTACT	CORRUPT	COZENER	CRISPED
CONTAIN	CORSAGE	CRABBED	CRISPER
CONTEMN	CORSAIR	CRACKED	CRISPIN
CONTEND	CORSLET	CRACKER	CRISPLY
CONTENT	CORTEGE	CRACKLE	CROAKED
CONTEST	CORVINE	CRADLED	CROAKER
CONTEXT	COSHING	CRAGGED	CROCHET
CONTORT	COSIEST	CRAKING	CROCKED
CONTOUR	COSSACK	CRAMMED	CROCKET
CONTROL	COSTARD	CRAMMER	CROESUS
CONTUSE	COSTING	CRAMPED	CROFTER
CONVENE	COSTIVE	CRAMPON	CROODLE
CONVENT	COSTUME	CRANAGE	CROOKED
CONVERT	COTERIE	CRANIAL	CROONED
CONVICT	COTTAGE	CRANING	CROONER
CONVOKE	COTTONY	CRANIUM	CROPFUL
COOKERY	COUCHED	CRANKED	CROPPED
COOKING	COUGHED	CRANKLE	CROPPER
COOLEST	COULDST	CRASHED	CROQUET
COOLING	COUNCIL	CRASHER	CROSSED
COOLISH	COUNSEL	CRATING	CROSSLY
COOPING	COUNTED	CRAUNCH	CROWBAR
CO-OPTED	COUNTER	CRAVING	CROWDED
CO-PILOT	COUNTRY	CRAWLED	CROWING
COPIOUS	COUPLED	CRAWLER	CROWNED
COPPERY	COUPLER	CRAZIER	CRUCIAL
COPPICE	COUPLET	CRAZILY	CRUCIFY
COPPING	COURAGE	CRAZING	CRUDELY
COPYING	COURANT	CREAKED	CRUDEST
COPYIST	COURIER	CREAMED	CRUDITY
CORACLE	COURSED	CREASED	CRUELTY
CORBEAU	COURSER	CREATED	CRUISED
CORBEIL	COURTED	CREATOR	CRUISER
CORDAGE	COURTER	CREEPER	CRUMBED
CORDATE	COURTLY	CREMATE	CRUMBLE
CORDIAL	COUTEAU	CREMONA	CRUMBLY
CORDING	COUVADE	CRENATE	CRUMPED
CORDITE	COVERED	CREOSOL	CRUMPET
CORINTH	COVETED	CRESSET	CRUMPLE
CORKAGE	COW-BANE	CRESTED	CRUPPER
CORKING	COW-CALF	CREVICE	CRUSADE
CORK-LEG	COWERED	CRIBBED	CRUSADO
CORN-COB	COWHERD	CRICKED	CRUSHED
CORNEAL	COWHIDE	CRICKET	CRUSHER
CORNICE	COWLICK	CRIMPED	CRUSTED
CORNISH	COWLIKE	CRIMSON	CRY-BABY

CRYPTIC	CUSTODY	DASTARD	DECRIAL
CRYSTAL	CUSTOMS	DATABLE	DECRIED
CUBBING	CUT-AWAY	DAUBING	DECRIER
CUBBISH	CUTICLE	DAUNTED	DECROWN
CUBICAL	CUTLASS	DAUPHIN	DEDUCED
CUBICLE	CUTLERY	DAWDLED	DEEDING
CUBITAL	CUTTING	DAWDLER	DEEMING
CUBITED	CUT-WORM	DAWNING	DEEPEST
CUCKOLD	CYCLING	DAY-BOOK	DEEP-SEA
CUDDLED	CYCLIST	DAY-STAR	DEFACED
CUE-BALL	CYCLONE	DAY-TIME	DEFACER
CUFFING	CYCLOPS	DAY-WORK	DEFAMED
CUIRASS	CYNICAL	DAZZLED	DEFAMER
CUISINE	CYPRESS	DEAD-END	DEFAULT
CULLING	CYPRIAN	DEAD-EYE	DEFENCE
CULPRIT	CYPRIOT	DEADISH	DEFIANT
CULTURE	CZARISM	DEAD-SET	DEFICIT
CULVERT		DEALING	DEFILED
CUMULUS	**D—7**	DEANERY	DEFILER
CUNEATE	DABBING	DEAREST	DEFINED
CUNNING	DABBLED	DEATHLY	DEFINER
CUPPING	DABBLER	DEBACLE	DEFLATE
CUPRITE	DABSTER	DEBASED	DEFLECT
CURABLE	DAFTEST	DEBASER	DEFRAUD
CURACAO	DAGGLED	DEBATED	DEFUNCT
CURATOR	DAISIED	DEBATER	DEFYING
CURBING	DALLIED	DEBAUCH	DEGLAZE
CURDING	DALLIER	DEBITED	DEGRADE
CURDLED	DAMAGED	DEBOUCH	DE-ICING
CURE-ALL	DAMMING	DECADAL	DEIFIED
CURETTE	DAMNIFY	DECAGON	DEIFORM
CURIOUS	DAMNING	DECANAL	DEIGNED
CURLING	DAMOSEL	DECAPOD	DEISTIC
CURRANT	DAMPING	DECAYED	DELAYED
CURRENT	DAMPISH	DECAYER	DELAYER
CURRIED	DANCING	DECEASE	DELETED
CURRIER	DANDIFY	DECEIVE	DELIGHT
CURRISH	DANDLED	DECENCY	DELILAH
CURSING	DANELAW	DECIBEL	DELIMIT
CURSIVE	DANGLED	DECIDED	DELIVER
CURSORY	DANGLER	DECIDER	DELOUSE
CURTAIL	DANKISH	DECIMAL	DELPHIC
CURTAIN	DANTEAN	DECKING	DELTAIC
CURTANA	DAPPLED	DECKLED	DELUDED
CURTEST	DARKEST	DECLAIM	DELUDER
CURTSEY	DARKISH	DECLARE	DELUGED
CURVATE	DARLING	DECLINE	DELVING
CURVING	DARNING	DECODED	DEMERIT
CUSHION	DARTING	DECORUM	DEMESNE
CUSSING	DASHING	DECOYED	DEMIGOD
CUSTARD	DASH-POT	DECREED	DEMISED

DEMODED	DEVALUE	DINNING	DISUSED
DEMONIC	DEVELOP	DIOCESE	DITCHED
DEMONRY	DEVIATE	DIORAMA	DITCHER
DENIZEN	DEVILRY	DIOXIDE	DITHERY
DENOTED	DEVIOUS	DIPLOMA	DIURNAL
DENSELY	DEVISED	DIPOLAR	DIVERGE
DENSEST	DEVISEE	DIPPING	DIVERSE
DENSITY	DEVISER	DIPTERA	DIVIDED
DENTING	DEVISOR	DIREFUL	DIVIDER
DENTIST	DEVOLVE	DIRTIED	DIVINER
DENTOID	DEVOTED	DIRTIER	DIVISOR
DENTURE	DEVOTEE	DIRTILY	DIVORCE
DENUDED	DEW-DROP	DISABLE	DIVULGE
DENYING	DEW-FALL	DISAVOW	DIZZIED
DEPLETE	DEWLESS	DISBAND	DIZZIER
DEPLORE	DEXTRAL	DISCARD	DIZZILY
DEPLUME	DIABOLO	DISCERN	DOCKAGE
DEPOSAL	DIAGRAM	DISCOID	DOCKING
DEPOSED	DIALECT	DISCORD	DODGERY
DEPOSIT	DIALLED	DISCOUS	DODGING
DEPRAVE	DIAMOND	DISCUSS	DOESKIN
DEPRESS	DIARCHY	DISDAIN	DOFFING
DEPRIVE	DIARIST	DISEASE	DOG-BANE
DEPUTED	DIBBLED	DISEUSE	DOG-CART
DERANGE	DICE-BOX	DISGUST	DOG-DAYS
DERATED	DICKENS	DISHFUL	DOG-FISH
DERIDED	DICTATE	DISHING	DOGGING
DERIDER	DICTION	DISJOIN	DOGGISH
DERIVED	DIDDLED	DISLIKE	DOGHEAD
DERRICK	DIDDLER	DISMAST	DOG-HOLE
DERVISH	DIE-HARD	DISMISS	DOGLIKE
DESCANT	DIETARY	DISOBEY	DOG-NAIL
DESCEND	DIETING	DISPARK	DOG-ROSE
DESCENT	DIFFUSE	DISPART	DOG'S-EAR
DESERVE	DIGGING	DISPLAY	DOG-STAR
DESIRED	DIGITAL	DISPONE	DOLEFUL
DESIRER	DIGNIFY	DISPORT	DOLLIED
DESPAIR	DIGNITY	DISPOSE	DOLPHIN
DESPISE	DIGRESS	DISPUTE	DOLTISH
DESPITE	DILATED	DISRATE	DOMINIE
DESPOIL	DILATER	DISROBE	DONATOR
DESPOND	DILEMMA	DISROOT	DONNING
DESSERT	DILUENT	DISRUPT	DONNISH
DESTINE	DILUTED	DISSECT	DONSHIP
DESTINY	DILUTER	DISSENT	DOOMING
DESTROY	DIMETER	DISTAFF	DOORMAT
DETERGE	DIMMING	DISTANT	DOORWAY
DETINUE	DIMMISH	DISTEND	DORMANT
DETRACT	DIMNESS	DISTICH	DORMICE
DETRAIN	DIMPLED	DISTORT	DOSSIER
DETRUDE	DINGING	DISTURB	DOTTIER

DOTTING	DRIBLET	DUENESS	EARTHED
DOUBLED	DRIFTED	DUFFING	EARTHEN
DOUBLET	DRIFTER	DUKEDOM	EARTHLY
DOUBTED	DRILLED	DULCIFY	EASEFUL
DOUBTER	DRINKER	DULLARD	EASIEST
DOUCEUR	DRIPPED	DULLEST	EAST-END
DOUCHED	DRIVING	DULLING	EASTERN
DOUGHTY	DRIZZLE	DULLISH	EASTING
DOUREST	DRIZZLY	DUMPING	EATABLE
DOUSING	DROLLED	DUMPISH	EBB-TIDE
DOUTING	DRONING	DUNCIAD	EBONISE
DOVECOT	DRONISH	DUNGEON	EBONITE
DOWABLE	DROOLED	DUNNAGE	EBRIOUS
DOWAGER	DROOPED	DUNNING	ECHELON
DOWDILY	DROPLET	DUNNISH	ECHOING
DOWERED	DROP-NET	DUNNOCK	ECLIPSE
DOWNING	DROPPED	DUPABLE	ECLOGUE
DOWSING	DROPPER	DURABLE	ECOLOGY
DRABBER	DROUGHT	DURABLY	ECONOMY
DRACHMA	DROWNED	DURANCE	ECSTASY
DRACULA	DROWNER	DUSKIER	EDDYING
DRAFTED	DROWSED	DUSKILY	EDENTAL
DRAGGED	DRUBBED	DUSKISH	EDIFICE
DRAGGLE	DRUBBER	DUST-BIN	EDIFIED
DRAG-MAN	DRUDGED	DUSTIER	EDIFIER
DRAG-NET	DRUDGER	DUSTING	EDITING
DRAGOON	DRUGGED	DUSTMAN	EDITION
DRAINED	DRUGGER	DUST-PAN	EDUCATE
DRAINER	DRUGGET	DUTEOUS	EDUCING
DRAPERY	DRUIDIC	DUTIFUL	EFFACED
DRAPING	DRUMMED	DWARFED	EFFECTS
DRAPPIE	DRUMMER	DWELLED	EFFENDI
DRASTIC	DRUNKEN	DWELLER	EGALITY
DRATTED	DRY-DOCK	DWINDLE	EGG-COSY
DRAUGHT	DRY-EYED	DYNAMIC	EGG-FLIP
DRAWBAR	DRY-FOOT	DYNASTY	EGOTISE
DRAWING	DRYNESS	E—7	EGOTISM
DRAWLED	DRY-SHOD	EAGERLY	EGOTIST
DRAWLER	DUALISM	EANLING	EJECTED
DRAW-NET	DUALIST	EAR-ACHE	EJECTOR
DRAYAGE	DUALITY	EAR-DROP	ELAPSED
DRAYMAN	DUBBING	EAR-DRUM	ELASTIC
DREADED	DUBIETY	EAR-HOLE	ELATING
DREAMED	DUBIOUS	EARLDOM	ELATION
DREAMER	DUCALLY	EARLESS	ELBOWED
DREDGED	DUCHESS	EARLIER	ELDERLY
DREDGER	DUCKING	EARMARK	ELECTED
DRESDEN	DUCTILE	EARNEST	ELECTOR
DRESSED	DUDGEON	EARNING	ELECTRO
DRESSER	DUELLED	EARRING	ELEGANT
DRIBBLE	DUELLER	EARSHOT	ELEGIAC

ELEGISE	ENCLASP	ENTERIC	ERUPTED
ELEGIST	ENCLAVE	ENTHRAL	ESCAPED
ELEMENT	ENCLOSE	ENTHUSE	ESCAPER
ELEVATE	ENCLOUD	ENTICED	ESCHEAT
ELEVENS	ENCORED	ENTICER	ESPARTO
ELF-LOCK	ENCRUST	ENTITLE	ESPOUSE
ELIDING	ENDEMIC	ENTRAIN	ESPYING
ELISION	ENDIRON	ENTRANT	ESQUIRE
ELLIPSE	ENDLESS	ENTREAT	ESSAYED
ELOPING	ENDLONG	ENTRUST	ESSENCE
ELUDING	ENDMOST	ENTWINE	ESTUARY
ELUSION	ENDORSE	ENTWIST	ETCHING
ELUSIVE	ENDOWED	ENURING	ETERNAL
ELUSORY	ENDOWER	ENVELOP	ETHICAL
ELYSIAN	ENDUING	ENVENOM	ETONIAN
ELYSIUM	ENDURED	ENVIOUS	EUGENIC
EMANATE	ENDURER	ENVIRON	EUPHONY
EMBARGO	ENDWAYS	ENVYING	EUTERPE
EMBASSY	ENDWISE	EPAULET	EVACUEE
EMBLAZE	ENERGIC	EPERGNE	EVADING
EMBOSOM	ENFORCE	EPICARP	EVANGEL
EMBOWER	ENFRAME	EPICURE	EVASION
EMBOXED	ENGAGED	EPIGRAM	EVASIVE
EMBRACE	ENGAGER	EPISODE	EVENING
EMBROIL	ENGINED	EPISTLE	EVERTED
EMBROWN	ENGLISH	EPITAPH	EVICTED
EMENDED	ENGORGE	EPITHET	EVICTOR
EMERALD	ENGRAFT	EPITOME	EVIDENT
EMERGED	ENGRAIN	EPOCHAL	EVIL-EYE
EMINENT	ENGRAVE	EQUABLE	EVINCED
EMITTED	ENGROSS	EQUABLY	EVOKING
EMOTION	ENGUARD	EQUALLY	EVOLVED
EMOTIVE	ENHANCE	EQUATED	EWE-LAMB
EMPALED	ENJOYED	EQUATOR	EXACTED
EMPANEL	ENLACED	EQUERRY	EXACTER
EMPEROR	ENLARGE	EQUINOX	EXACTLY
EMPIRIC	ENLIVEN	ERASING	EXACTOR
EMPLANE	ENNOBLE	ERASURE	EXALTED
EMPOWER	ENOUNCE	ERECTED	EXAMINE
EMPRESS	ENQUIRE	ERECTER	EXAMPLE
EMPTIED	ENQUIRY	ERECTLY	EXCERPT
EMPTIER	ENRAGED	ERELONG	EXCISED
EMULATE	ENROBED	EREMITE	EXCITED
EMULOUS	ENSLAVE	ERMINED	EXCITER
ENABLED	ENSNARE	ERODENT	EXCLAIM
ENACTED	ENSTAMP	ERODING	EXCLUDE
ENCAGED	ENSUING	EROSION	EXCUSED
ENCASED	ENSURED	EROSIVE	EXECUTE
ENCAVED	ENTAMED	ERRATIC	EXEMPLA
ENCHAIN	ENTENTE	ERRATUM	EXERTED
ENCHANT	ENTERED	ERUDITE	EXHALED

EXHAUST	FAIREST	FEBRILE	FIG-LEAF
EXHIBIT	FAIRING	FEDERAL	FIGMENT
EXHUMED	FAIRISH	FEEDING	FIG-TREE
EXIGENT	FAIR-WAY	FEELING	FIGURAL
EXILING	FALLACY	FEE-TAIL	FIGURED
EXISTED	FALLING	FEIGNED	FIGWORT
EXPANSE	FALSELY	FEINTED	FILBERT
EX-PARTE	FALSEST	FELLING	FILCHED
EXPENSE	FALSIFY	FELONRY	FILCHER
EXPIATE	FALSITY	FELSPAR	FILINGS
EXPIRED	FANATIC	FELTING	FILLING
EXPLAIN	FANCIED	FELUCCA	FILM-FAN
EXPLODE	FANFARE	FEMORAL	FILMING
EXPLOIT	FAN-MAIL	FENCING	FINABLE
EXPLORE	FANNING	FENDING	FINALLY
EXPOSED	FANTAIL	FEOFFEE	FINANCE
EXPOSER	FANTAST	FERMENT	FINDING
EXPOUND	FANTASY	FERNERY	FINESSE
EXPRESS	FAR-AWAY	FERN-OWL	FINICAL
EXPUNGE	FARCEUR	FERRATE	FINICKY
EXTINCT	FARCING	FERRIED	FINLESS
EXTRACT	FARMERY	FERROUS	FINNISH
EXTREME	FARMING	FERRULE	FIRE-ARM
EXTRUDE	FARMOST	FERTILE	FIRE-BAR
EXUDING	FARRAGO	FERVENT	FIRE-BOX
EXULTED	FARRIER	FERVOUR	FIREDOG
EYE-BALL	FARTHER	FESTIVE	FIREFLY
EYE-BOLT	FASCISM	FESTOON	FIREMAN
EYE-BROW	FASCIST	FETCHED	FIREPAN
EYE-HOLE	FASHING	FETLOCK	FIRSTLY
EYE-LASH	FASHION	FEVERED	FISHERY
EYELESS	FAST-DAY	FEWNESS	FISHILY
EYE-SHOT	FASTEST	FIANCEE	FISHING
EYE-SORE	FASTING	FIBBING	FISH-OIL
EYE-WASH	FATALLY	FIBROID	FISSILE
F—7	FATEFUL	FIBROUS	FISSION
FACETED	FAT-HEAD	FIBSTER	FISSURE
FACTION	FATIGUE	FIBULAR	FITMENT
FACTORY	FATNESS	FICTILE	FITNESS
FACTUAL	FATTEST	FICTION	FITTING
FACULTY	FATTISH	FICTIVE	FIXABLE
FADDISH	FATUITY	FIDDLED	FIXEDLY
FADDIST	FATUOUS	FIDDLER	FIXTURE
FADE-OUT	FAULTED	FIDGETY	FIZZING
FAGGING	FAWNING	FIELDED	FIZZLED
FAIENCE	FEARFUL	FIELDER	FLACCID
FAILING	FEARING	FIERCER	FLAG-DAY
FAILURE	FEASTED	FIERILY	FLAGGED
FAINTED	FEASTER	FIFTEEN	FLAKING
FAINTER	FEATHER	FIFTHLY	FLAMING
FAINTLY	FEATURE	FIGHTER	FLANEUR

FLANGED	FLORIST	FOOLING	FOUNDED
FLANKED	FLOTAGE	FOOLISH	FOUNDER
FLANKER	FLOTANT	FOOTBOY	FOUNDRY
FLANNEL	FLOTSAM	FOOTING	FOWLING
FLAPPED	FLOUNCE	FOOTLED	FOX-HUNT
FLAPPER	FLOURED	FOOTMAN	FOXLIKE
FLARING	FLOUTED	FOOTPAD	FOX-TAIL
FLASHED	FLOUTER	FOOT-ROT	FOX-TROT
FLASHER	FLOWERY	FOOTWAY	FRAGILE
FLATLET	FLOWING	FOPPERY	FRAILLY
FLATTEN	FLUENCY	FOPPISH	FRAILTY
FLATTER	FLUFFED	FORAGED	FRAME-UP
FLAVOUR	FLUKILY	FORAGER	FRAMING
FLAWING	FLUKING	FORAYED	FRANKED
FLAYING	FLUMMOX	FORBADE	FRANKLY
FLECKED	FLUNKEY	FORBEAR	FRANTIC
FLECKER	FLUSHED	FORBORE	FRAUGHT
FLEDGED	FLUSTER	FORCEPS	FRAYING
FLEECED	FLUTING	FORCING	FRAZZLE
FLEECER	FLUTIST	FORDING	FREAKED
FLEEING	FLUTTER	FORDONE	FRECKLE
FLEETED	FLUVIAL	FOREARM	FRECKLY
FLEETER	FLY-AWAY	FOREIGN	FREEDOM
FLEETLY	FLY-BOOK	FORELEG	FREEING
FLEMING	FLY-FLAP	FOREMAN	FREEMAN
FLEMISH	FLY-HALF	FORERAN	FREESIA
FLESHED	FLY-LEAF	FORERUN	FREEZER
FLESHER	FLY-OVER	FORESAW	FREIGHT
FLESHLY	FLY-PAST	FORESEE	FRESHEN
FLEURET	FLY-TRAP	FORETOP	FRESHER
FLEXILE	FOALING	FOREVER	FRESHET
FLEXING	FOAMING	FORFEIT	FRESHLY
FLEXION	FOBBING	FORFEND	FRETFUL
FLEXURE	FOCUSED	FORGAVE	FRET-SAW
FLICKED	FOE-LIKE	FORGERY	FRETTED
FLICKER	FOG-BANK	FORGING	FRIABLE
FLIGHTY	FOGGIER	FORGIVE	FRIEZED
FLIPPED	FOGGILY	FORGONE	FRIGATE
FLIPPER	FOGGING	FORKING	FRILLED
FLIRTED	FOG-HORN	FORLORN	FRINGED
FLITTED	FOILING	FORMATE	FRISIAN
FLITTER	FOISTED	FORMING	FRISKED
FLIVVER	FOLDING	FORMULA	FRISKER
FLOATED	FOLIAGE	FORSAKE	FRITTED
FLOATER	FOLIATE	FORSOOK	FRITTER
FLOCKED	FOLLIES	FORTIFY	FRIZZED
FLOGGED	FONDANT	FORTUNE	FRIZZLE
FLOODED	FONDEST	FORWARD	FROCKED
FLOORED	FONDLED	FORWENT	FROGGED
FLOORER	FONDLER	FOULARD	FROG-MAN
FLOPPED	FOOLERY	FOULING	FRONDED

FRONTAL	G—7	GAS-OVEN	GIGGLER
FRONTED	GABBING	GASPING	GILDING
FROSTED	GABBLED	GAS-PIPE	GIMBALS
FROTHED	GABBLER	GAS-RING	GIN-FIZZ
FROWARD	GADDING	GASSING	GINGERY
FROWNED	GADDISH	GASTRIC	GINGHAM
FRUITED	GAEKWAR	GATEMAN	GIN-SHOP
FRUITER	GAFFING	GATEWAY	GIRAFFE
FUCHSIA	GAGGING	GATLING	GIRDING
FUDDLED	GAINFUL	GAUDERY	GIRDLED
FUDDLER	GAINING	GAUDILY	GIRDLER
FUDGING	GAINSAY	GAUGING	GIRLISH
FUEHRER	GALATEA	GAULISH	GIRTHED
FUELLED	GALILEE	GAUNTLY	GIZZARD
FULCRUM	GALILEO	GAUNTRY	GLACIAL
FULGENT	GALLANT	GAVOTTE	GLACIER
FULLEST	GALLEON	GAYNESS	GLADDEN
FULL-PAY	GALLERY	GAYSOME	GLADDER
FULSOME	GALLING	GAZELLE	GLAD-EYE
FUMBLED	GALLOWS	GAZETTE	GLAMOUR
FUMBLER	GALUMPH	GEARING	GLANCED
FUNDING	GAMBIST	GELDING	GLARING
FUNERAL	GAMBLED	GELIDLY	GLASSES
FUNGOID	GAMBLER	GEMMING	GLAZIER
FUNGOUS	GAMBOGE	GENERAL	GLAZING
FUNKING	GAMEFUL	GENERIC	GLEAMED
FUNNILY	GAME-LEG	GENESIS	GLEANED
FUNNING	GANGING	GENETIC	GLEANER
FURBISH	GANGLIA	GENITAL	GLEEFUL
FURCATE	GANGWAY	GENOESE	GLIDING
FURIOSO	GAPPING	GENTEEL	GLIMMER
FURIOUS	GARAGED	GENTIAN	GLIMPSE
FURLING	GARBAGE	GENTILE	GLINTED
FURLONG	GARBLED	GENTLER	GLISTEN
FURNACE	GARFISH	GENUINE	GLISTER
FURNISH	GARGLED	GEOLOGY	GLITTER
FURRIER	GARLAND	GEORDIE	GLOATED
FURRING	GARMENT	GERMANE	GLOBATE
FURTHER	GARNISH	GESTAPO	GLOBING
FURTIVE	GAROTTE	GESTURE	GLOBOID
FUSIBLE	GARPIKE	GETABLE	GLOBOSE
FUSSIER	GAS-BUOY	GET-AWAY	GLOBULE
FUSSILY	GAS-COAL	GETTING	GLOOMED
FUSSING	GAS-COKE	GHASTLY	GLORIED
FUSS-POT	GASEITY	GHERKIN	GLORIFY
FUSTIAN	GASEOUS	GHILLIE	GLOSSED
FUSTIER	GAS-FIRE	GHOSTLY	GLOSSER
FUZZIER	GASHING	GIBLETS	GLOTTIC
FUZZLED	GAS-LIME	GIDDILY	GLOTTIS
	GAS-MAIN	GIFTING	GLOWING
	GAS-MASK	GIGGLED	GLUCOSE

GLUE-POT	GRABBER	GREENLY	GRUNTER
GLUMMER	GRABBLE	GREETED	GRUYERE
GLUTTED	GRACING	GREMLIN	GUARDED
GLUTTON	GRADATE	GRENADE	GUDGEON
GNARLED	GRADELY	GREY-HEN	GUELDER
GNARRED	GRADING	GREYISH	GUERDON
GNASHED	GRADUAL	GREYLAG	GUESSED
GNAWING	GRAFTED	GRIDDED	GUESSER
GNOSTIC	GRAFTER	GRIDDLE	GUICHET
GOADING	GRAINED	GRIEVED	GUIDAGE
GO-AHEAD	GRAINER	GRIFFIN	GUIDING
GOATISH	GRAMMAR	GRIFFON	GUILDER
GOBBLED	GRAMPUS	GRILLED	GUILDRY
GOBBLER	GRANARY	GRIMACE	GUIPURE
GOBELIN	GRANDAD	GRIMING	GULLERY
GODDESS	GRANDAM	GRIMMER	GULLIED
GODETIA	GRANDEE	GRINDER	GULLING
GODHEAD	GRANDER	GRINNED	GUM-BOIL
GODHOOD	GRANDLY	GRIPING	GUM-BOOT
GODLESS	GRANDMA	GRIPPED	GUMDROP
GODLIER	GRANGER	GRIPPER	GUMMING
GODLIKE	GRANITE	GRISTLE	GUM-TREE
GODLILY	GRANTED	GRISTLY	GUNBOAT
GODSEND	GRANTEE	GRITTED	GUN-DECK
GODSHIP	GRANTER	GRIZZLE	GUN-FIRE
GODWARD	GRANTOR	GRIZZLY	GUNNERY
GOGGLED	GRANULE	GROANED	GUNNING
GOGGLES	GRAPERY	GROCERY	GUN-ROOM
GOITRED	GRAPHIC	GROOMED	GUNSHOT
GOLFING	GRAPNEL	GROOVED	GUN-SITE
GOLIATH	GRAPPLE	GROPING	GUNWALE
GONDOLA	GRASPED	GROSSER	GURGLED
GONGING	GRASPER	GROSSLY	GURNARD
GOOD-BYE	GRASSED	GROUNDS	GUSHING
GOOD-DAY	GRATIFY	GROUPED	GUSTILY
GOODISH	GRATING	GROUPER	GUTTING
GOODMAN	GRAVELY	GROUSED	GUZZLED
GOOSERY	GRAVEST	GROUSER	GUZZLER
GORDIAN	GRAVIED	GROUTED	GYMNAST
GORGING	GRAVITY	GROWING	GYRATED
GORILLA	GRAVURE	GROWLED	
GORMAND	GRAZIER	GROWLER	H—7
GORSEDD	GRAZING	GROWN-UP	HABITAT
GOSLING	GREASED	GRUBBED	HABITED
GOSSIPY	GREASER	GRUBBER	HABITUE
GOUACHE	GREATER	GRUDGED	HACKBUT
GOUGING	GREATLY	GRUDGER	HACKING
GOULASH	GRECIAN	GRUFFER	HACKLED
GOURMET	GRECISM	GRUFFLY	HACKNEY
GOUTILY	GRECIZE	GRUMBLE	HACK-SAW
GRABBED	GREENER	GRUNTED	HADDOCK

HAFTING	HARKING	HEALTHY	HERITOR
HAGGARD	HARMFUL	HEAPING	HEROINE
HAGGISH	HARMING	HEARING	HEROISM
HAGGLED	HARMONY	HEARKEN	HEROIZE
HAGGLER	HARNESS	HEARSAY	HERONRY
HAILING	HARPING	HEARTED	HERRING
HAIR-CUT	HARPIST	HEARTEN	HERSELF
HAIR-OIL	HARPOON	HEATHEN	HESSIAN
HAIRPIN	HARRIED	HEATING	HEXAGON
HALBERD	HARRIER	HEAVE-TO	HEXAPOD
HALCYON	HARSHER	HEAVIER	HICKORY
HALF-PAY	HARSHLY	HEAVILY	HIDALGO
HALFWAY	HARVEST	HEAVING	HIDEOUS
HALF-WIT	HASHING	HEBRAIC	HIDE-OUT
HALIBUT	HASHISH	HECKLED	HIGGLED
HALOGEN	HASSOCK	HECKLER	HIGGLER
HALTING	HASTIER	HECTARE	HIGHDAY
HALVING	HASTILY	HEDGING	HIGHEST
HALYARD	HASTING	HEDONIC	HIGH-HAT
HAMBURG	HATABLE	HEEDFUL	HIGHWAY
HAMMOCK	HATCHER	HEEDING	HILLIER
HAMSTER	HATCHET	HEELING	HILLMAN
HAMULAR	HATEFUL	HEEL-TAP	HILLOCK
HANDBAG	HATLESS	HEFTIER	HILLTOP
HANDFUL	HAT-RACK	HEFTILY	HIMSELF
HANDIER	HAUBERK	HEIGH-HO	HINNIED
HANDILY	HAUGHTY	HEINOUS	HINTING
HANDING	HAULAGE	HEIRDOM	HIPPING
HANDLED	HAULIER	HEIRESS	HIRABLE
HANDLER	HAULING	HELICAL	HIRCINE
HANDSAW	HAUNTED	HELICON	HIRSUTE
HANG-DOG	HAUNTER	HELL-CAT	HISSING
HANGING	HAUTBOY	HELLENE	HISTORY
HANGMAN	HAUTEUR	HELLISH	HITCHED
HANG-NET	HAWKBIT	HELPFUL	HITTING
HANSARD	HAWKING	HELPING	HITTITE
HAPLESS	HAWK-OWL	HEMLOCK	HOARDED
HAP'ORTH	HAY-BAND	HEMMING	HOARDER
HAPPIER	HAYCOCK	HENBANE	HOAXING
HAPPILY	HAYFORK	HEN-COOP	HOBBLED
HARBOUR	HAY-LOFT	HENNAED	HOBNAIL
HARDEST	HAYRICK	HENNERY	HOGGING
HARDIER	HAYSEED	HENPECK	HOGGISH
HARDILY	HAY-WARD	HENWIFE	HOGWASH
HARDISH	HAYWIRE	HEPATIC	HOGSWEED
HARD-PAN	HAZIEST	HERBAGE	HOISTED
HARDSET	HEADILY	HERBARY	HOISTER
HARD-WON	HEADING	HERBIST	HOLDALL
HAREING	HEADMAN	HERBOUS	HOLDING
HARE-LIP	HEADWAY	HERDING	HOLIDAY
HARICOT	HEALING	HERETIC	HOLIEST

HOLLAND	HUFFILY	IDYLLIC	INANITY
HOLM-OAK	HUFFING	IGNEOUS	INAPTLY
HOLSTER	HUFFISH	IGNITED	INBEING
HOMERIC	HUGGING	IGNITER	INBOARD
HONESTY	HULKING	IGNOBLE	INBOUND
HONEYED	HULLING	IGNOBLY	INBREAK
HONITON	HUMANLY	IGNORED	INBREED
HONKING	HUMBLED	ILL-BRED	INCENSE
HOODING	HUMBLER	ILLEGAL	INCHING
HOODLUM	HUMDRUM	ILL-FAME	INCISED
HOOFING	HUMERUS	ILLICIT	INCISOR
HOOKING	HUMIDLY	ILLNESS	INCITED
HOOPING	HUMMING	ILL-TIME	INCLINE
HOOTING	HUMMOCK	ILLUMED	INCLUDE
HOPEFUL	HUMULUS	ILL-USED	INCOMER
HOPKILN	HUNCHED	ILL-WILL	INCUBUS
HOPLITE	HUNDRED	IMAGERY	INCURVE
HOPPING	HUNTING	IMAGINE	INDEXED
HOP-POLE	HURDLED	IMAGING	INDITED
HOP-VINE	HURDLER	IMBIBED	INDOORS
HORIZON	HURLING	IMBIBER	INDRAWN
HORMONE	HURRIED	IMBRUED	INDUCED
HORNBAR	HURRIER	IMBUING	INDULGE
HORNING	HURTFUL	IMITATE	INEPTLY
HORNISH	HURTLED	IMMENSE	INERTIA
HORN-OWL	HUSBAND	IMMERSE	INERTLY
HORRIFY	HUSHABY	IMMORAL	INEXACT
HOSANNA	HUSHING	IMMURED	INFANCY
HOSIERY	HUSKING	IMPALED	INFANTA
HOSPICE	HUSTLED	IMPASSE	INFANTE
HOSTAGE	HUSTLER	IMPEACH	INFERNO
HOSTESS	HUTMENT	IMPEDED	INFIDEL
HOSTILE	HYDRANT	IMPERIL	INFIELD
HOSTLER	HYDRATE	IMPETUS	INFIXED
HOT-FOOT	HYGIENE	IMPIETY	INFLAME
HOTNESS	HYMNIST	IMPINGE	INFLATE
HOTSPUR	HYMNODY	IMPIOUS	INFLECT
HOTTEST		IMPLANT	INFLICT
HOT-WALL		IMPLIED	INFUSED
HOUNDED	I—7	IMPLORE	INFUSER
HOUSAGE	IBERIAN	IMPOSED	INGENUE
HOUSING	ICEBERG	IMPOSER	INGOING
HOVERED	ICEBOAT	IMPOUND	INGRATE
HOVERER	ICE-FLOE	IMPRESS	INGRESS
HOWBEIT	ICEPACK	IMPREST	INHABIT
HOWDY-DO	ICE-RINK	IMPRINT	INHALED
HOWEVER	ICHABOD	IMPROVE	INHALER
HOWLING	ICINESS	IMPULSE	INHERED
HUDDLED	IDEALLY	IMPUTED	INHERIT
HUDDLER	IDIOTIC	IMPUTER	INHIBIT
HUELESS	IDOLISE	INANELY	INHUMAN

INITIAL	IRIDIUM	JEZEBEL	JUMBLED
INJURED	IRKSOME	JIBBING	JUMBLER
INJURER	IRONING	JIB-BOOM	JUMPING
INKHORN	ISHMAEL	JIGGING	JUNIPER
INKLING	ISLAMIC	JIGGLED	JUNKMAN
INKWELL	ISOLATE	JILTING	JUPITER
INLACED	ISOTOPE	JIM-CROW	JURY-BOX
INLAYER	ISSUING	JINGLED	JURY-MAN
INNINGS	ISTHMUS	JITTERS	JUSSIVE
INQUEST	ITALIAN	JITTERY	JUSTICE
INQUIRE	ITALICS	JOBBERY	JUSTIFY
INQUIRY	ITCHING	JOBBING	JUTTING
INSHORE	ITEMISE	JOBLESS	JUVENAL
INSIDER	ITERATE	JOCULAR	
INSIGHT	IVORIED	JOGGING	K—7
INSIPID	IVY-BUSH	JOGGLED	KAMERAD
INSPECT		JOG-TROT	KATYDID
INSPIRE		JOINDER	KEENEST
INSTALL	J—7	JOINERY	KEENING
INSTANT	JABBING	JOINING	KEEPING
INSTEAD	JACINTH	JOINTED	KENTISH
INSULAR	JACKASS	JOINTER	KESTREL
INSULIN	JACKDAW	JOINTLY	KETCHUP
INSURED	JACKING	JOISTED	KEYBOLT
INSURER	JACKPOT	JOLLIER	KEYED-UP
INTEGER	JACK-TAR	JOLLIFY	KEYHOLE
INTENSE	JACOBIN	JOLLILY	KEY-NOTE
INTERIM	JADEDLY	JOLLITY	KEY-RING
INTONED	JAGGING	JOLTING	KHAMSIN
INTRUDE	JAILING	JONQUIL	KHEDIVE
INTRUST	JAMMING	JOSTLED	KICKING
INTWINE	JANGLED	JOTTING	KICK-OFF
INURING	JANITOR	JOUNCED	KIDDING
INVADED	JANUARY	JOURNAL	KILLING
INVADER	JARRING	JOURNEY	KILL-JOY
INVALID	JASMINE	JOUSTED	KILN-DRY
INVEIGH	JAVELIN	JOYLESS	KINDEST
INVERSE	JAWBONE	JOY-RIDE	KINDLED
INVIOUS	JAZZING	JUBILEE	KINDRED
INVITED	JEALOUS	JUDAISM	KINETIC
INVITER	JEERING	JUDAIST	KINGCUP
INVOICE	JEHOVAH	JUDAISE	KINGDOM
INVOKED	JELLIED	JUDGING	KING-PIN
INVOKER	JELLIFY	JUGGING	KINKING
INVOLVE	JERICHO	JUGGINS	KINLESS
INWARDS	JERKING	JUGGLED	KINSHIP
INWOVEN	JESTFUL	JUGGLER	KINSMAN
IODISED	JESTING	JUGULAR	KIRTLED
IONISED	JETTIED	JUICIER	KISSING
IRACUND	JETTING	JU-JITSU	KITCHEN
IRANIAN	JEWELRY	JUKE-BOX	KNACKER

KNAPPED	LANDTAG	LEAGUER	LEXICAL
KNAPPER	LAND-TAX	LEAKAGE	LEXICON
KNARLED	LANGUID	LEAKING	LIAISON
KNAVERY	LANGUOR	LEANDER	LIBERAL
KNAVISH	LANKIER	LEANEST	LIBERTY
KNEADED	LANOLIN	LEANING	LIBRARY
KNEE-CAP	LANTERN	LEAPING	LICENCE
KNEE-PAN	LANYARD	LEARNED	LICENSE
KNIFING	LAPPING	LEARNER	LICITLY
KNITTED	LAPPISH	LEASHED	LICKING
KNITTER	LAPSING	LEASING	LIDLESS
KNOBBED	LAPWING	LEATHER	LIE-ABED
KNOBBLY	LARCENY	LEAVING	LIFTING
KNOCKED	LARDING	LECTERN	LIGATED
KNOCKER	LARGELY	LECTION	LIGHTED
KNOCK-ON	LARGEST	LECTURE	LIGHTEN
KNOTTED	LARGISH	LEEMOST	LIGHTER
KNOUTED	LARKING	LEERILY	LIGHTLY
KNOW-ALL	LASHING	LEERING	LIGNIFY
KNOWING	LASHKAR	LEE-SIDE	LIGNITE
KNUCKLE	LASSOED	LEE-TIDE	LIGNOSE
KNURLED	LASTING	LEEWARD	LIKABLE
KOUMISS	LATAKIA	LEGALLY	LIKENED
KREMLIN	LATCHED	LEGATEE	LILY-PAD
KRISHNA	LATCHET	LEGGING	LIMBATE
KURSAAL	LATENCY	LEGIBLE	LIMBING
	LATERAL	LEGIBLY	LIME-PIT
	LATERAN	LEG-IRON	LIMINAL
L—7	LATHING	LEGLESS	LIMITED
LABIATE	LATTICE	LEG-PULL	LIMITER
LACKING	LATVIAN	LEISURE	LIMNING
LACONIC	LAUDING	LEMMING	LIMPING
LACQUER	LAUGHED	LENDING	LINCTUS
LACTATE	LAUNDER	LENGTHY	LINEAGE
LACTOSE	LAUNDRY	LENIENT	LINEATE
LADLING	LAW-BOOK	LENTOID	LINEMAN
LADY-DAY	LAWLESS	LEONINE	LINGUAL
LAGGARD	LAW-LORD	LEOPARD	LINKAGE
LAGGING	LAW-SUIT	LEOTARD	LINKBOY
LAKELET	LAXNESS	LEPROSY	LINKING
LAMBENT	LAYERED	LEPROUS	LINSEED
LAMBING	LAYETTE	LESBIAN	LION-CUB
LAMBKIN	LAYLAND	LET-DOWN	LIONESS
LAMINAR	LAZIEST	LETTING	LIONISM
LAMMING	LAZY-BED	LETTISH	LIONISE
LAMP-LIT	LEACHED	LETTUCE	LIPPING
LAMPOON	LEADING	LEUCOMA	LIQUATE
LAMPREY	LEAFAGE	LEVELLY	LIQUEFY
LANCERS	LEAFING	LEVERED	LIQUEUR
LANCING	LEAFLET	LEVERET	LISPING
LANDING	LEAGUED	LEVYING	LISSOME

LISTING	LONG-RUN	LUMPIER	MALAISE
LITERAL	LOOKING	LUMPING	MALARIA
LITHELY	LOOKOUT	LUMPISH	MALAYAN
LITHIUM	LOOMING	LUNATIC	MALISON
LITHOID	LOOPING	LUNCHED	MALLARD
LITOTES	LOOSELY	LUNETTE	MALLING
LITURGY	LOOSING	LUNGING	MALMSEY
LIVABLE	LOOTING	LURCHED	MALTESE
LIVENED	LOPPING	LURCHER	MALTING
LIVE-OAK	LORDING	LURKING	MALTMAN
LIVERED	LORELEI	LUSHING	MAMMARY
LOADING	LORINER	LUSTFUL	MAMMOTH
LOAFING	LOSABLE	LUSTIER	MANACLE
LOAMING	LOTTERY	LUSTILY	MANAGED
LOANING	LOTTING	LUSTING	MANAGER
LOATHED	LOUDEST	LYCHNIS	MANAKIN
LOATHER	LOUNGED	LYDDITE	MANATEE
LOATHLY	LOUNGER	LYING-IN	MANCHET
LOBBIED	LOURING	LYINGLY	MANDATE
LOBBING	LOUSILY	LYNCHED	MANDREL
LOBELIA	LOUTISH	LYRICAL	MANDRIL
LOBSTER	LOVABLE		MANGLED
LOBULAR	LOW-BORN	M—7	MANGLER
LOCALLY	LOW-BRED	MACABRE	MANGOLD
LOCATED	LOWDOWN	MACADAM	MANHOLE
LOCKAGE	LOWERED	MACAQUE	MANHOOD
LOCKING	LOW-GEAR	MACHETE	MAN-HOUR
LOCK-JAW	LOWLAND	MACHINE	MAN-HUNT
LOCK-OUT	LOW-LIFE	MADDEST	MANIKIN
LODGING	LOWLILY	MADDING	MANILLA
LOFTIER	LOWNESS	MADEIRA	MANITOU
LOFTILY	LOW-TIDE	MADNESS	MANKIND
LOFTING	LOYALLY	MADONNA	MANLESS
LOG-BOOK	LOYALTY	MAESTRO	MANLIKE
LOGGING	LOZENGE	MAGENTA	MAN-MADE
LOGICAL	LUCENCY	MAGGOTY	MANNING
LOGLINE	LUCERNE	MAGICAL	MANNISH
LOG-REEL	LUCIDLY	MAGINOT	MAN-ROPE
LOG-ROLL	LUCIFER	MAGNATE	MANSARD
LOG-SHIP	LUCKIER	MAGNETO	MANSION
LOGWOOD	LUCKILY	MAGNIFY	MANTLED
LOLLARD	LUFFING	MAHATMA	MANTLET
LOLLING	LUGGAGE	MAHJONG	MAN-TRAP
LOMBARD	LUGGING	MAIL-BAG	MANURED
LONG-AGO	LUGMARK	MAILING	MANX-CAT
LONGBOW	LUGSAIL	MAIL-VAN	MAPPING
LONGEST	LUGWORM	MAIMING	MAPPIST
LONG-HOP	LULLABY	MAINOUR	MARABOU
LONGING	LULLING	MAINTOP	MARBLED
LONGISH	LUMBAGO	MAJESTY	MARCHED
LONG-LEG	LUMINAL	MALACCA	MARCHER

MARINER	MAY-POLE	MICROHM	MISDEEM
MARITAL	MAY-TIME	MIDLAND	MISDOER
MARKING	MAY-WEED	MID-LIFE	MISDONE
MARLINE	MAZURKA	MIDMOST	MISERLY
MARLING	MEADOWY	MIDRIFF	MISFALL
MARLPIT	MEANDER	MIDWIFE	MISFIRE
MARQUEE	MEANEST	MIGRANT	MISFORM
MARQUIS	MEANING	MIGRATE	MISGAVE
MARRIED	MEASLED	MILDEST	MISGIVE
MARRING	MEASLES	MILDEWY	MISHEAR
MARROWY	MEASURE	MILEAGE	MISJOIN
MARSALA	MEAT-TEA	MILFOIL	MISLAID
MARSHAL	MECHLIN	MILIARY	MISLEAD
MARTIAL	MEDDLED	MILITIA	MISLIKE
MARTIAN	MEDDLER	MILKILY	MISNAME
MARTINI	MEDIATE	MILKING	MISRATE
MARTLET	MEDICAL	MILKMAN	MISREAD
MARXIAN	MEETING	MILKSOP	MISRULE
MARXISM	MEISSEN	MILL-DAM	MISSAID
MARXIST	MELANGE	MILLIER	MISSEEM
MASHING	MELODIC	MILLING	MISSEND
MASH-TUB	MELTING	MILLION	MISSENT
MASKING	MEMENTO	MIMESIS	MISSILE
MASONIC	MENACED	MIMETIC	MISSING
MASONRY	MENACER	MIMICAL	MISSION
MASSAGE	MENDING	MIMICRY	MISSIVE
MASSEUR	MEN-FOLK	MINARET	MISTAKE
MASSING	MENTHOL	MINCING	MISTELL
MASSIVE	MENTION	MINDFUL	MISTERM
MASTERY	MERCERY	MINDING	MISTFUL
MASTIFF	MERCURY	MINERAL	MISTILY
MASTING	MERGING	MINERVA	MISTIME
MASTOID	MERITED	MINGLED	MISTRAL
MATADOR	MERLING	MINGLER	MISTUNE
MATCHED	MERMAID	MINIBUS	MISUSED
MATCHET	MERRIER	MINIKIN	MITHRAS
METALOT	MERRILY	MINIMAL	MIXABLE
MATINEE	MESEEMS	MINIMUM	MIXEDLY
MATTING	MESHING	MINIMUS	MIXTURE
MATTOCK	MESSAGE	MINSTER	MIZZLED
MATURED	MESSIAH	MINTING	MOANFUL
MAUDLIN	MESSING	MINUTED	MOANING
MAULING	METHANE	MIOCENE	MOBBING
MAUNDER	METONIC	MIRACLE	MOBBISH
MAWKISH	METTLED	MISCALL	MOBSMAN
MAXIMAL	MEWLING	MISCAST	MOCKERY
MAXIMUM	MEXICAN	MISCITE	MOCKING
MAYFAIR	MIASMAL	MISCUED	MOCK-SUN
MAY-LILY	MIAUING	MISDATE	MODALLY
MAY-MORN	MIAULED	MISDEAL	MODESTY
MAYORAL	MICROBE	MISDEED	MODICUM

MODISTE	MOUTHER	MUTABLY	NEIGHED
MODULUS	MOVABLE	MUTANDA	NEITHER
MOHICAN	MOVABLY	MUTTONY	NEMESIS
MOIDORE	MUCKING	MUZZILY	NEOLOGY
MOILING	MUD-BATH	MUZZLED	NEPOTIC
MOISTEN	MUD-CART	MYNHEER	NEPTUNE
MOLE-RAT	MUDDIED	MYSTERY	NERVING
MOLLIFY	MUDDIER	MYSTIFY	NERVOUS
MOLLUSC	MUDDILY		NEST-EGG
MONARCH	MUDDING	**N—7**	NESTING
MONEYED	MUDDLED	NABBING	NESTLED
MONGREL	MUD-FISH	NAGGING	NESTLER
MONIKER	MUD-FLAT	NAILERY	NET-BALL
MONITOR	MUD-HOLE	NAILING	NET-CORD
MONKISH	MUD-LARK	NAIVELY	NETTING
MONOCLE	MUEZZIN	NAIVETE	NETTLED
MONSOON	MUFFING	NAKEDLY	NETTLER
MONSTER	MUFFLED	NAMABLE	NETWORK
MONTHLY	MUFFLER	NANKEEN	NEURINE
MOOCHED	MUGGING	NAPHTHA	NEUROSE
MOODILY	MUGGINS	NAPLESS	NEUTRAL
MOONING	MUGGISH	NAPPING	NEUTRON
MOONISH	MUGWUMP	NARRATE	NEW-BORN
MOONLIT	MULATTO	NARWHAL	NEWGATE
MOORAGE	MULCHED	NASALLY	NEW-MADE
MOOR-HEN	MULCTED	NASCENT	NEWNESS
MOORING	MULLING	NASTIER	NEWSBOY
MOORISH	MULLION	NASTILY	NEWSMAN
MOOTING	MUMBLED	NATTIER	NIAGARA
MOPPING	MUMBLER	NATTILY	NIBBLED
MORALLY	MUMMERY	NATURAL	NIBBLER
MORDANT	MUMMIED	NATURED	NIBLICK
MORELLO	MUMMIFY	NAUGHTY	NICKING
MORNING	MUMMING	NAZI-ISM	NIGELLA
MOROCCO	MUMPING	NEAREST	NIGGARD
MORPHIA	MUMPISH	NEATEST	NIGGLED
MORTISE	MUNCHED	NEBULAE	NIGGLER
MORTIFY	MUNCHER	NEBULAR	NIGHTIE
MOSELLE	MUNDANE	NECKING	NIGHTLY
MOTORED	MURKIER	NECKLET	NIMBLER
MOTTLED	MURKILY	NECKTIE	NINE-PIN
MOULDED	MURRAIN	NEEDFUL	NINTHLY
MOULDER	MUSCLED	NEEDIER	NIPPERS
MOULTED	MUSETTE	NEEDILY	NIPPIER
MOUNDED	MUSHING	NEEDING	NIPPIES
MOUNTED	MUSICAL	NEEDLED	NIPPING
MOUNTER	MUSK-RAT	NEGATED	NIRVANA
MOURNED	MUSTANG	NEGLECT	NITRATE
MOURNER	MUSTARD	NEGLIGE	NITROUS
MOUSING	MUSTILY	NEGRESS	NOBBLED
MOUTHED	MUTABLE	NEGROID	NOBBLER

NOBLEST	NUTTING	OFFHAND	ORDINAL
NO-CLAIM	NUT-TREE	OFFICER	ORDINEE
NODATED	NUZZLED	OFFSIDE	OREADES
NODDING		OGREISH	ORGANIC
NODULAR	O—7	OIL-CAKE	ORIFICE
NODULED	OAFLIKE	OIL-SHOP	ORIGAMI
NOGGING	OAK-LEAF	OIL-SKIN	OROLOGY
NOISILY	OAKLING	OIL-WELL	ORPHEAN
NOISING	OARFISH	OLDNESS	ORPHEUS
NOISOME	OARLOCK	OLDSTER	ORTOLAN
NOMADIC	OARSMAN	OLD-TIME	OSCULAR
NOMINAL	OAT-CAKE	OLYMPIA	OSMANLI
NOMINEE	OAT-MEAL	OLYMPIC	OSTEOID
NON-ACID	OBELISK	OLYMPUS	OSTRICH
NONAGON	OBESITY	OMINOUS	OTTOMAN
NONPLUS	OBEYING	OMITTED	OURSELF
NONSTOP	OBLIGED	OMNIBUS	OUSTING
NONSUCH	OBLIGEE	OMNIFIC	OUT-BACK
NON-SUIT	OBLIGER	ONE-EYED	OUTBRAG
NOONDAY	OBLIGOR	ONEFOLD	OUTCAST
NORFOLK	OBLIQUE	ONENESS	OUTCOME
NORWICH	OBLOQUY	ONERARY	OUTCROP
NOSE-BAG	OBSCENE	ONEROUS	OUTDARE
NOSEGAY	OBSCURE	ONESELF	OUTDONE
NOSTRIL	OBSERVE	ONE-STEP	OUTDOOR
NOSTRUM	OBTRUDE	ONGOING	OUTFACE
NOTABLE	OBVERSE	ONWARDS	OUTFALL
NOTABLY	OBVIATE	OPACITY	OUTFLOW
NOTANDA	OBVIOUS	OPALINE	OUTGOER
NOTCHED	OCARINA	OPALISE	OUTGROW
NOTEDLY	OCCIPUT	OPEN-AIR	OUTHAUL
NOTHING	OCCLUDE	OPENING	OUTLAND
NOTICED	OCEANIA	OPERATE	OUTLAST
NOURISH	OCEANIC	OPINING	OUTLEAP
NOVELTY	OCTAGON	OPINION	OUTLIER
NOWHERE	OCTAVUS	OPOSSUM	OUTLINE
NOXIOUS	OCTETTE	OPPIDAN	OUTLIVE
NUCLEAR	OCTOBER	OPPOSED	OUTLOOK
NUCLEUS	OCTOPOD	OPPOSER	OUTMOST
NUDGING	OCTOPUS	OPPRESS	OUTMOVE
NULLIFY	OCTUPLE	OPTICAL	OUTPACE
NULLITY	OCULIST	OPTIMUM	OUTPLAY
NUMBERS	ODDMENT	OPULENT	OUTPOST
NUMBING	ODDNESS	ORATING	OUTPOUR
NUMERAL	ODORANT	ORATION	OUTRAGE
NUNNERY	ODOROUS	ORATORY	OUTRIDE
NUNNISH	ODYSSEY	ORBITAL	OUTRODE
NUPTIAL	OEDIPUS	ORCHARD	OUTSAIL
NURSERY	OFFENCE	ORDERED	OUTSELL
NURSING	OFFERED	ORDERER	OUTSIDE
NURTURE	OFFERER	ORDERLY	OUTSIZE

OUTSOLD	PACKING	PAPRIKA	PAUSING
OUTSPAN	PACKMAN	PAPULAR	PAWNING
OUTSTAY	PADDING	PAPYRUS	PAYABLE
OUTTALK	PADDLED	PARABLE	PAY-BILL
OUTVOTE	PADDLER	PARADED	PAY-BOOK
OUTWALK	PADDOCK	PARADOX	PAY-DIRT
OUTWARD	PADLOCK	PARAGON	PAY-LIST
OUTWEAR	PADRONE	PARAPET	PAY-LOAD
OUTWORK	PAGEANT	PARASOL	PAYMENT
OUTWORN	PAILFUL	PARBOIL	PAY-ROLL
OVARIAN	PAINFUL	PARCHED	PEACHED
OVATION	PAINING	PARESIS	PEACHER
OVERACT	PAINTED	PARETIC	PEACOCK
OVERALL	PAINTER	PARKING	PEA-FOWL
OVER-ATE	PAIRING	PARLOUR	PEAKING
OVERAWE	PALADIN	PARLOUS	PEAKISH
OVERBID	PALATAL	PARODIC	PEALING
OVERBUY	PALAVER	PARQUET	PEARLED
OVERDID	PALETOT	PARRIED	PEASANT
OVERDUE	PALETTE	PARSING	PEA-SOUP
OVEREAT	PALFREY	PARSLEY	PEAT-BOG
OVERFAR	PALLING	PARSNIP	PEAT-HAG
OVERJOY	PALMARY	PARTAKE	PEBBLED
OVERLAP	PALMATE	PARTIAL	PECCANT
OVERLAY	PALMERY	PARTING	PECCAVI
OVERLIE	PALMING	PARTNER	PECKING
OVERMAN	PALMIST	PARVENU	PECKISH
OVERPAY	PALM-OIL	PASCHAL	PECTATE
OVERPLY	PALPATE	PASSAGE	PECTINE
OVERRAN	PALSIED	PASSING	PEDDLED
OVERRUN	PANACEA	PASSION	PEDDLER
OVERSEA	PANACHE	PASSIVE	PEDICEL
OVERSEE	PANCAKE	PASS-KEY	PEDICLE
OVERSET	PANDEAN	PASSMAN	PEELING
OVERSEW	PANDORA	PASTERN	PEEPING
OVERTAX	PANICKY	PASTIME	PEERAGE
OVERTLY	PANNAGE	PASTING	PEERESS
OVERTOP	PANNIER	PASTURE	PEERING
OVIDIAN	PANNING	PATBALL	PEEVISH
OVOIDAL	PANOPLY	PATCHED	PEGASUS
OVOLOGY	PAN-PIPE	PATCHER	PEGGING
OWL-LIKE	PANSIED	PATELLA	PELAGIC
OXIDATE	PANTHER	PATHWAY	PELICAN
OXIDISE	PANTIES	PATIENT	PELISSE
OXONIAN	PANTILE	PATNESS	PELTING
	PANTING	PATRIOT	PENALLY
	PAPALLY	PATTERN	PENALTY
P—7	PAPERED	PATTING	PENANCE
PACIFIC	PAPERER	PAUCITY	PENATES
PACKAGE	PAPILLA	PAULINE	PENDANT
PACK-ICE	PAPOOSE	PAUNCHY	PENDENT

PENGUIN	PETRIFY	PIG-WASH	PITYING
PEN-NAME	PETROUS	PIKELET	PIVOTAL
PENNANT	PETTILY	PIKEMAN	PIVOTED
PENNIED	PETTING	PILEATE	PLACARD
PENNING	PETTISH	PILGRIM	PLACATE
PENSION	PETUNIA	PILLAGE	PLACEBO
PENSIVE	PEW-RENT	PILL-BOX	PLACING
PENTODE	PFENNIG	PILLING	PLACKET
PEOPLED	PHAETON	PILLION	PLAFOND
PEPPERY	PHALANX	PILLORY	PLAGUED
PEPSINE	PHANTOM	PILLOWY	PLAGUER
PEPTICS	PHARAOH	PILOTED	PLAINER
PEPTONE	PHARYNX	PIMENTO	PLAINLY
PERCEPT	PHILTRE	PIMPLED	PLAITED
PERCHED	PHINEAS	PINCERS	PLAITER
PERCHER	PHOEBUS	PINCHED	PLANARY
PERCUSS	PHOENIX	PINCHER	PLANING
PERDURE	PHONATE	PINFOLD	PLANISH
PERFECT	PHONICS	PINGING	PLANKED
PERFIDY	PHOTISM	PINGUID	PLANNED
PERFORM	PHRASED	PINGUIN	PLANNER
PERFUME	PHRENIC	PINHOLE	PLANTAR
PERFUSE	PHYSICS	PINK-EYE	PLANTED
PERGOLA	PIANIST	PINKING	PLANTER
PERHAPS	PIANOLA	PINKISH	PLASHED
PERIAPT	PIASTRE	PINNACE	PLASTER
PERIDOT	PIBROCH	PINNATE	PLASTIC
PERIQUE	PICADOR	PINNING	PLATEAU
PERIWIG	PICCOLO	PINT-POT	PLATING
PERJURE	PICKAXE	PIONEER	PLATOON
PERJURY	PICKING	PIOUSLY	PLATTED
PERKIER	PICKLED	PIP-EMMA	PLATTER
PERKILY	PICQUET	PIPERIC	PLAUDIT
PERKING	PICTISH	PIPETTE	PLAY-BOX
PERMUTE	PICTURE	PIPLESS	PLAY-BOY
PERPLEX	PIEBALD	PIPPING	PLAY-DAY
PERRIER	PIECING	PIQUANT	PLAYFUL
PERSEUS	PIERAGE	PIQUING	PLAYING
PERSIAN	PIERCED	PIRATED	PLEADED
PERSIST	PIERCER	PIROGUE	PLEADER
PERSONA	PIERROT	PISCARY	PLEASED
PERSPEX	PIFFLED	PITAPAT	PLEASER
PERTAIN	PIG-EYED	PITCHED	PLEATED
PERTURB	PIGGERY	PITCHER	PLEDGED
PERUSAL	PIGGING	PITCOAL	PLEDGEE
PERUSED	PIGGISH	PITEOUS	PLEDGER
PERUSER	PIG-IRON	PITFALL	PLENARY
PERVADE	PIG-LEAD	PIT-HEAD	PLENISH
PERVERT	PIGMENT	PITHILY	PLENIST
PESTLED	PIGSKIN	PITIFUL	PLEROMA
PETERED	PIGTAIL	PITTING	PLEURAL

PLEXURE	POMMARD	POUNCED	PREVAIL
PLIABLE	POMPOUS	POUNDED	PREVENT
PLIABLY	PONIARD	POUNDER	PREVIEW
PLIANCY	PONTIFF	POURING	PREYING
PLIMSOL	PONTOON	POUTING	PRICING
PLODDED	POOH-BAH	POVERTY	PRICKED
PLODDER	POOLING	POWDERY	PRICKER
PLOPPED	POOPING	POWERED	PRICKLE
PLOTTED	POOREST	PRAETOR	PRICKLY
PLOTTER	POOR-LAW	PRAIRIE	PRIDIAN
PLUCKED	POPCORN	PRAISED	PRIDING
PLUCKER	POPEDOM	PRAISER	PRIMACY
PLUGGED	POP-EYED	PRALINE	PRIMAGE
PLUGGER	POPPIED	PRANCED	PRIMARY
PLUMAGE	POPPING	PRANGED	PRIMATE
PLUMBED	POPPLED	PRANKED	PRIMELY
PLUMBER	POP-SHOP	PRATIES	PRIMING
PLUMING	POPULAR	PRATING	PRIMULA
PLUMMET	PORCINE	PRATTLE	PRINKED
PLUMPED	PORK-PIE	PRAYING	PRINTED
PLUMPER	PORT-BAR	PREACHY	PRINTER
PLUMPLY	PORTEND	PREBEND	PRISING
PLUNDER	PORTENT	PRECEDE	PRITHEE
PLUNGED	PORTICO	PRECEPT	PRIVACY
PLUNGER	PORTIFY	PRECISE	PRIVATE
PLUVIAL	PORTING	PREDATE	PRIVILY
PLUVIUS	PORTION	PREDICT	PRIVITY
PLY-WOOD	PORTRAY	PREDOOM	PRIZING
POACHED	POSSESS	PREEMPT	PROBANG
POACHER	POSTAGE	PREENED	PROBATE
POETESS	POST-BAG	PREFACE	PROBING
POINTED	POST-BOY	PREFECT	PROBITY
POINTER	POST-DAY	PRELACY	PROBLEM
POISING	POSTERN	PRELATE	PROCEED
POLE-AXE	POSTING	PRELECT	PROCESS
POLE-CAT	POSTMAN	PRELUDE	PROCTOR
POLEMIC	POSTURE	PREMIER	PROCURE
POLENTA	POST-WAR	PREMISE	PRODDED
POLICED	POTABLE	PREMISS	PRODDER
POLITER	POTENCY	PREMIUM	PRODIGY
POLITIC	POT-HERB	PREPAID	PRODUCE
POLLACK	POT-HOLE	PREPARE	PRODUCT
POLLARD	POT-HOOK	PRESAGE	PROFANE
POLL-AXE	POT-LUCK	PRESENT	PROFESS
POLLING	POT-SHOT	PRESIDE	PROFFER
POLL-MAN	POTTAGE	PRESSED	PROFILE
POLL-TAX	POTTERY	PRESSER	PROFUSE
POLLUTE	POTTING	PRESUME	PROGENY
POLYGON	POUCHED	PRETEND	PROGRAM
POLYPUS	POULARD	PRETEXT	PROJECT
POMFRET	POULTRY	PRETZEL	PROLATE

PROLONG	PUFFING	PYROSIS	QUININE
PROMISE	PUFFIER	PYROTIC	QUINTET
PROMOTE	PUFFILY	PYRRHIC	QUIPPED
PRONELY	PUGMILL	PYTHIAD	QUITTAL
PRONGED	PUG-NOSE	PYTHIAN	QUITTED
PRONOUN	PULLING		QUITTER
PROOFED	PULLMAN	**Q—7**	QUI-VIVE
PROPHET	PULL-OUT	QUACKED	QUIXOTE
PROPOSE	PULPING	QUAFFED	QUIZZED
PROPPED	PULPOUS	QUAFFER	QUIZZER
PROSAIC	PULSATE	QUAILED	QUONDAM
PROSIFY	PULSING	QUAKING	QUOTING
PROSILY	PUMPAGE	QUALIFY	
PROSING	PUMPING	QUALITY	**R—7**
PROSODY	PUMPKIN	QUANTIC	RABIDLY
PROSPER	PUNCHED	QUANTUM	RACCOON
PROTEAN	PUNCHER	QUARREL	RACKETY
PROTECT	PUNCTUM	QUARTAN	RACKING
PROTEGE	PUNGENT	QUARTER	RACQUET
PROTEIN	PUNNING	QUARTET	RADDLED
PROTEST	PUNSTER	QUASHED	RADIANT
PROTEUS	PUNTING	QUASSIA	RADIATE
PROUDER	PURGING	QUAVERY	RADICAL
PROUDLY	PURITAN	QUEENED	RADICLE
PROVERB	PURLIEU	QUEENLY	RADIOED
PROVIDE	PURLING	QUEERER	RAFFISH
PROVINE	PURLOIN	QUEERLY	RAFFLED
PROVING	PURPLED	QUELLED	RAFFLER
PROVISO	PURPORT	QUELLER	RAGEFUL
PROVOKE	PURPOSE	QUEROUS	RAG-FAIR
PROVOST	PURRING	QUERIED	RAGGING
PROWESS	PURSING	QUERIST	RAGTIME
PROWLED	PURSUED	QUESTED	RAG-WEED
PROWLER	PURSUER	QUESTER	RAGWORT
PROXIMO	PURSUIT	QUESTOR	RAIDING ·
PRUDENT	PURVIEW	QUIBBLE	RAIL-CAR
PRUDERY	PUSHFUL	QUICKEN	RAILING
PRUDISH	PUSHING	QUICKER	RAILWAY
PRUNING	PUSTULE	QUICKIE	RAIMENT
PRUSSIC	PUTREFY	QUICKLY	RAINBOW
PRYTHEE	PUTTIED	QUIESCE	RAINING
PSALTER	PUTTING	QUIETED	RAISING
PSYCHIC	PUZZLED	QUIETEN	RAKE-OFF
PUBERTY	PUZZLER	QUIETER	RALLIED
PUBLISH	PYGMEAN	QUIETLY	RAMADAN
PUCKISH	PYJAMAS	QUIETUS	RAMBLED
PUDDING	PYRAMID	QUILLED	RAMBLER
PUDDLED	PYRETIC	QUILTED	RAMEKIN
PUDDLER	PYREXIA	QUILTER	RAMEOUS
PUDDOCK	PYRITES	QUINARY	RAMLINE
PUERILE	PYRITIC	QUINATE	RAMMING

RAMPAGE	REALISM	REDOUBT	REGULUS
RAMPANT	REALIST	REDOUND	REHOUSE
RAMPART	REALITY	REDPOLL	REIGNED
RAMPING	REALLOT	REDRAFT	REINING
RAMPION	REALTOR	REDRAWN	REINTER
RANCHED	RE-ANNEX	REDRESS	REISSUE
RANCHER	REAPING	REDSKIN	REJOICE
RANCOUR	REAPPLY	RED-TAPE	REJOINT
RANGERS	REARGUE	REDUCED	REJUDGE
RANGING	REARING	REDUCER	RELABEL
RANKEST	REARISE	REDWING	RELAPSE
RANKING	REARMED	REDWOOD	RELATED
RANKLED	RE-AROSE	REEKING	RELATER
RANSACK	REAWAKE	RE-ELECT	RELATOR
RANTING	REBATED	REELING	RELAXED
RAPHAEL	REBIRTH	RE-ENACT	RELAYED
RAPIDLY	REBLOOM	RE-ENDOW	RELEASE
RAPPING	REBORED	RE-ENJOY	RELIANT
RAPPORT	REBOUND	RE-ENTER	RELIEVE
RAPTURE	REBUILD	RE-ENTRY	RELIGHT
RAREBIT	REBUILT	RE-EQUIP	RELIVED
RASHEST	REBUKED	RE-ERECT	RELUMED
RASPING	REBUKER	REEVING	RELYING
RATABLE	RECEDED	REFEREE	REMAINS
RATAFIA	RECEIPT	REFINED	REMARRY
RATATAT	RECEIVE	REFINER	REMBLAI
RATCHED	RECHEAT	REFLECT	REMNANT
RATCHET	RECITAL	REFLOAT	REMODEL
RATTING	RECITED	REFORGE	REMORSE
RATTLED	RECITER	RE-FOUND	REMOTER
RATTLER	RECKING	REFRACT	REMOULD
RAT-TRAP	RECLAIM	REFRAIN	REMOUNT
RAUCOUS	RECLAME	REFRAME	REMOVAL
RAVAGED	RECLASP	REFRESH	REMOVED
RAVINED	RECLINE	REFUGEE	REMOVER
RAWHIDE	RECLOSE	REFUSAL	RENAMED
RAWNESS	RECLUSE	REFUSED	RENDING
RAYLESS	RECOUNT	REFUSER	RENEWAL
REACHED	RECOVER	REFUTED	RENEWED
REACHER	RECROSS	REFUTER	RENT-DAY
REACTED	RECRUIT	REGALED	RENTIER
REACTOR	RECTIFY	REGALIA	RENTING
READIED	RECTORY	REGALLY	REORDER
READIER	RECURVE	REGATTA	REPAINT
READILY	RED-COAT	REGENCY	REPAPER
READING	REDDEST	REGIMEN	REPINED
READMIT	REDDISH	REGNANT	REPINER
READOPT	RED-EYED	REGORGE	REPLACE
READORN	RED-FISH	REGREET	REPLANT
REAGENT	RED-HEAD	REGRESS	REPLETE
REALISE	REDNESS	REGULAR	REPLEVY

REPLICA	RETAKEN	RICKETY	ROGUERY
REPLIED	RETINUE	RIDDING	ROGUISH
REPLIER	RETIRAL	RIDDLED	ROILING
REPOINT	RETIRED	RIDDLER	ROISTER
REPOSAL	RETOUCH	RIFLING	ROLLICK
REPOSED	RETRACE	RIFTING	ROLLING
REPOSER	RETRACT	RIGGING	ROMANCE
REPRESS	RETREAD	RIGHTED	ROMANIC
REPRINT	RETREAT	RIGHTEN	ROMAUNT
REPRISE	RETRIAL	RIGHTER	ROMPERS
REPROOF	RETRIED	RIGHTLY	ROMPING
REPROVE	RETYPED	RIGIDLY	ROMPISH
REPRUNE	REUNIFY	RIMLESS	RONDEAU
REPTILE	REUNION	RIMMING	ROOFING
REPULSE	REUNITE	RINDING	ROOKERY
REPUTED	REURGED	RINGING	ROOKING
REQUEST	REVALUE	RINGLET	ROOMAGE
REQUIEM	REVELRY	RINSING	ROOMFUL
REQUIRE	REVENGE	RIOTING	ROOMIER
REQUITE	REVENUE	RIOTOUS	ROOMILY
REREDOS	REVERED	RIPCORD	ROOMING
RESCIND	REVERIE	RIPOSTE	ROOSTED
RE-SCORE	REVERSE	RIPPING	ROOSTER
RESCUED	REVERSI	RIPPLED	ROOTING
RESCUER	REVILED	RISIBLE	ROPEWAY
RESEIZE	REVILER	RISIBLY	ROSEATE
RESERVE	REVISAL	RISKIER	ROSE-BAY
RESHAPE	REVISED	RISKING	ROSE-BOX
RESIDED	REVISER	RISOTTO	ROSE-BUD
RESIDER	REVISIT	RISSOLE	ROSETTE
RESIDUE	REVIVAL	RIVALRY	ROSIEST
RESOLVE	REVIVED	RIVETED	ROSTRUM
RESOUND	REVIVER	RIVETER	ROTATED
RESPECT	REVOKED	RIVIERA	ROTATOR
RE-SPELL	REVOLVE	RIVULET	ROTTING
RE-SPELT	REVVING	ROAD-HOG	ROTUNDA
RESPIRE	REWRITE	ROADMAN	ROUGHED
RESPITE	REWROTE	ROAD-MAP	ROUGHEN
RESPLIT	REYNARD	ROADWAY	ROUGHER
RE-SPOKE	RHEMISH	ROAMING	ROUGHLY
RESPOND	RHENISH	ROARING	ROULADE
RESTAMP	RHODIAN	ROASTED	ROULEAU
RESTATE	RHOMBUS	ROASTER	ROUNDED
REST-DAY	RHUBARB	ROBBERY	ROUNDEL
RESTFUL	RHYMING	ROBBING	ROUNDER
RESTING	RHYMIST	ROCKERY	ROUNDLY
RESTIVE	RIBBING	ROCKIER	ROUND-UP
RESTOCK	RIBLESS	ROCKILY	ROUSING
RESTORE	RIBSTON	ROCKING	ROUTINE
RESUMED	RICHEST	RODLIKE	ROUTING
RESURGE	RICKETS	ROE-BUCK	ROWDIER

ROWDILY
ROWLOCK
ROYALLY
ROYALTY
RUB-A-DUB
RUBBING
RUBBISH
RUB-DOWN
RUBICON
RUCHING
RUCKING
RUCKLED
RUCTION
RUDDIER
RUDDILY
RUFFIAN
RUFFING
RUFFLED
RUINING
RUINOUS
RUMBLED
RUMBLER
RUMMAGE
RUMNESS
RUMPLED
RUNAWAY
RUNNING
RUPTURE
RURALLY
RUSHING
RUSH-MAT
RUSSETY
RUSSIAN
RUSTIER
RUSTILY
RUSTING
RUSTLED
RUSTLER

S—7
SABBATH
SACKAGE
SACKBUT
SACKFUL
SACKING
SACRIST
SADDEST
SADDLED
SADDLER
SAD-EYED
SADIRON

SADNESS
SAFFRON
SAGGING
SAILING
SAINTED
SAINTLY
SALIENT
SALLIED
SALLOWY
SALSIFY
SALT-BOX
SALTIER
SALTING
SALTIRE
SALTISH
SALT-PAN
SALT-PIT
SALUTED
SALVAGE
SALVING
SAMOVAR
SAMOYED
SAMPLED
SAMPLER
SAMURAI
SANCTUM
SANCTUS
SANDBAG
SAND-BOX
SAND-BOY
SAND-EEL
SAND-FLY
SAND-PIT
SAPHEAD
SAPIENT
SAPLESS
SAPLING
SAPPHIC
SAPPING
SAP-WOOD
SARACEN
SARCASM
SARCOMA
SARDINE
SATANIC
SATCHEL
SATIATE
SATIETY
SATINET
SATIRIC
SATISFY

SAUCIER
SAUCILY
SAUCING
SAUNTER
SAURIAN
SAUROID
SAUSAGE
SAVAGED
SAVANNA
SAVE-ALL
SAVELOY
SAVINGS
SAVIOUR
SAVOURY
SAWDUST
SAW-FISH
SAW-MILL
SAW-WORT
SAXHORN
SCABIES
SCABRID
SCALDED
SCALENE
SCALING
SCALLOP
SCALPED
SCALPEL
SCALPER
SCAMPED
SCAMPER
SCANDAL
SCANNED
SCANTLE
SCANTLY
SCAPULA
SCARCER
SCARFED
SCARIFY
SCARING
SCARLET
SCARPED
SCARRED
SCATHED
SCATTER
SCAUPER
SCENERY
SCENTED
SCEPTIC
SCEPTRE
SCHEMED
SCHEMER

SCHERZO
SCHOLAR
SCHOLIA
SCIATIC
SCIENCE
SCISSOR
SCOFFED
SCOFFER
SCOLDED
SCOLLOP
SCOOPED
SCOOPER
SCOOTED
SCOOTER
SCORIFY
SCORING
SCORNED
SCORNER
SCORPIO
SCOURED
SCOURER
SCOURGE
SCOWLED
SCRAGGY
SCRAPED
SCRAPER
SCRAPPY
SCRATCH
SCRAWLY
SCRAWNY
SCREECH
SCREEVE
SCREWED
SCREWER
SCRIBAL
SCRIBED
SCRIBER
SCROOGE
SCRUBBY
SCRUFFY
SCRUMPY
SCRUNCH
SCRUPLE
SCUDDED
SCUFFLE
SCULLED
SCULLER
SCUPPER
SCUTATE
SCUTTLE
SCYTHED

SEA-BANK	SEA-WING	SERFAGE	SHATTER
SEA-BEAR	SEA-WOLF	SERFDOM	SHAVIAN
SEA-BEET	SEA-WORM	SERIATE	SHAVING
SEA-BIRD	SECEDED	SERINGA	SHEAFED
SEA-BOAT	SECEDER	SERIOUS	SHEARER
SEA-CALF	SECLUDE	SERPENT	SHEATHE
SEA-CARD	SECONDO	SERRATE	SHEAVED
SEA-COAL	SECRECY	SERRIED	SHEBEEN
SEA-COCK	SECRETE	SERVANT	SHEDDER
SEA-COOK	SECTILE	SERVIAN	SHEERED
SEA-CROW	SECTION	SERVICE	SHEETED
SEA-DACE	SECULAR	SERVILE	SHELLAC
SEA-FIRE	SECURED	SERVING	SHELLED
SEA-FISH	SECURER	SESSION	SHELLER
SEA-FOAM	SEDUCED	SET-BACK	SHELTER
SEA-FOLK	SEDUCER	SET-DOWN	SHELTIE
SEA-FOOD	SEEABLE	SETTING	SHELVED
SEA-FOWL	SEEDBED	SETTLED	SHERBET
SEA-GATE	SEEDILY	SETTLER	SHERIFF
SEA-GIRT	SEEDING	SEVENTH	SHEWING
SEA-GULL	SEED-LAC	SEVENTY	SHIFTED
SEA-HARE	SEED-OIL	SEVERAL	SHIFTER
SEA-HAWK	SEEKING	SEVERED	SHIKARI
SEAKALE	SEEMING	SEVERER	SHIMMER
SEA-KING	SEEPAGE	SEXLESS	SHINGLE
SEA-LARK	SEETHED	SEXTAIN	SHINGLY
SEA-LEGS	SEGMENT	SEXTANT	SHINING
SEALERY	SEIZING	SEXTILE	SHINNED
SEA-LILY	SEIZURE	SHACKLE	SHIP-BOY
SEA-LINE	SELF-FED	SHADIER	SHIPFUL
SEALING	SELFISH	SHADILY	SHIP-MAN
SEA-LION	SELLING	SHADING	SHIPPED
SEA-MARK	SELTZER	SHADOWY	SHIPPER
SEA-MILE	SELVAGE	SHAFTED	SHIP-WAY
SEAMING	SEMATIC	SHAGGED	SHIRKED
SEA-MOSS	SEMI-GOD	SHAKILY	SHIRKER
SEA-PIKE	SEMINAL	SHAKING	SHIRRED
SEA-PORT	SEMIPED	SHALLOP	SHIVERY
SEARING	SEMITIC	SHALLOT	SHOALED
SEA-RISK	SENATOR	SHALLOW	SHOCKED
SEA-ROOM	SENDING	SHAMBLE	SHOCKER
SEA-SALT	SEND-OFF	SHAMING	SHOEING
SEASICK	SENEGAL	SHAMMED	SHOE-TIE
SEASIDE	SENSING	SHAMMER	SHOOING
SEA-SLUG	SENSORY	SHAMPOO	SHOOTER
SEATING	SENSUAL	SHAPELY	SHOP-BOY
SEA-VIEW	SEPTATE	SHAPING	SHOPMAN
SEA-WALL	SEQUENT	SHARING	SHOPPED
SEAWARD	SEQUOIA	SHARPEN	SHOPPER
SEAWEED	SERBIAN	SHARPER	SHORING
SEA-WIFE	SERENER	SHARPLY	SHORTED

SHORTEN	SILENUS	SKIPPED	SLINGER
SHORTER	SILICIC	SKIPPER	SLIPPED
SHOTGUN	SILICON	SKIPPET	SLIPPER
SHOTTED	SILK-HAT	SKIRLED	SLIPWAY
SHOUTED	SILKIER	SKIRTED	SLITHER
SHOUTER	SILKILY	SKIRTER	SLITTED
SHOVING	SILK-MAN	SKITTER	SLITTER
SHOW-BOX	SILLIER	SKITTLE	SLOBBER
SHOWERY	SILLILY	SKIVING	SLOE-GIN
SHOWILY	SILTING	SKULKED	SLOGGED
SHOWING	SILVERN	SKY-BLUE	SLOGGER
SHOWMAN	SILVERY	SKY-HIGH	SLOPING
SHREDDY	SIMILAR	SKYLARK	SLOPPED
SHRILLY	SIMPLER	SKYLINE	SLOTTED
SHRINED	SINCERE	SKYSAIL	SLOUCHY
SHRIVEL	SINEWED	SKYWARD	SLOWEST
SHRIVEN	SINGING	SLABBED	SLOWING
SHROUDS	SINGLED	SLABBER	SLUBBER
SHRUBBY	SINGLET	SLACKED	SLUDGER
SHUDDER	SINKING	SLACKEN	SLUGGED
SHUFFLE	SINLESS	SLACKER	SLUICED
SHUNNED	SINNING	SLACKLY	SLUMBER
SHUNNER	SINUATE	SLAKING	SLUMMER
SHUNTED	SINUOUS	SLAMMED	SLUMPED
SHUNTER	SIPPING	SLANDER	SLURRED
SHUT-EYE	SIRGANG	SLANGED	SLYNESS
SHUTTER	SIRLOIN	SLANTED	SMACKED
SHUTTLE	SIROCCO	SLANTLY	SMACKER
SHYLOCK	SISTINE	SLAPPED	SMARTED
SHYNESS	SITTING	SLASHED	SMARTEN
SHYSTER	SITUATE	SLASHER	SMARTER
SIAMESE	SIXFOLD	SLATING	SMARTLY
SIBLING	SIXTEEN	SLAVERY	SMASHED
SICK-BAY	SIXTHLY	SLAVING	SMASHER
SICK-BED	SIZABLE	SLAVISH	SMASH-UP
SICKEST	SIZZLED	SLAYING	SMATTER
SICKISH	SKATING	SLEDDED	SMEARED
SIDEARM	SKEPFUL	SLEDGED	SMELLED
SIDECAR	SKEPTIC	SLEEKED	SMELLER
SIDLING	SKETCHY	SLEEKER	SMELTED
SIFFLED	SKIDDED	SLEEKLY	SMELTER
SIFTING	SKIFFLE	SLEEPER	SMICKER
SIGHING	SKILFUL	SLEETED	SMILING
SIGHTED	SKILLED	SLEIGHT	SMIRKED
SIGHTER	SKILLET	SLENDER	SMITING
SIGHTLY	SKIMMED	SLICING	SMITTEN
SIGNIFY	SKIMMER	SLICKER	SMOKIER
SIGNING	SKIMPED	SLIDDER	SMOKILY
SIGNORA	SKINFUL	SLIDING	SMOKING
SIGNORY	SKINNED	SLIMILY	SMOOTHE
SILENCE	SKINNER	SLIMMER	SMOTHER

M.C.D.—21

SMUDGED	SO-AND-SO	SOUREST	SPHERED
SMUDGER	SOAPBOX	SOURING	SPHERIC
SMUGGLE	SOAPING	SOURISH	SPICERY
SNAFFLE	SOARING	SOUSING	SPICILY
SNAGGED	SOBBING	SOUTANE	SPICING
SNAGGER	SOBERED	SOUTHER	SPIDERY
SNAKING	SOBERLY	SOU'WEST	SPIKING
SNAKISH	SOCIETY	SOZZLED	SPILLED
SNAPPED	SOCKEYE	SPACIAL	SPILLER
SNAPPER	SOCKING	SPACING	SPINACH
SNARING	SOFTEST	SPANGLE	SPINATE
SNARLED	SOFTISH	SPANGLY	SPINDLE
SNARLER	SOIGNEE	SPANIEL	SPINDLY
SNATCHY	SOILING	SPANISH	SPINNER
SNEAKED	SOJOURN	SPANKED	SPINNEY
SNEAKER	SOLACED	SPANKER	SPIRANT
SNEERED	SOLDIER	SPANNED	SPIRING
SNEERER	SOLICIT	SPANNER	SPIRTED
SNEEZED	SOLIDLY	SPARELY	SPITING
SNICKED	SOLIDUS	SPARING	SPITTED
SNICKER	SOLOIST	SPARKED	SPITTER
SNIFFED	SOLOMON	SPARKLE	SPITTLE
SNIFFLE	SOLUBLE	SPARRED	SPLASHY
SNIFTED	SOLVENT	SPARROW	SPLAYED
SNIFTER	SOLVING	SPARTAN	SPLEENY
SNIGGER	SOMATIC	SPASTIC	SPLENIC
SNIGGLE	SOMEHOW	SPATIAL	SPLICED
SNIPING	SOMEONE	SPATTER	SPLODGE
SNIPPED	SONGFUL	SPATULA	SPLODGY
SNIPPER	SONSHIP	SPAWNED	SPLOTCH
SNIPPET	SOOTHED	SPAWNER	SPOILED
SNOOKER	SOOTHER	SPEAKER	SPOILER
SNOOPED	SOOTING	SPEARED	SPONDEE
SNOOPER	SOPHISM	SPEARER	SPONGED
SNOOZED	SOPHIST	SPECIAL	SPONGER
SNOOZER	SOPPING	SPECIES	SPONSAL
SNORING	SOPRANO	SPECIFY	SPONSON
SNORTED	SORCERY	SPECKED	SPONSOR
SNORTER	SORDINE	SPECKLE	SPOOFED
SNOUTED	SORITES	SPECTRA	SPOOLED
SNOW-ICE	SORORAL	SPECTRE	SPOONED
SNOWILY	SOROSIS	SPEEDED	SPORRAN
SNOW-MAN	SORRILY	SPEEDER	SPORTED
SNUBBED	SORTING	SPEED-UP	SPORTER
SNUBBER	SOTTISH	SPELLED	SPOTTED
SNUFFED	SOUFFLE	SPELLER	SPOTTER
SNUFFER	SOULFUL	SPELTER	SPOUSAL
SNUFFLE	SOUNDLY	SPENCER	SPOUTED
SNUGGLE	SOUNDED	SPENDER	SPOUTER
SOAKAGE	SOUNDER	SPEWING	SPRAYED
SOAKING	SOUPCON	SPHERAL	SPRAYEY

SPRIGGY	STAMPED	STERILE	STOWING
SPRIGHT	STAMPER	STERNAL	STRANGE
SPRINGE	STAND-BY	STERNER	STRATUM
SPRINGY	STANDER	STERNLY	STRATUS
SPRUCED	STAND-TO	STERNUM	STRAYED
SPUMING	STAND-UP	STETSON	STRAYER
SPUN-OUT	STAPLED	STEWARD	STREAKY
SPURNED	STAPLER	STEWING	STREAMY
SPURNER	STARCHY	STEWPAN	STRETCH
SPURRED	STARDOM	STEWPOT	STREWED
SPURRER	STARING	STICKER	STRIATE
SPURREY	STARKLY	STICKLE	STRIKER
SPURTED	STARLIT	STIFFEN	STRINGY
SPURTLE	STARRED	STIFFER	STRIPED
SPUR-WAY	STARTED	STIFFLY	STRIVEN
SPUTTER	STARTER	STIFLED	STRIVER
SPY-BOAT	STARTLE	STILLED	STROKED
SPY-HOLE	STARVED	STILLER	STROKER
SQUABBY	STATANT	STILTED	STROPHE
SQUALID	STATELY	STILTON	STUBBED
SQUALLY	STATICS	STIMULI	STUBBLE
SQUALOR	STATING	STINGER	STUBBLY
SQUARED	STATION	STINKER	STUCK-UP
SQUASHY	STATIST	STINTED	STUDDED
SQUATTY	STATUED	STINTER	STUDENT
SQUEEZE	STATURE	STIPEND	STUDIED
SQUELCH	STATUTE	STIPPLE	STUFFED
SQUIFFY	STAUNCH	STIRRED	STUFFER
SQUIRED	STAVING	STIRRER	STUMBLE
STABBED	STAYING	STIRRUP	STUMPED
STABBER	STEALER	STOCKED	STUMPER
STABLED	STEALTH	STOICAL	STUNNED
STACKED	STEAMED	STOKING	STUNNER
STACKER	STEAMER	STOMACH	STUNTED
STADIUM	STEELED	STONILY	STUPEFY
STAFFED	STEEPED	STONING	STUTTER
STAGERY	STEEPEN	STOOGED	STYGIAN
STAGGER	STEEPER	STOOKED	STYLING
STAGING	STEEPLE	STOOPED	STYLISE
STAIDLY	STEEPLY	STOOPER	STYLISH
STAINED	STEERED	STOP-GAP	STYLIST
STAINER	STEERER	STOPPED	STYLITE
STAITHE	STELLAR	STOPPER	STYLOID
STAKING	STEMLET	STORAGE	STYMIED
STATELY	STEMMED	STORIED	SUASION
STALEST	STENCIL	STORING	SUASIVE
STALKED	STENTOR	STORMED	SUASORY
STALKER	STEPNEY	STORMER	SUAVELY
STALLED	STEPPED	STOUTER	SUAVITY
STAMINA	STEPPER	STOUTLY	SUBACID
STAMMER	STEP-SON	STOWAGE	SUBBING

SUBDEAN	SUMMARY	SWAGMAN	SYMPTOM
SUBDUAL	SUMMERY	SWAHILI	SYNAXIS
SUBDUCT	SUMMING	SWALING	SYNCOPE
SUBDUED	SUMMONS	SWALLOW	SYNESIS
SUBDUER	SUMPTER	SWAMPED	SYNODAL
SUBEDIT	SUN-BATH	SWANKED	SYNONYM
SUBFUSC	SUNBEAM	SWAPPED	SYRINGA
SUB-HEAD	SUN-BEAT	SWARDED	SYRINGE
SUBJECT	SUN-BIRD	SWARMED	T—7
SUBJOIN	SUNBURN	SWARTHY	TABASCO
SUBLATE	SUN-DIAL	SWASHED	TABINET
SUBLIME	SUNDOWN	SWASHER	TABLEAU
SUBRENT	SUN-FISH	SWATTED	TABLING
SUBSALT	SUNLESS	SWATTER	TABLOID
SUBSIDE	SUNNING	SWAYING	TABOOED
SUBSIDY	SUNRISE	SWEALED	TABULAR
SUBSIGN	SUNSPOT	SWEARER	TACITLY
SUBSIST	SUNWARD	SWEATED	TACKING
SUBSOIL	SUNWISE	SWEATER	TACKLED
SUBSUME	SUPPING	SWEDISH	TACTFUL
SUBTEND	SUPPLED	SWEEPER	TACTICS
SUBTILE	SUPPORT	SWEETEN	TACTILE
SUBTLER	SUPPOSE	SWEETER	TACTION
SUBTYPE	SUPREME	SWEETLY	TACTUAL
SUBURBS	SURCOAT	SWELLED	TADPOLE
SUBVENE	SURDITY	SWELTER	TAFFETA
SUBVERT	SURFACE	SWELTRY	TAGGING
SUCCEED	SURFEIT	SWERVED	TAIL-END
SUCCESS	SURGENT	SWERVER	TAILING
SUCCOUR	SURGEON	SWIFTER	TAINTED
SUCCUMB	SURGERY	SWIFTLY	TAKE-OFF
SUCKING	SURGING	SWIGGED	TAKINGS
SUCKLED	SURLIER	SWILLED	TALIPED
SUCKLER	SURLILY	SWILLER	TALIPES
SUCROSE	SURLOIN	SWIMMER	TALKIES
SUCTION	SURMISE	SWINDLE	TALKING
SUFFICE	SURNAME	SWINERY	TALLBOY
SUFFUSE	SURPASS	SWINGED	TALLEST
SUGARED	SURPLUS	SWINGER	TALLIED
SUGGEST	SURTOUT	SWINISH	TALLIER
SUICIDE	SURVIVE	SWIPING	TALLISH
SUITING	SUSPECT	SWIRLED	TALLOWY
SULKIER	SUSPEND	SWISHED	TALLY-HO
SULKILY	SUSPIRE	SWISHER	TALONED
SULKING	SUSTAIN	SWIZZLE	TAMABLE
SULLAGE	SUTURAL	SWOLLEN	TAMBOUR
SULLENS	SUTURED	SWOONED	TANGENT
SULLIED	SWABBED	SWOOPED	TANGLED
SULPHUR	SWABBER	SWOPPED	TANGOED
SULTANA	SWADDLE	SWOTTED	TANKAGE
SUMLESS	SWAGGER	SYLPHID	TANKARD

TANNAGE	TEEMING	THAWING	TIDE-WAY
TANNATE	TEENAGE	THEATRE	TIDIEST
TANNERY	TELERGY	THEOREM	TIDINGS
TANNING	TELLING	THERAPY	TIE-BEAM
TANTRUM	TEMPERA	THEREAT	TIERCEL
TAPERED	TEMPEST	THEREBY	TIGHTEN
TAPIOCA	TEMPLAR	THEREIN	TIGHTER
TAPPING	TEMPLED	THEREOF	TIGHTLY
TAPROOM	TEMPLET	THEREON	TIGRESS
TAPROOT	TEMPTED	THERETO	TIGRISH
TAPSTER	TEMPTER	THERMAL	TILBURY
TARDIER	TENABLE	THERMOS	TILLAGE
TARDILY	TENANCY	THESEUS	TILLING
TARNISH	TENDING	THICKEN	TILTING
TARRIED	TENDRIL	THICKER	TIMBREL
TARRIER	TENFOLD	THICKET	TIME-LAG
TARRING	TENSELY	THICKLY	TIMEOUS
TARTISH	TENSEST	THIEVED	TIMIDLY
TARTLET	TENSILE	THIMBLE	TIMOTHY
TASKING	TENSION	THINKER	TIMPANI
TASTIER	TENSITY	THINNED	TIMPANO
TASTILY	TENTHLY	THINNER	TINDERY
TASTING	TENT-PEG	THIRDLY	TINFOIL
TATTERY	TENUITY	THIRSTY	TINGING
TATTING	TENUOUS	THISTLE	TINGLED
TATTLED	TERMING	THISTLY	TINIEST
TATTLER	TERMINI	THITHER	TINKING
TAUNTED	TERMITE	THOLING	TINKLED
TAUNTER	TERNARY	THOUGHT	TINKLER
TAURINE	TERNATE	THREADY	TIN-MINE
TAUTEST	TERRACE	THRIFTY	TINNING
TAXABLE	TERRAIN	THRIVED	TIN-TACK
TAX-FREE	TERRENE	THRIVEN	TINTAGE
TAXI-CAB	TERRIER	THRIVER	TINTING
TAXYING	TERRIFY	THROATY	TINTYPE
TEA-CAKE	TERRINE	THRONAL	TINWARE
TEACHER	TERSELY	THRONED	TIP-CART
TEA-COSY	TERTIAN	THROUGH	TIPPING
TEA-GOWN	TESTACY	THROWER	TIPPLED
TEA-LEAF	TESTATE	THUMBED	TIPPLER
TEAMING	TESTIER	THUMPED	TIPSILY
TEARFUL	TESTIFY	THUMPER	TIPSTER
TEARING	TESTILY	THUNDER	TIPTOED
TEA-ROSE	TESTING	THYROID	TISSUED
TEASING	TETANUS	THYSELF	TITANIA
TEA-TIME	TEXTILE	TIARAED	TITANIC
TEA-TREE	TEXTUAL	TIBETAN	TITHING
TECHNIC	TEXTURE	TICKING	TITLARK
TEDDING	THALIAN	TICKLED	TITLING
TEDIOUS	THANAGE	TICKLER	TITMICE
TEEMFUL	THANKED	TIDDLER	TITULAR

TOADIED	TORTURE	TRAMWAY	TRINITY
TOASTED	TORYISM	TRANCED	TRINKET
TOASTER	TOSSILY	TRANSIT	TRINKLE
TOBACCO	TOSSING	TRANSOM	TRIOLET
TOBYMAN	TOSSPOT	TRANTER	TRIPLED
TOCCATA	TOTALLY	TRAPEZE	TRIPLET
TODDLED	TOTTERY	TRAPPED	TRIPOLI
TODDLER	TOTTING	TRAPPER	TRIPPED
TOE-NAIL	TOUCHED	TRASHED	TRIPPER
TOGGERY	TOUCHER	TRAVAIL	TRIREME
TOILFUL	TOUGHEN	TRAWLED	TRISECT
TOILING	TOUGHLY	TRAWLER	TRITELY
TOLLAGE	TOURING	TREACLE	TRIUMPH
TOLL-BAR	TOURISM	TREACLY	TRIVIAL
TOLLING	TOURIST	TREADER	TROCHEE
TOLLMAN	TOURNEY	TREADLE	TRODDEN
TOMBOLA	TOUSING	TREASON	TROLLED
TOMFOOL	TOUSLED	TREATED	TROLLER
TOMPION	TOUTING	TREATER	TROLLEY
TONGUED	TOWARDS	TREBLED	TROLLOP
TONIGHT	TOWBOAT	TREEING	TROOPED
TONNAGE	TOWERED	TREFOIL	TROOPER
TONNEAU	TOWLINE	TREKKED	TROPICS
TONSURE	TOWNISH	TREKKER	TROTTED
TONTINE	TOW-PATH	TRELLIS	TROTTER
TOOLING	TOW-ROPE	TREMBLE	TROUBLE
TOOTHED	TOYSHOP	TREMBLY	TROUNCE
TOOTING	TOYSOME	TREMOLO	TROUPER
TOOTLED	TRACERY	TRESTLE	TROWING
TOPARCH	TRACHEA	TRIABLE	TRUANCY
TOP-BOOT	TRACING	TRIBUNE	TRUCKED
TOPCOAT	TRACKED	TRIBUTE	TRUCKER
TOP-HOLE	TRACKER	TRICEPS	TRUCKLE
TOPIARY	TRACTOR	TRICKED	TRUDGED
TOPICAL	TRADING	TRICKER	TRUFFLE
TOP-KNOT	TRADUCE	TRICKLE	TRUMPED
TOPLESS	TRAFFIC	TRICKLY	TRUMPET
TOP-MAST	TRAGEDY	TRICKSY	TRUNCAL
TOP-MOST	TRAILED	TRICORN	TRUNDLE
TOPPING	TRAILER	TRIDENT	TRUSSED
TOPPLED	TRAINED	TRIFLED	TRUSTED
TOPSAIL	TRAINEE	TRIFLER	TRUSTEE
TOP-SIDE	TRAINER	TRIFORM	TRUSTER
TOPSMAN	TRAIPSE	TRIGAMY	TRY-SAIL
TOP-SOIL	TRAITOR	TRIGGER	TRYSTED
TORCHON	TRAJECT	TRILLED	TSARINA
TORMENT	TRAM-CAR	TRILOGY	TSARIST
TORNADO	TRAMMEL	TRIMMED	T-SQUARE
TORPEDO	TRAMPED	TRIMMER	TUBBING
TORRENT	TRAMPER	TRINARY	TUBBISH
TORSION	TRAMPLE	TRINGLE	TUBULAR

TUCKING	TWISTER	UNCIVIL	UNICITY
TUCK-OUT	TWITTED	UNCLASP	UNICORN
TUESDAY	TWITTER	UNCLEAN	UNIDEAL
TUFTING	TWOFOLD	UNCLEAR	UNIFIED
TUG-BOAT	TWONESS	UNCLOAK	UNIFIER
TUGGING	TWOSOME	UNCLOSE	UNIFORM
TUITION	TWO-STEP	UNCLOUD	UNITARY
TUMBLED	TYNWALD	UNCOUTH	UNITING
TUMBLER	TYPHOID	UNCOVER	UNJOINT
TUMBREL	TYPHOON	UNCROSS	UNKEMPT
TUMIDLY	TYPHOUS	UNCROWN	UNKNOWN
TUMULAR	TYPICAL	UNCTION	UNLACED
TUMULUS	TYRANNY	UNDATED	UNLADEN
TUNABLE	TZARINA	UNDEIFY	UNLATCH
TUNABLY	U—7	UNDERDO	UNLEARN
TUNEFUL	UKULELE	UNDERGO	UNLEASH
TUNNAGE	ULULATE	UNDOING	UNLIMED
TUNNERY	ULYSSES	UNDRAPE	UNLINED
TURBINE	UMBERED	UNDRAWN	UNLIVED
TURFING	UMBRAGE	UNDRESS	UNLOOSE
TURGENT	UMBROSE	UNDRIED	UNLOVED
TURGITE	UMPIRED	UNDYING	UNLUCKY
TURKISH	UMPTEEN	UNEARTH	UNMANLY
TURMOIL	UNACTED	UNEATEN	UNMARRY
TURNCAP	UNAGING	UNEQUAL	UNMEANT
TURNERY	UNAIDED	UNEXACT	UNMEWED
TURNING	UNAIRED	UNFADED	UNMIXED
TURNKEY	UNAPTLY	UNFAITH	UNMOIST
TURN-OUT	UNARMED	UNFILED	UNMORAL
TUSSLED	UNASKED	UNFITLY	UNMOULD
TUSSOCK	UNAWARE	UNFIXED	UNMOVED
TUSSORE	UNBAKED	UNFOUND	UNNAMED
TUTELAR	UNBEGUN	UNFROCK	UNNERVE
TUTORED	UNBLIND	UNFUSED	UNNOTED
TWADDLE	UNBLOCK	UNGIVEN	UNOILED
TWANGED	UNBLOWN	UNGLUED	UNOWNED
TWANGLE	UNBOSOM	UNGODLY	UNPAVED
TWANKED	UNBOUND	UNGUENT	UNPERCH
TWEAKED	UNBOWED	UNHANDY	UNPLAIT
TWEEDLE	UNBRACE	UNHAPPY	UNPLUMB
TWEENIE	UNBRAID	UNHARDY	UNQUIET
TWELFTH	UNBUILT	UNHASTY	UNRAKED
TWIDDLE	UNBURNT	UNHEARD	UNRAVEL
TWIGGED	UNCAGED	UNHEEDY	UNREADY
TWINGED	UNCANNY	UNHINGE	UNREEVE
TWINING	UNCARED	UNHIRED	UNRIVET
TWINKLE	UNCASED	UNHITCH	UNROBED
TWINNED	UNCEDED	UNHIVED	UNROYAL
TWIRLED	UNCHAIN	UNHOPED	UNRULED
TWIRLER	UNCHARY	UNHORSE	UNSATED
TWISTED	UNCINAL	UNHOUSE	UNSCREW

UNSEXED	UPBORNE	VAMOOSE	VERONAL
UNSHORN	UPBRAID	VAMPING	VERSIFY
UNSHOWN	UPDATED	VAMPIRE	VERSING
UNSIZED	UPENDED	VANDYKE	VERSION
UNSLING	UPGRADE	VANESSA	VERTIGO
UNSLUNG	UPHEAVE	VANILLA	VERVAIN
UNSOLID	UPLYING	VANNING	VESICLE
UNSOUND	UPRAISE	VANTAGE	VESTIGE
UNSPELL	UPRIGHT	VANWARD	VESTING
UNSPENT	UPRISEN	VAPIDLY	VESTRAL
UNSPIED	UPSTAGE	VAPOURS	VETERAN
UNSPIKE	UPSTART	VAPOURY	VETOING
UNSPILT	UPSURGE	VARIANT	VIADUCT
UNSPLIT	UPSWEEP	VARIATE	VIBRANT
UNSPOIL	UP-TRAIN	VARIETY	VIBRATE
UNSTACK	UPWARDS	VARIOUS	VIBRATO
UNSTAID	URALITE	VARMINT	VICEROY
UNSTEEL	URANITE	VARNISH	VICIOUS
UNSTICK	URANIUM	VARSITY	VICTORY
UNSTUCK	URGENCY	VARYING	VICTUAL
UNSWEET	USELESS	VASTEST	VIEWING
UNSWEPT	USHERED	VATICAN	VILLAGE
UNSWORN	USUALLY	VAULTED	VILLAIN
UNTAKEN	USURPED	VAULTER	VILLEIN
UNTAMED	USURPER	VAUNTED	VINEGAR
UNTAXED	UTENSIL	VEERING	VINTAGE
UNTHINK	UTILISE	VEHICLE	VINTNER
UNTILED	UTILITY	VEILING	VIOLATE
UNTIRED	UTOPIAN	VEINING	VIOLENT
UNTRIED	UTTERED	VEINOUS	VIOLIST
UNTRULY	UTTERER	VELLUMY	VIRGATE
UNTRUSS	UTTERLY	VELOURS	VIRTUAL
UNTRUTH	UXORIAL	VELVETY	VISAGED
UNTUNED		VENALLY	VIS-A-VIS
UNTWINE	V—7	VENDING	VISCOUS
UNTWIST	VACANCY	VENISON	VISIBLE
UNTYING	VACATED	VENOMED	VISIBLY
UNURGED	VACATOR	VENTAGE	VISITED
UNUSUAL	VACCINE	VENTAIL	VISITOR
UNVEXED	VACUITY	VENTING	VISORED
UNVOWED	VACUOLE	VENT-PEG	VITALLY
UNWAGED	VACUOUS	VENTRAL	VITAMIN
UNWEARY	VAGRANT	VENTURE	VITIATE
UNWEAVE	VAGUELY	VERANDA	VITRIFY
UNWIRED	VAGUEST	VERBENA	VITRINE
UNWOOED	VAINEST	VERBOSE	VITRIOL
UNWOUND	VALANCE	VERDANT	VIVIDLY
UNWOVEN	VALIANT	VERDICT	VIXENLY
UNWRUNG	VALIDLY	VERDURE	VOCABLE
UNYOKED	VALUING	VERGING	VOCALLY
UNZONED	VALVATE	VERIEST	VOICING

VOIDING	WAREFUL	WEAKEST	WHARFED
VOLCANO	WARFARE	WEALDEN	WHARVES
VOLTAGE	WARHOOP	WEALTHY	WHATNOT
VOLTAIC	WARIEST	WEANING	WHEATEN
VOLUBLE	WARLIKE	WEARIED	WHEEDLE
VOLUBLY	WARLOCK	WEARIER	WHEELED
VOLUTED	WAR-LORD	WEARILY	WHEELER
VOTABLE	WARMEST	WEARING	WHEEZED
VOUCHED	WARMING	WEARISH	WHELPED
VOUCHEE	WARNING	WEATHER	WHEREAS
VOUCHER	WARPATH	WEAVING	WHEREAT
VOYAGED	WARPING	WEBBING	WHEREBY
VOYAGER	WARRANT	WEB-FOOT	WHEREIN
VULGATE	WARRING	WEBSTER	WHEREOF
VULPINE	WARRIOR	WEB-TOED	WHEREON
VULTURE	WARSHIP	WEDDING	WHERESO
	WAR-SONG	WEDGING	WHERETO
W—7	WART-HOG	WEDLOCK	WHETHER
WADDING	WAR-WORN	WEEDING	WHETTED
WADDLED	WASHING	WEEKDAY	WHETTER
WADDLER	WASH-OUT	WEEK-END	WHIFFED
WAFERED	WASH-POT	WEENING	WHIFFLE
WAFTING	WASH-TUB	WEEPING	WHILING
WAGERED	WASP-FLY	WEFTAGE	WHIMPER
WAGGERY	WASPISH	WEIGHED	WHIMSEY
WAGGING	WASSAIL	WEIGHER	WHINING
WAGGISH	WASTAGE	WEIGHTY	WHIPPED
WAGGLED	WASTING	WEIRDER	WHIPPER
WAGONER	WASTREL	WEIRDLY	WHIPPET
WAGTAIL	WATCHED	WELCOME	WHIP-SAW
WAILING	WATCHER	WELDING	WHIP-TOP
WAISTED	WATCHET	WELFARE	WHIRLED
WAITING	WATERED	WELLING	WHIRRED
WAIVING	WATERER	WELL-MET	WHIRLER
WAKEFUL	WATTLED	WELL-OFF	WHISKER
WAKENED	WAVELET	WELL-SET	WHISKEY
WAKENER	WAVERED	WELL-WON	WHISPER
WALKING	WAVERER	WELSHED	WHISTLE
WALLABY	WAX-BILL	WELSHER	WHITELY
WALL-EYE	WAX-DOLL	WELTING	WHITEST
WALLING	WAX-MOTH	WENDING	WHITHER
WALLOON	WAX-PALM	WESTERN	WHITING
WALTZED	WAX-TREE	WESTING	WHITISH
WALTZER	WAX-WING	WET-DOCK	WHITLOW
WANGLED	WAXWORK	WETNESS	WHITSUN
WANNESS	WAY-BILL	WETTEST	WHITTLE
WANNISH	WAY-MARK	WETTING	WHIZZED
WANTAGE	WAYSIDE	WETTISH	WHIZZER
WARBLED	WAYWARD	WHACKED	WHOEVER
WARBLER	WAYWISE	WHACKER	WHOOPEE
WARDING	WAYWORN	WHALING	WHOOPED

WHOOPER	WIZENED	WRIGGLY	ZONALLY
WHOPPED	WOBBLED	WRINGER	ZONULAR
WHOPPER	WOBBLER	WRINKLE	ZOOIDAL
WHORLED	WOESOME	WRINKLY	ZOOLITE
WIDENED	WOLF-CUB	WRITHED	ZOOLOGY
WIDENER	WOLF-DOG	WRITING	ZOOMING
WIDGEON	WOLFISH	WRITTEN	
WIDOWED	WOLF-NET	WRONGED	A—8
WIDOWER	WOLFRAM	WRONGER	ABASHING
WIELDED	WOMANLY	WRONGLY	ABATABLE
WIELDER	WOOD-ANT	WROUGHT	ABATTOIR
WIGGERY	WOODCUT	WRYNECK	ABDICANT
WIGGING	WOODMAN	WRYNESS	ABDICATE
WIGGLED	WOOLLEN	WYCH-ELM	ABDUCTED
WIGGLER	WOOLMAN		ABDUCTOR
WIGLESS	WOOMERA	X—7	ABERDEEN
WILD-CAT	WORDILY	X-RAYING	ABERRANT
WILDEST	WORDING		ABERRATE
WILDING	WORDISH	Y—7	ABETMENT
WILDISH	WORK-BAG	YANKING	ABETTING
WILIEST	WORK-BOX	YAPPING	ABEYANCE
WILLING	WORK-DAY	YARDAGE	ABHORRED
WILLOWY	WORKING	YARD-ARM	ABHORRER
WILTING	WORKMAN	YARDING	ABJECTLY
WIMPLED	WORK-SHY	YARD-MAN	ABJURING
WINCHED	WORLDLY	YARNING	ABLATION
WINDAGE	WORMING	YASHMAK	ABLATIVE
WIND-BAG	WORN-OUT	YAWNING	ABLENESS
WINDIER	WORRIED	YEARNED	ABLUTION
WINDILY	WORRIER	YELLING	ABNEGATE
WINDING	WORSHIP	YELLOWY	ABNORMAL
WINDROW	WORSTED	YELPING	ABORTING
WINDSOR	WOTTING	YEW-TREE	ABORTION
WINE-BAG	WOULD-BE	YIDDISH	ABORTIVE
WINGING	WOULDST	YIELDED	ABRADING
WINGLET	WOUNDED	YORKIST	ABRASION
WINKING	WOUNDER	YOUNGER	ABRASIVE
WINNING	WRANGLE	YOWLING	ABRIDGED
WINSOME	WRAPPED	YULE-LOG	ABROGATE
WIRE-MAN	WRAPPER		ABSENTED
WIRE-WAY	WREAKED	Z—7	ABSENTEE
WISHFUL	WREAKER	ZANYISM	ABSENTLY
WISTFUL	WREATHE	ZEALFUL	ABSINTHE
WITCHED	WREATHY	ZEALOUS	ABSOLUTE
WITHERS	WRECKED	ZEOLITE	ABSOLVED
WITHOUT	WRECKER	ZESTFUL	ABSOLVER
WITLESS	WRESTED	ZESTING	ABSONANT
WITLING	WRESTER	ZINCOID	ABSORBED
WITNESS	WRESTLE	ZIONISM	ABSTRACT
WITTIER	WRICKED	ZIONIST	ABSTRUSE
WITTILY	WRIGGLE	ZIPPING	ABSURDLY

ABUNDANT	ADENOIDS	AFFORDED	ALIENISM
ABUSABLE	ADEPTION	AFFOREST	ALIENIST
ABUTMENT	ADEQUACY	AFFRIGHT	ALIGHTED
ABUTTING	ADEQUATE	AGAR-AGAR	ALIGNING
ACADEMIC	ADHERENT	AGEDNESS	ALKALINE
ACANTHUS	ADHERING	AGGRIEVE	ALKALOID
ACCEDING	ADHESION	AGITATED	ALLAYING
ACCENTED	ADHESIVE	AGITATOR	ALL-CLEAR
ACCEPTED	ADJACENT	AGLIMMER	ALLEGING
ACCEPTER	ADJOINED	AGNATION	ALLEGORY
ACCEPTOR	ADJUDGED	AGNOSTIC	ALLELUIA
ACCIDENT	ADJURING	AGONISED	ALLERGIC
ACCOLADE	ADJUSTER	AGRARIAN	ALLEYWAY
ACCORDED	ADJUTANT	AGREEING	ALL-FIRED
ACCOSTED	ADMIRING	AGRIMONY	ALL-FOURS
ACCOUTRE	ADMITTED	AGRONOMY	ALLIANCE
ACCREDIT	ADMIXING	AIGRETTE	ALLOCATE
ACCRUING	ADMONISH	AIRBORNE	ALLOTTED
ACCURACY	ADOPTING	AIR-BRAKE	ALLOWING
ACCURATE	ADOPTION	AIR-BRICK	ALLOYING
ACCURSED	ADOPTIVE	AIRCRAFT	ALLSPICE
ACCUSANT	ADORABLE	AIREDALE	ALLUDING
ACCUSING	ADORABLY	AIRFIELD	ALLURING
ACCUSTOM	ADORNING	AIR-GRAPH	ALLUSION
ACERBATE	ADROITLY	AIRINESS	ALLUSIVE
ACERBITY	ADSCRIPT	AIR-LINER	ALLUSORY
ACESCENT	ADULATED	AIR-PILOT	ALLUVIAL
ACHIEVED	ADULATOR	AIRPLANE	ALLUVION
ACIDNESS	ADVANCED	AIR-POWER	ALLUVIUM
ACIDOSIS	ADVERTED	AIR-SCREW	ALMIGHTY
ACONITIC	ADVISING	AIR-SHAFT	ALPHABET
ACORN-CUP	ADVISORY	AIR-SPACE	ALPINIST
ACOUSTIC	ADVOCACY	AIR-STRIP	ALSATIAN
ACQUAINT	ADVOCATE	AIRTIGHT	ALTERING
ACQUIRED	ADVOWSON	ALACRITY	ALTHOUGH
ACRIDITY	AERATING	ALARM-GUN	ALTITUDE
ACRIMONY	AERATION	ALARMING	ALTRUISM
ACROSTIC	AERIALLY	ALARMIST	ALTRUIST
ACTINISM	AERIFIED	ALBACORE	AMARANTH
ACTIVATE	AERIFORM	ALBANIAN	AMASSING
ACTIVELY	AERONAUT	ALBINISM	AMAZEDLY
ACTIVITY	AEROSTAT	ALDEHYDE	AMBITION
ACTUALLY	AESTHETE	ALDERMAN	AMBROSIA
ACTUATED	AFFECTED	ALEATORY	AMBULANT
ADAPTING	AFFIANCE	ALEHOUSE	AMBULATE
ADAPTIVE	AFFINITY	ALFRESCO	AMBUSHED
ADDENDUM	AFFIRMED	ALGERIAN	AMENABLE
ADDICTED	AFFIRMER	ALGORISM	AMENABLY
ADDITION	AFFIXING	ALHAMBRA	AMENDING
ADDUCING	AFFLATUS	ALICANTE	AMERICAN
ADDUCTOR	AFFLUENT	ALIENATE	AMETHYST

AMICABLE	ANTEDATE	APPROVER	ASCENDED
AMICABLY	ANTELOPE	APTEROUS	ASCIDIUM
AMMONIAC	ANTENNAE	APTITUDE	ASCORBIC
AMMONITE	ANTENNAL	AQUARIUM	ASCRIBED
AMORTISE	ANTERIOR	AQUARIUS·	ASH-STAND
AMOUNTED	ANTEROOM	AQUATINT	ASPERITY
AMPHIBIA	ANTIBODY	AQUEDUCT	ASPERSED
AMPUTATE	ANTIDOTE	AQUIFORM	ASPHODEL
AMUSABLE	ANTIMONY	AQUILINE	ASPHYXIA
ANABASIS	ANTI-NAZI	ARACHNID	ASPIRANT
ANACONDA	ANTIPHON	ARBITRAL	ASPIRATE
ANAGLYPH	ANTIPOLE	ARBOREAL	ASPIRING
ANALYSED	ANTIPOPE	ARBOURED	ASSAILED
ANALYSER	ANTI-TANK	ARCADIAN	ASSASSIN
ANALYSIS	ANTITYPE	ARCHAISM	ASSAYING
ANALYTIC	ANTLERED	ARCHDUKE	ASSEMBLE
ANARCHIC	ANYTHING	ARCHIVES	ASSENTED
ANATHEMA	ANYWHERE	ARCHNESS	ASSERTED
ANATOMIC	APERIENT	ARCTURUS	ASSESSED
ANCESTOR	APERITIF	ARDENTLY	ASSESSOR
ANCESTRY	APERTURE	ARGONAUT	ASSIGNED
ANCHORED	APHIDIAN	ARGUABLE	ASSIGNEE
ANCHORET	APHORISM	ARGUFIED	ASSIGNOR
ANDERSON	APHORIST	ARGUMENT	ASSISTED
ANECDOTE	APIARIST	ARIDNESS	ASSONANT
ANEURISM	APICALLY	ARMAMENT	ASSORTED
ANEURYSM	APOLLYON	ARMATURE	ASSUAGED
ANGELICA	APOLOGIA	ARMCHAIR	ASSUMING
ANGERING	APOPLEXY	ARMORIAL	ASSURING
ANGLICAN	APOSTASY	ARMOURED	ASSYRIAN
ANGRIEST	APOSTATE	ARMOURER	ASTERISK
ANIMATED	APPALLED	AROMATIC	ASTEROID
ANIMATOR	APPARENT	AROUSING	ASTONISH
ANISETTE	APPEALED	ARPEGGIO	ASTRAGAL
ANNALIST	APPEARED	ARQUEBUS	ASTUTELY
ANNAMITE	APPEASED	ARRANGED	ATABRINE
ANNEALED	APPEASER	ARRANTLY	ATHELING
ANNELIDA	APPENDED	ARRAYING	ATHENIAN
ANNEXING	APPENDIX	ARRESTED	ATHLETIC
ANNOTATE	APPETITE	ARRIVING	ATLANTIC
ANNOUNCE	APPLAUSE	ARROGANT	ATLANTIS
ANNOYING	APPLE-PIE	ARROGATE	ATOMISED
ANNUALLY	APPLIQUE	ARSONIST	ATOMISER
ANNULATE	APPLYING	ARTERIAL	ATONABLE
ANNULLED	APPOSITE	ARTESIAN	ATREMBLE
ANODISED	APPRAISE	ARTFULLY	ATROCITY
ANOINTED	APPRISED	ARTICLED	ATROPINE
ANSERINE	APPRIZED	ARTIFICE	ATTACHED
ANSWERED	APPROACH	ARTISTIC	ATTACKED
ANT-EATER	APPROVAL	ARTISTRY	ATTACKER
ANTECEDE	APPROVED	ASBESTOS	ATTAINED

ATTENDED	BACKBITE	BANTLING	BAULKING
ATTESTED	BACK-BONE	BAPTISED	BAVARIAN
ATTICISM	BACK-CHAT	BARATHEA	BEACHING
ATTIRING	BACK-DOOR	BARBARIC	BEAD-WORK
ATTITUDE	BACK-DROP	BARBECUE	BEAMLESS
ATTORNEY	BACKFIRE	BARBERRY	BEARABLE
ATTUNING	BACK-HAND	BARBETTE	BEARABLY
AUDACITY	BACK-LASH	BARBICAN	BEARDING
AUDIENCE	BACK-ROOM	BARDLING	BEARINGS
AUDITING	BACKSIDE	BAREBACK	BEARLIKE
AUDITION	BACK-STEP	BAREFOOT	BEARSKIN
AUDITORY	BACKWARD	BARGEMAN	BEATIFIC
AUGURING	BACKWASH	BARITONE	BEAUTIFY
AUGUSTAN	BACONIAN	BARNABAS	BEAVERED
AUGUSTLY	BACTERIA	BARNACLE	BECALMED
AURICULA	BACTRIAN	BARN-DOOR	BECHAMEL
AURIFORM	BADGERED	BARNYARD	BECHANCE
AUSTRIAN	BADINAGE	BAROLOGY	BECKONED
AUTARCHY	BAFFLING	BARONAGE	BECOMING
AUTOCRAT	BAGUETTE	BARONESS	BEDAUBED
AUTO-DA-FE	BAKELITE	BARONIAL	BED-CHAIR
AUTO-DYNE	BALANCED	BAROUCHE	BEDECKED
AUTOGYRO	BALANCER	BARRACKS	BEDEWING
AUTOMATA	BALDNESS	BARRATOR	BEDIMMED
AUTONOMY	BALL-COCK	BARRATRY	BED-LINEN
AUTUMNAL	BALLISTA	BARRENLY	BEDMAKER
AVAILING	BALLOTED	BARTERED	BEDPLATE
AVENGING	BALLROOM	BARTERER	BED-QUILT
AVERAGED	BALLYHOO	BARYTONE	BED-STAFF
AVERRING	BALLYRAG	BASALTIC	BEDSTEAD
AVERSELY	BALMORAL	BASEBALL	BEDSTRAW
AVERSION	BALUSTER	BASELESS	BED-TABLE
AVIATION	BANALITY	BASE-LINE	BEE-BREAD
AVIFAUNA	BANDAGED	BASEMENT	BEE-EATER
AVOIDING	BANDANNA	BASENESS	BEEFIEST
AVOWABLE	BANDEAUX	BASILICA	BEER-PUMP
AVOWABLY	BANDITTI	BASILISK	BEERSHOP
AVOWEDLY	BANDSMAN	BASKETRY	BEE'S-WING
AWAITING	BANDYING	BASS-DRUM	BEETLING
AWAKENED	BANISHED	BASS-HORN	BEETROOT
AWARDING	BANISTER	BASSINET	BEFITTED
AXLE-TREE	BANJOIST	BASS-TUBA	BEFLOWER
	BANK-BILL	BASS-VIOL	BEFOGGED
B—8	BANK-BOOK	BASTARDY	BEFOOLED
BABBLING	BANK-NOTE	BASTILLE	BEFOULED
BABY-FACE	BANK-RATE	BATAVIAN	BEFRIEND
BABY-FARM	BANKRUPT	BATHROOM	BEGGARED
BABYHOOD	BANNERET	BATSWING	BEGGARLY
BACCARAT	BANNEROL	BATTENED	BEGINNER
BACCHANT	BANTERED	BATTERED	BEGOTTEN
BACHELOR	BANTERER	BATTLING	BEGRIMED

BEGRUDGE	BESTREWN	BIRD'S-EYE	BLITZING
BEGUILED	BESTRIDE	BIRD-SONG	BLIZZARD
BEHAVING	BESTRODE	BIRTHDAY	BLOATING
BEHEADED	BETAKING	BIRTHDOM	BLOCKADE
BEHEMOTH	BETA-RAYS	BISECTED	BLOCKING
BEHOLDEN	BETEL-NUT	BISECTOR	BLOOD-HOT
BEHOLDER	BETIDING	BISEXUAL	BLOODIED
BEHOVING	BETRAYAL	BITINGLY	BLOODILY
BELABOUR	BETRAYED	BITTERLY	BLOODING
BELAYING	BETRAYER	BI-WEEKLY	BLOOD-RED
BELCHING	BETTERED	BLABBING	BLOOMERS
BELIEVED	BEVELLED	BLACKCAP	BLOOMING
BELIEVER	BEVERAGE	BLACK-FLY	BLOSSOMY
BELITTLE	BEWAILED	BLACK-GUM	BLOTCHED
BELLBIND	BEWARING	BLACKING	BLOTTING
BELL-BIRD	BEWIGGED	BLACKISH	BLOWBALL
BELL-BUOY	BEWILDER	BLACKLEG	BLOW-HOLE
BELLOWED	BIBLICAL	BLACKOUT	BLOW-PIPE
BELL-PULL	BIBULOUS	BLAMABLE	BLUDGEON
BELL-ROPE	BICAUDAL	BLAMABLY	BLUE-BACK
BELL-TENT	BICKERED	BLAMEFUL	BLUEBELL
BELLWORT	BICOLOUR	BLANCHED	BLUEBIRD
BELLYFUL	BICYCLED	BLANDEST	BLUEBOOK
BELLYING	BIDDABLE	BLANDISH	BLUECOAT
BELONGED	BIENNIAL	BLANKEST	BLUE-EYED
BEMOANED	BIGAMIST	BLANKING	BLUEFISH
BENCHING	BIGAMOUS	BLASTING	BLUENESS
BENDABLE	BIG-BONED	BLATANCY	BLUENOSE
BENEDICK	BIGNONIA	BLAZONED	BLUFFEST
BENEDICT	BILBERRY	BLEACHED	BLUFFING
BENEFICE	BILL-BOOK	BLEAKEST	BLUISHLY
BENIGNLY	BILLETED	BLEAKISH	BLUNTING
BENJAMIN	BILL-HEAD	BLEATING	BLUNTISH
BENUMBED	BILLHOOK	BLEEDING	BLURRING
BEQUEATH	BILLIARD	BLENCHED	BLURTING
BERATING	BILLOWED	BLENDING	BLUSHFUL
BERBERRY	BILLY-BOY	BLENHEIM	BLUSHING
BEREAVED	BILLY-CAN	BLESSING	BLUSTERY
BERGAMOT	BINDWEED	BLIGHTED	BOARDING
BERI-BERI	BINNACLE	BLIGHTER	BOASTFUL
BERRYING	BINOMIAL	BLIMPERY	BOASTING
BESIEGED	BIOGRAPH	BLINDAGE	BOAT-HOOK
BESIEGER	BIOMETRY	BLINDEST	BOATRACE
BESMIRCH	BIOSCOPE	BLINDING	BOBBINET
BESOTTED	BIRCHING	BLINDMAN	BOBOLINK
BESOUGHT	BIRDBATH	BLINKERS	BODLEIAN
BESPOKEN	BIRD-CAGE	BLINKING	BODY-LINE
BESSEMER	BIRDCALL	BLISSFUL	BOG-BERRY
BESTIARY	BIRDLIKE	BLISTERY	BOG-EARTH
BESTOWAL	BIRD-LIME	BLITHELY	BOGEYISM
BESTOWED	BIRD-SEED	BLITHEST	BOGEYMAN

BOGGLING	BOUILLON	BRIDLING	BULLDOZE
BOG-WHORT	BOUNCING	BRIEFING	BULLETIN
BOHEMIAN	BOUNDARY	BRIGHTEN	BULLFROG
BOLDNESS	BOUNDING	BRIGHTLY	BULL-HEAD
BOLTHOLE	BOWINGLY	BRIMLESS	BULL-RING
BOLT-ROPE	BOWSPRIT	BRIMMING	BULL'S-EYE
BOMB-FREE	BOX-PLEAT	BRINDLED	BULLYING
BONA-FIDE	BOYISHLY	BRINE-PAN	BULLYRAG
BONDMAID	BRACELET	BRINE-PIT	BUMMAREE
BONDSMAN	BRACKISH	BRINGING	BUNCHING
BONE-IDLE	BRADBURY	BRISLING	BUNDLING
BONELESS	BRADSHAW	BRISTLED	BUNGALOW
BONHOMIE	BRAGGART	BROACHED	BUNG-HOLE
BONIFACE	BRAGGING	BROADEST	BUNGLING
BONNETED	BRAIDING	BROADISH	BUNKERED
BONSPIEL	BRAIN-FAG	BROCADED	BUOYANCY
BOOBYISH	BRAINING	BROCCOLI	BURBERRY
BOOBYISM	BRAIN-PAN	BROCHURE	BURDENED
BOOHOOED	BRAISING	BROILING	BURGLARY
BOOKCASE	BRAKEMAN	BROKENLY	BURGLING
BOOK-CLUB	BRAKE-VAN	BROODING	BURGUNDY
BOOK-DEBT	BRAMBLED	BROOKING	BURROWED
BOOKLAND	BRANCHED	BROOKLET	BURSTING
BOOKLESS	BRANDIED	BROUGHAM	BUSH-BABY
BOOK-MARK	BRANDING	BROWBEAT	BUSH-BUCK
BOOK-NAME	BRANDISH	BROWLESS	BUSHVELD
BOOK-POST	BRAND-NEW	BROWNING	BUSINESS
BOOKSHOP	BRASSARD	BROWNISH	BUSYBODY
BOOKWORM	BRASS-HAT	BROWSING	BUSYNESS
BOOSTING	BRASSICA	BRUISING	BUTCHERY
BOOT-HOOK	BRAWLING	BRUNETTE	BUTTERED
BOOT-JACK	BRAZENED	BRUSHING	BUTTONED
BOOT-LACE	BRAZENLY	BRUSSELS	BUTTRESS
BOOT-LAST	BREACHED	BRYOLOGY	BY-PASSED
BOOTLESS	BREAKAGE	BUBBLING	BYRONISM
BOOT-TREE	BREAKING	BUCKBEAN	BY-STREET
BORDEAUX	BREASTED	BUCKETED	
BORDERED	BREATHED	BUCKHORN	
BORDERER	BREATHER	BUCKJUMP	C—8
BORECOLE	BREECHED	BUCKLING	CABIN-BOY
BORROWED	BREECHES	BUCKSHEE	CABOODLE
BORROWER	BREEDING	BUCK-SHOT	CABOTAGE
BOTANIST	BRETHREN	BUCKSKIN	CABRIOLE
BOTCHERY	BREVIARY	BUDDHISM	CABSTAND
BOTCHING	BREWSTER	BUDDHIST	CACHALOT
BOTHERED	BRIBABLE	BUDGETED	CACKLING
BOTTLING	BRICKBAT	BUFFETED	CADENCED
BOTTOMED	BRICKING	BUILDING	CADILLAC
BOTTOMRY	BRICK-RED	BULKHEAD	CAERLEON
BOTULISM	BRICK-TEA	BULKIEST	CAFFEINE
BOUFFANT	BRIDGING	BULL-CALF	CAJOLERY

CAJOLING	CAPSICUM	CATCHFLY	CHAFFING
CAKESHOP	CAPSULAR	CATCHING	CHAINING
CAKE-WALK	CAPTIOUS	CATEGORY	CHAIR-BED
CALABASH	CAPTURED	CATERING	CHAIRING
CALAMINE	CAPUCHIN	CATHEDRA	CHAIRMAN
CALAMITY	CAPYBARA	CATHOLIC	CHALDRON
CALCINED	CARAPACE	CATILINE	CHALICED
CALCULUS	CARBOLIC	CATONIAN	CHALKING
CALENDAR	CARBONIC	CAT'S-FOOT	CHALK-PIT
CALENDER	CARBURET	CAT'S-MEAT	CHAMPING
CALF-LOVE	CARDAMOM	CAT'S-TAIL	CHAMPION
CALFSKIN	CARD-CASE	CAULDRON	CHANCERY
CALIBRED	CARDIGAN	CAULKING	CHANCING
CALIPASH	CARDINAL	CAUSALLY	CHANDLER
CALIPERS	CAREENED	CAUSERIE	CHANGING
CALL-BIRD	CAREERED	CAUSEUSE	CHANTING
CALLIOPE	CAREFREE	CAUSEWAY	CHAPBOOK
CALL-NOTE	CARELESS	CAUTIOUS	CHAPELRY
CALL-OVER	CARESSED	CAVALIER	CHAPERON
CALMNESS	CAREWORN	CAVATINA	CHAPITER
CAMBERED	CARILLON	CAVE-BEAR	CHAPLAIN
CAMBRIAN	CARINATE	CAVERNED	CHAPPING
CAMELLIA	CARNIVAL	CAVILLED	CHARCOAL
CAMISOLE	CAROLINE	CAVORTED	CHARGING
CAMOMILE	CAROLLED	CELERIAC	CHARLOCK
CAMPAIGN	CAROUSAL	CELERITY	CHARMING
CAMP-FIRE	CAROUSED	CELIBACY	CHARRING
CAM-SHAFT	CARPETED	CELIBATE	CHARTING
CAM-WHEEL	CARRIAGE	CELLARER	CHARTISM
CANADIAN	CARRIOLE	CELLARET	CHARTIST
CANAILLE	CARRYING	CELLULAR	CHASSEUR
CANALISE	CART-LOAD	CEMENTED	CHASTELY
CANASTER	CARYATID	CEMETERY	CHASTISE
CANDIDLY	CASCADED	CENOTAPH	CHASTITY
CANDYING	CASE-BOOK	CENSORED	CHASUBLE
CANE-MILL	CASEMATE	CENSURED	CHATTELS
CANISTER	CASEMENT	CENTAURY	CHATTING
CANKERED	CASE-SHOT	CENTRING	CHAUFFER
CANNIBAL	CASHMERE	CEPHALIC	CHEATING
CANNONED	CASKETED	CERAMICS	CHECKERS
CANOEIST	CASTANET	CERASTES	CHECKING
CANONISE	CASTAWAY	CERBERUS	CHECK-OUT
CANOODLE	CAST-IRON	CEREBRAL	CHEEKING
CANOPIED	CASTLING	CEREBRUM	CHEEPING
CANTERED	CASTRATE	CEREMENT	CHEERFUL
CANTICLE	CASUALLY	CEREMONY	CHEERILY
CAPACITY	CASUALTY	CERULEAN	CHEERING
CAPERING	CATACOMB	CERVICAL	CHEMICAL
CAPITANO	CATALYST	CESAREAN	CHENILLE
CAPITATE	CATAPULT	CESSPOOL	CHERUBIC
CAPRIOLE	CATARACT	CETACEAN	CHERUBIM

CHESHIRE	CINCHONA	CLIMATIC	COARSELY
CHESSMAN	CINNABAR	CLIMBING	COARSEST
CHESTING	CINNAMON	CLINCHED	COASTING
CHESTNUT	CIPHERED	CLINGING	COBBLING
CHEVYING	CIRCLING	CLINICAL	COBWEBBY
CHIASMUS	CIRCULAR	CLINKING	COCKADED
CHICANED	CITATION	CLIPPERS	COCKATOO
CHICK-PEA	CITY-BRED	CLIPPING	COCK-CROW
CHILDBED	CIVET-CAT	CLIQUISH	COCKEREL
CHILDISH	CIVILIAN	CLOAKING	COCK-EYED
CHILDREN	CIVILITY	CLOCKING	COCKLING
CHILIASM	CIVILISE	CLODDISH	COCKSPUR
CHILIAST	CLACKING	CLOGGING	COCKSURE
CHILLIER	CLAIMANT	CLOISTER	COCKTAIL
CHILLING	CLAIMING	CLOSE-CUT	CODDLING
CHILTERN	CLAM-BAKE	CLOSETED	CODIFIED
CHIMAERA	CLAMPING	CLOTHIER	CO-EDITOR
CHIMERIC	CLANGING	CLOTHING	COERCING
CHINAMAN	CLANGOUR	CLOTTING	COERCION
CHIN-CHIN	CLANKING	CLOUDILY	COERCIVE
CHINKING	CLANNISH	CLOUDING	COFFERED
CHIPMUNK	CLANSHIP	CLOUDLET	COFFINED
CHIPPING	CLANSMAN	CLOUTING	COGENTLY
CHIRPING	CLAPPING	CLOWNERY	COGITATE
CHIRRING	CLAPTRAP	CLOWNING	COGNOMEN
CHIT-CHAT	CLARENCE	CLOWNISH	COG-WHEEL
CHIVALRY	CLARINET	CLUBBING	COHERENT
CHLORATE	CLASHING	CLUBBISH	COHERING
CHLORIDE	CLASPING	CLUB-FOOT	COHESION
CHLORINE	CLASSIER	CLUB-LAND	COHESIVE
CHLOROUS	CLASSIFY	CLUB-MOSS	COIFFEUR
CHOICELY	CLASSING	CLUB-ROOM	COIFFING
CHOIR-BOY	CLASSMAN	CLUB-ROOT	COIFFURE
CHOLERIC	CLASS-WAR	CLUB-RUSH	COINCIDE
CHOOSING	CLAVICLE	CLUCKING	COINLESS
CHOPPING	CLAYMORE	CLUELESS	COLANDER
CHOP-SUEY	CLEANING	CLUMPING	COLDNESS
CHORALLY	CLEANSED	CLUMSIER	COLE-SLAW
CHORTLED	CLEANSER	CLUMSILY	COLEWORT
CHORUSED	CLEAR-CUT	CLUTCHED	COLISEUM
CHOW-CHOW	CLEAREST	COACH-BOX	COLLAPSE
CHRISTEN	CLEARING	COACHDOG	COLLARED
CHROMIUM	CLEAVAGE	COACHFUL	COLLARET
CHUCKING	CLEAVING	COACHING	COLLATED
CHUCKLED	CLEMATIS	COACHMAN	COLLATOR
CHUMP-END	CLEMENCY	COACTIVE	COLLEGER
CHURLISH	CLENCHED	CO-AGENCY	COLLIDED
CHURNING	CLERICAL	COALESCE	COLLIERY
CICATRIX	CLEVERER	COAL-HOLE	COLLOQUY
CICERONE	CLEVERLY	COAL-MINE	COLLUDED
CIDER-CUP	CLICKING	COAL-SHIP	COLONIAL

COLONISE	CONFUSED	COPULATE	CRABBING
COLONIST	CONFUTED	COPY-BOOK	CRACKING
COLOSSAL	CONGRESS	COPYHOLD	CRACK-JAW
COLOSSUS	CONGREVE	COQUETRY	CRACKLED
COLOURED	CONJOINT	COQUETTE	CRACKNEL
COLUMNAR	CONJUGAL	CORDUROY	CRACK-POT
COLUMNED	CONJUNCT	CORDWAIN	CRADLING
COMATOSE	CONJURED	CORN-BEEF	CRAFTIER
COMBINED	CONJURER	CORNEOUS	CRAFTILY
COME-BACK	CONJUROR	CORNERED	CRAMMING
COMEDIAN	CONNIVED	CORPORAL	CRAMPING
COMMANDO	CONNOTED	CORRIDOR	CRANE-FLY
COMMENCE	CONQUEST	CORRODED	CRANKING
COMMERCE	CONSERVE	CORSELET	CRANNIED
COMMONER	CONSIDER	CORSICAN	CRASHING
COMMONLY	CONSOLED	CORUNDUM	CRAVENLY
COMMUNAL	CONSOMME	CORVETTE	CRAWFISH
COMMUNED	CONSPIRE	COSINESS	CRAWLING
COMMUTED	CONSTANT	COSMETIC	CRAYFISH
COMPARED	CONSTRUE	COSSETED	CRAYONED
COMPETED	CONSULAR	COSTLIER	CRAZIEST
COMPILED	CONSUMED	COST-PLUS	CREAKING
COMPILER	CONSUMER	COSTUMED	CREAMERY
COMPLAIN	CONTANGO	CO-TENANT	CREAMING
COMPLETE	CONTEMPT	COTSWOLD	CREASING
COMPLIED	CONTENTS	COTTAGER	CREATING
COMPOSED	CONTINUE	COTTONED	CREATION
COMPOSER	CONTRACT	COUCHANT	CREATIVE
COMPOUND	CONTRARY	COUCHING	CREATURE
COMPRESS	CONTRAST	COUGHING	CREDENCE
COMPRISE	CONTRITE	COUNTESS	CREDIBLE
COMPUTED	CONTRIVE	COUNTING	CREDIBLY
COMPUTER	CONTUSED	COUPLING	CREDITED
CONCEDED	CONVENED	COURSING	CREDITOR
CONCEIVE	CONVENER	COURTESY	CREEPING
CONCERTO	CONVERGE	COURTIER	CREMATED
CONCLAVE	CONVERSE	COURTING	CREOSOTE
CONCLUDE	CONVEXLY	COUSINLY	CRESCENT
CONCOURS	CONVEYED	COVENANT	CRESTING
CONCRETE	CONVEYOR	COVENTRY	CRETONNE
CONDENSE	CONVINCE	COVERAGE	CREVASSE
CONDOLED	CONVOKED	COVERING	CRIBBAGE
CONDONED	CONVOYED	COVERLET	CRIBBING
CONDUCED	CONVULSE	COVERTLY	CRIMINAL
CONFETTI	COOEEING	COVETING	CRIMPING
CONFIDED	COOK-SHOP	COVETOUS	CRINGING
CONFINED	COOLNESS	COWARDLY	CRINKLED
CONFLICT	COOPERED	COWERING	CRIPPLED
CONFOUND	CO-OPTING	COWHOUSE	CRITERIA
CONFRERE	CO-OPTION	CO-WORKER	CRITICAL
CONFRONT	COPPERED	COXSWAIN	CRITIQUE

CROAKING	CURTNESS	DATE-PLUM	DECODING
CROCKERY	CURTSIED	DAUGHTER	DECORATE
CROCKING	CUSPIDOR	DAUNTING	DECOROUS
CROMLECH	CUSTOMER	DAUPHINE	DECOYING
CROOKING	CUT-GLASS	DAWDLING	DECREASE
CROONING	CUTHBERT	DAYBREAK	DECREPIT
CROPPING	CUTPURSE	DAYDREAM	DECRYING
CROSS-BAR	CUT-WATER	DAYLIGHT	DEDICATE
CROSSBOW	CYCLAMEN	DAY-TO-DAY	DEDUCING
CROSSCUT	CYCLE-CAR	DAZZLING	DEDUCTED
CROSSING	CYCLICAL	DEAD-BEAT	DEEDPOLL
CROTCHED	CYCLONIC	DEADENED	DEEMSTER
CROTCHET	CYLINDER	DEAD-HEAD	DEEPENED
CROUCHED	CYNICISM	DEAD-HEAT	DEEP-LAID
CROUPIER	CYNOSURE	DEADLIER	DEERSKIN
CROWDING	CZARITZA	DEAD-LINE	DEFACING
CROWFOOT		DEADLOCK	DEFAMING
CROWNING		DEADNESS	DEFEATED
CRUCIBLE	D—8	DEAD-WOOD	DEFENDED
CRUCIFIX	DABBLING	DEAFENED	DEFENDER
CRUISING	DAB-CHICK	DEAFNESS	DEFERRED
CRUMBLED	DAEDALUS	DEANSHIP	DEFIANCE
CRUMPLED	DAFFODIL	DEARNESS	DEFILING
CRUNCHED	DAFTNESS	DEATH-BED	DEFINING
CRUSADED	DAINTILY	DEBARRED	DEFINITE
CRUSADER	DAIRYING	DEBASING	DEFLATED
CRUSHING	DAIRYMAN	DEBATING	DEFOREST
CRUSTILY	DALES-MAN	DEBILITY	DEFORMED
CRUTCHED	DALLYING	DEBITING	DEFRAYAL
CUBIFORM	DALMATIA	DEBONAIR	DEFRAYED
CUCUMBER	DAMAGING	DEBUNKED	DEFTNESS
CUDDLING	DAMNABLE	DEBUTANT	DEGRADED
CUL-DE-SAC	DAMOCLES	DECADENT	DEIFYING
CULINARY	DAMPENED	DECAMPED	DEIGNING
CULPABLE	DAMPNESS	DECANTED	DEJECTED
CULPABLY	DANDIEST	DECANTER	DEJEUNER
CULTURED	DANDLING	DECAYING	DELAYING
CULVERIN	DANDRUFF	DECEASED	DELECTUS
CUMBRIAN	DANDYISH	DECEIVED	DELEGACY
CUPBOARD	DANDYISM	DECEIVER	DELEGATE
CUPIDITY	DANGLING	DECEMBER	DELETING
CUPREOUS	DANSEUSE	DECENTLY	DELETION
CURATIVE	DAPPLING	DECIDING	DELICACY
CURATORY	DARINGLY	DECIMATE	DELICATE
CURBLESS	DARKENED	DECIPHER	DELIRIUM
CURDLING	DARKLING	DECISION	DELIVERY
CURELESS	DARKNESS	DECISIVE	DELOUSED
CURRENCY	DARK-ROOM	DECK-HAND	DELPHIAN
CURRICLE	DATELESS	DECLARED	DELUDING
CURRYING	DATE-LINE	DECLASSE	DELUGING
CURSEDLY	DATE-PALM	DECLINED	DELUSION

DELUSIVE	DESERTED	DIASTOLE	DISCOUNT
DEMAGOGY	DESERTER	DIATOMIC	DISCOVER
DEMANDED	DESERVED	DIATONIC	DISCREET
DEMARCHE	DESIGNED	DIATRIBE	DISEASED
DEMEANED	DESIGNER	DIBBLING	DISGORGE
DEMENTED	DESIRING	DICKERED	DISGRACE
DEMENTIA	DESIROUS	DICTATED	DISGUISE
DEMERARA	DESISTED	DICTATOR	DISHEVEL
DEMIJOHN	DESOLATE	DIDACTIC	DISINTER
DEMISING	DESPATCH	DIDDLING	DISJOINT
DEMOBBED	DESPISED	DIETETIC	DISLIKED
DEMOCRAT	DESPOTIC	DIFFERED	DISLODGE
DEMOLISH	DESTINED	DIFFRACT	DISLOYAL
DEMONIAC	DETACHED	DIFFUSED	DISMALLY
DEMONISM	DETAILED	DIGESTED	DISMAYED
DEMPSTER	DETAINED	DIGGINGS	DISMOUNT
DEMURELY	DETECTED	DIGITATE	DISORDER
DEMURRED	DETECTOR	DIHEDRAL	DISOWNED
DENARIUS	DETERRED	DILATING	DISPATCH
DENATURE	DETESTED	DILATION	DISPENSE
DENIABLE	DETHRONE	DILATORY	DISPERSE
DENOTING	DETONATE	DILIGENT	DISPIRIT
DENOUNCE	DETRITUS	DILUTING	DISPLACE
DENUDING	DEUCEDLY	DILUTION	DISPOSAL
DEPARTED	DEVALUED	DILUVIAL	DISPOSED
DEFENDED	DEVIATED	DIMINISH	DISPROOF
DEPICTED	DEVILISH	DIMPLING	DISPROVE
DEPILATE	DEVILISM	DINER-OUT	DISPUTED
DEPLETED	DEVILLED	DING-DONG	DISQUIET
DEPLORED	DEVISING	DINGIEST	DISROBED
DEPLOYED	DEVOLVED	DINORNIS	DISSOLVE
DEPONENT	DEVONIAN	DINOSAUR	DISSUADE
DEPORTED	DEVOTING	DIOCESAN	DISTANCE
DEPORTEE	DEVOTION	DIORAMIC	DISTASTE
DEPOSING	DEVOURED	DIPLOMAT	DISTINCT
DEPRAVED	DEVOUTLY	DIRECTED	DISTRACT
DEPRIVED	DEWBERRY	DIRECTLY	DISTRAIN
DEPUTING	DEWINESS	DIRECTOR	DISTRAIT
DEPUTISE	DEXTROSE	DIRTIEST	DISTRESS
DERAILED	DEXTROUS	DIRTYING	DISTRICT
DERANGED	DIABETES	DISABLED	DISTRUST
DERATING	DIABETIC	DISABUSE	DISUNION
DERELICT	DIABOLIC	DISAGREE	DISUNITE
DERIDING	DIAGNOSE	DISALLOW	DISUNITY
DERISION	DIAGONAL	DISARMED	DITCHING
DERISIVE	DIALLING	DISARRAY	DITHERED
DERISORY	DIALOGUE	DISASTER	DITTY-BAG
DERIVING	DIAMETER	DISBURSE	DITTY-BOX
DEROGATE	DIANTHUS	DISCIPLE	DIVE-BOMB
DESCRIBE	DIAPASON	DISCLAIM	DIVERGED
DESCRIED	DIASTASE	DISCLOSE	DIVERTED

DIVESTED	DOORLESS	DRAWABLE	DRY-GOODS
DIVIDEND	DOOR-NAIL	DRAWBACK	DRY-NURSE
DIVIDING	DOOR-POST	DRAWBOLT	DRY-PLATE
DIVINELY	DOOR-STEP	DRAW-GEAR	DRY-POINT
DIVINITY	DORMANCY	DRAWLING	DRY-STONE
DIVISION	DORMOUSE	DRAW-LINK	DUCHESSE
DIVORCED	DORSALLY	DRAW-WELL	DUCKBILL
DIVORCEE	DOTARDLY	DREADFUL	DUCK-HAWK
DIVULGED	DOTINGLY	DREADING	DUCKLING
DIZZYING	DOTTEREL	DREAMFUL	DUCK-MOLE
DOCILITY	DOUBLETS	DREAMILY	DUCK'S-EGG
DOCKYARD	DOUBLING	DREAMING	DUCK-SHOT
DOCTORED	DOUBLOON	DREARILY	DUCK-WEED
DOCTRINE	DOUBTFUL	DREDGING	DUELLING
DOCUMENT	DOUBTING	DRENCHED	DUELLIST
DODDERED	DOUCHING	DRESSING	DUETTING
DODDERER	DOUGHBOY	DRIBBLED	DUETTIST
DOGBERRY	DOUGHNUT	DRIBBLET	DUKELING
DOG-EARED	DOUM-PALM	DRIFT-ICE	DUKERIES
DOGESHIP	DOURNESS	DRIFTING	DUKESHIP
DOG-FACED	DOVECOTE	DRIFT-NET	DULCIMER
DOGGEDLY	DOVE-EYED	DRIFT-WAY	DULL-EYED
DOGGEREL	DOVELIKE	DRILLING	DULLNESS
DOG-HOUSE	DOVETAIL	DRINKING	DUMB-BELL
DOG-LATIN	DOWDYISH	DRIPPING	DUMBNESS
DOGMATIC	DOWDYISM	DRIVABLE	DUMB-SHOW
DOG'S-BODY	DOWELLED	DRIZZLED	DUMPLING
DOG'S-MEAT	DOWEL-PIN	DROLLERY	DUNGAREE
DOG'S-NOSE	DOWERING	DROOLING	DUNG-CART
DOG-TIRED	DOWNCAST	DROOPING	DUNG-FORK
DOGTOOTH	DOWNCOME	DROP-GOAL	DUNG-HILL
DOG-WATCH	DOWNFALL	DROPPING	DUODENAL
DOLDRUMS	DOWNHILL	DROPSIED	DUODENUM
DOLLED-UP	DOWNLAND	DROPWORT	DUOLOGUE
DOLOMITE	DOWN-LINE	DROUGHTY	DURATION
DOLOROSO	DOWNPOUR	DROWNING	DUST-CART
DOLOROUS	DOWNWARD	DROWSILY	DUST-COAT
DOMELIKE	DOXOLOGY	DROWSING	DUST-HOLE
DOMESDAY	DOZINESS	DRUBBING	DUTCHMAN
DOMESTIC	DRAFTING	DRUDGERY	DUTIABLE
DOMICILE	DRAGGING	DRUDGING	DUTY-FREE
DOMINANT	DRAGGLED	DRUGGING	DUTY-PAID
DOMINATE	DRAG-HOOK	DRUGGIST	DWARFING
DOMINEER	DRAG-HUNT	DRUIDISM	DWARFISH
DOMINION	DRAGOMAN	DRUMFIRE	DWELLING
DOMINOES	DRAINAGE	DRUMFISH	DWINDLED
DONATING	DRAINING	DRUMHEAD	DYE-HOUSE
DONATION	DRAMATIC	DRUMMING	DYE-STUFF
DOOMSDAY	DRAM-SHOP	DRUNKARD	DYNAMICS
DOOR-BELL	DRAUGHTS	DRY-CLEAN	DYNAMISM
DOOR-KNOB	DRAUGHTY		DYNAMIST

DYNAMITE	EGYPTIAN	EMENDING	ENFILADE
DYNASTIC	EIGHTEEN	EMERGENT	ENFOLDED
	EIGHTHLY	EMERGING	ENFORCED
E—8	EJECTING	EMERITUS	ENGAGING
EAGLE-OWL	EJECTION	EMERSION	ENGENDER
EARPHONE	EJECTIVE	EMIGRANT	ENGINEER
EARTHING	ELAPSING	EMIGRATE	ENGRAVED
EARTH-NUT	ELATEDLY	EMINENCE	ENGRAVER
EASEMENT	ELBOWING	EMISSARY	ENGULFED
EASINESS	ELDORADO	EMISSION	ENHANCED
EASTERLY	ELDRITCH	EMISSIVE	ENJOINED
EASTWARD	ELECTING	EMITTING	ENJOYING
EAU-DE-VIE	ELECTION	EMPHASIS	ENLACING
EBENEZER	ELECTIVE	EMPHATIC	ENLARGED
EBONISED	ELECTRIC	EMPLANED	ENLARGER
ECLECTIC	ELECTRON	EMPLOYED	ENLISTED
ECLIPSED	ELEGANCE	EMPLOYEE	ENMESHED
ECLIPTIC	ELEGANCY	EMPLOYER	ENNOBLED
ECONOMIC	ELEGIAST	EMPORIUM	ENORMITY
ECSTATIC	ELEGISED	EMPTYING	ENORMOUS
EDENTATA	ELEPHANT	EMPURPLE	ENOUNCED
EDENTATE	ELEVATED	EMPYREAN	ENQUIRED
EDGE-TOOL	ELEVATOR	EMULATED	ENQUIRER
EDGEWAYS	ELEVENTH	EMULATOR	ENRAGING
EDGEWISE	ELF-CHILD	EMULSIFY	ENRICHED
EDGINESS	ELICITED	EMULSINE	ENROLLED
EDIFYING	ELIGIBLE	EMULSION	ENSCONCE
EDITRESS	ELIGIBLY	EMULSIVE	ENSHRINE
EDUCABLE	ELLIPSIS	ENABLING	ENSHROUD
EDUCATED	ELLIPTIC	ENACTING	ENSLAVED
EDUCATOR	ELONGATE	ENACTION	ENSNARED
EDUCIBLE	ELOQUENT	ENACTIVE	ENSURING
EDUCTION	ELSEWISE	ENCAMPED	ENTAILED
EEL-GRASS	ELVISHLY	ENCASHED	ENTANGLE
EEL-SPEAR	EMACIATE	ENCASING	ENTERING
EERINESS	EMANATED	ENCIRCLE	ENTHRONE
EFFACING	EMBALMED	ENCLOSED	ENTHUSED
EFFECTED	EMBALMER	ENCOMIUM	ENTICING
EFFICACY	EMBANKED	ENCORING	ENTIRELY
EFFLUENT	EMBARKED	ENCROACH	ENTIRETY
EFFLUVIA	EMBATTLE	ENCUMBER	ENTITLED
EFFUSING	EMBEDDED	ENCYCLIC	ENTOMBED
EFFUSION	EMBEZZLE	ENDANGER	ENTR'ACTE
EFFUSIVE	EMBITTER	ENDEARED	ENTRAILS
EGG-PLANT	EMBLAZON	ENDORSED	ENTRANCE
EGG-SHELL	EMBODIED	ENDOWING	ENTREATY
EGG-SLICE	EMBOLDEN	ENDURING	ENTRENCH
EGG-SPOON	EMBOLISM	ENERGISE	ENTWINED
EGG-TOOTH	EMBOSSED	ENERVATE	ENVELOPE
EGG-WHISK	EMBRACED	ENFACING	ENVIABLE
EGOISTIC	EMBUSSED	ENFEEBLE	ENVIABLY

ENVIRONS
ENVISAGE
EOLITHIC
EPHEMERA
EPICERIE
EPICYCLE
EPIDEMIC
EPIGRAPH
EPILEPSY
EPILOGUE
EPIPHANY
EPISODIC
EQUALISE
EQUALITY
EQUALLED
EQUATING
EQUATION
EQUIPAGE
EQUIPPED
ERASABLE
ERECTING
ERECTION
EREWHILE
ERUPTING
ERUPTION
ERUPTIVE
ESCALADE
ESCALLOP
ESCAPADE
ESCAPING
ESCAPISM
ESCAPIST
ESCHEWED
ESCORTED
ESCULENT
ESOTERIC
ESPALIER
ESPECIAL
ESPOUSAL
ESPOUSED
ESSAYING
ESSAYISH
ESSAYIST
ESTEEMED
ESTIMATE
ESTRANGE
ESURIENT
ETCETERA
ETERNITY
ETHEREAL
ETHNICAL

ETRUSCAN
EUGENICS
EULOGISE
EULOGIST
EUPHONIC
EURASIAN
EUROPEAN
EVACUATE
EVADABLE
EVENNESS
EVENSONG
EVENTFUL
EVENTIDE
EVENTUAL
EVERMORE
EVERSION
EVERTING
EVERYDAY
EVERYONE
EVICTING
EVICTION
EVIDENCE
EVILDOER
EVINCING
EVOLVING
EXACTING
EXACTION
EXALTING
EXAMINED
EXAMINEE
EXAMINER
EXCAVATE
EXCEEDED
EXCEPTED
EXCHANGE
EXCISING
EXCISION
EXCITING
EXCLUDED
EXCUSING
EXECRATE
EXECUTED
EXECUTOR
EXEMPLAR
EXEMPTED
EXEQUIES
EXERCISE
EXERTING
EXERTION
EXHALING
EXHORTED

EXHUMING
EXIGENCY
EXISTENT
EXISTING
EX-LIBRIS
EXORCISE
EXORCISM
EXPANDED
EXPECTED
EXPEDITE
EXPENDED
EXPERTLY
EXPIATED
EXPIRING
EXPLICIT
EXPLODED
EXPLORED
EXPLORER
EXPONENT
EXPORTED
EXPORTER
EXPOSING
EXPOSURE
EXPUNGED
EXTENDED
EXTENSOR
EXTERIOR
EXTERNAL
EXTOLLED
EXTORTED
EXTRUDED
EXULTANT
EXULTING
EYEGLASS
EYE-PIECE
EYE-TEETH
EYE-TOOTH
EYE-WATER

F—8
FABULOUS
FACE-ACHE
FACELESS
FACE-LIFT
FACIALLY
FACILELY
FACILITY
FACTIOUS
FACTOTUM
FADELESS
FADINGLY

FAINTEST
FAINTING
FAINTISH
FAIRNESS
FAITHFUL
FALCONER
FALCONET
FALCONRY
FALDERAL
FALLIBLE
FALLOWED
FALSETTO
FALTERED
FAMILIAR
FAMISHED
FAMOUSLY
FANCIFUL
FANCYING
FANDANGO
FANGLESS
FANLIGHT
FANTASIA
FARCICAL
FAREWELL
FAR-FLUNG
FARINOSE
FARMYARD
FARRIERY
FARROWED
FARTHEST
FARTHING
FASCISTA
FASCISTI
FASTENED
FASTNESS
FATALISM
FATALIST
FATALITY
FATHERED
FATHERLY
FATHOMED
FATIGUED
FATTENED
FAUBOURG
FAULTILY
FAULTING
FAUTEUIL
FAVOURED
FEARLESS
FEARSOME
FEASIBLE

FEASIBLY	FILCHING	FLAGGING	FLOODLIT
FEASTING	FILIALLY	FLAGRANT	FLOORING
FEATHERY	FILIGREE	FLAG-SHIP	FLOPPILY
FEATURED	FILLETED	FLAMBEAU	FLOPPING
FEBRUARY	FILMGOER	FLAMINGO	FLORALLY
FECKLESS	FILM-STAR	FLANKING	FLORENCE
FEDERATE	FILTERED	FLAP-JACK	FLORIDLY
FEEBLISH	FILTHIER	FLAPPING	FLOTILLA
FEED-PIPE	FILTHILY	FLASHILY	FLOUNCED
FEIGNING	FILTRATE	FLASHING	FLOUNDER
FEINTING	FINALIST	FLATFISH	FLOURING
FELICITY	FINALITY	FLATFOOT	FLOURISH
FELLSIDE	FINANCED	FLAT-IRON	FLOUTING
FELO-DE-SE	FINDABLE	FLATNESS	FLOWERED
FEMININE	FINENESS	FLAT-RACE	FLOWERET
FEMINISE	FINE-SPUN	FLATTERY	FLUENTLY
FEMINISM	FINESSED	FLATTEST	FLUFFING
FEMINIST	FINGERED	FLATTISH	FLUIDITY
FENCIBLE	FINISHED	FLAT-WORM	FLUMMERY
FEROCITY	FINISHER	FLAUNTED	FLUORIDE
FERRETED	FIRE-BACK	FLAUTIST	FLUORINE
FERRYING	FIRE-BALL	FLAWLESS	FLURRIED
FERRYMAN	FIRE-BOMB	FLAX-LILY	FLUSHING
FERVENCY	FIRECLAY	FLAX-SEED	FLUSTERY
FERVIDLY	FIREDAMP	FLEA-BANE	FLYBLOWN
FESTALLY	FIRE-HOSE	FLEA-BITE	FLY-MAKER
FESTERED	FIRELOCK	FLECKING	FLY-PAPER
FESTIVAL	FIRE-PLUG	FLEECING	FLY-SHEET
FETCHING	FIRESHIP	FLEETEST	FLYWHEEL
FETTERED	FIRESIDE	FLEETING	FOAMLESS
FEUDALLY	FIRE-STEP	FLETCHER	FOCUSING
FEVERFEW	FIREWOOD	FLEXIBLE	FOG-BOUND
FEVERING	FIRMNESS	FLEXIBLY	FOGGIEST
FEVERISH	FISHABLE	FLICKING	FOLDEROL
FEVEROUS	FISH-BALL	FLIGHTED	FOLDLESS
FIBROSIS	FISH-CAKE	FLIM-FLAM	FOLIAGED
FIDDLING	FISH-GLUE	FLIMSIES	FOLIATED
FIDELITY	FISH-HAWK	FLIMSILY	FOLKLAND
FIDGETED	FISH-HOOK	FLINCHED	FOLKLORE
FIELD-DAY	FISH-MEAL	FLINGING	FOLK-SONG
FIELD-GUN	FISH-POND	FLIP-FLAP	FOLK-TALE
FIELDING	FISH-SKIN	FLIP-FLOP	FOLLICLE
FIENDISH	FISH-TAIL	FLIPPANT	FOLLOWED
FIERCELY	FISHWIFE	FLIPPING	FOLLOWER
FIERCEST	FISSURED	FLIRTING	FOMENTED
FIFTIETH	FITFULLY	FLITTING	FONDLING
FIGHTING	FIVEFOLD	FLOATING	FONDNESS
FIGURANT	FIXATION	FLOCK-BED	FOODLESS
FIGURINE	FIXATIVE	FLOCKING	FOOLSCAP
FIGURING	FIZZLING	FLOGGING	FOOTBALL
FILAMENT	FLABBILY	FLOODING	FOOT-BATH

FOOTFALL	FORESTRY	FREENESS	FUNCTION
FOOTGEAR	FORETELL	FREE-PORT	FUNDABLE
FOOTHILL	FORETOLD	FREE-SHOT	FUNDLESS
FOOTHOLD	FOREWARN	FREE-WILL	FUNEREAL
FOOTLESS	FOREWORD	FREEZING	FUNK-HOLE
FOOTLING	FORGIVEN	FRENZIED	FURBELOW
FOOTMARK	FORGOING	FREQUENT	FURLOUGH
FOOTNOTE	FORMALIN	FRETTING	FURROWED
FOOTPATH	FORMALLY	FRETWORK	FURTHEST
FOOT-RACE	FORMERLY	FREUDIAN	FUSELAGE
FOOT-ROPE	FORMLESS	FRICTION	FUSILIER
FOOTRULE	FORMULAE	FRIENDLY	FUTILELY
FOOTSLOG	FORSAKEN	FRIESIAN	FUTILITY
FOOTSORE	FORSOOTH	FRIGHTEN	FUTURISM
FOOTSTEP	FORSWEAR	FRIGIDLY	FUTURIST
FOOTWEAR	FORSWORE	FRILLING	FUTURITY
FOOTWORN	FORSWORN	FRINGING	
FOOZLING	FORTIETH	FRIPPERY	**G—8**
FORAGING	FORTRESS	FRISKILY	GABBLING
FORAYING	FORTUITY	FRISKING	GABLE-END
FORBORNE	FORWARDS	FRIZZLED	GADABOUT
FORCEDLY	FOSTERED	FROCKING	GADZOOKS
FORCEFUL	FOUGASSE	FRONTAGE	GAINSAID
FORCIBLY	FOULNESS	FRONTIER	GAITERED
FORDABLE	FOUL-PLAY	FRONTING	GALACTIC
FOREBEAR	FOUNDING	FROSTILY	GALILEAN
FOREBODE	FOUNTAIN	FROSTING	GALLIPOT
FORECAST	FOURFOLD	FROTHILY	GALLOPED
FOREDECK	FOURSOME	FROTHING	GALLOWAY
FOREDONE	FOURTEEN	FROU-FROU	GALVANIC
FOREDOOM	FOURTHLY	FROWNING	GAMBLING
FOREFOOT	FOXGLOVE	FRUCTIFY	GAMECOCK
FOREGONE	FOXHOUND	FRUGALLY	GAME-LAWS
FOREHAND	FOXINESS	FRUIT-BUD	GAMENESS
FOREHEAD	FRACTION	FRUIT-FLY	GAMESTER
FORELAND	FRACTURE	FRUITFUL	GANGLION
FORELOCK	FRAGMENT	FRUITING	GANGRENE
FOREMAST	FRAGRANT	FRUITION	GANGSTER
FOREMOST	FRAILISH	FRUITLET	GANYMEDE
FORENAME	FRAME-SAW	FRUMPISH	GAOLBIRD
FORENOON	FRANKING	FUDDLING	GAPINGLY
FORENSIC	FRANKISH	FUELLING	GARBLING
FOREPART	FRANKLIN	FUGITIVE	GARDENED
FOREPEAK	FRAULEIN	FULL-BACK	GARDENER
FORESAID	FREAKISH	FULL-FACE	GARDENIA
FORESAIL	FRECKLED	FULLNESS	GARE-FOWL
FORESEEN	FREEBORN	FULL-STOP	GARGANEY
FORESHIP	FREED-MAN	FUMBLING	GARGLING
FORESHOW	FREEHAND	FUMELESS	GARGOYLE
FORESTAY	FREEHOLD	FUMIGANT	GARISHLY
FORESTER	FREE-LOVE	FUMIGATE	GARNERED

GARRETED	GLASSILY	GOODLIER	GRIMACED
GARRISON	GLAUCOMA	GOODNESS	GRIMALDI
GARROTTE	GLAUCOUS	GOODWIFE	GRIMMEST
GARTERED	GLEAMING	GOODWILL	GRIMNESS
GASIFIED	GLEANING	GOOGLIES	GRINDING
GAS-LIGHT	GLIBNESS	GOOSE-EGG	GRINNING
GAS-METER	GLIMPSED	GORGEOUS	GRIPPING
GAS-MOTOR	GLINTING	GOSSAMER	GRISELDA
GASOLINE	GLISSADE	GOSSIPED	GRITTING
GAS-STOVE	GLOAMING	GOURMAND	GRIZZLED
GAS-TIGHT	GLOATING	GOVERNED	GROANING
GATELESS	GLOBULAR	GOVERNOR	GROG-SHOP
GATE-POST	GLOBULIN	GOWNSMAN	GROOMING
GATHERED	GLOOMILY	GRABBING	GROOVING
GAUNTLET	GLORIOUS	GRACEFUL	GROSBEAK
GAZETTED	GLORYING	GRACIOUS	GROUNDED
GEAR-CASE	GLOSSARY	GRADATED	GROUNDER
GELATINE	GLOSSILY	GRADIENT	GROUPING
GENDARME	GLOSSING	GRADUATE	GROUSING
GENERATE	GLOWERED	GRAFTING	GROUTING
GENEROUS	GLOW-WORM	GRAINING	GROWABLE
GENETICS	GLOXINIA	GRANDDAD	GROWLING
GENIALLY	GLUMMEST	GRANDEST	GRUBBIER
GENITIVE	GLUMNESS	GRANDEUR	GRUBBING
GENOCIDE	GLUTTING	GRANDSON	GRUDGING
GEOMETRY	GLUTTONY	GRANTING	GRUESOME
GEORGIAN	GNASHING	GRANULAR	GRUMBLED
GERANIUM	GOAL-LINE	GRAPHITE	GRUMBLER
GERMANIC	GOATHERD	GRAPPLED	GUARDIAN
GESTURED	GOAT-MOTH	GRASPING	GUARDING
GHOULISH	GOATSKIN	GRASSING	GUERILLA
GIANTESS	GOAT'S-RUE	GRATEFUL	GUERNSEY
GIBBERED	GOBBLING	GRATUITY	GUIDABLE
GIBINGLY	GODCHILD	GRAVAMEN	GUIDANCE
GIDDIEST	GOD-SPEED	GRAVELLY	GUILEFUL
GIGANTIC	GOFFERED	GRAYLING	GUILTILY
GIGGLING	GOGGLING	GREASILY	GULF-WEED
GIG-LAMPS	GOINGS-ON	GREASING	GULLIBLE
GILT-EDGE	GOLD-DUST	GREATEST	GULLIVER
GIMCRACK	GOLDENLY	GREEDILY	GUMPTION
GINGERLY	GOLDFISH	GREENERY	GUM-RESIN
GIN-SLING	GOLD-FOIL	GREEN-FLY	GUN-LAYER
GIRDLING	GOLD-LACE	GREENING	GUNMETAL
GIRLHOOD	GOLD-LEAF	GREENISH	GUNSMITH
GIVE-AWAY	GOLDLESS	GREEN-TEA	GUNSTOCK
GLADDEST	GOLD-MINE	GREETING	GURGLING
GLADIOLI	GOLD-SIZE	GREYNESS	GUTTERED
GLADNESS	GOLF-CLUB	GRID-BIAS	GUTTURAL
GLADSOME	GOLGOTHA	GRIDIRON	GUZZLING
GLANCING	GOLLYWOG	GRIEVOUS	GYMKHANA
GLASSFUL	GONENESS	GRILLING	GYRATING

GYRATION	HANGER-ON	HEADLAND	HERITAGE
GYRATORY	HANGNAIL	HEADLESS	HERMETIC
	HANG-OVER	HEADLINE	HESITANT
H—8	HANKERED	HEADLONG	HESITATE
HABITUAL	HAPPENED	HEAD-REST	HESPERUS
HACIENDA	HAPPIEST	HEADSHIP	HIAWATHA
HAGGLING	HARA-KIRI	HEAD-WIND	HIBERNIA
HAIRLESS	HARANGUE	HEAD-WORK	HIBISCUS
HAIRLINE	HARASSED	HEARABLE	HICCOUGH
HALF-BACK	HARDBAKE	HEARTILY	HICCUPED
HALF-BOOT	HARDENED	HEATHERY	HIGH-BALL
HALF-BRED	HARDIEST	HEAT-SPOT	HIGHBORN
HALF-COCK	HARDNESS	HEAT-WAVE	HIGHBRED
HALF-DEAD	HARDSHIP	HEAVENLY	HIGHBROW
HALF-DONE	HARDTACK	HEAVIEST	HIGHLAND
HALF-FACE	HARDWARE	HECKLING	HIGH-LIFE
HALF-MAST	HARDWOOD	HECTORED	HIGHNESS
HALF-MOON	HAREBELL	HEDGEHOG	HIGH-ROAD
HALF-NOTE	HARMLESS	HEDGE-HOP	HIGH-SPOT
HALF-PAST	HARMONIC	HEDGEROW	HIGH-TIDE
HALF-SEAS	HARRIDAN	HEEDLESS	HI-JACKED
HALF-TIME	HARROWED	HEELBALL	HI-JACKER
HALF-TINT	HARRYING	HEFTIEST	HILARITY
HALF-TONE	HASTENED	HEIGHTEN	HILL-FOLK
HALL-MARK	HASTINGS	HEIRLESS	HILL-FORT
HALLOOED	HATBRUSH	HEIRLOOM	HILLOCKY
HALLOWED	HATCHERY	HELLENIC	HILLSIDE
HALTERED	HATCHING	HELL-FIRE	HINDERED
HAMMERED	HATCHWAY	HELMETED	HINDMOST
HAMPERED	HATSTAND	HELMLESS	HINDUISM
HANDBALL	HAT-TRICK	HELMSMAN	HIP-JOINT
HANDBELL	HAUNTING	HELPLESS	HIRELING
HANDBILL	HAUSFRAU	HELPMATE	HISTORIC
HANDBOOK	HAWAIIAN	HELPMEET	HITCHING
HANDCART	HAWFINCH	HELVETIA	HITHERTO
HANDCUFF	HAWK-EYED	HEMP-SEED	HOARDING
HANDGRIP	HAWK-MOTH	HENCHMAN	HOARSELY
HANDHOLD	HAWTHORN	HEN-HOUSE	HOBBLING
HANDICAP	HAY-FEVER	HEN-ROOST	HOCK-TIDE
HAND-LINE	HAY-FIELD	HEPTAGON	HOGMANAY
HANDLING	HAY-MAKER	HEPTARCH	HOGSHEAD
HANDLOOM	HAY-STACK	HERALDED	HOISTING
HAND-MADE	HAZARDED	HERALDIC	HOLDFAST
HANDMAID	HAZEL-NUT	HERALDRY	HOLINESS
HANDMILL	HAZINESS	HERCULES	HOLLANDS
HAND-PICK	HEADACHE	HERD-BOOK	HOLLOWED
HAND-POST	HEADACHY	HERDSMAN	HOLLOWLY
HANDRAIL	HEAD-BAND	HEREDITY	HOLYROOD
HANDSOME	HEAD-BOOM	HERE-UNTO	HOMEBORN
HAND-WORK	HEADGEAR	HERE-UPON	HOMEBRED
HANDYMAN	HEADIEST	HEREWITH	HOME-FARM

HOMELAND	HOVERING	IDEALISE	IMPERIAL
HOMELESS	HOWITZER	IDEALISM	IMPETIGO
HOMELIKE	HUCKSTER	IDEALIST	IMPINGED
HOME-MADE	HUDDLING	IDEALITY	IMPISHLY
HOMESICK	HUDIBRAS	IDENTIFY	IMPLICIT
HOMESPUN	HUGENESS	IDENTITY	IMPLORED
HOMEWARD	HUGUENOT	IDEOLOGY	IMPLYING
HOMICIDE	HUMANELY	IDLENESS	IMPOLITE
HONESTLY	HUMANISE	IDOLATER	IMPORTED
HONEY-BEE	HUMANISM	IDOLATRY	IMPORTER
HONEYDEW	HUMANIST	IDOLISED	IMPOSING
HONEY-POT	HUMANITY	IGNITING	IMPOSTOR
HONORARY	HUMBLING	IGNITION	IMPOTENT
HONOURED	HUMIDIFY	IGNOMINY	IMPRISON
HOODWINK	HUMIDITY	IGNORANT	IMPROPER
HOOFLESS	HUMILITY	IGNORING	IMPROVED
HOOF-MARK	HUMMOCKY	ILL-BLOOD	IMPROVER
HOOK-WORM	HUMORIST	ILL-FATED	IMPUDENT
HOOLIGAN	HUMOROUS	ILL-TIMED	IMPUGNED
HOOP-IRON	HUMOURED	ILL-TREAT	IMPUNITY
HOPELESS	HUMPBACK	ILLUDING	IMPURELY
HOPINGLY	HUNGERED	ILLUMINE	IMPURITY
HORNBEAM	HUNGRILY	ILLUSION	IMPUTING
HORNBILL	HUNTRESS	ILLUSIVE	INACTION
HORNLESS	HUNTSMAN	ILLUSORY	INACTIVE
HORNPIPE	HURDLING	IMAGINED	INASMUCH
HOROLOGY	HURRYING	IMBECILE	INCENSED
HORRIBLE	HURTLING	IMBIBING	INCEPTOR
HORRIBLY	HUSHED-UP	IMITABLE	INCHOATE
HORRIDLY	HUSH-HUSH	IMITATED	INCIDENT
HORRIFIC	HUSKIEST	IMITATOR	INCISELY
HORSE-BOX	HUSTINGS	IMMANENT	INCISING
HORSE-BOY	HUSTLING	IMMATURE	INCISION
HORSE-CAR	HYACINTH	IMMERSED	INCISIVE
HORSE-FLY	HYDRATED	IMMINENT	INCISORY
HORSEMAN	HYDROGEN	IMMINGLE	INCITING
HOSE-PIPE	HYGIENIC	IMMOBILE	INCLINED
HOSE-REEL	HYMN-BOOK	IMMODEST	INCLUDED
HOSPITAL	HYPERION	IMMOLATE	INCOMING
HOSTELRY	HYPHENED	IMMORTAL	INCREASE
HOTCHPOT	HYPNOSIS	IMMUNISE	INCUBATE
HOTELIER	HYPNOTIC	IMMUNITY	INCURRED
HOTHOUSE	HYSTERIA	IMPACTED	INCURVED
HOT-PLATE	I—8	IMPAIRED	INDEBTED
HOT-PRESS	ICE-BOUND	IMPALING	INDECENT
HOUNDING	ICE-CREAM	IMPARITY	INDENTED
HOUR-HAND	ICE-FIELD	IMPARTED	INDEXING
HOUSE-BOY	ICE-HOUSE	IMPEDING	INDIAMAN
HOUSE-DOG	ICE-PLANT	IMPELLED	INDICATE
HOUSE-FLY	ICE-WATER	IMPELLER	INDICTED
HOUSE-TAX	ICE-YACHT	IMPENDED	INDIGENT

INDIRECT	INQUIRER	INVITING	JEALOUSY
INDITING	INSANELY	INVOICED	JEANETTE
INDOLENT	INSANITY	INVOKING	JEJUNELY
INDUCING	INSCRIBE	INVOLVED	JELLYBAG
INDUCTED	INSECURE	INWARDLY	JEOPARDY
INDULGED	INSERTED	IODISING	JEREMIAD
INDUSTRY	INSIGNIA	IOLANTHE	JEREMIAH
INEDIBLE	INSISTED	IREFULLY	JEROBOAM
INEQUITY	INSOLENT	IRISHISM	JERRICAN
INEXPERT	INSOMNIA	IRONBARK	JEST-BOOK
INFAMOUS	INSOMUCH	IRONCLAD	JET-BLACK
INFANTRY	INSPIRED	IRON-GREY	JET-PLANE
INFECTED	INSPIRER	IRONICAL	JETTISON
INFERIOR	INSPIRIT	IRONSIDE	JEWELLED
INFERNAL	INSTANCE	IRONWARE	JEWELLER
INFERRED	INSTINCT	IRONWOOD	JEWISHLY
INFESTED	INSTRUCT	IRONWORK	JEW'S-HARP
INFINITE	INSULATE	IRRIGATE	JIGGERED
INFINITY	INSULTED	IRRITANT	JIGGLING
INFIRMLY	INSURING	IRRITATE	JIGMAKER
INFLAMED	INTAGLIO	ISABELLE	JINGLING
INFLATED	INTEGRAL	ISLAMISM	JINGOISM
INFLATOR	INTENDED	ISLAMITE	JOCKEYED
INFORMAL	INTENTLY	ISLANDED	JOCOSELY
INFORMED	INTERACT	ISLANDER	JOCOSITY
INFORMER	INTER-COM	ISOBARIC	JOCUNDLY
INFRA-RED	INTEREST	ISOLATED	JODHPURS
INFRINGE	INTERIOR	ISOTHERM	JOGGLING
INFUSING	INTERLAY	ISSUABLE	JOHANNES
INFUSION	INTERMIX	ISTHMIAN	JOINTING
INFUSIVE	INTERNAL	ITERATED	JOINTURE
INHALANT	INTERNED		JOKINGLY
INHALING	INTERNEE	J—8	JOLLIEST
INHERENT	INTERPOL	JABBERED	JONATHAN
INHERING	INTERRED	JACKAROO	JONGLEUR
INHESION	INTERVAL	JACKETED	JOSTLING
INIMICAL	INTIMACY	JACOBEAN	JOUNCING
INIQUITY	INTIMATE	JACOBITE	JOUSTING
INITIATE	INTONING	JACQUARD	JOVIALLY
INJECTED	INTREPID	JAGGEDLY	JOYFULLY
INJECTOR	INTRIGUE	JAILBIRD	JOYOUSLY
INJURING	INTRUDER	JAMBOREE	JOY-STICK
INKINESS	INUNDATE	JANGLING	JUBILANT
INK-MAKER	INVADING	JAPANESE	JUDGMENT
INK-STAND	INVASION	JAPANNED	JUDICIAL
INLAYING	INVASIVE	JAPONICA	JUGGLERY
INNATELY	INVEIGLE	JAUNDICE	JUGGLING
INNOCENT	INVENTED	JAUNTIER	JUGO-SLAV
INNOVATE	INVENTOR	JAUNTILY	JULIENNE
INNUENDO	INVESTED	JAUNTING	JUMBLING
INQUIRED	INVESTOR	JAVANESE	JUNCTION

JUNCTURE	KNUCKLED	LARKSPUR	LEE-SHORE
JUNKETED	KOHINOOR	LARRIKIN	LEFT-HAND
JUSTNESS	KOHLRABI	LARRUPED	LEFTWARD
JUVENILE	KOTOWING	LASSOING	LEFT-WING
		LATCH-KEY	LEGALISE
		LATENESS	LEGALISM
K—8	L—8	LATENTLY	LEGALIST
KANGAROO	LABELLED	LATHERED	LEGALITY
KEDGEREE	LABOURED	LATHWORK	LEGATION
KEEL-HAUL	LABOURER	LATINISE	LEG-BREAK
KEENNESS	LABURNUM	LATINISM	LEMONADE
KEEPSAKE	LACERATE	LATINIST	LENGTHEN
KERCHIEF	LACE-WING	LATINITY	LENIENCE
KEROSENE	LACK-A-DAY	LATITUDE	LENIENCY
KEYBOARD	LACKEYED	LATTERLY	LENT-LILY
KEY-MONEY	LACROSSE	LATTICED	LESSENED
KEYSTONE	LADDERED	LAUDABLE	LETHARGY
KICKABLE	LADLEFUL	LAUDABLY	LETTERED
KICKSHAW	LADYBIRD	LAUDANUM	LEVELLED
KID-GLOVE	LADYLIKE	LAUGHING	LEVELLER
KILOGRAM	LADY-LOVE	LAUGHTER	LEVERAGE
KILOWATT	LADYSHIP	LAUNCHED	LEVERING
KINDLIER	LAKE-LAND	LAUREATE	LEVIABLE
KINDLING	LAMBENCY	LAVA-LIKE	LEVITATE
KINDNESS	LAMB-LIKE	LAVATORY	LEWDNESS
KING-CRAB	LAMBSKIN	LAVENDER	LEWISITE
KINGLIKE	LAMENESS	LAVISHED	LIBATION
KINGPOST	LAMENTED	LAVISHLY	LIBELLED
KINGSHIP	LAMINATE	LAWFULLY	LIBERATE
KINKAJOU	LAMPLESS	LAWGIVER	LIBERIAN
KINSFOLK	LAMP-POST	LAW-MAKER	LIBRETTO
KIPPERED	LAND-CRAB	LAWYERLY	LICENSED
KISS-CURL	LANDFALL	LAXATIVE	LICENSEE
KNAPPING	LAND-GIRL	LAYERING	LIEGEMAN
KNAPSACK	LANDLADY	LAZINESS	LIFE-BELT
KNAPWEED	LANDLESS	LEACHING	LIFEBOAT
KNEADING	LANDLORD	LEADSMAN	LIFEBUOY
KNEE-DEEP	LANDMARK	LEAFLESS	LIFELESS
KNEE-HIGH	LANDRAIL	LEANNESS	LIFELIKE
KNEELING	LANDSLIP	LEAP-FROG	LIFE-LINE
KNICKERS	LANDSMAN	LEAP-YEAR	LIFELONG
KNIGHTED	LANDWARD	LEARNING	LIFE-PEER
KNIGHTLY	LANDWEHR	LEASABLE	LIFE-RAFT
KNITTING	LAND-WIND	LEASHING	LIFE-SIZE
KNITWEAR	LANGUAGE	LEATHERY	LIFE-TIME
KNOCKING	LANGUISH	LEAVENED	LIFE-WORK
KNOCK-OUT	LANKIEST	LEAVINGS	LIFTABLE
KNOTLESS	LAPELLED	LEBANESE	LIGAMENT
KNOTTIER	LAPIDARY	LECTURED	LIGATURE
KNOTTING	LAP-JOINT	LECTURER	LIGHTING
KNOUTING	LARBOARD	LEE-BOARD	LIGHTISH
KNOWABLE	LARGESSE		

LIKEABLE	LOBBYIST	LOVELOCK	MAIL-BOAT
LIKENESS	LOCALISE	LOVELORN	MAIL-CART
LIKENING	LOCALISM	LOVE-NEST	MAIL-CLAD
LIKEWISE	LOCALITY	LOVESICK	MAIN-DECK
LILLIPUT	LOCATING	LOVESOME	MAINLAND
LIME-FREE	LOCATION	LOVINGLY	MAINMAST
LIME-KILN	LOCK-GATE	LOWERING	MAINSAIL
LIMERICK	LOCKSMAN	LOYALIST	MAINSTAY
LIME-TREE	LOCUTION	LUBBERLY	MAINTAIN
LIME-WASH	LODESTAR	LUCIDITY	MAINYARD
LIMITING	LODGINGS	LUCKIEST	MAJESTIC
LINCHPIN	LODGMENT	LUCKLESS	MAJOLICA
LINEALLY	LOG-CABIN	LUCKY-DIP	MAJORITY
LINEARLY	LOG-CANOE	LUKEWARM	MALAPROP
LINESMAN	LOITERED	LUMBERED	MALARIAL
LINGERED	LOITERER	LUMINARY	MAL-DE-MER
LINGERIE	LOLLIPOP	LUMINOUS	MALIGNED
LINGUIST	LOLLOPED	LUMPFISH	MALINGER
LINIMENT	LONDONER	LUNCHEON	MALODOUR
LINNAEUS	LONESOME	LUNCHING	MALT-KILN
LINOLEUM	LONGBOAT	LUNG-FISH	MALT-MILL
LINOTYPE	LONGHAND	LURCHING	MALTREAT
LIONISED	LONG-LEGS	LUSCIOUS	MALTSTER
LIP-STICK	LONG-SHIP	LUSTIEST	MALT-WORM
LIQUIDLY	LONG-SLIP	LUSTROUS	MANACLED
LIQUORED	LONG-STOP	LUTHERAN	MAN-CHILD
LISTENED	LONG-TERM	LYCH-GATE	MAN-EATER
LISTENER	LONGWAYS	LYNCHING	MAN-HATER
LISTEN-IN	LONGWISE	LYNCH-LAW	MAN-HOURS
LISTLESS	LONICERA	LYNX-EYED	MAN-OF-WAR
LITERACY	LOOKER-ON	LYRE-BIRD	MAN-POWER
LITERARY	LOOP-HOLE	LYRICISM	MANDAMUS
LITERATE	LOOP-LINE		MANDARIN
LITERATI	LOOSE-BOX	**M—8**	MANDATOR
LITIGANT	LOOSENED	MACARONI	MANDIBLE
LITIGATE	LOP-SIDED	MACAROON	MANDOLIN
LITTERED	LORD-LIKE	MACERATE	MANDRAKE
LITTLE-GO	LORDLING	MACHINED	MANDRILL
LITTORAL	LORD'S-DAY	MACKEREL	MANELESS
LIVE-AXLE	LORDSHIP	MADDENED	MANFULLY
LIVE-BAIT	LORIKEET	MADELINE	MANGLING
LIVELONG	LOSINGLY	MADHOUSE	MANGROVE
LIVENING	LOTHARIO	MADRIGAL	MANIACAL
LIVE-RAIL	LOUDNESS	MAGAZINE	MANICURE
LIVERIED	LOUNGING	MAGICIAN	MANIFEST
LIVERISH	LOVEBIRD	MAGNESIA	MANIFOLD
LIVE-WIRE	LOVE-KNOT	MAGNETIC	MANNERLY
LOAD-LINE	LOVELACE	MAGNOLIA	MANORIAL
LOANABLE	LOVELESS	MAHARAJA	MANTILLA
LOATHING	LOVE-LIFE	MAHOGANY	MANTLING
LOBBYING	LOVELILY	MAIDENLY	MANUALLY

MANURING	MAYORESS	METRICAL	MISGUIDE
MARATHON	MAZINESS	MIDDLING	MISHEARD
MARAUDER	MEAGRELY	MIDNIGHT	MISHMASH
MARBLING	MEAL-TIME	MIDSHIPS	MISJUDGE
MARCHING	MEAL-WORM	MIGHTILY	MISNAMED
MARGINAL	MEANNESS	MIGRAINE	MISNOMER
MARGRAVE	MEANTIME	MIGRATED	MISOGAMY
MARIGOLD	MEASURED	MIGRATOR	MISOGYNY
MARINADE	MEAT-SAFE	MILANESE	MISPLACE
MARINATE	MECHANIC	MILDEWED	MISPRINT
MARITIME	MEDDLING	MILDNESS	MISQUOTE
MARJORAM	MEDIATED	MILE-POST	MISRULED
MARKEDLY	MEDIATOR	MILITANT	MISSHAPE
MARKETED	MEDICATE	MILITARY	MISSPELL
MARKSMAN	MEDICINE	MILK-MAID	MISSPELT
MARMOSET	MEDIEVAL	MILK-WEED	MISSPEND
MAROCAIN	MEDIOCRE	MILL-HAND	MISSPENT
MAROONED	MEDITATE	MILLIARD	MISSTATE
MARQUESS	MEEKNESS	MILLIBAR	MISTAKEN
MARQUISE	MEETNESS	MILLINER	MISTEACH
MARRIAGE	MEGALITH	MILLPOND	MISTIMED
MARRYING	MELLOWED	MILLRACE	MISTITLE
MARSH-GAS	MELLOWLY	MILTONIC	MISTRESS
MARSH-HEN	MELODEON	MIMICKED	MISTRIAL
MARSH-TIT	MELODISE	MINATORY	MISTRUST
MARTELLO	MELODIST	MINCE-PIE	MISTUNED
MARTINET	MEMBERED	MINDLESS	MISUSAGE
MARTYRED	MEMBRANE	MINGLING	MISUSING
MARZIPAN	MEMORIAL	MINIMISE	MITIGATE
MASSACRE	MEMORISE	MINISTER	MITTENED
MASSAGED	MEM-SAHIB	MINISTRY	MIZZLING
MASSEUSE	MENACING	MINORITY	MNEMONIC
MASTERED	MENDABLE	MINOTAUR	MOBILITY
MASTERLY	MENTALLY	MINSTREL	MOBILIZE
MAST-HEAD	MERCHANT	MINUTELY	MOCCASIN
MASTLESS	MERCIFUL	MINUTEST	MOCKABLE
MASTODON	MERICARP	MINUTIAE	MODELLED
MATCH-BOX	MERIDIAN	MINUTING	MODELLER
MATCHING	MERINGUE	MIRRORED	MODERATE
MATERIAL	MERITING	MIRTHFUL	MODERATO
MATERIEL	MERRIEST	MISAPPLY	MODESTLY
MATERNAL	MESSMATE	MISCARRY	MODIFIED
MATHILDA	MESS-ROOM	MISCHIEF	MODIFIER
MATRONLY	MESSUAGE	MISCOUNT	MODISHLY
MATTERED	METALLED	MISCUING	MODULATE
MATTRESS	METALLIC	MISDATED	MOISTURE
MATURELY	METAPHOR	MISDEALT	MOLASSES
MATURING	METEORIC	MISDOING	MOLE-CAST
MATURITY	METERAGE	MISDRAWN	MOLE-HILL
MAVERICK	METHINKS	MISERERE	MOLE-SKIN
MAY-QUEEN	METHODIC	MISFIRED	MOLECULE

MOLESTED
MOLLUSCA
MOMENTUM
MONARCHY
MONASTIC
MONDAINE
MONETARY
MONEYBOX
MONGOOSE
MONITORY
MONKEYED
MONKFISH
MONKHOOD
MONOCLED
MONOGAMY
MONOGRAM
MONOLITH
MONOPOLY
MONORAIL
MONOTONE
MONOTONY
MONOTYPE
MONOXIDE
MONSIEUR
MONUMENT
MOOCHING
MOONBEAM
MOONCALF
MOONFACE
MOONFISH
MOONLESS
MOORCOCK
MOORFOWL
MOORLAND
MOOT-HALL
MOOTABLE
MOQUETTE
MORALIST
MORALITY
MORALIZE
MORATORY
MORAVIAN
MORBIDLY
MOREOVER
MORIBUND
MOROCCAN
MOROSELY
MORPHEAN
MORPHEUS
MORPHINE
MORTALLY

MORTARED
MORTGAGE
MORTISED
MORTUARY
MOSQUITO
MOSS-CLAD
MOSS-ROSE
MOTHERED
MOTHERLY
MOTIONED
MOTIVATE
MOTOR-BUS
MOTOR-CAR
MOTORING
MOTORIST
MOTORMAN
MOTTLING
MOUFFLON
MOULDING
MOULTING
MOUNDING
MOUNTAIN
MOUNTIES
MOUNTING
MOURNFUL
MOURNING
MOUSE-EAR
MOUTHFUL
MOUTHING
MOVELESS
MOVEMENT
MOVINGLY
MUCHNESS
MUCILAGE
MUCK-HEAP
MUCK-RAKE
MUDDLING
MUDDYING
MUDGUARD
MUFFLING
MULBERRY
MULCHING
MULCTING
MULE-DEER
MULETEER
MULISHLY
MULTIPLE
MULTIPLY
MUMBLING
MUNCHING
MUNIMENT

MUNITION
MURALLED
MURDERED
MURDERER
MURIATED
MURMURED
MUSCATEL
MUSCULAR
MUSHROOM
MUSICIAN
MUSINGLY
MUSK-BALL
MUSK-DEER
MUSK-PEAR
MUSK-PLUM
MUSK-ROSE
MUSKETRY
MUSQUASH
MUSTERED
MUTATION
MUTENESS
MUTILATE
MUTINEER
MUTINIED
MUTINOUS
MUTTERED
MUTUALLY
MUZZLING
MYCELIUM
MYCOLOGY
MYOSOTIS
MYRMIDON
MYSTICAL
MYTHICAL
N—5
NACREOUS
NAIL-FILE
NAINSOOK
NAMELESS
NAMESAKE
NAPOLEON
NARCISSI
NARCOSIS
NARCOTIC
NARGHILE
NARRATED
NARRATOR
NARROWED
NARROWER
NARROWLY
NATATION

NATATORY
NATIONAL
NATIVELY
NATIVITY
NATTERED
NATTIEST
NATURISM
NATURIST
NAUSEATE
NAUSEOUS
NAUTICAL
NAUTILUS
NAVIGATE
NAVY-BLUE
NAZARENE
NAZARITE
NAZIFIED
NEARNESS
NEATHERD
NEATNESS
NEBULOUS
NECKBAND
NECKBEEF
NECKLACE
NEEDLESS
NEEDLING
NEGATING
NEGATION
NEGATIVE
NEGLIGEE
NEGROISM
NEIGHING
NEO-LATIN
NEOPHYTE
NEPALESE
NEPOTISM
NESTLING
NETTLING
NEURITIS
NEUROSIS
NEUROTIC
NEW-COMER
NEWS-HAWK
NEWS-REEL
NEWS-ROOM
NIBBLING
NIBELUNG
NICENESS
NICKNAME
NICOTINE
NIGGLING

NIGHT-CAP	NOWADAYS	OCCUPANT	OPEN-EYED
NIGHT-JAR	NUDENESS	OCCUPIED	OPEN-WORK
NIGHT-MAN	NUGATORY	OCCUPIER	OPENCAST
NIGHT-OWL	NUISANCE	OCCURRED	OPENNESS
NIHILISM	NUMBERED	OCHREOUS	OPERA-HAT
NIHILIST	NUMBNESS	OCTOROON	OPERATED
NIHILITY	NUMERARY	OCTUPLET	OPERATIC
NINEFOLD	NUMERATE	OCULARLY	OPERATOR
NINEPINS	NUMEROUS	ODIOUSLY	OPERETTA
NINETEEN	NUMSKULL	ODOMETER	OPIUM-DEN
NITRATED	NUPTIALS	OERLIKON	OPPONENT
NITROGEN	NURSLING	OFF-BREAK	OPPOSING
NOBBLING	NURTURED	OFF-PRINT	OPPOSITE
NOBILITY	NUT-BROWN	OFF-SHOOT	OPTICIAN
NOBLEMAN	NUT-HATCH	OFF-SHORE	OPTIMISM
NOBLESSE	NUTMEGGY	OFF-STAGE	OPTIMIST
NOCTURNE	NUTRIENT	OFFENDED	OPTIONAL
NOISETTE	NUTSHELL	OFFENDER	OPULENCE
NOMADISM	NUZZLING	OFFERING	ORACULAR
NOMINATE		OFFICIAL	ORANGERY
NON-CLAIM	O—8	OFTTIMES	ORATORIO
NON-ELECT	OAK-APPLE	OHMMETER	ORCADIAN
NON-JUROR	OBDURACY	OILCLOTH	ORDAINED
NON-MORAL	OBDURATE	OIL-FIELD	ORDERING
NON-PARTY	OBEDIENT	OIL-GLAND	ORDINARY
NON-RIGID	OBEISANT	OIL-PAPER	ORDNANCE
NON-TOXIC	OBITUARY	OIL-PRESS	ORGANDIE
NON-UNION	OBJECTED	OIL-SKINS	ORGANISM
NONESUCH	OBJECTOR	OILINESS	ORGANIST
NONSENSE	OBLATION	OILSTONE	ORGANISE
NOONTIDE	OBLATORY	OINTMENT	ORIENTAL
NORMALCY	OBLIGANT	OLD-TIMER	ORIENTED
NORMALLY	OBLIGATE	OLD-WORLD	ORIGINAL
NORSEMAN	OBLIGATO	OLEANDER	ORNAMENT
NORTHERN	OBLIGING	OLEASTER	ORNATELY
NORTHING	OBLIVION	OLIPHANT	ORPHANED
NORTHMAN	OBSCURED	OLIVE-OIL	ORTHODOX
NOSE-DIVE	OBSERVED	OLYMPIAD	OSCULANT
NOSE-RING	OBSERVER	OLYMPIAN	OSCULATE
NOSEBAND	OBSESSED	OLYMPICS	OSSIFIED
NOSELESS	OBSOLETE	OMELETTE	OTOSCOPE
NOTANDUM	OBSTACLE	OMISSION	OUTBOARD
NOTATION	OBSTRUCT	OMISSIVE	OUTBOUND
NOTCHING	OBTAINED	OMITTING	OUTBREAK
NOTEBOOK	OBTRUDED	OMPHALOS	OUTBURST
NOTELESS	OBTUSELY	ONCE-OVER	OUTCLASS
NOTICING	OBVIATED	ONCOMING	OUTDOING
NOTIFIED	OCCASION	ONE-HORSE	OUTDOORS
NOTIONAL	OCCIDENT	ONE-SIDED	OUTFACED
NOVELIST	OCCLUDED	ONLOOKER	OUTFIELD
NOVEMBER	OCCULTLY	OOLOGIST	OUTFLANK

OUTFLASH	OVERCAST	OVERSHOE	PAMPERED
OUTFLING	OVERCOAT	OVERSHOT	PAMPHLET
OUTFLOWN	OVERCOLD	OVERSIDE	PANCAKED
OUTFLUSH	OVERCOME	OVERSIZE	PANCREAS
OUTGOING	OVERDONE	OVERSLIP	PANDERED
OUTGROWN	OVERDOSE	OVERSOLD	PANELLED
OUTHOUSE	OVERDRAW	OVERSTAY	PANGOLIN
OUTLAWED	OVERDREW	OVERSTEP	PANICKED
OUTLAWRY	OVERFAST	OVERTAKE	PANORAMA
OUTLEAPT	OVERFEED	OVERTASK	PANTHEON
OUTLEARN	OVERFILL	OVERTIME	PAPERING
OUTLINED	OVERFISH	OVERTONE	PARABOLA
OUTLIVED	OVERFLOW	OVERTURE	PARABOLE
OUTLYING	OVERFOLD	OVERTURN	PARADING
OUTMARCH	OVERFOND	OVERWASH	PARADISE
OUTPACED	OVERFULL	OVERWEAR	PARAFFIN
OUTPOWER	OVERGIVE	OVERWIND	PARAKEET
OUTRAGED	OVERGROW	OVERWORK	PARALLAX
OUTRANGE	OVERHAND	OVERWORN	PARALLEL
OUTREACH	OVERHANG	OXIDIZED	PARALYSE
OUTRIDER	OVERHAUL	OX-PECKER	PARAMOUR
OUTRIGHT	OVERHEAD	OX-TONGUE	PARANOIA
OUTSHINE	OVERHEAR		PARASITE
OUTSHONE	OVERHEAT	**P—8**	PARAVANE
OUTSIDER	OVERJUMP	PACIFIED	PARCHING
OUTSLEEP	OVERKIND	PACIFIER	PARDONED
OUTSLEPT	OVERLAID	PACIFISM	PARENTAL
OUTSLIDE	OVERLAIN	PACIFIST	PARGETED
OUTSMART	OVERLAND	PACK-LOAD	PARGETER
OUTSPEAK	OVERLEAF	PACK-MULE	PARISIAN
OUTSPENT	OVERLEAP	PACKETED	PARLANCE
OUTSPOKE	OVERLOAD	PADDLING	PARLEYED
OUTSTAND	OVERLOCK	PAGANISE	PARMESAN
OUTSTARE	OVERLONG	PAGANISH	PARODIED
OUTSTOOD	OVERLOOK	PAGANISM	PARODIST
OUTSTRIP	OVERLORD	PAGINATE	PAROXYSM
OUTSWEAR	OVERMUCH	PAINLESS	PARRYING
OUTVALUE	OVERNEAT	PAINTING	PARTAKEN
OUTVENOM	OVERNICE	PAKISTAN	PARTERRE
OUTVOTED	OVERPAID	PALATIAL	PARTHIAN
OUTWARDS	OVERPASS	PALATINE	PARTICLE
OUTWEIGH	OVERRAKE	PALE-EYED	PARTISAN
OVEN-BIRD	OVERRATE	PALE-FACE	PART-SONG
OVERALLS	OVERRIDE	PALENESS	PASSABLE
OVERARCH	OVERRIPE	PALISADE	PASSABLY
OVERAWED	OVERRULE	PALL-MALL	PASS-BOOK
OVERBEAR	OVERSEAS	PALLIATE	PASSER-BY
OVERBOIL	OVERSEEN	PALLIDLY	PASSOVER
OVERBOLD	OVERSEER	PALM-TREE	PASSPORT
OVERBUSY	OVERSELL	PALPABLE	PASSWORD
OVERCAME	OVERSEWN	PALPABLY	PASTICHE

PASTILLE	PENKNIFE	PHTHISIS	PITIABLY
PASTORAL	PENN'ORTH	PHYSICAL	PITILESS
PASTURED	PENOLOGY	PHYSIQUE	PITTANCE
PATCHING	PENT-ROOF	PIANETTE	PIVOT-MAN
PATENTED	PENTAGON	PICAROON	PIVOTING
PATENTEE	PEN-WIPER	PICKETED	PIXY-RING
PATENTOR	PENWOMAN	PICKLING	PLACATED
PATERNAL	PEOPLING	PICKLOCK	PLACEMAN
PATHETIC	PEPPERED	PICK-ME-UP	PLACIDLY
PATHLESS	PERCEIVE	PICKWICK	PLAGIARY
PATIENCE	PERCHING	PICTURED	PLAGUILY
PATTERED	PERFORCE	PIERCING	PLAGUING
PATTY-PAN	PERFUMED	PIFFLING	PLAITING
PAVEMENT	PERIANTH	PIG-FACED	PLANGENT
PAVILION	PERICARP	PIKEHEAD	PLANKING
PAWNSHOP	PERILOUS	PILASTER	PLANKTON
PAY-CLERK	PERIODIC	PILCHARD	PLANLESS
PAY-SHEET	PERISHED	PILFERED	PLANNING
PEACEFUL	PERJURED	PILLAGED	PLANTAIN
PEACHING	PERMEATE	PILLARED	PLANTING
PEA-GREEN	PERMUTED	PILLOWED	PLANTLET
PEARMAIN	PERORATE	PILOTAGE	PLASHING
PEASECOD	PEROXIDE	PILOTING	PLATEFUL
PEAT-MOOR	PERSONAL	PIN-WHEEL	PLATFORM
PEAT-MOSS	PERSPIRE	PINAFORE	PLATINIC
PECTORAL	PERSUADE	PINCE-NEZ	PLATINUM
PECULIAR	PERTNESS	PINCHERS	PLATONIC
PEDAGOGY	PERUSING	PINCHING	PLATTING
PEDALLED	PERUVIAN	PINE-CLAD	PLATYPUS
PEDANTIC	PERVADED	PINE-CONE	PLAYABLE
PEDANTRY	PERVERSE	PINE-WOOD	PLAYBILL
PEDDLERY	PESTERED	PING-PONG	PLAYBOOK
PEDDLING	PESTLING	PININGLY	PLAYGOER
PEDESTAL	PETERING	PINIONED	PLAYMATE
PEDICURE	PETERMAN	PINK-EYED	PLAYSOME
PEDIGREE	PETITION	PIN-MAKER	PLAYTIME
PEDIMENT	PETRONEL	PIN-MONEY	PLEACHED
PEEP-HOLE	PETULANT	PINNACLE	PLEADING
PEEP-SHOW	PHALANGE	PINPOINT	PLEASANT
PEERLESS	PHANTASM	PIPE-CASE	PLEASING
PEIGNOIR	PHANTASY	PIPE-CLAY	PLEASURE
PEKINESE	PHARISEE	PIPE-FISH	PLEATING
PELLAGRA	PHARMACY	PIPE-LINE	PLEBEIAN
PELL-MELL	PHEASANT	PIPE-RACK	PLECTRUM
PELLUCID	PHILOMEL	PIPE-WORK	PLEDGING
PEMMICAN	PHONE-BOX	PIQUANCY	PLEIADES
PENALISE	PHONETIC	PIRATING	PLETHORA
PENCHANT	PHOSGENE	PISCATOR	PLEURISY
PENDULUM	PHOSPHOR	PISTOLET	PLIANTLY
PENELOPE	PHRASING	PITCHING	PLIGHTED
PENITENT	PHRYGIAN	PITIABLE	PLIOCENE

PLODDING	POND-WEED	POULTICE	PRETTILY
PLOPPING	PONTIFEX	POUNCING	PREVIOUS
PLOTTING	PONTIFIC	POUNDAGE	PRICKING
PLOUGHED	PONY-SKIN	POUNDING	PRICKLED
PLUCKILY	POOH-POOH	POWDERED	PRIDEFUL
PLUCKING	POOL-ROOM	POWERFUL	PRIESTLY
PLUGGING	POOR-LAWS	POW-WOWED	PRIGGERY
PLUG-UGLY	POORNESS	PRACTICE	PRIGGISH
PLUMBAGO	POOR-RATE	PRACTISE	PRIMATES
PLUMB-BOB	POPELING	PRAISING	PRIMEVAL
PLUMBING	POPINJAY	PRANCING	PRIMNESS
PLUM-CAKE	POPISHLY	PRANDIAL	PRIMROSE
PLUM-DUFF	POPULACE	PRANGING	PRINCELY
PLUMELET	POPULATE	PRATTLED	PRINCEPS
PLUMPEST	POPULOUS	PREACHED	PRINCESS
PLUMPING	POROSITY	PREACHER	PRINTING
PLUNGING	PORPHYRY	PREAMBLE	PRIORESS
PLURALLY	PORPOISE	PRECEDED	PRIORITY
PLUTARCH	PORRIDGE	PRECINCT	PRISONER
PLUTONIC	PORTABLE	PRECIOUS	PRISTINE
PLUVIOUS	PORTHOLE	PRECLUDE	PRIZEMAN
POACHING	PORTIERE	PREDATED	PROBABLE
POCHETTE	PORTLAND	PRE-ELECT	PROBABLY
POCKETED	PORTRAIT	PREENING	PROCEEDS
POCKMARK	POSEIDON	PRE-ENTRY	PROCLAIM
POETICAL	POSINGLY	PRE-EXIST	PROCURED
POETIZED	POSITION	PREFACED	PRODDING
POIGNANT	POSITIVE	PREFIXED	PRODIGAL
POIGNARD	POSSIBLE	PREGNANT	PRODUCED
POINTING	POSSIBLY	PREJUDGE	PRODUCER
POISONED	POSTABLE	PRELUDED	PROFANED
POISONER	POST-CARD	PREMIERE	PROFILED
POLARITY	POST-DATE	PREMISED	PROFITED
POLARIZE	POST-FREE	PREMISES	PROFOUND
POLE-JUMP	POST-HORN	PRENATAL	PROGRESS
POLE-STAR	POSTICHE	PRENTICE	PROHIBIT
POLEMICS	POSTMARK	PREPARED	PROLAPSE
POLICING	POST-PAID	PRESAGED	PROLIFIC
POLISHED	POSTPONE	PRESCIND	PROLIXLY
POLITELY	POST-TIME	PRESENCE	PROLOGUE
POLITICS	POSTURED	PRESERVE	PROMISED
POLLUTED	POTATION	PRESIDED	PROMOTED
POLONIUM	POTENTLY	PRESS-BOX	PROMOTER
POLTROON	POTHERED	PRESSING	PROMPTED
POLYGAMY	POT-HOUSE	PRESSMAN	PROMPTER
POLYGLOT	POT-PLANT	PRESSURE	PROMPTLY
POLYGRAM	POTSHERD	PRESTIGE	PRONG-HOE
POMANDER	POT-STICK	PRE-STUDY	PROOFING
POMPEIAN	POT-STILL	PRESUMED	PROPERLY
PONDERED	POTTERED	PRETENCE	PROPERTY
POND-LILY	POUCHING	PRETTIFY	PROPHECY

PROPHESY	PUPATION	QUEASILY	RAFTSMAN
PROPOSAL	PUPPETRY	QUEEN-BEE	RAG-PAPER
PROPOSED	PUPPYISH	QUEENING	RAG-WHEEL
PROPOSER	PUPPYISM	QUEEREST	RAGGEDLY
PROPOUND	PURBLIND	QUEERING	RAGINGLY
PROPPING	PURCHASE	QUEERISH	RAGSTONE
PROROGUE	PURENESS	QUELLING	RAILHEAD
PROSEMAN	PURIFIED	QUENCHED	RAILLERY
PROSPECT	PURPLING	QUENCHER	RAILROAD
PROTEGEE	PURPLISH	QUERYING	RAINBAND
PROTOCOL	PURPOSED	QUESTFUL	RAINBIRD
PROTOZOA	PURSEFUL	QUESTING	RAINCOAT
PROTRACT	PURSE-NET	QUESTION	RAINDROP
PROTRUDE	PURSLANE	QUEUEING	RAINFALL
PROVABLE	PURSUANT	QUIBBLED	RAINLESS
PROVABLY	PURSUING	QUICKEST	RAKEHELL
PROVIDED	PURVEYED	QUICKSET	RAKISHLY
PROVINCE	PURVEYOR	QUIDNUNC	RALLYING
PROVOKED	PUSHBALL	QUIETEST	RAMADHAN
PROWLING	PUSHBIKE	QUIETUDE	RAMBLING
PRUDENCE	PUSS-MOTH	QUILLING	RAMIFIED
PRUNELLA	PUSS-TAIL	QUILL-PEN	RAMPAGED
PRUSSIAN	PUSSY-CAT	QUILTING	RAMPANCY
PRYINGLY	PUTTYING	QUIPPING	RAM'S-HORN
PSALMIST	PUZZLING	QUIRKING	RANCHERO
PSALMODY	PYRIFORM	QUISLING	RANCHING
PSALTERY	PYROXENE	QUIT-RENT	RANCHMAN
PTOMAINE		QUITTING	RANCIDLY
PUBLICAN	**Q—8**	QUIXOTIC	RANDOMLY
PUBLICLY	QUACKERY	QUIXOTRY	RANKLING
PUCKERED	QUACKING	QUIZZERY	RANKNESS
PUDDLING	QUACKISH	QUIZZING	RANSOMED
PUFF-BALL	QUADRANT	QUOTABLE	RAPACITY
PUFF-PUFF	QUADRATE	QUOTIENT	RAPE-SEED
PUG-FACED	QUADRIGA		RAPIDITY
PUGILISM	QUADROON	**R—8**	RAREFIED
PUGILIST	QUAFFING	RABBETED	RARENESS
PUISSANT	QUAGMIRE	RABELAIS	RASCALLY
PULINGLY	QUAILING	RABIDITY	RASHNESS
PULLOVER	QUAINTER	RACE-CARD	RATAPLAN
PULSATOR	QUAINTLY	RACE-GOER	RATEABLE
PUMP-ROOM	QUAKERLY	RACINESS	RATE-BOOK
PUNCHEON	QUANDARY	RACK-RENT	RATIFIED
PUNCHING	QUANTITY	RACKETED	RATIONAL
PUNCTUAL	QUARRIED	RADIALLY	RATIONED
PUNCTURE	QUARTERN	RADIANCE	RAT'S-BANE
PUNGENCY	QUARTERS	RADIATED	RAT'S-TAIL
PUNINESS	QUASHING	RADIATOR	RATTLING
PUNISHED	QUATORZE	RADIOING	RAVAGING
PUNITIVE	QUATRAIN	RAFFLING	RAVELLED
PUNITORY	QUAVERED	RAFTERED	RAVENING

RAVENOUS	RECLOTHE	REFUSING	RELIGION
RAVINGLY	RECOILED	REFUTING	RELISHED
RAVISHED	RECOINED	REGAINED	RE-LIVING
RAW-BONED	RE-COLOUR	REGALING	RE-LOADED
RE-ABSORB	RE-COMMIT	REGALITY	REMAINED
RE-ACCUSE	RE-CONVEY	REGARDED	REMAKING
REACHING	RECORDED	RE-GATHER	REMANENT
REACTION	RECORDER	REGICIDE	RE-MANNED
REACTIVE	RECOUPED	REGILDED	REMARKED
READABLE	RECOURSE	REGIMENT	REMARQUE
READABLY	RECOVERY	REGIONAL	REMEDIAL
RE-ADJUST	RECREANT	REGISTER	REMEDIED
RE-AFFIRM	RECREATE	REGISTRY	REMEMBER
REALIZED	RECURRED	REGNANCY	REMINDED
REALNESS	RECURVED	RE-GROUND	REMINDER
RE-APPEAR	RED-FACED	REGROWTH	REMISSLY
REAR-RANK	RED-SHIRT	REGULATE	REMITTAL
RE-ARMING	REDDENED	RE-HANDLE	REMITTED
REARMOST	REDEEMED	REHASHED	RE-MODIFY
REARWARD	REDEEMER	REHEARSE	REMOTELY
RE-ASCEND	REDIRECT	RE-HEATED	REMOVING
RE-ASCENT	RE-DIVIDE	RE-HOUSED	RENAMING
REASONED	RED-NOSED	REIGNING	RENDERED
RE-ASSERT	REDOLENT	RE-IGNITE	RENEGADE
RE-ASSESS	REDOUBLE	RE-IMPORT	RENEWING
RE-ASSIGN	REDSHANK	REIMPOSE	RENOUNCE
REASSURE	REDUCING	REINDEER	RENOVATE
RE-ATTACH	RE-DYEING	RE-INFECT	RENOWNED
RE-ATTAIN	RE-ECHOED	RE-INFUSE	RENTABLE
REBATING	REED-MACE	RE-INSERT	RENT-FREE
REBELLED	REED-STOP	RE-INSURE	RENT-ROLL
RE-BOILED	REEF-KNOT	RE-INVEST	RE-NUMBER
REBUFFED	REELABLE	REISSUED	RE-OBTAIN
REBUKING	RE-EMBARK	REJECTED	RE-OCCUPY
REBURIED	RE-EMBODY	REJOICED	RE-OPENED
REBUTTAL	RE-EMERGE	REJOINER	RE-OPPOSE
REBUTTED	RE-ENLIST	RE-JUDGED	RE-ORDAIN
RECALLED	RE-EXPORT	REKINDLE	REPAIRED
RECANTED	REFASTEN	RELANDED	REPAIRER
RECEDING	REFERRED	RELAPSED	REPARTEE
RECEIVED	REFILLED	RELATING	REPASSED
RECEIVER	REFINERY	RELATION	REPAYING
RECENTLY	REFINING	RELAXING	REPEALED
RECESSED	REFITTED	RELAYING	REPEATED
RECHARGE	REFLEXED	RELEASED	REPEATER
RECISION	REFORGED	RELEGATE	REPELLED
RECITING	REFORMED	RELEVANT	REPENTED
RECKLESS	REFORMER	RELIABLE	REPINING
RECKONED	REFRAMED	RELIABLY	REPLACED
RECLINED	REFUNDED	RELIANCE	RE-PLEDGE
RECLOSED		RELIEVED	REPLYING

RE-POLISH	RE-STRIKE	RHOMBOID	ROLY-POLY
REPORTED	RESULTED	RHYTHMIC	ROMANCED
REPORTER	RESUMING	RIBALDRY	ROMANCER
REPOSING	RE-SUMMON	RIBBONED	ROMANISE
RE-POTTED	RETAILED	RICHNESS	ROMANISH
REPRIEVE	RETAILER	RICKSHAW	ROMANIST
REPRISAL	RETAINED	RICOCHET	ROMANTIC
REPROACH	RETAINER	RIDDANCE	ROOD-BEAM
REPROVAL	RETAKING	RIDDLING	ROOD-LOFT
REPROVED	RETARDED	RIDEABLE	ROOD-TREE
RE-PRUNED	RETICENT	RIDICULE	ROOFLESS
REPTILIA	RETICULE	RIFENESS	ROOF-TREE
REPUBLIC	RETIRING	RIFF-RAFF	ROOSTING
REPUGNED	RETORTED	RIFLEMAN	ROOT-BEER
REPULSED	RE-TOSSED	RIGADOON	ROOT-CROP
RE-PURIFY	RETRACED	RIGHTFUL	ROOT-HAIR
REPUTING	RETRENCH	RIGHTING	ROOTLESS
REQUIRED	RETRIEVE	RIGIDITY	ROPE-WALK
REQUITAL	RETROACT	RIGOROUS	ROPE-YARN
REQUITED	RE-TRYING	RING-BARK	ROPINESS
RE-ROOFED	RETURNED	RING-BOLT	ROSARIAN
RE-SCORED	RE-UNITED	RINGBONE	ROSARIUM
RESCRIPT	REVALUED	RING-DOVE	ROSE-BUSH
RESCUING	REVAMPED	RINGWORM	ROSE-GALL
RESEARCH	REVEALED	RIPARIAN	ROSE-HUED
RESEATED	REVEILLE	RIPENESS	ROSE-KNOT
RESEMBLE	REVELLED	RIPPLING	ROSEMARY
RESENTED	REVELLER	RISKIEST	ROSE-PINK
RESERVED	REVENGED	RITUALLY	ROSE-ROOT
RESETTLE	REVEREND	RIVALLED	ROSE-TREE
RESIDENT	REVERENT	RIVER-BED	ROSETTED
RESIDUAL	REVERING	RIVER-GOD	ROSE-WOOD
RESIDUUM	REVERSAL	RIVER-HOG	ROSE-WORM
RESIGNED	REVERSED	RIVER-MAN	ROSINESS
RESISTED	RE-VETTED	RIVETING	ROSINING
RE-SOLDER	REVIEWED	ROAD-BOOK	ROSIN-OIL
RESOLUTE	REVIEWER	ROADLESS	ROTARIAN
RESOLVED	REVILING	ROADSIDE	ROTATING
RESONANT	REVISING	ROADSTER	ROTATION
RE-SORTED	REVISION	ROASTING	ROTATIVE
RESOURCE	REVIVIFY	ROBUSTLY	ROTATORY
RESOWING	REVIVING	ROCK-ALUM	ROT-GRASS
RESPIRED	REVOKING	ROCK-CAKE	ROTIFERA
RESPONSE	REVOLTED	ROCK-DOVE	ROTTENLY
RE-STATED	REVOLVED	ROCKETED	ROUGHAGE
REST-CURE	REVOLVER	ROCKLESS	ROUGH-DRY
RESTLESS	REWARDED	ROCK-ROSE	ROUGH-HEW
RESTORED	RE-WORDED	ROCK-SALT	ROUGHING
RESTORER	RHAPSODY	ROCK-WORK	ROUGHISH
RESTRAIN	RHEOSTAT	ROGATION	ROULETTE
RESTRICT	RHETORIC	ROLL-CALL	ROUND-ARM

ROUNDERS	SADDENED	SAND-BIRD	SAW-FRAME
ROUNDING	SADDLERY	SAND-CRAB	SAW-GRASS
ROUNDISH	SADDLING	SAND-DUNE	SAW-HORSE
ROUNDLET	SADDUCEE	SAND-FISH	SAW-TABLE
ROUND-TOP	SADFACED	SAND-FLEA	SCABBARD
ROUTEING	SAGACITY	SAND-HILL	SCABIOSA
ROVINGLY	SAGAMORE	SAND-IRON	SCABIOUS
ROWDYISH	SAGENESS	SAND-REED	SCABROUS
ROWDYISM	SAGO-PALM	SAND-REEL	SCAFFOLD
ROWELLED	SAILABLE	SAND-ROLL	SCALABLE
ROYALISM	SAIL-BOAT	SAND-SHOT	SCALDING
ROYALIST	SAILLESS	SAND-STAR	SCALPING
RUBBISHY	SAIL-LOFT	SAND-TRAP	SCAMPING
RUBICUND	SAIL-PLAN	SAND-WASP	SCAMPISH
RUCKSACK	SAIL-ROOM	SANDWICH	SCANNING
RUDENESS	SAIL-YARD	SAND-WORM	SCANSION
RUDIMENT	SAINFOIN	SAND-WORT	SCANTIES
RUEFULLY	SALACITY	SANENESS	SCANTILY
RUFFLING	SALAD-OIL	SANGUINE	SCAPULAR
RUGGEDLY	SALADING	SANITARY	SCARCELY
RUINABLE	SALARIED	SANSKRIT	SCARCITY
RUINATED	SALEABLE	SAPIDITY	SCARFING
RULELESS	SALEABLY	SAPIENCE	SCARF-PIN
RULINGLY	SALE-ROOM	SAPPHIRE	SCARLESS
RUMANIAN	SALESMAN	SARABAND	SCARRING
RUMBLING	SALE-WORK	SARATOGA	SCATHING
RUMINANT	SALIENCE	SARDONIC	SCAVENGE
RUMINATE	SALIFIED	SARDONYX	SCENARIO
RUMMAGED	SALINITY	SARGASSO	SCENE-MAN
RUMOURED	SALLYING	SARSENET	SCENT-BAG
RUMPLING	SALMONET	SASH-CORD	SCENT-BOX
RUNABOUT	SALOPIAN	SATANISM	SCEPTRED
RUNAGATE	SALT-BUSH	SATANITY	SCHEDULE
RUNNER-UP	SALTLESS	SATIABLE	SCHEMING
RURALISE	SALT-LICK	SATIATED	SCHILLER
RURALISM	SALT-MINE	SATIRIST	SCHNAPPS
RURALIST	SALTNESS	SATIRIZE	SCHOOLED
RURALITY	SALT-WELL	SATURATE	SCHOONER
RUSHLIKE	SALT-WORT	SATURDAY	SCIATICA
RUSTLESS	SALUTARY	SAUCEBOX	SCIMITAR
RUSTLING	SALUTING	SAUCEPAN	SCISSORS
RUTHLESS	SALVABLE	SAUTERNE	SCOFFING
RYE-GRASS	SALVAGED	SAVAGELY	SCOLDING
	SAMENESS	SAVAGERY	SCOOP-NET
S—8	SAMPHIRE	SAVAGING	SCOOPING
SABOTAGE	SAMPLING	SAVANNAH	SCOOTING
SABOTEUR.	SANCTIFY	SAVEABLE	SCORCHED
SACKLESS	SANCTION	SAVINGLY	SCORCHER
SACK-RACE	SANCTITY	SAVOURED	SCORNFUL
SACREDLY	SAND-BANK	SAVOYARD	SCORNING
SACRISTY	SAND-BATH	SAWBONES	SCORPION

SCOTCHED	SEACOAST	SEDIMENT	SENTIENT
SCOT-FREE	SEA-CRAFT	SEDITION	SENTINEL
SCOTSMAN	SEA-DEVIL	SEDUCING	SENTRY-GO
SCOTTISH	SEA-EAGLE	SEDULITY	SEPARATE
SCOURGED	SEAFARER	SEDULOUS	SEPTETTE
SCOURING	SEA-FIGHT	SEED-CAKE	SEPTUPLE
SCOUTING	SEA-FRONT	SEED-COAT	SEQUENCE
SCOWLING	SEA-FROTH	SEED-CORN	SERAGLIO
SCRABBLE	SEAGOING	SEED-GALL	SERAPHIC
SCRAGGED	SEA-GREEN	SEED-LEAF	SERAPHIM
SCRAGGLY	SEA-HEATH	SEEDLESS	SERENADE
SCRAMBLE	SEA-HOLLY	SEEDLING	SERENATA
SCRAPING	SEA-HORSE	SEED-PLOT	SERENELY
SCRAPPED	SEA-HOUND	SEEDSMAN	SERENEST
SCRATCHY	SEA-LEVEL	SEEDTIME	SERENITY
SCRAWLED	SEAL-SKIN	SEESAWED	SERGEANT
SCREAMED	SEAMANLY	SEETHING	SERIALLY
SCREAMER	SEAMIEST	SEIDLITZ	SERIATIM
SCREECHY	SEAMLESS	SEIGNEUR	SERJEANT
SCREENED	SEAMSTER	SEIGNIOR	SERRATED
SCREEVER	SEA-NYMPH	SEIZABLE	SERVITOR
SCREWING	SEA-PERCH	SELECTED	SET-PIECE
SCRIBBLE	SEA-PLANE	SELECTOR	SETTLING
SCRIBING	SEA-PLANT	SELF-HEAL	SEVERELY
SCRIMPED	SEA-PURSE	SELF-HELP	SEVERING
SCRIMPLY	SEARCHED	SELFLESS	SEVERITY
SCROFULA	SEARCHER	SELF-LIKE	SEWERAGE
SCROUNGE	SEA-ROVER	SELF-LOVE	SEWER-GAS
SCRUB-OAK	SEASCAPE	SELF-MADE	SEXTETTE
SCRUBBED	SEA-SHELL	SELF-PITY	SEXTUPLE
SCRUBBER	SEA-SHORE	SELFSAME	SEXUALLY
SCRUPLED	SEA-SHRUB	SELF-WILL	SFORZATO
SCRUTINY	SEA-SNAIL	SELLABLE	SHABBIER
SCUDDING	SEA-SNAKE	SELVEDGE	SHABBILY
SCUFFLED	SEASONED	SEMANTIC	SHACKING
SCULLERY	SEA-TROUT	SEMESTER	SHACKLED
SCULLING	SEA-WATER	SEMI-NUDE	SHADDOCK
SCULLION	SEA-WOMAN	SEMINARY	SHADIEST
SCULPTOR	SEA-WRACK	SEMINOLE	SHADOWED
SCUMBLED	SECATEUR	SEMITISM	SHAFTING
SCURRIED	SECEDING	SEMITONE	SHAGREEN
SCURRIES	SECLUDED	SEMOLINA	SHAMBLES
SCURVILY	SECONDED	SEMPSTER	SHAMEFUL
SCUTTLED	SECONDLY	SENILITY	SHAMMING
SCYTHIAN	SECRETED	SENNIGHT	SHAMROCK
SEA-ACORN	SECRETLY	SENORITA	SHANGHAI
SEA-ADDER	SECURELY	SENSEFUL	SHANKING
SEA-BEAST	SECURING	SENSIBLE	SHARP-CUT
SEABOARD	SECURITY	SENSIBLY	SHARPING
SEABORNE	SEDATELY	SENSUOUS	SHARP-SET
SEA-BREAM	SEDATIVE	SENTENCE	SHEARING

SHEATHED
SHEAVING
SHEDDING
SHEEP-DIP
SHEEPDOG
SHEEPFLY
SHEEPISH
SHEEP-PEN
SHEEP-RUN
SHEERING
SHEER-LEG
SHEETING
SHELDUCK
SHELLING
SHELVING
SHEPHERD
SHERATON
SHIELDED
SHIFTILY
SHIFTING
SHILLING
SHIMMING
SHIN-BONE
SHINGLED
SHINGLES
SHINNING
SHIPLESS
SHIPLOAD
SHIPMATE
SHIPMENT
SHIPPING
SHIP-WORM
SHIPYARD
SHIREMAN
SHIRKING
SHIRTING
SHIVERED
SHOCKING
SHOEBILL
SHOEHORN
SHOELACE
SHOELESS
SHOOTING
SHOP-BELL
SHOP-GIRL
SHOPPING
SHOPWORN
SHORTAGE
SHORT-CUT
SHORT-LEG
SHORT-RIB

SHOT-HOLE
SHOT-SILK
SHOULDER
SHOUTING
SHOW-BILL
SHOW-CARD
SHOW-CASE
SHOW-DOWN
SHOWERED
SHOW-ROOM
SHOW-YARD
SHRAPNEL
SHREDDED
SHREWDLY
SHREWISH
SHRIEKED
SHRILLED
SHRIMPED
SHRIMPER
SHRINKER
SHROUDED
SHRUGGED
SHUCKING
SHUFFLED
SHUNNING
SHUNTING
SHUT-DOWN
SHUTTING
SIBERIAN
SIBILANT
SIBILATE
SICILIAN
SICKENED
SICKLILY
SICK-LIST
SICKNESS
SICK-ROOM
SIDE-ARMS
SIDE-BEAM
SIDE-COMB
SIDE-DISH
SIDE-DRUM
SIDE-LINE
SIDELING
SIDE-LOCK
SIDELONG
SIDE-NOTE
SIDEREAL
SIDE-SHOW
SIDE-SLIP
SIDESMAN

SIDE-STEP
SIDE-VIEW
SIDEWALK
SIDEWAYS
SIFFLEUR
SIFFLING
SIGHTING
SIGNABLE
SIGNALLY
SIGNIEUR
SIGNLESS
SIGN-POST
SILENCED
SILENCER
SILENTLY
SILICATE
SILK-WORM
SILLABUB
SILURIAN
SILVANUS
SIMMERED
SIMPERED
SIMPLIFY
SIMULANT
SIMULATE
SINCIPUT
SINECURE
SINFULLY
SINGABLE
SINGEING
SINGLING
SING-SING
SING-SONG
SINGULAR
SINISTER
SINK-HOLE
SIPHONAL
SIPHONIC
SIPHONED
SISTERLY
SISYPHUS
SITUATED
SIXPENCE
SIXTIETH
SIZEABLE
SIZINESS
SIZZLING
SKEAN-DHU
SKELETAL
SKELETON
SKETCHED

SKEWBALD
SKEWERED
SKIDDING
SKIM-MILK
SKIMMING
SKIMPING
SKIN-DEEP
SKINLESS
SKINNING
SKIP-JACK
SKIPPING
SKIRLING
SKIRMISH
SKIRTING
SKITTISH
SKITTLES
SKULKING
SKULL-CAP
SKUNKISH
SKYLIGHT
SKY-PILOT
SKYSCAPE
SLABBING
SLACKING
SLAMMING
SLANGILY
SLANGING
SLANTING
SLAP-BANG
SLAP-DASH
SLAPJACK
SLAPPING
SLASHING
SLATE-AXE
SLATTERN
SLAVERED
SLAVONIC
SLEDGING
SLEEPILY
SLEEPING
SLEETING
SLIDABLE
SLIGHTLY
SLIMMING
SLIMNESS
SLINGING
SLINKING
SLIP-KNOT
SLIPPERY
SLIPPING
SLIPSHOD

SLITHERY	SNAPPING	SOCIALLY	SOREHEAD
SLITTING	SNAPPISH	SOCKETED	SORENESS
SLIVERED	SNAPSHOT	SOCKLESS	SORORITY
SLOGGING	SNARLING	SOCRATES	SORROWED
SLOP-BOWL	SNATCHED	SODDENED	SORTABLE
SLOP-PAIL	SNATCHER	SOFTENED	SOUCHONG
SLOPPING	SNEAKING	SOFT-EYED	SOUGHING
SLOTHFUL	SNEERING	SOFTLING	SOULLESS
SLOTTING	SNEEZING	SOFTNESS	SOUNDING
SLOUCHED	SNICKING	SOFT-SOAP	SOUR-EYED
SLOUGHED	SNIFFING	SOFT-WOOD	SOURNESS
SLOVENLY	SNIPPETY	SOILLESS	SOUR-PUSS
SLOWNESS	SNIPPING	SOIL-PIPE	SOUTHERN
SLOW-WORM	SNIP-SNAP	SOLACING	SOUTHPAW
SLUGGARD	SNIVELLY	SOLARIUM	SOUVENIR
SLUGGING	SNOBBERY	SOLATIUM	SOZZLING
SLUGGISH	SNOBBISH	SOLDERED	SPACIOUS
SLUICING	SNOOPING	SOLDIERY	SPADILLE
SLUMMING	SNOOZING	SOLECISE	SPALPEEN
SLUMPING	SNORTING	SOLECISM	SPANDREL
SLURRING	SNOWBALL	SOLECIST	SPANGLED
SLUTTISH	SNOWBIRD	SOLEMNLY	SPANKING
SLY-BOOTS	SNOWBOOT	SOLENESS	SPANLESS
SMACKING	SNOWDROP	SOLENOID	SPANNING
SMALL-ALE	SNOWFALL	SOLIDIFY	SPAN-ROOF
SMALLEST	SNOWLESS	SOLIDITY	SPARERIB
SMALLISH	SNOWLIKE	SOLITARY	SPARKING
SMALLPOX	SNOWLINE	SOLITUDE	SPARKLER
SMARTING	SNOW-SLED	SOLSTICE	SPARKLET
SMASHING	SNOWSHOE	SOLUTION	SPARRING
SMEARING	SNUBBING	SOLVABLE	SPARSELY
SMELLING	SNUBBISH	SOLVENCY	SPAVINED
SMELTING	SNUB-NOSE	SOMBRERO	SPAWNING
SMIRCHED	SNUFFBOX	SOMEBODY	SPEAKING
SMIRKING	SNUFFERS	SOMERSET	SPEARING
SMOCKING	SNUFFLED	SOMESUCH	SPEARMAN
SMOKABLE	SNUGGERY	SOMETIME	SPECIFIC
SMOKE-BOX	SNUGGING	SOMEWHAT	SPECIMEN
SMOKE-DRY	SNUGGLED	SOMNIFIC	SPECIOUS
SMOOTHED	SNUGNESS	SONATINA	SPECKING
SMOOTHLY	SOAPBALL	SONG-BIRD	SPECKLED
SMORZATO	SOAPSUDS	SONG-BOOK	SPECTRAL
SMOTHERY	SOAP-TEST	SONGLESS	SPECTRUM
SMOULDER	SOAP-TREE	SONGSTER	SPEEDIER
SMUDGING	SOAPWORT	SON-IN-LAW	SPEEDILY
SMUGGLED	SOB-STUFF	SONORITY	SPEEDING
SMUGGLER	SOBRANJE	SONOROUS	SPEEDWAY
SMUGNESS	SOBRIETY	SOOTHING	SPELLING
SNACK-BAR	SO-CALLED	SORBONNE	SPEND-ALL
SNAFFLED	SOCIABLE	SORCERER	SPENDING
SNAGGING	SOCIABLY	SORDIDLY	SPERM-OIL

SPHAGNUM	SPRINKLE	STAGNATE	STELLATE
SPHERICS	SPRINTED	STAINING	STEMLESS
SPHEROID	SPRINTER	STAIR-ROD	STEMMING
SPHERULE	SPROCKET	STAIRWAY	STEPPING
SPICCATO	SPRUCELY	STALKING	STERLING
SPICE-BOX	SPRUCIFY	STALL-FED	STERNWAY
SPIFFING	SPRUCING	STALLING	STICKING
SPIKELET	SPUN-YARN	STALLION	STICKLER
SPILLING	SPUR-GALL	STALWART	STIFFISH
SPILLWAY	SPUR-GEAR	STAMENED	STIFLING
SPINDLED	SPURIOUS	STAMPEDE	STIGMATA
SPINNING	SPURLESS	STAMPING	STILETTO
SPINSTER	SPURNING	STANDARD	STILLING
SPIRACLE	SPURRING	STANDING	STIMULUS
SPIRALLY	SPURTING	STANDISH	STINGILY
SPIRITED	SPY-GLASS	STAND-OFF	STINGING
SPITEFUL	SPY-MONEY	STAND-PAT	STING-RAY
SPITFIRE	SQUABBLE	STANHOPE	STINKPOT
SPITTING	SQUADRON	STAPLING	STINTING
SPITTOON	SQUALLED	STARCHED	STIPPLED
SPLASHED	SQUANDER	STAR-DUST	STIRRING
SPLATTER	SQUARELY	STAR-FISH	STITCHED
SPLAYING	SQUARING	STAR-GAZE	STOCKADE
SPLENDID	SQUARISH	STARLESS	STOCKIER
SPLICING	SQUASHED	STAR-LIKE	STOCKILY
SPLINTER	SQUATTED	STARLING	STOCKING
SPLITTER	SQUATTER	STARRING	STOCKIST
SPLOTCHY	SQUAWKED	STARTING	STOCKMAN
SPLUTTER	SQUAWMAN	STARTLED	STOCKPOT
SPOILING	SQUEAKED	STARVING	STOICISM
SPOLIATE	SQUEAKER	STARWEED	STOLIDLY
SPONGING	SQUEALED	STARWORT	STONE-PIT
SPOOFING	SQUEEGEE	STATUARY	STOOKING
SPOOKISH	SQUEEZED	STATURED	STOOPING
SPOONFUL	SQUEEZER	STAY-BOLT	STOP-COCK
SPOONILY	SQUIBBED	STAY-LACE	STOPPAGE
SPOONING	SQUIGGLE	STAYSAIL	STOPPING
SPORADIC	SQUINTED	STEADIED	STORABLE
SPORTFUL	SQUIREEN	STEADILY	STORMING
SPORTING	SQUIRING	STEADING	STOWAWAY
SPORTIVE	SQUIRMED	STEALING	STRADDLE
SPOTLESS	SQUIRREL	STEALTHY	STRAGGLE
SPOTTING	SQUIRTED	STEAMING	STRAIGHT
SPOUTING	STABBING	STEAM-TUG	STRAINED
SPRAGGED	STABLING	STEELING	STRAINER
SPRAINED	STACCATO	STEEL-PEN	STRAITEN
SPRAWLED	STACKING	STEEPING	STRANDED
SPRAYING	STAFFING	STEEPLED	STRANGER
SPREADER	STAGGERS	STEERAGE	STRANGLE
SPRIGGED	STAGHORN	STEERING	STRAPPED
SPRINGER	STAGNANT	STEINBOK	STRATEGY

STRATIFY	SUB-GRADE	SUPERMAN	SWERVING
STRAYING	SUB-GROUP	SUPER-TAX	SWIFTEST
STREAKED	SUB-HUMAN	SUPINELY	SWIGGING
STREAMED	SUB-LEASE	SUPPLANT	SWILLING
STREAMER	SUBMERGE	SUPPLIED	SWIMMING
STRENGTH	SUB-ORDER	SUPPLIER	SWINDLED
STRESSED	SUBORNED	SUPPOSED	SWINDLER
STRETCHY	SUBPOENA	SUPPRESS	SWINGING
STREWING	SUB-POLAR	SURCEASE	SWIRLING
STRICKEN	SUBSERVE	SURENESS	SWISHING
STRICTLY	SUBSIDED	SURETIES	SWITCHED
STRIDENT	SUBTITLE	SURF-BOAT	SWOONING
STRIDING	SUBTLETY	SURFACED	SWOOPING
STRIKING	SUBTRACT	SURGICAL	SWOPPING
STRINGED	SUBURBAN	SURMISED	SWORD-ARM
STRIPING	SUBURBIA	SURMOUNT	SWORD-CUT
STRIPPED	SUCCINCT	SURNAMED	SWOTTING
STRIPPER	SUCHLIKE	SURPLICE	SYBARITE
STROKING	SUCKLING	SURPRISE	SYCAMORE
STROLLED	SUDDENLY	SURROUND	SYLLABIC
STROLLER	SUFFERED	SURVEYED	SYLLABLE
STRONGLY	SUFFERER	SURVEYOR	SYLLABUS
STROPPED	SUFFICED	SURVIVAL	SYMBOLIC
STRUGGLE	SUFFIXED	SURVIVED	SYMMETRY
STRUMMED	SUFFRAGE	SURVIVOR	SYMPATHY
STRUMPET	SUFFUSED	SUSPENSE	SYMPHONY
STRUTTED	SUGARING	SWABBING	SYNDROME
STRUTTER	SUICIDAL	SWADDLED	SYNOPSIS
STUBBING	SUITABLE	SWAMPING	SYSTEMIC
STUBBLED	SUITABLY	SWAMP-OAK	
STUBBORN	SUITCASE	SWAN-LIKE	T—8
STUCCOED	SULLENLY	SWAN-NECK	TABBY-CAT
STUD-BOLT	SULLYING	SWANNERY	TABLEAUX
STUD-BOOK	SULPHATE	SWANKING	TABLEFUL
STUDDING	SULPHIDE	SWAPPING	TABOOING
STUD-FARM	SULPHITE	SWARMING	TABULATE
STUDIOUS	SULPHURY	SWASTIKA	TACITURN
STUDWORK	SUMMONED	SWATHING	TACKLING
STUDYING	SUNBURNT	SWATTING	TACTICAL
STUFFING	SUNBURST	SWEARING	TACTLESS
STULTIFY	SUNDERED	SWEATILY	TAFFRAIL
STUMBLED	SUN-DRIED	SWEATING	TAIL-BOOM
STUMPING	SUNDRIES	SWEEPING	TAILLESS
STUNNING	SUNLIGHT	SWEEP-NET	TAILORED
STUNTING	SUN-PROOF	SWEET-BAY	TAIL-RACE
STUPIDLY	SUNSHADE	SWEETING	TAIL-ROPE
STURDILY	SUNSHINE	SWEETISH	TAINTING
STURGEON	SUNSHINY	SWEET-OIL	TAKINGLY
SUB-AGENT	SUPERBLY	SWEET-PEA	TALENTED
SUBDUING	SUPERHET	SWEET-SOP	TALISMAN
SUB-GENUS	SUPERIOR	SWELLING	TALKABLE

TALLNESS	TEETOTUM	THICKSET	TIDEMILL
TALLYING	TEHEEING	THIEVERY	TIDES-MAN
TALLYMAN	TELEGRAM	THIEVING	TIDINESS
TAMARIND	TELEVISE	THIEVISH	TIGER-CAT
TAMARISK	TELLTALE	THINGAMY	TIGERISH
TAMEABLE	TEMERITY	THINKING	TIGHT-WAD
TAMELESS	TEMPERED	THINNESS	TILLABLE
TAMENESS	TEMPLATE	THINNEST	TILT-YARD
TAMPERED	TEMPORAL	THINNING	TIMBERED
TANGIBLE	TEMPTING	THINNISH	TIME-BALL
TANGIBLY	TENACITY	THIRSTED	TIME-BILL
TANGLING	TENANTED	THIRTEEN	TIME-BOOK
TANNABLE	TENANTRY	THOLE-PIN	TIME-CARD
TANTALUS	TENDENCY	THORACIC	TIME-FUSE
TAPERING	TENDERED	THOROUGH	TIMELESS
TAPESTRY	TENDERLY	THOUSAND	TIME-WORK
TAPEWORM	TENEMENT	THRALDOM	TIMEWORN
TARBOOSH	TENON-SAW	THRASHED	TIMIDITY
TARRAGON	TENTACLE	THREADED	TIMOROUS
TARRYING	TERMINAL	THREATEN	TINCTURE
TARTARIC	TERMINUS	THREE-PLY	TINGLING
TARTNESS	TERMLESS	THRESHED	TINKERED
TASTABLE	TERRACED	THRESHER	TINKLING
TASTE-BUD	TERRAPIN	THRILLED	TINPLATE
TASTEFUL	TERRIBLE	THRILLER	TINSELLY
TATTERED	TERRIBLY	THRIVING	TINSMITH
TATTLING	TERRIFIC	THROBBED	TINSTONE
TATTOOED	TERTIARY	THRONGED	TINTLESS
TAUNTING	TESTABLE	THROSTLE	TIPPLING
TAUTENED	TESTATOR	THROTTLE	TIPSTAFF
TAUTNESS	TEST-CASE	THROWING	TIRELESS
TAVERNER	TEST-TUBE	THRUMMED	TIRESOME
TAWDRILY	TETCHILY	THUDDING	TITANIUM
TAXATION	TETHERED	THUGGERY	TITIVATE
TEA-CADDY	TETRAGON	THUMBING	TITMOUSE
TEA-CHEST	TETRARCH	THUMB-POT	TITTERED
TEACHING	TEUTONIC	THUMPING	TITULARY
TEA-CLOTH	TEXT-BOOK	THUNDERY	TOAD-FLAX
TEA-HOUSE	THAILAND	THURSDAY	TOADYING
TEAMSTER	THALLIUM	THWACKED	TOADYISH
TEAMWORK	THANKFUL	THWARTED	TOADYISM
TEA-PARTY	THANKING	TICK-BEAN	TOBOGGAN
TEA-PLANT	THATCHED	TICKETED	TODDLING
TEA-SPOON	THATCHER	TICKLING	TOGETHER
TEA-TABLE	THEMATIC	TICKLISH	TOILSOME
TEARDROP	THEOLOGY	TICK-TICK	TOILWORN
TEAR-DUCT	THEORISE	TICK-TOCK	TOLBOOTH
TEARLESS	THEORIST	TIDEGATE	TOLERANT
TEENAGER	THESPIAN	TIDELESS	TOLERATE
TEETHING	THICKEST	TIDE-LOCK	TOLL-GATE
TEETOTAL	THICKISH	TIDEMARK	TOM-NODDY

TOMAHAWK	TRAGICAL	TRIAXIAL	TRUTHFUL
TOMBLESS	TRAILING	TRIBUNAL	TRYSTING
TOMMY-BAR	TRAIL-NET	TRICKERY	TSARITSA
TOMMY-GUN	TRAINING	TRICKILY	TUBERCLE
TOMMY-ROT	TRAIN-OIL	TRICKING	TUBEROSE
TOMORROW	TRAIPSED	TRICKLED	TUBEROUS
TONALITY	TRAMPING	TRICOLOR	TUCKSHOP
TONELESS	TRAMPLED	TRICYCLE	TUG-OF-WAR
TONSURED	TRAMROAD	TRIFLING	TUMBLING
TOOTHFUL	TRANCING	TRILLING	TUNELESS
TOOTLING	TRANQUIL	TRILLION	TUNGSTEN
TOP-DRESS	TRANSACT	TRIMMING	TUNING-IN
TOP-HEAVY	TRANSEPT	TRIMNESS	TURBANED
TOP-NOTCH	TRANSFER	TRIPLANE	TURBIDLY
TOPPLING	TRANSFIX	TRIPLETS	TURF-CLAD
TOREADOR	TRANSHIP	TRIPLING	TURGIDLY
TORPIDLY	TRANSMIT	TRIPPING	TURKOMAN
TORTILLA	TRAP-BALL	TRIPTYCH	TURMERIC
TORTOISE	TRAP-DOOR	TRIUMVIR	TURNCOAT
TORTUOUS	TRAPPING	TRIVALVE	TURNCOCK
TORTURED	TRAPPIST	TROLLING	TURNDOWN
TORTURER	TRASHILY	TROLLOPY	TURNOVER
TOTALISE	TRAVERSE	TROMBONE	TURNPIKE
TOTALITY	TRAVESTY	TROOPING	TURNSPIT
TOTTERED	TRAWLING	TROPHIES	TURRETED
TOUCHILY	TREACLED	TROPICAL	TUSSOCKY
TOUCHING	TREADING	TROTTING	TUTELAGE
TOUGHEST	TREADLED	TROUBLED	TUTELARY
TOUGHISH	TREASURE	TROUNCED	TUTORAGE
TOUSLING	TREASURY	TROUSERS	TUTORIAL
TOWERING	TREATING	TROUTLET	TUTORING
TOWN-HALL	TREATISE	TRUANTLY	TWANGING
TOWNLESS	TREBLING	TRUCKAGE	TWEAKING
TOWNSHIP	TRECENTO	TRUCKING	TWEEZERS
TOWNSMAN	TREE-CRAB	TRUDGEON	TWIDDLED
TOWN-TALK	TREE-DOVE	TRUDGING	TWIDDLER
TOXAEMIA	TREE-FERN	TRUE-BLUE	TWIGGING
TOXICANT	TREE-FROG	TRUE-BORN	TWILIGHT
TOXICITY	TREELESS	TRUE-BRED	TWILLING
TOYISHLY	TREE-NAIL	TRUE-LOVE	TWIN-BORN
TRACHEAL	TREKKING	TRUENESS	TWINKLED
TRACHEAN	TREMBLED	TRUMPERY	TWIRLING
TRACKAGE	TREMBLER	TRUMPING	TWISTING
TRACKING	TRENCHED	TRUNCATE	TWITCHED
TRACKMAN	TRENCHER	TRUNDLED	TWITTING
TRACKWAY	TRENDING	TRUNKFUL	TWO-EDGED
TRACTILE	TRESPASS	TRUNNION	TWO-FACED
TRACTION	TRIALITY	TRUSSING	TWO-PENCE
TRACTIVE	TRIANGLE	TRUSTFUL	TWOPENNY
TRACTORY	TRIARCHY	TRUSTILY	TWO-SIDED
TRADUCED	TRIASSIC	TRUSTING	TWO-SPEED

TYMPANIC	UNCAPPED	UNEARNED	UNITEDLY
TYMPANUM	UNCASING	UNEASILY	UNIVALVE
TYPE-HIGH	UNCAUGHT	UNENDING	UNIVERSE
TYPIFIED	UNCHASTE	UNERRING	UNIVOCAL
TYROLEAN	UNCHEWED	UNEVENLY	UNJOINED
TYROLESE	UNCLENCH	UNFADING	UNJOYFUL
TYRRANIC	UNCLOSED	UNFAIRLY	UNJOYOUS
	UNCLOTHE	UNFASTEN	UNJUDGED
U—8	UNCLOUDY	UNFENCED	UNJUSTLY
UBIQUITY	UNCOATED	UNFILLED	UNKINDLY
UDOMETER	UNCOCKED	UNFIXING	UNKINGLY
UGLINESS	UNCOILED	UNFOLDED	UNLACING
ULTERIOR	UNCOINED	UNFORCED	UNLARDED
ULTIMATA	UNCOMBED	UNFORMED	UNLASHED
ULTIMATE	UNCOMELY	UNFOUGHT	UNLAWFUL
ULULATED	UNCOMMON	UNFRAMED	UNLEARNT
UMBRELLA	UNCOOKED	UNFROZEN	UNLIKELY
UNABASED	UNCORKED	UNFURLED	UNLOADED
UNABATED	UNCOSTLY	UNGAINLY	UNLOCKED
UNAFRAID	UNCOUPLE	UNGENTLE	UNLOOSED
UNAMAZED	UNCTUOUS	UNGENTLY	UNLOVELY
UNAMUSED	UNCURBED	UNGIFTED	UNLOVING
UNATONED	UNCURLED	UNGILDED	UNMAKING
UNAVOWED	UNDAMPED	UNGIRDED	UNMANNED
UNAWARES	UNDEFIED	UNGIVING	UNMAPPED
UNBACKED	UNDENTED	UNGLAZED	UNMARKED
UNBARBED	UNDERACT	UNGLOVED	UNMARRED
UNBARRED	UNDERAGE	UNGLUING	UNMASKED
UNBATHED	UNDERARM	UNGROUND	UNMELTED
UNBEATEN	UNDERBID	UNGUIDED	UNMILKED
UNBELIEF	UNDERCUT	UNGULATA	UNMILLED
UNBIASED	UNDER-DOG	UNGULATE	UNMOCKED
UNBIDDEN	UNDERFED	UNGUMMED	UNMODISH
UNBLAMED	UNDERLAY	UNHANDED	UNMOORED
UNBLOODY	UNDERLET	UNHANGED	UNMOVING
UNBOILED	UNDERLIE	UNHARMED	UNNERVED
UNBOLTED	UNDER-LIP	UNHASPED	UNOPENED
UNBOOTED	UNDERPAY	UNHEATED	UNPACKED
UNBOUGHT	UNDERPIN	UNHEDGED	UNPAIRED
UNBRACED	UNDERTOW	UNHEEDED	UNPEELED
UNBRIDLE	UNDEVOUT	UNHEROIC	UNPEGGED
UNBROKEN	UNDIMMED	UNHINGED	UNPENNED
UNBUCKLE	UNDIPPED	UNHOOKED	UNPICKED
UNBUDDED	UNDIVINE	UNHORSED	UNPINNED
UNBUOYED	UNDOCKED	UNHOUSED	UNPLACED
UNBURDEN	UNDOUBLE	UNICYCLE	UNPOISED
UNBURIED	UNDRAPED	UNIFYING	UNPOSTED
UNBURNED	UNDREAMT	UNIMBUED	UNPRETTY
UNBUTTON	UNDULANT	UNIONISM	UNPRICED
UNCAGING	UNDULATE	UNIONIST	UNPROVED
UNCALLED	UNDULOUS	UNIQUELY	UNPRUNED

UNRAISED	UNTHAWED	USURPING	VENTURED
UNREASON	UNTHREAD	UTILIZED	VERACITY
UNREELED	UNTHROWN	UTTERING	VERANDAH
UNROBING	UNTIDILY	UXORIOUS	VERBALLY
UNROLLED	UNTILLED		VERBATIM
UNROOFED	UNTIMELY	V—8	VERBIAGE
UNROUTED	UNTINGED	VACATING	VERDANCY
UNRUFFLE	UNTIRING	VACATION	VERDERER
UNSADDLE	UNTOWARD	VAGABOND	VERIFIED
UNSAFELY	UNTRACED	VAGRANCY	VERMOUTH
UNSALTED	UNTUCKED	VAINNESS	VERONESE
UNSEALED	UNTURFED	VALANCED	VERONICA
UNSEATED	UNTURNED	VALENCIA	VERTEBRA
UNSEEDED	UNTWINED	VALERIAN	VERTICAL
UNSEEING	UNVALUED	VALETING	VESTMENT
UNSEEMLY	UNVARIED	VALHALLA	VESUVIAN
UNSETTLE	UNVEILED	VALIDATE	VEXATION
UNSHADED	UNVENTED	VALIDITY	VEXINGLY
UNSHAKEN	UNVERSED	VALOROUS	VIBRATED
UNSHAVED	UNVOICED	VALUABLE	VIBRATOR
UNSHAVEN	UNWANTED	VAMOOSED	VIBURNUM
UNSLAKED	UNWARILY	VANADIUM	VICARAGE
UNSMOKED	UNWARMED	VANGUARD	VICINITY
UNSOCIAL	UNWARNED	VANISHED	VICTORIA
UNSOILED	UNWASHED	VANQUISH	VICTUALS
UNSOLDER	UNWEDDED	VAPIDITY	VIEWABLE
UNSOLVED	UNWEEDED	VAPORIZE	VIEWLESS
UNSORTED	UNWIELDY	VAPOROUS	VIGILANT
UNSOUGHT	UNWISELY	VARIABLE	VIGNETTE
UNSPARED	UNWONTED	VARIABLY	VIGOROSO
UNSPEEDY	UNWORTHY	VARIANCE	VIGOROUS
UNSPIKED	UNYOKING	VARICOSE	VILENESS
UNSPOILT	UPHEAVAL	VASCULAR	VILIFIED
UNSPOKEN	UPLIFTED	VASELINE	VILLAGER
UNSTABLE	UPRAISED	VASTNESS	VILLAINY
UNSTATED	UPRISING	VAULTING	VINE-CLAD
UNSTEADY	UPROOTED	VAUNTING	VINE-GALL
UNSTITCH	UPSTAIRS	VEGETATE	VINEGARY
UNSTRUNG	UPSTREAM	VEHEMENT	VINEYARD
UNSUITED	UPSTROKE	VELOCITY	VIOLABLE
UNSURELY	UPTHRUST	VENALITY	VIOLATOR
UNSWAYED	UPTURNED	VENDETTA	VIOLENCE
UNTACKED	UPWARDLY	VENDIBLE	VIPERINE
UNTANGLE	URBANITY	VENDIBLY	VIPERISH
UNTANNED	URBANISE	VENEERED	VIPEROUS
UNTAPPED	URGENTLY	VENERATE	VIRGINAL
UNTASTED	URSIFORM	VENETIAN	VIRGINIA
UNTAUGHT	URSULINE	VENGEFUL	VIRILITY
UNTENDED	USEFULLY	VENOMOUS	VIRTUOSO
UNTESTED	USHERING	VENT-HOLE	VIRTUOUS
UNTETHER	USURIOUS	VENT-PLUG	VIRULENT

VISCERAL	WALTZING	WAYLEAVE	WHIPCORD
VISCOUNT	WANDERER	WEAKENED	WHIPHAND
VISIGOTH	WANGLING	WEAK-EYED	WHIPLASH
VISITANT	WANTONLY	WEAKLING	WHIPPING
VISITING	WARBLING	WEAKNESS	WHIRLING
VITALITY	WAR-DANCE	WEARABLE	WHIRRING
VITALISE	WARDMOTE	WEARYING	WHISKING
VITIATED	WARDRESS	WEED-HOOK	WHISTLED
VITREOUS	WARDROBE	WEEDLESS	WHITE-HOT
VIVACITY	WARD-ROOM	WEIGHING	WHITENED
VIVARIUM	WARDSHIP	WEIGHTED	WHITTLED
VIVA-VOCE	WAR-HORSE	WELCOMED	WHIZZING
VIVIFIED	WARINESS	WELDABLE	WHODUNIT
VIVISECT	WARMNESS	WELL-BORN	WHOOPING
VIXENISH	WARPAINT	WELL-BRED	WHOPPING
VOCALIST	WAR-PLANE	WELLDOER	WICKEDLY
VOCALITY	WARRANTY	WELL-HEAD	WIDE-EYED
VOCALIZE	WAR-WEARY	WELL-HOLE	WIDENESS
VOCATION	WAR-WHOOP	WELL-KNIT	WIDENING
VOCATIVE	WASHABLE	WELLNIGH	WIDOWING
VOIDABLE	WASHAWAY	WELL-READ	WIELDING
VOLATILE	WASHBALL	WELLSIAN	WIFEHOOD
VOLCANIC	WASHBOWL	WELL-TO-DO	WIFELESS
VOLITION	WASP-BITE	WELL-WORN	WIFELIKE
VOLLEYED	WASTEFUL	WELSHING	WIGGLING
VOLPLANE	WATCHDOG	WELSHMAN	WIGMAKER
VOMITING	WATCHFUL	WEREWOLF	WILD-FIRE
VORACITY	WATCHING	WESLEYAN	WILD-FOWL
VOTARESS	WATCH-KEY	WESTERLY	WILDNESS
VOUCHING	WATCHMAN	WESTWARD	WILFULLY
VOYAGEUR	WATERCAN	WET-NURSE	WILINESS
VULGARLY	WATER-HEN	WHACKING	WILLOWED
	WATER-ICE	WHALEMAN	WINCHMAN
W—8	WATERING	WHALE-OIL	WINDFALL
WADDLING	WATERMAN	WHANGHEE	WINDLASS
WAFERING	WATER-RAM	WHANGING	WINDLESS
WAGELESS	WATER-RAT	WHARFAGE	WINDMILL
WAGERING	WATER-TAP	WHARFING	WINDOWED
WAGGLING	WATERWAY	WHATEVER	WINDPIPE
WAGGONER	WATT-HOUR	WHEATEAR	WIND-PUMP
WAGONFUL	WATTLING	WHEEDLED	WINDWARD
WAGON-LIT	WAVELESS	WHEELING	WINE-CASK
WAINSCOT	WAVELIKE	WHEEZILY	WINELESS
WAITRESS	WAVERING	WHEEZING	WINESKIN
WAKENING	WAVINESS	WHELPING	WING-CASE
WALKABLE	WAXCLOTH	WHENEVER	WINGLESS
WALK-OVER	WAXLIGHT	WHEREVER	WINNOWED
WALLAROO	WAX-PAPER	WHETTING	WINTERED
WALL-EYED	WAXWORKS	WHIMBREL	WINTERLY
WALLOPED	WAYFARER	WHINCHAT	WIRELESS
WALLOWED	WAYGOOSE	WHINNIED	WIRE-WORM

WIRINESS	WOUNDING	ABDICATED	ACTUALITY
WISEACRE	WRACKING	ABDOMINAL	ACTUARIAL
WISHBONE	WRANGLED	ABDUCTING	ACTUATION
WISTARIA	WRANGLER	ABDUCTION	ACUTENESS
WITHDRAW	WRAPPING	ABHORRENT	ADAPTABLE
WITHDREW	WRATHFUL	ABHORRING	ADDICTING
WITHERED	WREAKING	ABIDINGLY	ADDICTION
WITHHELD	WREATHED	ABJECTION	ADDRESSED
WITHHOLD	WRECKAGE	ABNEGATED	ADDRESSEE
WIZARDLY	WRECKING	ABOLITION	ADDUCIBLE
WIZARDRY	WRENCHED	ABOMINATE	ADDUCTION
WOEFULLY	WRESTING	ABOUNDING	ADDUCTIVE
WOLF-FISH	WRESTLED	ABRIDGING	ADENOIDAL
WOLF-SKIN	WRESTLER	ABROGATED	ADENOTOMY
WOMANISH	WRETCHED	ABSCINDED	ADHERENCE
WONDERED	WRIGGLED	ABSCONDED	ADJACENCY
WONDROUS	WRINGING	ABSENTING	ADJECTIVE
WOOD-ACID	WRINKLED	ABSOLVING	ADJOINING
WOODBINE	WRISTLET	ABSORBENT	ADJOURNED
WOODCOCK	WRITHING	ABSORBING	ADJUDGING
WOODLAND	WRONGFUL	ABSTAINER	ADJUNCTLY
WOODLARK	WRONGING	ABSTINENT	ADJUSTING
WOODLESS		ABSURDITY	ADMIRABLE
WOOD-LICE	**X—8**	ABUNDANCE	ADMIRABLY
WOODMOTE	XYLONITE	ABUSIVELY	ADMIRALTY
WOOD-PULP		ACCENTING	ADMISSION
WOOD-SHED	**Y—8**	ACCEPTING	ADMISSIVE
WOODSMAN	YACHTING	ACCESSION	ADMISSORY
WOOD-VINE	YEAR-BOOK	ACCESSORY	ADMITTING
WOODWORK	YEARLING	ACCLIVITY	ADMIXTURE
WOOD-WORM	YEARNING	ACCOMPANY	ADOPTABLE
WOOD-WREN	YELLOWED	ACCORDING	ADOPTEDLY
WOOINGLY	YEOMANLY	ACCORDION	ADORATION
WOOLSACK	YEOMANRY	ACCOUNTED	ADORNMENT
WOOLWORK	YIELDING	ACCRETION	ADRENALIN
WORD-BOOK	YODELLED	ACCRETIVE	ADULATING
WORDLESS	YOKELESS	ACCUSABLE	ADULATION
WORKABLE	YOUNGEST	ACETYLENE	ADULATORY
WORKADAY	YOUNGISH	ACHIEVING	ADULTERER
WORKGIRL	YOURSELF	ACIDIFIED	ADULTNESS
WORKROOM	YOUTHFUL	ACIDIFIER	ADUMBRATE
WORKSHOP	YUGO-SLAV	ACIDULATE	ADVANCING
WORMCAST	YULETIDE	ACIDULOUS	ADVANTAGE
WORMGEAR		ACOUSTICS	ADVENTIST
WORM-HOLE	**Z—8**	ACQUIESCE	ADVENTURE
WORMLIKE	ZEPPELIN	ACQUIRING	ADVERBIAL
WORMWOOD		ACQUITTAL	ADVERSARY
WORRYING	**A—9**	ACQUITTED	ADVERSELY
WORSENED	ABANDONED	ACRIDNESS	ADVERSITY
WORSTING	ABASEMENT	ACROBATIC	ADVERTENT
WORTHILY	ABASHMENT	ACROPOLIS	ADVERTING
	ABATEMENT		

ADVERTISE	AIR-VESSEL	AMAZINGLY	ANGLICISM
ADVISABLE	AIR-WORTHY	AMAZONIAN	ANGLIFIED
ADVISABLY	AITCH-BONE	AMBERGRIS	ANGOSTURA
ADVOCATED	ALABASTER	AMBIGUITY	ANGRINES
AERODROME	ALARM-BELL	AMBIGUOUS	ANGUISHED
AEROMOTOR	ALARM-POST	AMBITIOUS	ANGULARLY
AEROPLANE	ALBATROSS	AMBLINGLY	ANGULATED
AESTHETIC	ALCHEMIST	AMBROSIAL	ANIMALISE
AESTIVATE	ALCOHOLIC	AMBROSIAN	ANIMALISM
AETIOLOGY	ALECONNER	AMBULANCE	ANIMATING
AFFECTING	ALERTNESS	AMBUSCADE	ANIMATION
AFFECTION	ALETASTER	AMBUSHING	ANIMOSITY
AFFECTIVE	ALGEBRAIC	AMENDABLE	ANNEALING
AFFIANCED	ALIENABLE	AMENDMENT	ANNOTATED
AFFIDAVIT	ALIENATED	AMIDSHIPS	ANNOTATOR
AFFILIATE	ALIGHTING	AMOROUSLY	ANNOUNCER
AFFIRMING	ALIGNMENT	AMORPHISM	ANNOYANCE
AFFLATION	ALIMENTAL	AMORPHOUS	ANNUITANT
AFFLICTED	ALIMENTED	AMORTIZED	ANNULARLY
AFFLUENCE	ALINEMENT	AMOUNTING	ANNULATED
AFFORDING	ALKALISED	AMPERSAND	ANNULLING
AFFRONTED	ALLAYMENT	AMPHIBIAN	ANNULMENT
AFOREHAND	ALLELUIAH	AMPHIBOLE	ANOINTING
AFORESAID	ALLEMANDE	AMPLENESS	ANOMALISM
AFORETIME	ALLEVIATE	AMPLIFIED	ANOMALOUS
AFRICAANS	ALLIGATED	AMPLIFIER	ANONYMOUS
AFTER-CARE	ALLIGATOR	AMPLITUDE	ANOPHELES
AFTERGLOW	ALLITERAL	AMPUTATED	ANSWERING
AFTER-LIFE	ALLOCATED	AMPUTATOR	ANTARCTIC
AFTERMATH	ALLOTTING	AMUSEMENT	ANTECEDED
AFTERNOON	ALLOWABLE	AMUSINGLY	ANTEDATED
AFTER-PART	ALLOWABLY	ANALGESIA	ANTENATAL
AFTERWARD	ALLOWANCE	ANALOGISE	ANTHELION
AGGRAVATE	ALLOWEDLY	ANALOGIST	ANTHOLOGY
AGGREGATE	ALMOND-OIL	ANALOGOUS	ANTIPATHY
AGGRESSOR	ALMSHOUSE	ANALYSING	ANTIPHONY
AGGRIEVED	ALOES-WOOD	ANARCHISM	ANTIPODAL
AGITATION	ALONGSIDE	ANARCHIST	ANTIPODES
AGONISING	ALOOFNESS	ANATOMISE	ANTIQUARY
AGONISTIC	ALPENHORN	ANATOMIST	ANTIQUATE
AGREEABLE	ALTAR-TOMB	ANCESTRAL	ANTIQUELY
AGREEABLY	ALTERABLE	ANCHORAGE	ANTIQUITY
AGREEMENT	ALTERABLY	ANCHORING	ANTITOXIC
AGRONOMIC	ALTERCATE	ANCHORITE	ANTITOXIN
AIMLESSLY	ALTERNATE	ANCHOR MAN	ANXIOUSLY
AIR-ENGINE	ALTIMETER	ANCIENTLY	APARTHEID
AIR-FILTER	ALTO-VIOLA	ANCILLARY	APARTMENT
AIR-FUNNEL	ALUMINIUM	ANECDOTAL	APARTNESS
AIR-INTAKE	AMARYLLIS	ANGEL-FISH	APATHETIC
AIR-JACKET	AMASSABLE	ANGELICAL	APERITIVE
AIR-POCKET	AMAZEMENT	ANGLICISE	APHORISED

APISHNESS	ARM'S-REACH	ASSURABLE	AUTONOMIC
APOCRYPHA	ARRAIGNED	ASSURANCE	AUXILIARY
APOLOGISE	ARRANGING	ASSUREDLY	AVAILABLE
APOLOGIST	ARRESTING	ASTHMATIC	AVAILABLY
APOSTOLIC	ARROGANCE	ASTOUNDED	AVALANCHE
APPALLING	ARROW-HEAD	ASTRADDLE	AVERAGELY
APPARATUS	ARROWROOT	ASTRAKHAN	AVERAGING
APPEALING	ARSENICAL	ASTROLABE	AVERTEDLY
APPEARING	ARSENIOUS	ASTROLOGY	AVOCATION
APPEASING	ARTEMISIA	ASTRONOMY	AVOCATIVE
APPELLANT	ARTHRITIC	ASYMMETRY	AVOIDABLE
APPELLATE	ARTHRITIS	ATAVISTIC	AVOIDANCE
APPENDAGE	ARTICHOKE	ATHANASIA	AVUNCULAR
APPENDANT	ARTICULAR	ATHEISTIC	AWAKENING
APPENDING	ARTIFICER	ATHENAEUM	AWARDABLE
APPERTAIN	ARTILLERY	ATHLETICS	AWESTRUCK
APPETISER	ARTLESSLY	ATLANTEAN	AWFULNESS
APPLAUDED	ASCENDANT	ATOMISING	AWKWARDLY
APPLE-JACK	ASCENDENT	ATONEMENT	AXIOMATIC
APPLE-JOHN	ASCENDING	ATROCIOUS	
APPLIANCE	ASCENSION	ATROPHIED	B—9
APPLICANT	ASCERTAIN	ATTACHING	BABYLONIC
APPLICATE	ASCRIBING	ATTACKING	BACCHANAL
APPOINTED	ASHAMEDLY	ATTAINDER	BACCHANTE
APPORTION	ASPARAGUS	ATTAINING	BACILLARY
APPRAISAL	ASPERATED	ATTAINTED	BACKBOARD
APPRAISED	ASPERSING	ATTEMPTED	BACKPIECE
APPREHEND	ASPERSION	ATTENDANT	BACKSIGHT
APPRISING	ASPHALTIC	ATTENDING	BACK-SLANG
APPROBATE	ASPIRATED	ATTENTION	BACK-SLIDE
APPROVING	ASSAILANT	ATTENTIVE	BACKSTAFF
AQUILEGIA	ASSAILING	ATTENUATE	BACKWARDS
ARABESQUE	ASSAULTED	ATTESTING	BACKWATER
ARACHNOID	ASSAYABLE	ATTICISED	BACKWOODS
ARBITRARY	ASSEMBLED	ATTRACTED	BADGERING
ARBITRATE	ASSENTING	ATTRIBUTE	BADMINTON
ARBORETUM	ASSERTING	ATTRITION	BAGATELLE
ARCHANGEL	ASSERTION	AUBERGINE	BAILIWICK
ARCH-DRUID	ASSERTIVE	AUDACIOUS	BAKEHOUSE
ARCHDUCAL	ASSESSING	AUGMENTED	BAKESTONE
ARCHDUCHY	ASSIDUITY	AUSTERELY	BAKSHEESH
ARCH-ENEMY	ASSIDUOUS	AUSTERITY	BALALAIKA
ARCHETYPE	ASSIGNING	AUSTRALIA	BALANCING
ARCH-FIEND	ASSISTANT	AUTHENTIC	BALCONIED
ARCHITECT	ASSISTING	AUTHORESS	BALD-PATED
ARCHIVIST	ASSOCIATE	AUTHORISE	BALEFULLY
ARDUOUSLY	ASSOILING	AUTHORITY	BALKINGLY
ARGENTINE	ASSONANCE	AUTOCRACY	BALLASTED
ARGUFYING	ASSORTING	AUTOGRAPH	BALLERINA
ARMADILLO	ASSUAGING	AUTOMATIC	BALLISTIC
ARMISTICE	ASSUETUDE	AUTOMATON	BALLOT-BOX

BALLOTING	BEAN-STALK	BENGALESE	BISHOPRIC
BALL-POINT	BEARDLESS	BENIGHTED	BLABBERED
BAMBOOZLE	BEATIFIED	BENIGNANT	BLACKBALL
BANDAGING	BEATITUDE	BENIGNITY	BLACKBIRD
BANDEROLE	BEAU-IDEAL	BENZOLINE	BLACKCOCK
BANDICOOT	BEAU-MONDE	BEREAVING	BLACKENED
BANDOLIER	BEAUTEOUS	BERYLLIUM	BLACKHEAD
BANEFULLY	BEAUTIFUL	BESEECHED	BLACK-JACK
BANISHING	BECALMING	BESETTING	BLACK-LEAD
BANQUETED	BECKONING	BESIEGING	BLACK-LIST
BANQUETTE	BEDAZZLED	BESMEARED	BLACKMAIL
BAPTISING	BEDECKING	BESOTTING	BLACKNESS
BAPTISMAL	BEDFELLOW	BESPATTER	BLADEBONE
BARBARIAN	BEDLAMITE	BESTIALLY	BLAEBERRY
BARBARISM	BEDRAGGLE	BESTIRRED	BLAMELESS
BARBARITY	BEDRIDDEN	BESTOWING	BLANCHING
BARBAROUS	BEDSPREAD	BETHOUGHT	BLANDNESS
BARBECUED	BEECHMAST	BETHUMBED	BLANKETED
BARBERING	BEEFEATER	BETOKENED	BLANKNESS
BAREBONED	BEEFLOWER	BETRAYING	BLASPHEME
BAREFACED	BEEFSTEAK	BETROTHAL	BLASPHEMY
BARGAINED	BEELZEBUB	BETROTHED	BLATHERED
BARLEY-MOW	BEER-MONEY	BETTERING	BLAZONING
BARMECIDE	BEFALLING	BEVELLING	BLEACHING
BAROGRAPH	BEFITTING	BEWAILING	BLEAR-EYED
BAROMETER	BEFOGGING	BEWITCHED	BLEMISHED
BARONETCY	BEFOOLING	BICKERING	BLENCHING
BARRELLED	BEFOULING	BICYCLING	BLESSEDLY
BARRICADE	BEGETTING	BICYCLIST	BLETHERED
BARRISTER	BEGGARING	BIFURCATE	BLIGHTING
BAR-TENDER	BEGINNING	BIGOTEDLY	BLINDFOLD
BARTERING	BEGRIMING	BILATERAL	BLINDNESS
BASHFULLY	BEGRUDGED	BILINGUAL	BLINDWORM
BASILICAN	BEGUILING	BILLABONG	BLISTERED
BASILICON	BEHAVIOUR	BILLETING	BLOCKADED
BASKETFUL	BEHEADING	BILLIARDS	BLOCKHEAD
BAS-RELIEF	BEHOLDING	BILLOWING	BLOOD-BATH
BASTINADO	BELEAGUER	BILLY-COCK	BLOOD-HEAT
BASTIONED	BELIEVING	BILLY-GOAT	BLOODLESS
BATH-BRICK	BELITTLED	BIMONTHLY	BLOOD-SHED
BATH-CHAIR	BELL-GLASS	BINDINGLY	BLOODSHOT
BATH-METAL	BELLICOSE	BINOCULAR	BLOODWORM
BATTALION	BELL-METAL	BINOMINAL	BLOODYING
BATTENING	BELLOWING	BIOGRAPHY	BLOSSOMED
BATTERING	BELL-PUNCH	BIOLOGIST	BLOTCHING
BATTLE-AXE	BELLYBAND	BIONOMICS	BLUBBERED
BATTLE-CRY	BELLY-ROLL	BIPARTITE	BLUEBEARD
BAWDINESS	BELONGING	BIRTHMARK	BLUE-BERRY
BAYONETED	BELVEDERE	BIRTHRATE	BLUE-BLACK
BAY-WINDOW	BEMOANING	BISECTING	BLUE-BLOOD
BEAN-FEAST	BENEFITED	BISECTION	BLUESTONE

BLUFFNESS
BLUNDERED
BLUNTNESS
BLUSTERED
BLUSTERER
BOANERGES
BOARDABLE
BOARHOUND
BOAR-SPEAR
BOASTLESS
BOAT-HOUSE
BOATSWAIN
BOB-SLEIGH
BOBTAILED
BODYGUARD
BOG-MYRTLE
BOLD-FACED
BOLOGNESE
BOLSHEVIK
BOLSTERED
BOMB-AIMER
BOMBARDED
BOMBARDON
BOMBASTIC
BOMBAZINE
BOMB-PROOF
BOMBSHELL
BOMBSIGHT
BONDSLAVE
BONDWOMAN
BONNETING
BONNINESS
BON-VIVANT
BOOBY-TRAP
BOOKISHLY
BOOKMAKER
BOOK-PLATE
BOOKSTALL
BOOKSTAND
BOOKSTORE
BOOMERANG
BOORISHLY
BORDERING
BORROWING
BOSPHORUS
BOTANICAL
BOTHERING
BOTTOMING
BOULEVARD
BOUNDLESS
BOUNTEOUS

BOUNTIFUL
BOURGEOIS
BOWER-BIRD
BOW-LEGGED
BOW-STRING
BOW-STRUNG
BOW-WINDOW
BOXING-DAY
BOX-OFFICE
BOYCOTTED
BRACKETED
BRACTLESS
BRAINLESS
BRAINWAVE
BRAKELESS
BRAKES-MAN
BRAMBLING
BRANCHING
BRANCHLET
BRASS-BAND
BRASSERIE
BRASSIERE
BRAZENING
BRAZILIAN
BRAZIL-NUT
BREACHING
BREADLESS
BREAD-ROOM
BREAKABLE
BREAKDOWN
BREAKFAST
BREAKNECK
BREASTPIN
BREATHING
BREECHING
BREWHOUSE
BRIAR-ROOT
BRIC-A-BRAC
BRICK-CLAY
BRICKDUST
BRICK-KILN
BRICKWORK
BRICKYARD
BRIDECAKE
BRIDELESS
BRIDESMAN
BRIDEWELL
BRIDLE-WAY
BRIEFLESS
BRIEFNESS
BRIGADIER

BRILLIANT
BRIMSTONE
BRIQUETTE
BRISKNESS
BRISTLING
BRITANNIC
BRITTLELY
BRITTLING
BROACHING
BROADBEAN
BROADBILL
BROADBRIM
BROADCAST
BROADENED
BROADNESS
BROADSIDE
BROADWAYS
BROADWISE
BROCADING
BROKERAGE
BRONCHIAL
BROOD-MARE
BROOKWEED
BROTHERLY
BROWNNESS
BRUMMAGEM
BRUSH-WOOD
BRUTALISE
BRUTALITY
BRUTISHLY
BRYTHONIC
BUCCANEER
BUCKBOARD
BUCKETFUL
BUCKETING
BUCKHOUND
BUCK'S-HORN
BUCKTHORN
BUCKTOOTH
BUCKWAGON
BUCK-WHEAT
BUDGETING
BUFFETING
BUGLE-CALL
BULGARIAN
BULGINESS
BULKINESS
BULL-FIGHT
BULLFINCH
BULLY-BEEF
BULWARKED

BUMBLE-BEE
BUMBLEDOM
BUMPINESS
BUMPTIOUS
BUOYANTLY
BURDENING
BURGEONED
BURLESQUE
BURLINESS
BURNISHED
BURROWING
BUSHINESS
BUTCHERED
BUTTERCUP
BUTTERFLY
BUTTERING
BUTTONING
BUXOMNESS
BUZZINGLY
BY-PASSAGE
BY-PRODUCT
BYSTANDER
BYZANTINE

C—9
CABALLERO
CABLEGRAM
CABRIOLET
CACOPHONY
CADDIS-FLY
CADETSHIP
CAESARIAN
CAFETERIA
CAIRNGORM
CALABOOSE
CALCIFIED
CALCINING
CALCULATE
CALENDULA
CALIBRATE
CALIPHATE
CALLA-LILY
CALLIPERS
CALLOSITY
CALLOUSLY
CALORIFIC
CALVINISM
CALVINIST
CAMBERING
CAMPANILE
CAMPANULA

CAMP-FEVER	CARNIVORA	CAUTERISE	CHAR-A-BANC
CAMPSTOOL	CAROLLING	CAUTIONED	CHARACTER
CANALISED	CAROUSING	CAVALCADE	CHARINESS
CANCELLED	CARPENTER	CAVENDISH	CHARIVARI
CANCEROUS	CARPENTRY	CAVERNOUS	CHARLATAN
CANDIDACY	CARPETING	CAVILLING	CHARLOTTE
CANDIDATE	CARPINGLY	CAVORTING	CHARTERED
CANDIFIED	CARRIABLE	CEASELESS	CHARTLESS
CANDLEMAS	CARTESIAN	CEILINGED	CHASEABLE
CANDYTUFT	CARTHORSE	CELANDINE	CHASTENED
CANE-SUGAR	CARTILAGE	CELEBRANT	CHASTISED
CANE-CHAIR	CARTOUCHE	CELEBRATE	CHATTERED
CANKER-FLY	CARTRIDGE	CELEBRITY	CHAUFFEUR
CANKERING	CARTWHEEL	CELESTIAL	CHEAPENED
CANKEROUS	CASHEWNUT	CELESTINE	CHEAPNESS
CANNON-BIT	CASHIERED	CELLARAGE	CHEATABLE
CANNONADE	CASSEROLE	CELLARMAN	CHECKMATE
CANNONING	CASSOWARY	CELLULOID	CHECK-REIN
CANONICAL	CASTIGATE	CELLULOSE	CHEEK-BONE
CANONISED	CASTILIAN	CEMENTING	CHEERLESS
CANOODLED	CASTOR-OIL	CENSORIAL	CHEESEFLY
CANOPYING	CASTRATED	CENSORING	CHEESEVAT
CANTABILE	CAST-STEEL	CENSURING	CHEMISTRY
CANTALOUP	CASUISTIC	CENTENARY	CHEQUERED
CANTERING	CASUISTRY	CENTIGRAM	CHERISHED
CANTINGLY	CATACLYSM	CENTIPEDE	CHEVALIER
CANVASSED	CATALEPSY	CENTRALLY	CHICANERY
CANVASSER	CATALOGUE	CENTRE-BIT	CHICANING
CAPACIOUS	CATALYSER	CENTURION	CHICKADEE
CAPARISON	CATALYSIS	CEREBRATE	CHICKLING
CAPILLARY	CATALYTIC	CERTAINLY	CHICKWEED
CAPITALLY	CATAMARAN	CERTAINTY	CHIDINGLY
CAPITULAR	CATAMOUNT	CERTIFIED	CHIEFLESS
CAPRICCIO	CATARRHAL	CERTITUDE	CHIEFTAIN
CAPRICORN	CATCHABLE	CESSATION	CHILBLAIN
CAPSIZING	CATCH-CROP	CETACEOUS	CHILDHOOD
CAPTAINCY	CATCHMENT	CHAFFERED	CHILDLESS
CAPTIVATE	CATCHPOLE	CHAFFINCH	CHILDLIKE
CAPTIVITY	CATCHWEED	CHAFFLESS	CHILLNESS
CAPTURING	CATCHWORD	CHAGRINED	CHINA-CLAY
CARBONATE	CATECHISE	CHAIN-GANG	CHINA-ROSE
CARBONISE	CATECHISM	CHAINLESS	CHINASHOP
CARBUNCLE	CATECHIST	CHAIN-MAIL	CHINATOWN
CARDBOARD	CATERWAUL	CHAINWORK	CHINAWARE
CAREENING	CATHEADED	CHALLENGE	CHIROPODY
CAREERING	CATHEDRAL	CHAMELEON	CHISELLED
CAREFULLY	CAUCASIAN	CHAMFERED	CHITTERED
CARESSING	CAUSALITY	CHAMPAGNE	CHOCK-FULL
CARMELITE	CAUSATION	CHANDLERY	CHOCOLATE
CARNALITY	CAUSATIVE	CHANGEFUL	CHOP-HOUSE
CARNATION	CAUSELESS	CHAPTERED	CHORISTER

CHORTLING	CLOCK-GOLF	COETERNAL	COMBATIVE
CHORUSING	CLOCKWISE	COEXISTED	COMBINING
CHRISTIAN	CLOCKWORK	COFFEE-BUG	COMFORTED
CHRISTMAS	CLOG-DANCE	COFFEE-CUP	COMFORTER
CHROMATIC	CLOISONNE	COFFEE-POT	COMICALLY
CHROMATIN	CLOISTERS	COFFERDAM	COMINFORM
CHRYSALIS	CLOSENESS	COGITABLE	COMINTERN
CHUCKLING	CLOSETING	COGITATED	COMMANDED
CHURCHILL	CLOTH-HALL	COGNATION	COMMANDER
CHURCHING	CLOTHYARD	COGNISANT	COMMENCED
CHURCHMAN	CLOUDLESS	COGNITION	COMMENDED
CICATRICE	CLOUDLINE	COGNITIVE	COMMENSAL
CICÁTRISE	CLOUT-NAIL	COHABITED	COMMENTED
CIGARETTE	CLOVE-PINK	COHEIRESS	COMMINGLE
CINERARIA	CLUBBABLE	COHERENCE	COMMISSAR
CINGALESE	CLUBHOUSE	COHERENCY	COMMITTAL
CIPHERING	CLUSTERED	COHERITOR	COMMITTED
CIPHER-KEY	CLUTCHING	COINCIDED	COMMITTEE
CIRCUITED	CLUTTERED	COLCHICUM	COMMODITY
CIRCULATE	COACH-WORK	COLD-CREAM	COMMONAGE
CIRRHOSIS	COAGULANT	COLLAPSED	COMMOTION
CIVILISED	COAGULATE	COLLARING	COMMOVING
CLAIMABLE	COAL-BLACK	COLLATING	COMMUNING
CLAMBERED	COALESCED	COLLATION	COMMUNION
CLAMOROUS	COALFIELD	COLLEAGUE	COMMUNISE
CLAMOURED	COAL-HOUSE	COLLECTED	COMMUNISM
CLAPBOARD	COALITION	COLLECTOR	COMMUNIST
CLARENDON	COAL-MINER	COLLEGIAN	COMMUNITY
CLARET-CUP	COARSENED	COLLIDING	COMMUTING
CLARIFIED	COASTLINE	COLLIMATE	COMPACTED
CLARIONET	COASTWISE	COLLISION	COMPACTLY
CLASSIBLE	COATFROCK	COLLOCATE	COMPANION
CLASSICAL	COAXINGLY	COLLODION	COMPARING
CLATTERED	COBDENISM	COLLOIDAL	COMPASSED
CLEANLILY	COBDENITE	COLLOTYPE	COMPASSES
CLEANNESS	COBWEBBED	COLLUSION	COMPELLED
CLEANSING	COCHINEAL	COLLUSIVE	COMPELLING
CLEARANCE	COCK-A-HOOP	COLLUSORY	COMPETENT
CLEAR-EYED	COCKFIGHT	COLONELCY	COMPETING
CLEARNESS	COCKHORSE	COLONISED	COMPLAINT
CLEAVABLE	COCKINESS	COLONNADE	COMPLETED
CLEMENTLY	COCKROACH	COLORIFIC	COMPLEXLY
CLENCHING	COCKSCOMB	COLOSSEUM	COMPLIANT
CLERGYMAN	COCK'S-FOOT	COLOUR-BOX	COMPLYING
CLERK-LIKE	COCK'S-HEAD	COLOURING	COMPONENT
CLERKSHIP	COCOA-BEAN	COLOURIST	COMPORTED
CLIENTELE	COCOA-PLUM	COLOURMAN	COMPOSING
CLIMACTIC	COCO-DE-MER	COLTSFOOT	COMPOSITE
CLIMBABLE	CODIFYING	COLUMBIAN	COMPOSTED
CLINCHING	COEQUALLY	COLUMBINE	COMPOSURE
CLOAKROOM	COERCIBLE	COMBATANT	COMPRISED

COMPUTING	CONGRUOUS	CONTUMELY	CORPORATE
CONCAVELY	CONICALLY	CONTUSING	CORPOREAL
CONCAVITY	CONJOINED	CONTUSION	CORPOSANT
CONCEALED	CONJUGATE	CONUNDRUM	CORPULENT
CONCEDING	CONJURING	CONVENING	CORPUSCLE
CONCEITED	CONNECTED	CONVERGED	CORRECTED
CONCEIVED	CONNECTOR	CONVERSED	CORRECTLY
CONCERNED	CONNEXION	CONVERTED	CORRECTOR
CONCERTED	CONNIVING	CONVEXITY	CORRELATE
CONCIERGE	CONNOTING	CONVEYING	CORRODING
CONCISELY	CONNUBIAL	CONVICTED	CORROSION
CONCLUDED	CO-NOMINEE	CONVINCED	CORROSIVE
CONCOCTED	CONQUERED	CONVIVIAL	CORRUGATE
CONCORDAT	CONQUEROR	CONVOKING	CORRUPTED
CONCOURSE	CONSCIOUS	CONVOLUTE	CORTICATE
CONCRETED	CONSCRIBE	CONVOYING	CORTISONE
CONCUBINE	CONSCRIPT	CONVULSED	CORUSCATE
CONCURRED	CONSENSUS	COOK-HOUSE	COSMOGONY
CONCUSSED	CONSENTED	COOPERAGE	COSMOLOGY
CONDEMNED	CONSERVED	CO-OPERATE	COSSETING
CONDENSED	CONSIGNED	COOPERING	COSTUMIER
CONDENSER	CONSIGNEE	COPARTNER	COTANGENT
CONDIGNLY	CONSIGNOR	CO-PATRIOT	COTILLION
CONDIMENT	CONSISTED	COPESTONE	COTTER-PIN
CONDITION	CONSOLING	COPIOUSLY	COTTON-GIN
CONDOLING	CONSONANT	COPPERING	COTTONING
CONDONING	CONSORTED	COPPERISH	COTYLEDON
CONDUCING	CONSPIRED	COPSE-WOOD	COUNTABLE
CONDUCIVE	CONSTABLE	COPYRIGHT	COUNTERED
CONDUCTED	CONSTANCY	COQUETTED	COUNTLESS
CONDUCTOR	CONSTRAIN	CORALLINE	COUNTRIFY
CONFERRED	CONSTRICT	CORALLITE	COURT-CARD
CONFESSED	CONSTRUCT	CORALLOID	COURTEOUS
CONFESSOR	CONSTRUED	CORAL-REEF	COURTESAN
CONFIDANT	CONSULATE	CORBELLED	COURTLIKE
CONFIDENT	CONSULTED	CORDELIER	COURTSHIP
CONFIDING	CONSUMING	CORDIALLY	COURT-YARD
CONFIGURE	CONTAGION	COREOPSIS	COVERTURE
CONFINING	CONTAINED	CORIANDER	COWARDICE
CONFIRMED	CONTAINER	CORKSCREW	COXCOMBRY
CONFLUENT	CONTENTED	CORMORANT	CRAB-APPLE
CONFORMED	CONTESTED	CORN-BREAD	CRABBEDLY
CONFUGIAN	CONTINENT	CORNCRAKE	CRACKLING
CONFUSING	CONTINUAL	CORNELIAN	CRAFTSMAN
CONFUSION	CONTINUED	CORNERING	CRAMP-IRON
CONFUTING	CONTINUUM	CORNFLOUR	CRANBERRY
CONGEALED	CONTORTED	CORN-POPPY	CRANKCASE
CONGENIAL	CONTOURED	CORN-SALAD	CRAPULENT
CONGESTED	CONTRALTO	CORNSTALK	CRAPULOUS
CONGRUENT	CONTRIVED	COROLLARY	CRASSNESS
CONGRUITY	CONTUMACY	CORONETED	CRAYONING

CRAZINESS	CRUSADING	DAISY-BUSH	DECANTING
CREAM-LIKE	CRUSTACEA	DALLIANCE	DECEITFUL
CREAM-LAID	CRYPTOGAM	DALMATIAN	DECEIVING
CREAM-WOVE	CUBICALLY	DAMASCENE	DECENNIAL
CREDITING	CUCKOLDED	DAMOCLEAN	DECENNIUM
CREDULITY	CUDGELLED	DAMPENING	DECEPTION
CREDULOUS	CULMINATE	DAMPISHLY	DECEPTIVE
CREMATING	CULTIVATE	DANDELION	DECIDABLE
CREMATION	CULTURING	DANDIFIED	DECIDEDLY
CRENATURE	CULTURIST	DANGEROUS	DECIDUOUS
CREPITANT	CUMBERING	DANNEBROG	DECILLION
CREPITATE	CUNEIFORM	DANTESQUE	DECIMALLY
CRESCENDO	CUNNINGLY	DAREDEVIL	DECIMATED
CRETINISM	CUP-BEARER	DARKENING	DECIMETRE
CREVICING	CUPRESSUS	DARTINGLY	DECK-CHAIR
CRIMELESS	CURBSTONE	DARWINIAN	DECK-HOUSE
CRIMSONED	CURIOSITY	DARWINISM	DECLAIMED
CRINKLING	CURIOUSLY	DASH-BOARD	DECLARANT
CRINOLINE	CURLINESS	DASTARDLY	DECLARING
CRIPPLING	CURLINGLY	DATUM-LINE	DECLINING
CRISPNESS	CURRENTLY	DAUNTLESS	DECLIVITY
CRITERION	CURRISHLY	DAVENPORT	DECOCTION
CRITICISE	CURRYCOMB	DAY-LABOUR	DECOLLETE
CRITICISM	CURSORIAL	DAY-SCHOOL	DECOMPLEX
CROCHETED	CURSORILY	DAY-SPRING	DECOMPOSE
CROCODILE	CURTAILED	DEACONESS	DECONTROL
CROOKBACK	CURTAINED	DEAD-ALIVE	DECORATED
CROOKEDLY	CURTILAGE	DEADENING	DECORATOR
CROQUETTE	CURTSYING	DEAFENING	DECOY-DUCK
CROSSBEAM	CURVATURE	DEATH-BLOW	DECREASED
CROSSBILL	CURVETTED	DEATHLESS	DECREEING
CROSS-EYED	CUSHIONED	DEATHLIKE	DECREMENT
CROSS-FIRE	CUSTODIAN	DEATH-MASK	DECUMBENT
CROSS-HEAD	CUSTOMARY	DEATH-RATE	DECUSSATE
CROSSNESS	CUTANEOUS	DEATH-ROLL	DEDICATED
CROSSROAD	CUTICULAR	DEATH-TRAP	DEDUCIBLE
CROSS-WIND	CUTTER-BAR	DEATH-WARD	DEDUCTING
CROSSWISE	CUT-THROAT	DEBARRING	DEDUCTION
CROSS-WORD	CUTTINGLY	DEBATABLE	DEDUCTIVE
CROTCHETY	CYCLOPEAN	DEBAUCHED	DEEPENING
CROUCHING	CYCLORAMA	DEBENTURE	DEEP-TONED
CROWBERRY	CYNICALLY	DEBOUCHED	DEFALCATE
CROW'S-FEET	CYTOPLASM	DEBUTANTE	DEFAULTED
CROW'S-FOOT		DECADENCE	DEFAULTER
CROW'S-NEST		DECAGONAL	DEFEATING
CROW-STONE		DECALCIFY	DEFEATISM
CRUCIFIED	D—9	DECALITRE	DEFECTION
CRUCIFORM	DACHSHUND	DECALOGUE	DEFECTIVE
CRUMBLING	DAEDALIAN	DECAMERON	DEFENDANT
CRUMPLING	DAIRY-FARM	DECAMETRE	DEFENDING
CRUNCHING	DAIRY-MAID	DECAMPING	DEFENSIVE

DEFERENCE DEPARTURE DESPERATE DIAGNOSED
DEFERRING DEPASTURE DESPISING DIAGNOSIS
DEFIANTLY DEPENDANT DESPOILED DIALECTAL
DEFICIENT DEPENDENT DESPONDED DIALECTIC
DEFINABLE DEPENDING DESPOTISM DIAL-PLATE
DEFINABLY DEPICTING DESTINING DIAPERING
DEFLATING DEPILATED DESTITUTE DIAPHRAGM
DEFLATION DEPLENISH DESTROYED DIARRHOEA
DEFLECTED DEPLETING DESTROYER DICHOTOMY
DEFLECTOR DEPLETION DESUETUDE DICHROMIC
DEFLEXION DEPLETIVE DESULTORY DICKERING
DEFOLIATE DEPLETORY DETACHING DICTATING
DEFORMING DEPLORING DETAILING DICTATION
DEFORMITY DEPLOYING DETAINING DICTATORY
DEFRAUDED DEPLUMING DETECTING DIDACTICS
DEFRAYING DEPORTING DETECTION DIESINKER
DEISTICAL DEPOSITED DETECTIVE DIETETICS
DEJECTING DEPOSITOR DETENTION DIETITIAN
DEJECTION DEPRAVING DETERRING DIFFERENT
DELEGATED DEPRAVITY DETERGENT DIFFERING
DELICIOUS DEPRECATE DETERMINE DIFFICILE
DELIGHTED DEPRESSED DETERRENT DIFFICULT
DELIMITED DEPRIVING DETERRING DIFFIDENT
DELINEATE DEPTHLESS DETESTING DIFFLUENT
DELIRIOUS DEPUTISED DETHRONED DIFFUSING
DELIVERED DERAILING DETONATED DIFFUSION
DELIVERER DERANGING DETONATOR DIFFUSELY
DEMAGOGIC DERIVABLE DETRACTED DIFFUSIVE
DEMAGOGUE DERIVABLY DETRACTOR DIGESTING
DEMANDANT DERMATOID DETRAINED DIGESTION
DEMANDING DEROGATED DETRIMENT DIGESTIVE
DEMARCATE DERRING-DO DETRITION DIGITALIN
DEMEANING DERRINGER DEVASTATE DIGITALIS
DEMEANOUR DESCANTED DEVELOPED DIGNIFIED
DEMI-MONDE DESCENDED DEVELOPER DIGNITARY
DEMISSION DESCRIBED DEVIATION DIGRESSED
DEMITTING DESCRYING DEVIL-FISH DILATABLE
DEMOCRACY DESECRATE DEVILLING DILIGENCE
DEMULCENT DESERTING DEVILMENT DILUTEDLY
DEMURRAGE DESERTION DEVIOUSLY DIMENSION
DEMURRANT DESERVING DEVISABLE DIMORPHIC
DEMURRING DESICCANT DEVITRIFY DINGINESS
DENIGRATE DESICCATE DEVOLUTED DINING-CAR
DENOUNCED DESIGNATE DEVOLVING DIPHTHONG
DENSENESS DESIGNING DEVONPORT DIPLOMACY
DENTATION DESIRABLE DEVOURING DIPTEROUS
DENTISTRY DESIRABLY DEWLAPPED DIRECTING
DENTITION DESISTING DEXTERITY DIRECTION
DEODORANT DESOLATED DEXTEROUS DIRECTIVE
DEODORISE DESPAIRED DIABOLISM DIRECTORY
DEPARTING DESPERADO DIAERESIS DIREFULLY

DIRIGIBLE	DISLOCATE	DISTILLER	DOWERLESS
DIRTINESS	DISLODGED	DISTORTED	DOWN-GRADE
DIRT-TRACK	DISMANTLE	DISTRAINT	DOWNINESS
DISABLING	DISMASTED	DISTURBED	DOWNRIGHT
DISABUSED	DISMAYING	DISUNITED	DOWN-WARDS
DISACCORD	DISMEMBER	DITHERING	DRABBLING
DISAFFECT	DISMISSAL	DITHYRAMB	DRACONIAN
DISAFFIRM	DISMISSED	DIURNALLY	DRAFTSMAN
DISAGREED	DISOBEYED	DIVAGATED	DRAGGLING
DISAPPEAR	DISOBLIGE	DIVERGENT	DRAGON-FLY
DISARMING	DISOWNING	DIVERGING	DRAINABLE
DISAVOWAL	DISPARAGE	DIVERSELY	DRAINPIPE
DISAVOWED	DISPARATE	DIVERSIFY	DRAMATISE
DISBANDED	DISPARITY	DIVERSION	DRAMATIST
DISBARRED	DISPELLED	DIVERSITY	DRAWN-WORK
DISBELIEF	DISPENSED	DIVERTING	DRAY-HORSE
DISBRANCH	DISPENSER	DIVESTING	DREAM-LAND
DISBUDDED	DISPERSAL	DIVIDABLE	DREAM-LESS
DISBURDEN	DISPERSED	DIVIDEDLY	DREAM-LIKE
DISBURSED	DISPLACED	DIVISIBLE	DRENCHING
DISCARDED	DISPLAYED	DIVISIBLY	DRIBBLING
DISCERNED	DISPLEASE	DIVORCING	DRIFT-LESS
DISCHARGE	DISPORTED	DIVULGING	DRIFT-WOOD
DISCLOSED	DISPOSING	DIZZINESS	DRINKABLE
DISCOLOUR	DISPRAISE	DOCK-CRESS	DRINKLESS
DISCOMFIT	DISPROVED	DOCTORATE	DRIPSTONE
DISCOURSE	DISPUTANT	DOCTORING	DRIVELLED
DISCOVERY	DISPUTING	DOCTRINAL	DRIZZLING
DISCREDIT	DISRATING	DODDERING	DROMEDARY
DISCUSSED	DISREGARD	DODECAGON	DROP-SCENE
DISDAINED	DISRELISH	DOGGINESS	DROPSICAL
DISEMBARK	DISREPAIR	DOGMATISE	DRUM-MAJOR
DISEMBODY	DISREPUTE	DOGMATISM	DRUM-STICK
DISENGAGE	DISROBING	DOGMATIST	DRUNKENLY
DISENTAIL	DISROOTED	DOG'S-TOOTH	DRYASDUST
DISENTOMB	DISRUPTED	DOG-VIOLET	DRYSALTER
DISFAVOUR	DISSECTED	DOLEFULLY	DUALISTIC
DISFIGURE	DISSEMBLE	DOLTISHLY	DUBIOUSLY
DISGORGED	DISSENTED	DOMICILED	DUBITABLE
DISGRACED	DISSENTER	DOMINANCE	DUBITABLY
DISGUISED	DISSERVED	DOMINICAL	DUCK-BOARD
DISGUSTED	DISSIPATE	DO-NOTHING	DUCK'S-FOOT
DISH-CLOTH	DISSOLUTE	DOOR-PLATE	DUCTILELY
DISH-CLOUT	DISSOLVED	DOOR-STONE	DUCTILITY
DISH-COVER	DISSONANT	DORMITORY	DUMB-BELLS
DISHONEST	DISSUADED	DOSS-HOUSE	DUMBFOUND
DISHONOUR	DISTANCED	DOUBTLESS	DUMPINESS
DISHWATER	DISTANTLY	DOUGHTILY	DUMPISHLY
DISINFECT	DISTEMPER	DOVE'S-FOOT	DUNGEONED
DISJOINED	DISTENDED	DOWDINESS	DUODECIMO
DISLIKING	DISTILLED	DOWELLING	DUODENARY

DUPLICATE	EJACULATE	EMOTIONAL	ENJOYMENT
DWINDLING	EJECTMENT	EMPHASISE	ENLARGING
DYNAMICAL	ELABORATE	EMPIRICAL	ENLIGHTEN
DYNAMITED	ELBOW-ROOM	EMPLOYING	ENLISTING
DYSENTERY	ELDERSHIP	EMPOWERED	ENLIVENED
DYSPEPSIA	ELDER-WINE	EMPTINESS	ENMESHING
DYSPEPTIC	ELECTORAL	EMULATING	ENOUNCING
DYSTROPHY	ELECTRESS	EMULATION	ENQUIRING
E—9	ELECTRIFY	EMULATIVE	ENRAPTURE
EAGERNESS	ELECTRODE	ENACTMENT	ENRICHING
EAGLE-EYED	ELEGANTLY	ENAMELLED	ENROLLING
EARLINESS	ELEMENTAL	ENAMOURED	ENROLMENT
EARMARKED	ELEVATING	ENCASHING	ENSCONCED
EARNESTLY	ELEVATION	ENCAUSTIC	ENSHRINED
EARTHWARD	ELEVATORY	ENCHANTED	ENSLAVING
EARTHWORK	ELICITING	ENCIRCLED	ENSNARING
EARTHWORM	ELIMINATE	ENCLASPED	ENTAILING
EASEFULLY	ELLIPSOID	ENCLOSING	ENTANGLED
EAST-ENDER	ELOCUTION	ENCLOSURE	ENTERTAIN
EASY-CHAIR	ELONGATED	ENCOMPASS	ENTHRONED
EASY-GOING	ELOPEMENT	ENCOUNTER	ENTHUSING
EAVESDROP	ELOQUENCE	ENCOURAGE	ENTITLING
EBONISING	ELSEWHERE	ENCRUSTED	ENTOURAGE
EBULLIENT	ELUCIDATE	ENDEARING	EN-TOUT-CAS
ECCENTRIC	EMACIATED	ENDEAVOUR	ENTRANCED
ECLIPSING	EMANATING	ENDLESSLY	ENTREATED
ECONOMICS	EMANATION	ENDOCRINE	ENTRECHAT
ECONOMISE	EMBALMING	ENDORSING	ENTREMETS
ECONOMIST	EMBANKING	ENDOSPERM	ENTRUSTED
ECTOPLASM	EMBARGOED	ENDOWMENT	ENTWINING
EDELWEISS	EMBARKING	ENDURABLE	ENUMERATE
EDITORIAL	EMBARRASS	ENDURABLY	ENUNCIATE
EDUCATING	EMBATTLED	ENDURANCE	ENVELOPED
EDUCATION	EMBEDDING	ENERGETIC	ENVENOMED
EFFECTING	EMBELLISH	ENERGISER	ENVIOUSLY
EFFECTIVE	EMBEZZLED	ENERVATED	ENVISAGED
EFFECTUAL	EMBEZZLER	ENFEEBLED	ENVOYSHIP
EFFICIENT	EMBODYING	ENFILADED	ENWRAPPED
EFFLUENCE	EMBOSSING	ENFOLDING	EPAULETTE
EFFLUVIUM	EMBOWERED	ENFORCING	EPHEMERAL
EFFLUXION	EMBRACING	ENGINE-MAN	EPICENTRE
EFFULGENT	EMBRASURE	ENGIRDING	EPICUREAN
EGLANTINE	EMBROIDER	ENGIRDLED	EPICURISM
EGREGIOUS	EMBROILED	ENGRAVING	EPICYCLIC
EGRESSION	EMBRYONIC	ENGROSSED	EPIDERMAL
EIDER-DOWN	EMENDATOR	ENGULFING	EPIDERMIC
EIDOGRAPH	EMERGENCE	ENHANCING	EPIDERMIS
EIGHTFOLD	EMERGENCY	ENIGMATIC	EPIGRAPHY
EIGHTIETH	EMINENTLY	ENJOINING	EPILEPTIC
EIGHTSOME	EMOLLIENT	ENJOYABLE	EPISCOPAL
EIRENICON	EMOLUMENT	ENJOYABLY	EPISTOLIC

EPITOMISE	EVANESCED	EXECUTIVE	EXTENDING
EQUALISED	EVANGELIC	EXECUTORY	EXTENSILE
EQUALISER	EVAPORATE	EXECUTRIX	EXTENSION
EQUALLING	EVASIVELY	EXEMPLARY	EXTENSIVE
EQUIPMENT	EVENTUATE	EXEMPLIFY	EXTENUATE
EQUIPOISE	EVERGLADE	EXEMPTION	EXTOLLING
EQUIPPING	EVERGREEN	EXEMPTIVE	EXTORTING
EQUITABLE	EVERYBODY	EXERCISED	EXTORTION
EQUIVOCAL	EVIDENTLY	EXFOLIATE	EXTRACTED
ERADICATE	EVOCATION	EXHALABLE	EXTRACTOR
ERECTNESS	EVOLUTION	EXHAUSTED	EXTRADITE
ERRAND-BOY	EXACTABLE	EXHIBITED	EXTREMELY
ERRONEOUS	EXACTNESS	EXHIBITOR	EXTREMISM
ERSTWHILE	EXAMINING	EXHORTING	EXTREMIST
ERUDITELY	EXCALIBUR	EXISTENCE	EXTREMITY
ERUDITION	EXCAVATED	EX-OFFICIO	EXTRICATE
ESCALADED	EXCAVATOR	EXOGAMOUS	EXTRINSIC
ESCALATOR	EXCEEDING	EXOGENOUS	EXTRUDING
ESCHEATED	EXCELLENT	EXONERATE	EXTRUSION
ESCORTING	EXCELSIOR	EXORCISED	EXUBERANT
ESPERANTO	EXCEPTING	EXPANDING	EXUBERATE
ESPIONAGE	EXCEPTION	EXPANSILE	EXUDATION
ESPLANADE	EXCEPTIVE	EXPANSION	EXULTANCY
ESPOUSING	EXCESSING	EXPANSIVE	EYE-BRIGHT
ESQUIRING	EXCESSIVE	EXPATIATE	EYE-OPENER
ESSENTIAL	EXCHANGED	EXPECTANT	
ESTABLISH	EXCHANGER	EXPECTING	F—9
ESTAMINET	EXCHEQUER	EXPEDIENT	FABRICATE
ESTEEMING	EXCISABLE	EXPEDITED	FACE-CLOTH
ESTIMABLE	EXCISEMAN	EXPENDING	FACE-GUARD
ESTIMABLY	EXCITABLE	EXPENSIVE	FACSIMILE
ESTIMATOR	EXCLAIMED	EXPIATING	FACTITIVE
ESTOPPING	EXCLUDING	EXPIATION	FACTORIAL
ESTRANGED	EXCLUSION	EXPIATORY	FACTORISE
ESTREATED	EXCLUSIVE	EXPLAINED	FADDINESS
ESTUARINE	EXCORIATE	EXPLETIVE	FAGGOTING
ETERNALLY	EXCREMENT	EXPLICATE	FAILINGLY
ETHICALLY	EXCRETION	EXPLOITED	FAINTNESS
ETHIOPIAN	EXCRETIVE	EXPLORING	FAIRY-LAMP
ETHNOLOGY	EXCRETORY	EXPLOSION	FAIRYLAND
ETIOLATED	EXCULPATE	EXPLOSIVE	FAIRY-LIKE
ETIQUETTE	EXCURSION	EXPORTING	FAIRY-TALE
ETYMOLOGY	EXCURSIVE	EXPOUNDED	FALDSTOOL
EUCHARIST	EXCUSABLE	EXPRESSED	FALERNIAN
EUCLIDEAN	EXCUSABLY	EXPRESSLY	FALLOPIAN
EULOGIZED	EXECRABLE	EXPULSION	FALLOWING
EUPHEMISE	EXECRABLY	EXPULSIVE	FALSEHOOD
EUPHEMISM	EXECRATED	EXPUNGING	FALSENESS
EUPHONIUM	EXECUTANT	EXPURGATE	FALSIFIED
EVACUATED	EXECUTING	EXQUISITE	FALTERING
EVALUATED	EXECUTION	EXTEMPORE	FAMISHING

FANATICAL
FANCY-FREE
FANTAILED
FANTASTIC
FARMHOUSE
FARMSTEAD
FARROWING
FASCIATED
FASCINATE
FASHIONED
FASTENING
FATEFULLY
FATHERING
FATHOMING
FATIGUING
FATTENING
FATTINESS
FAULTLESS
FAVOURING
FAVOURITE
FAWNINGLY
FEARFULLY
FEATHERED
FEATURING
FEBRIFUGE
FECUNDITY
FEDERATED
FEELINGLY
FEE-SIMPLE
FEIGNEDLY
FELONIOUS
FEMINISED
FENCELESS
FENESTRAL
FENLANDER
FERMENTED
FEROCIOUS
FERRETING
FERROTYPE
FERRYBOAT
FERTILELY
FERTILISE
FERTILITY
FERVENTLY
FESTERING
FESTIVELY
FESTIVITY
FESTOONED
FETIDNESS
FETISHISM
FETTERING

FEUDALISE
FEUDALISM
FEUDALITY
FEUDATORY
FIBRELESS
FIBRIFORM
FICTIONAL
FIDDLE-BOW
FIDGETING
FIDUCIARY
FIELDFARE
FIELDSMAN
FIERINESS
FIFE-MAJOR
FIFTEENTH
FILIATION
FILIGREED
FILLETING
FILLIPING
FILMINESS
FILTERING
FILTRATED
FINANCIAL
FINANCIER
FINANCING
FINEDRAWN
FINESSING
FINGERING
FINICALLY
FINICKING
FINISHING
FIRE-ALARM
FIREBRAND
FIREBRICK
FIRECREST
FIRE-EATER
FIRE-GUARD
FIRE-IRONS
FIRE-LIGHT
FIREPLACE
FIREPROOF
FIREWATER
FIRMAMENT
FIRSTBORN
FIRST-FOOT
FIRST-HAND
FIRST-RATE
FISH-CURER
FISHERMAN
FISHINESS
FISH-KNIFE

FISH-SPEAR
FISSILITY
FISTULOUS
FITTINGLY
FITTING-UP
FIXEDNESS
FLACCIDLY
FLAGELLUM
FLAGEOLET
FLAGRANCY
FLAG-STAFF
FLAG-STONE
FLAMBEAUX
FLAMELESS
FLAMINGLY
FLANNELLY
FLARINGLY
FLATTENED
FLATTERED
FLATTERER
FLAUNTING
FLAVOROUS
FLAVOURED
FLEETNESS
FLESHLESS
FLICKERED
FLIGHTILY
FLINCHING
FLINT-LOCK
FLIPPANCY
FLITTERED
FLOATABLE
FLOOD-GATE
FLOOD-MARK
FLOOD-TIDE
FLOORLESS
FLORIDITY
FLOTATION
FLOUNCING
FLOWERING
FLOWERPOT
FLOWINGLY
FLUCTUATE
FLUIDNESS
FLUKINESS
FLUMMOXED
FLUOR-SPAR
FLURRYING
FLUSHNESS
FLUSTERED
FLUTE-LIKE

FLUTTERED
FLUXIONAL
FLY-BITTEN
FLYING-FOX
FLYING-JIB
FLY-POWDER
FOAMINGLY
FODDERING
FOGGINESS
FOG-SIGNAL
FOLIATION
FOLK-DANCE
FOLLOWING
FOMENTING
FOOLHARDY
FOOLISHLY
FOOLPROOF
FOOTBOARD
FOOT-FAULT
FOOTPLATE
FOOT-POUND
FOOTPRINT
FOOTSTALK
FOOTSTOOL
FOPPISHLY
FORAGE-CAP
FORASMUCH
FORBIDDEN
FORCELESS
FORCEMEAT
FORCE-PUMP
FOREARMED
FOREBODED
FORE-CABIN
FORECLOSE
FORECOURT
FOREDATED
FOREFRONT
FOREGOING
FOREIGNER
FORE-JUDGE
FORESHEET
FORESHORE
FORESHOWN
FORE-SIGHT
FORESTALL
FORETASTE
FORETOKEN
FOREWOMAN
FORFEITED
FORGATHER

FORGETFUL	FRECKLING	FULSOMELY	GARNISHED
FORGIVING	FREEBOARD	FUMIGATED	GARNISHEE
FORLORNLY	FREELIVER	FUNGICIDE	GARNISHER
FORMALISE	FREEMASON	FUNICULAR	GARNITURE
FORMALISM	FREESTONE	FUNNELLED	GARRETEER
FORMALIST	FREE-WHEEL	FUNNINESS	GARROTTED
FORMALITY	FREIGHTED	FURBISHED	GARROTTER
FORMATION	FREIGHTER	FURIOUSLY	GARRULITY
FORMATIVE	FRENCHIFY	FURNISHED	GARRULOUS
FORMULARY	FRENCHMAN	FURNISHER	GARTERING
FORMULATE	FREQUENCY	FURNITURE	GAS-BURNER
FORMULISM	FRESHENED	FURROWING	GAS-CARBON
FORMULIST	FRESHNESS	FURTHERED	GASCONADE
FORSAKING	FRETFULLY	FURTHERER	GAS-COOKER
FORTHWITH	FRIBBLING	FURTIVELY	GAS-ENGINE
FORTIFIED	FRICASSEE	FUSILLADE	GASEOUSLY
FORTITUDE	FRICATIVE	FUSSINESS	GAS-FITTER
FORTNIGHT	FRIGHTFUL	FUSTIGATE	GAS-HOLDER
FORTUNATE	FRIGIDITY	FUSTINESS	GASIFYING
FORTY-FIVE	FRITTERED		GAS-MANTLE
FORWARDED	FRIVOLITY	**G—9**	GASOMETER
FORWARDLY	FRIVOLOUS	GABARDINE	GASPINGLY
FOSSILISE	FRIZZLING	GABERDINE	GAS-RETORT
FOSSORIAL	FROCK-COAT	GADDINGLY	GASTRITIS
FOSTERAGE	FROG-MARCH	GAINFULLY	GASTROPOD
FOSTERING	FROGMOUTH	GAINSAYER	GATE-HOUSE
FOSTER-SON	FROG-SPAWN	GAITERING	GATE-MONEY
FOUNDERED	FROLICKED	GALACTOSE	GATHERING
FOUNDLING	FRONTAGER	GALANTINE	GAUCHERIE
FOUNDRESS	FRONTWARD	GALINGALE	GAUDINESS
FOUR-HORSE	FROSTBITE	GALLANTRY	GAUNTNESS
FOURPENCE	FROSTLESS	GALLERIED	GAVELKIND
FOURPENNY	FROWARDLY	GALLICISE	GAZETTEER
FOUR-SCORE	FRUCTUOUS	GALLICISM	GAZETTING
FOXHUNTER	FRUGALITY	GALLINULE	GEAR-WHEEL
FOXTAILED	FRUIT-CAKE	GALLIVANT	GELIGNITE
FRACTIOUS	FRUIT-TREE	GALLOPING	GEMMATION
FRACTURED	FRUSTRATE	GALLOPADE	GENEALOGY
FRAGILELY	FRUTICOSE	GALL-STONE	GENERALLY
FRAGILITY	FRYING-PAN	GALVANISE	GENERATED
FRAGRANCE	FUGACIOUS	GALVANISM	GENERATOR
FRAGRANCY	FULFILLED	GALVANIST	GENIALITY
FRAILNESS	FULGURITE	GAMBOLLED	GENTEELLY
FRAMEWORK	FULL-BLOWN	GAMMA-RAYS	GENTILITY
FRANCHISE	FULL-DRESS	GAMMONING	GENTLEMAN
FRANCISCA	FULL-FACED	GANG-BOARD	GENUFLECT
FRANGIBLE	FULL-GROWN	GANGRENED	GENUINELY
FRANKNESS	FULL-PITCH	GARDENING	GEOGRAPHY
FRATERNAL	FULL-SWING	GARIBALDI	GEOLOGISE
FRAUDLESS	FULMINANT	GARLANDED	GEOLOGIST
	FULMINATE	GARNERING	GEOMETRIC

GERFALCON	GLITTERED	GRAND-AUNT	GRIZZLING
GERMANDER	GLOBE-FISH	GRAND-DUKE	GROOMSMAN
GERMANISM	GLOBOSITY	GRANDIOSE	GROPINGLY
GERMANIUM	GLORIFIED	GRAND-JURY	GROSSNESS
GERMICIDE	GLOWERING	GRANDNESS	GROTESQUE
GERMINANT	GLOWINGLY	GRANDSIRE	GROUNDAGE
GERMINATE	GLUCOSIDE	GRAND-SLAM	GROUND-ASH
GERUNDIAL	GLUEYNESS	GRANULATE	GROUNDING
GERUNDIVE	GLUTINOUS	GRANULOUS	GROUND-IVY
GESTATION	GLYCERIDE	GRAPESHOT	GROUNDNUT
GESTATORY	GLYCERINE	GRAPEVINE	GROUND-OAK
GESTURING	GNAWINGLY	GRAPPLING	GROUNDSEL
GET-AT-ABLE	GOATISHLY	GRASPABLE	GROVELLED
GHOSTLIKE	GO-BETWEEN	GRASS-LAND	GRUELLING
GHOST-MOTH	GODFATHER	GRASSLESS	GRUFFNESS
GIANTLIKE	GODLESSLY	GRASS-PLOT	GRUMBLING
GIBBERING	GODLINESS	GRATIFIED	GRUNDYISM
GIBBERISH	GODMOTHER	GRATINGLY	GUARANTEE
GIDDINESS	GODPARENT	GRATITUDE	GUARANTOR
GIFT-HORSE	GOFFERING	GRAVELESS	GUARD-BOAT
GILL-COVER	GOLDCLOTH	GRAVELLED	GUARDEDLY
GILT-EDGED	GOLDCREST	GRAVEL-PIT	GUARDLESS
GIMLETING	GOLDEN-ROD	GRAVENESS	GUARD-ROOM
GIN-PALACE	GOLDFINCH	GRAVEYARD	GUARDSHIP
GINGERADE	GOLDSMITH	GRAVITATE	GUARDSMAN
GINGER-ALE	GOLF-LINKS	GREATCOAT	GUERRILLA
GINGER-POP	GONDOLIER	GREATNESS	GUESSABLE
GINGLYMUS	GOODNIGHT	GREENBACK	GUESSWORK
GIRANDOLE	GOOSANDER	GREEN-EYED	GUEST-WISE
GIRL-GUIDE	GOOSEFOOT	GREENGAGE	GUIDE-BOOK
GIRLISHLY	GOOSENECK	GREENHORN	GUIDELESS
GIRONDIST	GOOSE-STEP	GREENNESS	GUIDE-POST
GLACIATED	GOOSEWING	GREENROOM	GUIDE-RAIL
GLADDENED	GORGONIAN	GREENSAND	GUIDE-ROPE
GLADIATOR	GOSPELLER	GREENWICH	GUILDHALL
GLADIOLUS	GOSSAMERY	GREENWOOD	GUILELESS
GLADSTONE	GOSSIPING	GREGORIAN	GUILLEMOT
GLAIREOUS	GOTHAMITE	GRENADIER	GUILLOCHE
GLAMOURED	GOUTINESS	GRENADINE	GUILTLESS
GLANDULAR	GOVERNESS	GREYBEARD	GUINEA-PIG
GLARINGLY	GOVERNING	GREYHOUND	GUMMINESS
GLASSLIKE	GRABBLING	GREYSTONE	GUN-BARREL
GLASSWARE	GRACE-NOTE	GRIEVANCE	GUNCOTTON
GLASS-WORK	GRACILITY	GRILL-ROOM	GUNPOWDER
GLASSWORT	GRADATING	GRIMACING	GUNRUNNER
GLENGARRY	GRADATION	GRIMALKIN	GUSHINGLY
GLIDINGLY	GRADATORY	GRIMINESS	GUSTATORY
GLIMMERED	GRADGRIND	GRIPINGLY	GUTTERING
GLIMPSING	GRADUALLY	GRISAILLE	GYMNASIUM
GLISSADED	GRADUATED	GRIST-MILL	GYROSCOPE
GLISTENED	GRADUATOR	GRITSTONE	

H—9	HARDFACED	HEART-WOOD	HIGH BLOWN
HABITABLE	HARDIHOOD	HEATH-CLAD	HIGH-FLIER
HABITABLY	HARDINESS	HEATH-COCK	HIGHFLOWN
HABITUATE	HARDSHELL	HEAVINESS	HIGH-FLYER
HACKNEYED	HARLEQUIN	HEBRIDEAN	HIGH-TONED
HAGGARDLY	HARMFULLY	HECTOGRAM	HIGH-WATER
HAGGISHLY	HARMONICA	HECTORING	HILARIOUS
HAGIOLOGY	HARMONICS	HEDGELESS	HILLINESS
HAG-RIDDEN	HARMONISE	HEEDFULLY	HINDERING
HAILSTONE	HARMONIST	HEEL-PIECE	HINDRANCE
HAILSTORM	HARMONIUM	HEFTINESS	HINDSIGHT
HAIRBROOM	HARNESSED	HEINOUSLY	HINTINGLY
HAIR-BRUSH	HARROVIAN	HEIR-AT-LAW	HIPPOCRAS
HAIR-CLOTH	HARROWING	HELIOGRAM	HISSINGLY
HAIRINESS	HARSHNESS	HELLEBORE	HISTOLOGY
HALF-BLOOD	HARTSHORN	HELLENIAN	HISTORIAN
HALF-BOUND	HARVESTED	HELLENISE	HOAR-FROST
HALF-BREED	HARVESTER	HELLENISM	HOARINESS
HALF-CASTE	HASTINESS	HELLENIST	HOAR-STONE
HALFCROWN	HATCHMENT	HELLBOUND	HOBGOBLIN
HALFPENNY	HATEFULLY	HELLISHLY	HOBNOBBED
HALF-PRICE	HAUGHTILY	HEMICYCLE	HOCUSSING
HALF-ROUND	HAVERSACK	HEMSTITCH	HODOMETER
HALF-SHAFT	HAWK-EAGLE	HENPECKED	HOGBACKED
HALF-TIMER	HAWK-NOSED	HEPATITIS	HOGGISHLY
HALLOWEEN	HAWKSBILL	HEPTARCHY	HOLLANDER
HALTERING	HAWSE-HOLE	HERALDING	HOLLOWING
HALTINGLY	HAYMAKING	HERBALIST	HOLLYHOCK
HAMADRYAD	HAZARDING	HERBARIUM	HOLOCAUST
HAMPERING	HAZARDOUS	HERBIVORE	HOLOGRAPH
HAMSTRING	HEAD-DRESS	HERCULEAN	HOLSTERED
HAMSTRUNG	HEADFRAME	HEREABOUT	HOLYSTONE
HANDBRACE	HEADLINES	HEREAFTER	HOMEBOUND
HANDCUFFS	HEADLIGHT	HERETICAL	HOMESTEAD
HANDGLASS	HEADMONEY	HERITABLE	HOMICIDAL
HANDINESS	HEADPHONE	HERITABLY	HOMOLOGUE
HANDIWORK	HEADPIECE	HERMITAGE	HOMONYMIC
HANDPRESS	HEADSTALL	HERONSHAW	HOMOPHONE
HANDSCREW	HEADSTOCK	HESITANCY	HOMOPHONY
HANDSPIKE	HEADSTONE	HESITATED	HOMOPTERA
HANKERING	HEALINGLY	HETERODOX	HONEY-BEAR
HANSEATIC	HEALTHFUL	HEXACHORD	HONEYCOMB
HAPHAZARD	HEALTHILY	HEXAGONAL	HONEYLESS
HAPPENING	HEARKENED	HEXAMETER	HONEYMOON
HAPPINESS	HEARTACHE	HEXASTYLE	HONEYWORT
HARANGUED	HEARTBURN	HEXATEUCH	HONORIFIC
HARBINGER	HEARTENED	HIBERNATE	HONOURING
HARBOURED	HEARTFELT	HIBERNIAN	HOOKNOSED
HARDBOARD	HEARTHRUG	HIDEBOUND	HOPEFULLY
HARD-BOUND	HEARTLESS	HIDEOUSLY	HOPGARDEN
HARDENING	HEART-SICK	HIERARCHY	HOP-PICKER

HOP-PILLOW	HURTFULLY	IMAGELESS	IMPORTING
HOP-POCKET	HUSBANDED	IMAGINARY	IMPORTUNE
HOP-SCOTCH	HUSBANDRY	IMAGINING	IMPOSABLE
HOREHOUND	HUSHMONEY	IMBROGLIO	IMPOSTURE
HOROSCOPE	HUSKINESS	IMITATING	IMPOTENCE
HOROSCOPY	HYBRIDISE	IMITATION	IMPOTENCY
HORRIFIED	HYBRIDISM	IMITATIVE	IMPOUNDED
HORSEBACK	HYBRIDITY	IMMANENCE	IMPRECATE
HORSE-BEAN	HYDRANGEA	IMMEDIACY	IMPRESSED
HORSEHAIR	HYDRAULIC	IMMEDIATE	IMPRINTED
HORSELESS	HYDROLOGY	IMMENSELY	IMPROMPTU
HORSEMEAT	HYDROSTAT	IMMENSITY	IMPROVING
HORSEPLAY	HYDROXIDE	IMMERSING	IMPROVISE
HORSEPOND	HYMNOLOGY	IMMERSION	IMPRUDENT
HORSERACE	HYPERBOLA	IMMIGRANT	IMPUGNING
HORSESHOE	HYPERBOLE	IMMIGRATE	IMPULSION
HORSETAIL	HYPERICUM	IMMINENCE	IMPULSIVE
HORSEWHIP	HYPHENING	IMMODESTY	IMPUTABLE
HOSTELLER	HYPNOLOGY	IMMORALLY	INABILITY
HOSTILELY	HYPNOTISM	IMMOVABLE	INAMORATO
HOSTILITY	HYPNOTIST	IMMOVABLY	INANIMATE
HOT-HEADED	HYPOCAUST	IMMUNISED	INANITION
HOTTENTOT	HYPOCRISY	IMMUTABLE	INAPTNESS
HOUR-GLASS	HYPOCRITE	IMMUTABLY	INARCHING
HOUSE-BOAT	HYSTERICS	IMPACTING	INAUDIBLE
HOUSEHOLD		IMPACTION	INAUDIBLY
HOUSE-LEEK		IMPAIRING	INAUGURAL
HOUSELESS	I—9	IMPARTIAL	INAURATED
HOUSEMAID	ICELANDER	IMPARTING	INCAPABLE
HOUSEROOM	ICELANDIC	IMPASSION	INCAPABLY
HOUSEWIFE	ICHNEUMON	IMPASSIVE	INCARNATE
HOUSEWORK	ICHTHYOID	IMPATIENS	INCENSING
HOWSOEVER	ICONOLOGY	IMPATIENT	INCENSORY
HUCKABACK	IDEALISED	IMPEACHED	INCENTIVE
HUFFINESS	IDENTICAL	IMPEDANCE	INCEPTION
HUFFISHLY	IDEOGRAPH	IMPELLENT	INCEPTIVE
HUMANISED	IDIOMATIC	IMPELLING	INCESSANT
HUMANKIND	IGNORAMUS	IMPENDENT	INCIDENCE
HUMANNESS	IGNORANCE	IMPENDING	INCIPIENT
HUMBLE-BEE	IGUANODON	IMPERFECT	INCLEMENT
HUMBLE-PIE	ILLEGALLY	IMPERIOUS	INCLINING
HUMBUGGED	ILLEGIBLE	IMPETUOUS	INCLUDING
HUMILIATE	ILLEGIBLY	IMPINGING	INCLUSION
HUMMOCKED	ILL-HUMOUR	IMPIOUSLY	INCLUSIVE
HUMOURING	ILLIBERAL	IMPLANTED	INCOGNITO
HUNCHBACK	ILLICITLY	IMPLEMENT	INCOMMODE
HUNDREDTH	ILL-JUDGED	IMPLICATE	INCORRECT
HUNGARIAN	ILL-NATURE	IMPLORING	INCORRUPT
HUNGERING	ILLOGICAL	IMPLOSION	INCREASED
HURRICANE	ILL-TIMING	IMPOLITIC	INCREMENT
HURRIEDLY	ILLUMINED	IMPORTANT	INCUBATED

INCUBATOR	INFECTION	INNOVATOR	INTERCEPT
INCULCATE	INFECTIVE	INOCULATE	INTERDICT
INCULPATE	INFERENCE	INODORATE	INTERFERE
INCUMBENT	INFERRING	INODOROUS	INTERFOLD
INCURABLE	INFERTILE	INORGANIC	INTERFUSE
INCURABLY	INFESTING	INQUIRING	INTERJECT
INCURIOUS	INFIRMARY	INSATIATE	INTERLACE
INCURRING	INFIRMITY	INSCRIBED	INTERLAID
INCURSION	INFLAMING	INSENSATE	INTERLARD
INCURSIVE	INFLATING	INSERTING	INTERLEAF
INCURVING	INFLATION	INSERTION	INTERLINE
INDECENCY	INFLECTED	INSETTING	INTERLOCK
INDECORUM	INFLEXION	INSIDIOUS	INTERLOPE
INDELIBLE	INFLICTED	INSINCERE	INTERLUDE
INDELIBLY	INFLOWING	INSINUATE	INTERMENT
INDEMNIFY	INFLUENCE	INSIPIDLY	INTERNING
INDEMNITY	INFLUENZA	INSISTENT	INTERNODE
INDENTING	INFOLDING	INSISTING	INTERPLAY
INDENTION	INFORMANT	INSOLENCE	INTERPOSE
INDENTURE	INFORMING	INSOLUBLE	INTERPRET
INDICATED	INFRINGED	INSOLVENT	INTERRING
INDICATOR	INFURIATE	INSPANNED	INTERRUPT
INDICTING	INFUSIBLE	INSPECTED	INTERSECT
INDIGENCE	INFUSORIA	INSPECTOR	INTERVENE
INDIGNANT	INGENIOUS	INSPIRING	INTERVIEW
INDIGNITY	INGENUITY	INSTALLED	INTERWOVE
INDISPOSE	INGENUOUS	INSTANCED	INTESTACY
INDOLENCE	INGESTION	INSTANTLY	INTESTATE
INDRAUGHT	INGLENOOK	INSTIGATE	INTESTINE
INDUCTING	INGRAINED	INSTILLED	INTIMATED
INDUCTION	INGROWING	INSTITUTE	INTONATED
INDUCTIVE	INHABITED	INSULARLY	INTRICACY
INDULGING	INHERENCE	INSULATED	INTRICATE
INDULGENT	INHERITED	INSULATOR	INTRIGUED
INDURATED	INHERITOR	INSULTING	INTRINSIC
→ INDWELLED	INHIBITED	INSURABLE	INTRODUCE
INEBRIATE	INHUMANLY	INSURANCE	INTROVERT
INEBRIETY	INITIALLY	INSURGENT	INTRUDING
INEFFABLE	INITIATED	INTEGRANT	INTRUSION
INEFFABLY	INJECTING	INTEGRATE	INTRUSIVE
INELASTIC	INJECTION	INTEGRITY	INTUITION
INELEGANT	INJURIOUS	INTELLECT	INTUITIVE
INEPTNESS	INJUSTICE	INTENDANT	INUNCTION
INERRABLE	INKBOTTLE	INTENSELY	INUNDATED
INERRABLY	INKHOLDER	INTENSIFY	INUREMENT
INERRANCY	INNERMOST	INTENSION	INUTILITY
INERTNESS	INNERVATE	INTENSITY	INVALIDED
INFANTILE	INNKEEPER	INTENSIVE	INVECTIVE
INFANTINE	INNOCENCE	INTENTION	INVEIGHED
INFATUATE	INNOCUOUS	INTERBRED	INVEIGLED
INFECTING	INNOVATED	INTERCEDE	INVENTING

INVENTION
INVENTIVE
INVENTORY
INVERSELY
INVERSION
INVERTING
INVESTING
INVIDIOUS
INVIOLATE
INVISIBLE
INVISIBLY
INVOICING
INVOLUCRE
INVOLVING
INWROUGHT
IRASCIBLE
IRASCIBLY
IRKSOMELY
IRONBOUND
IRONMOULD
IRONSMITH
IRONSTONE
IRRADIANT
IRRADIATE
IRREGULAR
IRRIGATED
IRRITABLE
IRRITABLY
IRRITANCY
IRRITATED
IRRUPTION
ISINGLASS
ISLAMITIC
ISOLATING
ISOLATION
ISOMETRIC
ISOSCELES
ISRAELITE
ITALICISE
ITERATING
ITERATION
ITERATIVE
ITINERANT
ITINERARY
ITINERATE

J—9
JACARANDA
JACK-KNIFE
JACK-PLANE

JACK-SNIPE
JACK-STRAW
JACK-TOWEL
JACQUERIE
JANISSARY
JANSENISM
JANSENIST
JARRINGLY
JAY-WALKER
JEALOUSLY
JEERINGLY
JELLYFISH
JENNETING
JESSAMINE
JESTINGLY
JEWELLERY
JEWEL-LIKE
JOBMASTER
JOCULARLY
JOINTEDLY
JOINT-HEIR
JOINTRESS
JOLLINESS
JOLLYBOAT
JOLTINGLY
JOSS-HOUSE
JOSS-STICK
JOURNEYED
JOVIALITY
JOYLESSLY
JOCUNDITY
JUDAS-TREE
JUDGEMENT
JUDGESHIP
JUDICIARY
JUDICIOUS
JUICELESS
JUICINESS
JUMPINESS
JUNIORITY
JURIDICAL
JUSTICIAR
JUSTIFIED
JUTTINGLY
JUVENILIA
JUXTAPOSE

K—9
KENNELLED
KENTLEDGE
KERBSTONE

KERNELLED
KIDNAPPED
KIDNAPPER
KILDERKIN
KILN-DRIED
KILOLITRE
KILOMETRE
KINGCRAFT
KINSWOMAN
KIPPERING
KITCHENER
KITTENISH
KITTIWAKE
KNAVISHLY
KNEADABLE
KNEE-PIECE
KNIFE-EDGE
KNIFE-REST
KNIGHTAGE
KNIGHTING
KNITTABLE
KNOCKDOWN
KNOTGRASS
KNOWINGLY
KNOWLEDGE
KNUCKLING
KYMOGRAPH

L—9
LABELLING
LABORIOUS
LABOURING
LABYRINTH
LACE-CORAL
LACE-FRAME
LACERATED
LACHRYMAL
LACTATION
LAGGINGLY
LAIRDSHIP
LAMB'S-WOOL
LAMELLATE
LAMENTING
LAMINATED
LAMPBLACK
LAMPLIGHT
LAMPOONED
LANCEWOOD
LAND-AGENT
LANDAULET
LAND-FORCE

LANDGRAVE
LANDOWNER
LANDSCAPE
LAND-SHARK
LANDSLIDE
LANGUIDLY
LANKINESS
LANTHANUM
LAODICEAN
LARCENOUS
LARGENESS
LARGHETTO
LASSITUDE
LASTINGLY
LATERALLY
LATHERING
LATTICING
LAUDATION
LAUDATORY
LAUGHABLE
LAUGHABLY
LAUNCHING
LAUNDERER
LAUNDRESS
LAURELLED
LAVISHING
LAWGIVING
LAWLESSLY
LAWMAKING
LAWMONGER
LAWNMOWER
LAY-FIGURE
LAZARETTO
LEADINGLY
LEAFINESS
LEAF-METAL
LEAF-MOULD
LEAFSTALK
LEAKINESS
LEAN-FACED
LEAPINGLY
LEARNABLE
LEARNEDLY
LEASEHOLD
LEASTWAYS
LEASTWISE
LEAVENING
LECHERING
LECHEROUS
LECTURING
LEERINGLY

LEGALISED	LIMPIDITY	LONG-DOZEN	MAELSTROM
LEGENDARY	LIMPINGLY	LONGEVITY	MAFFICKED
LEGER-LINE	LINCRUSTA	LONG-FIELD	MAGICALLY
LEGIONARY	LINEALITY	LONGINGLY	MAGNESIAN
LEGISLATE	LINEAMENT	LONGITUDE	MAGNESIUM
LEISURELY	LINEATION	LOOSENESS	MAGNETISE
LEIT-MOTIF	LINGERING	LOQUACITY	MAGNETISM
LENGTHILY	LION-HEART	LORGNETTE	MAGNETITE
LENIENTLY	LIONISING	LOUSINESS	MAGNIFICO
LEPROUSLY	LIQUATING	LOUTISHLY	MAGNIFIED
LESSENING	LIQUATION	LOVE-APPLE	MAGNITUDE
LETHARGIC	LIQUEFIED	LOVE-CHILD	MAHARANEE
LETTER-BOX	LIQUIDATE	LOVE-FEAST	MAHOMEDAN
LETTERING	LIQUIDITY	LOWERMOST	MAILCOACH
LEUCOCYTE	LIQUORICE	LOWLANDER	MAIL-GUARD
LEVANTINE	LIQUORISH	LOWLINESS	MAIL-TRAIN
LEVANTING	LISPINGLY	LOW-MINDED	MAIN-BRACE
LEVELLING	LISTENING	LOW-NECKED	MAINSHEET
LEVELNESS	LITERALLY	LUBRICANT	MAJORDOMO
LEVIATHAN	LITERATIM	LUBRICATE	MAJORSHIP
LEVITICUS	LITHENESS	LUBRICITY	MAKE-PEACE
LIABILITY	LITHESOME	LUBRICOUS	MAKESHIFT
LIBELLING	LITHOLOGY	LUCIDNESS	MALACHITE
LIBELLOUS	LITHOTINT	LUCK-PENNY	MALADROIT
LIBERALLY	LITHOTYPE	LUCRATIVE	MALARIOUS
LIBERATED	LITIGABLE	LUCUBRATE	MALFORMED
LIBERATOR	LITIGATED	LUCULLIAN	MALICIOUS
LIBERTINE	LITIGIOUS	LUDICROUS	MALIGNING
LIBRARIAN	LITTERING	LUMBERMAN	MALIGNANT
LIBRATION	LITURGIST	LUMBRICAL	MALIGNITY
LICENSING	LIVERWORT	LUMPISHLY	MALLEABLE
LICHENOUS	LIVERYMAN	LUNISOLAR	MALLEOLUS
LIFEBLOOD	LIVIDNESS	LUSTFULLY	MALMAISON
LIFEGUARD	LOADSTONE	LUSTINESS	MAMMALIAN
LIGHTABLE	LOAF-SUGAR	LUXURIANT	MAMMALOGY
LIGHTENED	LOATHSOME	LUXURIATE	MANNIFORM
LIGHTLESS	LOBSCOUSE	LUXURIOUS	MANACLING
LIGHTNESS	LOCKSMITH	LYMPHATIC	MAN-AT-ARMS
LIGHTNING	LOCOMOTOR		MANCUNIAN
LIGHTSHIP	LODESTONE	M—9	MANDATORY
LIGHT-YEAR	LODGEABLE	MACCABEAN	MANDOLINE
LILACEOUS	LOFTINESS	MACCABEES	MANDUCATE
LIME-JUICE	LOGARITHM	MACEDOINE	MANGANESE
LIMELIGHT	LOGICALLY	MACERATED	MANGINESS
LIMESTONE	LOGISTICS	MACHINATE	MAN-HANDLE
LIME-WATER	LOGOGRIPH	MACHINERY	MANIFESTO
LIMITABLE	LOGOMACHY	MACHINING	MANLINESS
LIMITEDLY	LOINCLOTH	MACHINIST	MANNEQUIN
LIMITLESS	LOITERING	MACROCOSM	MANNERISM
LIMNOLOGY	LOLLOPING	MADDENING	MANNISHLY
LIMOUSINE	LONGCLOTH	MADREPORE	MANOEUVRE

MANOMETER	MEALINESS	MESMERISE	MILLEPEDE
MANY-SIDED	MEANDERED	MESMERISM	MILLIGRAM
MARAUDING	MEANINGLY	MESSENGER	MILLINERY
MARCASITE	MEANWHILE	MESSIANIC	MILLIONTH
MARCHPANE	MEASURING	MESSINESS	MILLIPEDE
MARESCHAL	MEATINESS	METABOLIC	MILLSTONE
MARGARINE	MECHANICS	METALLING	MILL WHEEL
MARGINING	MECHANISE	METALLISE	MIMICKING
MARINATED	MECHANIST	METALLIST	MINCEMEAT
MARITALLY	MEDALLION	METALLOID	MINCINGLY
MARKET-DAY	MEDALLIST	METAMERIC	MINEFIELD
MARKETING	MEDIAEVAL	METAPLASM	MINELAYER
MARMALADE	MEDIATING	METEOROID	MINIATURE
MARMOREAL	MEDIATION	METHODISM	MINIMISED
MAROONING	MEDIATORY	METHODIST	MINT-JULEP
MARQUETRY	MEDICABLE	METHOUGHT	MINT-SAUCE
MARROWFAT	MEDICALLY	METHYLATE	MINUTE-GUN
MARROWISH	MEDICATED	METHYLENE	MIRRORING
MARSHLAND	MEDICINAL	METROLOGY	MIRTHLESS
MARSUPIAL	MEDULLARY	METRONOME	MISALLIED
MARTIALLY	MEGAPHONE	MEZZANINE	MISATTEND
MARTINMAS	MEGASCOPE	MEZZOTINT	MISBECAME
MARTYRING	MELANOSIS	MICACEOUS	MISBECOME
MARTYRDOM	MELIORISM	MICROBIAL	MISBEHAVE
MARVELLED	MELLOWING	MICROCOSM	MISBELIEF
MASCULINE	MELODIOUS	MICROFILM	MISCALLED
MASSACRED	MELODRAMA	MICROTOME	MISCHANCE
MASSAGING	MELPOMENE	MICROVOLT	MISCREANT
MASSIVELY	MELTINGLY	MIDDLEMAN	MISDATING
MASTERDOM	MEMORABLE	MIDDLINGS	MISDIRECT
MASTERFUL	MEMORABLY	MIDINETTE	MISEMPLOY
MASTERING	MEMORANDA	MID-STREAM	MISERABLE
MASTICATE	MEMORISED	MID-SUMMER	MISERABLY
MATCHLESS	MENAGERIE	MIDWIFERY	MISFORMED
MATCHLOCK	MENDACITY	MIDWINTER	MISGIVING
MATCHWOOD	MENDELIAN	MIGRATING	MISGOTTEN
MATERNITY	MENDELISM	MIGRATION	MISGOVERN
MATRIARCH	MENDICANT	MIGRATORY	MISGUIDED
MATRICIDE	MENDICITY	MILDEWING	MISHANDLE
MATRIMONY	MENNONITE	MILESTONE	MISINFORM
MATRONAGE	MENSHEVIK	MILITANCY	MISJOINED
MATTERING	MENTALITY	MILITATED	MISJUDGED
MAULSTICK	MENTIONED	MILK-FEVER	MISLAYING
MAUNDERED	MERCENARY	MILK-FLOAT	MIS-MANAGE
MAUSOLEUM	MERCILESS	MILKINESS	MISMARKED
MAWKISHLY	MERCURIAL	MILK-PUNCH	MISNAMING
MAXILLARY	MERCUROUS	MILK-TOOTH	MISPLACED
MAXIMISED	MERCY-SEAT	MILK-VETCH	MISQUOTED
MAYFLOWER	MERGANSER	MILL-BOARD	MISRATING
MAYORALTY	MERRIMENT	MILLENARY	MISREPORT
MEADOW-RUE	MERRINESS	MILLENIAL	MISRULING

MISSHAPED	MONOCHORD	MUDDINESS	NASEBERRY
MISSHAPEN	MONOCOQUE	MULLIONED	NASTINESS
MISSIONER	MONOCULAR	MULTIFORM	NATURALLY
MISSTATED	MONODRAMA	MULTITUDE	NAUGHTILY
MISTAKING	MONOGRAPH	MUMCHANCE	NAUSEATED
MISTAUGHT	MONOLOGUE	MUMMIFIED	NAVELWORT
MISTIMING	MONOMANIA	MUMMIFORM	NAVICULAR
MISTINESS	MONOMETER	MUNDANELY	NAVIGABLE
MISTITLED	MONOPLANE	MUNICIPAL	NAVIGATED
MISTLETOE	MONOTONIC	MUNITIONS	NAVIGATOR
MISTUNING	MONOTREME	MURDERING	NECESSARY
MITHRAISM	MONSIGNOR	MURDERESS	NECESSITY
MITIGATED	MONSTROUS	MURDEROUS	NECK-CLOTH
MNEMONICS	MOODINESS	MURKINESS	NECKLACED
MNEMOSYNE	MOON-DAISY	MURMURING	NECK-PIECE
MOANFULLY	MOONLIGHT	MURMUROUS	NECTARINE
MOBILISED	MOONRAKER	MUSCADINE	NEEDFULLY
MOCKINGLY	MOONSHINE	MUSCOVITE	NEEDINESS
MODELLING	MOONSHINY	MUSEFULLY	NEEDLEFUL
MODERATED	MOONSTONE	MUSHINESS	NEEDLE-GUN
MODERATOR	MORALISED	MUSICALLY	NEFARIOUS
MODERNISE	MORBIDITY	MUSIC-BOOK	NEGATIVED
MODERNISM	MORDACITY	MUSIC-HALL	NEGLECTED
MODERNIST	MORDANTLY	MUSK-APPLE	NEGLIGENT
MODERNITY	MORMONISM	MUSKETEER	NEGOTIATE
MODIFYING	MORTALITY	MUSKINESS	NEGROHEAD
MODULATED	MORTGAGED	MUSK-MELON	NEIGHBOUR
MODULATOR	MORTGAGEE	MUSK-SHREW	NEOLITHIC
MOISTENED	MORTGAGOR	MUSSULMAN	NEPENTHES
MOISTNESS	MORTIFIED	MUSTACHIO	NEPTUNIAN
MOLECULAR	MORTISING	MUSTERING	NERVELESS
MOLE-SHREW	MOSCHATEL	MUSTINESS	NERVOUSLY
MOLESTING	MOSS-GROWN	MUTILATED	NEURALGIA
MOLETRACK	MOSSINESS	MUTINYING	NEURALGIC
MOLLIFIED	MOTHERING	MUTUALITY	NEURATION
MOLLUSCAN	MOTIONING	MUZZINESS	NEUROLOGY
MOMENTARY	MOTOR-BOAT	MYSTICISM	NEUROPATH
MOMENTOUS	MOULDABLE	MYSTIFIED	NEUROTOMY
MONARCHAL	MOULDERED	MYTHICISE	NEUTRALLY
MONARCHIC	MOULD-LOFT	MYTHOLOGY	NEVERMORE
MONASTERY	MOULD-WARP		NEWSPAPER
MONDAYISH	MOUND-BIRD	N—9	NEWTONIAN
MONETISED	MOUNTABLE	NAILBRUSH	NICKNAMED
MONEYLESS	MOUSE-HOLE	NAKEDNESS	NICTITATE
MONEYWORT	MOUSE-HUNT	NAMEPLATE	NIGGARDLY
MONGERING	MOUSE-TAIL	NARCISSUS	NIGHT-CLUB
MONGOLIAN	MOUSE-TRAP	NARRATING	NIGHT-FALL
MONKEYING	MOUSTACHE	NARRATION	NIGHT-GOWN
MONKEY-NUT	MOUTHLESS	NARRATIVE	NIGHT-HAWK
MONKSHOOD	MUCKINESS	NARROWING	NIGHT-LESS
MONOBASIC	MUCK-SWEAT	NASALISED	NIGHT-LINE

NIGHTMARE	O—9	ODDFELLOW	ORDAINING
NIGHT-SOIL	OAST-HOUSE	ODOROUSLY	ORDINANCE
NINETIETH	OBBLIGATO	ODOURLESS	ORGANZINE
NIPPINGLY	OBEDIENCE	OENOTHERA	ORGIASTIC
NITRIFIED	OBEISANCE	OFFENSIVE	ORIENTATE
NOBLENESS	OBESENESS	OFFERABLE	ORIFLAMME
NOCTURNAL	OBEYINGLY	OFFERTORY	ORIGINATE
NOISELESS	OBFUSCATE	OFFHANDED	ORPHANAGE
NOISINESS	OBJECTIFY	OFFICERED	ORTHODOXY
NOISOMELY	OBJECTION	OFFICIANT	OSCILLATE
NOMINALLY	OBJECTIVE	OFFICIATE	OSCULATED
NOMINATED	OBJURGATE	OFFICINAL	OSSIFYING
NOMINATOR	OBLIGATED	OFFICIOUS	OSTEOLOGY
NONENTITY	OBLIQUELY	OFFSPRING	OSTEOPATH
NONILLION	OBLIQUITY	OFTENNESS	OSTRACISE
NONPAREIL	OBLIVIOUS	OIL-COLOUR	OTHERNESS
NON-SEXUAL	OBLONGISH	OIL-ENGINE	OTHERWISE
NONSUITED	OBNOXIOUS	OLEOGRAPH	OUT-AND-OUT
NORMALISE	OBSCENELY	OLEOMETER	OUTBRAVED
NORMALITY	OBSCENITY	OLEORESIN	OUTERMOST
NORTH-EAST	OBSCURANT	OLFACTORY	OUTFACING
NORTHERLY	OBSCURELY	OLIGARCHY	OUTGROWTH
NORTHWARD	OBSCURING	OLIGOCENE	OUT-JOCKEY
NORTH-WEST	OBSCURITY	OLIVE-YARD	OUTLANDER
NORWEGIAN	OBSEQUIAL	OMBUDSMAN	OUTLASTED
NOSEPIECE	OBSERVANT	OMINOUSLY	OUTLAWING
NOSTALGIA	OBSERVING	OMISSIBLE	OUTLEAPED
NOSTALGIC	OBSESSION	ON-LICENCE	OUTLINING
NOTEPAPER	OBSTETRIC	ONSETTING	OUTLIVING
NOTIFYING	OBSTINACY	ONSLAUGHT	OUTMANNED
NOTORIETY	OBSTINATE	OPALESCED	OUTNUMBER
NOTORIOUS	OBTAINING	OPALISING	OUT-OF-DOOR
NOURISHED	OBTRUDING	OPERATING	OUTPACING
NOVELETTE	OBTRUSION	OPERATION	OUTPLAYED
NOVICIATE	OBTRUSIVE	OPERATISE	OUTRAGING
NOVITIATE	OBVERSION	OPERATIVE	OUTRANGED
NOXIOUSLY	OBVERSELY	OPPORTUNE	OUTRIDDEN
NULLIFIED	OBVERTING	OPPOSABLE	OUTRIDING
NUMBERING	OBVIATING	OPPRESSED	OUTRIGGED
NUMERABLE	OBVIOUSLY	OPPRESSOR	OUTRIGGER
NUMERALLY	OCCIPITAL	OPTOMETER	OUTSAILED
NUMERATED	OCCLUDING	OPTOPHONE	OUTSPOKEN
NUMERATOR	OCCLUSION	OPULENTLY	OUTSPREAD
NUMERICAL	OCCULTISM	OPUSCULUM	OUTSTARED
NURSEMAID	OCCUPANCY	ORANGEADE	OUT-TALKED
NURTURING	OCCUPYING	ORANGE-MAN	OUTVALUED
NUTRIMENT	OCCURRING	ORANGE-PIP	OUTVOTING
NUTRITION	OCTAGONAL	ORATORIAL	OUTWARDLY
NUTRITIVE	OCTENNIAL	ORBICULAR	OUTWITTED
NUTTINESS	OCTILLION	ORCHESTRA	OUTWORKED
NYSTAGMUS	ODALISQUE	ORCHIDIST	OVERACTED

OVERAWING	PAGEANTRY	PAROCHIAL	PEDALLING
OVERBLOWN	PAINFULLY	PARODYING	PEDICULAR
OVERBOARD	PALANQUIN	PAROTITIS	PEDOMETER
OVERBUILD	PALATABLE	PARQUETRY	PEEVISHLY
OVERCLOUD	PALAVERED	PARRICIDE	PEKINGESE
OVERCROWD	PALE-FACED	PARSIMONY	PELLITORY
OVERDOING	PALISADED	PARSONAGE	PENALISED
OVERDOSED	PALLADIAN	PARTAKING	PEN-AND-INK
OVERDRAFT	PALLADIUM	PARTHENON	PENCILLED
OVERDRAWN	PALLIASSE	PARTIALLY	PENDRAGON
OVERDRIVE	PALLIATED	PARTITION	PENDULOUS
OVERHASTY	PALM-HOUSE	PARTITIVE	PENETRATE
OVERJOYED	PALMISTRY	PARTNERED	PENHOLDER
OVERLADEN	PALPITATE	PARTRIDGE	PENINSULA
OVERLEAPT	PAMPERING	PASSENGER	PENITENCE
OVERLYING	PANCAKING	PASSERINE	PENNIFORM
OVERNIGHT	PANDERING	PASSIVELY	PENNILESS
OVERPOWER	PANEGYRIC	PASSIVITY	PENNYWISE
OVERPROOF	PANELLING	PASTORALE	PENNYWORT
OVERRATED	PANHANDLE	PASTURAGE	PENSIONED
OVERREACH	PANOPLIED	PASTURING	PENSIONER
OVERRULED	PANORAMIC	PATCHOULI	PENSIVELY
OVERSHOOT	PANSLAVIC	PATCHWORK	PENTAGRAM
OVERSIGHT	PANTALOON	PATENTING	PENTECOST
OVERSLEEP	PANTHEISM	PATERNITY	PENTHOUSE
OVERSPEND	PANTHEIST	PATHOLOGY	PENURIOUS
OVERSTATE	PANTINGLY	PATIENTLY	PEPPERBOX
OVERSTOCK	PANTOMIME	PATRIARCH	PEPPERING
OVERTAKEN	PAPER-MILL	PATRICIAN	PERCEIVED
OVERTHROW	PAPILLARY	PATRICIDE	PERCHANCE
OVERTRUMP	PARABOLIC	PATRIMONY	PERCHERON
OVERVALUE	PARACHUTE	PATRIOTIC	PERCOLATE
OVERWHELM	PARACLETE	PATRISTIC	PERCUSSED
OVERWOUND	PARAGRAPH	PATROLLED	PERDITION
OVIPAROUS	PARALYSED	PATRONAGE	PEREGRINE
OWNERSHIP	PARALYSIS	PATRONESS	PERENNIAL
OXIDATION	PARALYTIC	PATRONISE	PERFECTED
OXIDISING	PARAMOUNT	PATTERING	PERFECTLY
OXYGENATE	PARASITIC	PATTERNED	PERFERVID
OXYGENIZE	PARATAXIS	PAUPERISE	PERFORATE
OXYGENOUS	PARBOILED	PAUSINGLY	PERFORMED
OYSTER-BED	PARBUCKLE	PAYMASTER	PERFORMER
	PARCELLED	PEACEABLE	PERFUMERY
P—9	PARCHMENT	PEACEABLY	PERFUMING
PACEMAKER	PARDONING	PEA-JACKET	PERIMETER
PACHYDERM	PAREGORIC	PEARL-WORT	PERIPHERY
PACIFYING	PARENTAGE	PEASANTRY	PERISCOPE
PACKETING	PARGETING	PECULATED	PERISHING
PACKHORSE	PARHELION	PECUNIARY	PERISTYLE
PADLOCKED	PARLEYING	PEDAGOGIC	PERJURING
PAGANISED	PARLEYVOO	PEDAGOGUE	PERMANENT

PERMEABLE	PHOSPHATE	PLACARDED	PLUTONIUM
PERMEABLY	PHOSPHINE	PLACATING	PNEUMATIC
PERMEATED	PHOSPHITE	PLACE-KICK	PNEUMONIA
PERMITTED	PHOTO-PLAY	PLACIDITY	PNEUMONIC
PERMUTING	PHOTO-STAT	PLAINNESS	POCKETING
PERORATED	PHRENETIC	PLAIN-SONG	POETASTER
PERPENDED	PHYSICIAN	PLAINTIFF	POIGNANCY
PERPETUAL	PHYSICIST	PLAINTIVE	POINTEDLY
PERPLEXED	PHYSICKED	PLANE-IRON	POINTLESS
PERSECUTE	PICKABACK	PLANETARY	POINTSMAN
PERSEVERE	PICKETING	PLANETOID	POISONOUS
PERSIMMON	PICTORIAL	PLANTABLE	POKERWORK
PERSISTED	PICTURING	PLASTERED	POLARIZED
PERSONAGE	PIECEMEAL	PLASTERER	POLEMICAL
PERSONATE	PIECE-WORK	PLATEMARK	POLE-VAULT
PERSONIFY	PIER-GLASS	PLATE-RACK	POLICEMAN
PERSONNEL	PIETISTIC	PLATINISE	POLISHING
PERSPIRED	PIGHEADED	PLATITUDE	POLITESSE
PERSUADED	PIGMENTAL	PLATONISE	POLITICAL
PERTAINED	PIGNORATE	PLATONISM	POLLINATE
PERTINENT	PIKESTAFF	PLATONIST	POLLUTING
PERTURBED	PILFERING	PLAUSIBLE	POLLUTION
PERVADING	PILLAR-BOX	PLAUSIBLY	POLONAISE
PERVASION	PILLORIED	PLAY-ACTOR	POLYANDRY
PERVASIVE	PILLOWING	PLAYFULLY	POLYGONAL
PERVERTED	PILOT-BOAT	PLAYGOING	POLYSTYLE
PESSIMISM	PILOTFISH	PLAYHOUSE	POMMELLED
PESSIMIST	PIMPERNEL	PLAYTHING	POMPADOUR
PESTERING	PINCHBECK	PLEACHING	POMPOSITY
PESTILENT	PINEAPPLE	PLEASANCE	POMPOUSLY
PESTOLOGY	PINIONING	PLENARILY	PONDERING
PETERSHAM	PINNACLED	PLENITUDE	PONDEROUS
PETRIFIED	PIONEERED	PLENTEOUS	POOR-HOUSE
PETROLEUM	PIPESTONE	PLENTIFUL	POPPY-COCK
PETTICOAT	PIPISTREL	PLEURITIC	POPULARLY
PETTINESS	PIQUANTLY	PLIGHTING	POPULATED
PETTISHLY	PIRATICAL	PLINTHITE	PORBEAGLE
PETULANCE	PIROUETTE	PLOUGHBOY	PORCELAIN
PHAGOCYTE	PISCATORY	PLOUGHING	PORCUPINE
PHALANGER	PISCIFORM	PLOUGHMAN	PORRINGER
PHALAROPE	PISTACHIO	PLUMBLINE	PORTATIVE
PHARISAIC	PITCHFORK	PLUMB-RULE	PORTENDED
PHENOMENA	PITCH-PINE	PLUMELESS	PORTERAGE
PHILANDER	PITCHPIPE	PLUMPNESS	PORTERESS
PHILATELY	PITEOUSLY	PLUNDERED	PORTFOLIO
PHILIPPIC	PITHECOID	PLURALISE	PORTRAYAL
PHILOLOGY	PITHINESS	PLURALISM	PORTRAYED
PHLEBITIS	PITIFULLY	PLURALIST	POSSESSED
PHONETICS	PITUITARY	PLURALITY	POSSESSOR
PHONOGRAM	PITYINGLY	PLUS-FOURS	POST-DATED
PHONOLOGY	PIZZICATO	PLUTOCRAT	POST-ENTRY

POSTERIOR	PREDICTED	PRIESTESS	PRONENESS
POSTERITY	PREDOOMED	PRIMARILY	PRONOUNCE
POST-HASTE	PRE-ENGAGE	PRIMATIAL	PROOFLESS
POST-NATAL	PREFACING	PRIMITIVE	PROPAGATE
POSTPONED	PREFATORY	PRINCEDOM	PROPELLED
POSTULANT	PREFERRED	PRINCIPAL	PROPELLER
POSTULATE	PREFIGURE	PRINCIPIA	PROPHETIC
POSTURING	PREFIXING	PRINCIPLE	PROPONENT
POTASSIUM	PREFORMED	PRINTLESS	PROPOSING
POTBOILER	PREGNANCY	PRINTSHOP	PROPRIETY
POTENTATE	PREJUDGED	PRISMATIC	PROROGUED
POTENTIAL	PREJUDICE	PRIVATEER	PROSCRIBE
POT-POURRI	PRELATURE	PRIVATELY	PROSECUTE
POTTERING	PRELUDING	PRIVATION	PROSELYTE
POULTERER	PRELUSIVE	PRIVILEGE	PROSINESS
POULTICED	PREMATURE	PROBATION	PROSODIST
POUNCE-BOX	PREMISING	PROBATIVE	PROSPERED
POURBOIRE	PREMOTION	PROBOSCIS	PROSTRATE
POURPOINT	PREOCCUPY	PROCEDURE	PROTECTED
POWDER-BOX	PREOPTION	PROCEEDED	PROTECTOR
POWDERING	PREORDIAN	PROCESSED	PROTESTED
POWERLESS	PREPACKED	PROCLITIC	PROTHESIS
POWER-LOOM	PREPARING	PRO-CONSUL	PROTOTYPE
POW-WOWING	PREPAYING	PROCREANT	PROTOZOAN
PRACTICAL	PRESAGING	PROCREATE	PROTOZOIC
PRACTISED	PRESBYTER	PROCURING	PROTRUDED
PRAGMATIC	PRESCIENT	PRODUCING	PROUDNESS
PRATINGLY	PRESCRIBE	PROFANELY	PROVENDER
PRATTLING	PRESCRIPT	PROFANING	PROVIDENT
PRAYERFUL	PRESENTED	PROFANITY	PROVIDING
PRAYINGLY	PRESENTLY	PROFESSED	PROVISION
PREACHIFY	PRESERVED	PROFESSOR	PROVISORY
PREACHING	PRESERVER	PROFFERED	PROVOKING
PREAMBLED	PRESIDENT	PROFILING	PROXIMATE
PREBENDAL	PRESIDING	PROFITEER	PROXIMITY
PRECEDENT	PRESSGANG	PROFITING	PRUDENTLY
PRECEDING	PRESSMARK	PROFUSELY	PRUDISHLY
PRECENTOR	PRESS-ROOM	PROFUSION	PRURIENCE
PRECEPTOR	PRESSWORK	PROGNOSIS	PRURIENCY
PRECIPICE	PRESUMING	PROGRAMME	PSALMODIC
PRECISELY	PRETENDED	PROJECTED	PSEUDONYM
PRECISIAN	PRETENDER	PROJECTOR	PSORIASIS
PRECISION	PRETERITE	PROLIXITY	PSYCHICAL
PRECLUDED	PRETTYISH	PROLOGUED	PSYCHOSIS
PRECOCITY	PREVAILED	PROLONGED	PTARMIGAN
PRECURSOR	PREVALENT	PROMENADE	PTOLEMAIC
PREDATING	PREVENTED	PROMINENT	PUBESCENT
PREDATORY	PREVISION	PROMISING	PUBLICISE
PREDESIGN	PRICELESS	PROMOTING	PUBLICIST
PREDICANT	PRICKLING	PROMOTION	PUBLICITY
PREDICATE	PRIDELESS	PROMPTING	PUBLISHED

PUBLISHER	PYRAMIDAL	QUOTATION	RAVELLING
PUCKERING	PYROGENIC	QUOTELESS	RAVISHING
PUERILELY	PYROLATRY	R—9	RAZORBACK
PUERILITY	PYROMANCY	RABBETING	RAZORBILL
PUERPERAL	PYROMANIA	RABBINATE	RAZOREDGE
PUFF-ADDER	PYROMETER	RABBINISM	RAZORFISH
PUFFINESS	PYROXYLIC	RABBINIST	REACHABLE
PUFFINGLY	PYROXYLIN	RABBITING	REACTANCE
PUGNACITY		RABIDNESS	READDRESS
PUISSANCE	Q—9	RACEHORSE	READINESS
PULLULATE	QUADRATIC	RACIALISM	READJOURN
PULMONARY	QUADRATED	RACKETEER	READOPTED
PULMONATE	QUADRILLE	RACKETING	READORNED
PULPINESS	QUADRUPED	RACONTEUR	READY-MADE
PULSATING	QUADRUPLE	RADIALITY	REALISING
PULSATILE	QUAKERISH	RADIANTLY	REALISTIC
PULSATION	QUAKERISM	RADIATING	REALLEGED
PULSATIVE	QUAKINGLY	RADIATION	REANIMATE
PULSATORY	QUALIFIED	RADIATIVE	REANNEXED
PULSELESS	QUARRYING	RADICALLY	REAPPLIED
PULVERISE	QUARRYMAN	RADIOGRAM	REAPPOINT
PUNCHBOWL	QUARTERED	RADIOLOGY	REAR-GUARD
PUNCTILIO	QUARTERLY	RAFTERING	REARRANGE
PUNCTUATE	QUARTETTE	RAG-PICKER	REASONING
PUNCTURED	QUARTZITE	RAIL-FENCE	REASSURED
PUNGENTLY	QUASIMODO	RAILINGLY	REAVOWING
PUNISHING	QUAVERING	RAIN-GAUGE	REBAPTISE
PUPILLARY	QUEEN-POST	RAININESS	REBELLING
PUPPYHOOD	QUEERNESS	RAINPROOF	REBELLION
PURCHASED	QUENCHING	RAIN-WATER	REBINDING
PURCHASER	QUERULOUS	RAMIFYING	REBLOOMED
PURGATION	QUIBBLING	RAMPAGING	REBOILING
PURGATIVE	QUICKENED	RAMPANTLY	REBOUNDED
PURGATORY	QUICKLIME	RAMPARTED	REBUFFING
PURIFYING	QUICKNESS	RANCIDITY	REBURYING
PURITANIC	QUICKSAND	RANCOROUS	REBUTTING
PURLOINED	QUICKSTEP	RANSACKED	RECALLING
PURPORTED	QUICK-TIME	RANSOMING	RECANTING
PURPOSELY	QUIESCENT	RANTINGLY	RECAPTURE
PURPOSING	QUIESCING	RAPACIOUS	RECASTING
PURPOSIVE	QUIETENED	RAPIDNESS	RECEIPTED
PURSUANCE	QUIETNESS	RAPTORIAL	RECEIVING
PURULENCE	QUINQUINA	RAPTUROUS	RECENSION
PURVEYING	QUINTETTE	RAREE-SHOW	RECEPTION
PUSHINGLY	QUINTUPLE	RAREFYING	RECEPTIVE
PUSTULATE	QUIT-CLAIM	RASCALITY	RECESSING
PUTREFIED	QUITTABLE	RASPATORY	RECESSION
PUTRIDITY	QUITTANCE	RASPBERRY	RECESSIVE
PUZZLEDOM	QUIVERING	RATEPAYER	RECHARGED
PYORRHOEA	QUIXOTISM	RATIONALE	RECHERCHE
PYRACANTH	QUIZZICAL	RATIONING	RECIPIENT

RECKONING	REDOLENCE	REGARDING	RELOADING
RECLAIMED	REDOUBLED	REGICIDAL	RELUCTANT
RECLINATE	REDOUBTED	REGILDING	REMAINDER
RECLINING	REDOUNDED	REGISTRAR	REMAINING
RECLOSING	REDRAFTED	REGORGING	REMANDING
RECLOTHED	REDRAWING	REGRANTED	REMANNING
RECOALING	REDRESSED	REGRADING	REMARKING
RECOASTED	REDUCIBLE	REGRETFUL	REMARRIED
RECOGNISE	REDUCTION	REGRETTED	REMEDYING
RECOILING	REDUNDANT	REGULARLY	REMINDFUL
RECOINING	RE-ECHOING	REGULATED	REMINDING
RECOLLECT	RE-ELECTED	REGULATOR	REMISSION
RECOMBINE	RE-EMERGED	REHANDLED	REMISSIVE
RECOMMEND	RE-ENACTED	REHANGING	REMITTING
RECOMPILE	RE-ENFORCE	REHASHING	REMOULDED
RECOMPOSE	RE-ENTERED	REHEARING	REMOUNTED
RECONCILE	RE-ENTRANT	REHEARSAL	REMOVABLE
RECONDITE	RE-EXAMINE	REHEARSED	RENASCENT
RECONFIRM	REFASHION	RE-HEATING	RENDERING
RECONQUER	REFECTION	REHOUSING	RENDITION
RECONVENE	REFECTORY	REICHSTAG	RENEWABLE
RECONVERT	REFERENCE	RE-IGNITED	RENOVATED
RECORDING	REFERRING	REIMBURSE	RENOVATOR
RECOUNTED	REFILLING	REINFORCE	REOPENING
RECOUPING	REFINEDLY	REINSTALL	REORDERED
RECOVERED	REFITMENT	REINSTATE	REPACKING
RECREANCY	REFITTING	REINSURED	REPAINTED
RECREATED	REFLECTED	REISSUING	REPAIRING
RECREMENT	REFLOATED	REITERATE	REPARABLE
RECROSSED	REFLOWING	REJECTING	REPARABLY
RECRUITED	REFOLDING	REJECTION	REPASSING
RECTANGLE	REFORGING	REJECTIVE	REPASTING
RECTIFIED	REFORMING	REJOICING	REPAYABLE
RECTIFIER	REFORMIST	REJOINDER	REPAYMENT
RECTITUDE	REFORTIFY	REJOINING	REPEALING
RECTORATE	RE-FOUNDED	REJOINTED	REPEATING
RECTORIAL	REFRACTED	REJUDGING	REPELLENT
RECUMBENT	REFRACTOR	REKINDLED	REPELLING
RECURRENT	REFRAINED	RELANDING	REPENTANT
RECURRING	REFRAMING	RELAPSING	REPENTING
RECURVATE	REFRESHED	RELAXABLE	REPERTORY
RECURVING	REFRESHER	RELEASING	REPLACING
REDACTING	REFULGENT	RELEGATED	REPLAITED
REDACTION	REFUNDING	RELENTING	REPLANTED
REDBREAST	REFURBISH	RELETTING	REPLEDGED
REDDENING	REFURNISH	RELEVANCE	REPLENISH
REDEEMING	REFUSABLE	RELEVANCY	REPLETION
REDELIVER	REFUTABLE	RELIEVING	REPLY-PAID
RED-HANDED	REGAINING	RELIGIOUS	REPOINTED
REDINGOTE	REGARDANT	RELIQUARY	REPORTAGE
RED-LETTER	REGARDFUL	RELISHING	REPORTING

REPOSEFUL	RESONANCE	RETROVERT	RIVALLING
REPOSSESS	RESONATED	RETURNING	RIVERSIDE
REPOTTING	RESONATOR	REUNIFIED	ROAD-HOUSE
REPREHEND	RESORBENT	REUNITING	ROADSTEAD
REPRESENT	RESORBING	REVALUING	ROARINGLY
REPRESSED	RESORTING	REVAMPING	ROCK-BASIN
REPRIEVED	RESOUNDED	REVEALING	ROCK-BOUND
REPRIMAND	RESPECTED	REVELLING	ROCK-CRESS
REPRINTED	RESPECTER	REVENGING	ROCKETING
REPROBATE	RE-SPELLED	REVERENCE	ROCKINESS
REPRODUCE	RESPIRING	REVERSELY	ROGUISHLY
REPROVING	RESPONDED	REVERSING	ROISTERED
REPRUNING	RESTAMPED	REVERSION	ROISTERER
REPTILIAN	RESTATING	REVERTING	ROLLICKED
REPUBLISH	RESTEMMED	REVETMENT	ROMANCING
REPUDIATE	RESTFULLY	REVETTING	ROMANISED
REPUGNANT	REST-HOUSE	REVICTUAL	ROMPISHLY
REPULSING	RESTIVELY	REVIEWING	ROOMINESS
REPULSION	RESTOCKED	REVISITED	ROOTSTOCK
REPULSIVE	RESTORING	REVIVABLE	ROPEMAKER
REPUTABLE	RESTRAINT	REVOCABLE	ROQUEFORT
REPUTABLY	RESULTANT	REVOCABLY	ROSACEOUS
REPUTEDLY	RESULTING	REVOLTING	ROSE-APPLE
REQUESTED	RESURGENT	REVOLVING	ROSE-NOBLE
REQUIRING	RESURRECT	REVULSION	ROSE-WATER
REQUISITE	RETAILING	REVULSIVE	ROSINANTE
REQUITING	RETAINING	REWARDING	ROTOGRAPH
RE-READING	RETALIATE	REWORDING	ROTUNDITY
RESCINDED	RETARDING	REWRITING	ROUGH-CAST
RE-SCORING	RETENTION	REWRITTEN	ROUGHENED
RESEATING	RETENTIVE	RHAPSODIC	ROUGH-HEWN
RESECTION	RETEXTURE	RHEUMATIC	ROUGHNESS
RESELLING	RETICENCE	RHINOLOGY	ROUGH-SHOD
RESEMBLED	RETICULAR	RHUMB-LINE	ROUNDED-UP
RESENDING	RETICULUM	RHYMELESS	ROUNDELAY
RESENTFUL	RETORTING	RHYMESTER	ROUNDHEAD
RESERVING	RETORTION	RICE-PAPER	ROUNDNESS
RESERVIST	RETORTIVE	RIDERLESS	ROUNDSMAN
RESETTING	RETOSSING	RIDGE-POLE	ROUSINGLY
RESETTLED	RETOUCHED	RIDICULED	ROWDINESS
RESHIPPED	RETRACING	RIGHTEOUS	ROWELLING
RESIDENCE	RETRACTED	RIGHT-HAND	RUDDINESS
RESIDENCY	RETRACTOR	RIGHTNESS	RUFFIANLY
RESIDUARY	RETREATED	RIGMAROLE	RUINATION
RESIGNING	RETRIEVED	RING-FENCE	RUINOUSLY
RESILIENT	RETRIEVER	RINGLETED	RUMINATED
RESISTANT	RETRIMMED	RING-OUZEL	RUMMAGING
RESISTING	RETROCEDE	RING-STAND	RUMOURING
RESOLUBLE	RETRODDEN	RIOTOUSLY	RUPTURING
RESOLVENT	RETROFLEX	RITUALISM	RUSSOPHIL
RESOLVING	RETROUSSE	RITUALIST	RUSTICATE

RUSTICITY	SANDPAPER	SCHOOLBOY	SEAFARING
RUSTINESS	SANDPIPER	SCHOOLING	SEA-LAWYER
RUTHENIUM	SANDSTONE	SCHOOLMAN	SEA-LETTER
	SANGFROID	SCIENTIAL	SEA-NETTLE
S—9	SANHEDRIN	SCIENTIST	SEARCHING
SACCHARIC	SAPIDNESS	SCINTILLA	SEA-ROBBER
SACCHARIN	SAPIENTLY	SCISSORED	SEA-ROCKET
SACKCLOTH	SAPPINESS	SCLEROSIS	SEASONING
SACRAMENT	SARCASTIC	SCLEROTIC	SEA-SQUIRT
SACRARIUM	SARTORIAL	SCORBUTIC	SEA-URCHIN
SACRIFICE	SASSAFRAS	SCORCHING	SEAWORTHY
SACRILEGE	SASSENACH	SCORIFIED	SEBACEOUS
SACRISTAN	SATELLITE	SCOTCHING	SECESSION
SADDENING	SATIATING	SCOTCHMAN	SECLUDING
SADDLE-BAG	SATIATION	SCOUNDREL	SECLUSION
SADDLEBOW	SATINWOOD	SCRAGGILY	SECLUSIVE
SAFEGUARD	SATIRICAL	SCRAGGING	SECONDARY
SAFETY-PIN	SATIRISED	SCRAMBLED	SECONDING
SAFFLOWER	SATISFIED	SCRAMBLER	SECRETARY
SAFFRONED	SATURATED	SCRAPPING	SECRETING
SAGACIOUS	SATURNIAN	SCRAPBOOK	SECRETION
SAGE-BRUSH	SATURNINE	SCRAP-HEAP	SECRETIVE
SAGITTATE	SAUCEBOAT	SCRATCHED	SECRETORY
SAILCLOTH	SAUCINESS	SCRAWLING	SECTARIAL
SAILMAKER	SAUNTERER	SCREAMING	SECTARIAN
SAIL-PLANE	SAVOURING	SCREECHED	SECTIONAL
SAINT-LIKE	SAVOURILY	SCREENING	SECULARLY
SALACIOUS	SAXIFRAGE	SCREWBALL	SEDENTARY
SALE-PRICE	SAXOPHONE	SCRIBBLED	SEDITIOUS
SALICYLIC	SCALELESS	SCRIBBLER	SEDUCTION
SALIENTLY	SCALINESS	SCRIMMAGE	SEDUCTIVE
SALIFYING	SCALLOPED	SCRIMPING	SEED-GRAIN
SALIVATED	SCALLYWAG	SCRIMSHAW	SEEDINESS
SALLOWISH	SCANTLING	SCRIPTURE	SEED-PEARL
SALLYPORT	SCANTNESS	SCRIVENER	SEEMINGLY
SALTATION	SCAPEGOAT	SCROUNGED	SEE-SAWING
SALTATORY	SCAPEMENT	SCROUNGER	SEGMENTAL
SALTISHLY	SCAPULARY	SCRUBBING	SEGMENTED
SALT-MARSH	SCARECROW	SCRUM-HALF	SEGREGATE
SALTPETRE	SCARF-RING	SCRUMMAGE	SEIGNIORY
SALT-WATER	SCARIFIER	SCRUPLING	SELECTING
SALUBRITY	SCATTERED	SCRUTATOR	SELECTION
SALVARSAN	SCAVENGER	SCUFFLING	SELECTIVE
SALVATION	SCENTLESS	SCULPTURE	SELFISHLY
SAMARITAN	SCEPTICAL	SCUMBLING	SELVEDGED
SANCTUARY	SCHEDULED	SCURRYING	SEMANTICS
SANDALLED	SCHEMATIC	SCUTCHEON	SEMAPHORE
SAND-BLAST	SCHILLING	SCUTTLING	SEMBLANCE
SAND-BLIND	SCHNORKEL	SEA-ANCHOR	SEMIBREVE
SANDGLASS	SCHOLARLY	SEA-BREACH	SEMICOLON
SANDINESS	SCHOLIAST	SEA-BREEZE	SEMI-FLUID

SEMILUNAR	SHAKINESS	SHOWINESS	SINGLETON
SEMINATED	SHALLOWLY	SHOW-PLACE	SINISTRAL
SEMIVOCAL	SHAMBLING	SHREW-MOLE	SINLESSLY
SEMIVOWEL	SHAMELESS	SHRIEKING	SINUOSITY
SENESCENT	SHAMPOOED	SHRILLING	SINUOUSLY
SENESCHAL	SHAPELESS	SHRIMPING	SIPHONAGE
SENIORITY	SHARPENED	SHRIMP-NET	SIPHONING
SENSATION	SHARPNESS	SHRINKAGE	SISYPHEAN
SENSELESS	SHATTERED	SHRINKING	SITUATION
SENSITISE	SHEAR-LEGS	SHROUDING	SIXFOOTER
SENSITIVE	SHEATHING	SHRUBBERY	SIXTEENTH
SENSORIAL	SHEEPCOTE	SHRUBLESS	SKEDADDLE
SENSORIUM	SHEEPFOLD	SHRUGGING	SKETCHILY
SENSUALLY	SHEEP-HOOK	SHUDDERED	SKETCHING
SENTENCED	SHEEPSKIN	SHUFFLING	SKEW-WHIFF
SENTIMENT	SHEEPWALK	SIBILANCE	SKILFULLY
SENTRY-BOX	SHEER-HULK	SIBYLLINE	SKINFLINT
SEPARABLE	SHELDRAKE	SICCATIVE	SKYROCKET
SEPARABLY	SHELLBACK	SICKENING	SLABSTONE
SEPARATED	SHELL-FISH	SIDEBOARD	SLACKENED
SEPARATOR	SHIELDING	SIDEBURNS	SLACKNESS
SEPTEMBER	SHIFTLESS	SIDE-LIGHT	SLANDERED
SEPTENARY	SHINGLING	SIDE-TABLE	SLANTWISE
SEPULCHRE	SHINTOISM	SIDETRACK	SLAPSTICK
SEQUACITY	SHIPMONEY	SIGHINGLY	SLATINESS
SEQUESTER	SHIPOWNER	SIGHTLESS	SLAUGHTER
SERENADED	SHIPSHAPE	SIGHTSEER	SLAVE-LIKE
SERMONISE	SHIPWRECK	SIGNAL-BOX	SLAVERING
SERRATION	SHIRTLESS	SIGNAL-GUN	SLAVISHLY
SERVIETTE	SHIVERING	SIGNALIZE	SLAVONIAN
SERVILELY	SHOEBLACK	SIGNALLED	SLEEPLESS
SERVILITY	SHOEBRUSH	SIGNALMAN	SLEIGHING
SERVITUDE	SHOEMAKER	SIGNATORY	SLENDERLY
SESSIONAL	SHOPWOMAN	SIGNATURE	SLIDE-RULE
SETACEOUS	SHORELESS	SIGN-BOARD	SLIGHTING
SET-SQUARE	SHOREWARD	SIGNIFIED	SLIMINESS
SEVEN-FOLD	SHORTCAKE	SIGNORINA	SLIP-COACH
SEVENTEEN	SHORTENED	SILENCING	SLIPPERED
SEVENTHLY	SHORTFALL	SILICATED	SLITHERED
SEVERABLE	SHORTHAND	SILICEOUS	SLIVERING
SEVERALLY	SHORT-HOSE	SILKINESS	SLOBBERED
SEVERALTY	SHORTNESS	SILLINESS	SLOP-BASIN
SEVERANCE	SHORT-SLIP	SILVER-FOX	SLOPINGLY
SEXENNIAL	SHOTPROOF	SILVERING	SLOUCH-HAT
SEXUALITY	SHOULDERS	SIMILARLY	SLOUCHING
SFORZANDO	SHOVELLED	SIMMERING	SLOUGHING
SHACKLING	SHOVELFUL	SIMPLETON	SLOWCOACH
SHADINESS	SHOVEL-HAT	SIMULATED	SLOW-MATCH
SHADOWING	SHOVELLER	SINCERELY	SLUMBERED
SHAFTLESS	SHOWBREAD	SINCERITY	SMALL-ARMS
SHAKEDOWN	SHOWERING	SINGINGLY	SMALL-BEER

SMALLNESS	SOLARISED	SPEARMINT	SPRINGING
SMARTENED	SOLDERING	SPECIALLY	SPRINGBOK
SMARTNESS	SOLDIERLY	SPECIALTY	SPRING-GUN
SMILELESS	SOLEMNISE	SPECIFIED	SPRINKLED
SMILINGLY	SOLEMNITY	SPECKLESS	SPRINKLER
SMIRCHING	SOLICITED	SPECKLING	SPRINTING
SMOCKLESS	SOLICITOR	SPECTACLE	SPROUTING
SMOKE-BOMB	SOLIDNESS	SPECTATOR	SPUR-ROYAL
SMOKELESS	SOLILOQUY	SPECULATE	SPUR-WHEEL
SMOKINESS	SOLITAIRE	SPEECH-DAY	SPUTTERED
SMOOTHING	SOMETHING	SPEECHFUL	SQUABBLED
SMOTHERED	SOMETIMES	SPEECHIFY	SQUALIDLY
SMUG-FACED	SOMEWHERE	SPELLABLE	SQUALLING
SMUGGLING	SOMNOLENT	SPERMATIC	SQUASHING
SMUTCHING	SONNETEER	SPHERICAL	SQUATTING
SNAFFLING	SOOTINESS	SPHINCTER	SQUAWKING
SNAIL-LIKE	SOPHISTRY	SPICINESS	SQUEAKING
SNAKE-BIRD	SOPHOMORE	SPIKENARD	SQUEALING
SNAKE-ROOT	SOPORIFIC	SPILLIKIN	SQUEAMISH
SNAKEWEED	SORCERESS	SPINDLING	SQUEEZING
SNAKE-WOOD	SORRINESS	SPINDRIFT	SQUELCHED
SNATCHING	SORROWFUL	SPINELESS	SQUIGGLED
SNICKERED	SORROWING	SPINNAKER	SQUINTING
SNIFFLING	SORTILEGE	SPINNERET	SQUIRMING
SNIGGERED	SOSTENUTO	SPIRALITY	SQUIRTING
SNIVELLED	SOTTISHLY	SPIRITING	STABILISE
SNOWBERRY	SOTTO-VOCE	SPIRITUAL	STABILITY
SNOWBLIND	SOUBRETTE	SPLASHING	STABLEBOY
SNOW-BOUND	SOULFULLY	SPLAY-FOOT	STABLEMAN
SNOWDRIFT	SOUNDLESS	SPLENDOUR	STACKYARD
SNOWFIELD	SOUNDNESS	SPLENETIC	STAGE-PLAY
SNOWFLAKE	SOUP-PLATE	SPLINTERY	STAGGERED
SNOW-GOOSE	SOUTHDOWN	SPLINTING	STAGHOUND
SNOWSTORM	SOUTH-EAST	SPLIT-RING	STAGINESS
SNUB-NOSED	SOUTHERLY	SPOKESMAN	STAGNANCY
SNUFFLING	SOUTHWARD	SPOLIATED	STAGNATED
SNUGGLING	SOUTH-WEST	SPONSORED	STAIDNESS
SOAPINESS	SOU'-WESTER	SPOON-BAIT	STAINLESS
SOAPSTONE	SOVEREIGN	SPOONBILL	STAIRCASE
SOARINGLY	SPADE-WORK	SPOON-FEED	STAIR-HEAD
SOBERNESS	SPAGHETTI	SPORE-CASE	STAKE-BOAT
SOBRIQUET	SPANGLING	SPORTLESS	STALACTIC
SOCIALISE	SPARENESS	SPORTSMAN	STALEMATE
SOCIALISM	SPARINGLY	SPOUT-HOLE	STALENESS
SOCIALIST	SPARKLING	SPOUTLESS	STALKLESS
SOCIALITE	SPASMODIC	SPRAGGING	STAMMERED
SOCIALITY	SPATTERED	SPRAINING	STAMMERER
SOCIOLOGY	SPATULATE	SPRAWLING	STAMP-DUTY
SODA-WATER	SPEAKABLE	SPREADING	STAMPEDED
SOFTENING	SPEAK-EASY	SPRIGGING	STANCHING
SOJOURNED	SPEARHEAD	SPRIGHTLY	STANCHION

STARBOARD	STIPULATE	STRATAGEM	SUBMERGED
STARCHING	STIRABOUT	STRATEGIC	SUBMITTED
STARGAZER	STITCHERY	STREAKING	SUBNORMAL
STARINGLY	STITCHING	STREAMING	SUBORNING
STARLIGHT	STOCKADED	STREAMLET	SUBSCRIBE
STAR-SHELL	STOCK-DOVE	STRENUOUS	SUBSCRIPT
STARTLING	STOCK-FISH	STRESSING	SUBSERVED
STATELESS	STOCKINET	STRETCHED	SUBSIDING
STATEMENT	STOCKINGS	STRETCHER	SUBSIDISE
STATE-ROOM	STOCKLESS	STRIATION	SUBSISTED
STATESMAN	STOCKWHIP	STRICTURE	SUBSTANCE
STATIONED	STOCKYARD	STRINGENT	SUBTENANT
STATIONER	STOICALLY	STRINGING	SUBTENDED
STATISTIC	STOKEHOLD	STRIPLING	SUBVERTED
STATUETTE	STOLIDITY	STRIPPING	SUCCEEDED
STATUTORY	STOMACHAL	STROLLING	SUCCENTOR
STAUNCHED	STOMACHER	STROMATIC	SUCCESSOR
STAYMAKER	STOMACHIC	STRONG-BOX	SUCCOTASH
STEADFAST	STONECHAT	STRONTIUM	SUCCOURED
STEADYING	STONE-COLD	STROPPING	SUCCULENT
STEAMBOAT	STONECROP	STRUCTIVE	SUCCUMBED
STEAMPIPE	STONE-DEAD	STRUGGLED	SUCKERING
STEAMSHIP	STONE-DEAF	STRUMMING	SUDORIFIC
STEEL-CLAD	STONELESS	STRUTTING	SUFFERING
STEELYARD	STONE-PINE	STRYCHNIC	SUFFICING
STEEPENED	STONEWALL	STUCCOING	SUFFIXING
STEEPNESS	STONINESS	STUD-GROOM	SUFFOCATE
STEERABLE	STOOL-BALL	STUD-HORSE	SUFFRAGAN
STEERSMAN	STOPPERED	STUDIEDLY	SUFFUSING
STELLATED	STOP-PRESS	STUMBLING	SUFFUSION
STERILISE	STOP-WATCH	STUPEFIED	SUGAR-BEET
STERILITY	STOREROOM	STUPIDITY	SUGAR-CANE
STERNMOST	STORESHIP	STUTTERER	SUGARLESS
STERNNESS	STORMCOCK	STYLISHLY	SUGAR-LOAF
STERNPOST	STORM-CONE	STYLOBATE	SUGAR-MILL
STEVEDORE	STORMSAIL	SUB-AGENCY	SUGAR-MITE
STEWARDLY	STORTHING	SUBALTERN	SUGAR-PINE
STEWARTRY	STORYBOOK	SUBCOSTAL	SUGARPLUM
STIFFENED	STOUTNESS	SUBDEACON	SUGGESTED
STIFFENER	STOVEPIPE	SUBDIVIDE	SULKINESS
STIFFNESS	STRADDLED	SUB-EDITOR	SULPHURIC
STIGMATIC	STRAGGLED	SUBFAMILY	SUMMARILY
STILL-BORN	STRAGGLER	SUBJACENT	SUMMARISE
STILL-LIFE	STRAINING	SUBJECTED	SUMMATION
STILLNESS	STRANDING	SUBJOINED	SUMMING-UP
STILL-ROOM	STRANGELY	SUBJUGATE	SUMMONING
STIMULANT	STRANGLED	SUBLIMATE	SUMPTUARY
STIMULATE	STRANGLER	SUBLIMELY	SUMPTUOUS
STINGLESS	STRAPPADO	SUBLIMITY	SUNBONNET
STINKBOMB	STRAPPING	SUBLUNARY	SUNFLOWER
STIPPLING	STRAPWORK	SUBMARINE	

SUNSTROKE	SWINISHLY	TAILORESS	TENANTING
SUPERFINE	SWITCHING	TAILORING	TENDERING
SUPERHEAT	SWITCHMAN	TAILPIECE	TENSENESS
SUPERPOSE	SWIVEL-EYE	TALBOTYPE	TENTATIVE
SUPERSEDE	SWIVELLED	TALKATIVE	TEPEFYING
SUPERVENE	SWORDBELT	TALLOWING	TEPIDNESS
SUPERVISE	SWORDBILL	TALLY-CARD	TEREBINTH
SUPPLIANT	SWORD-CANE	TALLYSHOP	TERMAGANT
SUPPLYING	SWORDFISH	TALMUDIST	TERMINATE
SUPPORTED	SWORDHILT	TAMPERING	TERRACING
SUPPORTER	SWORD-LILY	TANGERINE	TERRIFIED
SUPPOSING	SWORDSMAN	TANTALIZE	TERRITORY
SUPPURATE	SYBARITIC	TAP-DANCER	TERRORISE
SUPREMACY	SYCOPHANT	TARANTULA	TERRORISM
SUPREMELY	SYLLABARY	TARDINESS	TERRORIST
SURCHARGE	SYLLABIFY	TARNISHED	TERSENESS
SURCINGLE	SYLLABLED	TARPAULIN	TESTAMENT
SURFACING	SYLLEPSIS	TARTAREAN	TESTATRIX
SURLINESS	SYLLOGISE	TASSELLED	TESTIFIED
SURMISING	SYLLOGISM	TASTELESS	TESTIMONY
SURNAMING	SYLPH-LIKE	TATTERING	TESTINESS
SURPASSED	SYMBIOSIS	TATTOOING	TETHERING
SURPRISED	SYMBIOTIC	TAUTENING	TETRALOGY
SURRENDER	SYMBOLISE	TAUTOLOGY	TETRARCHY
SURROGATE	SYMBOLISM	TAWNINESS	TEXTUALLY
SURVEYING	SYMBOLIST	TAXIDERMY	THANKLESS
SURVIVING	SYMMETRIC	TAXIMETER	THATCHING
SUSPECTED	SYMPHONIC	TEACHABLE	THEOCRACY
SUSPENDED	SYMPHYSIS	TEASELLED	THEOCRASY
SUSPENDER	SYMPOSIUM	TECHNICAL	THEOMACHY
SUSPICION	SYNAGOGUE	TECHNIQUE	THEOMANCY
SUSTAINED	SYNCOPATE	TEDIOUSLY	THEORISED
SWADDLING	SYNDICATE	TELEGRAPH	THEOSOPHY
SWAGGERED	SYNODICAL	TELEMETER	THEREFORE
SWALLOWED	SYNONYMIC	TELEOLOGY	THEREFROM
SWAN'S-DOWN	SYNOPTIST	TELEPATHY	THEREINTO
SWARTHILY	SYNOVITIS	TELEPHONE	THEREUNTO
SWEET-CORN	SYNTHESIS	TELEPHONY	THEREUPON
SWEETENED	SYNTHETIC	TELEPHOTO	THEREWITH
SWEETMEAT	SYRINGING	TELEPRINT	THERMIDOR
SWEETNESS	SYSTEMISE	TELESCOPE	THESAURUS
SWEET-SHOP		TELLINGLY	THICKENED
SWELTERED	T—9	TELLURIUM	THICKNESS
SWIFTNESS	TABLATURE	TELLUROUS	THICK-KNEE
SWIMMERET	TABLELAND	TEMPERATE	THICK-SKIN
SWINDLING	TABLE-TALK	TEMPERING	THIGH-BONE
SWINEHERD	TABULARLY	TEMPORARY	THINKABLE
SWING-BOAT	TABULATED	TEMPORISE	THIRSTILY
SWING-DOOR	TACTICIAN	TEMPTRESS	THIRSTING
SWINGEING	TACTILITY	TENACIOUS	THIRTIETH
SWINGLING	TAILBOARD	TENACULUM	THORNBACK

THORNBUSH	TOAD-STONE	TRAITRESS	TRI-WEEKLY
THORNLESS	TOAD-STOOL	TRAMPLING	TROOPSHIP
THRASHING	TOAST-RACK	TRANSCEND	TROUBLING
THREADING	TOLERABLE	TRANSFORM	TROUBLOUS
THREEFOLD	TOLERABLY	TRANSFUSE	TROUNCING
THRESHING	TOLERANCE	TRANSIENT	TROUSERED
THRESHOLD	TOLERATED	TRANSLATE	TROUSSEAU
THRIFTILY	TOLL-BOOTH	TRANSMUTE	TROWELLED
THRILLING	TOMBSTONE	TRANSPIRE	TRUCKLING
THROBBING	TONSORIAL	TRANSPORT	TRUCULENT
THRONGING	TOOTHACHE	TRANSPOSE	TRUMPETER
THROTTLED	TOOTH-LESS	TRAPEZIUM	TRUNCATED
THROWSTER	TOOTH-PICK	TRAPEZOID	TRUNDLING
THRUMMING	TOOTHSOME	TRATTORIA	TRUNK-HOSE
THRUSTING	TOPICALLY	TRAUMATIC	TUGGINGLY
THUMB-MARK	TORMENTED	TRAVELLER	TUMESCENT
THUMB-NAIL	TORMENTIL	TRAVERSED	TUNEFULLY
THUMB-RACK	TORMENTOR	TREACHERY	TUNNELLED
THUNDERED	TORPEDOED	TREADMILL	TURBINATE
THUNDERER	TORPIDITY	TREASURED	TURBULENT
THWACKING	TORPIFIED	TREASURER	TURFINESS
THWARTING	TORREFIED	TREATMENT	TURF-SPADE
TICKETING	TORSIONAL	TREE-PIPIT	TURGIDITY
TIDEGAUGE	TORTURING	TRELLISED	TURNIP-FLY
TIDE-TABLE	TORTUROUS	TREMBLING	TURNSTONE
TIDE-WATER	TOTTERING	TREMULOUS	TURNTABLE
TIGER-LILY	TOUCHABLE	TRENCHANT	TURPITUDE
TIGER-MOTH	TOUCH-HOLE	TRENCHING	TURQUOISE
TIGER-WOOD	TOUCH-WOOD	TREPANNED	TUTORSHIP
TIGHTENED	TOUGHENED	TRIATOMIC	TWADDLING
TIGHTNESS	TOUGHNESS	TRIBALISM	TWENTIETH
TIGHT-ROPE	TOWELLING	TRIBESMAN	TWIDDLING
TIMBERMAN	TOWN-CLERK	TRIBUNATE	TWINKLING
TIMEPIECE	TOWN-CRIER	TRIBUTARY	TWISTABLE
TIME-TABLE	TOWN-HOUSE	TRICKLING	TWITCHING
TIMIDNESS	TOWN-MAJOR	TRICKSTER	TWITTERED
TIMOCRACY	TOWNSFOLK	TRICUSPID	TWO-HANDED
TINCTURED	TRACEABLE	TRIENNIAL	TWO-MASTED
TINDERBOX	TRACKLESS	TRIGAMIST	TYMPANIST
TINKERING	TRACTABLE	TRIHEDRAL	TYPEMETAL
TINSELLED	TRACTABLY	TRIHEDRON	TYPICALLY
TIPSINESS	TRADEMARK	TRILINEAR	TYPIFYING
TIPSY-CAKE	TRADESMAN	TRILITHON	TYRANNISE
TIREDNESS	TRADE-WIND	TRILOBATE	TYRANNOUS
TITILLATE	TRADITION	TRILOBITE	
TITIVATED	TRADUCING	TRINOMIAL	U—9
TITRATION	TRAGEDIAN	TRISECTED	UGLIFYING
TITTERING	TRAINABLE	TRITENESS	ULCERATED
TITTLE-BAT	TRAINBAND	TRIUMPHAL	ULTIMATUM
TITULARLY	TRAIN-MILE	TRIUMPHED	ULULATING
TOADEATER	TRAIPSING	TRIVIALLY	ULULATION

UMBELLATE UNCOUNTED UNEARTHED UNINVOKED
UMBILICAL UNCOUTHLY UNEARTHLY UNIPAROUS
UMBILICUS UNCOVERED UNEATABLE UNISEXUAL
UNABASHED UNCROPPED UNELECTED UNITARIAN
UNACCUSED UNCROSSED UNENGAGED UNIVALENT
UNACTABLE UNCROWDED UN-ENGLISH UNIVERSAL
UNADAPTED UNCROWNED UNENVIOUS UNJOINTED
UNADOPTED UNCURLING UNEQUABLE UNKNOTTED
UNADORNED UNDAMAGED UNEQUALLY UNKNOWING
UNADVISED UNDAUNTED UNEXCITED UNLASHING
UNALLOYED UNDECEIVE UNEXERTED UNLATCHED
UNALTERED UNDECIDED UNEXPIRED UNLEARNED
UNAMENDED UNDEFILED UNEXPOSED UNLEASHED
UNAMIABLE UNDEFINED UNFAILING UNLIGHTED
UNAMUSING UNDERDONE UNFEELING UNLIMITED
UNANIMITY UNDERFEED UNFEIGNED UNLOADING
UNANIMOUS UNDERFOOT UNFITNESS UNLOCATED
UNASHAMED UNDERGONE UNFITTING UNLOCKING
UNASSURED UNDERHAND UNFLEDGED UNLOOSING
UNBARRING UNDERHUNG UNFOLDING UNLOVABLE
UNBEKNOWN UNDERLAID UNFOUNDED UNLUCKILY
UNBENDING UNDERLAIN UNFROCKED UNMANNING
UNBINDING UNDERLINE UNFURLING UNMANURED
UNBLOCKED UNDERLING UNGALLANT UNMARRIED
UNBLUNTED UNDERMINE UNGIRDING UNMASKING
UNBOLTING UNDERMOST UNGRANTED UNMATCHED
UNBOSOMED UNDERPAID UNGRUDGED UNMERITED
UNBOUNDED UNDERPART UNGUARDED UNMINDFUL
UNBRACING UNDERPLOT UNGUMMING UNMOORING
UNBRIDLED UNDERRATE UNHANDILY UNMOULDED
UNBRUISED UNDERSELL UNHANDLED UNMOUNTED
UNBUCKLED UNDERSHOT UNHAPPILY UNMOURNED
UNBUCKLES UNDERSIGN UNHARMFUL UNMUFFLED
UNCANNILY UNDERSOLD UNHATCHED UNMUSICAL
UNCAPPING UNDERTAKE UNHEALTHY UNMUZZLED
UNCEASING UNDERTONE UNHEEDFUL UNNAMABLE
UNCERTAIN UNDERTOOK UNHEEDING UNNATURAL
UNCHANGED UNDERVEST UNHELPFUL UNNERVING
UNCHARGED UNDERWEAR UNHINGING UNNOTICED
UNCHARTED UNDERWENT UNHITCHED UNOBVIOUS
UNCHECKED UNDERWOOD UNHOOKING UNOFFERED
UNCLAIMED UNDERWORK UNHOPEFUL UNOPPOSED
UNCLEARED UNDESIRED UNHORSING UNORDERED
UNCLIPPED UNDILUTED UNHURTFUL UNORDERLY
UNCLOGGED UNDIVIDED UNIFORMLY UNPACKING
UNCLOSING UNDOUBTED UNIMPEDED UNPAINFUL
UNCLOTHED UNDRAINED UNIMPLIED UNPAINTED
UNCLOUDED UNDREAMED UNINDUCED UNPEGGING
UNCOILING UNDRESSED UNINJURED UNPENNING
UNCONCERN UNDULATED UNINSURED UNPERUSED
UNCORKING UNDUTIFUL UNINVITED UNPICKING

UNPIERCED	UNSHAPELY	UNWITTILY	VASSALAGE
UNPINNING	UNSHEATHE	UNWOMANLY	VEERINGLY
UNPITYING	UNSHIPPED	UNWORLDLY	VEGETABLE
UNPLAITED	UNSHRIVEN	UNWORRIED	VEHEMENCE
UNPLANTED	UNSIGHTLY	UNWOUNDED	VEHICULAR
UNPLEADED	UNSINKING	UNWRAPPED	VELVETEEN
UNPLEASED	UNSKILFUL	UNWREATHE	VENEERING
UNPLEDGED	UNSKILLED	UNWRECKED	VENERABLE
UNPLUGGED	UNSOUNDLY	UNWRITTEN	VENERABLY
UNPLUMBED	UNSPARING	UNWROUGHT	VENERATED
UNPOINTED	UNSPOILED	UPANISHAD	VENGEANCE
UNPOPULAR	UNSPOTTED	UPBRAIDED	VENIALITY
UNPOTABLE	UNSTAINED	UPHEAVING	VENTILATE
UNPRAISED	UNSTAMPED	UPHOLDING	VENTRALLY
UNPRESSED	UNSTINTED	UPHOLSTER	VENTRICLE
UNPRINTED	UNSTOPPED	UPLIFTING	VENTURING
UNQUIETLY	UNSTRIPED	UPPER-HAND	VERACIOUS
UNREALITY	UNSTUDIED	UPPERMOST	VERBALISE
UNREBUKED	UNSULLIED	UPRIGHTLY	VERBASCUM
UNREFINED	UNTACKING	UPROOTING	VERBOSELY
UNREFUTED	UNTAINTED	UPSETTING	VERBOSITY
UNRELATED	UNTAMABLE	UPTURNING	VERDANTLY
UNRENEWED	UNTANGLED	USELESSLY	VERDIGRIS
UNRESCUED	UNTEMPTED	USHERETTE	VERDUROUS
UNRESTFUL	UNTENABLE	USUALNESS	VERIDICAL
UNRESTING	UNTHANKED	UTILISING	VERIFYING
UNREVISED	UNTIRABLE	UTTERANCE	VERITABLE
UNREVIVED	UNTOUCHED	UTTERMOST	VERITABLY
UNREVOKED	UNTRAINED		VERMICIDE
UNRIDDLED	UNTRIMMED	V—9	VERMICULE
UNRIGGING	UNTRODDEN	VACCINATE	VERMIFORM
UNRIPENED	UNTUCKING	VACILLATE	VERMIFUGE
UNRIPPING	UNTUTORED	VADE-MECUM	VERMILION
UNROLLING	UNTWINING	VAGUENESS	VERMINOUS
UNROASTED	UNTWISTED	VAINGLORY	VERRUCOSE
UNROUNDED	UNUSUALLY	VALANCING	VERSATILE
UNRUFFLED	UNVACATED	VALENTINE	VERSIFIER
UNRUMPLED	UNVARYING	VALIANTLY	VERSIFORM
UNSADDLED	UNVEILING	VALIDATED	VERTEBRAL
UNSALABLE	UNVISITED	VALUATION	VESICULAR
UNSAVOURY	UNWAKENED	VALUELESS	VESTIBULE
UNSCANNED	UNWARLIKE	VAMOOSING	VESTIGIAL
UNSCATHED	UNWATCHED	VAMPIRISM	VESTRYMAN
UNSCOURED	UNWATERED	VANDALISM	VEXATIOUS
UNSCREWED	UNWEARIED	VANISHING	VIABILITY
UNSEALING	UNWEAVING	VAPORISED	VIBRATING
UNSEATING	UNWEIGHED	VAPOURING	VIBRATION
UNSELFISH	UNWELCOME	VARIATION	VICARIATE
UNSETTLED	UNWILLING	VARIEGATE	VICARIOUS
UNSEVERED	UNWINDING	VARIOUSLY	VICENNIAL
UNSHACKLE	UNWINKING	VARNISHED	VICEREGAL

VICIOUSLY	VULGARISM	WATER-FLAG	WHALEBOAT
VICTIMISE	VULGARITY	WATERFLEA	WHALEBONE
VICTORIAN	VULNERARY	WATERFOWL	WHATSOE'ER
VICTORINE	VULTURINE	WATER-GALL	WHEEDLING
VIEW-POINT	VULTURISH	WATER-HOLE	WHEEL-BASE
VIGILANCE	VULTURISM	WATERLESS	WHEREFORE
VIGILANTE	VULTUROUS	WATERLINE	WHEREINTO
VINACEOUS		WATERMARK	WHEREUNTO
VINDICATE	W—9	WATERMILL	WHEREUPON
VINOMETER	WAGGISHLY	WATER-POLO	WHEREWITH
VIOLATING	WAGNERIAN	WATER-RAIL	WHETSTONE
VIOLATION	WAGONETTE	WATER-RATE	WHICHEVER
VIOLENTLY	WAILINGLY	WATERSHED	WHIFFLING
VIOLINIST	WAISTBAND	WATERSIDE	WHIMPERED
VIRGILIAN	WAISTBELT	WATER-TANK	WHIMSICAL
VIRGINIAN	WAISTCOAT	WATER-VOLE	WHININGLY
VIRGINITY	WAIST-DEEP	WATERWEED	WHINNYING
VIRTUALLY	WAITINGLY	WATERWORN	WHINSTONE
VIRULENCE	WAKEFULLY	WATTMETER	WHIPGRAFT
VISCIDITY	WAKE-ROBIN	WAVEMETER	WHIPPER-IN
VISCOSITY	WALL-FRUIT	WAXWORKER	WHIPSNAKE
VISCOUNTY	WALLOPING	WAYFARING	WHIPSTOCK
VISIONARY	WALLOWING	WAYWARDLY	WHIRLIGIG
VISITABLE	WALLPAPER	WAYZGOOSE	WHIRLPOOL
VISUALIZE	WALL-PLATE	WEAKENING	WHIRLWIND
VITALISED	WALL-SIDED	WEAK-KNEED	WHISKERED
VITIATING	WALPURGIS	WEALTHILY	WHISPERED
VITIATION	WANDERING	WEARILESS	WHISPERER
VITRIFIED	WAREHOUSE	WEARINESS	WHISTLING
VITRIOLIC	WARNINGLY	WEARISOME	WHITEBAIT
VIVACIOUS	WARRANTED	WEATHERED	WHITEBEAM
VIVIDNESS	WARRANTEE	WEATHERLY	WHITEFISH
VIVIFYING	WARRANTOR	WEB-FOOTED	WHITEHEAD
VIZIERATE	WASHBOARD	WEDGEWISE	WHITE-HEAT
VOCALISED	WASHERMAN	WEDNESDAY	WHITE-IRON
VOICELESS	WASH-HOUSE	WEED-GROWN	WHITENESS
VOL-AU-VENT	WASHINESS	WEEPINGLY	WHITENING
VOLLEYING	WASHSTAND	WEEVILLED	WHITETAIL
VOLPLANED	WASPISHLY	WEIGHABLE	WHITEWASH
VOLTE-FACE	WASSAILED	WEIGHTILY	WHITEWING
VOLTMETER	WASTELESS	WEIGHTING	WHITEWOOD
VOLUNTARY	WASTE-PIPE	WEIRDNESS	WHITTLING
VOLUNTEER	WATCHCASE	WELCOMING	WHIZZBANG
VOODOOISM	WATCHFIRE	WELCOMELY	WHOLENESS
VORACIOUS	WATCHWORD	WELLBEING	WHOLESALE
VOUCHSAFE	WATERBIRD	WELL-HOUSE	WHOLESOME
VULCANISE	WATERBUCK	WELL-TIMED	WHOSOEVER
VULCANISM	WATERBUTT	WELL-WATER	WIDEAWAKE
VULCANITE	WATERCART	WESTERING	WIDOWHOOD
VULGARIAN	WATERFALL	WESTERNER	WIELDABLE
VULGARISE	WATER-FERN	WESTWARDS	WILLINGLY

WILLOWISH	WITTINESS	WORKHOUSE	**X—9**
WILSONITE	WITTINGLY	WORKMANLY	XANTHIPPE
WINDHOVER	WOEBEGONE	WORK-TABLE	XYLOPHONE
WINDINESS	WOLFISHLY	WORKWOMAN	
WINDINGLY	WOLF-HOUND	WORLDLING	**Y—9**
WINDOW-BOX	WOLF'S-BANE	WORLDWIDE	YACHTSMAN
WINEGLASS	WOLF'S-CLAW	WORMEATEN	YANKEEISM
WINE-PRESS	WOLVERINE	WORM-WHEEL	YARDSTICK
WINE-STONE	WOMANHOOD	WORRIMENT	YAWNINGLY
WINKINGLY	WOMANKIND	WORSENING	YELLOWING
WINNINGLY	WOMAN-LIKE	WORTHLESS	YELLOWISH
WINNOWING	WOMENFOLK	WOUNDLESS	YESTERDAY
WINSOMELY	WOMENKIND	WOUND-WORT	YGGDRASIL
WINTERING	WONDERING	WRANGLING	YORKSHIRE
WIREDRAWN	WONDERFUL	WREATHING	YOUNGLING
WIRE-GAUZE	WOOD-ASHES	WRENCHING	YOUNGSTER
WISTFULLY	WOODBLOCK	WRESTLING	
WITCH-HUNT	WOODCHUCK	WRIGGLING	**Z—9**
WITHDRAWN	WOODCRAFT	WRINKLING	ZEALOUSLY
WITHERING	WOOD-HOUSE	WRISTBAND	ZIGZAGGED
WITHSTAND	WOODINESS	WRONGDOER	ZIRCONIUM
WITHSTOOD	WOODLAYER	WRY-NECKED	ZOOGRAPHY
WITLESSLY	WOODLOUSE	WYCH-HAZEL	ZOOLOGIST
WITNESSED	WOOD-NYMPH		ZOOPHYTIC
WITTICISM	WORDINESS		

NOTES

NOTES